February 15–19, 2014
Orlando, Florida, USA

Association for
Computing Machinery

Advancing Computing as a Science & Profession

PPoPP'14

Proceedings of the 2014 ACM SIGPLAN Symposium on
Principles and Practice of Parallel Programming

Sponsored by:
ACM SIGPLAN

Supported by:
IBM Research and Oracle Labs

Association for Computing Machinery

Advancing Computing as a Science & Profession

The Association for Computing Machinery
2 Penn Plaza, Suite 701
New York, New York 10121-0701

ISBN: 978-1-4503-2656-8 (Digital)

ISBN: 978-1-4503-3096-1 (Print)

Additional copies may be ordered prepaid from:

ACM Order Department
PO Box 30777
New York, NY 10087-0777, USA

Phone: 1-800-342-6626 (USA and Canada)
+1-212-626-0500 (Global)
Fax: +1-212-944-1318
E-mail: acmhelp@acm.org
Hours of Operation: 8:30 am – 4:30 pm ET

Printed in the USA

Chairs' Welcome

It is our great pleasure to welcome you to the *19th ACM Symposium on Principles and Practice of Parallel Programming – PPoPP'14*. PPoPP is a forum for leading work on all aspects of parallel programming, including foundational and theoretical aspects, techniques, tools, and practical experiences. Given the rise of parallel architectures into the consumer market (desktops, laptops, and mobile devices), we made an effort to attract work that addresses new parallel workloads, techniques and tools that attempt to improve the productivity of parallel programming, and work towards improved synergy with such emerging architectures.

In 2014, PPoPP will again be co-located with the *20th IEEE International Symposium on High Performance Computer Architecture* (HPCA-2014) and *2014 International Symposium on Code Generation and Optimization* (CGO-2014). Our joint events will take place in sunny Orlando, Florida, providing both a mid-winter escape from colder climates and also an opportunity for children and family-friendly activities.

Our call for papers was enthusiastically answered with 184 submissions from academia, industry and national research facilities from all geographies. The PPoPP'14 Program Committee and external reviewers diligently evaluated each of the papers carefully and, after a rebuttal period and an in-person meeting, selected 28 papers for formal presentation at the symposium. An additional 17 submissions were selected for presentation at the Poster Session. Two joint (with HPCA and CGO) keynotes, by Mark Hill (University of Wisconsin-Madison) and Norm Rubin (NVIDIA), and a PPoPP keynote by Kunle Olukotun (Stanford University) complete our technical program.

Putting together PPoPP'14 was a team effort. First of all, we would like to thank the authors and keynotes for providing the content of the technical program. We would like to express our gratitude to the Program Committee and external reviewers, who worked very hard in reviewing papers and providing suggestions for their improvements. We would like to thank our Local Chair, Mark Heinrich, for all his efforts in making sure the participants have a pleasant and exciting stay during our symposium, and our Workshops and Tutorials Chair, Lawrence Rauchwerger, for putting together an excellent selection of workshops and tutorials related to parallel programming. Our thanks also go to our Publicity Chair, Basilio Fraguela, our Web Chair, Gokul Kandiraju, our Submissions Chair, Gong Su, and our Finance Chair, Kaoutar El Maghraoui, for their efforts in making PPoPP'14 a reality. We also want to thank the generous financial support from Oracle Labs (sponsor of the Poster Session) and IBM Research, which helped offset the costs of the symposium. Finally, we want to thank the staff of ACM, Sheridan Communications and the Hyatt Regency Orlando, for their hard work under tight deadlines and all the members of the PPoPP Steering Committee for their guidance during the organization of the conference.

We hope that you will find PPoPP'14 an interesting and thought-provoking symposium, and that this event will provide you with a valuable opportunity to share ideas with other researchers and practitioners from institutions around the world.

José Moreira   **James Larus**
PPoPP'14 General Chair   *PPoPP'14 Program Chair*
IBM Research, USA   *EPFL, Switzerland*

Table of Contents

Session Order 11: Non-Blocking Data Structures Session

Session Chair: James Larus *(EPFL)*

Poster Session

PPoPP 2014 Symposium Organization

General Chair: José Moreira *(IBM Research, USA)*

Program Chair: James Larus *(EPFL, Switzerland)*

Local Chair: Mark Heinrich *(University of Central Florida, USA)*

Workshops and Tutorials Chair: Lawrence Rauchwerger *(Texas A&M University, USA)*

Publicity Chair: Basilio Fraguela *(Universidade da Coruña, Spain)*

Web Chair: Gokul Kandiraju *(IBM Research, George Mason Institute, USA)*

Submissions Chair: Gong Su *(IBM Research, USA)*

Finance Chair: Kaoutar El Maghraoui *(IBM Research, USA)*

Steering Committee Chair: Calin Cascaval *(Qualcomm, USA)*

Steering Committee: Mary Hall *(University of Utah, USA)*
David Padua *(University of Illinois at Urbana-Champaign, USA)*
Keshav Pingali *(University of Texas at Austin, USA)*
J. Ramanujam *(Louisiana State University, USA)*
P. Sadayappan *(The Ohio State University, USA)*
Pen-Chung Yew *(Academia Sinica, Taiwan)*

Additional reviewers:

Vikram Adve
Gagan Agrawal
Kunal Agrawal
Sadaf Alam
Saman Amarasinghe
Scott Baden
Michael Bond
Daniel Cederman
Dhruva Chakrabarti
Barbara Chapman
Arun Chauhan
Daniel Chavarría-Miranda
Albert Cohen
Bronis de Supinski
Angela Demke Brown
Brian Demsky
Dave Dice
Mattan Erez
Thomas Fahringer
Michael Garland
Maria Garzaran
Phillip Gibbons
Yuxiong He
Huynh Phung Huynh
Michael Isard
Jungwon Kim
Jens Knoop
Uli Kremer
Sriram Krishnamoorthy
James Larus
Seyong Lee
Jaejin Lee
Yossi Lev
Zhiyuan Li
Dong Li
Kamesh Madduri

Naoya Maruyama
Mario Mendez-Lojo
Samuel Midkiff
Eliot Moss
Frank Mueller
Todd Mytkowicz
Santosh Nagarakatte
Satish Narayanasamy
Rupesh Nasre
Dimitrios Nikolopoulos
David O'Hallaron
David Padua
Vijay Pai
Scott Pakin
Victor Pankratius
Kaushik Rajan
Sanjay Rajopadhye
Zvonimir Rakamaric
Lawrence Rauchwerger
Kamil Rocki
Saday Sadayappan
Michael Scott
Koushik Sen
Marc Shapiro
Tatiana Shpeisman
Arrvindh Shriraman
Stephen Siegel
Marc Snir
Michelle Strout
Gong Su
Kenjiro Taura
Cheng Wang
Kyle Wheeler
Xiaodong Zhang
Huiyang Zhou

PPoPP 2014 Sponsor & Supporters

Sponsor:

Supporters: IBM **Research**

Oracle Labs

21st Century Computer Architecture

CGO/HPCA/PPoPP 2014 Keynote

Mark D. Hill

Computer Sciences Department
University of Wisconsin-Madison
markhill@cs.wisc.edu

Abstract

This talk has two parts. The first part will discuss possible directions for computer architecture research, including architecture as infrastructure, energy first, impact of new technologies, and cross-layer opportunities. This part is based on a 2012 Computing Community Consortium (CCC) whitepaper effort led by Hill, as well as other recent National Academy and ISAT studies. See: http://cra.org/ccc/docs/init/21stcenturyarchitecturewhitepaper.pdf

The second part of the talk will discuss one or more examples of cross-layer research advocated in the first part. For example, our analysis shows that many "big-memory" server workloads, such as databases, in-memory caches, and graph analytics, pay a high cost for page-based virtual memory: up to 50% of execution time wasted. Via small changes to the operating system (Linux) and hardware (x86-64 MMU), this work reduces execution time these workloads waste to less than 0.5%. The key idea is to map part of a process's linear virtual address space with a new incarnation of segmentation, while providing compatibility by mapping the rest of the virtual address space with paging.

Categories and Subject Descriptors   C. [Computer Systems Organization], D. [Software].

General Terms   Algorithms, Measurement, Performance, Design, Economics, Reliability, Security, Languages, Verification.

Keywords   computer systems; architecture; programming methods; performance; energy; new technology.

Biography

Mark D. Hill (http://www.cs.wisc.edu/~markhill) is the Gene M. Amdahl Professor of Computer Sciences and Electrical & Computer Engineering at the University of Wisconsin--Madison, where he also co-leads the Wisconsin Multifacet project. His research interests include parallel computer system design, memory system design, computer simulation, and transactional memory. He earned a PhD from University of California, Berkeley. He is an ACM Fellow, a Fellow of the IEEE, co-inventor on 30+ patents, and ACM SIGARCH Distinguished Service Award recipient. His accomplishments include teaching more than 1000 students, having 40 Ph.D. progeny so far, developing the 3C cache miss taxonomy (compulsory, capacity, and conflict), and co-developing "sequential consistency for data-race free" that serves as a foundation of the C++ and Java memory models.

PPoPP'14, February 15–19, 2014, Orlando, Florida, USA.
ACM 978-1-4503-2656-8/14/02.
http://dx.doi.org/10.1145/2555243.2558890

PREDATOR: Predictive False Sharing Detection

Tongping Liu

School of Computer Science
University of Massachusetts Amherst
tonyliu@cs.umass.edu

Chen Tian   Ziang Hu

Huawei US R&D Center
Chen.Tian@huawei.com,
Ziang.Hu@huawei.com

Emery D. Berger

School of Computer Science
University of Massachusetts Amherst
emery@cs.umass.edu

Abstract

False sharing is a notorious problem for multithreaded applications that can drastically degrade both performance and scalability. Existing approaches can precisely identify the sources of false sharing, but only report false sharing actually observed during execution; they do not generalize across executions. Because false sharing is extremely sensitive to object layout, these detectors can easily miss false sharing problems that can arise due to slight differences in memory allocation order or object placement decisions by the compiler. In addition, they cannot predict the impact of false sharing on hardware with different cache line sizes.

This paper presents PREDATOR, a predictive software-based false sharing detector. PREDATOR generalizes from a single execution to precisely predict false sharing that is latent in the current execution. PREDATOR tracks accesses within a range that could lead to false sharing given different object placement. It also tracks accesses within *virtual cache lines*, contiguous memory ranges that span actual hardware cache lines, to predict sharing on hardware platforms with larger cache line sizes. For each, it reports the exact program location of predicted false sharing problems, ranked by their projected impact on performance. We evaluate PREDATOR across a range of benchmarks and actual applications. PREDATOR identifies problems undetectable with previous tools, including two previously-unknown false sharing problems, with no false positives. PREDATOR is able to immediately locate false sharing problems in MySQL and the Boost library that had eluded detection for years.

Categories and Subject Descriptors D.1.3 [*Software*]: Concurrent Programming–Parallel Programming; D.4.8 [*Software*]: Operating Systems–Performance

PPoPP '14,   February 15–19, 2014, Orlando, Florida, USA.
Copyright © 2014 ACM 978-1-4503-2656-8/14/02... $15.00.
http://dx.doi.org/10.1145/2555243.2555244

General Terms   Performance, Measurement

Keywords   False Sharing, Multi-threaded

1. Introduction

While writing correct multithreaded programs is often challenging, making them scale can present even greater obstacles. Any contention can impair scalability or even cause applications to run slower as the number of threads increases.

False sharing is a particularly insidious form of contention. It occurs when two threads update logically-distinct objects that happen to reside on the same cache line. The resulting coherence traffic can degrade performance by an order of magnitude [4]. Unlike sources of contention like locks, false sharing is often invisible in the source code, making it difficult to find.

As cache lines have grown larger and multithreaded applications have become commonplace, false sharing has become an increasingly important problem. Performance degradation due to false sharing has been detected across the software stack, including inside the Linux kernel [5], the Java virtual machine [8], common libraries [19] and widely-used applications [20, 23].

Recent work on false sharing detection falls short in several dimensions. Some introduce excessive performance overhead, making them impractical [9, 16, 26]. Most do not report false sharing precisely and accurately [9–11, 16, 24, 28], and some require special OS support or only work on a restricted class of applications [17, 21].

In addition, all of these systems share one key limitation: they can only report *observed* cases of false sharing. As Nanavati et al. point out, false sharing is sensitive to where objects are placed in cache lines and so can be affected by a wide range of factors [21]. For example, using the gcc compiler *accidentally* eliminates false sharing in the Phoenix linear_regression benchmark at certain optimization levels, while LLVM does not do so at any optimization level. A slightly different memory allocation sequence (or different memory allocator) can reveal or hide false sharing, depending on where objects end up in memory; using a different hardware platform with different addressing or cache line sizes can have the same effect. All of this means that existing tools cannot root out potentially devastating cases of false sharing that could arise with different inputs, in different execution environments, and on different hardware platforms.

This paper makes the following contributions:

- **Predictive False Sharing Detection:** This paper introduces *predictive false sharing analysis*, an approach that can *predict* potential false sharing that does not manifest in a given run but may appear—and greatly degrade application performance—in a slightly different execution environment. Predictive false sharing detection thus overcomes a key limitation of previous detection tools.

- **A Practical and Effective Predictive False Sharing Detector:** This paper presents PREDATOR, a prototype predictive false sharing detector that combines compiler-based instrumentation with a runtime system. PREDATOR not only *detects* but also *predicts* potential false sharing problems. PREDATOR operates with reasonable overhead (average: $6\times$ performance, $2\times$ memory). It is the first false sharing tool able to automatically and precisely uncover false sharing problems in real applications, including MySQL and the Boost library.

2. False Sharing Detection

We first describe PREDATOR's false sharing detection mechanism, which comprises both compiler and runtime system components. Section 3 then explains how PREDATOR predicts potential false sharing based on a single execution.

2.1 Overview

False sharing occurs when two threads simultaneously access logically independent data in the same cache line, and where at least one of the accesses is a write. For the purposes of exposition, we assume that each thread runs on a distinct core with its own private cache.

We observe that if a thread writes a cache line after other threads have accessed the same cache line, this write operation most likely causes at least one cache invalidation. It is this invalidation traffic that leads to performance degradation due to false sharing. To identify the root cause of such traffic due to false sharing, PREDATOR tracks cache invalidations of all cache lines, and ranks the severity of performance degradation of any detected false sharing problems according to the number of cache invalidations.

To track cache invalidations, PREDATOR relies on compiler instrumentation to track accesses to memory. While a compiler can easily identify read or write accesses, it cannot know how and when those instructions are being executed, since that depends on a specific execution, input, and runtime environment.

Therefore, PREDATOR combines compiler instrumentation with a runtime system to track cache invalidations. The compiler instruments memory accesses with calls to the runtime system that notify it when an access occurs (see Section 2.2), and the runtime system collects and analyzes these accesses to detect and report false sharing (see Section 2.3).

2.2 Compiler Instrumentation

PREDATOR relies on LLVM to perform instrumentation at the intermediate representation level [15]. It traverses all functions one by one and searches for memory accesses to global and heap variables. For each memory access, PREDATOR inserts a function call to invoke the runtime system with the memory access address and access type (read or write). PREDATOR currently omits accesses to stack variables by default because stack variables are normally used for thread local storage and therefore do not normally introduce false sharing. However, instrumentation on stack variables can always be turned on if desired.

The instrumentation pass is placed at the very end of the LLVM optimization passes so that only those memory accesses surviving all previous LLVM optimization passes are instrumented. This technique, which can drastically reduce the number of instrumentation calls, is similar to the one used by AddressSanitizer [27].

2.3 Runtime System

PREDATOR's runtime system collects every memory access via the functions calls inserted by the compiler's instrumentation phase. It analyzes possible cache invalidations due to possibly interleaved reads and writes. Finally, PREDATOR precisely reports any performance-degrading false sharing problems it finds. For global variables involved in false sharing, PREDATOR reports their name, address and size; for heap objects, PREDATOR reports the callsite stack for their allocations, their address and size. In addition, PREDATOR provides word granularity access information for those cache lines involved in false sharing, including which threads accessed which words. This information can further help users diagnose and fix false sharing instances.

2.3.1 Tracking Cache Invalidations

PREDATOR only reports those global variables or heap objects on cache lines with a large number of cache invalidations. It is critical that PREDATOR track cache invalidations precisely in order to provide accurate reports of the location of false sharing instances. PREDATOR achieves this goal by maintaining a two entry cache history table for every cache line. In this table, each entry has two fields: the thread ID and access type (read or write). The thread ID is used to identify the origin of each access. As stated earlier, only accesses from different threads can cause cache invalidations.

For every new access to a cache line L, PREDATOR checks L's history table T to decide whether there is a cache invalidation based on the following rules. Note that table T only has two statuses: full and not full. There is no "empty" status since every cache invalidation should replace this table with the current write access.

- For each read access R,
  - If T is full, there is no need to record this read access.
  - If T is not full and another existing entry has a different thread ID, then PREDATOR records this read and its thread by adding a new entry to the table.
- For each write access W,
  - If T is full, then W can cause a cache invalidation since at least one of two existing entries has a different thread ID. After recording this invalidation, PREDATOR updates the existing entry with W and its thread.
  - If T is not full, PREDATOR checks whether W and the existing entry have the same thread ID. If so, W cannot cause a cache invalidation, so PREDATOR updates the existing entry with W. Otherwise, PREDATOR identifies an invalidation on this line caused by W. After recording this invalidation information, PREDATOR updates the existing entry with W and its thread.

2.3.2 Reporting False Sharing

Once cache lines with many cache invalidations have been detected, PREDATOR needs to perform further analysis to differentiate actual false sharing from true sharing. True sharing, e.g., multiple threads updating the same counter in a cache line, can also cause many cache invalidations.

In order to report false sharing precisely and accurately, PREDATOR employs the following mechanisms:

Distinguishing False from True Sharing. PREDATOR keeps track of access information for each word on those cache lines involved in false sharing: how many reads or writes to each word by which thread. When a word is accessed by multiple threads, PREDATOR marks the origin of this word as a shared access and does not track threads for further accesses to it. This approach lets PREDATOR accurately distinguish false sharing from true sharing in the reporting phase. It also helps diagnose where actual false sharing occurs when there are multiple fields or multiple objects in the same cache line, as this can greatly reduce the manual effort required to fix the false sharing problems.

Callsite Tracking for Heap Objects. In order to precisely report the origins of heap objects with false sharing problems, PREDATOR maintains detailed information so it can report source code level information for each heap object. To obtain callsite information, PREDATOR intercepts all memory allocations and de-allocations, and relies on the `backtrace()` function in the `glibc` library to obtain the whole callsite stack. PREDATOR also avoids pseudo false sharing (false positives) caused by memory reuse because it updates recording information at memory de-allocations for those objects without false sharing problems; heap objects involved in false sharing are never reused.

Optimizing Metadata Lookup. For every access, PREDATOR needs to look up the corresponding cache line's meta-

data in order to store detailed information or update access counters. Because this operation is so frequent, lookups need to be very efficient. Like AddressSanitizer [27] and other systems [22, 28], PREDATOR uses a shadow memory mechanism to store metadata for every piece of application data. Thus, PREDATOR can compute and locate corresponding metadata directly via address arithmetic.

Custom Memory Allocation. In order to efficiently support shadow memory, PREDATOR uses a predefined starting address and fixed size for its heap. It also contains a custom memory allocator, which is built with Heap Layers [2] using a "per-thread-heap" mechanism similar to that used by Hoard [1]. In this allocator, memory allocations from different threads never occupy the same physical cache line, which automatically prevents false sharing among different objects. However, using this custom memory allocator implies that false sharing caused by a memory allocator cannot be detected by PREDATOR. It is straightforward to solve such false sharing problems by using an allocator like Hoard that avoids this kind of false sharing.

2.4 Optimizations

Tracking every memory access can be extremely expensive. PREDATOR utilizes the following mechanisms to further reduce overhead.

2.4.1 Threshold-Based Tracking Mechanism

PREDATOR aims to detect false sharing that significantly degrades performance. Since cache invalidations are the root cause of performance degradation and only writes can possibly introduce cache invalidations, cache lines with a small number of writes are never a significant performance bottleneck. For this reason, PREDATOR only tracks cache invalidations once the number of writes to a cache line crosses a predefined threshold, which we refer to as the *TrackingThreshold*. Until this threshold is reached, PREDATOR only tracks the number of writes on a cache line while skipping tracking for reads. This mechanism reduces runtime and memory overhead at the same time.

PREDATOR maintains two arrays in shadow memory: *CacheWrites* tracks the number of memory writes to every cache line, and *CacheTracking* tracks detailed information for each cache line once the number of writes on a cache line exceeds the *TrackingThreshold*. If the threshold is not reached, there is no need to check the corresponding *CacheTracking* entry.

To avoid expensive lock operations, PREDATOR uses atomic instruction to increment the *CacheWrites* counter for each cache line. Once the number of writes of a cache line reaches the predefined threshold, PREDATOR allocates space to track detailed cache invalidations and word accesses. PREDATOR also uses an atomic compare-and-swap to set the cache tracking address for this cache line in the shadow mapping. After *CacheWrites* on a cache line have

```
void HandleAccess(unsigned long addr, bool isWrite) {
unsigned long cacheIndex = addr>>CACHELINE_SIZE_SHIFTS;
CacheTrack *track = NULL;

if (CacheWrites[cacheIndex] < TRACKING_THRESHOLD) {
if (isWrite) {
if (ATOMIC_INCR(&CacheWrites[cacheIndex])
>= TRACKING_THRESHOLD) {
track = allocCacheTrack();
ATOMIC_CAS(&CacheTracking[cacheIndex], 0, track));
}
}
} else {
track = CacheTracking[index];
if (track) {
// Track cache invalidations and detailed accesses
track->handleAccess(addr, isWrite);
}
}
}
```

Figure 1. Pseudo-code for PREDATOR's memory access instrumentation.

crossed the *TrackingThreshold*, PREDATOR tracks all read and write accesses to this cache line.

2.4.2 Selective Compiler Instrumentation

PREDATOR relies on instrumentation to provide memory access information to the runtime system and detects false sharing based on the sequences of memory accesses to every cache line. The performance overhead of doing this is proportional to the degree of instrumentation: more instrumentation means higher performance overhead. PREDATOR's design makes it possible to trade performance and accuracy as needed.

Currently, PREDATOR only adds instrumentation once for each type of memory access on each address in the same basic block. This selective instrumentation does not normally affect the effectiveness of detection. Because PREDATOR aims to detect cases of false sharing with many cache invalidations, less tracking inside a basic block can induce fewer cache invalidations, but this does not affect the overall behavior of cache invalidations.

To further improve performance, PREDATOR could easily be extended to support more flexible instrumentation:

- PREDATOR could selectively instrument both reads and writes or only writes. Instrumenting only writes reduces overhead while detecting write-write false sharing, as SHERIFF does [17].

- PREDATOR can be set to instrument or skip specific code or data. For example, the user could provide a blacklist so that given modules, functions or variables are not instrumented. Conversely, the user could provide a whitelist so that only specified functions or variables are instrumented.

2.4.3 Sampling Mechanism

As Section 2.4.1 describes, once the number of writes on a cache line exceeds the *TrackingThreshold*, every access must

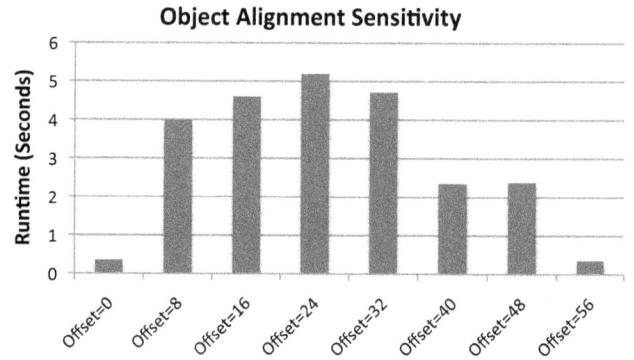

Figure 2. Performance of the linear_regression benchmark from the Phoenix benchmark suite. Performance is highly sensitive to the offset of the starting address of the (potentially) falsely-shared object from the start of the cache line.

be tracked to store details such as word access information, the access count, and the cache access history table of this cache line. When a cache line is involved in false or true sharing, updating those counters can exacerbate the impact of sharing on performance: not only is there an invalidation on an application cache line, but there is also at least another cache invalidation caused by updating the metadata of the corresponding cache lines.

To further reduce performance overhead, PREDATOR only samples the first specified number of accesses of each sampling interval for problematic cache lines. Currently, PREDATOR maintains an access counter for each cache line and only tracks the first $10,000$ out of every 1 million accesses to a cache line (a 1% sampling rate).

3. False Sharing Prediction

This section further motivates predictive false sharing and explains how to support it in the runtime system.

3.1 Overview

False sharing can depend on the alignment of objects and corresponding cache lines. Figure 2 demonstrates the impact of placement on linear_regression, a benchmark from the Phoenix benchmark suite. For this benchmark, when the offset of the starting address between the potentially falsely-shared object and corresponding cache lines is 0 or 56 bytes, there is no false sharing. When the offset is 24 bytes, we see the most severe performance effect caused by false sharing. The performance difference between these two scenarios can be as great as $15\times$.

Existing detection tools only report observed false sharing. In this case, they would miss a severe false sharing problem that could occur in the wild if the offset of the starting address was 0 bytes or 56 bytes in their test environment. PREDATOR overcomes this shortcoming by accurately predicting potential false sharing.

PREDATOR predicts *potential false sharing*, the type of false sharing that does not manifest in the current execution but may appear and greatly affect programs' performance in a slightly different environment.

Figure 3 presents a simplified overview of how false sharing can be triggered by different environments. In this figure, two rectangles with different patterns represent two portions of the same object, updated by different threads. In Figure 3(a), there is no false sharing when thread T1 only updates cache line 1 and T2 only updates cache line 2. However, false sharing appears in each of the following cases, even with the same access pattern:

- **Doubling the cache line size.** (Figure 3(b)) When the size of a cache line doubles, both T1 and T2 access the same cache line, leading to false sharing.

- **Different object starting addresses.** (Figure 3(c)) If the starting address of the object is not aligned with the starting address of the first cache line, T1 and T2 can update the second cache line simultaneously, causing false sharing.

PREDATOR predicts whether programs can have potential false sharing in either of these two scenarios. These scenarios capture the impact of any change in the execution environment, such as a different hardware platform or a different memory allocation sequence.

3.2 Basic Prediction Workflow

PREDATOR focuses exclusively on potential false sharing that can cause performance problems. Its implementation is based on two key observations. First, only accesses to adjacent cache lines can lead to potential false sharing: that is, they introduce cache invalidations when the cache line size or an object's starting address changes. Second, only when false sharing introduces a large number of cache invalidations can it degrade performance.

Based on these two observations, PREDATOR employs the following workflow to detect potential false sharing. Note that the detection optimizations listed in Section 2.4 apply directly to prediction as well.

1. Track the number of writes to different cache lines.

2. When the number of writes to a cache line L reaches *TrackingThreshold*, track detailed read and write accesses for every word in both cache line L and its adjacent cache lines.

3. When the number of writes to a cache line L crosses a second threshold (the *PredictionThreshold*), identify whether there exists false sharing in L and its adjacent cache lines by analyzing word access information collected in Step 2. Section 3.3 describes this process.

4. If potential false sharing is found, continue to track cache line invalidations to confirm it. Section 3.4 discusses the details.

3.3 Searching for Potential False Sharing

To predict potential false sharing in the cases when either the hardware cache line size doubles or when object placement changes, we first introduce the concept of a *virtual cache line*. A virtual cache line is a contiguous memory range that spans one or more physical cache lines.

Using virtual cache lines lets PREDATOR predict potential false sharing in both of the scenarios mentioned above. When the hardware cache line size doubles, a virtual line is composed of two original contiguous cache lines and the first cache line has an even index number. Thus, only cache lines $2*i$ and $2*i+1$ can form a virtual line. To predict false sharing due to different starting addresses, a virtual line can have the same size as physical lines, but can be positioned arbitrarily: unlike actual cache lines, the starting address of a virtual cache line does not need to be multiple of the cache line size. For instance, a 64-byte long virtual line can consist of the range $[0, 64)$ bytes or $[8, 72)$ bytes.

To search for potential false sharing problems, PREDATOR searches for a hot access pair on line L and its adjacent cache lines by analyzing the detailed word access information collected in Step 2. A hot access in a cache line refers to a word whose number of read or write accesses is larger than the average number of accesses to each word of cache line L. For every hot access X in cache line L, PREDATOR searches for another hot access Y in L's previous cache line or next cache line satisfying the following conditions: (1) X and Y reside in the same virtual line; (2) at least one of X or Y are a write access; and (3) X and Y are issued by different threads.

Whenever it finds such a pair X and Y, PREDATOR identifies potential performance-degrading false sharing whenever the number of cache invalidations caused by X and Y, at a possible virtual line, is greater than the average number of accesses on each word of L. This approach is based on a the same observation as in detection: *if a thread writes a virtual line after other threads have accessed the same virtual line, this write operation most likely causes at least one cache invalidation.* PREDATOR conservatively assumes that accesses from different threads occurs in an interleaved manner; that is, it assumes that the schedule exposes false sharing. This approach ensures that PREDATOR does not miss any potential false sharing cases.

After identifying possible false sharing, PREDATOR goes to Step 4 to verify whether this is an actual false sharing problem.

3.4 Verifying Potential False Sharing

PREDATOR verifies potential false sharing by tracking cache invalidations of a problematic virtual line.

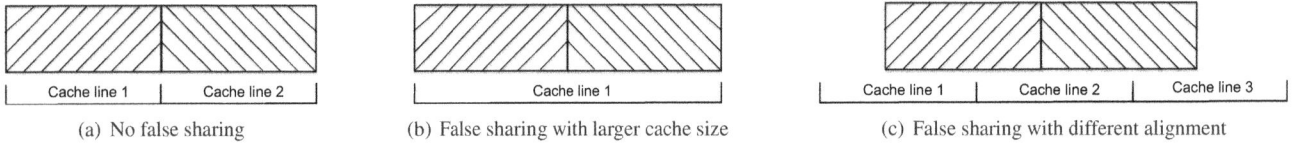

| (a) No false sharing | (b) False sharing with larger cache size | (c) False sharing with different alignment |

Figure 3. False sharing under different scenarios (see Section 3.1).

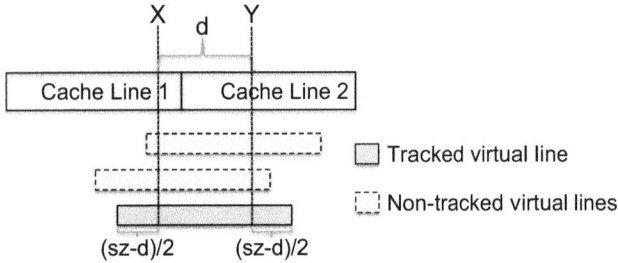

Figure 4. Determining a virtual line with size sz according to hot accesses (see Section 3.4).

For potential false sharing caused by double cache line size, as described in Section 3.3, a virtual line is always composed of cache line with index $2 * i$ and $2 * i + 1$. PREDATOR tracks cache invalidations on the virtual line on which false sharing has been discovered.

However, for the case of a change in starting address, two hot accesses with a distance less than the cache line size can form multiple virtual lines. There is thus an additional step required to determine which virtual line needs to be tracked.

Given two words with the hot accesses shown in Figure 4, PREDATOR leaves the same space before X and after Y in determining a virtual line. That is, the virtual line starting at location $X - ((sz - d)/2)$ and ending at $Y + ((sz - d)/2)$ is tracked. This choice allows tracking more possible cache invalidations caused by adjacent accesses to X and Y. Since adjusting the starting address of a virtual line has the same effect as adjusting the starting address of an object in detecting false sharing, all cache lines related to the same object must be adjusted at the same time. PREDATOR then tracks cache invalidations based on these adjusted virtual lines.

4. Experimental Evaluation

This section answers the following questions:

- How effective is PREDATOR at detecting and predicting false sharing (§ 4.1)?

- What is PREDATOR's overhead, in terms of execution time (§ 4.2) and memory (§ 4.3)?

- How sensitive is PREDATOR to different sampling rates (§ 4.4)?

Experimental Platform. All evaluations are performed on a quiescent Intel Core 2 dual-processor system equipped with 16GB RAM. Each processor is a 4-core 64-bit Intel Xeon running at 2.33 GHz, with a 4MB shared L2 cache and 32KB private L1 cache. The underlying operating system is an unmodified CentOS 5.5, running with Linux kernel version 2.6.18-194.17.1.el5. We use glibc version 2.5 and LLVM version 3.2. All applications were compiled as 64-bit executables with the optimization level set to $-O1$ in order to maintain accurate source code line number information.

Evaluated Applications. This paper evaluates two popular benchmark suites, Phoenix (with large input) [25] and PARSEC (with simlarge input) [3]. We were unable to include two of the benchmarks. LLVM does not compile Facesim successfully, reporting an undefined template. Canneal compiles but then aborts unexpectedly. We also evaluate PREDATOR on six real applications: MySQL, Boost, Memcached, aget, pbzip2 and pfscan.

4.1 Detection and Prediction Effectiveness

For every detected or predicted false sharing problem, PREDATOR reports source code information and detailed memory access information. Figure 5 shows an example for the linear_regression benchmark. This report shows that the heap object starting with $0x40000038$ potentially causes numerous cache invalidations. The allocation callsite is provided to help locate culprits. In addition, PREDATOR also reports word-level access information of this object, which makes it possible for the developer to identify where and how false sharing occurs. From this information, we can see that this instance is a latent false sharing problem predicted by PREDATOR, since different threads are accessing different hardware cache lines.

4.1.1 Benchmarks

Table 1 provides detection results across the Phoenix and PARSEC benchmark suites. The first column lists the programs with false sharing problems. The second column shows precisely where the problem is. Because all discovered false sharing occurs inside heap objects, we present callsite source code information here. The third column, *New*, indicates whether this false sharing was newly discovered by PREDATOR. A checkmark in the following two columns indicates whether the false sharing was identified without prediction and/or with prediction. The final column, *Improvement*, presents the performance improvement after fixing false sharing.

```
FALSE SHARING HEAP OBJECT: start 0x40000038 end 0x40000238 (with size 200).
Number of accesses: 5153102690; Number of invalidations: 175020; Number of writes: 13636004.

Callsite stack:
  ./stddefines.h:53
  ./linear_regression-pthread.c:133

Word level information:
  ......
    Address 0x40000070 (line 16777217): reads 339508  writes 339507 by thread 1
    Address 0x40000080 (line 16777218): reads 2716059 writes 0       by thread 2
  ......
    Address 0x400000b0 (line 16777218): reads 339507  writes 339508 by thread 2
    Address 0x400000c0 (line 16777219): reads 2716061 writes 0       by thread 3
    Address 0x400000c8 (line 16777219): reads 339507  writes 0       by thread 3
```

Figure 5. An example report by PREDATOR indicating false sharing in the linear_regression benchmark.

Benchmark	Source Code	New	Without Prediction	With Prediction	Improvement
histogram	histogram-pthread.c:213	✔	✔	✔	46.22%
linear_regression	linear_regression-pthread.c:133			✔	1206.93%
reverse_index	reverseindex-pthread.c:511		✔	✔	0.09%
word_count	word_count-pthread.c:136		✔	✔	0.14%
streamcluster	streamcluster.cpp:985		✔	✔	7.52%
streamcluster	streamcluster.cpp:1907	✔	✔	✔	4.77%

Table 1. False sharing problems in the Phoenix and PARSEC benchmark suites.

As the table shows, PREDATOR reveals two previously unknown false sharing problems. It is the first tool to detect false sharing problems in histogram and in line 1908 of streamcluster. In histogram, multiple threads simultaneously modify different locations of the same heap object, thread_arg_t. Padding this data structure eliminates false sharing and improves performance by around 46%. In streamcluster, multiple threads simultaneously access and update the same `bool` array, switch_membership. Simply changing all elements of this array to a `long` type reduces the false sharing and improves performance by about 4.7%.

Other false sharing problems reported here were also discovered by previous work [17]. We do not see significant performance improvement for the reverse_index and word_count benchmarks. They are reported here because the number of cache invalidations in these two programs crosses our predefined threshold. Increasing PREDATOR's reporting threshold would avoid reporting these cases, which are relatively insignificant. Nonetheless, it is worth noting that these two benchmarks do indeed have false sharing problems, which can be confirmed by the word-level information generated by PREDATOR.

The streamcluster benchmark has another false sharing problem located at line 985. Different threads repeatedly update the work_mem object. The authors of streamcluster were clearly aware of this issue and provide a CACHE_LINE macro for padding. Unfortunately, the default value of this macro is set to 32 bytes, which is smaller than the actual cache line size of the experimental machine. Setting it to 64 bytes instead improves performance by about 7.5%.

The linear_regression benchmark has an unusually severe false sharing problem. Fixing it improves performance by more than 12×. In this benchmark, different threads repeatedly update their thread-specific locations inside the tid_args object inside a tight loop. Interestingly, Nanavati et al. observe that this false sharing problem occurs when using clang and disappears when using gcc with the -O2 and -O3 optimization levels [21]. However, we observe a different result when using our version of clang and the custom memory allocator: the false sharing problem *does not occur at all* because the offset of the starting address of the potentially falsely-shared object and the start of cache line is 56 bytes (see Figure 2). As we discuss below, PREDATOR's prediction mechanism identifies this latent false sharing problem, highlighting the value of predictive detection.

4.1.2 Real Applications

We evaluate PREDATOR's effectiveness on several widely-used real applications. These applications include a MySQL, a database server [20]; Boost, a standard C++ library [19]; Memcached, a distributed memory object caching system; aget, a download accelerator; pbzip2, a parallel bzip2 file compressor; and pfscan, a parallel file scanner.

MySQL-5.5.32 and boost-1.49.0 are known to have false sharing problems. The other applications we examine (memcached-1.4.15, aget-0.4.1 and pbzip2-1.1.6) do not have any known false sharing problems.

MySQL's false sharing problem caused a significant scalability problem and was very difficult to identify. According to the architect of MySQL, Mikael Ronstrom, "we had gathered specialists on InnoDB..., participants from MySQL

```
struct
{
  pthread_t tid;   POINT_T *points;
  int num_elems;   long long SX;
  long long SY;    long long SXX;
  long long SYY;   long long SXY;
} lreg_args;

void * lreg_thread ( void * args_in ) {
  struct lreg_args * args = args_in ;
  for(i=0; i<args->num_elems; i++) {
    args->SX+=args->points[i].x;
    args->SXX+=args->points[i].x*args->points[i].x;
    args->SY+=args->points[i].y;
    args->SYY+=args->points[i].y*args->points[i].y;
    args->SXY+=args->points[i].x*args->points[i].y;
  }
}
```

Figure 6. The false sharing problem inside the linear_regression benchmark: multiple threads simultaneously update their entries in lreg_args.

support... and a number of generic specialists on computer performance...", "[we] were able to improve MySQL performance by 6× with those scalability fixes" [20]. The false sharing inside Boost is caused by the usage of a spinlock pool. Different threads may utilize different spinlocks located in the same cache line in this case. Fixing it brings a 40% performance improvement. PREDATOR is able to pinpoint the false sharing locations in both MySQL and the Boost library. For the other four applications, PREDATOR does not identify any severe false sharing problems.

4.1.3 Prediction Effectiveness

In this section, we describe in detail our experience with a particular benchmark that demonstrates the value of our approach. We use the linear_regression benchmark as a case study for the following reasons: (1) the false sharing problem of this benchmark cannot be detected without prediction; (2) false sharing severely degrades performance when it actually occurs. Hence, it is a serious problem that should always be detected.

Figure 6 shows the data structure and the source code experiencing false sharing. The size of this data structure, lreg_args, is 64 bytes when the program is compiled to a 64-bit binary. For this benchmark, the main thread allocates an array containing as many elements as the number of underlying hardware cores. Each element is a lreg_args type with 64 bytes. This array is then passed to different threads (lreg_thread function) so that each thread only updates its thread-dependent area. False sharing occurs if two threads happen to update data in the same cache line.

Figure 2 shows how sensitive linear_regression's performance is to different starting addresses of a falsely-shared object. When the offset is 0 or 56 bytes, this benchmark achieves its optimal performance and has no false sharing. When the offset is 24 bytes, the benchmark runs around 15× slower because of false sharing.

4.2 Performance Overhead

Figure 7 presents runtime overhead for using PREDATOR. All measurements are based on the average of 10 runs, excluding the maximum and minimum values. PREDATOR imposes an average of 5.4× performance overhead. There is no noticeable difference on performance whether the prediction mechanism is enabled or not.

Five of these (histogram, kmeans, bodytrack, ferret, and swaptions), have more than 8× performance overhead. The histogram benchmark runs more than 26× slower because tracking detailed accesses to cache lines with false sharing exacerbates the false sharing effect (see Section 2.4.3). Although bodytrack and ferret have no false sharing, PREDATOR detects numerous cache lines with writes that exceed the *TrackingThreshold*, causing it to track detailed access information. We have not identified the exact cause of PREDATOR's high performance overhead for kmeans.

As expected, PREDATOR imposes relatively little overhead for I/O-bound applications (matrix_multiply, blackscholes, x264, aget, Memcached, pbzip2, and pfscan).

4.3 Memory Overhead

Figure 9 and 8 present PREDATOR's relative and absolute memory overhead, respectively. We compute PREDATOR's physical memory consumption via the proportional set size (PSS) obtained from the /proc/self/smaps file [14]. We periodically collect this data and use the sum of all memory mappings as the total physical memory usage of running an application.

PREDATOR imposes less than 50% memory overhead for 17 out of 22 applications. For swaptions and aget, PREDATOR introduces high *relative* memory overhead because their original memory footprints are extraordinarily small: both have sub-megabyte footprints. MySQL's increase in memory consumption, from 132 MB to 512 MB, is due to PREDATOR's heap organization, which does not aggressively reclaim memory held by individual threads. In all cases where PREDATOR's imposes substantial memory overhead, the applications continue to comfortably fit into RAM on modern platforms.

4.4 Sensitivity to Different Sampling Rates

Section 2.4.3 describes PREDATOR's sampling approach to reduce tracking overhead. This section evaluates the effect of different sampling rates on performance and effectiveness. Note that running an application with different sampling rates does not affect its memory usage.

The default sampling rate used by PREDATOR is 1%. To test PREDATOR's sensitivity to this choice, we evaluate performance on a representative subset of the benchmarks with two other sampling rates: 0.1% and 10%. Figure 10 presents the results. As expected, PREDATOR introduces lower performance overhead at lower sampling rates. Even when using the 0.1% sampling rate, PREDATOR is still able to detect

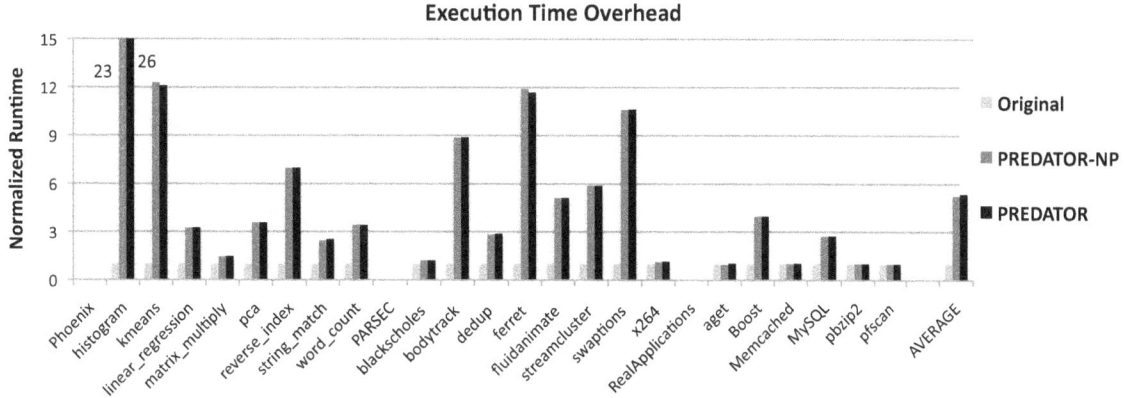

Figure 7. Execution time overhead of PREDATOR with and without prediction (PREDATOR-NP).

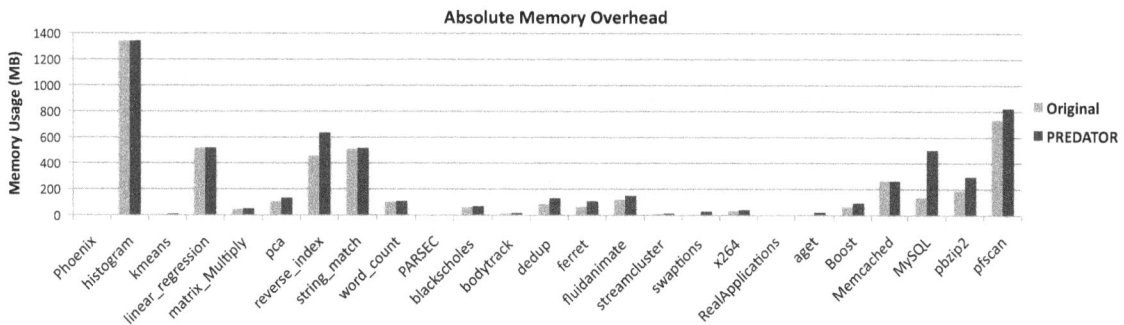

Figure 8. Absolute physical memory usage overhead with PREDATOR.

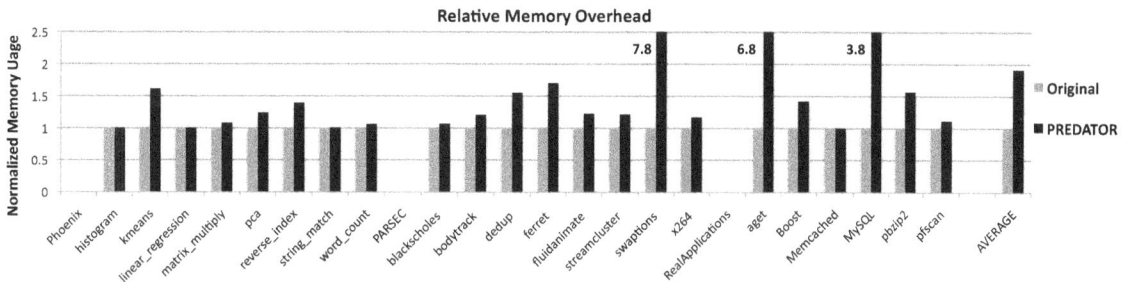

Figure 9. Relative physical memory usage overhead with PREDATOR.

all false sharing problems reported here, although it reports a lower number of cache invalidations.

5. Discussion

5.1 Instrumentation Selection

Dynamic binary instrumentation and compiler-based instrumentation are two alternative approaches for performing instrumentation [12]. They exhibit different tradeoffs of performance and generality. Dynamic binary instrumentors, such as Valgrind [22], Pin [18], and DynamoRIO [6], typically analyze the program's code just before execution in order to insert instrumentation. They introduce significant performance overhead, mostly caused by run-time encoding and decoding, but the fact that they operate directly on bi-

naries makes them extremely convenient. By contrast, compiler instrumentation inserts instrumentation in the compilation phase, which requires re-compilation of all source code. PREDATOR employs compiler-based instrumentation both because of its better performance and its greater flexibility, as discussed in Section 2.4.2.

5.2 Effectiveness

Several factors can affect PREDATOR's ability to identify false sharing.

Different Inputs. Different inputs trigger distinct executions of a program. If a specific input does not exercise the code with false sharing problems, PREDATOR cannot necessarily detect them. However, PREDATOR does generalize

11

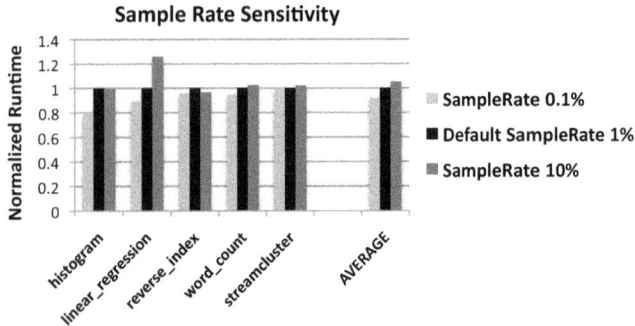

Figure 10. Sampling rate sensitivity (execution time).

over inputs to find latent false sharing problems on those exercised code. When any reasonably representative set of inputs are exercised, as is required by any testing regime, PREDATOR can effectively predict false sharing.

Input Size. Input size may affect detection results. As discussed in Section 2.4, PREDATOR introduces several threshold values to reduce tracking overhead, which can be adjusted as needed. If the input size is so small that it cannot generate enough false sharing events to cross the predefined thresholds, then the detection mechanism will not be triggered. In such cases, PREDATOR will miss actual cases of false sharing. However, realistically large inputs should be enough to trigger PREDATOR's detection mechanisms. In our experience, running applications for at least 150 seconds is sufficient to expose false sharing problems.

Hardware Independence. PREDATOR's compiler-based approach make it independent of the underlying hardware platform. This approach increases generality, but may lead it to over-report false sharing. PREDATOR conservatively assumes that different threads are running on different cores and detects false sharing problems based on possible cache invalidations. However, if multiple threads involved in false sharing are on the same core, then there will be no performance impact.

6. Future Work

We have identified several directions along which PREDATOR could be enhanced.

Use Across the Software Stack. PREDATOR's architecture should in principle let it detect and predict false sharing in the entire software stack, including hypervisors, operating systems, libraries, and applications using different threading libraries.

Improved Performance. PREDATOR currently imposes approximately 6× performance overhead. In the current implementation, every memory access is instrumented with a library call to notify the runtime system. A library call entails not only normal function call overhead but also Global Offset Table (GOT) and/or Procedure Linkage Table (PLT)

lookup overhead. We plan to improve PREDATOR's performance by inserting relevant code directly, rather than via function calls.

Suggest Fixes. Finally, we would like to enhance PREDATOR's reporting. We believe that leveraging memory trace information will make it possible for PREDATOR to prescribe fixes to the programmer to help them eliminate false sharing.

7. Related Work

This section describes related work in detecting or preventing false sharing; no prior work predicts false sharing.

7.1 False Sharing Detection

Schindewolf et al. designed a tool based on the SIMICS functional simulator to report different kinds of cache usage information, such as cache misses and cache invalidations [26]. Pluto relies on the Valgrind dynamic instrumentation framework to track the sequence of memory read and write events on different threads, and reports a worst-case estimation of possible false sharing [9]. Similarly, Liu uses Pin to collect memory access information, and reports total cache miss information [16]. These tools impose about $100 - 200\times$ performance overhead.

Zhao et al. present a tool based on the DynamoRIO framework to detect false sharing and other cache contention problems for multithreading programs [28]. It uses a shadow memory technique to maintain memory access history and detects cache invalidations based on the ownership of cache lines. However, it can only support at most 8 threads. In addition, it cannot differentiate cold cache misses from actual false sharing problems.

Intel's performance tuning utility (PTU) uses Precise Event Based Sampling (PEBS) hardware support to detect false sharing problems [10, 11]. PTU cannot distinguish true sharing from false sharing. In addition, PTU aggregates memory accesses without considering memory reuse and access interleavings, leading to numerous false positives. Sanath et al. designed a machine learning based approach to detect false sharing problems. They train their classifier on mini-programs and apply this classifier to general programs [13]. Instead of instrumenting memory accesses, this tool relies on hardware performance counters to collect memory accesses events. This approach operates with extremely low overhead but ties false sharing detection to a specific hardware platform.

In addition to their individual disadvantages, all approaches discussed above share a common shortcoming: they cannot pinpoint the exact location of false sharing in the source code, so programmers must manually examine the source code to identify problems.

Pesterev et al. present DProf, a tool that help programmers identify cache misses based on AMD's instruction-based sampling hardware [24]. DProf requires manual annotation to locate data types and object fields, and cannot detect false sharing when multiple objects reside on the same cache line.

7.2 False Sharing Prevention

Jeremiassen and Eggers use a compiler transformation to automatically adjust the memory layout of applications through padding and alignment citefalseshare:compile. Chow et al. alter parallel loop scheduling in order to avoid false sharing [7]. These approaches only works for regular, array-based scientific code.

Berger et al. describe Hoard, a scalable memory allocator that can reduce the possibility of false sharing by making different threads use different heaps [1]. Hoard cannot avoid false sharing problem in global variables or within a single heap object: the latter appears to be the primary source of false sharing problems.

7.3 False Sharing Detection and Prevention

SHERIFF provides two tools to handle false sharing based on its "threads-as-processes" framework [17]. SHERIFF's detection tool reports false sharing accurately and precisely with only 20% performance overhead. However, it can only detect write-write false sharing, and only works for programs that use the `pthreads` library. It can also break programs that communicate across different threads with stack variables or *ad hoc* synchronizations. These shortcomings limit SHERIFF's usefulness for real-world applications. PREDATOR can detect all kinds of false sharing and imposes no limitations on the kind of applications it works on.

SHERIFF's prevention tool prevents false sharing altogether, eliminating the need for programmer intervention. However, in programs with many synchronization calls, the overhead imposed by SHERIFF could lead to performance degradation.

Plastic leverages the sub-page granularity memory remapping facility provided by the Xen hypervisor to detect and tolerate false sharing automatically [21]. However, the sub-page memory remapping mechanism is not currently supported by most existing operating systems, reducing its generality. In addition, Plastic cannot pinpoint the exact source of false sharing. In order to utilize Plastic's prevention tool, a program has to run on the Xen hypervisor, limiting the applicability of their prevention technique.

8. Conclusion

This paper introduces *predictive false sharing detection*, and presents a prototype system that performs this detection called PREDATOR. By collecting and analyzing information through instrumented reads and writes, the runtime system detects false sharing based on cache invalidations and only reports those potentially causing severe performance degradation. PREDATOR predicts potential false sharing that could be caused by a change of hardware cache line size or the starting addresses of objects. By identifying latent false

sharing problems that can occur in the wild but which are unobserved in the test environment, PREDATOR overcomes a key limitation of all previous false sharing detection approaches.

Our evaluation shows that PREDATOR can effectively detect and predict several previously unknown and existing false sharing problems in two popular benchmark suites, Phoenix and PARSEC. We also evaluate PREDATOR on six real applications. It successfully detects two known false sharing problems inside MySQL and the Boost library. Fixing these false sharing problems improves performance by $6\times$ and 40%, respectively.

Acknowledgments

This material is based upon work supported by the National Science Foundation under Grant No. 1012195-CCF. The authors thank Junjie Gu for his assistance with LLVM. The authors also thank Charlie Curtsinger, Dimitar Gochev, John Altidor and the anonymous reviewers for their helpful suggestions during the development of this work. Tongping Liu was supported by an internship while at Huawei US Research Center.

References

[1] E. D. Berger, K. S. McKinley, R. D. Blumofe, and P. R. Wilson. Hoard: A scalable memory allocator for multithreaded applications. In *Proceedings of the International Conference on Architectural Support for Programming Languages and Operating Systems (ASPLOS-IX)*, pages 117–128, Cambridge, MA, Nov. 2000.

[2] E. D. Berger, B. G. Zorn, and K. S. McKinley. Composing high-performance memory allocators. In *Proceedings of the ACM SIGPLAN 2001 conference on Programming language design and implementation*, PLDI '01, pages 114–124, New York, NY, USA, 2001. ACM.

[3] C. Bienia and K. Li. PARSEC 2.0: A new benchmark suite for chip-multiprocessors. In *Proceedings of the 5th Annual Workshop on Modeling, Benchmarking and Simulation*, June 2009.

[4] W. J. Bolosky and M. L. Scott. False sharing and its effect on shared memory performance. In *SEDMS IV: USENIX Symposium on Experiences with Distributed and Multiprocessor Systems*, pages 57–71, Berkeley, CA, USA, 1993. USENIX Association.

[5] S. Boyd-Wickizer, A. T. Clements, Y. Mao, A. Pesterev, M. F. Kaashoek, R. Morris, and N. Zeldovich. An analysis of Linux scalability to many cores. In *Proceedings of the 9th USENIX Conference on Operating Systems Design and Implementation*, OSDI '10, pages 1–8, Berkeley, CA, USA, 2010. USENIX Association.

[6] D. Bruening, T. Garnett, and S. Amarasinghe. An infrastructure for adaptive dynamic optimization. In *Proceedings of the international symposium on Code generation and optimization: feedback-directed and runtime optimization*, CGO '03, pages 265–275, Washington, DC, USA, 2003. IEEE Computer Society.

[7] J.-H. Chow and V. Sarkar. False sharing elimination by selection of runtime scheduling parameters. In *ICPP '97: Proceedings of the international Conference on Parallel Processing*, pages 396–403, Washington, DC, USA, 1997. IEEE Computer Society.

[8] David Dice. False sharing induced by card table marking. https://blogs.oracle.com/dave/entry/false_sharing_induced_by_card, February 2011.

[9] S. M. Günther and J. Weidendorfer. Assessing cache false sharing effects by dynamic binary instrumentation. In *WBIA '09: Proceedings of the Workshop on Binary Instrumentation and Applications*, pages 26–33, New York, NY, USA, 2009. ACM.

[10] Intel Corporation. *Intel Performance Tuning Utility 3.2 Update*, November 2008.

[11] Intel Corporation. Avoiding and identifying false sharing among threads. http://software.intel.com/en-us/articles/avoiding-and-identifying-false-sharing-among-threads/, February 2010.

[12] T. Iskhodzhanov, R. Kleckner, and E. Stepanov. Combining compile-time and run-time instrumentation for testing tools. *Programmnye produkty i sistemy*, 3:224–231, 2013.

[13] S. Jayasena, S. Amarasinghe, A. Abeyweera, G. Amarasinghe, H. De Silva, S. Rathnayake, X. Meng, and Y. Liu. Detection of false sharing using machine learning. In *Proceedings of SC13: International Conference for High Performance Computing, Networking, Storage and Analysis*, SC '13, pages 30:1–30:9, New York, NY, USA, 2013. ACM.

[14] Justin L. A way to determine a process's "real" memory usage, i.e. private dirty RSS? http://stackoverflow.com/questions/118307/a-way-to-determine-a-processs-real-memory-usage-i-e-private-dirty-rss, October 2011.

[15] C. Lattner and V. Adve. LLVM: A compilation framework for lifelong program analysis & transformation. In *Proceedings of the International Symposium on Code Generation and Optimization: Feedback-directed and Runtime Optimization*, CGO '04, pages 75–, Washington, DC, USA, 2004. IEEE Computer Society.

[16] C.-L. Liu. False sharing analysis for multithreaded programs. Master's thesis, National Chung Cheng University, July 2009.

[17] T. Liu and E. D. Berger. SHERIFF: Precise detection and automatic mitigation of false sharing. In *Proceedings of the 2011 ACM International Conference on Object-Oriented Programming Systems Languages and Applications*, OOPSLA '11, pages 3–18, New York, NY, USA, 2011. ACM.

[18] C.-K. Luk, R. Cohn, R. Muth, H. Patil, A. Klauser, G. Lowney, S. Wallace, V. J. Reddi, and K. Hazelwood. Pin: Building customized program analysis tools with dynamic instrumentation. In *Proceedings of the 2005 ACM SIGPLAN Conference on Programming Language Design and Implementation*, PLDI '05, pages 190–200, New York, NY, USA, 2005. ACM.

[19] mcmcc. False sharing in boost::detail::spinlock pool? http://stackoverflow.com/questions/11037655/false-sharing-in-boostdetailspinlock-pool, June 2012.

[20] Mikael Ronstrom. Mysql team increases scalability by >50mysql 5.6 labs release april 2012. http://mikaelronstrom.blogspot.com/2012/04/mysql-team-increases-scalability-by-50.html, April 2012.

[21] M. Nanavati, M. Spear, N. Taylor, S. Rajagopalan, D. T. Meyer, W. Aiello, and A. Warfield. Whose cache line is it anyway?: operating system support for live detection and repair of false sharing. In *Proceedings of the 8th ACM European Conference on Computer Systems*, EuroSys '13, pages 141–154, New York, NY, USA, 2013. ACM.

[22] N. Nethercote and J. Seward. Valgrind: a framework for heavyweight dynamic binary instrumentation. In *Proceedings of the 2007 ACM SIGPLAN conference on Programming language design and implementation*, PLDI '07, pages 89–100, New York, NY, USA, 2007. ACM.

[23] K. Papadimitriou. Taming false sharing in parallel programs. Master's thesis, University of Edinburgh, 2009.

[24] A. Pesterev, N. Zeldovich, and R. T. Morris. Locating cache performance bottlenecks using data profiling. In *EuroSys '10: Proceedings of the 5th European conference on Computer systems*, pages 335–348, New York, NY, USA, 2010. ACM.

[25] C. Ranger, R. Raghuraman, A. Penmetsa, G. Bradski, and C. Kozyrakis. Evaluating MapReduce for multi-core and multiprocessor systems. In *HPCA '07: Proceedings of the 2007 IEEE 13th International Symposium on High Performance Computer Architecture*, pages 13–24, Washington, DC, USA, 2007. IEEE Computer Society.

[26] M. Schindewolf. Analysis of cache misses using SIMICS. Master's thesis, Institute for Computing Systems Architecture, University of Edinburgh, 2007.

[27] K. Serebryany, D. Bruening, A. Potapenko, and D. Vyukov. AddressSanitizer: a fast address sanity checker. In *Proceedings of the 2012 USENIX Annual Technical Conference*, USENIX ATC'12, pages 28–28, Berkeley, CA, USA, 2012. USENIX Association.

[28] Q. Zhao, D. Koh, S. Raza, D. Bruening, W.-F. Wong, and S. Amarasinghe. Dynamic cache contention detection in multi-threaded applications. In *The International Conference on Virtual Execution Environments*, Newport Beach, CA, Mar 2011.

Concurrency Testing Using Schedule Bounding: an Empirical Study *

Paul Thomson, Alastair F. Donaldson, Adam Betts

Imperial College London
{paul.thomson11,afd,abetts}@imperial.ac.uk

Abstract

We present the first independent empirical study on schedule bounding techniques for systematic concurrency testing (SCT). We have gathered 52 buggy concurrent software benchmarks, drawn from public code bases, which we call SCTBench. We applied a modified version of an existing concurrency testing tool to SCTBench to attempt to answer several research questions, including: How effective are the two main schedule bounding techniques, preemption bounding and delay bounding, at bug finding? What challenges are associated with applying SCT to existing code? How effective is schedule bounding compared to a naive random scheduler at finding bugs? Our findings confirm that delay bounding is superior to preemption bounding and that schedule bounding is more effective at finding bugs than unbounded depth-first search. The majority of bugs in SCTBench can be exposed using a small bound (1-3), supporting previous claims, but there is at least one benchmark that requires 5 preemptions. Surprisingly, we found that a naive *random* scheduler is at least as effective as schedule bounding for finding bugs. We have made SCTBench and our tools publicly available for reproducibility and use in future work.

Categories and Subject Descriptors D.2.4 [*Software Engineering*]: Software/Program Verification; D.2.5 [*Software Engineering*]: Testing and Debugging

Keywords Concurrency; systematic concurrency testing; stateless model checking; context bounding

---

* This work was supported by an EPSRC-funded PhD studentship and the EU FP7 STEP project CARP (project number 287767).

1. Introduction

In recent years, researchers have shown great interest in systematic techniques for testing concurrent programs [7, 12, 26, 32, 34, 36] to expose concurrency bugs—software defects (such as crashes, deadlocks, assertion failures, memory safety errors and errors in algorithm implementation) that arise directly or indirectly as a result of concurrent execution. This is motivated by the rise of multicore systems [31], the ineffectiveness of traditional testing for detecting and reproducing concurrency bugs due to nondeterminism [19], and the desire for automatic, precise analysis, which is hard to achieve using static techniques [1].

Systematic concurrency testing (SCT) [7, 12, 26, 32, 34], also known as *stateless model checking* [12], is used to find and reproduce bugs in multi-threaded software. It has been implemented in a variety of tools, including CHESS [26] and Verisoft [12]. The technique involves repeatedly executing a multi-threaded program, controlling the scheduler so that a different schedule is explored on each execution. This process continues until all schedules have been explored, or until a time or schedule limit is reached. The analysis is highly automatic, has no false-positives and bugs can be reproduced by forcing the bug-inducing schedule.

Assuming a nondeterministic scheduler, the number of possible thread interleavings for a concurrent program is exponential in the number of execution steps, so exploring all schedules for large programs using SCT is infeasible. To combat this schedule explosion, *schedule bounding* techniques have been proposed, which reduce the number of thread schedules that are considered with the aim of preserving schedules that are likely to induce bugs. *Preemption bounding* [23] bounds the number of preemptive context switches that are allowed in a schedule. *Delay bounding* [7] bounds the number of times a schedule can deviate from the scheduling decisions of a given deterministic scheduler. During concurrency testing, the bound on preemptions or delays can be increased iteratively, so that all schedules are explored in the limit; the intention is that interesting schedules are explored within a reasonable resource budget. Schedule bounding has two additional benefits, regardless of bug finding ability. First, it produces simple counterexample traces; a trace with a small number of preemptions is likely to be easy to understand. This property has been used in trace simplification [15, 16]. Secondly, it gives bounded coverage guarantees; if the search manages to explore all schedules with at most c preemptions, then any undiscovered bugs in the program require at least $c + 1$ preemptions. A guarantee of this kind provides some indication of the necessary complexity and probability of occurrence of any bugs that might remain, and recent works on concurrent software verification employ schedule bounding to improve tractability [6, 20].

The hypothesis that preemption and delay bounding are likely to be effective is based on empirical evidence suggesting that many interesting concurrency bugs require only a small number of preemptive context switches to manifest [7, 23, 26]. Prior work has also shown that delay bounding improves on preemption bounding, allowing additional bugs to be detected [7]. However, these works have focused on a particular set of C# and C++ programs that target the Microsoft Windows operating system, most of which are not publicly available. Additionally, these works do not explicitly show that schedule bounding provides benefit over a naive random scheduler for finding bugs.[1]

We believe that these exciting and important claims about the effectiveness of schedule bounding would benefit from further scrutiny using a wider range of publicly available applications. To this end, we present the first independent, fully reproducible empirical study of schedule bounding techniques for SCT. We have put together SCTBench, a set of 52 publicly available benchmarks amenable to systematic concurrency testing, gathered from a combination of stand-alone multi-threaded test cases, and test cases drawn from 13 distinct applications and libraries. These are benchmarks that have been used in previous work to evaluate concurrency testing tools, with a few additions. Our study is based on an extended version of Maple [36], an open source concurrency testing tool. Our aim was to answer the following questions over a large and varied set of benchmarks:

- Can we find the known bugs in the publicly available benchmark suites using SCT?

- How do preemption and delay bounding compare in their effectiveness at finding concurrency bugs?

- How effective is schedule bounding compared to a naive random scheduler at finding bugs?

- How easy is it to apply SCT to various existing code bases in practice?

- Can we find examples of concurrency bugs that require more than three preemptions (the largest number of preemptions required to expose a bug in previous work [7])?

---

[1] We note that [23] plots the state (partial-order) coverage of preemption bounding against a technique called "random" on a single benchmark, but the details of this and the bug finding ability are not mentioned.

1.1 Main findings and contribution

We now summarise the main findings of our study. The conclusions we draw of course only relate to the 52 benchmarks in SCTBench, but this does include publicly available benchmarks used in prior work to evaluate concurrency testing tools. We forward-reference the Venn diagrams of Figure 2, which are discussed in detail in §6. These diagrams provide an overview of our results in terms of the bug-finding ability of the various techniques we study: iterative preemption bounding (IPB), iterative delay bounding (IDB), depth-first search with no schedule bound (DFS) and naive random scheduling (Rand). For each method evaluated, a limit of 10,000 schedules per benchmark is used.

Schedule bounding is similar to naive random scheduling in terms of bug-finding ability. Our assumption prior to this study was that a naive random scheduler would not be effective at finding bugs. This claim is not made explicitly in prior work, but neither is it addressed; prior work (such as [7, 23, 26]) only includes depth-first search or preemption bounding as a baseline for finding bugs.[1] Our findings, summarised in Figure 2b, contradict this assumption: the bugs in 44 benchmarks were found by *both* schedule bounding and a naive random scheduler within 10,000 executions. Schedule bounding and random scheduling each found one additional, distinct, bug. The random scheduler almost always led to faster bug detection than with schedule bounding. This raises two important questions: Does schedule bounding actually aid in bug finding, compared to more naive approaches? Are the benchmarks used to evaluate concurrency testing tools (captured by SCTBench) representative of real-world concurrency bugs? Our findings indicate that the answer to at least one of these questions must be "no". As noted above, schedule bounding provides several benefits regardless of bug finding ability which are not questioned by our findings.

Many bugs can be found via a small (1-3) schedule bound. Schedule bounding exposed each bug in 45 of the 52 benchmarks and the highest preemption bound required in these cases was three. Thus, a large majority of the bugs in SCT-Bench can be found with a small schedule bound. This supports previous claims [7, 23, 26]. It also adds weight to the argument that bounded guarantees provided by schedule bounding are useful. However, we note that one benchmark is reported to require a minimum of five preemptions for the bug to manifest. A straightforward depth-first search with no schedule bounding exposed bugs in 33 benchmarks, all of which were also found with schedule bounding.

Delay bounding beats preemption bounding. Delay bounding found all of the 38 bugs that were found by preemption bounding, plus seven that were not (see Figure 2a).

SCT can be difficult to apply. Many interesting benchmarks could not be included in our study, as they use nondeterministic features or additional synchronisation that is not modelled or controlled appropriately by most SCT tools. This includes network communication, multiple processes, signals (other than pthread condition variables) and event libraries.

Additionally, we found several program modules that could not easily be tested in isolation due to direct dependencies on system functions and other program modules. Thus, creating isolated tests suitable for SCT may require significant effort, especially for those who are not developers of the software under test.

Data races are common. Many benchmarks feature a large number of data races that are not regarded as bugs. Treating them as errors would be too easy for benchmarking purposes, as they are very common. For the study, we explore the interleavings arising from sequentially consistent outcomes of racy memory accesses in order to expose bugs such as assertion failures and incorrect output.

Bugs may not be detected without additional checks. Some concurrency bugs manifest as out-of-bound memory accesses, which do not always cause a crash. Tools need to check for these, otherwise bugs may be missed or manifest nondeterministically, even when the required thread schedule is executed. Performing such checks reliably and efficiently is non-trivial.

Trivial benchmarks. We argue that certain benchmarks used in prior work are "trivial" (based on certain properties – see Table 2) and cannot meaningfully be used to compare the performance of competing techniques. Instead, they provide a minimum baseline for any respectable concurrency testing technique. For example, the bugs in 19 benchmarks were exposed 50% of the time when using a random scheduler, with 10,000 runs. In nine of these cases, the bugs were exposed 100% of the time.

Non-trivial benchmarks. We believe most benchmarks from the CHESS, PARSEC and RADBench suites, as well as the `misc.safestack` benchmark, present a non-trivial challenge for concurrency testing tools. Furthermore, these represent real bugs, not synthetic tests. Future work can use these challenging benchmarks to show the improvement obtained over schedule bounding and other techniques.

1.2 SCTBench and reproducibility of our study

To make our study fully reproducible, we provide the 52 benchmarks (SCTBench), our scripts and the modified version of Maple used in our experiments, online:

```
http://sites.google.com/site/sctbenchmarks
```

We believe SCTBench will be valuable for future work on concurrency testing in general and SCT in particular. Each benchmark is directly amenable to SCT and exhibits a concurrency bug.

As discussed further in §5, our results are given in terms of number of terminal schedules, not time, which allows them to be easily compared with other work and tools.

2. Systematic Concurrency Testing

Systematic concurrency testing (SCT) works by repeatedly executing a concurrent program using a custom scheduler, forcing a different thread schedule to be explored on each execution. Execution is serialised, so that concurrency is emulated by interleaving instructions from different threads. It is assumed that the only source of nondeterminism is from the scheduler so that repeated execution of the same schedule always leads to the same program state. Nondeterminism such as user input, network communication, etc. must be fixed or modelled. This continues until all schedules have been explored, or until a time or schedule limit is reached. The search space is over schedules; unlike model checking, program states are not represented. This is appealing because the state of real software is large and difficult to capture.

A schedule $\alpha = \langle \alpha(1), \ldots, \alpha(n) \rangle$ is a list of thread identifiers. We use the following shorthands for lists: $length(\alpha) = n$; $\alpha \cdot t = \langle \alpha(1), \ldots, \alpha(n), t \rangle$; $last(\alpha) = \alpha(n)$. The element $\alpha(i)$ refers to the thread that is executing at step i in the execution of the multi-threaded program, where step 1 is the first step. For example, the schedule $\langle T0, T0, T1, T0 \rangle$ specifies that, from the initial state, two steps are executed in the context of $T0$, one step in $T1$ and then a step in $T0$. A step corresponds to a particular thread executing a *visible* operation [12], such as a synchronisation operation or shared memory access, followed by a finite sequence of invisible operations until immediately before the next visible operation. Considering interleavings involving non-visible operations is unnecessary when checking safety property violations, such as deadlocks and assertion failures [12]. The point just before a visible operation, where the scheduler decides which thread to execute next, is called a *scheduling point*. Let $enabled(\alpha)$ denote the set of enabled threads (those that are not blocked, and so can execute) in the state reached by executing α. We say that the state reached by α is a *terminal state* when $enabled(\alpha) = \emptyset$. A schedule that reaches a terminal state is referred to as a *terminal schedule*.

Context switches A *context switch* occurs in a schedule when execution switches from one thread to another. Formally, step i in α is a context switch if and only if $\alpha(i) \neq \alpha(i-1)$. The context switch is *preemptive* if and only if $\alpha(i-1) \in enabled(\langle \alpha(1), \ldots, \alpha(i-1) \rangle)$. In other words, the thread executing step $i-1$ remained enabled after that step. Otherwise, the context switch is *non-preemptive*.

Preemption bounding Preemption bounding [23] bounds the number of preemptions in a schedule. Let the preemption count PC of a schedule be defined recursively; a schedule of length zero or one has no preemptions, otherwise:

$$PC(\alpha \cdot t) = \begin{cases} PC(\alpha) + 1 & \text{if } last(\alpha) \neq t \wedge last(\alpha) \in enabled(\alpha) \\ PC(\alpha) & \text{otherwise} \end{cases}$$

With a preemption bound of k, any schedule α with $PC(\alpha) > k$ will not be explored.

```
T0                         T1    T2    T3
a)create(T1,T2,T3)  b)x=1  d)z=1  e)assert x==y
                    c)y=1
```

Figure 1: Simple multi-threaded program.

Example 1. *Consider Figure 1, which shows a simple multi-threaded program. T0 launches three threads concurrently and is then disabled. All variables are initially zero and threads execute until there are no statements left. We refer to the visible actions of each thread via the statement labels (a, b, c, etc.) and we (temporarily) represent schedules as a list of labels. Note that 'a' cannot be preempted, as there are no other threads to switch to. A schedule with zero preemptions is $\langle a, b, c, e, d \rangle$. Note that, for example, e is not a preemption because T1 has no more statements and so is considered disabled after c. A schedule that causes the assertion to be violated is $\langle a, b, e \rangle$, which has one preemption at operation e. The bug will not be found with a preemption bound of zero, but will be found with any greater bound.*

Delay bounding A *delay* conceptually corresponds to blocking the thread that would be chosen by the scheduler at a scheduling point, which forces the next thread to be chosen instead. The blocked thread is then immediately re-enabled. Delay bounding [7] bounds the number of delays in a schedule, given an otherwise deterministic scheduler. Executing a program under the deterministic scheduler (without delaying) results in a single terminal schedule – this is the only terminal schedule that has zero delays.

In the remainder of this paper we assume the deterministic scheduler that is non-preemptive and when blocked chooses the next enabled thread in thread creation order in a round-robin fashion. We assume this instantiation of delay bounding because it has been used in previous work [7] and is straightforward to explain and implement.

The following is a definition of delay bounding assuming the non-preemptive round robin scheduler. Assume that each thread id is a non-negative integer, numbered in order of creation; the initial thread has id 0, and the last thread created has id $N - 1$. For two thread ids $x, y \in \{0, \ldots, N - 1\}$, let $distance(x, y)$ be the unique integer $d \in \{0, \ldots, N - 1\}$ such that $(x + d) \bmod N = y$. Intuitively, this is the "round-robin distance" from x to y. For example, given four threads $\{0, 1, 2, 3\}$, $distance(1, 0)$ is 3. For a schedule α and a thread id t, let $delays(\alpha, t)$ yield the number of delays required to schedule thread t at the state reached by α:

$$delays(\alpha, t) = |\{x : 0 \leq x < distance(last(\alpha), t) \\ \wedge (last(\alpha) + x) \bmod N \in enabled(\alpha)\}|$$

This is the number of enabled threads that are skipped when moving from $last(\alpha)$ to t. For example, let $last(\alpha) = 3$, $enabled(\alpha) = \{0, 2, 3, 4\}$ and $N = 5$. Then, $delays(\alpha, 2) = 3$ because threads 3, 4 and 0 are skipped (but not thread 1, because it is not enabled).

Define the delay count DC of a schedule recursively; a schedule of length zero or one has no delays, otherwise:

$$DC(\alpha \cdot t) = DC(\alpha) + delays(\alpha, t)$$

With a delay bound of k, any schedule α with $DC(\alpha) > k$ will not be explored.

The set of schedules with at most c delays is a subset of the set of schedules with at most c preemptions. Thus, delay bounding reduces the number of schedules by at least as much as preemption bounding.

Example 2. *Consider Figure 1 once more. Assume thread creation order $\langle T0, T1, T2, T3 \rangle$. The assertion can also fail via: $\langle a, b, d, e \rangle$, with one delay/preemption at d. However, a preemption bound of one yields 11 terminal schedules, while a delay bound of one yields only 4 (note that an assertion failure is a terminal state). Now assume that T2 comprises the same statements as T1, which we label as: f) x=1; g) y=1. Now, the assertion cannot fail with a delay bound of one because two delays must occur so that T1 and T2 do not both execute all their statements. For example, $\langle a, b, e \rangle$ exposes the bug, but executing e uses two delays. However, note that this schedule only has one preemption, so the assertion can still fail under a preemption bound of one. Adding an additional n threads between T1 and T3 (in the creation order) with the same statements as T1 will require n additional delays to expose the bug, while still only one preemption will be needed. Empirical evidence [7] suggests that adversarial examples like this are not common in practice. Our results (§6) also support this.*

Theoretical Complexity Upper-bounds for the number of terminal schedules produced by SCT techniques are described in [7, 23]. In summary, assume at most n threads and at most k execution steps in each thread. Of those k, at most b steps block (cause the executing thread to become disabled) and i steps do not block. Complete search is exponential in n and k, and thus infeasible for programs with a large number of execution steps. With a scheduling bound of c, preemption bounding is exponential in c (a small value), n (often, but not necessarily, a small value) and b (usually much smaller than k). Crucially, it is no longer exponential in k. Delay bounding is exponential only in c (a small value). Thus, it performs well (in terms of number of schedules) even when programs create a large number of threads.

Finding bugs The intuition behind schedule bounding is that it greatly reduces the number of schedules, but still allows many bugs to be found [7, 23, 26]. The reasoning is that only a *few* preemptions are needed at the *right* places in order to enforce an ordering that causes the bug to manifest. Performing a preemption elsewhere will have little impact. A complete depth-first search becomes infeasible as the execution length increases due to the large number of context switches, many of which are likely to be irrelevant.

Iterative schedule bounding Schedule bounding can be performed iteratively [23], where all schedules with zero preemptions or delays are all executed, followed by those with one preemption or delay, etc. until there are no more schedules or a time or schedule limit is reached. In the limit, all schedules are explored. Thus, iterative schedule bounding creates a partial-order in which to explore schedules: schedule α will be explored before schedule α' if $PC(\alpha) < PC(\alpha')$, while there is no predefined exploration order between schedules with equal preemption counts. The partial order for iterative delay bounding with respect to DC is analogous. Thus, iterative schedule bounding is a heuristic that aims to expose buggy schedules before the time or schedule limit is reached, based on the hypothesis discussed above.

In this study, we perform iterative schedule bounding to compare preemption and delay bounding.

3. Modifications to Maple

We chose to use a modified version of the Maple tool [36] to conduct our experimental study. Maple is a concurrency testing tool framework for pthread [21] programs. It uses the dynamic instrumentation library, PIN [22], to test binaries without the need for recompilation. One of the modules, *systematic*, is a re-implementation of the CHESS [26] algorithm for preemption bounding. The main reason for using Maple, instead of CHESS, is that it targets pthread programs. This allows us to test a wide variety of open source multi-threaded benchmarks and programs. Previous evaluations [7, 23, 26] focus on C# programs and C++ programs that target the Microsoft Windows operating system, most of which are not publicly available. In addition, CHESS requires re-linking the program with a test function that can be executed repeatedly; this requires resetting the global state (e.g. resetting the value of global variables) and joining any remaining threads, which can be non-trivial. In contrast, Maple can test native binaries out-of-the-box, by restarting the program for each terminal schedule that is explored, although a downside of this approach is that it is slower. Checking for data races is also supported by Maple; as discussed in §5, this is important for identifying visible operations. The public version of CHESS can only interleave memory accesses in native code if the user adds special function calls before each access.[2]

Delay bounding We modified Maple to add support for delay bounding, following a similar design to the existing support for preemption bounding. At each scheduling point, Maple conceptually constructs several schedules consisting of the current schedule concatenated with an enabled thread t. These are added to a set and will be explored on subsequent executions. If switching to thread t will cause the delay bound to be exceeded (as explained in §2), the schedule is not added to the set.

---

[2]See "Why does wchess not support /detectraces?" at http://social.msdn.microsoft.com/Forums/en-us/home?forum=chess

Depth-first search Even with a schedule bound, there are many possible orders in which to explore schedules. Maple's systematic mode only supports a depth-first search, as this allows a stack to be used to efficiently record which schedules still need to be explored. Since the stack is deeply ingrained in Maple's data structures and algorithms, we did not attempt to implement other search strategies. We note that the initial terminal schedule explored by iterative preemption bounding, iterative delay bounding and unbounded depth-first search is the same for all techniques (a non-preemptive round-robin schedule). We discuss the impact of depth-first search on our study further in §5.

Random scheduler Maple also includes a naive random scheduler mode, where, at each scheduling point, one enabled thread is randomly chosen from the set of enabled threads to execute a visible operation. Unlike schedule fuzzing, where randomisation is used to peturb the OS scheduler, this yields truly (pseudo-)random schedules because scheduling nondeterminism is fully controlled. No information is saved by the random scheduler for subsequent executions, so it is possible that the same schedule will be explored multiple times over many runs. This could be rectified by modifying Maple to record a history of schedules during random scheduling, but such a change would not be straightforward due to the way in which the tool is designed. As a result, with random scheduling the search cannot "complete", even for programs with a small number of schedules.

We include random scheduling as a baseline for non-systematic approaches, and to provide further insight on the complexity of the benchmarks.

Maple algorithm The default concurrency testing used by Maple (which we refer to as the *Maple algorithm*) is not systematic: it performs several profiling runs, recording patterns of inter-thread dependencies through shared-memory accesses [36]. From the recorded patterns, it predicts possible alternative interleavings that may be feasible, which are referred to as interleaving idioms. It then performs *active* runs, influencing thread scheduling to attempt to force untested interleaving idioms, until none remain or they are all deemed infeasible (using heuristics). Although the focus of our study is on SCT techniques, we also compare with the Maple algorithm since it is readily available in the tool.

4. Benchmark Collection

We have collected a wide range of pthread benchmarks from previous work and other sources. Table 1 summarises the benchmark suites (with duplicates removed), indicating where it was necessary to skip benchmarks due to the difficulty of applying SCT, or otherwise. "Non-buggy" means there were no existing bugs documented and we did not find any during our examination of the benchmark. We now provide details of the benchmark suites (§4.1) and barriers to the application of SCT identified through our benchmark gathering exercise (§4.2).

Benchmark set	Benchmark types	# used	# skipped
CB	Test cases for real applications	3	17 networked applications.
CHESS	Test cases for several versions of a work stealing queue	4	0
CS	Small test cases and some small programs	29	24 were non-buggy.
Inspect	Small test cases and some small programs	1	28 were non-buggy.
Miscellaneous	Test case for lock-free stack and a debugging library test case	2	0
PARSEC	Parallel workloads	4	29 were non-buggy.
RADBenchmark	Tests cases for real applications	6	5 Chromium browser; 4 networking.
SPLASH-2	Parallel workloads	3	9 (see text)

Table 1: An overview of the benchmark suites used in the study.

4.1 Details of benchmark suites

Concurrency Bugs (CB) Benchmarks [35] Includes buggy versions of programs such as `aget` (a file downloader) and `pbzip2` (a file compressions tool). We modified `aget`, modelling certain network functions to return data from a file and to call its interrupt handler asynchronously. Many benchmarks were skipped due to the use of networking, multiple processes and signals (`apache`, `memcached`, `MySQL`).

CHESS [26] A set of test cases for a work stealing queue, originally implemented for the Cilk multithreaded programming system [10] under Windows. The `WorkStealQueue` (WSQ) benchmark has been used frequently to evaluate concurrency testing tools [4, 23–27]. After manually translating the benchmarks to use pthreads and C++11 atomics, we found a bug in two of the tests that caused heap corruption, which always occurred when we ran the tests natively (without Maple). We fixed this bug and SCT revealed another bug that is much rarer, which we use in the study.

Concurrency Software (CS) Benchmarks [6] Examples used to evaluate the ESBMC tool [6], including small multithreaded algorithm test cases (e.g. bank account transfer, circular buffer, dining philosophers, queue, stack), a file system benchmark and a test case for a Bluetooth driver. These tests included unconstrained inputs. None of the bugs are input dependent, so we selected reasonable concrete values. We had to remove or define various ESBMC-specific functions to get the benchmarks to compile.

Inspect Benchmarks [34] Used to evaluate the INSPECT concurrency testing tool. We skipped `swarm_isort64` that did not terminate after five minutes when performing data race detection (see §5). There were no documented bugs, and testing all benchmarks revealed a bug in only one benchmark, `qsort_mt`, which we include in the study.

Miscellaneous We encountered two individual test cases, which we include in the study. The `safestack` test case, which was posted to the CHESS forums[3] by Dmitry Vyukov, is a lock-free stack designed to work on weak-memory models. The bug exposed by the test case also manifests under sequential consistency, so it should be detectable by existing

SCT tools. Vyukov states that the bug requires at least three threads and at least five preemptions. Previous work reported a bug that requires three preemptions [7], which was the first bug found by CHESS that required that many preemptions.

The `ctrace` test case, obtained from the authors of [18], exposes a bug in the ctrace multithreaded debugging library.

PARSEC 2.0 Benchmarks [2] A collection of multithreaded programs from many different areas. We used `ferret` (content similarity search) and `streamcluster` (online clustering of an input stream), both of which contain known bugs. We created three versions of `streamcluster`, each containing a distinct bug. One of these is from an older version of the benchmark and another was a previously unknown bug which we discovered during our study (see §4.2). We configured the `streamcluster` benchmarks to use non-spinning synchronisation and added a check for incorrect output. All benchmarks use the "test" input values (the smallest) with two threads, except for `streamcluster2`, where the bug requires three threads.

RADBenchmark [17] Consists of 15 tests that expose bugs in several applications. The 6 benchmarks we use test parts of Mozilla SpiderMonkey (the Firefox JavaScript engine) and the Mozilla Netscape Portable Runtime Thread Package, which are suitable for SCT. The others were skipped due to use of networking and multiple processes. Several tested the Chromium browser; the use of a GUI leads to nondeterminism that cannot be controlled or modelled by any SCT tools we know of. Some of the benchmarks were stress tests; we reduced the number of threads and other parameters as much as possible.

SPLASH-2 [33] Three of these benchmarks have been used in previous work [4, 29]. SPLASH-2 requires a set of macros to be provided; the bugs are caused by a set that fail to include the "wait for threads to terminate" macro. Thus, all the bugs are similar. For this reason, we just use the three benchmarks from previous work, even though the macros are likely to cause issues in the other benchmarks. We added assertions to check that all threads have terminated as expected. We reduce the values of input parameters, such as the number of particles in `barnes` and the size of the matrix in `lu`, so the tests complete quickly on our implementation, without exhausting memory. We discuss this further in §6.

---

[3]See "Bug with a context switch bound 5" at `http://social.msdn.microsoft.com/Forums/en-US/home?forum=chess`

4.2 Effort Required For SCT

We encountered a range of issues when trying to apply systematic concurrency testing to the benchmarks. These are general limitations of SCT, not of our method specifically, and all SCT tools that we know of would have similar issues.

Environment modelling System calls that interact with the environment, and hence can give nondeterministic results, must be modelled or fixed to return deterministic values. Similarly, functions that can cause threads to become enabled or disabled must be handled specially, as they affect scheduling decisions. This includes the forking of additional processes, which requires both modelling and engineering effort to make the testing tool work across different processes. For the above reasons, a large number of benchmarks in the CB and RADBenchmark suites had to be skipped because they involve testing servers, using several processes and network communication. Modelling network communication and testing multiple processes are both nontrivial tasks. We believe the difficulty of controlling various sources of nondeterminism is a key issue in applying SCT to existing code bases. In contrast, non-systematic techniques (discussed in §7) are able to handle such nondeterminism.

Isolated concurrency testing An alternative approach to modelling nondeterminism is to create isolated tests, similar to unit testing, but with multiple threads. Unfortunately, we found that many programs are not designed in a way that makes this easy. An example is the Apache httpd webserver; the server module that we inspected had many dependencies on other parts of the server and directly called system functions, making it difficult to create an isolated test case. Developers test the server as a whole; network packets are sent to the server by a script running in a separate process.

Many applications in the CB benchmarks use global variables and function-static variables that are scattered throughout several source files. These would need to be handled carefully with some SCT tools like CHESS, that require a repeatable function to test, in which the state must be reset when the function returns. This is not a problem for Maple, which restarts the test program for every schedule explored.

Memory safety We found that certain concurrency bugs manifest as out-of-bounds memory accesses, which do not always cause a crash. We implemented an out-of-bounds memory access detector on top of Maple, which allowed us to detect a previously unknown bug in the PARSEC suite, which is tested in the `streamcluster3` benchmark. Detecting certain types of out-of-bound memory accesses, such as accesses to the stack or data segments, is difficult, as information about the bounds of these regions is lost during compilation. Thus, our implementation had many false positives. However, a more serious issue was that the extra instrumentation code caused a slow-down of up to 8x; Maple's existing information on allocated memory was not designed to be speed-efficient. We disabled the out-of-bound access

detector in our experiments, but we note that a production quality SCT tool would require an efficient method for detecting out-of-bound accesses to automatically identify this important class of bug. We manually added assertions to detect out-of-bound accesses in the `streamcluster3` benchmark and in `fsbench_bad` in the CS benchmarks. Out-of-bound accesses to synchronisation objects, such as mutexes, are still detected. This proved to be useful in `pbzip2` from the CS benchmarks.

Data races We found that 33 of the 52 benchmarks contained data races. There are many compelling arguments against the tolerance of data races [3], and technically, according to the C++11 standard, the existence of a data race in a C++ program means that the behaviour of the *entire* program is undefined. Nevertheless, in practice, programs that exhibit races are often compiled in predictable ways by standard compilers so that many data races are not regarded as bugs by software developers. A particular pattern we noticed was that data races often occur on flags used in ad-hoc busy-wait synchronisation, where one thread keeps reading a variable until the value changes. In principle the "benign" races could be rectified through the use of C++11 relaxed atomics, the "busy wait" use of data races could be formalised using C++11 acquire/release atomics, and synchronisation operations could be added to eliminate the buggy cases. However, telling the difference between benign and buggy data races is non-trivial in practice [18, 28]. We explain how we treat data races in our study in §5.

Output checking The bugs in the benchmarks `CB.aget` and `parsec.streamcluster2`, lead to incorrect output. Thus, we added extra code to read the output file and trigger an assertion failure when incorrect; the output checking code for the `CB.aget` was provided as a separate program, which we added to the benchmark. Several of the PARSEC and SPLASH benchmarks do not verify their output, greatly limiting their usefulness as test cases.

5. Experimental Method

Our experimental evaluation aims to compare a straightforward depth-first search (DFS), iterative preemption bounding (IPB), iterative delay bounding (IDB) and the use of a naive random scheduler (Rand). We also test the default Maple algorithm (MapleAlg). Bugs are deadlocks, crashes or assertion failures (including those that identify incorrect output). Each benchmark contains a concurrency bug and goes through the following phases:

Data Race Detection Phase When checking safety properties, it is sound to only consider scheduling points before each synchronisation operation, such as locking a mutex, as long as execution aborts with an error as soon as a data race is detected [26]. This greatly reduces the number of schedules that need to be considered. However, treating data races as errors is not practical for this study due to the large number of data races in the benchmarks (see §4.2), which would make bug-finding trivial and arguably not meaningful.

As in previous work [36], we circumvent this issue by performing dynamic data race detection to identify a reasonable subset of load and store instructions that participate in data races. We treat these instructions as visible operations during SCT. For each benchmark, we execute Maple in its data race detection mode ten times, without controlling the schedule. Each racy instruction (stored as an offset in the binary) is treated as a visible operation in the IPB, IDB, DFS and Rand phases. We also tried detecting races during SCT, but this caused an additional slow-down of up to 8x, as Maple's race detector is not optimised for this scenario.

Thus SCT explores nondeterminism arising due to sequentially consistent outcomes of a subset of the possible data races for a concurrent program. Bugs found by this method are real (there are no false-positives), but bugs that depend on relaxed memory effects or data races not identified dynamically will be missed. We do not believe these missed bugs threaten the validity of our comparison of IPB, IDB, DFS and Rand, since the same information about data races is used by all of these techniques; the set of racy instructions could be considered as part of the benchmark.

An alternative to under-approximation would be to use static analysis to over-approximate the set of racy instructions. We did not try this, but speculate that imprecision of static analysis would lead to many instructions being promoted to visible operations, causing schedule explosion.

Iterative Preemption Bounding (IPB) Phase We next perform SCT on the benchmark using iterative preemption bounding, with a schedule limit. By repeatedly executing the program, restarting after each execution, we first explore all terminal schedules that have zero preemptions, followed by all schedules that have one preemption, etc. until either the schedule limit is reached, all schedules have been explored or a bug is found. If a bug is found, the search does not terminate immediately; the remaining schedules within the current preemption bound are explored (for our set of benchmarks, it was always possible to complete this exploration without exceeding the schedule limit). As explained in §3, this allows us to check whether non-buggy schedules could exceed the schedule limit when an underlying search strategy other than depth-first search is used.

We use a limit of 10,000 terminal schedules to enable a full experimental run over our large set of benchmarks to complete on a cluster within 24 hours. We chose to use a schedule limit instead of a time limit because there are many factors and potential optimisation opportunities that can affect the time needed for a benchmark to complete, and the cluster we have access to shares its machines with other jobs, making accurate time measurement difficult. On the other hand, the number of terminal schedules explored cannot be improved upon, without changing key aspects of the search algorithms themselves. By measuring the number of sched-

ules, our results can potentially be compared with other algorithms and future work that use different implementations with different overheads.

Iterative Delay Bounding (IDB) Phase This phase is identical to the previous, except delay bounding is used instead of preemption bounding.

Depth-First Search (DFS) Phase We perform a depth-first search, with no schedule bounding and a limit of 10,000 terminal schedules. This provides a point of comparison for schedule bounding.

Random scheduler (Rand) Phase We run each benchmark 10,000 times using Maple's naive random scheduler mode. This allows us to compare the systematic techniques against a straightforward non-systematic technique.

Maple Algorithm (MapleAlg) Phase We test each benchmark using the Maple algorithm. This algorithm terminates based on its own heuristics; we enforced a time limit of 24 hours per benchmark.

Notes on depth-first search and partial order reduction As discussed in §3, the SCT methods we evaluate are built on top of Maple's default depth-first search strategy. Although depth-first search is just one possible search strategy, and different strategies could give different results, we argue that this is not important in our study. First, if the depth-first search biases the search for certain benchmarks, then both schedule bounding algorithms are likely to benefit or suffer equally from this. Second, iterative schedule bounding explores *all* schedules with c preemptions/delays before *any* schedule with $c + 1$ preemptions/delays. This means that when the first schedule with $c + 1$ preemptions/delays is considered, exactly the same set of schedules, regardless of search strategy, will have been explored so far. If a bug is revealed at bound c then, by enumerating all schedules with bound c (as described above), we can determine the worst case number of schedules that might have to be explored to find a bug, accounting for an adversarial search strategy.

Partial-order reduction (POR) [11] is a commonly used technique in concurrency testing [9, 11, 24, 26]. We do not attempt to study the various POR techniques, to avoid an explosion of combinations of methods and because the relationship between POR and schedule bounding is complex and the topic of recent and ongoing work [5, 14, 24].

6. Experimental Results

Experimental platform We conducted our experiments on a Linux cluster, with Red Hat Enterprise Linux Server release 6.4, an x86_64 architecture and gcc 4.7.2. Our modified version of Maple is based on the latest commit [4]. The benchmarks, scripts and the modified version of Maple used in our experiments can be obtained from `http://sites.google.com/site/sctbenchmarks`.

---

[4] `http://github.com/jieyu/maple` commit at Sept 24, 2012

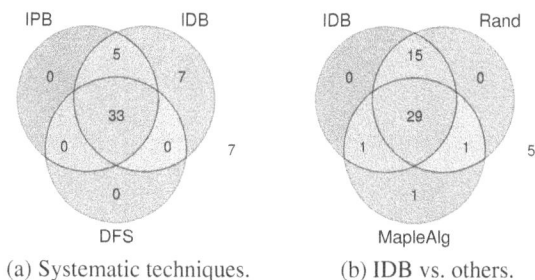

| (a) Systematic techniques. | (b) IDB vs. others. |

Figure 2: Venn diagram showing number of benchmarks in which the bugs were found with the various techniques.

Overview of results   The Venn diagrams in Figure 2 give a concise summary of the bug-finding ability of the techniques. When we say that a technique found x bugs, we mean that the technique found each bug in x benchmarks.

Figure 2a summarises the bugs found by the systematic techniques. IPB was superior to DFS, finding all 33 bugs found by DFS, plus an additional 5. IDB beat both DFS and IPB, finding all 38 bugs found by these techniques, plus an additional 7. The bugs in 7 benchmarks were missed by all systematic techniques, which we discuss below.

Figure 2b shows the bugs found by schedule bounding (IDB), a naive random scheduler (Rand) and the default Maple algorithm (MapleAlg). The bugs in 44 benchmarks were found by both IDB and Rand. IDB and Rand each found 1 additional, distinct, bug. Thus, these techniques performed similarly in terms of number of bugs found. We discuss this surprising result in detail below. MapleAlg found 31 bugs that were found by the other techniques, plus 1 additional bug. However, it missed 15 bugs that were found by the other techniques. There were 5 bugs missed by *all* techniques, but 3 of these are identical to benchmarks in which we did find bugs, except that they run a larger number of threads; the remaining 2 benchmarks, `radbench.bug1` and `misc.safestack`, are discussed below.

Detailed results   The full set of experimental data gathered for our benchmarks is shown in Table 3. We use *schedules* to refer to *terminal schedules*, for brevity. As explained in §5, we focus on the number of schedules explored rather than time taken for analysis. The execution of a single benchmark during SCT varied between 1-7 seconds depending on the benchmark; there was negligible variance between runtimes for multiple executions of the same benchmark. The longest time taken to perform ten data race detection runs for a single benchmark was five minutes, but race detection was significantly faster in most cases. Race detection could be made more efficient using an optimised, state-of-the-art method. Because race analysis results are shared between all systematic techniques and Rand, the time for race analysis is not relevant when comparing these methods.

For each benchmark, *# threads* and *# max enabled threads* show the total number of threads launched and the

Property	# benchmarks
Bug found with DB $= 0$	14
Total terminal schedules $< 10,000$	16
$> 50\%$ of random schedules were buggy	19
Every random schedule was buggy	9

Table 2: Benchmarks where bug-finding is arguably trivial.

maximum number of threads simultaneously enabled at any scheduling point, respectively, over all runs of the benchmark. The *# max scheduling points* column shows the maximum number of visible operations for which more than one thread was enabled, over all systematic testing. The smallest preemption or delay bound required to find the bug for a benchmark, or the bound reached (but not fully explored) if the schedule limit was hit, is indicated by *bound*; *# schedules to first bug* shows the number of schedules that were explored up to and including the detection of a bug for the first time; *# schedules* shows the total number of schedules that were explored; *# new schedules* shows how many of these schedules have exactly *bound* preemptions (for IPB) or delays (for IDB); *# buggy schedules* shows how many of the total schedules explored exhibited the bug. As explained in §5, when a bug is found, we continue to explore all buggy and non-buggy schedules within the preemption or delay bound; the schedule limit was never exceeded while doing this. An L entry denotes 10,000 (the schedule limit discussed in §5). When no bugs were found, the bug-related columns contain ✗. We indicate by *% buggy*, the percentage of schedules that were buggy out of the total number of schedules explored during DFS. We prefix the percentage with a '*' when the schedule limit was reached, in which case the percentage does not apply to *all* schedules.

For the Rand results, the *# schedules* column is omitted, as it is always 10,000. Note that *# schedules to first bug* and *# buggy schedules* may contain duplicate schedules.

For the Maple algorithm, we report whether the bug was found (*found?*), the total number of (not necessarily distinct) schedules explored, as chosen by the algorithm's heuristics, and the total time in seconds for the algorithm to complete. Benchmarks 32, 33 and 34 caused Maple to livelock, so the 24 hour time limit was exceeded. We indicate this with '-'.

Benchmark Properties   The *# max enabled threads* and *# max scheduling points* columns from Table 3 can be used to estimate the total number of schedules and, perhaps, the complexity of the benchmark. With at most n enabled threads and at most k scheduling points, there are at most n^k terminal schedules. On the other hand, if most of the schedules are buggy (see the *% buggy* column in Table 3) then the number of schedules is not necessarily a good indication of bug complexity. For example, `CS.din_phil3_sat` has a relatively high number of schedules, but since 87% of them are buggy, this bug is trivial to find. Of course, the majority of benchmarks cannot be explored exhaustively, and estimating the percentage of buggy schedules from the partial

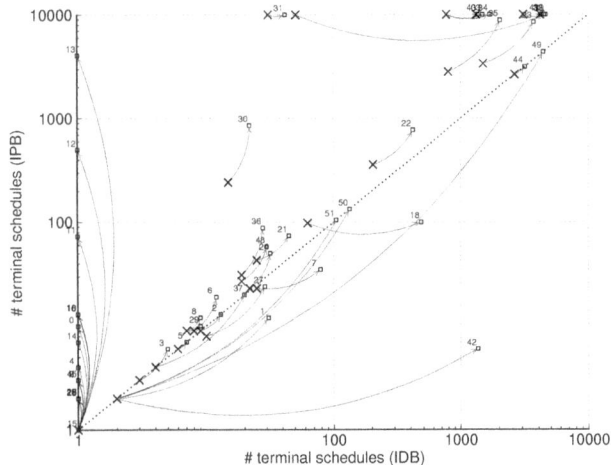

Figure 3: Shows # schedules to the first bug (cross) connected to the total # schedules (square), up to the bound that found the bug. Squares are labelled with the benchmark id.

Figure 4: Shows total # non-buggy schedules (cross) connected to the total # schedules (square), up to the bound that found the bug. Squares are labelled with the benchmark id.

DFS results is problematic because DFS is biased towards exploring deep context switches.

Table 2 provides some further insight into the complexity of the benchmarks, using properties derived from Table 3. Bugs found with a delay bound of zero will always be found on the initial schedule for IPB, IDB and DFS, as they all initially execute the same schedule. Any technique based on this same depth-first schedule will also find the bug immediately. It could be argued that this schedule is effective at finding bugs, or that the bugs in question are trivial, since the schedule includes minimal interleaving (there are no preemptions). Benchmarks with fewer than 10,000 terminal schedules (for DFS) will always be exhaustively explored by all systematic techniques, so the bug will always be found. Techniques can still be compared on how quickly they find the bugs. Bugs that were exposed more than 50% of the time when using the random scheduler could arguably be classified as "easy-to-find". Bugs that were exposed 100% of the time when using the random scheduler are almost certainly trivial to detect; indeed, Table 3 shows that all of these benchmarks were buggy for all schedules over *all* techniques, suggesting that these bugs are not even schedule-dependent.

In our view the relatively trivial nature of some of the bugs exhibited by our benchmarks has not been made clear in prior works that study these examples. We regard these easy-to-find bugs as having value only in providing a minimum baseline for any respectable concurrency testing technique. Failure to detect these bugs would constitute a major flaw in a technique; detecting them does not constitute a major achievement.

IPB vs. IDB Figure 3 compares IPB and IDB by plotting data from the following columns in Table 3: *# schedules to*

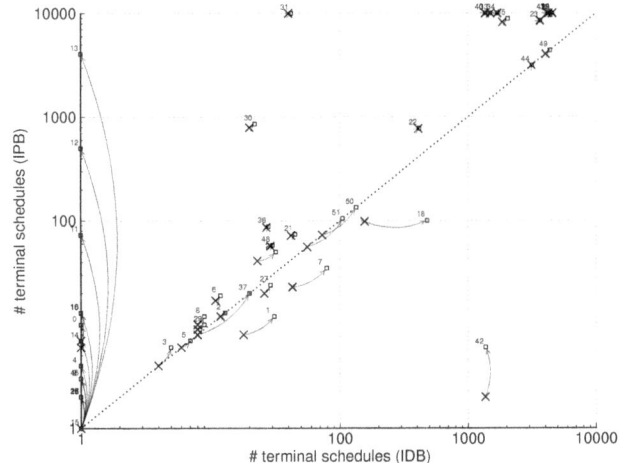

first bug (as a cross) and *# schedules* (as a square). Each benchmark, for which at least one technique found a bug, is depicted as a line connecting a cross and a square. Where the bug was not found by one of the techniques, this is indicated with a cross at 10,000 (the schedule limit discussed in §5). Each square is labelled with its benchmark *id* from Table 3. The cross indicates which technique was faster at finding the bug (with depth-first search as the underlying search strategy); crosses below/above the diagonal indicate that IPB/IDB was faster. The square indicates how many schedules exist with a bound less than or equal to the bound that found the bug. For example, when exploring benchmark 30 with IPB, the first buggy schedule was found after 243 schedules. The search continues until all 856 schedules with at most one preemption have been explored (bound at which the bug was found). Since the search terminated before reaching the schedule limit, we know that the bug would be found even if we were using an underlying search strategy other than depth-first search. Notice that a number of benchmarks appear at $(x, 10,000)$, with $x < 10,000$: this is where IPB failed to find a bug and IDB succeeded.

The bug-finding ability of the techniques in Figure 3 is tied to the underlying depth-first search. It is possible that this might cause one of the techniques to "get lucky" and find a bug quickly, while another search order could lead to many additional non-buggy schedules being considered before a bug is found. To avoid this implementation-dependent bias, in Figure 4 we consider the *worst-case* bug-finding ability. Each cross plots, for IDB and IPB, the total number of schedules within the bound exposing the bug that are *not* buggy. This corresponds to the difference between the *# schedules* and *# buggy schedules* columns presented in Table 3, and represents the worst-case number of schedules that might

24

have to be explored to find a bug, given an unlucky choice of search ordering. The squares are the same as in Figure 3.

Overall, IDB finds all bugs found by IPB, plus seven that were missed. In Figure 3, most crosses fall on or above the diagonal, showing that IDB was as fast or faster than IPB in terms of number of schedules to the first bug. The same is mostly true for the squares, showing that IDB generally leads to a smaller total number of schedules than IPB. In the worst case (Figure 4), some crosses fall under the line, but most are still very close, or represent a small number of schedules (less than 100) where the difference between the techniques is negligible. An outlier is benchmark 42 where, in the worst case, IPB requires 3 schedules to find the bug, while IDB requires 1366 schedules. Table 3 shows that the bug does not require any preemptions, but requires at least one delay; this difference greatly increases the number of schedules for IDB. We believe this can be explained as follows. First, there must be a small number of blocking operations, leading to a very small number of schedules with a preemption bound of zero. Second, the bug in question requires that when two particular threads are started and reach a particular barrier, the "master" thread (the thread that was created before the other) does *not* leave the barrier first. With zero preemptions, the non-master thread can be chosen at the first blocking operation (as any enabled thread can be chosen). With zero delays, only the master thread can be chosen, as one delay is required to skip over the master thread. Thus, this is an example where IDB performs worse than IPB. Nevertheless, IDB is still able to find the bug within the schedule limit.

The CS.reorder_X_bad benchmark (where X is the number of threads launched – see Table 3) is the adversarial delay bounding example given in §2; the smallest delay bound required for the bug to manifest is incremented as the thread count is incremented. However, IDB still performs better than IPB, as the number of schedules in IPB increases exponentially with the thread count. Furthermore, this is a synthetic benchmark for which the bug is found quickly by both techniques with a low thread count.

Effectiveness of random scheduling   Rand performed similarly to IDB in terms of bugs found (Figure 2b). Over *all* the benchmarks, it can be seen in Table 3 that Rand was nearly always similar to or much faster than IDB in terms of *# schedules to first bug*. This said, for any particular benchmark the *# schedules to first bug* value for Rand should be treated with caution due to the role of randomness in selecting the bug-inducing schedule.

We had not anticipated that a random scheduler would be so effective at finding bugs. A possible intuition for this is as follows. If a bug can be exposed with just one delay, say, then there is a single key preemption that exposes the bug. Any schedule where (a) the key preemption occurs, and (b) additional preemptions are irrelevant to the bug, will also expose the bug. There may be many such schedules and thus a good chance of exposing the bug through random

scheduling. More generally, if a bug can be exposed with a small delay or preemption count, there may be a high probability that a randomly selected schedule will expose the bug. On the other hand, radbench.bug2 (discussed below) requires three preemptions but was still found by Rand.

The CHESS benchmarks, used for evaluation in the introduction of preemption bounding [23], test several versions of a work stealing queue. Depth-first search fails for chess.WSQ, while IPB succeeds (as in prior work). However, Rand is also able to find the bug; prior work did not compare against a random scheduler in terms of bug finding ability. The remaining CHESS benchmarks are more complex (lock-free) versions of chess.WSQ, which were also used in prior work. IPB and DFS fail on these, while IDB and Rand are, again, both successful in finding the bugs. Rand found the bugs in fewer terminal schedules than IDB and IPB for all the CHESS benchmarks.

The bug in the parsec.ferret benchmark is missed by Rand, but found by IDB. The bug requires a thread to be preempted early in the execution and not rescheduled until other threads have completed their tasks. Since Rand is very likely to reschedule the thread, it is not effective at finding this bug. For IDB, only one delay is required, but, as seen in Table 3, only one buggy schedule was found; thus, the delay must occur at a specific visible operation.

The bug in radbench.bug4 is missed by IDB, but found by Rand. The bug is caused by a shared mutex being lazily initialised by two threads at once, without synchronisation. This can lead to a double-unlock or similar error. From Table 3, it can be seen that this bug requires more than one delay. The benchmark has a relatively large number of scheduling points, such that the number of schedules with at most two delays exceeds the schedule limit.

There are several benchmarks for which the percentage of buggy schedules encountered during DFS (see *% buggy* in Table 3) is very similar to the percentage of buggy schedules observed for Rand. For example, 4% vs. 5% in CB.stringbuffer-jdk1.4, and 14% vs. 10% in CS.account_bad: However, there are counter-examples: CS.carter01_bad: 2% vs. 48%; CS.deadlock01_bad: 6% vs. 40%. Since the majority of benchmarks cannot be explored exhaustively and DFS is biased towards exploring deep context switches, it is impossible to estimate the percentage of buggy schedules for most of the benchmarks.

Comparison with the default Maple algorithm   As shown in Figure 2b, MapleAlg missed 15 bugs that were found by the other techniques, and found 32 bugs, including 1 that was missed by the others. MapleAlg is impressive considering the low number of schedules it explores. For example, all other techniques missed the bug in radbench.bug5 after 10,000 terminal schedules. In contrast, MapleAlg found it after just 14 schedules. MapleAlg attempts to force certain patterns of inter-thread accesses (or *interleaving idioms*) that might lead to concurrency bugs. This allows it to expose many bugs quickly. It is possible that the bugs it misses require interleaving idioms that are not included in MapleAlg.

Discussion No technique found the bugs in 19, 20 and 28. However, these bugs can be exposed using a lower number of threads (as shown by the other versions of these benchmarks), so these results are arguably less useful.

The schedule bounding results reveal that the bug in `radbench.bug2` requires at least three delays or preemptions. The benchmark was modified to use just two threads in total and IPB and IDB explored the same schedules. This matches largest number of preemptions required to expose a bug found in previous work [7]. However, the `misc.safestack` benchmark reportedly requires five preemptions and three threads in order for the bug to manifest. We reproduced the bug using Relacy[5], a weak memory data race detector that performs either systematic or random search for C++ programs that use C++ atomics.

The bug in `radbench.bug1` requires a thread to be preempted after destroying a hash table and a second thread to access the hash table, causing a crash. From the description, the bug *may* only require one delay, but it is likely that the large number of scheduling points is what pushes this bug out of reach of all the techniques tested.

As explained in §4.1, we reduced the input values in the SPLASH-2 benchmarks; this resulted in fewer scheduling points and allowed our data race detector to complete, without exhausting memory. Due to these changes, the results are not directly comparable with other experiments that use the SPLASH-2 benchmarks (unless parameters are similarly reduced). However, the bugs are found by all systematic techniques after just two schedules; this would be the same, regardless of parameter values. Therefore, the *# schedules to first bug* data are accurate.

7. Related Work

To our knowledge, ours is the first independent empirical study to compare schedule bounding techniques. Background and related work on systematic schedule bounding was discussed in §2. We now discuss other relevant approaches to reducing thread schedules in order to find bugs.

Partial-order reduction (POR) [11] reduces the number of schedules that need to be explored without missing errors. It relies on the fact that executions are a partial-order of operations, and explores only *one* schedule of each partial-order. Dynamic POR [9] computes persistent sets [11] during systematic search; as *dependencies* between operations are detected, additional schedules are considered. Happens-before graph caching [24, 26] is similar to state-hashing [13], except the partial-order of synchronisation operations is used as an approximation of the state, resulting in a reduction similar to sleep-sets [11]. The combination of dynamic POR and schedule bounding is the topic of recent research [5, 14, 24].

[5] http://www.1024cores.net/home/relacy-race-detector

The PCT algorithm [4] executes programs using a randomised priority-based scheduler. A bounded number of priority change points are inserted at random depths during the execution, forcing certain thread interleavings. Crucially, the depths of the change points are chosen *uniformly* over the length of the execution, unlike a traditional random scheduler that makes a random choice at every execution step. This allows bugs to be detected with a probability that is inverse exponential in the number of change points c. It allows bugs with $c + 1$ ordering constraints to be found; this number is shown empirically to be small for many interesting concurrency bugs. The parallel PCT algorithm [27] improves on this work by allowing parallel execution of many threads, as opposed to always serialising execution.

In addition to PCT, there has been a wide-range of work on other non-systematic approaches, including [29, 30, 32, 36]. Like parallel PCT, these approaches are appealing as they allow parallel execution of many threads and can handle complex synchronisation and nondeterminism.

Our study has briefly touched on dynamic race detection issues. A discussion of this wide area is out of scope here, but we refer to [8] for the state-of-the-art.

8. Conclusions and Future Work

We have presented the first independent empirical study on schedule bounding techniques for systematic concurrency testing. Our most surprising finding is that a naive *random* scheduler performs at least as well the more sophisticated iterative schedule bounding approach, when trying to expose bugs within 10,000 terminal schedules. This may indicate that the benchmarks typically used to evaluate concurrency testing tools are not adequate, as they contain bugs that can be found fairly easily through random search. On the other hand, we have proposed an intuition for why bugs that can be exposed with few preemptions may be exposed by a high percentage of schedules, and thus are amenable to exposure through randomisation.

Our findings confirm results in previous work: that schedule bounding is superior to depth-first search; many, but not all, bugs can be found using a small schedule bound; and delay bounding beats preemption bounding.

In future work we plan to expand SCTBench to conduct larger studies, and to study additional methods, such as various partial-order reduction techniques that reduce the number of schedules explored during systematic testing, as well as non-systematic approaches to concurrency testing.

Acknowledgements We are grateful to the PPoPP reviewers for their useful comments, and especially to reviewer #1 who suggested that we try random scheduling, which led to interesting results. We are also grateful for feedback on this work from Ethel Bardsley, Nathan Chong, Pantazis Deligiannis, Tony Field, Jeroen Ketema and Shaz Qadeer.

id	name	# threads	# max enabled threads	# max scheduling points	IPB bound	IPB # sched to first bug	IPB # schedules	IPB # new schedules	IPB # buggy schedules	IDB bound	IDB # sched to first bug	IDB # schedules	IDB # new schedules	IDB # buggy schedules	DFS # sched to first bug	DFS # schedules	DFS # buggy schedules	DFS % buggy	Rand # sched to first bug	Rand # buggy schedules	Maple found?	Maple # schedules	Maple total time (seconds)
0	CB.aget-bug2	4	3	23	0	1	10	10	4	0	1	1	1	1	1	L	6698	*66%	2	4874	✓	17	37
1	CB.pbzip2-0.9.4	4	4	38	0	2	12	12	4	1	2	31	30	13	2	L	6245	*62%	1	4263	✓	4	20
2	CB.stringbuffer-jdk1.4	2	2	6	2	9	13	8	1	2	9	13	8	1	7	24	1	4%	5	577	✓	9	7
3	CS.account_bad	4	3	5	0	3	6	6	2	1	3	5	4	1	3	28	4	14%	3	1089	✓	20	12
4	CS.arithmetic_prog_bad	3	2	20	0	1	4	4	4	0	1	1	1	1	1	L	L	*100%	1	L	✓	1	1
5	CS.bluetooth_driver_bad	2	2	9	1	6	7	6	1	1	6	7	6	1	36	177	10	5%	45	562	✗	11	7
6	CS.carter01_bad	5	3	14	1	9	19	16	2	1	8	12	11	1	8	1708	49	2%	3	4898	✓	6	5
7	CS.circular_buffer_bad	3	2	26	1	23	35	32	12	2	25	79	56	36	20	3991	2043	51%	3	9013	✗	17	12
8	CS.deadlock01_bad	3	2	8	1	9	12	9	2	1	7	9	8	1	10	46	3	6%	1	4095	✗	7	5
9	CS.din_phil2_sat	3	2	17	0	1	3	3	3	0	1	1	1	1	1	5336	4686	87%	1	9700	✓	1	1
10	CS.din_phil3_sat	4	3	25	0	1	13	13	13	0	1	1	1	1	1	L	8710	*87%	1	9270	✓	1	1
11	CS.din_phil4_sat	5	4	36	0	1	73	73	73	0	1	1	1	1	1	L	9353	*93%	1	8756	✓	1	1
12	CS.din_phil5_sat	6	5	39	0	1	501	501	501	0	1	1	1	1	1	L	L	*100%	1	L	✓	1	1
13	CS.din_phil6_sat	7	6	49	0	1	4051	4051	4051	0	1	1	1	1	1	L	L	*100%	1	L	✓	1	1
14	CS.din_phil7_sat	8	7	10	0	1	7	7	7	0	1	1	1	1	1	924	924	100%	1	L	✓	1	1
15	CS.fsbench_bad	28	27	155	0	1	1	1	1	0	1	1	1	1	1	L	L	*100%	1	L	✓	1	1
16	CS.lazy01_bad	4	3	7	0	1	13	13	6	0	1	1	1	1	1	118	81	68%	1	6018	✓	1	1
17	CS.phase01_bad	3	2	6	0	1	2	2	2	0	1	1	1	1	1	17	17	100%	1	L	✓	1	1
18	CS.queue_bad	3	2	61	1	98	100	97	2	2	63	482	420	326	43	L	6405	*64%	1	9996	✓	2	1
19	CS.reorder_10_bad	11	10	38	0	✗	L	L	0	4	✗	L	3217	0	✗	L	0	*0%	✗	0	✗	11	7
20	CS.reorder_20_bad	21	20	87	0	✗	L	L	0	3	✗	L	6916	0	✗	L	0	*0%	✗	0	✗	11	7
21	CS.reorder_3_bad	4	3	10	1	43	74	61	2	2	25	45	35	3	126	2494	23	<1%	25	270	✗	10	7
22	CS.reorder_4_bad	5	4	14	1	359	774	701	3	3	205	417	330	7	6409	L	4	*<1%	9	63	✗	11	8
23	CS.reorder_5_bad	6	5	18	1	3378	8483	7982	4	4	1513	3681	2843	15	✗	L	0	*0%	123	22	✗	11	7
24	CS.stack_bad	3	2	31	1	23	50	47	9	1	22	32	31	9	22	L	512	*5%	1	5877	✗	10	8
25	CS.sync01_bad	3	2	2	0	1	2	2	2	0	1	1	1	1	1	6	6	100%	1	L	✓	1	1
26	CS.sync02_bad	3	2	9	0	1	2	2	2	0	1	1	1	1	1	88	88	100%	1	L	✓	1	1
27	CS.token_ring_bad	5	4	8	0	8	24	24	4	2	10	29	22	3	8	280	57	20%	6	1103	✓	5	4
28	CS.twostage_100_bad	101	100	792	0	✗	L	L	0	2	✗	L	9304	0	✗	L	0	*0%	✗	0	✗	11	9
29	CS.twostage_bad	3	2	8	1	9	10	7	1	1	7	9	8	1	13	87	3	3%	5	837	✓	8	5
30	CS.wronglock_3_bad	5	4	22	1	243	856	783	66	1	15	22	21	2	3233	L	94	*<1%	8	3010	✓	6	4
31	CS.wronglock_bad	9	8	46	0	✗	L	L	0	1	31	42	41	2	✗	L	0	*0%	5	3065	✓	6	4
32	chess.IWSQ	3	3	120	1	✗	L	9997	0	2	3077	4466	4351	192	✗	L	0	*0%	1496	15	✗	7	-
33	chess.IWSQWS	3	3	1497	1	✗	L	9997	0	1	773	1498	1497	1	✗	L	0	*0%	2	646	✗	9	-
34	chess.SWSQ	3	3	1697	1	✗	L	9997	0	1	773	1698	1697	1	✗	L	0	*0%	140	85	✗	7	-
35	chess.WSQ	3	3	90	2	2814	8852	8626	640	2	801	2048	1974	192	✗	L	0	*0%	355	8	✗	12	12
36	inspect.qsort_mt	3	3	33	1	31	88	84	2	1	19	28	27	1	✗	L	0	*0%	132	108	✗	142	102
37	misc.ctrace-test	3	2	19	1	4	20	19	12	1	4	20	19	12	4	20	12	60%	2	2641	✓	1	1
38	misc.safestack	4	3	114	1	✗	L	9987	0	3	✗	L	5958	0	✗	L	0	*0%	✗	0	✗	23	16
39	parsec.ferret	11	11	24453	0	✗	L	L	0	1	51	4575	4574	1	✗	L	0	*0%	✗	0	✗	27	205
40	parsec.streamcluster	5	2	1373	1	✗	L	9994	0	1	1336	1372	1371	10	✗	L	0	*0%	2	7122	✗	1	2
41	parsec.streamcluster2	7	3	4177	0	✗	L	L	0	1	4155	4177	4176	20	✗	L	0	*0%	31	347	✗	24	149
42	parsec.streamcluster3	5	2	1373	0	2	6	6	4	1	2	1369	1368	4	2	L	6078	*60%	4	3435	✓	1	1
43	radbench.bug1	4	3	14214	1	✗	L	9962	0	1	✗	L	9999	0	✗	L	0	*0%	✗	0	✗	629	8797
44	radbench.bug2	2	2	41	3	2647	3154	2808	8	3	2647	3154	2808	8	✗	L	0	*0%	2267	5	✗	220	804
45	radbench.bug3	3	2	239	0	1	3	3	3	0	1	1	1	1	1	L	L	*100%	1	L	✗	32	96
46	radbench.bug4	3	2	209	2	✗	L	9658	0	2	✗	L	9852	0	✗	L	0	*0%	377	9	✓	16	23
47	radbench.bug5	7	3	856	1	✗	L	9936	0	2	✗	L	9210	0	✗	L	0	*0%	✗	0	✓	14	18
48	radbench.bug6	3	3	29	1	27	58	55	1	1	19	30	29	1	✗	L	0	*0%	12	1306	✗	34	39
49	splash2.barnes	2	2	4408	1	2	4378	4377	326	1	2	4378	4377	326	2	L	2484	*24%	3	4982	✓	1	1
50	splash2.fft	2	2	136	1	2	134	133	61	1	2	134	133	61	2	L	7429	*74%	2	6214	✓	2	2
51	splash2.lu	2	2	114	1	2	105	104	49	1	2	105	104	49	2	L	4993	*49%	1	9741	✓	2	3

Table 3: Experimental results for systematic concurrency testing using iterative preemption bounding (IPB), iterative delay bounding (IDB) and unbounded depth-first search (DFS), and non-systematic testing with a naive random scheduler (Rand) and using the Maple algorithm (MapleAlg). Entries marked 'L' indicate 10,000, our schedule limit. A '✗' indicates that no bug was found. In the MapleAlg results, '-' indicates that the Maple tool timed out after 24 hours. A percentage prefixed with '*' does not apply to *all* schedules, only those that were explored via DFS before the schedule limit was reached.

References

[1] A. Bessey et al. A few billion lines of code later: using static analysis to find bugs in the real world. *Commun. ACM*, 53(2): 66–75, 2010.

[2] C. Bienia. *Benchmarking Modern Multiprocessors*. PhD thesis, Princeton University, 2011.

[3] H.-J. Boehm. How to miscompile programs with "benign" data races. In *HotPar*, pages 1–6, 2011.

[4] S. Burckhardt, P. Kothari, M. Musuvathi, and S. Nagarakatte. A randomized scheduler with probabilistic guarantees of finding bugs. In *ASPLOS*, pages 167–178, 2010.

[5] K. E. Coons, M. Musuvathi, and K. S. McKinley. Bounded partial-order reduction. In *OOPSLA*, pages 833–848, 2013.

[6] L. Cordeiro and B. Fischer. Verifying multi-threaded software using SMT-based context-bounded model checking. In *ICSE*, pages 331–340, 2011.

[7] M. Emmi, S. Qadeer, and Z. Rakamarić. Delay-bounded scheduling. In *POPL*, pages 411–422, 2011.

[8] C. Flanagan and S. N. Freund. FastTrack: efficient and precise dynamic race detection. In *PLDI*, pages 121–133, 2009.

[9] C. Flanagan and P. Godefroid. Dynamic partial-order reduction for model checking software. In *POPL*, pages 110–121, 2005.

[10] M. Frigo, C. E. Leiserson, and K. H. Randall. The implementation of the Cilk-5 multithreaded language. In *PLDI*, pages 212–223, 1998.

[11] P. Godefroid. *Partial-Order Methods for the Verification of Concurrent Systems*. Springer, 1996.

[12] P. Godefroid. Model checking for programming languages using VeriSoft. In *POPL*, pages 174–186, 1997.

[13] G. J. Holzmann. On limits and possibilities of automated protocol analysis. In *PSTV*, pages 339–344, 1987.

[14] G. J. Holzmann and M. Florian. Model checking with bounded context switching. *Formal Asp. Comput.*, 23(3):365–389, 2011.

[15] J. Huang and C. Zhang. An efficient static trace simplification technique for debugging concurrent programs. In *SAS*, pages 163–179, 2011.

[16] N. Jalbert and K. Sen. A trace simplification technique for effective debugging of concurrent programs. In *FSE*, FSE '10, pages 57–66, 2010.

[17] N. Jalbert, C. Pereira, G. Pokam, and K. Sen. RADBench: a concurrency bug benchmark suite. In *HotPar*, pages 1–6, 2011.

[18] B. Kasikci, C. Zamfir, and G. Candea. Data races vs. data race bugs: telling the difference with Portend. In *ASPLOS*, pages 185–198, 2012.

[19] B. Křena, Z. Letko, T. Vojnar, and S. Ur. A platform for search-based testing of concurrent software. In *PADTAD*, pages 48–58, 2010.

[20] A. Lal and T. W. Reps. Reducing concurrent analysis under a context bound to sequential analysis. *Formal Methods in System Design*, 35(1):73–97, 2009.

[21] B. Lewis and D. J. Berg. *Multithreaded programming with Pthreads*. Prentice-Hall, 1998.

[22] C.-K. Luk et al. Pin: building customized program analysis tools with dynamic instrumentation. In *PLDI*, pages 190–200, 2005.

[23] M. Musuvathi and S. Qadeer. Iterative context bounding for systematic testing of multithreaded programs. In *PLDI*, pages 446–455, 2007.

[24] M. Musuvathi and S. Qadeer. Partial-order reduction for context-bounded state exploration. Technical Report MSR-TR-2007-12, Microsoft Research, 2007.

[25] M. Musuvathi and S. Qadeer. Fair stateless model checking. In *PLDI*, pages 362–371, 2008.

[26] M. Musuvathi et al. Finding and reproducing Heisenbugs in concurrent programs. In *OSDI*, pages 267–280, 2008.

[27] S. Nagarakatte, S. Burckhardt, M. M. Martin, and M. Musuvathi. Multicore acceleration of priority-based schedulers for concurrency bug detection. In *PLDI*, pages 543–554, 2012.

[28] S. Narayanasamy et al. Automatically classifying benign and harmful data races using replay analysis. In *PLDI*, pages 22–31, 2007.

[29] S. Park, S. Lu, and Y. Zhou. CTrigger: exposing atomicity violation bugs from their hiding places. In *ASPLOS*, pages 25–36, 2009.

[30] K. Sen. Race directed random testing of concurrent programs. In *PLDI*, pages 11–21, 2008.

[31] H. Sutter and J. Larus. Software and the concurrency revolution. *ACM Queue*, 3(7):54–62, 2005.

[32] C. Wang, M. Said, and A. Gupta. Coverage guided systematic concurrency testing. In *ICSE*, pages 221–230, 2011.

[33] S. C. Woo et al. The SPLASH-2 programs: characterization and methodological considerations. In *ISCA*, pages 24–36, 1995.

[34] Y. Yang, X. Chen, and G. Gopalakrishnan. Inspect: A run-time model checker for multithreaded C programs. Technical Report UUCS-08-004, University of Utah, 2008.

[35] J. Yu and S. Narayanasamy. A case for an interleaving constrained shared-memory multi-processor. In *ISCA*, pages 325–336, 2009.

[36] J. Yu, S. Narayanasamy, C. Pereira, and G. Pokam. Maple: a coverage-driven testing tool for multithreaded programs. In *OOPSLA*, pages 485–502, 2012.

Trace Driven Dynamic Deadlock Detection and Reproduction

Malavika Samak

Indian Institute of Science, Bangalore

malavika@csa.iisc.ernet.in

Murali Krishna Ramanathan

Indian Institute of Science, Bangalore

muralikrishna@csa.iisc.ernet.in

Abstract

Dynamic analysis techniques have been proposed to detect *potential* deadlocks. Analyzing and comprehending each potential deadlock to determine whether the deadlock is feasible in a real execution requires significant programmer effort. Moreover, empirical evidence shows that existing analyses are quite imprecise. This imprecision of the analyses further *void* the manual effort invested in reasoning about *non-existent* defects.

In this paper, we address the problems of imprecision of existing analyses and the subsequent manual effort necessary to reason about deadlocks. We propose a novel approach for deadlock detection by designing a dynamic analysis that intelligently leverages execution traces. To reduce the manual effort, we replay the program by making the execution follow a schedule *derived* based on the observed trace. For a real deadlock, its feasibility is automatically verified if the replay causes the execution to deadlock.

We have implemented our approach as part of WOLF and have analyzed many large (upto 160KLoC) Java programs. Our experimental results show that we are able to identify 74% of the reported defects as true (or false) positives automatically leaving very few defects for manual analysis. The overhead of our approach is negligible making it a compelling tool for practical adoption.

Categories and Subject Descriptors D.2.5 [*Software Engineering*]: Testing and Debugging; D.2.4 [*Software Engineering*]: Software/Program Verification

Keywords deadlock detection; dynamic analysis; concurrency

1. Introduction

Traditional software testing to ensure the correctness of multi-threaded programs is inadequate due to the limitations associated with checking the correctness of the program across all possible interleavings [20]. This has resulted in the design of a number of program analysis techniques for detecting concurrency bugs [3, 8, 9, 14, 17, 22, 26, 29, 35]. The defects detected by dynamic analyses are highly likely to be real bugs because the analyses operate on real program execution data. Nevertheless, the analyses still suffer from false positives i.e., they report a defect when there is indeed no problem. Therefore, a programmer needs to analyze and comprehend a defect report to determine its correctness which can be time consuming. Practical experience [2, 19] shows that programmers adapt program analysis tools widely if the results are precise and actionable. Hence, the combination of imprecise analysis and the subsequent manual effort required to verify the correctness of the reported defects can lead to poor deployment of dynamic analysis tools, in spite of the sophisticated machinery employed to detect rare problems.

Deadlocks in multi-threaded programs are frustrating due to their ability to bring the system to a grinding halt in a nondeterministic fashion [16]. Existing state of the art dynamic analyses [3, 14] use cycle detection on a global lock graph to detect a deadlock. The nodes in the graph represent the lock instances. An edge, labelled t, between any two nodes u and v, represents the acquisition of lock v while holding lock u by thread t. A cycle in the global lock graph is considered a potential deadlock if the edge labels in the cycle are unique.

Even though cycles in the lock graph point to potential deadlocks, these deadlocks may *never* manifest in a real execution. For example, if two threads t_1 and t_2 acquire locks ℓ_1 and ℓ_2 in opposite order respectively, then the lock graph contains two edges – an edge from ℓ_1 to ℓ_2 and an edge from ℓ_2 to ℓ_1. Observe that a deadlock is only possible if the acquisitions by t_1 and t_2 overlap in some schedule. Because existing detectors do not consider the *complete* history prior to the relevant lock acquisitions, they report any cycle as a deadlock, even though the lock acquisitions by t_1 and t_2 *never* overlap. Identifying overlaps can be challenging as the corresponding threads may not communicate directly with each other. Even if there is an overlap, the detected deadlock may still not be real for a variety of reasons including infeasible interleavings.

As we mentioned above, significant programmer effort is also necessary to comprehend the defects reported by these approaches. Therefore, to address this problem, apart from detecting potential deadlocks, DeadlockFuzzer [14] goes a step further and attempts to reproduce the deadlocks in a real execution. For each potential deadlock, the program is re-executed by *fuzzing* the schedule appropriately to make the execution deadlock. If the re-execution deadlocks, then the deadlock is considered a real defect. Otherwise, the classification of the deadlock is *unknown*. While a necessary first step in reducing the tedious process of comprehending the reported defects, their approach manages to automatically reproduce only 8% of the reported defects [14][1].

A detected deadlock can be easily classified as real (or true positive) in the presence of just *one* deadlocking re-execution. Unlike true positives, for a detected deadlock to be classified as a false positive, a re-execution of the program with *any* schedule should not cause the execution to deadlock. Unfortunately, this goes back to the original problem of exhaustive search of the interleavings. Moreover, even for real defects, because the trace data generated during the detection process is not leveraged, random schedules are generated to cause a deadlocking execution. This strategy may be ineffective as it may not result in the intended deadlock. This ineffective exploration of schedules associated with a deadlock, along with the presence of a large number of false positives, leaves a significant number of *unknown* defects to be comprehended manually.

In this paper, we address both the problems: (a) imprecision of existing dynamic deadlock detection approaches and (b) poor automatic reproducibility of a potential deadlock. We design a novel, scalable and more precise dynamic deadlock detection approach that intelligently leverages trace data to identify *real* deadlocks. We extend the instrumentation for deadlock detection to keep track of time stamps of lock acquisitions and releases, apart from recording the operations. Each thread also maintains a vector of timestamp pairs, that presents the thread's view of the execution times of the other threads.

We build a Pruner that effectively uses this additional data to identify code regions from different threads that can never overlap, thereby pruning potential deadlocks reported in these regions. The remaining deadlocks along with the trace data are consumed by the Generator. The Generator generates a *synchronization dependency graph*, G_s, for each deadlock. The lock acquisitions leading to the deadlocking acquisitions made in the original execution of the program form the nodes of this graph. An edge between two nodes u and v in the graph denotes that the lock acquisition at u must

happen before the acquisition at v. The edges are generated systematically so that following the order specified in G_s will result in a deadlocking re-execution. If G_s contains a cycle, then the associated deadlock can *never* manifest in a real execution for the path explored (i.e., any different schedule on the same trace will never lead to a deadlocking execution). Therefore, potential deadlocks with a cycle in their corresponding synchronization dependency graphs are also eliminated as false positives automatically.

For the potential set of deadlocks that are output by the Generator, we attempt to re-execute the program on the same input so that all dependencies in G_s corresponding to the deadlock under consideration are satisfied. We build a Replayer for this purpose that monitors the thread operations and systematically pauses or enables different threads according to the dependencies in G_s. If the Replayer attempts to replay a potential deadlock and the re-execution results in the same deadlock, then it classifies the potential deadlock as *real*. If it is unable to reproduce the deadlock after a pre-determined number of attempts, the deadlock is classified as *unknown* and left for manual comprehension.

We have implemented all the above components as part of WOLF and analyzed large Java programs (upto 160KLoC). Applying WOLF on these benchmarks shows that it detects a number of deadlocks. It eliminates 18.5% (12 out of 65) of the reported defects as false positives and automatically confirms 68% (36 out of 53 defects) of the remaining potential defects as real deadlocks. Our experimental results also show the ability of the Replayer to reproduce a given deadlock reliably. The runtime overhead of WOLF for detecting the deadlocks is quite negligible. The average time to automatically reproduce a deadlock ranges from 3 to 50 seconds approximately.

This paper makes the following technical contributions:

- We design a novel and scalable algorithm that uses vector clocks and cycle detection effectively and leverages trace data to detect deadlocks precisely.

- We propose a replay algorithm that runs the program using the synchronization dependency graph generated from the recorded trace so as to deadlock the execution. The reproduction of the deadlock automatically confirms the correctness of the reported defect.

- We implement these algorithms as part of WOLF which takes as input the program under consideration and a set of test inputs and outputs a list of automatically confirmed deadlocks.

- We demonstrate the effectiveness of WOLF by applying it on large benchmarks (upto 160KLoC) and show that it not only reports deadlocks but also identifies 74% of the overall reported defects as true (or false) positives automatically.

---

[1] In our experiments, their approach is able to reproduce approximately 35% of the reported defects as we count the number of problematic source locations instead of the number of cycles. Refer Section 4.3 for more details.

2. Motivation

In this section, we demonstrate using examples that existing dynamic deadlock detection approaches, that are trace agnostic, suffer from false positives. We also show that using a randomized schedule to reproduce a real deadlock need not always succeed leaving even real bugs for manual comprehension and motivate the problems addressed in this paper.

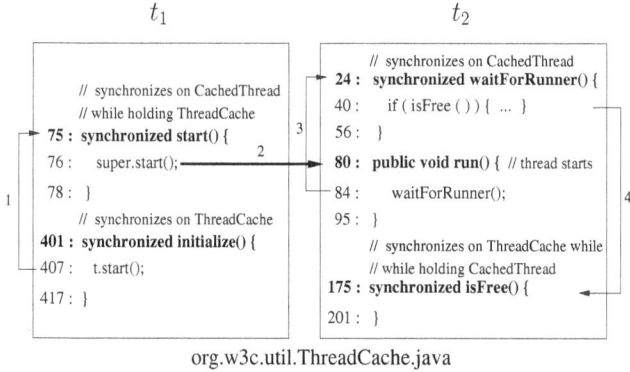

Figure 1. False deadlock reported by `iGoodLock` [14]. t_1 acquires lock on TC, an instance of `ThreadCache`, at line 401 and on CT, an instance of `ThreadCache`, at line 75. t_2 acquires the locks on the same objects in the opposite order at lines 24 and 175 respectively. Deadlock can never manifest because t_1 *always* starts t_2.

Figure 1 presents code fragment from `Jigsaw 2.2.6`, a web server, executed by two threads t_1 and t_2. Initially, t_1 executes and acquires a lock on an instance of `ThreadCache`, TC, at line 401. Subsequently, it acquires a lock on an instance of `CachedThread`, CT, at line 75 while still holding TC. Deadlock detectors based on cycle detection will create two nodes TC and CT corresponding to the two lock acquisitions and add an edge, labelled t_1, between them to represent the nested lock acquisition. Eventually, t_2 also executes and acquires locks on CT and TC at lines 24 and 175 respectively. An edge between CT and TC is added and is labelled t_2. Due to the presence of a cycle in the lock graph and the edges carrying labels of different threads, a potential deadlock is reported by existing state of the art detectors.

On closer examination, however, we observe that this deadlock can never happen in reality. This is because t_1 starts thread t_2 at line 76 while holding locks TC and CT. For the deadlock under consideration to manifest between t_1 and t_2, it is necessary that one of the locks must be held by t_2. This is *impossible* on any interleaving of the two threads as both the locks are already held by t_1. t_2 can acquire CT only after t_1 relinquishes it. Therefore, the deadlock detected on this set of lock acquisitions can be eliminated as a false positive. Moreover, we emphasize that any attempt to reproduce the detected (false) deadlock will obviously fail leaving this defect to be manually evaluated.

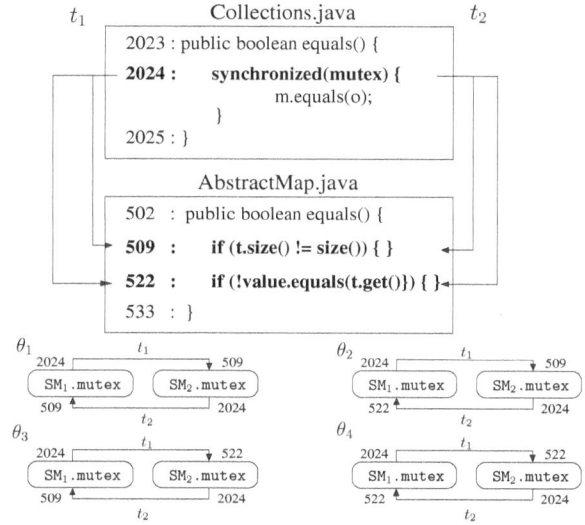

Figure 2. Cycle θ_4 is a false positive. The cycle cannot be reproduced in *any* interleaving. $t.\texttt{size()}$ and $t.\texttt{get()}$ synchronize on $t.\texttt{mutex}$ and their implementations are not shown here for ease of presentation.

Even when there is no total ordering of lock acquisitions, the sequence of lock acquisitions leading to the deadlocking acquisitions can make the deadlock infeasible. This is demonstrated by the code fragment given in Figure 2. Consider cycle θ_4 shown in the Figure. Let SM_1 and SM_2 be instances of `SynchronizedMap` with instance field `mutex`. Thread t_1 acquires locks on $SM_1.\texttt{mutex}$ and $SM_2.\texttt{mutex}$ at lines 2024 and 522 respectively. When thread t_2 acquires the same locks in the opposite order at lines 2024 and 522 respectively, then existing deadlock detectors report the presence of a potential deadlock. This indeed could be a real deadlock but for the presence of an interim lock acquisition in method `size` invoked at line 509 that lies in between these two lock acquisitions.

Thread t_1 acquires and releases a lock on $SM_2.\texttt{mutex}$, when the method `size` is invoked in `AbstractMap` at line 509. Therefore, if the underlying detector analyzes the trace leading to θ_4 it can potentially eliminate the reported deadlock as false because it will never manifest in a real execution. To elaborate further, let us assume t_1 acquires the lock on $SM_1.\texttt{mutex}$ at line 2024. Thread t_2 cannot go beyond line 509 resulting in cycle θ_1 or cycle θ_3 manifesting based on whether t_1 already invoked `size` or not. A similar argument can be made to show that even when t_2 is executed first, only cycles θ_1 and θ_2 can manifest. In other words, there is no schedule where θ_4 can be reproduced and thus the potential deadlock indicated by it can be safely eliminated as a false positive.

Because of the presence of false positives discussed above, any attempt to reproduce these *non-existent* bugs will obviously fail. These defects need to be comprehended

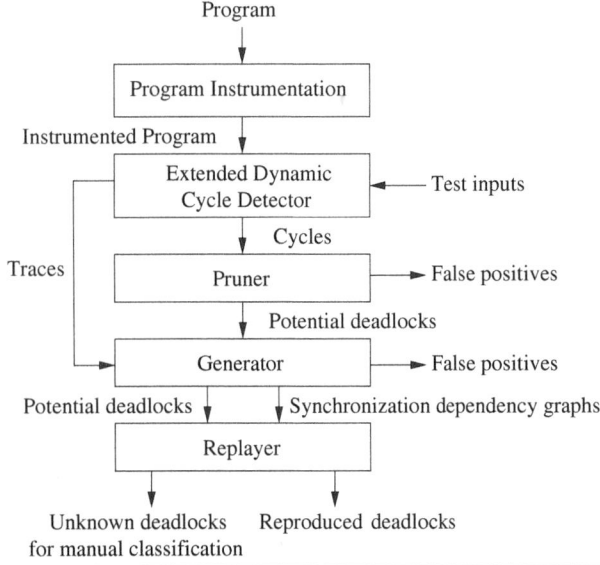

Figure 3. Architecture of WOLF

manually and because they require nuanced reasoning about threads and schedules, it can make the entire process tedious and time consuming. Notwithstanding the problems with false positives, even if a real defect needs to be automatically reproduced, existing tools [14] may not reliably reproduce the defect.

Consider a real deadlock between threads t_1 and t_2 indicated by cycle θ_2 in Figure 2. In the process of re-executing the program to reproduce a deadlock based on cycle θ_2, if a context switch happens such that t_1 always acquires lock on $\text{SM}_1.\text{mutex}$ at line 2024 before t_2 can acquire lock at line 509, then thread t_2 will always be blocked at line 509. This prevents the deadlock indicated by cycle θ_2 from manifesting and the deadlock indicated by cycle θ_1 to be reproduced. While the deadlock is indeed real, the randomized scheduling can potentially *bias* the schedules in favor of deadlocks that happen earlier in the code to manifest always, thus motivating the need for a systematic approach. We show, empirically, that maintaining a dependency of the lock acquisitions across threads indeed results in a higher number of real deadlocks being reproduced automatically.

3. Design

The overall system architecture of our trace aware dynamic deadlock detection tool named WOLF is shown in Figure 3. We broadly divide the system into four major components – Extended Dynamic Cycle Detector, Pruner, Generator and Replayer.

Extended Dynamic Cycle Detector analyzes the execution of the program on a set of test inputs and identifies cycles in the global lock graph as potential deadlocks. In this work, we use iGoodlock [14] to build the base Detector and extend it to get better precision. In the extended detector, the trace containing the lock acquisitions for each test

input is also recorded. Pruner takes the potential deadlocks as input and filters the false positives based on the timestamps. The filtered set of potential deadlocks along with the recorded trace are input to the Generator. For each deadlock and its associated trace, the Generator builds a *synchronization dependency graph*. The presence of a cycle in this graph indicates that the corresponding deadlock is false. Otherwise, the Replayer attempts to reproduce the potential deadlock by executing the program on the test input that enabled the Detector to detect the deadlock in the first place. Replayer executes the program by ensuring that the dependencies in the synchronization dependency graph associated with the potential deadlock are satisfied to cause the execution to deadlock appropriately. If the deadlock cannot be reproduced after multiple trials, the tool indicates that the defect needs to be analyzed manually. The rest of this section describes each component in detail.

3.1 Background

We initially explain the operations in the program that are handled by our analysis and give a brief background on iGoodLock [14] which is used as the base detector in WOLF.

- $Lock(\ell)$: Executing thread acquires lock on ℓ.
- $Unlock(\ell)$: Executing thread releases lock on ℓ.
- $t.start()$: Executing thread starts thread t and both the threads can execute in parallel thereon.
- $t.join()$: Executing thread waits till thread t finishes executing all its instructions.

We consider a thread t makes a deadlocking acquisition if it attempts to acquire a lock and potentially gets into a cyclic dependency with one or more threads resulting in all the threads waiting on each other.

To detect cycles in an execution σ, the detector maintains a lock dependency relation D_σ, where D_σ is a set of tuples (t, L_t, ℓ, C_t). During execution σ, if thread t acquires a lock on ℓ while holding locks in L_t creating a context C_t, then a tuple $\eta = (t, L_t, \ell, C_t)$ is added to D_σ. The context C_t is a sequence of execution indices[2] representing instructions that correspond to the acquisition of currently held locks given by L_t. We define functions $\text{thread}(\eta)$, $\text{lock}(\eta)$ and $\text{lockset}(\eta)$ that return t, ℓ and L_t respectively. For any tuple η_i, we define μ_i as a function which maps each lock contained in lockset L_t of η_i to its corresponding execution index in C_t.

The detector uses D_σ to detect potential deadlocks. We define a potential deadlock, $\theta = \{\eta_1, \eta_2 \ldots \eta_n\}$, where

- For every η_i, η_{i+1} in θ, $\text{lock}(\eta_i) \in \text{lockset}(\eta_{i+1})$ and $\text{lock}(\eta_n) \in \text{lockset}(\eta_1)$. Every thread in cycle attempts to acquire a lock that is acquired by some other thread.

---

[2] Identifies instructions, objects and threads across runs.

- For every η_i, η_j in θ, where $i \neq j$, lockset(η_i) $\cap$ lockset$(\eta_j) = \emptyset$ and thread$(\eta_i) \neq$ thread(η_j). There are no guard locks present for the cycle and each thread contributes to only one edge in the cycle.

For more details on cycle detection and how execution indices are determined, we refer the reader to [14]. We elucidate the basic deadlock detection process using an example and use it as a running example to demonstrate the application of our approach subsequently.

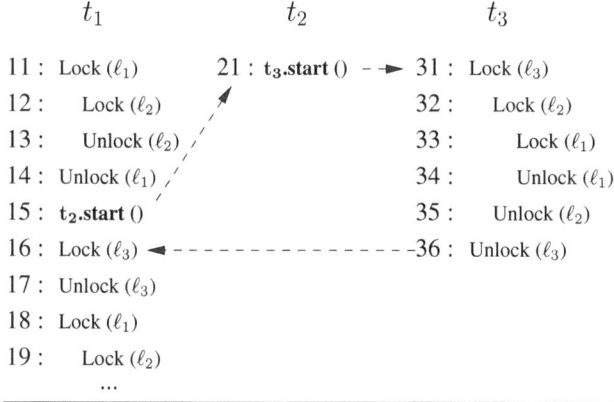

t_1	t_2	t_3
11 : Lock (ℓ_1)	21 : t_3.start ()	31 : Lock (ℓ_3)
12 : Lock (ℓ_2)		32 : Lock (ℓ_2)
13 : Unlock (ℓ_2)		33 : Lock (ℓ_1)
14 : Unlock (ℓ_1)		34 : Unlock (ℓ_1)
15 : t_2.start ()		35 : Unlock (ℓ_2)
16 : Lock (ℓ_3)		36 : Unlock (ℓ_3)
17 : Unlock (ℓ_3)		
18 : Lock (ℓ_1)		
19 : Lock (ℓ_2)		
...		

Figure 4. Illustrative example

$\eta_1 = (1,\{\},\ell_1,\{11\})$	$\eta_1' = (1,\{\},\ell_1,\{11\},1)$
$\eta_2 = (1,\{\ell_1\},\ell_2,\{11,12\})$	$\eta_2' = (1,\{\ell_1\},\ell_2,\{11,12\},1)$
$\eta_3 = (3,\{\},\ell_3,\{31\})$	$\eta_3' = (3,\{\},\ell_3,\{31\},1)$
$\eta_4 = (3,\{\ell_3\},\ell_2,\{31,32\})$	$\eta_4' = (3,\{\ell_3\},\ell_2,\{31,32\},1)$
$\eta_5 = (3,\{\ell_3,\ell_2\},\ell_1,\{31,32,33\})$	$\eta_5' = (3,\{\ell_3,\ell_2\},\ell_1,\{31,32,33\},1)$
$\eta_6 = (1,\{\},\ell_3,\{16\})$	$\eta_6' = (1,\{\},\ell_3,\{16\},2)$
$\eta_7 = (1,\{\},\ell_1,\{18\})$	$\eta_7' = (1,\{\},\ell_1,\{18\},2)$
$\eta_8 = (1,\{\ell_1\},\ell_2,\{18,19\})$	$\eta_8' = (1,\{\ell_1\},\ell_2,\{18,19\},2)$

Figure 5. Left: D_σ generated by iGoodLock. Right: D_σ generated by Extended Dynamic Cycle Detector.

Figure 4 presents a code fragment with threads t_1, t_2 and t_3, and locks ℓ_1, ℓ_2 and ℓ_3. Assume the numbers to the left of the instructions are the execution indices (and not line numbers). According to the Figure, t_1 acquires a lock on ℓ_1 by executing instruction with index 11. Tuple η_1 is added to D_σ to capture this acquisition. Later, t_1 acquires a lock on ℓ_2 and η_2 is added to D_σ. The other instructions are executed and subsequently t_3 acquires locks on ℓ_3, ℓ_2 and ℓ_1 in that order and tuples η_3, η_4, η_5 are added to D_σ accordingly. The state of D_σ after all instructions are executed is shown on the left side of Figure 5. When the program terminates, the detector analyzes D_σ and detects two cycles θ_1 and θ_2, where $\theta_1 = \{\eta_2, \eta_5\}$ and $\theta_2 = \{\eta_8, \eta_5\}$.

θ_1 is a false deadlock because there is no feasible schedule where t_3 begins its execution before t_1 acquires lock ℓ_2 at instruction 12. This is because there is a total order between instructions at 21 and 31 due to $t_3.start()$ and the total order between instructions at 31 and 32 due to program order. θ_2 can become a real deadlock, even though it involves the

same threads and locks as θ_1. The existing detector is ordering agnostic and outputs both cycles as potential deadlocks. We address this limitation by extending the cycle detection and describe it in the next section.

3.2 Extended Dynamic Cycle Detector

To improve the precision of detection, each thread maintains a time stamp, which is initially $\bot$. We use $\bot$ to indicate that the thread has not started. The value of the time stamp is updated to one when the thread begins its execution. The time stamp of thread t is increased by one whenever t executes a $t'.start()$ or $t'.join()$ for some thread t'. This represents the creation of a total order among a few instructions of t and t'. If t starts t', all the instructions executed by t prior to the start precedes every instruction executed by t'. Similarly, on a $t'.join()$ by t, all the instructions executed by t' always happens before every instruction executed by t after the join. We use the timestamps to identify non-overlapping range of instructions.

For every thread pair (t, t'), there can be a maximum of two non-overlapping regions between t and t'. Therefore, to identify the boundaries of the non-overlapping regions, we maintain an ordered pair of timestamps. Each thread maintains a vector of these ordered pairs presenting the boundaries of the non-overlapping regions.

We extend the definition of $\eta \in D_\sigma$ from the previous section to encode the timestamp as well. η is now defined as $(t, L_t, \ell, C_t, \tau_t)$, where τ_t is the time stamp of thread t, when it acquired a lock on ℓ, while holding locks in set L_t with context C_t. We *index* each thread in the system to a unique value in $\{1 \ldots |T|\}$. Also, every thread t maintains a *vector clock* V_t, a set of ordered pairs, whose cardinality is $|T|$. The ordered pair $(S, J) = V_t(t')$, represents t's view of thread t' and is defined as follows:

1. S: the time stamp of t' such that all operations in t' at timestamp less than S will always be completed before thread t begins its execution. In other words, no instruction in t' with timestamp less than S will *ever* overlap with any instruction in t.

2. J: the time stamp of t such that all operations in t at timestamp greater than or equal to J will always execute after thread t' has joined. In other words, no instruction in t with timestamp greater than or equal to J will *ever* overlap with any instruction in t'.

The detector is also extended to maintain two more global states, τ and V.

- $\tau: T \to N \cup \{\bot\}$, a map from a thread to its timestamp, which is initially $\bot$.
- $V: T \to (\{N \cup \bot\} \times \{N \cup \bot\})^{|T|}$, a map from a thread to its vector clock, where each ordered pair is initially $(\bot, \bot)$.

Algorithm 1 Extended Dynamic Cycle Detector

Input: Instrumented program, Test input
Output: Set of potential deadlocks, Θ

1: $D_\sigma \leftarrow \emptyset, Enabled \leftarrow T, Terminated \leftarrow \emptyset$;
2: **for** each i in $[1, |T|]$ **do**
3:    $C_i \leftarrow \emptyset; L_i \leftarrow \emptyset; \tau_i = \bot$;
4: **end for**
5: **for** each i, j in $[1, |T|]$ **do**
6:    $V_i(j) \leftarrow (\bot, \bot)$
7: **end for**
8: **while** $Enabled \neq \emptyset$ **do**
9:    $t_p \leftarrow$ a random thread from $Enabled$
10:    $s \leftarrow$ next statement to be executed by t_p
11:    **if** $\tau_p = \bot$ **then** $\tau_p \leftarrow 1$ **end if**
12:    **if** s is nil **then** Move t_p from $Enabled$ to $Terminated$
13:    **else if** s is $t_c.start()$ **then**
14:       $\tau_p \leftarrow \tau_p + 1; \tau_c \leftarrow 1$
15:       **for** each i in $[1, |T|]$ **do** /* updating V_c */
16:          /* Has thread t_i already joined?*/
17:          **if** $V_p[i].J \neq \bot$ **then** $V_c[i].J = \tau_c$ **end if**
18:          /*Time stamps of t_i that are always in past for t_c*/
19:          **if** $i = p$ **then** $V_c[p].S \leftarrow \tau_p$
20:          **else** $V_c[i].S \leftarrow V_p[i].S$ **end if**
21:       **end for**
22:    **else if** s is $t_c.join()$ **then**
23:       $\tau_p \leftarrow \tau_p + 1$
24:       **for** each i in $[1, |T|]$ **do** /* Has t_i already joined?*/
25:          **if** $i = c$ or $(V_c[i].J \neq \bot$ and $V_p[i].J = \bot)$ **then**
26:             $V_p[i].J \leftarrow \tau_p$
27:          **end if**
28:       **end for**
29:    **else if** s is lock(ℓ) **then**
30:       $idx \leftarrow$ execution index of s.
31:       Push ℓ to L_p and idx to C_p
32:       Add $\eta \leftarrow \{t_p, L_p, \ell, C_p, \tau_p\}$ to D_σ.
33:    **else if** s is unlock(ℓ) **then**
34:       Pop from L_p and C_p.
35:    **end if**
36:    Execute statement s
37: **end while**
38: $\Theta \leftarrow$ Detected cycles in D_σ /*standard cycle detection*/

Algorithm 1 presents the set of actions that are performed by the detector during execution. The set $Enabled$ is initialized to include all the active threads in the system. When a thread t_p starts another thread t_c, the time stamps of t_p and t_c are incremented by one and set to one respectively. The child thread t_c's vector clock V_c is also updated. The child thread t_c's S values are copied from the parent thread t_p's vector clock. We perform this operation because the instructions by threads that finished before t_p began its execution are obviously completed before t_c begins its execution. If J value is set to a value other than $\bot$ in $V_p(t')$, for some thread t', then the J value in $V_c(t')$ is set to τ_c. We perform this operation because if t_p cannot currently overlap with t' due to an execution of $t'.join()$ in *some* thread (not necessarily by t_p due to transitivity), then any thread started by t_p sub-

sequently can never overlap with the instructions in t'. In a similar fashion, other actions are designed for the rest of the operations. Once the program exits, the cycles in the dependency set D_σ are detected.

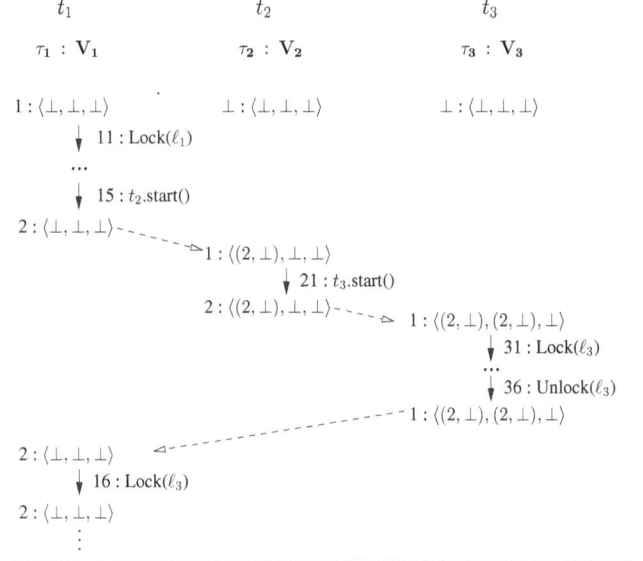

Figure 6. Time stamp calculation. At the end of the execution, $V = \{V_1, V_2, V_3\}$, where $V_1 = \langle \bot, \bot, \bot \rangle$, $V_2 = \langle (2, \bot), \bot, \bot \rangle$ and $V_3 = \langle (2, \bot), (2, \bot), \bot \rangle$

We revisit the example from Figure 4 to show the modified η values. The modified η values (denoted as η') of D_σ are given on the right side of Figure 5. Figure 6 details the change in the timestamps and the vector clocks of each thread. For ease of presentation, we shorthand the ordered pair $(\bot, \bot)$ to $\bot$. We also do not show changes to C_t, L_t and D_σ as the operations on them are the same as in the base detector algorithm. Furthermore, we elide showing the uninteresting operations where timestamps or vector clocks are not affected.

When t_1 starts, its timestamp is set to one. When t_1 calls $t_2.start()$, the timestamp of t_1 is increased to two and the timestamp of t_2 is set to one. t_2's vector clock is also updated such that the value of $V_2(1)$ is $(2, \bot)$ and the rest of the ordered pairs remain unchanged. Subsequently when t_2 performs $t_3.start()$, the time stamps of t_2 and t_3 are incremented and the vector clock of t_3 is updated as shown in the Figure. Even though t_2 starts t_3, the latter manages to get the information pertaining to the timestamp of t_1. Moreover, there are no changes in V_1 as shown by $\bot$ values. The updates to the remaining timestamp and vector clock values follow Algorithm 1.

The detector detects the same cycles that were detected previously (as discussed in Section 3.1), albeit with additional information. We now have two cycles θ_1' and θ_2' where $\theta_1' = \{\eta_2', \eta_5'\}$ and $\theta_2' = \{\eta_8', \eta_5'\}$.

3.3 Pruner

Armed with the additional information, `Pruner` applies Algorithm 2 on the potential defects and filters false positives.

Algorithm 2 Pruner

Input: Potential deadlocks Θ and vector clock V
Output: Result Map, R: $\Theta \rightarrow$ {`False`, `Unknown`}
1: **for** each cycle $\theta = \{\eta_1, \eta_2 \ldots \eta_n\}$ in Θ **do**
2:    R$[\theta] \leftarrow$ `Unknown`
3:    **for** each (η_i, η_j) in θ where $i \neq j$ **do**
4:       Let t_i be `thread`(η_i) and t_j be `thread`(η_j)
5:       **if** $V_i(j).\texttt{S} > \eta_j.\tau$ **then**
6:          /* Thread t_i hasn't started */
7:          R$[\theta] \leftarrow$ `False`
8:       **else if** $V_i(j).\texttt{J} \neq \perp$ and $V_i(j).\texttt{J} \leq \eta_i.\tau$ **then**
9:          /* Thread t_j has already joined */
10:         R$[\theta] \leftarrow$ `False`
11:       **end if**
12:    **end for**
13: **end for**

For a given cycle $\theta = \{\eta_1, \eta_2 \ldots \eta_n\}$, every pair (η_i, η_j) is checked to find if the cycle is feasible. If $t_i = $ `thread`(η_i) and $t_j = $ `thread`(η_j), then it is initially checked whether thread t_i always starts only after thread t_j made the deadlocking acquisition. Next we check whether thread t_j has always exited before thread t_i made its deadlocking acquisition. If either of these checks succeed, then the potential deadlock is marked as `False`. If both the checks fail for every such pair then the cycle is classified as a potential deadlock by `Pruner`.

Cycle θ'_1 is marked as false positive because $V_3(1).\texttt{S}$ equals 2 and $\eta'_2.\tau$ equals one and therefore the first conditional check in Algorithm 2 succeeds. The other potential deadlock, θ'_2 is still `Unknown` and forms the input to the `Generator`.

3.4 Generator

The potential deadlocks output by the `Pruner` along with the corresponding execution traces form the input to the `Generator`. `Generator` captures all the synchronization dependencies from the trace that need to be satisfied for a potential deadlock to become a real deadlock and generates a synchronization dependency graph accordingly. If a cycle is detected in this graph, then the deadlock is eliminated as a false positive. For an acyclic graph, the `Generator` outputs the synchronization dependency graph.

We now describe the process of generating a synchronization dependency graph, G_s. The execution indices of the lock acquisitions in D_σ, the execution trace, form the nodes in G_s. An edge (u, v) in G_s indicates that the acquisition at u must execute before acquisition at v. Let θ be a potential deadlock containing tuples $\{\eta_{t_1}, \eta_{t_2},..., \eta_{t_n}\}$ found in D_σ. Let $T_\theta = \{t_1, t_2, \ldots, t_n\}$, be the threads involved in cycle θ. We define $D'_\sigma \subset D_\sigma$ as the set of tuples leading upto the deadlocking acquisition in every thread t in T_θ. D'_σ is

---
Algorithm 3 Generator

Input: Cycle θ, Execution trace D'_σ
Output: Result Map, R : $\Theta \rightarrow$ {`False`, `Unknown`}.
1: $\theta \leftarrow \{\eta_1, \eta_2, \ldots, \eta_n\}$
2: Let T_θ be the set of threads in cycle θ
3: R$[\theta] \leftarrow$ `Unknown`
4: **for** every pair $\eta_i, \eta_j \in \theta$ where $i \neq j$ **do** /* add type-D edges */
5:    **if** `lock`$(\eta_i) \in$ `lockset`(η_j) **then**
6:       vertex $v \leftarrow ($`thread`$(\eta_i), \mu_i($`lock`$(\eta_i)),$ `lock`$(\eta_i))$;
7:       vertex $u \leftarrow ($`thread`$(\eta_j), \mu_j($`lock`$(\eta_i)),$ `lock`$(\eta_i))$;
8:       $V_s \leftarrow V_s \cup \{u, v\}; E_s \leftarrow E_s \cup \{(u, v)\}$
9:    **end if**
10: **end for**
11: **for** each $\eta_i \in \theta$ **do** /* add type-C edges */
12:    **for** each ℓ_k in `lockset`(η_i) **do**
13:       vertex $v \leftarrow ($`thread`$(\eta_i), \mu_i(\ell_k), \ell_k)$.
14:       $V_s \leftarrow V_s \cup \{v\}$
15:       **for** each tuple η_x in D'_σ **do**
16:          **if** `lock`$(\eta_x) = \ell_k$ **then**
17:             vertex $u \leftarrow ($`thread`$(\eta_x), \mu_x(\ell_k), \ell_k)$.
18:             $V_s \leftarrow V_s \cup \{u\}; E_s \leftarrow E_s \cup \{(u, v)\}$
19:          **end if**
20:       **end for**
21:    **end for**
22: **end for**
23: **for** each thread t_i in T_θ **do** /* add type-P edges */
24:    **for** each pair of consecutive tuples η_j, η_k by t_i in D'_σ **do**
25:       vertex $u \leftarrow (t_i, \mu_j($`lock`$(\eta_j)),$ `lock`$(\eta_j))$
26:       vertex $v \leftarrow (t_i, \mu_k($`lock`$(\eta_k)),$ `lock`$(\eta_k))$
27:       $V_s \leftarrow V_s \cup \{u, v\}$; $E_s \leftarrow E_s \cup \{(u, v)\}$
28:    **end for**
29: **end for**
30: **if** G_s is cyclic **then** R$[\theta] \leftarrow$ `False` **end if**

---

defined because all acquisitions by a thread t after the potentially deadlocking acquisition in the original run are irrelevant for the deadlock under consideration to be reproduced. Three types of edges are added to G_s.

1. *type-D* edge: For every $\eta_{t_i}, \eta_{t_{i+1}}$ in cycle θ such that $\ell_i = $ `lock`(η_{t_i}) and $\ell_i \in $ `lockset`$(\eta_{t_{i+1}})$, add edge $(\mu_{t_{i+1}}(\ell_i), \mu_{t_i}(\ell_i))$. This represents the necessary condition for the deadlock to happen. Informally, each thread in the cycle needs to acquire a lock and wait for another lock for the deadlock to manifest.

2. *type-C* edge: For each lock ℓ_j in `lockset`$(\eta_{t_i}), \forall t_i \in T_\theta$, $\forall \eta_x$ in D'_σ, if `thread`$(\eta_x) \neq t_i$ and `lock`$(\eta_x) = \ell_j$, then add edge $(\mu_x(\ell_j), \mu_{t_i}(\ell_j))$. This captures the fact that a lock ℓ_j in the lockset should be acquired by t_i only after every thread $t_j \in T_\theta$ has made necessary acquisitions on ℓ_j, setting up the deadlocking context.

3. *type-P* edge: For every pair of tuples η_i, η_j in D'_σ s.t `thread`$(\eta_i) = $ `thread`(η_j), if tuples η_i, η_j are added successively by `thread`(η_i), add edge $(\mu_i($`lock`$(\eta_i))$, $\mu_j($`lock`$(\eta_j)))$. This represents the program order edges.

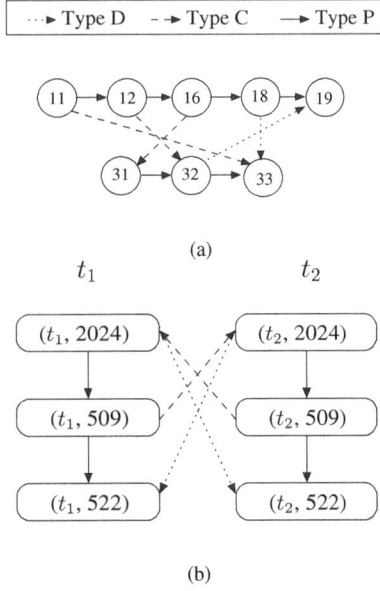

Figure 7. (a) The synchronization dependency graph for the code fragment from Figure 4 with different types of edges illustrated. (b) G_s for cycle θ_4 from Figure 2 that contains a cycle - $\{(t_1, 2024) \rightarrow (t_1, 509) \rightarrow (t_2, 2024) \rightarrow (t_2, 509) \rightarrow (t_1, 2024)\}$

We illustrate the different types of edges in G_s with an example. Consider cycle θ_2' from the running example in Figure 4. $\theta_2' = \{\eta_8', \eta_5'\}$ is declared by the Pruner as a potential deadlock. A potential deadlock between t_1 and t_2 exists when the threads hold locks ℓ_1 (at 18) and ℓ_2 (at 32) respectively and attempt to acquire ℓ_2 (at 19) and ℓ_1 (at 33) respectively. We add the *type-D* edges, the necessary condition for the deadlock to manifest, (18,33) and (32,19) to G_s as shown in Figure 7(a). Subsequently, we add *type-C* edges (16,31), (12,32) and (11,33) to the graph. This is because the pairs of locations (16,31), (12,32) and (11,33) acquire the same locks and the locks acquired at indices 31, 32 and 33 are present as part of t_2's context. If the lock at 31 is acquired and held by t_2 even before t_1 can acquire it at 16, then the deadlock indicated by θ_2' cannot be reproduced. Lastly, *type-P* edges (11,12), (12,16), (16,18), (18,19), (31,32) and (32,33) are added to denote the program order.

The algorithm for constructing G_s is given in Algorithm 3. Each vertex in G_s is a tuple with three elements that include the thread identifier, the execution index of the lock operation and the lock. As shown in Algorithm 3, type-D, type-C and type-P edges are added in that order and a cycle detection performed on G_s. If a cycle exists in G_s, then the potential deadlock is declared as a false positive. Otherwise, G_s is used by the Replayer to deadlock the execution.

The absence of a cycle in G_s (shown in Figure 7(a)), corresponding to θ_2', denotes its feasibility in practice. Poten-

Algorithm 4 Replayer

Input: $G_s(V_s, E_s)$: Synchronization dependency graph
$\quad\quad\quad\theta$: a potential deadlock cycle.
Output: Result Map, R : $\Theta \rightarrow \{\texttt{Deadlock, Unknown}\}$
1: $Paused \leftarrow \emptyset, Enabled \leftarrow T, Terminated \leftarrow \emptyset$
2: $BlockedInstr \leftarrow \emptyset, \texttt{R}[\theta] \leftarrow \texttt{Unknown}$
3: Let T_θ be the set of threads in cycle θ
4: **while** $Enabled \cup Paused \neq \emptyset$ **do**
5:     **if** $Enabled = \emptyset$ **then**
6:         Move a random thread t' from $Paused$ to $Enabled$.
7:     **end if**
8:     $t_i \leftarrow$ random thread from $Enabled$.
9:     $s \leftarrow$ next statement to be executed by t_i.
10:     **if** s is nil **then**
11:         move t_i from $Enabled$ to $Terminated$
12:     **end if**
13:     **if** $t_i \notin T_\theta$ **then**
14:         Execute s; Goto the beginning of the loop
15:     **end if**
16:     **if** s is Lock (ℓ) **then**
17:         Vertex $v \leftarrow (t_i, idx, \ell)$ /*idx is execution index of s*/
18:         **if** $\exists u$ in V_s, s.t $(u, v) \in E_s$ and $u.t \neq v.t$ **then**
19:             Add v to $BlockedInstr$
20:             Move t_i to $Paused$ and goto beginning of the loop
21:         **else**
22:             Remove every vertex u in V_s that reaches v
23:             Remove all the edges incident on u
24:             **for** every a in $BlockedInstr$ **do**
25:                 **if** $\nexists b$ in V_s, s.t $(b, a) \in E_s$ and $b.t \neq a.t$ **then**
26:                     Remove vertex a from $BlockedInstr$
27:                     Move thread $a.t$ from $Paused$ to $Enabled$
28:                 **end if**
29:             **end for**
30:         **end if**
31:     **end if**
32:     Execute statement s
33:     **if** execution deadlocked at the exact location **then**
34:         $\texttt{R}[\theta] \leftarrow \texttt{Deadlock}$
35:     **end if**
36: **end while**

tially, it can be reproduced if the dependencies in G_s are satisfied. Figure 7(b) presents a contrasting scenario and shows a cyclic G_s for the fourth cycle shown in Figure 2. We infer that the fourth cycle can never result in a deadlock because of the cyclic G_s.

3.5 Replayer

The potential deadlocks output by the Generator form the input to the Replayer along with the corresponding synchronization dependency graphs. To reproduce a deadlock automatically, the Replayer executes the program following the dependencies given by G_s. Algorithm 4 presents an approach that monitors and attempts to drive the execution to a deadlock. Edges in G_s are gradually eliminated as and when the dependencies are satisfied (or no longer exist). The program is run on the test input on which the potential deadlock was detected. If the thread attempts to acquire a lock at some execution index, and if there is no incoming edge to the node representing the execution index in G_s, the lock acquisition is permitted and once after acquisition all edges emanating from the node are removed. If the lock acquisition is not permitted then the thread needs to wait for atleast one acquisition by some other thread and the Replayer pauses the current thread until the acquisition happens. The Replayer also ensures that if a thread skips a specific execution index by following a different path, the edges from the node corresponding to the skipped execution index is also removed. Very rarely, all threads are paused when at least one of the threads can make progress. In that unlikely scenario, the Replayer chooses a random thread from the set of paused threads to execute. If none of the threads can make progress indicating a deadlock and if this deadlock corresponds to the potential deadlock that the Replayer set out to reproduce, then the potential deadlock is considered to be automatically verified as a *real* deadlock.

We now illustrate the application of Algorithm 4 on the running example from Figure 4 using the associated G_s (see Figure 7(a)). The Replayer randomly selects either t_1 or t_3 to execute. Since t_3 is not yet active, it selects t_1 and executes upto 15 thus removing edges (11,12), (12,16), (11,33) and (12,32) from G_s. At this point, both t_1 and t_3 are eligible to execute. Assuming t_3 is chosen randomly, t_3 attempts to acquire a lock on ℓ_3 at index 31. However, this acquisition is not allowed until t_1 acquires the lock at index 16 because of the dependency denoted by G_s. Therefore, the Replayer pauses t_3 and chooses t_1 for execution. As there are no dependencies in the updated G_s pertaining to index 16, t_1 acquires the lock at index 16. Subsequently, the dependencies (16,31) and (16,18) are removed from G_s. The removal of these dependencies enable t_3 to become active again. Subsequently, if t_3 attempts to acquire the lock at index 33 before t_1 acquires the lock at index 18, the execution of t_3 will be perturbed appropriately. Eventually, the execution proceeds until t_1 and t_3 are blocked at indices 19 and 33 respectively indicating the presence of a real deadlock.

While the above example shows the Replayer following the dependencies in G_s, it is also flexible when the dependencies are not satisfiable to ensure progress. For the same example, consider a run where t_1 executes 11,12 and 18 and skips 16 due to a conditional (possible due to other interleavings). In this case, the Replayer detects the change in the control flow of t_1 and automatically removes dependencies (16,31) and (16,18) from G_s enabling t_3 to execute again.

4. Implementation and Evaluation

We have implemented WOLF in Java to analyze Java applications. The implementation builds on top of the iGoodLock [14] framework which uses Soot [32] for code instrumen-

tation. The implementation of the Extended Detector, Pruner and Generator components of WOLF is straightforward and follows the respective algorithms described in the previous section. For the implementation of the Replayer component, WOLF implements a *monitor* thread that observes the synchronization operations performed by threads which are expected to deadlock. The threads are assigned a unique identifier during detection. During replay, we use the same assignment strategy to identify corresponding threads across runs. Therefore we monitor only k threads for a deadlock involving k threads. Monitoring only the selected threads enables us to drive the execution along the designated schedule without having to pause more threads than are necessary. The monitor thread pauses the selected threads at different synchronization points based on the synchronization dependency graph.

4.1 Experimental setup

We analyze large Java benchmarks (upto 160KLoC) to evaluate WOLF. All the experiments were conducted on a Ubuntu-12.04 desktop running on a 3.5 Ghz Intel Core i7 processor with 16GB RAM. The benchmarks used for the evaluation include a simple and fast cache for Java objects (cache4j), a leading edge web server platform (Jigsaw), a Java logging library (jakarta-log4j.1.2.8) and implementations of Java Collections. To show the effectiveness of our approach, we compare our approach with DeadlockFuzzer [14], a state of the art randomized tool for identifying real deadlocks. For each benchmark and for each test input, the program is executed twice – DeadlockFuzzer analyzes one execution and WOLF analyzes the other.

4.2 Results

The results of our experiments are given in Table 1. It tabulates the benchmarks used for our experiments, their sizes, statistics pertaining to the kinds of deadlocks, the number of deadlocks detected initially and the effectiveness of our approach compared to the state of the art. WOLF classifies approximately 18.5% of the deadlocks as false positives across all benchmarks. We manually verified that the defects reported as false positives are indeed false. The tool also reproduces significantly higher number of deadlocks (55.4%) compared to DeadlockFuzzer (35.4%) as seen from the table. We account this higher reproducibility of our approach to two factors – the use of the synchronization dependency graph to drive the execution and the pausing of only selected threads during execution. In contrast, DeadlockFuzzer uses a completely randomized approach for reproducing the deadlocks and also pauses all threads with the required abstraction. The elimination of false positives and higher reproducibility rate of WOLF leaves *only* 26% of defects for manual comprehension.

We use *hit rate* to measure the reliability of our approach to reproduce a given deadlock. A hit is considered to occur

Benchmark	LoC	S_L	V_s	Detection Time Slowdown	Detected Defects	False Positives			True Positives		Unknown	
						WOLF		DF	WOLF	DF	WOLF	DF
						Pr	Gen					
cache4j	3,897	–	–	1.32	0	0	0		0	0	0	0
Jigsaw	160,388	11	1486	1.23	30	7	0		6	3	17	27
Java Logging	4248	10	20	1.07	2	0	0		2	1	0	1
ArrayList	17,633	4	4	1.86	6	0	0	–	6	3	0	3
Stack		4.5	6	2.01	6	0	0		6	3	0	3
LinkedList		4	4	1.98	6	0	0		6	3	0	3
HashMap	18,911	4	4	2.19	3	0	1		2	2	0	1
TreeMap		4	4	2.17	3	0	1		2	2	0	1
WeakHashMap		4	4	2.24	3	0	1		2	2	0	1
LinkedHashMap		4	4	2.32	3	0	1		2	2	0	1
IdentityHashMap		4.5	4	2.09	3	0	1		2	2	0	1
Cumulative count					65	12 (18.5%)			36 (55.4%)	23 (35.4%)	17 (26.1%)	42 (64.6%)

Table 1. Experimental results. S_L: Average length of the stack trace, V_s: Average number of vertices in G_s, DF: DeadlockFuzzer, Pr: Pruner, Gen: Generator.

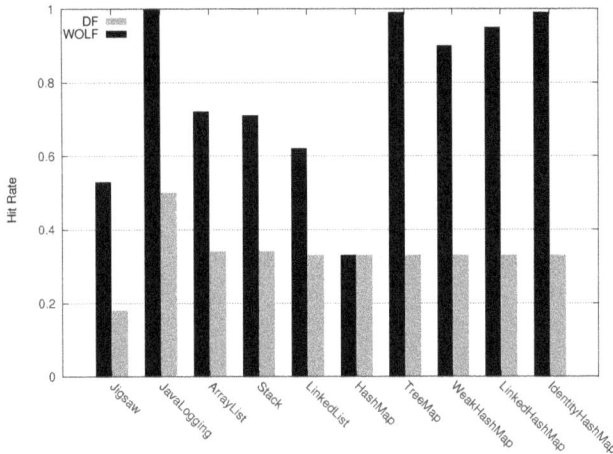

Figure 8. The hit rate of reproducing a deadlock averaged over 100 runs per potential deadlock.

if the replay results in a deadlock on which it was expected to deadlock. More specifically, if the deadlock that need to be reproduced has locks that are acquired from specific source code locations and the reproduced execution also acquired locks (or attempts to acquire locks) at the same locations, we consider that a hit. If the execution deadlocks at a different point, it is not considered a hit. For each benchmark and for each deadlock reported, we attempt to reproduce the deadlock by running the `Replayer` 100 times. We count the number of times a deadlock that is expected is reproduced in the execution. We use this count to calculate the hit rate. Figure 8 shows our approach has a higher hit rate than `DeadlockFuzzer` across all benchmarks. Even when both approaches are able to reproduce the deadlocks (e.g., `TreeHashMap`, `WeakHashMap`), the observed hit rate of our approach is higher. We attribute the higher hit rate of our approach to its ability to drive the execution through a previously observed synchronization schedule more reliably. However, observe that the `Replayer` drives the execution

according to dependencies in G_s and the threads have the freedom to execute other instructions in any order. This non-determinism accounts for the hit rate being less than one with our approach.

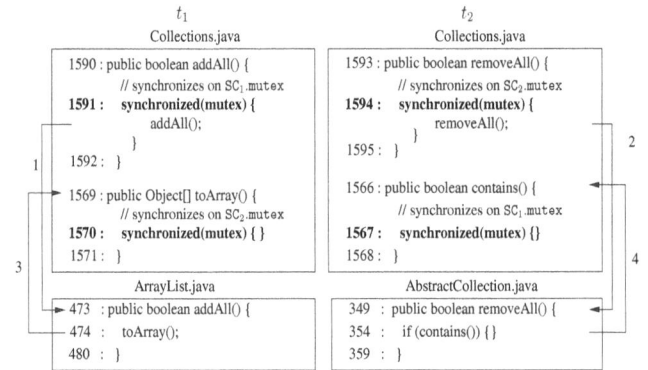

Figure 9. True deadlock reported in Java Collections. `WOLF` reliably reproduces this deadlock automatically whereas `DeadlockFuzzer` never reproduced the deadlock in 100 runs.

We are able to detect many critical deadlocks. For example, not only are we able to detect the defect reported in bug 24159 [3] in `Java Logging`, but also we are able to reproduce the deadlocking execution with a hit rate of one. We use a true deadlock reported in Java Collections to elaborate on the underlying reason for the higher hit rate of our approach. Figure 9 shows a code fragment where a deadlock exists between threads t_1 and t_2. SC_1 and SC_2 are two instances of class `SynchronizedCollection`, where `mutex` is a field. The deadlock happens when t_1 acquires a lock on SC_1.`mutex` at line 1591, t_2 acquires a lock on SC_2.`mutex` at line 1594 and then each thread attempts to acquire the other lock at lines 1570 and 1567 respectively. Surprisingly, `DeadlockFuzzer` was never able to reproduce this dead-

---

[3] https://issues.apache.org/bugzilla/show_bug.cgi?id=24159

38

Benchmark	Cycles	False Positives		True Positives		Unknown	
		WOLF	DF	WOLF	DF	WOLF	DF
Jigsaw	265	83		97	35	85	230
Java Logging	2	0		2	1	0	1
ArrayList	9	0		9	3	0	6
Stack	9	0	-NA-	9	3	0	6
LinkedList	9	0		9	3	0	6
HashMap	4	1		3	3	0	1
TreeMap	4	1		3	3	0	1
WeakHashMap	4	1		3	3	0	1
LinkedHashMap	4	1		3	3	0	1
IdentityHashMap	4	1		3	3	0	1
Cumulative count	314	88 (28.03%)		141 (44.90%)	60 (19.10%)	85 (27.07%)	254 (80.89%)

Table 2. Comparison of `WOLF` and `DeadlockFuzzer` (`DF`) based on the number of detected cycles.

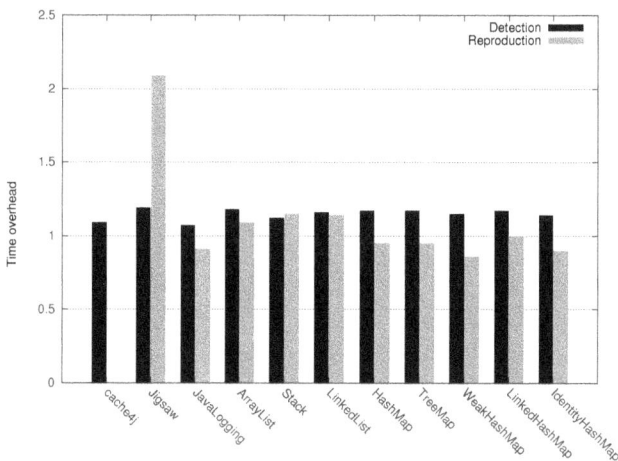

Figure 10. The detection and reproduction time overheads of `WOLF` normalized to the time taken by `DeadlockFuzzer`.

lock (in 100 runs) even though `WOLF` reliably reproduced this deadlock.

On careful examination, we find that t_2 executes the same sequence of operations as t_1 before it executes the operations shown in the Figure. Since, in `DeadlockFuzzer`, t_1 and t_2 have the same abstraction and the approach does not take the dependency constraints into account, t_2 is incorrectly paused at line 1570 causing a different deadlock (corresponding to different source locations) to be reproduced. Comparatively, as `WOLF` differentiates t_1 and t_2, it does not pause t_2 at line 1570. Moreover, as it uses the synchronization dependency graph to drive the execution, it pauses t_1 before line 1591 so that t_2 executes all the operations upto line 1594 causing the deadlock to be reproduced reliably.

Inspite of higher data generation and consumption, the additional overhead introduced by our tool is minimal. In Table 1, we present the slowdown due to deadlock detection as compared to running the uninstrumented program. We observe that the slowdown varies from 1.07x to 2.3x. Figure 10 also shows the relative detection and reproduction time overheads of `WOLF` as compared to `DeadlockFuzzer`. For de-

tection, which includes both `Pruner` and `Generator`, our tool introduces approximately 10% relative slowdown across all the benchmarks. The relative overhead of the `Replayer` ranges from 0.8x for `WeakHashMap` to 2.1x for `Jigsaw`. We attribute the better performance to the ability of `WOLF` to not pause unnecessarily. The extra overhead with `Jigsaw` is because their approach deadlocks at the same source points on many runs and fails to reproduce many deadlocks. In contrast, our tool explores newer regions to reproduce the deadlock resulting in a higher overhead. In absolute terms, the average amount of time taken to reproduce a deadlock ranges from approximately 3 seconds (for `ArrayList`) to 50 seconds (for `Jigsaw`). We believe the overhead incurred in automatically identifying a deadlock is tolerable given the costs associated with manual comprehension.

According to Table 1, the average length of the stack trace ranges from 4 to 11. These numbers point to the tediousness associated with manually reasoning about detected deadlocks. Even for a deadlock involving two threads and two locks, there will be two stack traces and a programmer needs to understand the semantics of multiple procedures to identify whether the reported deadlock can happen in a real execution. The average number of nodes in G_s, the synchronization dependency graph, ranges from 4 to 1486. The number gives the number of lock acquisitions that need to be made before a deadlock can happen. A completely random approach for generating a schedule has poor probability of reproducing a deadlock because failing to acquire even one of the locks in G_s appropriately may result in the deadlock not being detected. These statistics corroborate the underlying reason for designing the various algorithms presented in this paper.

4.3 Dynamic Defect Enumeration

The defect count reported in Table 1 corresponds to the unique source code locations of the deadlocking lock acquisitions by the respective threads. In contrast, in [14], the authors report the number of cycles in the lock graph. In other words, if there are two cycles in a lock graph and the nodes (or lock acquisitions) in the cycles correspond to the same source locations, they count it as two defects whereas we count it as one in this paper. We believe our counting is more appropriate because when the defects need to be fixed, a programmer will have to make changes to a specific source code location. Furthermore, to show a problem exists at a specific source location, it is sufficient to reproduce one deadlocking execution for that source location. Also, using cycles to count the overall defects penalizes both the approaches unnecessarily based on the number of dynamic occurrences of the defective source code location in a run.

For a better understanding, we also provide a comparison of both the tools, where each cycle is counted as a separate defect, in Table 2. Even using this metric of evaluation, WOLF significantly outperforms DeadlockFuzzer. The former classifies 28% of cycles as false positives and reproduces 44.9% of cycles, leaving around 27% of cycles for manual classification. On the other hand, the latter reproduces *only* 19.1% of cycles leaving 80.9% of cycles for manual analysis.

4.4 Discussion

Our design to reduce the false positives is inspired by other successful program analysis tools [2]. Since our approach is based on dynamic analysis, the quality of the results will be a function of the test inputs. For detecting concurrency bugs, it also becomes a function of the explored schedules. Therefore, a limitation of our approach is that it may consider real bugs as false due to incomplete traces. While our experimental results show that all the false positives reported by WOLF are indeed false, incomplete traces is still a valid concern – a concern that we share with other popular and useful dynamic analysis tools [6]. To elaborate further, in Figure 4, eliminating cycle θ_1' can be incorrect if there exists some unexplored execution path where t_3 is started by some other thread t_4 (instead of t_2). We can address this limitation in two ways. Integrate WOLF with other complementary tools – *viz.*, automatic test input generators [10, 24, 30] and effective schedule explorers [20]. Furthermore, the reported deadlocks can also be ranked based on the output of WOLF, so that the detected false positives are ranked the lowest instead of being eliminated.

WOLF reports 26% of the defects as *unknown* and a number of these defects are indeed false positives. These false positives exist due to data dependency which ensures that certain code regions never overlap. Currently, WOLF does not explore data dependency associated with the executions and we plan to address this in the future.

5. Related Work

Our approach for developing a precise technique for deadlock detection is inspired by the foundational work of Joshi *et al.* [14]. As we have shown in our experimental results, we propose an approach that is more precise and is able to reproduce deadlocks more reliably. In MagicFuzzer [3], Cai and Chan improve the scalability and efficiency of cycle detection by pruning the lock dependency graph and apply their algorithm on C/C++ programs. The modifications mentioned in MagicFuzzer can be easily incorporated in WOLF and with appropriate instrumentation, WOLF can be extended to C/C++ programs. Joshi *et al.* [15] also propose a dynamic analysis for detecting generalized deadlocks that specifically involve communication patterns. We focus on resource deadlocks in this paper. There are a number of static analysis approaches [22, 33] that are designed for detecting deadlocks. Static analysis techniques suffer from higher false positive rate [14]. Furthermore, automatically reproducing a deadlock based on a static analysis report is significantly harder.

Empirical evidence shows that vector clock [18] based concurrency bug detection tools are effective. Pozniansky and Schuster design an algorithm for detecting race conditions in multi-threaded programs [27]. The memory accesses and operations on locks are instrumented to compute the *happens-before* relation and race conditions are detected. FastTrack [8] makes this process more efficient by identifying appropriate locations where the vector can be reduced to a scalar. The pruning phase of our approach to identify non-overlapping regions of execution is motivated by these algorithms. However, we do not instrument memory accesses unlike these algorithms. Therefore, the overhead introduced by using vector clocks is negligible (approximately 10% overhead).

Replaying the execution by perturbing the schedule to automatically verify the correctness of the reported defects is an active area of research [1, 3, 14, 23, 26, 28]. Narayanasamy *et al.* [23] provide a replay approach for differentiating between real and benign races by changing the order of problematic memory accesses in the replay. Pradel and Gross [28] execute code sequentially whenever they observe a problem in a concurrent execution to verify whether the problem is due to concurrency. Our approach shares the same ideals of these pioneering approaches, i.e., reduce the amount of manual work that needs to be performed by a programmer to understand defects and concentrate on real bugs.

To improve the reliability of concurrent programs, many techniques based on manipulating schedules are proposed [5, 7, 11, 12, 31]. Cui *et al.* [4, 5, 34] propose schedule specialization to guard against bugs caused due to non-determinism. Huang and Zhang [11] design a tool PECAN to generate a feasible schedule for access anomalies in programs that use locks in a nested way. Farzan *et al.* [7] propose an approach for identifying alternative interleavings that detect null pointer dereferences in concurrent programs using SMT solvers. Sinha and Wang [31] differentiate between intra-thread and inter-thread semantics to reduce the number of possible interleavings that need to be explored. Here, we manipulate the schedule for a different purpose.

Reproducing the bugs that manifest occasionally in multi-threaded executions is an important problem [12, 25]. These approaches are applicable after a bug has manifested in a real execution as opposed to detecting the bugs proactively. CHESS [20] systematically explores thread interleavings by adopting a context-bounded algorithm to detect concurrency bugs. Other testing approaches targeted towards concurrent applications [13, 21, 36] are complementary to the design of WOLF.

6. Conclusions

We present the design and implementation of WOLF, a dynamic analysis tool for detecting deadlocks. WOLF leverages the trace of an execution to automatically identify false positives. Moreover, the tool uses the trace and attempts to reproduce a deadlock so as to verify the correctness of a reported defect without manual intervention. We analyze large Java benchmarks (upto 160KLoC) and our experimental results show that WOLF easily outperforms the state of the art detection tools by identifying three quarters of the reported defects as real (or false) deadlocks automatically.

Acknowledgments

We thank the anonymous reviewers for their useful feedback. We are grateful to Koushik Sen for providing the experimental benchmarks and test harnesses that are used in our experiments. This project is supported in part by Ministry of Human Resources and Development (Government of India), Microsoft Research India and Google India.

References

[1] S. Bensalem, J.-C. Fernandez, K. Havelund, and L. Mounier. Confirmation of deadlock potentials detected by runtime analysis. In *Proceedings of the 2006 Workshop on Parallel and Distributed Systems: Testing and Debugging*, PADTAD '06.

[2] A. Bessey, K. Block, B. Chelf, A. Chou, B. Fulton, S. Hallem, C. Henri-Gros, A. Kamsky, S. McPeak, and D. Engler. A few billion lines of code later: Using static analysis to find bugs in the real world. *Commun. ACM*, 53(2).

[3] Y. Cai and W. K. Chan. Magicfuzzer: Scalable deadlock detection for large-scale applications. In *Proceedings of the 2012 International Conference on Software Engineering*, ICSE 2012.

[4] H. Cui, J. Wu, C.-C. Tsai, and J. Yang. Stable deterministic multithreading through schedule memoization. In *Proceedings of the 9th USENIX Conference on Operating Systems Design and Implementation*, OSDI'10.

[5] H. Cui, J. Wu, J. Gallagher, H. Guo, and J. Yang. Efficient deterministic multithreading through schedule relaxation. In *Proceedings of the Twenty-Third ACM Symposium on Operating Systems Principles*, SOSP, 2011.

[6] M. D. Ernst, J. H. Perkins, P. J. Guo, S. McCamant, C. Pacheco, M. S. Tschantz, and C. Xiao. The daikon system for dynamic detection of likely invariants. *Sci. Comput. Program.*, 69(1-3).

[7] A. Farzan, P. Madhusudan, N. Razavi, and F. Sorrentino. Predicting null-pointer dereferences in concurrent programs. In *Proceedings of the ACM SIGSOFT 20th International Symposium on the Foundations of Software Engineering*, FSE '12.

[8] C. Flanagan and S. N. Freund. Fasttrack: Efficient and precise dynamic race detection. In *Proceedings of the 2009 ACM SIGPLAN Conference on Programming Language Design and Implementation*, PLDI '09.

[9] C. Flanagan, S. N. Freund, and J. Yi. Velodrome: A sound and complete dynamic atomicity checker for multithreaded programs. In *Proceedings of the 2008 ACM SIGPLAN Conference on Programming Language Design and Implementation*, PLDI '08.

[10] P. Godefroid, N. Klarlund, and K. Sen. Dart: Directed automated random testing. In *Proceedings of the 2005 ACM SIGPLAN Conference on Programming Language Design and Implementation*, PLDI '05.

[11] J. Huang and C. Zhang. Persuasive prediction of concurrency access anomalies. In *Proceedings of the 2011 International Symposium on Software Testing and Analysis*, ISSTA '11.

[12] J. Huang, C. Zhang, and J. Dolby. Clap: Recording local executions to reproduce concurrency failures. In *Proceedings of the 34th ACM SIGPLAN Conference on Programming Language Design and Implementation*, PLDI '13.

[13] V. Jagannath, M. Gligoric, D. Jin, Q. Luo, G. Rosu, and D. Marinov. Improved multithreaded unit testing. In *Proceedings of the 19th ACM SIGSOFT Symposium and the 13th European Conference on Foundations of Software Engineering*, ESEC/FSE '11.

[14] P. Joshi, C.-S. Park, K. Sen, and M. Naik. A randomized dynamic program analysis technique for detecting real deadlocks. In *Proceedings of the 2009 ACM SIGPLAN Conference on Programming Language Design and Implementation*, PLDI '09.

[15] P. Joshi, M. Naik, K. Sen, and D. Gay. An effective dynamic analysis for detecting generalized deadlocks. In *Proceedings of the Eighteenth ACM SIGSOFT International Symposium on Foundations of Software Engineering*, FSE, 2010.

[16] H. Jula, D. Tralamazza, C. Zamfir, and G. Candea. Deadlock immunity: Enabling systems to defend against deadlocks. In *Proceedings of the 8th USENIX Conference on Operating Systems Design and Implementation*, OSDI'08.

[17] V. Kahlon, Y. Yang, S. Sankaranarayanan, and A. Gupta. Fast and accurate static data-race detection for concurrent programs. In *Proceedings of the 19th international conference on Computer aided verification*, CAV'07.

[18] L. Lamport. Time, clocks, and the ordering of events in a distributed system. *Commun. ACM*, 21(7):558–565, July 1978.

[19] S. McPeak, C.-H. Gros, and M. K. Ramanathan. Scalable and incremental software bug detection. In *Proceedings of the 2013 9th Joint Meeting on Foundations of Software Engineering*, ESEC/FSE 2013.

[20] M. Musuvathi and S. Qadeer. Iterative context bounding for systematic testing of multithreaded programs. In *Proceedings*

of the 2007 ACM SIGPLAN Conference on Programming Language Design and Implementation, PLDI '07.

[21] S. Nagarakatte, S. Burckhardt, M. M. Martin, and M. Musuvathi. Multicore acceleration of priority-based schedulers for concurrency bug detection. In *Proceedings of the 33rd ACM SIGPLAN Conference on Programming Language Design and Implementation*, PLDI '12.

[22] M. Naik, C.-S. Park, K. Sen, and D. Gay. Effective static deadlock detection. In *Proceedings of the 31st International Conference on Software Engineering*, ICSE '09.

[23] S. Narayanasamy, Z. Wang, J. Tigani, A. Edwards, and B. Calder. Automatically classifying benign and harmful data races using replay analysis. In *Proceedings of the 2007 ACM SIGPLAN Conference on Programming Language Design and Implementation*, PLDI '07.

[24] C. Pacheco and M. D. Ernst. Randoop: Feedback-directed random testing for java. In *Companion to the 22Nd ACM SIGPLAN Conference on Object-oriented Programming Systems and Applications Companion*, OOPSLA '07.

[25] S. Park, Y. Zhou, W. Xiong, Z. Yin, R. Kaushik, K. H. Lee, and S. Lu. Pres: Probabilistic replay with execution sketching on multiprocessors. In *Proceedings of the ACM SIGOPS 22Nd Symposium on Operating Systems Principles*, SOSP '09.

[26] S. Park, S. Lu, and Y. Zhou. Ctrigger: Exposing atomicity violation bugs from their hiding places. In *Proceedings of the 14th International Conference on Architectural Support for Programming Languages and Operating Systems*, ASPLOS XIV, 2009.

[27] E. Pozniansky and A. Schuster. Efficient on-the-fly data race detection in multithreaded c++ programs. In *Proceedings of the Ninth ACM SIGPLAN Symposium on Principles and Practice of Parallel Programming*, PPoPP '03.

[28] M. Pradel and T. R. Gross. Fully automatic and precise detection of thread safety violations. In *Proceedings of the 33rd ACM SIGPLAN Conference on Programming Language Design and Implementation*, PLDI '12.

[29] S. Savage, M. Burrows, G. Nelson, P. Sobalvarro, and T. Anderson. Eraser: a dynamic data race detector for multithreaded programs. *ACM Trans. Comput. Syst.*, 15(4):391–411, Nov. 1997.

[30] K. Sen and G. Agha. Cute and jcute: Concolic unit testing and explicit path model-checking tools. In *Proceedings of the 18th International Conference on Computer Aided Verification*, CAV '06.

[31] N. Sinha and C. Wang. On interference abstractions. In *Proceedings of the 38th Annual ACM SIGPLAN-SIGACT Symposium on Principles of Programming Languages*, POPL '11.

[32] R. Vallee-Rai, E. Gagnon, L. Hendren, P. Lam, P. Pominville, and V. Sundaresan. Optimizing java bytecode using the soot framework: Is it feasible? In *In International Conference on Compiler Construction, LNCS 1781*, pages 18–34, 2000.

[33] A. Williams, W. Thies, and M. D. Ernst. Static deadlock detection for java libraries. In *ECOOP 2005-Object-Oriented Programming*. Springer Berlin Heidelberg.

[34] J. Wu, Y. Tang, G. Hu, H. Cui, and J. Yang. Sound and precise analysis of parallel programs through schedule specialization. In *Proceedings of the 33rd ACM SIGPLAN Conference on Programming Language Design and Implementation*, PLDI '12.

[35] C. Ye, S. C. Cheung, W. K. Chan, and C. Xu. Detection and resolution of atomicity violation in service composition. In *Proceedings of the the 6th Joint Meeting of the European Software Engineering Conference and the ACM SIGSOFT Symposium on The Foundations of Software Engineering*, ESEC-FSE '07.

[36] J. Yu, S. Narayanasamy, C. Pereira, and G. Pokam. Maple: A coverage-driven testing tool for multithreaded programs. In *Proceedings of the ACM International Conference on Object Oriented Programming Systems Languages and Applications*, OOPSLA '12.

Efficient Search for Inputs Causing High Floating-point Errors

Wei-Fan Chiang   Ganesh Gopalakrishnan   Zvonimir Rakamarić   Alexey Solovyev

School of Computing,
University of Utah,
Salt Lake City, UT 84112, USA
{wfchiang,ganesh,zvonimir,monad}@cs.utah.edu

Abstract

Tools for floating-point error estimation are fundamental to program understanding and optimization. In this paper, we focus on tools for determining the input settings to a floating point routine that maximizes its result error. Such tools can help support activities such as precision allocation, performance optimization, and auto-tuning. We benchmark current abstraction-based precision analysis methods, and show that they often do not work at scale, or generate highly pessimistic error estimates, often caused by non-linear operators or complex input constraints that define the set of legal inputs. We show that while concrete-testing-based error estimation methods based on maintaining shadow values at higher precision can search out higher error-inducing inputs, suitable heuristic search guidance is key to finding higher errors. We develop a heuristic search algorithm called Binary Guided Random Testing (BGRT). In 45 of the 48 total benchmarks, including many real-world routines, BGRT returns higher guaranteed errors. We also evaluate BGRT against two other heuristic search methods called ILS and PSO, obtaining better results.

Keywords   Sequential and parallel programming; floating-point error estimation methods; guided search.

1. Introduction

Computational errors caused by limited precision implementations of floating-point routines are a central concern in high-performance computing at all levels of scale ranging from high-end supercomputers through hand-held electronics. Researchers often allocate limited precision to gain higher performance, and study this trade-off using existing tools (e.g., [12, 31, 36]). Others have studied the effect of parallelization strategy selection in the limited-precision context, given that it has a direct impact on the effective shape of expression trees (e.g., [2, 3, 9, 15, 16]).

There are many challenges in developing a general-purpose tool for computing the worst error-causing inputs. The program structure as well as the operations employed can span a huge variety. Consequently, the output can exhibit high sensitivity to input values as well as internal loss of precision. Closed-form solutions for errors, or broadly applicable error-compensation techniques, are virtually impossible to develop except in special domains (e.g., [25]). Short of exhaustive search, there are no obvious ways to find the *worst error-causing inputs*. However, since realistic programs are quite complex and large, exhaustive search is infeasible. The novel approach we propose is based on *heuristic-guided search*, and we provide a new tool S^3FP (input-space Sour-Spot Searcher for Floating-Point) in support of this work. S^3FP can generate *guaranteed lower-bounds on imprecision*. To the best of our knowledge, this is the first tool of its kind, which computes guaranteed high lower bounds for many real-world programs, including library functions within Magma [34], implementations of FFT [39], benchmark suites such as Parboil [39], and also components of active projects (e.g., Uintah [33], where, after significant performance tuning, the developers sought our help to check for precision loss). S^3FP may also be used, for example, as an assistant while publishing floating-point routines in a library—by tagging it with the *guaranteed lower-bound* on relative error that a programmer can expect. Furthermore, it may find uses in auto-tuning compilers where the search (for algorithms or implementations) may be based both on performance and precision [2].

Automatic determination of inputs that cause high errors[1] can be useful in many settings. In Precimonious [36], the allocation of precision is based on manually provided training inputs; the work in this paper can help automate this aspect. In recent work [17], the authors report their initial efforts on proving safe separation zones for aircrafts using the PVS theorem prover, and how these proofs were re-done for finite-precision implementations in C. The authors employed the static analysis tool Gappa [12] for estimating bounds on variable values. We show in this paper that tools such as Gappa can often generate pessimistic results, and therefore, it is possible that the separation proofs will not carry over.[2] In these cases, S^3FP can help confirm at least some of the Gappa findings as genuine, allowing designers to probe further and refine their algorithm.

Related Work.   Many existing tool-based approaches for precision estimation are based on static analysis, as supported by tools such as Gappa [12] or SmartFloat [11]. While the use of Satisfiability Modulo Theories (SMT) based tools is possible for more precise estimation, we have not come across any such tools. Ideas combining symbolic techniques and heuristics have been studied, but not applied to the domain of imprecision analysis. (We later study in §3.5 one of the algorithms used in previous work called PSO [38].) Static analysis based precision estimation can yield pessimistic results (very high values of estimated relative error). This problem becomes worse when non-linear operations are present, or

PPoPP '14,   February 15–19, 2014, Orlando, FL, USA.
Copyright © 2014 ACM 978-1-4503-2656-8/14/02...$15.00.
http://dx.doi.org/10.1145/2555243.2555265

---

[1] In §2, we define the term *relative error* and explain why we choose this as our uniform metric (barring a few exceptions) for benchmarking.

[2] The authors of [17] reported no such failure of proof carry-over, although in personal conversation they agreed it was possible.

Benchmark	Operators Used
Microbenchmarks	$\{+,-,/\}$
Reductions (BR,IBR,IBR^K)	$\{+,-\}$
DQMOM	$\{+,-,/\}$ (exp unrolled)
FFT	$\{sin, cos, +, -, *, /\}$
LU and QR decomp, matrix mult.	$\{+,-,*,/\}$

Table 1: Operators Used in our Benchmarks

Tool	Benchmark 1	Benchmark 2	Benchmark 3
Gappa	Inf	7.7548e-16	NA
SmartFloat	1.0362e-15	NA	NA
SMT	4.9960e-15	Timeout	2.4367e-14

Table 2: Experimental Results for Microbenchmarks. 'NA' stands for the tool not handling the case correctly (see text). Timeout is set to one hour.

when certain inputs are semantically related (we demonstrate these through microbenchmarks in §2).

We believe that a practical way to handle large problem sizes, complex code structures, as well as non-linear operators is to employ some kind of *search* over input configurations—mappings of inputs to real-number intervals (e.g., for a two-input function, a configuration may be: $i_1 \mapsto [0.5, 0.6], i_2 \mapsto [1.5, 2.5]$). Our main contribution is a search method called Binary Guided Random Testing (BGRT) for locating inputs that (heuristically) cause the highest floating-point errors ("worst inputs"). For comparison, we also implemented two other guided search methods to locate the (inputs causing the) highest error: the first is based on Iterated Local Search (ILS, [32]) and the second on Particle Swarm Optimization (PSO, [26]). Our results are now summarized over 48 experiments (Table 1 lists our benchmarks and the operators used in them):

- Unguided Random Testing (URT) found the highest error in 3 of the 48 experiments.
- BGRT found the highest error in 39 of the 48 experiments.
- ILS found the highest error in 5 of the 48 experiments.
- PSO found the highest error in 1 of the 48 experiments.
- Also, compared to URT:
  - BGRT found higher error in 45 of the 48 experiments.
  - ILS found higher error in 32 of the 48 experiments.
  - PSO found higher error in 22 of the 48 experiments.

To eliminate biases in terms of implementation, we confirmed that BGRT produces these higher relative error values *both* for the same overall runtime as well as for the same number of search steps (Tables 6, 7, 8, and 10). Clearly, much like other search based algorithms (e.g., Boolean satisfiability solvers), there is ample opportunity to further tune the heuristics of BGRT, now that we have proposed one choice that appears to outperform previous methods. In summary, our main contributions are these:

- We evaluate static analysis and SMT-based approaches for precision, and for the first time bring out their pros and cons.
- We offer BGRT as our current best choice for guided random search, and evaluate it on real-world benchmarks (e.g., Parboil), libraries (e.g., Magma), and sequential applications (e.g., linear solver of DQMOM).
- We release the S^3FP tool on our website [37] to help parallel programmers conduct error analysis in practice.

2. Background and Microbenchmarking

We introduce error metrics commonly used in floating-point error estimation followed by a microbenchmark-based study of various existing tools, and finally our precision estimation techniques based on shadow values.

The two most common indicators of floating-point error are *absolute error* and *relative error*. For a program P whose output is O, we use $O_\mathbb{R}$ to denote P's output which is calculated under infinite precision. We use $O_\mathbb{F}$ to denote P's output which is calculated under finite precision (such as 32-bit floating-point arithmetic). The absolute error of P on its output O is then $|O_\mathbb{F} - O_\mathbb{R}|$. The relative error on the output O is $|(O_\mathbb{F} - O_\mathbb{R})/O_\mathbb{R}|$. When estimating relative error, the case of $O_\mathbb{R} = 0$ (which causes the relative error to become undefined) must be properly handled. In

this paper, we employ a padding constant, defining relative error as $|(O_\mathbb{F} - O_\mathbb{R})/max(O_\mathbb{R}, \delta)|$ similar to that employed in [5]. We choose $\delta = 10^{-3}$, keeping it sufficiently away from 0 while being relatively small with respects to the magnitudes of outputs in our experiments.

We observe that floating-point precision has been approached either through the metric of absolute error or relative error. For example, SmartFloat reports relative errors by default. On the other hand, Precimonious [36], an automatic floating-point bit-width allocation tool, measures absolute error by default. In our work, we select relative error as our default metric of floating-point error because, compared to absolute error, the scale of relative error is not related to the scales of the precise ($O_\mathbb{R}$) and the imprecise ($O_\mathbb{F}$) values. This property of relative error is helpful in pinpointing and isolating those instructions that introduce the most floating-point error in a program.

Recently, some floating-point precision estimation efforts have focused on detecting specific phenomena such as *catastrophic cancellation* [5, 29]. BGRT can complement such efforts.

There are three main approaches for abstract analysis of floating-point precision: interval arithmetic, affine arithmetic, and satisfiability modulo theories (SMT). Abstract analysis over-approximates floating-point error. It is generally used when verifying safety criteria such as separation proofs for aircraft [17].

Interval arithmetic tools [12, 14] are usually combined with proof assistants such as Coq [10] to work as lemma generators [6, 7]. Interval arithmetic based approaches tend to produce pessimistic results when computed values are interdependent (e.g., when one value is generated as the sum of two inputs $x + y$ and the other as $x - y$, their sum must be recognized as $x + x$). This situation is illustrated in Fig. 1a and further explained later in this section.

Some interval arithmetic tools such as Gappa employ expression re-writing to improve this situation. Affine arithmetic tools [11, 31] handle input dependencies better. However, when applied to precision analysis of programs, they cannot smoothly handle path conditions. While SMT [24, 27] based approaches[3] do not have these limitations, they are, however, limited by scalability. While SMT has recently been used for floating-point exception detection [4], their approach does not help with error estimation.

We use four benchmarks, three microbenchmarks and one real-world benchmark, to illustrate the limitations of abstract analysis.

- We selected one tool from each abstract analysis approach to measure the worst-case relative errors on the outputs of the four benchmarks.
- For interval arithmetic approach, we selected Gappa [12].
- For affine arithmetic approach, we selected SmartFloat [11].

---

[3] An approach to encode floating-point round-off errors was published in [24], and the method of using binary search for bounding floating-point numbers was published in [27]. A single tool combining these is what we implemented; we have not encountered such a tool by others, yet.

(a) Microbenchmark 1

```
1: double x_0 ← [1.0, 2.0], x_1 ← [1.0, 2.0],
   x_2 ← [1.0, 2.0]
2: double p_0 ← (x_0 + x_1) − x_2
3: double p_1 ← (x_1 + x_2) − x_0
4: double p_2 ← (x_2 + x_0) − x_1
5: double sum ← (p_0 + p_1) + p_2
6: compute error: sum // (x_0 + x_1) + x_2
```

(b) Microbenchmark 2

```
1: double sum ← 0.0, x_0 ← [1.0, 3.0], ...,
   x_7 ← [1.0, 3.0]
2: for i = 0 to 7 do
3:     sum ← sum + x_i
4: end for
5: assume 1.0 ≤ x_0 ... x_7 ≤ 2.0
6: compute error: sum
```

(c) Microbenchmark 3

```
1: double x ← [−1.0, 1.0], y ← [−1.0, 1.0]
2: assume x ≥ y + 0.1 ∧ y ≥ 0.0  //
   (x − y) > 0
3: double z = (x + y)/(x − y) // divide-by-
   zero is impossible
4: compute error: z
```

Figure 1: Microbenchmarks

Tool	$O_{\mathbb{R}}$	$O_{\mathbb{F}}$	Rel. Error
Gappa	$[-9e+10, 9e+10]$	$[-9e+10, 9e+10]$	7.3186e+09
SmartFloat	$[-9e+10, 9e+10]$	$[-9e+10, 9e+10]$	2.2207e-11
SMT	$[-9e+05, 9e+05]$	$[-9e+05, 9e+05]$	Timeout

Table 3: Results Returned by Abstract Analysis Tools on DQMOM. Timeout is set to one hour.

- For SMT approach, we built our own tool that uses Z3 [13] as its underlying solver. (The ideas of building this SMT based tool are proposed in [24, 27]).

- Table 2 shows the worst-case relative errors detected by tools for our microbenchmarks.

- Table 3 shows output ranges and the worst-case relative errors detected by tools for our real-world benchmark.

Microbenchmark 1 (see Fig. 1a) illustrates the scenario that interval arithmetic approaches could return pessimistic results. Without thoroughly considering the dependencies among p_0, p_1, and p_2, the range of sum is $[0, 9]$. (The true range is $[3, 6]$.) When calculating the relative error of sum, 0 is considered to be a possible value of the precise sum. Thus, interval arithmetic tools, which cannot precisely reason about variable dependencies, could report infinite as the bound of the sum's relative error.

Microbenchmark 2 (see Fig. 1b) illustrates the scalability problem of SMT (timeout in Table 2). Also, this microbenchmark contains a condition, encoded using the **assume** statement, which SmartFloat cannot handle. In particular, note that SmartFloat provides predicate functions, called *possibly* and *certainly*, to check whether a condition is possibly true or certainly true. In the microbenchmark, SmartFloat could check that $1.0 \le x_0 \ldots x_7 \le 2.0$ is true at line 5. However, SmartFloat cannot take the condition (on line 5) into account when computing floating-point error. Thus we report 'NA' as SmartFloat's result for this microbenchmark.

Microbenchmark 3 (see Fig. 1c) illustrates the scenario that mixes conditions and non-linear operations. Both Gappa and SmartFloat were unable to handle this microbenchmark. To the best of our knowledge, Gappa, a state-of-the-art interval arithmetic tool, relies on saturation based solving to handle additional conditions in measuring floating-point error. In our experiments with this microbenchmark, Gappa failed to find the bounds of $x - y$. On the other hand, given its precision, SMT successfully handled such scenario.

Table 3 shows the results of using abstract analysis tools to measure the range of the output values (computed both under finite and infinite precision) and the relative error of DQMOM. (We introduce DQMOM in §4.1.) We can observe that both interval and affine arithmetic tools, namely Gappa and SmartFloat, returned overly pessimistic results. We manually calculated the range of the outputs and verified that SMT's results were equal to our manually generated answers. Thus we can conclude that SMT has potential to

P	A program
$I_1 \ldots I_n$	Input variables of P
$R_1 \ldots R_n$	Value ranges (provided by users)
$R_i{}^{p/q}$ $p, q \in \mathbb{N}, 0 \le p < q$	If $R_i = [x, y]$ then $R_i{}^{p/q} = \left[x + \frac{(y-x)*p}{q}, x + \frac{(y-x)*(p+1)}{q}\right]$
$C_1 \ldots C_n$	Configurations: functions from input vars to their ranges
$Eval : P \times C \times \mathbb{N} \mapsto \mathbb{F}$	Evaluation of a program under a configuration
URT	Unguided Random Testing
BGRT	Binary Guided Random Testing
ILS	Iterated Local Search
PSO	Particle Swarm Optimization
RT	Random Testing; one of {URT, BGRT, ILS, PSO}
GRT	Guided Random Testing; one of {BGRT, ILS, PSO}

Table 4: Terminology and Notations

precisely measure floating-point error. However, when estimating the relative error for DQMOM, SMT was limited by its scalability.

To summarize, we conclude that the interval-arithmetic-based approach for floating-point precision measurement cannot handle input dependencies well (illustrated in Fig. 1a). The affine-arithmetic-based approach cannot estimate floating-point error while considering additional conditions (illustrated in Figs. 1b and 1c). On the other hand, the SMT-based approach could overcome both of these limitations. However, it is limited by its scalability (illustrated in Fig. 1c and Table 3). Therefore, when measuring floating-point precision for parallel programs, we consider none of the three approaches is a suitable solution.

3. Guided Random Testing

3.1 Terminology and Notations

We now introduce terminology and notations common to all our guided-search discussions (see Table 4).

Shadow Value Execution. Given a program P and its legal (intended) range of inputs, we execute P under the given precision setting, and also conduct a higher ("infinite") precision execution.[4] Given these outputs of P, we can compute the absolute/relative errors, as described in §2.

---

[4] Given the high difficulty of correctly modifying all external benchmarks to the same higher precision, we sometimes have ended up choosing 64 bits and sometimes 128 bits for our "infinite" precision. However, within each comparative study, we employ only one high-precision allocation.

$$\left\{\begin{array}{l} I_0 \mapsto [0.0, 1.0] \\ I_1 \mapsto [0.0, 1.0] \\ I_2 \mapsto [0.0, 1.0] \\ I_3 \mapsto [0.0, 1.0] \\ I_4 \mapsto [0.0, 1.0] \\ I_5 \mapsto [0.0, 1.0] \\ I_6 \mapsto [-1.0, 1.0] \\ I_7 \mapsto [-1.0, 1.0] \\ I_8 \mapsto [-1.0, 1.0] \end{array}\right\}$$

k	Rel. Error
10^1	3.7270e-07
10^2	1.6205e-06
10^3	1.4213e-05
10^4	1.6553e-04
10^5	2.7246e-04
10^6	8.6022e-04

(a) Original Configuration   (b) Evaluation Results

Figure 2: Original Configuration of DQMOM and its Evaluation Results

Valid Input. Here we describe how a *valid* input is found. For an input variable I_i of a program P, there is a corresponding (floating-point) value range R_i that contains all possible values of I_i. If I_1 is the only input of P, a valid input is a random value in R_1. If P has multiple input variables $I_1 \ldots I_n$, a valid input is a random sampling, one from each range $R_1 \ldots R_n$. We often denote R_i by $[x, y]$ where $x \leq y$. A sub-range $R_i^{p/q}$, where $0 \leq p < q$, is a subset of R_i defined by

$$\left[x + \frac{(y - x) * p}{q}, x + \frac{(y - x) * (p + 1)}{q} \right]$$

Configuration. A *configuration* is a function from program inputs to ranges of values. For two configurations, c_x and c_y, c_y is *tighter* than c_x if they have the same domain (input variables) and for every i in this domain, $c_y(i)$ is contained in $c_x(i)$. In our work, we assume that users supply the initial configurations, starting from which the search proceeds seeking the tightest configuration that maximizes error (within resource limits, and perhaps finding a local maximum).

Evaluation of a Configuration. During GRT, an initial configuration will be recursively divided into tighter configurations. (The intuition and the algorithm are introduced in §3.4.) We need to *evaluate* (tighter) configurations and compare them through shadow value computations. More specifically, for a configuration C, we sample k valid inputs from C and also perform shadow value execution k times on the program P. From the k measured floating-point errors, we use the highest one as the evaluation result. Function $Eval$ takes a program, a configuration, and an integer as its arguments. For example, $Eval(P, C, k)$ evaluates the given configuration C by performing shadow value execution k times on P, and reports the highest measured floating-point error. Finally, one configuration is chosen as "better" based on such comparisons.

3.2 Intuition behind Guided Random Testing

In this section, we give an intuitive description of GRT methods, using the Direct Quadrature Method of Moments benchmark (DQMOM, detailed in §4.1) as an illustrative example. First, Fig. 2a shows the initial (user-given) configuration of DQMOM mapping 9 program inputs $I_0 \ldots I_8$ into their ranges. Fig. 2b shows its evaluation results (highest relative error obtained) after the shown number of evaluations (trials) going from $10^1 \ldots 10^6$. As is to be expected, the higher the k parameter in $Eval(P, C, k)$, the higher is the generated relative error. Fig. 3 illustrates the intuition further with two experiments: Exp_1 and Exp_2. For each experiment, we find a "good" and "bad" configuration to replace the initial configuration, and then we evaluate both. Note that both good and bad configurations are tighter than the initial configuration. Figs. 3a and 3b show the bad and good configurations of Exp_1 and Exp_2, respectively. Fig. 3c gives the highest computed relative errors for these four configurations. Figs. 3d and 3e plot the comparison of

the computed relative errors for the original configuration, and the bad and good configurations of the two experiments. From these two plots we can observe the following:

- With higher number of iterations k, the exhibited error increases.
- The choice of the initial configuration matters.
- After only a few iterations (i.e., 10–100), it is possible to select a better/worse error inducing configuration.

The search heuristics we have experimented with attempt to capitalize on these observations.

3.3 Unguided Random Testing

Algorithm 1 Unguided Random Testing

1: **Input:** P, C_{init}
2: **Output:** Computed highest floating-point error
3: $WorstErr \leftarrow 0.0$
4: **while** has resources **do**
5:      $CurrErr \leftarrow Eval(P, C_{init}, 1)$
6:      **if** $CurrErr > WorstErr$ **then**
7:          $WorstErr \leftarrow CurrErr$
8:      **end if**
9: **end while**
10: **return** $WorstErr$

Unguided random testing takes as input a program to measure floating-point error for and its initial configuration. Then it just repeatedly samples inputs from the initial configuration and computes the highest floating-point error by performing shadow value executions. Algo. 1 shows the pseudocode of unguided random testing. It basically repeatedly calls the evaluation function $Eval$ until running out of the given resource limit (runtime or the total number of shadow value executions).

3.4 Binary Guided Random Testing

In this section, we describe our custom binary guided random testing (BGRT) algorithm, which is the best guiding heuristic we discovered so far. BGRT takes the initial configuration, and iteratively zooms into tighter configurations that result in higher error. Each BGRT iteration starts with an configuration (not necessary the initial), enumerates some of its tighter configurations, and selects the one that (locally) maximizes the error. The selected tighter configuration starts the next BGRT iteration. With a certain probability, we also allow restarts to the user-given initial configuration so that we prevent getting stuck in a local maximum.

To explain how BGRT enumerates tighter configurations, we first introduce some helper routines. $PartConf$ randomly partitions a configuration into two non-empty configurations such that the domains are mutually exclusive and exhaustive with respect to the domain of the incoming configuration. For example, c_q and c_r could be one possible result of $PartConf(c_p)$:

$$c_p: \left\{\begin{array}{l} I_0 \mapsto [-1, 1] \\ I_1 \mapsto [0.1, 0.2] \\ I_2 \mapsto [-0.2, -0.1] \end{array}\right\} \quad \begin{array}{l} c_q: \left\{\begin{array}{l} I_0 \mapsto [-1, 1] \\ I_2 \mapsto [-0.2, -0.1] \end{array}\right\} \\ c_r: \left\{ I_1 \mapsto [0.1, 0.2] \right\} \end{array}$$

We define the *upper half* and the *lower half* configurations of an incoming configuration c as $\overset{\frown}{c}$ and $\underset{\smile}{c}$, respectively. The upper half is obtained by changing each range (say R_i) of the incoming configuration to its upper half sub-range (i.e., $R_i^{1/2}$). Examples of the upper and the lower halves of the configuration c_p are as follows:

$$\overset{\frown}{c_p}: \left\{\begin{array}{l} I_0 \mapsto [0, 1] \\ I_1 \mapsto [0.15, 0.2] \\ I_2 \mapsto [-0.15, -0.1] \end{array}\right\} \quad \underset{\smile}{c_p}: \left\{\begin{array}{l} I_0 \mapsto [-1, 0] \\ I_1 \mapsto [0.1, 0.15] \\ I_2 \mapsto [-0.2, -0.15] \end{array}\right\}$$

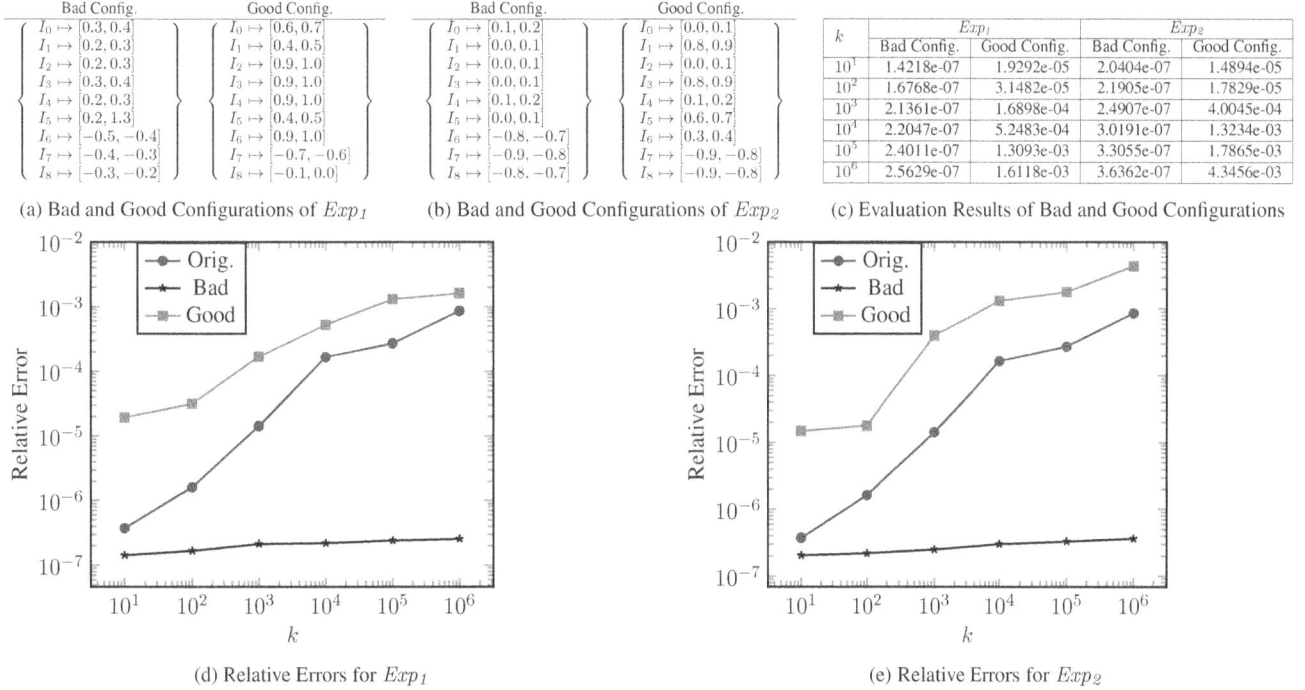

Bad Config.	Good Config.
$\begin{cases} I_0 \mapsto [0.3, 0.4] \\ I_1 \mapsto [0.2, 0.3] \\ I_2 \mapsto [0.2, 0.3] \\ I_3 \mapsto [0.3, 0.4] \\ I_4 \mapsto [0.2, 0.3] \\ I_5 \mapsto [0.2, 1.3] \\ I_6 \mapsto [-0.5, -0.4] \\ I_7 \mapsto [-0.4, -0.3] \\ I_8 \mapsto [-0.3, -0.2] \end{cases}$	$\begin{cases} I_0 \mapsto [0.6, 0.7] \\ I_1 \mapsto [0.4, 0.5] \\ I_2 \mapsto [0.9, 1.0] \\ I_3 \mapsto [0.9, 1.0] \\ I_4 \mapsto [0.9, 1.0] \\ I_5 \mapsto [0.4, 0.5] \\ I_6 \mapsto [0.9, 1.0] \\ I_7 \mapsto [-0.7, -0.6] \\ I_8 \mapsto [-0.1, 0.0] \end{cases}$

(a) Bad and Good Configurations of Exp_1

Bad Config.	Good Config.
$\begin{cases} I_0 \mapsto [0.1, 0.2] \\ I_1 \mapsto [0.0, 0.1] \\ I_2 \mapsto [0.0, 0.1] \\ I_3 \mapsto [0.0, 0.1] \\ I_4 \mapsto [0.1, 0.2] \\ I_5 \mapsto [0.0, 0.1] \\ I_6 \mapsto [-0.8, -0.7] \\ I_7 \mapsto [-0.9, -0.8] \\ I_8 \mapsto [-0.8, -0.7] \end{cases}$	$\begin{cases} I_0 \mapsto [0.0, 0.1] \\ I_1 \mapsto [0.8, 0.9] \\ I_2 \mapsto [0.0, 0.1] \\ I_3 \mapsto [0.8, 0.9] \\ I_4 \mapsto [0.1, 0.2] \\ I_5 \mapsto [0.6, 0.7] \\ I_6 \mapsto [0.3, 0.4] \\ I_7 \mapsto [-0.9, -0.8] \\ I_8 \mapsto [-0.9, -0.8] \end{cases}$

(b) Bad and Good Configurations of Exp_2

k	Exp_1 Bad Config.	Exp_1 Good Config.	Exp_2 Bad Config.	Exp_2 Good Config.
10^1	1.4218e-07	1.9292e-05	2.0404e-07	1.4894e-05
10^2	1.6768e-07	3.1482e-05	2.1905e-07	1.7829e-05
10^3	2.1361e-07	1.6898e-04	2.4907e-07	4.0045e-04
10^4	2.2047e-07	5.2483e-04	3.0191e-07	1.3234e-03
10^5	2.4011e-07	1.3093e-03	3.3055e-07	1.7865e-03
10^6	2.5629e-07	1.6118e-03	3.6362e-07	4.3456e-03

(c) Evaluation Results of Bad and Good Configurations

(d) Relative Errors for Exp_1

(e) Relative Errors for Exp_2

Figure 3: Two Experiments Illustrating the Intuition behind GRT

These are both tighter configurations with respect to the incoming configuration.

$NextGen$ (in Algo. 2) is a function that takes an configuration ($conf$) and enumerates a set of its tighter configurations (held by $nextg$) to explore. $NextGen$ first partitions $conf$ into two configurations c_x and c_y. Then it finds the upper and lower halves of the two partitions and permutes them. Such divide-and-permute will be repeated N_{part} times, which is one of the parameters of BGRT. Note that $\widehat{c_x} \cup \widehat{c_y} = \widehat{conf}$. Thus, we add the upper and the lower halves of $conf$ into $nextg$ once in the beginning of $NextGen$. In $NextGen$, we use $\cup$ to denote the union of the two tighter configurations (with disjoint domains) into one configuration. We use $\uplus$ to denote forming a set of configurations (discriminated union).

Algo. 2 shows our BGRT algorithm. A BGRT iteration is shown from lines 16–30. The starting configuration of a BGRT iteration is $LocalConf$, and it is used to enumerate tighter configurations ($NextConfs$) at line 17. From the enumerated tighter configurations, we choose the one whose evaluation results in the highest error (lines 18–24). The number of shadow value executions k is also a parameter of BGRT. Lines 25–27 keep track of the all-time highest floating-point error in $WorstErr$. Line 29 resets the starting configuration to the user-given initial configuration if BGRT decides to restart.

3.5 Other Guided Random Search Strategies

Beside BGRT, we have also implemented and explored two other GRT strategies: iterated local search (ILS) and particle swarm optimization (PSO). However, our experimental results currently show that ILS and PSO do not usually find higher floating-point errors than BGRT. The reason why we explored ILS and PSO is that they have been successful in finding (heuristically) optimal solutions for other problems. ILS is used in a framework called ParamILS [22] that automatically searches for optimal parameter settings of algorithms. It defines neighborhood relationships between models in

a search space, and searches for the optimal model by iteratively evaluating selected models and their neighbors. PSO is used in a randomized constraint solver called CORAL [38] that is capable of finding floating-point models for given floating-point constraints. It keeps track of a group of models with their evaluation results, finds the next group to explore based on the current group, and reports the optimal among all explored models. In this paper, we omit the details of our implementations of ILS and PSO; those details can be found on our website [37].

4. Experimental Results

To assess the effectiveness of the four proposed random search techniques, namely URT, BGRT, ILS, and PSO, we implemented them in our prototype tool S^3FP and compared on our benchmark suite. The benchmark suite includes both sequential and parallel programs. Our sequential benchmarks comprise of balanced reduction (BR), imbalanced reduction (IBR), and direct quadrature method of moments (DQMOM). Although DQMOM itself is sequential, we extracted it from a parallel computational framework [33]. Our parallel benchmarks are well-known GPU primitives including fast Fourier transform (FFT), LU decomposition (LU), QR decomposition (QR), and matrix multiplication (MM). FFT is taken from Parboil parallel benchmark set (v0.2) [39]; LU, QR, and MM are from Magma library (v1.4.0) [34].

All examples in our benchmark suite perform 32-bit floating-point arithmetic. To be able to perform shadow value execution, we created higher precision versions employing 64- or 128-bit

	Sequential BR	Sequential IBR	Sequential DQMOM	Parallel (GPU) FFT	Parallel (GPU) LU	Parallel (GPU) QR	Parallel (GPU) MM
Original	32	32	32	32	32	32	32
High Prec.	128	128	128	128	64	64	64

Table 5: Benchmark Precisions Used in Shadow Value Execution

Algorithm 2 Binary Guided Random Testing

1: **Input:** P, C_{init}, k, N_{part}
2: **Output:** Computed highest floating-point error
3:
4: **procedure** $NextGen(conf)$
5:     $nextg \leftarrow \overbrace{conf} \uplus conf$
6:     **for** $i = 1$ to N_{part} **do**
7:         $(c_x,\ c_y) = PartConf(conf)$
8:         $nextg \leftarrow nextg \uplus \left(\overbrace{c_x} \cup \underbrace{c_y} \right) \uplus \left(\underbrace{c_x} \cup \overbrace{c_y} \right)$
9:     **end for**
10:     **return** $nextg$
11: **end procedure**
12:
13: $WorstErr, LocalErr \leftarrow 0.0$
14: $LocalConf \leftarrow C_{init}$
15: **while** has resources **do**
16:     $LocalErr \leftarrow 0.0$
17:     $NextConfs \leftarrow NextGen(LocalConf)$
18:     **for** $c \in NextConfs$ **do**
19:         $err \leftarrow Eval(P, c, k)$
20:         **if** $err > LocalErr$ **then**
21:             $LocalErr \leftarrow err$
22:             $LocalConf \leftarrow c$
23:         **end if**
24:     **end for**
25:     **if** $LocalErr > WorstErr$ **then**
26:         $WorstErr \leftarrow LocalErr$
27:     **end if**
28:     **if** random restart **then**
29:         $LocalConf \leftarrow C_{init}$
30:     **end if**
31: **end while**
32: **return** $WorstErr$

	Algo.	IBR^K (2048)	BR (2048)	IBR (2048)	DQMOM (960)
Exp_1	URT^p	3.6151e-03	1.4106e-02	1.1035e-01	8.8729e-03
	$BGRT^p$	**2.7132e-01**	**9.6636e-01**	**4.4229e+01**	**6.0333e+00**
	ILS^p	2.5134e-02	4.3401e-01	5.0068e-01	4.6705e-02
	PSO^p	8.6183e-03	1.4833e-01	5.2374e-02	1.0133e-02
Exp_2	URT^p	3.1396e-02	3.5851e-01	3.2051e-01	2.4357e-03
	$BGRT^p$	**2.9659e-01**	**8.0504e-01**	**1.3488e+01**	**1.8198e+00**
	ILS^p	2.1614e-02	7.9974e-02	5.2502e-02	7.6498e-03
	PSO^p	3.1449e-02	2.7312e-01	9.4350e-01	5.9729e-03

Table 7: Relative Errors for Sequential Benchmarks. The number of allowed shadow value executions is set to 10^6.

floating-point arithmetic. Table 5 summarizes the floating-point bit-width of the original benchmarks and their higher precision versions. Although various versions of the benchmarks compute with different bit-widths, S^3FP generates only 32-bit floating-point numbers as inputs. Using exclusively 32-bit floating-point inputs guarantees that, when doing shadow value execution, the original and higher precision version are executed on identical inputs. If we used higher bit-width (i.e., 64- or 128-bit) inputs instead, we would immediately lose precision when type casting to 32-bit inputs for the original benchmarks, and the two executions would potentially diverge.

Outputs of most of our benchmarks are arrays or matrices, and hence defining relative errors for such benchmarks is not trivial. Our strategy for measuring relative errors for such benchmarks is to select one of the output array/matrix elements as a representative output, and measure only its relative error. This manual selection process is based on our study of the benchmarks: we chose the elements which are calculated using the highest number of floating-point operations since these are likely to exhibit the largest relative errors.

To perform a meaningful comparison of our random testing methods, we relied on measuring (or limiting) two different resources. The first resource is elapsed time, where we would limit the allocated running time (i.e., set a time out) to, for example, one hour. This gives us a good estimate of how well the proposed random testing techniques work in practice. However, it includes potential algorithm and implementation overheads. The

second resource we measure is the total number of times a shadow value execution is repeated. This demonstrates the power of RT techniques under the assumption that all have the same algorithm/implementation overhead.

We have implemented in S^3FP both sequential and parallel versions of all four runtime testing methods. In our tables with results, URT, BGRT, ILS, and PSO denote single-core implementations, while URT^p, $BGRT^p$, ILS^p, and PSO^p denote multi-core implementations. We parallelized URT^p by allowing simultaneous calls of $Eval(P, c_i, 1)$. $BGRT^p$, ILS^p, and PSO^p are parallelized by allowing a call of $Eval(P, c_i, k)$ to simultaneously perform shadow value executions. However, our current multi-core implementations can only be applied to sequential benchmarks. We will explore more parallelism in GRT implementations and apply them to parallel benchmarks in our future work.

4.1 Results for Sequential Benchmarks

Our benchmark suite contains four sequential programs. The sequential balanced reduction (BR) simulates parallel reduction [18], while the sequential imbalanced reduction (IBR) simulates multiple threads accumulating values using atomic operations. Since we have not fully investigated how non-deterministic thread interleavings affect floating-point precision, we converted parallel reductions into sequential versions to perform this comparison. This allows us to compare IBR^K, IBR, and BR. These examples are further discussed in §5. IBR^K is a variant of IBR that employs the more precise Kahan summation [25]. In our experiments, all BR and IBR input variables are initially mapped to ranges $[-100, 100]$.

The direct quadrature method of moments (DQMOM) is a core function of a combustion simulation component of Uintah computational framework [33]. DQMOM models the transform of particle density between moments, converts the transform as a linear system $AX = B$, and solves the system. In our initial configuration of DQMOM, the first 3/5 input variables are mapped to $[0.0, 1.0]$ and the last 2/5 input variables are mapped to $[-1.0, 1.0]$.

Table 6 gives the (highest) relative errors discovered by the four random testing methods on our sequential benchmarks within one hour time budget. In the table, "# SVE" denotes the total number of shadow value executions. (A call to $Eval(P, c_i, k)$ is counted as k shadow value executions.) The input size (the number of input variables) of each benchmark is given in parentheses next to the benchmark name. For each benchmark, we compared the four methods twice (denoted as Exp_1 and Exp_2), and highlighted the highest relative error using bold font. Table 7 shows the results of running RT methods with the same number of shadow value executions (10^6). From Tables 6 and 7, we can observe that BGRT usually returns the highest errors. Fig. 4 plots the results in Table 6.

4.2 Results for Parallel Benchmarks

For our parallel benchmarks, we have verified that their computational results (and hence, our error estimation) are unaffected by thread schedules, based on the following lines of reasoning. First, we assume the absence of data races (checking for races using tools

	Algo.	BR (512)		IBR (512)		DQMOM (240)	
		rel. error	# SVE	rel. error	# SVE	rel. error	# SVE
Exp_1	URT^P	2.7416e-02	1.2*10⁶	1.8757e-01	1.2*10⁶	8.8585e-03	1.2*10⁶
	BGRT^P	**4.3774e-01**	1.1*10⁶	**3.5947e+00**	1.2*10⁶	**1.0000e+00**	1.2*10⁶
	ILS^P	8.4400e-02	8.8*10⁵	2.9171e-01	8.7*10⁵	1.1611e-02	1.1*10⁶
	PSO^P	1.5789e-02	1.0*10⁶	2.7611e-02	1.0*10⁶	8.6954e-03	1.1*10⁶
Exp_2	URT^P	2.1344e-01	1.2*10⁶	4.1944e-01	1.2*10⁶	4.1150e-02	1.2*10⁶
	BGRT^P	**3.6824e-01**	1.1*10⁶	**1.7659e+00**	1.1*10⁶	**1.0000e+00**	1.2*10⁶
	ILS^P	1.3739e-02	8.8*10⁵	6.5749e-02	8.7*10⁵	8.2554e-02	1.1*10⁶
	PSO^P	3.5282e-02	1.0*10⁶	1.1199e-01	1.0*10⁶	1.5171e-02	1.1*10⁶

(a) Small Input Size

	Algo.	BR (2048)		IBR (2048)		DQMOM (960)	
		rel. error	# SVE	rel. error	# SVE	rel. error	# SVE
Exp_1	URT^P	1.4106e-02	6.4*10⁵	1.1035e-01	6.5*10⁵	8.8723e-03	6.6*10⁵
	BGRT^P	**9.6636e-01**	6.1*10⁵	**4.4229e+01**	6.1*10⁵	**1.0000e+00**	6.4*10⁵
	ILS^P	4.3401e-01	2.2*10⁵	5.0068e-01	2.2*10⁵	2.0105e-02	4.3*10⁵
	PSO^P	3.9677e-02	4.6*10⁵	4.4608e-02	4.6*10⁵	1.0133e-02	5.9*10⁵
Exp_2	URT^P	1.1031e-02	6.4*10⁵	7.3680e-02	6.4*10⁵	2.4357e-03	6.6*10⁵
	BGRT^P	**8.0504e-01**	6.0*10⁵	**6.8056e+00**	6.1*10⁵	**4.4318e-01**	6.4*10⁵
	ILS^P	7.9974e-02	2.2*10⁵	4.8452e-02	2.0*10⁵	2.7101e-03	4.3*10⁵
	PSO^P	2.7312e-01	4.6*10⁵	9.4350e-01	4.6*10⁵	5.9729e-03	5.9*10⁵

(b) Large Input Size

Table 6: Relative Errors for Sequential Benchmarks. Time budget is set to one hour.

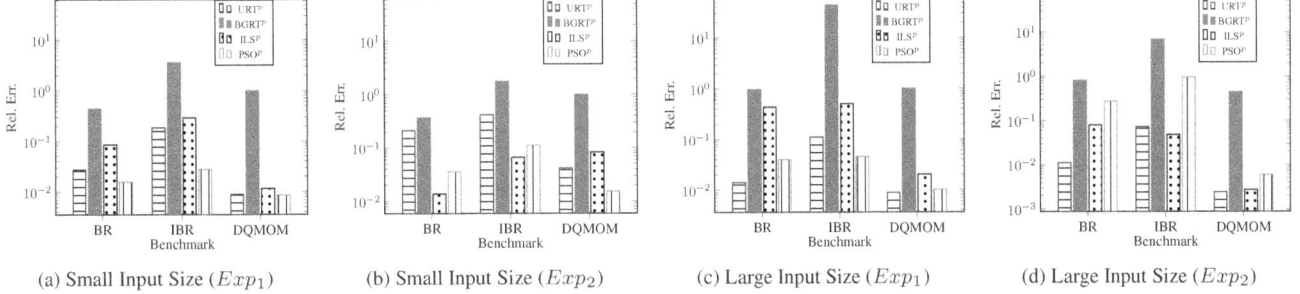

(a) Small Input Size (Exp_1) (b) Small Input Size (Exp_2) (c) Large Input Size (Exp_1) (d) Large Input Size (Exp_2)

Figure 4: Relative Errors for Sequential Benchmarks. Time budget is set to one hour.

	Algo.	FFT (512)		LU (256)		QR (256)		MM (770)	
		rel. error	# SVE	rel. error	# SVE	rel. error	# SVE	rel. error	# SVE
$Exp.1$	URT	1.9481e-02	8.0*10⁴	6.8969e-03	4.8*10⁴	**3.5228e-02**	4.8*10⁴	3.5777e-04	4.8*10⁴
	BGRT	**2.3552e-02**	8.0*10⁴	**1.7481e-02**	4.9*10⁴	3.0875e-02	4.5*10⁴	**1.2014e+01**	4.8*10⁴
	ILS	3.8490e-03	7.9*10⁴	9.3943e-03	4.9*10⁴	3.9905e-04	4.8*10⁴	2.0271e-02	4.8*10⁴
	PSO	4.7028e-03	8.0*10⁴	1.2302e-03	4.8*10⁴	1.2890e-02	4.2*10⁴	7.0844e-04	4.7*10⁴
$Exp.2$	URT	7.0919e-03	8.0*10⁴	6.2447e-04	4.9*10⁴	5.0282e-03	4.8*10⁴	2.1496e-03	4.9*10⁴
	BGRT	2.0740e-02	8.0*10⁴	**1.8670e-02**	4.9*10⁴	6.1168e-02	4.7*10⁴	**2.5339e+00**	4.8*10⁴
	ILS	**2.8143e-02**	8.1*10⁴	5.3179e-03	4.9*10⁴	2.2136e-03	4.8*10⁴	1.0493e-03	4.8*10⁴
	PSO	1.2055e-02	8.0*10⁴	1.3823e-03	4.8*10⁴	**2.0000e+00**	4.7*10⁴	1.9052e-03	4.8*10⁴

(a) Small Input Size

	Algo.	FFT (2048)		LU (1024)		QR (1024)		MM (3074)	
		rel. error	# SVE	rel. error	# SVE	rel. error	# SVE	rel. error	# SVE
$Exp.1$	URT	9.9671e-03	7.7*10⁴	1.1942e-03	4.8*10⁴	3.2723e-02	4.6*10⁴	1.0016e-02	4.6*10⁴
	BGRT	3.4312e-02	7.6*10⁴	**2.6197e-02**	4.8*10⁴	**1.9540e-01**	4.6*10⁴	**3.1161e+00**	4.6*10⁴
	ILS	**6.8418e-02**	7.5*10⁴	3.3736e-03	4.7*10⁴	2.1083e-02	4.7*10⁴	1.6710e-01	4.4*10⁴
	PSO	3.5419e-03	7.6*10⁴	2.8987e-03	4.7*10⁴	4.3618e-02	4.1*10⁴	8.6908e-04	4.1*10⁴
$Exp.2$	URT	1.9560e-03	7.7*10⁴	1.1742e-03	4.8*10⁴	**1.6825e-01**	4.7*10⁴	1.5422e-02	4.6*10⁴
	BGRT	1.2580e-02	7.6*10⁴	**2.5969e-02**	4.8*10⁴	1.0213e-01	4.6*10⁴	**1.7881e-01**	4.6*10⁴
	ILS	**4.4445e-02**	7.5*10⁴	7.9298e-03	4.8*10⁴	3.9839e-02	4.7*10⁴	7.6199e-03	4.4*10⁴
	PSO	1.4056e-02	7.5*10⁴	9.3751e-03	4.7*10⁴	8.1161e-02	4.6*10⁴	3.2531e-03	4.5*10⁴

(b) Large Input Size

Table 8: Relative Errors for Parallel Benchmarks. Time budget is set to one hour.

such as [30] is future work). Second, we have manually verified that there are no schedule-dependent reduction operations (automation of these checks is future work).

All input variables of our parallel (GPU) benchmarks are initially mapped to $[-100, 100]$. Table 8 shows the computed relative errors for our parallel benchmarks given one hour time limit. We can observe that BGRT returns the highest relative errors in most of our experiments with parallel benchmarks. When limiting the

number of shadow value executions as resource, BGRT still works the best among all four RT techniques (see Table 10). Fig. 5 plots the results from Table 8.

In Table 8, the largest input matrix size is 32×32. However, we observed that if the LU and QR benchmarks are called with these sizes, they directly call LAPACK [1] routines to *sequentially* compute the results. Table 9 show the results of applying larger input matrix size (1200×1200) that triggers GPU (paral-

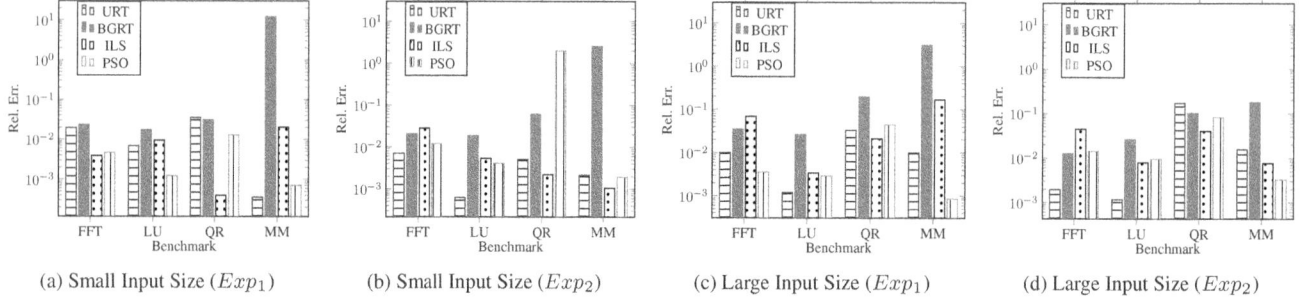

(a) Small Input Size (Exp_1) (b) Small Input Size (Exp_2) (c) Large Input Size (Exp_1) (d) Large Input Size (Exp_2)

Figure 5: Relative Errors for Parallel Benchmarks. Time budget is set to one hour.

	Algo.	LU (1440000)		QR (1440000)	
		rel. error	# SVE	rel. error	# SVE
$Exp.1$	URT	8.1670e-04	1630	1.4829e-01	2600
	BGRT	**5.3323e-02**	1440	**2.0008e+00**	2130
	ILS	6.4743e-03	1210	7.3494e-02	1670
	PSO	3.9983e-03	1160	1.8321e-02	1580
$Exp.2$	URT	3.0200e-03	1630	1.9998e+00	2600
	BGRT	**2.1163e-02**	1440	**2.0009e+00**	2140
	ILS	6.1338e-05	1210	8.9875e-03	1670
	PSO	1.7010e-02	1160	9.2871e-03	1570

Table 9: Relative Errors for LU and QR with Large Input Matrices. Time budget is set to one hour.

		FFT (2048)	LU (1024)	QR (1024)	MM (3074)
Exp_1	URT	9.9671e-03	1.1942e-03	3.2723e-02	1.0016e-02
	BGRT	3.4312e-02	**2.6197e-02**	**1.9540e-01**	**3.1161e+00**
	ILS	**4.0819e-02**	3.3736e-03	3.6521e-02	1.6710e-01
	PSO	3.5419e-03	3.1306e-03	4.3618e-02	8.6908e-04
Exp_2	URT	1.9560e-03	1.1742e-03	**1.6825e-01**	1.5422e-02
	BGRT	3.1750e-03	**2.5969e-02**	1.0213e-01	**1.7881e-01**
	ILS	**3.8323e-02**	7.9298e-03	3.9839e-02	2.7150e-02
	PSO	1.4056e-02	9.3751e-03	8.1161e-02	3.2531e-03

Table 10: Relative Errors for Parallel Benchmarks. The number of allowed shadow value executions is set to $5 * 10^4$.

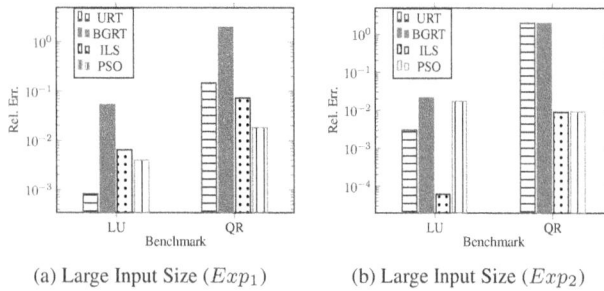

(a) Large Input Size (Exp_1) (b) Large Input Size (Exp_2)

Figure 6: Relative Errors for Parallel Benchmarks with 1200×1200 Input Matrices. Time budget is set to one hour.

lel) computations in LU and QR. Fig. 6 plots the results from Table 9. For the LU benchmark which performs LU decomposition, $A = P \times L \times U$, we calculate the product of P, L, and U, and measure the precision on one of the elements in the produced matrix. This precaution is required because the permutation matrices (Ps) computed by different precision versions may be different.

Note that in our experiments in §4.1 and §4.2 we only compute relative errors. However, we also performed limited experiments showing that BGRT also successfully generates higher absolute errors than URT. Table 11 gives the computed absolute errors for our parallel benchmarks with time out set to one hour. BGRT still returns the higher errors than URT in most of the experiments.

4.3 Discussion

From our experimental results we can observe that BGRT found the highest floating-point error 39 times out of 48 experiments total. The intuition behind such success of BGRT is that it could often "zoom in" to a certain configuration that potentially causes high floating-point error. By observing Figs. 3d and 3e, we could make a hypothesis: bad inputs (inputs that result in low errors) and good inputs (inputs that result in high errors) are not equally spaced in the input domain. In other words, for a configuration, there may exist a tighter configuration that contains many good inputs. On the other hand, there may exist a tighter configuration that contains many bad inputs. BGRT iteratively applies this hypothesis and iteratively searches for "better" configurations Our experimental results empirically show that the intuition is useful for measuring floating-point error in practice. However, ILS and PSO do not follow this hypothesis: when they encounter a configuration that is evaluated to high error, they try to find a similar, but not a tighter configuration, to explore. (Two configurations are similar if they have the same domain and map most of the input variables to the same ranges. But for those input variables which are mapped to different ranges, those ranges are mutually exclusive.)

Finally, note that the algorithm tuning parameters of BGRT, ILS, and PSO in our experiments were manually explored (e.g., k and N_{part} in BGRT, see Algo. 2). In particular, we manually varied parameter settings for the GRT techniques and chose the best one for our experiments. Admittedly, applying different parameter settings to different GRT techniques could give them different capabilities of generating floating-point errors. We plan to investigate automatic methods for tuning GRT parameters in our future work.

5. Applications

Combining Random Testing with Automatic Performance Tuning. Automatic tuning tools (e.g., [28, 36]) increase program performance by lowering floating-point bit-width of input variables or instruction operands while at the same time satisfying a user-provided precision constraint. The constraint is usually in the form of an upper bound on floating-point error. A common approach to checking whether a tuned program satisfies the precision constraint is to concretely execute it with user-given or randomly generated inputs. However, such inputs may not result in highly imprecise outputs of the program. Consequently, the tuned programs may frequently violate the expected precision constraint in practice. Our

	Algo.	FFT (512) abs. error	LU (256) abs. error	QR (256) abs. error	MM (770) abs. error
Exp_1	NRT	9.8124e-05	2.7483e-05	2.0435e-03	5.7346e-01
	BGRT	**1.2366e-04**	**2.9065e-04**	**1.3575e-02**	**3.3573e+01**
Exp_2	NRT	**1.0980e-04**	2.6175e-05	5.0654e-03	6.8767e-01
	BGRT	1.0325e-04	**1.3049e-03**	**2.8785e-02**	**3.1175e+00**

(a) Small Input Size

	Algo.	FFT (2048) abs. error	LU (1024) abs. error	QR (1024) abs. error	MM (3074) abs. error
Exp_1	NRT	1.5593e-04	**7.3125e-04**	**4.1454e-02**	1.6142e+00
	BGRT	**1.6951e-04**	3.5286e-04	1.1190e-02	**8.6679e+00**
Exp_2	NRT	1.5268e-04	9.5654e-05	1.9666e-03	1.2067e+00
	BGRT	**1.5341e-04**	**1.2441e+00**	**5.7901e-03**	**8.0260e+00**

(b) Large Input Size

Table 11: Absolute Error for Parallel Benchmarks. Time budget is set to one hour.

GRT approach could provide inputs that result in highly imprecise outputs to such automatic performance tuning tools. Hence, using GRT the final tuned programs are expected to violate the precision constraint in practice much less frequently.

Input Generation for Floating-point Error Detection. Recently proposed tools [5, 29] pin-point the critical instructions of a program that cause high floating-point errors. They employ shadow value execution and keep track of each value's shadow value. By comparing the original and shadow values they can find the source of floating-point imprecision. However, such technique highly depends on provided inputs: if the inputs result in precise outputs, the tools may not accurately point out the imprecision-causing instructions. Our GRT approach could enumerate inputs resulting in highly imprecise outputs, thereby increasing precision of floating-point error detection.

Algorithm Comparison. Mathematically analyzing numerical errors of algorithms is a tedious process, and it is not feasible that algorithm designers perform it for their every new algorithm. We believe that our random testing methods would provide the designers with solid empirical data about the numerical error of their algorithms. Publishing such data with an algorithm would in turn help programmers to select algorithms based on the numerical precision needs of their software. For example, Table 7 shows a comparison of three reductions: balanced (BR), imbalanced (IBR), and Kahan summation (IBR^K). The reductions calculate the summation of a set of 32-bit floating-point values. However, Kahan summation uses an additional 32-bit floating-point number to hold round-off value which "compensates" floating-point error. Such compensated summation is suggested to be a more precise way to summarize floating-point values [20]. Indeed, in Table 7 all random testing methods reported that Kahan summation has lower relative floating-point error than the other two. A programmer could rely on such data to make a more informative choice when exploring various trade-offs involving floating-point precision. We plan to investigate how to use GRT to more accurately compare numerical precision among various classes of algorithms.

6. Future Work

Combining Random Testing with Input Constraint Generation. A weakness of our current GRT methods, including BGRT, ILS, and PSO, is that they do not guarantee path coverage. In other words, given a set of randomly generated inputs, there may exist some program paths which are not traversed using these inputs. However, if there exists a path which could generate highly imprecise results, it is highly likely to be traversed sufficiently many times by our methods. Otherwise, the final floating-point error of the program may be heavily under-approximated. (Figs. 3d and 3e suggest that the fewer traversals of a path, the lower the floating-point error detected from it will be.)

A potential approach to improving path coverage of GRT methods is combining them with weakest precondition [21] inference, and related symbolic input generation techniques [8]. These techniques can help GRT methods generate equal number of inputs for each path, or even bias toward some designated paths. For example, one can generate input constraints that help reach specific program points. The difficulty of reasoning about floating-point values (not well-supported by current SMT tools) may be overcome by upcoming progress in SMT, and perhaps also by approximating the reasoning (perhaps sufficient to bias search).

Fair Floating-point Range Division. BGRT, ILS, and PSO divide floating-point ranges into sub-ranges with various granularity. For example, when generating the "upper half" of a configuration (see §3.4), we divide each range in half. For example, we divide $[2.0, 32.0]$ into $[2.0, 17.0]$ and $[17.0, 32.0]$. However, based on IEEE-754 standard [23], floating-point numbers are not equally spaced between the largest and the smallest floating-point numbers. Hence, the number of floating-point numbers in $[2.0, 17.0]$ is not equal to the number of floating-point numbers in $[17.0, 32.0]$. (In fact, $[2.0, 17.0]$ contains more floating-point numbers.) A side-effect of such unfair division is that we may bias some floating-point numbers to be chosen as input values. A *fair* division on $[2.0, 32.0]$ is $[2.0, 8.0]$ and $[8.0, 32.0]$ such that the two sub-ranges contain the same amount of floating-point numbers. Our preliminary experiments are not conclusive to show that such fair division could result in finding higher floating-point error—we are planning to explore this direction further.

Compositional Random Testing. Random testing could sometimes be expensive, in particular when even one run of the program under test takes a long time. In addition, input size could be very large as well. For example, Table 12 shows our experimental results for the parallel FFT from the NAS Parallel Benchmarks (NPB), MPI version [35]. The input of this benchmark contains about 0.5 million floating-point numbers, while the number of shadow value executions performed in an hour is about $8.5 * 10^2$. Hence, only a tiny fraction of the input space can be covered in an hour, which is sometimes not enough to find a satisfactory floating-point error. These are some challenges for GRT to detect high floating-point error for large-scale programs. A potential solution is to extract critical functions using a custom static analysis, and then focus RT only on those. For example, a large FFT program (Cooley-Tukey FFT [19]) recursively breaks down discrete Fourier transforms (DFTs) into smaller DFTs, and then gathers their results. We could potentially precisely measure the floating-point error for DFT, and leverage it to compositionally estimate the floating-point error of the whole program. We will further investigate such compositional GRT approaches for handling large scale programs.

Acknowledgements

Thanks to Alan Humphrey, Brandon Gibson and Martin Berzins for providing us the DQMOM benchmark from the Uintah Framework. Chiang was supported in part by an Nvidia Graduate Fellowship and Gopalakrishnan by the SUPER (super-scidac.org). Additional support was provided by NSF grants ACI 1148127, CCF 1255776, CCF 1302449 and CCF 1346756.

	Algo.	FFT (524288)			
		rel. err.	# SVE	|abs. err.|	# SVE
Exp_1	URT	**4.9803e-07**	870	8.8437e+00	880
	BGRT	4.6859e-07	830	**1.6545e+01**	790
Exp_2	URT	**5.6224e-07**	870	**9.9878e+00**	870
	BGRT	5.3524e-07	840	9.6160e+00	760

Table 12: Experimental Results on a Large Scale Program: Parallel FFT of the NAS Parallel Benchmarks (NPB)

References

[1] E. Anderson, Z. Bai, C. Bischof, L. S. Blackford, J. Demmel, J. J. Dongarra, J. Du Croz, S. Hammarling, A. Greenbaum, A. McKenney, and D. Sorensen. *LAPACK Users' Guide (3rd Ed.)*. SIAM: Society for Industrial and Applied Mathematics, 1999.

[2] J. Ansel, C. Chan, Y. L. Wong, M. Olszewski, Q. Zhao, A. Edelman, and S. Amarasinghe. Petabricks: a language and compiler for algorithmic choice. In *ACM SIGPLAN Conference on Programming Language Design and Implementation (PLDI)*, pages 38–49, 2009.

[3] D. H. Bailey and J. M. Borwein. Highly parallel, high-precision numerical integration, 2005.

[4] E. T. Barr, T. Vo, V. Le, and Z. Su. Automatic detection of floating-point exceptions. In *ACM SIGPLAN-SIGACT Symposium on Principles of Programming Languages (POPL)*, pages 549–560, 2013.

[5] F. Benz, A. Hildebrandt, and S. Hack. A dynamic program analysis to find floating-point accuracy problems. In *ACM SIGPLAN Conference on Programming Language Design and Implementation (PLDI)*, pages 453–462, 2012.

[6] S. Boldo and G. Melquiond. Flocq: A unified library for proving floating-point algorithms in Coq. In *IEEE Symposium on Computer Arithmetic*, pages 243–252, 2011.

[7] S. Boldo, J.-C. Filliâtre, and G. Melquiond. Combining Coq and Gappa for certifying floating-point programs. In *Intelligent Computer Mathematics*, pages 59–74. Springer-Verlag, 2009.

[8] C. Cadar and K. Sen. Symbolic execution for software testing: three decades later. *Communications of the ACM*, 56(2):82–90, Feb. 2013.

[9] W.-F. Chiang, G. Gopalakrishnan, Z. Rakamarić, D. H. Ahn, and G. L. Lee. Determinism and reproducibility in large-scale HPC systems. In *Workshop on Determinism and Correctness in Parallel Programming (WoDet)*, 2013.

[10] Coq. The Coq proof assistant. http://coq.inria.fr/.

[11] E. Darulova and V. Kuncak. Trustworthy numerical computation in Scala. In *Conference on Object-Oriented Programming Systems (OOPSLA)*, pages 325–344, 2011.

[12] F. de Dinechin, C. Q. Lauter, and G. Melquiond. Assised verification of elementary functions using Gappa. In *ACM Symposium on Applied computing (SAC)*, pages 1318–1322, 2006.

[13] L. De Moura and N. Bjørner. Z3: An efficient SMT solver. In *International Conference on Tools and Algorithms for the Construction and Analysis of Systems (TACAS)*, pages 337–340, 2008.

[14] D. Delmas, E. Goubault, S. Putot, J. Souyris, K. Tekkal, and F. Védrine. Towards an industrial use of FLUCTUAT on safety-critical avionics software. In *Workshop on Formal Methods for Industrial Critical Systems (FMICS)*, pages 53–69, 2009.

[15] J. Demmel and H. D. Nguyen. Numerical reproducibility and accuracy at exascale. In *IEEE Symposium on Computer Arithmetic*, pages 235–237, 2013.

[16] J. W. Demmel. Trading off parallelism and numerical stability. Technical Report UCB/CSD-92-702, EECS Department, University of California, Berkeley, 1992.

[17] A. Goodloe, C. Muñoz, F. Kirchner, and L. Correnson. Verification of numerical programs: From real numbers to floating point numbers. In *NASA Formal Methods Symposium (NFM)*, pages 441–446, 2013.

[18] M. Harris. *Optimizing parallel reduction in CUDA*. NVIDIA Developer Technology, 2007.

[19] M. Heideman, D. Johnson, and C. Burrus. Gauss and the history of the fast Fourier transform. *ASSP Magazine, IEEE*, 1(4):14–21, 1984.

[20] N. J. Higham. *Accuracy and Stability of Numerical Algorithms (2nd Ed.)*. SIAM: Society for Industrial and Applied Mathematics, 2002.

[21] C. A. R. Hoare. An axiomatic basis for computer programming. *Communications of the ACM*, 12(10):576–580, 1969.

[22] F. Hutter, H. H. Hoos, and T. Stützle. Automatic algorithm configuration based on local search. In *National Conference on Artificial Intelligence*, pages 1152–1157, 2007.

[23] IEEE Task P754. *ANSI/IEEE 754-1985, Standard for Binary Floating-Point Arithmetic*. IEEE, 1985.

[24] F. Ivancic, M. K. Ganai, S. Sankaranarayanan, and A. Gupta. Numerical stability analysis of floating-point computations using software model checking. In *IEEE/ACM Intl. Conference on Formal Methods and Models for Codesign (MEMOCODE)*, pages 49–58, 2010.

[25] W. Kahan. Pracniques: Further remarks on reducing truncation errors. *Communications of the ACM*, 8(1):40–, Jan. 1965.

[26] J. Kennedy. Particle swarm optimization. In *Encyclopedia of Machine Learning*, pages 760–766. Springer-Verlag, 2010.

[27] A. B. Kinsman and N. Nicolici. Finite precision bit-width allocation using SAT-modulo theory. In *Conference on Design, Automation and Test in Europe (DATE)*, pages 1106–1111, 2009.

[28] M. O. Lam, J. K. Hollingsworth, B. R. de Supinski, and M. P. LeGendre. Automatically adapting programs for mixed-precision floating-point computation. In *International Conference on Supercomputing (ICS)*, pages 369–378, 2013.

[29] M. O. Lam, J. K. Hollingsworth, and G. W. Stewart. Dynamic floating-point cancellation detection. *Parallel Computing*, 39(3):146–155, 2013.

[30] P. Li, G. Li, and G. Gopalakrishnan. Parametric flows: automated behavior equivalencing for symbolic analysis of races in CUDA programs. In *International Conference on High Performance Computing, Networking, Storage and Analysis (SC)*, pages 29:1–29:10, 2012.

[31] M. D. Linderman, M. Ho, D. L. Dill, T. H. Y. Meng, and G. P. Nolan. Towards program optimization through automated analysis of numerical precision. In *IEEE/ACM International Symposium on Code Generation and Optimization (CGO)*, pages 230–237, 2010.

[32] H. R. Lourenço, O. C. Martin, and T. Stutzle. Iterated local search. *arXiv preprint math/0102188*, 2001.

[33] J. Luitjens, B. Worthen, M. Berzins, and T. C. Henderson. *Petascale Computing Algorithms and Applications*, chapter Scalable parallel AMR for the Uintah multiphysics code, pages 67–82. Chapman and Hall/CRC, 2007.

[34] MAGMA. The MAGMA library. http://icl.cs.utk.edu/magma/index.html.

[35] NPB. The NAS parallel benchmarks (NPB). http://www.nas.nasa.gov/publications/npb.html.

[36] C. Rubio-González, C. Nguyen, H. D. Nguyen, J. Demmel, W. Kahan, K. Sen, D. H. Bailey, C. Iancu, and D. Hough. Precimonious: Tuning assistant for floating-point precision. In *International Conference on High Performance Computing, Networking, Storage and Analysis (SC)*, pages 27:1–27:12, 2013.

[37] S3FP. Guided random testing for floating-point error estimation. https://sites.google.com/site/grt4fperror/.

[38] M. Souza, M. Borges, M. d'Amorim, and C. S. Păsăreanu. CORAL: Solving complex constraints for symbolic Pathfinder. In *NASA Formal Methods Symposium (NFM)*, pages 359–374, 2011.

[39] J. A. Stratton, C. Rodrigues, I.-J. Sung, N. Obeid, L.-W. Chang, N. Anssari, G. D. Liu, and W.-m. W. Hwu. Parboil: A revised benchmark suite for scientific and commercial throughput computing. *Center for Reliable and High-Performance Computing*, 2012.

X10 and APGAS at Petascale

Olivier Tardieu[1], Benjamin Herta[1], David Cunningham[2] *, David Grove[1], Prabhanjan Kambadur[1],
Vijay Saraswat[1], Avraham Shinnar[1], Mikio Takeuchi[3], Mandana Vaziri[1]

[1]IBM T. J. Watson Research Center
[2]Google Inc.
[3]IBM Research - Tokyo

{tardieu,bherta,groved,pkambadu,vsaraswa,shinnar,mvaziri}@us.ibm.com, dcunnin@google.com, mtake@jp.ibm.com

Abstract

X10 is a high-performance, high-productivity programming language aimed at large-scale distributed and shared-memory parallel applications. It is based on the Asynchronous Partitioned Global Address Space (APGAS) programming model, supporting the same fine-grained concurrency mechanisms within and across shared-memory nodes.

We demonstrate that X10 delivers solid performance at petascale by running (weak scaling) eight application kernels on an IBM Power 775 supercomputer utilizing up to 55,680 Power7 cores (for 1.7 Pflop/s of theoretical peak performance). We detail our advances in distributed termination detection, distributed load balancing, and use of high-performance interconnects that enable X10 to scale out to tens of thousands of cores.

For the four HPC Class 2 Challenge benchmarks, X10 achieves 41% to 87% of the system's potential at scale (as measured by IBM's HPCC Class 1 optimized runs). We also implement K-Means, Smith-Waterman, Betweenness Centrality, and Unbalanced Tree Search (UTS) for geometric trees. Our UTS implementation is the first to scale to petaflop systems.

Categories and Subject Descriptors   D.1.3 [*Programming Techniques*]: Concurrent Programming—distributed programming; D.3.3 [*Programming Languages*]: Language Constructs and Features—concurrent programming structures, control structures

Keywords   X10; APGAS; scalability; performance

---

* Work done while employed at IBM T. J. Watson Research Center.

1. Overview

X10 is a high-performance, high-productivity programming language developed at IBM.[1] It is a class-based, strongly-typed, garbage-collected, object-oriented language [32, 33]. To support concurrency and distribution, X10 uses the Asynchronous Partitioned Global Address Space programming model (APGAS [31]). This model introduces two key concepts – places and asynchronous tasks – and a few mechanisms for coordination. With these, APGAS can express both regular and irregular parallelism, message-passing-style and active-message-style computations, fork-join and bulk-synchronous parallelism. In contrast to hybrid models like MPI+OpenMP, the same constructs underpin both intra- and inter-place concurrency.

Both its modern, type-safe sequential core and simple programming model for concurrency and distribution contribute to making X10 a high-productivity language in the HPC and Big Data spaces. User productivity is further enhanced by providing tools such as an Eclipse-based IDE (X10DT) and a source-level debugger.

In this paper, we focus on enabling X10 applications to run at very large scale. We demonstrate that X10 and APGAS deliver performance at petascale for regular and irregular kernels. We present experimental results for eight kernels.[2] We implement the four HPC Class 2 Challenge benchmarks: *HPL*, *FFT*, *RandomAccess*, and *Stream Triad* [17], as well as *Smith-Waterman* [37], *Betweenness Centrality* (BC) [5], *K-Means* [22], and *Unbalanced Tree Search* (UTS) [25]. These programs are compiled using X10's native backend,[3] and run on a large IBM Power 775 system with a theoretical peak performance of 1.7 Pflop/s.

---

[1] X10 was developed as part of the IBM "Productive, Easy-to-use, Reliable Computing System" project (PERCS [41]), supported by the DARPA High Productivity Computer Systems initiative (HPCS [11]).

[2] The X10 tool chain and the benchmark codes are publicly available at http://x10-lang.org.

[3] X10 is implemented with two backends. On the *managed* backend, X10 compiles into Java and runs on (a cluster of) JVMs. On the *native* backend, X10 compiles into C++ and generates a native binary for execution on scale-out systems.

For the four HPC Challenge benchmarks, X10 today achieves 41% to 87% of the system's potential at scale as reported by IBM's *optimized runs* entry to the HPC Class 1 Challenge in November 2012 [16]. Our K-Means and Smith-Waterman implementations scale linearly with the number of compute nodes (weak scaling). Our UTS implementation for geometric trees also scales linearly. To the best of our knowledge, it is the first implementation of UTS to scale to petaflop systems. Our BC implementation, which is being actively developed, is able to process 245 Billion edges per second using 47,040 cores.

All applications are written to run with minimal intra-place concurrency. We have separately done work on schedulers for intra-place concurrency [13, 40], but the results reported here do not reflect the integration of these schedulers with the scale-out stack. We leave this for future work.

All applications, except UTS, are implemented using a classic SPMD approach. For these applications, data is statically partitioned and computations are statically scheduled. For UTS, dynamic distributed load balancing is indispensable. We had to significantly revise and extend the lifeline-based load balancing algorithm from Saraswat et al. [35] to make it scale to tens of thousands of Power7 cores. While we recently added dynamic load balancing to our BC implementation, the results we report here predate this change.

Contributions. The contributions of this paper are:

- We demonstrate that the APGAS programming model delivers performance at petascale for both regular and irregular kernels.

- We show experimental results for eight kernel benchmarks implemented in X10 and running on a petaflop Power 775 system. We provide detailed performance analyses and, for the four HPC Challenge benchmarks, we compare X10 performance to the best implementations available.

- We describe our solutions to the distributed termination detection problem at scale – the implementation of X10's *finish* construct – and the effective use of high-performance interconnects in X10.

- We present a novel distributed load balancing algorithm for UTS derived from [35]. To the best of our knowledge, our implementation is the first that can effectively load balance UTS on geometric trees at petascale.

Outline. The next two sections review the core concepts of the X10 programming language (Section 2) and describe the key innovations necessary to allow them to perform at scale (Section 3). After describing the hardware and software configuration in Section 4, we discuss the implementation and performance results for each kernel in turn: we review the HPC Challenge benchmarks in Section 5, UTS in Section 6, and the remaining codes in Section 7. We discuss related work in Section 8 and conclude in Section 9.

2. The X10 Language

Like Java, X10 is a strongly-typed, garbage-collected, class-based, object-oriented programming language with single-class multiple-interface inheritance. To support concurrency and distribution, X10 introduces a few key concepts. We briefly review the core Asynchronous Partitioned Global Address Space programming model (APGAS [31]) that is at the heart of the X10 programming model.

2.1 APGAS Concepts

A *place* is a collection of data and worker threads operating on the data, typically realized as an operating system process. A single X10 computation typically runs over a large collection of places. The notion of places is reified in the language: if S is a statement, then `at(p) S` is a statement that shifts to place p to execute S. Similarly, `at(p) e` evaluates the expression e at place p. The expression `here` evaluates to the current place. The expression `GlobalRef(someObject)` computes a global reference to `someObject` that can be passed freely from place to place but only dereferenced at the `home` place of the reference, that is, the place of `someObject`.

Asynchrony is fundamental to the language: if S is a statement then `async S` is a statement which runs S as a separate, concurrent *activity*. Dually, the `finish S` statement executes S and waits for all activities transitively spawned during the execution of S to terminate before continuing.

Additional concurrency control is provided by the statement `when(c) S` which executes S in a single uninterrupted step when the condition c is true. An optimized unconditional form of `when`, `atomic S`, is also provided.

Other X10 features such as asynchronous memory transfers and dynamic barriers (*clocks*) can be viewed as particular patterns of use of these constructs.

An X10 program consists of at least one class definition with a `main` method. The number n of places available to a particular execution (0 to $n-1$) and the mapping from places to nodes is specified by the user at launch time using MPI-like controls. The execution starts with the execution of the `main` method at `Place(0)`. Other places are initially idle.

2.2 APGAS Idioms

The power of X10's core APGAS constructs lies in that, for the most part, they can be nested freely. Combinations of these constructs provide for MPI-like message passing, SPMD computation, active-message-style computation, bulk synchronous parallel computation, overlap between computation and communication, fork-join recursive parallel decomposition, etc. Formal semantics for these constructs have been developed in [8, 20, 33].

Remote evaluation is simply:

```
val v = at(p) evalThere(arg1, arg2); // blocking
```

We can combine `at` and `async` to obtain active messages:

```
at(p) async runThere(arg1, arg2); // non-blocking
```

We can combine `finish` and `async` to compute Fibonacci numbers with recursive parallel decomposition:

```
def fib(n:Int):Int {
  if (n < 2) return n;
  val f1:Int; val f2:Int;
  finish {
    // f1 and f2 are computed in parallel
    async f1 = fib(n-1);
    f2 = fib(n-2);
  }
  return f1+f2;
}
```

In the next example, one activity is spawned in each place to run some startup code. The `finish` construct works across places to ensures the initialization completes in each place before the main body runs:

```
class Foo {
  public static def main(args:Rail[String]) {
    finish for(p in Place.places()) {
      at(p) async {
        ... // startup code
    } }
    ... // main body
} }
```

Parallel, possibly distributed tasks can be synchronized with clocks. In this example, the clock ensures that loop iterations are synchronized across places:

```
clocked finish for (p in Place.places()) {
  at(p) clocked async for (val i in 0..9) {
    ... // loop body
    Clock.advanceAll(); // global barrier
} }
```

Below, we use a `GlobalRef` and `atomic` updates to compute the average system load across all places:

```
val acc = new Cell[Double](0.0);
val ref = GlobalRef[Cell[Double]](acc);
finish for(p in Place.places()) at(p) async {
  val load = MyUtils.systemLoad(); // at place p
  at(ref.home) async atomic ref() += load;
}
val averageLoad = acc()/Place.MAX_PLACES;
```

X10's compiler and runtime systems understand asynchrony and places and support them. For instance, the type checker tracks occurrences of GlobalRefs to ensure these are dereferenced in the proper places. In the last example, it verifies that `ref` is only accessed at place `ref.home`.

The compiler also analyzes the bodies of `at` statements and expressions to identify inter-place data dependencies and instructs the X10 runtime to serialize data accordingly.[4] In this example, the value of `load` is serialized from place `p` to place `ref.home` as part of the execution of `at(ref.home)`.

---

[4] Data reachable from the body of an `at` is implicitly copied from the source to the destination place of the `at`. `GlobalRef`s can be used to obtain remote references instead.

For bulk copies, such as array copies, X10's standard libraries offer dedicated APIs such as the `Array.asyncCopy` method, which minimize local memory transfers. An array `asyncCopy` is treated exactly as if it were an `async`. Its termination is simply tracked by the enclosing `finish`, making it easy to overlap communication and computation:

```
finish {
  // srcArray is local, dstArray is remote
  Array.asyncCopy(srcArray, 0, dstArray, 0, size);
  computeLocally(); // while sending the data
}
```

A great deal more information on X10 can be found online at `http://x10-lang.org` including the language specification [32], programmer's guide [34], and a collection of tutorials and sample programs.

2.3 Productivity

X10's productivity results from the combination of object-orientedness, strong typing, memory safety, a simple programming model for concurrency and distribution (APGAS), and tooling (Eclipse-based IDE and debugger).

The same `finish` construct is employed to track the termination of a large number of asynchronous tasks (local or remote) as well as the delivery of a single message or anything in-between. The same asynchronous tasks are used for distributing computations or data or both simultaneously across nodes. In this paper, we demonstrate that such an economy of means does not preclude scalable performance while providing a significant productivity boost. An in-depth productivity analysis however is beyond the scope of this paper. See Section 8 for references on this topic.

3. X10 at Scale

In this section, we discuss the key innovations and extensions that are needed to successfully scale X10 and the APGAS programming model to very large systems.

3.1 Scalable Finish

The X10 language places no restrictions on the ability of the programmer to combine and nest `at` and `async` statements within a `finish`. Implementing X10's `finish` construct therefore requires a distributed termination protocol that can handle arbitrary patterns of distributed task creation and termination.

Because networks can reorder control messages, fully general distributed termination detection algorithms become prohibitively expensive with scale. In particular, the default `finish` implementation in X10 uses $O(n^2)$ space where n is the number of places involved. It may also flood the network interface of the place of the activity waiting on the `finish` construct.

Collective communications such as barriers in large distributed systems are optimized in hardware and/or software. We need to do the same for `finish`.

Finish optimizations. We augment the X10 runtime to dynamically optimize `finish` by optimistically assuming that it is local (within a single place) and then dynamically switching to a more expensive distributed algorithm the first time an activity governed by the `finish` executes an `at`. Furthermore, the runtime automatically coalesces and compresses the control messages used by the termination detection algorithm.

In addition to these general dynamic optimizations, the runtime provides implementations of distributed `finish` that are specialized to common patterns of distributed concurrency for which there exist more efficient implementations. Currently we recognize five such patterns:

FINISH_ASYNC a finish governing a single activity, possibly remote. E.g.,

```
finish at(p) async S;
finish { async S1; S2 } // with S2 sequential
```

FINISH_HERE a finish governing a round trip. E.g.,

```
h=here; finish at(p) async {S1; at(h) async S2;}
```

FINISH_LOCAL a finish governing local activities. For instance, if S does not spawn remote activities,

```
finish for(i in 1..n) async S;
```

FINISH_SPMD a finish governing the execution of remote activities that do not spawn subactivities outside of a `finish`. E.g.,

```
finish for(p in places) at(p) async finish S;
```

FINISH_DENSE a finish governing activities with dense or irregular communication graphs. E.g.,

```
finish for(p in places) at(p) async {
  finish for(q in places) at(q) async S;
}
```

In this example, there is direct communication between any two places in `places`.

Each one of our benchmark programs uses a subset of these specialized distributed termination detection algorithms. The optimized implementations start to make a difference with hundreds of X10 places and become critical with thousands of places or more.

SPMD codes typically exploit three of these implementations: FINISH_SPMD for the "root" finish governing the parallel execution of the "main" activity in each place, FINISH_ASYNC for "puts" and FINISH_HERE for "gets". Codes exploiting intra-place concurrency can benefit from FINISH_LOCAL (even if the default algorithm already does a pretty good job in this case). Codes with lots of peer-to-peer communications use FINISH_DENSE in place of FINISH_HERE. This is the case for instance of the distributed load balancer in the Unbalanced Tree Search code (see be-low), as it permits an idle place to directly request work from randomly selected places in a fully decentralized manner.

For the first four patterns, the termination detection algorithms are actual specializations of the default algorithm. For instance, for FINISH_SPMD, the runtime knows it needs to wait for exactly n termination messages if n remote activities were spawned. In contrast to the default case, the order, source place, or content of each message is irrelevant.

Dense, irregular communication graphs are always a challenge. Network stacks of supercomputers tend to be optimized for traditional, regular workloads and are of course very concerned with latency. For instance the Power 775 network stack favors communication graphs with low out-degree. Detecting the termination of a large number of irregular activities across a large number of places is therefore not something these stacks are designed to do well out of the box. First, there is no regularity to exploit. Second, optimizing for latency is just wrong as the latency of the *last* control message is the only one that matters. But the network stack has no way of knowing this.

This is where the FINISH_DENSE implementation comes to the rescue. It uses software routing techniques to shape the traffic of control messages into something more natural, more idiomatic to the network stack. For now, it simply compensates for the fact that we run multiple X10 places per compute node by routing all communications through one master place in each node. A finish control message going from place p to q is routed via places $p - p\%b$ then $q - q\%b$ then q where b is the number of places per node (up to 32).

In the future, it will be interesting to see if such a latency-trading traffic-shaping approach is beneficial to other architectures as well, and whether more sophisticated routing strategies can further improve performance.

Implementation selection. We have prototyped a fully automatic compiler analysis that is capable of detecting many of the situations where these patterns are applicable. For instance, it correctly classifies the various occurrences of `finish` in our HPL code into instances of FINISH_SPMD, FINISH_ASYNC, and FINISH_HERE.

Unfortunately, we have not been able to turn this prototype into a finished product yet. Therefore, in our current system, opportunities to apply these specialized `finish` implementations are still guided by programmer supplied annotations – pragmas – such as:

```
@Pragma(Pragma.FINISH_ASYNC) finish at(p) async S;
```

As future work, we intend to further "harden" this analysis to the point where it can be robustly applied as part of the X10 compiler's standard optimization package. Ultimately, we do not want the end-user to worry about `finish` implementation selection at all.

We also intend to make the specialization mechanism extensible and let expert users develop efficient implementations tailored to particular concurrency patterns and/or specific network topologies.

3.2 Scalable Broadcast

Iterating sequentially over many places to send identical or similar messages (as we naively do in the examples of Section 2) can waste valuable time and flood the network. We developed a `PlaceGroup` library for efficiently managing large groups of places. In particular, we support efficient broadcast over place groups using spawning trees in order to parallelize and distribute the task creation overhead. It also efficiently handles the detection of the broadcast completion by means of nested `FINISH_SPMD` blocks.

3.3 High-Performance Interconnects

As expected from supercomputers, the Power 775 *Torrent* interconnect supports additional communication mechanisms beyond basic point-to-point "fifo" primitives.

To make it possible to adapt to a wide range of interconnects, the X10 runtime has a layered structure. At the lower level, the X10 Runtime Transport (X10RT) API provides a common interface to transports such as IBM's PAMI transport, MPI, and TCP/IP sockets.

We add support for RDMAs and collectives to X10RT (see below). An implementation of X10RT however is only required to provide basic point-to-point primitives. We provide an emulation layer to handle the more advanced APIs when not natively supported. We surface them in the X10's standard libraries as follows.

Collectives. X10 teams – the `x10.util.Team` class – offer capabilities similar to HPC collectives, such as Barrier, All-Reduce, Broadcast, All-To-All, etc. Some networks support these multi-way communication patterns in hardware including some simple calculations on the data. When the X10 runtime is configured for these systems, the X10 team operations map directly to the hardware implementations available, offering performance that cannot be matched by point-to-point messages. When unavailable, our emulation layer kicks in.

RDMAs. RDMA (Remote Direct Memory Access) hardware, such as the Torrent or InfiniBand, enables the transfer of segments of memory from one machine to another without local copies and without the involvement of the CPU or operating system. This technology significantly reduces the latency of data transfers, and frees the CPU to do other work while the transfer is taking place.

We modify the `Array.asyncCopy` implementation to take advantage of RDMAs. We also surface the "GUPS" RDMA feature of the Torrent, which enables atomic remote memory updates (e.g., XOR a memory location with an argument data word).

Congruent Memory Allocator. To use RDMA or collectives, the application needs to register the memory segments eligible for transfer with the network hardware. Moreover, the task initiating the communication must typically know the effective address of each memory segment involved (both source and destination). We implement a "congruent" memory allocator to allocate arrays backed by registered memory segments (outside of the control of the garbage collector). When using the same allocation sequence in every place, this allocator can be configured for symmetric allocation in order return the same sequence of addresses everywhere.

The Torrent, even more than the CPU, is very sensitive to TLB misses. It is therefore important (essential for RandomAccess) that these memory segments are backed by large pages so as to minimize the number of TLB entries. Our congruent memory allocator makes use of large pages if supported and enabled on the system.

Importantly for productivity, the allocation, garbage collection, or use of regular data is not affected at all. Congruent arrays do not behave differently from regular arrays after their initial allocation except of course for supporting extra communication primitives. Ultimately, we only want the end-user to designate arrays for congruent allocation. Everything else should then be handled automatically by the runtime system.

3.4 Scalable Load Balancing

Because irregular workloads are becoming the norm rather than the exception, there is a demand for dynamic distributed load balancing techniques. By applying dynamic distributed load balancing, a runtime system can effectively dynamically distribute or redistribute computationally-intensive tasks across CPU cores within and across shared-memory nodes to maximize utilization.

Saraswat et al. have developed a global load balancing library in X10 (GLB) based on insights from the Unbalanced Tree Search scheduler they described in [35]. GLB takes care of distributed rebalancing by permitting idle places to "steal" work from other places. The choice of the victim sequence is key to the scalability of distributed work stealing: who to try steal from, when, how often, when to back off, etc. GLB handles this.

In Section 6, we describe generic improvements to the load balancer as well as UTS-specific optimizations that make it possible to scale this highly-unbalanced workload to petascale systems for the first time. We have recently integrated the generic elements of this new scheduler to the GLB library and implemented UTS and BC using GLB [43].

4. The Power 775 System

We gathered our performance results on a Power7-based Power 775 supercomputer named Hurcules [29, 30].

The smallest building block of the machine is called an *octant* or simply a host. An octant is composed of a quad-chip module containing four eight-core 3.84 Ghz Power7 processors, one optical connect controller chip (codenamed *Torrent*), and 128 GB of memory. The peak bi-directional bandwidth between any two chips is 96 GB/s (direct link).

A single octant has a peak performance of 982 Gflop/s, a peak memory bandwidth of 512 GB/s, and a peak bi-directional interconnect bandwidth of 192 GB/s. Each octant forms a single SMP node running an operating system image. One physical *drawer* consists of eight octants. Four drawers are connected together to form a *supernode.*

The full machine we used for our measurements contains 56 supernodes, with 1740 octants (55,680 cores) available for computation. This gives the system a theoretical peak of 1.7 Pflop/s. For some benchmarks, we only used 32,768 cores because our implementations require the number of cores to be a power of two. For others (Section 7), we only had access to 47,040 cores due to operational constraints.

Interconnect. The Power 775 system is organized into a two-level direct-connect topology [2] with "L" links connecting every pair of octants within a supernode and "D" links connecting every pair of supernodes in the system.

1. Every octant in a drawer is connected to every other octant of this drawer using a "L" Local link (LL) with a peak bandwidth of 24 GB/s in each direction.

2. Every octant in a supernode is connected to every other octant in the other three drawers of this supernode using a "L" Remote link (LR) with a peak bandwidth of 5 GB/s in each direction.

3. Every supernode is connected to every other supernode using "D" links – eight of them in the current configuration for a combined peak bandwidth of 80 GB/s in each direction.

As a result, any two octants are at most three hops away (L-D-L). We configure the routing protocol for "direct striped" routes with MP_RDMA_ROUTE_MODE=hw_direct_striped. Intra-supernode messages only use a single L link (LL or LR). Inter-supernode messages only use the direct D links between the two supernodes (in addition to L links within these supernodes if needed) but are permitted to spread across all eight parallel D links.

In order to understand the bandwidth characteristics of a system partition of a given size, one has to account for two factors: the number and peak bandwidth of the various links (LL, LR, and D) as well as the peak interconnect bandwidth of each octant. Please refer to [38] for a thorough bandwidth analysis. In short, as we scale from one octant to a drawer to a supernode to the full system, we will observe three performance modes:

• With one supernode or less, the cross-section bandwidth is limited by the peak interconnect bandwidth of each individual octant.

• With a few supernodes, the cross-section bandwidth is limited by the aggregated D link bandwidth.

• With many supernodes, the cross-section bandwidth is again limited by the per-octant interconnect bandwidth.

In particular, there is a sharp drop in All-To-All bandwidth per octant when going from one supernode to two supernodes, followed by a slow recovery when further increasing the number of supernodes, followed by a plateau.

Software Configuration. Each of the octants runs RedHat Enterprise Linux 6.1 and uses the IBM Parallel Active Messaging Interface (PAMI) for network communication.

We compiled the benchmark programs using native X10 version 2.2.3 with and compiled the resulting C++ files with xlC version 11 with the -qinline -qhot -O3 -q64 -qarch=auto -qtune=auto compiler options. For the FFT and HPL kernels we used native implementations of key numerical routines from FFTE and IBM ESSL respectively. Our UTS code calls a native C routine to compute SHA1 hashes.

We executed the programs in a mode in which each X10 place contained a single worker thread (X10_NTHREADS=1) on which the X10 runtime scheduler dispatched the activities for that place. Moreover each core in the system supported exactly one X10 place. To minimize OS jitter, each X10 place was bound to a specific core (by setting X10RT_CPUMAP).

In the remainder of the paper, we use the terms place and core interchangeably to measure scale. A node or octant or host has 32 cores and runs 32 places.

While we always rely on PAMI to communicate among places even if they belong to the same octant, PAMI itself leverages shared memory to optimize intra-node communications.

We report results with all optimizations turned on for all benchmarks. Unfortunately, we did not have sufficient time allocated on this supercomputer to assess the benefits of our techniques on a per-optimization or per-benchmark basis. For some of these optimizations however (including FINISH_DENSE in UTS, scalable broadcast in the HPCC benchmarks, RDMA-based All-To-All collective in FFT), we observed that the runs at scale do not terminate (in any reasonable amount of time) without the optimization.

5. HPC Challenge Benchmarks

The HPC Challenge benchmark collection was designed not only to better characterize the capabilities of supercomputers than a single measurement can (Class 1 competition), but also to provide an opportunity to compare programming languages and models for concurrency and distribution (Class 2 competition) [17]. In the Class 2 competition, entries are judged for both performance and elegance.

In 2012, IBM entered both the Class 1 and Class 2 competition for this Power 775 system. IBM's Class 1 implementations are intended to demonstrate the highest performance achievable by this system [30]. They are written in a mix of C and assembly code. They are specifically tailored for the Power 775 architecture and carefully hand- and auto-tuned. They interface directly with the hardware device drivers bypassing the entire network stack. They rely on ad-hoc benchmark-specific communication protocols. They are intrinsically non-modular, i.e., cannot be composed into larger application codes. In contrast, the X10 implementations we entered into the Class 2 competition are built upon a common network stack and a few constructs (finish, async, at) that can be composed arbitrarily. The X10 code has been tuned for Power 775 to a much lesser extent, and runs unchanged on commodity clusters.

The implementations and performance results we describe in this section are essentially those obtained for our winning 2012 Class 2 entry to the HPC Challenge [39] with minor updates. We first discuss our implementations of the four benchmarks, then analyze and compare X10 performance with IBM's optimized runs as reported in IBM's 2012 Class 1 entry [15, 16].

5.1 Implementation

Our SPMD-style implementations of the four benchmarks mimic the main attributes of the reference implementations. We discuss each benchmark in turn.

Global HPL. Global HPL measures the floating point rate of execution for solving a linear system of equations. Performance is measured in Gflop/s.

Our implementation features a two-dimensional block-cyclic data distribution, a right-looking variant of the LU factorization with row-partial pivoting, and a recursive panel factorization. It lacks however various refinements of the reference implementation such as configurable look-ahead, configurable recursion depth in the panel factorization, and configurable collective communications. We simply use default PAMI collectives (via X10's Team class).

Our implementation uses a collection of idioms for communication: asynchronous array copies for row fetch or swap and teams for barriers, row and column broadcast, and pivot search. We take advantage of finish pragmas to make sure the compiler and runtime recognize that a row swap is a simple message exchange for instance.

Global RandomAccess. Global RandomAccess measures the system's ability to update random memory locations in a table distributed across the system, by performing XOR operations at the chosen locations with random values. Because the memory is spread across all the places, any update to a random location is likely to be an update to memory located at a remote place, not the local place. Performance is measured by how many Gup/s (Giga Updates Per Second) the system can sustain.

Our implementation takes advantage of congruent memory allocation to obtain a distributed array backed by large pages where the per-place array fragment is at the same address in each place. It then uses the Torrent's "GUPS" RDMA for the remote updates.

Global FFT. Global FFT performs a 1D discrete Fourier transform on an array of double-precision complex values.

The source and destination arrays are evenly distributed across the system. FFT stresses the floating point units, network, and memory subsystems. Performance is measured in Gflop/s.

Our implementation alternates non-overlapping phases of computation and communication on the array viewed as a 2D matrix: global transpose, per-row FFTs, global transpose, multiplication with twiddle factors, per-row FFTs, and global transpose. The global transposition is implemented with local data shuffling, followed by an All-To-All collective, and then finally another round of local data shuffling.

EP Stream. EP Stream (Triad) measures sustainable local memory bandwidth. It performs a scaled vector sum with two source vectors and one destination vector. Performance is measured in GB/s.

Our implementation of this benchmark follows a straightforward SPMD style of programming. The main activity launches an activity at every place using a PlaceGroup broadcast. These activities then allocate and initialize the local arrays, perform the computation, and verify the results. The backing storage for the arrays is allocated using huge pages to enable efficient usage of TLB entries.

5.2 Performance Results

For all runs, places are mapped to hosts in groups of 32. In particular, runs with 32 places or less use a single host. We run with up to 32,768 places in power-of-two increments. For Stream, we also run with the full system: 55,680 places. We use a constant per-place amount of memory (weak scaling). The exact amount is chosen in accordance with the HPC Challenge guidelines.

For every benchmark, we the same X10 implementation for all runs. In particular, our single-core "sequential" runs still use the full, distributed, parallel X10 code.

We plot the resulting performance curves in Figure 1. For each kernel we plot both the aggregated performance as well as the per-core performance (per-host for RandomAccess). We'll discuss the later four kernels in Sections 6 and 7.

Class 1 Comparison. In Table 1, we compare our performance results with IBM's HPC Class 1 optimized runs on the system [16].

Unfortunately, the comparison at scale is only indirect since the reference runs were obtained with larger core counts, which were not available to us. In addition, our FFT, HPL, and RandomAccess implementations require the number of cores to be powers of two. We compare the per-core performance for the largest X10 and Class 1 runs. Due to the nature of the benchmarks (for HPL and Stream) and the architecture of the network (for RandomAccess and FFT), we believe the Class 1 per-core performance results should be relatively stable between 32K and 64K cores.[5]

---

[5] An earlier Class 1 submission for a smaller 1470-host Power 775 system [15] show results within 7% of the more recent 1989-host submission [16] we use for comparison purposes.

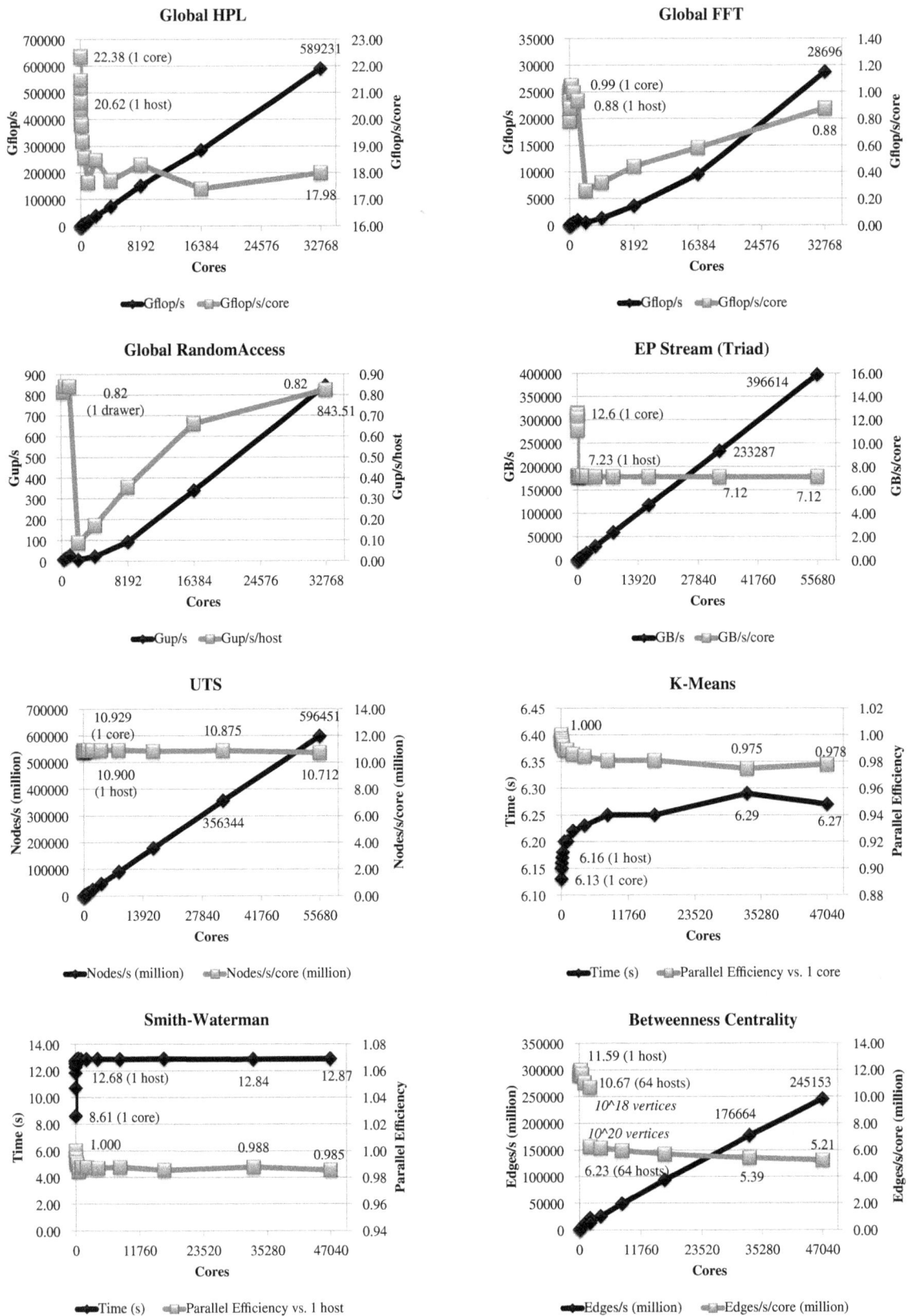

Figure 1. X10 Performance Results

Global HPL. We use about 55% of the memory of each host and a block size of 360. With 32,768 places, we measure an aggregated performance of about 589 Tflop/s, that is, about 60% of the theoretical peak of 1,024 hosts, which amounts to about 70% of the effective `DGEMM` peak performance (ESSL).

The single-core performance is 22.38 Gflop/s. The single-host performance is 20.62 Gflop/s/core. The performance at scale is 17.98 Gflop/s/core. Hence, the X10 code achieves a relative efficiency of 80% at scale. The efficiency drops primarily when scaling from 1 to 1,024 cores. Above 1,024 cores, the efficiency curve flattens. The seesaw is an artifact of the switch from a $n*n$ to a $2n*n$ block cyclic distribution for even and odd powers of two.

X10 achieves about 85% of the performance of the Class 1 run at scale (Gflop/s/core), which divides a matrix of approximately the same size across 1,989 hosts instead of 1,024.

Global RandomAccess. The per-place table size is fixed at 2 GB for a total of 64 GB per host, that is, half of the available memory. We plot results for eight hosts (one drawer) and above.

We measure 0.82 Gup/s/host at both end of the spectrum, that is, with 8 hosts and with 1,024 hosts. In either case, the per-host interconnect bandwidth is the bottleneck, hence the "perfect" relative efficiency. In-between the per-host Gup/s number is significantly lower because the cross-section bandwidth becomes a bottleneck as discussed in Section 4. For smaller runs (4 hosts or less, not plotted), other network bottlenecks come into play (switching, beyond the scope of this paper), and the performance per host is lower. These phases are intrinsic to the interconnect and can be observed also with the Class 1 or UPC code.

Overall, the performance of the X10 code matches the performance of the UPC code for the same benchmark, as well as the performance of a direct C implementation against PAMI. In comparison, the reference code (which bypasses PAMI) achieves 1.02 Gup/s/host at scale.

Global FFT. For even powers, each place uses 2 GB of memory. For odd powers, only 1 GB is used. Hence either half or a quarter of the memory of the host.

With one place, we measure 0.99 Gflop/s. At scale, the rate reduces to 0.88 Gflop/s per core. In-between, as we observed for RandomAccess, the per-core performance is significantly hindered by the relatively low cross-section bandwidth.

We only achieve about 41% of the per-core Class 1 performance at scale. The primary bottleneck lies in our sequential code. On Power 775, the All-To-All time represents only a small fraction of FFT's total execution time. Unfortunately, we did not have sufficient time on the system to hand- or auto-tune our sequential code (data shuffle and 1D FFT) or to experiment with computation communication overlap.

EP Stream. We use 1.5 GB of memory per place.

The per-place memory bandwidth decreases as the number of places per host increases. It drops from 12.6 GB/s with one place to 7.23 GB/s with 32 places due to the QCM architecture for a total of 231.5 GB/s for a single host. Our single-host measurements match the performance of the reference OpenMP EP Stream (Triad) implementation.

With 32 places and above, the per-place memory bandwidth is essentially constant. The total system bandwidth at 55,680 places (1,740 hosts) is about 397 TB/s, which exceeds 98% of 1,740 times the single-host bandwidth. We attribute the 2%-loss to jitter and synchronization overheads.

Our single-host number represents about 87% of the Class 1 result, which takes advantage of Power7 prefetching instructions that we do not. It may be possible to use xlC to generate assist threads for data prefetching for this benchmark and others, but we have not yet experimented with doing so.

Summary. As shown in Table 1, our relative performance compared to the Class 1 runs varies from 41% for FFT to 87% for Stream. As discussed earlier, due to configuration discrepancies these numbers are only estimates. Nevertheless, we believe that they demonstrate that X10 can deliver solid performance at scale even compared to the best codes tuned by IBM's best experts.

In Table 2, we compute that the per-host performance at scale of the X10 code never drops below 87% of the single-host performance for any of these four benchmarks.

We select this particular comparison as our main scalability metric for two reasons. First, the performance scaling from one core to one host is not expected to be linear in general as the memory bandwidth does not scale linearly due to bus contention. Second, the performance per host for partitions of intermediate size is gated by the cross-section bandwidth bottleneck for communication-bound benchmarks.

6. Unbalanced Tree Search

The workload in any of the four HPC Class 2 Challenge benchmarks can be partitioned statically across a distributed system effectively. We now consider a benchmark that is not amenable to such static partitioning but requires advanced dynamic distributed load balancing techniques to scale to large distributed systems.

The Unbalanced Tree Search benchmark measures the rate of traversal of a tree generated on the fly using a splittable random number generator. For this work, we used a *fixed geometric law* for the random number generator with branching factor $b_0 = 4$ and seed $r = 19$, and tree depth d varying from 14 with one place to 22 at scale (weak scaling).

> The nodes in a geometric tree have a branching factor that follows a geometric distribution with an expected value that is specified by the parameter $b_0 > 1$. The parameter d specifies its maximum depth cut-off,

Benchmark	X10 Implementation		HPC Class 1 Optimized Runs		Relative Performance
	Cores	Performance at Scale	Cores	Performance at Scale	
Global HPL	32,768	589.231 Tflop/s	63,648	1343.67 Tflop/s	85%
Global RandomAccess	32,768	843.58 Gup/s	63,648	2020.77 Gup/s	81%
Global FFT	32,768	28,696 Gflop/s	62,208	132,658 Gflop/s	41%
EP Stream (Triad)	32	231.481 GB/s	32	264.156 GB/s	87%

Table 1. Performance Comparisons for the HPC Class 2 Challenge Benchmarks

Benchmark	Performance of the X10 Implementation		Host Count	Relative Efficiency
	With One Host	At Scale	At Scale	
Global HPL	20.62 Gflop/s/core	17.98 Gflop/s/core	1,024	87%
Global RandomAccess	0.82 Gup/s/host	0.82 Gup/s/host	1,024	100%
Global FFT	0.88 Gflop/s/core	0.88 Gflop/s/core	1,024	100%
EP Stream (Triad)	7.23 GB/s/core	7.12 GB/s/core	1,740	98%
UTS	10.900 M nodes/s/core	10.712 M nodes/s/core	1,740	98%
K-Means	6.16s run time	6.27s run time	1,470	98%
Smith-Waterman	12.68s run time	12.87s run time	1,470	98%
Betweenness Centrality	11.59 M edges/s/core	5.21 M edges/s/core	1,470	45%

Table 2. Relative Efficiency: Performance at Scale versus Single-Host Performance (for the Same X10 Implementation)

beyond which the tree is not allowed to grow ... The expected size of these trees is $(b_0)^d$, but since the geometric distribution has a long tail, some nodes will have significantly more than b_0 children, yielding unbalanced trees. [25]

The depth cut-off makes it possible to estimate the size of the trees and guess parameters for a target execution time, but should not be used to predict subtree sizes. In other words, all nodes are to be treated equally for load balancing purposes, irrespective of the current depth.

6.1 Implementation

Our implementation follows from [35]. It uses global work-stealing with random steals followed by lifeline steals and hyper-cubes for the lifeline graphs.

Lifeline-based Global Work Stealing. Every worker (one per place) maintains a list of pending nodes to process (nodes not counted yet). Each worker primarily processes its own list. If the list becomes empty, the idle worker attempts to steal nodes from another worker. Steal attempts are first random – a victim worker is randomly selected – and synchronous – the thief wait for the attempt to complete either successfully – the victim list was not empty – or unsuccessfully – the victim was also idle. Past a few random attempts, the thief falls back to a fixed precomputed list of victims called lifelines, sends requests to these and dies. Lifelines have memory. If a request for work cannot be served immediately because the lifeline itself is idle, then if the lifeline later manages to obtain new nodes to process, it will split these nodes between itself and others as requested, resuscitating dead workers in the process.

Intuitively, random attempts are very effective at distributing work when most workers are busy, whereas lifelines are effective at propagating work quickly when many workers are idle. Lifeline "edges" are organized in graphs with both low diameters and low degree such as hyper-cubes to co-minimize the distance between any two workers and the number of lifeline requests in flight.

Because workers die when unsuccessful at random steals the overall termination of the counting can be implemented with a single `finish` construct. Each worker is implemented with one `async` task. Resuscitation is also one `async` task.

Work is initially distributed from the root worker in one tree-shaped wave. See [35] for more details.

Refinements. We first improve the scalability beyond [35] by (i) further reducing the overhead of termination detection, (ii) shaping the network traffic, and (iii) improving the work-queue implementation.

We use the `FINISH_DENSE` algorithm for the root `finish` responsible for detecting the termination of the tree traversal. We use an algorithm akin to `FINISH_HERE` to detect the termination of steal attempts – outgoing request followed by incoming response.[6] The root `finish` only accounts for the initial work distribution as well as the redistribution along lifelines but is oblivious to rebalancing operations resulting from successful random steal attempts.

We precompute for each place a set of potential victims with no more than 1,024 elements to bound the out-degree of the communication graph. We observe a severe degradation of the network performance at scale without such a bound.

---

[6] We could use the standard `FINISH_HERE` algorithm instead, but we have not yet rewritten our UTS code to confirm that the performance is the same.

We adopt a more compact representation of the nodes remaining to be processed in a place, by directly representing intervals of siblings in the tree as intervals (lower, upper bounds) instead of using expanded lists of nodes.

Finally, to counteract the bias introduced by the depth cutoff, a thief steals fragments of every interval in the work list. There are few of them since we traverse the tree depth first.

The last two changes are tailored for UTS for shallow trees and make a tremendous difference for these, but are not likely to help as much for deep and narrow trees. The earlier improvements however are applicable to distributed work stealing in general. We include them in the GLB library (see Section 3.4).

6.2 Performance Results

We run from one to 32,768 places in power-of-two increments and then at scale with 55,680 places. Figure 1 shows the total number of nodes processed per second as well as the per-place processing rate. We increase the depth of the tree from 14 with one place to 22 with 55,680 places so as to obtain runs of duration ranging from 90 to 200 seconds.

The per-place processing rate varies from 10.929 million nodes per second for one place to 10.712 million nodes per second at scale. The single-place performance is identical to the performance of the sequential implementation (no parallelism, distribution, or load balancing). The distributed implementation at scale achieves 98% parallel efficiency.

At scale, we traverse a tree of 69,312,400,211,958 nodes in 116s, that is, about 596 billion nodes/s. As part of this traversal, we compute 17,328,102,175,815 SHA1 hashes (for random number generation). In contrast, the algorithm from [35] achieves its peak performance with a few thousand cores and slows down to a crawl beyond that due to overwhelming termination detection overheads and network contention. We tried traversing the same tree at scale with the original algorithm and had to kill the run after an hour.

7. Other Benchmarks

In this section, we briefly review the three remaining kernels: K-Means, Smith-Waterman, and Betweenness Centrality.

K-Means. K-Means clustering aims to partition n points in a d-dimensional space into k clusters so as to minimize the average distance to cluster centroids. We implement Lloyd's algorithm [21]. Given arbitrary initial centroids, it iteratively refines the clusters and centroids.

We partition the points across p places. In parallel at each place, we classify the points by nearest centroid and compute the average positions of the per-place points in each cluster. Then we use two All-Reduce collectives to compute the averages across all places. They provide updated centroids for the next iteration.

We run with $40000p$ points with p places and 4096 clusters (dimension 12). We measure the running time for 5 iterations. It varies from 6.13s with one place to 6.27s with

47,040 places. Efficiency versus a single place never drops below 97%.

Smith-Waterman. The Smith-Waterman algorithm is a dynamic programming algorithm to compute the best possible alignment (partial match) of a short DNA sequence against a long DNA sequence.

We parallelize the computation by splitting the long sequence into overlapping fragments and computing in parallel the best match of the short sequence against each fragment. The best overall match is the best of the best matches.

We run with a short string of 4000 elements and a long string with $40000p$ elements. We report the running time for 5 iterations of the benchmark. We measure 8.61s for one place, 12.68s for one host (32 places), and 12.87s at scale with 47,040 places. The running time increases from 1 to 32 places because of memory bus contention. Scaling out from one host to 1,470 hosts we only lose 2% efficiency.

Betweenness Centrality. Betweenness centrality measures the "centrality" of a node in a graph, i.e., the number of shortest paths from all vertices to all others that pass through that node. We compute this measure for each node in an undirected R-MAT graph [6] using Brandes' algorithm [5].

Since even a small graph incurs a significant amount of computation, we replicate the graph in every place. We randomly partition the vertices across places. Each place is responsible for computing the centrality measure for all its vertices. These computations are local and independent.

We run with one host up to 1,470 hosts. Because BC is not amenable to perfect weak scaling, we consider two different problem instances. With 2,048 places or less, we consider a graph with 2^{18} vertices and 2^{21} edges. With 2,048 places or more, we consider a graph with 2^{20} vertices and 2^{23} edges. At scale we traverse 245 Billion edges per second.

There is a significant performance drop at 2,048 places when we increase the problem size, due – we speculate – to the increased footprint of the graph. With a fixed-size graph between 32 and 2,048 places, the number of traversed edges per place and per second reduces from 11.59 million to 10.67 million. With the larger graph, we measure 6.23 million edges/s/place with 2,048 places and 5.21 million with 47,040 places. Therefore, while the measured relative efficiency is only 45% at scale (Table 2), the "corrected" efficiency is 77% if we discount the performance drop due to the switch to a larger graph.

The remaining 23% primarily results from increasing unbalance. The computation of the centrality measure takes a variable amount of time depending on the vertex position in the graph. By randomizing the partition, we can mitigate this unbalance, but only to a degree. The smaller the parts, the higher the imbalance.

Since we collected these results, we have implemented BC on top of the GLB library to dynamically distribute the load across all places [43]. The resulting code has better efficiency.

8. Related Work

We structure the discussion of related work around the three main contributions of this paper: scalability of APGAS constructs, performance evaluation of high-productivity programming models, and algorithmic advances for dynamic distributed load balancing in the context of the Unbalanced Tree Search problem.

APGAS scalability. Our work on scalable `finish` is related to prior work in the Charm parallel programming system to develop a scalable algorithm for quiescence detection [36]. As in X10, Charm's core execution model combines asynchronous distributed tasks with the ability to determine when a collection of tasks has completed. Charm++ supports the ability to detect completion of a set of tasks or global quiescence of the entire computation [19]. Algorithmically, Charm's *Counting* algorithm and the *Task Balancing* algorithm [4] used by X10 as the most general implementation of `finish` make different time/space trade-offs. The Counting algorithm uses asymptotically fewer counters, but requires two phases to detect termination. Each phase involves communicating with all the tasks in scope. This is ill-suited for X10 where termination detection scopes are numerous, usually nested, and overlap places. Additionally, we have developed specialized algorithms for commonly occurring usage patterns `finish`.

The Co-Array Fortran 2.0 `finish` construct also ensures the global completion of a set of asynchronous tasks [23]. Because CAF is SPMD-centric, its `finish` is designed for this special case, specified as a collective operation, and implemented with rounds of termination detection as in Charm++. X10's `finish` is not limited to SPMD patterns, but we provide a specialized implementation for the SPMD case (FINISH_SPMD pragma).

Chapel also incorporates distributed asynchronous tasks and finish-like synchronization with its `begin`, `on` and `sync` constructs [9]. The techniques we have developed for scaling `finish` should be applicable to Chapel.

Productivity and performance. As illustrated by the submissions to the HPC Challenge Class 2 competitions [14], there has been significant prior work on improving the performance and scalability of high-productivity programming models. Performance results on machines ranging from hundreds to tens of thousands of nodes have been reported for PGAS languages such as Co-Array Fortran [23], UPC [1], Chapel [7], and X10 [39] and for programming models such as Charm++ [18] and XcalableMP [24]. The results we report in this paper represent significantly higher levels of absolute performance and/or scalability than was achieved in previous systems.

X10's productivity has been modeled as well as empirically studied by IBM as part of the HPCS PERCS project [12] and independently by X10 users [27]. While type or memory safety have the same productivity benefits at small and large scale, prior productivity analyses have not confirmed or refuted the value of APGAS constructs at very large scale. With this work, we demonstrate that these constructs do perform at very large scale, hence continue to deliver productivity to the programmer.

Our congruent memory allocator is similar to many symmetric memory allocators. It permits data structures to be at predictable but not necessary identical addresses in each place. This helps maximizing TLB utilization when multiple places are running on the same node. The IBM UPC implementation studied approaches for scalable congruent memory allocation and developed the Shared Variable Directory as one such scalable technique [3]. Our approach is more restricted, but does demonstrate how custom memory allocation can be integrated into a type safe and mostly garbage-collected programming language.

UTS. UTS, an excellent example of an irregular application, was first described by Prins et al. [28]. Olivier and Prins [26] provided the first scalable implementation of UTS on clusters that provided up to 80% efficiency on 1,024 nodes. To this end, they employed a custom application-level load balancer along with optimizations such as one-sided communications and novel termination detection techniques. Dinan et al. [10] provide a framework for global load balancing, which was used to achieve speedups on 8196 processors. Global load balancing and termination detection facilities were provided to express irregular applications. By reserving one core per compute node on the cluster exclusively for lock and unlock operations, this framework allowed threads to steal work asynchronously without disrupting the victim threads. However, the cost paid was a static allocation (one core out of every eight) for communication. This results in lower throughput because the thread is not available for user-level computations. Saraswat et al. [35] introduced lifeline-based global load balancing and showed 87% efficiency on 2048 nodes. An implementation of the life-line algorithm in Co-Array Fortran achieved 58% efficiency at 8192 nodes [23]. A more recent UTS code using CAF 2.0 `finish` construct achieves a 74% parallel efficiency on 32,768 Jaguar cores [42]. In comparison, our code reaches 98% parallel efficiency with 55,680 Power7 cores.

Work-stealing schedulers have been developed for X10 both in the context of intra- and inter-node load balancing. For the intra-node case, pure runtime techniques have been developed [13] as well as compiler-supported techniques [40]. For the inter-node case, the GLB library based on the scheduler developed for UTS in [35] enables the automated distributed load balancing of locality-insensitive tasks using global work stealing.

We have recently incorporated our improvements to the UTS scheduler to the GLB library and implemented Betweenness Centrality on top of GLB [43]. We were able to confirm that GLB can effectively balance BC and improve its efficiency at scale.

9. Summary

We implemented eight application kernels in X10 and ran them at scale on a petaflop Power 775 supercomputer. Excluding Betweenness Centrality, we measure an efficiency at scale (for 1,024 hosts or more) consistently above 87% of the single-host efficiency. For the four HPC Class 2 Challenge benchmarks, X10 achieves 41% to 87% of the top performance numbers reported for this system.

We show that X10's `finish` construct for distributed termination detection delivers performance at scale. We use `finish` to block for the delivery of a single asynchronous message, wait for the termination of a regular SPMD-style distributed computation, or control a distributed load balancing kernel, among other things. We believe there is a great productivity benefit in having a unique, universal, yet scalable mechanism for termination detection.

We show that hardware-accelerated communication primitives like RDMAs and collectives can be integrated into X10 via libraries and that accounting for low-level memory requirements can be achieved without crippling X10's automated memory management and safety.

To the best of our knowledge, our UTS implementation for geometric trees is the first to scale to petaflop systems. Asynchrony and distributed termination detection are essential to any scalable UTS implementation. We believe that the X10 language and tools gave us the ability to experiment with the UTS code like no other programming model would, ultimately giving us the keys to performance at scale.

We focus on scale out: we want as many places as possible to stress our `finish` implementations, etc. Therefore, we run with one place per core and implement the benchmark codes with minimal intra-place concurrency. A more natural APGAS implementation however would take advantage of intra-place concurrency, run with only one or a few places per host, and probably perform marginally better.

While collecting our performance results, we observed many times the practical benefits of the asynchronous programming style advocated for by X10. If a single core is not performing optimally, a statically scheduled code like HPL suffers greatly. With UTS however, there is no measurable impact as the load is dynamically pulled from the bad core.

Acknowledgments

This material is based upon work supported by the Defense Advanced Research Projects Agency under its Agreement No. HR0011-07-9-0002.

Earlier versions of the code presented here were worked on by Sreedhar Kodali, Ganesh Bikshandi, Pradeep Varma, Krishna Venkat and other colleagues.

We would like to thank all our colleagues on the PERCS project who made the collection of the performance results possible. We would especially like to thank Kevin Gildea, Vickie Robinson, Pat Esquivel, Pat Clarke, George Almasi, Gabriel Tanase, and Ram Rajamony.

References

[1] G. Almási, B. Dalton, L. L. Hu, F. Franchetti, Y. Liu, A. Sidelnik, T. Spelce, I. G. Tanase, E. Tiotto, Y. Voronenko, and X. Xue. 2010 IBM HPC Challenge Class II Submission, Nov. 2010.

[2] B. Arimilli, R. Arimilli, V. Chung, S. Clark, W. Denzel, B. Drerup, T. Hoefler, J. Joyner, J. Lewis, J. Li, N. Ni, and R. Rajamony. The PERCS high-performance interconnect. In *Proceedings of the 2010 18th IEEE Symposium on High Performance Interconnects*, HOTI '10, pages 75–82, Washington, DC, USA, 2010. IEEE Computer Society.

[3] C. Barton, C. Casçaval, G. Almási, Y. Zheng, M. Farreras, S. Chatterje, and J. N. Amaral. Shared memory programming for large scale machines. In *Proceedings of the 2006 ACM SIGPLAN conference on Programming language design and implementation*, PLDI '06, pages 108–117, New York, NY, USA, 2006. ACM.

[4] S. M. Blackburn, R. L. Hudson, R. Morrison, J. E. B. Moss, D. S. Munro, and J. Zigman. Starting with termination: a methodology for building distributed garbage collection algorithms. In *Proceedings of the 24th Australasian conference on Computer science*, ACSC '01, pages 20–28, Washington, DC, USA, 2001. IEEE Computer Society.

[5] U. Brandes. A faster algorithm for betweenness centrality. *Journal of Mathematical Sociology*, 25:163–177, 2001.

[6] D. Chakrabarti, Y. Zhan, and C. Faloutsos. R-mat: A recursive model for graph mining. In *In SDM*, 2004.

[7] B. Chamberlain, S.-E. Choi, M. Dumler, T. Hildebrandt, D. Iten, V. Litvinov, G. Titus, C. BaAaglino, R. Sobel, B. Holt, and J. Keasler. Chapel HPC Challenge Entry: 2012, Nov. 2012.

[8] S. Crafa, D. Cunningham, V. Saraswat, A. Shinnar, and O. Tardieu. Semantics of (Resilient) X10. http://arxiv.org/abs/1312.3739, Dec. 2013.

[9] Cray. Chapel language specification version 0.93. Apr. 2013.

[10] J. Dinan, D. B. Larkins, P. Sadayappan, S. Krishnamoorthy, and J. Nieplocha. Scalable work stealing. In *SC '09: Proceedings of the Conference on High Performance Computing Networking, Storage and Analysis*, pages 1–11, New York, NY, USA, 2009. ACM.

[11] J. Dongarra, R. Graybill, W. Harrod, R. Lucas, E. Lusk, P. Luszczek, J. Mcmahon, A. Snavely, J. Vetter, K. Yelick, S. Alam, R. Campbell, L. Carrington, T.-Y. Chen, O. Khalili, J. Meredith, and M. Tikir. DARPA's HPCS Program: History, Models, Tools, Languages. In M. V. Zelkowitz, editor, *Advances in COMPUTERS High Performance Computing*, volume 72 of *Advances in Computers*, pages 1 – 100. Elsevier, 2008.

[12] K. Ebcioglu, V. Sarkar, T. El-Ghazawi, and J. Urbanic. An experiment in measuring the productivity of three parallel programming languages. In *P-PHEC workshop, held in conjunction with HPCA*, February 2006.

[13] D. Grove, O. Tardieu, D. Cunningham, B. Herta, I. Peshansky, and V. Saraswat. A performance model for X10 applications: what's going on under the hood? In *Proceedings of the 2011*

ACM SIGPLAN X10 Workshop, X10 '11, pages 1:1–1:8, New York, NY, USA, 2011. ACM.

[14] HPC Challenge Awards Competition. `http://www.hpcchallenge.org/`.

[15] HPC Challenge Benchmark Record 482. `http://icl.cs.utk.edu/hpcc/hpcc_record.cgi?id=482`, July 2012.

[16] HPC Challenge Benchmark Record 495. `http://icl.cs.utk.edu/hpcc/hpcc_record.cgi?id=495`, Nov. 2012.

[17] HPC Challenge Benchmarks. `http://icl.cs.utk.edu/hpcc/`.

[18] L. V. Kalez, A. Arya, A. Bhatele, A. Gupta, N. Jain, P. Jetley, J. Lifflander, P. Miller, Y. Sun, R. Venkataramanz, L. Wesolowski, and G. Zheng. Charm++ for Productivity and Performance, Nov. 2011.

[19] P. P. Laboratory. The Charm++ Parallel Programming System Manual. Technical Report Version 6.4, Department of Computer Science, University of Illinois, Urbana-Champaign, 2013.

[20] J. K. Lee and J. Palsberg. Featherweight X10: a core calculus for async-finish parallelism. In *Proceedings of the 15th ACM SIGPLAN Symposium on Principles and Practice of Parallel Programming*, PPoPP '10, pages 25–36, New York, NY, USA, 2010. ACM.

[21] S. Lloyd. Least squares quantization in PCM. *IEEE Trans. Inf. Theor.*, 28(2):129–137, Sept. 2006.

[22] J. MacQueen. Some methods for classification and analysis of multivariate observations. Proc. 5th Berkeley Symp. Math. Stat. Probab., Univ. Calif. 1965/66, 1, 281-297 (1967)., 1967.

[23] J. Mellor-Crummey, L. Adhianto, G. Jin, M. Krentel, K. Murthy, W. Scherer, and C. Yang. Class II Submission to the HPC Challenge Award Competition Coarray Fortran 2.0, Nov. 2011.

[24] M. Nakao, H. Murai, T. Shimosaka, and M. Sato. XcalableMP 2012 HPC Challenge Class II Submission, Nov. 2012.

[25] S. Olivier, J. Huan, J. Liu, J. Prins, J. Dinan, P. Sadayappan, and C.-W. Tseng. UTS: an unbalanced tree search benchmark. In *Proceedings of the 19th international conference on Languages and compilers for parallel computing*, LCPC'06, pages 235–250, Berlin, Heidelberg, 2007. Springer-Verlag.

[26] S. Olivier and J. Prins. Scalable dynamic load balancing using UPC. In *ICPP '08: Proceedings of the 2008 37th International Conference on Parallel Processing*, pages 123–131, Washington, DC, USA, 2008. IEEE Computer Society.

[27] J. Paudel and J. N. Amaral. Using the Cowichan problems to investigate the programmability of X10 programming system. In *Proceedings of the 2011 ACM SIGPLAN X10 Workshop*, X10 '11, pages 4:1–4:10, New York, NY, USA, 2011. ACM.

[28] J. Prins, J. Huan, B. Pugh, C.-W. Tseng, and P. Sadayappan. UPC Implementation of an Unbalanced Tree Search Benchmark. Technical Report 03-034, Univ. of North Carolina at Chapel Hill, October 2003.

[29] D. Quintero, K. Bosworth, P. Chaudhary, R. G. da Silva, B. Ha, J. Higino, M.-E. Kahle, T. Kamenoue, J. Pearson, M. Perez, F. Pizzano, R. Simon, and K. Sun. *IBM Power Systems 775 for AIX and Linux HPC Solution.* IBM, 2012.

[30] R. Rajamony, M. W. Stephenson, and W. E. Speight. The Power 775 Architecture at Scale. In *Proceedings of the 27th International ACM Conference on International Conference on Supercomputing*, ICS '13, pages 183–192, New York, NY, USA, 2013. ACM.

[31] V. Saraswat, G. Almasi, G. Bikshandi, C. Cascaval, D. Cunningham, D. Grove, S. Kodali, I. Peshansky, and O. Tardieu. The Asynchronous Partitioned Global Address Space Model. In *AMP'10: Proceedings of The First Workshop on Advances in Message Passing*, June 2010.

[32] V. Saraswat, B. Bloom, I. Peshansky, O. Tardieu, and D. Grove. The X10 language specification, v2.2.3. Aug. 2012.

[33] V. Saraswat and R. Jagadeesan. Concurrent clustered programming. In *Concur'05*, pages 353–367, 2005.

[34] V. Saraswat, O. Tardieu, D. Grove, D. Cunningham, M. Takeuchi, and B. Herta. A brief introduction to X10 (for the high performance programmer). `http://x10.sourceforge.net/documentation/intro/latest/html/`, Feb. 2013.

[35] V. A. Saraswat, P. Kambadur, S. Kodali, D. Grove, and S. Krishnamoorthy. Lifeline-based global load balancing. In *Proceedings of the 16th ACM Symposium on Principles and Practice of Parallel Programming*, PPoPP '11, pages 201–212, 2011.

[36] A. B. Sinha, L. V. Kale, and B. Ramkumar. A dynamic and adaptive quiescence detection algorithm. Technical Report 93-11, Parallel Programming Laboratory, Department of Computer Science , University of Illinois, Urbana-Champaign, 1993.

[37] T. Smith and M. Waterman. Identification of common molecular subsequences. *Journal of Molecular Biology*, 147(1):195 – 197, 1981.

[38] G. Tanase, G. Almási, E. Tiotto, M. Alvanos, A. Ly, and B. Dalton. Performance analysis of the IBM XL UPC on the PERCS architecture. Technical Report RC25360, IBM Research, Mar. 2013.

[39] O. Tardieu, D. Grove, B. Bloom, D. Cunningham, B. Herta, P. Kambadur, V. A. Saraswat, A. Shinnar, M. Takeuchi, and M. Vaziri. X10 for Productivity and Performance at Scale, Nov. 2012.

[40] O. Tardieu, H. Wang, and H. Lin. A work-stealing scheduler for X10's task parallelism with suspension. In *Proceedings of the 17th ACM SIGPLAN symposium on Principles and Practice of Parallel Programming*, PPoPP '12, pages 267–276, 2012.

[41] Wikipedia. PERCS. `http://en.wikipedia.org/w/index.php?title=PERCS`, 2011.

[42] C. Yang, K. Murthy, and J. Mellor-Crummey. Managing Asynchronous Operations in Coarray Fortran 2.0. In *IEEE 27th International Symposium on Parallel Distributed Processing (IPDPS)*, pages 1321–1332, 2013.

[43] W. Zhang, O. Tardieu, D. Grove, B. Herta, T. Kamada, V. Saraswat, and M. Takeuchi. GLB: Lifeline-based Global Load Balancing Library in X10. `http://arxiv.org`, Dec. 2013.

Resilient X10

Efficient failure-aware programming

David Cunningham[2] *, David Grove[1], Benjamin Herta[1], Arun Iyengar[1], Kiyokuni Kawachiya[3],
Hiroki Murata[3], Vijay Saraswat[1], Mikio Takeuchi[3], Olivier Tardieu[1]

[1]IBM T. J. Watson Research Center
[2]Google Inc.
[3]IBM Research - Tokyo

dcunnin@google.com, {groved,bherta,aruni,vsaraswa,tardieu}@us.ibm.com, {kawatiya,mrthrk,mtake}@jp.ibm.com

Abstract

Scale-out programs run on multiple processes in a cluster. In scale-out systems, processes can fail. Computations using traditional libraries such as MPI fail when any component process fails. The advent of Map Reduce, Resilient Data Sets and MillWheel has shown dramatic improvements in productivity are possible when a high-level programming framework handles scale-out and resilience automatically.

We are concerned with the development of general-purpose languages that support resilient programming. In this paper we show how the X10 language and implementation can be extended to support resilience. In Resilient X10, places may fail asynchronously, causing loss of the data and tasks at the failed place. Failure is exposed through exceptions. We identify a *Happens Before Invariance Principle* and require the runtime to automatically repair the global control structure of the program to maintain this principle. We show this reduces much of the burden of resilient programming. The programmer is only responsible for continuing execution with fewer computational resources and the loss of part of the heap, and can do so while taking advantage of domain knowledge.

We build a complete implementation of the language, capable of executing benchmark applications on hundreds of nodes. We describe the algorithms required to make the language runtime resilient. We then give three applications, each with a different approach to fault tolerance (replay, dec-

---

* Work done while employed at IBM T. J. Watson Research Center.

PPoPP '14, February 15–19, 2014, Orlando, Florida, USA.
Copyright © 2014 ACM 978-1-4503-2656-8/14/02...$15.00.
http://dx.doi.org/10.1145/2555243.2555248

imation, and domain-level checkpointing). These can be executed at scale and survive node failure. We show that for these programs the overhead of resilience is a small fraction of overall runtime by comparing to equivalent non-resilient X10 programs. On one program we show end-to-end performance of Resilient X10 is ∼100x faster than Hadoop.

Categories and Subject Descriptors D.3.3 [*Programming Languages*]: Language Constructs and Features—Frameworks

Keywords X10, Distributed, Parallel, Resilience

1. Introduction

Scale out programs run on multiple processes in a cluster. In scale-out systems, processes can fail. They run out of memory, the node they are running on may lose power, overheat, or suffer a software failure.

Computations using traditional libraries such as MPI fail when any component process fails. If the mean time between failures (MTBF) of a single node is 6 months, a 24 hour job running on 1000 nodes has less than 1% chance of successful completion. Supercomputers are generally designed to be significantly more reliable than commodity clusters; nevertheless, resilience is a serious issue at extremely large scales.

Traditionally, long-lived multi-node applications have addressed node failure only via application-level checkpointing. This is *ad hoc*, error prone, problematic when the amount of state to be saved is large, and not applicable (or inefficient) in certain cases. For instance, for some machine learning applications a reasonable recovery strategy is to ignore the work assigned to the failed node and proceed to completion with the remaining nodes. We call this (checkpoint-free) strategy *decimation*. Depending on the algorithm, it may also be possible to proceed by recovering state from neighbors, from the original input files, through replay of work, or some combination of the above.

More recently, the advent of Map Reduce [12, 29], Resilient Data Sets [32], Pregel [17] and MillWheel [2] has shown the dramatic improvement in productivity possible when a high-level programming framework handles scale-out and resilience automatically. Nevertheless, the underlying programming model for which resilience is provided is very limited in these cases. Performance is a significant problem, and derivative frameworks such as M3R [25] improve performance but at the cost of loss of resilience.

We are concerned with the development of general-purpose, imperative languages that support resilient programming.[1] Over the last ten years, the X10 programming language [6, 22] has been developed as a simple, clean, but powerful and practical programming model for scale out computation. Its underlying programming model, the APGAS (Asynchronous Partitioned Global Address Space) programming model [23], is organized around the two notions of *places* and *asynchrony*. A place is an abstraction of shared, mutable data and worker threads operating on the data, typically realized as an operating system process. A single APGAS computation consists of hundreds, potentially tens of thousands of places. Asynchrony is provided through a single block-structured control construct, `async S`. If S is a statement, then `async S` is a statement that executes S in a separate thread of control (*activity* or *task*). Dually, `finish S` executes S, and waits for all tasks spawned (recursively) during the execution of S to terminate, before continuing. Memory locations in one place can contain references (*global refs*) to locations at other places. To use a global ref, the `at (p) S` statement must be used. It permits the current task to change its place of execution to p, execute S at p and return, leaving behind tasks that may have been spawned during the execution of S. The termination of these tasks is detected by the `finish` within which the at statement is executing. The values of variables used in S but defined outside S are serialized, transmitted to p, and de-serialized to reconstruct a binding environment in which S is executed. Constructs are provided for unconditional (`atomic S`) and conditional (`when (c) S`) atomic execution. Finally, Java-style non-resumptive exceptions (`throw`, `try/catch`) are supported. If an exception is not caught in an `async`, it is propagated to the enclosing `finish` statement. Since there may be many such exceptions, they appear wrapped in a `MultipleExceptions` exception.

The power of X10 lies in that these constructs can nest arbitrarily, almost without restriction[2]. A diverse variety of distributed control and communication idioms (e.g. recursive parallelism, active messaging, single process multiple data, accelerator off-load, remote memory transfers etc.) can be realized just through particular combinations of `async/at/finish/when`. Indeed, the usefulness of X10 for scale-out programming has been amply demonstrated. Large portions of the X10 runtime are written in X10. [28] presents

benchmark results on over 50,000 cores, with performance comparable to MPI (in some cases significantly better). [25] develops a main memory implementation of Hadoop with significant performance improvements over Hadoop. [24] presents a novel, high performance algorithm for unbalanced tree search that leverages `finish`. [18] presents a large, sophisticated, computational chemistry code written in X10. [11] develops a graph library in X10. [10, 13, 14] present results on the productivity of programming in X10.

In this paper, we show how the X10 language and implementation can be modified to support resilience. Because of the orthogonality of the core X10 constructs, this is conceptually straightforward. A place p may fail at any time, with the loss of its heap and tasks. Any `at(p) S` executing at a place q will see a `DeadPlaceException` (DPE). Any attempt to launch an `at(p) S` at p will also throw a DPE. Global refs pointing to locations hosted at p now "dangle", but they can only be dereferenced via an `at (p) S`, which will throw a DPE.

However, X10 permits arbitrary nesting of `async/at/finish`. Hence when a place p fails, one or more tasks running at other places may be in the middle of executing an `at (p) S` and, conversely, code running at the dead place p may be in the middle of running `at (q) T` statements at other (non-failed) places q. What should be done about such cross-place dependencies?

Let $u = $ `at (p) S` be a statement running at r, and S (running at p) contain a sub-statement $v = $ `at (q) T`, for $p \neq q$. We will call v a *non-local child task* of u. Note that v may have been launched within an arbitrarily nested `finish/async` sub-statements of u. What should be done with such "orphan" tasks when the spawning place (p) fails? We argue that it is unwise to track down and terminate such tasks. Asynchronous termination of tasks can leave the heap at different unfailed places in an inconsistent and unknown state. Tasks should either run to completion or not at all. However, we insist on a key design principle, the *Happens Before Invariance (HBI) Principle*:

> *Failure of a place should not alter the happens before relationship between statement instances at the remaining places.*

This guarantee permits the Resilient X10 programmer to write code secure in the knowledge that even if a place fails, changes to the heap at non-failed places will happen in the order specified by the original (unfailed) program. Failure of a place p will cause loss of data and control state at p but will not affect the concurrency structure of the remaining code.

As described below, this principle requires that the X10 runtime maintain some information about the control (`finish/async`) graph at every place in *resilient storage* (storage that outlasts the failure of a place). This information is used to repair the `finish` and at control dependency structure across places so as to correctly implement the HBI Principle.

---

[1] Erlang is an example of a general-purpose language supporting resilience that is not imperative.

[2] X10 restricts the `atomic S` and `when(c) S` constructs so that S may not dynamically execute `at (p) T`, `finish T` or `when (c) T` constructs.

Thus, Resilient X10 is obtained from X10 by permitting places to fail asynchronously, exposing failure through exceptions, and ensuring that the X10 runtime repairs the global control structure of the executing program to correctly implement the HBI Principle. In related work [8], we develop a formal semantics for Resilient X10 as a derivative of the formal semantics of X10. The semantics is presented as a transition system over configurations that are pairs $\langle s, g \rangle$ of a statement s (representing the tree of all tasks running in all places) and the global heap g. To model Resilient X10, this semantics need only be extended by a single rule that permits a place to fail asynchronously. g is changed to a g' that is the same as g except that all the state of p is lost. s is rewritten in a single step to a new statement s' that represents the loss of all tasks running at p and repairs the structure of the remaining tasks so that the HBI Principle (and an associated Exception Masking Principle) are preserved.

This paper presents the design and implementation of Resilient X10. Resilient X10 was implemented by modifying the X10 runtime and core libraries. Because the source language was unchanged, the X10 compiler is unchanged. The Resilient X10 programmer essentially writes X10 code, but with the awareness that DPEs may be thrown. User code may catch these exceptions and take appropriate recovery steps, based on domain specific information (e.g., discard lost state, reload from resilient storage, recompute, recover from neighbors, etc.). Note that a Resilient X10 program can run on an X10 implementation without change, and behaves just like an identical X10 program (such programs abort when a place fails). An X10 program can run on a Resilient X10 implementation without change, but may see DPEs on place failure. In summary, the contributions of this paper are:

1. The design and implementation of Resilient X10, which we believe to be the first implementation of a real, general-purpose, imperative programming language that allows applications to handle node failure without significant loss of scalability, performance, or productivity.

2. An evaluation of the overhead and scalability of our implementation for a variety of concurrency patterns.

3. A demonstration of the flexibility of Resilient X10 via benchmarks that handle failure in diverse ways. In particular, we identify decimation, an idiom that is applicable in many relaxed computing [5] settings, and which can be very simply and elegantly expressed in Resilient X10.

4. A comparison of sparse matrix dense vector multiply implementations showing that the end-to-end performance of Resilient X10 is $\sim$100x faster than Hadoop.

Section 2 continues with a more detailed comparison to existing work. Section 3 is a deeper discussion of the language design and programming idioms. Section 4 describes our implementation. Section 5 gives performance analysis and describes Resilient X10 applications, and Section 6 concludes.

2. Related Work

Hadoop [9, 29] handles failures invisibly, by writing *all* data out to a resilient disk store (HDFS) after each MapReduce job, and at key intermediate points. Hadoop, while relatively easy to program, is also restrictive in the types of algorithms it can support. Resilient X10 gives more flexibility to the programmer, both in how distributed programs are written, as well as giving the programmer control over how to cope with failures.

The Spark framework [32] uses Resilient Distributed Datasets, which provides a read-only collection of objects partitioned across multiple nodes. RDDs offer more flexibility and performance over Hadoop MapReduce, because all data does not need to be re-written to disk between each phase of the computation, and the programmer has more control over what data is persisted vs discarded. But Spark's programming model is much closer to MapReduce than a general programming language such as X10.

The Charm++ programming system [21] for distributed systems supports distributed termination detection as well as fault-tolerance via checkpoint/restart, but the user is responsible for combining the two safely. Typically checkpointing only happens at global synchronization points with no outstanding asynchronous processing. A similar approach, X10-FT, checkpoints the X10 state at the granularity of AP-GAS language constructs [31]. In contrast, Resilient X10 precisely defines the semantics of termination detection in the presence of failures. This makes it possible to continue executing in spite of failures without reverting to a checkpoint, while preserving the execution order of all surviving tasks.

Lifflander et al. [16] propose three fault-tolerant algorithms for detecting distributed termination for a core programming model and failure model similar to ours (asynchronous tasks, single root, fail-stop failures). They consider a single termination scope whereas we support multiple finish scopes (side-by-side or nested) thus providing more expressive power. In their algorithms, the shape of the spawn tree dictates the flow of control messages of the distributed termination detection as well as the layout of the redundant storage of the control state. A parent process is responsible for handling the failure of its children (possibly transitively), but the opposite is not possible. The memory overhead of fault tolerance is therefore not balanced across processes. In contrast, we decouple the resiliency implementation from the application structure. For instance, we provide an implementation where the task management state is centralized and another where it is distributed across all the nodes.

Containment domains [7] are a methodology whereby the programmer can provide fault tolerance in a modular fashion by choosing to either mask or report faults at the module boundary. In Resilient X10 it is easy for the programmer to follow this methodology. Masking errors means catching exceptions within a module and employing some internal redundant application-level computation/storage to return the correct result despite the failure. If that is not possible, the error can be reported by either simply not catching the exception (which may expose details of the module's implementation) or preferably by catching it and rethrowing a more abstract version that better matches the module's API.

3. Language Design and Examples

A complete but simple Resilient X10 program, a Monte Carlo application that calculates π, is given in Figure 1. Execution begins at place zero. Because of this, place zero typically has a special role of communicating the result to the user, so we assume it can never fail (if it does fail, the whole execution is torn down)[3]. From there, the application is free to spawn tasks on other places. In this example, an asynchronous task is created at every place (Lines 9, 11), tries a number of random samples (Lines 14–18), and communicates its result back to place 0 using a global ref[4] (Lines 20–25). If a place dies during this work, its task throws a DeadPlaceException (DPE) which is silently caught (Line 26). The last few lines (Lines 28–30) will therefore execute when all the work is either completed or dead. If places die before they communicate back, then they contribute no result, and the accumulated number of tested samples is correspondingly lower. Thus losing a place will cause the computed value of π to be less accurate.

This simple example does not show-case the full expressive power of Resilient X10. In particular Resilient X10 is unique in allowing the arbitrary nesting of finish and at. This allows blocking for distributed termination within a task, which is not supported by Charm++ [21]. This allows two levels of concurrency for distributed multicore programming, and the writing of libraries that internally use finish. It also allows divide-and-conquer parallelism where each invocation of a recursive method waits for the termination of its recursive calls before returning control [19]. In the context of this rich concurrency, Resilient X10 attempts to make handling errors as easy as possible without compromising performance.

The Happens Before Invariance (HBI) Principle means programmers need not be concerned with subtle concurrency bugs due to failed synchronization. In the following three examples, place p fails during the execution of S.

In this example, Resilient X10 ensures that R is executed after S, as in regular X10:

```
try {
    at (p) { at (q) S; ... }
} catch (e:DPE) { } R
```

---

[3] This means the MTBF of the system is the same as the MTBF of a single node, which we consider to be acceptable given the prevalence of divide-and-conquer and the convenience of orchestrating and completing the execution at a single root node. We discuss this further in Section 6.

[4] In the at block, any outer scope variables may be *captured*. All captured variables are copied deeply to the target place. Global refs override copying to enable the creation of cross-place references.

```
1:  import x10.util.Pair;
2:  import x10.util.Random;
3:  public class ResilientMontePi {
4:      static val ITERS = 10000000 / Place.MAX_PLACES;
5:      public static def main (args : Rail[String]) {
6:          // (points_in_circle, samples)
7:          val cell = new Cell(Pair[Long,Long](0, 0));
8:          val cell_gr = GlobalRef(cell);
9:          finish for (p in Place.places()) async {
10:             try {
11:                 at (p) {
12:                     val rand = new Random(System.nanoTime());
13:                     var total : Long = 0;
14:                     for (iter in 1..ITERS) {
15:                         val x = rand.nextDouble(),
16:                             y = rand.nextDouble();
17:                         if (x*x + y*y <= 1.0) total++;
18:                     }
19:                     val total_ = total;
20:                     at (cell_gr) async atomic {
21:                         // add our result to global total
22:                         val the_cell = cell_gr();
23:                         the_cell(Pair(the_cell().first+total_,
24:                                       the_cell().second+ITERS));
25:                     } }
26:             } catch (e:DeadPlaceException) { /* just ignore */ }
27:         } /* end of finish */
28:         val samples = cell().second;
29:         val pi = (4.0 * cell().first) / samples;
30:         Console.OUT.println("pi = "+pi+" (samples: "+samples+")");
31: } }
```

Figure 1. Computing π with the Monte Carlo method.

Adding async means R may execute in parallel with S. In Resilient X10, the termination of S is detected by the outer (implicit, not shown) finish as in regular X10:

```
try {
    at (p) { at (q) async S; ... }
} catch (e:DPE) { } R
```

Resilient X10 preserves the ordering guarantees from X10 by ensuring that R is executed *after* S, even though the finish governing S executes in a failed place:

```
try {
    at (p) { finish at (q) async S; ... }
} catch (e:DPE) { } R
```

In the examples above, what if S throws a user-defined exception? In regular X10 it would propagate to the closest catch block. However in the event of failure, the run-time representation of part of that control stack is now lost. We cannot tell whether the exception would have been caught in this lost part of the stack. Our options are: (1) Propagate the exception around the failure. (2) Drop the exception. (3) Make the control stack resilient. We decided that option 1 would be too surprising for programmers, since suppressed exceptions would never escape in regular X10. We chose option (2) to avoid the overhead and complexity of (3). The semantics of option (2) are actually quite reasonable. We give the programmer guarantees about synchronization, but we do not attempt to recover that task's exception output. A user-defined exception is never lost without there being at least one DPE appearing in its place, so the user-defined exception can be considered to be masked, rather than lost; we call this the *Exception Masking Principle*. Note that in the second example, the presence of the async means that any exception thrown by S will be routed directly to the outer finish, thus is not propagated through p and is not lost.

In summary, loss of place p will cause loss of the heap at p, loss of (most of) the control state at p and also masks any exceptions that would have been propagated through p.

3.1 Resilient Storage

A resilient store is a data structure that internally stores data in a manner that survives node failure. This can involve replication in another node's memory or on disk. Storing in memory is faster, but has space overhead. However it is attractive because the application is self-contained. Either way has a performance overhead, so use of resilient stores should be limited to critical data that cannot be recovered by other means. Another useful application of resilient stores is infrequent checkpoints of application state.

Resilient in-memory stores can be easily implemented in Resilient X10. A class can be designed that provides a simple interface to read and write to the store. The implementation of that class will then update one or more backups behind the scenes. If a synchronous update is not required, the `async` construct can be used. This can provide better performance with fewer consistency guarantees. As in collection libraries, we expect that there will not be one resilient store for all potential uses. Instead there will be a few different stores abstracted into utility libraries, as well as applications occasionally implementing specialized versions with particular properties. Using the resilient storage, we have prototyped several resilient-aware libraries such as a resilient `DistArray`. The design, implementation, and usage of resilient data structures is an area of current research.

4. Implementation

Implementing Resilient X10 required significant work at all levels of the X10 runtime. Failure of remote nodes is discovered at the lowest level (the communication layer) and propagated up the stack. Special termination detection algorithms needed to be written in order to implement the HBI Principle.

4.1 X10RT

The X10 runtime has the ability to use one of several communications libraries, depending on network it is running on. A common API (X10RT) exists within the X10 runtime for abstracting the different libraries [30]. X10RT implementations exist that support running on top of TCP/IP sockets, shared memory, MPI, or PAMI [20].

Node failure is handled by current MPI and PAMI by ending the entire program. Therefore, it is not possible to constructively handle failure by building on top of MPI and PAMI. However, the sockets backend gave us the freedom to handle the failure of individual connections.[5] We therefore built Resilient X10 on top of sockets. We could support

---

[5] In sockets backend, 1-to-1 connections are established between each pair of communicating places.

future implementations of MPI and PAMI if they provide appropriate failure notifications.

We extended the sockets implementation thus: Upon detection of a dead place (via a communication error or a configurable timeout), we clean up the link to that place, mark it as dead, and continue running. The message send API is asynchronous, which meant the failure to send a message could not be synchronously communicated up the stack. Instead, we added an API call to return the number of dead places (which never decreases) as well as calls to query the life/death status of arbitrary places. The typical use of this API by the X10 runtime involves checking whether the remote place has died while waiting for a message from that place. The runtime can thus tell if it is never going to receive the message and yield an error. The other X10RT backends (MPI, PAMI) continue to force an abort of the entire application upon the detection of a dead place, and so their implementations of the new methods never report a place death.

4.2 Finish

The `finish S` construct blocks until all tasks spawned by S have terminated. Since it is not statically known how many tasks there will be, where they will be running, and for how long, implementing finish requires a distributed termination detection algorithm. Regular X10 already has such an algorithm. Typically, an X10RT message from the spawning task to the *finish home* (the place on which the finish was created) records new tasks, and an X10RT message from the task's place to the home place is used to notify that a task has terminated. Often, global refs are used to reference the finish representation from a remote task.

A variety of finish implementations take advantage of particular patterns of concurrency. The default finish is optimized to locally cache updates and only update the home upon local quiescence. Other implementations are specialized for single remote tasks or SPMD-style workloads. However none of these implementations are resilient. If a place dies, these finish implementations forever wait for termination messages from the dead place.

We implemented 3 new finish implementations for Resilient X10. All are based on an abstract algorithm that maintains counters and can be described assuming its own state is resilient. The implementations differ in how the resilient storage is achieved.

Each implementation is realized with a *finish object* that is created at the opening brace of the finish. The ending brace of the finish is compiled to a `wait()` call on the object. Finish objects are used both for the *explicit* finish statements that occur in the code, and to implement the synchronous semantics of the `at` construct by spawning the remote task under an *implicit* finish. New tasks are governed by the closest enclosing explicit finish. When a finish object is copied across the network, the remote copy acts as a proxy that allows implicit communication but otherwise can be considered an alias of the original finish object.

```
public class FinishObject {
    public static def make(parent:FinishObject) : FinishObject;
    public def wait() : void; // may throw MultipleExceptions
    public def fork(src:Place, dst:Place) : void;
    public def begin(src:Place, dst:Place) : Boolean;
    public def join(dst:Place) : void;
    public def pushExc(e:Exception) : void;
}
```

Figure 2. Runtime API of a finish implementation.

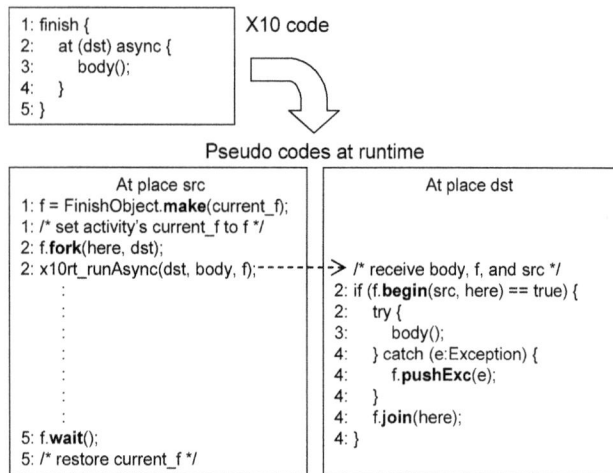

Figure 3. How the finish APIs are called.

The runtime maintains two stacks of finish states per task. The *synchronization* stack can be peeked to find the closest synchronization point. This is the closest implicit finish that is not outside of an `async`, otherwise it is the closest explicit finish. The *explicit* stack can be peeked to find the closest explicit finish, which governs new `asyncs`. In regular X10, only the explicit stack was needed. The synchronization stack is used for *adoption*, which will be explained shortly.

Any task can peek at either of these stacks to obtain the relevant finish object. As tasks are spawned and terminate, they call methods on the relevant finish object which internally communicates with the waiting task via X10RT messages and/or shared storage. The finish object API is shown in Figure 2.

Figure 3 shows how these APIs are used for executing an asynchronous task and waiting for its termination. When spawning a remote task[6], the finish object on the top of the explicit stack is used. The `fork()` method is called by the `src` place, and then an X10RT message is sent to create the remote task. Since the message is asynchronous, the `src` place then advances to the next program statement. When the X10RT message is received by the `dst` place, `begin()` is called, and if this returns `true` then the task is concurrently executed. If not, the message is silently discarded which happens when the source place died after transmission but before reception of the message. When the task terminates at

dst, `join()` is called. A given finish implementation may, within these methods, communicate with the finish home place using more X10RT messages. If an exception from the task is uncaught, it is communicated just before the `join()` call, via the `pushExc()` call. If there are any such exceptions, they are combined into a `MultipleExceptions` object which is thrown from the `wait()` call after termination. In the case of an implicit finish, the `MultipleExceptions` can only contain a single exception, so this is unwrapped and thrown as normal, thus propagating the exception through the `at` construct.

Conceptually, the finish state objects encapsulate counters that record what tasks are running where. We call this the *live* counter set. It also stores the exceptions accumulated via `pushExc()`. The `wait()` call returns control only when the counters representing non-dead places are zero. The dead counters are used to generate `DeadPlaceException` (DPE) objects which are added to the user-generated exceptions. The space overhead of the live counter set is $O(n)$ in the number of places per each active finish object.

In addition to this, if src dies after calling `fork()` but before dst calls `begin()`, then it is possible the message was not completely transmitted and the task is lost even though dst is still alive. Thus, the finish implementation must record the messages in transit between each pair of places. Such messages can be lost if either src or dst dies. If src dies, the message is silently dropped, but if dst dies, a DPE is generated. This ensures we get one DPE per task that was running at the time of the place death. Conceptually this is a 2-dimensional matrix, but the representation need not be $O(n^2)$ in memory overhead since it is very sparse (the number of messages in transit is limited by the size of network buffers). We call these the *transit* counters.

If src dies after sending the message, but before dst calls `begin()`, it is possible the finish will terminate and the task could execute on dst after the termination of the finish, violating the happens-before relationship. This is why we have the `begin()` call return `false` in this case, to prevent the execution of a task when it has been assumed to be lost.

The above semantics are sufficient for properly handling and reporting place failure, so long as the finish home place does not die. In that event, we call the tasks under that finish (which may be at other places that are still live) *orphaned*. The *parent* finish, which is determined when each finish is created by peeking the synchronous stack, must not assume that all tasks under it have terminated just because its counters are zero, because these counters do not record orphaned tasks. To solve this problem, if a place dies and there were active finishes on that place, the closest parent finish that is still alive must *adopt* these orphaned tasks. Broadly, this means exceptions are discarded, and the counters (both live and transit) from the dead finish are merged into its own

---
[6] Local task creation is exactly the same, except `src = dst`

72

counters[7]. This work is done during the `wait()` call, before checking the counters for termination.

To handle the case where these adopted tasks die (due to further place failures), we must ensure the generated DPEs, like any other exceptions, should not make it to the adopting finish. This difference in behavior means we need two sets each of live and transit counters. One set of counters records the non-adopted tasks, and is used both for termination detection and to generate DPEs upon place death. The other set of counters records adopted tasks and is only used for termination detection.

The orphaned tasks themselves must send subsequent finish updates to the adopting finish rather than to the dead finish, and these operations will modify the adopted counters. This can be achieved by setting a flag on the adopted finish during the adoption process, and leaving a forwarding reference. Any updates that must occur after the finish has died but before it has been adopted by the parent finish can simply update the dead finish state as usual. Both adopted and non-adopted counters from the dead finish are merged into the adopted counters of the adopting finish. To minimize the overhead, there is no built-in support for a user-level task to know whether it is adopted or not. However, if such knowledge is needed in specific cases, it could be implemented at the application (or framework) level on top of the basic primitives provided by Resilient X10.

In summary, a resilient finish implementation must record the tasks running directly under the finish, as well as adopting tasks from dead child finishes. It must record user-generated exceptions and generated DPEs for its immediate child tasks, while dropping them from adopted child tasks. The space overhead for a finish implementation is $O(n)$ assuming the transit matrix remains sparse. Having described how tasks are to be managed in the context of failure, we now describe 3 ways of using resilient storage to maintain the finish states.

4.2.1 Place-Zero-Based Finish

The simplest way to ensure that the finish state survives place failure is to store everything at place 0, which is assumed to never fail. This means every finish operation initiated by a place other than 0 involves a synchronous communication to 0. This is a bottleneck and requires more communication. However it is simple and performs reasonably well up to hundreds of nodes in common cases.

Place 0 contains a database of every finish state in the execution. Each finish state has a field indicating the home place and a field pointing to the parent finish, as well as all the counters. When place 0 discovers some other place has died, it scans the whole list, looking for finishes on the dead place. Each that it finds is adopted up to the nearest non-dead finish, by chasing the `parent` field.

We experimented with a simple 2-D array for the transit matrix, and a sparse representation based on the standard X10 standard library hash map. At the scales measured, the space overhead was negligible in both cases. Finish states are removed from the database (allowing garbage collection) when they terminate.

4.2.2 ZooKeeper-Based Finish

To provide a more scalable finish implementation, we tried to leverage ZooKeeper [15] to implement the required resilient storage. This seemed reasonable since ZooKeeper is touted for reliable task management in a cluster environment. Like a file system, ZooKeeper exposes a hierarchical database where each *znode* holds arbitrary data. In the ZooKeeper-based finish, all finish states are stored within ZooKeeper so can survive the death of places without depending on place 0 and should be more scalable.

X10 is implemented via translation to either Java (*Managed X10*) or C++ (*Native X10*). Currently, communication with the ZooKeeper server is implemented using Managed X10's Java interoperability framework [26, 27]. Therefore, the ZooKeeper-based finish is available only for Managed X10. The Native X10 implementation is left as future work.

Naive znode mapping: We considered two ways of mapping a finish state to znodes. The first method represents each counter of a finish state as a znode which holds the integer value, as shown in Figure 4(a). For each FinishState, a znode `FinishState-ID` is created, which holds various information for the finish state such as home ID, parent finish state ID and adopted flag. Under this FinishState znode, znodes `active` and `transit` are prepared, each of which contains znodes which hold corresponding counter values.

For example, a znode "`transit/0to1`" contains the number of tasks being created by place 0 at place 1 and a znode "`live/1`" contains the number of tasks being executed at place 1 under this finish. To reduce initialization overhead, these counter znodes are created dynamically when they are first used. Since the counter value may be modified in parallel from multiple places, a special znode "`lock`" is prepared for mutual exclusion. We use a lock mechanism provided in [3] with some modifications. Another znode "`excs`" is used to hold exception information.

The counter znodes are incremented and decremented by contacting the ZooKeeper server in each of the finish API methods. The `wait()` call blocks until all the counter znodes become zero. This logic is implemented by utilizing the *Watcher callback* mechanism of ZooKeeper. We evaluated the naive znode mapping and discovered it to be 50 times slower than the place zero implementation when creating an task.

Optimized znode mapping: In the naive znode mapping, the processing of `fork()`, `begin()`, and `join()` needed *multiple* ZooKeeper operations, each of which needs synchronous communication with the ZooKeeper server(s). To

---

[7] Note that the states of finish objects are stored in a resilient storage and are accessible even after the finish home place is dead.

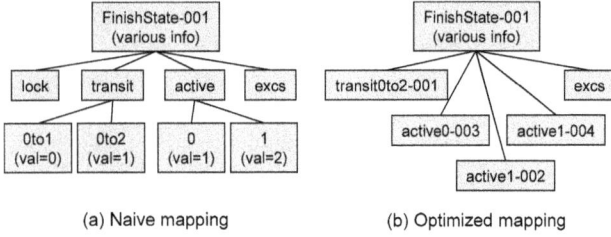

Figure 4. Mappings of a finish state to znodes.

ZooKeeper operation	Time
`create`	0.56 msec
`create` (with SeqNo)	0.58 msec
`delete`	0.33 msec
`exists`	0.34 msec
`getData`	0.49 msec
`setData`	0.57 msec
`lock`	1.43 msec
`unlock`	0.34 msec

Table 1. Cost of ZooKeeper operations.

minimize the overhead in ZooKeeper-based finish, we implemented another mapping of finish state optimized for ZooKeeper. This variation utilizes a ZooKeeper function that creates a znode with unique sequence number, enabled by specifying "`CreateMode.PERSISTENT_SEQUENTIAL`" for `ZooKeeper.create`. As shown in Figure 4(b), counter values are represented as the *number* of znodes rather than held in the znodes.

In `fork(S,D)` processing, a znode "`transitStoD-`*SeqNo*" is created, where *SeqNo* is assigned by ZooKeeper server. The sequence number is passed to the destination place D along with the task being created. In `begin(S,D)` processing, a znode "`liveD-`*SeqNo*" is created, then the passed znode "`transitStoD-`*SeqNo*" is deleted. In `join(D)`, the znode "`liveD-`*SeqNo*" is deleted. Since unique sequence numbers are assigned by ZooKeeper server, lock operations are not necessary for these processings. The `wait()` call waits until all of the `transit` and `live` znodes under the finish state are deleted. This blocking operation is also implemented by watching for znode deletion through the Watcher mechanism. Through this new mapping, the number of ZooKeeper operations necessary to spawn a task was reduced to 4 (`create` for `fork()`, `create` and `delete` for `begin()`, and `delete` for `join()`).

When we benchmarked this implementation, we discovered it was considerably faster than the naive mapping. However, it was still 13 times slower than the place-zero-based finish. To identify the reason of this overhead, we implemented a ZooKeeper-specific microbenchmark to measure the cost of ZooKeeper operations in our testing environment. The numbers were measured on the system described in Section 5 using IBM J9 Java VM [4] for Linux x86_64, version 7.0 SR6. We used ZooKeeper server version 3.4.5. To obtain a bound on the best possible performance we ran ZooKeeper on the same machine as the X10 program and used a ram disk for the snapshot storage of ZooKeeper. Table 1 summarizes our results.

Our experiments showed that each ZooKeeper operation takes 0.3 to 1.4 msec. The result is consistent with the numbers shown in a ZooKeeper paper [15], which states that the latency of a synchronous `create` operation is 1.2–1.4 msec. In our most efficient mapping to znodes, 4 ZooKeeper operations (2 `create` (with SeqNo) and 2 `delete`) are necessary for spawning one task. The total cost of these operations are

1.82 msec, which indicates that the slowness of ZooKeeper-based finish is a directed result of the cost of ZooKeeper operations.

For sufficiently large tasks, these overheads do not matter. However many X10 programs use fine-grained concurrency and small messages. We believe that, as a general-purpose resilient disk-backed database, ZooKeeper is too heavyweight to be the basis of termination detection in X10. After this experience, we decided to implement our own resilient store with the performance characteristics we needed.

4.2.3 Distributed Resilient Finish

The final finish implementation is an attempt to improve on the place-zero bottleneck by using an X10-level resilient storage for the finish state instead of relying on the implicit resilience of place 0. While this requires storing all the state in more than one place, this extra cost should be a constant factor overhead, and it can be done in a distributed manner that scales well. Moreover, implementing the resiliency within X10 avoids any out-of-process overheads and allows us to influence performance by controlling the manner in which the data is stored. However creating a resilient store within a finish implementation is harder than described in Section 3.1, because it must be built on top of X10RT messaging primitives instead of the high level APGAS primitives.

The basic idea is to store the finish at its home place, with a backup at some other place (more backups could be used for more resiliency but also more cost). If the home place happens to be place 0, then there is no need for a backup, and the implementation behaves like the place-zero-based finish. Otherwise, another place is chosen to contain a synchronized replica of the finish state. If both the master and the backup die, there is a fatal system-wide error. Otherwise, the finish implementation will transparently handle the fault. Currently, the next place is chosen for the backup, but more sophisticated algorithms could be used based on some model of failure correlation. The backup is accessed only to (1) receive updates from the master to keep it in sync, (2) receive updates from child tasks after the master had died but before adoption, (3) facilitate adoption. Every operation on the master internally performs a synchronous communication with the backup. This adds extra latency to the operation but ensures that the backup contains the most up-to-date information.

Because the backup is only used for termination detection if the finish home place dies, the backup need only store the data required to allow adoption by another finish. The backup therefore need not distinguish between regular and adopted counters, so to save memory it stores the pointwise sum of the master's two counter sets. After adoption, the backup is tagged with a forwarding pointer and is essentially inert. Another optimization is local tasks need not be backed up. This is because they die with the finish, so they never need to be adopted.

Each place has a *backup* table that can be used to find the backup of a given master if that master is dead. The table maps the master identity (the global ref to the master) to the backup object. Thus, if some task fails to communicate with the master because that place is dead, it can instead find the backup by searching other places' backup tables. The search can be accelerated if the backup place is chosen using a deterministic algorithm. This is an example of a global ref to a dead place being useful even though it cannot be dereferenced. The global ref still has a hash code and can be tested for equality with other global refs; thus it can be used to index a hash map. The fatal error for loss of master and backup arises when an exhaustive search (every place) does not find the backup.

With the distributed implementation, care must be taken when the master and backup are lost and a fatal error needs to be raised. Storing a list of child finishes at each finish (instead of a single parent pointer) means that even if master and backup disappear, the dangling pointer from the parent will indicate something has gone wrong. If a place dies, each finish checks if any of its child finishes were on that place. If so, the child pointer is used by the parent to find the backup and adopt the tasks. If a backup cannot be found, the fatal error is raised.

The finishes in the system thus form a distributed tree of masters and backups, with tasks referencing the masters, as shown in Figure 5. If a master is lost, one can still use the master reference to access the backup through the backup table. Thus the tree remains implicitly connected despite the loss of either M_n or B_n (but not both) for all n. When a parent finish adopts a child finish, it modifies its own list of child finishes by replacing the dead finish with the dead finish's child finishes. This process is repeated until all child finishes are alive, thus eliminating the dead finishes from the tree and ensuring there is no single point of failure. For example, if M_2 were to die, the tree would be modified such that M_2's tasks were governed by M_1 and M_1 would have M_3 and M_4 as child finishes.

5. Evaluation

We evaluate the practicality of the language design by writing one microbenchmark and three benchmark applications,

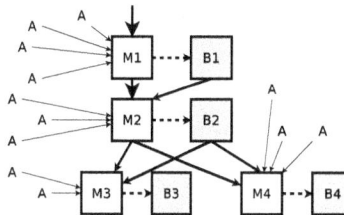

Figure 5. Distributed resilient finish tree.

each with a different approach to achieving resiliency. The microbenchmark tests the overhead of our X10-based finish implementations (compared to the regular algorithm). The applications show end-to-end running time and scalability, with and without resiliency.

Our benchmarking system is a 23 node AMD64 Linux cluster, each node having 16G RAM and 2 quad core AMD Opteron 2356 processors. The nodes are linked by gigabit ethernet, and are divided between two bladecenters. In this section we use Native X10 (the X10 C++ backend).

5.1 Microbenchmark

Just like X10, Resilient X10 supports arbitrary nesting of APGAS constructs. This makes the implementation challenging and can require significant runtime bookkeeping to orchestrate the running tasks and preserve the HBI Principle during failures. Therefore it is necessary to investigate both the constant overheads of this approach and identify potential scalability problems. To measure the overhead we wrote a number of microbenchmarks, each of which stresses the finish implementation in a different way. The microbenchmarks contain empty tasks, so only the termination detection overhead is measured. We tested many patterns but the differences we found can be illustrated with 3 of these in particular, shown in Figure 6.

The left benchmark spawns a single task at each place under a single finish (fan-out), and each of these tasks sends a single message back to the finish home place. This is of interest because it is a common pattern in our applications, e.g., Figure 1. The middle benchmark is a fan-out where each task creates its own local finish that governs 100 local tasks. This pattern occurs when using two levels of concurrency to both scale out and make use of multicore architectures. The right benchmark is a fan-out with each task doing another fan-out within a nested finish. This last case involves n^2 tasks and shows the non-scalability of the place-zero-based finish.

To demonstrate scalability on a machine that is closer to a typical supercomputer, we also ran these benchmarks on 13 node, 32 core per node *Power775* cluster, enabling a max of 416 places. These results are shown on the bottom row of graphs in Figure 6. We used the MPI backend of X10RT to take advantage of the cluster's very fast interconnect. This was possible because we were not testing failure, only overhead (the underlying HPC network library does not support

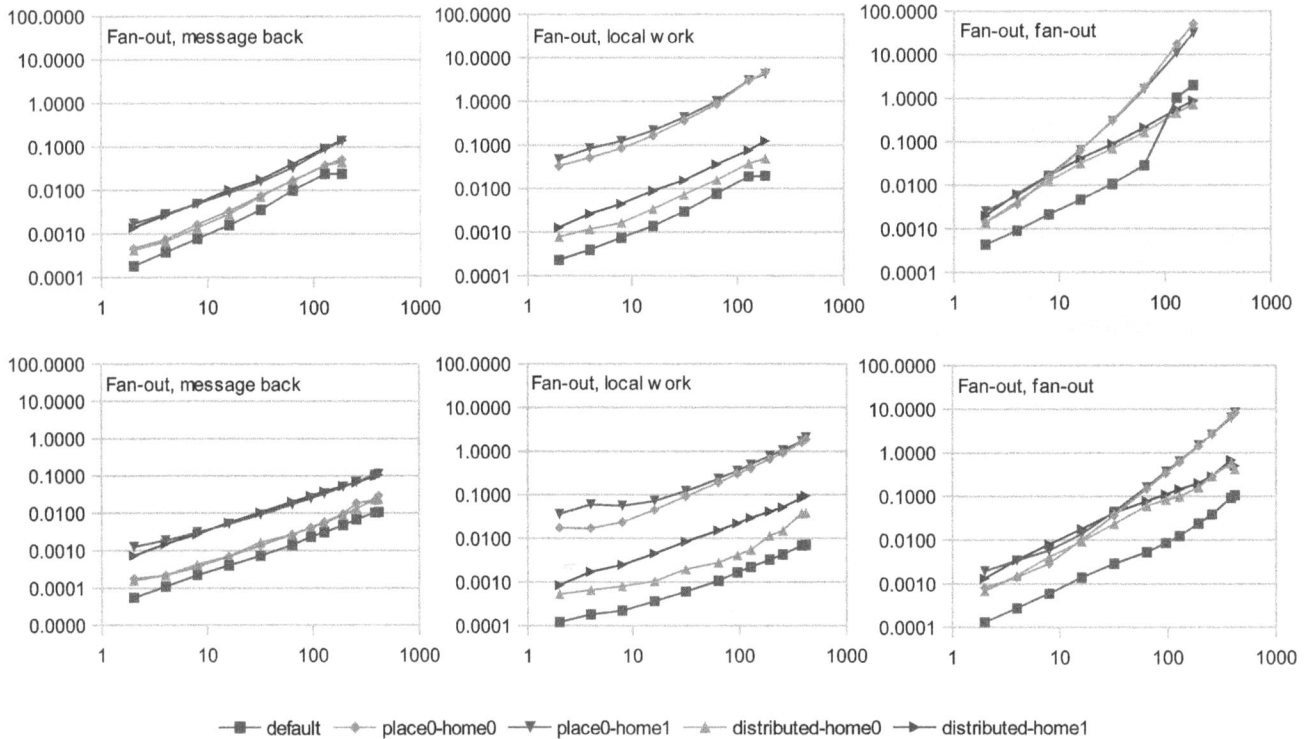

Figure 6. Scalability of the finish implementations, for different concurrency patterns. The top row of graphs are results from our 23 node AMD64 Linux cluster (max 184 places); the bottom row of graphs are results from a 13 node IBM Power775 cluster (max 416 places). The X axis is the number of places, the Y axis is the execution time in seconds.

failure). We hope that our work on Resilient X10 will motivate the development of HPC network libraries that handle failures so we can use them in the future.

We ran 5 experiments per benchmark. We compared the non-resilient (default), the place-zero-based and the distributed resilient finishes. Since the resilient implementations have different behaviors depending on whether the home is 0 or some other place, we ran the tests based at both place 0 and place 1. The results expose some qualitative differences between the implementations.

Firstly, there is a cost to resiliency. This is because resilient finish implementations require more synchronous communication because failure can preempt the execution at any time. In the left hand case, the two resilient implementations are similar in performance, but the need to store state in a resilient store (when finish is based outside of place 0) costs an order of magnitude in performance. In the middle case, the weakness of the place-zero-based implementation becomes clear: The distributed implementation is optimized to not store local tasks in the backup. However, the place-zero-based implementation must always communicate with place 0 even when managing local tasks. The final benchmark shows the place-zero-based implementation scaling very poorly because n^2 messages contend at place 0.

Exploiting our base assumption that place 0 will not fail, some communication is avoided for finishes based at place 0. This is why "home0" configurations showed slightly better performance than "home1" (i.e., non place 0 home). However, putting more work in place 0 can easily become a scalability bottleneck. It also depends on the application whether the `finishes` can be scattered among places.

In summary, there is measurable but manageable cost to resiliency. The place-zero-based implementation performs well enough in some cases but in general the distributed implementation is faster and more scalable.

5.2 Iterative sparse matrix dense vector multiply

This application represents a kernel found in a diverse range of analytics applications, including GNMF (Gaussian non-negative matrix factorization) and page rank. It was particularly interesting to us, because we had access to a Hadoop implementation of this algorithm that performed well within the Hadoop framework. This allowed direct comparison of Resilient X10 performance with Hadoop.

The input is an $N \times N$ sparse matrix (0.1% of elements are non-zero) of doubles, G, and a dense vector of N Doubles, V. The algorithm computes $U = G \times V$ and then U is used in place of V in the next iteration. Thus, the matrix remains constant for the whole execution but the vector converges to the end result. For benchmarking purposes we run for a fixed number (30) of iterations instead of testing convergence. Our input is randomly generated between 0 and 1. Both matrix and vector are blocked with a factor of 1000.

Since Hadoop only offers end-to-end (job) timings and does not separate disk I/O from other overheads, we implemented a full application capable of reading the input matrices and writing the resulting vector to disk. We used GPFS instead of HDFS, since GPFS manifests as an OS-level filesystem and thus the data was accessible using X10's standard I/O library. Rather than parse the file metadata from the Hadoop SequenceFileFormat, we wrote a Hadoop program to write out the data to a simpler format that we then read in the X10 program. The metadata is a negligible proportion of the file size so this does not affect our results.

This is not a computationally dense benchmark. During the matrix multiply, each matrix element is read from memory and has only one multiply-add instruction performed on it. Yet it is desirable to use more than one node because G will not fit in the memory of a single node. Therefore G is partitioned into $N/1000$ row blocks, and the multiplication work associated with these row blocks is divided across the available nodes as evenly as possible. The initial V is loaded from disk by place zero at initialization time. At each iteration, the places load any fragment of G they need but have not already loaded. Ignoring failures, this means G is loaded only once at the first iteration. When failures occur, the work assigned to dead places is reassigned, so places will load these new parts of G when they are first needed. When G is known to be ready, the input V is broadcast to all nodes. Each place uses all of V and its fragments of G to compute corresponding fragments of U. Finally the fragments of U are then concatenated at place zero to become the next iteration's V.

When distributed in the above manner on our cluster, the algorithm is network-bound as each place receives a full copy of V each iteration. For this reason we chose to use one worker thread and one place per node. There is not enough computational work to justify using more cores, and creating more places per node would just mean sharing RAM and network bandwidth. For the smallest data sizes, it may be possible to do the whole computation on one node to get better absolute performance. However we are primarily interested in investigating the scalability of the computation when the matrix (G) cannot fit in one node. Therefore all measurements are performed with the data distributed.

When a place fails, we lose its portion of G, the input V and its partially computed U. The loss of V is immaterial since that is duplicated on every other place. The partial loss of G is not a problem since it is never modified, and the lost fragments still exist on disk. The only real loss is the partial U which cannot be recovered without replaying that work.

Our implementation responds to place failure as follows: Any/all DPEs are caught together at the finish block for that

Size	Hadoop	X10	Res. X10	1 Dead Place
100K	3301	12	12	14
200K	3390	20	19	20
400K	3563	32	30	32
800K	5392	73	70	76
1M	6820	96	96	105
1.2M	8737	128	129	142
1.5M	12559	180	182	199
2M	21773	293	290	317
2.5M	33664	434	438	480
3M	52075	596	595	656

Table 2. End-to-end duration (seconds) for 30 iterations of sparse matrix dense vector multiply over the 23 nodes (23 places). In the final column, a place was killed at iteration 15; the longer execution time reflects the recovery and completion of the program with fewer nodes.

iteration. If there are any failures, the work assigned to the dead places is reassigned, all U are discarded and the last iteration is replayed with the new work assignment (missing out the dead nodes).[8] The execution then continues for the remaining iterations. Since G is now spread across fewer nodes, each place must have spare RAM to accommodate place failures. The cost of a failed place can be broken down: The previous iteration is lost, the remaining places must load their newly assigned parts of G from disk. Finally, each future iteration is slower due to each place having more work to do. Thus, the cost of place failure depends on the number of failures and when they occur.

In order to further improve the performance of the Resilient X10 version, we implemented the broadcast of V each iteration using a broadcast tree instead of naive iteration to each place. One must avoid dead places, so we modify the tree to avoid routing through places that have no work assigned. Our solution was simply to delete nodes of the tree and merge their children into the parent. A method that preserves the depth of the tree is future work.

In Table 2, we give the end-to-end times for various matrix sizes, running on our full cluster (23 nodes, 23 places). Hadoop is on average 100x slower than X10, due to excessive disk I/O. The cost of Resilient X10 as opposed to regular X10 is lost in the noise, and the cost of recovering from the a single node failure half way through execution is 10%.

In the case of size 3M, the Resilient X10 end-to-end time (596 seconds) breaks down into 273 seconds reading the matrix form disk, and 11 seconds per iteration. Clearly if the number of iterations were increased, the performance gap between X10 and Hadoop would increase. The 536 lines of code in this benchmark break down as follows: I/O: 33%, matrix/vector block data structures and multiply:

---

[8] Partial replay for faster recovery can be implemented, but we focused here on the non-failure overheads. Our long term vision is that such details would be handled by various frameworks depending on the resiliency model.

29%, distribution/concurrency control: 21%, command line options: 11%, failure handling: 6%.

We hope these results show that while Hadoop can be a good choice for certain large data traversals, it is not suitable for general-purpose cluster programming.

5.3 K-Means

The K-Means benchmark is a distributed implementation of Lloyd's algorithm. The problem is to find the k centroids that approximate the distribution of n points, where n is much larger than k. Arbitrarily, we chose our points to be $4D$ and represented with Floats.

The algorithm starts with guessed positions for the k centroids, and iteratively refines them. Each iteration, each centroid's new position is calculated by averaging the points for whom that centroid was closest. The algorithm is distributed by splitting the points evenly across places, and replicating the cluster positions across every place. Each iteration, each place uses its local points to calculate a partial average for the new cluster locations, and these are then aggregated to form the new clusters for the next iteration.

We chose this problem because it allows an approach to resilient programming that we call *decimation*. If a place dies, we simply use the remaining state to continue executing. This makes sense because in analytics, the input points are not precise, and likely to already be a sampling of a real phenomenon. The loss of an arbitrary but small percentage of that input should therefore yield an equivalent result. Other algorithms that operate on a sampled input dataset would also apply, such as any Monte Carlo problem.

The benefit of decimation is that error recovery is essentially instantaneous and the running time is unaffected by failures. If the input data is ordered in any meaningful way then loss of a contiguous portion of it could yield a substantially different result, but this can be fixed by storing the data in a random order. If failures are anticipated then the amount of input data can be over-provisioned to control the error bounds.

Implementing the decimation technique in Resilient X10 means catching and ignoring any DPEs that arise, and modifying the output to inform the user that the result is approximate due to place death. This requires only a few lines of code to be added to a regular implementation of K-Means in X10. We show the performance of the implementation in Figure 7. We execute the implementation on Resilient X10 (using the place 0 implementation of finish) and on regular X10. The measurements were done for 1 to 184 places allocated on the 23 nodes in a round-robin manner. The scaling is close to linear for the non-resilient case, and about 10% slower with the Resilient X10 runtime. The performance is not affected by failures.

5.4 Resilient Heat Transfer

The heat transfer application computes the diffusion of heat through a two-dimensional grid (represented with an array

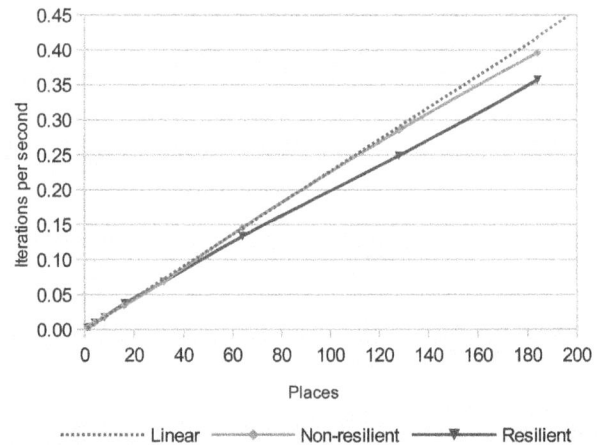

Figure 7. Strong scaling of K-Means ($n = 184000000$, $k = 100$), for 1 to 184 places over the 23 nodes.

of Double). The algorithm iteratively updates heat values by averaging the values from neighboring points (i.e. by performing a stencil computation – a common HPC pattern). Usually the computation is run until convergence but for benchmarking purposes we ran a fixed number of iterations.

The array of heat values is distributed across multiple places. Each place contains a *front* and *back* array. Each iteration, one of them is assigned to, while the other stores the last iteration's result. These arrays are 2 elements bigger in each dimension, so that they can store the *skirt*, i.e. the values they need from their neighbors. The skirt is updated via communication between places, each iteration.

While the matrix multiply benchmark had a large amount of state, most of it (G) was not updated during execution. This allowed recovery to proceed by reloading it from the original input files. Heat transfer also has a large amount of state, but this state is frequently updated during execution. A different approach to resiliency is thus required.

For resilience, the heat values array is periodically checkpointed into a resilient store. We chose a single backup in a neighboring place's RAM. This is easier and faster than disk I/O and means the application is self-contained, but has more memory overhead. Other variations are possible.

Upon failure, all state outside the resilient store is discarded. The data is recovered from the resilient store and redistributed according to a new distribution over the remaining nodes. Execution then continues from the last checkpoint iteration. The frequency of checkpointing can be customized. Depending on the speed of the network, the problem size, and the expected frequency of failures, it is possible to tune the checkpoint frequency to give the best end-to-end time. Infrequent checkpoints reduce checkpointing overhead, but require more CPU time to recover from failure.

In order to survive failure during the checkpointing operation, it is necessary to keep both old and new checkpoints

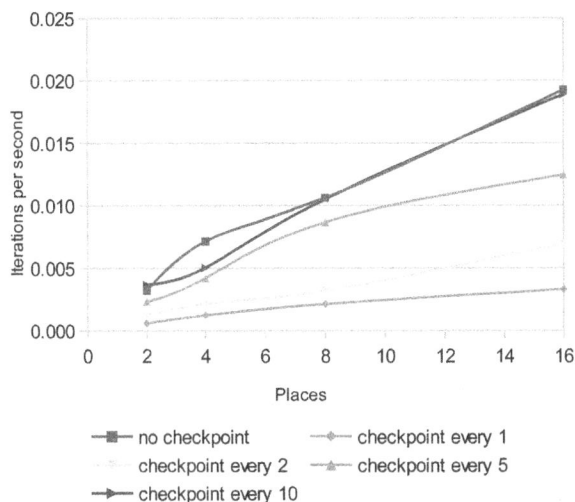

Figure 8. Strong scaling of heat transfer (16384×16384 grid) from 2 to 16 places with a variety of checkpointing frequencies.

in RAM until every place has finished checkpointing. This avoids the case where a place dies leaving its checkpoint not updated, but other places have completed their checkpoint. Recovering from that situation is impossible since there is no complete set of data for any given time point. This situation is analogous to using a disk storage, where the last checkpoint is not deleted until the new checkpoint is completely written. With our implementation, the space required is 3x that of the non-resilient version.

The stencil kernel is computationally non-intensive, so to avoid sharing the network interface we use 1 place per node. In Figure 8 we show the benchmark scaling to 16 nodes (16 places)[9] with a variety of checkpointing frequencies.

6. Conclusions and Future Work

We have designed and implemented an extension to X10 that allows general-purpose programming in an environment where node failure is common without compromising performance, scalability or productivity. We have made our implementation publicly available as part of the X10 2.4.1 open source release [1]. Resilient X10 preserves the happens before order of the original program, greatly simplifying the burden of handling node failures, while retaining performance transparency and allowing the programmer to use domain-specific knowledge to efficiently code resilient applications. We have measured the additional overhead of Resilient X10 in isolation, and found it to be modest, as well as scalable up to 416 places.

We have described three ways of writing resilient applications in X10. Replaying from disk is appropriate when there is a large amount of immutable state that can be recovered from the original input file. Decimation is appropriate for applications where an approximate result is acceptable; it is the simplest to achieve and also the fastest. Finally, if there is a large amount of mutable state then a resilient store can be implemented in Resilient X10 to allow state to be checkpointed in memory at neighboring nodes. Resilient X10 makes implementing such stores much easier than other languages, and they can also be provided as a utility library.

In the future, we would like to construct frameworks on top of Resilient X10 for transparent resilient programming in specialized programming models. A wide range of frameworks are possible: MapReduce, bulk synchronous parallelism, matrix processing, etc. Each should be easy to write on top of Resilient X10 since it provides a lot of the basic functionality required. Research into brand new paradigms for transparent resilient programming can also be conducted on top of Resilient X10.

We would also like to revisit our immortal place 0 design. One option is to decentralize the execution, allowing the code to start at every place and co-operate in a peer-to-peer fashion. Another option is to make place 0 transparently resilient (by synchronously checkpointing all the program state). This would allow relocating it upon failure, but would also cripple its performance. However that would not be a problem if the only work at place 0 is initialization, coordination and communication with the user. Extending basic distributed classes such as `DistArray` to make them resilient is also underway.

Finally, we would like to support adding new places during the execution as well as detecting failed places. This would allow nodes to be replaced, e.g. for online maintenance of highly available distributed applications such as web servers and databases.

Acknowledgments

We would like to thank Avraham Shinnar for his advice regarding the Hadoop comparison, Josh Milthorpe for helpful discussions about the fast multipole method and Silvia Crafa for discussions about semantics.

This work was funded in part by the Air Force Office of Scientific Research under Contract No. FA8750-13-C-0052.

References

[1] X10 web site, 2013. URL http://x10-lang.org/.

[2] T. Akidau, A. Balikov, K. Bekiroglu, S. Chernyak, J. Haberman, R. Lax, S. McVeety, D. Mills, P. Nordstrom, and S. Whittle. MillWheel: Fault-Tolerant Stream Processing at Internet Scale. In *Very Large Data Bases*, pages 734–746, 2013.

[3] Apache Software Foundation. ZooKeeper Recipes and Solutions, 2012. URL http://zookeeper.apache.org/doc/-current/recipes.html.

---

[9] Partitioning of the grid into equal squares is much harder for 23 nodes. To avoid additional communication overhead in the stencil algorithm by worse partitioning, we measured only 2, 4, 8 and 16 places.

[4] C. Bailey. Java Technology, IBM Style: Introduction to the IBM Developer Kit: An overview of the new functions and features in the IBM implementation of Java 5.0, 2006. URL http://www.ibm.com/developerworks/java/library/-j-ibmjava1.html.

[5] M. Carbin, D. Kim, S. Misailovic, and M. C. Rinard. Proving acceptability properties of relaxed nondeterministic approximate programs. In *Proceedings of the 33rd ACM SIGPLAN conference on Programming Language Design and Implementation*, PLDI '12, pages 169–180, 2012.

[6] P. Charles, C. Grothoff, V. Saraswat, C. Donawa, A. Kielstra, K. Ebcioglu, C. von Praun, and V. Sarkar. X10: an object-oriented approach to non-uniform cluster computing. In *OOPSLA*, pages 519–538, 2005.

[7] J. Chung, I. Lee, M. Sullivan, J. H. Ryoo, D. W. Kim, D. H. Yoon, L. Kaplan, and M. Erez. Containment Domains: A Scalable, Efficient, and Flexible Resilience Scheme for Exascale Systems. In *the Proceedings of SC'12*, November 2012.

[8] S. Crafa, D. Cunningham, V. Saraswat, A. Shinnar, and O. Tardieu. Semantics of (Resilient) X10. Dec. 2013. URL http://arxiv.org/abs/1312.3739.

[9] D. Cutting and E. Baldeschwieler. Meet Hadoop. In *O'Reilly Open Software Convention*, Portland, OR, 2007.

[10] C. Danis and C. Halverson. The Value Derived from the Observational Component in an Integrated Methodology for the Study of HPC Programmer Productivity. *Third Workshop on Productivity and Performance in High-End Computing*, page 11, 2006.

[11] M. Dayarathna, C. Houngkaew, H. Ogata, and T. Suzumura. Scalable performance of ScaleGraph for large scale graph analysis. In *HiPC*, pages 1–9. IEEE, 2012.

[12] J. Dean and S. Ghemawat. MapReduce: simplified data processing on large clusters. *Commun. ACM*, 51(1):107–113, Jan. 2008.

[13] K. Ebcioglu, V. Sarkar, T. El-Ghazawi, and J. Urbanic. An Experiment in Measuring the Productivity of Three Parallel Programming Languages. In *P-PHEC workshop, held in conjunction with HPCA*, February 2006.

[14] C. Halverson, C. B. Swart, J. P. Brezin, J. T. Richards, and C. M. Danis. The Value Derived from the Observational Component in an Integrated Methodology for the Study of HPC Programmer Productivity. *1st International Workshop on Software Engineering for Computational Science and Engineering*, 2008.

[15] P. Hunt, M. Konar, F. P. Junqueira, and B. Reed. ZooKeeper: wait-free coordination for internet-scale systems. In *Proceedings of the 2010 USENIX conference on USENIX annual technical conference*, pages 11–11, 2010.

[16] J. Lifflander, P. Miller, and L. Kale. Adoption Protocols for Fanout-Optimal Fault-Tolerant Termination Detection. In *18th ACM SIGPLAN Symposium on Principles and Practice of Parallel Programming*, PPoPP '13, February 2013.

[17] G. Malewicz, M. H. Austern, A. J. Bik, J. C. Dehnert, I. Horn, N. Leiser, and G. Czajkowski. Pregel: A system for large-scale graph processing. In *Proceedings of the 2010 ACM SIGMOD International Conference on Management of Data*, SIGMOD '10, pages 135–146, New York, NY, USA, 2010. ACM. ISBN 978-1-4503-0032-2. . URL http://doi.acm.org/10.1145/1807167.1807184.

[18] J. Milthorpe, V. Ganesh, A. P. Rendell, and D. Grove. X10 as a Parallel Language for Scientific Computation: Practice and Experience. In *IPDPS*, pages 1080–1088. IEEE, 2011.

[19] J. Milthorpe, A. P. Rendell, and T. Huber. PGAS-FMM: Implementing a distributed fast multipole method using the X10 programming language. *Concurrency and Computation: Practice and Experience*, pages n/a–n/a, 2013.

[20] PAMI Guide: http://tinyurl.com/pamiguide.

[21] Parallel Programming Laboratory. The Charm++ Parallel Programming System Manual. Technical Report version 6.4, Department of Computer Science , University of Illinois, Urbana-Champaign, 2013.

[22] V. Saraswat and R. Jagadeesan. Concurrent clustered programming. In *CONCUR 2005 - Concurrency Theory*, pages 353–367. Springer-Verlag, 2005.

[23] V. Saraswat, G. Almasi, G. Bikshandi, C. Cascaval, D. Cunningham, D. Grove, S. Kodali, I. Peshansky, and O. Tardieu. The Asynchronous Partitioned Global Address Space Model. In *The First Workshop on Advances in Message Passing (co-located with PLDI 2010)*, Toronto, Canada, June 2010.

[24] V. Saraswat, P. Kambadur, S. Kodali, D. Grove, and S. Krishnamoorthy. Lifeline-based global load balancing. In *Proceedings of the 16th ACM symposium on Principles and practice of parallel programming*, PPoPP '11, pages 201–212, 2011.

[25] A. Shinnar, D. Cunningham, V. Saraswat, and B. Herta. M3R: increased performance for in-memory Hadoop jobs. *Proc. VLDB Endow.*, 5(12):1736–1747, Aug. 2012.

[26] M. Takeuchi, Y. Makino, K. Kawachiya, H. Horii, T. Suzumura, T. Suganuma, and T. Onodera. Compiling X10 to Java. In *Proceedings of the 2011 ACM SIGPLAN X10 Workshop*, pages 3:1–3:10, 2011.

[27] M. Takeuchi, D. Cunningham, D. Grove, and V. Saraswat. Java interoperability in Managed X10. In *Proceedings of the third ACM SIGPLAN X10 Workshop*, pages 39–46, 2013.

[28] O. Tardieu, B. Herta, D. Cunningham, D. Grove, P. Kambadur, V. Saraswat, A. Shinnar, M. Takeuchi, and M. Vaziri. X10 and APGAS at Petascale. In *19th ACM SIGPLAN Symposium on Principles and Practice of Parallel Programming*, PPoPP '14, February 2014.

[29] T. White. *Hadoop: The Definitive Guide*. O'Reilly Media, Inc., 1st edition, 2009. ISBN 0596521979, 9780596521974.

[30] X10RT API: http://x10.sourceforge.net/x10rt/.

[31] C. Xie, Z. Hao, and H. Chen. X10-FT: transparent fault tolerance for APGAS language and runtime. In P. Balaji, M. Guo, and Z. H. 0001, editors, *PMAM*, pages 11–20. ACM, 2013.

[32] M. Zaharia, M. Chowdhury, M. J. Franklin, S. Shenker, and I. Stoica. Spark: cluster computing with working sets. In *Proceedings of the 2nd USENIX conference on Hot topics in cloud computing*, HotCloud'10, pages 10–10, 2010.

Portable, MPI-Interoperable Coarray Fortran

Chaoran Yang
Department of Computer Science
Rice University
chaoran@rice.edu

Wesley Bland
Math. and Comp. Sci. Division
Argonne National Laboratory
wbland@mcs.anl.gov

John Mellor-Crummey
Department of Computer Science
Rice University
johnmc@rice.edu

Pavan Balaji
Mathematics and Computer Science Division
Argonne National Laboratory
balaji@mcs.anl.gov

Abstract

The past decade has seen the advent of a number of parallel programming models such as Coarray Fortran (CAF), Unified Parallel C, X10, and Chapel. Despite the productivity gains promised by these models, most parallel scientific applications still rely on MPI as their data movement model. One reason for this trend is that it is hard for users to incrementally adopt these new programming models in existing MPI applications. Because each model use its own runtime system, they duplicate resources and are potentially error-prone. Such independent runtime systems were deemed necessary because MPI was considered insufficient in the past to play this role for these languages.

The recently released MPI-3, however, adds several new capabilities that now provide all of the functionality needed to act as a runtime, including a much more comprehensive one-sided communication framework. In this paper, we investigate how MPI-3 can form a runtime system for one example programming model, CAF, with a broader goal of enabling a single application to use both MPI and CAF with the highest level of interoperability.

Categories and Subject Descriptors D.3.2 [*Programming Languages*]: Language Classifications—Concurrent, distributed, and parallel languages; D.3.4 [*Programming Languages*]: Processors—Compilers, Runtime environments

Keywords Coarray Fortran; MPI; PGAS; Interoperability

PPOPP '14, February 15–19, 2014, Orlando, Florida, USA.
Copyright © 2014 ACM 978-1-4503-2656-8/14/02... $15.00.
http://dx.doi.org/10.1145/2555243.2555270

1. Introduction

Message Passing Interface (MPI) is the *de facto* standard for programming large-scale parallel programs today. There are several reasons for its success including a rich and standardized interface coupled with heavily optimized implementations on virtually every platform in the world. MPI's philosophy is simple: it's primary purpose is not to make simple programs easy to implement; rather, it is to make complex programs possible to implement.

In recent years a number of new programming models such as Coarray Fortran (CAF) [24], Unified Parallel C (UPC) [29], X10 [25], and Chapel [7] have emerged. These programming models feature a Partitioned Global Address Space (PGAS) where data is accessed through language load/store constructs that eventually translate to one-sided communication routines at the runtime layer. Together with the obvious productivity benefits of having direct language constructs for moving data, these languages also provide the potential for improved performance by utilizing the native hardware communication features on each platform.

Despite the productivity promises of these newer programming models, most parallel scientific applications are slow to adopt them and continue to use MPI as their data movement model of choice. One of the reasons for this trend is that it is not easy for programmers to incrementally adopt these new programming models in existing MPI applications. Because most of these new programming models have their own runtime systems, to incrementally adopt them, the user would need to initialize and use separate runtime libraries for each model within a single application. Not only does this duplicate the runtime resources, e.g. temporary memory buffers and metadata for memory segments, but it is also error-prone with a possibility for deadlock if not used in a careful and potentially in a platform-specific manner (more details to follow).

Why do we need Interoperable Programming Models?
Because of MPI's vast success in the parallel programming arena, a large ecosystem of tools and libraries has developed around it. There are high-level libraries using MPI for complex mathematical computations, I/O, visualization and data analytics, and almost every other paradigm used by scientific applications. One of the drawbacks of other programming models is that they do not enjoy such support, making it hard for applications to utilize them. For example, a new CAF application cannot directly utilize a math library (such as PETSc or Trillinos) that is written with MPI. Similarly, if one developed a high-performance FFT library in CAF, an MPI application cannot directly plug it in if the underlying runtime systems are not interoperable.

Such requirements are already seen in a number of scientific applications today. For example, in [23], Preissl et. al. identified that the Gyrokinetic Tokamak Simulation code that is based on MPI+OpenMP can naturally benefit from the language constructs in CAF that enable direct remote data accesses. Consequently, they modified their application to further hybridize it with MPI+CAF+OpenMP, and demonstrated performance improvements with such a model. QMCPACK [16], an MPI-based quantum monte-carlo package developed by Oak Ridge National Laboratory, and GFMC [17, 22], an MPI-based nuclear physics monte-carlo simulation developed by Argonne National Laboratory, both demonstrate such requirements as well. Specifically, both of these applications rely on large arrays that reside on each node for their core sequential computations, and they use MPI to communicate data between processes. As problem sizes grow, however, these arrays are becoming too large to reside on a single node, thus requiring the memory of multiple nodes to accommodate them. Hybridizing with MPI+CAF provides a natural extension for these MPI applications where they can simply define these arrays as CAF coarrays, allowing the runtime system to distribute them across nodes and convert load/store accesses of these arrays to remote data access operations.

Challenges in Interoperable Programming Models. There are several challenges in facilitating multiple programming models to interoperate with each other. Some of these aspects are related to the programming semantics and the execution model itself. For instance, for a programming model such as Chapel, which exposes a completely dynamic execution model where tasks can fork other tasks on demand, to interoperate with a more static model such as MPI, a clear definition of what the user is allowed to do needs to be specified. This part is not the focus of this paper. Instead we focus on interoperation of CAF and MPI, which have similar execution model semantics, with a number of images/processes that move data between each other.

Even for programming models with similar execution semantics, various challenges exist that make interoperability hard. For example, today, each programming model uses its

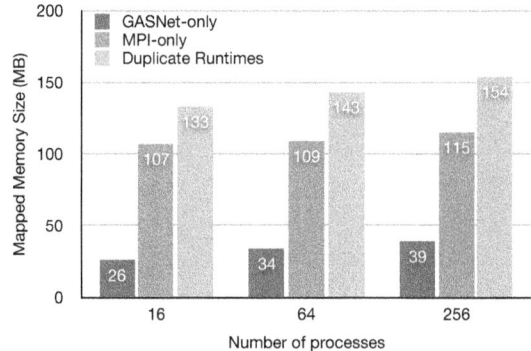

Figure 1. An example of memory usage when using both GASNet and MPI.

```
1  PROGRAM MAY_DEADLOCK
2  USE MPI
3
4  CALL MPI_INIT(IERR)
5  CALL MPI_COMM_RANK(MPI_COMM_WORLD, MY_RANK, IERR)
6
7  IF (MY_RANK .EQ. 0) THEN
8      A(:)[1] = A(:)
9  END IF
10
11 CALL MPI_BARRIER(MPI_COMM_WORLD, IERR)
12 CALL MPI_FINALIZE(IERR)
13 END PROGRAM
```

Figure 2. A CAF program that may deadlock because CAF cannot make progress when the process blocks in MPI.

own separate runtime system. For example, GASNet [5] is a common runtime system used by Berkeley UPC, CAF 2.0, and others. MPI, on the other hand, uses its own platform-specific runtime system. An application that uses multiple programming models would need to initialize and use multiple runtime systems in a single application, thus duplicating resources.

Figure 1 shows an example of the per-process memory usage when initializing both GASNet and MPI in an application.[1] The memory usage of both libraries grows along with the number of processes. The duplicated runtime resources reduce the resources available to an application, which will eventually hurt performance or prevent the application from running at a larger scale.

Using multiple runtime systems within a single application also makes it hard to reason about the correctness of codes. The semantics of an operation are often well-defined with respect to its own runtime system but are unclear when multiple runtime systems are used. For example, Figure 2 lists a simple CAF program that has the process with rank 0 perform a coarray write (line 8), then has every process participate in an **MPI_BARRIER** (line 11). Depending on the im-

---

[1] GASNet uses less memory than MPI because it saves data such as meta-data of memory segments in user-space buffers.

plementation of CAF, a coarray write operation may require the involvement of the target process to complete. Although such involvement is implicit, it requires the target process to make a runtime call to make progress internally. In this example, because the target process is likely to run into the **MPI_BARRIER** before seeing the write operation, the coarray write on process 0 may never complete. Some implementations of CAF may use a separate progress thread or have better support from the hardware allowing it to make asynchronous progress. This makes the scenario implementation-specific and even harder for users to debug.

Contributions of this paper. One possible solution to the interoperability issues described above is to use MPI as the runtime system for CAF, thus allowing all data movement to be funneled through a common runtime library. However, the use of MPI as a runtime system was previously deemed impossible for these PGAS programming models because MPI was considered inadequate to implement these models. Bonachea and Duell [6] put together a comprehensive list of reasons why the remote memory access (RMA) features introduced in the MPI-2 Standard fall short of the task of serving as a compilation target of PGAS languages. The recently released MPI-3 Standard, however, adds several new capabilities including a much more comprehensive one-sided communication (or RMA) model. These new additions not only address the critiques raised about MPI-2 RMA but also provide new functionality with performance benefits over existing PGAS runtime systems. But whether MPI-3 can live up to the goal of forming a runtime basis for PGAS programming models with these new additions is yet to be validated in practice.

In this paper, we investigate the capability of MPI in serving as the basis of a PGAS programming model such as CAF. We redesigned the runtime system of CAF 2.0, which was originally built on top of GASNet, to use MPI-3. The paper describes various design choices we made during this process. Further, we present the performance of CAF over MPI-3 relative to that of the original CAF implementation, and demonstrate that the MPI runtime system can achieve a comparable or better performance in several cases. We also point out some cases where the performance falls short of the existing implementation; in such cases we present a detailed analysis of the performance difference.

This paper is organized as follows: Section 2 presents an overview of CAF-2.0 and MPI-3 and serves as background knowledge for the later discussion of the paper. Section 3 describes the design of the CAF-MPI runtime system. In Section 4 we evaluate our implementation using three HPC Challenge Benchmarks [11] and the CGPOP miniapp [27], which uses both CAF and MPI. In Section 5 we discuss possible extensions to the MPI-3 RMA interface that may provide further benefits when using MPI as the basis of PGAS languages. We discuss related work in Section 6 and present a summary of our work in Section 7.

2. Overview of CAF and MPI-3

To make the paper relatively self-contained, this section briefly introduces the necessary context for this paper. We will give an overview of CAF [18] and MPI-3 [19]. For further background information, refer to the cited papers.

2.1 Coarray Fortran 2.0

We choose Coarray Fortran 2.0 (CAF 2.0) [18], developed by Rice University, as our PGAS programming model to test the new capabilities of MPI-3. CAF 2.0 is an open source implementation of CAF and also contains a richer set of PGAS extensions than CAF-1 that is integrated into the Fortran 2008 standard. CAF 2.0 better represents the semantics and requirements of modern PGAS languages and would provide a better picture of the appropriateness of MPI-3 as a basis for these models. We describe the PGAS extensions in CAF 2.0 that are not included in Fortran 2008 standard in this section.

Teams. In CAF 2.0, a team is a first-class entity that represents a group of processes, analogous to an MPI communicator. Teams in CAF 2.0 serve three purposes: (a) the set of images in a team serves as a domain onto which coarrays may be allocated; (b) a team provides a name space within which images can be indexed by their relative rank within that team; (c) a team provides an isolated domain for members of a team to communicate and synchronize collectively. When a CAF program starts, all images belong to the same team named TEAM_WORLD, and new teams can be created with the team_split operation.

Synchronization. CAF 2.0 provides a rich set of synchronization constructs. These constructs are designed to enable programmers to structure correct parallel programs while allowing maximum opportunity to hide communication latency with computation. These constructs were previously introduced by Yang et. al. in [32].

Pair-wise synchronization between process images in CAF 2.0 can be achieved with *events*, a first-class entity in CAF 2.0. An event must be initialized with event_init before any other operation can occur. Events can be allocated as coarrays to enable them to be posted by other process images. One posts an event with the event_notify operation. An event_wait operation blocks execution of the current thread until the event is posted. event_trywait is a non-blocking operation which tests whether an event is posted and returns immediately.

To synchronize asynchronous operations (described in the next subsection), CAF 2.0 provides two synchronization models: the *implicit synchronization* model, and the *explicit synchronization* model. All asynchronous operations in CAF 2.0 optionally accept event arguments. Asynchronous operations invoked with an event argument are *explicitly synchronized operations*. The events passed to asynchronous operations are notified by the runtime system when the synchronization point is reached. One can test or wait for the event to synchronize these operations.

One can also use the implicit synchronization model to synchronize asynchronous operations. CAF 2.0 provides `cofence` statements and `finish` blocks to serve this purpose. A `cofence` statement blocks the current thread until all asynchronous operations issued before the statement complete locally. More specifically, a `cofence` ensures all local buffers used by asynchronous operations issued previously are ready to be reused. A `cofence` also serves as a compiler barrier; operations are not allow to be reordered across a `cofence` statement.

`finish` is a block-structured global synchronization construct in CAF 2.0, demarcated by `finish` and `end finish` statements. `finish` in CAF 2.0 is similar to the `finish` block in X10; it ensures that all asynchronous operations issued within the block are globally complete before current thread exits from the block. However, unlike the `finish` statement in X10, a `finish` statement in CAF 2.0 is a collective operation. A `finish` statement takes a team variable, and each process image within the associated team should create a `finish` block that matches those of its teammates. When the thread exits from the block, all operations issued by all images within the team are globally complete. `finish` blocks can be nested within each other; this is useful because it allows asynchronous operations issued within the outer `finish` block to proceed while the process is waiting for the inner `finish` block to complete, which yields more opportunity for communication-computation overlapping.

Asynchronous operations. CAF 2.0 provides three categories of asynchronous operations: *asynchronous copy*, *asynchronous collectives*, and *function shipping*. Scherer et. al. and Yang provide detailed descriptions of these operations elsewhere [26, 31].

A `copy_async` operation transfers data from a buffer (the source) to another buffer (the destination) asynchronously. The source and destination may be local or remote coarrays. An asynchronous copy takes three optional event arguments: the predicate event, the source event, and the destination event. The copy may proceed after its predicate event is posted. The source event, when posted, indicates the source buffer is ready to be reused. Notification of the destination event indicates the data has been delivered to the destination; the destination is ready to be read.

Asynchronous collectives have similar functionality as their synchronous versions except that they are non-blocking. For example, `team_reduce_async` performs a reduction across a team asynchronously. An asynchronous collective takes two optional event arguments: the data completion event and the operation completion event. The data completion event indicates the local buffer is ready to be read, and the operation completion event indicates the local buffer is ready to be modified.

Function shipping is an new addition of CAF 2.0 that enables programmers to transfer computation to where data is located, rather than moving data towards computation. The design of CAF 2.0 function shipping mechanism allows the shipped function to perform the full range of CAF 2.0 operations, e.g., spawning more functions, performing blocking communications, and synchronization.

2.2 MPI-3 Remote Memory Access Extensions

The MPI-3 Standard improved the MPI-2 RMA functionality in a number of ways including the addition of atomic operations, request-generating RMA operations, new synchronization operations in passive target epochs, a new unified memory model, and new window types. This section serves as a introductory description of the features relevant to this paper.

One-sided atomic operations. MPI-3 RMA provides several operations that enable one to manipulate data in target windows atomically. **MPI_ACCUMULATE** and **MPI_GET_ACCUMULATE** operations allow remote atomic updates of data, with **MPI_GET_ACCUMULATE** further fetching the original remote data back to the origin. The MPI-3 Standard also defines **MPI_FETCH_AND_OP**, which is a special case of **MPI_GET_ACCUMULATE** for single element predefined datatypes (to provide a fast-path for such operations), and **MPI_COMPARE_AND_SWAP**, which provides a remote compare-and-swap operation.

Request-generating operations. MPI-3 adds 'R' versions of most of the RMA operations that return request handles, such as **MPI_RPUT**, **MPI_RGET**, and **MPI_RACCUMULATE**. The request handles returned by these operations can be later passed to MPI request completion routines, such as **MPI_WAIT**, to manage local completion of the operation. These request-generating operations may be used only in passive target synchronization epochs.

MPI-allocated windows. MPI-3 adds several new routines for creating windows. **MPI_WIN_ALLOCATE** allows the MPI implementation to allocate memory for a window, rather than using a user allocated buffer. When MPI allocates memory for a window, it has the opportunity to allocate special memory regions such as aligned memory segments across a group or shared memory regions, which reduces the overhead of RMA operations performed on that window. **MPI_WIN_ALLOCATE_SHARED** will allocate memory that is shared by all processes in the group of the communicator when the processes belong to the same shared-memory node. **MPI_WIN_CREATE_DYNAMIC** creates a window without memory attached; one can dynamically attach memory later with **MPI_WIN_ATTACH**.

Unified memory model. MPI-2 RMA assumes no coherence in the memory subsystem or network interface, resulting in logically distinct *public* and *private* copies of a window. This conservative model (the *separate* model) is a poor match for systems where coherent memory subsystems are available. The new *unified* memory model added in MPI-3 better exposes these hardware capabilities to the user. This assumption relaxes several restrictions present in the *separate* model such as access to non-overlapping regions in a window by an **MPI_PUT** and a regular store operation concurrently, thus allowing for higher concurrency in access to the window data.

Passive target synchronization. MPI-3 adds a pair of locking routines to lock and unlock all targets of a window simultaneously. With **MPI_WIN_LOCK_ALL**, finer-grained synchronization can be achieved, for example using request-generating operations described earlier in this section. Two new synchronization routines, **MPI_WIN_FLUSH** and **MPI_WIN_FLUSH_ALL**, were also added that allow the user to complete all operations initiated by an origin process to a specified target or to all targets.

3. Designing CAF over MPI-3

In this section, we describe the key details of a new implementation of CAF 2.0 using MPI-3 as its communication substrate. CAF 2.0 features that are trivial to implement with MPI, e.g., teams and collectives, are left out due to space constrains. In the rest of the paper, we will sometimes refer to our implementation of CAF as CAF-MPI and the original CAF 2.0 as CAF-GASNet.

3.1 Coarrays

Coarrays are the main addition of CAF to Fortran 95. Coarrays add a codimension to a plain Fortran array. The codimension indicates the process image on which an array is located. Coarrays on remote images can be accessed with a Fortran 95 array section syntax plus a codimension. Thus, reading from or writing to a remote coarray is a one-sided operation that is mapped naturally to **MPI_GET** and **MPI_PUT**.

The original CAF 2.0 runtime system represents a reference to a remote memory location with a (image_ID, address) tuple. Because MPI RMA hides the absolute address of a remote memory in the window object, and currently provides no interface to access this information, we augmented the tuple with a remote coarray location that includes with an window object and the offset from the start of the window. Thus, the new remote memory reference become a (window, rank, displacement) tuple.

CAF-MPI allocates coarrays using **MPI_WIN_ALLOCATE**. With **MPI_WIN_ALLOCATE**, an MPI implementation can potentially improve performance by allocating aligned memory segments or shared memory regions for the window.

The semantics of coarray read and write operations require the effect of the operation to be globally visible after the operation completes. Proper synchronization is needed to ensure this semantic. Because the active target synchronization model in MPI requires the participation of the tar-

get processes, it is more convenient to use the passive target synchronization model in CAF. With the new additions of synchronization routines in the MPI-3 passive target model, we can lock all targets with **MPI_WIN_LOCK_ALL** when a coarray is allocated. Blocking read and write operations in CAF-MPI use **MPI_WIN_FLUSH** to ensure remote completion. The target processes of a window are only unlocked when the coarray is deallocated.

3.2 Active Messages

Active Messages (AM) [30] are an integral component of GASNet. The CAF runtime system of makes heavy use of them in various places, e.g., function shipping and event mechanisms. For CAF-MPI, we implemented Active Messages using MPI's two-sided communication routines. Our design of the AM interface is a near-exact replica of the AM interface in the GASNet core API to maintain maximum compatibility with the original CAF 2.0 runtime system. GASNet's AM API consists of three categories of AM: the short Active Messages carry only a few integer arguments, the medium Active Message can carry an opaque data payload in addition to integer arguments, and the long Active Message can also carry an opaque data payload but user needs to specify a predetermined address in the target process's memory space to receive the data payload. The number of integer arguments that a short AM can carry can be queried with gasnet_AMMaxArgs() function; the size of the data payload a medium AM can carry can be queried with gasnet_AMMaxMedium(). Providing different APIs for different message sizes allows the compiler to generate more efficient code when the message size is known at compile time.

Since AMs are used in many places in CAF 2.0's runtime system, its performance is critical. To ensure a fast message injection rate for AM, we used **MPI_ISEND** to send all messages. Integer arguments of medium data payload are internally buffered to use **MPI_ISEND**, and waiting for local completion of the send operation is delayed until the next synchronization point. The data payload of long AMs are sent with an extra blocking **MPI_SEND**. Theoretically, this extra send could be replaced by an **MPI_PUT** operation to avoid the internal data buffering within MPI. However, because the current MPI standard does not provide a mechanism to notify the target on the arrival of an **MPI_PUT**, it is hard to ensure that the AM is invoked only after its data payload arrives. Hence we stayed with the **MPI_SEND** based design in our approach.

3.3 Asynchronous Operations

The original CAF 2.0's asynchronous progression model is based on a common progress engine that all aspects of the CAF runtime plug into. Thus, if a process is waiting on one CAF event, the runtime can make progress on other operations that are internally queued up. This progress model is similar to what most runtime systems, including MPI, use.

When redesigning CAF's runtime system with MPI, one of the restrictions we faced was with the asynchronous progress engine as it relates to MPI RMA operations. Specifically, the MPI-3 Standard does not provide a mechanism to test for remote completion for all MPI RMA operations. The 'R' versions of MPI RMA operations (e.g., **MPI_RPUT** and **MPI_RGET**) provide requests that can be tested or waited on for completion but completion of this request only refers to local completion for **MPI_RPUT** and **MPI_RACCUMULATE**, while it refers to both local and remote completion for **MPI_RGET** and **MPI_RGET_ACCUMULATE**. For remote completion of **MPI_PUT** and **MPI_ACCUMULATE**, MPI-3 only provides **MPI_WIN_FLUSH** and **MPI_WIN_FLUSH_ALL**, apart from the epoch close operations such as **MPI_WIN_LOCK** and **MPI_WIN_LOCK_ALL**. These operations can be blocking (e.g., when someone else is holding the lock) and do not have a request handler that can be used to test for their completion.

To workaround this issue, we use the following mapping of operations:

1. For one-sided communication operations, if no local or remote completion event is requested, we use **MPI_PUT** and **MPI_GET**.

2. If a local or remote completion event is requested for GET-style operations, we use **MPI_RGET** which returns an MPI request on which we can wait or test.

3. If only a local completion event is requested for a PUT-style operation, we use **MPI_RPUT** which returns an MPI request on which we can wait or test.

4. If a remote completion event is requested for a PUT-style operation, we use active messages (that are based on **MPI_SEND** and **MPI_RECV** as described in Section 3.2) to transfer data in the source buffer to the target process, copy data into the destination buffer, then post the destination event associated with the asynchronous operation. This option is obviously not as efficient as a direct **MPI_PUT** or **MPI_GET**, which can be implemented more efficiently on current network hardware. But it provides the necessary functionality. We will further discuss this limitation of MPI-3 and other possible solutions in Section 5.

3.4 Explicit Event Notification

There are two obvious approaches to implement the event mechanism in CAF-MPI. One approach is to leverage the newly added **MPI_FETCH_AND_OP** operation in MPI-3 to notify an event and use the **MPI_COMPARE_AND_SWAP** operation to busy-wait for the event to be posted in `event_wait`. The second approach is to use **MPI_ISEND** to notify an event and use **MPI_RECV** to wait for the event to be posted. The performance implication of these two methods are unclear at this point and may largely depend on the underlying MPI implementation. CAF-MPI used the second method

since the performance of **MPI_SEND** and **MPI_RECV** routines are more well-tuned to date, and a two-sided communication model fits more naturally the `event_notify` and `event_wait` model.

`event_wait` is a blocking operation; it blocks the process until the event being waited upon is posted. To be semantically correct, `event_wait` also forbids asynchronous operations in program order after an `event_wait` from being reordered to a position before the `event_wait` (i.e., it also functions as a compiler barrier). This restriction is guaranteed by the code generation process of CAF-MPI source-to-source translator. `event_wait` uses a blocking network polling operation to wait for a specific message to arrive; the polling operation internally uses MPI blocking receive. The benefit of using a blocking polling operation allows the MPI runtime to make progress internally to respond to other processes' requests.

The semantics of the `event_notify` operation specify that when a process posts the notification for an event, the target of the event can only see the notification after all previous operations issued by the notifying process are complete at their respective targets. However, the notification itself is nonblocking to avoid a possible deadlock situation caused by circular `event_wait` and `event_notify` chains. We implement `event_notify` with a release barrier and an short AM request. The release barrier holds a request handle to every asynchronous operation initiated locally. Upon `event_notify`, the release barrier waits to complete all its request handles with **MPI_WAITALL**; this ensures local completion of these operations. Furthermore, a **MPI_WIN_FLUSH_ALL** is required to ensure the remote completion of all previous operations. The actual notification in `event_notify` is performed by sending an AM request to the target process. We use an **MPI_ISEND** to avoid the deadlock possibility mentioned above.

3.5 `cofence` and `finish`

Thanks to the new additions of request-generating RMA operations in MPI-3, local completion of RMA operations can be easily waited upon using the request handles of RMA operations. The `cofence` statement takes an optional argument that a user can use to request local completion notification of PUT or GET operations. Thus, CAF-MPI runtime system internally maintains an array of request handles of implicitly synchronized PUT operations and another array of request handles of implicitly synchronized GET operations. The `cofence` statement translates to an **MPI_WAITALL** call for the local completion of these operations.

`finish` is implemented in the same way as in the original CAF implementation; it uses a distributed termination detection algorithm presented by Yang [31]. Yang's algorithm detects termination by repeatedly performing SUM reductions across a team to compute the global difference between the number of shipped functions and the number of completed functions shipped from others. Global termination occurs when a sum reduction yields zero for the difference. This algorithm uses n rounds of reductions in the worst case, where n is the length of the longest chain of function shipping calls in the `finish` block. We also implement a fast version of `finish` that can be used when function shipping is not used in an application. This version of `finish` involves calling **MPI_WIN_FLUSH_ALL** on every window that the local process has touched within the block followed by an **MPI_BARRIER** across the team associated with the `finish` block.

4. Evaluation

We have evaluated CAF-MPI on two platforms: Fusion, an InfiniBand cluster at Argonne National Laboratory, and Edison, a Cray XC30 system at Lawrence Berkeley National Laboratory. The hardware characteristics of these systems are given in Table 1. For each platform, we compare the performance of CAF-MPI with CAF-GASNet. We evaluate the performance of our implementation with three HPC Challenge Benchmarks: HPL, FFT, and RandomAccess [11]. These benchmarks exhibit different communication vs. computation ratios and data access patterns and thus can serve as representative examples for a wide range of applications. We also demonstrate the performance of CAF-MPI with the CGPOP miniapp, which uses both CAF and MPI simultaneously. All benchmarks are compiled with Intel compilers and optimization level "-O3" on both platforms.

4.1 RandomAccess Benchmark

The HPC Challenge RandomAccess benchmark evaluates the rate at which a parallel system can apply read-modify-write updates to randomly indexed entries in a distributed table. Performance of the RandomAccess benchmark is measured in Giga Updates Per second (GUP/s). GUP/s is calculated by identifying the number of table entries that were randomly updated in one second, divided by 1 billion (10^9).

The CAF 2.0 implementation of RandomAccess uses a software routing algorithm that uses a hypercube-based pattern of bulk communication to route updates to the process image co-located with the table index being updated. The CAF 2.0 primitives most heavily used in the RandomAccess benchmark are coarray `write` and `event_notify`.

Because the performance of RandomAccess benchmark largely depends on the performance of one-sided communication of the communication library used. The result of RandomAccess benchmark is a good indication of the overhead of the communication library on top of the underlying network hardware. Figure 3 shows the performance difference of RandomAccess between CAF-MPI and CAF-GASNet on Fusion. The CAF-GASNet version of RandomAccess outperforms the CAF-MPI version by a small constant factor up to 64 cores; this indicates that the overhead of the MPI-3 RMA implementation has a constant overhead for each operation which is higher than the overhead of GASNet RMA.

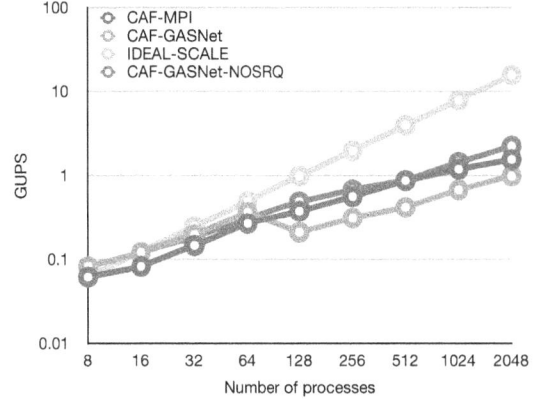

Figure 3. Performance of RandomAccess benchmark on Fusion.

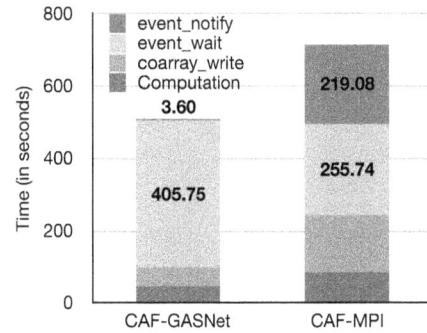

Figure 4. Time decomposition of RandomAccess on 2048 cores on Fusion.

CAF-GASNet's performance drops at 128 cores. Further investigation shows that this is caused by the use of the Shared Receive Queue (SRQ) in GASNet. The default configuration of GASNet library automatically enables SRQ as soon as doing so reduces the memory usage of GASNet. The effect of using SRQ in MVAPICH2 is not noticed in our experiment of up to 2048 cores. By disabling the use of SRQ in GASNet, CAF-GASNet performs roughly the same as CAF-MPI. The CAF-GASNet version shows slightly better scalability than the CAF-MPI version on 1024 and larger cores.

We profiled the 2048-core run of RandomAccess with HPCToolkit [2] to analyze CAF-MPI; the analysis results are shown in Figure 4. The CAF-MPI version of RandomAccess spends around 200 seconds in `event_notify` while the CAF-GASNet version spends almost none. This is because of how `event_notify` is implemented in these two libraries. In CAF-MPI, `event_notify` invokes **MPI_WIN_FLUSH_ALL** to ensure that all previously issued operations have been completed before performing the notification. The current implementation of **MPI_WIN_FLUSH_ALL** in all MPICH derivatives (including MVAPICH and Cray MPI) performs a flush operation on each process within the communicator; hence the execution time of **MPI_WIN_FLUSH_ALL** grows linearly with the number of processes. This is, of course, a

System	Nodes	Cores per Node	Memory per Node	Interconnect	MPI Version
Cluster (Fusion)	320	2 x 4	36GB	InfiniBand QDR	MVAPICH2-1.9
Cray XC30 (Edison)	5,200	2 x 12	64GB	Cray Aries	CRAY-MPICH-6.0.2

Table 1. Experimental platforms and system characteristics.

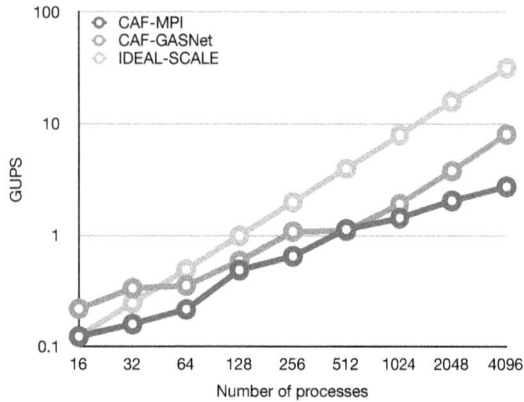

Figure 5. Performance of RandomAccess benchmark on Edison.

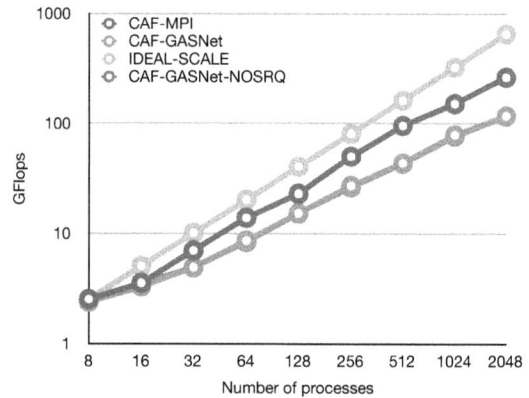

Figure 6. Performance of FFT benchmark on Fusion.

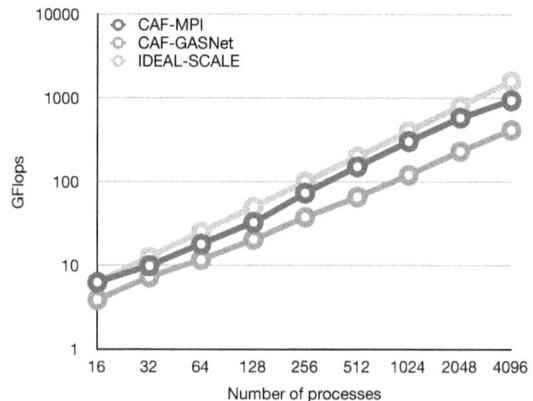

Figure 7. Performance of FFT benchmark on Edison.

simple performance scalability issue that can be addressed within the MPI implementation, but as of the writing of this paper, this issue exists.

The performance of RandomAccess on Edison, shown in Figure 5, tells roughly the same story as it does on Fusion. The MPI-3 RMA operations in Cray MPI are currently implemented internally with send and receive routines rather than directly leveraging RDMA support in the network. This causes a more obvious performance loss of CAF-MPI version of RandomAccess on Edison. Better implementations of MPI RMA on Cray platforms, such as foMPI [10], already exist and deliver performance competitive with CAF and UPC. However, the foMPI implementation is not integrated into Cray MPI yet.

4.2 FFT Benchmark

The HPC Challenge FFT benchmark measures the ability of a system to overlap computation and communication while calculating a very large Discrete Fourier Transform of size m. Performance of the FFT benchmark is measured in GFLOP/s, with calculated performance defined as $5\frac{m\log_2 m}{t}10^{-9}$, where m is the size of the DFT and t is the execution time in seconds. Parallel FFT algorithms have been well studied in the past [3, 13, 28].

The CAF 2.0 FFT implementation uses a radix-2 binary exchange formulation that consists of three parts: permutation of data to move each source element to the position that is its binary bit reversal; local FFT computation for as many layers of the DFT calculation as can fit in the memory of a single processor; and remote DFT computation for the layers that span multiple processor images. The CAF 2.0 FFT im-

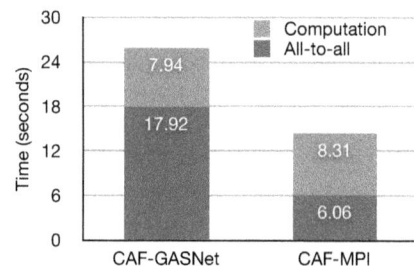

Figure 8. Time decomposition of FFT on 256 cores on Fusion.

plementation solely uses all-to-all operation for data movement.

Figures 6 and 7 show the performance of the FFT benchmark on Fusion and Edison, respectively. The CAF-MPI version consistently outperforms CAF-GASNet on both plat-

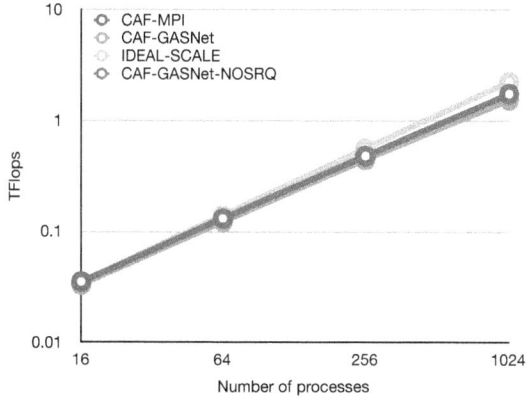

Figure 9. Performance of HPL benchmark on Fusion.

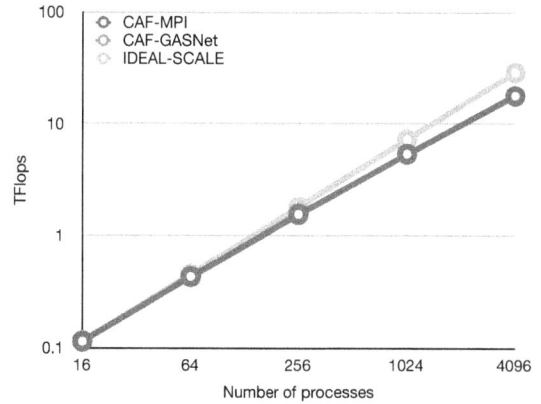

Figure 10. Performance of HPL benchmark on Edison.

forms at different scales. To analyze the performance difference of the two versions of FFT, we use HPCToolkit to profile the benchmark run on 256 cores on Fusion. Figure 8 illustrates how much of the execution time of FFT is spent in local computation and communication (all-to-all to be specific). We can see that the performance difference in two versions of FFT is caused largely by the performance of all-to-all operations used in CAF's runtime system. Because GASNet currently does not have collectives, CAF-GASNet implements alltoall operation with GASNet's PUT, GET, and Active Messages. This is not as well tuned as **MPI_ALLTOALL**, which has been used and well-optimized for many years on most computing platforms today.

4.3 HPL Benchmark

The High-Performance Linpack (HPL) [1] benchmark measures the ability of a system to deliver fast floating point execution while solving a system of linear equations. HPL is one of the most common implementations of parallel LU factorization for distributed memory systems. HPL has been previously ported to CAF 2.0 by Jin et. al. [12]. HPL differs greatly from the RandomAccess and FFT benchmarks described earlier because its performance is mostly dominated by computation rather than communication.

Figures 9 and 10 show the performance of HPL on Fusion and Edison, respectively. Between the two CAF implementations, HPL's performance difference is hardly noticeable. Because the performance of HPL benchmark is mostly computation bound, the performance difference of using different communication library has little effect on HPL's overall performance.

4.4 The CGPOP Miniapp

The CGPOP miniapp is the conjugate gradient solver from LANL POP 2.0, an important multi-agency code used for global ocean modeling and is a component within the Community Earth System Model. CGPOP is the performance bottleneck for the full POP application; it implements a version of conjugate gradient that uses a single inner product

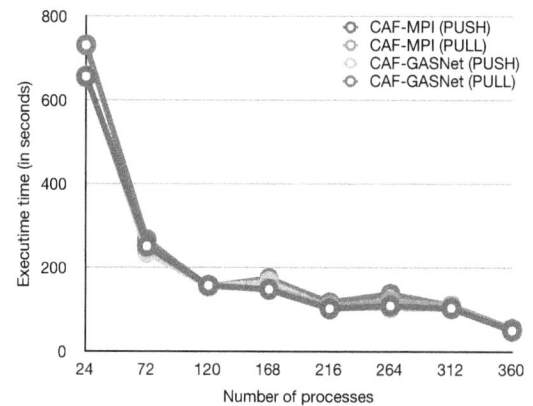

Figure 11. Performance of CGPOP on Fusion.

to iteratively solve for vector x in the equation $Ax = b$. The algorithm consists of a number of linear algebra computations interleaved with two communication steps. The `GlobalSum` function performs a 3-word vector reduction, while `UpdateHalo` function performs a boundary exchange between neighboring sub-domains. The CGPOP miniapp was ported to CAF for evaluating the performance gains of using a PGAS programming model for the performance critical part of POP. It is a hybrid MPI+CAF application that uses CAF coarray primitives for data exchange and **MPI_REDUCE** for reduction operations.

Figures 11 and 12 show the performance results of CGPOP on Fusion and Edison, respectively. On Edison, we can hardly see a difference in the performance of CGPOP between the two CAF implementations. On Fusion, the performance of the two CAF implementations only differs slightly when running on a small number of cores. Since both CAF versions of CGPOP use **MPI_REDUCE**, the only possible cause of performance difference in two versions of CGPOP is the use of PUT and GET operations used by CAF-MPI and CAF-GASNet. The lack of a performance difference indicates that both implementations are equally efficient in the raw **MPI_PUT** and **MPI_GET** operations.

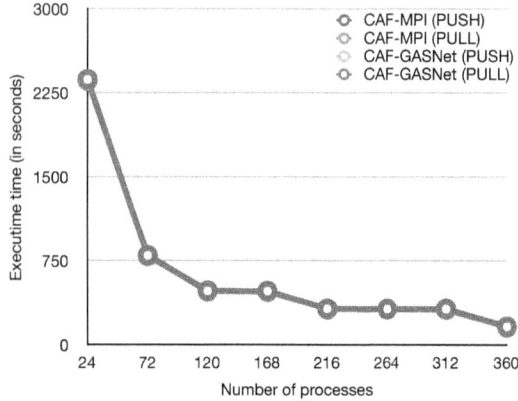

Figure 12. Performance of CGPOP on Edison.

5. Discussion

In this section, we discuss our findings during the process of redesigning CAF 2.0 runtime system to use MPI. Using MPI as the basis of a PGAS runtime system, such as CAF, reveals several advantages of using MPI over a low-level networking layer such as GASNet. We also discovered several features that the current MPI Standard lacks which can be useful in building a PGAS runtime system.

The benefits of MPI's rich interface. Compared with GASNet and other low-level networking layers, MPI provides a much richer set of API functions to support different high-level libraries, languages, and applications. We found this rich interface to be immensely time-saving when building a runtime system that delivers high performance across various platforms. For example, because GASNet does not have collectives, collective operations in CAF are hand-crafted in its runtime system on top of GASNet. Not only is this time consuming, but also based on our evaluation, not as performant as the MPI collectives. Because collectives in MPI are well-optimized over the years by different MPI implementations on different platforms, harnessing the performance benefits of these fully-optimized collectives in MPI is valuable for a programming model, such as CAF, which provides both one-sided and two-sided operations.

The need for Active Messages in MPI. One of the goals of building an interoperable runtime system for CAF is to allow the runtime system to make progress for both CAF and MPI when applications make blocking calls in either one. The current implementation of CAF-MPI can stay true to this goal for all parts of its runtime except active messages. Because we built the AM subsystem on top of **MPI_SEND** and **MPI_RECV**, the CAF-MPI runtime has to do further processing of a message to invoke the AM handler. The MPI runtime itself cannot invoke the handler. Thus, if the application is blocked inside an MPI call, no progress is made on such AM handlers.

Having AM support inside MPI can solve this problem. AMs are essential for building runtime systems for various programming models, especially for models such as X10,

Chapel, and CAF 2.0 that supports dynamic task parallelism. Zhao et. al. [33, 34] have made an effort in this direction to support MPI-interoperable Active Messages, but such a model is not a part of the current MPI Standard.

The need for non-blocking flush operation in MPI. In passive target epochs, the MPI Standard provides two routines: **MPI_WIN_FLUSH** and **MPI_WIN_FLUSH_ALL** for ensuring remote completion of RMA operations without closing the access epoch. These routines can be blocking calls (e.g., if another image is holding the lock). As discussed in Section 3.3, the blocking **MPI_WIN_FLUSH** operation eliminates the potential opportunity for overlapping the latency of communication with local computation. A nonblocking request-based version of **MPI_WIN_FLUSH**, such as **MPI_WIN_RFLUSH**, can solve this problem. The **MPI_WIN_RFLUSH** operation would start the flush process and return a request handle. The request handle can be later passed to MPI completion routines to wait/test for the completion of the operation.

6. Related Work

CAF and GASNet. CAF has been adopted by the Fortran 2008 committee as the parallel programming model in Fortran. GASNet [5] is a portable PGAS runtime used not only by CAF-2.0, but also by UPC and other parallel libraries. There has been previous work to implement GASNet using MPI, culminating in a GASNet conduit built on AM-MPI [4]. However, the AM-MPI implementation is dated and only uses MPI-1.1, which does not include many of the more recent MPI features which provide a much higher performing implementation, including RMA.

MPI+PGAS Implementations. There has been previous work to implement some PGAS-like libraries on top of MPI. Dinan et. al. [9] implemented the aggregate remote memory copy interface (ARMCI), the runtime layer for Global Arrays (GA) on top of MPI using one-sided communication. This work provided portability for GA to new systems which would previously require significant work to provide both an efficient one-sided MPI library and an efficient ARMCI implementation. Our work is similar, but with different goals. In this work, we want to understand the semantics and requirements of a full PGAS language, not just a high-level PGAS-like library. Specifically, a full PGAS language such as CAF enforces a large number of requirements on the MPI implementation, particularly with respect to active messages and event management, which are not required by Global Arrays.

Before this work, the same authors had made efforts to provide a hybrid MPI+UPC programming model [8]. Unified Parallel C (UPC) [29] is a PGAS library intended to simplify data sharing between processes by allowing them to share portions of their address space easily with each other. With the hybrid model between UPC and MPI, Dinan et. al.

demonstrated how applications could take advantage of both the large amount memory which becomes available when using UPC and the portability and existing libraries of MPI. As an example, an application could be written primarily in UPC, but could use an MPI library, such as ScaLAPACK to perform optimized, domain-specific work. However, that work only dealt with the semantic interactions between the two programming models and did not improve the runtime infrastructure of the models. That is, it still relied on each programming model using its own runtime system.

More work was done in this area by researchers at the Ohio State University [14] which was specific to MVAPICH. For this work, the authors unified the runtime systems of MVAPICH and UPC to create a single runtime which supported both programming models. While this work provides similar results to the work presented here, it is not portable across many MPI implementations and therefore requires that MVAPICH be available on the system, something which is not always possible given its reliance on InfiniBand.

Work to unify programming models has existed outside of purely PGAS languages. In 2011, Preissl et. al. [23] examined a communication model that integrated MPI, Fortran 2008 (Coarray Fortran), and OpenMP [21]. This work was specific to the Gyrokinetic Tokamak Simulation code but demonstrated the use of many communication libraries to implement different algorithms within the code. They focused on how PGAS/OpenMP combined could improve over a more traditional MPI+OpenMP algorithm.

Other MPI+X Hybrid Models. The MPI+OpenMP paradigm is just one example of a more classical hybridization of parallel libraries. It has been specifically targeted to improve on-node communication performance by taking advantage of shared address spaces with OpenMP, then switch to MPI when off-node communication is necessary. More recently, accelerators have entered the hybrid programming model space by introducing MPI+CUDA [20] or MPI+OpenCL [15] and allowing an MPI application to offload work to the GPU which can take advantage of the highly parallel architecture available on GPUs.

7. Conclusions and Future Work

In this paper, we demonstrated how MPI-3 can act as a runtime layer for CAF 2.0, thereby providing a basis for interoperability between the MPI and CAF, and reducing the runtime overhead introduced by having independent runtime systems. We demonstrated the new features introduced by MPI-3 and their applicability within a PGAS runtime system. We demonstrated that changing the runtime layer from GASNet to MPI introduces minimal overhead in some cases, and a performance improvement in instances where the CAF operations better map to MPI native operations. Finally, we outlined some improvements which could be adopted by future MPI Standards which would allow work like this to use

more optimized MPI operations than what was necessary for this work, such as Active Messages and **MPI_WIN_RFLUSH**.

As future work, we plan to look into several additions to our proposed CAF-MPI framework. One of the short-term goals that we plan to tackle are the performance issues that we identified within the MPI implementation, particularly with respect to the scalability of **MPI_WIN_FLUSH_ALL**. This would improve the performance of operations that rely heavily on CAF events, such as the RandomAccess benchmark.

As a slightly longer term goal, we plan to study the ability of **MPI_WIN_RFLUSH** and its applicability to CAF-MPI. We believe that such an implementation would allow us to move away from **MPI_SEND** and **MPI_RECV** almost entirely within the CAF-MPI runtime, except within active messages. We also plan to use this study as a motivating example to encourage the standardization of such a routine in the next MPI Standard.

Finally, we plan to investigate several applications that can benefit from a hybrid MPI+CAF framework. Two of the first applications we are planning to look at are QMCPACK and GFMC. As described in Section 1, these are existing MPI applications that have a tremendous potential to benefit from using coarrays that would allow their "local" data to be distributed across a small number of processes.

Acknowledgments

This work was supported by the U.S. Department of Energy, Office of Science, Advanced Scientific Computing Research, under Contract DE-AC02-06CH11357. We also thank Scott K. Warren and Dung X. Nguyen from Rice Group for porting CGPOP to CAF 2.0 and allowing us to use it for the evaluation of CAF-MPI.

References

[1] A. Petitet and R.C.Whaley and J.Dongara and A.Cleary. HPL - A Portable Implementation of the High-Performance Linpack. http://bit.ly/JtavrU, Sept. 2008.

[2] L. Adhianto, S. Banerjee, M. Fagan, M. Krentel, G. Marin, J. Mellor-Crummey, and N. R. Tallent. HPCTOOLKIT: tools for performance analysis of optimized parallel programs. *Concurr. Comput. : Pract. Exper.*, 22(6):685–701, 2010.

[3] R. C. Agarwal, F. G. Gustavson, and M. Zubair. A high performance parallel algorithm for 1-D FFT. In *Proceedings of the 1994 Conference on Supercomputing*, pages 34–40, Los Alamitos, CA, USA, 1994.

[4] D. Bonachea. Active Messages over MPI. URL http://bit.ly/14VZNOs.

[5] D. Bonachea. GASNet specification, v1.1. Technical Report UCB/CSD-02-1207, University of California at Berkeley, Berkeley, CA, USA, 2002.

[6] D. Bonachea and J. Duell. Problems with using MPI 1.1 and 2.0 as compilation targets for parallel language implementations. *Int. J. High Perform. Comput. Netw.*, 1(1-3):91–99, Aug. 2004. .

[7] B. Chamberlain, D. Callahan, and H. Zima. Parallel Programmability and the Chapel Language. *Intl. J. of High Performance Computing Applications*, 21(3):291–312, 2007. .

[8] J. Dinan, P. Balaji, E. L. Lusk, P. Sadayappan, and R. Thakur. Hybrid Parallel Programming with MPI and Unified Parallel C. In *7th ACM International Conference on Computing Frontiers*, Bertinoro, Italy, Apr. 2010.

[9] J. Dinan, P. Balaji, J. R. Hammond, S. Krishnamoorthy, and V. Tipparaju. Supporting the Global Arrays PGAS Model Using MPI One-Sided Communication. In *Proc. 26th Intl. Parallel and Distributed Processing Symp. (IPDPS)*, Shanghai, China, May 2012.

[10] R. Gerstenberger, M. Besta, and T. Hoefler. Enabling Highly-scalable Remote Memory Access Programming with MPI-3 One Sided. In *Proceedings of Intl. Conf. for High Perf. Computing, Networking, Storage and Analysis*, SC '13, pages 53:1–53:12, New York, NY, USA, 2013. URL http://bit.ly/1dCbxe2.

[11] HPC Challenge Benchmark. HPC challenge benchmark, July 2010. URL http://icl.cs.utk.edu/hpcc.

[12] G. Jin, J. Mellor-Crummey, L. Adhianto, W. N. Scherer III, and C. Yang. Implementation and Performance Evaluation of the HPC Challenge Benchmarks in Coarray Fortran 2.0. In *Proceedings of the 2011 IEEE Intl. Parallel & Distributed Processing Symposium*, IPDPS '11, pages 1089–1100, Washington, DC, USA, 2011. .

[13] S. L. Johnsson and R. L. Krawitz. Cooley-Tukey FFT on the Connection Machine. *In: Parallel Computing. Volume*, 18: 1201–1221, 1991.

[14] J. Jose, M. Luo, S. Sur, and D. K. Panda. Unifying UPC and MPI runtimes: experience with MVAPICH. In *Proceedings of the Fourth Conference on Partitioned Global Address Space Programming Model*, page 5. ACM, 2010.

[15] Khronos OpenCL Working Group. The OpenCL Specification, Version 2.0, July 2013. URL http://bit.ly/15tR61M.

[16] J. Kim, K. P. Esler, J. McMinis, M. A. Morales, B. K. Clark, L. Shulenburger, and D. M. Ceperley. Quantum energy density: Improved efficiency for quantum Monte Carlo calculations. *Physical Review B*, 88(3), 2013. .

[17] E. Lusk, S. Pieper, and R. Butler. More SCALABILITY, Less PAIN. *SciDAC Review*, (17):30–37, 2010. URL http://bit.ly/163sZtd.

[18] J. Mellor-Crummey, L. Adhianto, W. N. Scherer, III, and G. Jin. A new vision for Coarray Fortran. In *Proceedings of the 3rd Conf. on Partitioned Global Address Space Programing Models*, PGAS '09, pages 1–9, New York, NY, USA, 2009. ACM. .

[19] Message Passing Interface Forum. MPI Report 3.0, Sept. 2012. URL http://bit.ly/U1OwY2.

[20] J. Nickolls, I. Buck, M. Garland, and K. Skadron. Scalable Parallel Programming with CUDA. *Queue*, 6(2):40–53, Mar. 2008. ISSN 1542-7730. .

[21] OpenMP Architecture Review Board. OpenMP Application Program Interface Version 4.0, July 2013. URL http://bit.ly/13LNHtI.

[22] S. C. Pieper and R. B. Wiringa. QUANTUM MONTE CARLO CALCULATIONS OF LIGHT NUCLEI. *Annual Review of Nuclear and Particle Science*, 51(1):53–90, 2001. . URL http://bit.ly/143fd6u.

[23] R. Preissl, N. Wichmann, B. Long, J. Shalf, S. Ethier, and A. Koniges. Multithreaded Global Address Space Communication Techniques for Gyrokinetic Fusion Applications on Ultra-Scale Platforms. In *Proceedings of 2011 Int. Conf. for High Performance Computing, Networking, Storage and Analysis*, SC '11, pages 78:1–78:11, New York, NY, USA, 2011. ACM. ISBN 978-1-4503-0771-0. .

[24] J. Reid. Coarrays in Fortran 2008. In *Proceedings of the Third Conference on Partitioned Global Address Space Programing Models*, PGAS '09, pages 4:1–4:1, New York, NY, USA, 2009. ACM. ISBN 978-1-60558-836-0. .

[25] V. A. Saraswat, B. Bloom, I. Peshansky, O. Tardieu, and D. Grove. X10 Language Specification, Version 2.2, Sept. 2011. URL http://bit.ly/1431tse.

[26] W. N. Scherer, III, L. Adhianto, G. Jin, J. Mellor-Crummey, and C. Yang. Hiding latency in coarray fortran 2.0. In *Proceedings of the 4th Conf. on Partitioned Global Address Space Programming Model*, PGAS '10, pages 14:1–14:9, New York, NY, USA, 2010. ACM. ISBN 978-1-4503-0461-0. .

[27] A. Stone, J. Dennis, and M. M. Strout. The CGPOP Miniapp, Version 1.0. Technical Report CS-11-103, Colorado State University, July 2011.

[28] D. Takahashi and Y. Kanada. High-performance radix-2, 3 and 5 parallel 1-D complex FFT algorithms for distributed-memory parallel computers. *J. Supercomput.*, 15(2):207–228, 2000.

[29] UPC Consortium. UPC language specifications v1. 2. Technical report, Lawrence Berkeley National Laboratory, Berkeley, CA, USA, May 2005.

[30] T. von Eicken, D. E. Culler, S. C. Goldstein, and K. E. Schauser. Active messages: a mechanism for integrated communication and computation. *SIGARCH Comput. Archit. News*, 20:256–266, Apr. 1992. ISSN 0163-5964. .

[31] C. Yang. Function shipping in a scalable parallel programming model. Master's thesis, Department of Computer Science, Rice University, Houston, Texas, 2012.

[32] C. Yang, K. Murthy, and J. Mellor-Crummey. Managing asynchronous operations in coarray fortran 2.0. In *Proceedings of the 2013 IEEE International Symposium on Parallel Distributed Processing*, pages 1321–1332, 2013. .

[33] X. Zhao, P. Balaji, W. D. Gropp, and R. S. Thakur. MPI-Interoperable Generalized Active Messages. In *IEEE International Conference on Parallel and Distributed Systems (ICPADS)*, Dec. 2013.

[34] X. Zhao, D. Buntinas, J. A. Zounmevo, J. Dinan, D. Goodell, P. Balaji, R. Thakur, A. Afsahi, and W. Gropp. Toward Asynchronous and MPI-Interoperable Active Messages. In *CCGRID'13*, pages 87–94, 2013.

CUDA-NP: Realizing Nested Thread-Level Parallelism in GPGPU Applications

Yi Yang

Department of Computing Systems Architecture
NEC Laboratories America, Inc.
yyang@nec-labs.com

Huiyang Zhou

Department of Electrical and Computer Engineering
North Carolina State University
hzhou@ncsu.edu

Abstract

Parallel programs consist of series of code sections with different thread-level parallelism (TLP). As a result, it is rather common that a thread in a parallel program, such as a GPU kernel in CUDA programs, still contains both sequential code and parallel loops. In order to leverage such parallel loops, the latest Nvidia Kepler architecture introduces dynamic parallelism, which allows a GPU thread to start another GPU kernel, thereby reducing the overhead of launching kernels from a CPU. However, with dynamic parallelism, a parent thread can only communicate with its child threads through global memory and the overhead of launching GPU kernels is non-trivial even within GPUs.

In this paper, we first study a set of GPGPU benchmarks that contain parallel loops, and highlight that these benchmarks do not have a very high loop count or high degrees of TLP. Consequently, the benefits of leveraging such parallel loops using dynamic parallelism are too limited to offset its overhead. We then present our proposed solution to exploit nested parallelism in CUDA, referred to as CUDA-NP. With CUDA-NP, we initially enable a high number of threads when a GPU program starts, and use control flow to activate different numbers of threads for different code sections. We implemented our proposed CUDA-NP framework using a directive-based compiler approach. For a GPU kernel, an application developer only needs to add OpenMP-like pragmas for parallelizable code sections. Then, our CUDA-NP compiler automatically generates the optimized GPU kernels. It supports both the reduction and the scan primitives, explores different ways to distribute parallel loop iterations into threads, and effi-

ciently manages on-chip resource. Our experiments show that for a set of GPGPU benchmarks, which have already been optimized and contain nested parallelism, our proposed CUDA-NP framework further improves the performance by up to 6.69 times and 2.18 times on average.

Categories and Subject Descriptors D.3.3 [**Programming Languages**]: Processors – Compilers, Optimization.

General Terms Performance, Design, Experimentation, Languages.

Keywords GPGPU; nested parallelism; compiler; local memory;

1. Introduction

Parallel programs consist of series of code sections with different thread-level parallelism (TLP). Depending on application characteristics and the parallelization strategy, a parallel thread itself may contain both serial code and parallel loops. Such parallel loops inside a thread are referred to as nested thread-level parallelism. To exploit such nested parallelism in GPGPU (general purpose computation on graphics processing units) applications, the latest Nvidia Kepler architecture introduces the support for dynamic parallelism, which enables a GPU thread to invoke another kernel during execution. Although dynamic parallelism reduces the overhead of invoking a GPU kernel from a CPU, two key limitations remain. First, the communication between a parent thread and its child threads has to be through global memory variables. Second, launching a kernel from a GPU thread involves the device runtime [27] and has a non-trivial performance overhead.

In this paper, we first study a set of benchmarks to show that they contain parallel loops with relatively small loop counts. As a result, the benefits from parallelizing such loops using dynamic parallelism fail to overweigh its overhead. Then, we propose our solution, referred to as CUDA-NP, to exploit nested parallelism within GPGPU applications. Similar to dynamic parallelism, two fundamental challenges face CUDA-NP: (1) how to have different numbers of threads running in different code sections, and (2) how to enable low-latency data communication between a parent/master thread and its child/slave threads. To address these challenges, CUDA-NP first re-maps threads in a thread block (TB) into a one-dimension organization. Then, for each thread, referred to as a master thread, CUDA-NP adds a set of slave threads along a different dimension. The purpose of the slave threads is to help their master thread on its parallel loops. To do so, CUDA-NP introduces control flow to disable slave threads during sequential code sections. In CUDA-NP, low cost data communication between a master thread and its slave threads is achieved through registers or shared memory. In a way, CUDA-NP can be viewed as lightweight dynamic parallelism.

Our proposed CUDA-NP is implemented as a source-to-source compiler framework, which takes CUDA kernels with OpenMP-like directives as the input and outputs optimized CUDA kernels to exploit nested parallelism. This way, a GPGPU application developer only needs to add pragmas to identify parallel loops within a kernel to take advantage of CUDA-NP.

Our experimental results on Nvidia GTX 680 GPUs show our proposed CUDA-NP achieves remarkable performance gains, up to 6.69 times and 2.18 times on Our optimized code also consistently outperforms the highly optimized library CUBLAS V5.0 on the benchmarks matrix-vector multiplication and transpose-matrix-vector multiplication for different input sizes.

In summary, our work makes the following contributions. (1) We study a set of GPGPU applications and highlight the characteristics of their nested parallelism; (2) we propose simple pragmas and a set of optimization techniques to support nested parallelism; (3) we implement our CUDA-NP using a source-to-source compiler to relieve the programming complexity from application developers; and (4) we show that our proposed solution is highly effective and significantly improves the performance.

The remainder of the paper is organized as follows. In Section 2, we present a brief background on GPGPU architecture with a focus on Nvidia dynamic parallelism. We also analyze a set of GPGPU application to show the characteristics of their parallel loops. In Section 3, we present our compiler framework to exploit nested parallelism. The experimental methodology is addressed in the Section 4 and the results are presented in Section 5. Related works are discussed in Section 6. Section 7 concludes our paper.

2. Background

2.1 GPGPU Architecture and Programming Model

In order to achieve high computational throughput and memory bandwidth, GPGPU exploits many-core architectures and organizes the cores in a two-level hierarchy. First, a GPU contains multiple streaming multiprocessors (SMs) in Nvidia GPU architecture. An SM is also called a next generation SM (SMX) in Nvidia's latest Kepler architecture and is similar to a compute unit (CU) in AMD GPU architecture. Each SMX/CU in turn consists of multiple streaming processors (SPs) or thread processors (TPs). An SMX/CU can support thousands of threads running concurrently following the single-program multiple-data (SPMD) programming model.

In the CUDA programming model, the threads are also managed in a two-level hierarchy: thread grids and thread blocks (TBs). A GPGPU program, also called a kernel, is launched as a grid of TBs. A TB in turn contains multiple threads, which can have up-to-three-dimension thread identifiers (ids). In our compiler, we always map a multi-dimension thread id into a one-dimension one using the approach presented in Section 3.7. Therefore, in our subsequent discussions, we assume the input kernel has only one-dimensional threads in a TB.

GPGPU employs the single-instruction multiple-data (SIMD) model to amortize the cost of instruction decode and fetch. A small group of threads, referred to as a warp, share the same instruction pointer. The latest Nvidia Kepler architecture introduces a set of shuffle (shfl) instructions to enable the data exchange through registers for threads in the same warp. One shfl instruction used in this paper is __shfl(var, laneID, laneSize). For this instruction, a warp (32 threads) is partitioned into small groups with the group size as laneSize. Then, the laneID is used to specify the relative thread id in a group, and the var is the variable to be read. For example, the instruction __shfl(var, 0, 4) means that a warp contains 8 groups with a group size of 4 and all threads in the same group will read var from the first thread of the group. As a result, threads with id 0, 1, 2, and 3, belonging to the first group, read 'var' from thread 0; threads with id 4, 5, 6, and 7, read 'var' from thread 4; and so on. Compared to shared memory, which can be shared among all threads in the same TB, the shfl instructions have higher performance with the following two limitations. First, it can only be supported for the threads in the same warp. Second, threads can read a register from another thread in the same warp, but cannot write to a register of another thread.

The support for dynamic parallelism is introduced to Nvidia GPUs with compute capability 3.5. With dynamic parallelism, a GPU thread can launch a kernel during execution. Dynamic parallelism provides an easy way to develop GPU kernels for a program that contains nested parallelism without involving the host CPU. However, in order to achieve the high performance, the kernel launched by a GPU thread must have a very high number of threads to offset the overhead of launching a kernel. To illustrate the overhead of dynamic parallelism, we use the memory-copy micro-benchmark in our experiment on an Nvidia Tesla K20c GPU. To copy 64-million floats, the baseline micro-benchmark without dynamic parallelism achieves the bandwidth is 142 GB/s. Then, we observe that once we enable the compiler flag for dynamic parallelism, the original kernel without using dynamic parallelism can only achieve 63 GB/s. Such overhead is referred to as dynamic-parallelism-enabled kernel overhead [27]. Next, we modify the benchmark to make use of dynamic parallelism. In the dynamic parallelism version, we have a parent kernel and a child kernel. The parent kernel is launched once, but each thread of parent kernel will launch a child kernel. the child kernel can be launched many times. In the child kernel, each thread simply copies a float from the input to the output. If the number of threads of the parent kernel is m, and the number of threads of every child kernel launch is n, then m*n is the overall floats to be copied from the input to the output. We fix the value of m*n to 64 million and show the bandwidths for different m in Figure 1. Although the overall workload remains the same, the performance degrades rapidly when the number of child kernel launches increases. In other words, each kernel launch needs to have a high number of threads to achieve good performance. From Figure 1, we can see that when each child kernel launch has 16k threads, the overall memory copy bandwidth only reaches 34GB/s. This highlights the kernel launching overhead for dynamic-parallelism. Another limitation of dynamic parallelism is that the communication between the parent thread and its child threads has to be through global memory [27].

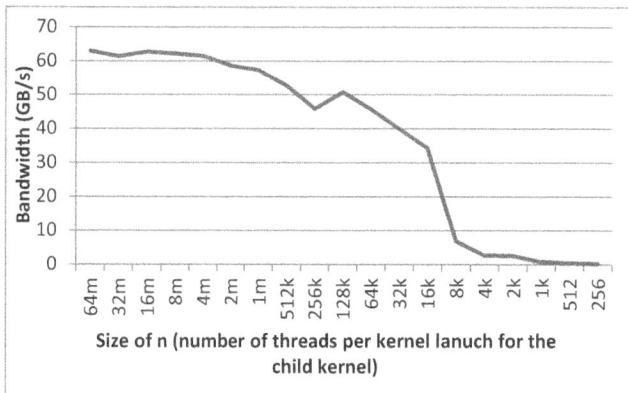

Figure 1. The throughput of the memory-copy micro-benchmark using dynamic parallelism.

2.2 Nested Parallelism in GPGPU Programs

GPGPU applications are typically highly parallelized due to the required TLP to hide high memory access latencies. Still, there exist parallel loops in the kernel code. As an example, Figure 2 shows the kernel code of transposed-matrix-vector multiplication (TMV). Each thread computes one element in the output vector. The loop between lines 4 and 5 reads one column of input matrix a and the vector b,

and performs the dot-product operation. This example illustrates common reasons for nested parallelism existed in GPU kernels.

```
1   __global__ void tmv(float *a, float*b, float* c, int w, int h){
2       float sum = 0;
3       int tx = threadIdx.x+blockIdx.x*blockDim.x;
4       for (int i=0; i<h; i++)
5           sum += a[i*w+tx]*b[i];
6       c[tx] = sum;
7   }
```

Figure 2. The kernel code of transposed-matrix-vector multiplication (TMV).

First, developers tend to view that there is already sufficient TLP. In the TMV example, the output vector c may have a high number of elements and further parallelization of the loop in Figure 2 may be considered not necessary. However, based on the characteristics of the applications, each thread may require too much resource to limit the number of threads that can run concurrently on each SMX, even though the overall number of threads of the application is indeed high enough.

Second, if a loop contains loop-carried dependencies, application developers may choose not to parallelize it. As shown in Figure 2, to parallelize the loop, the reduction primitive needs to be supported.

Third, if an application developer chooses to further parallelize some parallel loops in a kernel, he/she needs to understand the GPGPU architecture very well, in order to achieve good performance. For example, if a parallel loop is distributed among threads in the same warp, we should avoid workload imbalance due to the nature of SIMD execution. Another key factor is how to balance the resource usage among shared memory, register file and local memory. Therefore, in this paper, we argue for a compiler approach to exploit nested parallelism to relieve the application developers from the associated complexity.

Overall, the loop in Figure 2 showcases a common example in many benchmarks that contain parallel loops. An outstanding feature of a good candidate for leveraging nested parallelism is limited TLP due to the nature of the application or the heavy resource usage of each GPU

2.3 Characteristics of Nested Parallelism in GPGPU Programs

In order to understand available nested parallelism in GPGPU programs, we studied the benchmarks in Nvidia SDK [26], Rodinia [6] and GPGPUSim [2]. The detailed experimental methodology is discussed in Section 5. We list in Table 1 some benchmarks that contain nested parallelism. In the table, the first column (**Name**) contains the name of the benchmarks; the second column (**Input**) shows the input to each benchmark; the third column (**PL**) shows how many parallel loops exist in the kernel; the forth column (**LC**) shows the largest loop counts among these parallel loops; the fifth column (**R/S**) indicates if the loops contain the scan(S)/reduction(R) operations or not (X). We also show the resource usage including register file (**REG**), shared memory (**SM**) and local memory (**LM**) per thread for the baseline code (**BL**) and optimized versions (**OPT**) generated from CUDA-NP.

From Table 1, we can see that the benchmarks LE, LIB and CFD have intensive local memory usage to limit their performance, even though they do have relatively high numbers of concurrent threads running on each SMX; the benchmarks LU, MV, SS and BK have intensive shared memory usage, which limits the number of concurrent threads on each SMX; the benchmark MC has intensive usage of both shared memory and local memory; the remaining benchmarks, TMV and NN, do not have intensive resource usage. From these benchmarks, we can see that the loop counts of parallel loops are relatively small.

Table 1. Benchmarks

Name	Input	PL	LC	R/S	Bytes per thread (BL)			Bytes per thread(OPT)		
					REG	SM	LM	REG	SM	LM
MC	grid=8	4	12	X	252	288	40	144	36	0
LU	2048.dat	4	32	R	44	96	0	72	24	0
LE	testfile.avi	3	150	R	156	0	600	252	4	24
MV	2K*2K	1	32	R	100	132	0	100	34	0
SS	DIM=8K	2	8K	R	60	80	0	72	20	0
LIB	NPATH=256K	4	80	S	216	0	960	200	40	640
CFD	fvcorr.domn.193K	1	4	R	252	0	56	252	0	8
BK	2M	2	32	X	60	128	0	56	4	0
TMV	2K*2K	1	2K	R	88	0	0	64	4	0
NN	1K	1	1K	R	88	0	0	56	0	0

3. CUDA-NP: A Directive-Based Compiler Framework for Nested Parallelism

In this section, we present our CUDA-NP compiler framework to leverage nested parallelism. The input to our compiler is a CUDA kernel with OpenMP-like directives to denote parallel loops. The output of our compiler framework is the optimized kernel code. Figure 3 shows an example. The kernel with directives denoting the parallel loop is shown in Figure 3a and the optimized kernel using our proposed compiler is shown in Figure 3b. The first transformation on the input kernel is to increase the TB size. Given the hardware limit of GTX 680 GPUs, the maximal number of threads in a TB is 1024. So, the TB size is increased up to 1024 if the input kernel has a smaller TB size. As our compiler already re-maps the threads in a TB into a one-dimension organization, increasing the TB size is achieved by adding a new dimension. The newly introduced threads will be used to carry out the parallel loops in the input kernel. To differentiate the original threads from

the newly added ones, we refer to the original threads as 'master' threads and the newly added ones as 'slave' threads and we use 'master_id' and 'slave_id' as their thread ids along different dimensions. If the master threads are aligned in the X/Y dimension, slave threads will be added along the Y/X dimension, as discussed in Section 3.4. For the kernel shown in Figure 3, master_id is actually threadIdx.x and slave_id is threadIdx.y.

```
1   #define BLOCK_SIZE 16
2   __global__ void lud_perimeter(float *m, int matrix_dim, int
3   offset) {
4       __shared__ float
5       peri_row[BLOCK_SIZE][BLOCK_SIZE],
6       peri_col[BLOCK_SIZE][BLOCK_SIZE],
7       dia[BLOCK_SIZE][BLOCK_SIZE];
8       .......
9       int array_offset;
10      array_offset = offset*matrix_dim+offset;
11
12      // parallel loop
13      #pragma np parallel for
14      for (i=0; i < BLOCK_SIZE; i++)
15        peri_row[i][idx]= m[array_offset+
16          (blockIdx.x+1)*BLOCK_SIZE+matrix_dim*i];
17      ......
18  }
```

(a)   The input kernel

```
1   #define BLOCK_SIZE 16
2   __global__ void lud_perimeter_np(float *m, int matrix_dim,
3   int offset) {
4       __shared__ float
5       peri_row[BLOCK_SIZE][BLOCK_SIZE],
6       peri_col[BLOCK_SIZE][BLOCK_SIZE],
7       dia[BLOCK_SIZE][BLOCK_SIZE];
8       .......
9       int array_offset;
10      if (slave_id==0) { //slave_id == 0 means a master thread
11        array_offset = offset*matrix_dim+offset;
12      }
13      array_offset = read_from_master(array_offset);
14      for (i=slave_id; i < BLOCK_SIZE; i+=slave_size)
15        peri_row[i][idx]= m[array_offset+
16          (blockIdx.x+1)*BLOCK_SIZE+matrix_dim*i];
17      ......
18  }
```

(b)   The output kernel from CUDA-NP

Figure 3. The kernel 'lud_perimeter' before and after CUDA-NP optimizations.

The 'lud_perimeter' kernel in Figure 3a has only 32 threads in a TB and each TB needs 3kB shared memory. As a result, 16 thread blocks can run concurrently on each SMX on an Nvidia GTX 680 GPU, for which the shared memory is configured to 48kB per SMX. The line 13 in Figure 3a is the pragma indicating the subsequent loop can be parallelized. Then in the code optimized using CUDA-NP, as shown in Figure 3b, each TB has 32x8 threads, where the size of the X dimension is 32 and the size of the Y dimension is 8. However, we only allow 32 threads in a TB to be active for the sequential code such as line 10 in

Figure 3a in the kernel. For the parallel loops, such as those between line 14 and 16 in Figure 3a, all 256 threads per TB are active, and each thread processes one or more iterations of the loop. In other words, for each master thread, 7 slave threads are added to share its parallel workload. Note that the parameter '*slave_size*' is 8 as 8 threads (1 master + 7 slaves) will all work equally on the parallel loops.

Next, we use one example to illustrate why our optimized kernel improves performance, as shown in Figure 4. In Figure 4a, we assume each TB of the input kernel has 8 threads running through its whole lifetime. Then in the optimized kernel, each TB has 8*4 threads as shown in Figure 4b. However we have only 8 threads running for sequential codes, such as line 10 in Figure 3a, and 8*4 threads for loop sections, such as line 14 to line 16 in Figure 3a. These active threads that execute the sequential sections are the master threads, as they are very similar to original threads in the input kernel. But in the parallel loop sections, the workload of each thread in the input kernel will be distributed to the corresponding master thread and its slave as shown in the Figure 4b. The overall performance is improved due to higher TLP for parallel loops.

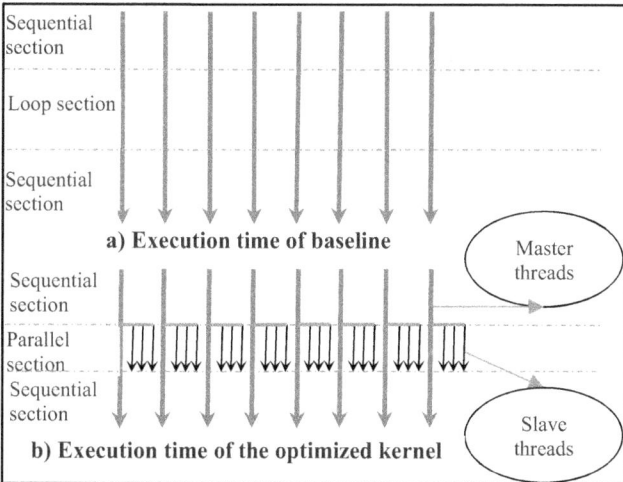

Figure 4. Execution paradigms to show why CUDA-NP works.

In the example in Figure 3, the master threads are aligned along the X dimension, i.e., the master id is threadIdx.x in the corresponding TB of the input kernel. When we generate the slave threads for a master thread, they share the same master id (i.e., threadIdx.x) but have different slave ids (i.e., threadIdx.y). Therefore, we actually use threads in different warps to work collaboratively for the workload of a master thread in the input kernel, since the warps are formed using consecutive thread ids. For example, the threads with two-dimension ids (1,0) to (1,7) in a TB of our optimized kernel perform the workload of the thread with id 1 in the TB of the original kernel. The thread with id (1,0) in the optimized kernel will be the

master thread corresponding to thread 1 in the original kernel and threads with ids (1,1) to (1,7) are its slave threads. These threads will be in different warps as the TB dimension is 32x8. Therefore, we refer to this way of distributing parallel loop iterations as **inter-warp NP**. Besides inter-warp NP, we can map the 'master_id' to threadIdx.y and map 'slave_id' to threadIdx.x. For example, we use threads with thread ids (0,1) to (7,1) in our optimized kernel to perform the workload of thread 1 in the original kernel. This way, we use threads within a warp to distribute the parallel loops. We refer to this way of thread id mapping or workload distribution as **intra-warp NP**.

As illustrated in Figure 3b, several key code transformations are performed by our proposed CUDA-NP compiler framework. In the sequential code sections, it introduces the control flow in line 10 to only allow the master threads to compute the variable '*array_offset*'. Since this variable is to be used in the parallel loop by slave threads, it needs to be broadcasted to the slave threads. A function called *read_from_master* is introduced for this purpose. In the parallel loop, it updates the loop iterator using slave ids and the number of slave threads (i.e., '*slave_size*') so that multiple slave threads can process multiple loop iterations in parallel. As the loop bound checking remains in the transformed code, this transformation is valid if the loop bound is determined at the runtime. Also, from this example, we can see that a key challenge of our code transformations is to handle the variables which are live cross a parallel section and a sequential section.

In Section 3.1, we discuss how our compiler handles scalar live-in variables. Section 3.2 addresses the scalar live-out variables. For live array-variables, if they reside in global memory or shared memory, they are already accessible by the master threads and their salve threads. So, in Section 3.3, we discuss our compiler transformation to deal with live array-variables, which are located in local memory. In Section 3.4, we summarize the tradeoffs between the two workload distribution schemes, intra-warp NP and inter-warp NP. In Section 3.5, we present the overall compiler algorithm for code transformations. Section 3.6 lists our proposed pragmas for NP. Section 3.7 discusses the preprocessing step of our compiler.

3.1 Scalar Inputs/Live-Ins to Parallel Sections

For a scalar variable defined in a sequential section and used in a subsequent parallel section, i.e., a live-in variable to the parallel section, we need to broadcast it from a master thread to its slave threads. The exception is that the variable is in the global memory which is already visible to all the threads. For example, as shown with line 15 in Figure 3a, the global memory array m can be directly accessed by slave threads. Shared memory has similar behavior and can be used directly by slave threads without additional code transformations.

The variables in the register file or local memory have to be broadcasted to slave threads as they are private to a master thread. We implement it using the function *read_from_master*. If we use intra-warp NP for Kepler GPUs, since the master and its slave threads are in the same warp, we can use the shfl instruction, *__shfl(var, 0, slave_size)*, to implement the *read_from_master* function. As explained in Section 2.1, for such a __shfl instruction, a warp threads first are partitioned into small groups with the group size of *slave_size*. Therefore, a group actually contains all the slave threads of a master thread for intra-warp NP. Then all threads within a group will read the value of *var* from the master thread, whose id (i.e., threadIdx.x % slave_size) is 0, in the small group. For inter-warp NP or intra-warp NP on GPUs that do not support __shfl instructions, *read_from_master* is implemented using shared memory. In this case, master threads first write values to shared memory, and then slave threads read from shared memory.

Instead of communicating through registers or shared memory, another way is to let all slave threads compute the live-in variables redundantly. Such redundant computation is also called uniform vector operations as they have the same input and output values for different threads [7]. If the overhead is only simple ALU computations like line 10 in Figure 3a, in general redundant computation can deliver better performance due to eliminating the shared memory usage and control flow. In our compiler, if an instruction's inputs are constant values or the output of a uniform vector instruction, this instruction will be executed by all slave threads redundantly. Otherwise, we let the master thread execute it and broadcast the result to slave threads.

3.2 Scalar Outputs/Live-Outs of Parallel Sections

Similarly to the live-ins of a parallel section, if a scalar output of a parallel section is in global memory or shared memory, we can just leave as it is, as it is already visible to the master threads. If a variable is in the register file or local memory, we have different scenarios to handle. One common scenario is a reduction or scan variable, for which we can generate the parallel implementations to retrieve the results from slave threads. We implement the reduction using shared memory for inter-warp NP or using the shfl instruction for intra-warp NP. For the scan implementation, we also use a similar approach to Nvidia CUDA SDK [26].

There are scenarios that an output of a parallel section is neither a reduction variable nor a scan variable. One such example is the code '*if (i==3) x = a[i];*' inside a parallel loop, where *i* is the loop iterator and the variable *x* is the used in later sequential sections. The problem with this code is that in our CUDA-NP scheme, each slave thread

has a local variable *x* and will execute the code. But it is supposed that only one slave thread will write the value to *x*, and the *x* of this slave thread needs to be transferred to the master thread. In such a case, we can make the initial value of *x* to be 0 so that a reduction operation on *x* can be used to retrieve the value from the slave threads.

3.3 Live Array-Variables Residing in Local Memory

Since the register file has a limited size and cannot be accessed as an indexed array, array variables residing in the local memory are used in some CUDA programs. As shown in Figure 5, the array *Grad* has to be spilled into local memory due to the register file size limitation. Such local memory accesses incur high pressure on the L1 cache and lead to poor performance.

```
1   #define NPOINTS 150
2   __global__ void ellipsematching_kernel(...) {
3       float Grad[NPOINTS]; //live array-variable in local memory
4       ……
5       #pragma np parallel for
6       for(n = 0; n < NPOINTS; n++) {
7           …...
8           Grad[n] = tex1Dfetch(t_grad_x,addr) * ……;
9       }
10      #pragma np parallel for reduction(+:sum)
11      for(n = 0; n < NPOINTS; n++) sum += Grad[n];
12      ave = sum / ((float) NPOINTS);
13
14      #pragma np parallel for reduction(+:var,ep)
15      for(n = 0; n < NPOINTS; n++) {
16          sum = Grad[n] - ave;
17          var += sum * sum;
18          ep += sum;
19      }
20      ……
21      if(((ave * ave) / var) > sGicov)
22          gicov[(i * grad_m) + j] = ave / sqrt(var);
23  }
```

Figure 5. The kernel with live array-variables in local memory.

We apply our CUDA-NP on the parallel loops marked with our CUDA-NP pragmas in Figure 5, and Figure 6 shows the code after our optimization. From Figure 6, we can see all parallel loops are distributed to multiple slave threads. For the loop starting from line 6 in Figure 5, each slave thread only needs to compute *NPOINTS/slave_size* iterations as shown from line 6 in Figure 6. As shown from line 7 in Figure 6, each iteration of the loop in a slave thread is mapped to an iteration of the loop of the baseline kernel before our optimization. This way, all iterations of the loop in the baseline are distributed to slave threads. The reduction or scan operations are also appended after the loops if the pragmas specify the reduction or scan clauses.

As we discussed in section 3.1, a local array is private to a thread, and not visible to other threads. However, in order for slave threads to process a parallel loop, this array has to be shared among those threads. Therefore, we need to replace a local array with a shared memory array or a global memory so as to make it visible to all threads. One exception is that a local array is accessed based on the loop iterator. For example, the parallel loops in Figure 5 always access the array *Grad* using the loop iterators. In this case, since each slave thread only needs to accesses part of the local array without interleaving, we can partition the local array into small ones and distribute each small array to one slave thread. Therefore, for a live local array, we can replace it with a global memory array, a shared memory array, or partition it into small local arrays as shown in Figure 6. Since these approaches only affect the accesses to local arrays, we differentiate them using two MACROs: *DEF_Grad* and *Grad(i),* in Figure 6a, 6b, and 6c so that the code in Figure 6d remains the same.

1. ***Replace a local array with a global memory array***: We first define a new global array and partition it such that each partition corresponds to the local array of a master thread. As shown in Figure 6a, the MACRO *DEF_Grad* partitions a new global memory array *Grad_g* based on the id of a master thread so that all slave threads of the master thread access the same partition.

2. ***Replace a local memory with a shared memory array***: In this case, we first declare a shared memory array. The size of its first dimension is the *master_size*, i.e., the number of master threads in a TB, and the size of its second dimension is the size of the local array. Then slave threads can access the shared memory based on its master thread id and the index of original local array. Since many benchmarks already use shared memory intensively, the potential issue of this approach is the increased usage of shared memory.

3. ***Partition a local array into smaller local arrays***: In Figure 6c, each slave thread only requires a smaller local array whose size is *NPOINTS/slave_size*. This approach requires a slave thread must only read and write its own local array after the partition.

Our framework employs the following policy to decide which option is to be used to replace a local array. First, if the local array meets all conditions to be partitioned into smaller ones, we choose option 3. Otherwise, the size of the local array is checked, and the shared memory is used to replace the local array, if the size of the local array is less than 384 byte. The reason for this choice is that assuming the local array size is 384 bytes and we can launch 8 slave threads for each master thread, 48Kbytes shared memory can support 128 master threads and 896 slave threads after our optimizations, which provides enough TLP on each SMX. If the shared memory is already used in the baseline, we also need to subtract such shared memory usage from 384 bytes to ensure that shared memory will not be the resource bottleneck for TLP. The last choice is to replace

the local array with one in global memory due to the high access latency.

```
#define DEF_Grad  float* Grad=Grad_g+ \
   (master_size*blockIdx.x)* NPOINTS+master_id
#define Grad(i) Grad[i*master_size]
```
   (a) Replace a local memory array with a global memory one
```
#define DEF_Grad  __shared__ float Grad[master_size][ NPOINTS]
#define Grad(i) Grad_sm[master_id][i]
```
   (b) Replace a local memory array with a shared memory one
```
#define DEF_Grad float Grad_reg[NPOINTS/slave_size]
#define Grad(i) Grad_reg[i%(slave_size)]
```
   (c) Partition a local array to small ones

```
1  #define NPOINTS 150
2  template<int slave_size>
3  __global__ void ellipsematching_kernel(..., float*Grad_g) {
4    DEF_Grad
5    ......
6    for(ni = 0; ni < NPOINTS/slave_size; ni++) {
7      n = ni*slave_size+slave_id;//map thread id to iteration
8      ......
9      Grad(n) = tex1Dfetch(t_grad_x,addr) * ......;
10   }
11   for(ni = 0; ni < NPOINTS/slave_size; ni++) {
12     n = ni*slave_size+ slave_id;
13     sum += Grad(n);
14   }
15   sum =reduction(sum);// reduction on slave threads
16   ave = sum / ((float) NPOINTS);
17
18   for(ni = 0; ni < NPOINTS/slave_size; ni++) {
19     n = ni*slave_size+ slave_id;
20     sum = Grad(n) - ave;
21     var += sum * sum;
22     ep += sum;
23   }
24   var =reduction(var);//
25   ep = reduction(ep);//
26   ......
27   if (slave_id==0)  // only master threads
28   if(((ave * ave) / var) > sGicov)
29     gicov[(i * grad_m) + j] = ave / sqrt(var);
30 }
```
   (d) Optimized code

Figure 6. Approaches to handle live array-variables in local memory.

3.4 Inter-Warp NP vs. Intra-Warp NP

The choice between inter-warp NP and intra-warp NP may have significant performance impact. Here, we summarize their tradeoffs. First, since threads in the same warp can use registers to exchange data, __shfl instructions can be used for communication and also the scan and reduction operations for intra-warp NP. As a result, the intra-warp NP may have less shared memory usage. Second, if the slave threads of a master thread have different workloads, the intra-warp NP will be worse than inter-warp NP due to control divergence. Third, intra-warp NP may have negative impact on memory coalescing as it changes the memory access pattern of the original kernel. In general, the master threads in the original kernel have adjacent thread ids and tend to access the global memory in a coalesced way. If we map these master thread ids into threadIdx.y as the intra-warp NP approach, these coalesced global memory accesses are broken. Forth, a similar issue may also happen for constant memory accesses when we use intra-warp NP. Considering line 11 in Figure 5, if the *Grad* is a constant array, threads in a warp will access the same address of *Grad* in the baseline. However, after intra-warp NP, slave threads of a master thread will access different addresses of the constant array. Such accesses cannot leverage the hardware broadcast logic and may hurt performance. Finally, to use the __shfl instructions, the number of slave threads for a master thread has to be (a 2's power -1), i.e., 1, 3, 7, 15. Otherwise, these slave threads might be in different warps.

```
NP_transformation(Kernel kernel)
    css = generateCodeSections(kernel)
    inter-warp or intra-warp thread map for kernel (Section 3.4)
    for cs in css:
        if cs is sequential:
            cs is master thread model
        if cs is a parallel loop:
            map each slave thread id to iterations of cs
            for each input in of cs:
                insert broadcast function for in before cs (Section 3.1)
            for each output out of cs:
                insert reduction or scan for out after cs (Section 3.2)
            for each live local memory array lm : (Section 3.3)
                map lm to global memory, shared memory or the
                    register file
```

Figure 7. The overall compiler algorithm of CUDA-NP.

3.5 Compiler Algorithm

Here, we summarize our CUDA-NP compiler algorithm, as shown in Figure 7. CUDA-NP takes a kernel as the input. It parses the kernel into a series of code sections. Each code section is either sequential or parallel. A parallel section is identified by the '*np*' pragma. First, we map the thread id of the input kernel to master and slave thread ids in the transformed kernel for either the inter-warp NP or intra-warp NP approach. Then, if a code section is sequential one, we generate the control flow to only allow the master threads to execute it. Redundant computations can be used in sequential sections depending on the characteristics of an instruction as discussed in Section 3.1. For parallel sections, all slave threads along with their master threads are active. For each parallel section, we also generate the code for its scalar input (Section 3.1) and the code for its scalar output (Section 3.2). The live local arrays have to be replaced with global/shared memory arrays, or partitioned into smaller local arrays, as discussed in Section 3.3.

3.6 Pragma

In order to reduce the programming complexity to leverage nested parallelism, we adapt the OpenMP pragmas for our

CUDA-NP framework. Most of CUDA-NP grammars are designed to be very similar to OpenMP pragmas on purpose. A developer can add '*#pragma np for*' to denote a parallel loop, and can also specify different clauses of the pragma. A *copy-in* clause defines the data which should be broadcasted from a master thread to its slave threads. If a *copy-in* clause is not available from users' pragmas, our compiler can automatically find the live-in variables defined before a parallel loop and make them to be broadcasted from a master thread to its slave threads. A *reduction/scan* clause defines the reduction or scan operations. Developers have the flexibility to specify the preferred number of slave threads (*number_threads*), whether the inter-warp NP or intra-warp NP is preferred (*NP_type*), and the targeted version of Nvidia CUDA compute capability (*sm_version*). Our current support for compute capability versions is mainly for the purpose of using shfl instructions. If the target version is less than 3, the shfl instruction cannot be used to guarantee correctness. If a developer does not provide such information, our compiler generates multiple versions to explore different numbers of slave threads, and different thread distribution approaches.

```
threadIdx_x ← threadIdx.z * blockDim.x * blockDim.y +
    threadIdx.y * blockDim.x + threadIdx.x
```
(a)   map three-dimension thread ids into one-dimension ones
```
threadIdx_x ← threadIdx.x % blockDim_x
threadIdx_y← (threadIdx.x/blockDim_x) % blockDim_y
threadIdx_z←threadIdx.x /(blockDim_x * blockDim_z)
```
(b)   map one-dimension thread ids into three-dimension ones

Figure 8. Mapping thread ids.

```
vertexInterp2(isoValue, v[0], v[1], ...);
vertexInterp2(isoValue, v[1], v[2], ...);
vertexInterp2(isoValue, v[2], v[3], ...),
......
vertexInterp2(isoValue, v[3], v[7], ...),
                (a) Sequential code
__constant__ int CS_0= {0,1,2,...,3}
__constant__ int CS_1= {1,2,3,...,7}
for (int i=0; i<12; i++)
    vertexInterp2(isoValue, v[CS_0[i]], v[CS_1[i]], ...);
            (b)  A loop converted from the code in (a)
```

Figure 9. Converting sequential code into a loop.

3.7 Preprocessors

The purpose of the preprocessors to our compiler is to generate the input source code suitable for our code optimizations.

1. ***Convert a TB with multi-dimensional threads into a TB with one-dimensional threads***: We use the mapping relationship shown in Figure 8 to map multi-dimension thread ids to one-dimension ones and vice versa. This transformation has limited performance impact since it does not change thread organizations within warps. In other words, the threads in a warp remain in a warp after

the transformation. Therefore, it does not affect memory coalescing or divergence.

2. ***Combine unrolled statements into a loop***: We found that sometimes the developers may manually unroll some loops. Since our compiler targets at parallel loops, for statements after unrolling, they can be combined into a parallel loop to take advantage of CUDA-NP. Figure 9a shows such an example, as the input of each statement cannot be mapped to an iterator of a loop directly. In our pre-processor, we put the non-linear indexes in constant buffers, and then access these indexes using loop iterator. This way, we can convert such sequential code into a parallel loop.

3. ***Pad arrays***: as shown in Figure 5, the size of the local memory array 'Grad' is 150, which is not multiple of 4,8,16, or 32. However, if we apply the inter-warp NP scheme, the number of slave threads of a master thread has to be (a 2's power number – 1) and the loop count needs to be a multiple of slave_size. In this case, we can pad the size of Grad to 160 and also increase the upper bound of the loop to 160 so that the loop counter is the multiple of 32. Then an additional control flow "*if (i<150)*' is added in the loop body to skip the padding data, where *i* is the loop iterator. Such padding may introduce workload imbalance among slave threads due to some idle iterations.

4. Experimental Methodology

To evaluate our proposed compiler, we perform our experiments on Nvidia GTX 680 GPUs with CUDA SDK 5.0. We let the CUDA runtime determine the shared memory usage automatically based on the resource requirement of each benchmark. Most benchmarks used in the experiments are from Nvidia SDK, GPGPUSim, and Rodinia benchmark suite. Among these benchmarks, MarchingCubes (MC) is from Nvidia SDK, and Libor (LIB) is from GPGPUSim. Lud (LU), Leukocyte (LE), Streamcluster (SS), Computational Fluid Dynamics (CFD), BucketSort (BK), and Nearest Neighbor (NN) are from Rodinia. The LE is the array order version [4], and BK is in the Hybrid Sort package. Since NN only uses one thread in each TB and has very poor performance, we first modify the TB configuration so that each TB has 32 threads, which is 2.89 times faster than the original version. Then we use this modified version as the baseline in our experiments. We use the optimized matrix-vector multiplication (MV) based on [42]. The TMV code is shown in Figure 1. In Table 1, as a comparison, we show the resource usage of our optimized benchmarks. For these benchmarks, we manually add the NP pragma to identify parallel loops.

We implement our proposed CUDA-NP in a source-to-source compiler using Cetus [20]. Our compiler has an auto-tuning mechanism to select from multiple choices, such as intra-warp NP or inter-warp NP, and different numbers of slave threads to be used to distribute parallel loop iterations.

5. Experimental Results

In Figure 10, we report the speedups of the optimized kernel generated by our compiler over the baseline. As shown in the figure, our proposed CUDA-NP can achieve from 1.36 to 6.69 times speedups. On average using the geometric mean (GM), our proposed CUDA-NP can achieve 2.18 times speedup among the ten benchmarks.

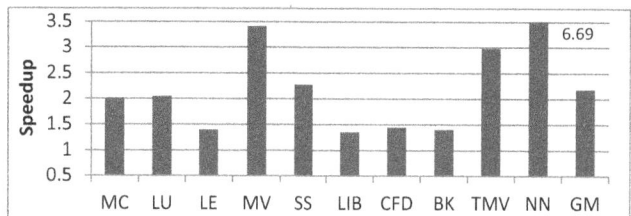

Figure 10. Speedups of our proposed CUDA-NP over baseline.

In order to better understand the impact of our CUDA-NP on these benchmarks, we show results for different slave_sizes coupled with either inter-warp NP or intra-warp NP in Figure 11. Among these benchmarks, LU and NN are the only cases that intra-warp NP achieves better performance than inter-warp NP. The main reason for LU is that the loops of LU are in the control flow 'master_id<16'. The intra-warp NP approach allocates slave threads in the same warp for a master thread. Assuming each master thread has 3 slave threads, each warp will contain only 8 master threads (8 master threads+24 slaves). These 8 master threads and their slaves will execute the same path. Therefore, control divergence disappears after intra-warp NP. Furthermore, when three slave threads are allocated to each master thread (i.e, slave_size=4), it achieves the best performance for both intra-warp NP and inter-warp NP, as it enables 2k threads per SMX based on the resource usage. For NN, the intra-warp NP version can access the global memory in a more coalesced manner while the impact of inter-warp NP is minor.

For other benchmarks, inter-warp NP always outperforms intra-warp NP. MC, LIB and LE have imbalanced workload among slave threads for intra-warp NP. For example, since the loop count of MC is 12, and if we allocate 7 slave threads for each master thread, then some slave threads have to take 2 iterations and others take 1 iteration. LIB and LE have similar behaviour to MC.

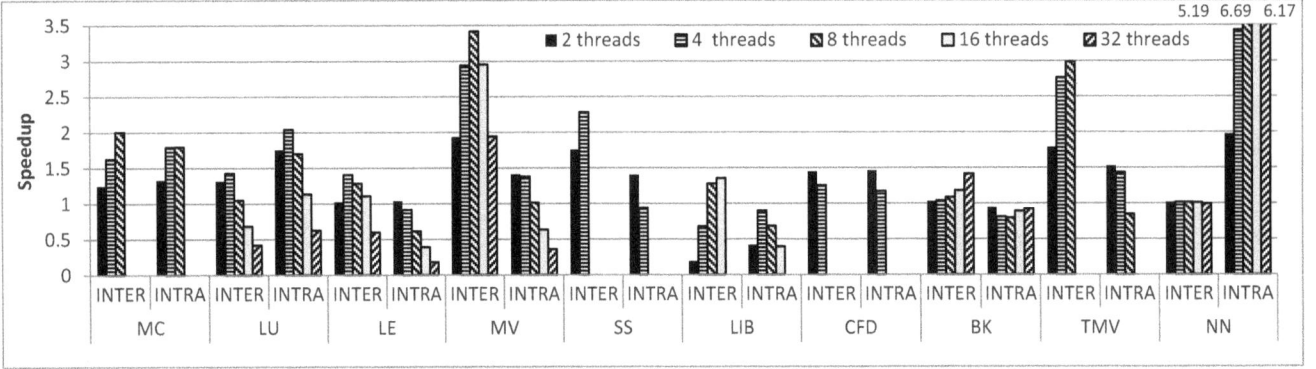

Figure 11. Performance comparison between inter-warp and intra-warp NP with different slave_sizes. Some slave_sizes are not applicable as the resulting TB size would exceed the maximal TB size.

The difference between inter-warp NP and intra-warp NP for CFD is minor, because the memory accesses of the baseline are not all coalesced and the loop iterations can be evenly distributed to slave threads.

From Figure 11, we can also see that in some cases, the performance degrades when the number of slave threads increases. This observation is consistent with the previous work [18] in that higher TLP is not always helpful.

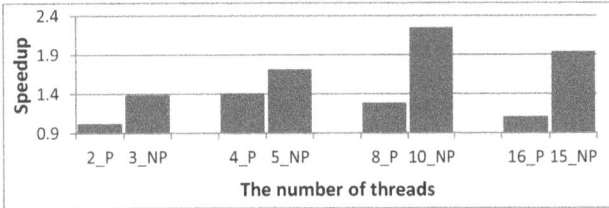

Figure 12. The impact of padding on LE.

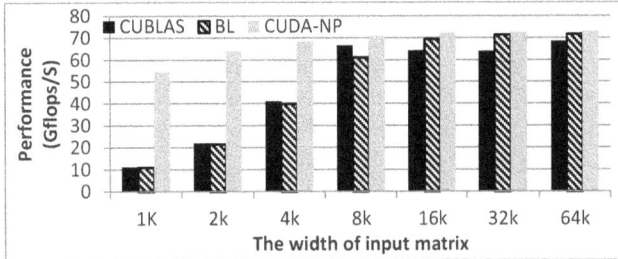

Figure 13. TMV results on GTX 680 for matrices with variable widths and a constant height (2k).

As we discussed previously, if the loop count of a parallel loop counter is not power of 2, we need to pad it to the multiple of power of 2 for intra-warp NP. However, for inter-warp NP, such limitation can be removed. Therefore in Figure 12, for the benchmark LE, we compare the results without padding to those with padding. The loop count of the baseline is 150. We choose to compare these results that have similar numbers of slave threads. If we compare 3 threads (no padding) to 2 threads (padding), 5 threads (no padding) to 4 threads (padding), 8 threads (padding) to 10 threads (no padding), 16 threads (padding) to 15 threads (no padding), we can see that the no-padding version (**NP**) always outperforms the padding version (**P**). The best optimized version can achieve 2.25 times speedup over the baseline.

Since the benchmarks TMV and MV are available in Nvidia CUBLAS library, we also compare our optimized version to CUBLAS V5.0 [25] in Figure 13 and Figure 14 on GTX 680 GPUs. We also include the SMM version for MV [42] in Figure 14 as a reference. In Figure 13, the height of input matrix is always 2k, and we vary the width of the input matrix. From this figure we can see that our baseline has similar performance to CUBLAS, and our CUDA-NP solution achieves significantly better performance. For matrices with smaller sizes, since the number of overall threads is determined by the width of input matrix, our approach enables more threads to occupy the SMXs and achieve even higher speedups. For example, if the input width is 1k, our CUDA-NP version delivers 4.9 times speedup over CUBLAS.

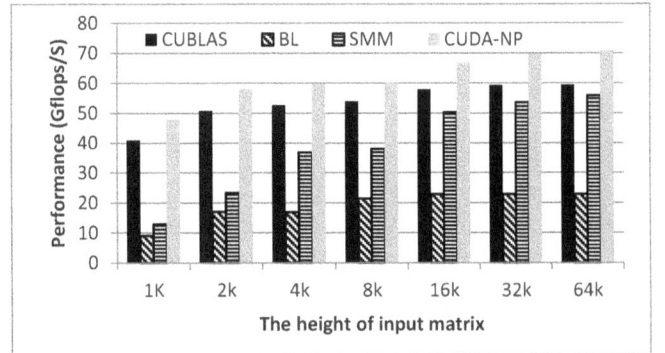

Figure 14. MV results on GTX 680 for matrices with variable heights and a constant width (2k).

We compare our result of MV to CUBLAS and SMM in Figure 14. The shared memory configuration is set to 48KB per SMX. We fix the width of input matrix to 2k and vary the height from 1k to 64k. The height determines the overall number of threads for the baseline. From Figure 14, we can see that our solution always outperforms both SMM and CUBLAS.

As discussed in Section 3.3, for a local memory array, we may replace it with an array in global memory/shared memory or partition it so that the small partitions can be allocated as registers. Among all benchmarks, we are able to apply such optimizations to LE and LIB. We show the performance results when using global memory, shared memory or register file to replace the local memory arrays for these two benchmarks in Figure 15. As show in the figure, using global memory does not help the performance, as the global memory is off-chip memory and the local memory can be cached through L1 cache. The performance of using shared memory depends on the usage of shared memory. Since the size of the local memory array of LE is about twice of the size of local memory array of LIB, we can see heavy shared memory usage for LE actually hurts the performance while we can observe the performance gains for LIB. Since the register file is much larger than shared memory, it works the best for both benchmarks.

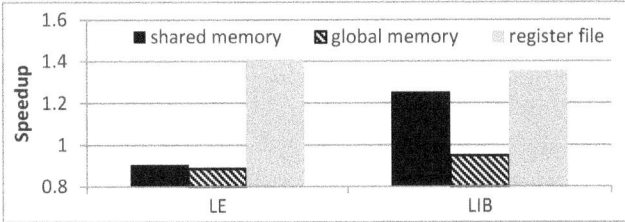

Figure 15. Comparing different ways to replace a local memory array.

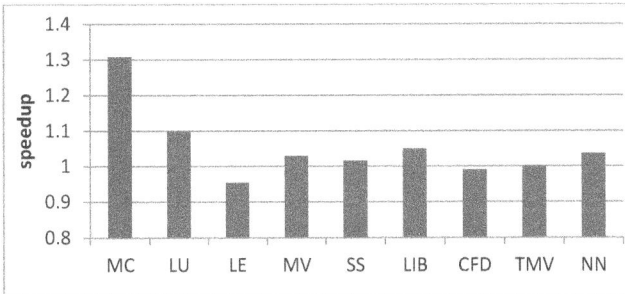

Figure 16. Speedup of using the shfl instruction over using shared memory for reduction or scan operations when applying intra-warp NP. The baseline is the best performing inter-warp NP version.

The benefit of using the __shfl instruction is shown in Figure 16. In the figure, we use the best inter-warp NP version as the baseline to be normalized to. Then we show the speedup of the version of using __shfl instruction for reduction or scan operations over the version of using shared memory. From this figure, we can see that the __shfl instruction is very useful for MC and LU. These two benchmarks have intensive shared memory usage, and using shared memory for reduction or scan operations can make it even more intensive. For other benchmarks, the impact of using __shfl instruction is minor as the scan or reduction primitive only takes a small amount of execution

time. We also see some small slowdowns, and consider the reason may be due to memory behaviour changes.

6. Related Work And Discussion

Many compiler frameworks [3][21][23][38][41] have been developed to utilize high-throughput GPGPU architecture. For example, OpenMPC [21] is proposed to transfer legacy OpenMP programs to GPGPU programs, and [41] translates the naïve GPU programs into optimized ones. Most of these works focuses on optimizing global memory accesses and enabling massive thread-level parallelism. To the best of our knowledge, nested parallelism has been overlooked and our solution is the first compiler approach to exploit it.

It is shown in [10] that using dynamic parallelism can improve the performance of the divide-and-conquer algorithms as the child kernels can be launched by the GPU instead of the CPU. However, they also observed slowdowns due to dynamic parallelism for regular applications such as K-mean.

Dynamic parallelism is more suitable for massive nested loops instead of benchmarks listed in the paper. Furthermore, dynamic parallelism may require additional development effort due to the communication between a child kernel and a parent kernel. For example, shared memory is used in the nested loops for benchmarks, MC, LU, MV, SS, and BK. In order to utilize dynamic parallelism, developers have to write the code to copy the data from shared memory to global memory so that the child kernel can access the data, and then copy the data from global memory back to shared memory. Such expensive memory copy introduces both performance overhead and code In comparison, our CUDA-NP solution eliminates such redundant communications. For the benchmarks, NN, LE, LIB, and CFD, we implemented dynamic parallelism versions, which show 28.92, 7.61, 13.45, 125.67 and 52.29 times slower than their original versions, respectively, due to the communication cost and the dynamic-parallelism-enabled kernel overhead. Using NN as an example, which has a parallel loop with a large loop count, if we choose to let each thread of parent kernel launch a child kernel to perform the parallel loop, the dynamic parallelism version is about 28.92 times slower, compared to the version without dynamic parallelism. Then, we manually optimize it by only using the first thread in a TB to start a child kernel to reduce the number of kernel launches. This version is still 3.25 times slower. Overall, for benchmarks used in this paper, dynamic parallelism cannot help the performance for benchmarks even with manual optimizations, as the available NP is too limited to offset the high overhead of dynamic parallelism.

Some recent works focus on identifying the best performing version in a large search space, either using analytical models [14] or auto-tuning [28]. Since CUDA-NP only generates a small number of versions, the optimal version can be found by testing these versions exhaustively. In other words, a simple auto-tuning can be used to find the optimal configuration. Furthermore, our experiments also reveal some key factors to find the optimal version for CUDA-NP. First, memory coalescing and intra-warp divergence can be used to determine the priority between intra-warp NP and inter-warp NP. Second, using 3 or 7 slave threads achieves close-to-optimal performance for all benchmarks in our study.

While many architectural improvements [24][28][35] and application optimizations [12][14][16][18] [29][31][32] [33][34][39][40][42][43][44] have been proposed for GPGPU programs, only few observe the potential of nested TLP in GPU programs. In [35] a hardware approach is proposed to create threads dynamically in the runtime to reduce the overhead of complex control flow, similar to Nvidia dynamic parallelism. In [14], a warp is used handle one job instead of one thread so as to reduce control divergence. However, in this paper, we show that inter-warp NP, i.e., distributing one master thread's workload into different warps, may be suitable for many benchmarks. Furthermore, compared to [14], our approach only requires an application developer to write pragmas instead of developing new programs. In addition, our compiler can also handle the reduction and scan variables and leverage the __shfl instructions.

Nested parallelism is specified as an option in the OpenMP and is supported in some implementations such as [22]. Compared to previous OpenMP studies [1][5][8][9] [10][11][13][36][37] on nested parallelism for CPUs, our solution is the first language extension to support nested parallelism for GPGPU platforms, and we show different ways to handle the scan and reduction operations, the inter-warp and intra-warp NP schemes, as well as careful resource managements on GPGPUs.

7. Conclusion

In this paper, we propose a novel compiler solution to leverage nested parallelism for GPGPU application. We observe that many benchmarks have relatively light nested parallelism, i.e., parallel loops with small loop counts, which cannot be effectively exploited using the recently introduced dynamic parallelism. Therefore, we propose to partition the code sections into sequential sections and parallel sections, and then enable different numbers of threads for sequential sections and parallel sections. In order to simplify application development, we implement our approach as a compiler framework to support directive-based nested parallelism. In our proposed CUDA-NP compiler framework, an application developer only needs to add OpenMP-like pragmas for parallel loops, and our compiler will generate the optimized code. Our compiler can

handle the reduction and scan variables, chooses either the intra-warp NP or inter-warp NP approach to distribute the parallel loop iterations, and automatically handle different types of live variables across code sections. Our performance results show significant performance gains and demonstrate the effectiveness of our proposed solution.

Acknowledgments

We thank the anonymous reviewers for their insightful comments to improve our paper. This work is supported by an NSF grant CCF-1216569 and a NSF CAREER award CCF-0968667. We also want to thank the ARC Cluster [16] for providing Nvidia K20c GPUs.

References

[1] E. Ayguadé, N. Copty, A. Duran, J. Hoeflinger, Y. Lin, F. Massaioli, X. Teruel, P. Unnikrishnan, and G. Zhang. The design of openmp tasks. In TPDS, 2009.

[2] A. Bakhoda, G. Yuan, W. W. L. Fung, H. Wong, and T. M. Aamodt. Analyzing CUDA workloads using a detailed GPU simulator. In ISPASS April 2009.

[3] M. M. Baskaran, U. Bondhugula, S. Krishnamoorthy, J. Ramanujam, A. Rountev, and P. Sadayappan. A Compiler Framework for Optimization of Affine Loop Nests for GPGPUs. In ICS, 2008.

[4] M. Boyer, D. Tarjan, S. T. Acton, and K. Skadron. Accelerating leukocyte tracking using CUDA: A case study in leveraging manycore coprocessors. In IPDPS 2009.

[5] HM. Bücker, A.Rasch, and A. Wolf. A class of OpenMP applications involving nested parallelism. In Proceedings of the 2004 ACM symposium on Applied computing, 2004.

[6] S. Che, M. Boyer, J. Meng, D. Tarjan, J. W. Sheaffer, S. H. Lee, and K. Skadron. Rodinia: A benchmark suite for heterogeneous computing. In IISWC 2009.

[7] S. Collange, D. Defour, and Y. Zhang. Dynamic detection of uniform and affine vectors in GPGPU computations. In ICPP, 2009.

[8] L. Dagum, and R. Menon. OpenMP: an industry standard API for shared-memory programming. Computational Science & Engineering, 1998.

[9] VV. Dimakopoulos, EH. Panagiotis, and GC. Philos.A microbenchmark study of OpenMP overheads under nested parallelism. In OpenMP in a New Era of Parallelism, 2008.

[10] J. DiMarco, and M. Taufer. Performance impact of dynamic parallelism on different clustering algorithms. In SPIE Defense, Security, and Sensing. International Society for Optics and Photonics, 2013.

[11] A. Duran, M. Gonzàlez, and J. Corbalán.Automatic thread distribution for nested parallelism in OpenMP. In ICS, 2005.

[12] N. Govindaraju, B. Lloyd, Y. Dotsenko, B. Smith, and J. Manferdelli. High performance discrete Fourier transforms on graphics processors. In Proc. Supercomputing, 2008.

[13] PE. Hadjidoukas, and VV. Dimakopoulos . Nested parallelism in the OMPI OpenMP/C compiler. In Euro-Par Parallel Processing, 2007.

[14] S. Hong and H. Kim. An analytical model for GPU architecture with memory-level and thread-level parallelism awareness. In Proc. International Symposium on Computer Architecture, 2009.

[15] S. Hong, S.K. Kim, T. Oguntebi, and K. Olukotun. Accelerating CUDA graph algorithms at maximum warp. In PPoPP 2011.

[16] http://moss.csc.ncsu.edu/~mueller/cluster/arc/

[17] B. Jang, D. Schaa, P. Mistry and D. Kaeli. Exploiting memory access patterns to improve memory performance in data-parallel architectures. In IEEE TPDS, 2010.

[18] O. Kayiran, A. Jog, M. T. Kandemir, C. R. Das. Neither More Nor Less: Optimizing Thread-level Parallelism for GPGPUs. In PACT, 2013.

[19] J. Kim, H. Kim, J. Lee, and J. Lee. Achieving a Single Compute Device Image in OpenCL for Multiple GPUs. In PPoPP, 2011.

[20] S. I. Lee, T. Johnson, and R. Eigenmann. Cetus – an extensible compiler infrastructure for source-to-source transformation. In LCPC, 2003

[21] S. Lee, S.-J. Min, and R. Eigenmann. OpenMP to GPGPU: A compiler framework for automatic translation and optimization. In Proc. In PPoPP, 2009

[22] C. Liao, O. Hernandez, B. Chapman, W. Chen and W. Zheng. OpenUH: An Optimizing, Portable OpenMP Compiler. In the 12th Workshop on Compilers for Parallel Computers, Spain, 2006.

[23] Y. Liu, E. Z. Zhang, amd X. Shen. A Cross-Input Adaptive Frame-work for GPU Programs Optimization. In IPDPS, 2009.

[24] V. Narasiman, C. Lee, M. Shebanow, R. Miftakhutdinov, O. Mutlu, and Y. Patt. Improving GPU Performance via Large Warps and Two-Level Warp Scheduling. In MICRO, 2011.

[25] Nvidia CUDA Toolkit 5.0 CUBLAS Library, 2013

[26] Nvidia GPU Computing SDK 5.0, 2013.

[27] Nvidia Programming Guide, CUDA Toolkit V5.5, 2013.

[28] P. M. Phothilimthana, J. Ansel, J. Ragan-Kelley, and S. Amarasinghe. Portable performance on heterogeneous architectures. In ASPLOS, 2013.

[29] B. Ren, G. Agrawal, J. R. Larus, T. Mytkowicz, T. Poutanen and W. Schulte. SIMD Parallelization of Applications that Traverse Irregular Data Structures. In CGO, 2013.

[30] T. G. Rogers, M.Connor, T. Aamodt, Cache-Conscious Wavefront Scheduling. In MICRO , 2012.

[31] S. Ryoo, C. I. Rodrigues, S. S. Stone, S. S. Baghsorkhi, S. Ueng, J. A. Stratton, and W. W. Hwu. Optimization space pruning for a multi-threaded GPU. In CGO, 2008.

[32] S. Ryoo, C. I. Rodrigues, S. S. Baghsorkhi, S. S. Stone, D. B. Kirk, and W.W. Hwu. Optimization principles and application performance evaluation of a multithreaded GPU using CUDA. In PPoPP, 2008.

[33] G. Ruetsch and P. Micikevicius, Optimize matrix transpose in CUDA. Nvidia, 2009.

[34] J. Sim, A. Dasgupta, H. Kim, and R. Vuduc, A Performance Analysis Framework for Identifying Performance Benefits in GPGPU Applications. In PPoPP, 2012.

[35] M. Steffen and J. Zambreno. Dynamic Thread Creation for Improving Processor Utilization on SIMT Streaming Processor Architectures. In MICRO, 2010.

[36] Y. Tanaka, K. Taura, M. Sato, and A. Yonezawa. Performance evaluation of OpenMP applications with nested parallelism. In Languages, Compilers, and Run-Time Systems for Scalable Computers, 2000.

[37] X. Tian, JP. Hoeflinger, G. Haab, Y.K. Chen, M. Girkar, and S. Shah. A compiler for exploiting nested parallelism in OpenMP programs. Parallel Computing, 2005.

[38] S. Ueng, M. Lathara, S. S. Baghsorkhi, and W. W. Hwu. CUDA-lite: Reducing GPU programming Complexity, In LCPC, 2008

[39] V. Volkov and J. W. Benchmarking GPUs to tune dense linear algebra. In Proc. Supercomputing, 2008.

[40] B. Wu, Z. Zhao, E. Zhang, Y. Jiang, and X. Shen. Complexity Analysis and Algorithm Design for Reorganizing Data to Minimize Non-Coalesced GPU Memory Accesses. In PPoPP, 2013.

[41] Y. Yang, P. Xiang, J. Kong and H. Zhou. A GPGPU Compiler for Memory Optimization and Parallelism Management. In PLDI, 2010.

[42] Y. Yang, P. Xiang, M. Mantor, N. Rubin, and H. Zhou. Shared Memory Multiplexing: A Novel Way to Improve GPGPU Throughput. In PACT, 2012.

[43] Y. Zhang, J. Cohen, and J. D. Owens. Fast Tridiagonal Solvers on the GPU. In PPoPP, 2010.

[44] E. Z. Zhang, Y. Jiang, Z. Guo, K. Tian, and X. Shen. On-the-fly elimination of dynamic irregularities for GPU computing. In ASPLOS, 2011.

yaSpMV: Yet Another SpMV Framework on GPUs

Shengen Yan

Institute of Software, Chinese
Academy of Sciences
University of Chinese Academy
of Sciences Beijing, China
North Carolina State University
Raleigh, NC

yanshengen@gmail.com

Chao Li

North Carolina State University
Raleigh, NC

cli17@ncsu.edu

Yunquan Zhang

State Key Lab of Computer
Architecture, Institute of
Computing Technology, Chinese
Academy of Sciences
Institute of Software, Chinese
Academy of Sciences
Beijing, China
zyq@ict.ac.cn

Huiyang Zhou

North Carolina State University
Raleigh, NC

hzhou@ncsu.edu

Abstract

SpMV is a key linear algebra algorithm and has been widely used in many important application domains. As a result, numerous attempts have been made to optimize SpMV on GPUs to leverage their massive computational throughput. Although the previous work has shown impressive progress, load imbalance and high memory bandwidth remain the critical performance bottlenecks for SpMV. In this paper, we present our novel solutions to these problems. First, we devise a new SpMV format, called blocked compressed common coordinate (BCCOO), which uses bit flags to store the row indices in a blocked common coordinate (COO) format so as to alleviate the bandwidth problem. We further improve this format by partitioning the matrix into vertical slices to enhance the cache hit rates when accessing the vector to be multiplied. Second, we revisit the segmented scan approach for SpMV to address the load imbalance problem. We propose a highly efficient matrix-based segmented sum/scan for SpMV and further improve it by eliminating global synchronization. Then, we introduce an auto-tuning framework to choose optimization parameters based on the characteristics of input sparse matrices and target hardware platforms. Our experimental results on GTX680 GPUs and GTX480 GPUs show that our proposed framework achieves significant performance improvement over the vendor tuned CUSPARSE V5.0 (up to 229% and 65% on average on GTX680 GPUs, up to 150% and 42% on average on GTX480 GPUs) and some most recently proposed schemes (e.g., up to 195% and 70% on average over clSpMV on GTX680 GPUs, up to 162% and 40% on average over clSpMV on GTX480 GPUs).

Categories and Subject Descriptors D.1.3 [**Concurrent Programming**]: Parallel programming

Keywords SpMV, Segmented Scan, BCCOO, OpenCL, CUDA, GPU, Parallel algorithms

PPoPP'14, February 15–19, 2014, Orlando, Florida, USA.
Copyright © 2014 ACM 978-1-4503-2656-8/14/02...$15.00.
http://dx.doi.org/10.1145/2555243.2555255

1. Introduction

Sparse matrix vector multiplication (SpMV) is a key linear algebra algorithm and is heavily used in many important application domains. As state-of-art many-core GPUs feature remarkably high computational throughput and memory access bandwidth, there has been strong interest in GPU-accelerated SpMV [1][6][7][12][14][15][16][17][21].

Although the sequential implementation of SpMV is fairly straightforward, its parallel implementation is challenging for two main reasons. First, the row-based parallelization, i.e., assigning one thread to compute the dot-product between one row of the matrix and the multiplied vector, although making logical sense, suffers from the load imbalance problem as non-zeros in a matrix may not be evenly distributed across different rows. Such a load imbalance problem is more severe in GPU architectures since the threads in a warp operate in the single-instruction multiple-data (SIMD) manner. Load imbalance among threads in a warp will result in control divergence and the execution time of all the threads in a warp will be forced to be equal to the longest running one. Second, SpMV puts high pressure on the memory hierarchy. The matrix data have low reuse as each non-zero element is only used once for computing the corresponding dot product. On the other hand, although the multiplied vector is reused as each non-empty row of the matrix will use it to compute a dot-product, the access pattern is irregular due to irregular locations of non-zeros in different rows. Such irregular accesses do not meet the GPU memory coalescing requirement, which means that different threads in a warp need to access the data in the same block, to achieve high memory access bandwidth.

Many approaches have been proposed to optimizing SpMV on multi-core CPUs and many-core GPUs. To reduce the memory footprint of sparse matrices, different formats have been proposed to leverage different characteristics of sparse matrices. It has been shown in [16] that among the existing formats, no single format can achieve the best performance and a cocktail format is proposed to combine the strengths of existing formats by partitioning a sparse matrix and applying different formats to different partitions. Given the different features of target hardware platforms and different characteristics of sparse matrices, offline auto-tuning or benchmarking is commonly used to improve the performance. Although previous work has achieved impressive performance improvement for SpMV, the load imbalance problem and the high memory bandwidth requirement remain the fundamental performance bottlenecks for SpMV. In this paper, we propose our novel solution to SpMV.

We first propose a new format for sparse matrices to alleviate the high memory bandwidth requirement of SpMV. Our new format is referred to as blocked compressed common coordinate (BCCOO) as it is built upon the common coordinate (COO) format. The BCCOO format extends the COO format with blocking to reduce the size for both row and column index arrays. Then, it uses bit-flags to drastically reduce the size of the row index array. To improve the cache hit rate for accessing the multiplied vector, we partition a sparse matrix into vertical slices and align the slices in a top-down manner before applying the BCCOO format. Such vertical partition-based BCCOO is referred to as the BCCOO+ format.

To address the load imbalance problem, we revisit the matrix-based segmented scan and design a new highly optimized segmented scan/sum kernel for SpMV. In our approach, each thread processes the same number of consecutive non-zero blocks and it performs *sequential* segmented scans/sums to generate partial sum results. This way, it avoids the workload imbalance problem and reduces the memory requirement on the row information associated with each thread. Then, each workgroup/thread block will run the parallel segmented scan on the last partial sum results computed from each of its threads. When the final dot-product results require accumulating partial sums across multiple workgroups/thread blocks, adjacent synchronization [24] is used to eliminate the overhead of global synchronization.

To further improve the performance of our SpMV kernel, we introduce an auto-tuning framework to explore optimization parameters for different sparse matrices and different platforms. Such optimization parameters include whether to use texture cache for multiplied vector, whether to perform transpose online or offline, the suitable block sizes for our proposed BCCOO/BCCOO+ format, the number of non-zero blocks to be processed by each thread, the number of threads in a workgroup, the size of shared memory (also called local memory in OpenCL [19]) or registers to be used for intermediate partial sums, etc. As these parameters form a large search space, we introduce a set of accelerations to reduce the auto-tuning time to a few seconds.

Our experiments on a set of 20 sparse matrices show that our proposed single format fits nearly all of the sparse matrices under our study. Compared to the vendor-tuned library CUSPARSE V5.0, our proposed scheme achieves performance improvement by up to 150% and 42% on average on GTX480 GPUs, up to 229% and 65% on average

on GTX680 GPUs. Compared to the clSpMV [16], which combines advantages of many existing formats, our proposed scheme achieves a performance gain of up to 162% and 40% on average on GTX480 GPUs, up to 195% and 70% on average on GTX680 GPUs.

The remainder of this paper is organized as follows. Section 2 presents our proposed BCCOO/BCCOO+ format for sparse matrices. Section 3 details our proposed customized matrix-based segmented scan/sum approach for SpMV. Section 4 summarizes our auto-tuning framework. The experimental methodology and the results are discussed in Sections 5 and 6, respectively. Section 7 addresses the related work. Section 8 concludes the paper.

2. The Block-based Compressed Common Coordinate (BCCOO) Format

Our proposed block-based compressed common coordinate format builds upon the common coordinate (COO) format. In this section, we first present the COO format as the background and then introduce our BCCOO format and its extension BCCOO+ format. For illustration, we use the matrix in Eq. 1 as a running example.

$$A = \begin{bmatrix} 0 & 0 & a & 0 & 0 & 0 & b & c \\ 0 & 0 & d & e & 0 & 0 & f & 0 \\ 0 & 0 & 0 & 0 & g & h & i & j \\ k & l & 0 & 0 & m & n & o & p \end{bmatrix} \quad \text{Eq. 1}$$

2.1 COO Format

The COO format is a widely used format for sparse matrices. It has explicit storage for the column and row indices for all non-zeros in a sparse matrix. For example, the matrix in Eq.1 can be represented with a row index array, a column index array, and a data value array, as shown in Figure 1.

Row_index = [0 0 0 1 1 1 2 2 2 2 3 3 3 3 3 3]
Col_index = [2 6 7 2 3 6 4 5 6 7 0 1 4 5 6 7]
Value = [a b c d e f g h i j k l m n o p]

Figure 1. The COO format of matrix A.

The parallelization strategy suitable with COO, as shown in previous work [1], is segmented scan/reduction. As highlighted in [1][16], the advantage of the COO format is that it does not suffer from the load imbalance problem and can achieve consistent performance over different types of sparse matrices. However, the key problem of the COO format is that it needs to explicitly store both the row index and the column index for every non-zero data element. Therefore, it has the worst memory footprint [16].

2.2 BCCOO Format

Our proposed BCCOO format extends the COO format in two ways. First, we incorporate the block-based format to the COO format. In block-based formats such as blocked ELLPACK and blocked CSR [7], a non-zero block is stored consecutively. This way, one block of data values will share the same row index and the same column index. Therefore, the storage overhead of the row index array and the column index array can be significantly reduced. For matrix A in Eq. 1, if a block size of 2x2 is used, the blocked COO (BCOO) format has the index arrays and the data value array shown in Figure 2.

Row_index = [0 0 1 1 1]

Col_index = [1 3 0 2 3]

$\text{Value} = \begin{pmatrix} [a \ 0 \ b \ c \ 0 \ 0 \ g \ h \ i \ j] \\ [d \ e \ f \ 0 \ k \ l \ m \ n \ o \ p] \end{pmatrix}$

Figure 2. The blocked COO format of matrix A with the block size of 2x2.

From Figure 2, we can see that there are 5 non-zero blocks. Both the row index array and the column index array have been reduced significantly. The first non-zero 2x2 block is $\begin{pmatrix} a & 0 \\ d & e \end{pmatrix}$ and its block-based row index and column index are 0 and 1, respectively. The next non-zero 2x2 block is $\begin{pmatrix} b & c \\ f & 0 \end{pmatrix}$ and its blocked-based row index and column index are 0 and 3, respectively. Note that in Figure 2, we use two data value arrays rather than a single array in Figure 1. The reason is that for a block size with the height larger than 1, we put different rows in different data value arrays such that both the row index and column index can be used directly to index the data in each of the value arrays. Such data arrangement is also helpful for contiguous memory accesses. The overhead of the BCOO format, which is shared among all block-based formats, is the zeros in the data value array when a non-zero block contains zeros.

Bit Flag = [1 0 1 1 0]

Col_index = [1 3 0 2 3]

$\text{Value} = \begin{pmatrix} [a \ 0 \ b \ c \ 0 \ 0 \ g \ h \ i \ j] \\ [d \ e \ f \ 0 \ k \ l \ m \ n \ o \ p] \end{pmatrix}$

Figure 3. The BCCOO format of matrix A with the block size of 2x2.

Our key extension to the COO format is to use a bit flag array to compress the row index array in a lossless manner. The bit flag array can be viewed simply as the result of a difference function being applied to the row index array. For a difference value larger than 1, we replace it with multiple 1s. Then, we flip 1s and 0s such that a bit value of '0' in the bit flag array represents a row stop, i.e., the corresponding value is the last non-zero in a row. A bit value of '1' represents that it is not the last non-zero in a row. The reason for such representation is that when we compute the partial sums for dot-product result, using the value '0' eliminates the condition check on the next non-zero for the end of a row (see Section 3.2). As our bit flag array provides lossless compression on the row index array, the row index information can be reconstructed from the bit flag array by accumulating the number of row stops. We refer to this format as blocked compressed COO (BCCOO). For matrix

A in Eq. 1, the BCCOO format is shown in Figure 3 with the block size of 2x2.

Compared to the BCOO format shown in Figure 2, the column index array and the data value arrays remain the same. The row index array becomes a bit vector of 5 bits. Assuming that integers are used for row indices, a compression ratio of 32 is achieved for the row index array.

In our implementation, in order to remove the control flow to check the end of the bit flag array, we pad it with bit '1' such that the length of the bit flag array is a multiple of the working set (i.e., number of non-zero blocks to be processed) of a workgroup.

Similar to row-index arrays, we can also try to reduce data transmission required for column index arrays using difference functions. In our approach, we first apply a segmented difference function on a column index array with each segment being the working set of each thread. This way, there is no inter-thread dependency when reconstructing the column indices. The resulting difference array is stored using the short data type instead of the regular integer type. If a difference value is beyond the range of a signed short, we replace it with a fixed value -1, which means that the original column index array needs to be accessed for this particular index.

$$B = \begin{bmatrix} 0 & 0 & a & 0 \\ 0 & 0 & d & e \\ 0 & 0 & 0 & 0 \\ k & l & 0 & 0 \\ 0 & 0 & b & c \\ 0 & 0 & f & 0 \\ g & h & i & j \\ m & n & o & p \end{bmatrix}$$

(a)

Bit Flag = [0 0 0 1 0]

Col_index = [1 0 3 2 3]   (uncompressed)

$\text{Value} = \begin{pmatrix} [a \ 0 \ 0 \ 0 \ b \ c \ g \ h \ i \ j] \\ [d \ e \ k \ l \ f \ 0 \ m \ n \ o \ p] \end{pmatrix}$

(b)

Figure 4. The BCCOO+ format of matrix A in Eq. 1. (a) The vertically sliced and rearranged matrix of matrix A. (b) The bit flag array, the column index array, and the data value arrays.

2.3 BCCOO+ Format

We also propose an extension to our BCCOO format to improve the locality of the accesses to the multiplied vector, referred to as the BCCOO+ format. In this format, we first partition a sparse matrix into vertical slices and then align the slices in a top-down manner. Then, we apply the BCCOO format on the vertically sliced and rearranged matrix with an exception on column indices. The column index array is generated based on the block coordinates in the original matrix rather than the transformed matrix as we need original column indices to locate the corresponding elements in the multiplied vector for dot-product operations.

For matrix A in Eq. 1, the vertically sliced and rearranged matrix becomes matrix B in Figure 4a if the number of slice is 2 and the slice width is 4. The BCCOO+ format of A is shown in Figure 4b when the block size 2x2 is used.

As shown in Figure 4, the bit flag array encodes that there is only one non-zero block in row 0, row 1, and row 2. Row 3, in contrast, contains 2 non-zero blocks. The column indices of these blocks, however, are determined from matrix A rather than matrix B. Taking the 2x2 block $\begin{pmatrix} g & h \\ m & n \end{pmatrix}$ as an example, it resides at column 2 in matrix A, which is why its column index value is 2 as shown in Figure 4b.

The benefit of BCCOO+ format can be illustrated with matrix-vector multiplication between matrix A and vector y, i.e., $A*\vec{y}$. Different rows in the same vertical slice, e.g., slice 0, will all use y[0]~y[3]. Similarly, all the rows in slice 1 will use y[4]~y[7] to compute the dot-product. As the block $\begin{pmatrix} g & h \\ m & n \end{pmatrix}$ is in slice 1, it needs to use y[4]~y[7], with the block size of 2x2, its column index of 2 provides the necessary information for indexing y[4] and y[5] from the vector $\vec{y}$.

$$A * \vec{y} = \begin{bmatrix} 0 & 0 & a & 0 \\ 0 & 0 & d & e \\ 0 & 0 & 0 & 0 \\ k & l & 0 & 0 \end{bmatrix} * \begin{bmatrix} y[0] \\ y[1] \\ y[2] \\ y[3] \end{bmatrix} + $$
$$\begin{bmatrix} 0 & 0 & b & c \\ 0 & 0 & f & 0 \\ g & h & i & j \\ m & n & o & p \end{bmatrix} * \begin{bmatrix} y[4] \\ y[5] \\ y[6] \\ y[7] \end{bmatrix}$$

Figure 5. Matrix-vector multiplication as a sum of the products between its vertical slices and the corresponding vector segments.

Since the BCCOO+ format breaks the original matrix into slices, after performing the matrix-vector multiplication on each slice, the intermediate results need to be combined to generate the final results. Using our running example of matrix A in Eq. 1, the derivation of $A*\vec{y}$ is shown in Figure 5. Therefore, when using the BCCOO+ format, it is necessary to use a temporary buffer to store the intermediate results and to invoke an additional kernel to combine them. Depending on the number of slices, the size of the temporary buffer can be large, thereby hurting the performance. As a result, the BCCOO+ format is not always preferred over the BCCOO format and we resort to auto-tuning to determine either the BCCOO or BCCOO+ format should be used.

2.4 Auxiliary Information for SpMV

To facilitate the computation of SpMV, the following information is computed and stored along with the BCCOO/BCCOO+ format. First, based on the number of non-zeros that each thread will process, we compute the location of the first result generated by each thread, i.e., the row index that the result belongs to. Using matrix C in Eq. 2

as an example, in which each element is a block of data. To simplify the discussion, we assume the block size as nx1. As discussed in Section 2.2, for a block size with the height larger than 1, each row will be stored in a separate value array. The BCCOO format of matrix C is shown in Figure 6a. As there are 16 non-zero data blocks, assuming each thread will process 4 non-zero blocks, we will compute the row index that the first result generated by each thread belongs to. Such information can be computed with a scan operation on the bitwise inverse of the bit flag array in the BCCOO format. In this example, thread 0 processes the first 4 non-zero data blocks A', B', C', and D' and its first computation result, i.e., A'*y', is part of the final result for the dot-product between row 0 and the multiplied vector. So, the result entry is set to 0. Similarly, thread 1 processes the next four non-zero blocks E', F', G', and H'. As block E' still belongs to row 0, the entry for the first result of thread 1 is set as 0.

$$C = \begin{bmatrix} A' & 0 & B' & 0 & C' & 0 & D' & E' \\ 0 & 0 & 0 & F' & 0 & 0 & G' & 0 \\ 0 & H' & 0 & I' & 0 & J' & 0 & 0 \\ 0 & K' & L' & M' & 0 & N' & O' & P' \end{bmatrix} \qquad \text{Eq.2}$$

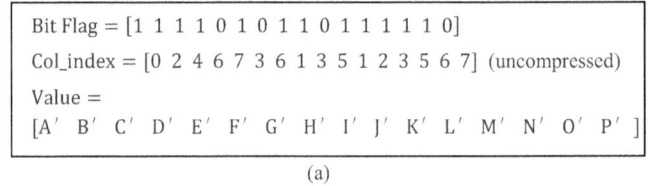

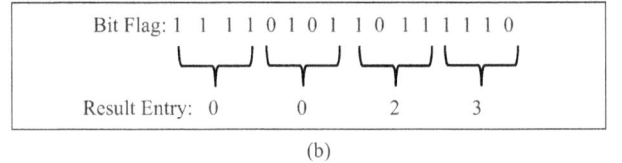

Bit Flag = [1 1 1 1 0 1 0 1 1 0 1 1 1 1 1 0]

Col_index = [0 2 4 6 7 3 6 1 3 5 1 2 3 5 6 7] (uncompressed)

Value =
[A' B' C' D' E' F' G' H' I' J' K' L' M' N' O' P']

(a)

Bit Flag: 1 1 1 1 0 1 0 1 1 0 1 1 1 1 1 0

Result Entry: 0   0   2   3

(b)

Figure 6. (a) The BCCOO format of Matrix C in Eq.2. (b) The example of compute the location of the first result generated by each thread, assuming that there are four threads and each thread processes four non-zero blocks.

Second, we perform a quick check to see whether we can skip the parallel segmented scan operation at the workgroup level. It is the case when each thread in a workgroup encounters a row stop, which results in the segment size being 1 for the parallel segmented scan.

3. An Efficient Matrix-based Segmented Sum/Scan for SpMV

With a sparse matrix stored in our BCCOO/BCCOO+ format, SpMV can be implemented in three logical steps: (1) read the data value arrays and multiply them with the corresponding vector values indexed by the *Col_index* array; (2) perform a segmented scan using the bit flag array from our BCCOO/BCCOO+ format; (3) write back the results to global memory. In our proposed scheme, all these three steps are implemented in a single kernel so as to minimize the kernel invocation overhead.

3.1 Segmented Scans

The segmented scan primitive scans multiple data segments that are stored together. A start flag array is typically used to identify the first element of a segment. We show an example of the inclusive segmented scan in Figure 7. Its start flag array is generated from the bit-flag array of the BCCOO format in Figure 6. The output of the inclusive segment scan is the '*Result*' array in Figure 7. Note that for SpMV, the complete segmented scan results are not necessary. Instead, the last sum of each segment is sufficient, as marked with underscores in the '*Result*' array. In other words, for SpMV, the segmented reduction/sum primitive can be used rather than the segmented scan primitive.

Input = [3 2 0 2 1 0 4 2 4 3 2 2 0 1 3 1]

Bit Flag = [1 1 1 1 0 1 0 1 1 0 1 1 1 1 1 0]

Start Flag = [1 0 0 0 0 1 0 1 0 0 1 0 0 0 0 0]

Result = [3 5 5 7 <u>8</u> 0 <u>4</u> 2 6 <u>9</u> 2 4 4 5 8 <u>9</u>]

Figure 7. An inclusive segmented scan with the start flags generated from the bit flag array in Figure 6(a).

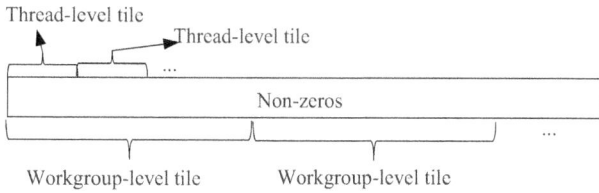

Figure 8. Even workload distribution: each workgroup/thread block works on a workgroup-level tile; each thread works on a thread-level tile of non-zero blocks.

Two main approaches have been proposed to parallelize the segmented scan primitive on GPUs. One is a tree-based approach [5], which builds a binary tree through different processing stages. The tree-based approach suffers from the load imbalance problem as different numbers of threads will be idle in different processing stages. Furthermore, it requires workgroup-level synchronization between stages as discussed in [8]. The other is a matrix-based approach, which is proposed to improve memory efficiency and overcome the load imbalance problem. Our proposed BCCOO/BCCOO+ format suits better with the matrix-based segmented scan and we further customize it for SpMV.

3.2 A Customized Matrix-based Segmented Sum/Scan for SpMV

3.2.1 Per-thread and per-workgroup working sets

In our segmented sum/scan approach for SpMV, the input non-zero blocks as well as the corresponding bit-flag array and the column index array are divided evenly among workgroups. The working set of each workgroup is referred to as a workgroup-level tile, which in turn will be divided evenly among the threads within the workgroup. The working set of a thread is referred to as a thread-level tile, as shown in Figure 8. The benefits of using a single thread to

process multiple consecutive non-zero blocks (e.g., 16) are two-folds. First, a single/few load(s) from the bit flag array (e.g., loading a single short type of data) will be sufficient to provide all the bit flag information. Compared to the previous approaches, which load the row index information for every non-zero, significant bandwidth will be saved. Second, each thread will perform the segmented scan in a sequential manner and may use a segmented sum instead of a segmented scan, which has fewer intermediate results to keep. Also, note that the bit flags in our BCCOO/BCCOO+ format are different from the start flags that are used in typical segmented scans as shown in Figure 7. Although the start flags can be derived from the bit flags, we choose to use the bit flags since it is straightforward to tell whether a segment ends from the bit flags. If the start flags were used, one needs to search for the next start to find the end of the current segment. It would be more complex when the non-zeros in a row span across multiple thread-level or workgroup-level tiles.

Since a thread-level tile may contain row stops, each thread will write its last partial sum into a temporary array, called 'last_partial_sums', based on its thread identifier (tid) within the workgroup. Then, a parallel scan will be performed on this last_partial_sums array. The start flags of the last_partial_sums array are generated by each thread as well. To handle the case when the non-zeros in a row span multiple workgroups/thread blocks, we leverage the recently proposed adjacent synchronization [24] to enable inter-workgroup communication while eliminating global synchronization.

3.2.2 Computing per-thread and per-workgroup partial sums

We design two strategies to compute intra-workgroup partial sums from a workgroup-level tile. Either suits for different types of sparse matrices. In the first strategy, each thread has an array, called '*intermediate_sums*', to keep all the intermediate sums of its thread-level tile. This intermediate_sums array can be stored in shared memory, registers, or split between shared memory and registers. This strategy works well if the lengths of the segments are very small, meaning that many rows in a sparse matrix have very small numbers of non-zeros. For matrix C in Eq. 2, assuming that each thread-level tile contains 4 non-zero blocks and there are 4 threads in a workgroup, the computation is illustrated in Figure 9. From the figure, we can see that each thread performs a sequential segmented scan, stores the results in its intermediate_sums array, and uses the last partial sum to update the corresponding entry of the last_partial_sums array, which locates in shared memory and is accessible by all the threads in a workgroup. If the last element of a thread-level tile is a row stop, the last partial sum of this thread is 0, as shown in thread 3 in Figure 9.

To facilitate memory accesses to the data value array, we can view it as a 2-dimension array with the width as the

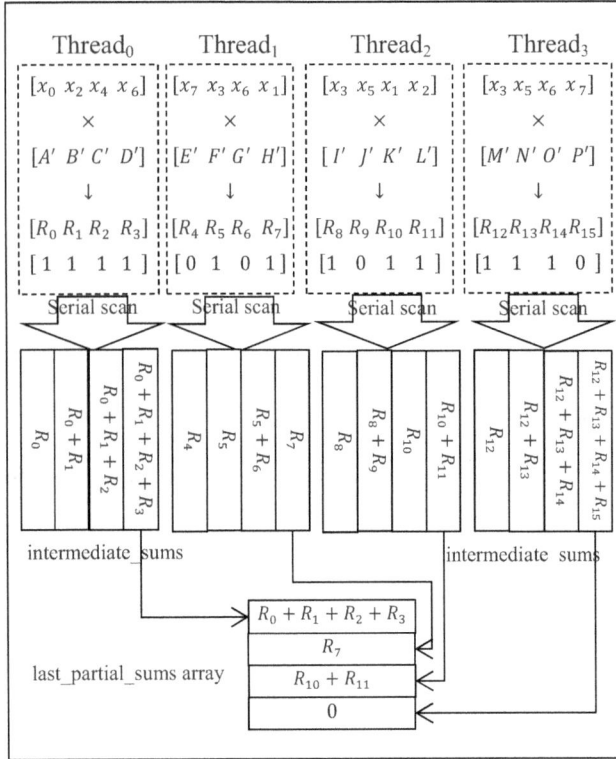

Figure 9. Computing segmented scans: strategy 1, which uses per-thread buffers, i.e., 'intermediate_sums' arrays to store intermediate sum results.

thread-level tile size. Then, with a transpose operation, which can be done either on-line or offline, the threads in a warp will access the data in a row-by-row manner, thereby satisfying the memory coalescing requirement. The same also applies to the col_index array. Offline transpose removes the need for a share memory buffer which is required for transpose. In comparison, with the on-line approach, the threads in a warp read one tile at a time in a coalesced manner and multiply with the corresponding vector elements, then store the results in a shared memory buffer still in the row-based manner. Later on, when performing the segmented scan, the threads read the buffer in a column-based manner. This way, better performance may be achieved due to improved locality from accesses to the multiplied vector if non-zeros in a row are close to each other.

In our second strategy, we allocate a result cache in shared memory to only store the sum of each segment. This strategy works better for long segments and also benefits from efficient memory writes as we can store the result cache to global memory in a coalesced way. With this strategy, the offline transpose is used to ensure coalesced memory reads from the value array and the col_index array. After performing the multiplication with vector elements, each thread carries out a segmented sum sequentially on its thread-level tile, using the bit flag array as the mask for the segments. All the segmented sums will be written to the

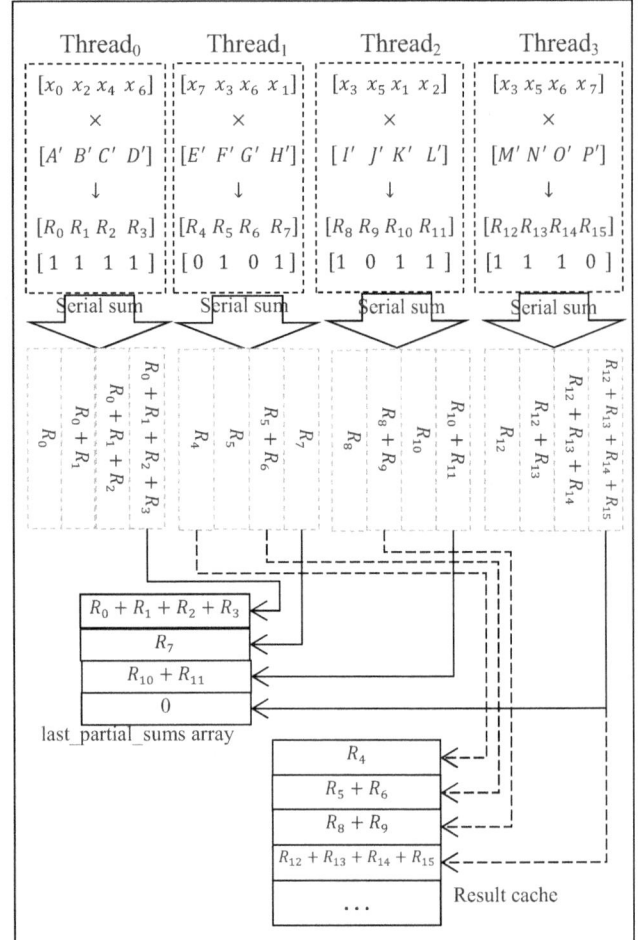

Figure 10. Computing segmented scan: strategy 2, which uses a per-workgroup result cache to store segmented sums. The dashed blocks mean that the intermediate sums are *not* stored.

result cache with the help of the first-result-entry information generated along with the BCCOO format. The process is illustrated in Figure 10 for matrix C in Eq. 2 assuming that the thread-level tile size is 4 and there are 4 threads in a workgroup. The first-result-entry information shown in Figure 6 is used for updating the result cache. For example, as shown in Figure 6 the first-result-entry for thread 1 and thread 2 is 0 and 2, respectively. Therefore, when thread 1 encounters the first row stop, i.e., the end of the first segment, it uses its current sum R4 to update the results cache entry 0. When thread 1 encounters the second row stop, it uses the sum R5+R6 to update the result cache entry 1. In a sense, the first-result-entry information computed along the BCCOO format partitions the result cache among different threads in a workgroup. In the case when the number of row stops in a workgroup-level tile is larger than the results cache size, the extra segmented sums will be stored in the result array in global memory, which will be re-accessed later to generate the final outputs. The same as the first strategy, each thread also writes its last partial sum to the last_partial_sums array. To generate the

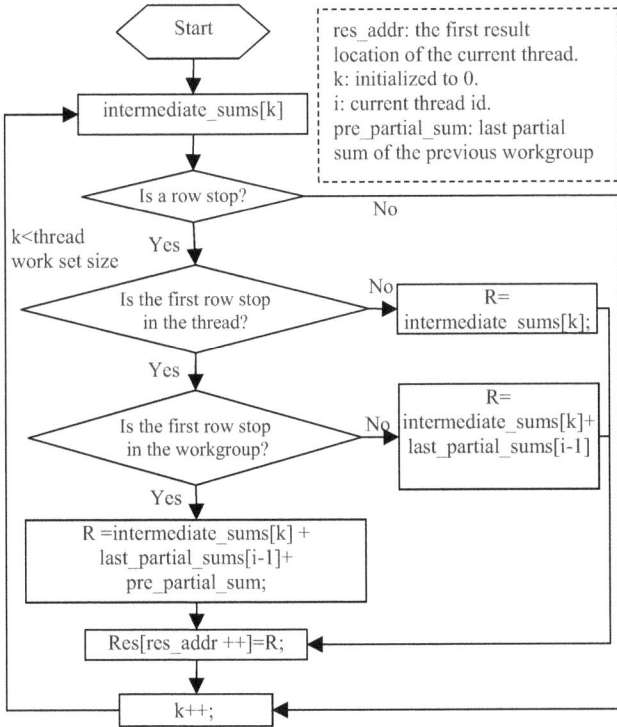

Figure 11. A flow chart of combining the partial sums from threads and workgroups: strategy 1.

start flags for the last_partial_sums array, in either strategy, each thread performs the simple check on whether its bit flags contain a 0. In other words, each thread checks whether there is a row stop in its thread-level tile. If so, its last partial sum should be a start for a segment in the last_partial_sums array. For the example in Figure 9 and Figure 10, the start flags are [0, 1, 1, 1] since all threads except thread 0 process a tile containing a row stop. After all threads in a workgroup update its last partial sum in the last_partial_sums array and generate the start flags, which is signaled with a workgroup-level synchronization or syncthreads(), the threads in the workgroup perform a parallel segmented scan using the scan algorithm in [18] and the results are also stored in the same last_partial_sums array. In our example in Figure 9 or Figure 10, this parallel scan can be skipped as all the segment sizes are 1.

3.2.3 Combining per-thread and per-workgroup partial sums

Next, we need to combine the results in the per-thread intermediate_sums arrays, the scanned result for the per-workgroup last_partial_sums array, and also the results from other workgroups to generate the final output of SpMV.

For our first strategy, each thread will go through its intermediate_sums array. For each element, it checks whether the corresponding bit flag is a row stop. If not, it means the corresponding result has already been incorporated into the sum of the segment. For a row stop, a thread further checks whether it is the first stop in its thread-level tile. If not, it means the thread-level tile contains the

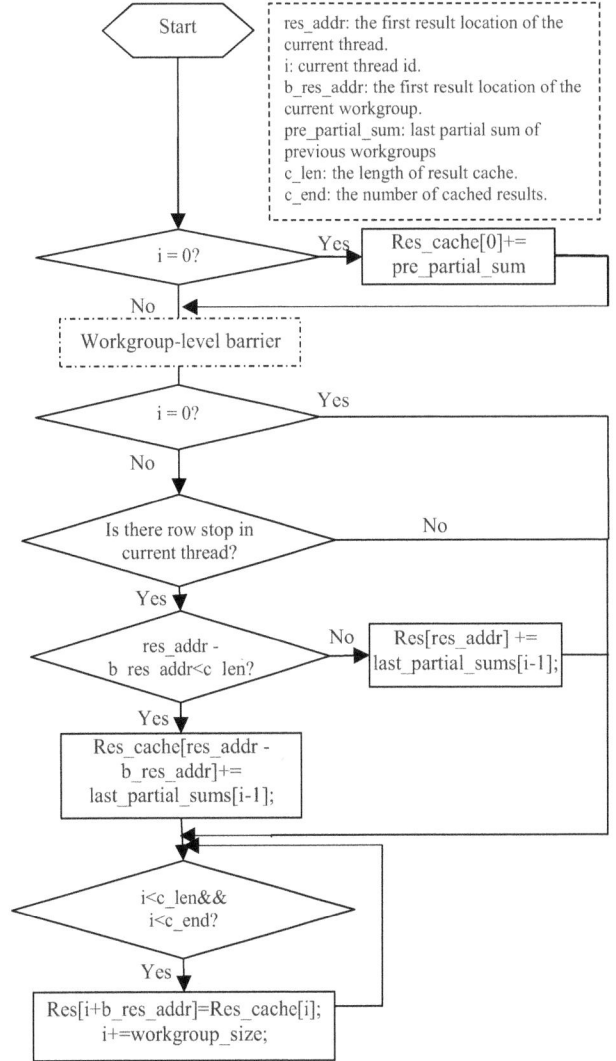

Figure 12. A flow chart of combining the partial sums from threads and workgroups: strategy 2

complete segment and the corresponding result is the final result. In the example shown in Figure 9, for thread 1, the entry in its intermediate_sums array containing (R_5+R_6) is such a case. If a row stop is the first in a thread-level tile (e.g., the entry containing R_4 for thread 1 in Figure 9), there are two possibilities. One is that the segment spans multiple threads within a workgroup. Then, the last_partial_sums array of the workgroup will be used to retrieve the last partial sum of the previous threads. For example, the entry containing $(R_0+R_1+R_2+R_3)$ in the last_partial_sums array will be added to R_4 of thread 1 in Figure 9. As the last_partial_sums array contains the scanned result of the original last partial sums of each thread, the entry *last_partial_sums[i-1]* (*i* the current thread id) already accumulates the partial sums of multiple threads for segments spanning multiple threads. The other possibility is that the segment spans multiple threads across workgroups. In this case, we also need to accumulate previous workgroups' last partial sum results. We resort to adjacent synchronization to avoid global synchronization as discussed in Section 3.2.4. In Figure 11, a flow chart of the kernel program is presented to illustrate the process discussed above.

For our second strategy, there are no per-thread intermediate sum arrays. Instead, there is a per-workgroup result cache and therefore threads in a workgroup rely on the first result location, which is produced along the BCCOO/BCCOO+ format, to process the result cache and the flow chart of the kernel code is presented in Figure 12. Each thread except thread 0 first checks whether there are row stops in its thread-level tile. If so, it means that the thread has generated some partial sums corresponding to the row stops. Here, each thread only needs to process the partial sum at the first row stop since it may be a part of a long segment spanning multiple thread-level tiles (e.g., R_4 in the result cache in Figure 10). For subsequent row stops in the thread, the partial sums in the result cache are already complete segment sums (e.g., R_5+R_6 in the result cache in Figure 10). Then, each thread except thread 0 checks whether its first partial sum is written in the result cache or in global memory depending on its first result position and the result cache size. As the last partial sum corresponding to the previous thread in the last_partial_sums array already accumulates the partial sums of multiple threads for segments spanning multiple threads, it is added to the result cache entry (e.g., $R_0+R_1+R_2+R_3$ from the last_partial_sums array is added to R_4 in the result cache in Figure 10). For thread 0, it updates result cache entry 0 with the last partial sum from the previous workgroup. To avoid data race at result cache entry 0, a workgroup-level synchronization is added after thread 0 processes the result cache entry 0. After the result cache is processed, it is written to global memory in a memory coalesced way by all threads together in a workgroup.

3.2.4 Accumulating partial sums across workgroups

As discussed in Section 3.2.3, for segments spanning multiple workgroups, the last workgroup, which contains the row stop, needs to accumulate previous workgroups partial sums. Here, we make an implicit assumption that the workgroup-level tiles are distributed to workgroups in-order. In other words, workgroup 0 processes the first tile; workgroup 1 processes the second tile; etc. Current GPUs dispatch workgroups in-order. Therefore, we can directly use the workgroup ids in the kernel. If a GPU dispatches workgroups out-of-order, workgroups can get such 'logic' workgroup ids from global memory using atomic fetch-and-add operations. This approach incurs small performance overhead, less than 2% in our experiments. To accumulate partial sums across workgroups, we use a global memory array 'Grp_sum'. The array is initialized to a special value (e.g., maximal floating-point number). This array is updated in a sequential manner. Workgroup 0 updates the first entry 'Grp_sum[0]' with its last partial sum. For a subsequent workgroup with id X, if it does not contain a row stop, it waits for the entry 'Grp_sum[X-1]' to be changed from the

initial value, i.e., updated by workgroup (X-1), and then updates 'Grp_sum[X]' with the sum of its last partial sum and 'Grp_sum[X-1]'. If a workgroup contains a row stop, it breaks such chained updates and directly updates 'Grp_sum[X]' with its last partial sum. This approach is called adjacent synchronization in [24].

4. Auto-Tuning Framework

As discussed in Sections 2 and 3, we propose a new format BCCOO and its variant BCCOO+ for sparse matrices, and two new strategies to compute segmented sums/scans for SpMV. To find the optimal solution for a sparse matrix, we build an auto-tuning framework to select the format, the computing strategy, as well as their associated parameters. Then, the OpenCL code is generated according to the selected parameters from this auto-tuning framework. We also use this framework to exploit the texture cache for the multiplied vector. Another optimization is that we use the 'unsigned short' data type for the col_index array if the width of a sparse matrix is less than 65535. In this case, there is no need to further compress the col_index array using the approach discussed in Section 2.2. The parameters that this framework explores are listed in Table 1. Note that when strategy 1 is used to compute the segmented scan, the thread-level tile size is the size of the immediate_sums array, which is the sum of the parameters, Reg_size and ShM_size.

Table 1. Tunable parameters of the auto-tuning framework.

Parameter Name		Possible Values
Matrix format		BCCOO, BCCOO+
Col_index compress		Yes, No
Block width		1, 2, 4
Block height		1, 2, 3, 4
Data type for the bit flag array		Unsigned char, unsigned short, unsigned int
Vertical slice number		1, 2, 4, 8, 16, 32
Transpose		Offline, online
Texture memory for multiplied vector		Yes, No
Workgroup size		64, 128, 256, 512
Strategy 1	Registers for the per-thread intermediate sums array (Reg_size)	0, 8, 16, 32
	Shared memory for the per-thread intermediate sums array (ShM_size)	0, 8, 16, 32
Strategy 2	Thread-level tile size	8,16,24,32,40,64,96,128
	Result cache size (multiple of the workgroup size)	1,2,3,4

As shown in Table 1, there are many parameters to tune, which form a relatively large search space for a sparse matrix on a particular hardware platform. In order to accelerate auto-tuning, we perform the following optimizations. First, we use GPUs to accelerate the translation from the COO format to the BCCOO/BCCOO+ format. Second, we cache compiled kernels in a hash table so that they can reused for difference matrices. Third, we prune the search space using the follow heuristics: since the memory footprint is highly dependent on block dimensions, we only need to select the block dimensions corresponding to the 4 smallest memory footprints. Fourth, we further reduce the search space by: always using the texture memory for the multiplied vector, always using offline transpose, limiting the result cache size to 1 and 2 for strategy 2, and setting the shared memory size as 0 for the per-thread intermediate sums array for strategy 1. With these optimizations, the average auto-tuning time is 12.8 seconds among the 20 matrices in our study, running on a desktop machine with an Intel(R) Core2 Quad CPU Q9650 @ 3.00GHz and an NVIDIA GTX680 GPU. Compared to the optimal results obtained from an exhaustive search of the parameters listed in Table 1, our auto-tuning results are identical to the optimal ones on GTX 680 GPUs. On GTX480 GPUs, however, the optimal configurations show 10.5% better performance for the matrix Epidemiology, which prefers no texture memory usage, and 11.1% better performance for the matrix Circuit, which prefers online transpose. Furthermore, a finer grain parameter selection may further improve performance. For example, a Thread-level tile size of 40 yields 5% better performance for the matrix Dense than our auto-tuning results on GTX480 GPUs.

Table 2. The sparse matrices used in the experiments.

Spyplot	Name	Size	Non-zeros (NNZ)	NNZ/Row
	Dense	2K * 2K	4000000	2000
	Protein	36K * 36K	4344765	119
	FEM/Spheres	83K * 83K	6010480	72
	FEM/Cantilever	62K * 62K	4007383	65
	Wind Tunnel	218K*218K	11634424	53
	FEM/Harbor	47K * 47K	2374001	59
	QCD	49K * 49K	1916928	39
	FEM/Ship	141K*141K	7813404	28
	Economics	207K*207K	1273389	6
	Epidemiology	526K*526K	2100225	4
	FEM/Accelerator	121K*121K	2620000	22
	Circuit	171K*171K	958936	6
	Webbase	1M * 1M	3105536	3
	LP	4K * 1.1M	11279748	2825
	Circuit5M	5.56M* 5.56M	59524291	11
	eu-2005	863K*863K	19235140	22
	Ga41As41H72	268K*268K	18488476	67
	in-2004	1.38M* 1.38M	16917053	12
	mip1	66K * 66K	10352819	152
	Si41Ge41H72	186K*186K	15011265	81

5. Experimental Methodology

We implemented our proposed scheme in OpenCL[19]. Our experiments have been performed on both an Nvidia GTX680 GPU and an Nvidia GTX480 GPU.

We use a total of 20 sparse matrices, 14 of them are from [23] and 6 of them are from [16]. Table 2 summarizes the information of the sparse matrices, including the size, total number of non-zeros, and number of non-zeros per row. These matrices have been widely used in previous works [1][7][12][16][23].

In our experiments, we also use CUSPARSE V5.0 [13], CUSP [1], and clSpMV [16] for performance comparisons. CUSPARSE supports three formats HYB, BCSR, and CSR. As the HYB format is a hybrid format combining the advantages of the ELL and COO formats, the row length of the ELL part is configurable. We manually searched the row length in a wide range and use the best performing one for each matrix. For the BCSR format in CUSPARSE, we also searched the block size for the best performance. For clSpMV, besides the COCKTAIL format, which uses different formats for different partitions of a matrix, we tested all the single formats and chose the best performing single format for each matrix. The same performance testing framework is used as in [16]. The code of our proposed framework is available at *http://code.google.com/p/yaspmv/*.

6. Experimental Results

In our first experiment, we evaluate the impact of our proposed BCCOO/BCCOO+ format on memory bandwidth. Since in our BCCOO/BCCOO+ format, all the information, including the bit flag array, the col_index array, the data value array, as well as the auxiliary information described in Section 2.4, is only read once, we assume that it is also the case for all the formats in comparison. Therefore, we can simply use the sum of the array sizes to show the memory footprint of each format. The results are shown in Table 3. As our auto-tuning framework selects the BCCOO+ format only for the matrix LP, we do not separate the BCCOO and the BCCOO+ format. For some sparse matrices, due to the high variance in the number of non-zeros in different row, the ELL format is not applicable (labeled 'N/A' in Table 3).

Table 3. The memory footprint size (MB) of different formats.

Name	COO	ELL	Cocktail	Best Single	BCCOO
Dense	48	32	17	17	17
Protein	52	59	40	34	21
FEM/Spheres	72	54	52	51	31
FEM/Cantilever	48	39	25	25	21
Wind Tunnel	140	314	78	78	65
FEM/Harbor	28	54	24	24	14
QCD	23	15	15	15	9
FEM/Ship	94	115	56	59	34
Economics	15	73	14	28	8
Epidemiology	25	17	17	17	14
FEM/Accelerator	31	79	26	25	17
Circuit	12	483	9	23	6
Webbase	37	N/A	29	138	27
LP	135	1927	91	91	85
Circuit5M	714	N/A	578	714	516
eu-2005	231	N/A	248	209	159
Ga41As41H72	222	1505	139	170	136
in-2004	203	N/A	209	203	132
mip1	124	N/A	66	54	51
Si41Ge41H72	180	983	118	135	105
Average	122	N/A	93	106	73

From Table 3, we can see that our proposed BCCOO/BCCOO+ format significantly reduces the storage size of various sparse matrices. On average, our proposed

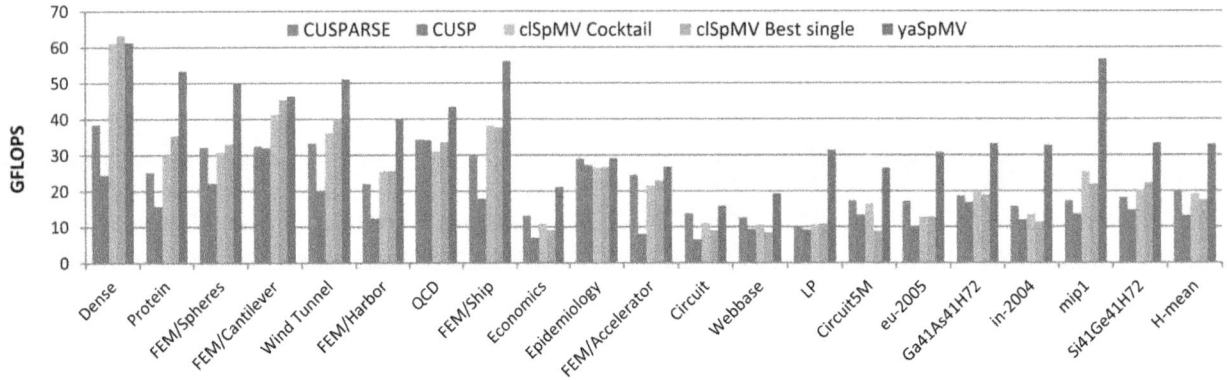

Figure 13. Performance comparison between our proposed scheme (labeled 'yaSpMV') and CUSPARSEV 5.0, CUSP, clSpMV-best single, and clSpMV-COCKTAIL on GTX680 GPUs.

BCCOO/BCCOO+ format reduces the storage size by 40% compared to the COO format, 31% compared to the best single format among all the 9 formats included in clSpMV, and 21% compared to the COCKTAIL format.

In the second experiment, we compare the performance of our proposed scheme to the state-of-art techniques. The results of GTX680 are shown in Figure 13 and the results of our proposed approach are labeled 'yaSpMV' in the figure. From the figure, we can see that our proposed approach outperforms the existing schemes for all the matrices except Dense. The Dense matrix prefers a block size of 2x8 as used in the BCSR format from the 'clSpMV best single' results. However, our auto-tuning framework limits the maximal block height is limited to 4, thereby achieving sub-optimal performance. Using the harmonic mean (H-mean) as the average throughput, our yaSpMV achieves an average performance improvement of 65% over CUSPARSE, 70% over clSpMV COCKTAIL, 88% over clSpMV best single, and 150% over CUSP. The highest performance improvement of yaSpMV achieved over clSpMV COCKTAIL is on matrix LP (195%). Compared to CUSPARSE, the highest performance gain of yaSpMV is

from the matrix mip1 (229%).

In the third experiment, we examine the performance contributions from different optimizations in our approach, including memory footprint reduction, efficient segmented sum/scan, adjacent synchronization to remove global synchronization, and fine-grain optimizations, which consist of (a) the use of the short data type for the col_index array and (b) early check to skip the parallel scan on a last_partial_sums array if each thread-level tile in a workgroup-level tile contains a row stop. The results are shown in Figure 14. We start with the COO format with a tree-based segment sum (labeled 'COO'). Then, we replace the COO format with our BCCOO/BCCOO+ format (labeled 'BCCOO'). Next, we replace the tree-based segmented sum with our proposed efficient matrix-based segment sum/scan (labeled 'Efficient segmented sum/scan') while using another kernel to accumulate partial sums across workgroups. We then use adjacent synchronization to replace this kernel (labeled 'adjacent synchronization') and add the fine-grain optimizations (labeled 'fine-gain optimizations'). From the figure, we can see that the main performance gains are from our proposed BCCOO/BCCOO+ format and our efficient segmented

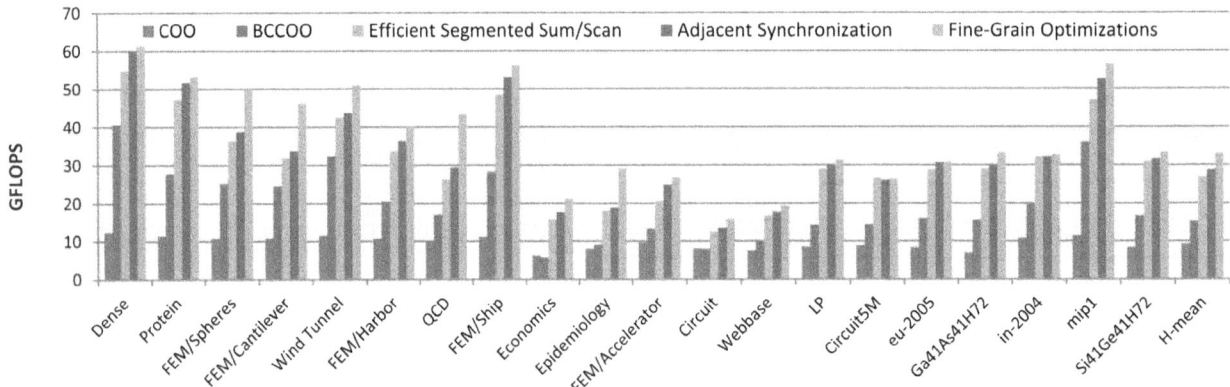

Figure 14. Performance Contributions from different optimization techniques (GTX680)

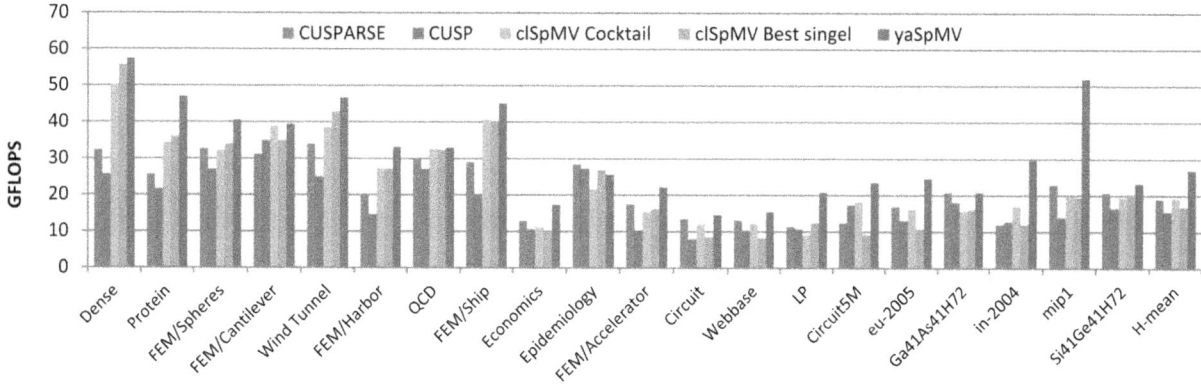

Figure 15. Performance comparison between our proposed scheme (labeled 'yaSpMV') and CUSPARSEV 5.0, CUSP, clSpMV-best single, and clSpMV-COCKTAIL on GTX480 GPUs.

sum/scan for SpMV.

We also evaluate the performance of SpMV on Nvidia GTX480 GPUs. The results are shown in Figure 15. Among the 20 sparse matrices, our proposed yaSpMV achieve significantly higher performance than existing approaches, up to 162% better than clSpMV COCKTAIL and up to 150% better than CUSPARSE. The only exception is the matrix Epidemiology. It has 4 non-zeros on each row and therefore is a perfect fit for the ELL format. For this matrix, our yaSpMV has a suboptimal performance of 25.5 GFLOPS. The best performing approach for this matrix, CUSPARSE, has a throughput of 28.5 GFLOPS. On average using the harmonic mean, our proposed yaSpMV achieves a performance improvement of 40% than clSpMV COCKTAIL, 60% over clSpMV best single, 74% over CUSP, and 42% over CUSPARSE.

7. Related Work

Sparse matrix-vector multiplication (SpMV) is so important that there have been numerous works optimizing its performance. We only discuss the most relevant ones here. Williams et al. present several optimizations for multicore platforms [23]. Kourtis et al. [11] proposed an Extended Compression Format (CSX) on shared memory systems. OSKI [22] is a library collection which provides low-level primitives for automatically tuned kernels on sparse matrices. Aydın Buluc et al. [3] introduced a compressed sparse blocks (CSB). Among the research works leveraging GPUs for SpMV, Bolz et al. first introduced the GPU for SpMV [6]. Bell and Garland implemented several well-known formats on Nvidia GPUs [1]. These formats include DIA, ELL, CSR, COO and a new hybrid format HYB, which combines the advantage of the ELL and COO formats. Vázquez et al. proposed a derivative format of ELLPACK, ELL-R [21]. They use an auxiliary array to store the row lengths. Alexander et al. proposed the Sliced ELL format (SELL) [12]. They horizontally partition the original matrix into several slices and different slices use different ELL padding lengths to reduce the filling zeros. Compared to the

ELL format, the ELL-R and SELL formats have less padding zeros while the workload may be imbalanced. Based on the CSR format, Kozaa et al. [10] proposed a Compressed Multiple-Row Storage Format for SpMV on GPUs. The advantage of this format is that the adjacent rows may be processed by the same thread, so the multiplied vector data could be reused. Sun et al. [17] proposed a CRSD format for diagonal sparse matrices. Choi et al. implemented the BCSR and BELL formats on GPUs [7]. A performance model driven framework is also proposed in [7] for performance auto-tuning of SpMV on GPUs. Su et al. [16] proposed the COCKTAIL format, which uses different formats to represent different partitions of a matrix. There are some works focusing on compression and reordering techniques as well [2][14]. The challenge of compression technique is the complexity of the decompression algorithm. The problem with the reordering technique is that it changes the inherent locality of the original matrix. A recent work by Tang et al. [20] studies bit-representations to compress index arrays. Similar to our work, a difference function is applied to index arrays. The difference from our proposed formats is that a bit packing scheme is then used to encode the delta values, which makes their decompression scheme more complicated than ours and also does not exploit the row stop information, when compressing row index arrays.

Blelloch et al. [4] first introduced the segmented operations to SpMV on vector multiprocessors. Harris [9] implemented the segmented scan based SpMV in the library CUDPP. Because they used a tree based scan algorithm, which has been shown to be inefficient [24], the performance is limited. Baskaran et al. [15] implemented a more efficient segmented scan based SpMV using the matrix based scan [8]. However, their scan-based implementation also is outperformed by their alternative implementations [15]. Bell and Garland implemented their COO format use the segmented reduction (scan) algorithm. However, due to the disadvantage of the COO format and the two-kernel implementation, the performance is not highly competitive.

117

Different from the previous works, we design the new BCCOO/BCCOO+ format to drastically reduce the bandwidth requirement. We also propose an efficient matrix-based segmented sum/scan for SpMV to maximize the benefit from our new BCCOO/BCCOO+ format on GPUs. Our algorithm only needs one kernel and explores a number of optimization techniques.

8. Conclusions

In this paper, we present yet another framework for SpMV on GPUs. First, we propose a new format, called blocked compressed common coordinate (BCCOO), for sparse matrices. The key idea is to extend the COO format with blocking and to use a bit flag array to replace the row index array. We also propose to vertically partition a sparse matrix before using the BCCOO format so as to improve the locality for accesses to the multiplied vector. Second, we revisit segmented scans for SpMV. We propose a highly efficient matrix-based segmented sum/scan for SpMV. Our matrix-based segmented sum/scan is closely coupled to our BCCOO/BCCOO+ format to reduce the memory bandwidth and achieve load balance. Our performance results from a set of 20 sparse matrices show that our proposed framework significantly advances the state-of-art of the highly important SpMV algorithm. It outperforms the vendor tuned CUSPARSE by up to 150% and 42% on average on GTX480 GPUs, by up to 229% and 65% on average on GTX680 GPUs. Compared to the clSpMV, our proposed scheme achieves a performance gain of up to 162% and 40% on average on GTX480 GPUs, up to 195% and 70% on average on GTX680 GPUs.

Acknowledgments

We would like to thank the anonymous reviewers for their insightful comments. This paper is supported in part by the National High-tech R&D Program of China (No.2012AA010902), an NSF project CCF-1216569, an NSF CAREER award CCF-0968667, and NSFC (No. 61272136, No. 61221062, No. 61100072).

References

[1] N. Bell and M. Garland. Implementing Sparse Matrix-Vector Multiplication on Throughput-Oriented Processors. SC, 2009.

[2] A. Buluç, S. Williams, L. Oliker and J. Demmel. Reduced-Bandwidth Multithreaded Algorithms for Sparse Matrix-Vector Multiplication. IPDPS, 2011.

[3] A. Buluc, J. T. Fineman, M. Frigo, J. R. Gilbert, and C. E. Leiserson Parallel sparse matrix-vector and matrix-transpose-vector multiplication using compressed sparse blocks. SPAA, 2009.

[4] G. E. Blelloch, M. A. Heroux and M. Zagha. Segmented Operations for Sparse Matrix Computation on Vector Multiprocessors. Tech. Rep. CMU-CS-93-173, School of Computer Science, Carnegie Mellon University, Aug 1993.

[5] G. E. Blelloch. Scans as Primitive Parallel Operations. IEEE Transactions on Computers, 1989.

[6] J. Bolz, I. Farmer, E. Grinspun and P. Schr¨oder. Sparse Matrix Solvers on the GPU: Conjugate Gradients and Multigrid. ACM Transactions on Graphics (TOG), July 2003.

[7] J. W. Choi, A. Singh and R. W. Vuduc. Model-driven Autotuning of Sparse Matrix-Vector Multiply on GPUs. PPoPP, 2010.

[8] Y. Dotsenko, N. K. Govindaraju, P.-P. Sloan, C. Boyd and J. Manferdelli. Fast Scan Algorithms on Graphics Processors. ICS, 2008.

[9] M. Harris, S. Sengupta, and J. D. Owens. CUDPP:CUDA Data Parallel Primitives Library. http://gpgpu.org/developer/cudpp

[10] Z. Koza, M. Matyka, S. Szkoda and L. Miroslaw. Compressed Multiple-Row Storage Format. CoRR 2008.

[11] K. Kourtis, V. Karakasis, G. Goumas and N. Koziris. CSX: An Extended Compression Format for SpMV on Shared Memory Systems. PPoPP, 2011.

[12] A. Monakov, A. Lokhmotov and A. Avetisyan. Automatically Tuning Sparse Matrix-Vector Multiplication for GPU Architectures. HiPEAC, 2010.

[13] Nvidia. CUSPARSE. https://developer.nvidia.com/ cusparse. http://docs.nvidia.com/cuda/cuda-c-programming-guide/index.html

[14] J. C. Pichel, F. F. Rivera, M. Fernández and A. Rodríguez. Optimization of sparse matrix–vector multiplication using reordering techniques on GPUs. Microprocessors and Microsystems, 36(2), 65–77, Mar 2012.

[15] M. M. Baskaran and R. Bordawekar. Optimizing Sparse Matrix-Vector Multiplication on GPUs using Compile-time and Run-time Strategies. Technical Report RC24704 (W0812-047), IBM, Dec 2008.

[16] B.-Y. Su and K. Keutzer. clSpMV: A Cross-Platform OpenCL SpMV Framework on GPUs. ICS, 2012.

[17] X. Sun, Y. Zhang, T. Wang, X. Zhang, L. Yuan and L. Rao. Optimizing SpMV for Diagonal Sparse Matrices on GPU. ICPP, 2011.

[18] S. Sengupta, M. Harris, Y. Zhang, and J. D. Owens. Scan primitives for GPU computing. In Graphics Hardware 2007.

[19] The Khronos OpenCL Working Group OpenCL. The Open Standard for Parallel Programming of Heterogeneous Systems. http://www.khronos.org/opencl/

[20] W. Tang et al., Accelerating sparse matrix-vector multiplication on GPUs using bit-representation-optimized schemes, SC 2013.

[21] F. Vázquez, J. J. Fernández and E. M. Garzón. A new approach for sparse matrix vector product on NVIDIA GPUs. Concurrency Computat.: Pract. Exper. Sep 2010.

[22] R. Vuduc, J. W. Demmel and K. A. Yelick. OSKI: A library of automatically tuned sparse matrix kernels. SciDAC 2005.

[23] S. Williams, L. Oliker, R. Vuduc, J. Shalf, K. A. Yelick and J. W. Demmel. Optimization of Sparse Matrix-Vector Multiplication on Emerging Multicore Platforms. SC, 2007.

[24] S. Yan, G. Long and Y. Zhang. StreamScan: Fast Scan Algorithms for GPUs without Global Barrier , PPoPP, 2013.

Singe: Leveraging Warp Specialization for High Performance on GPUs

Michael Bauer

Stanford University

mebauer@cs.stanford.edu

Sean Treichler

Stanford University

sjt@cs.stanford.edu

Alex Aiken

Stanford University

aiken@cs.stanford.edu

Abstract

We present Singe, a Domain Specific Language (DSL) compiler for combustion chemistry that leverages *warp specialization* to produce high performance code for GPUs. Instead of relying on traditional GPU programming models that emphasize data-parallel computations, warp specialization allows compilers like Singe to partition computations into sub-computations which are then assigned to different warps within a thread block. Fine-grain synchronization between warps is performed efficiently in hardware using producer-consumer named barriers. Partitioning computations using warp specialization allows Singe to deal efficiently with the irregularity in both data access patterns and computation. Furthermore, warp-specialized partitioning of computations allows Singe to fit extremely large working sets into on-chip memories. Finally, we describe the architecture and general compilation techniques necessary for constructing a warp-specializing compiler. We show that the warp-specialized code emitted by Singe is up to 3.75X faster than previously optimized data-parallel GPU kernels.

Categories D.1.3 [*Programming Techniques*]: Parallel Programming

Keywords warp specialization; warp-specializing compiler; GPU; DSL

1. Introduction

Current GPU programming models, such as OpenCL[10] and CUDA[1], support data-parallel computations where all threads execute the same instruction stream on arrays of data. However, the expansion of GPUs into general purpose computing has uncovered many applications which exhibit properties which make them challenging to map onto traditional data-parallel GPU programming models. For example, consider the domain of combustion science, which includes applications such as S3D[5, 11]. The physics and chemistry kernels for these combustion applications have three characteristics that make them difficult to optimize for GPUs:

- Large working sets: combustion kernels routinely require hundreds of live double-precision variables per physical point in discretized space. In a data-parallel model these working sets commonly exceed the small on-chip memory capacity allotted to each thread, resulting in register spilling, low occupancy, and under-utilization of math units.

PPoPP '14, Feburary 15-19, 2014, Orlando, FL, USA.
Copyright is held by the owner/author(s). Publication rights licensed to ACM.
ACM 978-1-4503-2656-8/14/02. . . $15.00.
http://dx.doi.org/10.1145/2555243.2555258

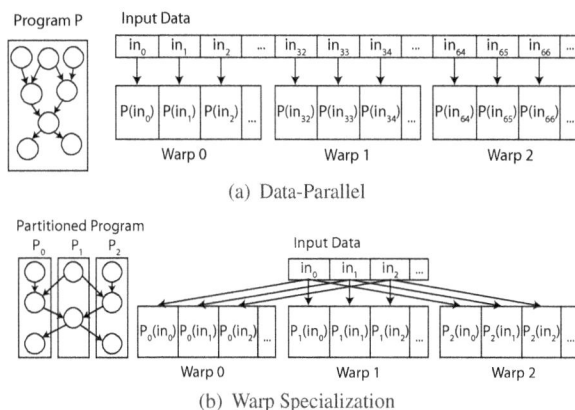

Figure 1. Contrasting GPU programming models.

- Irregular computations: combustion kernels often contain multiple phases with different computational characteristics. The large number of temporaries between phases necessitates that the phases be fused together into a single kernel. While some of these phases could be run in parallel, current data-parallel GPU programming models serialize these phases.

- Irregular data accesses: data accesses in combustion kernels are dependent both on the properties of the chemical mechanism as well as runtime values. Under many circumstances it is impossible for a data-parallel model to avoid memory divergence and shared memory bank conflicts.

In practice, many different scientific computing domains demonstrate some or all of the same characteristics as combustion. Achieving peak performance for these applications mandates finding alternative approaches to programming GPUs.

In this work we describe how *warp specialization* can be used as an alternative programming model for mapping irregular and large working set applications onto GPUs. Figure 1 illustrates the differences between the core data-parallel abstraction of current GPU programming models and warp specialization. In the data-parallel model, a collection of threads within a *thread block* all execute the same program over independent elements from arrays of input data. On the hardware, however, a thread block is broken into *warps* consisting of (typically) 32 threads which serve as the unit of scheduling. Warp specialization exploits the division of a thread block into warps to partition computations into sub-computations such that each sub-computation is executed by a different warp within a thread block. Carefully structured programs can handle irregularity by grouping threads into warps such that threads within a warp have good data-parallel behavior, even if threads in different warps do not. Warp specialization can also be used to partition extremely large working sets across multiple threads in different warps, keeping data on-chip and dramatically reducing the register pressure on an individual thread.

We describe the design and implementation of a Domain Specific Language (DSL) compiler capable of using warp specialization in conjunction with domain specific knowledge to better map challenging kernels onto GPU architectures. Our approach has been implemented in Singe, a DSL compiler for general combustion simulations. While Singe targets combustion specifically, the techniques described in this paper are general and can be adapted to other domains. We show that using these techniques, Singe generates warp-specialized code that achieves speedups up to 3.75X over heavily optimized but purely data-parallel combustion kernels.

In Section 2 we give a brief introduction to the mechanics of warp specialization. Each of the following sections describe one of our primary contributions.

- We present a case study of how Singe uses warp specialization to partition the three most expensive kernels in a real-world combustion application. We elucidate how warp-specialized partitioning addresses the critical performance bottlenecks in these kernels (Section 3).
- We describe the architecture of a warp-specializing compiler including the necessary algorithms for managing data placement, communication, and synchronization for general warp-specialized kernels (Section 4).
- We cover three general techniques for generating high performance warp-specialized code that are essential to avoiding instruction cache thrashing. We give code examples of how Singe employs these techniques (Section 5).
- We investigate the performance advantages conferred by warp specialization by examining the performance of the kernels emitted by Singe on both Fermi and Kepler GPUs for two different chemical mechanisms (Section 6).

Section 7 discusses implications of warp specialization, Section 8 describes related work, and Section 9 concludes.

2. Warp Specialization

While there are several APIs for programming GPUs, they all implement variations of the same programming model. We use CUDA as a proxy for the standard GPU programming model as it is the only interface that currently supports the fine-grain synchronization primitives necessary for warp specialization.

CUDA launches grids of thread blocks or *cooperative thread arrays* (referred to as CTAs for the remainder of the paper) on the GPU. This abstraction gives the hardware considerable flexibility when executing a CUDA application. In current GPUs, the threads within a CTA are broken into groups of 32 threads called *warps*. All threads within a CTA (and therefore also within a warp) execute the same program. If the threads within a warp *diverge* on a branch instruction, the streaming multiprocessor (SM) on which the warp is executing first executes the warp with all the threads not taking the branch masked off. After the taken branch is handled, the warp is re-executed for the not-taken branch with the complementary set of threads masked off from executing. Divergence is severely detrimental to program performance because it serializes potentially parallel thread execution within a warp.

The crucial insight for warp specialization is that while control divergence within a warp results in performance degradation, divergence between warps does not. A warp-specialized kernel is one in which dynamic branches, dependent on each thread's warp ID, create explicit inter-warp control divergence for the purpose of executing different code in each warp. As long as all threads within a warp execute the same instruction stream then the only execution overhead is the cost of the warp-specific branch instructions.

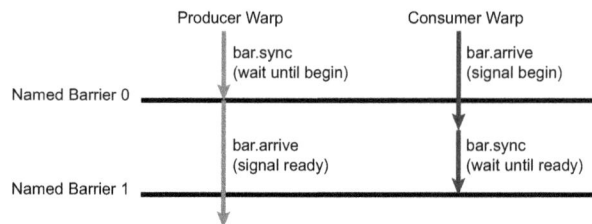

Figure 2. Producer-consumer named barriers example.

Warp-specialized programs also require more expressive synchronization mechanisms. In traditional CUDA programs synchronization is performed using barriers between all the threads within a CTA. However, by using inline PTX statements, a CUDA program has access to a more expressive set of intra-CTA synchronization primitives referred to as *named barriers*[2]. Named barriers provide two operations: *arrive* and *sync*. Arrive is a non-blocking operation which registers that a warp has arrived at a barrier and then continues execution. Sync is a blocking operation that waits until all the necessary warps have arrived or synced on the barrier.

Using arrive and sync operations, programmers can encode producer-consumer relationships in warp-specialized programs. Figure 2 illustrates using two named barriers to coordinate movement of data from a producer warp (red) to a consumer warp (blue) through a buffer in shared memory. The producer warp first waits for a signal from the consumer warp that the buffer is empty. The consumer warp signals the buffer is ready by performing a non-blocking arrive operation. Since the arrive is non-blocking, the consumer warp is free to perform additional work while waiting for the buffer to be filled. At some point the consumer warp blocks on the second named barrier waiting for the buffer to be full. The producer warp signals when the buffer is full using a non-blocking arrive operation on the second named barrier. It is important to note that named barriers support synchronization between arbitrary subsets of warps within a CTA, including allowing synchronization between a single pair of warps as in this example.

3. Warp-Specialized Partitioning

Warp-specialized partitioning provides a useful mechanism for DSL compilers when grappling with computations that exhibit both irregularity and large working sets. While warp-specialized partitioning is a useful tool, it is important to note that the particular method for partitioning a computation into specialized warps relies on both domain specific knowledge and the target architecture. Therefore the partitioning strategy must vary with each DSL compiler and we cannot provide a general partitioning algorithm. Instead, we provide a case study of coupling domain specific information with warp specialization to address performance problems in the domain of large and complex combustion applications. Subsequent sections will cover generally applicable techniques for mapping and scheduling computations after they have been partitioned using domain specific knowledge.

We begin with a brief overview of the combustion domain in Section 3.1. We then describe how warp-specialized partitioning is used by Singe to address the performance challenges inherent in the generation of three expensive combustion kernels: viscosity (Section 3.2), diffusion (Section 3.3) and chemistry (Section 3.4).

3.1 Combustion Chemistry

Combustion simulations are described by *chemical mechanisms* which consist of a set of *reactions* and the *species* involved in those reactions. Chemical species range from single elements to very large and complex hydro-carbons. Table 3 shows the characteristics of the Dimethyl Ether (DME) and n-Heptane mechanisms used in

Mechanism	Reactions	Species	QSSA	Stiff
DME	175	39	9	22
Heptane	283	68	16	27

Figure 3. Chemical Mechanisms

this paper. These mechanisms were chosen for their relevance in current combustion research[12].

Combustion mechanisms are described by a declarative data DSL based on the CHEMKIN[9] standard. A mechanism in this DSL is described by three input files:

- CHEMKIN file: a list of chemical reactions with stoichiometric coefficients and reaction models (see Figure 4)
- TRANSPORT file: a table of diffusion and viscosity coefficients for all chemical species
- THERMO file: a table of thermodynamic coefficients for all chemical species

Singe parses these files and emits CUDA code for each of the kernels necessary to simulate combustion of the specified chemical mechanism. Singe may also take an optional fourth input file describing the set of *quasi-steady-state approximation* (QSSA) and *stiffness* (Stiff) species. QSSA species arise out of techniques that reduce the total number of species across all phases of the simulation at the expense of additional computation during the chemistry phase of the application[12]. For example, in the heptane mechanism, the 16 QSSA species are removed from the original group of 68 so that only a total of 52 species must be simulated, while requiring a complex QSSA computation be performed in the chemistry kernel. Stiffness species allow the simulation to take longer time steps, but require additional computations be performed in the chemistry kernel. We describe how warp specialization handles both the QSSA and stiffness computations in Section 3.4.

Most combustion simulations operate on a three dimensional cartesian grid. Each point in the grid has an associated set of *fields* with each field laid out contiguously in a separate array to ensure coalescing of global memory loads. In most GPU combustion kernels[11], each thread is responsible for a single point in the cartesian grid, which conforms to the traditional data-parallel GPU programming model.

3.2 Viscosity

The viscosity kernel computes a viscosity coefficient for each point in the cartesian grid as a function of the temperature and molar fractions for each species. Per-species viscosities are first computed by taking the exponent of a per-species third order polynomial dependent on temperature (T):

$$vis_i(T) = e^{\eta_{i0} + \eta_{i1}*T + \eta_{i2}*T^2 + \eta_{i3}*T^3}$$

The final viscosity output ν for each cartesian grid point is then computed as an interaction of the viscosity of each species with every other species given by the following equation:

$$\nu = \sqrt{8} * \sum_{k=1}^{N} \left[\frac{x_k * vis_k}{\sum_{j=1}^{N} x_j * \frac{\left(1 + \sqrt{\frac{vis_k}{vis_j}} * \sqrt{\frac{m_j}{m_k}}\right)^2}{\sqrt{1 + \frac{m_k}{m_j}}}} \right]$$

where N is the number of species and x_i and m_i are the molar fraction and molecular mass of species i respectively. In an optimized CUDA implementation, this computation is performed in logarithmic space to reduce the dependency on square root and divide operations that are implemented using Newton's method in the absence of dedicated hardware on GPUs. After constant folding, for each of the N^2 pairs of species the viscosity kernel requires that 2

```
!1
  ch3+h(+m) = ch4(+m)  2.138e+15  -0.40  0.000E+00
          low / 3.310E+30 -4.00 2108. /
    troe/0.0  1.E-15  1.E-15  40./ h2/2/ h2o/5/
!2
  ch4+h  =  ch3+h2  1.727E+04  3.00  8.224E+03
    rev /  6.610E+02  3.00  7.744E+03 /
!3
  ch4+oh  =  ch3+h2o  1.930E+05  2.40  2.106E+03
    rev /  3.199E+04  2.40  1.678E+04 /
...
```

Figure 4. Example CHEMKIN input file to Singe.

double precision constants be loaded and that 2 double precision adds, 2 double precision multiplies, and 10 double precision fused multiply-add (DFMA) operations be performed.

The viscosity computation is embarrassingly parallel as each point in the grid can be computed independently, but it places a significant strain on several GPU resources. First, the working set for a cartesian grid point is difficult to fit on chip into a single thread's registers. For the heptane mechanism with 52 species, storing the molar fractions and per-species viscosity values requires 104 double precision values, which would require 208 registers on an NVIDIA GPU. Fermi GPUs only support 64 registers per thread, while Kepler GPUs support 256 but at the cost of extremely low warp occupancy and under-utilized math units. In this scenario, a data parallel GPU programming model forces the DSL compiler to choose between low-occupancy or spilling registers, which adds additional memory latency to the kernel.

A second problem encountered by the viscosity kernel has to do with the large number of constant values required for the computation. Every pair of species requires two different double precision constants. GPU architectures include constant caches, but their working set sizes are small. GPUs only have 8 KB of on-chip constant cache[1]. The DME and Heptane mechanisms require 13.9 and 42.4 KB of constants respectively. Loading constants for the viscosity kernel is therefore expensive since they are unlikely to hit in the constant cache. The problem of hiding these long-latency constant loads is exacerbated by the low occupancy of the kernel caused by the large working set described earlier.

Singe uses warp-specialized partitioning to solve both of these problems. The outer sum over the set of chemical species is broken into individual computations each of which is mapped to a different warp using the algorithm described in Section 4.1. Unlike data-parallel CUDA where each thread handles a single point, all of the warps in a CTA cooperate on a set of 32 points. A thread in lane l of warp w handles the per-species computations assigned to warp w for the l-th point. Warp specialization necessitates the sharing of data between warps, therefore the molar fractions and per-species viscosities are moved into shared memory. These values fit easily because each CTA is only handling 32 grid points at a time.

Partitioning the computation for warp specialization also provides a solution to the problem of storing the large number of constant values in on-chip memory. Since each warp is only performing a subset of the computation, it only requires a subset of the constant values. Furthermore, moving the working set to shared memory makes the registers available for storing constants. Using the constant deduplication optimization described in Section 5.2, warp specialization enables all the constant values to be stored in on-chip registers. At the end of the computation, all the warps reduce their values through shared memory and the threads in warp 0 perform the write of the resulting values for each point. Using warp specialization, Singe is able to partition the viscosity computation so that values better fit into the on-chip memories which we will show leads to significant performance gains in Section 6.

121

X	X	X	2
1	X	X	X
1	1	X	X
X	1	2	X

X	X	X	2	2
1	X	X	X	2
1	1	X	X	X
X	1	1	X	X
X	X	1	2	X

Figure 5. Diffusion partitioning between two warps for $N=4,5$.

3.3 Diffusion

The diffusion computation shares some characteristics with the viscosity computation which leads to similar challenges, but requires a more complex warp-specialized partitioning scheme. For every pair of species i and j, a diffusive constant is computed from the exponent of a third order polynomial dependent on the temperature T where δ is a NxNx4 matrix of coefficients.

$$d_{ij}(T) = e^{\delta_{ij0}+\delta_{ij1}*T+\delta_{ij2}*T^2+\delta_{ij3}*T^3}$$

The NxN matrix of these diffusive constants is then used in computing per-species diffusion outputs Δ_i:

$$mass = \sum_{j=1}^{N} m_j * x_j$$

$$clamp_i = max(\epsilon, x_i)$$

$$\Delta_i = \frac{P_{atmos}}{P} * \frac{-clamp_i * m_i + \sum_{j=1}^{N} clamp_j * m_j}{mass * \sum_{j=1}^{N} clamp_j * d_{ij}}$$

where N is the number of species, P is the pressure, P_{atmos} is atmospheric pressure, ϵ is the minimum molar fraction, and x_i and m_i are the molar fraction and molecular mass of species i respectively. Note that unlike the viscosity computation, which computed a single output value per point, the diffusion kernel computes one output value per species per point. Furthermore the d_{ij} matrix is symmetric with zeros along the diagonal which implies that less than half of the matrix must actually be computed. However, each d_{ij} must contribute to both Δ_i and Δ_j.

Like viscosity, diffusion suffers from the same large working set and constant problems. We again solve them using warp specialization, but with a different partitioning strategy. The NxN matrix of d_{ij} values is partitioned by column. Columns are offset by one from each other and only a subset of values in each column need be computed because of the symmetric nature of the matrix. For odd numbers of species, each column must compute $\lfloor \frac{N}{2} \rfloor$ d_{ij} values; for even numbers of species the first $\frac{N}{2}$ columns compute $\frac{N}{2}$ d_{ij} values and the second $\frac{N}{2}$ columns compute $\frac{N}{2} - 1$ d_{ij} values. Figure 5 shows the assignment of d_{ij} value computations for matrices with $N = 4$ and $N = 5$ for two warps. 'X' values indicate that the point need not be computed because its symmetric point about the diagonal has already been computed.

Warps are assigned adjacent columns to maximize locality. Each warp traverses its set of columns and maintains a partial sum for the species in each of its columns. Additional partial sums for each species are also maintained in shared memory. For a given row, the warp computes the d_{ij} values and reduces them into the partial sums stored in registers for each column. The warp also computes a row partial sum and reduces it into the location for the corresponding row species in shared memory. To avoid data races when accessing shared memory, named barriers are used to synchronize access to different regions of shared memory.

At the end of the computation, each warp reads the partial sums out of shared memory for the species that it owns and sums the results with the partial sums stored in the warp's registers. The

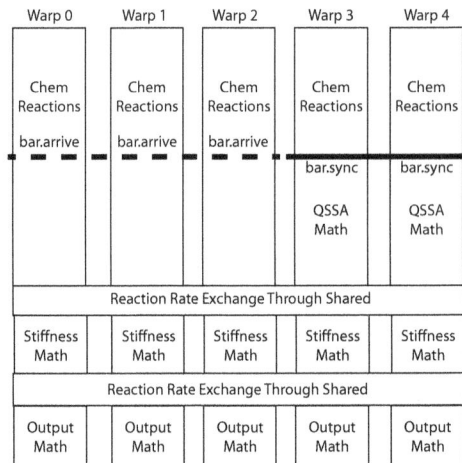

Figure 6. Warp specialization for chemistry kernel.

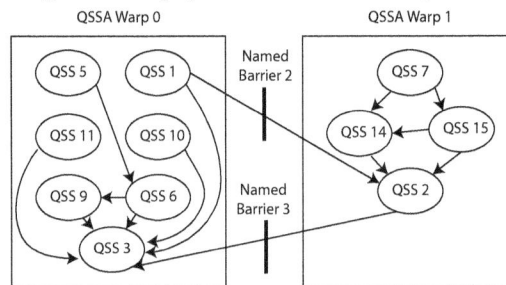

Figure 7. Example partitioning of heptane QSSA computation.

pressure scaling ratio is then applied and each warp writes out results for its owned species. In this scenario, the warp-specialized partitioning of the diffusion computation results in a hybrid storage of the working set using both shared memory and registers that enables additional parallelism to be extracted. We describe the algorithm for placing data in further detail in Section 4.1.

3.4 Chemistry

The chemistry computation is the most complex kernel that Singe emits because it requires multiple phases, some of which can execute in parallel. The first phase computes forward and reverse reaction rates for every reaction using an Arrhenius, Lindermann, or Landau-Teller reaction model[9], requiring between 6 and 15 double precision constants per reaction. The second phase computes the QSSA scaling factors and then applies them to all reactions involving a QSSA species. A similar computation is performed in the third phase for the stiff species. The output phase sums the contributions from each reaction and computes the resulting rate of change for each species based on stoichiometric coefficients.

While the chemistry kernel could be fissioned into separate kernels, each such kernel would read and write a forward and reverse reaction rate for every reaction at every point. Kernels for the heptane mechanism would each require 566 double precision reads and 566 double precision writes per cartesian grid point, which would be memory bandwidth limited and therefore slow.

Instead we employ warp-specialized partitioning to break apart the computation and the working set so it fits in on-chip memory. However, unlike viscosity and diffusion, for all interesting mechanisms the number of reaction rates is too large to store in shared memory. Instead we partition the reaction computations across warps and store the resulting forward and reverse reaction rates in each warp's registers. When reaction rates are needed for computa-

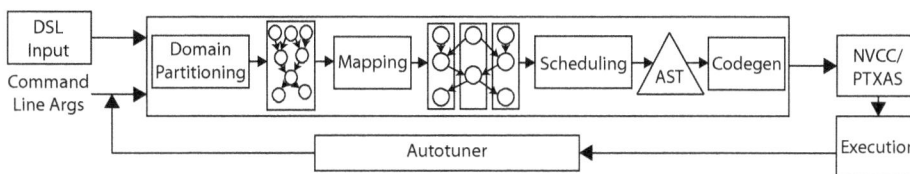

Figure 8. Architecture of a warp-specializing compiler.

tions, they are exchanged in passes by writing subsets of the rates into shared memory and having the needed values read out before progressing to the next pass. While this adds latency to the kernel, it is significantly less latency than going to off-chip global memory and well within the bandwidth limits of shared memory.

The chemistry kernel also suffers from another performance challenge: the QSSA phase is both computationally expensive and difficult to parallelize. Singe uses warp specialization at two different granularities to address this problem. First, the QSSA computation usually requires between half and two-thirds of the reaction rates. Singe assigns these reactions to warps first. A subset of the warps are then siphoned off to perform the QSSA computation while the remaining warps complete the reaction computations. Figure 6 shows an example of this partitioning of the warps for the chemistry kernel. A producer-consumer named barrier is used to indicate to the QSSA warps when the needed values from the non-QSSA warps have been written into shared memory. Note that because this barrier is non-blocking warp specialization enables the QSSA computation to be overlapped with the remaining reaction rate computations, which cannot be done in the data-parallel version of the kernel.

Warp specialization is also used to further parallelize the QSSA computation. The QSSA computation performs many divide operations and consequently requires between 20 and 60 DFMA operations for each QSSA species. Data dependences exist between species further complicating parallelization. Singe uses a heuristic for partitioning the directed acyclic graph (DAG) of a QSSA computation across a set of QSSA warps. For every edge that crosses a warp boundary, a producer-consumer named barrier is allocated. Figure 7 shows an example of one such partitioning for the QSSA computation for the heptane mechanism across two warps. In Section 4.2 we describe a general algorithm for synchronizing and scheduling these dataflow DAGs that avoids deadlock.

4. Warp-Specializing Compiler Architecture

We now describe the general architecture and compilation stages of a warp-specializing DSL compiler as seen in Figure 8. We are primarily interested in the transformations necessary for performing warp specialization and therefore assume a source-to-source compiler that will rely on a lower-level compiler like the PTX assembler to perform optimizations on sequential code within a single thread. Input for a warp-specializing compiler consists of a DSL file describing the computation to be performed and a set of command line flags indicating the number of warps to target as well as any explicit mapping decisions (described in Section 4.1).

Our experience with Singe has shown it is valuable for a warp-specializing compiler to generate correct code for any number of warps and choice of mapping decisions. This property enables autotuning and significantly reduces the complexity of the compiler by removing specialized logic for trying to compute an optimal mapping of a computation onto an arbitrary architecture. In practice, the search space for Singe was never more than a few hundred points because warp-specialized decisions dealt with very coarse-grained properties such as the number of target warps. Consequently, we used a brute-force exhaustive autotuning script to drive Singe when tuning our kernels.

The first stage of any warp-specializing compiler partitions the primary computation into sub-computations. As we have seen with the three kernels discussed in Section 3, how to partition and at what granularity is domain specific and will therefore be determined by each DSL compiler individually. The first stage outputs a dataflow graph with nodes corresponding to units of computation, which we refer to as *operations*, and edges indicating data dependences between operations. Section 4.1 describes the second stage of compilation which maps operations onto warps and determines where data is stored. The output of the second stage is another dataflow graph with each operation assigned to a specific warp and inputs and outputs of operations assigned either to registers or shared memory. The third compiler stage described in Section 4.2 performs named barrier placement and scheduling. The result of the third stage is an abstract syntax tree (AST) for each warp which encodes the chosen schedule and necessary synchronization for each warp's operations. Code is generated directly from these ASTs in the last compilation stage, but requires several non-standard traversal techniques which we cover in detail in Section 5.

4.1 Computation and Data Mapping

The mapping compilation stage is responsible for taking in an arbitrary dataflow graph of operations and mapping it onto the specified number of warps and available GPU memories. This is accomplished in two steps: first, operations must be assigned to warps, and second, the data values produced and consumed by operations must be assigned to one of the available software-managed on-chip GPU memories (e.g. registers, shared).

When performing the first step there are three primary (and often conflicting) metrics to consider when assigning operations to warps. First, the mapping stage should aim to achieve a balanced computational load across all the warps as imbalance can lead to under-utilized computational resources. In Singe, we use the number of floating point operations (FLOPS) in each operation as a proxy for computational load, and attempt to balance the total number of FLOPS assigned to each warp.

The second metric which must be balanced is the total registers required for each warp. The need for this metric is an artifact of the use of data-parallel programming models: current GPU architectures and compilers do not support per-warp register allocation schemas. Consequently, the warp requiring the most registers dictates the number of registers allocated for all warps in the kernel. If there is a large imbalance in required registers between warps, then significant fractions of the register file can go unused, limiting the total working set size for warp-specialized kernels and reducing total occupancy. In Singe, we assume intermediate values in an operation consume no registers because they are short-lived, but the values generated by operations consume registers as long as they are live. Singe stores values generated by an operation in the registers of the thread that computed the operation to avoid duplicating values and consuming additional registers.

The third metric which must be considered is locality. A warp-specializing compiler should attempt to maximize locality by minimizing the number of dataflow edges with operations assigned to different warps. This reduces the amount of communication that must occur through shared memory and also reduces the number of barrier synchronizations which must be performed.

123

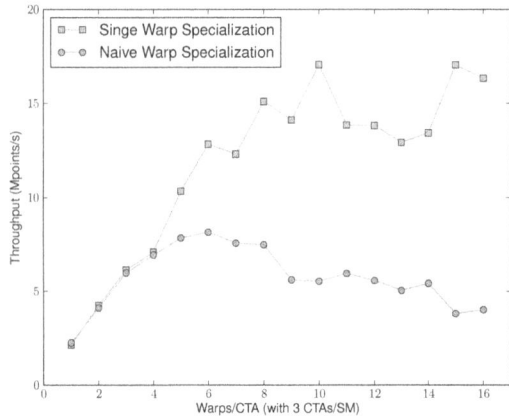

Figure 9. Comparison of warp-specialized code generation.

There are many possible algorithms for mapping operations onto warps that consider all three metrics, including some which may opt to use domain- or architecture-specific knowledge. The Singe compiler uses a general greedy algorithm for performing mapping. Operations are weighted based on their FLOP counts, register needs, and locality to warps based on the current mapping. Singe maps operations in order of cost from the most expensive to the least in a way that locally minimizes overall cost. Singe makes mapping visible to the autotuner by allowing weights to be assigned to each of the three metrics using command line flags. Exposing these design dimensions to the autotuner also significantly reduces the complexity of the compiler implementation.

The second step of mapping consists of assigning variables to registers or shared memory. A command line flag specifies the target number of CTAs per SM which places an upper bound on the amount of shared memory and number of registers available to any one CTA. Shared memory is considered first as it is usually the more constrained resource. There are three ways shared memory can be used by a warp-specializing compiler, each of which is illustrated by a Singe kernel:

- *Store* - there are few enough values shared between operations that they can all be stored in shared memory (viscosity).
- *Buffer* - due to extremely large working sets, values are kept in registers and shared memory is only used as a buffer for communicating values between different warps (chemistry).
- *Mixed* - some values are stored in shared memory, while the remaining fraction of shared memory functions as a buffer for communication between different warps (diffusion).

The choice of where to place data and how to use shared memory may also be application or architecture dependent. Singe uses a simple working set analysis that attempts to keep values in registers unless they are accessed by many threads in which case they are assigned to shared memory. If the total number of registers needed exceeds the number budgeted by the target number of CTAs, then Singe emits a warning indicating that spilling is likely to occur. Singe also makes the choice of data placement available to the autotuner via command line flags which specify how shared memory and registers should be employed.

4.2 Named Barrier Placement and Scheduling

Traditional data-parallel GPU programming models present a very simple coarse-grain barrier for synchronization within a CTA. Named barriers provide a finer granularity of synchronization between individual warps, but can lead to poor performance and deadlock if placed incorrectly. In this section we describe an algorithm

for placing named barrier synchronization calls that guarantees a deadlock-free schedule. We also present a class of transformations on the schedule that can safely be performed by the compiler during optimization passes.

In order to guarantee correct synchronization of communication between different warps we rely on the following algorithm:

1. Tag every data dependence between two operations assigned to different warps as requiring a *synchronization point*, with the producer warp needing to perform an arrival and the consumer warp needing to perform a wait.
2. Construct a partial order of the synchronization points based on their transitive data dependences.
3. Linearize the partial order of all synchronization points and then number each synchronization point, defining a total order on synchronization points.
4. For each warp, create a static schedule of all the operations in that warp that obeys operational data dependences and obeys the total ordering on synchronization points so that an operation with a lower numbered synchronization point comes before an operation with a higher numbered synchronization point.

We now prove that using this algorithm guarantees the existence of at least one schedule that is deadlock-free.

Theorem 1. A schedule for each warp that obeys the initial data dependences and a total ordering on synchronization points exists and is deadlock-free.

Proof. Initially the graph of operations is a DAG which defines a partial ordering on the operations. For every operation which requires a synchronization point we add an additional edge to every operation that requires a synchronization point with a larger number. By construction, these edges also obey the partial order of the original DAG since the total order on synchronization points was constrained by the original data dependences. Therefore a partial order still exists on the graph which guarantees that the graph is still a DAG. From any partial order, there exists at least one total ordering on all the operations. An initial schedule for a warp can be then be found by removing the operations assigned to each warp in order from any total ordering of all operations. The DAG nature of the resulting graph ensures the absence of any cycles on control resources which could result in deadlock and therefore the resulting schedule is deadlock-free. □

After an initial deadlock-free schedule has been generated for each warp, there are several re-ordering transformations permitted that do not invalidate Theorem 1.

- Operations arriving at a synchronization point can be re-ordered up the schedule arbitrarily far, or can be moved down the schedule if they are not re-ordered with respect to an operation that waits on a higher-numbered synchronization point.
- Operations waiting at a synchronization point can be re-ordered up the schedule if they are not re-ordered with respect to a lower-numbered synchronization point, or can be re-ordered down the schedule if they are not re-ordered with respect to operations on a higher-numbered synchronization point.

These two transformations on the schedule are useful for several purposes. First, they can be used to hoist operations which lie on the kernel's critical dataflow path so they are performed before less important operations. Second, using these transformation, multiple synchronization points between common sets of warps can be grouped together. This allows for bulk communication through shared memory between warps and reduces the total number of named barrier synchronizations. Singe uses scheduling heuristics to achieve both of these goals.

124

```
1   const int warp_id = (threadIdx.x >> 5);
2   const int lane_id = (threadIdx.x & 0x1f);
3   ...
4   if ((1 << warp_id) & 0x000005D7) {
5     int troe_idx = troe_index_0[0+step*step_stride][warp_id];
6     double fcent = scratch[TROE_OFFSET+troe_idx][lane_id];
7     double flogpr = log10(pr) − 0.4 − 0.67 * fcent;
8     double fdenom = 0.75 − 1.27 * fcent − 0.14 * flogpr;
9     double fquan = flogpr / fdenom;
10    fquan = fcent / (1.0 + fquan * fquan);
11    rr_f_0 = rr_kinf * pr/(1.0 + pr) * exp(fquan * DLn10);
12  } else {
13    rr_f_0 = rr_kinf * pr/(1.0 + pr);
14  }
```

Listing 1. Overlaid bit-mask code emitted by Singe.

After the schedule for each warp has been fixed, a warp-specializing compiler must map the set of synchronization points onto the set of 16 named barriers per SM available on both Fermi and Kepler architectures[1]. The problem of mapping synchronization points onto named barriers is isomorphic to the problem of register allocation for static single-assignment (SSA) code and can be performed in polynomial time[7]. In practice, only the heptane chemistry kernel has required the use of all 16 named barriers. The final output of this stage is a forest of ASTs (one AST for each warp) which codify the chosen schedule of operations and include code to perform the necessary synchronizations.

5. Warp-Specialized Code Generation

In this section we describe techniques for emitting high-performance warp-specialized code. The primary obstacle to overcome when generating warp-specialized code is the performance of the GPU's instruction cache. GPUs are built assuming all threads run the same code with minimal stretches of control divergence. The naïve code generation strategy of using a top-level switch statement on the warp ID to send each warp to a different block of code violates this assumption and results in severe performance degradation. Figure 9 (on previous page) shows a comparison of naïve warp-specialized code with code emitted by Singe for a DME viscosity kernel over a range of warps per CTA. The naïve approach begins thrashing the instruction cache at six different warp code paths, while the code emitted by Singe continues to improve with peaks for warp counts that evenly divide the number of species in the DME mechanism. It is therefore imperative that common code paths be maintained across warps and that branching on warp IDs be done at a fine enough granularity to avoid thrashing the instruction cache.

5.1 Overlaying Computation

In order to minimize instruction cache thrashing, a warp-specializing compiler must *overlay* code from different warps whenever warps are performing similar computations. To achieve this goal we modify the standard approach to generating code from an AST. Code generation from an AST traditionally involves traversing the AST from top to bottom, emitting code at a node and then emitting code for each of a node's children in program order. In a warp-specializing compiler, code must be generated from a forest of ASTs with each AST describing the code to be executed for a different warp. To generate code from this forest of ASTs, a warp-specializing compiler traverses all the ASTs simultaneously. As long as the AST nodes across all warps are identical (with the exception of different constant values and indexing offsets, discussed in Sections 5.2 and 5.3), the compiler emits a single instance of

```
1   __shared__ volatile double real_mirror[NUM_WARPS];
2   const int warp_id = (threadIdx.x >> 5);
3   const int lane_id = (threadIdx.x & 0x1f);
4   ...
5   if (lane_id == 3)
6     real_mirror[warp_id] = real_constants[0];
7   double arrhenius = real_mirror[warp_id] * vlntemp;
8   if (lane_id == 4)
9     real_mirror[warp_id] = real_constants[0];
10  arrhenius = __fma_rn(real_mirror[warp_id], ortc, arrhenius);
```

Listing 2. Example Fermi constant broadcasts.

```
1   int hi_part, lo_part;
2   hi_part = __shfl(__double2hiint(real_constants[0]),3,32);
3   lo_part = __shfl(__double2loint(real_constants[0]),3,32);
4   double arrhenius = __hiloint2double(hi_part,lo_part) * vlntemp;
5   hi_part = __shfl(__double2hiint(real_constants[0]),4,32);
6   lo_part = __shfl(__double2loint(real_constants[0]),4,32);
7   arrhenius = __fma_rn(__hiloint2double(hi_part,lo_part), ortc, arrhenius);
```

Listing 3. Example Kepler constant broadcasts.

code for all the warps in the kernel to execute[2]. When the structure of the ASTs differs, the compiler uses branches dependent on warp ID to differentiate code blocks for warps.

Singe uses two different approaches to branching on warp ID. In the first case, if there are no similarities between the code required for each warp, Singe emits an indirect branch dependent on warp ID to jump to the correct block of code for a given warp. For cases with longer sequences of instructions, the single indirect branch statement is fissioned into multiple indirect branch statements. In our experience this approach does not degrade performance provided the regions of code along each path of an indirect branch are less than a few hundred instructions long. Under these circumstance the instruction cache prefetching mechanism is capable of handling the inter-warp divergence.

In cases where there is still some structure shared among a subset of the warps, Singe uses bit-masks to indicate which warps should enter a block of code. Bit-masks are constructed using one-hot encoding with each bit in the mask indicating whether a warp should take the branch or not. Listing 1 shows an example of overlaid code generated by Singe for computing Laundau-Teller and Lindermann reaction rates simultaneously in the chemistry kernel. By overlaying code with bit-mask warp filters, Singe minimizes the number of different paths warps can take during execution, thereby improving performance of the GPU instruction cache.

In general we have found that branching many ways for a few hundred instructions or less, or only branching a few ways for longer stretches of code, is necessary to avoid thrashing the GPU's instruction cache. This is consistent with earlier results on using warp specialization that only contained two or three different warp-specialized code paths[3]. The penalty for thrashing the instruction cache is routinely performance degradation of an order of magnitude or worse. Therefore it is crucial that any warp-specializing compiler overlay warp-specialized code on current GPUs.

5.2 Constant Arrays and Constant Deduplication

One of the challenges in generating overlaid warp-specialized code is that often warps require different constant values. We describe a technique that avoids branching on different constant values.

After a computation has been partitioned for warp specialization, each warp requires only a subset of the total constants needed for the full computation. The DSL compiler can then allocate an array for storing the constants needed by each warp that is as large as the largest number of constants needed by any warp. The compiler emits code so that all warps access the same locations in the

---

[1] If the desired occupancy is more than one CTA per SM, then the maximum number of named barriers per CTA is 16 divided by the desired number of CTAs per SM since named barriers are a conserved resource and, similar to shared memory and registers, can restrict occupancy.

[2] Care must also be taken to standardize variable names wherever possible between different warps to avoid creating false AST differences.

125

Mechanism	Viscosity	Diffusion	Chemistry
DME	8	18	6
Heptane	28	28	8

Figure 10. Constant registers per thread on Kepler.

constant array at all times. After code generation is complete, the compiler lays out constants in memory to ensure the right values are in the correct locations of the array for each warp. In some cases for divergent code, this may involve emitting padding values into the array for some warps. However, the cost of loading a few padded values is small compared to the cost of dynamic branching.

In practice, we have discovered that these constant arrays are often quite large for a single warp and can consume more than an entire thread's worth of registers. We therefore have developed another optimization for deduplicating constants between the threads within a warp. All the threads within a warp require the same set of constants and a single thread can broadcast a constant value to the other threads within a warp with no synchronization. Instead of each thread holding all the constants required for computation, the constants for a warp are statically striped across the threads within a warp, requiring each thread hold only $\frac{1}{32}$ of all the constants. Whenever a constant is needed, it is broadcast from the owning thread to the other threads within the warp.

This broadcast takes different forms depending on the architecture. For Fermi GPUs, the broadcast is performed using an allocation of shared memory with one location per warp. One thread writes data into shared memory and then the other threads in the warp read the value; no explicit synchronization is required because all the threads within a warp execute in lock step. Listing 2 shows example code emitted by Singe employing this technique.

On Kepler GPUs the broadcast is performed more efficiently using *shuffle instructions*. Shuffle instructions allow an exchange of 32 bits between all threads in a warp. By breaking double precision constants into their upper and lower halves they can be broadcast from the owning thread and then re-assembled. The two shuffle instructions are faster on Kepler because they do not stall pipelined loads in the shared memory pipeline, which happens during the shared memory write for the Fermi broadcast. Listing 3 shows an example of exchanging constants using shuffle instructions.

Figure 10 shows the number of registers required per thread for storing constants values across both mechanisms on the Kepler architecture. Note that they are small enough to allow the majority of registers to remain free for general purpose computation while still holding more constants on chip than can even be addressed by the constant cache, let alone fit in its working set[1].

This approach to storing constant values in registers can yield further performance gains when coupled with a streaming execution model. When multiple sets of points are mapped onto a single CTA, the CTA performs a loop to handle all of its points. By hoisting the loads for the constants outside of this loop, a DSL compiler can amortize the cost of loading constants into registers, resulting in very low overhead constant access.

5.3 Warp Indexing

For applications with irregular memory access patterns, warp specialization can result in warps needing to access different locations in memory. One of the many examples of this occurring in Singe is in the stiffness computations for the chemistry kernel described in Section 3.4. Each of the different warps needs to load different diffusion rates from global memory and different molar fractions from shared memory. The need to access different memory locations by different warps runs counter to the DSL compiler's goal of overlaying as much code as possible. To support code overlay without dynamic branching, a compiler can use *warp indexing* constants when doing memory accesses.

```
1  __shared__ volatile double scratch[192][32];
2  const int lane_id = threadIdx.x & 0x1f;
3  ...
4  int index = __shfl(index_constants[0],1,32);
5  asm volatile("ld.global.nc.cg.f64 %0,_[%1];" : "=d"(stif_diffusion_0) :
6    "l"(diffusion_array+index*spec_stride) : "memory");
7  stif_mole_frac_0 = scratch[index][lane_id];
```

Listing 4. Stiffness warp indexing on Kepler.

Warp indexing is a technique where each warp stores integer offset values for indexing into memory that are specific to that warp. All warps can then perform their address calculations using the same index variable even though the variable stores different values for different warps. As with the constant arrays, this extra level of indirection enables the compiler to overlay warp-specialized code without requiring dynamic branching for irregular memory access patterns.

Similar to constant deduplication, if the number of warp indexing constants is large, they can be deduplicated by striping them across the threads within a warp using the same approach described in Section 5.2. The only difference is that the index constants are not directly involved in computation, but are instead only used for address indexing. Listing 4 shows an example of warp indexing on Kepler from the stiffness computation where the same index is used to load a diffusion value from global memory and a molar fraction from shared memory.

One important caveat to warp indexing is that it only applies to data that is stored in dynamically indexable GPU memories, specifically global, shared, and constant memories. Arrays allocated in registers are not dynamically indexable and any attempt to index them with a dynamic variable causes the CUDA compiler to spill the array to much slower local memory. Ideally future GPUs will allow dynamic indexing of the register file as well.

6. Experimental Results

In this section we quantify the performance gains that result from applying warp specialization in Singe. We compare against baseline versions of the kernels emitted by an earlier version of Singe in the traditional CUDA data-parallel programming model. The baseline versions of the kernels were fully optimized using a combination of domain- and architecture-specific optimizations, including the use of logarithmic-space computations, exposure of additional instruction level parallelism, and the use of LDG texture loads using inline PTX for higher memory bandwidth on the Kepler architecture. In addition, a brute-force autotuner exhaustively explored the space of occupancy-register tradeoffs on all architectures. Consequently, the baseline CUDA kernels were already up to 2X faster than the OpenACC versions currently used by the production version of S3D[11]. The same set of optimizations were also applied to the warp-specialized versions of the kernels to ensure that all performance gains are directly attributable to warp specialization.

All experiments were run on two different architectures. The first was an NVIDIA Tesla C2070 Fermi GPU with 14 SMs, a 1147 MHz SM clock frequency, and a 1494 MHz DRAM clock frequency. The second architecture was a Tesla K20c Kepler GPU with 13 SMs, a 705 MHz SM clock frequency, and a 2600 MHz DRAM clock frequency. ECC was disabled on both architectures to make the memory-bound baseline kernels perform as well as possible against the kernels emitted by Singe. Singe kernels are primarily limited by on-chip resources and therefore achieve even larger speedups relative to the baseline kernels with ECC enabled. All kernels were compiled with the default version of nvcc from CUDA 5.0 and were run with version 304.54 of the CUDA driver.

For all experiments, we report throughput for three different grid problem sizes 32^3, 64^3, and 128^3 to illustrate any scaling effects. Absolute times for each experiment can be computed by di-

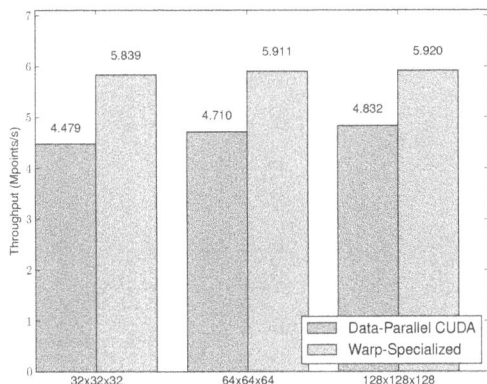

(a) Fermi

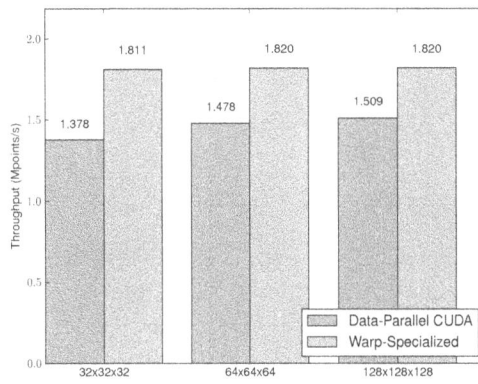

(b) Kepler

Figure 11. Viscosity performance results for DME.

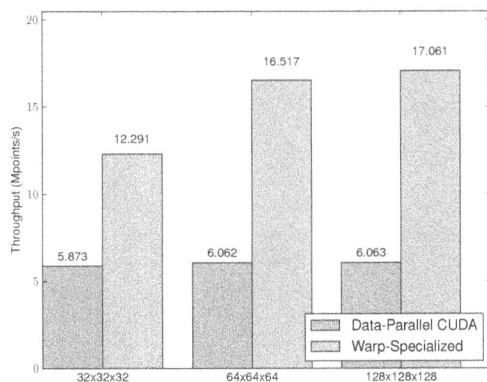

(a) Fermi

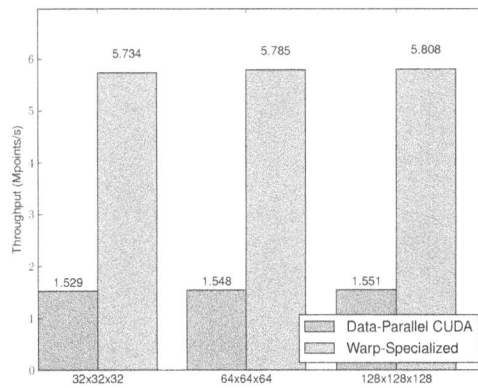

(b) Kepler

Figure 12. Viscosity performance results for heptane.

viding the number of points in each grid by the reported throughput. In all cases the reported throughput is computed using the harmonic mean of the throughputs for twenty iterations of each experiment. In addition to reporting performance results for each kernel, we also analyze the underlying SASS machine code for each kernel to determine the limiting factor for each of the different kernels.

6.1 Viscosity

Figures 11 and 12 show performance results comparing warp-specialized versions of the viscosity kernel to the baseline versions for the DME and heptane mechanisms respectively. Speedups for the warp specialization kernels ranged from 1.2X to 3.75X over the baseline kernels. Significantly larger speedups over the baseline versions were achieved on the Kepler architecture.

To understand the underlying reasons for these results we investigated the underlying SASS machine code generated for both the baseline and warp-specialized versions of the code. From the SASS we were able to determine the total number of double precision floating point operations required per warp for both the baseline and warp-specialized versions on Fermi and Kepler. For the DME mechanism on Fermi the baseline and warp-specialized kernels achieved 197.9 and 257.3 billion double precision floating point operations per second (GFLOPS) respectively; on Kepler they achieved 220.6 and 617.7 GFLOPS respectively.

Using these numbers along with an understanding of the Fermi and Kepler architectures we were able to discern the limiting factors for each kernel. In theory, a Fermi GPU can issue 1 DFMA instruction per SM every other clock cycle. For the C2070 GPU in these experiments this yields a theoretical math throughput of 513 GFLOPS. In practice, optimized Fermi kernels such as DGEMM can reach around 300 GFLOPS[1]. Achieving 257.3 GFLOPS on

the warp-specialized viscosity kernel is near optimal math throughput on Fermi when the overhead of dynamic branching and shared memory accesses are included. The baseline CUDA version however does not come as close to the practical peak math throughput for two reasons. First, the working set of molar fractions and per-species viscosities does not fit in registers and is spilled to local memory. Second, the large number of constants do not fit in the constant cache. Both these issues add latency and account for the slowdown relative to the warp-specialized kernels.

For the Kepler architecture, the theoretical math throughput is significantly higher. On Kepler each *quad* of an SM can issue one DFMA every other cycle, yielding a theoretical throughput of 1173 GFLOPS on a K20c with 13 SMs. The 617.7 GFLOPS achieved by the warp-specialized viscosity kernel is more than half of theoretical peak. We hypothesized that this kernel is actually limited by the throughput of DFMA operations whose third operand is loaded from the constant cache, which is the case for the 12 DFMA operations in the Taylor series expansion of the exponential function which dominates viscosity performance. To verify this hypothesis we modified Singe to emit an incorrect exponential function that instead relied on constants stored in registers. Experiments showed these kernels were capable of performance near 750 GFLOPS, indicating that our warp-specialized viscosity kernels were also compute-bound on Kepler. The baseline CUDA version improved marginally from Fermi, but still suffered from severe register spilling and constant cache misses. The highest performing baseline CUDA version used the larger on-chip register file on Kepler to avoid spilling and not to increase occupancy which meant that the latency of loading constants was still exposed.

These results demonstrate that warp specialization enables Singe to partition the viscosity kernel in a way that better maps

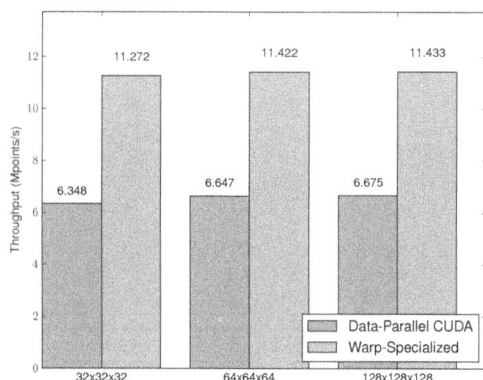

(a) Fermi

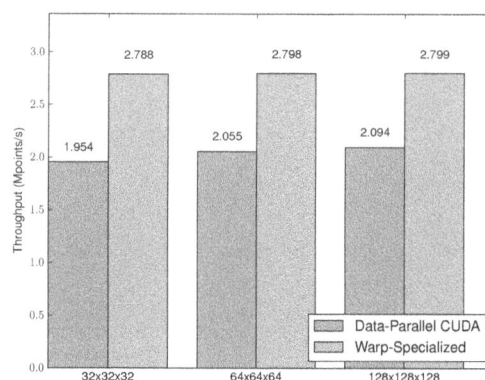

(b) Kepler

Figure 13. Diffusion performance results for DME.

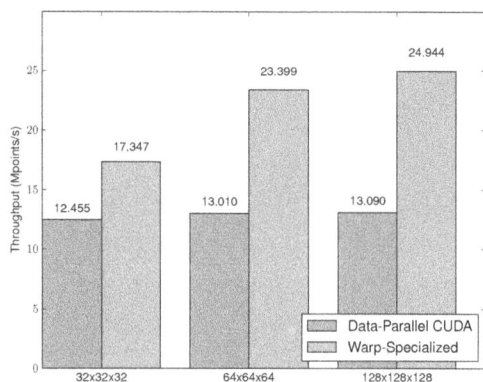

(a) Fermi

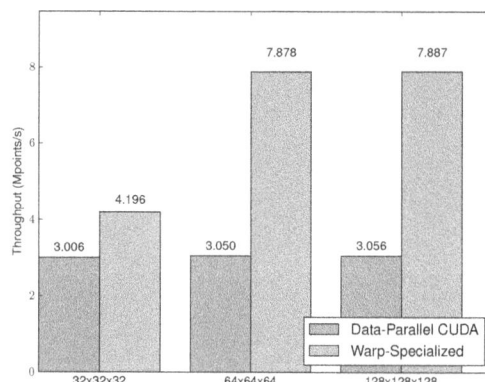

(b) Kepler

Figure 14. Diffusion performance results for heptane.

onto both Fermi and Kepler GPUs. Both warp-specialized kernels approach the limits of math throughput on their architectures. The higher potential math throughput on Kepler explains why the Kepler warp-specialized kernel performs significantly better than the Fermi warp-specialized kernel relative to the baseline.

6.2 Diffusion

Figures 13 and 14 show performance results for the diffusion kernels for the DME and heptane mechanisms respectively. Speedups for the warp-specialized kernels ranged from 1.33X to 2.58X over the baseline CUDA kernels. Again larger speedups were achieved on the Kepler architecture than the Fermi architecture due to the higher ceiling of math instruction throughput.

To confirm that the performance of the warp-specialized kernels was again limited by math throughput, we again analyzed the SASS machine code. We were surprised to discover that for the DME mechanism the warp-specialized version of the kernel was only achieving 212.8 GFLOPS on Fermi and 526.6 GFLOPS on Kepler. After examining the SASS, we determined that the degradation in performance was caused by the additional named barrier calls that were needed to synchronize access to the partial sums stored in shared memory. A larger number of barriers resulted in excessive cycles waiting for straggler warps to arrive at the barrier which consequently reduced math throughput. Unsafely removing the barriers resulted in performance around 250 GFLOPS on Fermi and 625 GFLOPS on Kepler, which is consistent with the actual peak math throughput observed in Section 6.1.

Another interesting effect can be observed in Figures 13(b) and 14(b). For smaller problem sizes the speedup over the baseline kernels is smaller. Due to the large number of constants required for the diffusion kernel, the cost of loading these constants into

registers is significant. However, for larger problem sizes it is more easily amortized. This effect is only noticeable on Kepler where the math performance is much higher and exposes the constant loading phase. A problem size of at least 64^3 is therefore required to fully amortize the cost of loading the constants into registers.

6.3 Chemistry

Figures 15 and 16 show performance results for the chemistry kernels for both the DME and heptane mechanisms respectively. Speedups for the warp-specialized kernels ranged from 1.01X to 1.50X over the baseline CUDA kernels. Unlike the viscosity and diffusion kernels, the performance characteristics of the chemistry kernels are very different. The very large working set places extreme pressure on the architectural resources of any GPU. Using warp specialization Singe was able to emit code using an alternative allocation of resources which yielded performance gains.

The baseline CUDA chemistry kernels spill significant amounts of memory due to the large working sets required. For the heptane mechanism 8736 bytes are spilled per thread on Fermi and 8500 bytes per thread are spilled on Kepler. With enough occupancy all this latency can be hidden, but results in a memory bandwidth limited kernel. After analyzing the SASS for the baseline CUDA kernels, we measured memory bandwidths of 85 GB/s on Fermi and 100 GB/s on Kepler, which are consistent with actual peak memory bandwidths for these architectures[3].

---

[3] We have measured read bandwidths of 165 GB/s on a Kepler K20c with five GDDR5 memory partitions when using LDG texture loads, but this path is not available to local memory since local memory is not constant. 100 GB/s load bandwidth is consistent with measured load bandwidths through the much smaller pipe in the L1 cache with only 13 SMs.

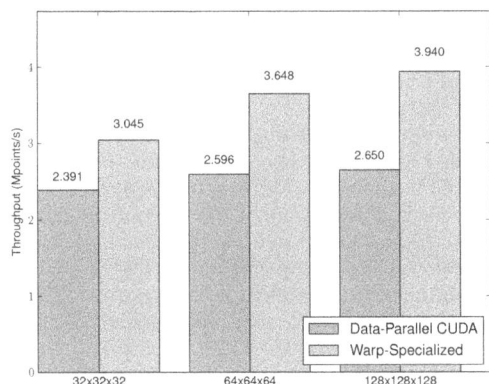

(a) Fermi

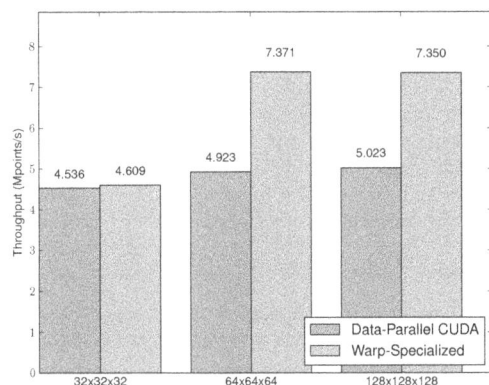

(b) Kepler

Figure 15. Chemistry performance results for DME.

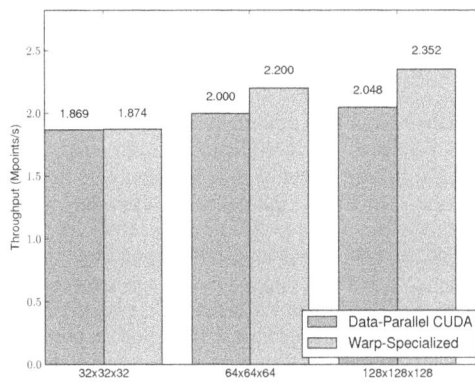

(a) Fermi

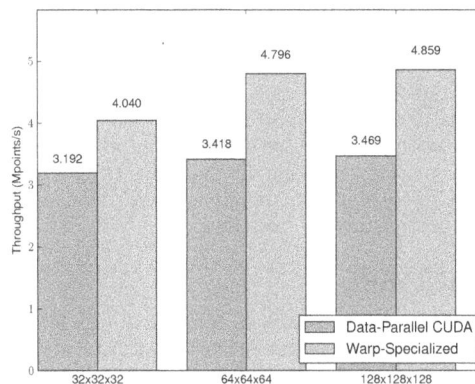

(b) Kepler

Figure 16. Chemistry performance results for heptane.

Alternatively, the warp-specialized kernels emitted by Singe for heptane spill only 276 bytes on Fermi and 44 bytes on Kepler (mostly infrequently accessed pointer data). Almost the entire working set of the computation including all forward and reverse reaction rates remain in registers at the cost that they must be repeatedly exchanged through shared memory. Neither the Fermi nor the Kepler warp-specialized kernels have enough warps to hide the 30 cycles of shared memory access latency with only 20 and 16 warps per SM respectively. As a result, the warp-specialized versions of the kernel are shared memory latency limited. However, the performance results demonstrate that this is significantly better than being global memory bandwidth limited.

7. Discussion

While we have shown that warp specialization is effective on NVIDIA GPUs, we believe that similar benefits could be realized on other wide-vector SIMD architectures, such as Intel's Xeon Phi. Conceptually, a warp is a single instruction stream issuing 32-wide vector instructions, which is not far removed from a thread on a Xeon Phi issuing 8-wide double-precision vector instructions. Instead of partitioning and mapping computations onto warps, computations could be mapped onto vectorized threads. Identical to warp specialization, the techniques presented in this paper could be used to fit large working sets into on-chip memories and handle irregularity. There are currently two absent hardware features on the Xeon Phi that inhibit this approach. First, there are no fast hardware synchronization primitives equivalent to named barriers present (heavy-weight software mutexes are currently necessary). Second, there are no on-chip software-managed memories to be used for fast data exchange buffers. Instead the hardware-managed

L1 cache must be used which is subject to interference and eviction by other data movement operations.

The presence of hardware-managed caches on GPUs also hinders the performance of warp-specializing compilers like Singe. Hardware-managed caches consume transistors which could have been used to fit larger working sets in on-chip software-managed memories. Hardware-managed caches are also difficult resources for compilers to reason about. An earlier version of Singe attempted to store the large number of constant values in the GPUs hardware-managed L2 cache. However, writes from other threads kept evicting constants off-chip despite Singe annotating all global writes with the PTX cache-streaming qualifier `cs`. The current Singe compiler completely ignores the L2 cache which wastes significant on-chip memory (768 KB on Fermi and 1536 KB on Kepler). Finally, hardware-managed caches add overhead to the kernels emitted by Singe both in terms of performance (tag look-ups on all memory accesses) and power (unnecessary data movement between cache levels). Ideally, future GPUs and other wide-vector architectures will consist primarily of software-managed caches which will enable compilers like Singe to directly orchestrate data movement leading to both higher performance and power efficiency.

The poor performance of current GPU instruction caches makes warp specialization infeasible without overlaying code paths. Instruction caches designed for handling many divergent warps in future GPUs would remove the need for overlaying code using the techniques described in Section 5. This would improve the performance of Singe kernels by significantly reducing the number of necessary warp-specific branch instructions. Additionally, it would greatly reduce the complexity of the code generation stage for warp-specializing compilers. It would also make writing warp-specialized code practical for human programmers.

Finally, a common misconception regarding warp specialization is that it will be made obsolete by Moore's law because more transistors in future chips will allow current large working sets to fit on-chip. Ideally, more on-chip storage could lead to higher occupancy and would only require a simple data-parallel programming model to achieve high performance. Unfortunately, this view fails to consider that many computational science domains, including combustion, cosmology, and molecular dynamics, all limit the scope of their simulations in order to execute efficiently on current hardware. For example, the combustion mechanisms described in this paper are considered *reduced* mechanisms because they only simulate tens of chemical species instead of the hundreds and thousands of species in real mechanisms[12]. In our experience, computational scientists will always use additional hardware to perform higher fidelity but more computationally expensive simulations instead of making current simulations perform better. As machines become more powerful, scientists will devise more complex simulations that place intense pressure on both programming systems and hardware. Under such conditions, data-parallel programming models such as CUDA, OpenCL, and especially OpenACC will struggle to take full advantage of future hardware. Ultimately, programming models such as warp specialization will become essential for managing large working sets, handling irregularity, and exploiting task-level parallelism to fully leverage forthcoming architectures for general purpose computing.

8. Related Work

The most closely related work to Singe is CudaDMA[3], a library that uses warp specialization to optimize data movement between on-chip and off-chip memories. CudaDMA kernels specialize warps into *compute warps* for application code, and *DMA warps* for data movement. Synchronization is performed via a simple interface using named barriers. There are many differences between CudaDMA and Singe. For example, with only two warp code paths, CudaDMA programs do not require Singe's optimizations to avoid instruction cache thrashing. As another example, all CudaDMA kernels use the same partitioning scheme: application code runs on compute warps and CudaDMA code executes on DMA warps. Avoiding the partitioning problem faced by Singe reduces the implementation complexity of CudaDMA. The focus is also different: CudaDMA is a general purpose library for CUDA users, while the techniques presented here are for warp-specializing compilers.

Green-Marl is a DSL and compiler for implementing graph analyses[8] on GPUs. The Green-Marl compiler makes use of the concept of virtualized warps to handle the irregularity inherent in graph algorithms. While the creation of virtualized warps is similar to the partitioning operation required for warp specialization, the Green-Marl compiler maps virtualized warps onto physical warps to conform to the data-parallel GPU programming model.

G-Streamline is a framework that dynamically detects computational and memory access irregularities in GPU kernels[14]. Using this information G-Streamline rewrites kernels on the fly to reduce the overheads associated with irregularity. In this work we've shown how warp-specializing DSL compilers like Singe can handle irregularity without any dynamic overheads.

Halide is a high-level DSL and autotuning framework for two dimensional image processing pipelines[13]. Halide performs many interesting optimization techniques for taking advantage of various GPU resources similar to how a DSL compiler might leverage warp specialization. However, Halide does not consider warp specialization as an approach for optimizing GPU programs.

There have been many DSL languages that target GPUs for high performance[4, 6, 8]. To the best of our knowledge, we are the only ones who demonstrate the necessary techniques for constructing a warp-specializing DSL compiler.

9. Conclusion

We have introduced warp specialization as an effective compiler technique for generating GPU code for applications with both irregular computation and memory accesses as well as large working sets. We have also presented Singe, a DSL compiler that leverages warp specialization in conjunction with domain specific knowledge to produce GPU combustion kernels that perform better than is possible in standard data-parallel GPU programming models. We described the general architecture and compilation techniques necessary for constructing a warp-specializing DSL compiler. Using warp specialization, Singe emits kernels that are up to 3.75X faster than previously optimized but purely data-parallel GPU code.

Acknowledgments

This work was supported by the ExaCT Combustion Co-Design Center via Los Alamos National Laboratory Subcontract No. 173315-1 through the U.S. Department of Energy Office of Advanced Scientific Computing Research under Contract No. DE-AC52-06NA25396. The authors thank the anonymous reviewers, our shepherd John Reppy, Elliott Slaughter, Zach DeVito, Michael Garland, Bryan Catanzaro, and Pat McCormick for their useful comments and suggestions. Special thanks go to Jackie Chen, Hemanth Kolla, and Tianfeng Lu for their detailed explanations and patience in answering questions regarding combustion science.

References

[1] CUDA programming guide version 5.5. http://docs.nvidia.com/cuda/cuda-c-programming-guide/index.html, 2013.

[2] Parallel thread execution ISA version 3.2. http://docs.nvidia.com/cuda/parallel-thread-execution/index.html, 2013.

[3] M. Bauer, H. Cook, and B. Khailany. CudaDMA: optimizing GPU memory bandwidth via warp specialization. SC '11, 2011.

[4] H. Chafi, A. K. Sujeeth, K. J. Brown, H. Lee, A. R. Atreya, and K. Olukotun. A domain-specific approach to heterogeneous parallelism. PPoPP, pages 35–46, 2011.

[5] J. H. Chen, A. Choudhary, B. de Supinski, M. DeVries, E. R. Hawkes, S. Klasky, W. K. Liao, K. L. Ma, J. Mellor-Crummey, N. Podhorszki, R. Sankaran, S. Shende, and C. S. Yoo. Terascale direct numerical simulations of turbulent combustion using S3D. *Computational Science and Discovery*, 2009.

[6] Z. DeVito, N. Joubert, F. Palacios, S. Oakley, M. Medina, M. Barrientos, E. Elsen, F. Ham, A. Aiken, K. Duraisamy, E. Darve, J. Alonso, and P. Hanrahan. Liszt: a domain specific language for building portable mesh-based pde solvers. SC, pages 9:1–9:12, 2011.

[7] S. Hack and G. Goos. Optimal register allocation for SSA-form programs in polynomial time. *Inf. Process. Lett.*, 2006.

[8] S. Hong, S. K. Kim, T. Oguntebi, and K. Olukotun. Accelerating CUDA graph algorithms at maximum warp. PPoPP, 2011.

[9] R. Kee, F. Rupley, and E. Meeks. CHEMKIN-III: A fortran chemical kinetics package for the analysis of gas-phase chemical and plasma kinetics. 1996.

[10] Khronos. The OpenCL Specification, Version 2.0. http://www.khronos.org/registry/cl/specs/opencl-2.0.pdf, 2013.

[11] J. M. Levesque, R. Sankaran, and R. Grout. Hybridizing S3D into an exascale application using OpenACC: an approach for moving to multi-petaflops and beyond. SC '12, pages 15:1–15:11, 2012.

[12] T. Lu and C. K. Law. Toward accommodating realistic fuel chemistry in large-scale computations. *Progress in Energy and Combustion Science*, pages 192 – 215, 2009.

[13] J. Ragan-Kelley, A. Adams, S. Paris, M. Levoy, S. Amarasinghe, and F. Durand. Decoupling algorithms from schedules for easy optimization of image processing pipelines. *ACM Trans. Graph.*, 2012.

[14] E. Z. Zhang, Y. Jiang, Z. Guo, K. Tian, and X. Shen. On-the-fly elimination of dyn. irregularities for GPU computing. ASPLOS, 2011.

Eliminating Global Interpreter Locks in Ruby through Hardware Transactional Memory

Rei Odaira

IBM Research – Tokyo

odaira@jp.ibm.com

Jose G. Castanos

IBM Research – T.J. Watson
Research Center

castanos@us.ibm.com

Hisanobu Tomari

University of Tokyo

tomari@is.s.u-tokyo.ac.jp

Abstract

Many scripting languages use a Global Interpreter Lock (GIL) to simplify the internal designs of their interpreters, but this kind of lock severely lowers the multi-thread performance on multi-core machines. This paper presents our first results eliminating the GIL in Ruby using Hardware Transactional Memory (HTM) in the IBM zEnterprise EC12 and Intel 4th Generation Core processors. Though prior prototypes replaced a GIL with HTM, we tested realistic programs, the Ruby NAS Parallel Benchmarks (NPB), the WEBrick HTTP server, and Ruby on Rails. We devised a new technique to dynamically adjust the transaction lengths on a per-bytecode basis, so that we can optimize the likelihood of transaction aborts against the relative overhead of the instructions to begin and end the transactions. Our results show that HTM achieved 1.9- to 4.4-fold speedups in the NPB programs over the GIL with 12 threads, and 1.6- and 1.2-fold speedups in WEBrick and Ruby on Rails, respectively. The dynamic transaction-length adjustment chose the best transaction lengths for any number of threads and applications with sufficiently long running times.

Categories and Subject Descriptors D.1.3 [**Programming Techniques**]: Concurrent Programming – Parallel programming

Keywords Global interpreter lock; hardware transactional memory; scripting language; lock elision

1. Introduction

Scripting languages such as Ruby [26] and Python [21] offer high productivity, but at the cost of slow performance.

PPoPP '14, February 15 - 19 2014, Orlando, FL, USA
Copyright © 2014 ACM 978-1-4503-2656-8/14/02...$15.00.
http://dx.doi.org/10.1145/2555243.2555247

The single-thread performance is limited because of interpreted execution, dynamic typing, and the support for meta-programming. Many projects [10,24,30] have attempted to overcome these limitations through Just-in-Time (JIT) compilation with type specialization.

Meanwhile, the multi-thread performance of the scripting languages is constrained by the Global Interpreter Lock (GIL), or the Giant VM Lock (GVL) in Ruby's terminology. Although each application thread is mapped to a native thread, only the one thread that acquires the GIL can actually run. At pre-defined yield points, each thread releases the GIL, yields the CPU to another runnable thread if any exists, and then reacquires the GIL. The GIL eases the programming of the interpreters' logic and the extension libraries because they do not need to worry about concurrency. In return, the GIL significantly limits the performance on multi-core systems. Some new implementations of the Ruby and Python languages [9,10,12,13] use complex fine-grained locking to remove the GIL. However, their class libraries still need to be globally protected to remain compatible with the original implementations of the languages.

Transactional memory has been proposed as an alternative to eliminate global locking without requiring the complex semantics of fine-grained locking. In transactional memory, a programmer encloses critical sections with transaction begin and end directives. A transaction is executed atomically so that its memory operations appear to be performed in a single step. Transactions can be executed concurrently as long as their memory operations do not conflict, so that transactional memory can outperform global locking. Although transactional memory is attractive for its potential concurrency, pure software implementations are slow [2].

Chipmakers in the industry regard transactional memory as a promising technology for parallel programming in the multi-core era and are designing or producing hardware for transactional memory, called Hardware Transactional Memory (HTM). Intel published documentation for an instruction set called Transactional Synchronization Extensions [8] and implemented it in the 4th Generation Core processor. IBM has released Blue Gene/Q and the main-frame zEnterprise EC12 (zEC12) with HTM support [5,27]. IBM also defined HTM extensions for POWER ISA [6] to be implemented in POWER8 [28]. These HTM implementations will offer effective concurrency with low overhead.

There have been previous studies [1,23,29] of replacing the GIL of a scripting language with HTM, but they measured only micro-benchmarks on simulators or on the limited HTM of Sun's Rock processor [3]. Therefore, these studies did not propose solutions to or even reveal many transaction aborts encountered when realistic programs are executed on less-restrictive HTM hardware.

This paper shows the empirical results of removing the GIL from Ruby and proposes dynamic transaction length adjustment to reduce transaction aborts and overhead. We used IBM's HTM implementation in zEC12 and Intel's implementation in the 4th Generation Core processor (Xeon E3-1275 v3). In addition to micro-benchmarks, we measured the NAS Parallel Benchmarks ported to Ruby [17], the WEBrick HTTP server attached in the Ruby distribution, and Ruby on Rails [25]. Our results are also applicable to other HTM implementations. Unlike the results [29] on Sun's Rock processor, the HTM implementations on which we experimented are similar to the generic ones proposed in the literature, e.g. [22].

Running these programs on the real HTM hardware revealed a tradeoff between transaction aborts and overhead. On the one hand, we desire long transactions as we amortize the overhead to begin and end each transaction. On the other hand, no HTM implementation allows for transactions of unlimited lengths, and longer transactions increase the amount of discarded work when a transaction aborts.

To balance the transaction aborts against the overhead, we propose a new technique to dynamically adjust the transaction lengths on a per-yield-point basis. As in the GIL, a transaction ends and begins at pre-defined transaction yield points, but it need not do so at every transaction yield point. We dynamically adjust the transaction lengths, i.e. how many yield points to skip, based on the abort statistics of the transactions started at each yield point.

Here are our contributions:

- We propose an algorithm for the GIL elimination that adjusts the transaction lengths at each yield point.
- We implemented and evaluated the GIL elimination on real machines that support HTM, using real-world applications in addition to micro-benchmarks.
- We eliminated the GIL from Ruby, going beyond prior work focusing on Python. We also removed transaction conflict points in the Ruby interpreter.

Section 2 describes the HTM implementations used in our studies and Section 3 explains Ruby's GIL implementation. Section 4 shows how we replaced the GIL with the HTM and then balanced the aborts against the overhead,

leading to the experimental results in Section 5. Section 6 covers related work. Section 7 concludes the paper.

2. HTM Implementations

We used the HTM implementations in the IBM mainframe zEC12 and the Intel 4th Generation Core processor (Xeon E3-1275 v3) for our studies. This section briefly describes the instruction set architectures supporting the HTM and their micro-architectures. A complete description of the HTM in zEC12 appeared in a paper [11]. The instruction set architectures of zEC12 and the 4th Generation Core processor are also available [7,8].

2.1 Instruction set architectures

In zEC12, each transaction begins with a TBEGIN instruction and is ended by a TEND instruction. In the 4th Generation Core processor, XBEGIN and XEND correspond to TBEGIN and TEND, respectively. If a transaction aborts, then the execution returns back to the instruction immediately after the TBEGIN in zEC12, while the argument of the XBEGIN specifies a relative offset to a fallback path.

A transaction can abort for various reasons. The most frequent causes include footprint overflows and conflicts. When the abort is transient, e.g. because of a conflict, simply retrying the transaction is likely to succeed. On persistent aborts, e.g. due to transaction footprint overflow, the program should cancel the execution of the transaction. The condition code in zEC12 and the EAX register in the 4th Generation Core processor report whether the abort is transient or persistent. A transaction can also be aborted by software with a TABORT (in zEC12) or an XABORT (in the 4th Generation Core processor) instruction.

2.2 Micro-architectures

The zEC12 Central Processor (CP) chip has 6 cores, and 6 CP chips are packaged in a multi-chip module (MCM). Up to 4 MCMs can be connected in a single cache-coherent system. Each core has 96-KB L1 and 1-MB L2 data caches. The 6 cores on a CP chip share a 64-MB L3 cache and the 6 CP chips share an off-chip 384-MB L4 cache included in the same MCM. Each core supports a single hardware thread. The cache line size is 256 bytes.

The Xeon E3-1275 v3 processor contains 4 cores and each core supports 2 simultaneous multi-threading (SMT) threads. Each core has 32-KB L1 data and 256-KB L2 unified caches. The 4 cores share an 8-MB L3 cache. The cache line size is 64 bytes.

The zEC12 HTM facilities are built on top of its cache structure. Each L1 data cache line is augmented with its own tx-read and tx-dirty bits. An abort is triggered if a cache-coherency request from another CPU conflicts with a transactionally read or written line. A special LRU-extension vector records the lines that are transactionally read but evicted from the L1. Thus the maximum read-set size is roughly the size of the L2. The transactionally written data is buffered in the Gathering Store Cache between the L1 and the L2/L3. The maximum write-set size is limited to this cache size, which is 8 KB.

The detailed design of the Xeon E3-1275 v3 processor's HTM has not been revealed, but it takes advantage of the cache structure, like zEC12. Our preliminary experiments showed that the maximum read-set size is 6 MB, and the maximum write-set size is about 19 KB.

3. Ruby Implementation

This section introduces the Ruby language and its original implementation, often called CRuby, and describes how the GIL works in CRuby. Our description is based on CRuby 1.9.3-p194.

3.1 The Ruby language and CRuby

Ruby is a modern object-oriented scripting language that is widely known as part of the Ruby on Rails Web application framework. Nevertheless, Ruby is a general-purpose language that has many features in common with other scripting languages such as JavaScript, Python, or Perl: a flexible, dynamic type system; meta-programming; closures; and an extensive standard runtime library.

The reference Ruby implementation [26] is called CRuby, which is written in the C language. The recent releases of CRuby use a stack-based virtual machine. Ruby code is compiled into an internal bytecode representation at runtime and is executed by an interpreter. CRuby does not have a JIT compiler.

3.2 The GIL in CRuby

The Ruby language supports multi-threaded programming through objects of the standard Thread class that synchronize through standard concurrency constructs like Mutex or ConditionVariable objects. Since CRuby 1.9, the interpreter supports native threads, where each Ruby application thread maps to a kernel thread. In our environments, each application thread corresponds to a Pthread.

Unfortunately, the concurrency is limited. The interpreter has a GIL, guaranteeing that only one application thread is executing in the interpreter at any given time. The GIL eliminates the need for concurrency programming in the interpreter and libraries. Unlike normal locking, which holds a lock only during part of the execution, the GIL is almost always held by one of the application threads during execution and is released only when necessary. An application thread acquires and releases the GIL when it starts and ends, respectively. It also releases the GIL when it is about to perform a blocking operation, such as I/O, and it acquires the GIL again after the operation is finished.

However, if the GIL were released only at the blocking operations, compute-intensive application threads could not be switched with one another at all. Therefore, at certain pre-defined points, the application thread yields the GIL by releasing the GIL, calling the sched_yield() system call to yield the CPU, and then acquiring the GIL again. To insure reaching a yield point within a finite time, CRuby sets yield points at loop back-edges and each exit of a method and block. Note that the yield points have nothing to do with the "yield" expression in the Ruby language.

As an optimization, each application thread does need not yield the GIL at every yield point, because the yield operation is heavy. To allow for occasional yields, CRuby runs a timer thread in background. It wakes up every 250 msec and sets a flag in the per-thread data structure of the running application thread. Each thread checks the flag at each yield point and yields the GIL only when it is set. In addition, if there is only one application thread, then no yield operations will be performed at all.

4. GIL Elimination through HTM

This section presents our algorithm for eliminating the GIL by using an HTM. Our algorithm is based on Transactional Lock Elision (TLE) [3,22]. Like TLE, our algorithm retains the GIL as a fallback mechanism. A thread first executes Ruby code as a transaction. If the transaction aborts, the thread can retry the transaction, depending on the abort reason. If the transaction aborts after several retries, the thread acquires the GIL to proceed.

Transactions should begin and end at the same points as where the GIL is acquired, released, and yielded, because those points are guaranteed as safe critical-section boundaries. However, our preliminary experiments showed the original yield points were too coarse-grained for the HTM, which caused footprint overflows. Thus we added new yield points as explained in Section 4.2.

4.1 Beginning and ending a transaction

Figure 1 shows the algorithm to begin a transaction. The GIL status is tracked by the global variable GIL.acquired, which is set to true when the GIL is acquired.

If there is no other live application thread in the interpreter, then the algorithm reverts to the GIL (Lines 2-3), because concurrency is unnecessary in this case. Otherwise, the algorithm first sets the length of the transaction to be executed (Line 5). This will be explained in Section 4.3.

Before beginning a transaction, the algorithm checks the GIL and if it has been acquired by some other thread, waits until it is released (Lines 6-8 and 40-48). This is not mandatory but an optimization.

The TBEGIN() function (Line 13) is a wrapper for the TBEGIN or XBEGIN instruction described in Section 2.1. The TBEGIN() function initially returns 0. If the transaction aborts, the execution returns back to within the TBE-GIN() function and then it returns an abort reason code.

Lines 14-15 are within the transaction. As in the original TLE, the transaction first reads the GIL (Line 15) into its transaction read set, so that later the transaction can be aborted if the GIL is acquired by another thread. The transaction must abort immediately if the GIL is already acquired, because otherwise the transaction could read data being modified.

Lines 16-37 are for abort handling. We describe Lines 17-20 in Section 4.3. If the GIL is acquired (Line 21), there is a conflict at the GIL. In the same way as in Lines 6-8, Lines 22-27 waits until the GIL is released. The algorithm first tries to use spin locking, but after GIL_RETRY_MAX-time aborts, it forcibly acquires the GIL (Line 27). If the abort is persistent, retrying the transaction will not succeed, so the execution immediately reverts to the GIL (Lines 28-29). For the transient aborts, we retry the transaction TRANSIENT_RETRY_MAX times before falling back on the GIL (Lines 31-35).

Ending a transaction is much simpler than beginning a transaction (Figure 2). The acquired GIL (Line 2) means this transaction has been executed not as a transaction but with the GIL being held. Thus the GIL must be released. Otherwise, the TEND or XEND instruction is issued.

4.2 Yielding a transaction

As described in Section 3.2, the original CRuby implementation has a timer thread to force yielding among the application threads. We no longer need the timer thread because the application threads are running in parallel using the HTM, but we still need the yield points. Without them, some transactions would last so long that there would be many conflicts and footprint overflows.

In our preliminary experiments, we found the original yield points were too coarse-grained for the HTM. As described in Section 3.2, the original CRuby sets yield points at branches and method and block exits. With only these yield points, most of the transactions abort due to store overflows. Therefore, we defined the following bytecode types as additional yield points: getlocal, getinstancevariable, getclassvariable, send, opt_plus, opt_minus, opt_mult, and opt_aref. The first three bytecode types are to read variables. The send bytecode invokes a method or a block. The opt_ variants perform their corresponding operations (plus, minus, multiplication, and array reference) but are optimized for certain types such as integer numbers. We chose these bytecodes because they appear frequently in bytecode sequences or they access much data in memory. This means that in the NAS Parallel Benchmarks, more than half of the bytecode instructions are now yield points.

We also need to guarantee that the new yield points are safe. In interpreters, the bytecode boundaries are natural

```
1.  transaction_begin(current_thread, pc) {
2.    if (there is no other live thread) {
3.      gil_acquire();
4.    } else {
5.      set_transaction_length(current_thread, pc);
6.      if (GIL.acquired) {
7.        if (spin_and_gil_acquire()) return;
8.      }
9.      transient_retry_counter = TRANSIENT_RETRY_MAX;
10.     gil_retry_counter = GIL_RETRY_MAX;
11.     first_retry = 1;
12.   transaction_retry:
13.     if ((tbegin_result = TBEGIN()) == 0) {
14.       /* transactional path */
15.       if (GIL.acquired) TABORT();
16.     } else { /* abort path */
17.       if (first_retry) {
18.         first_retry = 0;
19.         adjust_transaction_length(pc);
20.       }
21.       if (GIL.acquired) {
22.         gil_retry_counter--;
23.         if (gil_retry_counter > 0) {
24.           if (spin_and_gil_acquire()) return;
25.           else goto transaction_retry;
26.         }
27.         gil_acquire();
28.       } else if (is_persistent(tbegin_result)) {
29.         gil_acquire();
30.       } else {
31.         /* transient abort */
32.         transient_retry_counter--;
33.         if (transient_retry_counter > 0)
34.           goto transaction_retry;
35.         gil_acquire();
36.       }
37.     }
38.   }
39. }

40. spin_and_gil_acquire() {
41.   Spin for a while until the GIL is released;
42.   if (! GIL.acquired) return false;
43.   gil_acquire();
44.   return true;
45. }

46. gil_acquire() {
47.   /* Omitted. Original GIL-acquisition logic. */
48. }
```

Figure 1. Algorithm to begin a transaction.

yield points. Because the bytecode instructions can be generated in any order, it is unlikely that the interpreters internally have a critical section straddling a bytecode boundary. However, for applications that are incorrectly synchronized, such as those assuming the GIL can be yielded only at branches or method exits, the new yield points can change their behavior. Applications properly synchronized by using Mutex objects are not affected by our changes.

At each yield point, we call the transaction_yield() function in Figure 2, which simply calls the functions to end and begin transactions (Lines 12-13), but with two optimizations. First, as described in Section 3.2, no yield operation is performed if there is only one application thread (Line 9). Note that the GIL is used in this case (Line 3 of Figure 1). Second, a transaction does not yield at every yield point but only after a set number of yield points (using yield_point_counter) have been passed (Lines 10-11). This optimization is described in Section 4.3. Unlike the original

```
1.  transaction_end() {
2.      if (GIL.acquired) gil_release();
3.      else TEND();
4.  }

5.  gil_release() {
6.      /* Omitted.  Original GIL-release logic */
7.  }

8.  transaction_yield(current_thread, pc) {
9.      if (there is other live thread) {
10.         current_thread->yield_point_counter--;
11.         if (current_thread->yield_point_counter == 0) {
12.             transaction_end();
13.             transaction_begin(current_thread, pc);
14.         }
15.     }
16. }
```

Figure 2. Algorithm to end and yield a transaction.

GIL-yield operation, we do not need to call the sched_yield() system call, because the multiple threads are already running in parallel and the OS is scheduling them.

4.3 Dynamic transaction-length adjustment

As shown in Figure 2, each transaction will skip a predetermined number of yield points before it ends. This means that the transaction lengths vary with the granularity of the yield points. The length of a transaction means the number of yield points the transaction passes through plus one.

Tradeoff in transaction length

In general, there are three reasons the total abort overhead decreases as the transaction lengths shorten. First, the amount of work that becomes useless and has to be rolled-back at the time of an abort is smaller. Second, the probabilities of footprint overflows are smaller, because they depend on the amount of data accessed in each transaction. Third, if the execution reverts to the GIL, the serialized sections are shorter.

In contrast, the shorter the transactions are, the larger the relative overhead to begin and end the transactions. In particular, beginning a transaction suffers from the overhead of not only TBEGIN or XBEGIN but also the surrounding code in Figure 1.

The best transaction length depends on each yield point. If the intervals (i.e. the number of instructions) between the subsequent yield points are small, then the lengths of the transactions starting at the current yield point should be long. As another example, suppose there are three consecutive yield points, A, B, and C. If the code between B and C contains an instruction that is not allowed in transactions, e.g. a system call, then the length of any transaction starting at A should be one. If the length was two or more, the transactions would definitely abort.

Adjustment algorithm

We propose a mechanism to adjust the transaction lengths on a per-yield-point basis. The transaction length is initialized to a certain large number at each yield point. The abort

```
1.  set_transaction_length(current_thread, pc) {
2.      if (transaction length is constant) {
3.          current_thread->yield_point_counter =
                  TRANSACTION_LENGTH;
4.      } else {
5.          if (transaction_length[pc] == 0)
6.              transaction_length[pc] =
                      INITIAL_TRANSACTION_LENGTH;
7.          current_thread->yield_point_counter =
                  transaction_length[pc];
8.          if (transaction_counter[pc] < PROFILING_PERIOD)
9.              transaction_counter[pc]++;
10.     }

11. adjust_transaction_length(pc) {
12.     if (transaction length is NOT constant &&
13.         transaction_length[pc] > 1 &&
14.         transaction_counter[pc] <= PROFILING_PERIOD) {
15.         num_aborts = abort_counter[pc];
16.         if (num_aborts <= ADJUSTMENT_THRESHOLD) {
17.             abort_counter[pc] = num_aborts + 1;
18.         } else {
19.             transaction_length[pc] =
                    transaction_length[pc] * ATTENUATION_RATE;
20.             transaction_counter[pc] = 0;
21.             abort_counter[pc] = 0;
22.         }
23.     }
24. }
```

Figure 3. Algorithm to set and adjust a transaction.

ratios of the transactions starting at each yield point are monitored. If the abort ratio is above a threshold at a particular yield point, then the transaction length is shortened. This process continues during a profiling period until the abort ratio falls below the threshold.

The set_transaction_length() function in Figure 3 is invoked from Line 5 in Figure 1 before each transaction begins. The parameter pc is the program counter of the yield-point bytecode from which this transaction is about to start. If the Ruby interpreter is configured to use a constant transaction length, that constant value is assigned to the transaction length (yield_point_counter) at Line 3. Otherwise, the yield-point-specific length is assigned at Line 7. If it has not yet been initialized, then a pre-defined long length is assigned (Lines 5-6). To calculate the abort ratio, this function also counts the number of the transactions started at each yield point (Line 9). To avoid the overhead of monitoring the abort ratio after the program reaches a steady state, there is an upper bound for the counter (Line 8).

The adjust_transaction_length() function is called when a transaction aborts for the first time (Line 19 in Figure 1). If the transaction length has not yet reached the minimum value or 1 (Line 13), and if this is during a profiling period (Line 14), then the abort ratio is checked and updated (Lines 16-17). If the number of aborts in the transactions started from the current yield point exceeds a threshold (Line 16) before the PROFILING_PERIOD number of transactions began, then the transaction length is shortened (Line 19). The two counters to monitor the abort ratio are reset (Lines 20-21) to extend the profiling period.

Note that even when the execution reverts to the GIL, the length of the transaction is unchanged. If the current length is 3, for example, the current thread passes through 2 yield points and releases the GIL at the third one.

4.4 Conflict removal

To obtain better scalability with the HTM, any transaction conflicts must be removed. We fixed five major sources of conflicts in CRuby.

The most severe conflicts occurred at global variables pointing to the Ruby-thread structure of the running thread. Immediately after the GIL is acquired, the global variables point to the running thread. If multiple threads write to these variables every time any transaction begins, they will cause many conflicts. Therefore we moved these variables from the global scope to the Pthread thread-local storage.

The second source of severe conflicts is the head of the single global linked list of free objects. CRuby allocates each new object from the head of the list. This mechanism obviously causes conflicts in multi-threaded execution. We modified CRuby's memory allocator, so that each thread maintains a short thread-local free list. A specified number (256, in our implementation) of objects are moved in bulk from the global free list to the thread-local free list, and each new object is allocated on a thread-local basis.

Garbage collection (GC) is the third conflict point. The mark-and-sweep GC in CRuby is not parallelized. GC will cause conflicts if invoked from multiple transactions. Even if it is triggered from one transaction, the transaction size will overflow. This implies that GC is always executed with the GIL acquired. To mitigate this overhead, we reduced the frequency of GC by increasing the initial Ruby heap. We changed the initial number of free objects from 10,000 to 10,000,000, which corresponded to about 400 MB.

Fourth, inline caches cause aborts when they miss. CRuby searches a hash table to invoke a method or to access an instance variable. To cache the search result, a one-entry inline cache is collocated with each method-invocation and instance-variable-access bytecode. Since the inline caches are shared among threads, an update to an inline cache at the time of a cache miss can result in a conflict. For method invocations, we changed the caching logic so that each cache is filled only at the first miss. For instance-variable accesses, we reduced the cache misses by changing the inline cache guard. Originally, the cached content is used if the class of the object is the same as the class recorded in the cache when it is filled. However, the cached content is valid even when the classes are different, as long as the instance-variable table of the class of the object is the same as that of the recorded class. Therefore, we reduced the cache misses by using the instance-variable-table equality check instead of the class-equality check.

Finally, as we added frequently updated fields, such as yield_point_counter (Line 10 in Figure 2), to CRuby's thread structures, they began to cause false sharing. We avoided this by allocating the thread structures in dedicated cache lines.

Each of these conflict removals was limited to a few dozen modified lines in the source code.

5. Experimental Results

This section describes our implementation for zEC12 and the 4th Generation Core processor. Then our experimental results are presented for the Ruby NAS Parallel Benchmarks (NPB) [17], the WEBrick HTTP server, and Ruby on Rails [25].

5.1 Implementation

We implemented the algorithms and optimizations explained in Section 4 in CRuby 1.9.3-p194. CRuby ran on Linux 3.10.5 and the 4th Generation Core processor without any modifications. To run CRuby on zEC12, we ported it into the UNIX System Services (USS) of z/OS 1.13.

For the conflict resolutions in Sections 4.4, we also implemented the thread-local free lists in the original CRuby. We tested a back-port to the original CRuby of the global variable removal, and the changes in the inline caches, but found they degraded the performance. The new yield points (Section 4.2) were not added in the original CRuby because they would increase the overhead without any benefit. In all of the experiments, the initial Ruby heap size was set to 10,000,000, using the RUBY_HEAP_MIN_SLOTS environmental variable.

The values of TRANSIENT_RETRY_MAX and GIL_RETRY_MAX in Figure 1 were set to 3 and 16, respectively. In our preliminary experiments, it was unlikely that a transaction would ever succeed after 3-or-more consecutive transient aborts. In contrast, a thread should wait more patiently for the GIL release, because the GIL will eventually be released and the fallback to GIL is very slow. The INITIAL_TRANSACTION_LENGTH of Figure 3 was set to 255, and the PROFILING_PERIOD to 300. Unless set to extremely large values like 10,000, these constants did not affect the performance. The target abort ratio of the dynamic transaction-length adjustment was set to 1% on zEC12 and 6% on the 4th Generation Core processor, based on our preliminary experiments. The best target abort ratios are independent of the applications but depend on the HTM implementations, especially the abort costs. Accordingly, ADJUSTMENT_THRESHOLD (Line 16 in Figure 3) was set to 3 on zEC12 and 18 on the 4th Generation Core processor, which meant that the ADJUST-MENT_THRESHOLD / PROFILING_PERIOD = 3 / 300 = 1% on zEC12 and 18 / 300 = 6% on the 4th Generation Core processor. The ATTENUATION_RATE (Line 19 in Figure 3) was set to 0.75.

5.2 Experimental environments

The experimental zEC12 system was divided into multiple Logical PARtitions (LPARs), and each LPAR corresponds to a virtual machine. Our LPAR was assigned 12 cores, all running at 5.5 GHz. Our system for the 4th Generation Core processor has one Xeon E3-1275 v3 chip, running at 3.5 GHz. Its microcode version was 0x8. Although the systems were not totally dedicated to our experiments, no other process was running during our measurements, and the performance fluctuations were negligible.

The malloc() function in z/OS can cause many conflicts because it is not a thread-local allocator by default. When running with the HTM, we specified the HEAPPOOLS runtime option to enable thread-local allocation in malloc().

5.3 Benchmarks

We measured two micro-benchmarks, seven programs in the Ruby NPB, the WEBrick HTTP server, and Ruby on Rails. We ran them four times and took the averages.

As preliminary experiments, we created the two micro-benchmarks to assess how the HTM works for embarrassingly parallel programs. Figure 4 shows the workloads for each thread. The results showed good scalability for the HTM, while the GIL did not scale at all. The best HTM configurations for each benchmark achieved an 11- to 10-fold speedup over the GIL using 12 threads on zEC12 in the While and Iterator benchmarks, respectively.

The Ruby NPB [17] was translated from the Java version of the NPB version 3.0 [16]. It contains 7 programs, BT, CG, FT, IS, LU, MG, and SP. We chose the class size W for IS and MG and S for the other programs. With these sizes, the programs ran in 10 to 300 seconds.

The NPB programs are composed of serialized sections and multi-threaded sections. To investigate their scalability characteristics, we ran the Ruby NPB on JRuby 1.7.3 [12] as well as the original Java NPB. JRuby is an alternative implementation of the Ruby language written in Java. JRuby is suitable as a comparison target for HTM because it minimizes its internal scalability bottlenecks by using fine-grained locking instead of the GIL. Note that this means JRuby sacrifices its compatibility with CRuby, as discussed in Section 6. JRuby does not run on zEC12 because it does not support the EBCDIC character encoding. To measure the scalability up to 12 threads, we ran JRuby on a 12-core 2.93-GHz Intel Xeon X5670 machine (with hyper-threading disabled) running Linux 2.6.32 and HotSpot Server VM 1.7.0_06.

The Java NPB is useful for estimating the scalability of the application programs themselves, because the Java VM has even fewer VM-internal scalability bottlenecks than JRuby. We ran the Java NPB on the same Xeon X5670 machine, using the interpreter of IBM J9 VM 1.7.0 SR3. We disabled the JIT compiler because the class sizes of S

```
       While benchmark                Iterator benchmark

1.  def workload(numIter)      1.  def workload(numIter)
2.    x = 0                     2.    x = 0
3.    i = 1                     3.    (1..numIter).each do |i|
4.    while i <= numIter        4.      x += i
5.      x += i                  5.    end
6.      i += 1                  6.  end
7.    end
8.  end
```

Figure 4. Each thread's workloads in the two embarrassingly parallel micro-benchmarks.

and W were small. With the JIT compiler, the execution time was too short to outweigh the parallelization overhead.

WEBrick is the default HTTP server for Ruby on Rails. It is implemented in Ruby and is included in the CRuby distribution. It creates one Ruby thread for each incoming request and discards the thread after returning a response. We ran WEBrick version 1.3.1. To measure its scalability, we changed the number of HTTP clients simultaneously accessing WEBrick. Each run sent 30,000 requests for a 46-byte page from the same machine as the one running WEBrick. We took the peak throughput (requests per second) as the result of each run. The HTTP clients consumed less than 5% of the CPU cycles.

Ruby on Rails is a popular Web application framework in Ruby. Using Ruby on Rails version 4.0.0, we created an application to fetch a list of books from a database. We used SQLite3 as the database manager and WEBrick as the HTTP server. Ruby on Rails is thread-safe, but for backward compatibility it has a global lock to serialize the request processing. In our experiments, we disabled the global lock. The measurement method was the same as in WEBrick. We ran Ruby on Rails only on Xeon E3-1275 v3 because we encountered problems installing it in z/OS.

5.4 Results of the NAS Parallel Benchmarks

Figure 5 shows the throughput of the Ruby NAS Parallel Benchmarks on zEC12 and Xeon E3-1275 v3, normalized to GIL with 1 thread. The number of threads was set from 1 to 2, 4, 6, and 8 on Xeon E3-1275 v3, and to 12 on zEC12. HTM-1, -16, and -256 denote the fixed transaction lengths of 1, 16, and 256. These configurations correspond to Lines 2-3 in Figure 3. HTM-dynamic uses the dynamic transaction-length adjustment described in Section 4.3.

In zEC12, HTM-dynamic showed up to a 4.4-fold speedup in FT with 12 threads and at the minimum 1.9-fold speedups in CG, IS, and LU. From the four HTM configurations, HTM-dynamic was almost always the best or close to the best. HTM-dynamic was 18% faster than HTM-16 in FT with 12 threads. HTM-1 was worse than HTM-dynamic because of its larger overhead, although its abort ratios were lower. HTM-256 showed almost no scalability. Due to its long transaction lengths, its abort ratios were above 90%, and the execution almost always fell back on the GIL. HTM-16 was the best among the fixed-transaction-length

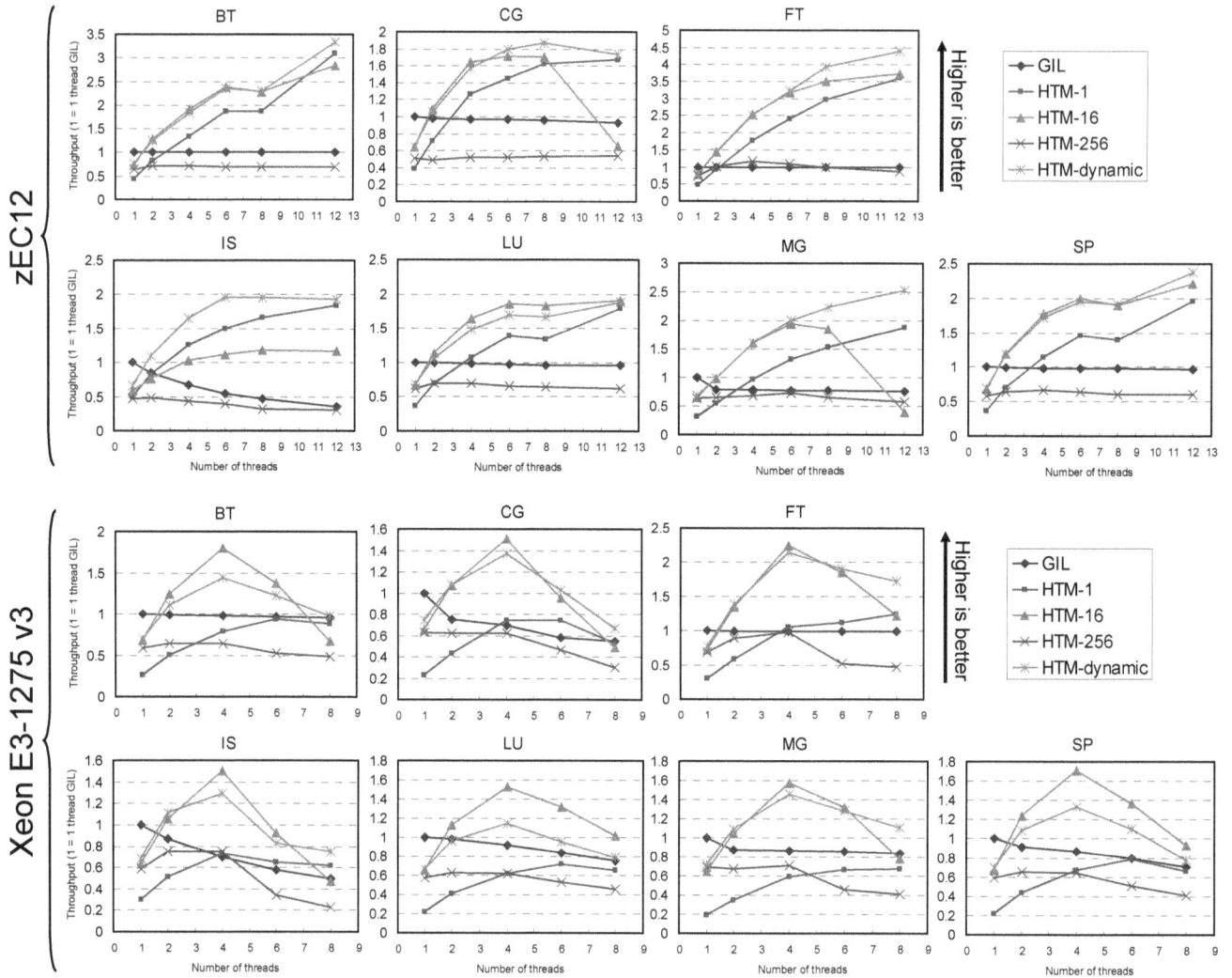

Figure 5. Throughput of the Ruby NAS Parallel Benchmarks on 12-core zEC12 (top) and 4-core 2-SMT Xeon E3-1275 v3 (bottom), normalized to the 1-thread GIL. HTM-1, -16, and -256 ran transactions of fixed lengths 1, 16, and 256. HTM-dynamic uses our proposed dynamic transaction-length adjustment.

configurations, but it incurred more conflict aborts as the number of threads increased.

In the 4-core Xeon E3-1275 v3 machine, HTM-16 showed the best throughput. Its speedups for up to 4 threads were almost the same as the corresponding speedups of HTM-dynamic on zEC12. Beyond 4 threads, HTM-16 did not scale using SMT, while HTM-1 did scale in some benchmarks. With SMT, HTM-16 suffered from many transaction footprint overflows because a pair of threads on the same core share the same caches, thus halving the maximum read- and write-set sizes.

HTM-dynamic did not scale better than HTM-16 in Xeon E3-1275 v3. This was due to the learning algorithm of Xeon E3-1275 v3's HTM. We found that the HTM in Xeon E3-1275 v3 changed its abort criteria for each transaction, based on the abort statistics. We created a test program to simulate our dynamic transaction-length adjustment.

gram to simulate our dynamic transaction-length adjustment. In each iteration, it sequentially wrote a specified amount of data to memory during a transaction. In one process, it first wrote 24 KB 10,000 times, and then 20 KB 10,000 times, and so on. We measured the transaction success ratios for each 100 iterations. Figure 6(a) shows the results. When the write-set size was shrunk from 20 KB to 16 KB and then to 12 KB, the success ratios did not jump sharply but instead increased gradually. It took about 5,000 iterations to reach a steady state. This implies that the HTM in Xeon E3-1275 v3 eagerly aborts a transaction that has suffered from many footprint overflows and thus cannot quickly adapt to change in the data set size.

This learning algorithm of Xeon E3-1275 v3's HTM can conflict with our dynamic transaction-length adjustment. The running times of the Ruby NPB were too short for both

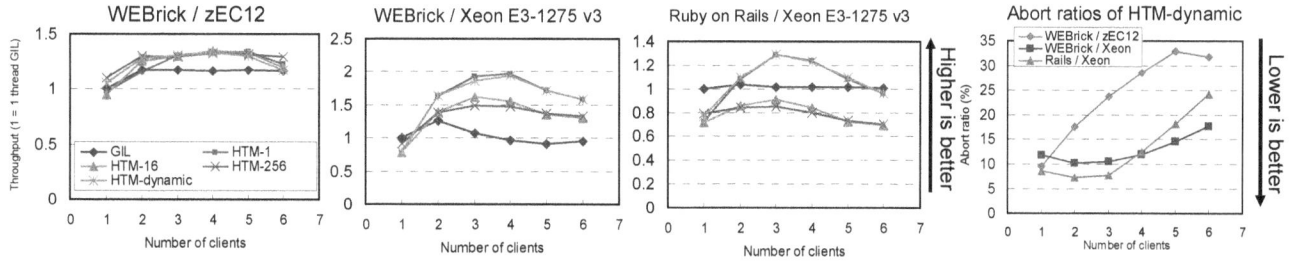

Figure 7. Throughput and abort ratios of the WEBrick HTTP server on 12-core zEC12, on 4-core 2-SMT Xeon E3-1275 v3, and Ruby on Rails on Xeon E3-1275 v3. The throughput results are normalized to the 1-thread GIL. HTM-1, -16, and -256 ran transactions of fixed lengths, and HTM-dynamic uses our proposed dynamic transaction-length adjustment.

the underlying HTM and our algorithm to reach a steady state. We ran the benchmarks longer by increasing the class sizes and confirmed HTM-dynamic was equal to or better than HTM-16. Figure 6(b) presents the results of BT with the class size W.

Without the new yield points described in Section 4.2, all of the benchmarks except for CG in the Ruby NPB suffered from more than 20% slowdowns compared with the GIL. Without the conflict removals in Section 4.4, the HTM provided no acceleration in any of the benchmarks.

5.5 Results of WEBrick and Ruby on Rails

Figure 7 shows the throughput and abort ratios of WEBrick and Ruby on Rails on zEC12 and Xeon E3-1275 v3. As described in Section 5.3, we ran Ruby on Rails only on Xeon E3-1275 v3. The throughput was normalized to GIL with 1 thread. We changed the number of concurrent clients from 1 to 6. In WEBrick, HTM-1 and HTM-dynamic achieved a 33% speedup on zEC12 and a 97% speedup on Xeon E3-1275 v3 (over 1-thread GIL). GIL also showed speedups of 17% and 26% on zEC12 and Xeon E3-1275 v3, respectively, because the GIL is released during I/O. As a result, HTM-1 and HTM-dynamic were faster than GIL by 14% and 57% on zEC12 and Xeon E3-1275 v3, respectively. Similarly, in Ruby on Rails, HTM-1 and HTM-dynamic improved the throughput by 24% over GIL. The throughput degraded when the number of clients was increased from 4 to 6, due to the rise in the abort ratio, as we explain in Section 5.6.

The HTM scaled worse on zEC12 than on Xeon E3-1275 v3, because many conflicts occurred in malloc(). As described in Section 5.2, we used a thread-local allocator, but there still remained conflict points. Due to these excessive conflicts, HTM-1 and HTM-dynamic did not show better throughput than HTM-16 and HTM-256 on zEC12.

Unlike the Ruby NPB, HTM-1 was the best or one of the best among the fixed transaction-length configurations in WEBrick and Ruby on Rails. HTM-dynamic also chose the best transaction lengths in these programs. In summary, with HTM-dynamic, the users do not need to specify different transaction lengths for different programs and numbers

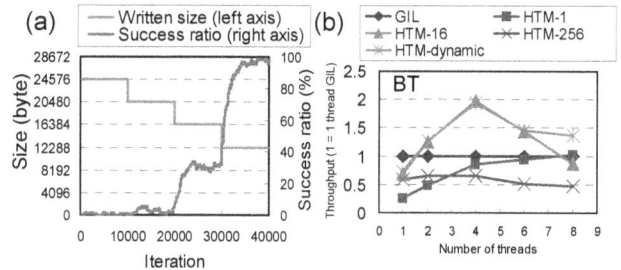

Figure 6. (a) Results of a test program shrinking the write-set size on Xeon E3-1275 v3. The transaction success ratio increased gradually when the size shrank. **(b)** Throughput of BT with a bigger class size (W) on Xeon E3-1275 v3. HTM-dynamic showed the best throughput.

of threads to obtain near optimal performance, as long as the programs run long enough on the Xeon E3-1275 v3. With 12 threads on zEC12, 40% of the frequently executed yield points had the transaction length of 1 in the Ruby NPB. That means HTM-dynamic effectively chose better lengths for the other points.

5.6 Further optimization opportunities

We present the abort ratios of HTM-dynamic in the rightmost part of Figure 7 and in Figure 8. In the Ruby NPB, the abort ratios were mostly below 2% on zEC12 and 7% on Xeon E3-1275 v3, indicating that HTM-dynamic adjusted the transaction lengths properly with the respective 1% and 6% target abort ratios (of Section 5.1). In WEBrick and Ruby on Rails, HTM-dynamic could not control the abort ratios because most of the transaction lengths reached 1 and could not be shortened further.

The cycle breakdowns of 12-thread HTM-dynamic on zEC12 in Figure 8 show that the time spent waiting for the GIL release was longer than the time for cycles wasted on aborted transactions. The cycle breakdown of IS does not represent the actual execution, because 79% of the time was spent in data initialization, which was outside of the measurement period.

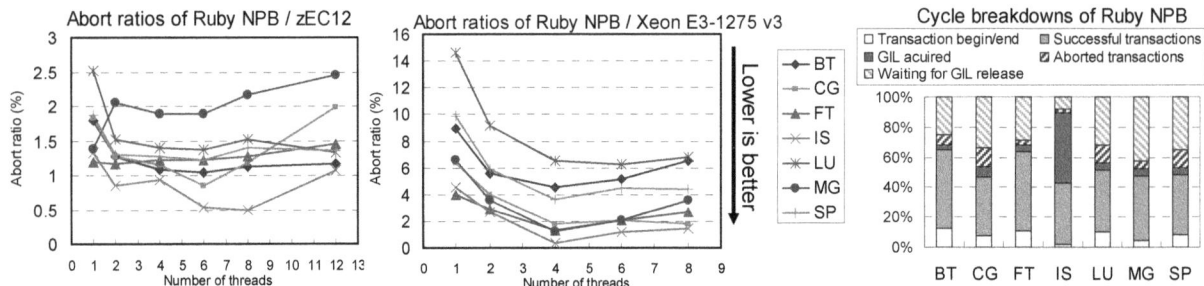

Figure 8. Abort ratios and cycle breakdowns (when running with 12 threads on zEC12) of HTM-dynamic in the Ruby NPB.

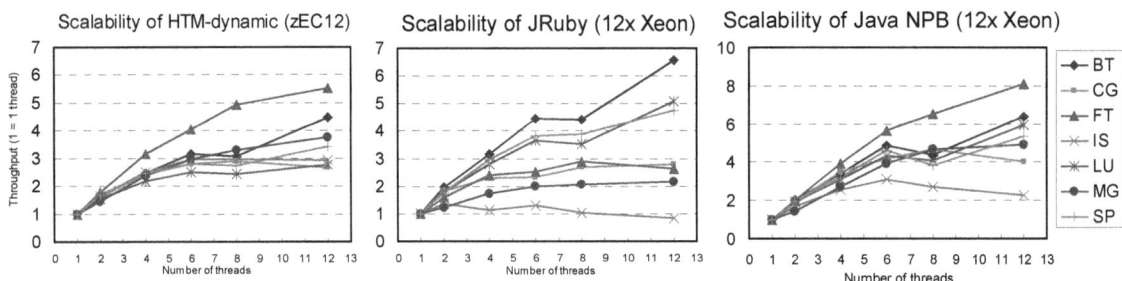

Figure 9. Scalability comparison of the Ruby NAS Parallel Benchmarks on HTM-dynamic/CRuby on 12-core zEC12, fine-grained locking/JRuby, and the Java NAS Parallel Benchmarks. JRuby and the Java version ran on 12-core Intel Xeon X5670 (no hyper-threading).

Investigation of the abort reasons that caused the GIL to be acquired revealed that read-set conflicts accounted for more than 80% for all of the Ruby NPB with 12 threads. Except for IS, more than 50% of those read-set conflicts occurred at the time of object allocation. Even with the thread-local free lists described in Section 4.4, the global free list still needed occasional manipulation. Also, when the global free list became empty, lazy sweeping of the heap was triggered and thus caused more conflicts. To overcome the conflicts in the object allocations, the global free list must be eliminated. When a thread-local free list becomes empty, the lazy sweeping should be done on a thread-local basis. GC should also be parallelized or thread-localized.

For WEBrick on zEC12, malloc() caused many conflicts, as described in Section 5.5. In WEBrick on Xeon E3-1275 v3 with 4-clients HTM-dynamic, footprint overflows and conflicts accounted for 34% and 29%, respectively, of the aborts that resulted in the GIL acquisition, but the CPU did not report the abort reasons for the others. In Ruby on Rails on Xeon E3-1275 v3 with 4-client HTM-dynamic, 87% of the aborts were due to transaction footprint overflows. Most of these aborts in WEBrick and Ruby on Rails occurred in the regular-expression library and method invocations. The regular expression library is written in C, so there is no yield point in it. A method invocation is a complex operation in CRuby, and since it is a single byecode, it does not have a yield point in it either. To reduce the aborts in the

library and method invocations, these operations should be split into multiple transactions.

The single-thread overhead of HTM-dynamic against the GIL was 18% to 35% in Figures 5 and 7. Aborts due to overflows and external interrupts occurred even with one thread, but there were three more overhead sources. First, the checking operation in Line 9 of Figure 2 and the new yield points described in Section 4.2 caused 5%-14% overhead. Second, as described in Section 4.4, we changed the logic of the method-invocation inline caches to reduce conflicts. This change degraded the single-thread performance by up to 5%. To avoid this degradation, HTM-friendly inline caches, such as thread-local caches, are required. Third, on zEC12, access to Pthread's thread-local storage accounted for 9% of the execution cycles on average. As explained in Section 4.4, we moved several global variables to the thread-local storage. Unfortunately, the access function, pthread_getspecific(), is not optimized in z/OS, but it is highly tuned in some environments, including Linux.

5.7 Scalability characterization

The abort ratios and cycle breakdowns of the Ruby NPB in Figure 8 had little correlation with the speedups in Figure 5. These facts suggest that although the speedups achieved by HTM-dynamic were limited by the conflicts at the time of object allocation, the differences among the programs were due to their inherent scalability characteristics.

In Figure 9, we compare the scalability of HTM-dynamic on zEC12, JRuby, and the Java NPB, from which

140

the Ruby NPB was translated. Figure 9 shows that even the Java NPB hit scalability bottlenecks and HTM-dynamic resembled the Java NPB in terms of the scalability. These results confirmed that the differences in the speedups by HTM-dynamic among the benchmarks originated from each program's own scalability characteristics. When compared with JRuby, HTM-dynamic achieved the same scalability on average: 3.6-fold with HTM-dynamic and 3.5-fold with JRuby, running 12 threads (not shown in Figure 9). We believe the characteristics of each benchmark were different between HTM-dynamic and JRuby because of JRuby's internal scalability bottlenecks.

6. Related Work

Riley et al. [23] used HTM to eliminate the GIL in PyPy, one of the implementations of the Python language. However, because they experimented with only two micro-benchmarks on a non-cycle-accurate simulator, it is hard to assess how their implementation would behave on a real HTM. Tabba [29] used the HTM of an early-access version of Sun's Rock processor to remove the GIL in the original Python interpreter. Although their measurements were on real hardware, they ran only three synthetic micro-benchmarks. Also, the HTM on Rock had a severe limitation in that transactions could not contain function returns or tolerate TLB misses. These prototype results cannot be extended to real-world applications. The GIL in Ruby was eliminated through HTM in our prior report [18]. This paper is the first to evaluate larger benchmarks including WEBrick and Ruby on Rails on two implementations of less-restrictive HTM, zEC12 and Xeon E3-1275 v3.

RETCON [1] applied speculative lock elision to the GIL in Python. The focus of the work was on reducing conflicts due to reference-counting GC by symbolic re-execution. However, because it was evaluated on a simulator supporting an unlimited transaction size, the aborts in the experiment were mostly due to conflicts. In our experience with a real HTM implementation, the effectiveness of GIL elimination is limited by overflows and other types of aborts, which calls for the dynamic transaction-length adjustment.

Dice et al. [3] evaluated a variety of programs using HTM on the Sun Rock processor. Wang et al. [31] measured the STAMP benchmarks [15] on the HTM in Blue Gene/Q. Neither of these evaluations covered GIL elimination for scripting languages.

Some alternative implementations of the Ruby and Python languages [9,10,12,13,24] use or are going to use fine-grained locking instead of the GIL. JRuby [12] maps Ruby threads to Java threads and then uses concurrent libraries and synchronized blocks and methods in Java to protect the internal data structures. However, JRuby has two types of incompatibility with CRuby. First, while some of the standard-library classes in CRuby are written in C and are im-plicitly protected by the GIL, JRuby rewrites them in Java and leaves them unsynchronized for performance reasons. Thus any multi-threaded programs that depend on the implicitly protected standard-library classes in CRuby may behave differently in JRuby. Second, because JRuby does not support CRuby-compatible extension libraries, it does not need the GIL to protect the thread-unsafe extension libraries. The current version 2.2.1 of Rubinius [24] uses fine-grained locking. However, the Rubinius support for the CRuby-compatible extension libraries conflicts with further removing the locks. In contrast, replacing the GIL with HTM creates no compatibility problems in the libraries and can yet increase scalability. PyPy is planning to eliminate the GIL through software transactional memory (STM) [20], but it is unclear whether the scalability improvement can offset the overhead of the STM.

Scripting languages other than Ruby and Python mostly do not have a GIL, but that is because they do not support shared-memory multi-thread programming, and thus their programming capabilities are limited on multi-core systems. Perl's ithreads clone the entire interpreter and its data when a thread is created, and any data sharing among threads must be explicitly declared as such [19]. The cloning makes a GIL unnecessary, but it is as heavy as fork() and restricts shared-memory programming. Lua [14] does not support multi-threading but uses coroutines. The coroutines switch among themselves by explicitly calling a yield function. This means they never run simultaneously and do not require a GIL. JavaScript (AKA ECMAScript) [4] does not support multi-threading, so the programs must be written in an asynchronous event-handling style.

7. Conclusion and Future Work

This paper shows the first empirical results of eliminating the Global Interpreter Lock (GIL) in a scripting language through Hardware Transactional Memory (HTM) to improve the multi-thread performance of realistic programs. We proposed a new automatic mechanism to dynamically adjust the transaction lengths on a per-yield-point basis. Our mechanism chooses a near optimal tradeoff point between the relative overhead of the instructions to begin and end the transactions and the likelihood of transaction conflicts and footprint overflows. We experimented on the HTM facilities in the mainframe processor IBM zEC12 and the Intel 4th Generation Core processor (Xeon E3-1275 v3). We evaluated the Ruby NAS Parallel Benchmarks (NPB), the WEBrick HTPP server, and Ruby on Rails. Our results show that HTM achieved up to a 4.4-fold speedup in the Ruby NPB, and 1.6-fold and 1.2-fold speedups in WEBrick and Ruby on Rails, respectively. The dynamic transaction-length adjustment chose the best transaction lengths. On Xeon E3-1275 v3, programs need to run long enough to benefit from the dynamic transaction-length adjustment.

From all of these results, we concluded that HTM is an effective approach to achieve higher multi-thread performance compared to the GIL.

Our techniques will be effective also in Python, because our GIL elimination and dynamic transaction-length adjustment do not depend on Ruby. Conflict removal can be specific to each implementation. For example, the original Python implementation (CPython) uses reference counting GC, which will cause many conflicts, while PyPy uses copying GC and thus is more suitable for the GIL elimination through HTM.

Acknowledgments

We would like to thank our colleagues in IBM Research for helpful discussions. We are also grateful to the anonymous reviewers for valuable comments.

References

[1] Blundell, C., Raghavan, A., and Martin, M. M. K. RETCON: transactional repair without replay. In *ISCA*, pp. 258-269, 2010.

[2] Cascaval, C., Blundell, C., Michael, M., Cain, H. W., Wu, P., Chiras, S., and Chatterjee, S. Software transactional memory: why is it only a research toy? *ACM Queue*, 6(5), pp. 46-58, 2008.

[3] Dice, D., Lev, Y., Moir, M., and Nussbaum, D. Early experience with a commercial hardware transactional memory implementation. In *ASPLOS*, pp. 157-168, 2009.

[4] ECMAScript. http://www.ecmascript.org/ .

[5] Haring, R. A., Ohmacht, M., Fox, T. W., Gschwind, M. K., Satterfield, D. L., Sugavanam, K., Coteus, P. W., Heidelberger, P., Blumrich, M. A., Wisniewski, R.W., Gara, A., Chiu, G. L.-T., Boyle, P.A., Chist, N.H., and Kim, C. The IBM Blue Gene/Q compute chip. *IEEE Micro*, 32(2), pp. 48-60, 2012.

[6] IBM. Power ISA Transactional Memory. Power.org, 2012.

[7] IBM. z/Architecture Principles of Operation Tenth Edition (September, 2012). http://publibfi.boulder.ibm.com/epubs/pdf/dz9zr009.pdf .

[8] Intel Corporation. Intel Architecture Instruction Set Extensions Programming Reference. 319433-012a edition, 2012.

[9] IronPython, http://ironpython.codeplex.com/ .

[10] IronRuby, http://www.ironruby.net/ .

[11] Jacobi, C., Slegel, T., and Greinder, D. Transactional memory architecture and implementation for IBM System z. In *MICRO 45*, 2012.

[12] JRuby, http://jruby.org/ .

[13] Jython, http://www.jython.org/ .

[14] Lua, http://www.lua.org/

[15] Minh, C. C., Chung, J., Kozyrakis, C., and Olukotun, K. STAMP: Stanford transactional applications for multi-processing. In *IISWC*, pp. 35-46, 2008.

[16] NAS Parallel Benchmarks, http://www.nas.nasa.gov/publications/npb.html .

[17] Nose, T. Ruby version of NAS Parallel Benchmarks 3.0. http://www-hiraki.is.s.u-tokyo.ac.jp/members/tknose/ .

[18] Odaira, R. and Castanos, J. G. Eliminating global interpreter locks in Ruby through hardware transactional memory. Research Report RT0950, IBM Research – Tokyo, 2013.

[19] Perl threads, http://perldoc.perl.org/perlthrtut.html .

[20] PyPy Status Blog. We need Software Transactional Memory. http://morepypy.blogspot.jp/2011/08/we-need-software-transactional-memory.html .

[21] Python programming language. http://www.python.org/ .

[22] Rajwar, R. and Goodman, J. R. Speculative lock elision: enabling highly concurrent multithreaded execution. In *MICRO*, pp. 294-305, 2001.

[23] Riley, N. and Zilles, C. Hardware transactional memory support for lightweight dynamic language evolution. In *Dynamic Language Symposium (OOPSLA Companion)*, pp. 998-1008, 2006.

[24] Rubinius, http://rubini.us/ .

[25] Ruby on Rails. http://rubyonrails.org/ .

[26] Ruby programming language, http://www.ruby-lang.org/ .

[27] Shum, C.-L. IBM zNext: the 3rd generation high frequency micro-processor chip. In *HotChips* 24, 2012.

[28] Stuecheli, J. Next Generation POWER microprocessor. In *HotChips* 25, 2013.

[29] Tabba, F. Adding concurrency in python using a commercial processor's hardware transactional memory support. *ACM SIGARCH Computer Architecture News*, 38(5), pp. 12-19, 2010.

[30] Tatsubori, M., Tozawa, A., Suzumura, T., Trent, S., Onodera, T. Evaluation of a just-in-time compiler retrofitted for PHP. In *VEE*, pp. 121-132, 2010.

[31] Wang, A., Gaudet, M., Wu, P., Ohmacht, M., Amaral, J. N., Barton, C., Silvera, R., Michael, M. M. Evaluation of Blue Gene/Q hardware support for transactional memories. In *PACT*, pp. 127-136, 2012.

Leveraging Hardware Message Passing
for Efficient Thread Synchronization

Darko Petrović   Thomas Ropars   André Schiper

Ecole Polytechnique Fédérale de Lausanne (EPFL), Switzerland

firstname.lastname@epfl.ch

Abstract

As the level of parallelism in manycore processors keeps increasing, providing efficient mechanisms for thread synchronization in concurrent programs is becoming a major concern. On cache-coherent shared-memory processors, synchronization efficiency is ultimately limited by the performance of the underlying cache coherence protocol. This paper studies how hardware support for message passing can improve synchronization performance. Considering the ubiquitous problem of mutual exclusion, we adapt two state-of-the-art solutions used on shared-memory processors, namely the server approach and the combining approach, to leverage the potential of hardware message passing. We propose HYBCOMB, a novel combining algorithm that uses both message passing and shared memory features of emerging hybrid processors. We also introduce MP-SERVER, a straightforward adaptation of the server approach to hardware message passing. Evaluation on Tilera's TILE-Gx processor shows that MP-SERVER can execute contended critical sections with unprecedented throughput, as stalls related to cache coherence are removed from the critical path. HYB-COMB can achieve comparable performance, while avoiding the need to dedicate server cores. Consequently, our queue and stack implementations, based on MP-SERVER and HYB-COMB, largely outperform their most efficient pure-shared-memory counterparts.

Categories and Subject Descriptors   D.1.3 [*Programming Techniques*]: Concurrent Programming

Keywords   combining; mutual exclusion; concurrent objects; message passing

PPoPP '14,   February 15–19, 2014, Orlando, Florida, USA.
Copyright © 2014 ACM 978-1-4503-2656-8/14/02... $15.00.
http://dx.doi.org/10.1145/2555243.2555251

1. Introduction

As industry is shifting toward manycore processors, it is increasingly important to put the constantly growing number of cores to good use. For some types of applications, for instance scale-out workloads typically found in data centers, this is not a problem because of their *embarrassingly parallel* nature. There are, however, applications whose parallelization requires significant effort, as they contain data or objects intensively *shared* by multiple threads. To ensure consistency, threads must access such shared parts of the program state in a synchronized fashion. Whether synchronization is implemented using critical sections (CSes) or nonblocking (lock-free) algorithms, it creates sequential bottlenecks that, because of *Amdahl's law*, ultimately limit application speedup. Indeed, recent studies show that optimizing contended CSes can significantly improve the performance of some workloads [17, 27]. Furthermore, fast synchronization on simple concurrent objects, such as queues, is key to the performance of parallelization frameworks [4]. It is therefore of great importance to understand the subtleties of synchronization and to continue making it more efficient.

At the same time, as parallel programming is becoming mainstream, it is desirable to provide *universal constructions* that enable non-experts to easily write highly-efficient concurrent code. In this work, we study universal constructions for executing contended CSes. The state of the art in this field is the *combining* synchronization technique [10, 11, 13, 24]. The key idea behind combining is that a thread, holding the lock on an object, should not immediately release it after executing its own CS. Instead, the thread executes a number of pending CSes of other threads as well, which minimizes the cost of lock handover and improves data locality. A more extreme version of this idea, sometimes referred to as *delegation* [8], is to earmark a special *server* thread and pin it to a certain processor core. The server thread does not run application code, but only executes CSes of other threads. Dedicating cores is less feasible if an application includes a large number of potentially contended concurrent objects.

A vast majority of work on thread synchronization, including existing universal constructions, assumes the shared memory programming model. Shared memory is often built using local caches and a complex *cache coherence protocol* [26], which makes the caches functionally invisible to the programmer. However, the performance impact of the cache coherence protocol on concurrent algorithms cannot be ignored [11, 13]. Optimizing concurrent code requires in-depth understanding of cache coherence protocols and memory consistency models. Vendors tend to hide their details, or provide them in informal or incomplete ways [23], which makes the task of designing efficient concurrent algorithms notoriously hard. On top of that, the future of cache coherence is uncertain: Some recent studies question the scalability of the traditional cache-coherent shared-memory approach and advocate the use of message passing [6, 16, 29]. As a result, there are experimental [16] as well as commercial [1, 2] processors with hardware support for sending application-level messages between processor cores.

Message passing offers explicit control over communication, so some studies call for complete redesign of software with message passing in mind, notably in the context of operating systems [6, 29]. The same can be advocated for thread synchronization: Indeed, some recent work presents concurrent objects that rely on message passing [8, 20]. A question that arises, however, is whether a full paradigm shift is necessary and justified. Although the problems of cache coherence are evident, we ought to precisely quantify advantages that message passing could provide. Also, even if message passing is advantageous, this does not mean coherent shared memory should be abandoned altogether. In support of this, there are arguments that on-chip cache coherence can scale to large core counts as its overhead in terms of traffic, storage, latency and energy can be made to increase very slowly with the number of cores [18].

Coherent shared memory and message passing coexist in some recent *hybrid* processors, such as Tilera's TILE-Gx processor family [2]. As such, it provides a large design space for synchronization primitives. It is also an ideal testbed to experimentally compare shared memory and message passing approaches. In this work, we consider the problem of contended CSes, and use TILE-Gx to study how hardware message passing can make their execution more efficient than with classic shared-memory techniques.

Our findings indicate that state-of-the-art solutions for efficient CS execution based on a server (RCL [17]) or a combiner (CC-SYNCH [11]) waste much time in CPU stalls resulting from activities related to cache coherence. When CSes are short, these stalls dominate all other overheads. To overcome this problem, we take advantage of hardware message passing and present two solutions: MP-SERVER, a simple server-based approach, and HYBCOMB, a universal construction based on the combining technique. Whereas adapting the server-based approach used in shared-memory systems to message passing is straightforward, the design of HYBCOMB involves significant algorithmic complexity.

As its name suggests, HYBCOMB is a *hybrid* algorithm that relies both on cache-coherent shared memory and hardware message passing for synchronization: Hardware message passing is used to exchange requests and responses between the combiner and other threads, while shared memory is used to manage combiner identity (which would be complex and inefficient to do using message passing).

We evaluate the performance of MP-SERVER and HYBCOMB, by implementing ubiquitous linearizable [15] concurrent objects, namely counters, queues, and stacks. Experiments with counters show that MP-SERVER outperforms CC-SYNCH and RCL by up to 4.3x. This is due to the fact that, in high concurrency levels, virtually no stalls remain on the critical path of the server. HYBCOMB also largely outperforms the pure-shared-memory solutions, and can achieve performance close to the one of MP-SERVER, while avoiding the need to dedicate cores. Compared to other queues and stacks, our new implementations on top of MP-SERVER and HYBCOMB reach up to 2x and 1.5x higher throughput respectively, shedding light on the advantages of hardware message passing for synchronization.

In summary, the contributions of this work are the following. We analyze the performance limitations of state-of-the-art solutions for efficient CS execution over cache-coherent shared memory in Section 3. In Section 4, we describe MP-SERVER and HYBCOMB, our two synchronization solutions based on hardware message passing. This includes the full specification and a proof sketch of HYBCOMB, which is, to the best of our knowledge, the first combining algorithm that exploits the hybrid nature of contemporary processors. Finally, we present an extensive evaluation of MP-SERVER and HYBCOMB in Section 5. On the example of linearizable counters, queues and stacks, we show that they perform significantly better than their most efficient known shared-memory counterparts.

2. System Model

We assume a set of T sequential threads that can communicate both by issuing operations to coherent shared memory and by directly exchanging messages.

Cache coherence. In the cache-coherent (CC) shared-memory model, threads operate on cached copies of shared variables. We assume a model adapted from the one by Sorin et al [26]. A processor chip is composed of single-threaded cores. Each core has its local, private data cache. All cores have access to a globally shared memory through an interconnection network. The cache coherence protocol maintains the *single-writer-multiple-reader* invariant: At any given time, either a single core has read-write access to a cached variable, or some cores have read-only access [26]. *Remote Memory References* (RMRs) are accesses to shared variables that involve communication on the interconnection network. In this model and assuming write-back caches, reading a shared variable generates an RMR if the core does not hold a copy of the variable in either mode. Writing a shared variable generates an RMR if the core does not hold a copy of the variable in read-write mode.

Shared-memory operations. The memory is an array of 64-bit locations. Similarly to most related studies, we assume that the memory is sequentially consistent. Supported operations on a memory location a are the standard *read(a)*, *write(a, v)* operations as well as some atomic read-modify-write operations, namely *FAA(a, v)* (fetch-and-add), *SWAP(a, v)* and *CAS(a, v_{old}, v_{new})* (compare-and-set[1]), with their standard definitions.

Message-passing operations. Each thread has its incoming FIFO message queue that stores 64-bit values (message queue hereafter). Supported operations are *send, receive* and *is_queue_empty*. The operation *send(i, M)* puts message M, which is a set of values $v_1, v_2, ..., v_n$, in the message queue of thread t_i. The *send* operation is asynchronous, *i.e.*, it may return before M is placed in the destination message queue. Message transmission time is bounded but unknown, *i.e.*, the time between a call to *send* and the moment when the message is placed in the corresponding queue is arbitrarily, but finitely long. If $|M| > 1$, values are placed in the destination message queue in the order $v_1, v_2, ..., v_n$. The operation *receive(k)* returns k values from the head of the local message queue. If there are fewer than k values in the queue, the operation blocks until k values are available. Operation *is_queue_empty()* returns true if the local message queue is empty.

3. Critical Sections over CC Shared Memory

This section details existing techniques for the efficient execution of highly-contended critical sections on cache-coherent processors. It explains how their performance is influenced by the underlying CC protocol.

On a CC processor, the number of RMRs generated by a synchronization algorithm should be minimized. Indeed, an RMR is typically orders of magnitude more expensive than an access to the local cache. This section shows that even the most efficient shared-memory synchronization techniques to implement mutual exclusion on a CS generate a constant number of RMRs per CS execution. Thus, their performance depends on the CC protocol.

Critical sections are usually implemented using locks. In this context, the basic technique to limit the number of RMRs is to introduce *local spinning* [19]: Each thread polls on a different variable which stays in its local cache, to limit the number of RMRs and avoid contention on the interconnection network. Queue locks provide local spinning [5, 19] and achieve an $O(1)$ RMR complexity per lock acquisition. In addition to local spinning, locality inside the CS can be optimized to further reduce the number of RMRs. The key idea is that, instead of moving the data associated with a CS

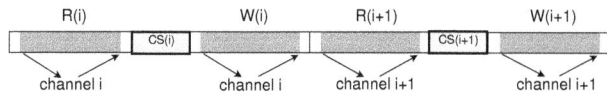

Figure 1. Mutual exclusion server – shared-memory implementation; $R(i)$, $W(i)$ – resp. reading from, writing to the channel of client i; $CS(i)$ – corresponding critical section; dark grey – server stalls (due to RMRs)

to the core that wants to execute the CS, the CS is executed on the core where the data are located. If contention is high, this results in a substantial performance increase over classic locks. We can identify two approaches that exploit this idea: the client-server approach [9, 17], and the combiner approach [10, 11, 13, 24].

Remote Core Locking (RCL) [17] is an efficient implementation of the client-server approach. A non-application thread (the server) is in charge of executing CSes. Application threads (clients) send requests to the server to execute a critical section on their behalf. Assuming that data accessed inside the CSes are never accessed by application threads outside the CSes, these data remain in the cache of the server, ensuring that the number of RMRs during CS execution is minimized. Ideally, the only RMRs that remain on the critical path of the CS execution are the ones related to synchronization between the clients and the server. Figure 1 illustrates the execution of an RCL server. For client-server communication in RCL, each client thread has a dedicated cache line, which it uses as a bi-directional channel. When client i wants to execute a CS, it writes its request to the cache line $channel_i$, and then spins on that cache line until it receives a reply from the server. The server first reads the request from $channel_i$ ($R(i)$ in Figure 1). Since the last access to $channel_i$ was from client i writing the request, this read triggers an RMR (server stalls are represented in dark grey). Then, the server executes the critical section ($CS(i)$). Finally, it writes to $channel_i$ to inform the client that the request has been processed ($W(i)$). This write triggers another RMR to invalidate the client's copy of the cache line. The figure assumes high load, *i.e.*, the server is never idle, and shows that in this case there are two RMRs at the RCL server per CS. Note that Figure 1 is somewhat simplified, since it assumes sequential consistency. On a real processor, the different RMRs might partially overlap, depending on the memory consistency model of the processor at hand, resulting in fewer CPU stalls. Nevertheless, these RMRs remain an important source of overhead even on a processor with weak memory consistency (see Section 5).

While keeping similar performance benefits, the combiner approach does not require dedicated servers [13]. When a thread gets a lock associated with a CS, it becomes a *combiner* and executes operations of other threads that are waiting to access this CS, in addition to its own. To prevent the combiner from starving if the number of operations of other threads to execute is high, the combiner role is handed

---
[1] The variant of compare-and-swap that returns a boolean.

over to another thread when the current combiner has served a predefined number of requests. CC-SYNCH [11] is, to our knowledge, the most efficient combiner-based approach. Since the combiner changes over time, the synchronization mechanism is more complex than in RCL. Nevertheless, while a thread is acting as a combiner, CC-SYNCH is similar to RCL with respect to RMRs: It generates one RMR to read a request from another thread, and then generates another RMR to inform that thread that the operation has been performed.

The server-based approach has the advantage of being simple and very efficient in cases where a small number of clearly identified CSes are highly contended [17]. On the other hand, combining is more flexible, which comes at the expense of requiring more complex synchronization between threads. Indeed, combiners adapt themselves automatically to the load: If a CS is highly contended, all the CPU cycles of one core will be temporarily allocated to it, but if no thread tries to execute a CS, no resources are consumed.

Both with RCL and CC-SYNCH, only two RMRs related to thread synchronization remain on the critical path of a CS execution. These two RMRs, however, can have a big impact on throughput if the code to execute in the CS itself contains few or no RMRs.

4. Critical Sections using Message Passing

We present two ways to leverage hardware support for message passing to execute critical sections efficiently. Taking the server approach, we first explain why hardware messaging can be beneficial in this context. Then we present a novel combining algorithm that uses both shared memory and hardware message passing for thread synchronization.

4.1 The Server Approach (MP-SERVER)

A client-server approach, such as RCL, is a natural fit for message passing. Indeed, RCL's client-server communication layer can be seen as an implementation of message passing over shared memory. Instead, we simply leverage hardware message passing support to implement client-server communication. We refer to this solution as MP-SERVER. Based on the model introduced in Section 2, Figure 2 explains why MP-SERVER may have better performance than its shared-memory counterpart. Compared to Figure 1, stalls can be avoided for two reasons. First, the server reads requests from the local message queue, without any remote actions that would cause it to stall. Second, the server does not wait for the actual message transmission to take place when it sends a response. When and how the messages are actually sent to their destinations is the responsibility of the underlying hardware message passing implementation. Therefore, if hardware message passing is used, we expect to be able to *completely remove* stalls related to synchronization from the critical execution path.

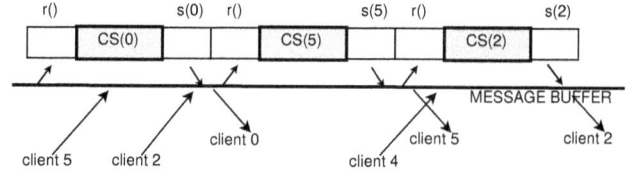

Figure 2. Mutual exclusion server – message-passing implementation; $r()$ – receive message; $s(t)$ – send message to thread t; request from client 0 is already available in the server's message queue

4.2 The Combiner Approach (HYBCOMB)

We now detail HYBCOMB, our combining algorithm tailored to take advantage of message passing. We start by describing the main principles of combining techniques over shared memory, to identify how message passing can be used to improve performance.

Main principles. In combining algorithms, threads interact for two purposes: (i) *electing* a combiner; (ii) exchanging information between the combiner and threads that have operations to be executed in mutual exclusion. In shared-memory combining algorithms [11, 13, 24], these two tasks are handled by a single shared object: a list of requests. To execute an operation, a thread adds a request to the list. The current combiner traverses the list to fetch and execute requests. When the current combiner wants to return, it hands over the combining role to the thread owning the next request in the list (if there are no requests to be executed, the next thread that inserts a request will become the combiner).

HYBCOMB uses hardware message passing for synchronization between the combiner and the other threads. As long as the combiner does not change, synchronization works as with MP-SERVER (Figure 2). Still, we use shared memory for managing combiner identity. In a nutshell, HYBCOMB works as follows: When a thread t wants to execute a request, it first checks the identity of the combiner through a shared variable. If a combiner is available and ready to handle the request, t sends a message to that combiner. If not, t tries to promote itself to a combiner, by executing CAS on the variable that keeps the combiner identity.

Managing combiner identity using message passing would be complex and probably inefficient. The main problem is that a thread acting as a combiner has to stop combining at some point, which must be synchronized with actions of other threads. To get its operation executed by a combiner, a thread has to get the identity of the combiner thread and send a request to it. If the combiner identity changes in the meantime, the operation will never get executed. Dealing with this problem using message-passing would require either a delegated thread (which is exactly what the combiner approach is trying to avoid), or intensive communication between threads (*e.g.*, broadcast).

Detailed description. Algorithm 1 describes HYBCOMB. The interface is the same as that of CC-SYNCH: When a thread wants to execute a critical section, it calls the *apply_op* method, providing a pointer to the function to execute and its arguments.[2] Note, however, that HYBCOMB is not just a simple adaptation of existing combining algorithms, where message passing is used instead of a shared list to make the combiner thread aware of the requests to execute. As already mentioned, using message passing requires us to be able to identify the combiner thread to which requests should be sent. This should be carefully handled, especially at the time the combiner changes. This problem does not exist in combining techniques fully based on shared memory since it is the combiner thread that fetches requests from a shared data structure.

The code executed by the active combiner are lines 23-43. Algorithm 1 ensures that these lines are executed in mutual exclusion, *i.e.*, that there is a single active combiner at a time. To manage combiner identity, a data structure called $Node$ is used. Each thread owns a reference to a different node (my_node). The id of the thread owning a node is saved in the field $Node.thread\_id$. Managing combiner identity is done using the shared pointer $last\_registered\_combiner$. To become a combiner (lines 17-21), a thread t tries to execute a CAS operation on $last\_registered\_combiner$ to make it point to its node. If the CAS succeeds, t keeps a pointer to the node corresponding to the previous $last\_registered\_combiner$ in its local variable $last\_reg$. This mechanism can be seen as building a logical queue where the head of the queue is the current active combiner and the tail is the $last\_registered\_combiner$, each thread in the queue having a reference to the predecessor in its $last\_reg$ variable. The $Node.combining\_done$ flag is used to synchronize the threads in the queue. Before starting executing as a combiner, a thread spins on the $combining\_done$ flag of its predecessor (line 19), which is set by the predecessor when it finishes combining (line 42).

Upon calling *apply_op*, a thread t first tries to register its request with $last\_registered\_combiner$. It does so by performing a fetch-and-increment on the $Node.n\_ops$ field of the corresponding node. This field guarantees that one combiner will receive and execute at most MAX_OPS requests of other threads. If the threshold MAX_OPS is not reached, t sends its request to the combiner using message passing (line 13), and waits for a response (line 14). If the last registered combiner cannot accept any new request, t tries to register itself as a combiner as already explained.

Once t becomes the active combiner, it first executes its own request (line 23). Then it reads messages from its message queue, processes requests and sends responses. When its message queue is empty, t decides to stop combining and announces it by writing MAX_OPS to its n_ops field.

---

[2] To make the presentation more concise, the shared-memory object on which the critical section is executed is implicit.

Algorithm 1 HYBCOMB combining algorithm – code for thread id

```
1:  const MAX_OPS {* max. operations per combiner *}
2:  type Node{thread_id: int, n_ops: int, combining_done: bool}

Global Variables:
3:  departed_combiner: Node ← {⊥, MAX_OPS, true}
4:  last_registered_combiner: Node ← departed_combiner

Local Variables:
5:  my_node: Node ← {id, MAX_OPS, false}

6:  apply_op (func_ptr, args)
7:      ops_completed ← 0
8:      loop
9:          last_reg ← last_registered_combiner
10:         {* try to register with last registered combiner *}
11:         if FAA(last_reg.n_ops, 1) < MAX_OPS then
12:             {* success. send message to combiner and wait *}
13:             send(last_reg.thread_id, {id, func_ptr, args})
14:             return receive(1)
15:         else
16:             {* failure. try to register as combiner *}
17:             if CAS(last_registered_combiner, last_reg, my_node)
                then
18:                 my_node.n_ops ← 0
19:                 while ¬last_reg.combining_done do
20:                     nop
21:                 break

22:     {* became combiner. do your own op first *}
23:     retval ← func_ptr(args)

24:     {* as long as message queue is not empty, handle requests *}
25:     while ¬is_queue_empty() do
26:         {sender_id, fptr, fargs} ← receive(3)
27:         send(sender_id, fptr(fargs))
28:         ops_completed ← ops_completed + 1

29:     {* close combining for new requests *}
30:     total_ops ← SWAP(my_node.n_ops, MAX_OPS)
31:     if total_ops > MAX_OPS then
32:         total_ops ← MAX_OPS

33:     {* serve remaining requests *}
34:     while ops_completed < total_ops do
35:         {sender_id, fptr, fargs} ← receive(3)
36:         send(sender_id, fptr(fargs))
37:         ops_completed ← ops_completed + 1

38:     {* exchange your node, inform next combiner and return *}
39:     my_node ← SWAP(departed_combiner, my_node)
40:     my_node.combining_done ← false
41:     my_node.thread_id ← id
42:     departed_combiner.combining_done ← true
43:     return retval
```

Since it does so using SWAP, it retains the old value of n_ops (in $total\_ops$), which is the total number of requests it has to serve as a combiner. It then finishes its combining round by serving the remaining requests, if any (lines 34-37).

Before returning, t must get the node it will use next time it calls *apply_op* (we want to avoid allocating a new node for every *apply_op* call). Obviously, t cannot use the same node because that requires the $combining\_done$ field to be

147

reset, but t cannot know when the next combiner will have read this field. As a solution, only one additional node is allocated for all n threads, and t gets the node that was used by the previous combiner (pointed by $departed\_combiner$) (lines 39-42)[3]: t knows that the $combining\_done$ field of this node can be reset since t was the thread spinning on this node. Finally, note that t must not reset the n_ops field of its new node at this point because other threads might still have an old reference to this node in their $last\_reg$ variable (lines 9-11): if n_ops were reset, these threads could send requests to t while it is not a combiner. Thus, t will reset n_ops only once it registers as a combiner again (line 18).

Additional comments. Before presenting the proof of correctness, we make a few remarks on the way HYBCOMB works. First, we can note that registering as a combiner (line 17) and resetting the n_ops counter (line 18) are not atomic. This does not affect the correctness of the algorithm. In the very unfortunate case where a thread t' executes the FAA at line 11 while t is between those two lines, t' will simply not manage to register its request with t, and so, will try to become the next combiner. This could merely result in a performance penalty as t would only have its own request to execute as a combiner. Results presented in Section 5 show that this rarely occurs in practice.

Note also that the first *while* loop in the request execution part (lines 25 to 28) is not necessary for correctness: The thread can decide to stop combining as soon as it has executed its own request. Still, this loop is beneficial for performance, as postponing the SWAP at line 30 increases the combining potential.

HYBCOMB uses a CAS operation like some other combining algorithms [13, 24], but unlike CC-SYNCH [11]. It is well known that CAS can impair performance (because it can repeatedly fail, causing contention) as well as fairness (a thread can starve if it executes CAS in a loop and persistently fails). We still choose to use CAS and not SWAP at line 17 for the following reasons: i) if SWAP is used and several threads try to register as combiners, they all succeed but some of them only have their own request to execute as a combiner, whereas with CAS only one thread manages to register as a combiner, and potentially execute all other requests; ii) the CAS is not expected to be a hot spot in HYBCOMB as it is only executed when a thread wants to register as a combiner. Experiments presented in Section 5 confirm the second point. If desired, a middle ground would be to use SWAP only if CAS fails several times.

Proof of correctness. Due to the space constraints, we only sketch the proof. The key idea is to show that Algorithm 1 maintains a logical queue of $Nodes$, denoted by CS_{queue}, (queue for entering the CS corresponding to lines 23 to 43) where each node represents a thread. The head

of the queue is the current combiner that executes the CS. Other nodes in the queue, if any, correspond to threads that want to become combiners, *i.e.*, to enter the CS. The operation $insert$ into CS_{queue} corresponds to a successful execution of CAS at line 17. The operation $remove$ from CS_{queue} corresponds to the execution of lines 39 to 43. Algorithm 1 maintains the following invariants related to CS_{queue}: (i) the tail of CS_{queue} is the node pointed to by the global variable $last\_registered\_combiner$ (line 4); (ii) $\forall n_t \in CS_{queue}$, node n_t corresponding to thread t, we have $last\_reg_t = n$, n being the predecessor of n_t in CS_{queue}; (iii) if $last\_reg_t.combining\_done = true$, then t is the head of CS_{queue}. We denote these invariants related to CS_{queue} by I_1. In addition to I_1, we consider the following invariants:

- I_2 :: For every thread t, $my\_node_t.thread\_id = id(t)$.
- I_3 :: There is at most one node n such that $n.combining\_done = true$;

Proposition 1. *I_1, I_2, I_3 are invariants of Algorithm 1.*

The proof is as follows. Let us denote by $I(x, y)$ the fact that I_1 to I_3 hold after x executions of $insert(CS_{queue})$ and y executions of $remove(CS_{queue})$. We prove that for all x, y, we have $I(x, y)$ by a double induction on x and y: first, we prove $I(1, 0)$ and $I(1, 1)$ (base step); second, we prove the induction step: $I(x, y) \Rightarrow I(x + 1, y)$ and $I(x, y) \Rightarrow I(x, y + 1)$ (if $x > y$).

Proposition 1 ensures lines 23 to 43 are executed in mutual exclusion (one combiner at a time). Then, the two lemmas

Lemma 1. *If for node n we have $n.n\_ops < MAX\_OPS$, then n is in CS_{queue}.*

Lemma 2. *If the message queue of thread t contains a request, then the node pointed to by my_node_t is in CS_{queue}.*

allow us to prove the following result:

Proposition 2. *At line 14, thread t cannot receive a request (i.e., t can only receive the response to the request sent at line 13).*

Mutual exclusion established by Proposition 1 together with Proposition 2 show that Algorithm 1 is *safe*. The linearizability of Algorithm 1, with respect to calls to $func\_ptr$, follows directly. For *liveness*, we need to prove additional results:

Lemma 3. *Every combiner t executes its own operation (line 23), and all the operations sent to it (at line 13); then t removes itself from CS_{queue}.*

Finally:

Proposition 3 (liveness). *Algorithm 1 is deadlock-free.*

If thread t wants to execute some operation op, then either t eventually gets the response (Lemma 3), or t tries to enter CS_{queue} (line 17). In the latter case, if t succeeds (executes CAS successfully), then it eventually executes op and leaves CS_{queue} (Lemma 3).

---

[3] The use of a SWAP operation at line 39 to exchange the two nodes is only for brevity. An atomic operation is not needed since these lines are executed in mutual exclusion anyway.

5. Evaluation

In this section we implement and thoroughly evaluate the algorithms presented in Sections 3 and 4. We begin by introducing the used hybrid processor and our experimental setup. Then we present experiments that evaluate different implementations of a concurrent counter. We then extend our analysis to more complex concurrent objects, namely queues and stacks. Finally, we discuss the generality of our results and their applicability to other platforms.

5.1 Platform

We use the Tilera TILE-Gx8036, which integrates 36 cores, works at 1.2 GHz and features complete hardware support for both coherent shared memory and message passing [2]. Software-wise, we use GCC 4.4.6 and version 2.6.40.38-MDE-4.1.0.148119 of Tilera's custom Linux kernel. The memory consistency model is relaxed compared to x86, so a careful use of memory fences is necessary to avoid inconsistency. Each core has a dedicated hardware message buffer, capable of storing up to 118 64-bit words. The message buffer of each core is 4-way multiplexed, which means that every per-core buffer can host up to four independent hardware FIFO queues, containing incoming messages. The User Dynamic Network (UDN) allows applications to exchange messages directly through the mesh interconnect, without OS intervention. While exchanging messages, a thread must be pinned to a core and registered to use the UDN (but it can unregister and freely migrate afterwards). When a message is sent from core A to core B, it is stored in the specified hardware queue of core B. The *send* operation is asynchronous and does not block, except in the following case. Since messages are never dropped, if a hardware queue is full, subsequent incoming messages back up into the network and may cause the sender to block. It is the programmer's responsibility to avoid deadlocks that can occur in such situations. When a thread executes *receive* on one of the four local queues, the first message from the queue is returned. If there are no messages, the thread blocks. Messages consist of one or multiple words.

5.2 Methodology and Setup

We have implemented MP-SERVER and HYBCOMB on the TILE-Gx, as well as two algorithms purely based on shared memory: the CC-SYNCH combining algorithm [11] and SHM-SERVER, a server approach. SHM-SERVER can be seen as a simplified version of RCL [17], since it implements the same core mechanism (an array of cache lines, one for each client), but lacks support for some advanced features, such as nested critical sections (note that this simplification does not decrease performance). The implementations have been carefully optimized and compiled with the O3 flag. Because of the relaxed memory model of the TILE-Gx, we have inserted memory fences where necessary to ensure correctness. We assume that shared data is accessed only inside

CSes, which holds for the concurrent objects we evaluate. A more conservative use of memory fences would be necessary when this is not the case [9]. To obtain the best possible performance, we augment all of the implementations with a simple interface that allows a thread to send a unique opcode of the CS to the servicing thread, rather than a function pointer. This allows the compiler to inline the function calls that the servicing thread makes for every CS, which results in a visible performance increase in most cases [9]. It is worth noting that the results are qualitatively the same without this optimization.

We use the methodology commonly found in related studies [11, 13, 21, 22]: In each experiment, a specified number of application threads repeatedly execute operations on a concurrent object. After every operation, a thread executes a random number of empty loop iterations (at most 50). This simulates local work and prevents *long runs*, in which a thread would execute bursts of operations on a concurrent object in its local cache. To minimize interference caused by context switching, we assume a uniprogrammed environment, where each thread runs on a separate core (multiprogramming is discussed in Section 6). We pin threads to cores in ascending order, i.e., thread i is pinned to core i. With server-based approaches (SHM-SERVER and MP-SERVER), the server code is executed by thread 0, and other threads execute application code (the server position has a negligible performance impact). In the case of HYBCOMB and CC-SYNCH, all threads run the same code. Unless otherwise stated, the maximum number of requests a thread can combine in HYBCOMB and CC-SYNCH is set to 200 (we analyze this choice later in this section). Every value reported in the graphs is an average over ten one-second runs.

5.3 Microbenchmarks

We first use each of the approaches to implement a simple object, a concurrent counter. Figure 3a shows the throughput of the counter implementations. The approaches that use hardware message passing are clearly faster: MP-SERVER is most efficient in all concurrency levels. Its reaches 4.3x higher throughput than SHM-SERVER, indicating that message passing supported natively is much more efficient than emulation over shared memory. When it comes to combining, HYBCOMB consistently outperforms CC-SYNCH. This is especially pronounced in higher concurrency levels, where HYBCOMB reaches about 2.5x higher throughput. CC-SYNCH and SHM-SERVER have very similar performance, indicating that CC-SYNCH manages to avoid dedicating cores at virtually no performance cost. On the other hand, the difference between MP-SERVER and HYBCOMB is much more visible. We will shortly identify the source of this difference, and explain how it can be minimized.

To give a more complete picture about performance, Figure 3b shows the average request latency observed by application threads. Again, MP-SERVER has by far the lowest latency even in low concurrency levels, indicating that

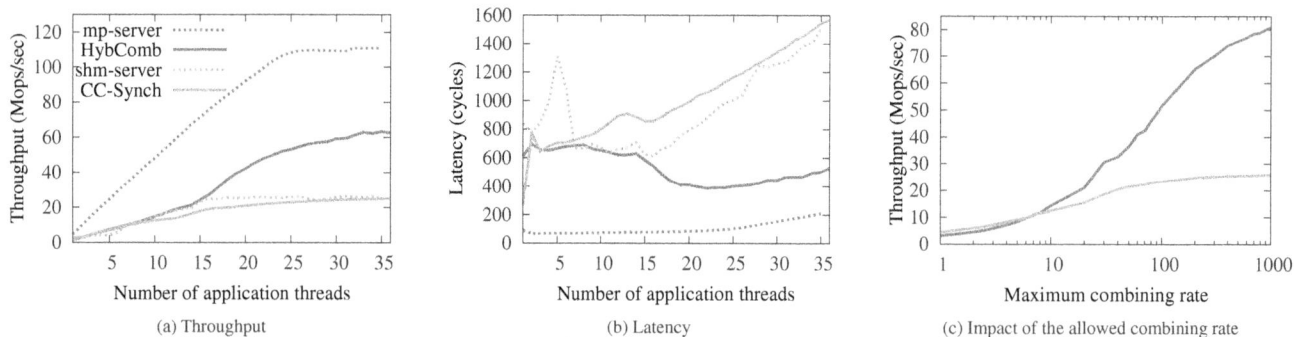

(a) Throughput   (b) Latency   (c) Impact of the allowed combining rate

Figure 3. Performance of a concurrent counter implemented using different synchronization techniques

hardware message passing is useful even latency-wise. HYBCOMB also has lower latency than CC-SYNCH and SHM-SERVER, which becomes especially visible as concurrency increases. The only noteworthy exception is single-threaded performance, where CC-SYNCH is better than HYBCOMB. We believe this is mainly because an isolated thread running CC-SYNCH executes only one atomic instruction per operation, whereas HYBCOMB executes three. Since atomic instructions on the TILE-Gx are not executed in the local cache but on memory controllers, this results in higher latency. As concurrency increases, the latency of both CC-SYNCH and HYBCOMB dips at one point before continuing to grow (between 14 and 17, resp. 14 and 24 application threads). This is due to more intensive combining, as we will confirm shortly.

One might question the choice of the maximum allowed combining rate (MAX_OPS). If MAX_OPS is too low, less combining is possible, which negatively affects throughput. On the other hand, increasing it above a certain limit does not increase throughput further, as the cost of combiner switching becomes negligible, but can result in higher latency observed by the combining thread. The optimal value heavily depends on the application needs and anticipated concurrency level. In Figure 3c, we examine how the maximum achievable throughput changes with MAX_OPS. Very high MAX_OPS values provide little benefit in terms of throughput of CC-SYNCH. On the other hand, as we increase MAX_OPS up to 1,000, the throughput of HYBCOMB continues to grow, barely showing signs of saturation. Combining is so fast with HYBCOMB, that the impact of combiner switching is visible even when MAX_OPS is high. This explains the difference between MP-SERVER and HYBCOMB observed in Figure 3a (recall that MAX_OPS is set to 200 there). The throughput of HYBCOMB levels off at about 88 Mops/sec, with MAX_OPS set to 5'000. Therefore, one can achieve nearly as high throughput with HYBCOMB as with MP-SERVER, if willing to trade the throughput increase for sporadic latency "hiccups" for some requests (when the requesting thread becomes a combiner). We have chosen a moderate value of 200 for our experiments, since it

already provides the highest possible throughput with CC-SYNCH and decent results with HYBCOMB.

Now we more precisely identify the reason for the observed performance improvement. Figure 4a shows the average number of CPU stalls per operation on the servicing thread under maximum load, as well as the total number of cycles per operation.[4] The advantage of HYBCOMB and MP-SERVER becomes clearer: The servicing thread is virtually never stalled, whereas CPU stalls account for more than 50% of the cycles of the servicing thread in CC-SYNCH and SHM-SERVER. There are no event counters that would provide more fine-grained information on the source of stalls, but we believe they mostly originate from the load-store unit, which has to wait for the cache coherence protocol to fetch data. This confirms the reasoning from Section 3: Cache-coherence related stalls are an important source of overhead, and hardware message passing is helpful in avoiding them.

Figure 4b shows the average combining rate with HYBCOMB and CC-SYNCH. Ideally, we expect it to reach MAX_OPS under high load. At the beginning, the actual combining rate steadily grows, and is approximately equal to the number of threads minus one. This is because a combiner manages to combine one request for all of the other threads. At that point, no thread has started the subsequent operation yet, so the combiner returns. As concurrency grows, more requests arrive at the combiner concurrently. As it takes more time to service them, there is more time for other requests to arrive before the combiner returns, and so forth. This circular effect leads to a sudden sharp increase in the combining rate, which explains the latency dip we observed in Figure 3b. As we can see in Figure 4b, in high concurrency levels CC-SYNCH reaches the desired combining rate, whereas HYBCOMB is slightly below it. This is because registering as a combiner and resetting the n_ops field are not atomic. As explained in Section 4.2, an unfortunate thread interleaving could leave one combiner with no work to do because a new

---

[4] To be able to use per-core event counters, only in this experiment we modified HYBCOMB and CC-SYNCH to have a fixed combiner for the whole run, which is equivalent to setting $MAX\_OPS = \infty$.

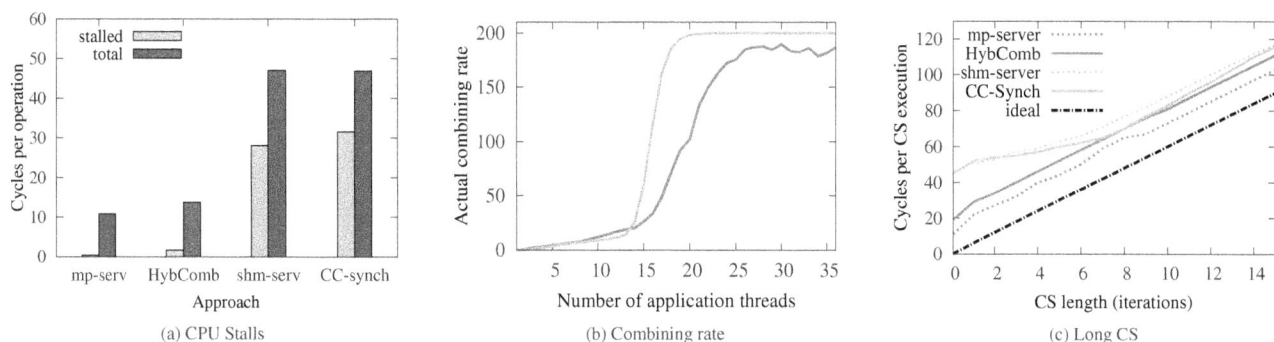

Figure 4. Analyzing the performance of the different synchronization techniques

thread would register as a combiner before any request is associated with the current one. However, we can see that this has only a marginal effect on the combining rate in practice: In spite of somewhat lower combining rate, HYBCOMB still has much better performance than CC-SYNCH (Figure 3).

To complete the analysis, we now examine what happens when the CS body is longer. We implement a CS in which the elements of an array are incremented in a loop (one increment per iteration). In Figure 4c, we vary the number of iterations and observe the average CS execution time (the dash-dot line is the time to execute the CS body without synchronization overheads). With MP-SERVER and HYBCOMB, the overhead due to synchronization is constant. The overhead of CC-SYNCH and SHM-SERVER initially decreases as the CS length increases. When the CS is short, their overhead is about 30 cycles higher than with MP-SERVER, which corresponds to the stalled cycles observed in Figure 4a. As the CS gets longer, the RMRs due to thread synchronization get partially overlapped with the CS execution, leading to fewer stalls. Hence, Figure 4c shows that MP-SERVER and HYB-COMB can lead to better performance mainly when CSes are short. At 15 loop iterations, the difference between the best (MP-SERVER) and the worst (SHM-SERVER) performer drops to about 10%, since the time to execute the CS body (which is the same with all of the implementations, if we ignore combiner switching) dominates the entry/exit overhead.

Finally, recall that HYBCOMB uses CAS, but the presented graphs indicate that this does not cause visible performance degradation. This is because, when concurrency is high, threads rarely execute CAS: They mostly send their requests to an active combiner. Indeed, we have measured as few as 0.1 executed CAS per operation (call to $apply\_op$) in high concurrency levels. This number is a bit higher when concurrency is not high enough to trigger high combining rates, but even then, there are not more than 0.7 CAS per operation in multithreaded executions. Regarding fairness, we have measured the ratio between the highest and lowest number of operations executed by some thread (so 1 denotes ideal fairness). Across the whole concurrency spectrum, the

highest value of this ratio with HYBCOMB is 1.2 and the average is 1.16. Even MP-SERVER, in which all requests are read from a hardware FIFO queue, has a ratio of nearly 1.1, only because some cores are nearer to the server, so they execute slightly more operations. Hence, the use of CAS in HYBCOMB does not impair fairness on this platform.

5.4 Queues and Stacks

Because of their ubiquity, concurrent linearizable queues and stacks have been extensively studied and they are typically used to evaluate the performance of universal synchronization constructions [10, 11, 13]. Following this observation, we implement some well-established queues and stacks from the literature and analyze their performance. With these experiments, we study an important use case where CSes are usually short. The implementations store 64-bit values, and are evaluated under balanced load.

Queues. One of the best-known blocking queues is the fine-grained Michael and Scott queue (MS-Queue) [21]. It is based on a linked list accessed using two CSes, so enqueues and dequeues can take place in parallel. Its performance mostly depends on the way CSes are implemented. We implement MS-Queue using HYBCOMB, CC-SYNCH, and the two server-based approaches (which requires two dedicated servers per queue instance). Besides the two-lock version, we implement the same queue using a single lock. We also test LCRQ [22], a nonblocking queue that takes advantage of the wide spectrum of atomic operations supported by x86 processors. The TILE-Gx supports most of the necessary instructions, so adapting the LCRQ code written in C for x86 was relatively easy.[5]

The queue performance is shown in Figure 5a. The single-lock MS-Queues ("-1" suffix in the legend) perform best. Among them, MP-SERVER and HYBCOMB are most efficient: They obtain respectively up to 2x and 1.5x higher throughput than the third best implementation. LCRQ, as

---

[5] We made the following modifications: the lacking bitwise test-and-set (BTAS) was replaced with a simple CAS loop; for lack of the 128-bit CAS (CAS2), we modified LCRQ to store 32-bit values, and used a 64-bit CAS.

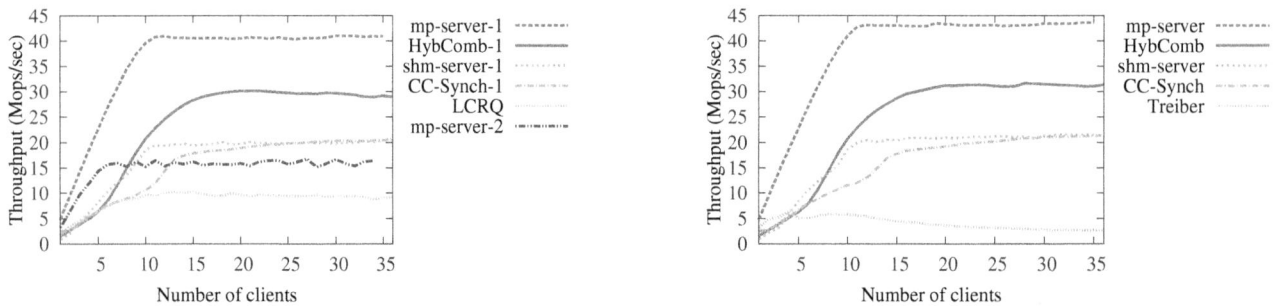

(a) **Queue.** X-1 – one-lock MS-Queue implemented using approach X; MP-SERVER-2 – two-lock MS-Queue, implemented using MP-SERVER; LCRQ – non-blocking queue as presented in [22]

(b) **Stack.** X – coarse-lock stack implemented using approach X; Treiber – nonblocking stack presented in [28]

Figure 5. Performance of concurrent queues and stacks under balanced load

well as the two-lock MS-Queue[6], level off sooner than the rest, which we now explain in more detail.

One might expect fine-grained locking to always outperform a coarse lock. However, fine-grained locking involves a tradeoff, since the additional synchronization it includes might outweigh the gain that comes from increasing parallelism [13]. Given Tilera's relaxed memory model, the enqueue and dequeue methods of the two-lock queue must be carefully coded if they can run in parallel – memory fences are necessary to ensure queue consistency. On this platform, it turns out that the necessity of inserting fences far outweighs the benefit from fine-grained access. Therefore, a simple sequential queue implemented using MP-SERVER or HYBCOMB yields best results.

In spite of its excellent performance on x86 [22], LCRQ is less efficient on the TILE-Gx. This is primarily because of the way atomic instructions work on this processor. Namely, there are two memory controllers in charge of executing them. This means that two atomic instructions might collide on the memory controller even if they have independent data sets. Because LCRQ executes many atomic instructions per queue operation, such *false serialization* is very frequent, resulting in performance degradation.

Stacks. The stack is known to be hard to parallelize, since both push and pop operations access its top. One way to obviate its seemingly inherent sequential nature is to use the the *elimination* technique [8, 25]: if a push and pop operation are executed concurrently, they can be *eliminated* to avoid accessing the stack. Still, if an operation cannot be eliminated, it has to access the top of the stack. As elimination is orthogonal to the content of this paper, we evaluate the performance of a non-elimination concurrent stack (which, of course, can be used to back up an elimination-based stack).

We evaluate five implementations: a sequential linked-list based stack, turned concurrent using MP-SERVER, HY-

BCOMB, CC-SYNCH and SHM-SERVER, as well as well-known Treiber's nonblocking stack [28]. Their performance is given in Figure 5b. MP-SERVER and HYBCOMB stacks are again the best performers – and the numbers nearly match those given in Figure 5a for the single-lock MS queue. This is not surprising, as both concurrent objects are represented as linked lists protected by a coarse lock. Treiber stack performance is inferior to that of the blocking implementations, because the head of the stack is accessed using CAS. This causes growing contention as concurrency increases, as most CAS operations repeatedly fail.

5.5 Discussion

One might wonder to what extent our results are processor-specific. To answer this question, we have measured the throughput of a concurrent counter implemented using CC-SYNCH and SHM-SERVER on two single-socket x86 processors: a 10-core Intel Xeon E7-L8867 (without and with Hyperthreading enabled), and a 6-core AMD Opteron 6176. In virtually all of the cases, peak throughput is significantly lower on x86. We have also measured the number of stalls per operation of the servicing thread (as in Figure 4a) and got proportionally larger numbers than on the TILE-Gx. Therefore, we believe MP-SERVER and HYBCOMB would outperform their purely shared-memory counterparts also on x86 hardware, if it provided native message passing support. Moreover, since there are more stalls on x86, the potential performance improvement is higher.

Still, it is noteworthy that we did observe some platform-specific effects. Since the implementation of atomic instructions differs on the TILE-Gx and the x86, algorithms that use them intensively (typically nonblocking ones) may behave differently. This is visible on the example of LCRQ, which has substantially higher throughput on the x86 processors than on the TILE-Gx. Also, because of the different memory consistency model, one-lock MS-Queue outperforms its two-lock counterpart on the TILE-Gx (cf. Figure 5a), in contrast to what we have observed on the Xeon

---

[6] To avoid clutter, we only present the MP-SERVER implementation of the two-lock queue. The other implementations have inferior performance.

and Opteron. Note, however, that these differences are specific to implementations of a certain concurrent object, a queue in this case. In other words, Figure 5a (showing queue performance) would look different on an x86, but the qualitative advantage of MP-SERVER and HYBCOMB over SHM-SERVER and CC-SYNCH, which is central to this paper, would in all likelihood remain the same.

Finally, the advantage provided by MP-SERVER and HYBCOMB is due to the way hardware message passing is implemented, and more specifically, to the fact that receive operations read from a local buffer, and that send operations are asynchronous. These features are not too specific, and so, we believe they can be easily provided by future implementations of hardware message passing. Note also that HYBCOMB depends a lot on the performance of the fetch-and-add instruction, since every client must execute it on the same variable before sending a request to the current combiner. Fetch-and-add on x86 processors is typically fast and scalable, since it is guaranteed to succeed [22].

6. Additional Considerations

This section discusses some practical aspects of our message-passing approaches.

Oversubscribing and thread migration. The results presented in Section 5 assume a uniprogrammed environment, with at most one thread pinned to a core. This is not an inherent limitation of the hardware message passing approaches. On the TILE-Gx, oversubscribing is easily achieved thanks to the possibility to multiplex the hardware queue of each core (cf. Section 5.1), which means that up to four threads can share a core and still have their exclusive message queue. With both MP-SERVER and HYBCOMB, application threads can freely migrate to another core in between requests, as long as they are able to reserve a hardware queue on that core. Upon making a request, a thread t is only expected to have a valid identifier, corresponding to its current core and hardware queue. As long as t remains pinned to the current core while its request is pending, other threads will be able to reach it using that identifier.

Deadlocks. Bearing in mind the limited capacity of the hardware message queues, another practical issue with message passing is the possibility of deadlocks, if messages back up in the network and block the sender. Obviously, the message queues of MP-SERVER clients or HYBCOMB non-combiner threads cannot overflow since they contain at most one message. Therefore, the servicing thread never blocks when sending a response to a request.

In our experiments, the message queue of a servicing thread cannot overflow, as it contains at most 35 3-word requests at any time, which fits in the message queue. More generally, overflows can happen if the hardware queue is not big enough to keep one request per application thread. In this case, some clients could be blocked when sending

a request, but this is not an issue since every such *send* is anyway immediately followed by a blocking *receive*.

7. Related Work

In Section 3, we detailed generic shared-memory constructions for implementing concurrent objects. This section gives an overview of other work studying message passing in the manycore context.

Due to the uncertain future of cache coherence, a great body of recent work studies manycores provided with hardware message passing such as the Tilera [2] and the Intel SCC [16]. It has been shown that message passing can help in achieving good performance in the implementation of transactional memory [12] and key-value stores [7]. In the 90's, Herlihy et al. showed, by simulating MIT's Alewife processor, that message-passing implementations of counting networks and combining trees are more efficient than their shared-memory counterparts [14]. In this paper, we leverage message passing to efficiently implement an arbitrary concurrent object, through universal constructions.

Some recent work also considers hardware augmentations for efficient mutual exclusion: token-based messaging over a dedicated network [3] and a custom instruction set and dedicated cores [27]. Our paper complements these studies by considering an off-the-shelf processor with generic hardware support for message passing, and providing synchronization completely in software.

Finally, similarly to RCL [17], recent work implements message passing over shared memory in the context of concurrent objects [8, 20], because of the explicit control over communication and improved data locality it provides. Our results show that in this case, performance is still limited by the underlying CC protocol, and that hardware message passing can provide a performance improvement.

8. Conclusion

Considering the problem of executing contended critical sections, we studied how hardware message passing can be used for efficient thread synchronization. We proposed two generic constructions tailored to take advantage of hardware message passing: MP-SERVER, a server-based approach, and HYBCOMB, a combiner-based approach. Experiments on Tilera's TILE-Gx processor show that MP-SERVER and HYBCOMB largely outperform their pure-shared-memory counterparts, when used to implement ubiquitous linearizable concurrent objects (counters, queues, stacks).

Our results show that hardware message passing can provide more efficient thread synchronization, and thus, improve the scalability of concurrent code. The hybrid design of HYBCOMB demonstrates that processors providing both CC shared memory and message passing are appealing, as they allow us to take the best of both worlds. However, it also illustrates that significant algorithmic effort can be necessary in order to exploit the resources of a hybrid machine.

Acknowledgments

We would like to thank EcoCloud[7] for providing access to the Tilera processor. Thanks also to Martin Biely, Omid Shahmirzadi and Vasileios Trigonakis for useful comments.

References

[1] Kalray. http://www.kalray.eu. Accessed: 15-12-2013.

[2] Tilera. http://www.tilera.com. Accessed: 15-12-2013.

[3] J. L. Abellán, J. Fernández, and M. E. Acacio. GLocks: Efficient Support for Highly-Contended Locks in Many-Core CMPs. In *Proceedings of the 2011 IEEE International Parallel & Distributed Processing Symposium*, 2011.

[4] S. Agathos, N. Kallimanis, and V. Dimakopoulos. Speeding up OpenMP tasking. In *Proceedings of the 18th international conference on Parallel Processing*, 2012.

[5] T. E. Anderson. The Performance of Spin Lock Alternatives for Shared-Memory Multiprocessors. *IEEE Transactions on Parallel and Distributed Systems*, 1(1):6–16, Jan. 1990.

[6] A. Baumann, P. Barham, P.-E. Dagand, T. Harris, R. Isaacs, S. Peter, T. Roscoe, A. Schüpbach, and A. Singhania. The multikernel: a new OS architecture for scalable multicore systems. In *Proc. of the ACM SIGOPS 22nd symposium on Operating systems principles*, 2009.

[7] M. Berezecki, E. Frachtenberg, M. Paleczny, and K. Steele. Many-core key-value store. In *Proceedings of the 2011 International Green Computing Conference and Workshops*, 2011.

[8] I. Calciu, J. Gottschlich, and M. Herlihy. Using elimination and delegation to implement a scalable numa-friendly stack. In *5th USENIX Workshop on Hot Topics in Parallelism*, 2013.

[9] J. Cleary, O. Callanan, M. Purcell, and D. Gregg. Fast asymmetric thread synchronization. *ACM Transactions on Architecture and Code Optimization*, 9(4):27:1–27:22, Jan. 2013.

[10] P. Fatourou and N. D. Kallimanis. A highly-efficient wait-free universal construction. In *Proceedings of the 23rd ACM symposium on Parallelism in algorithms and architectures*, 2011.

[11] P. Fatourou and N. D. Kallimanis. Revisiting the combining synchronization technique. In *Proceedings of the 17th ACM SIGPLAN symposium on Principles and Practice of Parallel Programming*, 2012.

[12] V. Gramoli, R. Guerraoui, and V. Trigonakis. TM2C: a software transactional memory for many-cores. In *Proceedings of the 7th ACM european conference on Computer Systems*, 2012.

[13] D. Hendler, I. Incze, N. Shavit, and M. Tzafrir. Flat combining and the synchronization-parallelism tradeoff. In *Proceedings of the 22nd ACM symposium on Parallelism in algorithms and architectures*, 2010.

[14] M. Herlihy, B.-H. Lim, and N. Shavit. Scalable concurrent counting. *ACM Transactions on Computer Systems*, 13(4):343–364, Nov. 1995.

[15] M. P. Herlihy and J. M. Wing. Linearizability: a correctness condition for concurrent objects. *ACM Trans. Program. Lang. Syst.*, 12(3):463–492, July 1990.

[16] J. Howard, S. Dighe, Y. Hoskote, S. Vangal, D. Finan, G. Ruhl, D. Jenkins, et al. A 48-core IA-32 message-passing processor with DVFS in 45nm CMOS. In *International IEEE Solid-State Circuits Conference Digest of Technical Papers*, 2010.

[17] J.-P. Lozi, F. David, G. Thomas, J. Lawall, and G. Muller. Remote core locking: migrating critical-section execution to improve the performance of multithreaded applications. In *Proceedings of the 2012 USENIX Annual Technical Conference*, 2012.

[18] M. Martin, M. Hill, and D. Sorin. Why on-chip cache coherence is here to stay. *Communications of the ACM*, 55(7):78–89, July 2012.

[19] J. M. Mellor-Crummey and M. L. Scott. Algorithms for scalable synchronization on shared-memory multiprocessors. *ACM Transactions on Computer Systems*, 9(1):21–65, Feb. 1991.

[20] Z. Metreveli, N. Zeldovich, and M. F. Kaashoek. CPHASH: a cache-partitioned hash table. In *Proceedings of the 17th ACM SIGPLAN symposium on Principles and Practice of Parallel Programming*, 2012.

[21] M. M. Michael and M. L. Scott. Simple, fast, and practical non-blocking and blocking concurrent queue algorithms. In *Proceedings of the fifteenth annual ACM symposium on Principles of distributed computing*, 1996.

[22] A. Morrison and Y. Afek. Fast concurrent queues for x86 processors. In *Proceedings of the 18th ACM SIGPLAN symposium on Principles and practice of parallel programming*, 2013.

[23] S. Owens, S. Sarkar, and P. Sewell. A better x86 memory model: x86-TSO. In *Proceedings of the 22nd International Conference on Theorem Proving in Higher Order Logics*, 2009.

[24] Y. Oyama, K. Taura, and A. Yonezawa. Executing parallel programs with synchronization bottlenecks efficiently. In *Proceedings of the International Workshop on Parallel and Distributed Computing for Symbolic and Irregular Applications*, 1999.

[25] N. Shavit and D. Touitou. Elimination trees and the construction of pools and stacks: preliminary version. In *Proceedings of the 7th annual ACM symposium on Parallel algorithms and architectures*, 1995.

[26] D. Sorin, M. Hill, and D. Wood. A Primer on Memory Consistency and Cache Coherence. *Synthesis Lectures on Computer Architecture*, 6(3):1–212, 2011.

[27] M. A. Suleman, O. Mutlu, M. Qureshi, and Y. Patt. Accelerating Critical Section Execution with Asymmetric Multicore Architectures. *IEEE Micro*, 30(1):60–70, Jan. 2010.

[28] R. K. Treiber. Systems Programming: Coping with Parallelism. Technical Report RJ 5118, IBM Almaden Research Center, Apr. 1986.

[29] D. Wentzlaff and A. Agarwal. Factored operating systems (fos): the case for a scalable operating system for multicores. *SIGOPS Operating Systems Review*, 43(2):76–85, Apr. 2009.

---

[7] http://www.ecocloud.ch

Well-Structured Futures and Cache Locality

Maurice Herlihy

Computer Science Department
Brown University
mph@cs.brown.edu

Zhiyu Liu

Computer Science Department
Brown University
zhiyu_liu@brown.edu

Abstract

In *fork-join parallelism*, a sequential program is split into a directed acyclic graph of tasks linked by directed dependency edges, and the tasks are executed, possibly in parallel, in an order consistent with their dependencies. A popular and effective way to extend fork-join parallelism is to allow threads to create *futures*. A thread creates a future to hold the results of a computation, which may or may not be executed in parallel. That result is returned when some thread *touches* that future, blocking if necessary until the result is ready.

Recent research has shown that while futures can, of course, enhance parallelism in a structured way, they can have a deleterious effect on cache locality. In the worst case, futures can incur $\Omega(PT_\infty + tT_\infty)$ deviations, which implies $\Omega(CPT_\infty + CtT_\infty)$ additional cache misses, where C is the number of cache lines, P is the number of processors, t is the number of touches, and T_∞ is the *computation span*. Since cache locality has a large impact on software performance on modern multicores, this result is troubling.

In this paper, however, we show that if futures are used in a simple, disciplined way, then the situation is much better: if each future is touched only once, either by the thread that created it, or by a later descendant of the thread that created it, then parallel executions with work stealing can incur at most $O(CPT_\infty^2)$ additional cache misses, a substantial improvement. This structured use of futures is characteristic of many (but not all) parallel applications.

Categories and Subject Descriptors C.4 [*Performance of Systems*]: Performance attributes; D.3.3 [*Language Constructs and Features*]: Concurrent programming structures

Keywords   scheduling; work stealing; futures; parallel programming; cache locality; performance bounds

PPoPP '14,   February 15–19, 2014, Orlando, Florida, USA.
Copyright © 2014 ACM 978-1-4503-2656-8/14/02. . . $15.00.
http://dx.doi.org/10.1145/2555243.2555257

1. Introduction

Futures [18, 19] are an attractive way to structure many parallel programs because they are easy to reason about (especially if the futures have no side-effects) and they lend themselves well to sophisticated dynamic scheduling algorithms, such as work-stealing [11] and its variations, that ensure high processor utilization. At the same time, however, modern multicore architectures employ complex multi-level memory hierarchies, and technology trends are increasing the relative performance differences among the various levels of memory. As a result, processor utilization can no longer be the sole figure of merit for schedulers. Instead, the *cache locality* of the parallel execution will become increasingly critical to overall performance. As a result, cache locality will increasingly join processor utilization as a criterion for evaluating dynamic scheduling algorithms.

Several researchers [1, 22] have shown, however, that introducing parallelism through the use of futures can sometimes substantially reduce cache locality. In the worst case, if we add futures to a sequential program, a parallel execution managed by a work-stealing scheduler can incur $\Omega(PT_\infty + tT_\infty)$ deviations, which, as we show, implies $\Omega(CPT_\infty + CtT_\infty)$ more cache misses than the sequential execution. Here, C is the number of cache lines, P is the number of processors, t is the number of touches, and T_∞ is the computation's *span* (or *critical path*). As technology trends cause the cost of cache misses to increase, this additional cost is troubling.

This paper makes the following three contributions. First, we show that if futures are used in a simple, disciplined way, then the situation with respect to cache locality is much better: if each future is touched only once, either by the thread that created it, or by a later descendant of that thread, then parallel executions with work stealing can incur at most $O(CPT_\infty^2)$ additional cache misses, a substantial improvement over the unstructured case. This result provides a simple way to identify computations for which introducing futures will not incur a high cost in cache locality, as well as providing guidelines for the design of future parallel computations. (Informally, we think these guidelines are natural, and correspond to structures programmers are likely to use anyway.) Our second contribution is to observe that when the scheduler has a choice between running the thread that created a future, and the thread that implements the future, running the future thread first provides better cache locality. Finally, we show that certain variations of structured computation also have good cache locality.

The paper is organized as follows. Section 2 describes the model for future-parallel computations. In Section 3, we describe parsimonious work-stealing schedulers, and briefly discuss their cache performance measures. In Section 4, we define some restricted forms of structured future-parallel computations. Among them, we highlight structured single-touch computations, which, we believe, are likely to arise naturally in many programs. In Section 5.1, we prove that work-stealing schedulers on structured single-touch computations incur only $O(CPT_\infty^2)$ additional cache misses, if a processor always chooses the future to execute first when it creates that future. We also prove this bound is tight within a factor of C. In section 5.2, we show that if a processor chooses the current thread over the future thread when it creates that future, then the cache locality of a structured single-touch computation can be much worse. In Section 6, we show that some other kinds of structured future-parallel computations also achieve relatively good cache locality. Finally, we present conclusions in Section 7.

2. Model

In *fork-join parallelism* [5, 6, 8], a sequential program is split into a directed acyclic graph of *tasks* linked by directed dependency edges. These tasks are executed in an order consistent with their dependencies, and tasks unrelated by dependencies can be executed in parallel. Fork-join parallelism is well-suited to dynamic load-balancing techniques such as *work stealing* [1–3, 9, 11–13, 15, 18–20].

A popular and effective way to extend fork-join parallelism is to allow threads to create *futures* [4, 7, 14, 18, 19]. A future is a data object that represents a *promise* to deliver the result of an asynchronous computation when it is ready. That result becomes available to a thread when the thread *touches* that future, blocking if necessary until the result is ready. Futures are attractive because they provide greater flexibility than fork-join programs, and they can also be implemented effectively using dynamic load-balancing techniques such as work stealing. Fork-join parallelism can be viewed as a special case of future-parallelism, where the spawn operation is an implicit future creation, and the sync operation is an implicit touch of the untouched futures created by a thread. Future-parallelism is more flexible than fork-join parallelism, because the programmer has finer-grained control over touches (joins).

2.1 Computation DAG

A thread creates a future by marking an expression (usually a method call) as a *future*. This statement spawns a new thread to evaluate that expression in parallel with the thread that created the future. When a thread needs access to the results of the computation, it applies a *touch* operation to the future. If the result is ready, it is returned by the touch, and otherwise the touching thread blocks until the result becomes ready. Without loss of generality, we will consider fork-join parallelism to be a special case of future-parallelism, where forking a thread creates a future, and joining one thread to another is a touch operation.

Our notation and terminology follow earlier work [1, 3, 11, 22]. A future-parallel computation is modeled as a *directed acyclic graph* (DAG). Each node in the DAG represents a task (one or more instructions), and an edge from node u to node v represents the dependency constraint that u must be executed before v. We follow the convention that each node in the DAG has in-degree and out-degree either 1 or 2, except for a distinguished *root node* with in-degree 0, where the computation starts, and a distinguished *final node* with out-degree 0, where the computation ends.

There are three types of edges:

- *continuation edges*, which point from one node to the next in the same thread,
- *future edges* (sometimes called *spawn* edges), which point from node u to the first node of another thread spawned at u by a future creation,
- *touch edges* (sometimes called *join* edges), directed from a node u in one thread t to a node v in another thread, indicating that v touches the future computed by t.

A *thread* is a maximal chain of nodes connected by continuation edges. There is a distinguished *main thread* that begins at the root node and ends at the final node, and every other thread t begins at a node with an incoming future edge from a node of the thread that spawns t. The last node of t has only one outgoing edge which is a touch edge directed to another thread, while other nodes of t may or may not have incoming and outgoing touch edges. A *critical path* of a DAG is a longest directed path in the DAG, and the DAG's *computation span* is the length of a critical path.

As illustrated in Figure 1, if a thread t_1 spawns a new thread t_2 at node v in t_1 (i.e., v has two out-going edges, a continuation edge and a future edge to the first node of t_2), then we call t_1 the *parent thread* of t_2, t_2 the *future thread* (of t_1) at v, and v the *fork* of t_2. A thread t_3 is a *descendant thread* of t_1 if t_3 is a future thread of t_1 or, by induction, t_3's parent thread is a descendant thread of t_1.

If there is a touch edge directed from node v_1 in thread t_1 to node v_2 in thread t_2 (i.e., t_2 touches a future computed by t_1), and a continuation edge directed from node u_2 in t_2 to v_2, then we call node v_2 a *touch of* t_1 by t_2, v_1 the *future parent* of v_2, u_2 the *local parent* of v_2, and t_1 the future thread of v_2. (Note that the touch v_2 is actually a node in thread t_2.) We call the fork of t_1 the *corresponding fork* of v_2.

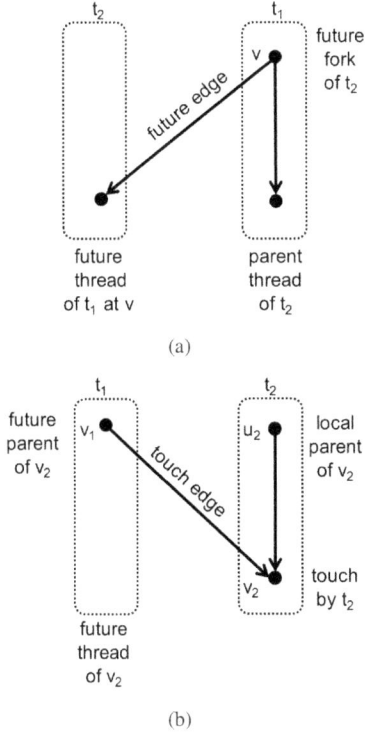

Figure 1. Node and thread terminology

Note that only touch nodes have in-degree 2. To distinguish between the two types of nodes with out-degree 2, forks and future parents of touches, we follow the convention of previous work that the children of a fork both have in-degree 1 and cannot be touches. In this way, a fork node has two children with in-degree 1, while a touch's future parent has a (touch) child with in-degree 2.

We follow the convention that when a fork appears in a DAG, the future thread is shown on the left, and the future parent on the right. (Note that this does not mean the future thread is chosen to execute first at a fork.) Similarly, the future parent of a touch is shown on the left, and the local parent on the right.

We use the following (standard) notation. Given a computation DAG, P is the number of processors executing the computation, t is the number of touches in the DAG, T_∞, the *computation span* (or *critical path*), is the length of the longest directed path, and C is the number of cache lines in each processor.

3. Work-Stealing and Cache Locality

In the paper, we focus on parsimonious work stealing algorithms [3], which have been extensively studied [1, 3, 10, 11, 22] and used in systems such as Cilk [9]. In a parsimonious work stealing algorithm, each processor is assigned a double-ended queue (deque). After a processor executes a node with out-degree 1, it continues to execute the next node if the next node is ready to execute. After the processor exe-

cutes a fork, it pushes one child of the fork onto the bottom of its deque and executes the other. When the processor runs out of nodes to execute, it pops the first node from the bottom of its deque if the deque is not empty. If, however, its deque is empty, it steals a node from the top of the deque of an arbitrary processor.

In our model, a cache is fully associative and consists of multiple *cache lines*, each of which holds the data in a *memory block*. Each instruction can access only one memory block. In our analysis we focus only on the widely-used *least-recently used* (LRU) cache replacement policy, but our results should apply to all *simple* cache replacement policies [1].

The *cache locality* of an execution is measured by the number of cache misses it incurs, which depends on the structure of the computation. To measure the effect on cache locality of parallelism, it is common to compare cache misses encountered in a sequential execution to the cache misses encountered in various parallel executions, focusing on the number of *additional* cache misses introduced by parallelism.

Scheduling choices at forks affect the cache locality of executions with work stealing. After executing a fork, a processor picks one of the two child nodes to execute and pushes the other into its deque. For a sequential execution, whether a choice results in a better cache performance is a characteristic of the computation itself. For a parallel execution of a computation satisfying certain properties, however, we will show that choosing future threads (the left children) at forks to execute first guarantees a relatively good upper bound on the number of additional cache misses, compared to a sequential execution that also chooses future threads first. In contrast, choosing the parent threads (the right children) to execute first can result in a large number of additional cache misses, compared to a sequential execution that also chooses parent threads first.

4. Structured Computations

Consider a sequential execution where node v_1 is executed immediately before node v_2. A *deviation* [22], also called a drifted node [1], occurs in a parallel execution if a processor P executes v_2, but not immediately after v_1. For example, p might execute v_1 after v_2, it might execute other nodes between v_1 and v_2, or v_1 and v_2 might be executed by distinct processors.

Spoonhower et al. [22] showed that a parallel execution of a future-parallel computation with work stealing can incur $\Omega(PT_\infty + tT_\infty)$ deviations. This implies a parallel execution of a future-parallel computation with work stealing can incur $\Omega(PT_\infty + tT_\infty)$ additional cache misses. With minor modifications in that computation (see Figure 2), a parallel execution can even incur $\Omega(CPT_\infty + CtT_\infty)$ additional cache misses.

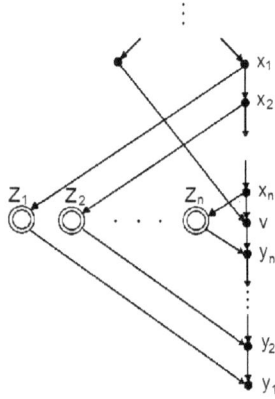

Figure 2. The interesting part of the bound is $\Omega(CtT_\infty)$. Figure 5 in [22] shows a DAG, as a building block of a worst-case computation, that can incur $\Omega(T_\infty)$ deviations because of one touch. We can replace it with the DAG in Figure 2, which can incur $\Omega(CT_\infty)$ additional cache misses due to one touch v (if the processor at a fork always chooses the parent thread to execute first), so that the worst-case computation in [22] can incur $\Omega(CtT_\infty)$ additional cache misses because of t such touches. This DAG is similar to the DAG in Figure 6(a) in this paper. The proof of Theorem 10 shows how a parallel execution of this DAG incurs $\Omega(CT_\infty)$ additional cache misses.

Our contribution in this paper is based on the observation that such poor cache locality occurs primarily when futures in the DAG are touched by threads created before the future threads computing these futures where created. As illustrated in Figure 3(a), a parallel execution of such a computation can arrive at a scenario where a thread touches a future before the future thread computing that future has been spawned. (As a practical matter, an implementation must ensure that such a touch does not return a reference to a memory location that has not yet been allocated.) We will show that such scenarios are avoided by *structured* future-parallel computations that follow certain simple restrictions.

DEFINITION 1. *A DAG is a* structured future-parallel computation *if, (1) for the future thread t of any fork v, the local parents of the touches of t are descendants of v, and (2) at least one touch of t is a descendant of the right child of v.*

There are two reasons we require that at least one touch of t is a descendant of the right child of v. First, it is natural that a computation spawns a future thread to compute a future because the computation itself later needs that value. At the fork v, the parent thread (the right child of v) represents the "main body" of the computation. Hence, the future will usually be touched either by the parent thread, or by threads spawned directly or indirectly by the parent thread.

Second, a computation usually needs a kind of "barrier" synchronization to deal with resource release at the end of the computation. Some node in the future thread t, usually

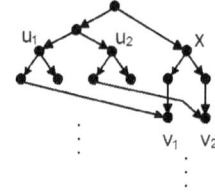

(a) A simplified version of the DAG in Spoonhower et al. [22] that can incur high cache overhead. Here, v_1 and v_2 are touches. Suppose a processor p_1 executes the root node, pushes the right child x of the root node into its deque, and then falls asleep. Now another processor p_2 steals x from p_1's deque and executes the subgraph rooted at x. Thus, v_1 and v_2 will be checked (to see if they are available) even before the corresponding future threads are spawned at u_1 and u_2.

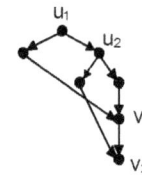

(b) In this structured computation, the touches v_1 and v_2 will not be checked until their corresponding future threads have been spawned at u_1 and u_2, respectively

Figure 3. Unstructured and Structured DAGs

the last node, should have an outgoing edge pointing to the "main body" of the computation to tell the main body that the future thread has finished. Without such synchronization, t and its descendants will be isolated from the main body of the computation, and we can imagine a dangerous scenario where the main body of the computation finishes and releases its resources while t or its descendant threads are still running.

In our DAG model, such a synchronization point is by definition a touch node, though it may not be a real touch. We follow the convention that the thread that spawns a future thread releases it, so the synchronization point is a vertex in the parent thread or one of its descendants. Another possibility is to place the synchronization point at the last node of the entire computation, which is the typically case in languages such as Java, where the main thread of a program is in charge of releasing resources for the entire computation. These two styles are essentially equivalent, and should have almost the same bounds on cache overheads. We will briefly discuss this issue in Section 6.2.

We consider how the following constraint affects cache locality.

DEFINITION 2. *A* structured single-touch *computation is a structured computation where each future thread spawned at a fork v is touched only once, and the touch node is a descendant of v's right child.*

By the definition of threads, the future parent of the only touch of a future thread is the last node of that future thread (the last node can also be a parent of a join node, but we don't distinguish between a touch node and a join node). We will show that work-stealing parallel executions of structured single-touch computations achieve significantly less cache overheads than unstructured computations.

In principle, a future could be touched multiple times by different threads, so structured single-touch computations are more restrictive structured computations in general. Nevertheless, the single-touch constraint is one that is likely to be observed by many programs. For example, as noted, the Cilk [9] language supports fork-join parallelism, a strict subset of the future-parallelism model considered here. If we interpret the Cilk [9] language's `spawn` statement as creating a future, and its `sync` statement as touching all untouched futures previously created by that thread, then Cilk programs (like all fork-join programs) are structured single-touch computations.

Structured single-touch computations encompass fork-join computations, but are strictly more flexible. Figure 4 presents two examples that illustrate the differences. If a thread creates multiple futures first and touches them later, fork-join parallelism requires they be touched (evaluated) in the reverse order. MethodA in Figure 4(a) shows the only order in which a thread can first create two futures and then touch them in a fork-join computation. This rules out, for instance, a program where a thread creates a sequence of futures, stores them in a priority queue, and evaluates them in some priority order. In contrast, our structured computations permit such futures to be evaluated by their creating thread or its descendants in any order.

Also, unlike fork-join parallelism, our notion of structured computation permits a thread to pass a future to a subroutine or descendant thread which touches that future, as illustrated in Figure 4(b). Our restrictions are: (1) only one thread can touch a future, and (2) the descendant thread that touches the future has to be created after the future. In fact, MethodC can even pass the future to a descendant of its own. In a fork-join computation, however, only the thread creating the future can touch it, which is much more restrictive. We believe these restrictions are easy to follow and should be compatible with how many people program in practice.

Belloch and Reid-Miller [7] observe that if a future can be touched multiple times, then complex and potentially inefficient operations and data structures are needed to correctly resume the suspended threads that are waiting for the touch. By contrast, the run-time support for futures can be significantly simplified if each future is touched at most once.

The single-touch constraint can be relaxed as follows.

DEFINITION 3. *A structured* local-touch *computation is one where each future thread spawned at a fork v is touched only at nodes in the parent thread of t, and these touches are descendants of the right child of v.*

Informally, the local touch constraint implies that a thread that needs the value of a future should create the future it-

```
void MethodA {
    Future x = some computation;
    Future y = some computation;
    a = y.touch();
    b = x.touch();
}
```

(a)

```
void MethodB {
    Future x = some computation;
    fork MethodC(x);
}
void MethodC(Future f){
    a = f.touch();
}
```

(b)

Figure 4. Two examples illustrating single-touch computations are more flexible than fork-join computations

self. Note that in a structured computation with local touch constraint, a future thread is now allowed to evaluate multiple futures and these futures can be touched at different times. Though allowing a future thread to compute multiple futures is not very common, Blelloch and Reid-Miller [7] point out that it can be useful for some future-parallel computations like pipeline parallelism [7, 9, 16, 17, 21]. We will show in Section 6.1 that work-stealing parallel executions of computations satisfying the local touch constraint also have relatively low cache overheads. Note that structured computations with both single touch and local touch constraints are still a superset of fork-join computations.

5. Structured Single-Touch Computations

5.1 Future Thread First at Each Fork

We now analyze cache performance of work stealing on parallel executions of structured single-touch computations. We will show that work stealing has relatively low cache overhead if the processor at a fork always chooses the future thread to execute first, and puts the parent future into its deque. For brevity, all the arguments and results in this section assume that every execution chooses the future thread at a fork to execute first.

LEMMA 4. *In the sequential execution of a structured single-touch computation, any touch x's future parent is executed before x's local parent, and the right child of x's corresponding fork v immediately follows x's future parent.*

Proof. By induction. Given a DAG, initially let S be an empty set and T the set of all touches. Note that

$$S \cap T = \emptyset \text{ and } S \cup T = \{\text{all touches}\}. \qquad (1)$$

Consider any touch x in T, such that x has no ancestors in T. (That is, x has no ancestor nodes that are also touches.) Let t be the future thread of x and v the corresponding fork. Note that x's future parent is the last node of t by definition. When the single processor executes v, the processor pushes v's right child into the deque and continues to execute thread t. By hypothesis, there are no touches by t, since any touch by t must be an ancestor of x. There may be some forks in t. However, whenever the single processor executes a fork in t, it pushes the right child of that fork, which is a node in t, into the deque and hence t (i.e., a node in t) is right below v's right child in the deque. Therefore, the processor will always resume thread t before the right child of v. Since there is no touch by t, all the nodes in t are ready to execute one by one. Thus, when the future parent of the touch x is executed eventually, the right child of v is right at the bottom of the deque. By the single touch constraint, the local parent of x is a descendant of the right child of v, so the local parent of x cannot be executed yet. Thus, the processor will pop the right child of v from the bottom of the deque to execute. Since this node is not a touch, it is ready to execute. Therefore, x satisfies the following two properties.

PROPERTY 5. *Its future parent is executed before its local parent.*

PROPERTY 6. *The right child of its corresponding fork immediately follows its future parent.*

Now set $S = S \cup \{x\}$ and $T = T - \{x\}$. Thus, all touches in S satisfy Properties 5 and 6. Note that Equation 1 still holds.

Now suppose that at some point all nodes in S satisfy Properties 5 and 6, and that Equation 1 holds. Again, we now consider a touch x in T, such that no touches in T are ancestors of x, i.e., all the touches that are ancestors of x are in S. Since the computation graph is a DAG, there must be such an x as long as T is not empty. Let t be the future thread of x and v the corresponding fork. If there are no touches by t, then x satisfies Properties 5 and 6, as shown above. Now assume there are touches by t. Since those touches are ancestors of x, they are all in S and hence they all satisfy Property 5. When the processor executes v, it pushes v's right child into the deque and starts executing t. Similar to what we showed above, when the processor gets to a fork in t, it will always push t into its deque, right below the right child of v. Thus, the processor will always resume t before the right child of v. When the processor gets to the local parent of a touch by t, we know the future parent of the touch has already been executed since the touch satisfies Property 5. Thus, the processor can immediately execute that touch and continue to execute t. Therefore, the processor will eventually execute the future parent of x while the right

child of t is still the next node to pop in the deque. Again, since the local parent of x is a descendant of the right child of v, the local parent of x as well as x cannot be executed yet. Therefore, the processor will now pop the right child of v to execute, and hence x satisfies Properties 5 and 6. Now we set $S = S \cup \{x\}$ and $T = T - \{x\}$. Therefore, all touches in S satisfy Properties 5 and 6, and Equation 1) also holds. By induction, we have $S = \{\text{all touches}\}$ and all touches satisfy Properties 5 and 6. $\qquad \square$

Acar *et al.* [1] have shown that the number of additional cache misses in a work-stealing parallel computation is bounded by the product of the number of deviations and the number of cache lines. It is easy to see that only two types of nodes in a DAG can be deviations: the touches and the child nodes of forks that are not chosen to execute first. Since we assume the future thread (left child) at a fork is always executed first, only the right children of forks can be deviations. Next, we bound the number of deviations incurred by a work-stealing parallel execution to bound its cache overhead.

LEMMA 7. *Let t be the future thread at a fork v in a structured single-touch computation. If t's touch x or v's right child u is a deviation, then either u is stolen or there is a touch by t which is a deviation.*

Proof. By Lemma 4, a touch is a deviation if and only if its local parent is executed before its future parent. Now suppose a processor p executes v and pushes u into its deque. Assume that u is not stolen and there are no touches by t that are deviations. Thus, u will stay in p's deque until p pops it out. The proof of this lemma is similar to that of Lemma 4. After p executes v, it moves to execute thread t. There are two possibilities that can make p move from t to another thread: when it executes a fork or the local parent of a touch. When it executes a fork, it will push t (the right child of the fork) into its deque, right below u. Since a thief processor always steals from the top of a deque, and by hypothesis u is not stolen, t cannot be stolen. Thus, p will always resume t before u and then u will become the next node in the deque to pop. When p executes the local parent of a touch by t, the future parent of that touch must have been executed, since we assume that touch is not a deviation. Thus, p can continue to execute that touch immediately and keep moving on in t. Therefore, p will finally get to the local parent of x and then pop u out from its deque, since x is a descendant of u and x cannot be execute yet. Hence, neither x nor u can be a deviation. $\qquad \square$

THEOREM 8. *If, at each fork, the future thread is chosen to execute first, then a parallel execution with work stealing incurs $O(PT_\infty^2)$ deviations and $O(CPT_\infty^2)$ additional cache misses in expectation on a structured single-touch computation, where (as usual) P is the number of processors involved*

160

in this computation, T_∞ is the computation span, and C is the number of cache lines.

Proof. Arora *et al.* have shown that in a parallel execution with work stealing, there are in expectation $O(PT_\infty)$ steals [3]. Now let us count how many deviations these steals can incur. A steal on the right child u of a fork v can make u and v's corresponding touch x_1 deviations. Suppose x_1 is a touch by a thread t_2, then the right child of the fork of t_2 and t_2's touch x_2 can be deviations. If x_2 is a deviation and x_2 is a touch by another thread t_3, then the right child of the fork of t_3 and t_3's touch x_3 can be deviation too. Note that x_2 is a descendant of x_1 and x_3 is a descendant of x_2. By repeating this observation, we can find a chain of touches $x_1, x_2, x_3, ..., x_n$, called a *deviation chain*, such that each x_i and the right child of the corresponding fork of x_i can be deviations. Since for each $i > 1$, x_i is a descendant of x_2, $x_1, x_2, x_3, ..., x_n$ is in a directed path in the computation DAG. Since the length of any path is at most T_∞, we have $n \le T_\infty$. Since each future thread has only one touch, there is only one deviation chain for a steal. Since there are $O(PT_\infty)$ steals in expectation in a parallel execution [3], we can find in expectation $O(PT_\infty)$ deviation chains and in total $O(PT_\infty^2)$ touches and right children of the corresponding forks involved, i.e., $O(PT_\infty^2)$ deviations involved.

Next, we prove by contradiction that no other touches or right children of forks can be deviations. suppose there is touch y, such that y or the right child of the corresponding fork of y is a deviation, and that y is not in any deviation chain. The right child of the corresponding fork of y can not be stolen, since by hypothesis y is not the first touch in any of those chains. Thus by Lemma 7, there is a touch y' by the future thread of y and y' is a deviation. Note that $y's$ cannot be in any deviation chain either. Otherwise y and the deviation chain y' is in will form a deviation chain too, a contradiction. Therefore, by repeating such "tracing back", we will end up at a deviation touch that is not in any deviation chain and has no touches as its ancestors. Therefore, there are no touches by the future thread of this touch, and the right child of the corresponding future fork of it is not stolen, contradicting Lemma 7.

The upper bound on the expected number of additional cache misses follows from the result of Acar *et al.* [1] that the number of additional cache misses in a work-stealing parallel computation is bounded by the product of the number of deviations and the number of cache lines. $\square$

The bound on the number of deviations in Theorem 8 is tight, and the bound on the number of additional cache misses is tight within a factor of C, as shown below in Theorem 9.

THEOREM 9. *If, at each fork node, the future thread is chosen to execute first, then a parallel execution with work stealing can incur $\Omega(PT_\infty^2)$ deviations and $\Omega(PT_\infty^2)$ addi-*

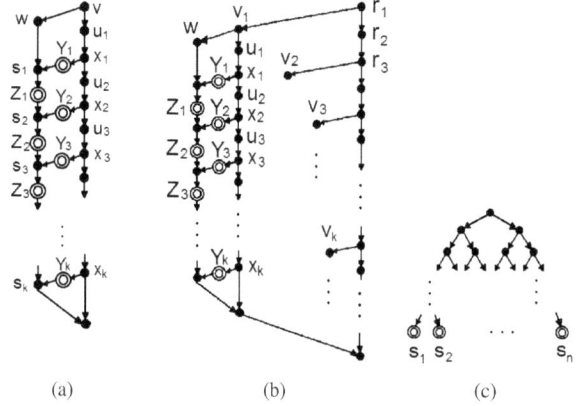

(a)   (b)   (c)

Figure 5. Figure (c) shows a DAG on which work stealing can incur $\Omega(PT_\infty^2)$ deviations and $\Omega(PT_\infty^2)$ additional cache misses. It uses the DAGs in (a) and (b) as building blocks.

tional cache misses on a structured single-touch computation, while the sequential execution of this computation incurs $O(PT_\infty^2/C)$ cache misses.

Proof. Figure 5(c) shows a computation DAG on which we can get the bounds we want to prove. The DAG in Figure 5(c) uses the DAGs in Figures 5(a) and 5(b) as building blocks. Let's look at Figures 5(a) first. Suppose there are two processors p_1 and p_2 executing the DAG in Figure 5(a). Suppose p_2 executes v, pushes u_1 into its deque, and then falls asleep before executing w. Now suppose p_1 steals u_1. For each $i \le k$, s_i or Z_i cannot be executed since w has not been executed yet. Now p_1 takes a solo run, executing $u_1, x_1, Y_1, u_2, x_2, Y_2, ..., x_k, Y_k$. After p_1 finishes, p_2 wakes up and executes the rest of the computation DAG. Note that the right (local) parent of s_i is executed before the left (future) parent of the touch is executed. Thus, by Lemma 4, each s_i is a deviation. Hence, this parallel execution incurs k deviations and the computation span of the computation is $\Theta(k)$.

Now let us consider a parallel execution of the computation in 5(b). For each $i \le k$, the subgraph rooted at v_i is identical to the computation DAG in 5(a) (except that the last node of the subgraph has an extra edge pointing to a node of the main thread). Suppose there are three processors p_1, p_2, and p_3 working on the computation. Assume p_2 executes r_1 and v_1 and then falls asleep when it is about to execute w. p_3 now steals r_2 from p_2 and then falls asleep too. Then p_1 steals u_1 from p_2's deque. Now p_1 and p_2 execute the subgraph rooted at v_1 in the same way they execute the DAG in 5(a). After p_1 and p_2 finish, p_3 wakes up, executes r_2. Now these three processors start working on the subgraph rooted at r_3 in the same way they executed the graph rooted at r_1. By repeating this, the execution ends up incurring k^2 deviations when all the k subgraphs are done.

161

Since the length of the path $r_1, r_2, r_3...$ on the right-hand side is $\Theta(k)$, the computation span of the DAG is still $\Theta(k)$.

Now we construct the final computation DAG, as in Figure 5(c). The "top" nodes of the DAG are all forks, each spawning a future thread. Thus, they form a binary tree and the number of threads increase exponentially. The DAG stops creating new threads at level $\Theta(\log n)$ when it has n threads rooted at $S_1, S_2, ..., S_n$, respectively. For each i, the subgraph rooted at S_i is identical to the DAG in 5(b). Suppose there are $3n$ processors working on the computation. It is easy to see n processors can eventually get to $S_1, S_2, ..., S_n$. Suppose they all fall asleep immediately after executing the first two nodes of S_i(corresponding to r_1 and v_1 in Figure 5(b)) and then each two of the rest $2n$ free processors join to work on the subgraph rooted at S_i, in the same way p_1, p_2 and p_3 did in Figure 5(b). Therefore, this execution will finally incur nk^2 deviations, while the computation span of the DAG is $\Theta(k + \log n)$. Therefore, by setting $n = P/3$, we get a parallel execution that incurs $\Omega(PT_\infty^2)$ deviations, when $\log P = O(k)$.

To get the bound on the number of additional cache misses, we just need to modify the graph in 5(a) as follows. For each $1 \leq i \leq k$, Y_i consists of a chain of C nodes $y_{i1}, y_{i2}, ..., y_{iC}$, where C is the number of cache lines. $y_{i1}, y_{i2}, ..., y_{iC}$ access memory blocks $m_1, m_2, ..., m_C$, respectively. Similarly, each Z_i consists of a chain of C nodes $z_{i1}, z_{i2}, ..., z_{iC}$. $z_{i1}, z_{i2}, ..., z_{iC}$ access memory blocks $m_C, m_{C-1}, ..., m_1$, respectively. all s_i access memory block m_C. For all $1 \leq i \leq k$, u_i and x_i both access memory block m_{C+1}. It does not matter which memory blocks the other nodes in the DAG access. For simplicity, assume the other nodes do not access memory. In the sequential execution, the single processor has $m_1, m_2, ..., m_C$ in its cache after executing v, w, u_1, x_1, Y_1, Z_1 and it has incurred $(C + 1)$ cache misses so far. Now it executes u_2 and x_2, incurring one cache miss at node u_2 by replacing m_C with m_{C+1} in its cache, since m_C is the least recently used block. When it executes Y_2 and Z_2, it only incurs one cache miss by replacing m_{C+1} with m_C at the last node of Y_2, y_{2C}. Likewise, it is easy to see that the sequential execution will only incur cache misses at nodes u_i and at the last nodes of Y_i for all i. Hence, the sequential execution incurs only $O(k + C)$ cache misses. When $k = \Omega(C)$, the sequential execution incurs only $O(k)$ cache misses.

Now consider the parallel execution by two processors p_1 and p_2 we described before. p_2 will incur only C cache misses, since Z_i and s_i only access m different blocks $m_1, m_2, ..., m_C$ and hence p_2 doesn't need to swap any memory blocks out of its cache. However, p_1 will incur lots of cache misses. After executing each Y_i, p_1 will execute u_{i+1}. Thus at u_{i+1}, one cache miss is incurred and m_1 is replaced with m_{C+1}, since m_1 is the least recently used block. Then, when p_1 executes the first node $y_{(i+1)1}$ in Y_i, , m_1 is not in its cache. Since m_2 now becomes the

least recently used memory block in p_1's cache, m_2 is replaced by m_1. Thus, m_2 will not be in the cache when it is in need at $y_{(i+1)2}$. Therefore, it is obvious that p_1 will incur a cache miss at each node in Y_i and hence incur Ck cache misses in total in the entire execution. Note that the computation span of this modified DAG is $\Theta(Ck)$, since each Z_i now has C nodes. Therefore, the sequential execution and the parallel execution actually incur $\Theta(T_\infty/C)$ and $\Theta(T_\infty)$, respectively, when $\log P = O(k)$. Therefore, if we use this modified DAG as the building blocks in 5(c), we will get the bound on the number of additional cache misses stated in the theorem. $\square$

5.2 Parent Thread First at Each Fork

In this section, we show that if the parent thread is always executed first at a fork, a work-stealing parallel execution of a structured single-touch computation can incur $\Omega(tT_\infty)$ deviations and $\Omega(CtT_\infty)$ additional cache misses, where t is the number of touches in the computation, while the corresponding sequential execution incurs only a small number of cache misses. This bound matches the upper bound for general, unstructured future-parallel computations [22][2]. This result, combined with the result in Section 5.1, shows that choosing the future threads at forks to execute first achieves better cache locality for work-stealing schedulers on structured single-touch computations.

THEOREM 10. *If, at each fork, the parent thread is chosen to execute first, then a parallel execution with work stealing can incur $\Omega(tT_\infty)$ deviations and $\Omega(CtT_\infty)$ additional cache misses on a structured single-touch computation, while the sequential execution of this computation incurs only $O(C + t)$ cache misses.*

Proof. The final DAG we want to construct is in Figure 7. It uses the DAGs in Figure 6 as building blocks. We first describe how a single deviation at a touch u_3 can incur $\Omega(T_\infty)$ deviations and $\Omega(CT_\infty)$ additional cache misses in Figure 6(a). In order to get the bound we want to prove, here we follow the convention in [1, 22] to distinguish between touches and join nodes in the DAG. More specifically, y_i is a join node, not a touch, for each $1 \leq i \leq n$. For each $1 \leq i \leq n$, node x_i accesses memory block m_1 and y_i accesses memory block m_{C+1}. Z_i consists of a chain of C nodes $z_{i1}, z_{i2}, ..., z_{iC}$, accessing memory blocks $m_1, m_2, ..., m_C$ respectively. All the other nodes do not access memory. Assume in the sequential execution a single processor p_1 executes the entire DAG in Figure 6(a). Suppose initially the left (future) parent of u_3 has already been executed. p_1 starts executing the DAG at u_1. Since p_1 always stays on the parent thread at a fork, it first pushes s into

---

[2]The bound on the expected number of deviations in [22] is actually $O(PT_\infty + tT_\infty)$. However, as pointed out in [22], a simple fork-join computation can get $\Omega(PT_\infty)$ deviations. Hence we focus on the more interesting part $\Omega(tT_\infty)$.

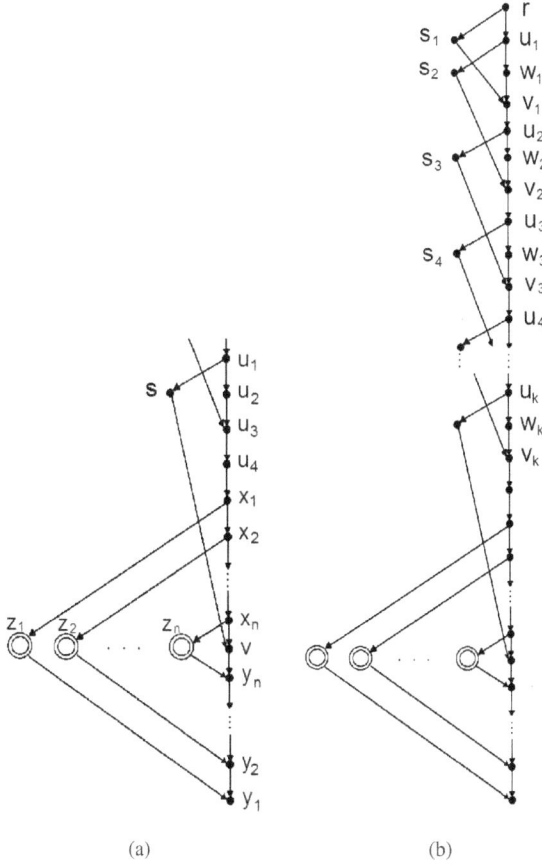

Figure 6. DAGs used by Figure 7 as building blocks.

out and executes all the nodes $z_{(n-1)1}, z_{(n-1)2}, ..., z_{(n-1)}C$ in Z_{n-1} one by one. When p_1 executes $z_{(n-1)1}$, it replaces m_2 with m_1, and when it executes $z_{(n-1)2}$, it replaces m_3 with m_2, and so on. The same thing happens to all Z_i and y_i. Thus, p_1 will incur a cache miss at every node afterwards, ending up with $\Omega(Cn)$ cache misses in total. Note that the computation span of this DAG is $T_\infty = \Theta(C + n)$. Thus, this execution with a deviation at u_3 incurs $\Omega(CT_\infty)$ cache misses when $n = \Omega(C)$. Moreover, all y_i are deviations and hence this execution incurs $\Omega(T_\infty)$ deviations.

Now let us see how a single steal at the beginning of a thread results in $\Omega(T_\infty)$ deviations and $\Omega(CT_\infty)$ cache misses at the end of the thread. Figure 6(b) presents such a computation. First we consider the sequential execution by a processor p_1. It is easy to check p_1 executes nodes in the order $r, u_1, w_1, s_2, s_1, v_1, u_2, w_2, v_2, u_3, w_3, s_4, s_3, v_3, u_4, ...$ The key observation is that w_i is executed before s_i is executed for any odd numbered i while w_i is executed after s_i is executed for any even numbered i. This statement can be proved by induction. Obviously, this holds for $i = 1$ and $i = 2$, as we showed before. Now suppose this fact holds for all $1, 2, ..., i$, for some even numbered i. Now suppose p_1 executes u_{i-1}. Then p_1 pushes s_i into its deque and executes w_{i-1}. Since we know w_{i-1} should be executed before s_{i-1}, s_{i-1} has not been executed yet. Moreover, s_{i-1} must already be in the deque before s_i was pushed into the deque, since s_{i-1}'s parent u_{i-2} has been executed and s_{i-1} is ready to execute. Now p_1 pops s_i to execute. Since v_i is not ready to execute, p_1 pops s_{i-1} and then executes s_{i-1}, v_{i-1}, u_i, and pushes s_{i+1} into the deque. Now p_1 continues to execute w_i, v_i, u_{i+1} and pushes s_{i+1} into its deque. Then p_i executes w_{i+1} and pops s_{i+2}, since v_{i+1} is not ready due to s_{i+1}. Now we can see w_{i+1} and s_{i+2} have been executed, but s_{i+1} and w_{i+2} not yet. Therefore, w_{i+1} is executed before s_{i+1} and w_{i+2} is executed after s_{i+2}. That is, the statement holds for $i + 1$ and $i + 2$, and hence the proof.

The subgraph rooted at u_k is identical to the graph in Figure 6(a), with v_k corresponding to u_3 in Figure 6(a). Therefore, if k is an even number, v_k's left parent has been executed when w_k is executed and hence the sequential execution will incur only $O(C)$ cache misses on the subgraph rooted at u_k.

Now consider a parallel execution of the DAG in 6(b) by two processors p_1 and p_2. p_1 executes r and pushes s_1 into its deque. p_2 immediately steals s_1 and executes it. Then p_2 falls asleep, leaving p_1 executing the rest of the DAG alone. It is easy to check p_1 will execute the nodes in the DAG in the order $u_1, w_1, v_1, u_2, w_2, s_3, s_2, v_2, u_3, w_3, v_3, u_4, s_4, ...$ It can be proved by induction that w_i is executed after s_i is executed for any odd numbered i while w_i is executed before s_i is executed for any even numbered i, which is opposite to the order in the sequential execution. The induction proof is similar to that of the previous observation in the sequential execution, so we omit the proof here. If k is an even number,

its deque, continues to execute u_2, u_3, u_4, and then executes $x_1, x_2, ..., x_n$ while pushing $z_{11}, z_{21}, ..., z_{n1}$ into its deque. Since v cannot be executed due to s, p_1 pops z_{n1} out of its deque and executes the nodes in Z_n. Then p_1 executes all the nodes in $Z_{n-1}, Z_{n-2}, ..., Z_1$, in this order. So far p_1 has only incurred C cache misses, since all the nodes it has executed only access memory blocks $m_1, ..., m_C$ and hence it did not need to swap any memory blocks out of its cache. Now p_1 executes s, v and then $y_n, y_{n-1}, ..., y_1$, incurring only one more cache miss by replacing m_1 with m_{C+1} at y_n. Hence, this execution incurs $O(C)$ cache misses in total. Note that the left parent of y_i is executed before the right parent y_i for all i.

Now assume in another execution by p_1, the left parent of u_3 is in p_1's deque when p_1 starts executing u_1. Thus, u_3 is a deviation with respect to the previous execution. Since u_3 is not ready to execute after p_1 executes u_2, p_1 pops s out of its deque to execute. Since v is not ready, p_1 now pops the left parent of u_3 to execute and then executes $u_3, u_4, x_1, x_2, ..., x_n, v$. Now p_1 pops z_{n1} out and executes all the nodes Z_n. Note that y_n is now ready to execute and the memory blocks in p_1's cache at the moment are $m_1, m_2, ..., m_C$. Now p_1 executes y_n, replacing the least recently used block m_1 with m_{C+1}. p_1 then pops $z_{(n-1)1}$

163

w_k will be executed before the left parent of v_k and hence this execution will incur $\Omega(T_\infty)$ deviations and $\Omega(CT_\infty)$ cache misses when $n = \Omega(C)$ and $n = \Omega(k)$.

The final DAG we want to construct is in Figure 7. This is actually a generalization of the DAG in Figure 6(b). Instead of having one fork u_i before each touch v_i, it has two forks u_i and x_i, for each i. After each touch v_i, the thread at y_i splits into two identical branches, touching the futures spawned at u_i and x_i, respectively. In this figure, we only depict the right branch and omit the identical left branch. As we can see, the right branch later has a touch v_{i+1} touching the future s_{i+1} spawned at the fork x_i. If we only look at the thread on the right-hand side, it is essentially the same as the DAG in Figure6(b). The sequential execution of this DAG by p_1 is similar to that in Figure6(b). The only difference is that p_1 at each y_i will execute the right branch and then the left branch recursively. Similarly, it can be proved by induction that w_i is executed before s_i is executed for any odd numbered i while w_i is executed after s_i is executed for any even numbered i. Obviously this also holds for each left branch. Now consider a parallel execution by two processors p_1 and p_2. p_1 first executes r. p_2 immediately steals s_1 and executes it and then sleeps forever. Now p_1 makes a solo run to execute the rest of the DAG. Again, we can prove by induction that w_i is executed after s_i is executed for any odd numbered i while w_i is executed before s_i is executed for any even numbered i, which is opposite to the order in the sequential execution. The proofs of the two observations above are a little more complicated than those for the DAG in Figure6(b), but the ideas are essentially the same. Due to space limits, we again omit the two induction proofs.

By splitting each thread into two after each y_i, the number of branches in the DAG increases exponentially. Suppose there are t touches in the DAG. Thus, there are eventually $\Theta(t)$ branches and the height of this structure is $\Theta(\log t)$. At the end of each branch is a subgraph identical to the DAG in Figure 6(a). Therefore, the parallel execution with only one steal can end up incurring $\Theta(tn)$ deviations and $\Theta(Ctn)$ cache misses. The sequential execution incurs only $\Theta(C+t)$ cache misses, since the sequential execution will incur only 2 cache misses by swapping m_{C+1} in and out at each branch, after it incurs C cache misses to load $m_1, m_2, ..., m_C$ at the first branch. hence, when $n = \Omega(\log t)$ and $n = \Omega(C)$, we get the bound stated in the theorem. $\qquad\square$

6. Other Kinds of Structured Computations

It is natural to ask whether other kinds of structured computations can also achieve relatively good cache locality. We now consider two alternative kinds of restrictions.

6.1 Structured Local-Touch Computations

In this section, we prove that work-stealing parallel executions of structured local-touch computations also have rela-

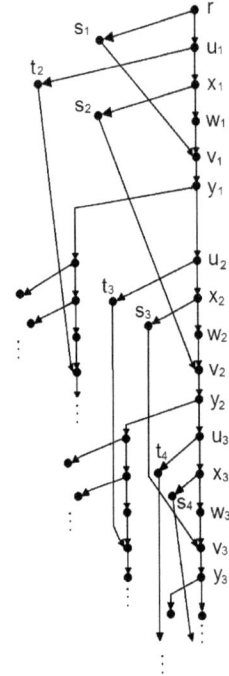

Figure 7. A DAG on which work stealing can incur $\Omega(tT_\infty)$ deviations and $\Omega(CtT_\infty)$ if it chooses parents threads to execute first at forks. This example uses the DAGs in Figure 6 as building blocks.

tively good cache locality, if the future thread is chosen to execute first at each fork. This result, combined with Theorems 8 and 10, implies that work-stealing schedulers for structured computations are likely better off choosing future threads to execute first at forks.

LEMMA 11. *In the sequential execution of a structured local-touch computation where the future thread at a fork is always chosen to execute first, any touch x's future parent is executed before x's local parent, and the right child of any fork v immediately follows the last node of the future thread spawned at v, i.e., the future parent of the last touch of the future thread.*

The proof is omitted because it is almost identical to the proof of Lemma 4.

THEOREM 12. *If the future thread at a fork is always chosen to execute first, then a parallel execution with work stealing incurs $O(PT_\infty^2)$ deviations and $O(CPT_\infty^2)$ additional cache misses in expectation on a structured local-touch computation.*

Proof. Let v be a fork that spawns a future thread t. Now we consider a parallel execution. Let p be a processor that executes v and pushes the right child of v into its deque. Suppose the right child of v is not stolen. Now consider the subgraph G' consisting of t and its descendant threads. Note that G' itself is a structured computation DAG with local touch constraint. Now p starts executing G'.

According to local touch constraint, the only nodes outside G' that connect to the nodes in G' are v and the touches of t, and c is the only node outside G' that the nodes in G' depend on. Now v has been executed and the touches of t are not ready to execute due to the right child of v. Hence, p is able to make a sequential execution on G' without waiting for any node outside to be done or jumping to a node outside, as long as no one steals a node in G' from p's deque. Since we assume the right child of v will not be stolen and any nodes in G' can only be pushed into p's deque below v, no nodes in G' can be stolen. Hence, G' will be executed by a sequential execution by p. Therefore, there are no deviations in G'. After p executed the last node in G', which is the last node in t, p pops the right child of v to execute. Hence, the right child of v cannot be a deviation either, if it is not stolen. That is, those nodes can be deviations only if the right child of v is stolen. Since there are in expectation $O(PT_\infty)$ steals in an parallel execution and each future thread has at most T_∞ touches, the expected number of deviations is bounded by $O(PT_\infty^2)$ and the expected number of additional touches is bounded by $O(CPT_\infty^2)$. □

6.2 Structured Computations with Super Final Nodes

As discussed in Section 4, in languages such as Java, the program's main thread typically releases all resources at the end of an execution. To model this structure, we add an edge from the last node of each thread to the final node of the computation DAG. Thus, the final node becomes the only node with in-degree greater than 2. Since the final node is always the last to execute, simply adding those edges pointing to the final node into a DAG will not change the execution order of the nodes in the DAG. It is easy to see that having such a super node will not change the upper bound on the cache overheads of the work-stealing parallel executions of a structured computation.

For structured computations with super final nodes, it also makes sense to relax slightly the single-touch constraint.

DEFINITION 13. *A structured single-touch computation with a super final node is one where each future thread t at a fork v has at least one and at most two touches, a descendant of v's right child and the super final node.*

In such a computation, a future thread can have the super final node as its only touch. This structure corresponds to a program where one thread forks another thread to accomplish a side-effect instead of computing a value. The parent thread never touches the resulting future, but the computation as a whole cannot terminate until the forked thread completes its work.

Now we prove that the parallel executions of structured single-touch computations with super final nodes also have relatively low cache overheads.

LEMMA 14. *In the sequential execution of a structured single-touch computation with a super final node, where the future thread at a fork is always chosen to execute first, any touch x's future parent is executed before x's local parent, and the right child of any fork v immediately follows the last node of the future thread spawned at v, i.e., the future parent of the last touch of the future thread.*

LEMMA 15. *Let t be the future thread at a fork v in a structured single-touch computation with a super final node. If a touch of t or v's right child u is a deviation, then either u is stolen or there is a touch by t which is a deviation.*

The proofs of these two lemmas are omitted because they are almost identical to the proofs of Lemma 4 and Lemma 7, respectively.

THEOREM 16. *If, at each fork, the future thread is chosen to execute first, then a parallel execution with work stealing incurs $O(PT_\infty^2)$ deviations and $O(CPT_\infty^2)$ additional cache misses in expectation on a structured single-touch computation with a super final node.*

Proof. The proof is similar to that of Theorem 8. The only difference is that if a touch by a thread t is a deviation, now the two touches of t can both be deviations, which could be a trouble for constructing the deviation chains. Fortunately, one of these two touches is the super final node, which is always the last node to execute and hence will not make the touches of other threads become deviations. Therefore, we can still get a unique deviation chain starting from a steal and hence the proof of Theorem 8 still applies here. □

7. Conclusions

We have focused primarily on structured single-touch computations, in which futures are used in a restricted way. We saw that for such computations, a parallel execution by a work-stealing scheduler that runs future threads first can incur at most $O(CPT_\infty^2)$ cache misses more than the corresponding sequential execution, a substantially better cache locality than the $\Omega(CPT_\infty + CtT_\infty)$ worst-case additional cache misses possible with unstructured use of futures. Although we cannot prove this claim formally, we think that these restrictions correspond to program structures that would occur naturally anyway in many (but not all) parallel programs that use futures. For example, Cilk [9] programs are structured single-touch computations, and that Belloch and Reid-Miller [7] observe that the single-touch requirement substantially simplifies implementations.

We also considered some alternative restrictions on future use, such as structured local-touch computations, and structured computations with super final nodes, that also incur a relatively low cache-locality penalty. In terms of future work, we think it would be promising to investigate how far these restrictions can be weakened or modified while still avoiding a high cache-locality penalty. We would also like to understand how these observations can be exploited by future compilers and run-time systems.

References

[1] Umut A. Acar, Guy E. Blelloch, and Robert D. Blumofe. The data locality of work stealing. In *Proceedings of the twelfth annual ACM symposium on Parallel algorithms and architectures*, SPAA '00, pages 1–12, New York, NY, USA, 2000. ACM.

[2] Kunal Agrawal, Yuxiong He, and Charles E. Leiserson. Adaptive work stealing with parallelism feedback. In *Proceedings of the 12th ACM SIGPLAN symposium on Principles and practice of parallel programming*, PPoPP '07, pages 112–120, New York, NY, USA, 2007. ACM.

[3] Nimar S. Arora, Robert D. Blumofe, and C. Greg Plaxton. Thread scheduling for multiprogrammed multiprocessors. In *Proceedings of the tenth annual ACM symposium on Parallel algorithms and architectures*, SPAA '98, pages 119–129, New York, NY, USA, 1998. ACM.

[4] Arvind, Rishiyur S. Nikhil, and Keshav K. Pingali. I-structures: data structures for parallel computing. *ACM Trans. Program. Lang. Syst.*, 11(4):598–632, October 1989.

[5] Guy E. Blelloch. Programming parallel algorithms. *Commun. ACM*, 39(3):85–97, March 1996.

[6] Guy E. Blelloch, Phillip B. Gibbons, and Yossi Matias. Provably efficient scheduling for languages with fine-grained parallelism. In *Proceedings of the seventh annual ACM symposium on Parallel algorithms and architectures*, SPAA '95, pages 1–12, New York, NY, USA, 1995. ACM.

[7] Guy E. Blelloch and Margaret Reid-Miller. Pipelining with futures. In *Proceedings of the ninth annual ACM symposium on Parallel algorithms and architectures*, SPAA '97, pages 249–259, New York, NY, USA, 1997. ACM.

[8] Robert D. Blumofe, Matteo Frigo, Christopher F. Joerg, Charles E. Leiserson, and Keith H. Randall. An analysis of dag-consistent distributed shared-memory algorithms. In *Proceedings of the eighth annual ACM symposium on Parallel algorithms and architectures*, SPAA '96, pages 297–308, New York, NY, USA, 1996. ACM.

[9] Robert D. Blumofe, Christopher F. Joerg, Bradley C. Kuszmaul, Charles E. Leiserson, Keith H. Randall, and Yuli Zhou. Cilk: an efficient multithreaded runtime system. In *Proceedings of the fifth ACM SIGPLAN symposium on Principles and practice of parallel programming*, PPOPP '95, pages 207–216, New York, NY, USA, 1995. ACM.

[10] Robert D. Blumofe and Charles E. Leiserson. Space-efficient scheduling of multithreaded computations. *SIAM J. Comput.*, 27(1):202–229, February 1998.

[11] Robert D. Blumofe and Charles E. Leiserson. Scheduling multithreaded computations by work stealing. *J. ACM*, 46(5):720–748, September 1999.

[12] F. Warren Burton and M. Ronan Sleep. Executing functional programs on a virtual tree of processors. In *Proceedings of the 1981 conference on Functional programming languages and computer architecture*, FPCA '81, pages 187–194, New York, NY, USA, 1981. ACM.

[13] David Chase and Yossi Lev. Dynamic circular work-stealing deque. In *Proceedings of the seventeenth annual ACM symposium on Parallelism in algorithms and architectures*, SPAA '05, pages 21–28, New York, NY, USA, 2005. ACM.

[14] Matthew Fluet, Mike Rainey, John Reppy, and Adam Shaw. Implicitly-threaded parallelism in manticore. In *Proceedings of the 13th ACM SIGPLAN international conference on Functional programming*, ICFP '08, pages 119–130, New York, NY, USA, 2008. ACM.

[15] Matteo Frigo, Charles E. Leiserson, and Keith H. Randall. The implementation of the cilk-5 multithreaded language. In *Proceedings of the ACM SIGPLAN 1998 conference on Programming language design and implementation*, PLDI '98, pages 212–223, New York, NY, USA, 1998. ACM.

[16] John Giacomoni, Tipp Moseley, and Manish Vachharajani. Fastforward for efficient pipeline parallelism: a cache-optimized concurrent lock-free queue. In *Proceedings of the 13th ACM SIGPLAN Symposium on Principles and practice of parallel programming*, PPoPP '08, pages 43–52, New York, NY, USA, 2008. ACM.

[17] Michael I. Gordon, William Thies, and Saman Amarasinghe. Exploiting coarse-grained task, data, and pipeline parallelism in stream programs. In *Proceedings of the 12th international conference on Architectural support for programming languages and operating systems*, ASPLOS XII, pages 151–162, New York, NY, USA, 2006. ACM.

[18] Robert H. Halstead, Jr. Implementation of multilisp: Lisp on a multiprocessor. In *Proceedings of the 1984 ACM Symposium on LISP and functional programming*, LFP '84, pages 9–17, New York, NY, USA, 1984. ACM.

[19] Robert H. Halstead, Jr. Multilisp: a language for concurrent symbolic computation. *ACM Trans. Program. Lang. Syst.*, 7(4):501–538, October 1985.

[20] D. A. Kranz, R. H. Halstead, Jr., and E. Mohr. Mul-t: a high-performance parallel lisp. In *Proceedings of the ACM SIGPLAN 1989 Conference on Programming language design and implementation*, PLDI '89, pages 81–90, New York, NY, USA, 1989. ACM.

[21] I-Ting Angelina Lee, Charles E. Leiserson, Tao B. Schardl, Jim Sukha, and Zhunping Zhang. On-the-fly pipeline parallelism. In *Proceedings of the 25th ACM symposium on Parallelism in algorithms and architectures*, SPAA '13, pages 140–151, New York, NY, USA, 2013. ACM.

[22] Daniel Spoonhower, Guy E. Blelloch, Phillip B. Gibbons, and Robert Harper. Beyond nested parallelism: tight bounds on work-stealing overheads for parallel futures. In *Proceedings of the twenty-first annual symposium on Parallelism in algorithms and architectures*, SPAA '09, pages 91–100, New York, NY, USA, 2009. ACM.

Time-Warp: Lightweight Abort Minimization in Transactional Memory

Nuno Diegues   Paolo Romano

INESC-ID / Instituto Superior Técnico, University of Lisbon, Portugal

ndiegues@gsd.inesc-id.pt   romano@inesc-id.pt

Abstract

The notion of permissiveness in Transactional Memory (TM) translates to only aborting a transaction when it cannot be accepted in any history that guarantees correctness criterion. This property is neglected by most TMs, which, in order to maximize implementation's efficiency, resort to aborting transactions under overly conservative conditions.

In this paper we seek to identify a sweet spot between permissiveness and efficiency by introducing the Time-Warp Multi-version algorithm (TWM). TWM is based on the key idea of allowing an update transaction that has performed stale reads (i.e., missed the writes of concurrently committed transactions) to be serialized by "committing it in the past", which we call a *time-warp* commit. At its core, TWM uses a novel, lightweight validation mechanism with little computational overheads. TWM also guarantees that read-only transactions can never be aborted. Further, TWM guarantees *Virtual World Consistency*, a safety property that is deemed as particularly relevant in the context of TM. We demonstrate the practicality of this approach through an extensive experimental study, where we compare TWM with four other TMs, and show an average performance improvement of 65% in high concurrency scenarios.

Categories and Subject Descriptors D.1.3 [*Software*]: Programming Techniques - Concurrent Programming

Keywords Software Transactional Memory; Spurious Abort; Permissiveness; Multi-Version

1. Introduction

The advent of multi-cores has motivated the research of paradigms aimed at simplifying parallel programming. Trans-

PPoPP '14,   February 15–19, 2014, Orlando, Florida, USA.
Copyright © 2014 ACM 978-1-4503-2656-8/14/02. . . $15.00.
http://dx.doi.org/10.1145/2555243.2555259

actional Memory [18] (TM) is probably one of the most prominent proposals in this sense. With TM, programmers are only required to identify *which* code blocks should run atomically, and not *how* concurrent access to shared state should be synchronized to enforce isolation. TMs guarantee correctness by aborting transactions that would otherwise generate unsafe histories [16, 19, 25].

TM implementations achieve this by tracking transparently which memory locations are accessed by transactions. This information is then used to detect conflicts, and possibly abort transactions with the objective of guaranteeing a safe execution. However, to minimize instrumentation's overhead, practical TM implementations suffer of *spurious aborts*, i.e. they abort transactions unnecessarily, even when they did not threaten correctness.

Indeed, existing literature on Software Transactional Memory (STM) has highlighted an inherent trade-off between the efficiency of a TM algorithm, and the number of spurious aborts it produces — the notion of permissiveness [17] was proposed precisely to capture this trade-off. A TM is permissive if it aborts a transaction only when the resulting history (without the abort) does not respect some target correctness criterion (e.g., serializability). Achieving permissiveness, however, comes at a non-negligible cost, both theoretically [21] and in practice [15]. Indeed, most state of the art TMs [9, 10, 13, 14] are far from being permissive, and resort to concurrency control algorithms that generate a large number of spurious aborts, but which have the advantage of allowing highly efficient implementations.

1.1 Problem

To illustrate the problem, consider an example consisting of a sorted linked-list as shown in Fig. 1. This list is accessed by update transactions that insert or remove an element, and by read-only transactions that try to find if a given element is in the list. Let us consider three transactions: a read-only transaction T_1 that seeks element D in the list; an update transaction T_2 that inserts item D; and an update transaction T_3 that removes item E. In the figure we also show a possible execution for the operations of each transaction, and the corresponding result, in a typical STM.

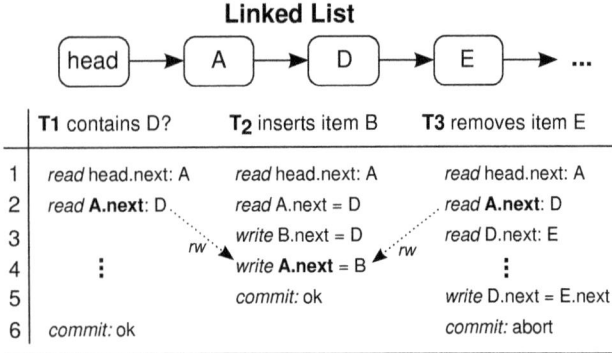

Figure 1. Possible executions accessing a sorted list.

One widely used form of reducing spurious aborts is by serializing a read-only transaction R before any concurrent update transaction. The intuition is that read-only transactions do not write to shared variables and, consequently, are not visible to other transactions. Thus T_1 is allowed to commit in the example — many STMs skip validation for read-only transactions at commit-time [10, 13, 14] because they can be safely serialized in the past.

Let us now consider T_3, which is an update transaction that modifies shared variables. The execution shown for T_3 dictates its abort in state of the art, *practical* STM algorithms, e.g. [9, 13]. To minimize overheads, these algorithms rely on a simple validation scheme, which allows update transactions to commit only if they can be serialized at the present time (6), i.e. after every other so far committed transaction. This validation mechanism has been systematically adopted by a number of STM algorithms (and database concurrency control schemes [2, 6]), for which reason we refer it as *classic validation* rule. In the example, when T_3 is validated at commit, the *next* pointer of element A is found to have been updated after T_3 read it, causing T_3 to abort. Notice, however, that this abort is spurious, given that T_3 could have been safely serialized "in the past", namely before T_2, yielding the equivalent sequential history $T_1 \rightarrow T_3 \rightarrow T_2$.

On the other hand, serializing update transactions in the past is not always possible, as their effects could have been missed by concurrently committed update transactions. This would be the case, for instance, if T_3 had also attempted to insert element C, missing the concurrent update of T_2 and overwriting B. In such a scenario, a cycle in the serialization graph would arise, and T_3 could not be spared from aborting. Overall, minimizing spurious aborts, in a practical way, requires designing algorithms capable of deciding *efficiently* (i.e., without checking the full conflict graph) when update transactions can be serialized in the past.

1.2 Contribution

In this paper we present an algorithm to efficiently tackle the problem identified above: Time-Warp Multi-version (TWM) is a multi-versioned STM that strikes a new balance between permissiveness and efficiency to reduce spurious aborts.

The key idea at the basis of TWM is to allow an update transaction that missed the write committed by a concurrent transaction T' to be serialized "in the past", namely before T'. Unlike TM algorithms that ensure permissiveness [21, 28], TWM exclusively tracks the direct conflicts (more precisely, anti-dependencies [2]) developed by a committing transaction, avoiding onerous validation of the entire conflicts' graph. Thus, TWM's novel validation is sufficiently lightweight to ensure efficiency, but it can also accept far more histories than state of the art, efficient TM algorithms that only allow the commit of update transactions "in the present" (using the *classic validation* rule).

Furthermore, our TWM algorithm provides *Virtual World Consistency* (VWC) [19], which is a safety criterion that provides consistency guarantees even on the snapshots observed by transactions that abort. This means that TWM prevents typical problems (such as infinite loops and run time exceptions) due to observing inconsistent values not producible in *any* sequential execution.

We present an extensive experimental study comparing TWM with four other STMs representative of different designs, guarantees and algorithmic complexities. This study was conducted on a large multi-core machine with 64 cores using several TM benchmarks. The results highlight gains up to $9\times$, with average gains across all benchmarks and compared TMs of 65% in high concurrency scenarios. The remainder of the paper is structured as follows. In Section 2 we discuss related work. Then we focus on describing the TWM algorithm in Section 3. We elaborate on the correctness of TWM in Section 4 and present our experimental study in Section 5. We conclude in Section 6.

2. Related Work

The growing interest in TM research has led to the development of STMs designed to maximize single-thread performance and reduce bookkeeping overhead [9, 10]. As a consequence, these algorithms are optimized for uncontended scenarios and end up rejecting a large number of serializable schedules (i.e., producing many spurious aborts). An interesting strategy in STMs has been to reduce spurious aborts only for read-only transactions. This idea has been formally characterized as mv-permissiveness [26], and has been used in both single-versioned [3] and multi-versioned [11, 22, 27] TM algorithms. Here, we seek to reduce spurious aborts even further than mv-permissiveness.

Several proposals were designed with the main concern of reducing spurious aborts, ultimately achieving permissiveness [17]. These works target different consistency criteria (serializability, virtual-world consistency, opacity) and pursue permissiveness using both probabilistic and deterministic techniques. Clearly, these design decisions have a strong impact on several important details of these algorithms. Nevertheless, it is still possible to coarsely distinguish them into two classes: i) algorithms [15, 21, 28] that instantiate the full transactions' conflict graph and ensure consistency by ensuring its acyclicity [25]; ii) algorithms [4, 8, 17] that determine the possible serialization points of transactions by using time intervals, whose bounds are dynamically adjusted based on the conflicts developed with other concurrent transactions. Concerning the first class of algorithms, which rely on tracking the full conflict graph, these are generally recognized (often by the same authors [15, 21]) to introduce a too large overhead to be used in practical systems. Analogous considerations apply to interval-based algorithms: as previously shown [17], and confirmed by our evaluation study, these algorithms have costly commit procedures, which hinder their viability in various practical scenarios.

The TWM algorithm leverages on the lessons learnt from prior art and identifies a sweet spot between efficiency (i.e., avoiding costly bookkeeping operations) and the ability to avoid spurious aborts: (1) TWM deterministically accepts many common patterns rejected by practical TM algorithms, by tracking only *direct* conflicts between transactions; and (2) it exploits multi-versioning to further reduce aborts and achieve mv-permissiveness.

TWM also shares commonalities with SSI [7], a technique that enhances snapshot isolation [5] DBMSs to provide serializability. In particular, both schemes track direct (anti-dependency [2]) conflicts between transactions to detect possible serializability violations. However, the two algorithms differ significantly both from a theoretical and a pragmatic standpoint. First, unlike TWM, SSI does not ensure mv-permissiveness (i.e., SSI can abort read-only transactions). Further, SSI was designed to be layered on top of, and guarantee interoperability with, a snapshot isolation concurrency control mechanism designed to operate in disk-based DBMS environments. Hence, SSI relies on techniques (e.g., a global lock-table that needs to be periodically garbage collected to avoid spurious aborts) that would have an unbearable overhead in a disk-less environment, such as in TM.

Finally, TWM draws inspiration from Jefferson's Virtual Time and Time-Warp concepts [20], which also aim at decoupling the real-time ordering of events from their actual serialization order. In Jefferson's work, however, Time-Warp is used to reconstruct a safe global state. In TWM, instead, the time-warp mechanism injects "back in time" the versions produced by transactions that observed an obsolete snapshot (to avoid aborting them).

3. The TWM algorithm

Before presenting TWM we introduce preliminary notations.

3.1 Preliminary Notations and Assumptions

As in typical Multi-Version Concurrency Control (MVCC) schemes, TWM maintains a set of versions for each data item k. We refer to data items as variables. A history $\mathcal{H}(\mathcal{S}, \ll)$ over a set of transactions $\mathcal{S}$ consists of two parts:

a partial order among the set of operations generated by the transactions in S and a version order, $\ll$, that is a total order on the committed versions of each k.

We denote with $\mathrm{DSG}(\mathcal{H})$ a Direct Serialization Graph over a history $\mathcal{H}$, i.e., a direct graph containing: a vertex for each committed transaction in $\mathcal{H}$; an edge from a vertex corresponding to a transaction T_i to a vertex corresponding to transaction T_j, if there exists a read/write/anti-dependency from T_i to T_j. These edges are labelled with the type of the dependency: (1) $A \xrightarrow{wr} B$ when B read-depends on A because it read one of A's updates; (2) $A \xrightarrow{ww} B$ when B write-depends on A because it overwrote one of A's updates; (3) $A \xrightarrow{rw} B$ when B anti-depends on A because A read a version of a variable for which B commits a new version.

Throughout the description of the algorithm we consider a model with strong atomicity [1]. Considering weak atomicity in multi-versioned TMs is an issue largely orthogonal to the focus of this paper (reducing spurious aborts), and therefore we assume that all accesses to shared variables are transactional and governed by the TM algorithm to ease presentation. We also assume that transactions are statically identified as being read-only. Dynamic, or compiler-assisted, identification of such transactions may be used to this purpose, and is also orthogonal to this work.

3.2 Algorithm Overview

Typical MVCC algorithms [6] allow read-only transactions to be serialized "in the past", i.e., before the commit event of any concurrent update transaction. Conversely, they serialize an update transaction T committing at time t "in the present", by: (1) ordering versions produced by T after all versions created by transactions committed before t; (2) performing the classic validation, which ensures that the snapshot observed by T is still up-to-date considering the updates generated by all transactions that committed before t. We note that this approach is conservative, as it guarantees serializability by systematically rejecting serializable histories in which T might have been safely serialized before T'.

The key idea in TWM is to allow an update transaction to sometimes commit "in the past", by ordering the data versions it produces before those generated by already committed, concurrent transactions. In this case we say that T performs a *time-warp* commit. An example illustrating the benefits of time-warp commits is shown in Fig. 2(a): by adopting a classic validation scheme, B would be aborted because it misses the writes issued by the two concurrent transactions A_1 and A_2; however, B could be safely serialized before both transactions that anti-depend on it, which is precisely what TWM allows for, by time-warp committing B.

To implement the time-warp abstraction efficiently, TWM orders the commit events of update transactions according to two totally ordered, but possibly diverging, time lines. The first time line reflects the *natural commit order* of transactions (or, briefly, *commit order*), which is obtained by

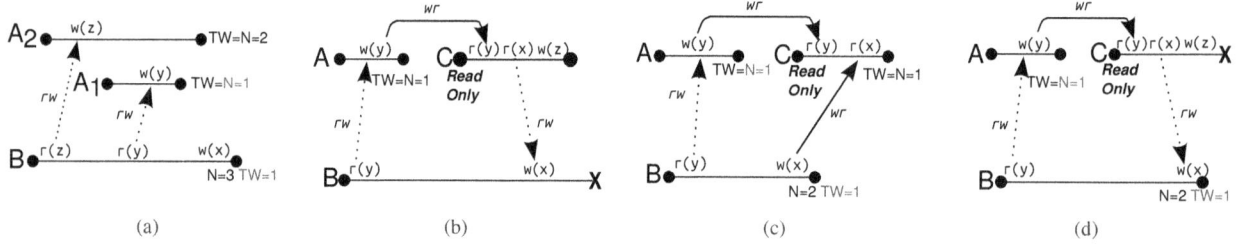

Figure 2. Example histories. The edges are labelled according to the operations they connect.

monotonically increasing a shared logical (i.e., scalar) clock and assigning the corresponding value to each committed transaction. TWM uses this time line to identify concurrent transactions and to establish the visible snapshot for a transaction upon its start. The actual transaction serialization order (and hence the version order) is instead determined by means of a second time line, which reflects what we call the *time-warp commit order* and that diverges from natural commit time order whenever a transaction performs a time-warp commit. TWM keeps track of the two time lines by associating each version of a variable with two timestamps, namely *natOrder* and *twOrder*, which reflect, respectively, the natural commit and the time-warp commit order of the transaction that created it.

We denote as $\mathcal{N}(T)$, resp. $\mathcal{TW}(T)$, the function (having the set of transactions that commit in $\mathcal{H}$ as domain, and $\mathbb{N}$ as co-domain) that defines the total order associated with the natural, resp. time-warp, commit order. Further, we write $T \prec_{\mathcal{N}} T'$, resp. $T \prec_{\mathcal{TW}} T'$, whenever $\mathcal{N}(T) < \mathcal{N}(T')$, resp. $\mathcal{TW}(T) < \mathcal{TW}(T')$.

We start by discussing how to determine the serialization order of transactions that perform a time-warp commit. Next we describe the transaction validation logic. Finally, we explain how read and write operations are managed.

Time-warp Commit: TWM establishes the time-warp order of a committed update transaction B ($\mathcal{TW}(B)$) as follows:

Rule 1. Consider that B misses the writes of a set of committed transactions A_S that executed concurrently with B (i.e., the transactions in A_S anti-depend on B). Let A be the first transaction in A_S according to the natural commit order. Then $\mathcal{TW}(B) = \mathcal{N}(A)$, which effectively orders B before the transactions in A_S, namely those whose execution B did not witness. The versions of each variable updated by B are timestamped with $\mathcal{TW}(B)$ and added to the versions' list according to the time-warp order.

The above rule is exemplified by the history illustrated in Fig. 2(a): as both A_1 and A_2 perform a regular commit, their time-warp order $\mathcal{TW}$ and natural commit order $\mathcal{N}$ coincide; conversely, as B time-warp commits due to anti-dependency edges developed towards A_1 and A_2, then B is serialized by TWM before A_1 (which commits before

A_2 according to $\mathcal{N}$), and is assigned a serialization order $\mathcal{TW}(B) = \mathcal{N}(A_1) = 1$.

Validation Rule: As we will see shortly, the version visibility rule of read-only transactions ensures that these can always be correctly serialized, without the need for any validation phase. Update transactions, conversely, undergo a validation scheme that aims at detecting a specific pattern in the DSG, named *triad*. A triad exists whenever there is transaction T that is both the source and target of anti-dependency edges from two transactions T' and T'' that are concurrent with T (where, possibly, $T' = T''$). We call T a *pivot*, and define the TWM validation scheme as follows:

Rule 2. A transaction fails its validation if, by committing, it would create a triad whose *pivot* time-warp commits.

In other words, TWM deterministically rejects schedules in which two conditions must happen: 1) a pivot transaction T misses the updates of a concurrent transaction T'; and 2) a concurrent transaction T'' (possibly T') misses in its turn the updates of the pivot transaction T. Note that the first condition corresponds to the classic validation rule, and that the second condition (which restricts the set of histories rejected by TWM) is what allows to reduce spurious aborts with respect to state of the art STMs.

Fig. 2(b) exemplifies Rule 2: when B is validated during its commit phase, TWM detects that B is the *pivot* of a triad including also A and C, and it would have to time-warp commit before A. Consequently, B is aborted; this history is indeed non-serializable. Note that B reaches that conclusion by checking solely the direct anti-dependencies it developed, hence avoiding expensive checks for cycles in the entire DSG. Moreover, a pivot must be an update transaction because a read-only transactions is never the target of an anti-dependency.

Read and Write operations: It remains to discuss how TWM regulates the execution of read and write operations. Write operations are privately buffered during transaction's execution phase, and are applied only at commit time, in case the transactions is successfully validated. To determine which versions of a variable a transaction should observe, TWM attributes to a transaction, upon its start, the current value of the shared logical clock. We call this value the start of a transaction ($\mathcal{S}(T)$). TWM uses distinct version visibility rules for read-only and update transactions:

Rule 3. If a read-only transaction T issues a read operation on a variable x, it returns the most recent version of x (according to the time-warp order) created by a transaction T', such that $\mathcal{TW}(T') \leq \mathcal{S}(T)$. If T is an update transaction, it is additionally required that $\mathcal{N}(T') \leq \mathcal{S}(T)$. This prevents update transactions from observing versions produced by concurrently time-warp committed transactions.

The rationale underlying the choice of using different visibility rules for read-only and update transactions is of performance nature. TWM is designed to guarantee that read-only transactions are never aborted. As a consequence, in order to preserve correctness, TWM must ensure that the snapshot observed by a read-only transaction T includes all transactions serialized before T, including time-warp committed ones (see transaction C in Fig. 2(c)). The trade-off is that, in order to be sheltered from the risk of abort, a read-only transaction T must perform visible reads to ensure that concurrent update transactions can detect anti-dependencies originating from T (necessary to implement Rule 2). Fig. 2(b) shows a scenario in which the read-only transaction C commits and, using visible reads, allows pivot B to detect a potential violation of Rule 2, and, hence, to abort. Fig. 2(d) highlights that, without visible reads, B would have no means of detecting a violation of Rule 2, and thus would have committed. In such case, it would be necessary to abort the read-only C (violating mv-permissiveness).

On the other hand, adopting visible reads for update transactions would not render them immune to aborts. Hence, TWM spares them from the cost of visible reads during their execution. Conversely, TWM adopts a lightweight approach ensuring that the snapshot visible for an update transaction T is determined upon its start, and prevent it from reading versions created by concurrent transactions that time-warped. This guarantees that the snapshot observed by T is equivalent to one producible by a serial history defined over a subset of the transactions in $\mathcal{H}$, even if T aborts.

3.3 Pseudo-Code Description

The pseudo-code of the TWM algorithm is reported in Algs. 1 and 2. In Table 1 we describe the metadata used in the pseudo-code for ease of readability.

Any transaction tx starts by reading the global logical clock (*globalClock*), which defines $\mathcal{S}(tx)$. In the READ operation we first check for a read-after-write. Otherwise, if the reader is a read-only transaction, it invokes function SEMIVISIBLEREAD in line 10. For a practical implementation we used a scalar for each variable (attribute *readStamp*). This scalar represents the latest global clock at which some transaction read the variable. This corresponds to a semi visible read scheme, as we do not track individually each reader as other more onerous approaches [4, 15, 17, 21]. To conclude the read operation, we iterate through the versions ordered by $\mathcal{TW}$ until a condition is satisfied that reflects Rule 3.

TWM avoids any validation for read-only transactions. For update transactions, the COMMIT function starts by validating the writes and reads as per Rule 2. When validating a write (function HANDLEWRITE) we first lock the variable and then verify if there existed a concurrent transaction that read any of the variables written by tx, meaning there is an anti-dependence from that reader to tx. When validating a read (function HANDLEREAD) we make the visible read (line 47). Then tx is said to be the source of an edge if tx read a variable and there exists a version for it that was committed after tx started. This means that such version was not in the snapshot of tx and thus an anti-dependency exists from tx to the transaction (say B) that produced that version. In such case, tx tries to *time-warp* commit and serialize before B. In the case that B had set its *source* flag during its previous commit, then tx now fails to commit (as exemplified in Fig. 2(d) with transaction C conducting the validation). In that case, note that B had time-warp committed, so if tx now committed as well, B would become a *pivot* breaking Rule 2. This check is also performed for update transactions during the read operation (line 16) in order to early abort them.

Also note that each anti-dependency, of which tx is the source, is stored locally during the commit procedure (line 54). This is used to implement the *time-warp* commit according to Rule 1 (see line 69). At this point tx aborts only if it raised both flags (source and target in line 64 and exemplified by Fig. 2(b) with B conducting the validation). Otherwise, $\mathcal{N}(tx)$ is computed by atomically incrementing the global clock and reading it. The new writes are committed and stamped with both $\mathcal{TW}(tx)$ (as its version) and $\mathcal{N}(tx)$ (as the time at which it was created). Function CREATENEWVERSION places each committed write in the list of versions by using $\mathcal{TW}(tx)$ to establish the order. Because this order is non-strict, there may occur *time-warp clashes* between transactions, i.e., $A =_{\mathcal{TW}} B$. For a set of transactions that *time-warp clash* and write to the same variable

Struct	Attribute	Description
Var	readStamp	*ts* of *globalClock* when this Var was last read
	latestVersion	pointer to the most recent Ver of this Var
Ver	value	the value of the version
	natOrder	*ts* of the *natural commit order* of the version
	twOrder	*ts* of the *time-warp order* of the version
	nextVersion	pointer to the version overwritten by this one
Tx	writeTx	false when this Tx is identified as read-only
	readSet	not used in read-only Tx
	writeSet	not used in read-only Tx
	start	*ts* of the *globalClock* when this Tx started
	source	true when another tx anti-depends on Tx
	target	true when Tx anti-depends on another tx
	natOrder	*ts* of the *natural commit order* of this Tx
	twOrder	*ts* of the *time-warp order* of this Tx

Table 1. Data structures used in TWM (*ts* = timestamp).

Pseudo-code 1 of TWM (1/2).

```
 1: BEGIN(Tx tx, boolean isWriteTx):
 2:    tx.start ← globalClock              ▷ corresponds to S(tx)
 3:    tx.writeTx ← isWriteTx

 4: READ(Tx tx, Var var):
 5:    if tx.writeTx then
 6:       if ∃ ⟨var, value⟩ ∈ tx.writeSet then
 7:          return value                  ▷ tx had already written to var
 8:       tx.readSet ← tx.readSet ∪ var    ▷ performed by update txs
 9:    else
10:       SEMIVISIBLEREAD(tx, var, globalClock)    ▷ read-only txs
11:    ▷ ensure a concurrent committer sees the visible read
12:    wait until not locked(var)
13:    Ver version ← var.latestVersion
14:    while (version.twOrder > tx.start) ∨        ▷ rule 3 for read-only tx
              (tx.writeTx ∧ version.natOrder > tx.start) do   ▷ write tx
15:       if (tx.writeTx ∧ version.natOrder ≠ version.twOrder) then
16:          abort(tx)                     ▷ early abort update tx due to rule 2
17:       version ← version.nextVersion
18:    return version.value

19: SEMIVISIBLEREAD(Tx tx, Var var, long ts):
20:    do
21:       long lastRead ← var.readStamp
22:    while lastRead < ts ∧ CAS(var.readStamp, lastRead, ts) = failed

23: WRITE(Tx tx, Var var, Value val):
24:    tx.writeSet ← (tx.writeSet \ ⟨var, _⟩ ) ∪ ⟨var, val⟩

25: CREATENEWVERSION(Tx tx, Var var, Value val):
26:    Ver newerVersion ← ⊥
27:    Ver olderVersion ← var.latestVersion
28:    while tx.twOrder < olderVersion.twOrder do
29:       newerVersion ← olderVersion
30:       olderVersion ← olderVersion.nextVersion
31:    if tx.twOrder = olderVersion.twOrder then
32:       return                           ▷ no tx will ever read this value, skip it
33:    Ver version ← ⟨val, tx.natOrder, tx.twOrder, tx, olderVersion⟩
34:    ▷ insert according to time-warp order...
35:    if newerVersion = ⊥ then
36:       var.latestVersion ← version      ▷ ...as the latest version
37:    else
38:       newerVersion.nextVersion ← version   ▷ ...or as an older version
```

Pseudo-code 2 of TWM (2/2).

```
39: HANDLEWRITE(Tx tx, Var var): ▷ check if tx is the target of an edge
40:    lock(var)
41:    ▷ lines 10, 12 and 40 ensure readers are visible to tx or blocked
42:    if var.readStamp ≥ tx.start then
43:       ▷ detect concurrent transactions that read var
44:       tx.target ← true

45: HANDLEREAD(Tx tx, Var var): ▷ check if tx is the source of an edge
46:    ▷ tx can now do visible reads without affecting its validation
47:    SEMIVISIBLEREAD(tx, var, globalClock)
48:    wait until not locked(var) by tx' ≠ tx
49:    ▷ check writes committed concurrently to tx's execution
50:    Ver version ← var.latestVersion
51:    while version.natOrder > tx.start do
52:       if version.natOrder ≠ version.twOrder then
53:          abort(tx)                     ▷ rule 2
54:       tx.antiDeps.add(version.natOrder)    ▷ used to compute TW(tx)
55:       tx.source ← true
56:       version ← version.nextVersion

57: COMMIT(Tx tx):
58:    if !tx.writeTx then
59:       return                           ▷ read-only txs never abort
60:    ▷ check for rw edges from/to concurrent txs
61:    ∀var ∈ tx.writeSet do: HANDLEWRITE(tx, var)
62:    ∀var ∈ tx.readSet do: HANDLEREAD(tx, var)
63:    if tx.target ∧ tx.source then
64:       abort(tx)                        ▷ rule 2
65:    tx.natOrder ← incAndFetch(globalClock)    ▷ compute N(tx)
66:    if (tx.antiDeps = ∅) then
67:       tx.twOrder ← tx.natOrder         ▷ TW(tx) = N(tx)
68:    else
69:       tx.twOrder ← min(tx.antiDeps)    ▷ compute TW(tx)
70:    ∀ ⟨var, value⟩ ∈ tx.writeSet do:
71:       CREATENEWVERSION(tx, var, value)
72:    releaseLock(var)
```

k, CREATENEWVERSION keeps only the update to k of the transaction T that has the least value for $\mathcal{N}$ (the other transactions execute line 32). In other words, the transactions in a *time-warp clash* are serialized in the inverse order of $\mathcal{N}$, because the one that happened earlier according to the natural commit order was missed by all others in the clash.

3.4 Garbage collection, privatization and lock-freedom

Garbage Collection: The *time-warp* commit mechanism does not raise particular issues for the garbage collection of versions. Indeed, it can rely on standard garbage collection algorithms for MVCC schemes that maintain any version that can possibly be read by an active transaction (as in different implementations in [14, 22, 27]). The key idea of those algorithms is the following: assume that T is the oldest active transaction, with $\mathcal{S}(T) = k$; then versions up to (and excluding) k can be garbage collected — note that the newest version is preserved regardless of this condition.

One may argue that a problematic scenario may arise if some update transaction U *time-warp committed* such that $\mathcal{TW}(U) < k$. For that to happen, there must exist some transaction Z concurrent with U such that: $U \xrightarrow{rw} Z$ and $\mathcal{N}(Z) < k$. But this is impossible because we assumed that T was the oldest active transaction, so Z could not be concurrent with U and obtain *natural commit order k*.

Privatization Safety: Recall that, in our assumptions, we precluded non-transactional accesses to simplify presentation. However, another relevant concern is that of privatization safety [23]. This implies that a transaction P should be able to safely make some shared data only available to it (privatizing it) and work on it without transactional barriers. The challenge here is to ensure that the thread executing P and concurrent transactions do not interfere with each other. However, similarly to the concern of garbage collection, *time-warping* does not present additional challenges to privatization. Existing approaches to support privatization, in fact, are based on the notion of *quiescence*, which forces privatizing transactions to wait for concurrent transactions to finish [22] (using, if possible, explicitly identified privatizing operations to minimize waiting). These techniques suffice to ensure that, once a privatizing transaction P has committed, no transaction can time-warp commit and serialize before P.

Lock-Freedom: Finally, recent work has motivated the adoption of lock-free synchronization schemes to obtain maximum scalability [14, 17], for which reason in the prototype implementation we have used the lock-free commit procedure of [14]. As this concern is orthogonal to our focus, we preserved a simpler presentation with locks, and delegate additional details to our technical report [12].

4. Correctness Arguments

In this section we provide arguments on the correctness of the TWM algorithm. We begin by discussing the serializability of committed transactions in TWM, by showing that the serializability graph of histories accepted by the TWM algorithm is acyclic.Next, we discuss the consistency guarantees provided also to non-committed transactions, namely Virtual World Consistency [19].

4.1 Rejecting Non-Serializable Histories

To prove serializability, we first define a strict total order ($\mathcal{O}$) on the transactions in the committed projection of $\mathcal{H}$ (noted $\mathcal{H}|C$), and then we show that any edge between two transactions in DSG($\mathcal{H}|C$) is compliant with $\mathcal{O}$. The strict total order $\mathcal{O}$ is obtained from the non-strict total order defined by $\mathcal{TW}$, which we recall can have ties in presence of time-warp clashes, breaking ties as follows. We order update transactions in $\mathcal{O}$ using the *time-warp order* and, whenever there is a *time-warp clash*, i.e., $A =_{\mathcal{TW}} B$, we use the natural commit order $\mathcal{N}$ as a tie breaker and serialize B before A in $\mathcal{O}$ iff $A \prec_{\mathcal{N}} B$. This results in a strict total order because $\mathcal{N}$ defines a strict total order as well. Any read-only transaction T is serialized in $\mathcal{O}$ according to $\mathcal{S}(T)$, which surely makes them coincide with some update transaction in $\mathcal{O}$. To tie-break, we place the read-only transactions always later than coinciding update transactions in $\mathcal{O}$. If two read-only transactions obtain the same value (because they started on the same snapshot), any deterministic function suffices as a tie break (for instance, the identifier of the thread that executed the transaction).

In order to prove the acyclicity of DSG($\mathcal{H}|C$), we show that for any committed transactions A and B such that $A \prec_{\mathcal{O}} B$, there cannot be any edge from B to A in the DSG. We prove this claim by contradiction, considering individually each type of edge. First, let us assume that $B \xrightarrow{ww} A \in$ DSG($\mathcal{H}|C$). According to function CREATENEWVERSION this is possible iff $B \prec_{\mathcal{TW}} A$. This, however, contradicts the assumption $A \prec_{\mathcal{O}} B$, because it implies that $A \preceq_{\mathcal{TW}} B$.

Now let us consider that $B \xrightarrow{wr} A$. First suppose that A is an update transaction. Then, according to line 14, A can read a version created by B iff $\mathcal{N}(B) \leq \mathcal{S}(A)$. However,

the time-warp commit timestamp of a transaction is always less or equal than its natural commit timestamp ($\mathcal{TW}(B) \leq \mathcal{N}(B)$); also, an update transaction A can only time-warp due to concurrent transactions, meaning they commit after $\mathcal{S}(A)$ and thus $\mathcal{S}(A) < \mathcal{TW}(A)$. Hence, we obtain $\mathcal{TW}(B) \prec \mathcal{TW}(A)$, contradicting the initial assumption. Now consider that A is a read-only transaction. Then, according to line 14, A can read a version created by B (concurrent with A's execution) iff $\mathcal{TW}(B) \leq \mathcal{S}(A)$. Given that A is a read-only transaction, $\mathcal{TW}(A) = \mathcal{S}(A)$, hence $\mathcal{TW}(B) \leq \mathcal{TW}(A)$. The case $\mathcal{TW}(B) < \mathcal{TW}(A)$ clearly contradicts the initial assumption. If $\mathcal{TW}(B) = \mathcal{TW}(A)$, then we note that A is a read-only transaction that clashes with B; according to the rules we used to derive $\mathcal{O}$ then A is ordered after B in $\mathcal{O}$, which again contradicts the initial assumption ($A \prec_{\mathcal{O}} B$).

Finally we consider that $B \xrightarrow{rw} A$. First assume that B is a read-only transaction. Then the version written by A is not visible to B iff $\mathcal{S}(B) < \mathcal{TW}(A)$. But since B is read-only, then $\mathcal{S}(B) = \mathcal{TW}(B)$, and we once again contradict the initial assumption. Assume now that B is an update transaction, for which we have two possible cases depending on whether B commits before or after A in the *natural commit order*. Consider the first case where $B \prec_{\mathcal{N}} A$. Then B performs some visible read in line 47; later A triggers the condition in line 42 and sets $A.target \leftarrow true$. Consequently A cannot *time-warp commit* or else both *target* and *source* flags would be true and A would abort in line 64. Then $\mathcal{TW}(B) < \mathcal{N}(A) = \mathcal{TW}(A)$, which is a contradiction with the initial assumed order. Lastly, consider the second case where $A \prec_{\mathcal{N}} B$. Then B triggers the condition in line 51. If A *time-warp commits*, then B aborts in line 53. Otherwise, B adds A to it's *antiDeps* set which results in $\mathcal{TW}(B) \leq (\mathcal{N}(A) = \mathcal{TW}(A))$ (according to line 69). The case where $B \prec_{\mathcal{TW}} A$ trivially violates our assumption. The tie-break in the *time-warp clash*, where $B =_{\mathcal{TW}} A$, is broken in the inverse *natural commit order* (recall $A \prec_{\mathcal{N}} B$), which also contradicts the assumption.

4.2 Virtual World Consistency

So far we have argued that TWM ensures serializability for committed transactions. But running (or already aborted) transactions are equally important in TWM because certain phenomena must be prevented with regard to them [16, 19]. If a transaction executing alone is correct, then it should be correct when faced with concurrency under a TM algorithm. This translates to a sense of consistency sufficiently strong in which hazards, such as infinite loops or divisions by zero, are avoided — this is considered an imperative requirement in TM algorithms [10, 16] and it is guaranteed by Virtual World Consistency [19].

VWC is a correctness criterion stronger than serializability, as it prevents transactions from observing snapshots that cannot be generated in any sequential history. Besides serializability for committed transactions, VWC also requires that, for every aborted or running transaction T, there is a legal linear extension of partial order $past(T)$, where $past(T)$ is obtained from the sub-graph of DSG($\mathcal{H}$) containing all the transactions on which T transitively depends, and removing any anti-dependencies. A legal linear extension of $past(T)$ is a linear extension $\widehat{S}(T)$ of $past(T)$ where every transaction $T' \in past(T)$ observes values written by the most recent transaction that precedes T' in $\widehat{S}(T)$.

Recall that we have argued the absence of cycles in DSG($\mathcal{H}|C$). Note that $past(T)$ is a subgraph of DSG($\mathcal{H}$), on which non-committed transactions are also considered; but they must be sinks in that subgraph (because anti-dependencies are removed) and thus we also argue that $past(T)$ is also acyclic. It then follows that a linear extension $\widehat{S}(T)$ of $past(T)$ must exist. $\widehat{S}(T)$ is legal because transactions read the most recent version committed according to $\mathcal{TW}$ (see line 14). But, since $past(T)$ respects the $\mathcal{TW}$ order, we get that T must be legal and so we argue that TWM provides VWC.

Another similar, albeit stronger, correctness criterion is that of opacity. In the following we discuss why TWM does not guarantee opacity [16], and then explain how TWM might be adapted to ensure this property. Briefly, the opacity specification requires 2 properties: O.1) the existence of an equivalent serial history $\mathcal{H}_S$ that preserves the real-time order of $\mathcal{H}$; O.2) that every transaction in $\mathcal{H}_S$ is legal. TWM does respect property O.1 (not shown here for space constraints). Concerning property O.2, we note that two concurrent transactions R and W can perceive two different serialization orders — this is a consequence of the different version visibility conditions in line 14 according to the nature of the transaction. These two orders, denoted respectively as $\mathcal{H}_S^R$ and $\mathcal{H}_S^W$ for transactions R and W, exist in case a third concurrent transaction A time-warp commits before R and W. In this case, A may be included in $\mathcal{H}_S^R$ but not included in $\mathcal{H}_S^W$. But then, in such case, TWM would abort W due to line 53, thus not endangering serializability. Then, this makes $\mathcal{H}_S^W$ a legal sequential history, but it is incompatible with the serial history equivalent to $\mathcal{H}$, which we denoted as $\mathcal{H}_S$. This is why TWM does not abide by property O.2.

We stress that the fact that $\mathcal{H}_S^R$ and $\mathcal{H}_S^W$ may not be compatible is acceptable by VWC. This is because any transaction in $\mathcal{H}_S^W$ that is not compatible with $\mathcal{H}_S$ aborts, and in VWC aborted transactions can observe legal linear extensions of different causal pasts. We also remark that it would be indeed relatively straightforward to adapt TWM to ensure property O.2, and hence opacity: it would be sufficient to homogenize the logic governing the execution of read operations for both read-only and update transactions, allowing update transactions to observe the snapshots generated by concurrent transactions and forcing them to use visible reads, just like read-only transactions. As discussed in Section 3, the choice of using non-visible reads for update trans-

actions is motivated by performance considerations. Indeed, by adopting VWC rather than opacity as reference correctness criterion, it is possible to maximize its efficiency via lightweight conflict tracking mechanisms, while still providing robust guarantees concerning the avoidance of unexpected errors due to inconsistent/partial reads.

5. Evaluation

In this section we experimentally evaluate the performance of a Java-based implementation of TWM. To access its merit, we compare it with four other STMs representative of different designs: (1) JVSTM [14] is multi-versioned and guarantees abort-freedom for read-only transactions; (2) TL2 [10] is a simpler TM based on timestamps and locks; (3) NOrec [9] uses a single word for metadata (a global lock), thus being even simpler than TL2; and (4) AVSTM [17] is also single-version, but on top of that it is also probabilistically permissive with regard to opacity. This allows to contrast TWM directly against a different design that minimizes spurious aborts (AVSTM); against TMs representative of single-thread efficient designs (TL2 and NOrec); and against a multi-versioned TM (JVSTM). Note that both JVSTM and AVSTM are lock-free (similarly to our prototype of TWM, as mentioned in Section 3.4), whereas TL2 and NOrec are lock-based. Finally, TWM and AVSTM exploit alternative mechanisms to validate transactions, whereas the others rely on the *classic validation*.

We used Java implementations for all the STMs, by obtaining the code for JVSTM from its public repository, TL2 and NOrec from their respective ports to the Deuce framework, and by porting AVSTM to Java. All implementations were modified to share a common interface that uses manual instrumentation relying on a concept similar to that of VBoxes [14]. This means that the benchmarks were manually instrumented to identify shared variables and transactions, resulting in an equal and fair environment for comparison of all TMs. We also identified read-only transactions in the benchmarks, and allowed implementations to take advantage of this when possible. This means that TWM, JVSTM and TL2 do not maintain read-sets for such transactions and their commit procedure needs no validation. NOrec requires the read-set for re-validation of a transaction T when the global clock has changed, and AVSTM requires it for an update transaction T that is committing to update the validity interval of concurrent transactions T' that read items committed by T.

In the following experimental study we seek to answer the following questions: (1) What is the performance difference of TWM to each of the other design class of STM? (2) Where does the difference in performance come from? (3) What is the overhead in reducing aborts with respect to the classic validation?

To answer the above questions, we conducted experiments on a variety of benchmarks and workloads. We first present results with a classic micro-benchmark for TM, namely Skip List. Then, we consider the more complex and realistic benchmarks from the STAMP suite [24][1]. STAMP contains a variety of transactions, with different sizes and contention levels. However, contrarily to the Skip List micro-benchmark, STAMP does not have read-only transactions, which is a disadvantage to multi-version TMs. The following results were obtained on a machine with four AMD Opteron 6272 processors (64 total cores), 32GB of RAM, running Ubuntu 12.04 and Oracle's JVM 1.7.0_15 and each data point corresponds to the average of 10 executions. Finally, we use use the geometric mean when we show averages over normalized result and use as abort rate metric the ratio of number of restarts to the number of executions (encompassing committed and restarted transactions).

5.1 Skip List

We begin by studying the behavior of time-warping in a traditional data-structure. As described in Section 1.1, concurrent traversals and modifications in data-structures, such as a skip-list, are perfect examples of the advantages of time-warping: a transaction T_1 modifying an element near the end of the list need not abort because a concurrent transaction T_2 modified an element in the beginning of the list and committed; TWM can automatically, and safely, commit T_1 before T_2, whereas *classic validation* precludes the commit of T_1.

For this micro-benchmark we used the source code available in the IntSet benchmark in the Deuce framework. We set up the skip-list with 100 thousand elements and 25% update transactions that either insert or remove an element. Fig. 3(a) shows the scalability results for this workload, where TWM performs best after 16 threads, and below that is competitive with the other TMs. At 64 cores TWM achieves the following speedups: 2.8× for TL2; 9.4× for NOrec; 4.3× for JVSTM; and 1.8× for AVSTM. It is actually interesting to assess that, at a low thread count, NOrec performs best. However, this difference quickly fades at a low thread count and its performance plunges due to the overly pessimistic validation procedure — this is visible on Fig. 3(b) where its abort rate quickly grows to approximately 70%. Note that JVSTM's update transactions incur in a significant cost due to the multi-version maintenance — this cost is amplified by the non-negligible percentage of update transactions, which have no advantage in the availability of multi-versions. TWM, instead, takes advantage of multi-versions even for update transactions due to time-warping.

Overall, as we can see in Fig. 3(b), the source of our gains is two-fold: TWM clearly aborts much less transactions than *classic validation* TMs; on the other hand, despite TWM aborting slightly more than AVSTM, it introduces a much lower overhead, as we will discuss in detail next.

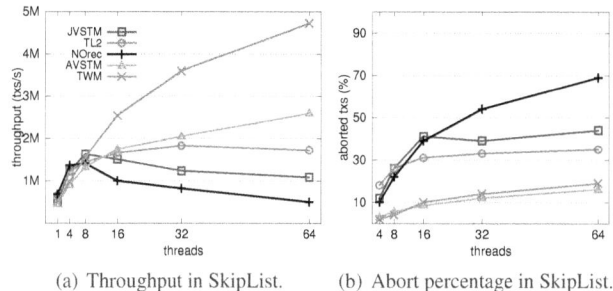

(a) Throughput in SkipList.   (b) Abort percentage in SkipList.

Figure 3. SkipList with 25% modifications.

5.2 Overhead Assessment

To better understand the nature of each design, we conducted worst-case experiments to assess the cost of reducing spurious aborts. We first conducted an experiment with two shared variables, both incremented once by every transaction, to create a scenario with very high contention, whose conflict patterns cannot be accommodated by the TWM algorithm (as well as by the other considered TMs).

We can see the throughput for this experiment in Fig. 4(a), where the slowdown of TWM is comparable to that of JVSTM and TL2, being 7% and 12% worse with respect to those two TMs. Both AVSTM and NOrec perform worse beyond 8 threads due to the internal validation procedures — we shall see this in detail next.

We also modified the SkipList micro-benchmark to have each thread modify an independent skip-list. Consequently, no transaction ever runs into conflicts, although they still activate the validation procedures as every transaction performs some writes. The results of this experiment are shown in Fig. 4(b). As expected, every TM is able to scale as this scenario is conflict-free. Moreover, the relative trends are consistent with those observed for the highly-contended scenario with the shared counters.

To better understand the previous results, we instrumented the prototypes to collect the time spent by transactions on each phase of the TM algorithm. Fig. 4(c) shows the results relative to the previous experiment. We considered four different phases: the *read* corresponds to time spent in read barriers; *readSet-val* and *writeSet-val* are the validations conducted by the transaction, including those at a commit-time and when executed during the transaction execution in the case of NOrec — note that the write-set validation only exists in the case of TWM and AVSTM; and finally *commit* corresponds to the rest of the time spent in the commit phase (for instance, writing-back, or helping other transactions in the case of lock-free schemes).

In this plot, we see that the commit is generally the main source of overhead as the threads increase. TL2 obtains the least overhead because transactions are conflict-free and the workload is write-intensive, which implies extra costs for schemes that minimize aborts and for multi-version algorithms. Initially, NOrec also benefits from these circum-

---

[1] Additional experiments are available in our technical report [12].

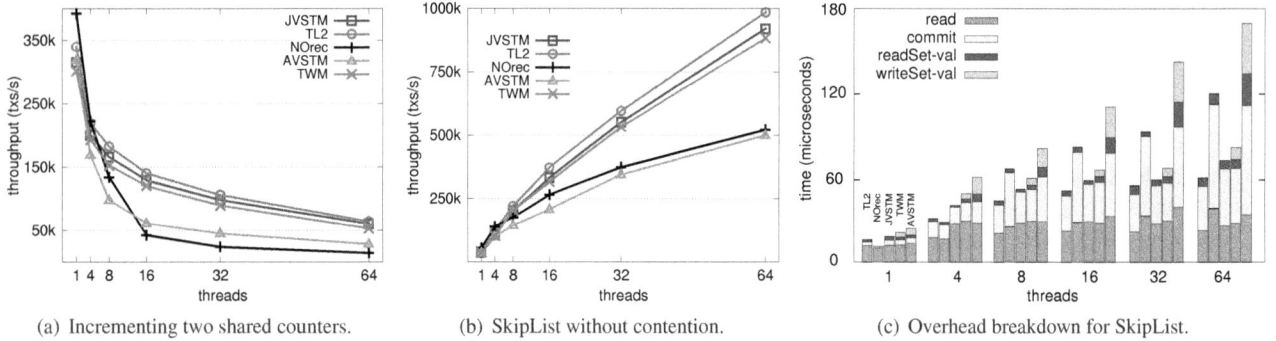

Figure 4. Overhead assessment with 100% writes.

stances to yield the least overhead. However, it quickly becomes less efficient as the global commit lock becomes a bottleneck and the commit time increases significantly due to threads waiting to commit. Moreover, its read-set validation time also increases because transactions re-validate the read-set when they notice the global clock has changed (due to an update transaction committing).

On the other hand, the lock-free schemes also incur in some overhead right from the start. Both TWM and AVSTM conduct additional validations that are useless in this scenario, as it is conflict-free, and are noticeably making them more expensive. Yet, TWM preserves the overheads rather low as the scale increases, whereas AVSTM suffers considerably as we reach 64 threads, making it the most expensive TM at that scale, slightly above NOrec. The main culprit for this cost in AVSTM is that a committing update transaction must possibly update metadata of every concurrent transaction. As a result of this onerous check, the commit and validations cost grow considerably with the number of threads.

Finally, we highlight that TWM's overheads are consistently close to those of JVSTM. They are also both higher than those of TL2 due to the management of multi-versions and lock-freedom guarantees. Yet, TWM manages to reduce spurious aborts with respect to both JVSTM and TL2. This illustrates the appeal of TWM, which escapes the overheads of aiming for permissiveness, while improving performance in high concurrency scenarios.

5.3 Application Benchmarks

In this section we present additional experiments with larger benchmarks to demonstrate the ability of TWM to reduce spurious aborts.

For that, we studied the performance of these TMs in STAMP, for which we used an existing port to Java in Deuce framework. Fig. 5 presents the time to complete each benchmark, excluding Yada (not available in the Java port) and Bayes (excluded given its non-determinism). Note that in these plots lower is better.

TWM behaves slightly worse than JVSTM and TL2 in both Intruder and Kmeans with an average slowdown of

7%. On the other benchmarks, it is either on par with the best TM (Genome, SSCA2, Vacation (low)) or it obtains improvements over all TMs (Labyrinth and Vacation (high)). We have manually inspected each benchmark to understand if there are opportunities for time-warp to reduce spurious aborts: this is the case for Genome, Labyrinth and Vacation. The other three only generate simple conflict patterns that cannot be surpassed with time-warping. Yet, TWM manages to perform among the best TMs in every benchmark. Conversely, AVSTM only obtains considerable improvements in Vacation (high), although it still performs worse than TWM.

Fig. 5(i) shows the geometric mean (and deviation) of the speedup of TWM relative to the other TMs across all the STAMP benchmarks. The overall trend is that TWM is more beneficial than *classic validation* TMs as the thread count increases. The average improvement across all the benchmarks is 31% over JVSTM, 12% over TL2, 16% over NOrec and 21% over AVSTM. Additionally, if we only consider the benchmarks with possibility of time-warping, TWM obtains an average improvement of 36% over JVSTM, 37% over TL2, 41% over NOrec, and 37% over AVSTM. Note that the gains over AVSTM are mostly due to a more efficient algorithm, rather than by abort reduction (as shown in Table 2).

6. Final remarks

This paper presented TWM, a novel multi-version algorithm that aims at striking a balance between permissiveness and efficiency. TWM exploits the key idea of allowing update transactions to be serialized "in the past", according to what we called a *time-warp* time line. This time line diverges from the natural commit order of transactions in order to allow update transactions to commit successfully (but in the past) despite having performed stale reads. Past solutions have tried to maximize permissiveness via costly and inefficient procedures. TWM explored a new validation strategy that results in less aborts, without hindering efficiency (e.g., by avoiding expensive checks of the transactions' dependency graph). Furthermore, TWM ensures mv-permissiveness and VWC. Our experiments comparing a variety of TMs evidenced the

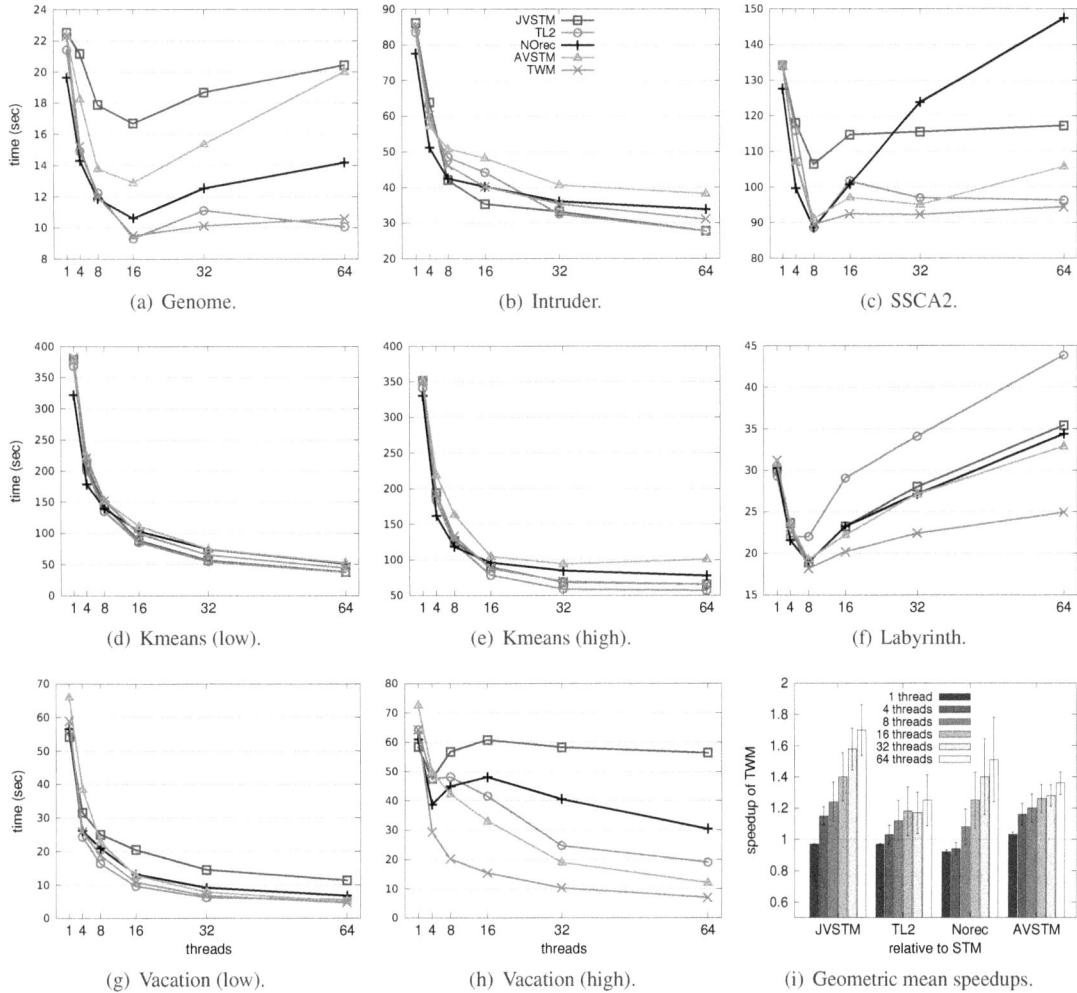

Figure 5. Scalability in the STAMP benchmarks.

	Benchmark									Threads				
STM	genome	intruder	kmeans-l	kmeans-h	labyrinth	ssca2	vac-l	vac-h	STM	4	8	16	32	64
TWM	3.8	3.8	1.4	4.2	8.8	10.5	6.4	17.8	TWM	1.2	4.4	6.6	9.9	15.7
JVSTM	15.4	3.2	1.6	4.9	12.3	11.3	12.1	41.1	JVSTM	1.8	7.0	10.2	15.7	21.2
TL2	12.1	4.8	3.8	3.4	13.8	11.7	10.0	41.4	TL2	2.6	6.5	11.4	16.1	20.9
NOrec	21.1	6.0	3.8	6.4	27.6	14.9	19.9	55.0	NOrec	3.4	9.6	18.6	24.9	34.0
AVSTM	13.0	3.5	2.6	4.8	10.4	11.5	9.4	18.9	AVSTM	2.5	5.5	8.6	12.7	17.6

Table 2. Average abort rate (%) across each STAMP benchmark (left) and each thread count (right).

merits of time-warping with an average improvement of 65% in high concurrency scenarios and gains extending up to 9×. Further, we showed that TWM introduces very limited overheads when faced with contention patterns that cannot be optimized using TWM. We opted for a multi-version scheme for time-warping, although part of our ideas can also be applied to single-versioned TMs. The extent to which that can be advantageous is interesting future work.

The recent release of hardware support for TM is another source of interesting open questions. Hardware vendors have opted for a paradigm of best-effort semantics for the first generation of Hardware TMs, in which no guarantee is given that a transaction will ever complete successfully. One of the main reasons for such weak semantics is the difficulty in dealing with arbitrarily large transactions, while preserving a simple hardware design. The proposed alternative is thus to use software fallback paths, namely to an STM implementation. Consequently, it is interesting to explore the integration of STM implementations with reduced spurious aborts, such as TWM, in the fallback paths for hardware implementations. The difficulty is in the efficient integration of both systems, which becomes more challenging with the metadata and validations conducted in such STM algorithms. We hope to provide answers to this problem in our future work.

Acknowledgements.

This work was supported by national funds through FCT — Fundação para a Ciência e Tecnologia — under project PEst-OE/EEI/LA0021/2013, and by specSTM project (PTDC/EIA-EIA/122785/2010).

References

[1] M. Abadi, T. Harris, and M. Mehrara. Transactional memory with strong atomicity using off-the-shelf memory protection hardware. In *Proceedings of the 14th Symposium on Principles and Practice of Parallel Programming*, PPoPP, pages 185–196, 2009.

[2] A. Adya. *Weak consistency: a generalized theory and optimistic implementations for distributed transactions*. PhD thesis, Massachusetts Institute of Technology, 1999.

[3] H. Attiya and E. Hillel. Single-version STMs can be multi-version permissive. In *Proceedings of the 12th International Conference on Distributed Computing and Networking*, ICDCN, pages 83–94, 2011.

[4] U. Aydonat and T. Abdelrahman. Relaxed Concurrency Control in Software Transactional Memory. *IEEE Transactions on Parallel and Distributed Systems*, 23(7):1312–1325, 2012.

[5] H. Berenson, P. Bernstein, J. Gray, J. Melton, E. O'Neil, and P. O'Neil. A critique of ANSI SQL isolation levels. In *Proceedings of SIGMOD*, pages 1–10, 1995.

[6] P. A. Bernstein, V. Hadzilacos, and N. Goodman. *Concurrency Control and Recovery in Database Systems*. Addison-Wesley Longman Publishing, Boston, MA, USA, 1987.

[7] M. Cahill, U. Röhm, and A. Fekete. Serializable isolation for snapshot databases. In *Proceedings of SIGMOD*, pages 729–738, 2008.

[8] T. Crain, D. Imbs, and M. Raynal. Read invisibility, virtual world consistency and probabilistic permissiveness are compatible. In *Proceedings of the 11th International Conference on Algorithms and Architectures for Parallel Processing*, ICA3PP, pages 244–257, 2011.

[9] L. Dalessandro, M. F. Spear, and M. L. Scott. NOrec: streamlining STM by abolishing ownership records. In *Proceedings of the 15th Symposium on Principles and Practice of Parallel Programming*, PPoPP, pages 67–78, 2010.

[10] D. Dice, O. Shalev, and N. Shavit. Transactional locking II. In *Proceedings of the 20th Symposium on Distributed Computing*, DISC, pages 194–208, 2006.

[11] N. Diegues and J. Cachopo. Practical Parallel Nesting for Software Transactional Memory. In *Proceedings of the 27th Symposium on Distributed Computing*, DISC, pages 149–163, 2013.

[12] N. Diegues and P. Romano. Enhancing permissiveness in transactional memory via time-warping. Technical Report 16, december 2013.

[13] P. Felber, C. Fetzer, and T. Riegel. Dynamic performance tuning of word-based software transactional memory. In *Proceedings of the 13th Symposium on Principles and Practice of Parallel Programming*, PPoPP, pages 237–246, 2008.

[14] S. M. Fernandes and J. Cachopo. Lock-free and scalable multi-version software transactional memory. In *Proceedings of the 16th Symposium on Principles and Practice of Parallel Programming*, PPoPP, pages 179–188, 2011.

[15] V. Gramoli, D. Harmanci, and P. Felber. On the Input Acceptance of Transactional Memory. *Parallel Processing Letters*, 20(1), 2010.

[16] R. Guerraoui and M. Kapalka. On the correctness of transactional memory. In *Proceedings of the 13th Symposium on Principles and Practice of Parallel Programming*, PPoPP, pages 175–184, 2008.

[17] R. Guerraoui, T. A. Henzinger, and V. Singh. Permissiveness in Transactional Memories. In *Proceedings of the 22nd Symposium on Distributed Computing*, DISC, pages 305–319, 2008.

[18] M. Herlihy and J. E. B. Moss. Transactional Memory: architectural support for lock-free data structures. In *Proceedings of the 20th International Symposium on Computer Architecture*, ISCA, pages 289–300, 1993.

[19] D. Imbs and M. Raynal. Virtual World Consistency: A condition for STM systems. *Theoretical Computer Science*, 444 (0):113–127, 2012.

[20] D. R. Jefferson. Virtual time. *ACM Transactions on Programming Languages Systems*, 7(3):404–425, July 1985.

[21] I. Keidar and D. Perelman. On avoiding spare aborts in transactional memory. In *Proceedings of the 21st Symposium on Parallelism in Algorithms and Architectures*, SPAA, pages 59–68, 2009.

[22] L. Lu and M. L. Scott. Generic Multiversion STM. In *Proceedings of the 27th Symposium on Distributed Computing*, DISC, pages 134–148, 2013.

[23] V. J. Marathe, M. F. Spear, and M. L. Scott. Scalable Techniques for Transparent Privatization in Software Transactional Memory. In *Proceedings of the 37th International Conference on Parallel Processing*, ICPP, pages 67–74, 2008.

[24] C. C. Minh, J. Chung, C. Kozyrakis, and K. Olukotun. STAMP: Stanford transactional applications for multi-processing. In *Symposium on Workload Characterization*, IISWC, pages 35–46, 2008.

[25] C. H. Papadimitriou. The serializability of concurrent database updates. *J. ACM*, 26(4):631–653, Oct. 1979.

[26] D. Perelman, R. Fan, and I. Keidar. On maintaining multiple versions in stm. In *Proceedings of the 29th Symposium on Principles of Distributed Computing*, PODC, pages 16–25, 2010.

[27] D. Perelman, A. Byshevsky, O. Litmanovich, and I. Keidar. SMV: Selective Multi-Versioning STM. In *Proceedings of the 25th Symposium on Distributed Computing*, DISC, pages 125–140, 2011.

[28] H. E. Ramadan, I. Roy, M. Herlihy, and E. Witchel. Committing conflicting transactions in an stm. In *Proceedings of the 14th Symposium on Principles and Practice of Parallel Programming*, PPoPP, pages 163–172, 2009.

Beyond Parallel Programming with Domain Specific Languages

Kunle Olukotun

Stanford University
kunle@stanford.edu

Abstract

Today, almost all computer architectures are parallel and heterogeneous; a combination of multiple CPUs, GPUs and specialized processors. This creates a challenging problem for application developers who want to develop high performance programs without the effort required to use low-level, architecture specific parallel programming models (e.g. OpenMP for CMPs, CUDA for GPUs, MPI for clusters). Domain-specific languages (DSLs) are a promising solution to this problem because they can provide an avenue for high-level application-specific abstractions with implicit parallelism to be mapped directly to low level architecture-specific programming models; providing both high programmer productivity and high execution performance.

In this talk I will describe an approach to building high performance DSLs, which is based on DSL embedding in a general purpose programming language, metaprogramming and a DSL infrastructure called Delite. I will describe how we transform DSL programs into efficient first-order low-level code using domain specific optimization, parallelism and locality optimization with parallel patterns, and architecture-specific code generation. All optimizations and transformations are implemented in Delite: an extensible DSL compiler infrastucture that significantly reduces the effort required to develop new DSLs. Delite DSLs for machine learning, data querying, graph analysis, and scientific computing all achieve performance competitive with manually parallelized C++ code.

Keywords domain specific languages, compilers, heterogeneous architectures, performance

Bio

Kunle Olukotun is a Professor of Electrical Engineering and Computer Science at Stanford University. Olukotun is a pioneer in chip multiprocessor (CMP) design and lead the Stanford Hydra CMP research project. Olukotun founded Afara Websystems to develop commercial high-throughput, low-power server systems with CMP technology. The Afara microprocessor, called Niagara, was acquired by Sun Microsystems. Later generation Niagara processors now power all Oracle SPARC-based servers. Olukotun currently directs the Stanford Pervasive Parallelism Lab (PPL) which seeks to proliferate the use of parallelism in all application areas using Domain Specific Languages (DSLs). Olukotun is an ACM Fellow and an IEEE fellow.

PPoPP '14, February 15–19, 2014, Orlando, Florida, USA.
Copyright is held by the owner/author(s).
ACM 978-1-4503-2656-8/14/02.
http://dx.doi.org/10.1145/2555243.2557966

Designing and Auto-Tuning Parallel 3-D FFT for Computation-Communication Overlap

Sukhyun Song

Department of Computer Science
University of Maryland, College Park
shsong@cs.umd.edu

Jeffrey K. Hollingsworth

Department of Computer Science
University of Maryland, College Park
hollings@cs.umd.edu

Abstract

This paper presents a method to design and auto-tune a new parallel 3-D FFT code using the non-blocking MPI all-to-all operation. We achieve high performance by optimizing computation-communication overlap. Our code performs fully asynchronous communication without any support from special hardware. We also improve cache performance through loop tiling. To cope with the complex trade-off regarding our optimization techniques, we parameterize our code and auto-tune the parameters efficiently in a large parameter space. Experimental results from two systems confirm that our code achieves a speedup of up to 1.76× over the FFTW library.

Categories and Subject Descriptors D.1.3 [*Programming Techniques*]: Concurrent Programming–Distributed Programming, Parallel Programming

Keywords Performance; 3-D FFT; MPI; Overlap; Non-Blocking; All-to-All; Auto-Tuning

1. Introduction

The Fast Fourier Transform (FFT) is widely used in many fields of science and engineering. Uses include signal processing, image processing, and differential equation solving. More specifically, high-performance scientific applications have recently used three-dimensional FFT (3-D FFT) to run astrophysical N-body simulations [21] and blood flow simulations [25].

There have been many research efforts to achieve high performance of 3-D FFT in distributed-memory parallel systems. Most of the approaches require all-to-all communi-

cation among parallel computing processes. For example, in the FFTW [2, 17] and P3DFFT [7, 24] libraries, each process exchanges a 3-D array with other processes using `MPI_Alltoall`, then performs local 1-D FFT computations on a newly assigned array. Researchers tried to increase the parallel 3-D FFT performance through computation-communication overlap. One example is Bell et. al's UPC code [9], which divides an input array into multiple small blocks and overlaps the computation on each block with the communication for other blocks. In this way, they could hide communication latency behind computation.

As the MPI library is widely and successfully used in the parallel computing community, it is important to design a parallel 3-D FFT code based on MPI and achieve portability as well as high performance. However, none of the prior overlap approaches effectively used the non-blocking `MPI_Ialltoall` operation described in the MPI-3.0 standard [16]. Kandalla et. al [22] implemented their own `MPI_Ialltoall` and used it to overlap computation and communication between multiple independent input arrays. Kandalla et. al's approach is not effective in many scientific applications because scientific simulations [21, 25] normally perform successive 3-D FFT operations on a single array. Hoefler et. al [18] also followed the MPI-3.0 standard, and successfully overlapped computation and communication on a single 3-D FFT operation. However, Hoefler et. al's implementation does not optimize computation-communication overlap.

In this paper, we describe a new parallel 3-D FFT code with `MPI_Ialltoall` that overlaps computation and communication to achieve high performance. Our design approach is similar to prior work by Bell et. al [9] and Hoefler et. al [18]. We divide an input array into multiple small blocks to overlap computation on one block with communication on other blocks. However, there are several unique characteristics of our design. First, we *optimize computation-communication overlap*. We hide communication behind as much computation as possible. Second, we design a *portable* code. We use `MPI_Test` for fully asynchronous communication [19] rather than rely on special hardware support or separate threads. Third, we also *optimize local computation*. We improve cache performance through loop tiling. Last, we *parameterize* our parallel 3-D FFT code. We can adjust the parameters and potentially cope with the complex trade-off regarding our optimization techniques.

To achieve the best performance of 3-D FFT, we *utilize auto-tuning*. Our new parallel 3-D FFT code contains many tunable parameters that can affect the performance. It is not feasible to hand-tune those parameters because the parameter space is very large (billions of possible configurations). Also, the optimal configuration may vary widely depending on system environment such as hardware, OS, and compiler. Thus, it will not work to tune in one system and reuse the optimal configuration for another. This paper also presents a method to find a good parameter configuration efficiently in the large parameter space. We integrate our parallel 3-D FFT code with the Active Harmony auto-tuning framework [28]. Our new contribution for auto-tuning is to introduce several techniques to help Active Harmony tune our FFT code fast and effectively.

The rest of the paper is organized as follows. We first provide background information in Section 2. Sections 3 and 4 describe how we design and auto-tune our parallel 3-D FFT code. Section 5 evaluates our approach with experiments. We describe the related work in Section 6. Finally, we conclude and discuss future work in Section 7.

2. Background and Assumptions

This section first reviews FFT computation. We then introduce a general method for parallel 3-D FFT. Last, we describe several basic assumptions underlying our design.

2.1 FFT

In mathematics, the Discrete Fourier Transform (DFT) converts a finite list of samples of a function into the list of coefficients of a finite combination of complex sinusoids. In other words, DFT converts a sampled function from the original time domain to the frequency domain. With an input array X of N complex numbers, a one-dimensional DFT produces an output array Y of N complex numbers. When $\omega_N = e^{-\frac{2\pi}{N}i}$, $Y[k]$ for $k = 0, 1, ..., N - 1$ is defined as follows:

$$Y[k] = \sum_{j=0}^{N-1} X[j]\omega_N^{jk} \qquad (1)$$

The Fast Fourier Transform (FFT) refers to an efficient algorithm to compute DFT. The Cooley-Tukey algorithm [10] is the most common FFT algorithm which takes $O(N \log N)$ for 1-D DFT on N complex numbers. FFTW [17] is a widely used software library that computes DFT using various FFT algorithms including the Cooley-Tukey. For the rest of this paper, we will use the term FFT to refer to the DFT computation as well as the algorithm for DFT.

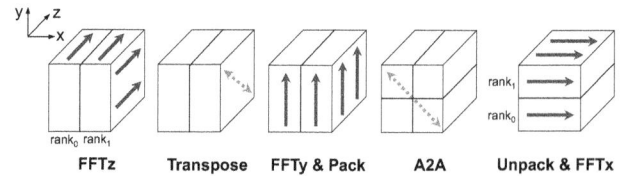

Figure 1. 1-D Decomposition Method for Parallel 3-D FFT

The d-dimensional FFT can be computed simply as the composition of a sequence of d sets of 1-D FFTs along each dimension. For example, 3-D FFT for N^3 complex numbers can be computed by three sets of N^2 1-D FFTs along each dimension.

2.2 1-D Decomposition Method for Parallel 3-D FFT

Our design for a parallel 3-D FFT that will be described in Section 3 basically follows the *1-D domain decomposition* method. The method is used by many parallel 3-D FFT codes [2, 9, 18]. We now describe the overall procedure of the 1-D domain decomposition method by defining seven steps in the procedure. Then in Section 3, we will present how we improve the procedure through computation-communication overlap.

Figure 1 shows the overall procedure of parallel 3-D FFT with 1-D domain decomposition. We parallelize 3-D FFT with p processes rank$_0$, rank$_1$, ..., rank$_{(p-1)}$, and Figure 1 shows an example of $p = 2$. An input 3-D array is divided equally into p arrays along the x dimension and assigned to each process. Then each process executes the following steps on each divided 3-D array:

1. **FFTz**: Compute 1-D FFTs along the z dimension. (Assume that elements on the z dimension are adjacent in memory.)

2. **Transpose**: Change the memory layout for the next step, so that elements on the y dimension are adjacent in memory.

3. **FFTy**: Compute 1-D FFTs along the y dimension.

4. **Pack**: Pack the 3-D array data into a buffer in preparation for all-to-all communication.

5. **A2A**: Perform blocking all-to-all communication among all p processes.

6. **Unpack**: Unpack the received data into the 3-D array with the new memory layout such that elements on the x dimension are adjacent in memory. After this step, the entire input 3-D array is divided into p arrays along the y dimension.

7. **FFTx**: Compute 1-D FFTs along the x dimension.

An alternative way to compute a parallel 3-D FFT is to use a 2-D domain decomposition. The 2-D domain decomposition method decomposes an input array along two

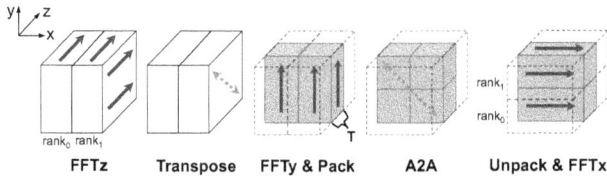

Figure 2. Our Approach for Parallel 3-D FFT

dimensions rather than one dimension. Accordingly, the method is more scalable than 1-D domain decomposition since we can use up to N^2 parallel computing processes for a 3-D FFT operation on N^3 complex numbers. However, 2-D decomposition requires two steps of all-to-all communication, which involves a highly complex communication pattern. So, depending on the system environment, 1-D decomposition can be a better choice than 2-D decomposition. In this paper, we focus on 1-D decomposition and compare the performance with other approaches that use a 1-D decomposition. We consider it as a future work to extend our method with the 2-D decomposition method.

2.3 Assumptions

First, this paper focuses on the *forward* transform that transforms X into Y in Equation 1. Our approach can be easily applied to transform Y backward into X.

Second, we only describe the *complex-to-complex* transform that takes an input array of complex numbers and produces an output array of complex numbers. There are special techniques [26] that can transform real numbers to complex numbers faster than the complex-to-complex transform. Our methods for computation-communication overlap is also applicable to the techniques for the real-to-complex transform.

Third, for simplicity, this paper only presents results for the case of $N_x \bmod p = 0$ and $N_y \bmod p = 0$, where an input 3-D array has N_x and N_y elements on the x and y dimensions, respectively, and p is the number of parallel processes. Note that our current code handles the general case whether N_x and N_y are divisible by p or not.

Last, we focus on the *in-place* transform and want the output to overwrite the input array. Our approach can be applied directly for the out-of-place transform where the output is written to a separate output array.

3. New Design of Parallel 3-D FFT

We improve the 1-D decomposition method by overlapping computation and communication. Our overlap strategy is similar to prior work by Bell et. al [9] and Hoefler et. al [18]. Each process divides an input array into small blocks and overlaps computation on one block with communication for other blocks. However, there are several unique contributions in our design. First, we overlap communication with as much computation as possible. For example, while Hoefler et. al's implementation [18] only overlaps the FFTy and

Pack steps with A2A, we also make progress for A2A during Unpack and FFTx. Second, we design a portable code that requires no support of hardware or separate threads for asynchronous communication progression [19]. Third, we also optimize local computation by improving cache performance through loop tiling [29]. Last, our code contains ten tunable parameters so that we can cope with the complex trade-off regarding our optimization techniques.

3.1 Overall Procedure

Figure 2 shows the overall procedure of our parallel 3-D FFT. Algorithms 1-3 describe pseudocodes for each process. Assume that an entire input 3-D array has N_x, N_y, and N_z elements (complex numbers) on the x, y, and z dimensions, respectively. So each of p processes is assigned a partial 3-D array of $\frac{N_x}{p} \times N_y \times N_z$ elements. The memory layout for the divided 3-D array in each process starts with x-y-z in the row-major order. So the elements on the z dimension are adjacent in memory.

Following the original 1-D decomposition method, Algorithm 1 first computes 1-D FFTs along the z dimension (FFTz) and rearranges the memory layout to z-x-y (Transpose). To achieve high performance for the FFTz step, we utilize the highly optimized code for 1-D FFT from the FFTW library. For the Transpose step, the FFTW *guru* interface is used to execute a high-performance routine of memory rearrangement.

We then continue to the next steps to fulfill computation-communication overlap. Each process first divides the input 3-D array into multiple small blocks along the z dimension as shown in Figure 2. We call each divided block a *communication tile*. We define a tile size parameter $\boldsymbol{T}$ to handle the trade-off between the overlap efficacy and the messaging efficiency. With small T, we can overlap many computations with communication but there would be a large overhead of exchanging many small-sized messages. If T gets bigger, there will be less overlap but higher efficiency for communication. Thus we should find a good value of T to achieve high performance. Section 4 will discuss the method to auto-tune T and other parameters of our 3-D FFT code. Each tile contains T elements on the z dimension. So the number of elements in each communication tile is equal to $\frac{N_x}{p} \times N_y \times T$.

We also define a window size parameter $\boldsymbol{W}$ to specify the degree of communication parallelism. It is also important to adjust W properly to utilize as many concurrent communication connections as possible.

For each communication tile, Algorithm 1 repeats the FFTy, Pack, A2A, Unpack, and FFTx steps. Note that, unlike the original 1-D decomposition method, Algorithm 1 uses the non-blocking MPI all-to-all operation (`MPI_Ialltoall` and `MPI_Wait`) for the A2A step. Thus we can overlap computation (FFTy, Pack, Unpack, and FFTx) on one communication tile with communication (A2A) for other tiles. Algorithm 2 describes a pseudocode for the FFTy and Pack

---

Algorithm 1: Parallel 3-D FFT on Each Process

---

1 FFTz: 1-D FFTs along the z dimension
2 Transpose: Change the memory layout from x-y-z to z-x-y
3 Divide an input array into $k = \lceil N_z/T \rceil$ tiles of size T along the z dimension
4 **for** $i \leftarrow 0$ **to** $k + W - 1$ **do**
5   **if** $i < k$ **then** FFTy and Pack on tile i
6   **if** $i \geq W$ **then** MPI_Wait on tile $(i - W)$
7   **if** $i < k$ **then** MPI_Ialltoall on tile i
8   **if** $i \geq W$ **then** Unpack and FFTx on tile $(i - W)$

Algorithm 2: FFTy and Pack on Tile i

---

1 Divide tile i into sub-tiles of size $P_x \times N_y \times P_z$ along the x and z dimensions
2 **foreach** *sub-tile* **do**
3   **foreach** *1-D array along the y dimension* **do**
4   FFTy: Compute 1-D FFT
5   Call MPI_Test on W previous tiles F_y times in total during this algorithm for tile i
6   Pack: Pack the current sub-tile into a buffer
7   Call MPI_Test on W previous tiles F_p times in total during this algorithm for tile i

---

Algorithm 3: Unpack and FFTx on Tile i

---

1 Divide tile i into sub-tiles of size $N_x \times U_y \times U_z$ along the y and z dimensions
2 **foreach** *sub-tile* **do**
3   Unpack: Unpack the current sub-tile from a buffer into the input array with the z-y-x memory layout
4   Call MPI_Test on W next tiles F_u times in total during this algorithm for tile i
5   **foreach** *1-D array along the x dimension* **do**
6   FFTx: Compute 1-D FFT
7   Call MPI_Test on W next tiles F_x times in total during this algorithm for tile i

---

steps on one communication tile, and Algorithm 3 describes Unpack and FFTx. Details of Algorithms 2 and 3 will be described in Section 3.4. After the Unpack step, the data in each communication tile are rearranged in memory to the z-y-x order, so that we can execute the FFTx step on 1-D arrays along the x dimension. Like the FFTz step, we rely on FFTW's optimized code of 1-D FFT for the FFTy and FFTx steps.

3.2 Computation-Communication Overlap

Figure 3 shows how Algorithm 1 overlaps computation and communication between tiles over time. W is set to be two as an example in the figure. The long dashed arrow represents a single control flow of each process during the for loop in Algorithm 1. Note that there are at most W tiles with active communication being executed. While the process is working on tile i for the FFTy and Pack steps, the all-to-all communication (A2A) for two previous tiles $(i - 2)$ and $(i - 1)$ takes place in the background. Also, when the process is working on tile i for Unpack and FFTx, the communication for two next tiles $(i + 1)$ and $(i + 2)$ goes on in the background. Likewise, during A2A on tile i, the previous two tiles are computed for Unpack and FFTx, and the next two tiles are computed for FFTy and Pack. A key characteristic of our design is that we optimize the performance by having all the computation steps (FFTy, Pack, Unpack and FFTx) overlapped with communication (A2A).

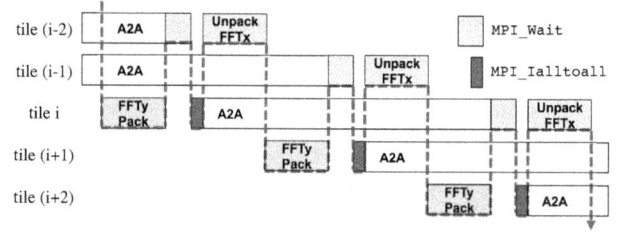

Figure 3. Computation-Communication Overlap between Communication Tiles over Time

3.3 Asynchronous Message Progression

In order to optimize the computation-communication overlap, *fully asynchronous communication* [19] is required for the A2A step. In other words, the non-blocking all-to-all communication should make progress while computation takes place. The first possible approach to ensure asynchronous message progression is to offload protocol processing to the communication hardware such as a programmable network interface card. Alternatively, we could maintain a thread on a separate CPU, so the thread can make progress for the all-to-all communication in the background. A third option is *manual progression*, which is to call MPI_Test periodically during the computation and let the MPI library make progress for the corresponding non-blocking all-to-all operation. We choose the manual progression method due to its greater portability. Accordingly, our code does not require any hardware support or separate threads for message progression.

It is important to determine the proper frequency of MPI_Test calls. Too high of frequency will incur unnecessary function call overhead, and too low of frequency will limit the progress of the all-to-all communication. To cope with the trade-off, we have four tunable parameters to adjust the frequency of MPI_Test calls. F_y defines the number of

MPI_Test calls during FFTy for one communication tile. F_p is the frequency parameter during the Pack step for one communication tile. Likewise, F_u is for Unpack, and F_x is for FFTx.

3.4 Loop Tiling for Pack and Unpack

Algorithm 2 describes the FFTy and Pack steps on each communication tile. To optimize the FFTy and Pack steps with respect to cache reuse, we tile the loop inside each communication tile. As shown in the left side of Figure 4, each communication tile is divided again into *sub-tiles* with P_x elements on the x dimension and P_z on the z dimension. So each sub-tile contains $P_x \times N_y \times P_z$ elements. Iterating over each sub-tile, we execute a 1-D FFT computation along the y dimension, then pack the result into a communication buffer. In this way, we can increase cache hit rate during Pack by reading the sub-tile information from the cache after FFTy. Note that, as described in Section 3.3, Algorithm 2 calls MPI_Test ($F_y + F_p$) times for asynchronous message progression.

Similarly to FFTy and Pack, we optimize Unpack and FFTx by using the loop tiling technique shown in Algorithm 3. Each communication tile is divided into sub-tiles along the y and z dimensions as shown in the right side of Figure 4. The size of each sub-tile is determined by two parameters U_y and U_z. Thus, we can increase cache hits during FFTx by reading the sub-tile information from the cache after Unpack. Algorithm 3 also calls MPI_Test ($F_u + F_x$) times for asynchronous message progression.

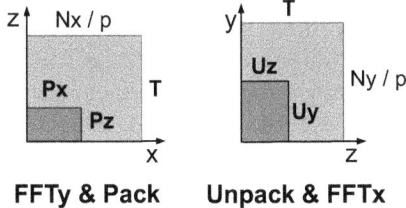

Figure 4. Loop Tiling for Improving Cache Performance

3.5 Improvement for the $N_x = N_y$ Case

As described in Section 3.1, the Transpose step changes the memory layout from x-y-z to z-x-y in preparation for FFTy. For the special case of an input array with $N_x = N_y$, we can improve the performance of Transpose by producing the new memory layout of x-z-y instead of z-x-y. The x-z-y rearrangement should be faster than the original z-x-y rearrangement as the former is simpler and has better cache reuse than the latter. Nonetheless, we cannot use the fast x-z-y rearrangement when $N_x \neq N_y$ because we use an in-place 3-D FFT and want the output to overwrite the input array. Suppose that Transpose produces the x-z-y layout for an input array with $N_x \neq N_y$ in Figure 2. Then it is impossible to match the memory area of a communication

tile before A2A with the memory area after A2A because we divide the input array into communication tiles along the z dimension. On the other hand, for a special input with $N_x = N_y$, we can have the same memory area for A2A source and destination data in each communication tile, by generating the y-z-x layout (as opposed to z-y-x) after A2A and Unpack. Thus, for the case of $N_x = N_y$, Transpose rearranges the memory layout from x-y-z to x-z-y, so that we can improve the overall 3-D FFT performance.

4. Auto-Tuning Method

This section describes how we achieve high performance of parallel 3-D FFT by utilizing auto-tuning techniques. Our parallel 3-D FFT code contains ten parameters as described in Section 3. Table 1 summarizes these parameters. To the best of our knowledge, our work is the first that auto-tunes a complex parameter space to optimize computation-communication overlap in parallel 3-D FFT. We first describe how we optimize the code sections that are performed by FFTW. We then justify why we should auto-tune the ten parameters in Table 1. We also introduce an auto-tuning software framework that we use to tune our code, and describe the general tuning procedure. Last, we present our main contribution for auto-tuning. We describe several novel techniques to auto-tune the 3-D FFT code fast and effectively.

4.1 Tuning 1-D FFTs and Transpose

As described in Section 3.1, we rely on the FFTW library for all 1-D FFT computations and the Transpose step. Before we auto-tune the ten parameters in Table 1, we first optimize the FFTW code performance through the auto-tuning feature of FFTW. We choose to use the FFTW_PATIENT option for FFTW tuning among three options. Since we want to achieve the best performance of parallel 3-D FFT, we do not use the FFTW_MEASURE option. FFTW_MEASURE tunes the FFTW library slightly less than FFTW_PATIENT. We do not run FFTW_EXHAUSTIVE because it takes too much time to auto-tune the FFTW library. With a few empirical tests, we found the code tuned with FFTW_PATIENT had the similar performance to FFTW_EXHAUSTIVE. Further details about the auto-tuning feature of FFTW can be found in [2, 17].

4.2 Why Should We Auto-Tune the Ten Parameters?

After the FFTW tuning is finished, we continue to auto-tune the parameters defined by our parallel 3-D FFT code. Figure 5 gives evidence that the ten parameters in Table 1 really affect the code's performance, so it is necessary to tune the parameters to achieve the high performance. To gauge the impact of those parameters, we measured the execution time of our 3-D FFT code for 200 random parameter configurations using 16 processes and an array with 256^3 elements. We exclude the FFTz and Transpose steps as those steps have the fixed performance regardless of parameter values. Figure 5 shows the cumulative distribution of the execution time. The x-axis represents the execution time, and

Table 1. Ten Tunable Parameters of Our Parallel 3-D FFT Code

parameter	meaning
T	the number of elements on the z dimension in one communication tile (tile size)
W	the maximum number of communication tiles involved in concurrent all-to-all communication (window size)
P_x	the number of elements on the x dimension in one sub-tile during Pack
P_z	the number of elements on the z dimension in one sub-tile during Pack
U_y	the number of elements on the y dimension in one sub-tile during Unpack
U_z	the number of elements on the z dimension in one sub-tile during Unpack
F_y	the number of `MPI_Test` calls during FFTy for one communication tile
F_p	the number of `MPI_Test` calls during Pack for one communication tile
F_u	the number of `MPI_Test` calls during Unpack for one communication tile
F_x	the number of `MPI_Test` calls during FFTx for one communication tile

the y-axis shows the cumulative fraction of 200 parameter configurations. The code performance widely varies around from 0.16 to 0.48 second (nearly $3\times$) depending on parameter configurations.

We also claim that since the parameter space is very large, we need to auto-tune the parameters rather than adjusting them manually. It is hard to define the size of the parameter space by a single number because the range of possible parameter values is dependent on various factors such as the input array size, the number of processes, and other parameter values. So we can consider a conservative case where each parameter only has ten possible values. In spite of the conservative calculation, we have a large number (10^{10}) of possible parameter configurations. Since it is not feasible to investigate all the configurations manually and exhaustively, we must find a smart and fast way to auto-tune the parameters and determine a good configuration.

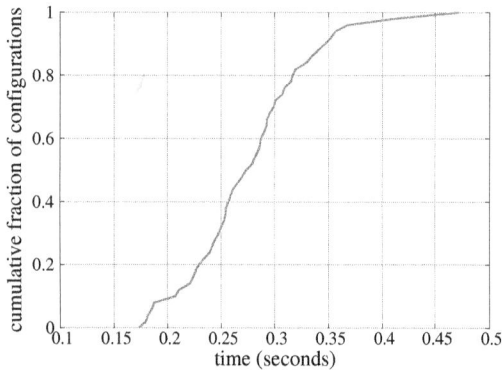

Figure 5. Cumulative Distribution of the 3-D FFT Execution Time for 200 Random Configurations (16 cores and 256^3 elements)

4.3 Active Harmony: An Auto-Tuning Framework

Active Harmony (AH) [11, 28] is a general software framework to auto-tune user-specified parameters for a tunable code. Figure 6 shows the overall procedure of how AH interacts with a tuning target (our parallel 3-D FFT code designed in Section 3). The AH server searches efficiently through a large parameter space and decides a parameter configuration

to be tested on the tuning target. The AH client receives a parameter configuration from the server, executes the tuning target with the received configuration, and reports the performance back to the server. This procedure is repeated until the search converges.

Although AH supports several different search strategies, we use the Nelder-Mead (NM) method [23] to search for a good parameter configuration as it is a commonly used optimization technique in many fields of science. NM uses the concept of a *simplex*, which is a polytope of $(d+1)$ vertices in d dimensions. For example, a simplex is a triangle in two dimensions. The AH client measures the performance of the tuning target at each point (or parameter configuration) on a simplex. NM generates a new test point by extrapolating the performance values measured at points on the simplex. Then NM replaces one of the simplex points with the new point. For example, for $(d+1)$ simplex points, NM can sometimes replace the worst simplex point W with a new point R such that R is reflected from W through the centroid of the remaining d points. The search procedure finishes when all the points on a simplex are close to each other, and can be considered to be converged to a single point. Further details about NM are described in [23].

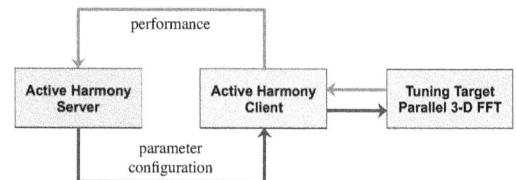

Figure 6. Auto-Tuning Procedure

4.4 Techniques for Effective and Fast Auto-Tuning

We now introduce several techniques to auto-tune the ten parameters in Table 1 effectively and fast. First, we *penalize an infeasible configuration*. The possible values of our parameters reside in a range that can be limited by other parameters. For example, the tile size T must be ≥ 1 and $\leq N_z$, and the sub-tile size P_z must be ≥ 1 and $\leq T$. However, the Nelder-Mead method of AH is originally designed to work in a multi-dimensional orthotope (hyperrectangle) parameter space. [1] So it is possible that the AH server provides a test configuration that contains *out-of-range* values, for example, P_z that is $> T$. To cope with an infeasible parameter configuration, we modify the AH client in the following way. When the AH client receives an infeasible configuration, it reports the worst performance value (infinity) immediately back to the AH server without executing the tuning target code. Then the AH server and the NM strategy will suggest another configuration that might be in a feasible area in the parameter space.

The second technique is to *reuse the prior performance data for fast tuning*. NM was originally designed to optimize a continuous function. To support the discrete integer domain of parameters, the AH server determines the closest integer point to a simplex point in a continuous domain. So the AH server can sometimes provide the same configuration even though it has been already tested before. To save tuning time, we maintain the history of tested configurations and utilize it when the AH client receives the previously tested configuration again.

The third technique is also about improving the auto-tuning speed. In the auto-tuning procedure, we can *skip executing the code section that is independent of the ten parameters*. Since the performance of the FFTz and Transpose steps is fixed regardless of a parameter configuration, the AH client does not execute FFTz and Transpose during the auto-tuning procedure.

Fourth is *search space reduction*. Instead of searching a whole set of all possible values of a parameter, we reduce a search space to a log scale and consider power-of-two values for testing. The minimum and maximum values are additionally considered for testing whether the value is a power of two or not. So, we can also take into account the boundary values in the original parameter space after reducing the search space. For example, when $N_z = 24$, T can be 1, 2, 4, 8, 16, or 24. As an exception, the log-scale reduction is not applied to W because there are few possible values for W.

Finally, we carefully construct the initial simplex that the NM uses. The initial simplex can affect the tuning time and the quality of the tuning result. Thus it is important to guess a good initial simplex so that NM can find the global minimum point in a short time without falling into local minimum points. In this paper we determine an initial simplex in the following way, and demonstrate its performance with experiments in Section 5. We need to investigate further how to determine a good initial simplex and leave it as an open question. We construct an initial simplex by first defining a

default point and determining the other ten points around the default point. We define the default point as follows. First, we set $T = N_z/16$ to guarantee some degree of computation-communication overlap. $W = 2$ is set to exploit some level of communication parallelism. Assuming that a cache size is equal to 256KB, we can fit 16K complex number elements in a cache. Assuming we use the cache to read/write a sub-tile for data-packing, we can have 8K complex numbers as a sub-tile size for Algorithm 2. Thus, we set $P_x = 8192/N_y$ and $P_z = 8192/N_y/P_x$. Similarly, it is set to be $U_y = 8192/N_x$ and $U_z = 8192/N_x/U_y$. We set $F_y = F_p = F_u = F_z = p/2$ where p is equal to the number of processes as `MPI_Ialltoall` requires more rounds of point-to-point communication as p increases.

5. Evaluation

We first show how fast our auto-tuned 3-D FFT is compared to two other approaches. Then we analyze where the improvement of our approach comes from. Last, we quantify why it is necessary to use an auto-tuning method for our 3-D FFT code.

5.1 Platforms and Comparison Models

We use two platforms for our experiments. The first platform, which is named **UMD-Cluster**, is a 64-node Linux cluster at the University of Maryland. Each node consists of two Intel Xeon 2.66GHz (SSE) cores. Each core has a 512KB L2 cache. We used one core per node in our experiments. A Myrinet 2000 interconnect is used to connect nodes. For a non-blocking all-to-all operation on UMD-Cluster, we use `NBC_Ialltoall` of the NBC library 1.1.1 [3, 20] on top of OpenMPI 1.4.1 [6]. The NBC library is designed compatible to the MPI-3.0 standard. FFTW 3.3.2 is used for 1-D FFT. We used `mpicxx` of OpenMPI 1.4.1 with the `-O2` option to compile all the libraries and codes.

The second platform, which is named **Hopper**, a Cray XE6 machine at NERSC [5]. Each node contains two twelve-core AMD MagnyCours 2.1GHz processors (153,216 cores total in the machine). Each core has its own L1 and L2 caches, with 64KB and 512KB, respectively. We used four cores per processor (eight cores per node) in our experiments. Nodes are connected via a Cray Gemini Network that forms a 3-D torus. For a non-blocking all-to-all operation on Hopper, we use `MPIX_Ialltoall` of the Cray Message Passing Toolkit 5.6.0 that is derived from the MPICH [4] implementation. FFTW 3.3.0.1 is used for 1-D FFT. We used the PGI C++ compiler with `-fast` option to compile all the codes except the underlying libraries. The FFTW and MPI libraries are already compiled and installed in the Hopper system.

We compare three different methods for parallel 3-D FFT. **FFTW** is the MPI-enabled FFTW library. We tune and optimize the parallel 3-D FFT computation of FFTW by using the `FFTW_PATIENT` option. The second approach is **NEW**,

---

[1] The developers of Active Harmony are currently implementing a constraint plugin that supports a non-hyperrectangle parameter space, but it was not ready when this paper was written.

Table 2. Parallel 3-D FFT Time (seconds)

(a) UMD-Cluster

p	N^3	FFTW	NEW	TH
16	256^3	0.369	0.245	0.319
16	384^3	1.207	0.725	1.063
16	512^3	2.948	1.966	2.514
16	640^3	5.927	3.515	5.234
32	256^3	0.189	0.153	0.197
32	384^3	0.653	0.477	0.644
32	512^3	1.580	1.119	1.520
32	640^3	3.129	2.158	3.061

(b) Hopper

p	N^3	FFTW	NEW	TH
16	256^3	0.096	0.087	0.106
16	384^3	0.322	0.293	0.354
16	512^3	0.836	0.693	0.885
16	640^3	1.636	1.428	1.725
32	256^3	0.061	0.046	0.061
32	384^3	0.189	0.146	0.198
32	512^3	0.475	0.340	0.488
32	640^3	0.920	0.747	0.930

(c) Hopper (large scale)

p	N^3	FFTW	NEW	TH
128	1280^3	2.426	1.638	2.505
128	1536^3	4.722	3.092	4.573
128	1792^3	8.029	5.115	7.746
128	2048^3	11.269	7.079	12.994
256	1280^3	1.373	0.920	1.389
256	1536^3	2.574	1.650	2.452
256	1792^3	4.781	2.850	4.253
256	2048^3	6.467	3.679	6.850

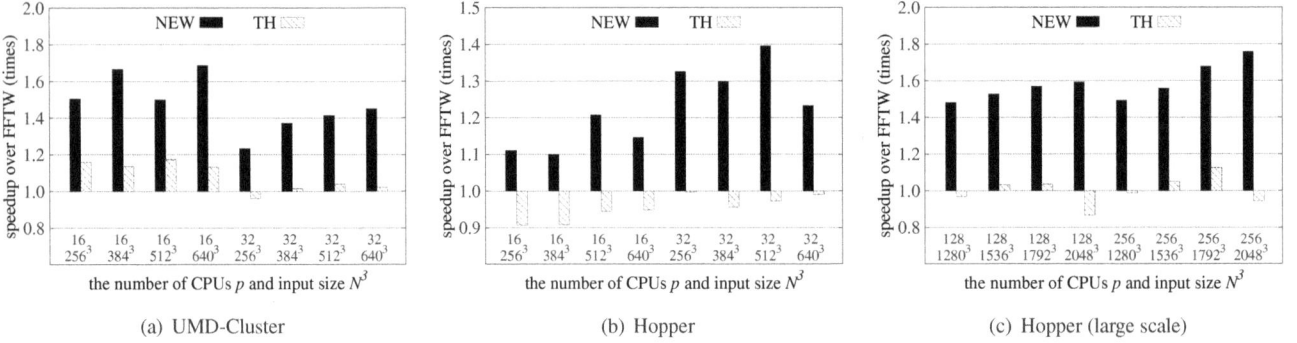

(a) UMD-Cluster   (b) Hopper   (c) Hopper (large scale)

Figure 7. Parallel 3-D FFT Speedup over FFTW

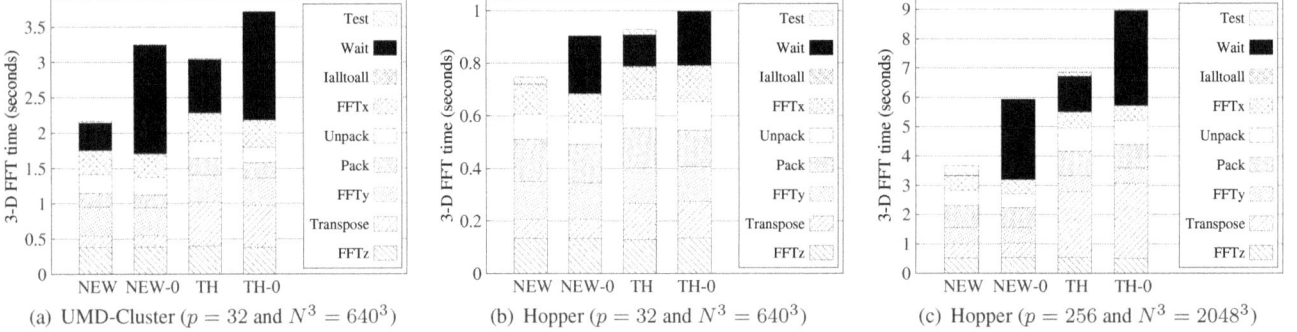

(a) UMD-Cluster ($p = 32$ and $N^3 = 640^3$)   (b) Hopper ($p = 32$ and $N^3 = 640^3$)   (c) Hopper ($p = 256$ and $N^3 = 2048^3$)

Figure 8. Performance Breakdown

which is our method described in Section 3. Since NEW relies on the FFTW library for some computations, we auto-tune those computations with the `FFTW_PATIENT` option. The major part of NEW is auto-tuned by the Nelder-Mead strategy of Active Harmony as described in Section 4. Last is **TH**, which is Hoefler et. al's parallel 3-D FFT kernel [18] that also implements computation-communication overlap with the MPI-3.0 standard. For fair comparison, we slightly optimized the original code. We auto-tune 1-D FFT computations with the `FFTW_PATIENT` flag on. Also, we parameterize the code with three parameters of a communication tile size, a window size, and a frequency of `MPI_Test` calls, then auto-tune the three parameters with Active Harmony similarly to NEW. Thus, TH is the combination of a prior

work for parallel 3-D FFT and our auto-tuning method described in Section 4. TH shows the higher performance than Hoefler et. al's original code.

5.2 Parallel 3-D FFT Performance

5.2.1 UMD-Cluster

Table 2(a) shows the 3-D FFT execution time of the three different approaches. p is the number of parallel computing processes. N is the number of elements on each dimension in a 3-D input array. So an input array contains N^3 complex numbers. To cope with the execution noise, we conducted five runs of auto-tuning each with five runs of 3-D FFT, and picked the best performance out of the 25 runs for each of the three algorithm being compared. For all different settings of p and N, NEW is faster than FFTW and TH. Figure 7(a) shows the speedup of NEW and TH over FFTW. NEW has speedup over FFTW of $1.23\times$ to $1.68\times$. On the other hand, TH, the other overlap approach, shows the maximum speedup of $1.17\times$ compared to FFTW, and there is even a setting such that TH is worse than FFTW.

To better explain the effectiveness of NEW, we break down the performance of NEW and TH for the $p = 32$ and $N^3 = 640^3$ configuration, and show the result in Figure 8(a). Two extra variants of FFT are examined. **NEW-0** is a non-overlapped version of NEW where W and all the frequency parameters are set to be zero with all the other parameters equal to NEW. Also, lines 6 and 7 in Algorithm 1 are replaced with MPI_Ialltoall and MPI_Wait on tile i. Likewise, **TH-0** is a non-overlapped version of TH. The all-to-all communication time for this setting is around 1.6 seconds as marked with Wait in NEW-0, and the "overlappable" computation time (FFTy, Pack, Unpack, and FFTx) is 1.2 seconds. NEW reduces the Wait time down to 0.4 seconds, which means NEW nearly achieves the perfect computation-communication overlap. This high degree of overlap explains why NEW is faster than FFTW. Since FFTW does not exploit non-blocking communication, the performance should be similar to NEW-0. On the other hand, TH performs a low degree of overlap and results in a long 1.3 seconds for Wait. This is because TH does not overlap the Unpack and FFTx steps with communications while NEW uses all the computation steps for overlap as described in Section 3. Also, we can see that NEW optimizes computation better than TH. First, as NEW utilizes the highly-optimized matrix transpose of FFTW, NEW shows a large improvement for Transpose compared to TH in Figure 8(a). Second, the time NEW spent for Pack and FFTx is shorter than that of TH, which is the result of the loop tiling technique of NEW.

It is interesting that NEW shows better performance for $p = 16$ than $p = 32$ in Figure 7(a). It is not easy to find the exact reason for this because we measured the performance as the speedup over FFTW, and we are not aware of the details of the FFTW behavior. However, assuming the NEW-0 approach should be close to FFTW, we can find a partial reason. For the best overlap, the computation time should be ideally equal to the communication time. We found that, on UMD-Cluster, the computation-communication time is balanced better at $p = 16$ than $p = 32$. The reason for the worse computation-communication balance at $p = 32$ is the high complexity of the all-to-all operation at high p. So, for example, NEW-0 of Figure 7(a) shows the larger communication (Wait) time than the computation time (FFTy, Pack, Unpack, and FFTx).

5.2.2 Hopper

We conducted the same experiment on Hopper as what we did on UMD-Cluster. Table 2(b) shows the 3-D FFT execution time on Hopper. Figure 7(b) shows the speedup of NEW and TH over FFTW. Figure 8(b) shows the perfor-

Table 3. Parameter Values Found via Auto-Tuning
(a) UMD-Cluster

p	N^3	T	W	P_x	P_z	U_y	U_z	F_y	F_p	F_u	F_x
16	256^3	32	3	8	2	16	4	32	8	8	16
16	384^3	16	2	16	1	16	2	16	16	8	16
16	512^3	64	3	16	2	16	2	32	16	32	32
16	640^3	32	3	16	1	16	2	16	16	16	16
32	256^3	64	3	8	8	8	4	64	8	16	64
32	384^3	32	2	12	2	8	2	32	8	8	16
32	512^3	32	2	16	4	16	4	64	8	8	16
32	640^3	32	2	8	1	8	1	16	16	16	16

(b) Hopper

p	N^3	T	W	P_x	P_z	U_y	U_z	F_y	F_p	F_u	F_x
16	256^3	32	3	16	2	8	2	16	16	16	32
16	384^3	32	3	24	1	24	2	16	16	16	16
16	512^3	64	3	32	1	16	2	64	64	64	64
16	640^3	64	3	16	2	16	2	64	32	64	32
32	256^3	64	2	8	4	8	4	64	16	16	64
32	384^3	64	3	12	2	8	2	128	32	64	128
32	512^3	128	3	16	2	8	4	128	64	32	64
32	640^3	64	3	16	2	16	2	64	64	64	64

(c) Hopper (large scale)

p	N^3	T	W	P_x	P_z	U_y	U_z	F_y	F_p	F_u	F_x
128	1280^3	256	4	10	2	8	2	512	128	256	512
128	1536^3	128	3	12	1	8	2	1024	128	128	1024
128	1792^3	128	4	14	1	8	2	256	128	128	512
128	2048^3	128	4	16	1	8	2	512	128	128	512
256	1280^3	256	4	5	4	2	8	1280	64	64	1024
256	1536^3	256	3	6	2	4	2	1024	128	256	1024
256	1792^3	256	3	7	2	4	2	512	128	256	1024
256	2048^3	512	3	8	2	4	2	2048	256	512	2048

mance breakdown for the setting of $p = 32$ and $N^3 = 640^3$. Like on UMD-Cluster, NEW is faster than TH with better optimized overlap and computation. But on Hopper, the speedup of NEW over FFTW ranges from $1.10\times$ to $1.40\times$, which is lower than the speedup on UMD-Cluster. This low speedup on Hopper comes from the relatively bad computation-communication time balance. For example, NEW-0 in Figure 8(b) shows a lower ratio of the Wait time than in Figure 8(a). This is because the Cray Gemini Network of Hopper is faster than the Myrinet 2000 on UMD-Cluster. Also, the intra-node communication between multiple cores in the same node on Hopper should be faster than the inter-node communication on UMD-Cluster. So the worse computation-communication time balance on Hopper limits the possibility of overlap and results in a relatively low speedup over FFTW. It is interesting that NEW shows worse performance for $p = 16$ than $p = 32$ in Figure 7(a). The reason for this difference on Hopper is the same as that on UMD-Cluster even though the result is opposite on UMD-Cluster. Due to the high complexity of the all-to-all operation, increasing p causes an increase in the ratio of the communication time to the computation time. So, the communication ratio at $p = 16$ is lower than that at $p = 32$. Since the communication ratio is already low at $p = 32$ because of the fast communication on Hopper, the lower communication ratio at $p = 16$ would results in a worse computation-communication balance.

We did the similar experiments on Hopper for larger scale settings with more cores and bigger input sizes. As seen in Table 2(c), Figure 7(c), and Figure 8(c), the trend is similar to the previous experiments on Hopper. We can see our approach NEW is still faster than FFTW and TH. The speedup of NEW over FFTW ranges from $1.48\times$ to $1.76\times$.

5.3 Auto-Tuning

As described in Section 4, the performance of our 3-D FFT widely varies depending on configurations. The varying performance in a large parameter space justifies why we need to auto-tune the 3-D FFT code.

5.3.1 Different Tuning Results on Different Systems

We found that the best parameter values in one system setting differ from those in another setting. Table 3 contains the auto-tuned parameter configurations of NEW that are used to create Table 2. The auto-tuned parameter configuration varies depending on system setting such as the underlying platform, input size, and the number of CPUs. The next question is how good is an auto-tuning result of the Nelder-Mead method, compared to random search. The tuning result for the setting of $p = 16$ and $N^3 = 256^3$ on UMD-Cluster ranks in the first percentile in the distribution of 200 random configurations in Figure 5. Although the Nelder-Mead method did not find the optimal configuration, its deterministic strategy works faster than the random search. For example, the Nelder-Mead method found the first percentile configuration after testing 35 configurations. However, the probability to find the point within 35 random configurations is only $1 - (1 - 0.01)^{35} \approx 30\%$.

5.3.2 Cross-Platform Test

We found that the tuning result from one platform does not work well for another platform. We executed the 3-D FFT code on UMD-Cluster with the tuning result from Hopper as in Table 3(b). The performance of this cross-platform test is named **CROSS** in Figure 9(a). NEW means the performance of the tuning result on UMD-Cluster, which should be the same as NEW in Figure 7(a). For all the settings, NEW is faster than CROSS. Specifically, NEW is around 10% faster than CROSS for $p = 32$ and $N^3 = 512^3$ on UMD-Cluster. Likewise, we have executed the 3-D FFT code on Hopper with the tuning result of the UMD-Cluster as in Table 3(a). The difference between NEW and CROSS in Figure 9(b) is more significant than that in Figure 9(a). NEW is around 20% faster than CROSS on Hopper when $p = 32$ and $N^3 = 512^3$. The best configuration for the UMD-Cluster is not the best on Hopper, and vice versa. Thus, it is necessary

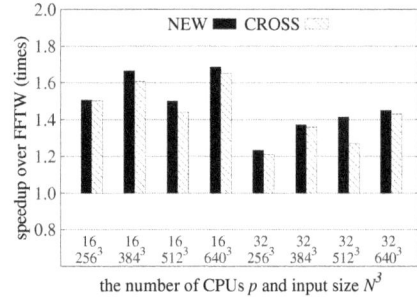

(a) UMD-Cluster

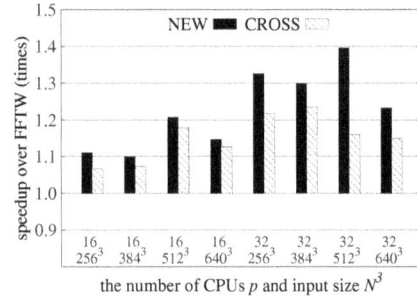

(b) Hopper

Figure 9. Cross-Platform Test

to auto-tune our 3-D FFT code for each different platform to achieve the best of its performance.

5.3.3 Auto-Tuning Time

Table 4 contains the time spent for auto-tuning to achieve the performance in Table 2. Although we focus on the 3-D FFT performance, it is not desirable to spend unacceptably long time on auto-tuning. NEW shows a comparable tuning speed to FFTW as NEW finds a good configuration faster for most of the cases. It takes less time for Active Harmony to tune TH than NEW because TH only has three parameters while NEW has ten. Fewer dimensions mean a small search space, and it is natural to find a good configuration quickly in a small search space.

6. Related Work

This section introduces several studies related to parallel 3-D FFT and describes how our approach is different from those studies.

FFTW [17] is the most popular library for FFT computations, and its MPI-enabled version supports parallel 3-D FFT. FFTW exploits no computation-communication overlap, which results in a relatively poor performance as shown in Section 5. P3DFFT [24], Ayala et. al [8], Takahashi [27], and Eleftheriou et. al [14] achieved high scalability with the high-dimensional domain decomposition technique. However, they did not include any computation-communication overlap. On the other hand, our approach increases the 3-

Table 4. Auto-Tuning Time (seconds)

(a) UMD-Cluster

p	N^3	FFTW	NEW	TH
16	256^3	22.569	16.443	5.732
16	384^3	60.859	27.178	13.279
16	512^3	87.568	123.993	30.916
16	640^3	202.134	197.916	71.724
32	256^3	14.388	11.385	3.768
32	384^3	44.795	28.489	7.834
32	512^3	67.426	45.308	25.124
32	640^3	174.081	73.263	52.897

(b) Hopper

p	N^3	FFTW	NEW	TH
16	256^3	11.413	9.091	2.221
16	384^3	37.786	17.342	17.984
16	512^3	69.912	43.718	27.020
16	640^3	249.358	87.573	22.857
32	256^3	6.614	6.467	1.382
32	384^3	23.317	155.975	10.425
32	512^3	41.969	165.527	6.666
32	640^3	188.474	38.279	15.027

(c) Hopper (large scale)

p	N^3	FFTW	NEW	TH
128	1280^3	461.240	140.986	34.474
128	1536^3	460.229	198.068	60.475
128	1792^3	484.678	335.273	83.986
128	2048^3	562.398	396.553	120.555
256	1280^3	400.582	80.085	17.172
256	1536^3	401.474	109.250	34.568
256	1792^3	414.020	144.743	46.684
256	2048^3	465.411	224.744	75.616

D FFT performance through computation-communication overlap.

Kandalla et. al [22] overlap the computation on one input array with the communication for other input arrays. This "inter-array" overlap is useful when there are many independent input arrays for 3-D FFT. However, scientific simulations [21, 25] normally need successive 3-D FFT computations over time on a single input array. In this case, our "intra-array" method is effective as we optimize computation-communication overlap inside each 3-D FFT operation. Also, Kandalla et. al's approach requires hardware support for asynchronous communication while our approach does not. 2DECOMP&FFT [1] follows Kandalla et. al's overlap method, so it naturally has the limitation of the inter-array overlap. Also, 2DECOMP&FFT is not optimized for asynchronous communication as they do not auto-tune the frequency of MPI_Test calls unlike our approach. Bell et. al [9] overlap computation and communication on a single input array. However, unlike our portable MPI-based approach, their code is written in UPC and requires hardware support for asynchronous communication. Also, the overlap may not be optimized because they use a fixed communication tile size. Fang et. al [15] lack portability as they use a specialized API for communication with special hardware support. Also, there is no auto-tuning of overlap-related parameters. Doi et. al [12] utilize multiple threads in a shared-memory parallel environment, and overlap computation and communication between different computing cores. On the other hand, we overlap the computation of one core with the communication of the same core. Hoefler et. al's approach [18] is the closest to our work, but it does not maximize computation-communication overlap, as shown with TH in Section 5.

Dotsenko et. al [13] auto-tuned the 3-D FFT computations on top of special GPU processors while our approach is more generalized based on MPI and CPU and focuses on computation-communication overlap.

7. Conclusions and Future Work

This paper has presented a novel method to optimize parallel 3-D FFT for computation-communication overlap. We first designed a portable parallel 3-D FFT code that uses the non-blocking MPI all-to-all operation and requires no hardware support for asynchronous communication. We then described a method to auto-tune the parameters of our 3-D FFT code in a large parameter space and optimize computation-communication overlap. With extensive experiments on two systems, we showed that our approach for parallel 3-D FFT maximized computation-communication overlap and performed faster than two existing approaches.

We are currently extending this work in several ways. First, we are improving the auto-tuning method. The quality and speed of the Nelder-Mead heuristic is dependent on how an initial simplex is defined. Although our definition of the initial simplex was successful, it is worth investigating if there exist other more effective initial simplex construction techniques. Also, we plan to try optimization strategies other than Nelder-Mead. Second, we intend to apply our overlap method to the 2-D domain decomposition technique. If successful, we could achieve high scalability with many computing cores as well as the high performance with the maximized computation-communication overlap. Finally, we plan to overlap additional computation and communication between multiple independent input arrays. The communication time can dominate the 3-D FFT performance at large scale where ran on many cores. So it would be helpful to overlap more communication time with computation. We are planning to find a method to achieve both intra-array and inter-array computation-communication overlap.

Acknowledgments

Support for this work was provided through Scientific Discovery through Advanced Computing (SciDAC) program funded by U.S. Department of Energy, Office of Science, Advanced Scientific Computing Research under award numbers ER25763 and ER26054.

We thank Torsten Hoefler for providing us with his parallel 3-D FFT code, which is used to evaluate our approach in Section 5. We are also grateful to Alan Sussman for reviewing this paper and providing helpful comments.

References

[1] 2decomp&fft. http://www.2decomp.org/.

[2] Fastest fourier transform in the west. http://www.fftw.org/.

[3] Libnbc - nonblocking mpi collective operations. http://htor.inf.ethz.ch/research/nbcoll/libnbc/.

[4] Mpich. http://www.mpich.org/.

[5] National energy research scientific computing center. http://www.nersc.gov/.

[6] Open mpi: Open source high performance computing. http://www.open-mpi.org/.

[7] Parallel three-dimensional fast fourier transforms. http://www.sdsc.edu/us/resources/p3dfft/.

[8] O. Ayala and L.-P. Wang. Parallel implementation and scalability analysis of 3d fast fourier transform using 2d domain decomposition. *Parallel Computing*, 39(1), Jan. 2013.

[9] C. Bell, D. Bonachea, R. Nishtala, and K. Yelick. Optimizing bandwidth limited problems using one-sided communication and overlap. In *Proceedings of the 20th International Parallel & Distributed Processing Symposium (IPDPS)*. IEEE Computer Society Press, 2006.

[10] J. W. Cooley and J. W. Tukey. An Algorithm for the Machine Calculation of Complex Fourier Series. *Mathematics of Computation*, 19(90), 1965.

[11] C. Ţăpuş, I.-H. Chung, and J. K. Hollingsworth. Active harmony: towards automated performance tuning. In *Proceedings of the 2002 ACM/IEEE International Conference for High Performance Computing, Networking, Storage and Analysis (SC)*. ACM Press, 2002.

[12] J. Doi and Y. Negishi. Overlapping methods of all-to-all communication and fft algorithms for torus-connected massively parallel supercomputers. In *Proceedings of the 2010 ACM/IEEE International Conference for High Performance Computing, Networking, Storage and Analysis (SC)*. IEEE Computer Society Press, 2010.

[13] Y. Dotsenko, S. S. Baghsorkhi, B. Lloyd, and N. K. Govindaraju. Auto-tuning of fast fourier transform on graphics processors. In *Proceedings of the 16th ACM symposium on Principles and practice of parallel programming (PPoPP)*. ACM, 2011.

[14] M. Eleftheriou, B. G. Fitch, A. Rayshubskiy, T. J. C. Ward, and R. S. Germain. Scalable framework for 3d ffts on the blue gene/l supercomputer: implementation and early performance measurements. *IBM J. Res. Dev.*, 49(2), Mar. 2005.

[15] B. Fang, Y. Deng, and G. J. Martyna. Performance of the 3d fft on the 6d network torus qcdoc parallel supercomputer. *Computer Physics Communications*, 176(8), 2007.

[16] M. P. I. Forum. Mpi: A message-passing interface standard version 3.0. http://www.mpi-forum.org/docs/mpi-3.0/mpi30-report.pdf.

[17] M. Frigo and S. G. Johnson. The design and implementation of FFTW3. *Proceedings of the IEEE*, 93(2), 2005. Special issue on "Program Generation, Optimization, and Platform Adaptation".

[18] T. Hoefler, P. Gottschling, and A. Lumsdaine. Brief announcement: Leveraging non-blocking collective communication in high-performance applications. In *Proceedings of the 20th annual symposium on Parallelism in algorithms and architectures (SPAA)*. ACM, 2008.

[19] T. Hoefler and A. Lumsdaine. Message progression in parallel computing - to thread or not to thread? In *Proceedings of the 2008 IEEE International Conference on Cluster Computing (CLUSTER)*, 2008.

[20] T. Hoefler, A. Lumsdaine, and W. Rehm. Implementation and performance analysis of non-blocking collective operations for mpi. In *Proceedings of the 2007 ACM/IEEE International Conference for High Performance Computing, Networking, Storage and Analysis (SC)*. ACM Press, 2007.

[21] T. Ishiyama, K. Nitadori, and J. Makino. 4.45 pflops astrophysical n-body simulation on k computer: the gravitational trillion-body problem. In *Proceedings of the 2012 ACM/IEEE International Conference for High Performance Computing, Networking, Storage and Analysis (SC)*. IEEE/ACM, Nov. 2012.

[22] K. Kandalla, H. Subramoni, K. Tomko, D. Pekurovsky, S. Sur, and D. K. Panda. High-performance and scalable non-blocking all-to-all with collective offload on infiniband clusters: a study with parallel 3d fft. *Computer Science*, 26(3-4), June 2011.

[23] J. A. Nelder and R. Mead. A simplex method for function minimization. *The Computer Journal*, 7(4), 1965.

[24] D. Pekurovsky. P3DFFT: A Framework for Parallel Computations of Fourier Transforms in Three Dimensions. *SIAM Journal on Scientific Computing*, 34(4), Aug. 2012.

[25] A. Rahimian, I. Lashuk, S. Veerapaneni, A. Chandramowlishwaran, D. Malhotra, L. Moon, R. Sampath, A. Shringarpure, J. Vetter, R. Vuduc, D. Zorin, and G. Biros. Petascale direct numerical simulation of blood flow on 200k cores and heterogeneous architectures. In *Proceedings of the 2010 ACM/IEEE International Conference for High Performance Computing, Networking, Storage and Analysis (SC)*. IEEE Computer Society Press, 2010.

[26] H. Sorensen, D. Jones, M. Heideman, and C. Burrus. Real-valued fast fourier transform algorithms. *IEEE Transactions on Acoustics, Speech and Signal Processing*, 35(6):849–863, 1987.

[27] D. Takahashi. An implementation of parallel 3-d fft with 2-d decomposition on a massively parallel cluster of multi-core processors. In *Parallel Processing and Applied Mathematics*, volume 6067 of *Lecture Notes in Computer Science*. Springer Berlin Heidelberg, 2010.

[28] A. Tiwari and J. K. Hollingsworth. Online adaptive code generation and tuning. In *Proceedings of the 25th International Parallel & Distributed Processing Symposium (IPDPS)*. IEEE Computer Society Press, 2011.

[29] M. Wolfe. More iteration space tiling. In *Proceedings of the 1989 ACM/IEEE International Conference for High Performance Computing, Networking, Storage and Analysis (SC)*, pages 655–664. ACM Press, 1989.

A Decomposition for In-place Matrix Transposition

Bryan Catanzaro

NVIDIA Research

bcatanzaro@nvidia.com

Alexander Keller

NVIDIA Research

akeller@nvidia.com

Michael Garland

NVIDIA Research

mgarland@nvidia.com

Abstract

We describe a decomposition for in-place matrix transposition, with applications to Array of Structures memory accesses on SIMD processors. Traditional approaches to in-place matrix transposition involve cycle following, which is difficult to parallelize, and on matrices of dimension m by n require $O(mn \log mn)$ work when limited to less than $O(mn)$ auxiliary space. Our decomposition allows the rows and columns to be operated on independently during in-place transposition, reducing work complexity to $O(mn)$, given $O(\max(m, n))$ auxiliary space. This decomposition leads to an efficient and naturally parallel algorithm: we have measured median throughput of 19.5 GB/s on an NVIDIA Tesla K20c processor. An implementation specialized for the skinny matrices that arise when converting Arrays of Structures to Structures of Arrays yields median throughput of 34.3 GB/s, and a maximum throughput of 51 GB/s.

Because of the simple structure of this algorithm, it is particularly suited for implementation using SIMD instructions to transpose the small arrays that arise when SIMD processors load from or store to Arrays of Structures. Using this algorithm to cooperatively perform accesses to Arrays of Structures, we measure 180 GB/s throughput on the K20c, which is up to 45 times faster than compiler-generated Array of Structures accesses.

In this paper, we explain the algorithm, prove its correctness and complexity, and explain how it can be instantiated efficiently for solving various transpose problems on both CPUs and GPUs.

Categories and Subject Descriptors E.1 [*Data Structures*]: Arrays; F.2.1 [*Analysis of Algorithms and Problem Complexity*]: Numerical Algorithms and Problems

1. Introduction

In-place matrix transposition is a well-studied problem, with papers being published on the subject from 1959 [11] until the present day [1]. In-place transposition for square matrices is straightforward, but for non-square matrices, the algorithms are more involved. Traditional approaches to in-place transposition operate by following cycles in the permutation induced by the transposition. Since storing cycle descriptors requires $O(mn)$ space, cycle following in-place algorithms with auxiliary storage requirements less than $O(mn)$ elements have work complexity $O(mn \log mn)$, due to the need to recompute the cycles as the transposition proceeds [3].

In this paper, we show how the in-place transposition problem can be decomposed into independent row-wise and column-wise permutations. By decomposing the transposition, we improve the algorithmic complexity by performing smaller permutations out-of-place. With $O(\max(m, n))$ auxiliary storage, our algorithm requires $O(mn)$ work, and requires no cycle following. Our algorithm works on arrays linearized in row-major or column-major order.

In contrast to traditional cycle following algorithms, which can be difficult to parallelize due to poorly distributed cycle lengths, our decomposed transposition is straightforward to parallelize, with perfect load balancing due to the regular structure of the decomposition.

Additionally, our algorithm enables efficient SIMD transpositions on the very small arrays that arise from vector memory operations on SIMD processors. When each lane of a SIMD processor requests a vector of data, the straightforward implementation accesses elements of the vectors sequentially, which results in strided memory accesses and dramatically reduced memory throughput. There are several techniques that can ameliorate this problem, and our algorithm creates a new alternative. Firstly, the data structure itself can be transposed in memory, which removes strided memory accesses. This technique is burdensome to programmers, and cannot be applied in many circumstances, such as when data structures are dictated due to interface constraints

This research was, in part, funded by the U.S. Government. The views and conclusions contained in this document are those of the authors and should not be interpreted as representing the official policies, either expressed or implied, of the U.S. Government.

or algorithmic requirements. Alternatively, programmers access the data in transposed order to ensure vectorized memory accesses, performing transpositions in on-chip memory to route the data to each SIMD lane. This technique is effective, but allocating on-chip memory in order to perform this transpose out-of-place can be difficult, especially when scarce on-chip memory resources are occupied with other tasks. Our transposition algorithm adds a new technique: perform the transposition in-place in the register file, without requiring additional on-chip memory.

This paper makes three main contributions. Firstly, we present and prove a new algorithm for in-place matrix transposition. We show it has optimal work complexity with reduced auxiliary storage requirements compared to traditional algorithms. Secondly, we discuss several practical implementations of this algorithm, on both parallel CPUs and GPUs, including optimizations to improve cache performance. Finally, we present an implementation that allows SIMD processors to efficiently perform arbitrary length vector memory loads and stores, without relying on scarce on-chip memory resources for an out-of-place transpose.

2. Decomposition

The core of our technique is a decomposition for in-place matrix transposition that reduces the overall transposition into a series of independent row and column permutations.

Traditional approaches to in-place transposition view the problem as a single, monolithic permutation of elements in an array. In contrast, our algorithm retains the natural view of the data as a two-dimensional array rather than as a linearized one-dimensional structure, operating on the rows and columns of the original array, until the data movement has been completed for the transposition. The data is then reinterpreted as a two-dimensional array with transposed dimensions.

Viewing the data as a two-dimensional array, the transposition can be accomplished in two directions, which we call "Rows to Columns" (R2C) and "Columns to Rows" (C2R). The R2C and C2R transposes are inverses of each other. These two permutations are illustrated in Figure 1.

We are not the first to view transposition in this manner, for example, see the description of Columnsort in Leighton [4], where the C2R permutation is called "transpose", and the R2C permutation is called "untranspose".

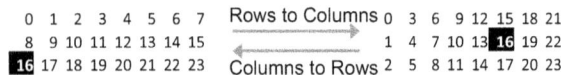

```
 0  1  2  3  4  5  6  7    Rows to Columns   0  3  6  9 12 15 18 21
 8  9 10 11 12 13 14 15    ──────────────→   1  4  7 10 13 16 19 22
16 17 18 19 20 21 22 23    Columns to Rows   2  5  8 11 14 17 20 23
```

Figure 1: C2R and R2C transpositions, $m = 3, n = 8$

We begin by discussing out-of-place versions of these transpositions, and showing how they relate to traditional matrix transposition.

Define the standard row-major linearization, where $l_{rm}(i, j)$ creates a linear index from a row and column index, and

$i_{rm}(l)$ and $j_{rm}(l)$ decompose a linear index into a row and column index, respectively.

$$l_{rm}(i, j) = j + in \tag{1}$$

$$i_{rm}(l) = \left\lfloor \frac{l}{n} \right\rfloor \tag{2}$$

$$j_{rm}(l) = l \bmod n \tag{3}$$

With the observation that $l_{rm}(i_{rm}(l), j_{rm}(l)) = l$.

And the standard column-major linearization:

$$l_{cm}(i, j) = i + jm \tag{4}$$

$$i_{cm}(l) = l \bmod m \tag{5}$$

$$j_{cm}(l) = \left\lfloor \frac{l}{m} \right\rfloor \tag{6}$$

With the observation that $l_{cm}(i_{cm}(l), j_{cm}(l)) = l$.

To define the R2C and C2R transpositions, we will use the following four functions:

$$s(i, j) = l_{rm}(i, j) \bmod m \tag{7}$$

$$c(i, j) = \left\lfloor \frac{l_{rm}(i, j)}{m} \right\rfloor \tag{8}$$

$$t(i, j) = \left\lfloor \frac{l_{cm}(i, j)}{n} \right\rfloor \tag{9}$$

$$d(i, j) = l_{cm}(i, j) \bmod n \tag{10}$$

We then define the transpositions:

$$A^{C2R}[i, j] = A[s(i, j), c(i, j)] \tag{11}$$

$$A^{R2C}[i, j] = A[t(i, j), d(i, j)] \tag{12}$$

Equations 11 and 12 define the transpositions in terms of gather operations. Since the C2R and R2C transpositions are inverses of each other, and scatter and gather transpositions are inverses of each other, we can also define the transpositions in terms of scatter operations:

$$A^{C2R}[t(i, j), d(i, j)] = A[i, j] \tag{13}$$

$$A^{R2C}[s(i, j), c(i, j)] = A[i, j] \tag{14}$$

For example, consider the element with value 16 highlighted in Figure 1, where $m = 3, n = 8$. On the left, this element is located at $i = 2, j = 0$, After the R2C transposition, the element is located at $i' = 1, j' = 5$. Looking at Equation 14, we can compute the destination indices: $i' = s(i, j) = (j + in) \bmod m = (0 + 2 \cdot 8) \bmod 3 = 1$, and $j' = c(i, j) = \left\lfloor \frac{j+in}{m} \right\rfloor = \left\lfloor \frac{0+2 \cdot 8}{3} \right\rfloor = 5$.

Now we show the connection between the R2C and C2R transposes and the linearized transposition problem.

Theorem 1. *The C2R transpose implements transposition for row-major arrays, and the R2C transpose implements transposition for column-major arrays.*

Proof. To prove this, we will examine linearized versions of a matrix A and its transpose A^T. We will show that the row-major linearization of A^T is equivalent to the row-major linearization of A^{C2R}.

By the definition of transposition,

$$A^T[i,j] = A[j,i] \tag{15}$$

Since A^T has dimensions $n \times m$, its indexing must be adjusted slightly. Define

$$i_{rm}^T(l) = \left\lfloor \frac{l}{m} \right\rfloor = j_{cm}(l) \tag{16}$$

$$j_{rm}^T(l) = l \bmod m = i_{cm}(l) \tag{17}$$

These equations are just Equations 2 and 3 with dimensions swapped.

Let A_{rm} be a row-major linearized representation of array A, indexed with $l \in [0, mn)$. Then

$$A_{rm}^T[l] = A_{rm}[l_{rm}(j_{rm}^T(l), i_{rm}^T(l))], \tag{18}$$

where we have linearized A^T and A, using the definition of transposition.

As defined in Equation 11,

$$A^{C2R}[i,j] = A[s(i,j), c(i,j)] \tag{19}$$

Linearizing,

$$A_{rm}^{C2R}[l] = A[l_{rm}(s(i_{rm}(l), j_{rm}(l)), c(i_{rm}(l), j_{rm}(l)))] \tag{20}$$

However:

$$
\begin{aligned}
s(i_{rm}(l), j_{rm}(l)) &= l_{rm}(i_{rm}(l), j_{rm}(l)) \bmod m \\
&= l \bmod m = j_{rm}^T(l)
\end{aligned}
$$

$$
\begin{aligned}
c(i_{rm}(l), j_{rm}(l)) &= \left\lfloor \frac{l_{rm}(i_{rm}(l), j_{rm}(l))}{m} \right\rfloor \\
&= \left\lfloor \frac{l}{m} \right\rfloor = i_{rm}^T(l)
\end{aligned}
$$

And so we can substitute to show

$$A_{rm}^{C2R}[l] = A[l_{rm}(j_{rm}^T(l), i_{rm}^T(l))] \tag{21}$$

Therefore, $A_{rm}^{C2R} = A_{rm}^T$. Symmetric reasoning shows $A_{cm}^{R2C} = A_{cm}^T$. $\qquad\square$

Theorem 2. *Swapping dimensions m and n before performing the transpose, the C2R transpose implements transposition for column-major arrays, and the R2C transpose implements transposition for row-major arrays.*

Proof. Defining versions of l_{cm}, i_{rm}, and j_{rm} where m and n have been swapped:

$$
\begin{aligned}
l_{cm}^s(i,j) &= & i + jn &= & l_{rm}(j,i) \\
i_{rm}^s(l) &= & \left\lfloor \frac{l}{m} \right\rfloor &= & i_{rm}^T(l) \\
j_{rm}^s(l) &= & l \bmod m &= & j_{rm}^T(l)
\end{aligned}
$$

The R2C transpose induces the following permutation:

$$
\begin{aligned}
A_{cm}^{R2C}[l] &= A_{cm}[l_{cm}(j_{cm}^T(l), i_{cm}^T(l))] \\
&= A_{cm}[l_{cm}(i_{rm}(l), j_{rm}(l))]
\end{aligned}
$$

If we swap m and n first, the resulting index expression is

$$
\begin{aligned}
l_{cm}^s(i_{rm}^s(l), j_{rm}^s(l)) &= l_{rm}(j_{rm}^s(l), i_{rm}^s(l)) \\
&= l_{rm}(j_{rm}^T(l), i_{rm}^T(l))
\end{aligned}
$$

Since this index expression is the same as in Equation 21, we see that if m and n are swapped before the transposition, the R2C permutation transposes a row-major array. Symmetric reasoning shows that swapping m and n before the transposition allows the C2R permutation to transpose a column-major array.

$\qquad\square$

We have described both the C2R and R2C transpositions and shown how they can both be used to transpose arrays of either row-major or column-major linearization.

3. Algorithm

The key insight in this work is that one need not consider the entire permutation required for performing the transposition in-place on an array. Instead, we can decompose the transposition into independent row-wise and column-wise permutations.

In this section, we prove that the decomposition underlying this technique is sound, and then present the algorithm. We will restrict our attention to the C2R transposition in this section, as the R2C transposition is merely the inverse of the C2R transposition.

As shown Equation 10, the destination column of element j in row i is:

$$d_i(j) = (i + jm) \bmod n \tag{22}$$

where we have fixed i for presentation purposes. We would like to perform row-wise permutations to send each element to the correct column required by the transposition. This can only be done if each element goes to a unique column, otherwise the row-wise operation is not a well-formed permutation, and the transposition is not decomposable.

However, in general, $d_i(j)$ is not bijective on $j \in [0, n)$, meaning each element does not go to a unique column, and so the row-wise operation is not a well-formed permutation.

In fact, $d_i(j)$ is periodic, which means there are guaranteed to be conflicts in the permutation. However, the periodicity of $d_i(j)$ gives us a clue as to how to remove these conflicts, as we will see.

Let the array have m rows and n columns. Define $c = \gcd(m,n)$, $a = \frac{m}{c}$, $b = \frac{n}{c}$.

Lemma 1. $\forall i \in \mathbb{Z}$, $d_i(j)$ *is periodic with period b.*

Proof. Given $j, k \in \mathbb{Z}$,

$$
\begin{aligned}
d_i(j + kb) &= \left(i + \left(j + k\frac{n}{c}\right)m\right) \bmod n \\
&= \left(i + jm + nk\frac{m}{c}\right) \bmod n \\
&= (i + jm + nka) \bmod n \\
&= (i + jm) \bmod n = d_i(j)
\end{aligned}
$$

Therefore, $d_i(j)$ is periodic with period b. $\quad\square$

Lemma 1 shows that if $c > 1$, multiple elements in each row will be sent to the same column, since in that case $b < n$. This means that the row-wise permutation that sends each element to the correct column does not exist if $c > 1$. However, note that if m and n are coprime, $c = 1$, and the period $b = n$. Later, we will prove that this means the decomposition is trivial in this case.

For the case when m and n are not coprime, we would like to find a set of column-wise permutations that ensure each element goes to a unique column. We must show that after these permutations, the destination column for each element is some new function $d_i'(j)$ that is bijective on the domain $[0,n)$.

Since $d_i(j)$ is periodic with period b, we adjust the array in groups of b columns to remove the conflicts. Consider rotating the columns of a matrix, by which we mean: for a column x of length m being rotated by k elements, the rotated column $x'[i] = x[(i+k) \bmod m]$. Consider rotating column j by $k = \lfloor \frac{j}{b} \rfloor$ elements, or equivalently, column j of the rotated array is gathered from the source array using index equation

$$
r_j(i) = \left(i + \left\lfloor \frac{j}{b} \right\rfloor\right) \bmod m \tag{23}
$$

Substituting, after rotating all columns of the array, the resulting destination column for each element of the new array is

$$
d_i'(j) = \left(\left(i + \left\lfloor \frac{j}{b} \right\rfloor\right) \bmod m + jm\right) \bmod n \tag{24}
$$

Our task is to prove that Equation 24 is a bijection, which will show that the rotations have removed conflicts, decomposing the transposition.

To do this, the following lemmas are useful.

Lemma 2. $\forall x, y \in \mathbb{N} \mid 0 \le x < b, 0 \le y < b,$ $mx \bmod n = my \bmod n$ *implies $x = y$.*

Proof. Proof by contradiction. Assume $\exists x, \exists y \mid 0 \le x < b, 0 \le y < b, x \neq y$ and also that $mx \bmod n = my \bmod n$. Substituting, $acx \bmod bc = acy \bmod bc$. By cancellability of congruences, this implies $ax \bmod \frac{bc}{\gcd(c,bc)} = ay \bmod \frac{bc}{\gcd(c,bc)}$. Since $\gcd(c, bc) = c$, then $ax \bmod b = ay \bmod b$ must be true. Since a and b are coprime, the modular multiplicative inverse of a and b exists. Therefore, $x \bmod b = y \bmod b$ must be true. Since we assumed $0 \le x < b$ and $0 \le y < b$, the modulus is extraneous, and so $x = y$. But this is a contradiction, since we assumed earlier that $x \neq y$. $\quad\square$

Lemma 3. *Let $S = \bigcup_{h=0}^{b-1} \{hm \bmod n\}$, and let $T = \bigcup_{h=0}^{b-1} \{hc\}$. Then $S = T$.*

Proof. By Lemma 2, we know $|S| = b$. We also know $|T| = b$ by inspection. Next, we show that $S \subseteq T$. To do this, we show that $\forall h \in [0, b), \exists k \in [0, b) \mid hm \bmod n = kc$. By the definition of modulus, $hac \bmod bc = hac - bc \lfloor \frac{hac}{bc} \rfloor = (ha - b \lfloor \frac{hac}{bc} \rfloor)c = kc$, where $k \in \mathbb{Z}$. To bound k, we note that since kc is a remainder with respect to bc, $0 \le k < b$. Accordingly, $S \subseteq T$, and since we already showed $|S| = |T|$, it must be true that $S = T$. $\quad\square$

Theorem 3. $d_i'(j)$ *is a bijection on $j \in [0,n)$ for any fixed $i \in [0,m)$.*

Proof. Observing that $\lfloor \frac{j}{b} \rfloor = l$ is constant for $j \in [lb, (l+1)b)$, we first analyze the sets

$$
\begin{aligned}
S_{i,l} &= \bigcup_{j=lb}^{(l+1)b-1} \{d_i'(j)\} \\
&= \bigcup_{j=lb}^{lb+b-1} \{((i+l) \bmod m + jm) \bmod n\} \\
&= \bigcup_{h=0}^{b-1} \{((i+l) \bmod m + (lb+h)m) \bmod n\} \\
&= \bigcup_{h=0}^{b-1} \{((i+l) \bmod m + hm) \bmod n\} \\
&= \bigcup_{h=0}^{b-1} \{((i+l) \bmod c + hm \bmod n) \bmod n\} \\
&= \bigcup_{h=0}^{b-1} \{(i+l) \bmod c + hm \bmod n\} \\
&= \bigcup_{h=0}^{b-1} \{(i+l) \bmod c + hc\},
\end{aligned}
$$

where we first replace $d_i'(j)$ by its definition, followed by removing the offset lb from the index, which allows one to cancel the resulting additive term

$$lbm \bmod n = lbac \bmod bc = 0$$

We then distribute the modulus over both remaining terms. We can replace the expression $((i + l) \bmod m) \bmod n$ by $(i + l) \bmod c$ by defining $k_m = \left\lfloor \frac{i+l}{m} \right\rfloor$ and $k_n = \left\lfloor \frac{i+l-k_m m}{n} \right\rfloor$, and $r = i + l - (k_m m + k_n n)$. Then

$$((i + l) \bmod m) \bmod n = r \text{ and } (i + l) \bmod c = r$$

due to $m = ac$ and $n = bc$. Noting that $(i + l) \bmod c \in [0, c)$, and $hac \bmod bc$ is kc, for $k \in [0, b)$, we see that $(i + l) \bmod c + hm \bmod n < bc = n$, so the external modulus is unnecessary. Then the last line follows from Lemma 3, noting that the term $(i + l) \bmod c$ is independent of h and so can we can replace the set $\bigcup_{h=0}^{b-1} \{hm \bmod n\}$ with $\bigcup_{h=0}^{b-1} \{hc\}$.

Now, for any fixed $i \in [0, m)$, the range of $d_i'(j)$ over the entire domain $[0, n)$ is

$$
\begin{aligned}
\bigcup_{j=0}^{n-1} \{d_i'(j)\} &= \bigcup_{l=0}^{c-1} S_{i,l} \\
&= \bigcup_{l=0}^{c-1} \bigcup_{h=0}^{b-1} \{hc + ((i + l) \bmod c)\} \\
&= [0, n)
\end{aligned}
$$

because $((i + l) \bmod c)$ enumerates all values in $[0, c)$ on the domain $l \in [0, c)$. Therefore $d_i'(j)$ is a bijection on $[0, n)$. $\square$

Note that for $c = \gcd(n, m) = 1$, $\left\lfloor \frac{i}{b} \right\rfloor = 0$, yielding

$$d_i'(j) = (i + jm) \bmod n = d_i(j)$$

This implies that if m and n are coprime, $d_i(j)$ is naturally bijective.

Theorem 4. *In-place transposition can be decomposed into independent row-wise and column-wise operations.*

Proof. Since $d_i'(j)$ is bijective on the domain $j \in [0, n)$, then after pre-rotating columns of the array, each element can be sent to a unique destination column during independent row-wise permutations. Once each element is in the correct destination column, it necessarily has a unique row to which it should be sent to complete the transposition. Since the indices in both steps are unique, the row and column wise permutations are decomposable. $\square$

We have already described the column-wise rotations, and given the set of independent row-wise permutations. Now we will give the column-wise permutations necessary to finish the transposition. Since the decomposition ensures each element is directed to the correct column via row-wise

permutations, we need only consider permuting elements within the columns.

For the C2R transposition, Equation 7 shows that the source row of element i in column j is

$$s_j(i) = (j + in) \bmod m \qquad (25)$$

However, since we rotated the original array to create $d_i'(j)$, the correct source row is a different function. Define:

$$s_j'(i) = \left(j + in - \left\lfloor \frac{i}{a} \right\rfloor \right) \bmod m \qquad (26)$$

Theorem 5. $s_j'(i)$ *computes the correct source row indices to complete the transposition.*

Proof. From Equation 8, the source column of element i in column j for a C2R transposition is

$$c_j(i) = \left\lfloor \frac{(j + in)}{m} \right\rfloor \qquad (27)$$

Also note that $\frac{mn}{c} = bm = an$. When we rotated the columns of the original array to enable the decomposition, we rotated groups of b columns together. Each of those b columns formed a subarray of bm elements. Now, examine groups of a rows of the array, each of which form subarrays of an elements. These subarrays have a one-to-one correspondence with the subarrays that were rotated earlier.

To see this, we will show that $\forall i \in [0, m), \forall j \in [0, n)$, $c_j(i) \in [kb, (k + 1)b)$, where $k = \left\lfloor \frac{i}{a} \right\rfloor$.

First, note that $c_j(i)$ is monotonic in both i and j, so we can bound it over a domain of interest by its values at the extrema of the domain. Decompose $i = ak + y$, where $k = \left\lfloor \frac{i}{a} \right\rfloor$, and note that due to the definition of k, $y \in [0, a)$. Accordingly, $c_0(ka) \leq c_j(ka) \leq c_j(i) \leq c_j((k+1)a-1) \leq c_{n-1}((k + 1)a - 1)$

Evaluating the bound,

$$
\begin{aligned}
c_0(ka) &= \left\lfloor \frac{0 + (ka)n}{m} \right\rfloor \\
&= \left\lfloor \frac{akb}{a} \right\rfloor = kb
\end{aligned}
$$

Similar reasoning shows that the upper bound $c_{n-1}((k + 1)a - 1) = (k + 1)b - 1$, Accordingly, over the domain $0 \leq j < n$, it must be true that $kb \leq c_j(i) < (k+1)b$. Then it is also true that over this domain, $\left\lfloor \frac{c_j(i)}{b} \right\rfloor = k$.

In other words, the source columns for all elements in group k were rotated by k elements.

k then establishes a one-to-one correspondence between subarrays comprised of the original columns of the array that were rotated by k places, and the rows of the array that are reading from those rotated columns.

Having established this correspondence, we need to adjust the source row indices to compensate for the rotation. Adding the term $-k = -\left\lfloor \frac{i}{a} \right\rfloor$ to the original $s_j(i)$ function counteracts this rotation. Accordingly, $s_j'(i)$ is the correct set of row indices to use for the column opersations. $\square$

Summarizing, the C2R algorithm is performed in three steps:

- If $\gcd(m, n) > 1$: Rotate columns by gathering from each column using $r_j(i)$ from Equation 23 into a temporary vector, then copy the result over the original column.

- Row shuffle: scatter each row into a temporary vector using indices $d'_i(j)$ from Equation 24, then copy the result over the original row.

- Column shuffle: gather from each column into a temporary vector using $s'_j(i)$ from Equation 26, then copy the result over the original column.

Combining these three steps leads to a straightforward statement of the C2R transposition algorithm, using out-of-place permutations in a temporary buffer of size $\max(m, n)$. This is presented as algorithm 1.

Algorithm 1 In-place C2R transposition of array A

---

if $\gcd(m, n) > 1$ **then**
  for j in $[0, n)$ **do**
    for i in $[0, m)$ **do**
      $tmp[i] = A[r_j(i), j]$ {Gather per eq. 23}
    end for
    for i in $[0, m)$ **do**
      $A[i, j] = tmp[i]$
    end for
  end for
end if
for i in $[0, m)$ **do**
  for j in $[0, n)$ **do**
    $tmp[d'_i(j)] = A[i, j]$ {Scatter per eq. 24}
  end for
  for j in $[0, n)$ **do**
    $A[i, j] = tmp[j]$
  end for
end for
for j in $[0, n)$ **do**
  for i in $[0, m)$ **do**
    $tmp[i] = A[s'_j(i), j]$ {Gather per eq. 26}
  end for
  for i in $[0, m)$ **do**
    $A[i, j] = tmp[i]$
  end for
end for

Figure 2 shows the state of a matrix as it is transposed using a C2R transposition. Each of the three steps corresponds to one of the three outermost loops in algorithm 1.

The R2C transposition algorithm is the inverse of the C2R algorithm. It can be derived by reversing the order of the permutation steps in the C2R algorithm and interchanging gather and scatter permutations.

Theorem 6. *The decomposed in-place transpose algorithm has optimal work complexity $O(mn)$, when given auxiliary space of $O(\max(m, n))$.*

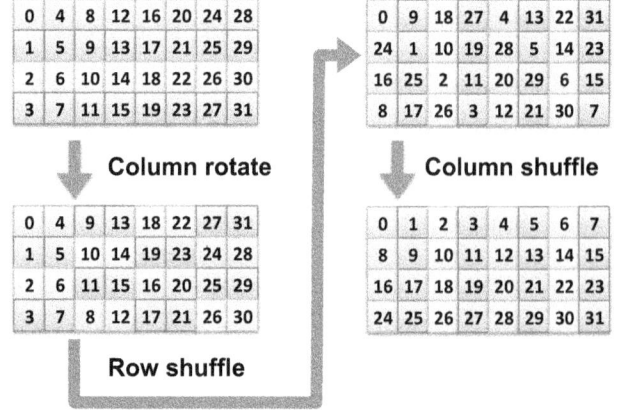

Figure 2: C2R transpose of 4×8 matrix

Proof. In the worst case, the algorithm reads and writes each element 6 times, performing row and column permutations out-of-place. This gives the work complexity of $O(mn)$, which is known to be optimal. The algorithm requires a temporary vector of size $\max(m, n)$ in order to carry out these out-of-place permutations. $\qquad\square$

4. Optimizations

The C2R transpose shown in algorithm 1 and its R2C inverse are defined in terms of both scatter and gather based permutations on both the rows and columns of the array. Practical considerations of these algorithms may motivate the use of alternative implementations. For example, gather based formulations are sometimes more efficient, or required due to functional restrictions. Additionally, we have found it useful to restrict the column operations: rather than allowing unrestricted column shuffles, we perform the column operations using a composition of two more restricted primitives. Restricting the column operations allows us to optimize memory access patterns, and enables the in-register implementation using SIMD instructions.

We also observe that we are free to choose either row-major or column-major linearization during C2R and R2C transposes, which is an important optimization.

Theorem 7. *The linearization assumed while performing C2R or R2C transposes does not affect the permutation they induce*

Proof. Let B represent a row-major array that is created by a C2R transposition using column-major indexing on a row-major array A.

$$B[l] = A_{rm}[l_{cm}(s(i_{cm}(l), j_{cm}(l)), c(i_{cm}(l), j_{cm}(l)))] \tag{28}$$

Noting that

$$l_{cm}\left(x \bmod m, \left\lfloor \frac{x}{m} \right\rfloor\right) = x \tag{29}$$

and substituting the C2R source equations from Equations 7 and 8, as well as from Equations 16 and 17 into the indexing function above,

$$
\begin{aligned}
l_{cm}(s(i_{cm}(l), j_{cm}(l)), c(i_{cm}(l), j_{cm}(l))) &= \\
l_{rm}(i_{cm}(l), j_{cm}(l)) &= \\
l_{rm}(j_{rm}^T(l), i_{rm}^T(l))
\end{aligned}
$$

This proves

$$
B[l] = A_{rm}^{C2R}[l] \tag{30}
$$

Similar reasoning holds for using row-major indexing on a column-major array. $\qquad\square$

Theorem 7 gives us the freedom to index arrays in row-major or column-major order, regardless of their native storage order. Although the intermediate state during the transposition differs depending on the choice of linearization used to perform C2R or R2C transposes, the fact that the final result does not depend on this choice simplifies implementation. This is an important performance optimization, since we can design the implementation so that row and column operations always run in fixed directions, regardless of whether the array was given to us in row or column major order. This enables us to optimize memory access patterns to fit cache lines.

4.1 Restricted Column Operations

Instead of implementing arbitrary column shuffles, we have found it useful to restrict column operations to column rotation and row permutation.

In column rotation, each column of the array is rotated by some rotation amount, such that the gather based index equation of the column operation is of the form $f_j(i) = (i + g(j)) \bmod m$.

In row permutation, all rows of the array are permuted, such that the gather based index equation of the column operation is of the form $f(i)$, with no dependence on the column index j. Since the rows are all permuted identically, the effect is a particular kind of column-wise permutation, where every column is permuted identically.

4.2 Columns to Rows Optimizations

As specified earlier, if $c > 1$, we first rotate by gathering indices $r_j(i)$ specified in Equation 23.

The row shuffle indices $d_i'(j)$ were specified as a scatter permutation in Equation 24. To transform it into a gather permutation, we must find its inverse $d_i'^{-1}(j)$.

We will use the modular multiplicative inverse function $\mathrm{mmi}(x, y)$, which is defined for coprime integers x and y:

$$
(x \cdot \mathrm{mmi}(x, y)) \bmod y = 1
$$

Define a helper function

$$
\mathrm{f}(i, j) = \begin{cases} j + i(n-1) & i - (j \bmod c) + c \le m \\ j + i(n-1) + m & i - (j \bmod c) + c > m \end{cases}
$$

and compute the modular multiplicative inverse $a^{-1} = \mathrm{mmi}(a, b)$. Then

$$
d_i'^{-1}(j) = \left(a^{-1} \left\lfloor \frac{\mathrm{f}(i, j)}{c} \right\rfloor \right) \bmod b + (\mathrm{f}(i, j) \bmod c) \cdot b \tag{31}
$$

To decompose the column shuffle given by $s_j'(i)$ in Equation 26 into a column rotation and a row permutation, we note that for gather-based permutation functions $f(i)$ and $g(i)$, gathering with indices $(f \circ g)(i)$ is equivalent to first gathering with indices $f(i)$, followed by a second gather with indices $g(i)$. Scatter-based permutations have the opposite ordering under composition. The column shuffle indices $s_j'(i)$ can be decomposed into a column rotation followed by a row permutation, where the column rotation is:

$$
p_j(i) = (i + j) \bmod m \tag{32}
$$

And the row permutation is:

$$
q(i) = \left(i \cdot n - \left\lfloor \frac{i}{a} \right\rfloor \right) \bmod m \tag{33}
$$

This decomposition of a column shuffle into these two more restricted primitives is correct because $(p_j \circ q)(i) = s_j'(i)$.

4.3 Rows to Columns Optimizations

The row shuffle step in the R2C transpose is simple when formulated as a gather, since it can just use $d_i'(j)$ directly without the need for inversion.

However, the gather-based indices for the row permute step require $q^{-1}(i)$. Compute the modular multiplicative inverse $b^{-1} = \mathrm{mmi}(b, a)$. Then

$$
q^{-1}(i) = \left(\left\lfloor \frac{c - 1 + i}{c} \right\rfloor b^{-1} \right) \bmod a + (((c-1)i) \bmod c) \cdot a \tag{34}
$$

Instead of perfoming a scatter rotation to invert the rotation in the C2R algorithm, we can do a gather rotation with inverted indices:

$$
p_j^{-1}(i) = (i - j) \bmod m \tag{35}
$$

And the final rotation indices are also inverted from the C2R pre-rotation indices:

$$
r_j^{-1}(i) = \left(i - \left\lfloor \frac{j}{b} \right\rfloor \right) \bmod m \tag{36}
$$

4.4 Arithmetic Strength Reduction

Evaluating the index equations, such as Equation 31, involves repeated calculations of integer division and integer modulus. We found a significant performance improvement by using a strength reduction technique that involves computing a fixed-point reciprocal, and then converting integer division into a multiplication by the reciprocal followed by a shift [10]. The modulus can then be computed with an additional multiplication and a subtraction. This technique amortizes the calculation of the reciprocal across many repeated divisions or modulus operations.

4.5 On-chip Row Shuffle

Implementing arbitrary row shuffle operations requires two passes over each row along with the use of temporary storage, as shown in algorithm 1. If on-chip storage is sufficient, whether in caches or in register files, we can perform row shuffle operations in a single pass, without writing the intermediate result to temporary storage in memory. For example, each streaming multiprocessor on the NVIDIA Tesla K20c processor contains 256 kB of register file—in practice we found we could use this storage to process rows with up to 29440 64-bit elements in a single pass.

4.6 Cache-aware Rotate

We can improve the performance of column rotations on the array by ensuring all cache-lines read and written to and from memory are utilized efficiently. We use a row-major linearization during the transpose operations, regardless of the native linearization of the array, in order to ensure that our indexing maps to cache-lines in a canonical way.

A naive column rotation would involve reading the column from memory, then storing it in rotated order to a temporary buffer, then copying the temporary buffer back over the original column. This utilizes cache-lines poorly, especially when neighboring columns are being rotated by different amounts.

Instead of performing the rotation in this manner, we break the rotation into two phases, both of which use no temporary storage and thus save the cost of reading and writing to a temporary buffer. The first phase performs a coarse rotation in place, using cycle following. The coarseness is determined by the size of the cache-line: if we rotate groups of columns together so that the a sub-row selected from this group is one cache-line wide, we improve the efficiency of reading and writing such a sub-row. The sub-row from such a group may span one cache-line, if it happens to be aligned to cache-line boundaries, or it may span two cache-lines if it is not aligned. If the size of one row of the array is evenly divisible by the cache-line size, we are guaranteed that all sub-rows will be aligned; otherwise some sub-rows will be aligned, and others will not. In any case, reading and writing sub-rows is much more efficient than reading and writing elements from each column independently.

Cycle-following for rotation is straightforward: when rotating a vector of m elements by r places, there are $z = \gcd(m, r)$ cycles, each of which with length $\frac{m}{z}$. The elements in these cycles are also straightforward to compute analytically: $l_y(x) = (y + x(m - r)) \bmod m$, for cycle $y \in [0, z)$, and element $x \in [0, \frac{m}{z})$. Having an analytic solution to the cycles makes it straightforward to perform the

coarse rotation, since there is no need to precompute cycle descriptors.

The goal of the coarse rotation is to ensure that the residual rotation for each column is bounded. This is true for the rotations we perform, since both $f(j) = \lfloor \frac{j}{b} \rfloor$ and $f(j) = j \bmod b$ have the property that $0 \le (f(j + w) - f(j)) \bmod m < w$, where w is the width of a sub-row, or the number of columns being rotated together.

Since the residual rotation is bounded, we can then proceed with a fine in-place rotation pass that reads in the array block by block, using on-chip memory to store blocks of the array, rotate it, and write it out block by block. This ensures off-chip memory bandwidth is efficiently utilized. The fine rotation pass for a block of columns can be omitted if the residual rotation amounts for all columns in a block are identically 0. This is often the case for the C2R prerotation or the R2C postrotation performed if $c > 1$, since $r(j) = \lfloor \frac{j}{b} \rfloor$ is a slow-changing function when $b > w$.

4.7 Cache-aware Row Permute

The row permute operation can be made cache-aware through cycle-following. We do not have an analytic solution for cycles resulting from $q(i)$ and $q^{-1}(i)$, so instead we compute the cycles dynamically and store them in our temporary memory. Since all rows are permuted identically, we have only one set of cycles to compute. The number of cycles of length greater than 1 element is bounded at $\frac{m}{2}$, and so we are guaranteed to have enough storage to hold the cycle leaders and cycle length descriptors. Because cycle-following is most naturally understood through scatter permutations, we use $q^{-1}(i)$ for the C2R permutation and $q(i)$ for the R2C permutation.

As with the cache-aware rotation, this primitive operates on groups of columns chosen such that one sub-row selected from such a group is the same size as a cache-line, ensuring that reading and writing a sub-row is efficient.

5. Implementation

To test our algorithm, we wrote parallel CPU and GPU implementations and compare them against contemporary in-place matrix transposition routines. Since an ideal matrix transpose would read the array once and write the array once, we calculate throughput in this section as

$$throughput(m, n, s, t) = \frac{2mns}{t} \qquad (37)$$

Where s is the size of an array element, and t is the time for the complete transposition.

5.1 Parallel CPU Implementation

Our CPU implementation of in-place matrix transposition is a straightforward OpenMP parallelization of algorithm 1. We performed two optimizations: using a completely gather based implementation using $d_i'^{-1}(j)$ during the row shuffles, and using arithmetic strength reduction to lower the cost of index calculations. We leave cache-aware optimizations for this implementation to future work.

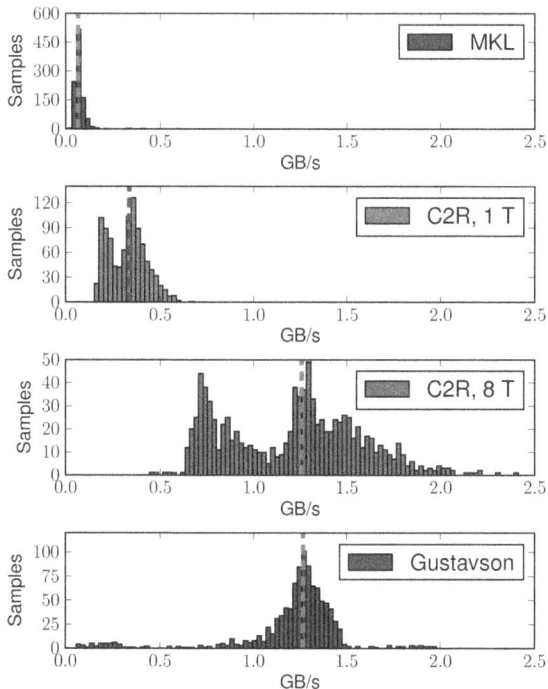

Figure 3: Throughput Histograms of In-Place Matrix Transposition CPU Implementations. Median throughput indicated with dashed line. 1 T indicates sequential execution, 8 T indicates execution with 8 threads.

Figure 3 shows histograms of in-place transpose throughput. We benchmarked transpose throughput on 1000 randomly sized matrices where m, n were chosen uniformly at random from the interval $[1000, 10000)$. Each array is comprised of 64-bit elements. We used an Intel Core i7 950 processor with 4 cores and 8 threads. We show performance for our method running sequentially, as well as with 8 threads. We also show performance of `mkl_dimatcopy()`, the corresponding method from the Intel MKL library, version 11.0.1 [2]. Median performance of our sequential implementation on this machine achieved 336 MB/s, which compares well to MKL's median performance of 67 MB/s. Additionally, since our algorithm parallelizes trivially, we were able to see a median performance of 1.26 GB/s when using 8 threads. In contrast `mkl_dimatcopy()` is not parallelized, likely due to the complexity of parallelizing traditional cycle-following algorithms. On this test set, the implementation described in Gustavson et al. [1] achieves median performance of 1.27 GB/s, including overhead for packing and unpacking the array into the tiled format required for use with their algorithm.

Median Throughputs	GB/s
Intel MKL	0.067
C2R, 1 Thread	0.336
C2R, 8 Threads	1.26
Gustavson et al. [1] (double)	1.27

Table 1: Median In-Place Transposition Throughputs on Intel Core i7 950 on Arrays of 64-bit Elements

Our performance is comparable to the performance described in Gustavson et al. [1], despite the simplicity of our implementation, which doesn't employ any of the cache-aware permutations we outlined earlier, and the complexity of Gustavson's implementation, which is highly optimized for cache accesses. Additionally, our algorithm has theoretical advantages over Gustavson's algorithm: our work complexity is $O(mn)$, while Gustavson's algorithm is $O(mn \log mn)$, given less than $O(mn)$ auxiliary space. Similarly to our algorithm, Gustavson's algorithm also requires $O(m)$ auxiliary space: arrays that are not conveniently tiled must be transformed through a packing and unpacking operation. These results are summarized in Table 1.

5.2 Parallel GPU Implementation

Our GPU implementation is also built using gather permutations, with strength reduction, and additionally uses the cache-aware permutations described in section 4.

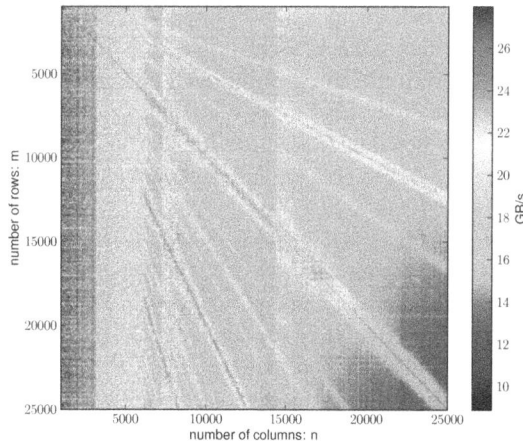

Figure 4: C2R Performance Landscape on Tesla K20c

Figure 4 shows a sampling of the performance landscape of the C2R algorithm for 250000 row-major arrays with sizes $m, n \in [1000, 25000]$. To better visualize structure, outlier samples that performed faster than the 99th percentile had their values clamped to the 99th percentile throughput. The high-performing band on the left of the graph shows that when the number of columns is small, a row fits in on-chip memory, significantly improving performance.

201

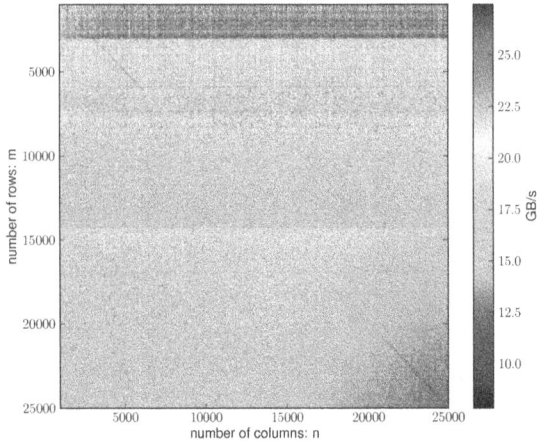

Figure 5: R2C Performance Landscape on Tesla K20c

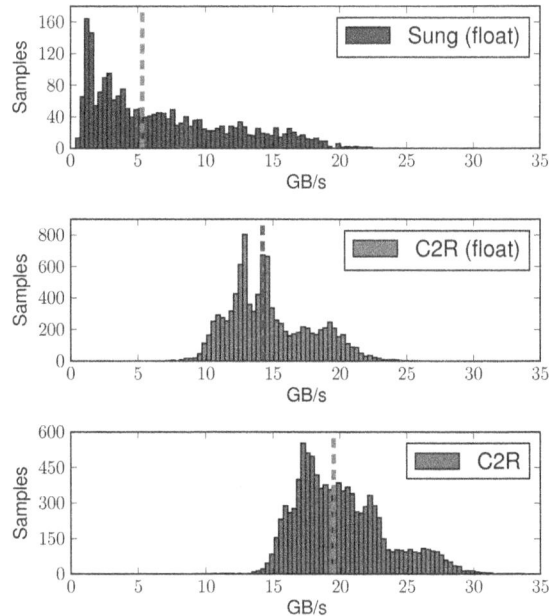

Figure 6: Throughput Histograms of In-Place Matrix Transposition GPU Implementations. Median throughput indicated with dashed line. (float) represents implementations operating on 32-bit elements

Figure 5 shows the same performance landscape sampling as Figure 4, but using the R2C algorithm, with fast outliers clamped as explained earlier. The high-performing band on the top of the graph shows that when the number of rows is small, an entire column fits in on-chip memory.

Since the C2R and R2C algorithms can both be used for transposing any array, but their performance characteristics differ, we combined them using a simple heuristic: if $m > n$, use the C2R algorithm, otherwise use the R2C algorithm. This improves the performance of our transposition routine and makes it more efficient than either the C2R algorithm or the R2C algorithm on their own.

Figure 6 shows a histogram of throughput results for several implementations running on the NVIDIA Tesla K20c processor. We benchmarked these implementations on arrays where m, n were chosen uniformly at random from the interval $[1000, 20000)$.

First, we benchmarked the implementation from Sung [6]. We tested this implementation on 2500 arrays, of which 2155 completed correctly and are reported in Figure 6. The algorithm published in Sung [6] operates on arrays in a tiled manner, with the restriction that the dimensions of the tile must evenly divide the dimensions of the array. However, it does not choose tile sizes automatically, but instead requires the user to supply them. In order to test this code on arbitrary arrays, we used the following heuristic: sort the factors of the array dimension, then starting with the smallest factors, multiply them until the tile dimension equals or exceeds some threshold t. The motivation behind this heuristic is to find a tile size that is not too small nor too large for the hardware.

For these experiments, we set $t = 72$, so that the maximum tile size was 72×72. We did not tune over the many possible tile sizes for each array, since autotuning over data-dependent parameters is not practical for many applications. We note this heuristic was able to replicate the maximum

performance of 20.8 GB/s reported in Sung [6] on an array of dimension 7200×1800, with tile size 32×72. Indeed, we saw performance of 22.35 GB/s on an array of dimension 7223×10368, with tile size 31×64.

As shown in Figure 6, the implementation published in Sung [6] achieves a median throughput of 5.33 GB/s, when operating on arrays of 32-bit elements. Tiled algorithms perform poorly on arrays with inconvenient dimensions, which explains why this measurement is lower than the throughput on the six arrays measured in Sung [6]. We also note that this implementation works only on arrays of 32-bit elements, and so its throughput can only be compared to other implementations that work on arrays of 32-bit elements. Additionally, we note that the implementation in Sung [6] has auxilary space requirement of $O(mn)$, since it may in the worst case require one bit per element of the array. Our asymptotically reduced auxiliary space requirement is an important advantage of our algorithm. We refer the reader to Sung et al. [8] for further development of this algorithm and implementation.

We also provide results for our algorithm. To make a direct comparison to Sung [6], we instantiated our algorithm for arrays of 32-bit elements, and measured a median throughput of 14.23 GB/s. When operating on arrays of 64-bit elements, our implementation measured a median throughput of 19.53 GB/s. The double-precision ar-

Median Throughputs	GB/s
Sung [6] (float)	5.33
C2R (float)	14.23
C2R (double)	19.53

Table 2: Median In-place Transposition Throughputs on NVIDIA Tesla K20c on Arrays of 32-bit Elements (float) and 64-bit Elements (double)

rays transpose at higher throughput because the unstructured reads of array elements required for our row shuffle operation are more efficient when operating on 64-bit elements. These results are summarized in Table 2.

6. SIMD Vector Memory Accesses

Many algorithms mapped onto SIMD processors require vector loads and stores. Programmers often strive to increase the amount of sequential work that can be mapped onto a SIMD lane, in order to reduce the algorithmic overhead of parallelization; this requires vector loads and stores because each SIMD lane is consuming or producing a vector of data. Similarly, directly operating on Arrays of Structures (AoS) is convenient for programmers, but also requires arbitrary length vector loads and stores, as each SIMD lane loads or stores a structure. Although most processors provide limited vector loads and stores for a few fixed datatypes, using them can be inconvenient and suboptimal, since the size of a desired vector load or store may not map cleanly to the vector loads and stores provided by the hardware. Using compiler generated loads and stores for arbitrarily sized vector accesses often interacts poorly with the memory subsystem, since the vector loads and stores are implemented as a sequential series of strided memory operations, leading to poor memory bandwidth utilization.

6.1 Data Layout Conversion

As we explained in the introduction, one technique for dealing with this problem is to convert Arrays of Structures into Structures of Arrays, to eliminate the strided memory accesses. Our algorithm can perform this conversion in-place. Consider an Array of Structures of m elements, each of which is a structure containing n fields. Then the data is laid out in memory as a row-major $m \times n$ array, and transposing it into an $n \times m$ array corresponds to the Structure of Arrays data layout.

This can be done directly with the array transposition implementation we outlined earlier, but it performs poorly in practice because it is parallelized expecting m and n to both be relatively large, and for data layout conversion one of the two dimensions (the structure size) is very small, while the other (the array dimension) is very large.

We created specialized implementations of the transpose algorithm for arrays where one of the dimensions is large and the other is very small. These implementations perform all column operations in on-chip memory, since we can guarantee that the number of rows is very small by choosing the C2R or R2C algorithm appropriately.

This specialization is faster than the general implementation we described earlier, thanks to its better use of on-chip memory.

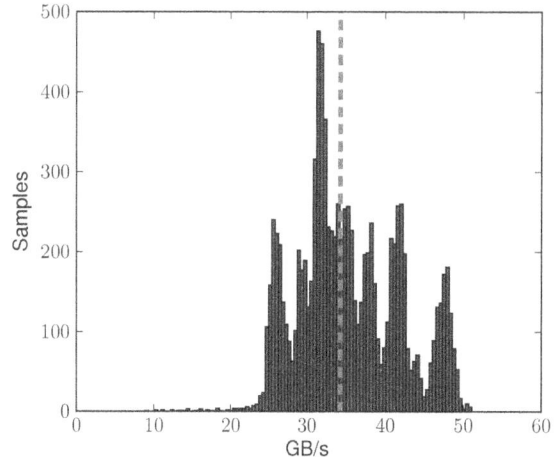

Figure 7: In-place transpose throughput for Array of Structure to Structure of Array conversion.

Figure 7 shows Array of Structures to Structures of Arrays conversion performance, where the structures are comprised of 64-bit elements. We tested performance on 10000 randomly sized Arrays of Structures, where the structure size was between $[2, 32)$ elements, and the number of structures in the array was between $[10^4, 10^7)$ We achieve median performance of 34.3 GB/s, and maximum performance of 51 GB/s.

6.2 SIMD Vector Memory Accesses

In some circumstances, Arrays of Structures do not need to be converted to Structures of Arrays at all: the transposition can be performed lazily as data is accessed. Our algorithm enables efficient, arbitrary length vector loads and stores, without the need to allocate on-chip memory to perform an out-of-place transpose.

Consider a SIMD vector of n SIMD lanes, each holding m items. This forms an array of dimension $m \times n$ in the register file. Using a shuffle instruction to interchange data between SIMD lanes, we can perform row shuffles, and using register operations locally to each SIMD lane, we can perform column operations. We will explain how this is done.

6.2.1 Row Shuffle

Most SIMD instruction sets provide a row shuffle that allows processing elements to communicate with other elements in their array. We can use this shuffle instruction directly to implement the row shuffles described in the algorithm. For

SIMD processors that do not provide a shuffle instruction, the shuffle can be simulated using a very small amount of on-chip memory that can hold one register for each SIMD lane.

6.2.2 Dynamic column rotation

In this primitive, each processing element rotates its vector by some distance, determined dynamically. Since each SIMD lane may rotate by a different amount, if this rotation were implemented with branching based on the rotation amount, this primitive would introduce SIMD divergence, dramatically reducing efficiency. To avoid this problem, we note that the rotation can be performed analogously to a barrel rotation implemented as a VLSI circuit. We can perform the rotation in-place in $\lceil \log_2 m \rceil$ steps, by statically iterating over the bits of the rotation amount, and conditionally rotating each SIMD lane's vectors by distance $d = 2^k$ at each step. This eliminates branches, even when each SIMD lane rotates its array by a different amount. This approach uses completely static register indexing, using conditional moves to perform the dynamic rotation. This comes at a cost: we must do $\lceil \log_2 m \rceil$ select instructions per element.

6.2.3 Static row permutation

In this primitive, each processing element statically permutes its vector in the same way. Since the permutation is statically known, and is constant for all processing elements, in many cases this permutation can be implemented statically without any hardware instructions: it is performed in the compiler by logically renaming elements in each column vector.

6.2.4 Implementation

This algorithm allows SIMD processors to read and write vectors of data at full memory bandwidth. Since n is constant for a given architecture, and m, the size of the structure in registers, is static, the task of computing indices can be simplified through careful strength reduction and static precomputation.

Figures 8 and 9 show the throughput vector loads and stores using this technique achieve on the NVIDIA Tesla K20c processor. The line marked "C2R" is using our transpose algorithm based on shuffle instructions to enable efficient memory accesses, and can achieve full memory bandwidth. The line marked "Vector" is using the native 128-bit vector loads and stores provided by the K20c processor. This can be efficient when the requested vector length is equal to 16 bytes, and is general more efficient than element wise loads and stores, but is not as efficient as performing the transpose. The line marked "Direct" uses compiler-generated element wise loads and stores. Figure 8 shows throughputs on unit-stride accesses, where each SIMD lane is loading or storing contiguous structures. The technique also works for random accesses to arrays of structures: in this case, indices must also be passed between SIMD lanes

```
T* ptr; //Private to each CUDA thread
coalesced_ptr<T> c_ptr(ptr);
T loaded = *c_ptr; //Load and R2C transpose
*c_ptr = value; //C2R Transpose and store
```

Figure 10: High level interface

using shuffles. For random access, throughput improves as the size of the structure approaches the cache-line width, as shown in Figure 9.

Our transpose mechanism enables higher throughput on all regimes, both when performing unit strided vector memory accesses, as well as when performing randomized vector memory addresses. The performance differential can be large, up to $45\times$ for the case of unit-stride vector stores, compared to compiler generated stores. These benchmarks illustrates the utility of this technique for processors such as the K20c.

Although we can achieve full memory bandwidth when performing transpositions in registers, there may still be cases where performing the transposition in memory is advantageous. Since our algorithm accommodates both the register-based transpose as well as the full storage transpose, the best solution for the particular application can be exploited.

6.2.5 Interface

Figure 10 shows a high level interface in CUDA C++ [5] that makes use of this transpose. Because the transpose does not require allocating on-chip memory, it is straightforward to create a `coalesced_ptr<T>` wrapper type that performs transpositions internally. Every CUDA thread has its own pointer pointing to a structure of type T that it wishes to load or store. Directly dereferencing this pointer would lead to the undesirable performance characteristics described in the previous section. However, simply wrapping this pointer in a `coalesced_ptr<T>` type ensures that all dereferences occur through transpositions, and are therefore efficient.

7. Related Work

As in-place matrix transposition is a well studied field, there are several important related works with which to relate our algorithm.

We already discussed Gustavson et al. [1] and Sung [6] in Section 5.

Tretyakov and Tyrtyshnikov [9] present an algorithm for in-place matrix transposition that has optimal work complexity of $O(mn)$ while requiring only $O(\min(m, n))$ auxiliary space. This algorithm was presented without any experimental results, but we note that it requires up to 24 swaps per element, which corresponds to reading and writing each element 48 times, since each swap involves 2 reads and 2 writes. Our algorithm requires reading and writing each el-

(a) Store Bandwidth

(b) Copy Bandwidth

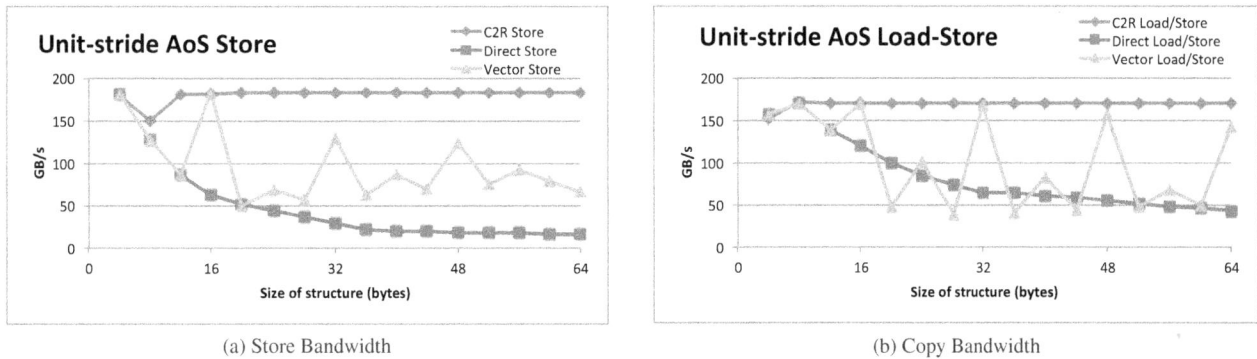

Figure 8: Unit-stride Array of Structures Access

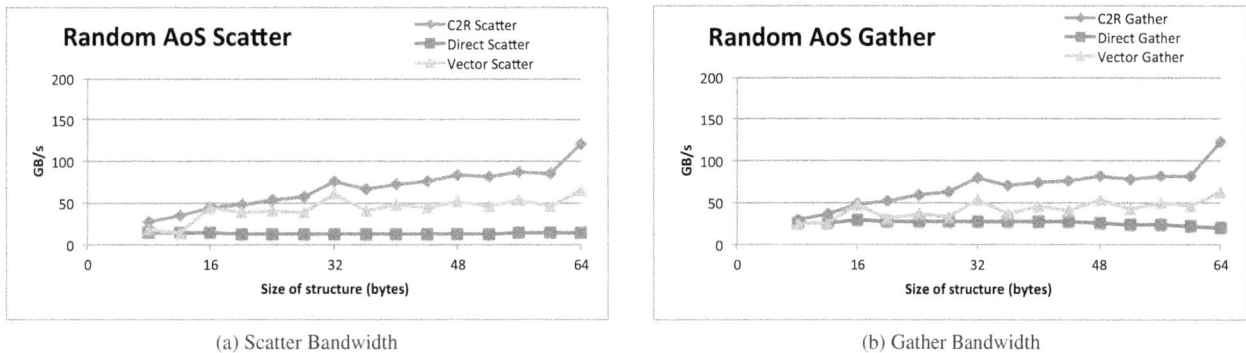

(a) Scatter Bandwidth

(b) Gather Bandwidth

Figure 9: Random Array of Structures Access

ement 6 times, in the worst case, which we believe gives it practical advantages. Additionally, the simplicity of our algorithm enables straightforward, efficient parallel implementation, as well as the in-register transpose that arises when SIMD processors perform vector memory accesses.

Sung et al. [7] propose a partial Arrays of Structures to Structures of Arrays transform. Because the cost of the full transposition using traditional algorithms is too high, the paper recommends modifying the program to use a hybrid Array of Structure of Tiled Array format, where the transposition cost is reduced by transposing tiles rather than elements of the array. As this introduces non-trivial complexity to the task of addressing elements of the array, the authors propose a compiler and runtime that hide this complexity from the programmer. In contrast, with our approach, we can afford to do the full transposition to convert to a true Structure of Arrays format, or alternatively, can leave the data in an Array of Structure format and perform SIMD transpositions as the data is loaded and stored.

8. Conclusion

In this paper, we have shown a decomposition for in-place matrix transposition. This decomposition has theoretical ad-

vantages compared to prior algorithms: it reduces work complexity of the transposition when auxiliary storage space is limited by reducing the scope of each permutation to a single row or column. The decomposition leads to a naturally parallel algorithm for in-place matrix transposition that has optimal work complexity of $O(mn)$, given auxiliary storage space of $O(\max(m, n))$. Our algorithm has either work or space complexity advantages over many published algorithms for in-place matrix transposition.

We have shown that the algorithm is correct, and given performance results showing its efficiency for several implementations on CPUs and GPUs. We have also shown how specializations of this algorithm can efficiently convert between Arrays of Structures and Structures of Arrays. Finally, the regular structure of our algorithm lends itself to an in-place transpose on the register file of a SIMD processor, which can allow access to Arrays of Structures at full memory bandwidth. Because the algorithm operates in-place, it is particularly easy to integrate into existing code, without requiring the user to allocate on-chip storage for the transposition. The software we have developed to illustrate this algorithm is publically available.

Acknowledgments

This research was funded in part by the DARPA PERFECT program and the U.S. Department of Energy FastForward program.

We wish to thank Manjunath Kudlur, Sean Treichler, Sean Baxter, John Owens, Brandon Lloyd, and Pace Nielsen for discussions that improved this work.

References

[1] F. Gustavson, L. Karlsson, and B. Kågström. Parallel and cache-efficient in-place matrix storage format conversion. *ACM Transactions on Mathematical Software*, 38(3):1–32, Apr. 2012. doi: 10.1145/2168773.2168775.

[2] Intel. Intel MKL, 2013. URL http://software.intel.com/en-us/intel-mkl.

[3] D. E. Knuth. *The Art of Computer Programming*, volume 3. Addison-Wesley, 1973. ISBN 0-201-03803-X.

[4] T. Leighton. Tight bounds on the complexity of parallel sorting. In *Proceedings of the Sixteenth Annual ACM Symposium on Theory of Computing*, STOC '84, pages 71–80, New York, NY, USA, 1984. ACM. doi: 10.1145/800057.808667.

[5] J. Nickolls, I. Buck, M. Garland, and K. Skadron. Scalable parallel programming with CUDA. *ACM Queue*, pages 40–53, Mar./Apr. 2008. doi: 10.1145/1365490.1365500.

[6] I.-J. Sung. *Data layout transformation through in-place transposition*. PhD thesis, University of Illinois, Department of Electrical and Computer Engineering, May 2013. URL http://hdl.handle.net/2142/44300.

[7] I.-J. Sung, G. D. Liu, and W.-M. W. Hwu. DL: A data layout transformation system for heterogeneous computing. In *Innovative Parallel Computing (InPar)*, May 2012. doi: 10.1109/InPar.2012.6339606.

[8] I.-J. Sung, J. Gómez-Luna, J. M. González-Linares, N. Guil, and W.-M. W. Hwu. In-place transposition of rectangular matrices on accelerators. In *Principles and Practices of Parallel Programming (PPoPP)*, PPoPP '14, 2014. doi: 10.1145/2555243.2555266.

[9] A. A. Tretyakov and E. E. Tyrtyshnikov. Optimal in-place transposition of rectangular matrices. *Journal of Complexity*, 25(4):377–384, Aug. 2009. doi: 10.1016/j.jco.2009.02.008.

[10] H. S. Warren. *Hacker's Delight*. Addison-Wesley Professional, 2002. ISBN 978-0-201-91465-8.

[11] P. F. Windley. Transposing matrices in a digital computer. *The Computer Journal*, 2(1):47–48, Jan. 1959. doi: 10.1093/comjnl/2.1.47.

In-Place Transposition of Rectangular Matrices on Accelerators

I-Jui Sung

MulticoreWare, Inc

ray@multicorewareinc.com

Juan Gómez-Luna

University of Córdoba

el1goluj@uco.es

José María González-Linares
Nicolás Guil

University of Málaga

{jgl, nguil}@uma.es

Wen-Mei W. Hwu

University of Illinois at Urbana-Champaign

w-hwu@illinois.edu

Abstract

Matrix transposition is an important algorithmic building block for many numeric algorithms such as FFT. It has also been used to convert the storage layout of arrays. With more and more algebra libraries offloaded to GPUs, a high performance in-place transposition becomes necessary. Intuitively, in-place transposition should be a good fit for GPU architectures due to limited available on-board memory capacity and high throughput. However, direct application of CPU in-place transposition algorithms lacks the amount of parallelism and locality required by GPUs to achieve good performance. In this paper we present the first known in-place matrix transposition approach for the GPUs. Our implementation is based on a novel 3-stage transposition algorithm where each stage is performed using an elementary tiled-wise transposition. Additionally, when transposition is done as part of the memory transfer between GPU and host, our staged approach allows hiding transposition overhead by overlap with PCIe transfer. We show that the 3-stage algorithm allows larger tiles and achieves 3X speedup over a traditional 4-stage algorithm, with both algorithms based on our high-performance elementary transpositions on the GPU. We also show our proposed low-level optimizations improve the sustained throughput to more than 20 GB/s. Finally, we propose an asynchronous execution scheme that allows CPU threads to delegate in-place matrix transposition to GPU, achieving a throughput of more than 3.4 GB/s (in-

cluding data transfers costs), and improving current multi-threaded implementations of in-place transposition on CPU.

Categories and Subject Descriptors G.4 [*Mathematics of Computing*]: MATHEMATICAL SOFTWARE—Parallel and vector implementations

Keywords GPU, Transposition, In-Place

1. Introduction

Matrix transposition converts an M-rows-by-N-columns array ($M \times N$ for brevity) to an N-rows-by-M-columns array. It is an important algorithmic building block with a wide range of applications from converting the storage layout of arrays to numeric algorithms, such as FFT and K-Means clustering, or computing linear algebra functions as defined by BLAS libraries.

FFT implementations typically carry out matrix transpositions before transforming each dimension [1]. This allows the transforms to access contiguous data, avoiding time-consuming strided memory accesses. K-Means clustering also benefits from transposition when partitioning thousands or even millions of descriptors in image classification applications [2], in which typical descriptors are multidimensional vectors with up to 256 components.

BLAS libraries, such as GotoBLAS [3] and Intel MKL [4], use matrix transposition extensively as well. For instance, MKL includes out-of-place and in-place transposition routines since release 10.1. Moreover, many level 2 and level 3 functions, such as matrix multiplication (`sgemm` and `dgemm`), include a parameter to specify that input matrices are transposed before executing the operation. When offloading these BLAS libraries to the GPU, an efficient transposition becomes important.

Since matrix transposition merely reorders the elements of a matrix, performance of matrix transposition is essentially determined by the sustained memory bandwidth of the system. This makes GPU an attractive platform to execute the transposition because of its sheer memory bandwidth (to its global memory) compared to CPUs. A GPU implementation of matrix transposition can be used to accelerate CPU transposition as well by transferring the matrix to GPU memory, transposing on GPU, and copying back the transposed matrix to CPU memory. Lastly, it can be used as a building block in more complex GPU applications.

Implementing out-of-place matrix transposition on GPU, that achieves high fraction of peak memory bandwidth, is well understood [5]. However, the memory capacity on GPU is usually a much more constrained resource than its CPU counterpart. If an out-of-place transposition is employed, only up to 50% of the total available GPU memory could be used to hold one or several matrices, that need to be transposed, since the out-of-place transposition has at least 100% spatial overhead. This leads to the need of a general in-place transposition library for the accelerator programming models.

To avoid the high spatial overhead of out-of-place transposition, in-place transposition can be employed, which means the resulting A^T occupies the same physical storage locations as A and there should not be much temporary storage required during transposition. The spatial overhead is either none (i.e. methods that do not require bit flags but with extra computations) [6] or at most a small fraction of the input size (one bit per element) [7].

Mathematically, in-place transposition is a permutation, that can be factored into a product of disjoint cycles [8]. These cycles are "chains" of shifting, where each data element is moved to a destination that is the original location of another data element. In the special case of square matrices, the shifting consists of simply swapping symmetric elements along the diagonal, while the diagonal elements remain in the same location. There are as many cycles as elements over (or under) the diagonal, and their length is two. Thus, the GPU implementation is straightforward. However, in the general case of rectangular matrices the number of cycles can be much lower, and their length is not uniform. These facts make parallelization a challenge. Obtaining a fast parallelization of matrix transposition requires the use of tiling, in order to take advantage of the spatial locality in scratchpads or cache memories. In this paper, we propose a new technique that tackles the general case of arbitrary rectangular matrices. Our proposal is "in-place" in the sense that A^T is placed in the same global memory space as A. Moreover, it does not need much temporary storage in global memory (except 0.1% or less overhead coordination bits), since tiles are temporarily stored in on-chip memories, which are of a very small and bounded size.

The contributions of this paper are as follows:

- This is, as of today, the first known in-place full transposition algorithm for general rectangular matrices on the GPU [9]. We present a full transposition on GPU that is a 4-stage technique based on Gustavson/Karlsson imple-

mentation [10, 11]. In each stage, elementary tiled-wise transpositions are carried out. These were developed by Sung et al. [12], but they did not explain how to use them to implement full transposition.

- We propose further a brand new 3-stage tiled transposition scheme that is optimized for GPUs [9], compared to 4-stage Gustavson/Karlsson transposition, plus insights to minimize the search space of tile sizes, which is crucial to obtain high throughput.

- We improve Sung's elementary transpositions by reducing memory contention due to atomic instructions, and by modifying the way the work is distributed among workgroups.

- We develop an asynchronous execution scheme that accelerates CPU matrix transposition by delegating the work to our GPU implementation. Further improvement is obtained by overlapping 2 stages of the GPU transposition with GPU-CPU transfer.

- We compare our in-place matrix transposition on GPU with state-of-the-art out-of-place and in-place implementations for multi-core and many-core CPUs, and discuss under which conditions executing transpositions on an accelerator is profitable.

Our 3-stage in-place transposition achieves on modern GPUs more than 20 GB/s of sustained throughput (calculated as twice the number of bytes of the matrix -once for reading the matrix and once for writing- divided by the total execution time). Moreover, a 3X speedup with respect to the baseline transposition (i.e, 4-stage Gustavson/ Karlsson-style implementation on GPU) is obtained. OpenCL codes of the baseline and the new 3-stage transpositions are publicly available[1].

From the CPU's perspective, our asynchronous execution scheme offers an effective throughput of more than 3.4 GB/s, that is, more than 20% faster than Gustavson/Karlsson implementation on a 6-core CPU. This scheme can be very profitable when in-place transposition is required on CPU due to the use of very large matrices and memory limitations. In these cases, our 3-stage GPU in-place transposition can be applied to transpose these matrices, whose size would be only limited by the GPU memory size.

The rest of the paper is organized as follows. Section 2 presents the related works in the field of matrix transposition on CPU and GPU. In Section 3, the matrix transposition is defined, and a basic GPU implementation is presented. Section 4 describes how the full in-place transposition of rectangular matrices can be carried out as a sequence of elementary transpositions. Section 5 explains the low-level optimizations on the elementary transpositions. Section 6 describes how our in-place transposition on GPU can be used to accelerate in-place transposition on CPU. Section 7

---

[1] https://bitbucket.org/ijsung/libmarshal/wiki/Home

presents the experimental results. Finally, the conclusions are stated.

2. Related Work

2.1 In-Place Transposition and Parallelization for CPUs

As indicated above, most of sequential in-place transposition algorithms can be classified as cycle-following. Berman [7] proposed a bit-table for tagging cycles that have been shifted, and it requires $O(MN)$ bits of workspace for transposing an $M \times N$ matrix. Windley [6] presented the notation of cycle-leaders as the lowest numbered element. Cate and Twigg [13] proved a theorem to compute the number of cycles in a transposition.

Achieving fast implementations of in-place transposition has attracted several research efforts. Recent works took a 4-stage approach [10, 11, 14], in order to improve cache locality. Moreover, Gustavson et al. [11] proposed parallelization for multicores up to 8-cores. They noticed load imbalance issues, even for the relatively small number of threads available on multicores compared to modern GPUs. To address this problem, they proposed greedy assignment of cycles to threads and, for long cycles, splitting the shifting a priori.

2.2 In-Place and Out-of-Place Transposition for GPUs

For many-core processors, previous work [5] studied optimizations for out-of-place transposition. Sung et al. [12] proposed the use of atomically-updated bit flags to solve the load-imbalance problem for GPUs and introduced elementary transposition routines that can be used to compose a multi-stage transposition. However, they do not specify how one would compose these elementary transpositions to obtain a full transposition.

Previous works on fast Fourier transform for the GPU such as [15] includes transposition to improve locality for global memory accesses; the authors did not specify whether the transposition is in-place or not, but we believe it is an out-of-place one. We also believe that their work can be enhanced by employing an in-place transposition algorithm such as ours to increase the maximum size of dataset allowed for GPU offloading.

3. Definition of Matrix Transposition

Assume that A is an $M \times N$ matrix, where $A(i,j)$ is the element in row i and column j. The transpose of A is an $N \times M$ matrix A^T, so that the columns of A are the rows of A^T, or formally $A(i,j) = A^T(j,i)$.

In a linearized row-major layout, $A(i,j)$ is in offset location $k = i \times N + j$. When transposing, $A(i,j)$ at offset k is moved to $A^T(j,i)$ at $k' = j \times M + i$ in the transposed array A^T. The formula for mapping from k to k' is:

$$k' = \begin{cases} k \times M \mod \mathcal{M}, & \text{if } 0 \leq k < \mathcal{M} \\ \mathcal{M}, & \text{if } k = \mathcal{M} \end{cases} \quad (1)$$

where $\mathcal{M} = M \times N - 1$ [11].

```
for(int k = wi_id; k < M * N - 1; k += wg_size){
    // Transpose in a temporary array
    int k1 = (k * M) % (M * N - 1);
    temp[k1] = matrix[k];
}
// Synchronization
barrier();
// Copy to global memory
for(int i = wi_id; i < M * N - 1; i += wg_size){
    matrix[i] = temp[i];
}
```

Figure 1. Code segment of in-place matrix transposition with barrier synchronization (BS). Input matrix `matrix` is located in global memory. The temporary array in local memory is `temp`. Each work-item `wi_id` belongs to a work-group size `wg_size`.

The expression in Equation (1) allows us to calculate the destination for a matrix element. Since we are moving elements in-place, the original element in the destination has to be saved and further shifted (according to the involved permutation) to the next location. This generates cycles or chains of shifting.

The former transformation can be implemented on GPU by assigning matrix elements to work-items (i.e., a thread in OpenCL terminology), as the code in Figure 1 shows. In this kernel, called Barrier-sync (BS), one work-group transposes a matrix that fits the on-chip memory (registers or local memory). Although this implementation does not directly apply to arrays larger than tens of kilobytes in size, it can be used as a building block when transposing larger matrices.

4. In-place Transposition of Rectangular Matrices

In a general implementation of in-place transposition of rectangular matrices, the cycles are generated using Equation (1). For instance, we can use a row-majored 5×3 matrix transposition example, i.e. $M = 5, N = 3, \mathcal{M} = M \times N - 1 = 14$. We start with element 1, or the location of $A(0,1)$. The content of element 1 should be moved to the location of element 5, or the location of $A^T(1,0)$. The original content at the location of element 5, or the location of $A(1,2)$, is saved before being overwritten and moved to location of element 11, or the location of $A^T(2,1)$; The original content at the location of element 11 to the location of element 13, and so on. Eventually, we will return to the original offset 1. This gives a cycle of (1 5 11 13 9 3 1). For brevity, we will omit the second occurrence of 1 and show the cycle as (1 5 11 13 9 3). The reader should verify that there are five such cycles in transposing a 5×3 row-majored matrix: (0) (1 5 11 13 9 3)(7)(2 10 8 12 4 6)(14).

Prior works [11] targeting multicores parallelize by assigning each cycle to a thread. As cycles by definition never

209

overlap, they are an obvious source of parallelism that could be exploited by parallel architectures. In [12] this implementation is called P-IPT. However, for massively parallel systems that require thousands of concurrently active threads to attain maximum parallelism, this form of parallelism alone is neither sufficient nor regular. In fact, for the vast majority of other cases the amount of parallelism from the sheer number of cycles is both much lower and varying except when $M = N$ or square arrays. Even for larger M and N, the parallelism coming from cycles can be low. Also, as proven by Cate and Twigg [13], the length of the longest cycle is always several times the lengths of other cycles. This creates significant load imbalance problem.

Sung et al. [12] have proposed an atomic-operation-based approach to coordinate the shifting to reduce load imbalance. The gist of their method, called PTTWAC, is to have multiple threads participating in the shifting of elements in one cycle, and use atomic operations to coordinate the shifting among threads. However, the problem is that modern GPUs lack bit-addressable atomic operations as the smallest addressable unit is a 4-byte word. As we shall show in Section 5, simulating atomic bit operations naïvely can lead to significant performance loss due to the conflicts among concurrent threads. In this regard, we have also been inspired by recent works on histogram calculation, which is a class of atomic-intensive application that has attracted many research efforts in the GPU computing community. They minimize the impact of atomic conflicts by replicating the histogram in local memory in combination with the use of padding [16] or a careful layout [17].

4.1 Full Transposition As a Sequence of Elementary Tiled Transpositions

Good locality is crucial for modern memory hierarchies. Therefore staged transpositions that trade locality with extra data movements can be favorable. A full transposition of a matrix can be achieved by a series of blocked transpositions in four stages [10, 11, 14]. As shown further, on a modern NVIDIA K20 GPU, a 4-stage Gustavson/Karlsson-style in-place transposition reaches around 7 GB/s with optimized blocked transposition whereas a single-stage in-place transposition only runs at 1.5 GB/s, due to poor locality.

A Gustavson/Karlsson style transposition first considers an $M \times N$ matrix as an $M' \times m$ by $N' \times n$ matrix where $M = M' \times m$ and $N = N' \times n$. Then the elementary transpositions are designed in such a way that they only swap adjacent dimensions among the four dimensions. In this case, the problem becomes finding a sequence of elementary transpositions to reach $N' \times n \times M' \times m$. We employ the factorial numbering system [18] to refer each stage: Table 1 lists possible permutations that refer to swapping of adjacent dimensions. Intuitively, each digit of the factorial number for a particular permutation can be thought as an item from an imaginary queue of items, with offset starting from zero for the leftmost element. If we insert items from the right

Table 1. Permutations in Factorial Numbering System.

#Dimensions	From	To	Factorial Num.	Sung's terminology [12]
3D	(A, B, C)	(A, C, B)	$010_!$	AoS-ASTA transpose
	(A, B, C)	(B, A, C)	$100_!$	SoA-ASTA transpose
4D	(A, B, C, D)	(B, A, C, D)	$1000_!$	
	(A, B, C, D)	(A, C, B, D)	$0100_!$	A instances of SoA-ASTA
	(A, B, C, D)	(A, B, D, C)	$0010_!$	$A \times B$ instances of AoS-ASTA

end of the queue and take the items from the left end of the queue, we maintain the original order. However, when an item reaches the left end, if we take its right neighbor instead for the next turn, we reverse the order between the two items. If we have 4 items, (A, B, C, D) in the queue, we can generate a sequence of 4 numbers by generating 0 whenever we remove the leftmost item (offset 0) and 1 for the item right to the leftmost item (offset 1). So if we reverse the order between B and C, we would generate $0100_!$, which is the factorial number for a permutation from (A, B, C, D) to (A, C, B, D).

The elementary transpositions were used by Sung et al. [12] to transform data layouts from Array-of-Structures (AoS) or Structure-of-Arrays (SoA) to an intermediate layout called Array-of-Structures-of-Tiled-Arrays (ASTA). Thus, Sung's implementation of transposition $010_!$ considers AoS as a $M' \times m \times N$ 3-D array (where N is the number of elements in each structure), and each of these $m \times N$ tiles is assigned one work-group (in OpenCL terminology), that is in charge of transposing the corresponding tile. Thus, their AoS-to-ASTA marshaling is essentially an elementary transposition that converts $M' \times m \times N$ (AoS) to $M' \times N \times m$ (ASTA). Similarly, their SoA to ASTA (i.e. transposition $100_!$) transformation essentially is from $N \times M' \times m$ (SoA) to $M' \times N \times m$ (ASTA), in which every m-element tile is treated as a super-element that is then shifted in order to obtain ASTA.

Figure 2 illustrates our 4-stage implementation of a full in-place transposition based on [10], which employs the mentioned elementary tiled transpositions. Initially, the matrix is considered as a 4D array. Then, the first stage applies transposition $0100_!$, that is, M' instances of transpositions of $m \times N'$ matrices that are formed by super-elements of size n. Although $m \times N'$ can be large, this stage always moves super-elements of size n that can be tuned to fit cache line and/or DRAM burst size, thus maintaining locality. The second stage employs $0010_!$ to transpose $M' \times N'$ instances of $n \times m$ matrices. This stage can be realized by holding a temporary array of $n \times m$ in fast on-chip memory of GPUs for each instance. The third stage, which applies the factorial $1000_!$, can be considered as one instance of transposition of an $N' \times M'$ array of super-element sized $n \times m$. The fourth stage is similar to the first one but with a different dimensionality.

4.2 3-Stage Full In-place Transposition on GPU

The transposition $1000_!$ in the 4-stage approach moves super-elements of $m \times n$ elements, so that its best perfor-

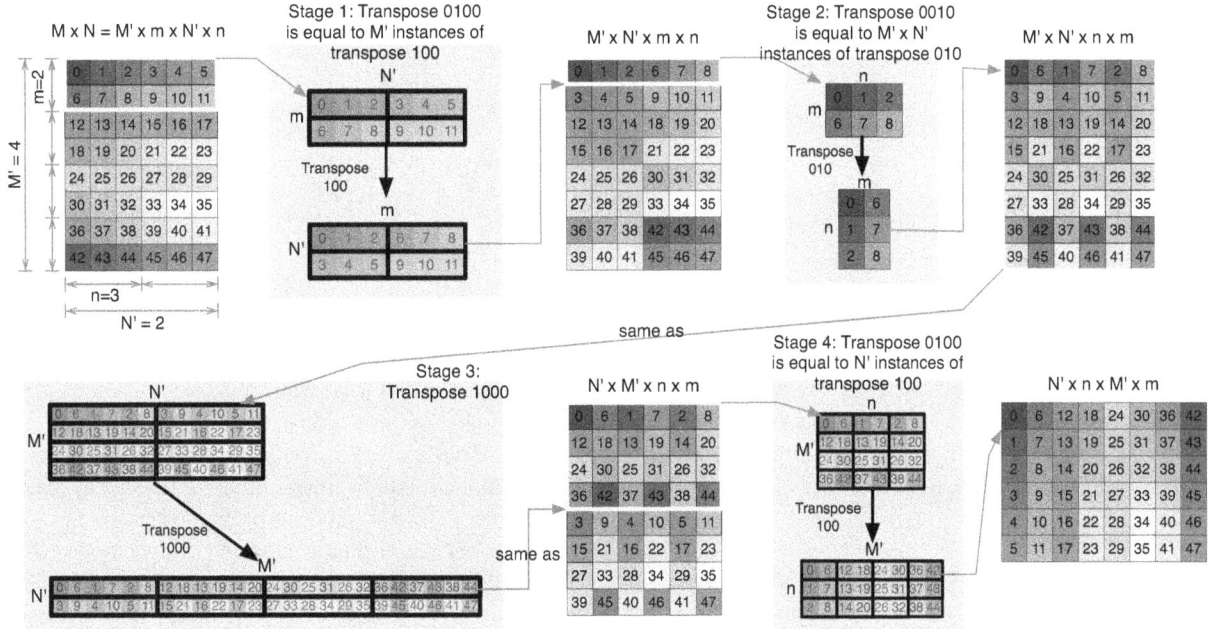

Figure 2. 4-stage full in-place transposition. In every figure, memory addresses increase from left to right and from top to bottom. Yellow halos indicate the part of the matrix that is brought into focus in the subsequent step. Black halos represent super-elements, which are shifted as a whole.

mance is obtained when these super-elements fit on-chip memory. Thus, values for m and n resulting in a high throughput for that transposition in stage 3, can perform poorly for transposition $0100_!$ in stage 1 and 4, where the size of the super-elements is only n and m, respectively.

To address this problem, we propose to eliminate the intermediate transposition $1000_!$ without sacrificing locality. One such improved 3-stage approach is:

1. Treat matrix $M \times N$ as a 3-dimensional array of $M \times N' \times n$. Perform transposition of n-sized super-elements, i.e. $M \times N' \times n$ to $N' \times M \times n$. This is transposition $100_!$.

2. Treat matrix $N' \times M \times n$ as a 4-dimensional array of $N' \times M' \times m \times n$. Perform $N' \times M'$ instances of transposition of $m \times n$ matrices, i.e. $N' \times M' \times m \times n$ to $N' \times M' \times n \times m$. This is transposition $0010_!$.

3. Perform N' instances of transposition of m-sized super-elements, i.e. $N' \times M' \times n \times m$ to $N' \times n \times M' \times m$. This is transposition $0100_!$.

In this improved algorithm, there are only three steps, and a much larger values of m and n can be used in the first and the third stage respectively for transposition $0100_!$ without overflowing the on-chip memory.

5. Performance Improvements for Elementary Transpositions

Sung et al. [12] suggests parallelization strategies that are useful for the elementary transpositions shown in the previ-

ous section. However, their transposition algorithms suffer from the following bottlenecks, if implemented literally. On the one hand, AoS-ASTA transformation is burdened by serious atomic memory contention. On the other hand, SoA-ASTA transformation has several limitations related to the work-group size, that are detailed below. In the following sections we describe improvements to those transposition building blocks.

5.1 Transposition $010_!$ (aka AoS-ASTA)

Sung et al. present two versions of transposition $010_!$: the first one is the fast Barrier-sync (BS) kernel, that we have already shown in Figure 1. As we also pointed out, for BS the tile size (the product of sizes of the lowest two dimensions) is limited, since it cannot exceed the size of on-chip memory accessible to a work-group (i.e., OpenCL local memory or register file). The second one is devised for large tiles and is based on the PTTWAC algorithm.

In their PTTWAC-based algorithm for large tiles, each work-item of a work-group shifts scalar values inside a tile directly from global memory. In order to ensure load balancing and coalesced global memory reads, adjacent work-items start to read adjacent elements and then follow the corresponding cycle. Recall that given a current element, the next one in the cycle is calculated by Equation (1).

One 1-bit flag per element per tile is stored in local memory, so that work-items can mark the elements they shift. When one work-item finds a previously set flag, it terminates. Sung et al. pack the flag bits in local memory 32-bit words using an intuitive layout. The local memory word

Flag_word, where the flag bit for element *Element_position* is stored, is given by Equation (2). *Element_position* stands for the one-dimensional index of an element within a tile.

$$Flag\_word = \left\lfloor \frac{Element\_position}{32} \right\rfloor \qquad (2)$$

Reading or setting a flag is a 1-bit atomic operation. Since the smallest hardware atomic operation size available is 32 bits wide, an atomic logic OR function is used to simulate bit-addressable atomics. This will cause conflicts among work-items updating flags in the same 32-bit word. Particularly burdening are intra-warp atomic conflicts[2], as explained by Gómez-Luna et al. [19]. In that work, the authors showed the latency is roughly increased by a factor equal to the number of colliding threads, which is called position conflict degree.

5.1.1 Spreading the Flag Bits

The position conflict degree can be diminished by spreading the flag bits over more local memory words. In Equation (3), the spreading factor stands for the reduction in the number of flag bits per local memory word. Thus, the maximum spreading factor is 32, unless the local memory available becomes a constraint [3].

$$Flag\_word = \left\lfloor \frac{Element\_position \times Spreading\_factor}{32} \right\rfloor \qquad (3)$$

5.1.2 Padding to Reduce Bank and Lock Conflicts

When using transposition $010_!$ in the second stage of the previously proposed full in-place transposition, the tile dimensions $m \times n$ are determined by the factors of the matrix dimensions $M \times N$. Thus, typical values m and n might be power-of-2. And recall that Equation (1) multiplies the offset by m. So a power-of-two value of m will cause new conflicts that are even more frequent when spreading the flags, as explained in Figure 3 (a) and (b). These new conflicts can be categorized as bank conflicts and lock conflicts [19]. Bank conflicts are due to concurrent reads or writes to different addresses in the same local memory bank. Lock conflicts are caused by the limited number of locks associated to atomic operations that are available in the hardware. This produces a similar effect to position conflicts.

Padding can be used to remove both types of conflicts. This optimization technique consists of keeping some memory locations unused, in order to shift the bank or lock accessed by concurrent threads. For instance, as the NVIDIA Fermi architecture contains 32 local memory banks and 1024 locks, inserting one unused location each 32 words

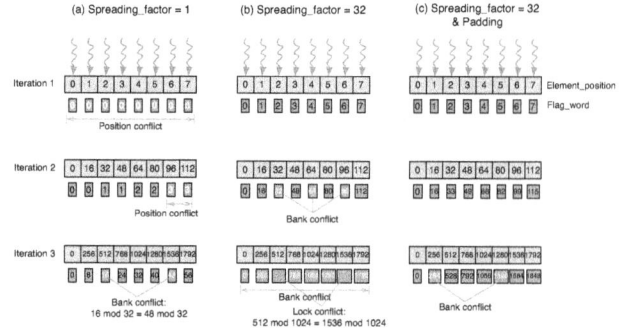

Figure 3. Consecutive work-items access consecutive elements in iteration 1. In the following iterations, the next elements in the cycle are computed with Equation (1). In this example, $m = 16$ and $n = 215$. Representative conflicts are highlighted: position conflicts (white), bank conflicts (yellow), lock conflicts (green). In case (a), the flag word is obtained through Equation (2). Many position conflicts appear. In case (b), the flag words are obtained with Equation (3). Position conflicts are removed, but bank and lock conflicts appear. 32 banks and 1024 locks are considered, as shown by Gómez-Luna et al. for NVIDIA Fermi architecture. In case (c), the use of padding avoids the lock conflicts and most bank conflicts.

will remove most bank and lock conflicts. This is shown in Figure 3 (c).

5.2 Transposition $100_!$ (aka SoA-ASTA)

Sung's implementation of SoA-ASTA transformation essentially converts from $N \times M' \times m$ to $M' \times N \times m$. Adjacent m elements are treated as a super-element that is then shifted in order to obtain the ASTA layout. Such a task is carried out by $N \times M'$ work-groups of m work-items. Thus, coordination between work-groups must be done with atomic operations on global memory. Hence, the shared-memory-oriented optimization techniques above are not applicable here.

Optimization efforts on this kernel can be oriented to overcome some limitations in Sung's implementation that are related to the fact that m is derived from the factors of the matrix dimensions:

1. The runtime imposes a maximum limit on the number of active work-groups in a GPU (e.g., 8 per *streaming multiprocessor* in NVIDIA Fermi). This entails low occupancy (i.e., the ratio of active work-items to the maximum possible number of active work-items) because of typical values of m (between 8 and 64). For instance, $m = 32$ means 16% occupancy for Fermi while the minimum recommended is 50% [20].

2. Every m that is not a multiple of the SIMD unit size[4] entails idle work-items, that is, further occupancy reduction.

---

[2] Warps are SIMD units in NVIDIA devices. AMD counterparts are called wavefronts.

[3] Practically, we could use any spreading factor up to 16, because 32 would entail 100% local memory overhead, that would allow us to use the faster BS kernel.

[4] NVIDIA's warp = 32 work-items; AMD's wavefront = 64 work-items.

3. If m is larger than the SIMD unit size, barriers are needed to synchronize the SIMD units belonging to the same work-group. This degrades performance, as SIMD units need to wait for each other.

4. The maximum possible m is limited to the maximum number of work-items per work-group (only 256 in AMD devices).

5.2.1 Improving Flexibility and Performance

The aforementioned limitations can be alleviated by using one SIMD unit to move m elements, instead of one work-group as in [12]. This increases occupancy, saves costly barriers, and expands the value range of m.

In Sung's implementation, each element of a super-element was temporally stored in one register per work-item. Since m might be longer than the SIMD unit size in our approach, local memory tiling is required in the pursuit of flexibility. First, each SIMD unit will need several iterations to store its m elements in local memory. Then, the SIMD unit will move its m elements to the new location in global memory.

Further performance improvement can be achieved for particular cases where m is a divisor or a multiple of the SIMD unit size using register tiling, because register accesses are faster than local memory accesses [21].

6. Using GPU Full In-place Transposition from CPU Host

The high memory bandwidth of GPUs makes them attractive to accelerate matrix transposition. Out-of-place matrix transposition on GPU [5] has demonstrated a very high throughput, but it is not suitable for large matrices, as it needs 100% memory overhead. In these cases, our 3-stage in-place approach can be employed. It is not strictly in-place by the definition from CPU's perspective as we are using 1X memory in the accelerator, but still the in-place algorithm works for datasets up to 100% of GPU accelerator's on-board memory theoretically. Thus, in-place matrix transposition is virtually executed on CPU, but physically executed on GPU. Figure 4 shows a high-level plan on how to implement this. The entire matrix must be transferred from CPU to GPU through the PCIe bus (1). Then, the in-place transposition is executed on GPU (2). Finally, the matrix is copied from GPU memory to the same location in CPU memory (3). The total execution time (including data transfers) will determine the effective throughput from CPU's perspective.

The use of several concurrent command queues can help us to accelerate this in-place matrix transposition. Using more than one command queue in OpenCL codes allows programmers to overlap data transfers and computation on a heterogenous system. This is a way to alleviate the bottleneck caused by data transfers.

OpenCL command queues are similar to CUDA streams, which were thoroughly studied in [22]. They are defined as sequences of operations that are executed in order, while

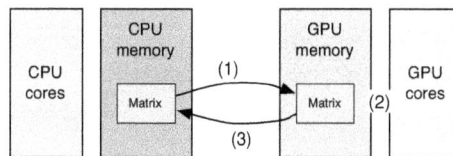

Figure 4. Scheme of an in-place matrix transposition on CPU memory using a GPU. In (1) the matrix is transferred to GPU memory. In-place matrix transpose is performed on GPU (2). In (3) the matrix is moved back to the same location in CPU memory.

different streams are executed asynchronously[5]. Data transfers and computation can be divided into a number of command queues. Thus, data transfers belonging to one command queue can be overlapped with computation belonging to a different command queue. Similar to the asynchronous scheme we propose below, in [23] data transfers are overlapped with memory layout reorganization kernels using CUDA streams.

As explained in Section 4.1, stages 2 and 3 in our 3-stage transposition execute independent instances of transpose $010_!$ and transpose $100_!$, respectively. These independent instances work with separate memory areas. Thus, they can be executed asynchronously: work-groups can be split into Q command queues (see Figure 5 (b) with $Q = 4$). This will allow us to overlap stages 2 and 3 and GPU-CPU transfer.

The number Q can range from 1 to a maximum number that still keeps the GPU multiprocessors busy (i.e., with the same occupancy as the synchronous execution) and leverages the PCIe bandwidth. Moreover, it should also be taken into account that the creation of multiple command queues entails an overhead.

Unfortunately, stage 1 (transpose $100_!$) cannot be overlapped with data transfers. This elementary transposition is made up of a number of cycles that shift super-elements across the entire memory space where the matrix is located. For this reason, transpose $100_!$ cannot be divided into independent command queues.

7. Experimental Results

Experiments in this section have been performed on two current NVIDIA devices and one AMD device, using single precision versions of the algorithms. NVIDIA GeForce GTX 580 with Fermi architecture has a peak bandwidth 192.4 GB/s. The recently released NVIDIA Tesla K20 with Kepler architecture achieves up to 208 GB/s. The AMD Radeon HD7750 Cape Verde has a peak memory bandwidth 72 GB/s.

7.1 Transposition $010_!$

The effect of spreading and padding on throughput has been measured with the same inputs used by Sung et al. [12] Fig-

---

[5] OpenCL also supports out-of-order execution within a command queue

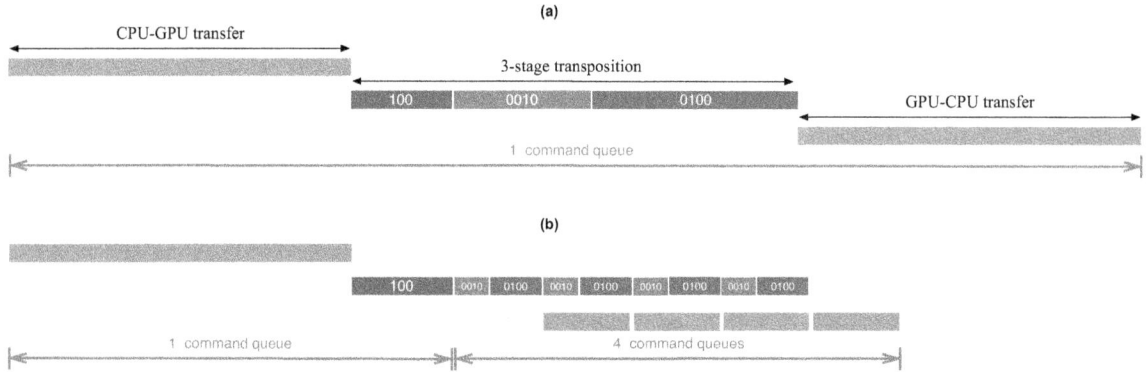

Figure 5. Timeline comparison. (a) Synchronous execution of the 3-stage in-place GPU transposition. (b) Asynchronous execution of the 3-stage in-place GPU transposition. Stages 2 and 3 and GPU-CPU transfer are divided into 4 command queues.

ure 6 shows the results on an NVIDIA Tesla K20 GPU. The experiment resizes matrices from $M' \times m \times n$ to $M' \times n \times m$. The reduction in the amount of position conflicts produces in average $1.77\times$ increased throughput. Moreover, the use of padding minimizes the bank and lock conflicts, so that 12% additional improvement is achieved. Some significant performance drops are noticeable when increasing the spreading factor (e.g., test problem bccstk31 with m equal to 32 and 64). These are caused by an occupancy value under 50%, due to the increase of local memory needs.

We have compared our optimized PTTWAC (with spreading and padding) to the original algorithm for n between 16 and 256 (in steps of 1) and m between 16 and 64 (in steps of 1). The average (minimum / maximum) speedup is 1.85 (1.36 / 3.49) on NVIDIA GeForce GTX 580, 1.79 (1.30 / 5.29) on NVIDIA Tesla K20, and 1.90 (1.15 / 3.34) on AMD Cape Verde.

The optimized PTTWAC has been compared to the P-IPT version [12], introduced in Section 1. P-IPT outperformed the original PTTWAC algorithm in some well load-balanced cases, but it is defeated by the optimized PTTWAC.

7.2 Transposition $100_!$

The new version of the transpose $100_!$ results in impressive speedups compared to Sung's original implementation on NVIDIA devices. Experiments resize from $N \times M' \times m$ to $M' \times N \times m$. We have tested with matrices of m between 16 and 64 (in steps of 1), and M' between 16 and 256 (in steps of 1). In order to obtain the highest throughput, the work-group size has been chosen to maximize the occupancy. Analyzing the need for registers and local memory, we noticed that the occupancy is limited on Fermi by the number of registers (22 registers per thread). Thus, the highest occupancy is obtained for 192 threads/block. On Kepler, such a limitation does not appear. The highest occupancy can be obtained with a number of threads per block that is a multiple of 128.

The average (minimum / maximum) speedup is equal to 2.95 (1.97 / 4.09) on GTX 580 and 2.58 (1.54 / 3.50) on

Table 2. Throughput of our 3-stage approach and Karlsson/-Gustavson 4-stage approach on a Kelper K20. Best performing tile sizes have been used. Both implementations include the low-level optimizations presented in Section 5.

	3-stage	4-stage (+fusion)
7200×1800	20.59 GB/s	7.11 (7.67) GB/s
5100×2500	18.49 GB/s	6.87 (7.38) GB/s
4000×3200	20.73 GB/s	7.23 (7.79) GB/s
3300×3900	18.80 GB/s	7.23 (7.79) GB/s
2500×5100	17.29 GB/s	6.86 (7.37) GB/s
1800×7200	18.70 GB/s	7.07 (7.60) GB/s

K20, when using local memory tiling. Register tiling can be applied for m that is multiple or divisor of the warp size. In these cases, performance further increases by 16% on GTX 580 and 23% on K20. The P-IPT version [12] is always outperformed by these new versions. Unfortunately, on AMD we did not observe speedups (albeit being more flexible, as explained in Section 5.2).

Figure 7.2 shows the throughput of transposition $100_!$ on K20 and Cape Verde for values of m and M' under 256. The best performance on K20 is obtained with m between 64 and 160. This range ensures enough work per work-item in the warp, and does not reduce the occupancy due to local memory needs for tiling. Similar results have been observed on GTX 580. On Cape Verde the best performance results occur with m over 128 (wavefront size doubles warp size). Local memory needs are not an issue, because the amount of local memory per wavefront is larger. To maximize occupancy, we typically use 40 wavefronts for 64 KB of local memory on Cape Verde [24], while 64 warps for 48 KB of local memory on K20 [20].

7.3 3-Stage and 4-Stage Transposition

Table 2 summarizes the throughput difference on a Tesla K20 of our 3-stage approach compared to the 4-stage version, which we have developed following the original ap-

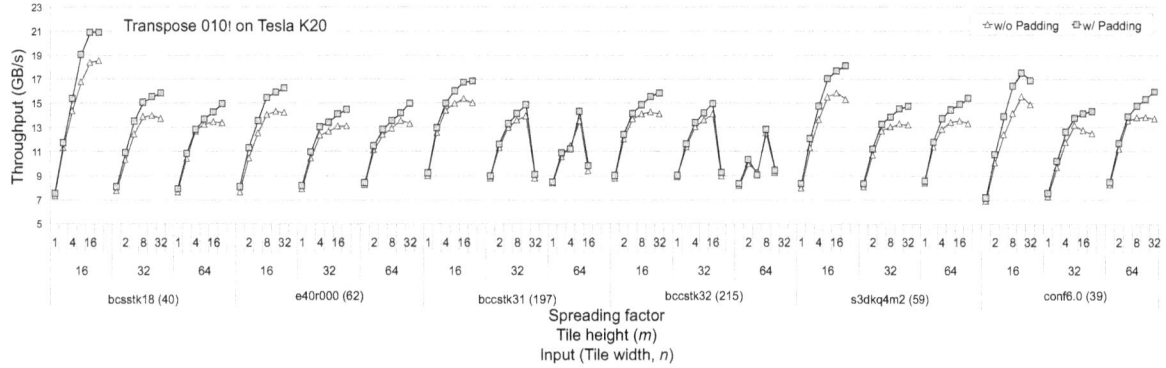

Figure 6. Effect of spreading and padding on Tesla K20. Transposition $010_!$ converts from $M' \times m \times n$ to $M' \times n \times m$. Six inputs are used [12]. The value within parentheses is the tile width n. Three values of the tile height m are tested (16, 32, 64). The spreading factor changes between 1 and 32 for every case.

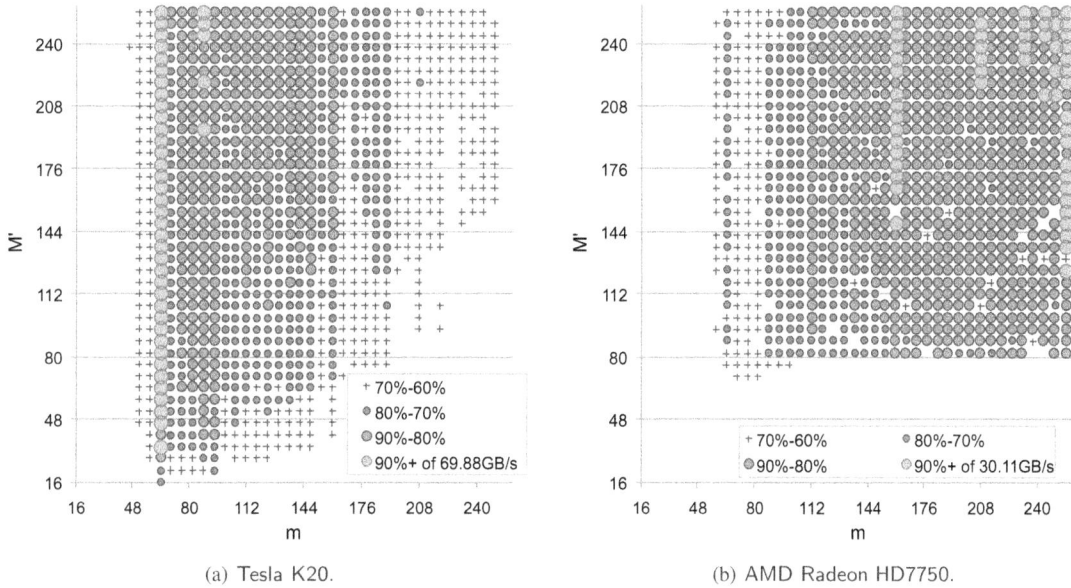

(a) Tesla K20.

(b) AMD Radeon HD7750.

Figure 7. Throughput (GB/s) of transpose $100_!$ for m and M' under 256. The experiment converts from $N \times M' \times m$ to $M' \times N \times m$.

proach by Gustavson [11] and Karlsson [10], using the dataset configuration from their paper. Both approaches are implemented using the same set of elementary transposition routines.

Note as also pointed out by Karlsson and Gustavson, the stage 2–3 in the 4-stage approach in Figure 2 could be fused. We present the throughput of their approach with fusion in the second column (values inside parentheses) of Table 2. The reason why our 3-stage method is significantly faster than the 4-stage method is not only eliminating one stage (which can be achieved by fusion in 4-stage approach anyway), but the 3-stage algorithm allows much bigger tile sizes which is crucial for transposition $100_!$ including derived $0100_!$, and $1000_!$. For Tesla K20, the throughput of transpositions $100_!$ et al., is dominated by tile size used: 12.5 GB/s

for tile size 8, 24.5 GB/s for tile size 16, 47.6 GB/s for tile size 32, 69 GB/s for tile size 64 on average. In fact, the best performing tile sizes (m, n) for transposing a 7200×1800 matrix is $(20, 16)$ for 4-stage transposition, but $(32, 72)$ for the 3-stage algorithm on a Tesla K20.

7.4 Choosing Tile Sizes for Full Transposition

Tile sizes are crucial to the throughput of full transposition. Naïvely, we could exhaustively search on all possible m and n combination and use the best one, but that is too time-consuming especially for M and N values having many possible dividends. We can prune the search space by taking into consideration these three factors: Transposition $100_!$ and $0100_!$ obtain a better throughput if the tile size is larger. This limits the stage 1 (tile size $= n$) and stage 3 (tile size

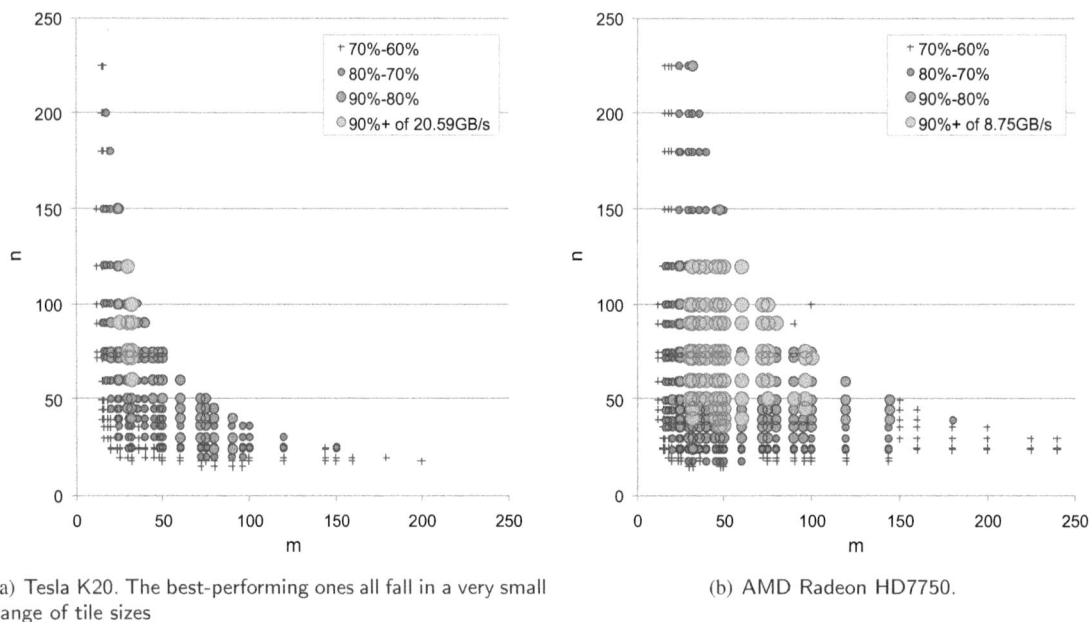

(a) Tesla K20. The best-performing ones all fall in a very small range of tile sizes

(b) AMD Radeon HD7750.

Figure 8. Tile Sizes versus Performance

$= m$). Transposition 0010₁ obtains a better throughput if the tile (in this case $m \times n$) fits into shared memory, because the barrier-synchronization kernel can be used.

Figure 8(a) plots some of the best combinations of tile sizes (m and n) in a 7200x1800 in-place transposition on one Tesla K20 (Kepler). The best ones achieved a throughput of 20.59 GB/s in an exhaustive search. It is clear that the tile sizes that lead to best throughput (80%+ of the best performing combinations) are actually within a very small subset roughly along the curve of $m \times n < 3600$ (which is roughly the shared memory capacity) and with mostly m and n around 60. Figure 8(b) shows a similar trend but on an AMD Radeon HD7750 (Cape Verde). We can see that for AMD GPUs the best performing combinations are also confined in a small region, but the shape is different from an NVIDIA GPU. For all three GPUs, a good guess for m and n will be from 50 to 100 with $m \times n$ less than the maximal shared memory capacity: this simple heuristic can yield at least 80% of the best throughput.

That exposes the only limitation of our algorithm. When the algorithm cannot choose a good tile size (e.g., prime-number dimensions), the throughput would be degraded [6].

7.5 Comparison to Matrix Transposition on CPU

We compare our 3-stage in-place transposition on GPU with Intel MKL [4] and Gustavson/Karlsson [11] out-of-place and in-place transpositions on CPU. From Intel MKL we use `mkl_somatcopy()` and `mkl_simatcopy()`, single precision

routines for out-of-place and in-place transposition, respectively. Gustavson/Karlson original implementations are double precision. We have moved them to single precision for a fair comparison. Figure 9 shows the throughput results for the best configurations. The same matrix sizes as in Section 7.3 have been used. CPU transposition implementations have run on a 6-core 3.47 GHz Intel Xeon W3690 and our 3-stage GPU in-place transposition on a Tesla K20.

It is remarkable that MKL in-place transposition is a sequential implementation. Thus, it achieves less than 0.1 GB/s, so that the corresponding column is not represented in the figure. MKL out-of-place transposition is a parallel implementation. Its throughput is not limited by the number of cores, but the memory bandwidth, since it does not scale for more than 4 threads. As it entails 100% memory overhead, its main drawback is that it is not suitable for applications in which the memory resources are constrained.

Gustavson/Karlsson implementations are also parallel and launch as many threads as CPU cores. The average throughput of their in-place transposition is 2.85 GB/s. Our 3-stage implementation on GPU is up to 6.7X faster than Gustavson/Karlsson's.

If our 3-stage implementation on GPU is used by a CPU thread, both data transfers (CPU-GPU and GPU-CPU) times must be added when using a synchronous execution scheme. For those matrix sizes, both transfers take around 15 ms to complete. Thus, the resulting average throughput from CPU's perspective is 2.87 GB/s, that is, slightly faster than Gustavson/Karlsson's method on CPU. Using an out-of-place transposition on GPU [5], instead of our 3-stage in-place approach, would only result in a minimally higher

---

[6] Contemporary to the preparation of this paper is another work [25] that addresses this limitation for a particular architecture (NVIDIA Kepler), obtaining a comparable performance.

Table 3. Assessment of in-place and out-of-place matrix transposition methods on CPU and GPU. Throughput figures are average results for the matrix sizes in Table 2. CPU codes have been tested on a 6-core Xeon, while GPU implementations have run on a Tesla K20.

Implementation	Executed on...	Throughput (GB/s)	CPU memory overhead	GPU memory overhead
Intel MKL out-of-place [4]	6 CPU cores	12.07	100%	-
Intel MKL in-place [4]	1 CPU core	< 0.1	0%	-
Gustavson/Karlsson out-of-place [11]	6 CPU cores	2.36	100%	-
Gustavson/Karlsson in-place [11]	6 CPU cores	2.85	0%	-
GPU out-of-place [5] + data transfers	GPU cores	3.57	0%	100%
3-stage GPU in-place + data transfers	GPU cores	3.43	0%	$\simeq 0\%$

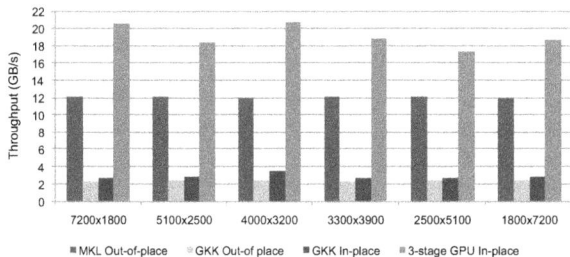

Figure 9. Throughput results for Intel MKL out-of-place transposition on CPU, Gustavson/Karlsson (GKK) out-of-place and in-place transposition on CPU, and 3-stage in-place transposition on GPU. The throughput of MKL in-place transposition is < 0.1 GB/s in all cases. CPU results have been obtained on a 6-core Xeon. GPU results correspond to a Tesla K20.

overall performance: data transfers are still the main performance bottleneck, even though the out-of-place transposition achieves more than 120 GB/s on a K20. Furthermore, our in-place approach has the additional advantage that it can transpose larger matrices, as it needs a negligible memory overhead.

7.6 Overlapping Stages 2 and 3 with GPU-CPU Transfer

As explained in Section 6, stages 2 and 3 of our 3-stage in-place GPU transposition can be overlapped with GPU-CPU data transfer. We have evaluated this asynchronous execution scheme with the same matrix sizes and all possible combinations of m and n (6444 tests).

In these tests, the asynchronous execution scheme (Q command queues) outperforms the synchronous execution scheme (1 command queue) by an average 9% and a maximum 24%. In the asynchronous execution, the best number Q is typically under 8. Larger values lower the resulting throughput because of the overhead derived from the creation of the command queues [22]. Such a throughput degradation is not attributable to an underutilization of either GPU resources (the occupancy value is maintained) or PCIe bandwidth (data transfers are still larger than 1 MB, which ensures a linear timing behavior of PCIe transfers [26]).

If only the best configurations are considered, the asynchronous execution scheme increases the effective average

throughput from CPU's perspective from 2.87 to 3.43 GB/s, that is, 19% improvement. Thus, this virtual in-place transposition achieves more than 20% speedup with respect to Gustavson/Karlsson in-place implementation on CPU.

As a summary, Table 3 compares all in-place and out-of-place implementations from CPU's perspective. Throughput results and memory overheads are presented.

It can be noticed that our 3-stage GPU in-place transposition has GPU memory overhead approximately equal to 0%. This is thanks to using on-chip memory for temporary storage. An insignificant global memory overhead is due to coordination bits in elementary transposition 100_1, as explained in Section 5.2. Such an overhead is negligible because only one bit per super-element is needed. Thus, it depends on the number of super-elements, not the size of the matrix. Assuming m and n between 50 and 100 (as indicated in Section 7.4), the overhead is less than 0.1%.

7.7 Testing our implementations on a non-GPU accelerator

As our 4-stage and 3-stage in-place matrix transpositions are implemented in OpenCL, we have tested them on a 60-core Intel Xeon Phi [27]. The average results of the best configurations for the matrix sizes in Table 2 are 2.81 and 5.02 GB/s for our 4-stage and our 3-stage implementations, respectively. Thus, the 3-stage approach improves throughput by 1.8X.

The lack of on-chip scratchpad memory on Xeon Phi makes these implementations not strictly in-place, since OpenCL local memory is emulated on the regular GDDR memory. We leave for future work an implementation with a reduced memory overhead.

8. Conclusion

We have presented the design and implementation of the first known general in-place transposition of rectangular matrices for modern GPUs. We have enhanced both the performance of building blocks proposed by earlier works as well as the overall staged approach. Combined with insights that lead to greatly improved performance of elementary tiled transformations, a new 3-stage approach that is efficient for the GPUs is presented and we have shown that this is much faster than traditional 4-step approaches. We have also observed that the tile size greatly affects performance of in-place transposition, especially for the GPUs since it can affect the algorithm choice due to hardware limitations of on-chip resources. Though the search space for tile sizes can be big, we have also identified pruning criteria that helps user to choose good tile sizes for current GPUs. Finally, we have proposed an asynchronous execution scheme that allows CPU threads to transpose in-place, obtaining 20% speedup to the fastest state-of-the-art in-place transposition for multi-core CPUs. As a future work, besides the above mentioned implementation for Xeon Phi, we plan to extend our work to multi-GPU environments. We believe that our efficient 3-stage approach can be used as a building block for a multi-GPU version.

Acknowledgments

This project was partly supported by the STARnet Center for Future Architecture Research (C-FAR), the DoE Vancouver Project (DE-FC02-10ER26004/DE-SC0005515), and the UIUC CUDA Center of Excellence. We also thank NVIDIA for a hardware donation to the University of Málaga under CUDA Research Center 2012-2013 Awards, and the Ministry of Education of Spain for financial support (TIN2010-16144). Access to Xeon Phi was kindly provided by J.R. Bilbao-Castro, and financed by a Ramón y Cajal fellowship by the Ministry of Economy and Competitiveness of Spain.

References

[1] Frigo, M., Johnson, S.: The design and implementation of fftw3. Proceedings of the IEEE **93**(2) (2005) 216–231

[2] Kohlhoff, K., Pande, V., Altman, R.: K-means for parallel architectures using all-prefix-sum sorting and updating steps. IEEE Transactions on Parallel and Distributed Systems **24**(8) (2013) 1602–1612

[3] Goto, K., Geijn, R.A.v.d.: Anatomy of high-performance matrix multiplication. ACM Trans. Math. Softw. **34**(3) (May 2008) 12:1–12:25

[4] Intel MKL: Intel Math Kernel Library (January 2013)

[5] Ruetsch, G., Micikevicius, P.: Optimizing matrix transpose in CUDA. (January 2009)

[6] Windley, P.F.: Transposing matrices in a digital computer. The Computer Journal **2**(1) (1959) 47–48

[7] Berman, M.F.: A method for transposing a matrix. J. ACM **5**(4) (October 1958) 383–384

[8] Hungerford, T.: Abstract algebra: an introduction. Saunders College Publishing (1997)

[9] Sung, I.J.: Data layout transformation through in-place transposition. PhD thesis, University of Illinois at Urbana-Champaign, Department of Electrical and Computer Engineering (May 2013) http://hdl.handle.net/2142/44300.

[10] Karlsson, L.: Blocked in-place transposition with application to storage format conversion. Technical report (2009)

[11] Gustavson, F., Karlsson, L., Kågström, B.: Parallel and cache-efficient in-place matrix storage format conversion. ACM Transactions on Mathematical Software **38**(3) (April 2012) 17:1–17:32

[12] Sung, I.J., Liu, G., Hwu, W.M.: DL: A data layout transformation system for heterogeneous computing. In: Innovative Parallel Computing, InPar. (May 2012) 1 –11

[13] Cate, E.G., Twigg, D.W.: Algorithm 513: Analysis of in-situ transposition [f1]. ACM Trans. Math. Softw. **3**(1) (March 1977) 104–110

[14] Kaushik, S.D., Huang, C.H., Johnson, J.R., Johnson, R.W., Sadayappan, P.: Efficient transposition algorithms for large matrices. In: Supercomputing. (November 1993)

[15] Dotsenko, Y., Baghsorkhi, S.S., Lloyd, B., Govindaraju, N.K.: Auto-tuning of fast fourier transform on graphics processors. In: Proceedings of the 16th ACM symposium on Principles and Practice of Parallel Programming. PPoPP '11, New York, NY, USA, ACM (2011) 257–266

[16] Gómez-Luna, J., González-Linares, J.M., Benavides, J.I., Guil, N.: An optimized approach to histogram computation on gpu. Machine Vision and Applications **24**(5) (2013) 899–908

[17] Van den Braak, G.J., Nugteren, C., Mesman, B., Corporaal, H.: GPU-vote: A framework for accelerating voting algorithms on GPU. In Kaklamanis, C., Papatheodorou, T., Spirakis, P., eds.: Euro-Par Parallel Processing. Volume 7484 of Lecture Notes in Computer Science. (2012) 945–956

[18] Knuth, D.E.: The Art of Computer Programming, Volume II: Seminumerical Algorithms, 2nd Edition. Addison-Wesley (1981)

[19] Gómez-Luna, J., González-Linares, J.M., Benavides, J.I., Guil, N.: Performance modeling of atomic additions on GPU scratchpad memory. IEEE Transactions on Parallel and Distributed Systems **24**(11) (2013) 2273–2282

[20] NVIDIA: CUDA C Programming Guide 5.0 (July 2012)

[21] Volkov, V., Demmel, J.W.: Benchmarking GPUs to tune dense linear algebra. In: Supercomputing, Piscataway, NJ, USA, IEEE Press (2008) 31:1–31:11

[22] Gómez-Luna, J., González-Linares, J.M., Benavides, J.I., Guil, N.: Performance models for asynchronous data transfers on consumer graphics processing units. Journal of Parallel and Distributed Computing **72**(9) (2012) 1117 – 1126 Accelerators for High-Performance Computing.

[23] Che, S., Sheaffer, J.W., Skadron, K.: Dymaxion: optimizing memory access patterns for heterogeneous systems. In: Proceedings of 2011 International Conference for High Performance Computing, Networking, Storage and Analysis. SC '11, New York, NY, USA, ACM (2011) 13:1–13:11

[24] AMD: ATI Stream SDK OpenCL Programming Guide (2010)

[25] Catanzaro, B., Keller, A., Garland, M.: A decomposition for in-place matrix transposition. In: Proceedings of the 19th ACM SIGPLAN Symposium on Principles and Practice of Parallel Programming. PPoPP '14 (February 2014)

[26] Boyer, M., Meng, J., Kumaran, K.: Improving GPU performance prediction with data transfer modeling. In: 2013 IEEE 27th International Parallel and Distributed Processing Symposium Workshops PhD Forum (IPDPSW). (2013) 1097–1106

[27] Intel: OpenCL design and programming guide for the Intel Xeon Phi coprocessor. (2013)

Parallelizing Dynamic Programming Through Rank Convergence

Saeed Maleki

Univerity of Illinois at
Urbana-Champaign
maleki1@illinois.edu

Madanlal Musuvathi

Microsoft Research
madanm@microsoft.com

Todd Mytkowicz

Microsoft Research
toddm@microsoft.com

Abstract

This paper proposes an efficient parallel algorithm for an important class of dynamic programming problems that includes Viterbi, Needleman-Wunsch, Smith-Waterman, and Longest Common Subsequence. In dynamic programming, the subproblems that do not depend on each other, and thus can be computed in parallel, form stages or *wavefronts*. The algorithm presented in this paper provides additional parallelism allowing multiple stages to be computed in parallel despite dependences among them. The correctness and the performance of the algorithm relies on rank convergence properties of matrix multiplication in the tropical semiring, formed with plus as the multiplicative operation and max as the additive operation.

This paper demonstrates the efficiency of the parallel algorithm by showing significant speed ups on a variety of important dynamic programming problems. In particular, the parallel Viterbi decoder is up-to $24\times$ faster (with 64 processors) than a highly optimized commercial baseline.

Categories and Subject Descriptors D.1.3 [*Concurrent Programming*]: Parallel programming; F.1.2 [*Modes of Computation*]: Parallelism and concurrency

Keywords Parallelism; Dynamic Programming; Tropical Semiring; Wavefront; Viterbi; Smith-Waterman;

1. Introduction

Dynamic programming [4] is a method to solve a variety of important optimization problems in computer science, economics, genomics, and finance. Figure 1 describes two such examples: Viterbi, which finds the most-likely path through a hidden-Markov model for a sequence of observations and LCS, which finds the longest common subsequence between

PPoPP '14, February 15–19, 2014, Orlando, Florida, USA.
Copyright © 2014 ACM 978-1-4503-2656-8/14/02...$15.00.
http://dx.doi.org/10.1145/2555243.2555264

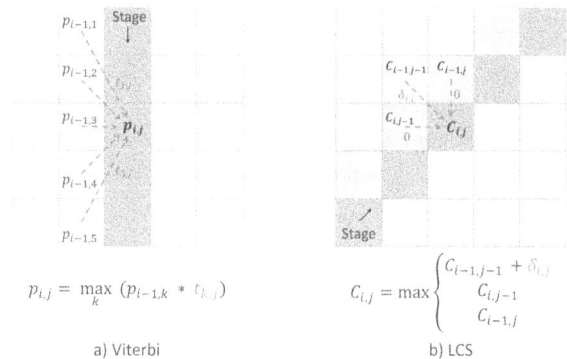

$$p_{i,j} = \max_k (p_{i-1,k} * t_{k,j})$$

a) Viterbi

$$C_{i,j} = \max \begin{cases} C_{i-1,j-1} + \delta_{i,j} \\ C_{i,j-1} \\ C_{i-1,j} \end{cases}$$

b) LCS

Figure 1: Dynamic programming examples with dependences between stages.

two input strings. Dynamic programming algorithms proceed by recursively solving a series of subproblems, usually represented as cells in a table as shown in the figure. The solution to a subproblem is constructed from solutions to an appropriate set of subproblems, as shown by the respective recurrence relation in the figure.

These data-dependences naturally group subproblems into *stages* whose solutions do not depend on each other. For example, all subproblems in a column form a stage in Viterbi and all subproblems in an anti-diagonal form a stage in LCS. A predominant method for parallelizing dynamic programming is *wavefront* parallelization [20], which computes all subproblems within a stage in parallel.[1]

In contrast, this paper breaks data-dependences *across* stages and fixes up incorrect values later in the algorithm. Therefore, this approach exposes parallelism for a class of dynamic programming algorithms we call *linear-tropical dynamic programming* (LTDP). A LTDP computation can be viewed as performing a sequence of matrix multiplications in the tropical semiring where the semiring is formed with $+$ as the multiplicative operator and $\max$ as the additive operator. This paper demonstrates that several important optimization problems such as Viterbi, LCS, Smith-Waterman,

---

[1] The definition of wavefront parallelism used here is more general and includes the common usage where a wavefront performs computations across logical iterations as in the LCS example in Figure 1(a).

and Needleman-Wunsch (the latter two are used in bioinformatics for sequence alignment) belong to LTDP. To efficiently break data-dependences across stages, the algorithm uses *rank convergence*, a property by which the rank of a sequence of matrix products in the tropical semiring is likely to converge to 1.

A key advantage of our parallel algorithm is its ability to simultaneously use both the coarse-grained parallelism across stages and the fine-grained wavefront parallelism within a stage. Moreover, the algorithm can reuse existing highly-optimized implementations that exploit wavefront parallelism with little modification. As a consequence, our implementation achieves multiplicative speed ups over existing implementations. For instance, the parallel Viterbi decoder is up-to $24\times$ faster with 64 cores than a state-of-the-art commercial baseline [25]. This paper demonstrates similar speed ups for other LTDP instances studied in this paper.

2. Background

In linear algebra, a matrix-vector multiplication maps a vector from an input space to an output space. If the matrix is of low rank, the matrix maps the vector to a subspace of the output space. In particular, if the matrix has rank 1, then it maps all input vectors to a *line* in the output space. These geometric intuitions hold even when one changes the meaning of the sum and multiplication operators (say to max and +, respectively), as long as the new meaning satisfies the following rules.

Semirings A semiring is a five-tuple $(D, \oplus, \otimes, \mathbb{0}, \mathbb{1})$, where D is the domain of the semiring that is closed under the additive operation $\oplus$ and the multiplicative operation $\otimes$. The two operations satisfy the following properties:

- $(D, \oplus, \mathbb{0})$ forms a commutative monoid with $\mathbb{0}$ as the identity
  - associativity: $\forall x, y, z \in D : (x \oplus y) \oplus z = x \oplus (y \oplus z)$
  - identity: $\forall x \in D : x \oplus \mathbb{0} = x$
  - commutativity: $\forall x, y \in D : x \oplus y = y \oplus x$
- $(D, \otimes, \mathbb{1})$ forms a monoid with $\mathbb{1}$ as the identity
  - associativity: $\forall x, y, z \in D : (x \otimes y) \otimes z = x \otimes (y \otimes z)$
  - identity: $\forall x \in D : x \otimes \mathbb{1} = \mathbb{1} \otimes x = x$
- $\otimes$ left- and right-distributes over $\oplus$
  - $\forall x, y, z \in D : x \otimes (y \oplus z) = (x \otimes y) \oplus (x \otimes z)$
  - $\forall x, y, z \in D : (y \oplus z) \otimes x = (y \otimes x) \oplus (z \otimes x)$
- $\mathbb{0}$ is an annihilator for $\otimes$
  - $\forall x \in D : x \otimes \mathbb{0} = \mathbb{0} \otimes x = \mathbb{0}$

Tropical Semiring The semiring $(\mathbb{R} \cup \{-\infty\}, \max, +, -\infty, 0)$ with the real numbers extended with $-\infty$ as the domain, max as the additive operation $\oplus$, and $+$ as the multiplicative

operation $\otimes$ is called the tropical semiring. All properties of a semiring hold with $-\infty$ as the additive identity $\mathbb{0}$ and 0 as the multiplicative identity $\mathbb{1}$. Alternately, one can reverse the sign of every element in the domain and change the additive operation to min.

Matrix Multiplication Let $A_{n \times m}$ denote a matrix with n rows and m columns with elements from the domain of the tropical semiring. Let $A[i, j]$ denote the element of A at the ith row and jth column. The matrix product of $A_{l \times m}$ and $B_{m \times n}$ is $A \odot B$, a $l \times n$ matrix defined such that

$$(A \odot B)[i, j] = \bigoplus_{1 \le k \le m} (A[i, k] \otimes B[k, j])$$
$$= \max_{1 \le k \le m} (A[i, k] + B[k, j])$$

Note, this is the standard matrix product with multiplication replaced by $+$ and addition replaced by $\max$.

The transpose of $A_{n \times m}$ is the matrix $A^{\mathsf{T}}_{m \times n}$ such that $\forall i, j : A^{\mathsf{T}}[i, j] = A[j, i]$. Using standard terminology, we will denote a $v_{n \times 1}$ matrix as the column vector $\vec{v}$, a $v_{1 \times n}$ matrix as the row vector $\vec{v}^{\mathsf{T}}$, and $x_{1 \times 1}$ matrix simply as the scalar x. This terminology allows us to extend the definition of matrix-matrix multiplication above to matrix-vector, scalar-matrix, and scalar-vector multiplication appropriately. Also, $\vec{v}[i]$ is the ith element of a vector $\vec{v}$. The following lemma follows from the associativity, distributivity, and commutativity properties of $\otimes$ and $\oplus$ in a semiring.

Lemma 1. *Matrix multiplication is associative in semirings*

$$(A \odot B) \odot C = A \odot (B \odot C)$$

Parallel Vectors Two vectors $\vec{u}$ and $\vec{v}$ are parallel in the tropical semiring, denoted as $\vec{u} \parallel \vec{v}$, if there exist scalars x and y such that $\vec{u} \odot x = \vec{u} \odot y$. Intuitively, parallel vectors in tropical semiring $\vec{u}$ and $\vec{v}$ differ by a constant offset. For instance, $[1\,0\,2]^{\mathsf{T}}$ and $[3\,2\,4]^{\mathsf{T}}$ are parallel vectors differing by an offset 2. Note that the definition above requires two scalars as $-\infty$ does not have a multiplicative inverse in the tropical semiring.

Matrix Rank The rank of a matrix $M_{m \times n}$, denoted by $\text{rank}(M)$, is the smallest number r such that there exist matrices $C_{m \times r}$ and $R_{r \times n}$ whose product is M. In particular, a rank-1 matrix is a product of a column vector and a row vector. There are alternate ways to define the rank of a matrix in semirings, such as the number of linearly independent rows or columns in a matrix. While such definitions coincide in fields (which have inverses for $\oplus$ and $\otimes$), they are not equivalent in semirings [7].

Lemma 2. *For any vectors $\vec{u}$ and $\vec{v}$ and a matrix A of rank 1, $A \odot \vec{u} \parallel A \odot \vec{v}$*

Intuitively, this lemma states that a rank-1 matrix maps all vectors to a line. If $\text{rank}(A) = 1$ then it is a product of some column vector $\vec{c}$ and a row vector $\vec{r}^{\mathsf{T}}$. For any vectors $\vec{u}$ and $\vec{v}$:

$$A \odot \vec{u} = (\vec{c} \odot \vec{r}^{\mathsf{T}}) \odot \vec{u} = \vec{c} \odot (\vec{r}^{\mathsf{T}} \odot \vec{u}) = \vec{c} \odot x_u$$
$$A \odot \vec{v} = (\vec{c} \odot \vec{r}^{\mathsf{T}}) \odot \vec{v} = \vec{c} \odot (\vec{r}^{\mathsf{T}} \odot \vec{v}) = \vec{c} \odot x_v$$

for appropriate scalars x_u and x_v. As an example, consider

$$A = \begin{bmatrix} 1 & 2 & 3 \\ 2 & 3 & 4 \\ 3 & 4 & 5 \end{bmatrix} \qquad \vec{u} = \begin{bmatrix} 1 \\ -\infty \\ 3 \end{bmatrix} \qquad \vec{v} = \begin{bmatrix} -\infty \\ 2 \\ 0 \end{bmatrix}$$

$A = [1\,2\,3]^{\mathsf{T}} \odot [0\,1\,2]$ is rank-1. $A \odot \vec{u} = [6\,7\,8]^{\mathsf{T}}$ and $A \odot \vec{v} = [4\,5\,6]^{\mathsf{T}}$ which are parallel with a constant offset 2. Also note that all rows in a rank-1 matrix are parallel to each other.

3. Linear-Tropical Dynamic Programming

Dynamic programming is a method for solving problems that have optimal substructure — the solution to a problem can be obtained from the solutions to a set of its overlapping subproblems. This dependence between subproblems is captured by a recurrence equation. Classic dynamic programming implementations solve the subproblems iteratively applying the recurrence equation in an order that respects the dependence between subproblems.

LTDP Definition A dynamic programming problem is linear-tropical dynamic programming (LTDP), if (a) the subproblems can be grouped into a sequence of stages such that the solution to a subproblem in a stage only depends on the solutions in the previous stage and (b) this dependence is linear in the tropical semiring. In other words, $s_i[j]$, the solution to subproblem j in stage i of LTDP, is given by the recurrence equation

$$s_i[j] = \max_k (s_{i-1}[k] + A_i[j,k]) \qquad (1)$$

for appropriate constants $A_i[j,k]$. This linear dependence allows us to view LTDP as computing a sequence of vectors $\vec{s}_1, \vec{s}_2, \ldots, \vec{s}_n$, where

$$\vec{s}_i = A_i \odot \vec{s}_{i-1} \qquad (2)$$

for an appropriate matrix of constants A_i derived from the recurrence equation. In this equation, we will call $\vec{s}_i$ as the *solution vector* at stage i and call A_i as the *transformation matrix* at stage i. Also, $\vec{s}_0$ is the initial solution vector obtained from the base case of the recurrence equation.

Predecessor Product Once all of the subproblems are solved, finding the solution to the underlying optimization problem of LTDP usually involves tracing the *predecessors* of subproblems. A predecessor of a subproblem is the subproblem for which the maximum in Equation 1 is reached. For ease of exposition, we define the *predecessor product* of a matrix A and a vector $\vec{s}$ as the vector $A \star \vec{s}$ such that

$$(A \star \vec{s})[j] = \arg\max_k (\vec{s}[k] + A[j,k])$$

```
1   LTDP_Seq (vector s₀, matrix A₁..Aₙ) {
2     vector pred[1..n];  vector res;
3     // forward
4     s = s₀;
5     for i in (1..n) {
6       pred[i] = Aᵢ ⋆ s; // pred[i] = p⃗ᵢ
7       s       = Aᵢ ⊙ s; // s = s⃗ᵢ
8     }
9     // backward
10    res[n+1] = 0;  // res = r⃗
11    for i in (n..1) {
12      res[i] = pred[i][res[i+1]];          }
13    return res;                             }
```

Figure 2: LTDP implementation that computes the stages sequentially. An implementation can possibly employ wavefront parallelization within a stage.

Note the similarity between this definition and Equation 1. We assume that ties in $\arg\max$ are broken deterministically. The following lemma shows that predecessor products do not distinguish between parallel vectors, a property that will be useful later.

Lemma 3. $\vec{u} \parallel \vec{v} \implies \forall A : A \star \vec{u} = A \star \vec{v}$

This follows from the fact that parallel vectors in the tropical semiring differ by a constant and that $\arg\max$ is invariant when a constant is added to all its arguments.

Sequential LTDP Figure 2 shows the *sequential* algorithm for LTDP phrased in terms of matrix multiplications and predecessor products. This algorithm is deemed sequential because it computes the stages one after the other based on the data-dependence in Equation 1. However, the algorithm can utilize wavefront parallelism to compute the solutions within a stage in parallel.

The inputs to the sequential algorithm are the initial solution vector $\vec{s}_0$ and transformation matrices $A_1, \ldots, A_n$, which respectively capture the base and inductive case of the LTDP recurrence equation. The algorithm consists of a forward phase and a backward phase. The forward phase computes the solutions in each stage $\vec{s}_i$ iteratively. In addition, it computes the predecessor product $\vec{p}_i$ that determines the predecessor for each solution in a stage. The backward phase iteratively follows the predecessors computed in the forward phase. The algorithm assumes that the first subproblem in the last stage, $\vec{v}_n[0]$, contains the desired solution to the underlying optimization problem. Accordingly, the backward phase starts with 0 in Line 10. The resulting vector res is the solution to the optimization problem at hand (e.g., the longest-common-subsequence of the two input strings).

The exposition above consciously hides a lot of details in the $\odot$ and $\star$ operators. An implementation does not need to represent the solutions in a stage as a vector and perform matrix-vector operations. It might statically know that the current solution depends on some of the subproblems in the previous stage (a sparse matrix) and only accesses those.

221

Finally, as mentioned above, an implementation might use wavefront parallelism to compute the solutions in a stage in parallel. All these implementation details are orthogonal to how the parallel algorithm described in this paper parallelizes across stages.

4. Parallel LTDP Algorithm

This section describes an efficient algorithm for parallelizing the sequential algorithm in Figure 2 across stages.

4.1 Breaking Data-Dependences Across Stages

Viewing LTDP computation as matrix multiplication in the tropical semiring provides a way to break data-dependences among stages. Consider the solution vector at the last stage $\vec{s}_n$. From Equation 2, we have

$$\vec{s}_n = A_n \odot A_{n-1} \dots A_2 \odot A_1 \odot \vec{s}_0$$

Standard techniques [11, 16] can parallelize this computation using the associativity of matrix multiplication. For instance, two processors can compute the partial products $A_n \odot \dots \odot A_{n/2+1}$ and $A_{n/2} \odot \dots \odot A_1$ in parallel, and multiply their results with $\vec{s}_0$ to obtain $\vec{s}_n$.

However, doing so converts a sequential computation that performs matrix-vector multiplications to a parallel computation that performs matrix-matrix multiplications. This results in a parallelization overhead linear in the size of the stages and thus requires linear number of processors to observe constant speed ups. In practice, the size of stages can easily be hundreds or larger and thus is not practical on real problems and hardware.

The key contribution of this paper is a parallel algorithm that avoids the overhead of matrix-matrix multiplications. This algorithms relies on the convergence of matrix rank in the tropical semiring as discussed below. Its exposition requires the following definition.

Partial Product For a given LTDP instance, the partial product $M_{i \to j}$, defined for stages $j \geq i$, is given by

$$M_{i \to j} = A_j \odot \dots A_{i+1} \odot A_i$$

Partial product determines how a later stage j depends on stage i as $\vec{s}_j = M_{i \to j} \odot \vec{s}_i$.

4.2 Rank Convergence

Rank of the product of two matrices is not greater than the rank of the individual matrices.

$$\text{rank}(A \odot B) \leq \min(\text{rank}(A), \text{rank}(B)) \qquad (3)$$

This is because, if $\text{rank}(A) = r$, then $A = C \odot R$ for some matrix C with r columns. Thus, $A \odot B = (C \odot R) \odot B = C \odot (R \odot B)$ implying that $\text{rank}(A \odot B) \leq \text{rank}(A)$. Similar argument shows that $\text{rank}(A \odot B) \leq \text{rank}(B)$.

Equation 3 implies that for stages $k \geq j \geq i$

$$\text{rank}(M_{i \to k}) \leq \text{rank}(M_{i \to j}) \leq \text{rank}(A_i)$$

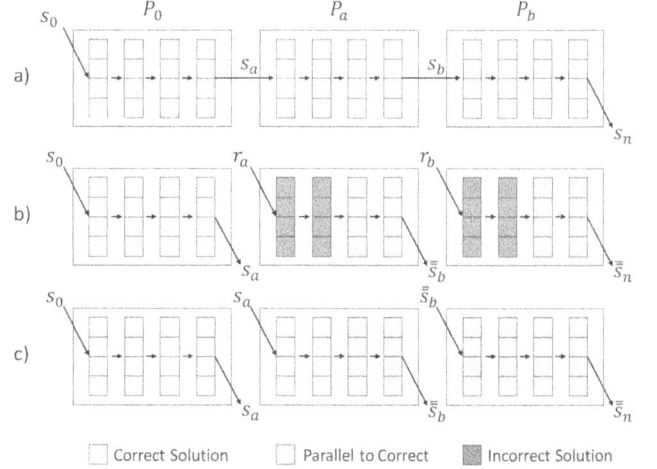

Figure 3: Parallelization algorithm using rank convergence.

In effect, as the LTDP computation proceeds, the rank of the partial products will never increase. Theoretically, there is a possibility that the ranks do not decrease. However, we have only observed this for carefully crafted problem instances that are unlikely to occur in practice. On the contrary, the rank of these partial products is likely to converge to 1, as will be demonstrated in Section 6.1.

Consider a partial product $M_{i \to j}$ whose rank is 1. Intuitively, this implies a *weak* dependence between stages i and j. Instead of the actual solution vector, $\vec{s}_i$, say the LTDP computation starts with a different vector $\vec{t}_i$ at stage i. From Lemma 2, the new solution vector at stage j, $\vec{t}_j = M_{i \to j} \odot \vec{t}_i$, is parallel to the actual solution vector $\vec{s}_j = M_{i \to j} \odot \vec{s}_i$. Essentially, the direction of the solution vector at stage j is independent of stage i. The latter stage only determines its magnitude. In the tropical semiring, where the multiplicative operator is $+$, this means that the solution vector at stage j will be off by a constant if one starts stage i with an arbitrary vector.

4.3 Parallel Algorithm Overview

The parallel algorithm uses this insight to break dependences between stages as shown pictorially in Figure 3. The figure uses three processors as an example. Figure 3(a) represents the forward phase of the sequential algorithm described in Figure 2. Each stage is represented as a vertical column of cells and an arrow between stages represents a multiplication with an appropriate transformation matrix. Processor P_0 starts from the initial solution vector s_0 and computes all its stages. Processor P_a waits for s_a, the solution vector in the final stage of P_0, in order to start its computation. Similarly, processor P_b waits for s_b the solution vector at the final stage of P_a.

In the parallel algorithm shown in Figure 3(b), processors P_a and P_b start from *arbitrary* solutions r_a and r_b respectively in parallel with P_0. Of course, the solutions for

```
1   LTDP_Par(vector s₀, matrix A₁..Aₙ) {
2     vector s[1..n];  vector pred[1..n];
3     vector conv;
4     // proc p owns stages (lₚ..rₚ]
5     ∀p: lₚ = n/P*(p-1); rₚ = n/P*p;
6     // parallel forward phase
7     parallel.for p in (1..P) {
8       local s = (p == 1 ? s₀ : nz);
9       for i in (lₚ+1..rₚ) {
10        pred[i]  = Aᵢ ⋆ s;
11        s = s[i] = Aᵢ ⊙ s;        }}
12    ----- barrier -----
13    do {  // till convergence (fix up loop)
14      parallel.for p in (2..P) {
15        conv[p] = false;
16        // obtain final soln from prev proc
17        s = s[lₚ];
18        for i in (lₚ+1..rₚ) {
19          pred[i] = Aᵢ ⋆ s;
20          s       = Aᵢ ⊙ s;
21          if( s is parallel to s[i] ) {
22            conv[p] = true;
23            break;                  }
24          s[i] = s;                }}
25      ----- barrier -----
26      conv = ⋀ conv[p];
                p
27    } while (!conv);
28
29    //parallel backward phase is in Figure 5
30    return Backward_Par(pred);
```

Figure 4: Parallel algorithm for the forward Pass of LTDP that relies on rank convergence for efficiency. All interprocessor communication is shown in magenta.

the stages computed by P_a and P_b will start out as completely wrong (shaded dark in the figure). However, if rank convergence occurs then these erroneous solution vectors will eventually become parallel to the actual solution vectors (shaded gray in the figure). Thus, P_a will generate some solution vector $\bar{\bar{s}}_b$ parallel to s_b and P_b will generate some solution vector $\bar{\bar{s}}_n$ parallel to s_n.

In a subsequent *fix up phase*, shown in Figure 3(c), P_a uses s_a computed by P_0 and P_b uses $\bar{\bar{s}}_b$ computed by P_1 to fix stages that are not parallel to the actual solution vector at that stage. After the fix up, the solution vectors at each stage are either the same as or parallel to the actual solution vector at those respective stages.

For LTDP, it is not necessary to compute the actual solution vectors. As parallel vectors generate the same predecessor products (Lemma 3), following the predecessors in Figure 3(c) will generate the same solution as the following the predecessors in Figure 3(a).

The next sections describe the parallel algorithm in more detail.

4.4 Parallel Forward Phase

The goal of the parallel forward phase in Figure 4 is to compute a solution vector s[i] at stage i that is *parallel* to the actual solution vector $\vec{s}_i$, as shown in Figure 3. During the execution of the algorithm, we say that a stage i has *converged* if s[i] computed by the algorithm is parallel to its actual solution vector $\vec{s}_i$.

The parallel algorithm splits the stages equally among P processors such that a processor p owns stages between l_p (exclusive) and r_p (inclusive), as shown in line 5. While processor 1 starts its computation from $\vec{s}_0$, other processors start from some vector nz (line 8). This initial vector can be arbitrary except none of its entries can be $\mathbb{0} = -\infty$. Section 4.5 explains the importance of this constraint.

The loop starting in line 9 is similar to the sequential forward phase (Figure 2) except that the parallel version additionally stores the computed s[i] needed in the convergence loop below.

Consider a processor $p \neq 1$ that owns stages $(l_p = l \ldots r = r_p]$. If there exists a stage k in $(l \ldots r]$ such that $\text{rank}(M_{l \to k})$ is 1, then stage k converges, irrespective of the initial vector nz (Lemma 2). Moreover, by Equation 3, $\text{rank}(M_{l \to j})$ is 1 for all stages j in $[k \ldots r]$, implying that these stages converge as well (Figure 3(b)). However, processor p is not cognizant of the actual solution vectors and, thus, does not know the value of k or whether such a k exists.

The fix up loop starting at line 13 (fix up phase in Figure 3(c)) fixes stages $i < k$. In this loop, processor p receives the vector at stage l computed by the previous processor $p - 1$. (Figure 4 shows all such interprocessor communication in magenta.) Processor p then updates s[i] for all stages till the new value becomes parallel to the old value of s[i] (line 21). This ensures that all stages owned by p have converged, under the assumption that stage l has converged.

In addition, the Boolean variable conv[p] indicates whether processor p advertised a converged value for its last stage to processor $p + 1$ at the beginning of the iteration. Thus, when conv (line 26) is true, all stages have converged. In the ideal case, every processor has a partial product with rank 1, and thus, the fix up loop executes exactly one iteration. Section 6 shows that we observe the best case for many practical instances.

Say, however, conv[p] is not true for processor p. This indicates that the stages $(l_p \ldots r_p]$ was not large enough to generate a partial product with rank 1. In the next iteration of the fix up phase, processor $p + 1$, in effect, searches for rank convergence in the wider range $(l_p \ldots r_{p+1}]$. The fix up loop iteratively combines the stages of the processors till all processors converge. In the worst case, the fix up loop executes $P - 1$ iterations and the parallel algorithm devolves to the sequential case.

Important to note is that even though the discussion above refers to partial products, the algorithm does not perform any matrix-matrix multiplications. Like the sequential algorithm, the presentation hides many implementation details in the $\star$ and $\odot$ operations (in lines 10,11,19,and 20). In fact, the parallel implementation can reuse efficient implementations of these operations, including those that use wavefront parallelism, from existing sequential implementations. Also, the computation of conv at line 26 is a standard reduce operation that is easily parallelized, if needed.

When compared to the sequential algorithm, the parallel algorithm has to additionally store s[i] per stage required to test for convergence in the fix up loop. If space is a constraint, then the fix up loop can be modified to *recompute* s[i] in each iteration, trading compute for space.

4.5 All-Non-Zero Invariance

A subtle issue with the correctness of the algorithm above is that starting the LTDP computation midway with an arbitrary initial vector nz could produce a zero vector (one with all $\mathbb{0} = -\infty$ entries) at some stage. If this happens, all subsequent stages will produce a zero vector resulting in an erroneous result. To avoid this, we ensure that nz is *all-non-zero*, i.e. none of its elements are $\mathbb{0} = -\infty$.

A transformation matrix A is non-trivial, if every row of A contains at least one nonzero entry. In Equation 1, the j row of matrix A_i captures how the subproblem j in stage i depends on the subproblems in stage $i - 1$. If *all* entries in this row are $-\infty$, then the subproblem j is forced to be $-\infty$ for any solution to stage $i - 1$. Such trivial subproblems can be removed from a given LTDP instance. So, we can safely assume that transformation matrices in LTDP instances are non-trivial.

Lemma 4. *For a non-trivial transformation matrix A,*

$$\vec{v} \text{ is all-non-zero} \implies A \odot \vec{v} \text{ is all-non-zero}$$

$(A \odot \vec{v})[i] = max_k(A[i,k] + \vec{v}[k])$. But $A[i,k] \neq -\infty$ for some k ensuring that at least one of the arguments to max is not $-\infty$. Here we rely on the fact that no element has an inverse under max, except $-\infty$. As such this lemma is not necessarily true in other semirings.

Thus, starting with a all-non-zero vector ensures that none of the stages result in a zero vector.

4.6 Parallel Backward Phase

Once the parallel forward phase is done, performing the sequential backward phase from Figure 2 will generate the right result, even though s[i] is not exactly the same as the correct solution $\vec{s}_i$. In many applications, the forward phase overwhelmingly dominates the execution time and parallelizing the backward phase is not necessary. If this is not the case, the backward phase can be parallelized using the same idea as the parallel forward phase as described below.

The backward phase recursively identifies the predecessor at stage i starting from stage n. One way to obtain

```
1   Backward_Par(vector pred[1..n]) {
2     vector res;      vector conv;
3     // proc p owns stages (l_p..r_p]
4     ∀p: l_p = n/P*(p-1); r_p = n/P*p;
5     // parallel backward phase
6     parallel.for p in (P..1){
7       // all processors start from 0
8       local x = 0;
9       for i in (r_p..l_p+1) {
10        x = res[i] = pred[i][x]; }}
11    ----- barrier -----
12    do {  // till convergence (fix up loop)
13      parallel.for p in (P-1..1) {
14        conv[p] = false;
15        // obtain final result from next proc
16        local x = res[r_p+1];
17        for i in (r_p..l_p+1) {
18          x = pred[i][x];
19          if (res[i] == x)
20            conv[p] = true;
21            break;           }
22          res[i] = x;            }
23      ----- barrier -----
24      conv = ⋀ conv[p];
              p
25    } while (!conv)
26    return res;                    }
```

Figure 5: Parallel algorithm for the backward phase of LTDP that relies on rank convergence for efficiency. All interprocessor communication is shown in magenta.

this predecessor is by iteratively looking up the predecessor products pred[i] computed during the forward phase. Another way to obtain this is through repeated matrix multiplication as $M_{i \leftarrow n} \star \vec{s}_i$, where $M_{i \leftarrow n}$ is the backward partial product $A_n \odot \ldots A_{i+1}$. Using the same rank convergence argument, the rank of $M_{i \leftarrow n}$ will converge to 1 for large enough number of matrices (small enough i). Lemma 5 below shows that the predecessor at stages beyond i do not depend on the initial value used for the backward phase.

Lemma 5. *For a matrix A of rank 1 and any vector $\vec{v}$, all elements of $A \star \vec{v}$ are equal.*

This lemma follows from the fact that the rows in a rank-1 matrix only differ by a constant and $\arg\max$ is invariant when an offset is added to all its arguments.

The algorithm in Figure 4 uses this insight for a parallel backward phase. Every processor starts the predecessor traversal from 0 (line 8) on the stages it owns. Each processor enters a fix up loop whose description and correctness mirror those of the forward phase above.

4.7 Optimizing using Delta Computation

The fix up loop in Figure 4 recomputes solutions s[i] for the initial stages for each processor. We have observed that the ranks of the partial products converges to a small rank *much faster* than to rank 1. Intuitively, the old and new values of s[i] are almost parallel to each other for these low-rank stages, but still the fix up loop redundantly updates all of their solutions. *Delta* computation optimizes this redundant computation.

Consider parallel vectors $[1, 2, 3, 4]^\intercal$ and $[3, 4, 5, 6]^\intercal$. Instead, if we represent the vector as the *delta* between adjacent entries along with the first entry, these vectors, represented as $[1, 1, 1, 1]^\intercal$ and $[3, 1, 1, 1]^\intercal$, are exactly the same except for the first entry. Extending this intuition, if the partial-product at a stage is low-rank, many (but not all) of the entries in the vectors will be the same when represented as deltas. If one modifies the recurrence Equation 1 to operate on deltas, then only the deltas that are different between the old and new values of `s[i]` need to be propagated to the next iteration. This optimization is crucial for instances, such as LCS and Needleman-Wunsch for which the number of solutions in a stage is large and the convergence to low-rank is much faster than the convergence to rank 1.

4.8 Rank Convergence Discussion

One can view solving a LTDP problem as computing shortest/longest paths in a graph. In this graph, each subproblem is a node and directed edges represent the dependences between subproblems. The weights on edges represent the constants $A_i[j, k]$ in Equation 1. In LCS for instance (Figure 1), each subproblem has incoming edges with weight 0 from the subproblem above and to its left, and an incoming edge with weight $\delta_{i,j}$ from its diagonal neighbor. Finding the optimal solution to the LTDP problem amounts to finding the longest path in this graph from the subproblem 0 in the last stage to subproblems in the first stage, given initial weights to the latter. Alternately, one can negate all the weights and change the max to a min in Equation 1 to view this as computing shortest paths.

Entries in the partial product $M_{l \to r}$ represent the cost of the shortest (or longest) path from a node in stage l to a node in stage r. The rank of this product is 1 if these shortest paths go through a single node in some stage between l and r. Road networks have this property. For instance, the fastest path from any city in Washington state to any city in Massachusetts is highly likely to go through Interstate I-90 that connects the two states. Routes that use I-90 are overwhelmingly better than those that do not; choices of the cities at the beginning and at the end do not drastically change how intermediate stages are routed. Similarly, if problem instances have optimal solutions that are overwhelmingly better than other solutions, one should expect rank convergence.

5. LTDP Examples

This sections shows four important optimization problems as LTDP — Viterbi, Longest Common Subsequence, Smith-Waterman, and Needleman-Wunsch. Our goal in choosing these particular problems is to provide an intuition on how problems with different structure can be viewed as LTDP.

Other problems are LTDP, but not evaluated in this paper, include dynamic time warping and seam carving.

Viterbi The Viterbi algorithm [30] finds the most likely sequence of states in a (discrete) hidden Markov model (HMM) for a given sequence of n observations. Its recurrence equation is shown in Figure 1(a). Here, $p_{i,j}$ represents the probability of the most likely state sequence ending in state j of the HMM that explains the first i observations. The meaning of the term $t_{k,j}$ is not important here (see [30]). The solution to a Viterbi instance is given by the maximum value of $p_{n,j}$ as we are interested in the most likely sequence ending in *any* HMM state.

The subproblems along a column in Figure 1(a) form a stage and they only depend on the subproblems in the previous column. This dependence is not directly in the desired form of Equation 1. But applying logarithm on both sides to the recurrence equation brings it to this form. By transforming the Viterbi instance into one that calculates log-probabilities instead of probabilities, we obtain a LTDP instance.

Invoking the parallel algorithm in Figure 4 requires one additional transformation. The algorithm assumes that the solution to LTDP is given by the first subproblem in the last stage n. To account for this, we introduce an additional stage $n + 1$ in which every subproblem is the maximum of all subproblems in stage n. Essentially, stage $n + 1$ is obtained from multiplying a matrix with 0 in all entries with stage n.

Longest Common Subsequence LCS finds the longest common subsequence of two input strings A and B [12]. The recurrence equation of LCS is shown in Figure 1 (b). Here, $C_{i,j}$ is the length of the longest common subsequence of the first i characters of A and the first j characters of B. Also, $\delta_{i,j}$ is 1 if the ith character of A is the same as the jth character of B and 0 otherwise. The LCS of A and B is obtained by following the predecessors from the bottom-rightmost entry in the table in Figure 1(b).

Some applications of LCS, such as the `diff` utility tool, are only interested in solutions that are at most a width w away from main diagonal - ensuring that the LCS is still reasonably similar to the input strings. For these applications, the recurrence relation can be modified such that $C_{i,j}$ is set to $-\infty$ whenever $|i - j| > w$. Using a smaller width also reduces the memory requirements of LTDP as the entire table need not be stored in memory. Smaller width limits the scope of wavefront parallelism due to smaller sizes of stages, which emphasizes the need for parallelizing across stages as proposed by this paper.

Grouping the subproblems of LCS into stages can be done in two ways, as shown in Figure 6. In the first approach, the stages correspond to anti-diagonals, such as the stage consisting of z_is in Figure 6 (a). This stage depends on two previous stages (on x_is and y_is) and does not strictly follow the rules of LTDP. One way to get around this is to define stages as overlapping pairs of anti-diagonals, like stages

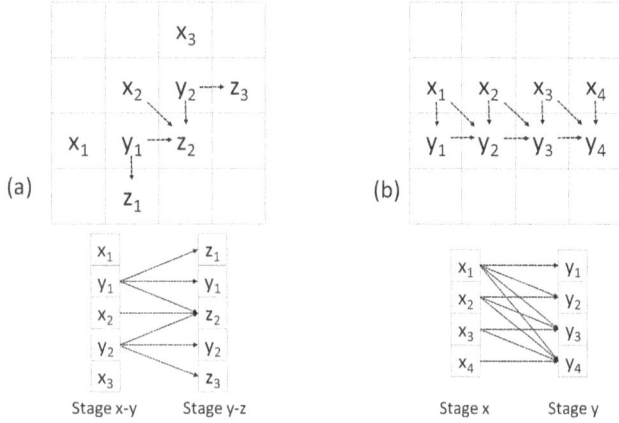

Figure 6: Two ways of grouping the subproblems in LCS into stages such that each stage only depends on one previous stage.

x-y and stage y-z in Figure 6 (a). Subproblems y_is are replicated in both stages, allowing stage y-z to depend only on stage x-y. While this representation has the downside of doubling the size of each stage, it can sometimes lead to efficient representation. For LCS, one can show that the difference between solutions to consecutive subproblems in a stage is either 1 or 0. This allows compactly representing the stage as a sequence of bits [13]).

In the second approach, the stages correspond to the rows (or columns) as shown in Figure 6 (b). The recurrence needs to be unrolled to avoid dependences between subproblems within a stage. For instance, y_i depends on all x_j for $j \leq i$. In this approach, since the final solution is obtained from the last entry, the predecessor traversal in Figure 2 has to be modified to start from this entry, say by adding an additional matrix at the end to move this solution to the first solution in the added stage.

Needleman-Wunsch   This algorithm [23] finds a *global* alignment of two input sequences, commonly used to align protein or DNA sequences. The recurrence equation is very similar to the one in LCS (Section 5).

$$ s_{i,j} = \max \begin{cases} s_{i-1,j-1} + m[i,j] \\ s_{i-1,j} - d \\ s_{i,j-1} - d \end{cases} $$

In this equation, $s_{i,j}$ is the score of the best alignment for the prefix of length i of the first input and the prefix of length j of the second input, $m[i,j]$ is the matching score for aligning the last characters of the respective prefixes, and d is the penalty for an insertion or deletion during alignment. The base cases are defined as $s_{i,0} = -i * d$ and $s_{0,j} = -j * d$.

Grouping subproblems into stages can done using the same approach as in LCS. Abstractly, one can think of LCS as an instance of Needleman-Wunsch for appropriate values of matching scores and insert/delete penalties. However, the

implementation details differ sufficiently enough for us to consider them as two different algorithms.

Smith-Waterman   This algorithm [26] performs a *local* sequence alignment, in contrast to Needleman-Wunsch. Given two input strings, Smith-Waterman finds the *substrings* of the input that have the best alignment, where longer substrings have a better alignment. In its simplest form, the recurrence equation is of the form

$$ s_{i,j} = \max \begin{cases} 0 \\ s_{i-1,j-1} + m[i,j] \\ s_{i-1,j} - d \\ s_{i,j-1} - d \end{cases} $$

Key difference from Needleman-Wunsch is the 0 term in max which ensures that alignments "restart" whenever the score goes to zero. Because of this term, the constants in A_i matrices in equation 1 need to be set accordingly. This slight change has significant difference to the convergence properties of Smith-Waterman as we will see later in Section 6.1. Our implementation uses a more complex recurrence equation that allows for affine gap penalties when aligning sequences [8].

Also, the solution to Smith-Waterman requires finding the maximum of all subproblems in all stages and performing a predecessor traversal from that subproblem. To account for this in our LTDP formulation, we add one "running maximum" subproblem per stage that contains the maximum of all subproblems in the current stage and previous stages.

6. Evaluation

This section evaluates the parallel LTDP algorithm on the four problems discussed in Section 5. Section 6.1 empirically evaluates the occurrence of rank convergence in practice. Section 6.3 evaluates scalability, speed up and efficiency of our implementation. Finally, Section 6.4 compares the parallel algorithm with wavefront parallelization.

6.1 LTDP Rank Convergence

Determining whether the LTDP parallel algorithm benefits a dynamic programming problem requires: 1) the problem to be LTDP (discussed in Section 4); 2) rank convergence happens in reasonable number of steps. This section demonstrates how rank convergence can be measured and evaluates it for the 4 LTDP problems discussed in Section 5.

Rank Convergence is an empirical property of a sequence of matrix multiplications that depends on both the LTDP recurrence relation in addition to the input. Table 1 empirically evaluates the number of steps required for rank convergence across different algorithms and inputs. For a LTDP instance, defined by the algorithm (Column 1) and input (Column 2), we first compute the actual solution vectors at each stage. Then, starting from a random all-non-zero vector at 200 different stages, we measured the number of steps required to generate a vector parallel to the actual solution vector (i.e.,

Steps to Converge to Rank-1		Min	Median	Max
Viterbi Decoder	Voyager: 2^6	22	40	104
	LTE: 2^6	18	30	62
	CDMA: 2^8	22	38	72
	MARS: 2^{14}	46	112	414
Smith-Waterman	Query-1: 603	2	6	24
	Query-2: 884	4	8	24
	Query-3: 1227	4	8	24
	Query-4: 1576	4	8	24
Needleman-Wunsch	Width: 1024	1,580	19,483	192,747
	Width: 2048	3,045	44,891	378,363
	Width: 4096	5,586	101,085	404,4374
	Width: 8192	12,005	267,391	802,991
LCS	Width: 8192	9,142	79,530	370,927
	Width: 16384	19,718	270,320	–
	Width: 32768	42,597	626,688	–
	Width: 65536	86,393	–	–

Table 1: Number of steps to converge to rank 1.

convergence). Columns 3,4, and 5 respectively show the minimum, median, and maximum number of steps needed for convergence. For each input, Column 2 specifies the computation width (the size of a stage or the size of each A_i matrices). Each algorithm has a specific definition of width: for Viterbi decoder, width is the number of states for each decoder, in Smith-Waterman, it is the size of each query, and in LCS and Needleman-Wunsch, it is a fixed-width around the diagonal of each stage. LCS never converged so we leave those entries blank. The rate of convergence is specific to the algorithm and input (i.e., Smith-Waterman converges fast while LCS sometimes does not converge) and, generally speaking, wider widths require more steps to converge. We will use this table later in Section 6.3 to explain scalability of out approach.

6.2 Environmental Setup

We conducted experiments on a shared memory machine and on a distributed memory machine. A shared memory machine favors fast communication and is ideal for wavefront approach. Likewise, a distributed machine has a larger number of processors and so we can better understand how our parallel algorithm scales. Next, we describe these two machines.

Distributed-Memory Machine: Stampede [27], a Dell PowerEdge C8220 Cluster with 6,400 nodes. At the time of writing this paper, Stampede is ranked 6th on the Top500 [28] list. Each node contains 2 8-core Intel Xeon E5-2600 processor @ 2.70 GHz (16 cores in total) and 32 GB of memory. The interconnect topology is a fat-tree, FDR InfiniBand interconnect. On this cluster, we used the MPI MVAPICH 2 library [21] and the Intel C/C++ compiler version 13.0.1 [14].

Shared-Memory Machine: an unloaded Intel 2.27GHz Xeon (E7) workstation with 40 cores (80 threads with hyperthreading) and 128GB RAM. We use the Intel C/C++ compiler (version 13.0.1) [14] and the Intel MPI library (version 4.1) [15].

We report scalability results on Stampede but results from the shared-memory machine are qualitatively similar. We used the shared-memory machine to compare our parallel algorithm with wavefront parallelization. Unless specified otherwise, the reported results are from Stampede runs.

We use MPI/OMP timer to measure process runtime. We do not measure setup costs — only the time it takes to execute one invocation of a LTDP problem. When we compare against a baseline, we modify that code to take the same measurements.

Finally, to get statistically significant results, we run each experiment multiple times and report the mean and 95% confidence interval of the mean when appropriate. We do not include confidence intervals in the graphs if they are small.

6.3 Parallel LTDP Benchmarks and Performance

This section evaluates the parallel algorithm on four LTDP problems. To substantiate our scalability results, we evaluate each benchmark across a wide variety of real-world inputs. We break the results down by the LTDP problem.

6.3.1 Viterbi Decoder

Viterbi decoder uses the Viterbi algorithm (Section 5) to communicate over noisy and unreliable channels, such as cell phone communications [30]. Given a potentially corrupted convolution-encoded message [24], Viterbi decoding finds the most likely unencoded message.

Baseline We used Spiral's [25] Viterbi decoder: a highly optimized (via auto-tuning) decoder that utilizes SIMD to parallelize decoding within a stage. To the best of our knowledge, there is no efficient multi-processor algorithm for Viterbi decoders since the amount of parallelism in each stage is limited.

Our Implementation Spiral code is heavily optimized and even small changes negatively affect performance. Therefore, the performance-critical internal loop of the Spiral code is used as a black box. Each processor starts from an arbitrary all-non-zero vector (except the first, which uses the initial vector) and uses Spiral to execute its set of stages. Each processor (except the last) then communicates its result to the next processor.

Data We use four real-world convolution codes; Voyager, the convolution codes used on NASA's deep space Voyager. Mars, the convolution codes used to communicate with NASA's mars rovers, and both CDMA and LTE, two convolution codes commonly used in modern cell-phone networks. For each of these 4 convolution codes, we investigate the impact of 4 network packet sizes (2048, 4096, 8192, and 16384), which determine the number of stages in the computation. For each size, we used Spiral's input generator to create 50 network packets.

Performance and Scalability Figure 7 shows the performance, the speed up, and the efficiency of each 4 decoders.

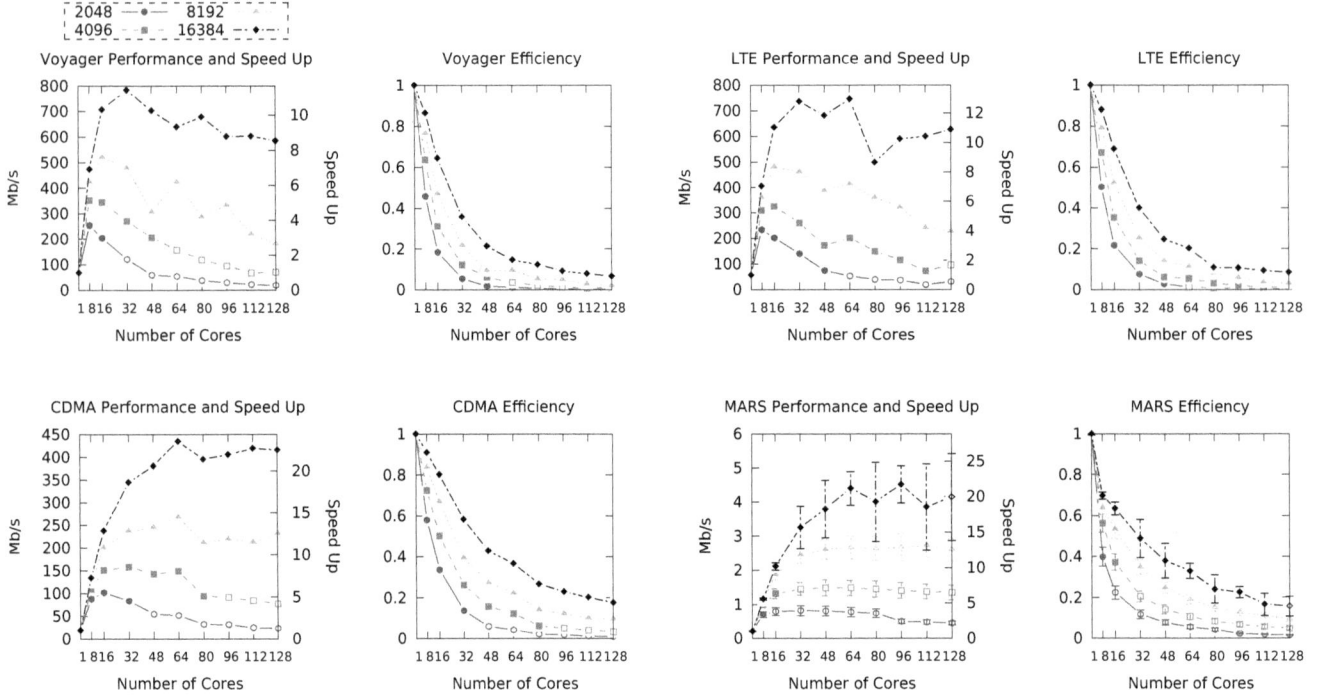

Figure 7: Performance (Mb/S), speed up and efficiency of 4 Viterbi decoders. The non-filled data points demonstrates where processors have too few iterations to converge to rank 1

To evaluate the impact of different decoder sizes, each plot has four lines (one per network packet size). A point (x, y) in a performance/speed up plot with the primary y-axis on left, gives the throughput y (the number of bits processed in a second) in megabits per second (Mb/S) as a function of the number of processors x used to perform the Viterbi Decoding. The same point with the secondary y-axis on right shows the speed up y with x number of processors over the sequential performance. Note that Spiral sequential performance at $x = 1$ is almost the same for different packet sizes. The filled data points in the plots show that convergence occurred in the first iteration of the fix-up loop in Figure 4 algorithm (i.e. each processor's stage is large enough for convergence). The non-filled data points show multiple iterations of the fix-up loop were required. Similarly, a point in an efficiency plot provides the speed up of our parallel implementation over the sequential performance of Spiral generated code divided by the number of processors. Each point is the mean of 50 random packets.

Figure 7 demonstrates (i) our approach provides significant speed ups over the sequential baseline and (ii) different convolution codes and network packet sizes have different performance characteristics. For example, with 64 processors, our CDMA Viterbi Decoder processing packets of size 16384 decodes at a rate of 434 Mb/S which is 24× faster than the sequential algorithm. Note that for the same network packet size and number of processors, our MARS decoder only processes at 4.4 Mb/S because the amount

of computation per bit (size of each stage) is significantly greater than CDMA.

The performance of our approach — and thus our speed up numbers — depend on the rate of rank convergence for each pair of convolution codes and network size as shown in Table 1. Larger network packet size provide better performance across all convolution codes (i.e., a network packet size of 16384 is *always* the fastest implementation, regardless of convolution code) because the amount of recomputation (i.e., the part of the computation that has not converged), as a proportion of the overall computation decreases with larger network packet size.

Also, as it can be seen in Figure 7, efficiency plots drop as the packet sizes decrease and this is again because the ratio of the amount of re-computation to the whole computation decreases. Note that with 48 processors, our algorithm for CDMA can reach efficiency of more than 0.4.

6.3.2 Smith-Waterman

As described in Section 5, Smith-Waterman is an algorithm for local sequence alignment [26] often used to align DNA/protein sequences.

Baseline We implemented the fastest known CPU version, Farrar's algorithm, which utilizes SIMD to parallelize within a stage [8].

Our Implementation Our parallel implementation of Smith-Waterman uses Farrar's algorithm as a black-box.

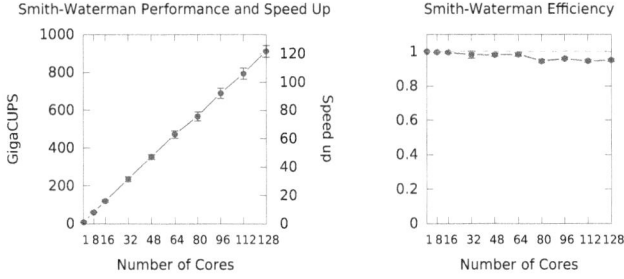

Figure 8: Smith-Waterman performance, speed up and efficiency

Data We aligned chromosomes 1, 2, 3 and 4 from the human reference genome hg19 as databases and four randomly selected expressed sequence tags as queries. All the inputs are publicly available to download from [22]. We report the average of performance across all combinations of DNA and query (16 in total).

Performance and Scalability A point (x, y) in the performance/speed up plot in Figure 8 with the primary y-axis on left, gives the performance y in Giga cell updates per second, or (GigaCUPS) as a function of the number of processors used to perform the Smith-Waterman alignment. GigaCUPS is a standard metric used in bioinformatics to measure the performance of DNA based sequence alignment problems and refers to the number of cells (in a dynamic programming table) updated per second. Similar to the Viterbi decoder plots, the secondary y-axis on the left show the speed up for each number of processors. We run Smith-Waterman on all combinations of 4 DNA databases and 4 DNA queries (we run each combination 5 times). Unlike the prior Viterbi results, we do not see large variability in performance as a function of the problem data. In other words, the DNA database and query pairs do not significantly impact our performance numbers. This can also be confirmed from Table 1 where the number of steps to converge to rank 1 is significantly smaller than a DNA database size which is more than 100 million long. Thus, we plot the average, across all combinations of DNA databases and queries.

The performance gain of our approach for this algorithm is significant: the efficiency plot in Figure 8 demonstrates that our approach has efficiency ~ 1 for any number of processors which means almost linear speed up with up-to 128 processors. This can be also confirmed from the performance/speed up plot. Our algorithm would scale more with more number of processors but we only report up-to 128 processors to keep Figure 8 consistent with the others.

6.3.3 Needleman-Wunsch

In contrast to Smith-Waterman, which performs a *local* alignment between two sequences, Needleman-Wunsch *globally* aligns two sequences and is often used in bioinformatics to align protein or DNA sequences [23].

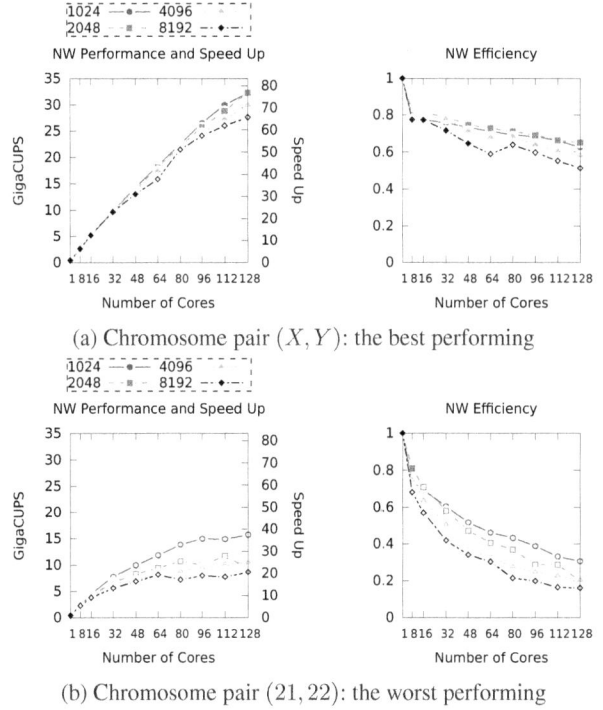

(a) Chromosome pair (X, Y): the best performing

(b) Chromosome pair $(21, 22)$: the worst performing

Figure 9: Performance, speed up and efficiency results of Needleman-Wunsch

Baseline We utilized SIMD parallelization *within* a stage for this benchmark by using the grouping technique shown in Figure 6 a.

Our Implementation We implemented the incremental optimization described in Section 4.7 using the baseline code.

Data We used 4 pairs of DNA sequences as inputs: Human Chromosomes $(17, 18)$, $(19, 20)$, $(21, 22)$ and (X, Y) from the human reference genome hg19. We only used the first 1 million elements of the sequences since Stampede does not have enough memory on a single node to store the cell values for the complete chromosomes. We also tried 4 different width sizes: 1024, 2048, 4096 and 8192 since we found that widths larger than 8192 do not affect the final alignment score.

Performance and Scalability Figure 9 shows the performance, speed up and efficiency of Needleman-Wunsch algorithm parallelized using our approach for two pairs of chromosomes: (X, Y) and $(21, 22)$. Instead of averaging performance numbers over all 4 pairs, we separated them and reported the best performing pair ((X, Y) in Figure 9a) and the worst performing pair ($(21, 22)$ in Figure 9b). This is because the performance varies significantly between different pairs as can be seen in Figures 9a and 9b. The figures show results for each of the width sizes: 1024, 2048, 4096 and 8192. Similar to the Viterbi decoder benchmark, filled/non-filled data points show whether convergence occurred in the first iteration of the fix up phase.

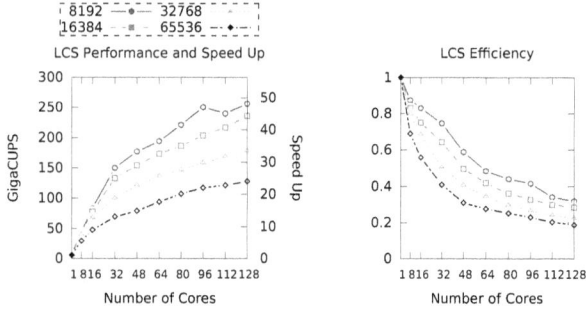

(a) Chromosome pair (X, Y): the best performing

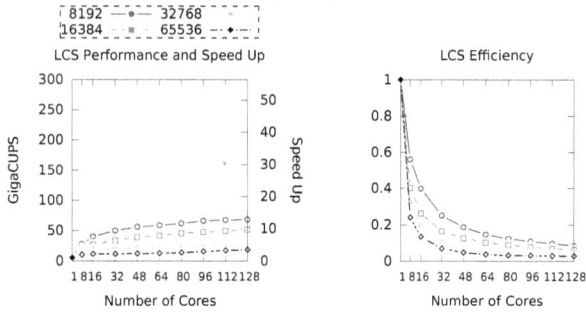

(b) Chromosome pair $(21, 22)$: the worst performing

Figure 10: Performance, speed up and efficiency results of Longest Common Subsequence

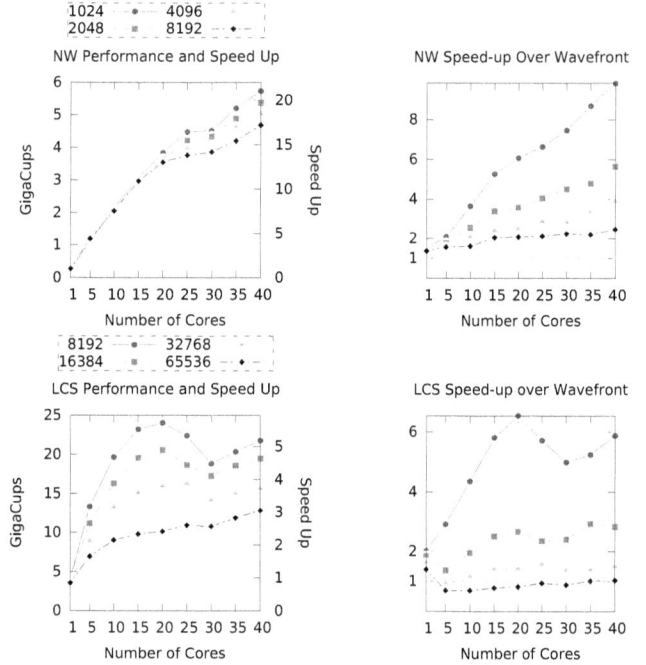

Figure 11: Performance/speed up results and comparison of LTDP and Wavefront for Needleman-Wunsch and LCS

The figures show great variability in performance for different inputs based on the variability in convergence. Also, as it can be seen from non-filled data points and Table 1, rank convergence in this benchmark is not as fast as in Viterbi decoder or Smith-Waterman.

In Figure 9, larger widths perform poorer than smaller ones since the convergence rate depends on the size of each stage in a LTDP instance. Note that we used the same sequence size (1 million element) for all plots.

6.3.4 LCS

Longest Common Subsequence is a method to find the largest subsequence common to two candidate sequences [12] (See Section 5 for description).

Baseline We adapted the fastest known single-core algorithm for LCS that exploits bit-parallelism to parallelize the computation *within* a column [6, 13]. This approach uses the the grouping technique shown in Figure 6 b.

Our Implementation Similar to Needleman-Wunsch, we implemented the incremental optimization described in Section 4.7 using the bit-parallel baseline code.

Data We used the same input data as with Needleman-Wunsch except that we used the following width range: 8192, 16384, 32768 and 65536. We report performance numbers in the same way as in Needleman-Wunsch.

Performance and Scalability The performance, speed up and efficiency plots in Figure 10 are very similar to Figure 9.

We used the same two pairs of chromosomes: (X, Y) and $(21, 22)$ as they are the best and worst performing pairs respectively. The 4 lines in each plot corresponds to one of following width sizes: 1024, 2048, 4096 and 8192. Likewise, the input pair has a great impact on rank convergence as it can be seen in Figure 10a and Figure 10b.

6.4 Wavefront vs LTDP

Our goal in this section is to directly compare across-stage parallelism with wavefront parallelism. We focus on Needleman-Wunsch and LCS as the size of the stages in Viterbi and Smith-Waterman is very small for wavefront parallelism to be viable. We should note that the two approaches are complementary. Exploring the optimal way to distribute a given budget of processors to simultaneously use across-stage parallelism and within-stage parallelism is left for future work. Furthermore, note that we implemented the best known wavefront algorithm for each of our benchmarks.

We used OpenMP for wavefront implementations and compared it with our MPI implementation used in our Stampede experiments above, but running on our shared-memory machine. This difference in implementation choice should at the worst bias the results against our parallel algorithm.

Wavefront for Needleman-Wunsch: We used tiling to group cells of the computation table and used SIMD in each tile. Wavefronts proceed along the anti-diagonal of these tiles. Tiling greatly reduces the number of barriers involved [19]. On the other hand, processing cells in a tile by utilizing SIMD has computation overhead over the baseline that we used for our parallel approach (without tiling). Therefore, the sequential performance of the baseline with tiling is slower than the baseline without tiling. We investigated different tiling parameters and chose the best performing configuration.

Wavefront for LCS: Similar to the baseline of Needleman-Wunsch, we tiled the cells. For computation in each cell, we used the same bit-parallelism to parallelize the computation within a column of each tile. Likewise, we parallelized computation of tiles that are in the same anti-diagonal.

Figure 11 compares the performance of our approach with an optimized wavefront based approach for both LCS and Needleman-Wunsch. The plots on the left in Figure 11 show the performance and speed up (over sequential non-tiled baseline) of our approach for Needleman-Wunsch and LCS. Plots on the right, a point (x, y) gives the speed up (y as runtime of wavefront divided by runtime of our approach) as we change the number of processors allocated to each approach (x). We plot 4 lines, one for each of four *widths*. Small widths are better for our approach (as wavefront approach incurs more barriers per unit of compute) while large widths are better for wavefront approach (as our approach is less likely to reach rank 1). As we add more processors, our approach utilizes each additional processor more efficiently than a wavefront based approach, particularly so when the width is small (i.e., our approach is $\sim 9\times$ faster than wavefront approach with 40 processors for Needleman-Wunsch and $\sim 6\times$ faster than wavefront approach for LCS with width size 8192).

7. Related Work

There has been a lot of prior work in parallelizing dynamic programming. Predominantly, implementations use wavefront parallelism to parallelize within a stage. In contrast, this paper exploits parallelism across stages in addition to wavefront parallelism. For instance, Martins et al. build a message passing based implementation of sequence alignment dynamic programs (i.e., Smith-Waterman and Needleman-Wunsch) using wavefront parallelism [19]. Our baseline for Needleman-Wunsch builds on this work.

Stivala et al. use an alternate strategy for parallelizing dynamic programming. They use a "top-down" approach that solves the dynamic programming problem by recursively solving the subproblems in parallel. To avoid redundant solutions to the same subproblem, they use a lock-free data structure that memorizes the result of the subproblems. This shared data structure makes it difficult to parallelize across multiple machines.

There is also a large body of theoretical work analyzing the parallel complexity of dynamic programming. Valient et al. [29] show that straight-line programs that compute polynomials in a field, which includes classical dynamic programming, belong to $\mathbf{NC}$, the class of asymptotically efficiently parallelizable problems. Subsequent work [3, 10] has improved both the time complexity and processor complexity of this result. These works view dynamic programming as finding a shortest path in an appropriate grid graph, computing all-pairs shortest paths in partitions of the graph in parallel, and combining the results from each partition efficiently. The works differ in how they use the structure of the underlying graph for efficiency. While it is not clear if these asymptotically efficient algorithms lead to efficient implementation, using the structure of the underlying computation for parallel efficiency is an inspiration for this work.

There are many dynamic programming problem specific implementations. For example, much like we do in this paper, LCS can exploit bit-parallelism (e.g., [1], [5], [13]). And, Aluru et al. describe a prefix-sum approach to LCS[2] which exploits the fact that LCS only uses binary values in its recurrence equation.

Smith-Waterman has been studied extensively due to its importance to DNA sequencing. This paper uses Farrar's SIMD implementation [8] on multi-core, however, prior work has also investigated other hardware (e.g., GPU [18] and FPGA [17]).

Due to its importance in telecommunications, there has been lots of work on parallel Viterbi decoding. Because this algorithm is often implemented in hardware, one simple approach to increase performance is to pipeline via systolic arrays (i.e. to get good throughput) and increase clock frequency (i.e., to get good latency) [9]. The closest approach to us is Fettweis and Meyr who frame Viterbi as linear operations on the tropical semiring and utilize the associativity of matrix-matrix multiplications. However, they suffer linear overheads of this approach which is hidden by adding more hardware.

8. Conclusions

This paper introduces a novel method for parallelizing a class of dynamic programming problems called linear-tropical dynamic programming problems, which includes important optimization problems such as Viterbi and longest-common subsequence. The algorithm uses algebraic properties of the tropical semiring to break data dependence efficiently.

Our implementations show significant speed ups over optimized sequential implementations. In particular, the parallel Viterbi decoding is up-to $24\times$ faster (with 64 cores) than a highly optimized commercial baseline.

While we evaluate our approach on a large shared memory multi-core machine, we expect equally impressive results on a wide variety of parallel hardware platforms (clusters, GPUs and even FPGAs).

Acknowledgments

This material is based upon work supported by the National Science Foundation under Grant No. CNS 1111407. The authors thank the Texas Advanced Computing Center for providing computation time on the Stampede cluster. We also thank Serdar Tasiran and anonymous reviewers for useful feedback on the paper.

References

[1] L. Allison and T. I. Dix. A bit-string longest-common-subsequence algorithm. *Information Processing Letters*, 23 (6):305–310, Dec. 1986.

[2] S. Aluru, N. Futamura, and K. Mehrotra. Parallel biological sequence comparison using prefix computations. *J. Parallel Distrib. Comput.*, 63(3):264–272, 2003. ISSN 0743-7315.

[3] A. Apostolico, M. J. Atallah, L. L. Larmore, and S. Mc-Faddin. Efficient parallel algorithms for string editing and related problems. *SIAM J. Comput.*, 19(5):968–988, 1990.

[4] R. Bellman. *Dynamic Programming*. Princeton University Press, 1957.

[5] M. Crochemore, C. S. Iliopoulos, Y. J. Pinzon, and J. F. Reid. A fast and practical bit-vector algorithm for the longest common subsequence problem. *Information Processing Letters*, 80(6):279 – 285, 2001.

[6] S. Deorowicz. Bit-parallel algorithm for the constrained longest common subsequence problem. *Fundamenta Informaticae*, 99(4):409–433, 2010.

[7] M. Develin, F. Santos, and B. Sturmfels. On the rank of a tropical matrix. *Combinatorial and computational geometry*, 52:213–242, 2005.

[8] M. Farrar. Striped Smith-Waterman speeds database searches six times over other SIMD implementations. *Bioinformatics*, 23(2):156–161, 2007.

[9] G. Fettweis and H. Meyr. Parallel Viterbi algorithm implementation: breaking the ACS-bottleneck. *IEEE Transactions on Communications*, 37(8):785–790, 1989.

[10] Z. Galil and K. Park. Parallel algorithms for dynamic programming recurrences with more than O(1) dependency. *Journal of Parallel and Distributed Computing*, 21(2):213–222, 1994.

[11] W. D. Hillis and G. L. Steele, Jr. Data parallel algorithms. *Communications of the ACM*, 29(12):1170–1183, Dec. 1986.

[12] D. S. Hirschberg. A linear space algorithm for computing maximal common subsequences. *Communications of the ACM*, 18(6):341–343, June 1975.

[13] H. Hyyro. Bit-parallel LCS-length computation revisited. In *In Proc. 15th Australasian Workshop on Combinatorial Algorithms*, pages 16–27, 2004.

[14] Intel C/C++ Compiler, http://software.intel.com/en-us/c-compilers, 2013.

[15] Intel MPI Library, http://software.intel.com/en-us/intel-mpi-library/, 2013.

[16] R. E. Ladner and M. J. Fischer. Parallel prefix computation. *Journal of the ACM*, 27(4):831–838, Oct. 1980.

[17] I. Li, W. Shum, and K. Truong. 160-fold acceleration of the Smith-Waterman algorithm using a field programmable gate array (FPGA). *BMC Bioinformatics*, 8(1):1–7, 2007.

[18] L. Ligowski and W. Rudnicki. An efficient implementation of Smith Waterman algorithm on GPU using CUDA, for massively parallel scanning of sequence databases. In *IEEE International Symposium on Parallel Distributed Processing (IPDPS)*, pages 1–8, 2009.

[19] W. S. Martins, J. B. D. Cuvillo, F. J. Useche, K. B. Theobald, and G. Gao. A multithreaded parallel implementation of a dynamic programming algorithm for sequence comparison. In *In Pacific Symposium on Biocomputing*, pages 311–322, 2001.

[20] Y. Muraoka. *Parallelism exposure and exploitation in programs*. PhD thesis, University of Illinois at Urbana-Champaign, 1971.

[21] MVAPICH: MPI over InfiniBand, http://mvapich.cse.ohio-state.edu/, 2013.

[22] National Center for Biotechnology Information, http://www.ncbi.nlm.nih.gov/, 2013.

[23] S. B. Needleman and C. D. Wunsch. A general method applicable to the search for similarities in the amino acid sequence of two proteins. *Journal of Molecular Biology*, 48: 443–453, 1970.

[24] W. W. Peterson and E. J. Weldon. *Error-Correcting Codes*. MIT Press: Cambridge, Mass, 1972.

[25] M. Püschel, J. M. F. Moura, J. Johnson, D. Padua, M. Veloso, B. Singer, J. Xiong, F. Franchetti, A. Gacic, Y. Voronenko, K. Chen, R. W. Johnson, and N. Rizzolo. SPIRAL: Code generation for DSP transforms. *Proceedings of the IEEE, Special issue on "Program Generation, Optimization, and Adaptation"*, 93:232–275, 2005.

[26] T. Smith and M. Waterman. Identification of common molecular subsequences. *Journal of Molecular Biology*, 147(1):195–197, 1981.

[27] *Stampede: Dell PowerEdge C8220 Cluster with Intel Xeon Phi coprocessors*. Texas Advanced Computing Center, http://www.tacc.utexas.edu/resources/hpc.

[28] Top500 Supercompute Sites, http://www.top500.org, 2013.

[29] L. G. Valiant, S. Skyum, S. Berkowitz, and C. Rackoff. Fast parallel computation of polynomials using few processors. *SIAM Journal of Computing*, 12(4):641–644, 1983.

[30] A. Viterbi. Error bounds for convolutional codes and an asymptotically optimum decoding algorithm. *IEEE Transactions on Information Theory*, 13(2):260–269, 1967.

Revisiting Loop Fusion in the Polyhedral Framework

Sanyam Mehta   Pei-Hung Lin   Pen-Chung Yew

Department of Computer Science and Engineering, University of Minnesota Twin Cities, USA

sanyam@cs.umn.edu   phlin@cs.umn.edu   yew@cs.umn.edu

Abstract

Loop fusion is an important compiler optimization for improving memory hierarchy performance through enabling data reuse. Traditional compilers have approached loop fusion in a manner decoupled from other high-level loop optimizations, missing several interesting solutions. Recently, the polyhedral compiler framework with its ability to compose complex transformations, has proved to be promising in performing loop optimizations for small programs. However, our experiments with large programs using state-of-the-art polyhedral compiler frameworks reveal suboptimal fusion partitions in the transformed code. We trace the reason for this to be lack of an effective cost model to choose a good fusion partitioning among the possible choices, which increase exponentially with the number of program statements.

In this paper, we propose a fusion algorithm to choose good fusion partitions with two objective functions - achieving good data reuse and preserving parallelism inherent in the source code. These objectives, although targeted by previous work in traditional compilers, pose new challenges within the polyhedral compiler framework and have thus not been addressed. In our algorithm, we propose several heuristics that work effectively within the polyhedral compiler framework and allow us to achieve the proposed objectives. Experimental results show that our fusion algorithm achieves performance comparable to the existing polyhedral compilers for small kernel programs, and significantly outperforms them for large benchmark programs such as those in the SPEC benchmark suite.

Categories and Subject Descriptors   D.3.4 [*Processors*]: Compilers, Optimization

PPoPP '14,   February 15–19, 2014, Orlando, Florida, USA.
Copyright © 2014 ACM 978-1-4503-2656-8/14/02... $15.00.
http://dx.doi.org/10.1145/2555243.2555250

Keywords   Loop fusion; Polyhedral framework; Data reuse; Coarse-grained parallelism

1. Introduction and Motivation

Over the last decade, computer microarchitecture has witnessed a shift from single-core, to the multi-core, and now to the many-core. Through this transition, the *memory wall* has remained a very challenging problem, where high memory latency limits system performance. In practice, there are various techniques employed to hide or reduce these high memory latencies, such as larger cache blocks, lock-up free caches, prefetching and simultaneous multithreading. However, each of these techniques increases the off-chip bandwidth. In such a scenario, loop fusion becomes particularly relevant as a compiler optimization that reduces memory latency through improving data reuse in on-chip caches, and also thus reduces the off-chip memory accesses. In addition to data reuse, it is imperative for loop fusion to preserve coarse-grained parallelism, especially in the wake of the current trend towards many cores on chip. In a compiler, effectively achieving these goals through loop fusion implies considering it in the context of other supporting compiler transformations such as loop interchange, skewing, etc.

In the past, there has been a significant amount of work [14, 22, 26, 31] on loop fusion. However, these works did not consider loop fusion in the context of other transformations. This misses some of the better solutions in various cases. For example, in the *gemver* benchmark shown in Figure 1(a), traditional compilers first identify outer parallel loops and then consider loops for fusion such that outer-loop or coarse-grained parallelism is not hurt. This approach cannot achieve fusion of statements S1 and S2 because of unsatisfied dependences (as shown in Figure 1(b)), and thus data reuse opportunity is lost. However, if loop fusion was considered in a manner coupled with outer-loop parallelism and loop interchange, legal fusion could be accomplished after interchanging loops i and j in the first loop nest as shown in Figure 1(c). As a result, the transformed program now achieves both data reuse and outer-level parallelism.

In addition, in the traditional compilers, the granularity of loop fusion is an entire loop nest. This again misses good solutions. For example, in the *swim* benchmark shown in Figure 2, the two loop nests cannot be entirely fused because

```
for (i=0; i<N; i++)  // parallel loop          for (i=0; i<N; i++)                              for (i=0; i<M; i++) {
  for (j=0; j<N; j++)                            for (j=0; j<N; j++)                              for (j=0; j<N; j++) {
   S1: B[i][j] = A[i][j] + u1[i]*v1[j]           S1: B[i][j] = A[i][j] + u1[i]*v1[j] + u2[i]*v2[j];   S1: UNEW[i+1][j] = UOLD[i+1][j]+C1*(Z[i+1][j+1]+Z[i+1][j])
                  + u2[i]*v2[j];                                                                         *(CV[i+1][j+1]+CV[i][j+1]+CV[i][j]+CV[i+1][j])-C2*(H[i+1][j]-H[i][j]);
                                                 S2: x[i] = x[i] + beta* B[i][i]*y[j];               S2: VNEW[i][j+1] = VOLD[i][j+1]-C1*(Z[i+1][j+1]+Z[i][j+1])
for (i=0; i<N; i++)  // parallel loop                                                                    *(CU[i+1][j+1]+CU[i][j+1]+CU[i][j]+CU[i+1][j])-C3*(H[i][j+1]-H[i][j]);
  for (j=0; j<N; j++)                            . . .                                               S3: PNEW[i][j] = POLD[i][j]-C2*(CU[i+1][j]-CU[i][j])
   S2: x[i] = x[i] + beta*B[j][i]*y[j];                                                                     -C3*(CV[i][j+1]-CV[i][j]);
                                                          (b)                                          }
for (i=0; i<N; i++) // parallel loop                                                                 }
   S3: x[i] = x[i] + z[i];                                                                           /*  Update of variables at grid boundary  (S4 - S12)  */
                                               for (i=0; i<N; i++)   // parallel loop              for (i=0; i<M; i++) {
for (i=0; i<N; i++) // parallel loop             for (j=0; j<N; j++)                                 for (j=0; j<N; j++) {
  for (j=0; j<N; j++)                             S1: B[j][i] = A[j][i] + u1[j]*v1[i] + u2[j]*v2[i];    S13: UOLD[i][j] = U[i][j]+ALPHA*(UNEW[i][j]-2*U[i][j]+UOLD[i][j]);
   S4: w[i] = w[i] + alpha*B[i][j]*x[j];          S2: x[i] = x[i] + beta* B[j][i]*y[j];                S14: VOLD[i][j] = V[i][j]+ALPHA*(VNEW[i][j]-2*V[i][j]+VOLD[i][j]);
                                                 . . .                                                 S15: POLD[i][j] = P[i][j]+ALPHA*(PNEW[i][j]-2*P[i][j]+POLD[i][j]);
            (a)                                             (c)                                        S16: U[i][j] = UNEW[i][j];
                                                                                                      S17: V[i][j] = VNEW[i][j];
                                                                                                      S18: P[i][j] = PNEW[i][j];
                                                                                                      }
                                                                                                    }
                                                                                                    /*  Update of variables at grid boundary  (S19 - S36)  */
```

Figure 1: (a) the *gemver* kernel; (b) illegal fusion; (c) legal fusion after loop interchange in the first loop-nest;

Figure 2: the *swim* benchmark

of dependences between some of the intermediate statements (S4-S12) and statements S13, S14 of the second loop nest. However, if the granularity of loop fusion was individual statements, statements S15 and S18 that are not dependent on any of the intermediate statements could be fused with statements S1-S3 in the first loop nest, as shown later in Figure 5(b).

The polyhedral compiler framework is markedly different from its traditional counterparts in that, it takes a *statement centric view* of the entire program as against a *loop-nest centric view*. This shift in the intermediate representation allows to simultaneously compose multiple high-level loop transformations and also to reduce the granularity of fusion from loop nests to individual statements. This enables finding effective fusion partitions that exploit data reuse in a global program context, those that are missed by the traditional compilers as shown in the above two examples. *However, this statement centric view also results in a very large search space of the possible fusion partitionings.* The size of the search space varies exponentially with the number of statements, or more precisely, with the number of Strongly Connected Components (SCCs). For example, for just the 3 statements S1-S3 in the first loop nest of *swim* that have no dependences between them, there can be 3! (=6) different ways in which they can be ordered. Further, for a particular ordering of statements (e.g., S2-S3-S1), there can be 2^{3-1} (=4) different partitionings[1], i.e. (S2|S3,S1), (S2,S3|S1), (S2|S3|S1), (S2,S3,S1), where '|' represents a fusion partition or, in other words, it implies that statements on either side belong to different loop nests. Thus, a total of 24 different fusion partitionings are possible for only 3 statements considered. Similarly, if statements S13-S18 in the second loop nest are considered, there are 90 possible orderings of statements[2], and for each ordering, there are 32

different fusion partitionings, resulting in a total of 2880 possible fusion partitionings. If all the 36 statements of the *swim* benchmark are considered, the search space of possible fusion partitionings becomes unmanageable.

This necessitates the need for an effective cost model to find a good fusion partitioning among all legal partitionings. However, incorporating useful optimization criteria within the polyhedral framework for this purpose is hard as the algorithms involved are computationally intensive [29], and the complexity increases exponentially with the number of statements. Our experiments show that the fusion model employed in the state-of-the-art polyhedral compiler frameworks [1, 2, 4, 7, 20] gives good performance only for kernel programs with few statements, but performs sub-optimally for larger programs such as those in SPEC benchmark suite. We also find that the iterative compilation framework leveraging the polyhedral model [27–29] cannot construct the search space of legal fusion partitionings for such large programs, as the algorithms employed are not scalable with the number of statements. In this paper, we propose a new cost model to tackle this important problem that has eluded the polyhedral compiler framework from effectively optimizing large programs.

The cost model employed by our fusion algorithm has 2 objective functions, (1) *maximize data reuse* in the fused loop nest, and (2) *preserve coarse-grained parallelism*, inherent in the source code. In our fusion algorithm, we achieve data reuse through the use of heuristics in a *pre-fusion* step that absolves the polyhedral framework from the responsibility of providing an objective function to guide loop fusion, and keeps the large programs tractable. This pre-fusion step blends effectively with the polyhedral framework and as a result, subsequent benefits of composing multiple loop optimizations can still be achieved. This pre-fusion step also helps us to consider input dependences while

---

[1] For any two consecutive statements, there exist 2 possibilities - they can either belong to the same loop nest or not. Since, there are a total of (n-1) pairs of consecutive statements for a total of n statements, there exist 2^{n-1} possible fusion partitionings.

[2] The number of orderings of statements is not 6! (=720) because there are dependences among statement pairs S13-S16, S14-S17 and S15-S18, respectively. As a result, some among the 720 total orderings are not legal.

evaluating data reuse and not just the true dependences that constitute real edges in the Data Dependence Graph.

The objective of maximizing data reuse, however, conflicts with preserving coarse-grained parallelism that is originally present in the source code. This is because merging multiple statements into the same loop nest may result in a dependence carried by the outer-loop, leading to a loss of outer-loop or coarse-grained parallelism. Thus, in our fusion algorithm, we detect the occurrence of such a dependence between two SCCs and distribute them into separate loop nests such that loss of data reuse is minimized and coarse-grained parallelism is preserved.

Our fusion algorithm is implemented within a source-to-source polyhedral compiler framework, PLuTo. We tested our fusion algorithm, called *wisefuse*, using 10 benchmarks from 3 different benchmark suites, with the large programs from SPEC and NAS Parallel (NP) benchmark suites and the small kernel programs from the Polybench [3] suite. Using our fusion algorithm within the polyhedral framework, we achieve a performance improvement ranging from 1.7X to 7.2X for these large benchmarks over state-of-the-art fusion algorithms leveraging the polyhedral model. We achieve an improvement of 5% to 18% over the Intel compiler for the same benchmarks. Results also demonstrate that our algorithm matches the performance achieved by existing polyhedral frameworks for the kernel programs from Polybench, and in some cases we achieve an improvement of as much as 2.1X due to coarse-grained parallelization.

The rest of the paper proceeds as follows. Section 2 introduces the polyhedral framework and particularly discusses loop fusion within the polyhedral framework. Section 3 formulates the loop fusion problem and describes the legality constraints for fusion, in the context of the polyhedral framework. Section 4 describes our loop fusion algorithm and discusses the heuristics used to achieve the aforementioned objectives. Section 5 compares and discusses the performance results of our fusion algorithm and other state-of-the-art algorithms. The related work is presented in Section 6 and we conclude in Section 7.

2. Background

This section introduces the polyhedral framework, the terminology and the concepts useful for understanding this work. This section lays particular emphasis on the fusion model within the polyhedral framework, and also discusses the state-of-the-art in the same.

2.1 The Polyhedral Framework

The polyhedral framework for compiler optimizations is a powerful mathematical framework based on parametric linear algebra and integer linear programming. It provides an effective intermediate representation that captures nearly all the complex high level optimizations performed by a traditional automatic parallelizing compiler.

The polyhedral framework performs loop transformations on a *Static Control Part* (SCoP), a maximal set of consecutive statements $(S_1, S_2, ..., S_n)$, where loop bounds and conditionals are affine functions of the surrounding loop iterators and parameters. The iteration domain of these loops enclosing the statements within a SCoP can be specified as a set of linear inequalities in the polyhedral framework. This set of linear inequalities defines a polyhedron, with each iteration of a loop represented by an integer point within this polyhedron. With such an abstraction, it is possible not only to obtain the exact dependences between statements, but also to model a composition of complex transformations as a single algebraic operation.

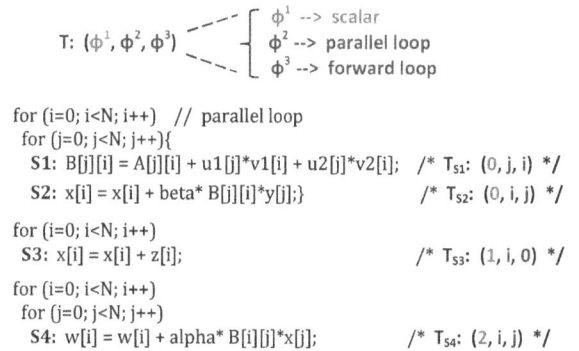

Figure 3: Statement-wise multidimensional affine function for the transformed *gemver* program

A dependence between two statement instances belonging to statements S_i and S_j respectively, is represented by a set of equalities and inequalities in the *dependence polyhedron*, $P_{e^{S_i \to S_j}}$, where $e^{S_i \to S_j} \in E$ is an edge in the Data Dependence Graph (DDG), $G = (V, E)$, with each vertex representing a statement. Since dependences among all loop iterations are considered, the dependence information in the DDG is *exact*. With this exact dependence information, the goal is to find a statement-wise multi-dimensional affine function (T) to represent a composition of loop transformations for the entire SCoP. Each dimension or level of this multi-dimensional affine function is represented by $\phi(\vec{i})$ and is defined as follows:

$$\phi_S(\vec{i_S}) = (c_S^1 \ c_S^2 \ ... \ c_S^{m_S})(\vec{i_S}) + c_S^0 \qquad (1)$$

where $\vec{i_S}$ is the loop iteration vector for statement S, and $c_S^0 ... c_S^{m_S}$ are constants. Figure 3 shows the multi-dimensional affine functions (T_{S1} through T_{S4}) for each of the four statements of the *gemver* benchmark, where each function has 3 dimensions or levels represented by ϕ^1, ϕ^2, and ϕ^3, respectively.

The one-dimensional affine transform (ϕ) for each statement can either specify a *loop hyperplane* or a *scalar dimension*. A *loop hyperplane* is an $n - 1$ dimensional subspace of an n dimensional space represented by the normal $(c_S^1 \ c_S^2 \ ... \ c_S^{m_S}) \neq \vec{0}$. A legal loop hyperplane corresponds to a loop in the transformed program. For example, for *gemver*, $\phi_{S2}^2 = (1 \ 0)(i \ j)^T = i$, and it represents a hyperplane that corresponds to the outermost loop (i-loop) for statement S2 as shown in Figure 3. A legal hyperplane does not violate any unsatisfied dependence, $e^{S_i \to S_j}$, at that loop level, i.e.

$$\phi_{S_j}(\vec{t}) - \phi_{S_i}(\vec{s}) \geq 0, \langle \vec{s}, \vec{t} \rangle \in P_{e^{S_i \to S_j}} \tag{2}$$

where $\vec{s}$ (source) and $\vec{t}$ (target) are instances of statements S_i and S_j, respectively. The above condition implies the loop hyperplane preserves the direction of dependences between any two instances of statements S_i and S_j. Since this condition was not satisfied for the *gemver* code shown earlier in Figure 1(b), the transformed code was incorrect.

In the polyhedral model, a fusion partitioning can be represented by a *scalar dimension* in the multi-dimensional affine function. For a scalar dimension, $c_S^1 = c_S^2 = ... = c_S^{m_s} = 0, \forall S$, and c_S^0 determines the partition number that the statement belongs to. The statements with the same value of c_S^0 belong to the same partition, or in other words, they are fused at that loop level. For example, for *gemver*, ϕ^1 represents a scalar dimension, and statements S1 and S2 both have $c_S^0 = 0$, and as a result, they are perfectly fused in the transformed *gemver* code shown in the figure. Since, c_S^0 is 1 and 2, respectively, for statements S3 and S4, they are distributed in the transformed code.

Thus, a multi-dimensional affine transform consists of multiple one-dimensional affine transforms representing legal loop hyperplanes interspersed by scalar dimensions. This multi-dimensional affine transform, because of the *convex combination* property, allows it to capture a sequence of simpler transformations such as coarse-grained parallelism, loop interchange, skewing, shifting, fusion and tiling. For example, in *gemver*, it allowed to capture parallelism, interchange and fusion in a single optimization step as seen in Figure 3.

2.2 Loop fusion and the polyhedral framework

The polyhedral framework finds legal statement-wise loop hyperplanes one loop-level at a time using an Integer Linear Programming (ILP) solver. If the ILP solver cannot find a solution at the current loop level because of unsatisfied dependences, a *cut* must be issued, represented by a scalar dimension. A *cut* between two SCCs essentially distributes them into different loop nests, thus satisfying certain dependences. The most important criteria in cutting SCCs is based on the dimensionality (depth of the enclosing loop nest) of the SCC, i.e. any two *consecutive* SCCs with different dimensionalities are cut first as they are least likely to aid data reuse. Thus, the initial ordering of the SCCs (we call, the *pre-fusion schedule*[3]) decides which SCCs remain fused and

which ones are distributed in the transformed code, and is therefore critical in achieving a good fusion partitioning with effective data reuse.

Loop fusion within the polyhedral framework thus involves three steps

1. finding the Strongly Connected Components (SCCs) in the Data Dependence Graph,

2. determining a legal (and good) pre-fusion schedule, and

3. finding legal statement-wise loop hyperplanes one loop level at a time. This involves issuing cuts (represented by scalar dimensions in the affine transform) between SCCs, whose relative ordering is determined in step 2.

SCCs that do not require to be cut to satisfy dependences end up in the same fusion partition after the above 3 steps. Thus, loop fusion is implicitly performed with the finding of the legal loop hyperplanes, in composition with other transformations.

2.3 Existing fusion models in the polyhedral framework

The state-of-the-art polyhedral frameworks (PLuTo [1], PoCC [2], PolyOpt [4], LLVM's Polly [25]) employ an effective cost function to find statement-wise loop hyperplanes that minimize communication volume among processors (or, reuse distance in sequential execution). However, there does not exist a useful cost function to find a good pre-fusion schedule that eventually guides loop fusion as explained above. The existing frameworks combine steps 1 and 2, i.e. they use a depth-first traversal of the DDG to find the SCCs and the resultant order also yields a *legal* (but not necessarily *good*) pre-fusion schedule. Existing frameworks do not also employ an optimization criteria for data reuse in step 3 as this would require incorporation of additional constraints in the ILP formulation for finding legal hyperplanes. This may render large programs intractable as these constraints increase exponentially with the number of statements. The pre-fusion schedule obtained from a depth-first traversal of the DDG has 2 drawbacks.

1. It does not attempt to order statements with the same dimensionality consecutively. This leads to sub-optimal fusion. For example, in the *swim* benchmark shown in Figure 2, the intermediate statements S4-S12 have a dimensionality of 1, and if any of these statements is ordered (in the pre-fusion schedule) between statements from the first loop nest and statements S13-S18, then a cut to find legal loop hyperplanes would prevent any possible fusion of these statements.

2. It does not order statements with an input dependence between them consecutively, or in other words, it does not consider data reuse through the input or the Read-After-Read (RAR) dependences. This is because the DDG (traversed to find SCCs) does not contain edges correspond-

---

[3] Pre-fusion schedule is called so, because this schedule or ordering of SCCs serves as a guideline for the fusion partitioning obtained in the final transformed program. A *fusion partitioning* is the partitioning of program statements into clusters of statements called *fusion partitions*, where each fusion partition represents a single loop nest.

```
for (j = 4; j <= ny+9-2; j++)  // parallel loop
  for (i = 4; i <= nx+9-3; i++)
    for (k = 4; k <= nz+9-3; k++)
      S1: ab[j][i][k] = uyb[j][i][k] * ((a[j-1][i][k] + a[j][i][k])
        + (a[j-2][i][k] + a[j+1][i][k]) + (a[j-3][i][k] + a[j+2][i][k]));

for (j = 4; j <= ny+9-3; j++)  // parallel loop
  for (i = 4; i <= nx+9-2; i++)
    for (k = 4; k <= nz+9-3; k++)
      S2: al[j][i][k] = uxl[j][i][k] * ((a[j][i-1][k] + a[j][i][k])
        + (a[j][i-2][k] + a[j][i+1][k]) + (a[j][i-3][k] + a[j][i+2][k]));

for (j = 4; j <= ny+9-3; j++)  // parallel loop
  for (i = 4; i <= nx+9-3; i++)
    for (k = 4; k <= nz+9-2; k++)
      S3: af[j][i][k] = uzf[j][i][k] * ((a[j][i][k-1] + a[j][i][k])
        + (a[j][i][k-2] + a[j][i][k+1]) + (a[j][i][k-3] + a[j][i][k+2]));

for (j = 4; j <= ny+9-3; j++)  // parallel loop
  for (i = 4; i <= nx+9-3; i++)
    for (k = 4; k <= nz+9-3; k++)
      S4: athird[j][i][k] = (af[j][i][k+1] - af[j][i][k]) + (al[j][i+1][k] -
        al[j][i][k]) + (ab[j+1][i][k] - ab[j][i][k]) + a[j][i][k];
                                                   (a)
```

```
/* prologue */
for (j = lb_j ; j <= ub_j ; j++)
  for (i = lb_i ; i <= ub_i ; i++)
    for (k = lb_k ; k <= ub_k ; k++) {
      S1: ab[j][i][k] = uyb[j][i][k] * ( .. );
      S2: al[j][i][k] = uxl[j][i][k] * ( .. );
      S3: af[j][i][k] = uzf[j][i][k] * ( .. );
                            backward
                            dependence
      S4: athird[j][i][k] = (af[j][i][k+1] - af[j][i][k]) + .. ;
  }
/* epilogue */
                                 (b)

/* prologue */
for (j = lb_j ; j <= ub_j ; j++)  // fwd-dep loop
  for (i = lb_i ; i <= ub_i ; i++)  // fwd-dep loop
    for (k = lb_k ; k <= ub_k ; k++) {
      S1: ab[j][i][k] = uyb[j][i][k] * ( .. );
      S2: al[j][i][k] = uxl[j][i][k] * ( .. );
      S3:   af[j][i][k] = uzf[j][i][k] * ( .. );
      S4:   athird[j-1][i-1][k-1] = (af[j-1][i-1][k]
forward        - af[j-1][i-1][k-1]) + ... ;
dependence
  }
/* epilogue */
                                 (c)
```

Figure 4: (a) Original source code for *advect*; (b) Fully fused *advect* without shifting (incorrect code); (c) Fully fused *advect* with shifting (correct code)

ing to the input dependences as such edges restrict parallelism. The input dependences are, nonetheless, crucial to achieve effective data reuse. For example, in the *swim* benchmark, if the input dependences between statements S1, S2 and S3 are not considered, they would not be ordered consecutively in the pre-fusion schedule. As a result, they would be distributed into different loop nests, leading to a loss of data reuse.

Thus, for effective loop fusion, steps 1 and 2 must be treated independently and there must be an effective cost model to determine a good pre-fusion schedule. Lack of a powerful cost model is a serious limitation in the existing polyhedral frameworks as a poorly chosen pre-fusion schedule impacts all the other transformations performed. The performance impact becomes more significant as the number of statements within a SCoP, and consequently, the number of possible pre-fusion schedules becomes larger.

3. Problem Formulation

Prior to formulating the problem, we identify the different scenarios that result from fusing two statements, each enclosed in separate loop nests. Here, we consider statements instead of loops, because of the statement-centric view held by the polyhedral compiler. Before fusion, there is either no dependence or a loop-independent dependence between any two statements. Fusion is clearly legal in the former case. In the latter case, however, fusing two statements (S_i and S_j) with a loop-independent dependence can lead to 3 different scenarios.

1. The dependence remains loop independent. In the polyhedral framework, this is represented by the condition,

$$\phi_{S_j}(\vec{t}) - \phi_{S_i}(\vec{s}) = 0, \langle \vec{s}, \vec{t} \rangle \in P_{e^{S_i \to S_j}} \quad (3)$$

Clearly, this does not violate the constraint in Equation (2), and thus fusing statements S_i and S_j is legal. Such a dependence allows the loop to be a parallel loop and is called a *precedence* or a *fusion-permitting dependence*.

2. The dependence can become a backward loop-carried dependence. This is represented by the condition,

$$\phi_{S_j}(\vec{t}) - \phi_{S_i}(\vec{s}) < 0, \langle \vec{s}, \vec{t} \rangle \in P_{e^{S_i \to S_j}} \quad (4)$$

This dependence violates the constraint in Equation (2), i.e. there is at least one instance or loop iteration that does not preserve the direction of the dependence, and thus fusing the two statements is illegal. Such a dependence is called a *fusion-preventing dependence*.

3. the dependence can become a forward loop-carried dependence. This is represented by the condition,

$$\phi_{S_j}(\vec{t}) - \phi_{S_i}(\vec{s}) > 0, \langle \vec{s}, \vec{t} \rangle \in P_{e^{S_i \to S_j}} \quad (5)$$

This dependence satisfies the constraint in Equation (2), i.e. it preserves the direction of the dependence, and thus leads to a legal fusion. However, it leads to a forward dependence or non-parallel loop. Although we call it a *precedence dependence* (following previous works), this dependence may also be considered as a *fusion-preventing dependence* if the goal is to preserve parallelism.

With this background on the different types of dependences, we next formulate the loop fusion problem.

In the past, the loop fusion problem has been formulated as a graph partitioning problem [14, 22], where the goal was to partition all loops into disjoint clusters, each cluster representing a set of loops to be fused. However, in the context of the polyhedral compiler framework that takes a statement-centric view, this formulation needs an adjustment in that each vertex of the graph corresponds to a *statement* instead of a *loop*. The relations between statements are represented by a directed acyclic graph $G = (V, E = F \cup \bar{F})$, where each statement corresponds to a vertex $v \in V$ of the graph. Edges in E are classified into *fusion-permitting edges* (edges in F) and *fusion-preventing edges* (edges in $\bar{F}$). The problem is thus formulated as one of finding a *fusion partitioning*, i.e partitioning V into clusters of statements that can be legally fused. The partitioning V is legal, subject to the following legality constraints. These constraints together ensure that all dependences are lexicographically positive.

1. Statements in the same SCC belong to the same fusion partition.

2. **Precedence constraint** - The ordering of SCCs in the partitioned graph (that corresponds to the the fused program) must respect all dependences between statements.

3. **Fusion-preventing constraint** - The fusion partitioning should not result in any loop-carried backward dependence, i.e. statements connected by an edge in $\bar{F}$ must belong to different fusion partitions.

To ensure the satisfaction of the first constraint, the first step in the fusion algorithm (listed in Section 2.2) involves determining SCCs in the source program. Satisfaction of this constraint is ensured by ordering SCCs instead of statements in the further steps that achieve some optimization criteria. The ordering of SCCs must satisfy the precedence constraint to ensure that a legal partitioning exists that leads to correct execution. Thus, the pre-fusion schedule that decides the initial ordering of SCCs (step 2 in the fusion algorithm) must satisfy the precedence constraint. However, a pre-fusion schedule that satisfies the precedence constraint may still lead to a partitioning where there is a loop carried backward dependence between two statement instances in a partition. Such a partitioning is not legal. For example, fusing all four statements of the *advect* benchmark as shown in Figure 4(b), leads to a loop-carried backward dependence, although the precedence constraint is satisfied.

In such a scenario, the polyhedral framework would either apply the *loop shifting* transformation to remove the backward dependence or issue a cut between statements to satisfy the dependence. In other words, *if the pre-fusion schedule satisfies the precedence constraint, then the polyhedral framework guarantees legal fusion partitioning that satisfies the fusion-preventing constraint.*

In case of the *advect* benchmark, legality is ensured through shifting S4 by 1 iteration and thus removing the backward dependence as shown in Figure 4(c). As a result

of applying the shifting transformation, the backward dependence from S4 to statements S1-S3 turns into a forward dependence from statements S1-S3 to S4. This renders the outer loops i and j as forward dependence loops, or in other words, coarse-grain parallelism is lost as shown in Figure 4(c).

Thus, the problem of loop fusion within the polyhedral framework can be formulated as one of finding a pre-fusion schedule that satisfies the precedence constraint. In addition to legality, the criteria for deciding good partitions is two-fold, maximizing *data reuse* and *parallelism*. In the following section, we propose a fusion algorithm that achieves precisely these two key objectives in the polyhedral framework.

4. Our Fusion Algorithm

As explained in previous sections, a pre-fusion schedule or the initial ordering of the SCCs has a significant bearing on the fusion partitioning achieved in the transformed program. In this section, we first describe our algorithm (Algorithm 1) for finding a good pre-fusion schedule and the heuristics underlying the algorithm. We use the same example of the *swim* benchmark shown in Figure 2 to elucidate our algorithm. We next describe Algorithm 2, which is used to achieve the second objective of preserving coarse-grained parallelism in the transformed code. We use the example of the *advect* benchmark introduced in Section 3 for the purpose of explanation.

4.1 Algorithm 1: Finding a good pre-fusion schedule

A good pre-fusion schedule is one that orders the SCCs so that, SCCs with significant reuse between them are merged in the same loop nest in the transformed code. In order to achieve a good pre-fusion schedule, the ordering of SCCs is done based on the following criteria:

- **Constraint:** The ordering must respect the precedence constraint among the SCCs
- **Heuristic 1:** SCCs that allow data reuse and have the same dimensionality are ordered consecutively
- **Heuristic 2:** SCCs are considered for re-ordering in the original program order

The above criteria does not necessarily lead to a fusion partitioning that maximizes data reuse, but it does lead to one that has significant data reuse.

Rationale for the chosen heuristics. As explained in Section 3, even with the satisfaction of the precedence constraint, there may be fusion preventing dependences between statements and hence some SCCs will need to be cut to satisfy those dependences. The heuristics chosen are such that they aim to minimize loss of reuse through these inevitable cuts. Since the first and the most important criteria of issuing a cut is based on the dimensionality of the SCCs, *heuristic 1* ensures that SCCs that have reuse remain immune to a cut with high probability. Also, since data reuse through input dependences is considered, we achieve better overall data reuse. This is possible mainly because we decouple the pre-fusion scheduling from the step where the DDG (with only true dependences) is traversed to find the SCCs. *Heuristic 2* allows more SCCs to be fused together into a single loop nest. The reason is that, if SCCs close to each other in original program order are fused, then it increases the probability of following SCCs to become legally fusable because the precedence constraint is satisfied. Also, SCCs that are close to each other tend to have higher reuse through reads to the same data items.

ALGORITHM 1: Finding a good pre-fusion schedule

1: **INPUT:**
   List of statements in the program: $S(1, ..., n)$
   Adjacency matrix representing true dependences:
   $adj(1,..,n)(1,..,n)$
   Adjacency matrix representing input dependences:
   $RARadj(1,..,n)(1,..,n)$
   List of statements belonging to an SCC that contains
   statement s: SCC_s
2: **begin**
3: Initialize id to 0
4: **for** each statement $s \in S$ **do**
5:   $visited(s) = 0$
6: **end for**
7: **for** each statement $s \in S$ **do**
8:   **if** $visited(s) = 0$ **then**
9:     $fusable = \emptyset$ {/* where $fusable$ is the list of
   statements, fusable with statement s */}
10:     **for** each statement $t \in SCC_s$ **do**
11:       $visited(t) = 1$
12:       $sccId(t) = id$
13:       Add t to $fusable$
14:     **end for**
15:     Increment id by 1
   {/* Lines 16, 17, 18 check for dimensionality,
   reuse and precedence constraint resp. */}
16:     **for** each statement $t \in S$ s.t. $visited(t) = 0 \wedge$
   $dimension(s) = dimension(t)$ **do**
17:       **if** $\exists\, i \in fusable$, s.t.
   $adj(i,j) = 1 \vee RARadj(i,j) = 1, \forall j \in SCC_t$
   then
18:         **if** $\nexists\, s' \in S$, s.t. $adj(s',t') \neq 0, \forall\, t' \in SCC_t$
   then
19:           **for** each statement $t' \in SCC_t$ **do**
20:             $visited(t') = 1$
21:             $sccId(t') = id$
22:             Add t' to $fusable$
23:           **end for**
24:           Increment id by 1
25:         **end if**
26:       **end if**
27:     **end for**
28:   **end if**
29: **end for**
30: **end**
31: **OUTPUT:** *Pre-fusion Schedule*

Explanation of the algorithm. In order to find a pre-fusion schedule, it is essential that the Strongly Connected Components are first extracted from the Data Dependence Graph. This is done using the Kosaraju's algorithm [30] as in existing polyhedral compiler frameworks. But, our fusion algorithm determines the pre-fusion schedule in a separate step. The choice of the pre-fusion schedule is made to meet the above-mentioned three criteria. For this purpose, Algorithm 1 begins a traversal of the DDG in program order. For a statement s thus 'visited', Algorithm 1 finds an 'unvisited' statement t (i.e. $visited(t) = 0$) with the same dimension and that also has data reuse with statements already marked as *fusable* with statement s. The algorithm further checks to see whether t satisfies the precedence constraint. The precedence constraint is satisfied if no statement t' belonging to the SCC that contains t (SCC_t) depends on an 'unvisited' statement node s', i.e. $adj(s',t') \neq 0$. If the precedence constraint is thus satisfied, all statements belonging to SCC_t are marked visited, assigned the next higher id than SCC_s and put into the set, *fusable*. This ensures that the reordering of SCCs achieved satisfies all 3 criteria. The heuristics used can be seen in play for the *swim* benchmark in Figure 5.

Figure 5 compares the pre-fusion schedule obtained from Algorithm 1 with that achieved by the state-of-the-art pre-fusion scheduling algorithm used in PLuTo. The other existing polyhedral compilers such as PoCC [2], PolyOpt [4], LLVM's Polly [25] all use the fusion algorithm described by Bondhugula et al. in their paper [10] and implemented in their tool, PLuTo. The fusion algorithm employed in PLuTO uses a depth-first traversal to find and order the SCCs. Figures 5(a) and (c) show the partial DDG for the same code excerpt of the *swim* benchmark shown earlier in Figure 2. The values in square brackets are the SCC *id* for the 36 statements of the *swim* benchmark, and are representative of the pre-fusion schedules chosen by Algorithm 1 and PLuTo, respectively. Since Algorithm 1 also considers reuse through the input dependences, the DDG in (a) also shows input dependences marked with dashed lines. Figures 5(b) and (d) show the transformed codes for *swim* generated from the pre-fusion schedules given by Algorithm 1 and PLuTo, respectively. From the figures, following observations can be made about the pre-fusion schedule obtained from Algorithm 1.

1. Statement S18 is scheduled immediately after statement S15 as there is an opportunity for reuse and the precedence constraint is satisfied. Since both S15 and S18 have the same dimensionality, they remain fused in the transformed code shown in Figure 5(b). This opportunity for reuse is missed by the fusion model used in PLuTo since statement S27 ($SCC_{id}=3$) with a different dimensionality is scheduled immediately after S15 ($SCC_{id}=2$), as shown in Figure 5(c).

2. Reuse through input dependences is considered. As a result, statements S1, S2 and S3 that have reuse through in-

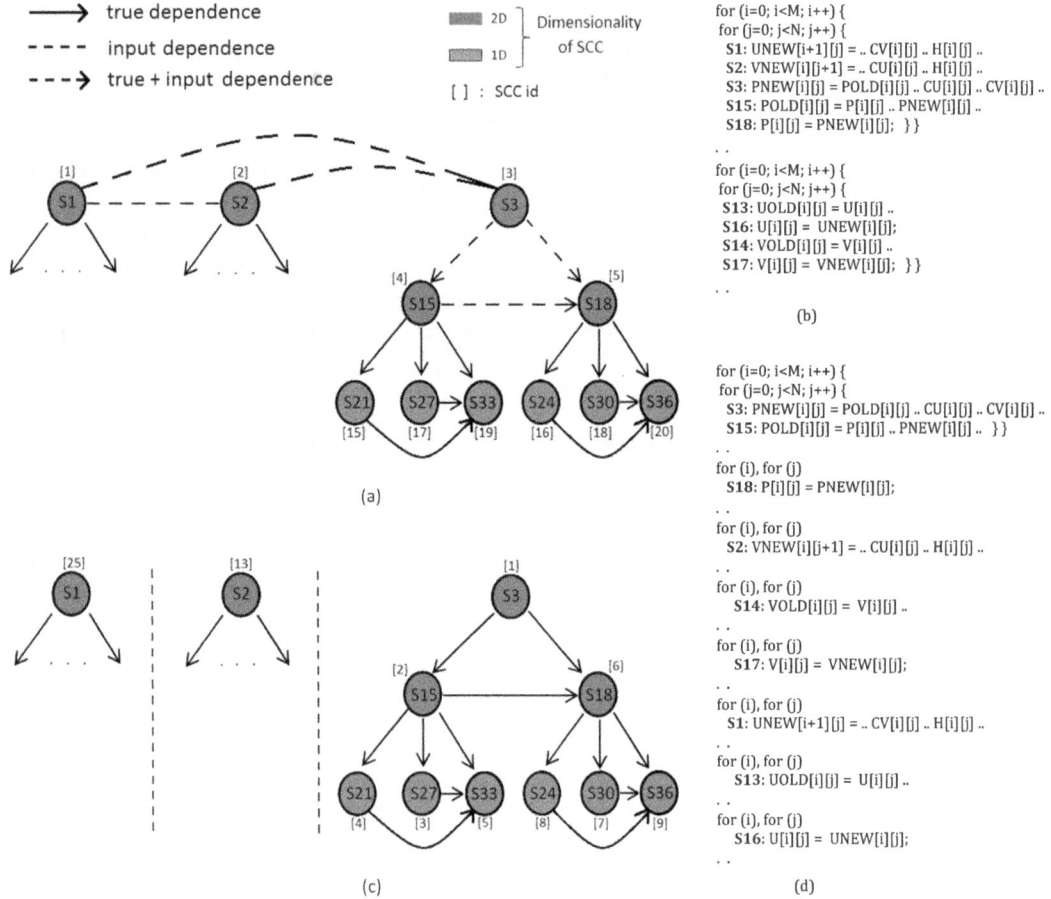

Figure 5: Our fusion model: (a) Partial DDG for *swim* and pre-fusion schedule from Algorithm 1; (b) Fused code corresponding to (a); (c) Pre-fusion schedule chosen by PLuTo; (d) Fused code corresponding to (c)

put dependences and the same dimensionality are ordered next to each other as shown in (a). This allows them to be fused in the transformed code as shown in (b). Again, this opportunity for significant data reuse is missed by PLuTo. It schedules these 3 statements separately because they are disconnected in the DDG as shown in (c).

3. Ordering SCCs that are close to each other in program order consecutively, allows more statements to be fused together in the same loop nest because of satisfaction of precedence constraint. For example, statements S1, S2 and S3 were considered in program order. Since S3 was already scheduled, it created the opportunity for statements S15 and S18 to also be fused in the same loop nest because the precedence constraint was satisfied. As a result, 5 statements could be fused together in the same loop nest as shown in (b), thus allowing significant data reuse. In contrast, a maximum of 2 statements are fused in a loop nest using the fusion model in PLuTo as shown in (d).

4. Statements S13, S16 and statements S14, S17 could not be fused with the other statements in the first loop nest, as

these statements depend on the intermediate statements (S4-S12, that update the variables at grid boundary). In other words, scheduling these statements with the other statements violates the precedence constraint and thus are distributed into a different loop nest.

4.2 Algorithm 2: Enabling Outer-level Parallelism

As explained in Section 2.2, in the polyhedral framework, legal statement-wise hyperplanes are found one loop-level at a time using an ILP solver. The cost function used aims to find a loop hyperplane that minimizes the communication traffic among processors. As a result, it first aims to find a hyperplane that involves no communication, i.e. an outer-parallel loop. If no communication-free hyperplane can be found, a pipelined-parallel (or, forward dependence) hyperplane with constant communication cost is found. This was seen in the case of *advect* benchmark as shown in Figure 4(c).

The pre-fusion schedule obtained from Algorithm 1 leads to a partitioning that is legal and achieves good reuse. However, this may deprive the transformed code of outer-loop parallelism because of the introduction of a forward dependence at the outermost loop, between two of the fused statements. Although, with the outermost loop becoming a forward-dependence loop, pipelined parallelism can still be achieved (for example, in the *advect* benchmark), but the performance can be far from optimal because of increased communication costs. Algorithm 2 thus aims to preserve parallelism in the outermost loop to enable a coarse-grained parallel code, although at a cost of some loss of data reuse.

ALGORITHM 2: Enabling outer-level parallelism
INPUT:
List of dependences in the program: $deps$
begin
{For the first non-serial loop hyperplane, h, found by the ILP solver}
for each dependence, $S_i \rightarrow S_j$, $\in deps$ **do**
  if $S_i \rightarrow S_j$ is not satisfied at loop-level $h \wedge$
  $\phi_{S_j}^h(\vec{t}) - \phi_{S_i}^h(\vec{s}) > 0, \langle \vec{s}, \vec{t} \rangle \in P_{e_{S_i \rightarrow S_j}}$ **then**
    Issue a cut between SCCs containing statements S_i and S_j
    Discard the found hyperplane, and solve for a new hyperplane with the updated DDG
  end if
end for
end
OUTPUT: Fusion with possible outer-level parallelism

For the pre-fusion schedule determined through Algorithm 1, the ILP solver starts finding legal loop hyperplanes. For the first non-serial[4] loop hyperplane thus found, Algorithm 2 checks for any unsatisfied forward-dependence at that loop level. A forward dependence between two statement instances is determined through the inequality in Equation 5. An existence of a forward-dependence implies a forward-dependence outermost loop. To satisfy the dependence and thus to generate a parallel outermost loop, we issue a cut between the dependent SCCs, and re-solve for a new hyperplane with the updated dependence information in the DDG. This may be repeated until all dependences are satisfied and outer-loop parallelism is restored. *Since we issue the cut between SCCs carrying the actual dependence and not arbitrarily, the transformed code is minimally distributed, or in other words, it suffers minimal loss of data reuse.* This can be seen in the transformed code for the *advect* benchmark generated from Algorithm 2 as shown in Figure 6. Statements S1, S2 and S3 are still merged in the same loop nest and enjoy reuse through reads, while only statement S4 is distributed into a different loop nest. Thus, coarse-grained parallelism is achieved with a minimal loss of reuse. The existing polyhedral frameworks, on the other hand, perform maximal fusion after loop shifting leading to loss of coarse-grained parallelism as shown in earlier in Figure 4(c).

---

[4] a serial loop hyperplane cannot be parallelized

```
for (t2=4; t2<=ny+6; t2++) // parallel loop
  for (t3=4;t3<=nx+6;t3++)
    for (t4=4;t4<=nz+6;t4++) {
      S1: ab[t2][t3][t4]= uyb[t2][t3][t4] * ( .. a[j][i][k] .. );
      S2: al[t2][t3][t4]= uxl[t2][t3][t4] * ( .. a[j][i][k] .. );
      S3: af[t2][t3][t4]= uzf[t2][t3][t4] * ( .. a[j][i][k] .. );
    }

/* Update of variables at grid boundary  */

for (t2=5; t2<=ny+7; t2++) // parallel loop
  for (t3=5;t3<=nx+7;t3++)
    for (t4=5;t4<=nz+7;t4++)
      S4: athird[t2-1][t3-1][t4-1] = (af[t2-1][t3-1][t4] - af[t2-1][t3-1][t4-1]) +...;
```

Figure 6: Transformed *advect* code generated using Algorithm 2

5. Experimental Evaluation

We implemented our fusion algorithm within PLuTo. We replaced its algorithm for finding the pre-fusion schedule with ours, and also incorporated our algorithm for preserving the coarse-grained parallelism. However, for the purpose of finding loop hyperplanes, we rely on the same cost function as used in PLuTo and described in [9].

5.1 Setup

Fusion Model	Description
Intel Compiler	Fusion within Intel compiler (baseline)
wisefuse	Our fusion model
smartfuse	The default fusion model in PLuTo. It uses heuristics to 'cut' or distribute SCCs into different loop nests
nofuse	Another fusion model implemented in PLuTo. It separates all SCCs into different loop nests.
maxfuse	Another fusion model implemented in PLuTo. It conservatively distributes SCCs into different loop nests

Table 1: Summary of the fusion models

We ran our experiments on an Intel Xeon processor (E5-2650) with 8 Sandy Bridge-EP cores, operating at 2.0GHz. The processor has private L1 (32KB per core) and L2 (256KB per core) caches and a 20MB shared L3 cache. The experimental results compare the performance between our fusion algorithm and the one used within PLuTo that employs three different fusion heuristics. We compare against all the three heuristics used. The reason for comparing with PLuTo, as explained before, is that various other automatic polyhedral frameworks such as [2, 4, 25] use the same fusion algorithm as in PLuTo, and others [5, 7] use its variants. Since PLuTo cannot parse Fortran code, we integrated our fusion model with PolyOpt/Fortran [4], a tool that uses ROSE compiler [6] frontend to parse Fortran code and relies on PLuTo to accomplish loop fusion. A summary of the different fusion models compared in this section is given in Table 1. The transformed code generated using different fusion models was compiled using the Intel compiler v13 (icc and ifort) as the backend compiler. The compile time options used with the Intel compiler were '-O3' and '-parallel'. The original source, automatically parallelized using the Intel compiler and with all high level optimizations including loop fusion enabled, was used as the base case for comparison.

5.2 Benchmarks

The benchmarks used in the experiments belong to three different benchmark suites. We chose large programs from the SPEC and the NAS Parallel (NP) benchmark suites. The small kernel programs were chosen mainly from Polybench and PLuTo. These are summarized in Table 2. In the table, the first five benchmarks correspond to the large programs, and the last five represent small kernel programs.

Benchmark	Benchmark Suite	Category	Problem Size
gemsfdtd	SPEC 2006	Computational Electromagnetics	Reference Input
swim	SPEC OMP	Shallow Water Modeling	Reference Input
applu	SPEC OMP	Computational Fluid Dynamics	Reference Input
bt	NPB	Block Tri-diagonal solver	CLASS C; $(162)^3$, dt = 0.0001
sp	NPB	Scalar Penta-diagonal solver	CLASS C; $(162)^3$, dt = 0.00067
advect	PLuTo	Weather modeling	nx=ny=nz=300
lu	Polybench	Linear Algebra	N=1500
tce	Polybench	Computational Chemistry	Standard; $(55)^3$
gemver	Polybench	Linear Algebra	N=1500
wupwise	SPEC OMP	Quantum Chromodynamics	Reference Input

Table 2: Summary of the benchmarks

5.3 Results and Discussion

Figure 7 shows the normalized performance with respect to the Intel compiler achieved using different fusion models on the different benchmarks considered. Each of the codes was run using all 8 cores on the test processor. The figure also shows the geometric mean (represented as GM in Figure 7) of the performance achieved by different fusion models over the 10 benchmarks - *wisefuse* achieves a performance improvement of 1.3X over the Intel compiler.

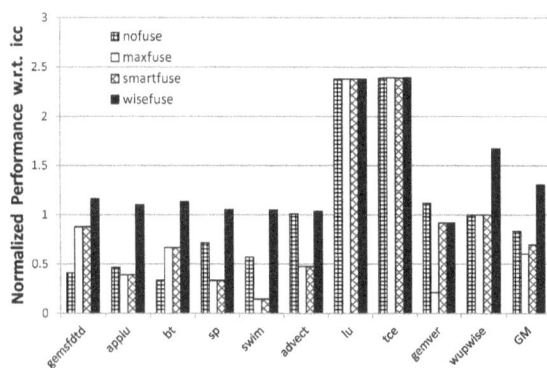

Figure 7: Results

For the purpose of discussing our experimental results, we divide the benchmarks into three categories, (1) the large benchmark programs, (2) the programs where fusion leads to a loss of parallelism, and (3) small kernel programs.

Large Benchmark Programs. Large programs tend to have multiple loop nests, with the potential to serve as ideal playground for the polyhedral compilers. However, ironically, none of the polyhedral frameworks has yet demonstrated success with large programs. As explained earlier, a fundamental reason for this is the lack of an effective cost model for loop fusion, which in turn hurts all other transformations.

Figure 7 shows that our fusion algorithm, *wisefuse*, achieves a performance improvement in the range of 1.7X to 7.2X as compared to *smartfuse* for the large programs, and an improvement of 5-18% over the Intel Compiler. It is important to note that This performance improvement is attributed to the better fusion partitioning achieved by *wisefuse*, with the amount of improvement achieved being a function of the reuse opportunity available in the source program. For large programs, only a part of the program usually provides fusion opportunity. For example, *wisefuse* improves UPMLupdatee and UPMLupdateh routines in *gemsfdtd* benchmark by nearly 1.5X, but the overall program by only 1.18X. Similar is the case with APPLU, SP and BT benchmarks. The following discussion provides further insight into the results obtained.

SCC ID	Dimensionality	Partitions in icc	Partitions in wisefuse	Partitions in smartfuse
1	3	1	1	6
2	3	1	1	6
3	3	1	1	6
4	2	2	2	5
5	2	2	2	5
6	3	3	3	6
7	3	3	1	6
8	3	3	1	6
9	3	3	1	4
10	3	3	1	4
11	3	3	1	4
12	2	4	2	3
13	2	4	2	3
14	3	5	1	4
15	3	5	3	4
16	3	5	1	4
17	3	5	1	2
18	3	5	1	2
19	3	5	1	2
20	2	6	2	1
21	2	6	2	1
22	3	7	1	2
23	3	7	1	2
24	3	7	3	2

total partitions

Figure 8: Partitioning achieved by different fusion models for the *gemsfdtd* benchmark (values in each column are spaced out for readability)

Figure 8 compares the fusion partitioning achieved by icc, *smartfuse* and *wisefuse*, for the *UPMLupdateh* subroutine in the *gemsfdtd* benchmark. The *UPMLupdateh* and another similar subroutine, *UPMLupdatee*, together account for 45% of the total execution time in *gemsfdtd*. In the figure, the second column shows the dimensionality of each SCC within *UPMLupdateh*, and columns 3 through 5 show the partition number to which each SCC belongs to, in the transformed codes obtained from different fusion strategies. The SCCs with the same partition number in the figure are fused in the same loop nest in the transformed code. It can be seen that *wisefuse* minimizes the number of partitions and thus, in effect achieves maximum reuse. All the SCCs fused together have reuse not only through true dependences but also through input dependences. The key to fusing more SCCs together is that *wisefuse* chooses a pre-fusion schedule such that SCCs with the same dimensionality are ordered next to each other, increasing the probability for them to be fused together into perfect loop nests. For example, all SCCs with a dimensionality of 2 are perfectly fused in the transformed *gemsfdtd* code generated using *wisefuse*.

Also, *wisefuse* employs another heuristic - it fuses SCCs close to each other in program order as such SCCs tend to reuse more data and this also leads to effective fusion. This was observed in *applu*, *bt* and *sp* benchmark applications, where *wisefuse* fused SCCs that belonged to the same pass (x-, y- or z-pass) and thus enjoyed excellent reuse through the input dependences. *Smartfuse* on the other hand, fused statements across different passes, which although led to reuse through the true dependences, deprived it from achieving better reuse among the SCCs close in program order. This led to overall poor reuse achieved through *smartfuse* in such programs.

For all the large programs, *icc* largely maintains the original program order and doesn't accomplish any fusion. This is because *icc* performs a pair-wise fusion [15], where pairs of loops are fused incrementally to prevent exponential cost of finding all fusion choices. However, when successive loops are of different dimensionality as in the *gemsfdtd* benchmark, *icc* does not fuse them. This is because fusing loop nests of different dimensionality does not lead to significant reuse and the fused nest may contain conditional statements that hinders compiler auto-vectorization. *Wisefuse*, instead, reorders statements such that those with (reuse and) the same dimensionality are ordered consecutively in a pre-fusion step for them to be considered for fusion. This allows us to achieve both global reuse (as seen in Figure 7) and is effectively vectorized by the backend compiler. As compared to *icc*, *smartfuse* generally performs worse due to lack of a cost model to determine a good pre-fusion schedule.

Programs with Conflict between Fusion and Parallelism. In the case of *advect* and *swim* benchmarks, a maximal fusion leads to a loss of outer-loop parallelism. In these benchmarks, *wisefuse* detects the SCCs that carry a forward dependence on the outer-loop and selectively distributes them to different loop nests as was shown earlier in Figure 6 for the *advect* benchmark. Both *smartfuse* and *maxfuse* fusion strategies apply maximal fusion in these cases resulting in a loss of outer-loop parallelism. Although the transformed codes generated by *smartfuse* and *maxfuse* fusion strategies are pipelined parallel, they perform worse than *wisefuse* because of the constant communication costs involved after the parallel execution of each wavefront. It is for the same reason that the transformed code generated by *wisefuse* scales better than *smartfuse*, and the performance gap increases with the increase in the number of processors.

Wisefuse also slightly outperforms *icc* (that achieves no fusion) because of the better reuse accomplished in each case.

Small Kernel Programs. Among the various small kernel programs from the Polybench benchmark suite, we chose *lu* and *tce* benchmarks as these two benchmarks particularly provide an opportunity for fusion and also reveal the limitations of the current non-polyhedral compilers. The *lu* benchmark implements the Gaussian elimination algorithm that converts a system of linear equations to a unit upper-triangular system. Thus, the *lu* benchmark exhibits a non-rectangular iteration space, or in other words, non-conformable loop bounds. As a result, *icc* adopts a conservative approach and does not achieve coarse-grained parallelization. The polyhedral frameworks, on the other hand, armed with exact dependence information, are able to find available parallelism even in benchmarks with non-rectangular iteration spaces such as *lu*. Both *smartfuse* and *wisefuse* achieve the same fusion partitioning and consequently the same performance, that is considerably better than *icc*.

The *tce* kernel appears in computational quantum chemistry problems. It contains 4 loop nests with significant reuse opportunity among statements. However, since each loop nest contains loops in different order, the non-polyhedral compilers such as *icc* cannot find a conformable pattern to accomplish loop fusion. The polyhedral compilers, on the other hand, find common loop hyperplanes for the different statements and thus achieve loop fusion. Again, both *wisefuse* and *smartfuse* yield similar fusion partitions. Similarly, for other benchmarks from the Polybench benchmark suite, *wisefuse* achieves the same fusion partitioning as *smartfuse*, proving the effectiveness of the heuristics employed by *wisefuse* even for small kernel programs.

The *gemver* benchmark considered earlier shows interesting behavior with different fusion models. Both *wisefuse* and *smartfuse* achieve identical fusion partitioning. However, they perform worse than both the *icc* and *nofuse* fusion models for the chosen problem size. The Intel compiler, like the *nofuse* fusion model does not accomplish any fusion, i.e. all 4 statements in *gemver* are left unfused. *Wisefuse* and *smartfuse* fuse statements S1 and S2 (shown earlier in Figure 3), but at the cost of spatial locality in the two statements. *Nofuse* outperforms *icc* as *icc* fails to achieve coarse-grained parallelism in the loop nest enclosing statement S2. It is for this reason that the fusion partitioning accomplished by *wisefuse* and *smartfuse* is still better than that achieved by *icc* as loss of coarse-grained parallelism in even one loop nest hurts scalability when the number of processors are increased.

Among small programs, we also chose the *wupwise* benchmark. Although from the SPEC OMP benchmark suite, 60% of its execution time is spent executing the *zgemm* subroutine, which is nothing but complex matrix-matrix multiplication. However, within the SPEC suite, it is written as a collection of imperfect nests (loop nests of different dimensionality) and also involves data-dependent control flow. Although a recent work [8] has made data-dependent control flow amenable for the polyhedral frameworks through the use of predicates, no available implementation exists for the same. We implemented the predication strategy as proposed in [8] and were thus able to optimize the *wupwise* benchmark. Since *wupwise* consists of imperfect nests, *wisefuse* distributes them into different perfect loop nests so as to achieve better data reuse. This results in a serial performance improvement of 20% over *icc*, that avoids loop distribution given imperfect nests. However, interestingly, the performance improvement goes up to 40% for 8 cores. This was because, loop distribution allowed it to selectively parallelize loop nests, as not all loops nests contain enough computation to benefit from the parallelization. Thus, this proved to be an additional advantage of using the heuristic that favors the fusion of SCCs with the same dimensionality.

6. Related Work

In this section, we present the related work on loop fusion in 2 phases - the work done prior to the advent of the polyhedral compilers, and work done within the domain of polyhedral compiler framework.

Loop fusion has been extensively studied in the compiler community as an effective optimization to improve data reuse since its advent in 1980's. Since then, loop fusion has been studied to achieve complementary goals of preserving parallelism, minimizing register pressure and minimizing synchronization. Kennedy et al. in [22] study loop fusion to preserve parallelism while minimizing synchronization. They also show that finding fusion partitions that maximize data reuse is an NP-hard problem, and provide a polynomial time solution to improve data reuse. In their formulation, Kennedy et al. represent data reuse by an edge between loops (nodes), whereas Ding and Kennedy [15] later gave another formulation based on the hyper graph where the computation units are represented as nodes, and each data array is represented as a hyper edge connecting all nodes where the array is accessed. These works thus treated the two problems of preserving parallelism and maximizing reuse independently. Singhai and McKinley in [31] consider these two problems together and use heuristics to find solutions that achieve good reuse and preserve parallelism. Megiddo and Sarkar in [26] target the same problem and show that optimal solutions can be found using their proposed integer programming formulation for problem sizes that occur in practice. In both of these works, the parallel loop nests are already identified and the problem reduces to merging loop nests such that parallelism is not hurt. This decoupling of loop fusion and parallelism misses certain good solutions. In addition, fusion and parallelism are sometimes enabled only after other loop transformations such as skewing, interchange, shifting, etc. are applied. This composition of high-level transformations is not facilitated within the traditional compiler frameworks, leading to the development of the polyhedral compiler framework.

The state-of-the-art fully automatic fusion algorithm [10] within the domain of polyhedral compilers is employed in the source-to-source compilation tool, PLuTo [1]. It subsumes previous work in affine scheduling [16, 17, 19, 21] and partitioning [23, 24] and overcomes their major limitation by incorporating an effective cost model for coarse-grained parallelization and data locality. The fusion algorithm employed within PLuTo is also used by various other polyhedral frameworks including PoCC, PolyOpt, LLVM's Polly and IBM's XL compiler. However, as discussed in our motivation to this work, it lacks a cost model to determine good pre-fusion schedules leading to suboptimal fusion partitions, especially for large programs with many statements. Recently, the fusion algorithm used in PLuTO was revised [11], that also aims to preserve coarse-grained parallelization while allowing loop fusion. However, their approach, in addition to relying on a suboptimal pre-fusion schedule, may lead to significant loss of reuse in order to preserve parallelism. This is because, unlike *wisefuse* that precisely distributes only the SCCs preventing parallelism to minimize loss of reuse, the proposed approach in [11] uses heuristics and may end up in excessive distribution to restore parallelism.

In order to find the best fusion partitioning, the authors in [27–29] have proposed iterative compilation framework leveraging the polyhedral model. The authors propose techniques to build a convex space of all legal and non-redundant fusion partitions, and an optimization algorithm to explore this space. This technique has been shown to find the optimal fusion schedule for small benchmark programs through iterative search. However, we observed that the iterative compilation framework fails to build the search space for even moderately sized programs because the search space grows exponentially with the size of the program. Our work in this paper proposes a fusion algorithm with a static cost model to achieve data reuse and preserve parallelism and thus helps to overcome this limitation, especially for programs with many statements.

In addition, URUK/WRaP-IT [13, 18] and CHiLL [12] are other well known tools that use the polyhedral representation to perform various high level optimizations. However, both of these tools are semi-automatic, and require transformations to be specified manually by an expert. The authors of URUK in [18] also achieve performance improvement for some large programs from the SPEC benchmark suite. Our fusion algorithm, on the other hand, demonstrates performance gains on such large programs through a fully automatic application of polyhedral techniques by incorporating an effective cost model for loop fusion.

7. Conclusion

In this work, we presented a loop fusion algorithm, *wisefuse*, with 2 objective functions - maximizing data reuse and preserving parallelism. To achieve data reuse, *wisefuse* employs certain heuristics in a pre-fusion step that work in consonance with the polyhedral framework and help to find good fusion partitions. In addition, *wisefuse* ensures that coarse-grained parallelism inherent in the source code remains preserved as aggressive loop fusion may lead to a loop-carried dependence on the outer-loop that prevents parallelism. Experimental results demonstrate that *wisefuse* achieves good fusion partitions not only for the small kernel programs but also the large benchmark programs. *Wisefuse* thus allows to overcome a major limitation in the existing polyhedral frameworks in handling large programs.

8. Acknowledgements

We would like to acknowledge NSF grants CNS-0834599 and CCF-0708822, and a special grant from the Asian Office of Aerospace Research and Development (AOARD-11-4092) for supporting this work.

References

[1] Pluto: An automatic parallelizer and locality optimizer for multicores. Available at http://pluto-compiler.sourceforge.net.

[2] Pocc: Polyhedral compiler collection. Available at http://www.cse.ohio-state.edu/~pouchet/software/pocc/.

[3] Polybench, . Available at http://www-roc.inria.fr/~pouchet/software/polybench/.

[4] Polyopt: a polyhedral optimizer for the rose compiler, . Available at http://www.cse.ohio-state.edu/~pouchet/software/polyopt/.

[5] R-stream compiler. Available at https://www.reservoir.com/?q=rstream.

[6] Rose compiler. Available at http://rosecompiler.org/.

[7] Ibm xl compiler. Available at http://ibm.com/software/awdtools/xlcpp/.

[8] M.-W. Benabderrahmane, L.-N. Pouchet, A. Cohen, and C. Bastoul. The polyhedral model is more widely applicable than you think. In *CC '2010*, pages 283–303, Paphos, Cyprus, Mar. . Springer Verlag.

[9] U. Bondhugula. *Effective Automatic Parallelization and Locality Optimization Using The Polyhedral Model*. PhD thesis, Ohio State University, 2010.

[10] U. Bondhugula, M. Baskaran, S. Krishnamoorthy, J. Ramanujam, A. Rountev, and P. Sadayappan. Automatic transformations for communication-minimized parallelization and locality optimization in the polyhedral model. In *CC'2008*, pages 132–146. Springer Berlin / Heidelberg, .

[11] U. Bondhugula, O. Gunluk, S. Dash, and L. Renganarayanan. A model for fusion and code motion in an automatic parallelizing compiler. In *PACT '2010*, pages 343–352. ACM, .

[12] C. Chen, J. Chame, and M. Hall. Chill: A framework for composing high-level loop transformations. *U. of Southern California, Tech. Rep*, pages 08–897, 2008.

[13] A. Cohen, M. Sigler, S. Girbal, O. Temam, D. Parello, and N. Vasilache. Facilitating the search for compositions of program transformations. In *ICS '05*, pages 151–160. ACM.

[14] A. Darte. On the complexity of loop fusion. In *PACT '99*, Washington, DC, USA. IEEE Computer Society.

[15] C. Ding and K. Kennedy. Improving effective bandwidth through compiler enhancement of global cache reuse. *JPDC*, 64(1):108 – 134, 2004.

[16] P. Feautrier. Some efficient solutions to the affine scheduling problem. i. one-dimensional time. *IJPP*, pages 313–347, 1992.

[17] P. Feautrier. Some efficient solutions to the affine scheduling problem. part ii. multidimensional time. *IJPP*, pages 389–420, 1992.

[18] S. Girbal, N. Vasilache, C. Bastoul, A. Cohen, D. Parello, M. Sigler, and O. Temam. Semi-automatic composition of loop transformations for deep parallelism and memory hierarchies. *IJPP*, 34:261–317, 2006.

[19] M. Griebl. *Automatic Parallelization of Loop Programs for Distributed Memory Architectures*. PhD thesis, University of Passau, 2004.

[20] T. Grosser, H. Zheng, R. Aloor, A. Simbürger, A. Größlinger, and L.-N. Pouchet. Polly-polyhedral optimization in llvm. In *IMPACT '2011*.

[21] W. Kelly and W. Pugh. Minimizing communication while preserving parallelism. In *ICS '1995*, pages 52–60. ACM Press.

[22] K. Kennedy and K. McKinley. Maximizing loop parallelism and improving data locality via loop fusion and distribution. In *LCPC*, volume 768 of *Lecture Notes in Computer Science*, pages 301–320. 1994.

[23] A. W. Lim and M. S. Lam. Maximizing parallelism and minimizing synchronization with affine partitions. *Parallel Computing*, 24:445 – 475, 1998.

[24] A. W. Lim, G. I. Cheong, and M. S. Lam. An affine partitioning algorithm to maximize parallelism and minimize communication. In *ICS '99*, pages 228–237. ACM.

[25] LLVM. Polly: Polyhedral optimizations for llvm. Available at http://polly.llvm.org/.

[26] N. Megiddo and V. Sarkar. Optimal weighted loop fusion for parallel programs. In *SPAA '97*, pages 282–291. ACM.

[27] L.-N. Pouchet, C. Bastoul, A. Cohen, and J. Cavazos. Iterative optimization in the polyhedral model: Part ii, multidimensional time. In *PLDI '08*, pages 90–100. ACM, .

[28] L.-N. Pouchet, C. Bastoul, A. Cohen, and N. Vasilache. Iterative optimization in the polyhedral model: Part i, one-dimensional time. In *CGO '07*, pages 144 –156, .

[29] L.-N. Pouchet, U. Bondhugula, C. Bastoul, A. Cohen, J. Ramanujam, P. Sadayappan, and N. Vasilache. Loop transformations: convexity, pruning and optimization. In *POPL '2011*, pages 549–562. ACM, .

[30] M. Sharir. A strong-connectivity algorithm and its applications in data flow analysis. *Computers & Mathematics with Applications*, 7(1):67–72, 1981.

[31] S. K. Singhai and K. S. McKinley. A parametrized loop fusion algorithm for improving parallelism and cache locality. *The Computer Journal*, 40(6):340–355, 1997.

Triolet: A Programming System that Unifies Algorithmic Skeleton Interfaces for High-Performance Cluster Computing

Christopher Rodrigues   Thomas Jablin   Abdul Dakkak   Wen-Mei Hwu

University of Illinois at Urbana-Champaign

{cirodrig, jablin, dakkak, w-hwu}@illinois.edu

Abstract

Functional algorithmic skeletons promise a high-level programming interface for distributed-memory clusters that free developers from concerns of task decomposition, scheduling, and communication. Unfortunately, prior distributed functional skeleton frameworks do not deliver performance comparable to that achievable in a low-level distributed programming model such as C with MPI and OpenMP, even when used in concert with high-performance array libraries. There are several causes: they do not take advantage of shared memory on each cluster node; they impose a fixed partitioning strategy on input data; and they have limited ability to fuse loops involving skeletons that produce a variable number of outputs per input.

We address these shortcomings in the Triolet programming language through a modular library design that separates concerns of parallelism, loop nesting, and data partitioning. We show how Triolet substantially improves the parallel performance of algorithms involving array traversals and nested, variable-size loops over what is achievable in Eden, a distributed variant of Haskell. We further demonstrate how Triolet can substantially simplify parallel programming relative to C with MPI and OpenMP while achieving 23–100% of its performance on a 128-core cluster.

Categories and Subject Descriptors   D.3.2 [*Programming Languages*]: Language Classifications—Applicative (functional) languages, Concurrent, distributed and parallel languages; D.3.4 [*Programming Languages*]: Processors—Optimization

Keywords   Algorithmic skeletons; Loop fusion; Parallel programming

PPoPP '14,   February 15–19, 2014, Orlando, Florida, USA.
Copyright is held by the owner/author(s). Publication rights licensed to ACM.
ACM 978-1-4503-2656-8/14/02... $15.00.
http://dx.doi.org/10.1145/http://dx.doi.org/10.1145/2555243.2555268

1. Introduction

Clusters of multicore computers are an inexpensive way to furnish parallel computing capacity. Data-parallel algorithmic skeletons—higher-order functions capturing common patterns of parallel computation—have been proposed as a simple, high-level interface for multicore [6, 12, 16, 19] and distributed [11, 15, 22] parallel programming. Skeletons decompose work into parallel tasks and distribute that work across a parallel machine, allowing a programmer to focus on what parallelization strategy to use from a skeleton library, rather than how it is implemented. Additionally, distributed functional skeletons send data and collect results from tasks, allowing programmers to focus on what data to use rather than how to move it between cluster nodes. Separating out the low-level details of parallelism allows developers to write parallel code that resembles sequential code, wherein the choice of parallel skeletons determines the details of parallel execution. However, while prior distributed functional skeleton frameworks have demonstrated their ease of use, they do not approach lower-level parallel programming models in absolute performance [14, 21].

For example, the molecular modeling application `cutcp` has a computationally demanding loop nest computing a floating-point histogram. It loops over a collection of atoms, visits all grid points near the atom, and updates the grid point with the electric potential induced by the atom. In idiomatic sequential Haskell, this could be written using a list comprehension as shown below, assuming suitable definitions of `floatHist`, `f`, and `gridPts`.

```
floatHist [f a r | a <- atoms, r <- gridPts a]
```

In the list comprehension, the generator `a <- atoms` loops over a list of atoms, the generator `r <- gridPts a` computes and loops over the grid points near each atom, and the call `f a r` computes the electrostatic potential induced by an atom at a grid point. The list of results is collected into a histogram by `floatHist`. A naïve attempt at parallelization might replace `floatHist` and the traversal of `atoms` by a distributed implementation written in Eden, a distributed extension of Haskell [15]. One could write a distributed `floatHist` function that partitions an input list across tasks and performs histogramming within each task and use it as shown below.

```
floatHistD (\x -> [f r x | r <- gridPts x]) atoms
```

This code demonstrates the attractive simplicity of algorithmic skeletons, but its per-thread performance is an order of magnitude lower than sequential C chiefly due to the overhead of list manipulation, indicating that there is substantial room for improvement.

A performance-oriented high-level programmer could optimize the parallelized code by writing custom skeletons that minimize network communication and implementing each task with imperative code manipulating unboxed arrays. Since the combination of Eden and high-performance array libraries has not been studied before, we evaluate this high-performance style as a reference point. These optimizations can indeed yield sequential performance within a small multiplicative factor of C. However, this kind of manual transformation is exactly what skeletons should make unnecessary. Moreover, scalability remains limited because Eden does not exploit sharing on each cluster node.

We identify and address three problems that cause distributed functional skeletons to fail to achieve high performance. First, irregular loops, where each element of an input data structure yields a dynamically determined number of outputs, cannot be fused and parallelized using prior loop representations. As in the example above, it is common to write a parallel loop as a multi-stage process of generating, then consuming a collection of temporary values. We use a novel representation of fusible, nested loops to isolate irregularity within inner loops, allowing irregular generation phases to be fused with consumers into a single parallel loop. Unlike prior methods, our representation balances support for random access to collections, needed to efficiently parallelize loops and implement index-based operations such as zip, with support for cheap opportunistic partitioning of collections, needed to fuse and parallelize irregular loops.

Second, we treat data distribution strategies separately from work distribution strategies, enabling a parallel skeletons to use a data distribution mechanism appropriate for their inputs. Prior data-parallel distributed skeleton frameworks performed both data and work distribution by partitioning a list or array of inputs across processors. For some algorithms, this may be inefficient due to the overhead of processing linked lists, because tasks can be implemented more efficiently on chunks of data than on individual elements, and/or because some input data are unnecessarily replicated for use in multiple loop iterations. Separating data distribution reduces the programmer effort and run-time overhead of reorganizing data before a parallel loop.

Third, skeletons need to be able to employ different algorithm implementations at the sequential, shared-memory, and distributed scales, taking advantage of in-place data structure updates at the sequential level and avoiding copying at the shared-memory level. Eden's scalability, in partic-ular, is limited by its inability to take advantage of shared memory to reduce communication cost. We utilize a two-level parallel architecture, with message passing across nodes and work-stealing thread parallelism in each node. Our parallel skeletons follow this two-level architecture, exploiting shared memory and in-place updates.

We have implemented these solutions in the library, compiler, and runtime of the Triolet programming language. We evaluate the performance and scalability of four programs written in Triolet, Eden, and C+MPI+OpenMP on a 128-core (8 nodes × 16 cores per node) cluster. Each of these benchmarks presents challenges that the Eden code must work around, whereas Triolet's library and runtime allow a cleaner expression of parallelism to achieve high performance. The C+MPI+OpenMP implementations, with their highly efficient low-level communication and synchronization, provide a reference point for estimating the overhead in Triolet's algorithms and runtime system. Triolet consistently yields higher parallel performance than Eden, achieves 23–100% of the performance of C+MPI+OpenMP versions, and yields a speedup up to 9.6–99× relative to simple loops in sequential C.

2. Overview

In typical data-parallel algorithmic skeleton libraries, each skeleton is a higher-order function containing a carefully implemented pattern of parallel communication and work distribution. Invoking a skeleton effectively instantiates and inserts code into a parallel loop. To conform their algorithm to an available skeleton, users of a library often have to regularize their algorithms and reorganize their data structures. These adaptations add complexity and overhead to parallel programs.

Triolet's skeleton library has a more modular design that builds parallel loops from loosely coupled components managing data movement, work distribution, result collection, and the composition of loops. Support for composition of nested loops accommodates irregular and nested parallel loops. The data movement component accommodates different looping patterns. The work distribution component supports block-based decomposition of multidimensional arrays for memory locality. By implementing library functions in terms of these components rather than parallel loops, the library permits simple source code to execute efficiently.

From an application developer's perspective, Triolet presents an extensible set of data-parallel higher-order functions that help manipulate aggregate data structures. A Triolet parallel loop resembles sequential Python code that uses list comprehensions and higher-order functions to manipulate lists. For example, a function for computing the dot product of two vectors could be defined as follows.

```
def dot(xs, ys):
    return sum(x*y for (x, y) in par(zip(xs, ys)))
```

This statement defines dot as a function of xs and ys. The body of dot calls the library functions zip, par, map, and sum to sum the elementwise product of xs and ys. The call of map arises from desugaring the list comprehension (...for...in...) [27], used here to mutiply the input lists elementwise after zipping them together. Loops execute sequentially by default. The call to par designates the loop as parallel, directing the library to use all available parallelism when computing the dot product.

Though not computationally intensive enough to benefit from cluster parallelism, dot exhibits scaling and efficiency challenges that also limit the performance of realistic workloads. Multiple library calls commonly express what should be a single parallel loop. In this case, Triolet fuses the calls of zip, map, par, and sum into a single loop to minimize communication and memory traffic. Input data should be identified and, if appropriate, partitioned across cluster nodes. Triolet partitions the arrays xs and ys into subarrays and distributes them to cluster nodes. Results from each thread should be aggregated locally within each node to minimize the cost of communicating results. Each thread computes its own private sum, and these are summed on each node, produce a single value per node that is sent back to the main thread. While dot has a relatively simple looping pattern, some algorithms loop over irregular or multidimensional iteration spaces, which adds complexity to loop fusion, work distribution, and result collection.

Triolet uses a library-driven approach to generating efficient parallel loops. Optimized, modular components are assembled into loops by library code, effectively decoupling loop optimizations from the design of the compiler. Compile-time optimization on user code often yields statically generated loops. Library-driven loop optimizations have been introduced previously [5, 7, 12], and Triolet adopts some of these techniques. Triolet's compiler incorporates a suite of general-purpose optimizations on a typed, functional intermediate language [17, 26]. The library uses this optimization infrastructure like a metaprogramming framework: library functions examine their arguments and assemble functions embodying the code to execute, and as long as this assembly process depends only on statically known information, that code will be built and simplified during compile-time optimizations. In the simplified program, the optimizer is often able to replace costly dynamic features such as anonymous functions and heap allocation by cheaper control flow and register-allocatable local variables.

Some library functions return lazily evaluated arrays, called *iterators*, to enable loop fusion. An iterator represents a collection of tasks, each of which computes some result values. Typical parallel iterator representations bear a close connection to parallel loops: the collection of tasks is encoded as a function of the loop counter (the loop body) together with a range of loop counter values (the iteration space) [1, 12]. This is an *indexed* iterator representation,

since elements are retrieved by index. In the parallel dot function, zip, par, and map return iterators. The call to zip represents a parallel loop whose body is the function $\lambda i \rightarrow \langle \text{xs}[i], \text{ys}[i] \rangle$ that, when called with a value for parameter i, retrieves the ith elements of both input arrays and tuples them together. (We use Haskell syntax for examples of code within the optimizer, and use brackets for array subscripting.) This iterator is passed to par, which leaves the loop body unchanged. The call to map constructs a new iterator whose body performs the work of zip (with the function call below), unpacks the result (with the case expression), and multiplies values:

$$\lambda k \rightarrow \textbf{case } (\lambda i \rightarrow \langle \text{xs}[i], \text{ys}[i] \rangle) \; k$$
$$\textbf{of } \langle x, y \rangle \rightarrow x * y$$

Compile-time optimizations eliminate the function call and temporary tuple, producing $\lambda k \rightarrow \text{xs}[k] * \text{ys}[k]$, which performs zip's array lookups followed immediately by map's multiplication. Thus, a carefully chosen iterator representation allows compile-time optimizations to fuse loops.

Indexed representations are not suited to parallelizing irregular loops, where the set of loop iterations to execute is determined dynamically. A common use of irregular parallelism is to generate many inputs, then conditionally skip inputs or expand them into multiple inputs for subsequent processing. This can be parallelized by partitioning the initial set of inputs evenly across parallel processes. To support this work distribution, a loop body should not implement the operation "get the nth intermediate result," which requires a communication phase to count intermediate results, but rather "get each intermediate result generated from the nth input." Each parallel process loops over a subset of inputs and, in an inner loop, generates and processes intermediate results from each input.

To provide the convenience of a shared memory programming interface on a cluster, iterator-based parallelization needs a way to automatically send data over the network. Prior iterator-based parallelization either assumes a shared memory for all parallel tasks [1, 12], sends each distributed task a copy of all objects that are referenced by its input [15, 22], or statically analyzes memory references to find the subarrays used by distributed tasks [11]. While the last approach has the potential to maximize performance by eagerly sending each task only the subset of data it needs, it is challenging to provide a static array reference analysis that yields precise results in the presence of higher-order functions and pointer data structures.

Triolet's library takes advantage of the access patterns implicit in higher-order function calls to partition arrays across parallel tasks without the need for strong compile-time analysis. Many algorithms employ regular array traversals that can be cleanly expressed as compositions of library calls. To track traversal patterns, each iterator contains a representation of both a set of parallel tasks and a set of input data.

Iterators include methods for extracting a subset, or *slice*, of the input. When a subset of tasks is sent to a cluster node, the corresponding slice of the input data is extracted and sent as well. This feature enables a parallel 2D block decomposition of dense matrix multiplication to be written in two lines of code. The matrix product AB is computed (after transposing B for faster memory access) by evaluating dot products of rows of A with rows of B^T:

```
zipped_AB = outerproduct(rows(A), rows(BT))
AB = [dot(u, v) for (u, v) in par(zipped_AB)]
```

Here, `dot` is taken to be defined as sequential code so that the computation of a single output block is sequential. The calls to the library function `rows` reinterpret the two-dimensional arrays A and B^T as one-dimensional iterators over array rows, where each array row is a one-dimensional iterator over elements. The zip-like library function `outerproduct` creates a 2D iterator paring rows of A with rows of B^T. Together, the functions on the first line determine a block distribution of input data. Iterators returned by `rows` associate each task with the corresponding array row. From these iterators, `outerproduct` associates each 2D matrix block with the rows of A and B corresponding, respectively, to the block's vertical and horizontal extent. When parallel tasks are launched by the comprehension on the second line of code, each task will be sent only the array rows that it needs to compute its output.

The library uses several techniques to efficiently execute parallel loops for multidimensional, nested, and irregular problems. Operations that compute a new value or array, such as `dot`'s summation or matrix multiplication's construction of the output array, loop over and execute an iterator's tasks and collect results. Nested and irregular iteration spaces are treated as a loop nest, and the library chooses a sequential or parallel implementation for each nesting level individually.

Due to the differences in communication costs over shared memory and over a network, many algorithms benefit from different inter-node and intra-node parallelization strategies. Unfortunately, the majority of existing programming languages and libraries either present a "flat" view of parallelism where all cores are equally remote from one another, as in Eden, or require developers to explicitly manage the distribution of work across levels, as in C with MPI and OpenMP. Triolet uses a two-level work distribution policy that first distributes large units of work to cluster nodes, then subdivides this work among cores within a node. Because library code cannot examine user code to decide whether a loop is worth paralellizing, it relies on user hints. The library functions `par` and `localpar` set a flag in an iterator to indicate that it should be parallelized across the entire system or across a single node, respectively. Single-node parallelization leverages shared memory to obtain speedup on loops that do very little work per byte of data, such as matrix transposition. A skeleton in the library consists of code that,

depending on the input iterator's parallelism hint, invokes low-level skeletons for distributing work across nodes, cores within a node, and/or sequential loop iterations in a task.

3. Implementation

This section describes how Triolet's library, compiler, and runtime execute algorithmic skeletons efficiently. Section 3.1 explains prior approaches to loop fusion. Section 3.2 explains how Triolet's iterators build on prior loop fusion techniques. Section 3.3 generalizes iterators for programming with multidimensional arrays. Section 3.4 describes how Triolet manages parallel tasks and communication.

3.1 Loop Fusion Background

Triolet builds on several existing loop fusion strategies in order to avoid the shortcomings of each. This section introduces these fusion strategies.

At the most basic level, a library may operate only on data structures whose contents are stored in memory, such as arrays. Each skeleton is a loop that reads its entire input and writes its entire output. Compilers may fuse loops by rewriting known patterns of function calls [2, 6, 20]. For example, any pair of calls to filter matching the pattern filter g (filter f a) can be fused by rewriting it to filter $(\lambda x \rightarrow f\ x\ \&\&\ g\ x)\ a$. The rewritten code does the work of both filter calls in one pass over a. Because this approach involves designing ad-hoc fusion rules for each pattern, its effectiveness is limited by a library implementor's ability to anticipate and make rules for all combinations of function calls. A more systematic approach is necessary to fuse a larger inventory of loops, especially as nested loops multiply the space of possible looping patterns.

In an imperative setting, loop fusion interleaves the execution of loops on an iteration-by-iteration basis [13]. However, loops with variable numbers of outputs, such as filter, have dependence patterns that can't be expressed purely in terms of loop iterations. In the example above, the first iteration of the second call to filter may depend on any iteration of the first call to filter. Consequently, iteration-based loop fusion techniques cannot fuse this example.

Triolet uses a relatively simple and robust approach to loop fusion that depends only on general-purpose compile-time optimizations. This approach uses what we call *virtual* data structures in place of some of a program's arrays. Several virtual data structure encodings, listed as the rows of Figure 1, have been developed to enable loop fusion. What they have in common is that they all contain a function that is called to compute the data structure's contents. Use of a function effectively defers computation until results are needed. General-purpose compile-time optimizations inline the function at the site where it is used, typically in a loop body, fusing loops.

The rest of this section presents the virtual data structures in Figure 1 and explains why each encoding has limited

	Parallel	Zip	Filter	Nested traversal	Mutation
Indexer	yes	yes	no	no	no
Stepper	no	yes	yes	slow	no
Fold	no	no	yes	yes	no
Collector	no	no	yes	yes	yes

Figure 1. Features of fusible virtual data structure encodings. A "no" means the feature cannot be used or its output is not fusible. A "slow" means the feature may be much less efficient than a handwritten loop.

applicability. We then introduce a new encoding used by Triolet that builds on these encodings to work around their limitations. We use as an example a list holding consecutive integers $[0, 1, 2]$. When used as the input to a skeleton, this list is analogous to a counted loop with three iterations.

Indexers   An indexer encoding consists of a size and a lookup function. The ith element of a data structure is retrieved by calling the lookup function with argument i. The example list would be encoded as the pair $\langle 3, \lambda i \to i \rangle$: the list's size is 3, and its ith element is i. Mapping a function f over this data structure builds a new virtual list whose lookup function calls the original lookup function, then calls f on the result: $\langle 3, \lambda j \to f ((\lambda i \to i) \ j) \rangle$, which the compiler simplifies to $\langle 3, f \rangle$. Summing the elements of this data structure proceeds by looping over all indices less than 3, calling the lookup function on each, and summing the results. The map function and many other indexer-based skeletons consist of straight-line code that builds an indexer. Loop fusion becomes a function inlining task, which is typically easier for compilers to accomplish than traditional loop transformations.

Since indexers allow any element to be retrieved independently of the others, indexers can be used in parallel loops. In C++, readable random access iterators fill the role of indexers. Thrust [1] and Repa [12] use indexers internally to generate fused parallel loops. Parallel loop bodies in functional languages [8, 23] resemble indexers, though they are special syntactic forms rather than ordinary functions.

While the random-access nature of indexers affords parallelism, it also makes indexers unsuitable for irregular loops or loops that write mutable data structures. The user of an indexer is free to choose how to execute the indexer's lookup function, making it difficult to predict side effects when an indexer is created. Triolet prevents such unpredictability by disallowing parallel access to mutable data structures. Functions that produce a variable number of outputs per input cannot be fused by encoding them with indexers. This includes the skeletons concatMap for nested traversal and filter for conditionally skipping elements. To retrieve a value at one index, one must compute some information about all lower indices, which wastes work. For instance, to look up the output at index 10, it's necessary to find the producers of all output elements up to index 10. The usual solution is to

precompute the necessary index information using a parallel scan, but because parallel scan is a multipass algorithm, fusion is impossible; all temporary values have to be saved to memory at some point.

Steppers   A stepper encoding is a coroutine that returns one data structure element each time it is run, until all elements have been extracted. Steppers are not parallelizable since it is only possible to retrieve the "next" element at any given time. In C++ and other imperative languages, readable forward traversal iterators play the role of steppers. The Haskell vector library, which provides high-performance sequential loops over arrays, uses the fusible stepper encoding presented by Coutts et al. [7]. In this encoding, a stepper is a data structure containing a suspended loop state and a function for stepping to the next loop iteration. The stepper function returns a result value holding the loop's result and the starting state of the next iteration, or else indicating that the last iteration has completed. Similarly to indexers, loop fusion extends a stepper with code that does further processing on the stepper's result and state.

Steppers are a fairly versatile sequential encoding. Their main drawback is that, although nested traversals are fusible, they are not reliably optimized to nested loops [7]. In our two Eden applications that use nested loops, using steppers was roughly a factor of two to five slower than imperative loop nests.

Folds   A data structure can be encoded as a function that folds over its elements in some predetermined order. The function calls a given worker function on each data structure element to update an accumulator. The list $[0, 1, 2]$ has the following fold encoding.

$$\lambda w \ z \to \textbf{let loop } i \ x = \textbf{if } i == 3$$
$$\textbf{then } x$$
$$\textbf{else loop } (i + 1) \ (w \ i \ x)$$
$$\textbf{in loop } 0 \ z$$

Its meaning is clearer after unrolling the loop to get $\lambda w \ z \to w \ 2 \ (w \ 1 \ (w \ 0 \ z))$, which calls w to update an accumulator with the values 0, 1, and 2 in turn. Nested traversals do not pose the same optimization trouble for folds that they do for steppers. In a nested traversal, the worker function passed into w calls another fold function that contains its own loop. Inlining moves the value of w to its callsite in the body of loop, bringing the inner fold function along to produce a nested loop.

Unlike indexers and steppers, the fold encoding offers no flexibility in execution order. A fold processes each data structure element in sequence without interruption. This inflexibility rules out fusion of zip skeletons, which pair up elements at corresponding indices in multiple data structures. A fused zip skeleton would read from each of several data structures in an interleaved fashion. It is a common pattern to store data in a structure-of-arrays format, then zip the arrays together in preparation for a loop that uses all the fields. Folds do not support this pattern.

Collectors A collector is an imperative variant of a fold. Instead of updating an accumulator, the worker function uses side effecting operations to update its output value. Collectors are used by Scala's collection library [20] and SkeTo [25]. Triolet uses collectors in sequential code for histogramming and for packing variable-length output skeletons' results into an array.

Conversions The rows of Figure 1 are ordered by how much the user of a virtual data structure can control its execution order. Indexers offer the greatest control, steppers offer less, and folds and collectors offer no control. A higher-control encoding can be converted to a lower-control one. Although no encoding supports zips and mutation, for instance, one could fuse histogram(n, map(f, zip(a, b))) by zipping and mapping over indexers, converting the result to a collector, and computing a histogram of the result. A collector that is created from indexer $\langle n, f \rangle$ loops over all indices up to n, calls f on each index, and passes the generated values to the worker function:

$$
\begin{aligned}
\mathsf{idxToColl} \, \langle n, f \rangle = \\
\quad \lambda w \; s \rightarrow \textbf{let } \mathrm{loop} \; i \; s_2 = \textbf{if } i == n \\
\qquad\qquad\qquad\qquad\qquad \textbf{then } s_2 \\
\qquad\qquad\qquad\qquad\qquad \textbf{else } \mathrm{loop} \; (i+1) \; (w \; (f \; i) \; s_2) \\
\quad \textbf{in } \mathrm{loop} \; 0 \; s
\end{aligned}
$$

However, this conversion removes the potential for parallelization, since a collector's use of side effects is not compatible with parallel execution.

Triolet's iterator library is layered on top of a library of fusible operations for manipulating each of these virtual data structures. We use conventional names for these library functions along with a subscript to indicate what encoding they are implemented for, e.g., $\mathsf{map}_{\mathsf{Idx}}$, $\mathsf{map}_{\mathsf{Step}}$, $\mathsf{map}_{\mathsf{Fold}}$, and $\mathsf{map}_{\mathsf{Coll}}$ are map functions over indexers, steppers, folds, and collectors. We use conversion functions named by their input and output encoding, such as $\mathsf{idxToColl}$.

3.2 Hybrid Iterators

There is at least one fusible encoding supporting every desirable feature in Figure 1, and this suggests that a hybrid encoding could overcome the limitations in the previous section. Triolet's iterator encoding represents a loop nest with either an indexer or stepper encoding at each nesting level. To illustrate, consider the computation of sum(filter(lambda x: x > 0), xs), which selects the positive numbers in array xs and sums them. Suppose xs has the value $[1, -2, -4, 1, 3, 4]$. The call to filter returns $[1, 1, 3, 4]$. For the implementation of sum, indexers are the only parallelizable, fusible form at our disposal so far. Using indexers, each thread is assigned a specific number of elements to process. For instance, one thread may sum the first

two values while the other sums the last two. Unfortunately, computing which index each output of filter resides at requires a complete pass through the data, making a fusible indexer encoding impossible.

A better fusion strategy is to partition the input array xs across threads and have each thread sequentially filter and sum one partition. The key to fusion is that our implementation of filter does not reassign indices, but rather produces either zero or one output at each index so that it is compatible with indexer-based parallelization and fusion. Conceptually, the call to filter transforms $[1, -2, -4, 1, 3, 4]$ into the nested list $[[1], [], [], [1], [3], [4]]$, then the call to sum partitions this nested list into $[[1], [], []]$ and $[[1], [3], [4]]$ and sums the two parts in parallel. By encoding the nested list as an indexer of steppers, we ensure that the filter computation is fused with the summation.

In general, a loop may have arbitrarily nested filter operations and/or traversals. Each level of nesting may produce a predetermined number of values using an indexer, or a variable number of values using a stepper. Thus an iterator can consist of an indexer containing values, a stepper containing values, an indexer containing iterators, or a stepper containing iterators. We name these cases IdxFlat, StepFlat, IdxNest, and StepNest and make them the constructors of the Iter data type:

$$
\begin{aligned}
\textbf{data } \mathsf{Iter} \; \alpha \; \textbf{where} \\
\quad \mathsf{IdxFlat} :: \mathsf{Idx} \; \alpha \rightarrow \mathsf{Iter} \; \alpha \\
\quad \mathsf{StepFlat} :: \mathsf{Step} \; \alpha \rightarrow \mathsf{Iter} \; \alpha \\
\quad \mathsf{IdxNest} :: \mathsf{Idx} \; (\mathsf{Iter} \; \alpha) \rightarrow \mathsf{Iter} \; \alpha \\
\quad \mathsf{StepNest} :: \mathsf{Step} \; (\mathsf{Iter} \; \alpha) \rightarrow \mathsf{Iter} \; \alpha
\end{aligned}
$$

Nested iterators can be understood as loop nests where all loops work together to produce a sequence of values.

Triolet's iterators are flexible enough to fuse all the difficult patterns in Figure 1, while also keeping indexer-based loops available so that they can be distributed across parallel tasks. Figure 2 shows Iter-based implementations of some common skeleton functions. The functions zip, filter, concatMap, and collect implement four of the five features from Figure 1. Section 3.4 addresses the remaining feature, parallelism. Reductions are illustrated by sum. Each function examines its input iterator's constructor (i.e., what loop structure was passed in), and executes code suitable for handling that loop structure. Thus, most functions in Figure 1 are defined by four equations, one for handling each constructor. A function's output loop structure is always determined solely by its input loop structure, ensuring that any composition of known function calls can be simplified statically. In the sum-of-filter example, iterating over the input array produces an IdxFlat term. The compiler inlines the implementation of filter for this form of iterator, which yields an IdxNest term as the argument to sum. The compiler inlines sum for this form of iterator, exposing a recursive call

$\mathsf{zip}\ (\mathsf{IdxFlat}\ xs)\ (\mathsf{IdxFlat}\ ys) = \mathsf{IdxFlat}\ (\mathsf{zip}_{\mathsf{Idx}}\ xs\ ys)$
$\mathsf{zip}\ xs\ ys = \mathsf{StepFlat}\ (\mathsf{zip}_{\mathsf{Step}}\ (\mathsf{toStep}\ xs)\ (\mathsf{toStep}\ ys))$
   where
       $\mathsf{toStep}\ (\mathsf{IdxFlat}\ xs) = \mathsf{idxToStep}\ xs$
       $\mathsf{toStep}\ (\mathsf{StepFlat}\ xs) = xs$
       $\mathsf{toStep}\ (\mathsf{IdxNest}\ xss) =$
          $\mathsf{concatMap}_{\mathsf{Step}}\ \mathsf{toStep}\ (\mathsf{idxToStep}\ xss)$
       $\mathsf{toStep}\ (\mathsf{StepNest}\ xss) = \mathsf{concatMap}_{\mathsf{Step}}\ \mathsf{toStep}\ xss$

$\mathsf{filter}\ f\ (\mathsf{IdxFlat}\ xs) =$
   $\mathsf{IdxNest}\ (\mathsf{map}_{\mathsf{Idx}}\ (\mathsf{StepFlat} \circ \mathsf{filter}_{\mathsf{Step}}\ f \circ \mathsf{unit}_{\mathsf{Step}})\ xs)$
$\mathsf{filter}\ f\ (\mathsf{StepFlat}\ xs) = \mathsf{StepFlat}\ (\mathsf{filter}_{\mathsf{Step}}\ f\ xs)$
$\mathsf{filter}\ f\ (\mathsf{IdxNest}\ xss) = \mathsf{IdxNest}\ (\mathsf{map}_{\mathsf{Idx}}\ (\mathsf{filter}\ f)\ xss)$
$\mathsf{filter}\ f\ (\mathsf{StepNest}\ xss) = \mathsf{StepNest}\ (\mathsf{map}_{\mathsf{Step}}\ (\mathsf{filter}\ f)\ xss)$

$\mathsf{concatMap}\ f\ (\mathsf{IdxFlat}\ xs) = \mathsf{IdxNest}\ (\mathsf{map}_{\mathsf{Idx}}\ f\ xs)$
$\mathsf{concatMap}\ f\ (\mathsf{StepFlat}\ xs) = \mathsf{StepNest}\ (\mathsf{map}_{\mathsf{Step}}\ f\ xs)$
$\mathsf{concatMap}\ f\ (\mathsf{IdxNest}\ xss) =$
   $\mathsf{IdxNest}\ (\mathsf{map}_{\mathsf{Idx}}\ (\mathsf{concatMap}\ f)\ xss)$
$\mathsf{concatMap}\ f\ (\mathsf{StepNest}\ xss) =$
   $\mathsf{StepNest}\ (\mathsf{map}_{\mathsf{Step}}\ (\mathsf{concatMap}\ f)\ xss)$

$\mathsf{collect}\ (\mathsf{IdxFlat}\ xs) = \mathsf{idxToColl}\ xs$
$\mathsf{collect}\ (\mathsf{StepFlat}\ xs) = \mathsf{stepToColl}\ xs$
$\mathsf{collect}\ (\mathsf{IdxNest}\ xss) =$
   $\lambda w\ s_1 \to \mathsf{idxToColl}\ xss\ (\lambda xs\ s_2 \to \mathsf{collect}\ xs\ w\ s_2)\ s_1$
$\mathsf{collect}\ (\mathsf{StepNest}\ xss) =$
   $\lambda w\ s_1 \to \mathsf{stepToColl}\ xss\ (\lambda xs\ s_2 \to \mathsf{collect}\ xs\ w\ s_2)\ s_1$

$\mathsf{sum}\ (\mathsf{IdxFlat}\ xs) = \mathsf{sum}_{\mathsf{Idx}}\ xs$
$\mathsf{sum}\ (\mathsf{StepFlat}\ xs) = \mathsf{sum}_{\mathsf{Step}}\ xs$
$\mathsf{sum}\ (\mathsf{IdxNest}\ xss) = \mathsf{sum}_{\mathsf{Idx}}\ (\mathsf{map}_{\mathsf{Idx}}\ \mathsf{sum}\ xss)$
$\mathsf{sum}\ (\mathsf{StepNest}\ xss) = \mathsf{sum}_{\mathsf{Step}}\ (\mathsf{map}_{\mathsf{Step}}\ \mathsf{sum}\ xss)$

Figure 2. Triolet iterator functions.

to sum that is also inlined:

$\mathsf{sum}\ (\mathsf{filter}\ f\ (\mathsf{IdxFlat}\ ys))$
$= \mathsf{sum}\ (\mathsf{IdxNest}\ (\mathsf{map}_{\mathsf{Idx}}\ (\mathsf{StepFlat} \circ \mathsf{filter}_{\mathsf{Step}}\ f \circ \mathsf{unit}_{\mathsf{Step}})\ ys))$
$= \mathsf{sum}_{\mathsf{Idx}}\ (\mathsf{map}_{\mathsf{Idx}}\ (\mathsf{sum} \circ \mathsf{StepFlat} \circ \mathsf{filter}_{\mathsf{Step}}\ f \circ \mathsf{unit}_{\mathsf{Step}})\ ys)$
$= \mathsf{sum}_{\mathsf{Idx}}\ (\mathsf{map}_{\mathsf{Idx}}\ (\mathsf{sum}_{\mathsf{Step}} \circ \mathsf{filter}_{\mathsf{Step}}\ f \circ \mathsf{unit}_{\mathsf{Step}})\ ys)$

Iterators are completely eliminated, leaving behind indexer and stepper code that further simplifies to a simple loop nest.

Zipping together two loops involves pairing up corresponding iterations. Since indexers allow elements to be retrieved by iteration number, flat indexers can be zipped into a new indexer. This preserves the potential parallelism in regular loops, such as when zipping arrays together. Other forms of iterator involve variable-length outputs and require scanning through outputs to find corresponding elements. These are zipped together sequentially using steppers. The variable-output functions filter and concatMap work similarly to each other. They add a level of loop nesting in order to preserve potential outer-loop parallelism and avoid the overhead of stepper-based nested traversals. Functions that consume iterators, like collect and sum, transform each level of nesting into a loop.

The functions in Figure 2 need to be inlined to enable subsequent optimizations. Compilers are normally reluctant to inline recursive functions, as doing so can blow up code size and/or execution time. We implement constructor-aware inlining control to inline recursive functions only when it would benefit subsequent optimization. We manually annotate library functions that should be inlined only when the compiler knows their Iter argument's constructor, which ensures that inlining only occurs when it would expose further optimization opportunities. Inlining eventually terminates because each level of recursion consumes one level of statically known loop nesting.

3.3 Multidimensional Iterators

So far, the Iter data type is good for variable-length and nested looping patterns, but is awkward for looping over multidimensional arrays. On the other hand, indexer-based libraries like Repa and loop-based functional languages like Single Assignment C are well-suited to loops over multidimensional arrays, but they do not support fusion of irregular loops. This section generalizes Iter for multidimensional loops and arrays.

Matrix transposition is an example of an algorithm that is awkward to write using one-dimensional arrays. The transpose of a matrix A can be defined by giving a loop that retrieves input matrix element `A[x,y]` for a given output position (`y`, `x`). For a given matrix A whose dimensions are `w` and `h`, this would be written `[A[x,y] for (y, x) in arrayRange((0,0), (h, w))]`. The functions `map` (implicitly called by the comprehension) and `arrayRange` are overloaded for multidimensional iteration spaces.

Simulating a multidimensional loop using one-dimensional iterators would introduce overhead. Expressing transposition in flattened form, using a 1D loop over a 1D array, would require expensive division and modulus operations to reconstruct the 2D indices x and y from a 1D loop index. Alternatively, using an array of arrays adds an additional pointer indirection to subsequent lookups.

We introduce a type class called Domain to characterize index spaces. Each index space is a type that is a member of Domain. One-dimensional organizations of data, as we have been discussing up until now, have type Seq. A value of type Seq holds an array length. Two-dimensional arrays have a width and a height, so a two-dimensional domain Dim2 holds a pair of integers.

data $\mathsf{Seq} = \mathsf{Seq}\ \mathsf{Int}$
data $\mathsf{Dim2} = \mathsf{Dim2}\ \mathsf{Int}\ \mathsf{Int}$

Each domain type d has an associated type Index d whose values identify individual indices within a domain. An Index Seq is an Int and an Index Dim2 is an $\langle\mathsf{Int}, \mathsf{Int}\rangle$.

Functions that deal with the indices represented by a domain, for instance by looping over a domain's indices, are overloaded for different domain types. The definition of class Domain, below, lists overloaded types and functions that are used in this paper.

class Domain d **where**
    type Index d
    idxToFold :: $(\alpha \to \beta \to \beta) \to \beta \to$ Idx $d\ \alpha \to \beta$
    idxToColl :: $(\alpha \to$ State $\to$ State$) \to$ Idx $d\ \alpha \to$
                State $\to$ State
    zipWith :: $(\alpha \to \beta \to \gamma) \to$ Iter $d\ \alpha \to$ Iter $d\ \beta \to$
                 Iter $d\ \gamma$

The functions idxToFold and idxToColl convert an indexer to a fold or collector that loops over all points in the domain. The function zipWith visits all points in the intersection of two domains.

We also generalize Idx to arbitrary domains d:

type Idx $d\ \alpha = \langle d,$ Index $d \to \alpha \rangle$

Finally, we generalize Iter over arbitrary domains. Every Idx α is converted to a Idx $d\ \alpha$, producing the following generalized algebraic data type.

data Iter $d\ \alpha$ **where**
    IdxFlat :: Idx $d\ \alpha \to$ Iter $d\ \alpha$
    StepFlat :: Step $\alpha \to$ Iter Seq α
    IdxNest :: Domain $d \Rightarrow$ Idx d (Iter Seq $\alpha) \to$ Iter Seq α
    StepNest :: Step (Iter Seq $\alpha) \to$ Iter Seq α

Only the IdxFlat constructor can create iterators of arbitrary domain types. It simply allows an Idx $d\ \alpha$ to be used through the Iter interface. The other three constructors contain variable-length traversals, which do not preserve array dimensionality—removing arbitrary elements of a 2D array does not in general yield a 2D array, for instance—so it does not make sense for them to build multidimensional iterators.

3.4 Parallelism

Triolet's runtime uses Threading Building Blocks for thread parallelism and MPI for distributed parallelism. We implement wrapper functions that expose these interfaces as generic parallel skeletons. On top of these wrappers, we layer high-level skeletons that allow users to select what degree of parallelism to use.

We add a field to Iter holding a flag to indicate what degree of parallelism to use. Users designate an iterator as parallel by calling `localpar` (for thread parallelism) or `par` (for distributed and thread parallelism) on it, thereby setting the flag. Parallel skeletons inspect the flag and invoke the appropriate distributed, threaded, and sequential functions. For instance, a distributed-parallel histogram performs a distributed reduction, which performs one threaded reduction per node, which sequentially builds one histogram per thread.

Triolet includes runtime facilities for serializing and deserializing objects to byte arrays. The compiler automatically generates serialization code from the definitions of algebraic data types. Functions are represented by heap-allocated closures and are also serialized. Serializing an object transitively serializes all objects that it references. Pointers to global data are serialized as a segment identifier and offset. Since the majority of serialized data typically resides in pointer-free arrays, such arrays are serialized using a block copy to minimize serialization time.

3.5 Array partitioning

In parallel array traversals, the library identifies what array subset a task will use and extracts the subset to send over the network. Consider the loop `sum(par(xs))`. If parallelized on two nodes, each node should receive half of the array xs. Iterating over xs produces an indexer function $\lambda i \to xs[i]$ that reads an element of xs, and loop fusion merges this with additional code from `sum`. Using the compiler-generated serialization, when the function is serialized and sent to cluster nodes, the function's reference to xs would drag the entire array along with it.

We enhance the functionality of indexers so that the library can partition arrays that are traversed in parallel. First, we reorganize indexers' lookup functions into a (potentially large) data source and a value-extracting function. In the example, the function $\lambda i \to xs[i]$ is reorganized into the source array xs and an extractor that takes the source as an additional parameter, $\lambda xs\ i \to xs[i]$. This function is cheap to serialize since it does not directly reference the array.

Then, we extend the indexer type with a method for extracting a data subset or *slice*. An indexer's slice method builds a new indexer whose data source holds only the data used by the extracted slice. When a distributed parallel loop partitions work across nodes, it extracts and sends the slice needed for each node's chunk of work. The slice extraction process extracts subarrays, which are serialized and sent by the runtime. This approach is flexible enough to efficiently handle common cases of regular array traversal. No copying overhead is introduced in inner loops since data sources are used in-place and an indexer's functions are typically inlined into their use sites. Data sources may involve multiple arrays, such as in the result of a call to `zip` or `outerproduct`, without requiring a step of data copying and reorganization.

4. Evaluation

To show how a solid skeleton framework can deliver high performance without burdening programmers, we have converted four Parboil benchmarks [24] into Triolet, Eden and C+MPI+OpenMP. For each benchmark, we normalize performance as speedup against sequential C to provide a measure of absolute performance. As a highly efficient implementation layer, the C+MPI+OpenMP serves as a useful reference point against which to evaluate the scalability and

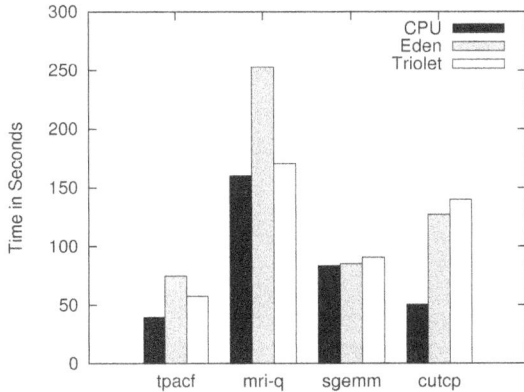

Figure 3. Sequential execution time of benchmarks.

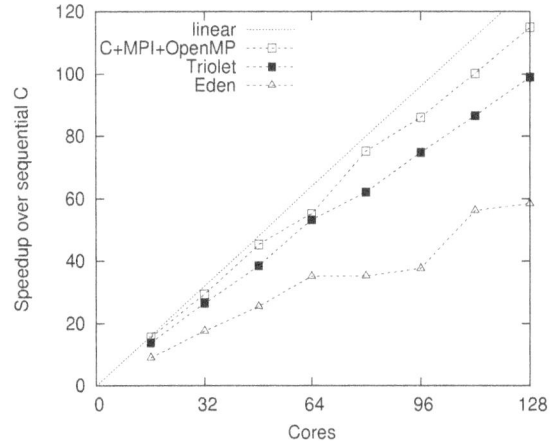

Figure 4. Scalability and performance of `mri-q` implemented in different languages.

parallel overhead of the high-level languages. We measure sequential execution time (Figure 3) to compare the efficiency of the code without communication overhead. We use similar parallelization strategies across languages in order to reveal the overhead imposed by each language.

C code is compiled with GCC 4.7.3 -O3. Eden code is compiled with GHC-Eden 7.6.1 -O2 with LLVM 3.2 as the backend. All three versions use OpenMPI as a distributed communication layer. Tests are run on a group of 8 Amazon EC2 cluster compute nodes with two 8-core Xeon E5-2670 processors per node (a total of 16 cores per node). Hyperthreading is disabled. Parboil includes a range of input problem sizes for each benchmark. We select data sets with a sequential C running time between 20 and 200 seconds. This is large enough for the C+MPI+OpenMP code to scale up to the full test system. Parallel times are the average of 5 runs.

4.1 Eden Overview

Eden is a distributed parallel extension of the Glasgow Haskell Compiler (GHC) [15]. Eden uses either MPI or PVM to create and communicate among parallel execution contexts. Processes do not share memory.

We write parallel loops using map and reduce skeletons with sequential tasks that manipulate unboxed arrays. In array manipulation code, we follow a high-level Haskell programming style using the vector and Repa libraries where possible. Where this is inefficient, we rewrite tasks to use imperative loops and mutable arrays: for nested loops that build histograms in `tpacf` and `cutcp`, and for performing random-access array writes when building a 2D array from subarrays in `sgemm`.

We implement parallel skeletons that use a two-level work distribution similar to Triolet and C+MPI+OpenMP. The main process distributes work to one process in each node, which further distributes work to other processes in the same node. This avoids the communication bottleneck with the main process in Eden's skeleton library, where the main process directly communicates with all other processes.

4.2 MRI-Q

The main loop of `mri-q` computes a non-uniform 3D inverse Fourier transform to create a 3D image. This computation is straightforward to parallelize. In Triolet, it can be distilled down to the following two lines of code.

```
[sum(ftcoeff(k, r) for k in ks)
  for r in par(zip3(x, y, z))]
```

This consists of a parallel map over image pixels, summing contributions from all frequency-domain samples. Although this code contains only a call to `par` to control parallelization, it yields parallel performance nearly on par with manually written MPI and OpenMP (Figure 4).

In Eden, we build arrays in chunked form, as lists of 1k-element vectors, so that the runtime can distribute subarrays to processors while still benefiting from efficient array traversal. Unfortunately, Eden loses performance across the entire range. Eden's backend misses a floating-point optimization on `sinf` and `cosf` calls, resulting in about 50% longer run time on a single thread (Figure 3). While Eden scales fairly well, tasks occasionally run significantly slower than normal. With more nodes, it is more likely that a task will be delayed, reducing the observed scalability.

C+MPI+OpenMP is the most verbose, dedicating more code to partitioning data across MPI ranks than to the actual numerical computation. While `mri-q`'s communication pattern fits MPI's scatter, gather, and broadcast primitives, these were not as efficient as the Triolet code; the fastest version used nonblocking, point-to-point messaging.

4.3 SGEMM

The scaled product αAB of two 4k by 4k-element matrices is computed in `sgemm`. We parallelize the multiplication after transposing matrices so that the innermost loop accesses contiguous matrix elements.

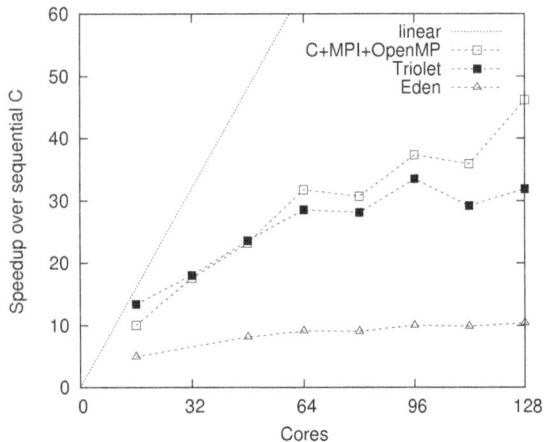

Figure 5. Scalability and performance of `sgemm` implemented in different languages.

```
 1  def correlation(size, pairs):
 2      values = (score(size, u, v)
 3                   for (u, v) in pairs))
 4      return histogram(size, values)
 5
 6  def randomSetsCorrelation(size, corr1, rands):
 7      empty = [0 for i in range(size)]
 8      def add(h1, h2):
 9          return [x + y for (x, y) in zip(h1, h2)]
10      return reduce(add, empty,
11                   par(corr1(r) for r in rands))
12
13  def selfCorrelations(size, obs, rands):
14      def corr1(rand):
15          indexed_rand = zip(indices(domain(rand)), rand)
16          pairs = localpar((u, v)
17                   for (i, u) in indexed_rand
18                   for v in rand[i+1:])
19          return correlation(size, pairs)
20      return randomSetsCorrelation(size, corr1, rands)
```

Figure 6. Triolet code of `tpacf`'s self-correlation loop

All three versions use a 2D block-based parallel decomposition that sends each worker only the input matrix rows that it needs to compute its output block. As discussed in Section 2, this data decomposition can be written using Triolet's `rows` and `outerproduct` library functions. Similar decompositions are written as part of the parallel C+MPI+OpenMP and Eden code. This took over 120 lines of code in each language, adding development complexity and detracting from the code's readability.

Transposition is a sequential bottleneck in Eden since it does too little work to parallelize profitably on distributed memory. We parallelize it over shared memory on a single node in Triolet and C+MPI+OpenMP. At 128 cores, transposition takes 35% of Eden's execution time.

All versions of the code exhibit limited scalability due to transposition time and communication time (Figure 5). C+MPI+OpenMP and Triolet spend similar amounts of time in communication and in parallel computation, resulting in similar performance. Triolet's performance stops rising toward 8 nodes as it spends more time constructing messages. At 8 nodes, 40% of Triolet's overhead relative to C+MPI+OpenMP is attributable to the garbage collector [3], which is slow when allocating objects comprising tens of megabytes. The garbage collection overhead was determined by comparing to the run time when libc `malloc` was substituted for garbage-collected memory allocation. The Eden code fails at 2 nodes because the array data is too large for Eden's message-passing runtime to buffer.

4.4 TPACF

The `tpacf` application analyzes the angular distribution of observed astronomical objects. It uses histogramming and nested traversals, presenting a challenge for conventional fusion frameworks. Three histograms are computed using different inputs. One loop compares an observed data set with itself; one compares it with several random data sets;

and one compares each random data set with itself. We parallelize across data sets and across elements of a data set.

Triolet allows the common code of the three loops to be factored out and written once. The function on lines 1–4 of Figure 6) contains the common part of all three histogram computations, dealing with correlating pairs of values taken from a pair of data sets. This code maps `score` over all given pairs of objects to compute a similarity between members of each pair and collects the results into a new histogram. On lines 6–11, `randomSetsCorrelation` computes a parallel histogram over a collection of random data sets. Parameter `corr1` computes a histogram from one random data set, and `rands` is an array of random data sets. The function body consists of a parallel reduction that computes histograms of individual data sets and adds them together.

The `selfCorrelations` of random data sets are computed in lines 13–20. The function `corr1` computes the self-correlation of one data set `rand` (lines 14–18). Self-correlation examines all unique pairs of values (`rand[i]`, `rand[j]`) where j > i. Lines 15–18 define a triangular loop building all unique pairs of elements (u, v) from `rand`. Line 19 computes a correlation histogram from these pairs. Line 20 runs `corr1` in parallel over the random data sets and sums the generated histograms. The other two parallel histogramming loops are defined similarly to `selfCorrelation`.

Triolet abstracts away the number of threads in the system, while the Eden and C+MPI+OpenMP contain additional code to adapt to the number of threads. The Eden code subdivides data in order to produce enough work to occupy all threads. The C+MPI+OpenMP code examines the number of threads in order to privatize histograms. For a pro-

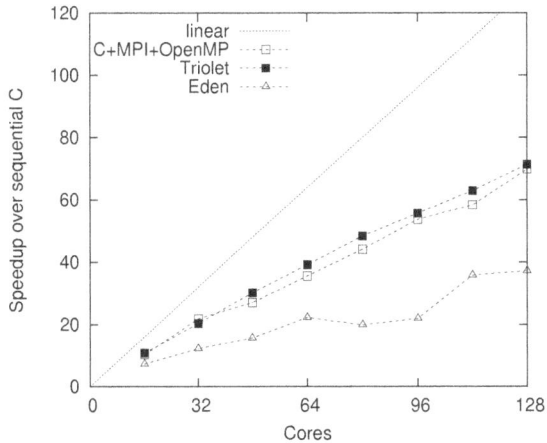

Figure 7. Scalability and performance of `tpacf` implemented in different languages.

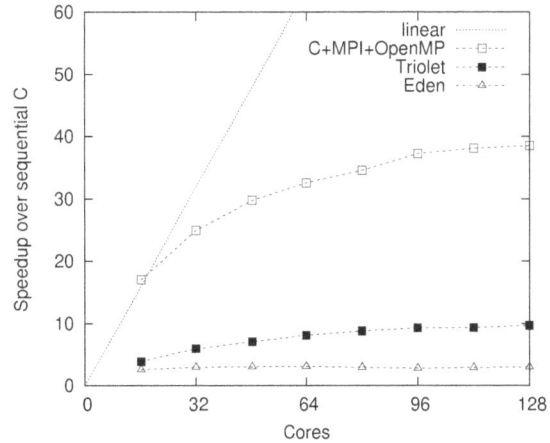

Figure 8. Scalability and performance of `cutcp` implemented in different languages.

grammer, identifying and inserting this code entails one or more iterations of performance optimization.

Triolet and C+MPI+OpenMP scale similarly (Figure 7). Triolet is slightly faster due to a more even distribution of computation time across nodes. Eden has somewhat worse sequential performance and a higher communication overhead.

4.5 CUTCP

The `cutcp` benchmark is taken from a molecular modeling application. It computes the electrostatic potential induced by a collection of charged atoms at all points on a grid. An atom's charge affects the potential at grid points within a distance c. The body of the computation is essentially a floating-point histogram: it loops over atoms, loops over nearby grid points, skips points that are not within distance c, and updates the grid at the remaining points. This computation is done by nested loops and conditionals in the C code or nested traversals in Triolet. Subsets of atoms are processed in parallel.

Performance of Triolet and C+MPI+OpenMP saturates quickly (Figure 8), as the overhead of summing the large output arrays dominates execution time. As in `sgemm`, Triolet has significant garbage collection overhead. Approximately 60% of Triolet's execution time at 8 nodes arises from allocation overhead.

5. Related Work

The use of higher-order functions as a parallel programming interface has a long history. Vector parallel languages extract fine-grained parallel loops from programs, then fuse them into larger tasks [2, 6]. The vector execution model maximizes load balancing and parallelism in irregular workloads, sometimes at the cost of high communication and memory overheads. Later work reduces these overheads in some

cases [4, 9]. Another line of development follows a *loop* execution model [8, 12, 23], related to or based on indexers.

Loop fusion has been achieved through iteration-based loop transformations [8, 23], compile-time deforestation [28], expression rewriting [2, 9, 18, 20], and virtual data structures [7, 12]. Delite [20] performs compiler-driven fusion and parallelization of nested traversals.

Algorithmic skeletons abstract out the communication and coordination aspects of parallel programs. Gonzalez [10] surveys recent work on algorithmic skeletons. Triolet's programming model is most similar to the data-parallel, distributed, functional algorithmic skeleton frameworks HDC [11], PMLS [22], and Eden [15]. These frameworks incorporate compile-time generation or library implementations of skeleton code for higher-order functions. Eden also provides low-level primitives for implementing new skeletons. These frameworks do not address irregular loops, do not combine shared memory with message passing, and (in PMLS and Eden) do not provide skeletons for array computation.

6. Conclusion

Functional algorithmic skeletons are a simple, high-level interface to parallel programming, but their overhead relative to lower-level programming models has limited their usefulness. Triolet demonstrates that the most severe performance limitations can be eliminated, yielding superior performance without increased programming complexity. On code that is not communication-bound, performance rivals that of C with MPI and OpenMP. The necessary changes to runtime behavior are familiar to low-level programmers: storing data in arrays, fusing loops, partitioning arrays across distributed tasks, and utilizing shared memory and in-place array updates. Triolet allows skeletons to make those changes under the hood through library enhancements, coupled with compiler and runtime support for data serialization and shared memory parallelism.

Acknowledgments

This project was partly supported by the STARnet Center for Future Architecture Research (C-FAR) and the DoE Vancouver Project (DE-FC02-10ER26004/DE-SC0005515).

References

[1] N. Bell and J. Hoberock. Thrust: A productivity-oriented library for CUDA. *GPU Computing Gems Jade Edition*, page 359, 2011.

[2] G. Blelloch, J. Hardwick, J. Sipelstein, M. Zagha, and S. Chatterjee. Implementation of a portable nested data-parallel language. *Journal of Parallel and Distributed Computing*, 21(1): 4–14, 1994.

[3] H. Boehm and M. Weiser. Garbage collection in an uncooperative environment. *Software—Practice & Experience*, 18(9): 807–820, 1988.

[4] B. Catanzaro, M. Garland, and K. Keutzer. Copperhead: Compiling an embedded data parallel language. In *Proc. ACM Symposium on Principles and Practice of Parallel Programming*, pages 47–56, 2011.

[5] M. Chakravarty and G. Keller. Functional array fusion. In *Proc. ACM International Conference on Functional Programming*, pages 205–216, 2001.

[6] M. Chakravarty, R. Leshchinskiy, S. Peyton Jones, G. Keller, and S. Marlow. Data Parallel Haskell: A status report. In *Proc. Workshop on Declarative Aspects of Multicore Programming*, pages 10–18, 2007.

[7] D. Coutts, R. Leshchinskiy, and D. Stewart. Stream fusion: From lists to streams to nothing at all. In *Proc. ACM International Conference on Functional Programming*, pages 315–326, 2007.

[8] J. T. Feo, D. C. Cann, and R. R. Oldehoeft. A report on the sisal language project. *Journal of Parallel and Distributed Computing*, 10(4):349–366, 1990.

[9] M. Fluet, M. Rainey, J. Reppy, and A. Shaw. Implicitly threaded parallelism in manticore. *Journal of Functional Programming*, 20(5–6):537–576, 2010.

[10] H. González-Vélez and M. Leyton. A survey of algorithmic skeleton frameworks: high-level structured parallel programming enablers. *Software: Practice and Experience*, 40(12): 1135–1160, 2010.

[11] C. Herrmann and C. Lengauer. HDC: A higher-order language for divide-and-conquer. *Parallel Processing Letters*, 10(2–3): 239–250, 2000.

[12] G. Keller, M. Chakravarty, R. Leshchinskiy, S. Peyton Jones, and B. Lippmeier. Regular, shape-polymorphic, parallel arrays in Haskell. In *Proc. ACM International Conference on Functional Programming*, pages 261–272, 2010.

[13] K. Kennedy and K. McKinley. Maximizing loop parallelism and improving data locality via loop fusion and distribution. In *Proc. International Workshop on Languages and Compilers for Parallel Computing*, pages 301–320, 1994.

[14] H.-W. Loidl, F. Rubio, N. Scaife, K. Hammond, S. Horiguchi, U. Klusik, R. Loogen, G. Michaelson, R. Peña, S. Priebe, Á. Rebón, and P. Trinder. Comparing parallel functional languages: Programming and performance. *Higher-Order and Symbolic Computation*, 16(3):203–251, 2003.

[15] R. Loogen, Y. Ortega-mallén, and R. Peña-marí. Parallel functional programming in Eden. *Journal of Functional Programming*, 15(3):431–475, 2005.

[16] E. Meijer. Confessions of a used programming language salesman. In *Proc. ACM Conference on Object-oriented Programming, Systems, Languages, and Applications*, pages 677–694, 2007.

[17] S. Peyton Jones. Compiling Haskell by program transformation: A report from the trenches. In *Proc. European Symposium on Programming*, pages 18–44, 1996.

[18] S. Peyton Jones, A. Tolmach, and T. Hoare. Playing by the rules: Rewriting as a practical optimisation technique in GHC. In *Proc. ACM Haskell Workshop*, pages 203–233, 2001.

[19] A. Prokopec, T. Rompf, P. Bagwell, and M. Odersky. A generic parallel collection framework. In *Euro-Par'11: Proceedings of the International Conference on Parallel Processing*, pages 136–147, 2011.

[20] T. Rompf, A. Sujeeth, N. Amin, K. Brown, V. Jovanovic, H. Lee, M. Jonnalagedda, K. Olukotun, and M. Odersky. Optimizing data structures in high-level programs: new directions for extensible compilers based on staging. In *Proc. ACM Symposium on Principles of Programming Languages*, pages 497–510, 2013.

[21] N. Scaife, G. Michaelson, and S. Horiguchi. Comparative cross-platform performance results from a parallelizing SML compiler. In *Proc. International Workshop on Implementation of Functional Languages*, pages 138–154, 2002.

[22] N. Scaife, S. Horiguchi, and G. M. P. Bristow. A parallel SML compiler based on algorithmic skeletons. *Journal of Functional Programming*, (4):615–650, 2005.

[23] S.-B. Scholz. Single Assignment C—efficient support for high-level array operations in a functional setting. *Journal of Functional Programming*, 3(6):1005–1059, 2003.

[24] J. Stratton, C. Rodrigues, I.-J. Sung, N. Obeid, L.-W. Chang, N. Anssari, G. Liu, and W.-M. Hwu. Parboil: A revised benchmark suite for scientific and commercial throughput computing. Technical Report IMPACT-12-01, University of Illinois at Urbana-Champaign, 2012.

[25] H. Tanno and H. Iwasaki. Parallel skeletons for variable-length lists in SkeTo skeleton library. In *Euro-Par 2009 Parallel Processing*, volume 5704 of *Lecture Notes in Computer Science*, pages 666–677. 2009.

[26] D. Tarditi, G. Morrisett, P. Cheng, C. Stone, R. Harper, and P. Lee. TIL: A type-directed optimizing compiler for ML. In *Proc. ACM Conference on Programming Language Design and Implementation*, pages 181–192, 1996.

[27] P. Wadler. List comprehensions. In S. Peyton Jones, editor, *The Implementation of Functional Programming Languages*, pages 127–138. Prentice Hall, 1987.

[28] P. Wadler. Deforestation: transforming programs to eliminate trees. *Theoretical Computer Science*, 73(2):231–248, 1988.

A Tool to Analyze the Performance of Multithreaded Programs on NUMA Architectures

Xu Liu   John Mellor-Crummey

Department of Computer Science MS 132, Rice University
P.O.Box 1892, Houston, TX 77251-1892
{xl10, johnmc}@rice.edu

Abstract

Almost all of today's microprocessors contain memory controllers and directly attach to memory. Modern multiprocessor systems support non-uniform memory access (NUMA): it is faster for a microprocessor to access memory that is directly attached than it is to access memory attached to another processor. Without careful distribution of computation and data, a multithreaded program running on such a system may have high average memory access latency. To use multiprocessor systems efficiently, programmers need performance tools to guide the design of NUMA-aware codes. To address this need, we enhanced the HPCToolkit performance tools to support measurement and analysis of performance problems on multiprocessor systems with multiple NUMA domains. With these extensions, HPCToolkit helps pinpoint, quantify, and analyze NUMA bottlenecks in executions of multithreaded programs. It computes derived metrics to assess the severity of bottlenecks, analyzes memory accesses, and provides a wealth of information to guide NUMA optimization, including information about how to distribute data to reduce access latency and minimize contention. This paper describes the design and implementation of our extensions to HPCToolkit. We demonstrate their utility by describing case studies in which we use these capabilities to diagnose NUMA bottlenecks in four multithreaded applications.

Categories and Subject Descriptors C.4 [*Performance of systems*]: Measurement techniques, Performance attributes; D.2.8 [*Metrics*]: Performance measures.

Keywords profiler, threads, NUMA, performance optimization, memory access pattern.

1. Introduction

As microprocessors have become faster and multiple cores per chip have become the norm, memory bandwidth has become an increasingly critical rate-limiting factor for system performance. For multiprocessor systems, scaling memory bandwidth proportional to processing power has led to designs in which microprocessors include memory controllers on chip. As a result, the aggregate memory bandwidth of systems scales with the number of microprocessors.

Multiprocessor systems in which some memory is locally-attached to each processor are known as Non-Uniform Memory Access (NUMA) architectures because it is faster for a microprocessor to access memory that is locally attached rather than memory attached to another processor. Some microprocessors, e.g., IBM's POWER7 [29], have NUMA organizations on-chip as well, with some cores having lower latency access to some directly-attached cache and/or memory banks than others. To simplify discussion of systems where NUMA effects may exist within and/or between microprocessors, we simply refer to cache/memory along with all CPU cores that can access it with uniform latency as a *NUMA domain*. There is not only a difference in latency when accessing data in local vs. remote NUMA domains, there is also a difference in bandwidth: cores typically have significantly higher bandwidth access to local cache/memory than remote.

Systems with multiple NUMA domains are challenging to program efficiently. Without careful design, multithreaded programs may experience significant performance losses when running on systems with multiple NUMA domains if they access remote data too frequently. On such systems, multithreaded programs achieve best performance when threads are bound to specific cores and each thread mostly processes data co-located in the same NUMA domain as the core in which it executes. In addition to latency, contention can also hurt the performance of multithreaded programs. If many of the data accesses performed by a mul-

PPoPP '14, February 15–19, 2014, Orlando, Florida, USA.
Copyright is held by the owner/author(s). Publication rights licensed to ACM.
ACM 978-1-4503-2656-8/14/02. . . $15.00.
http://dx.doi.org/10.1145/2555243.2555271

tithreaded program are remote, contention for limited bandwidth between NUMA domains can be a bottleneck. This problem can be particularly acute if a large data array is mapped to a single NUMA domain and many threads compete for the limited bandwidth in and out of that domain. This situation is more common than one might think. By default, today's Linux systems employ a "first-touch" policy to bind pages of memory newly-allocated from the operating system to memory banks directly attached to the NUMA domain where the thread that first accesses the page resides. As a result, if a single thread initializes a data array, but multiple threads process the data later, severe contention can arise.

Tailoring a program for efficient execution on systems with multiple NUMA domains requires identifying and adjusting data and computation layouts to minimize each thread's use of remote data and avoid contention for bandwidth between NUMA domains. Due to the myriad of opportunities for mis-steps, tools that can provide insight into NUMA-related performance losses are essential for guiding optimization of multithreaded programs.

There are two broad classes of techniques for identifying NUMA bottlenecks in a program: simulation and measurement. Tools such as MACPO [25] and NUMAgrind [32] use simulation to identify NUMA bottlenecks in a program. A drawback of tools that simulate all memory accesses is that they are slow, which makes them of limited use for programs with significant running time. To address this shortcoming, a new class of tools, e.g., ThreadSpotter [26], apply simulation sparingly to selected memory accesses to reduce execution overhead.

In contrast, measurement-based tools, such as TAU [27], Intel Vtune Amplifier [11], IBM Visual Performance Analyzer (VPA) [10], AMD CodeAnalyst [2], and CrayPat [8] can gather data to provide insight into NUMA performance at much lower cost. On today's microprocessor-based systems, such tools can monitor NUMA-related events using a microprocessor's on-chip Performance Monitoring Unit (PMU). These tools measure and aggregate NUMA-related events and associate them with source code contexts, such as functions and statements. We call this approach *code-centric analysis*. A shortcoming of code-centric measurement and analysis is that it often fails to provide enough guidance for NUMA optimization [24]. *Data-centric analysis* tools, which can provide deeper insight into NUMA bottlenecks, use advanced PMU capabilities to gather instruction and data address pairs to associate instructions that access memory with the variables that they touch. Existing data-centric tools, such as HPCToolkit [19–21], Memphis [24] and MemProf [15] can identify both instructions and variables that suffer from NUMA problems.

There are three principal shortcomings of existing tools for measurement-based data-centric analysis. First, since PMU support for data-centric analysis differs significantly across microprocessors from different vendors and even pro-

cessor generations, most data-centric tools only support only a single family of PMU designs. Second, these tools do not assess the impact of NUMA bottlenecks on overall program performance. Without such information, one may invest significant effort to improve the design of a code for NUMA systems to address measured inefficiencies and net only a small performance gain. Finally, while existing tools can identify NUMA-related bottlenecks, they fail to provide information to guide NUMA-aware code optimization.

To address these shortcomings, we developed a lightweight tool for measurement and analysis of performance problems on multicore and multiprocessor systems with multiple NUMA domains. Our profiler outperforms existing tools in three ways. First, our tool is widely applicable to nearly all modern microprocessor-based architectures. Second, we define several derived metrics that can be computed by tools to assess the severity of NUMA bottlenecks. These metrics can effectively identify whether NUMA-related performance losses in a program are significant enough to warrant optimization. Third, our tool analyzes memory accesses and provides a wealth of information to guide NUMA optimization, including information about how and where to distribute data to maximize local accesses and reduce memory bandwidth contention.

We describe case studies using four well-known multithreaded codes that highlight the capabilities of our tool and demonstrate their utility. For three of the programs, our tool provided unique insights unavailable with other tools. These guided us to code changes that yielded non-trivial performance improvements. In the course of our studies, we found, somewhat surprisingly, that stack variables sometimes play a significant role in NUMA bottlenecks. Another case study demonstrates the utility of our novel metrics for assessing the severity of NUMA bottlenecks.

The rest of the paper is organized as follows. Section 2 describes NUMA problems and introduces NUMA optimization strategies. Section 3 describes hardware support for data-centric measurement in modern microprocessors, which provides the foundation for our tool. Section 4 describes derived metrics our tool computes to quantify the impact of NUMA-related performance losses. Section 5 shows how we attribute metrics with different views for NUMA analysis. Section 6 describes how we efficiently pinpoint locations in the source code that need modification to effect NUMA-aware data distributions. Section 7 describes the implementation of our tool. Section 8 presents case studies that illustrate the use of our tool to identify and fix NUMA-related bottlenecks in four multithreaded programs. Section 9 discusses previous work on tools for NUMA performance analysis and distinguishes our work. Finally, Section 10 summarizes our conclusions and plans for future work.

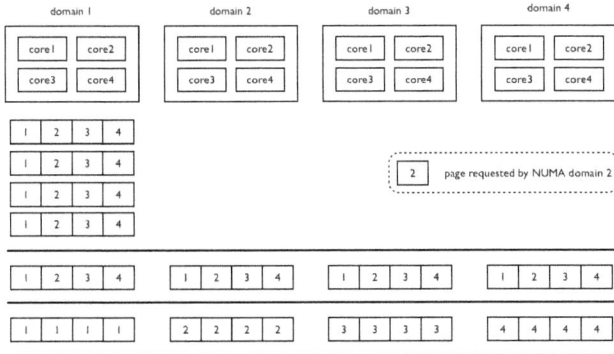

Figure 1. Three common data distributions in a program on a NUMA architecture. The first distribution allocates all data in NUMA domain 1. It suffers from both locality and bandwidth problems. The second distribution maps data to each of the NUMA domains and avoids centralized contention. The third distribution co-locates data with computation, which both maximizes low-latency local accesses and reduces bandwidth contention.

2. NUMA-aware program design

There are two causes of NUMA bottlenecks: excessive remote accesses and uneven distribution of requests to different NUMA domains. In modern processors, remote accesses have more than 30% higher latency than local accesses [28]. If one co-locates data in the same NUMA domain with a thread that manipulates it most frequently, the program can benefit from the fast local accesses. We use the term *co-location* to refer to the process of mapping part or all of a data object and the thread that accesses it most frequently to the same NUMA domain.

On the other hand, uneven distribution of memory accesses to NUMA domains can lead to contention and unnecessary bandwidth saturation in both on-chip and off-chip interconnects, caches, and memory controllers. Contention for interconnect and memory controller bandwidth has been observed to increase memory access latency by as much as a factor of five [7]. Instead of mapping large data objects to a single NUMA domain, in many cases one can reduce contention and associated bandwidth saturation by distributing large data objects across all NUMA domains. We call this optimization *contention reduction*.

Figure 1 illustrates various strategies for mapping data to NUMA domains and discusses the latency, contention, and performance issues associated with alternative distributions. One can identify excessive remote accesses to program data objects by measuring NUMA-related events using techniques described in the next section. One can identify contention by counting requests to different NUMA domains. Co-locating data and computation is the most powerful optimization as it reduces the need for bandwidth to remote domains, reduces bandwidth contention, and reduces latency by exploiting the lower latency and higher bandwidth access to local data. In cases where there is not a fixed binding between threads and data and/or concurrent computations may focus on only parts of a data object at a time, then using memory interleaving to avoid contention for a single NUMA domain may be beneficial. However, in some cases, using interleaving to balance memory requests to NUMA domains may hurt locality and performance [15, 21].

When data objects are not allocated using interleaved memory pages, the Linux "first touch" policy binds a new memory page obtained from the OS to a physical page frame managed by a memory controller when the page is first read or written. To ensure that data will be mapped to the proper NUMA domain, one must carefully design code that first touches each of the principal data structures in a multi-threaded program. To control allocation without completely refactoring an application, one can introduce an initialization pass right after a variable is allocated to control its page distribution.

To help application developers tailor a program for NUMA systems, application developers need tools that

- pinpoint the variables suffering from uneven memory requests, so one can use different allocation methods (e.g., interleaved allocation) to balance the memory requests,

- analyze the access patterns across threads to guide NUMA locality optimization, and

- identify where data pages are bounded to NUMA domains.

To our knowledge, no prior profiling tool provides all of these capabilities. In the next section, we describe address samplng—a key technique needed to build tools with these desired capabilities.

3. Address sampling

Address sampling, which involves collecting instruction and data address pairs to associate memory references with the data that they touch, is essential for profiling NUMA access patterns. PMUs on most recent processors from AMD, Intel, and IBM support address sampling. A processor can support efficient NUMA profiling *iff* it has the following three capabilities.

- It can record the effective address touched by a sampled instruction that accesses memory. It is important for this support to guarantee that memory accesses are uniformly sampled.

- It can sample memory-related events, such as load/store instructions and cache accesses/misses, as well as measure memory access latency. Such information is useful for quantifying NUMA-related bottlenecks.

- It can capture the precise instruction pointer for each sample. Special hardware support is required for correct attribution of access behavior to instructions on processors with out-of-order cores [9].

We know of five hardware-based address sampling techniques used in modern processors: instruction-based sampling (IBS) [9] in AMD Opteron and its successors, marked event sampling (MRK) [30] in IBM POWER5 and its successors, precise event-based sampling (PEBS) [12] in Intel Pentium 4 and its successors, data event address sampling (DEAR) [13] in Intel Itanium, and precise event-based sampling with load latency extension (PEBS-LL) [12] in Intel Nehalem and its successors.

Since support for address sampling is not universally available, e.g., on ARM processors. we developed a software-based strategy for address sampling that we call Soft-IBS. Soft-IBS can simulate address sampling with memory access instrumentation. Using an instrumentation engine based on LLVM [22], we instrument every memory access instruction using a function that captures the effective address and instruction pointer of the sampled instruction. The engine invokes an instrumentation stub function that our profiler overloads to monitor memory accesses. Rather than recording information for each memory access, our profiler records information for every n^{th} memory access, where the value of n can be selected when the profiler is launched.

These six address sampling mechanisms are the foundation for our NUMA profiling tool. The aforementioned hardware and software mechanisms for address sampling each have their own strengths and weaknesses for NUMA profiling. Naturally, the hardware mechanisms are much more efficient than Soft-IBS. In Section 8, we compare the overhead of address sampling with these various mechanisms.

4. NUMA metrics

Using information we gather with address sampling, we compute several metrics to gain insight into NUMA bottlenecks. In the next section, we describe metrics to identify remote accesses and imbalanced memory requests. These metrics can be computed with information gathered using any mechanism for address sampling. In Section 4.2, we describe some additional metrics that can be derived using information available from only some PMU implementations.

4.1 Identifying remote accesses and imbalanced requests

To understand remote accesses, our profiler computes two derived metrics: M_l and M_r. M_l is the number of sampled memory accesses touching the data in the *local* NUMA domain, while M_r is the number of sampled memory accesses touching the data in a *remote* NUMA domain. Unless $M_r \ll M_l$ for a code region, the code region may suffer from NUMA problems. To compute M_l and M_r, our tool needs two pieces of information for each address sample: the NUMA domain that is the target of an effective address and the NUMA domain of the thread performing the access. Our profiler uses the move_pages API from libnuma [14] to query the NUMA domain for the effective address. To

identify the NUMA domain for a thread, we have two mechanisms. With PMU support for address sampling, a sample includes the CPU ID performing the access. For Soft-IBS, we bind each thread to a core and maintain a static mapping between thread and CPU ID that we query at runtime. Our tool uses libnuma's numa_node_of_cpu to map the CPU ID to its NUMA domain. For each address sample, if the effective address and thread are in the same NUMA domain, we increment M_l; otherwise, we increment M_r.

To evaluate memory request balance, our tool counts the number of sampled memory accesses to each NUMA domain by each thread. As before, we identify the NUMA domain for an access using the libnuma move_pages API. If the aggregate number of accesses to some NUMA domains is much larger than others, the access pattern may cause memory bandwidth congestion.

By themselves, the aforementioned metrics can be misleading. For example, if a thread loads a variable allocated into its private cache and touches it frequently, though no further remote accesses occur, the M_r caused by this thread is high, because the variable is deemed in the remote NUMA domain by move_pages. Therefore, one needs to use other metrics to eliminate this bias. In the next section, we describe a latency-per-instruction metric, which can be computed on some architectures, that addresses this shortcoming.

4.2 NUMA latency per instruction

IBS and PEBS-LL support measuring the latency of remote accesses. When this information is available, our tool computes the NUMA latency per instruction to provide additional insight into NUMA bottlenecks. We compute the NUMA latency per instruction, lpi_{NUMA}, to quantify a NUMA bottleneck's impact on overall program performance. If a NUMA bottleneck's lpi_{NUMA} is small, even if M_r is large, NUMA optimization of the program can't improve performance much. Equation 1 defines lpi_{NUMA}.

$$
\begin{aligned}
lpi_{NUMA} &= \frac{l_{NUMA}}{I} \\
&= \frac{l_{NUMA}}{I_{NUMA}} \times \frac{I_{NUMA}}{I_{MEM}} \times \frac{I_{MEM}}{I}
\end{aligned} \tag{1}
$$

In the equation, l_{NUMA} is the total latency of all remote accesses (including remote caches and memory); I_{NUMA}, I_{MEM}, and I represent the number of remote accesses, memory accesses, and instructions executed, respectively. This metric can be computed for the whole program or any code region. The equation can be computed as the product of three terms: the average latency per remote access, the fraction of memory accesses that are remote, and the ratio of memory accesses per instruction executed. The resulting quantity indicates whether NUMA performance losses are significant for a code region.

Equation 2 shows how we approximate lpi_{NUMA} using address sampling with IBS.

$$lpi_{NUMA} \approx \frac{l^s_{NUMA}}{I^s} \quad (2)$$

l^s_{NUMA} is the accumulated latency for sampled remote accesses; I^s is the number of sampled instructions. Calculating lpi_{NUMA} this way yields an approximate value because l^s_{NUMA} and I^s are representative subsets of l_{NUMA} and I. Equation 3 shows how we approximate lpi_{NUMA} using address sampling with PEBS-LL.

$$lpi_{NUMA} \approx \frac{l^s_{NUMA}}{E^s_{NUMA}} \times \frac{E_{NUMA}}{I} \quad (3)$$

As PEBS-LL samples memory access events, we can obtain an absolute event number E_{NUMA} and an average latency per sampled remote access event $\frac{l^s_{NUMA}}{E^s_{NUMA}}$ for the whole program or any code region. With a conventional PMU counter, we can collect the absolute number of instructions I executed by the monitored program or any code region. Experimentally, we have found that if lpi_{NUMA} is larger than 0.1 cycle per instruction, the NUMA losses for a program or important code region are significant enough to warrant optimization.

5. Metric attribution

To help a user understand NUMA performance losses, our tool attributes metrics using three different approaches.

- *Code-centric* attribution correlates performance metrics to instructions, loops, and functions that have high access latency.

- *Data-centric* attribution associates performance metrics with variables that have high access latency.

- *Address-centric* attribution summarizes a thread's memory accesses, which is useful for understanding data access patterns.

Each attribution technique highlights different aspects of NUMA performance losses. Together, they provide deep insight into NUMA bottlenecks. We describe these attribution methods in the next two sections.

5.1 Code- and data-centric attribution

Using hardware or software support for address sampling, our tool can accurately attribute costs to both code and data. Our approach for code- and data-centric attribution leverages existing support in HPCToolkit [21].

For code-centric attribution, we determine the call path for each address sample by unwinding the call stack. We then associate NUMA metrics with the call path.

For data-centric attribution, we directly associate metrics with variables, including static variables and dynamically allocated heap data. Our tool identifies address ranges

associated with static variables by reading symbols in the executable and dynamically loaded libraries. We identify address ranges associated with heap-allocated variables by tracking memory allocations and frees. Our tool attributes each sampled heap variable access to the full calling context where the heap variable was allocated.

5.2 Address-centric attribution

Address-centric attribution provides insight into memory access patterns of each thread. Such information is needed by application developers to help them adjust data distributions to minimize NUMA overhead. Prior data-centric tools, e.g., [15, 21, 24], identify problematic code regions and data objects, but don't provide insight into data access patterns to guide optimization. Below, we first describe a naive address-centric attribution strategy and then introduce refinements to make this approach useful.

> For each memory access m to a variable x, e.g., an array, we compute the addresses that form the lower and upper bounds of the range accessed by m and update the lower and upper bounds of x accessed for each procedure along the call path to m. At analysis time, we plot the upper and lower bounds of the data range accessed by each thread for any variable in any calling context to gain insight into the data access patterns across threads for code executed in that context.

This approach is too simplistic to be useful. Often data ranges are accessed non-uniformly because of loops, conditionals, and indirect references. For some program regions, a hot variable segment may account for 90% of a thread's accesses, while other segments of this variable only account for 10%. Therefore, instead of computing the minimum and maximum effective addresses for the whole memory range allocated for the variable, we represent a variable's address range with a sequence of bins, each bin representing a subrange. We treat each bin as a separate synthetic variable that gets its own data- and address-centric attributions. As performance measurements are associated with individual bins, one can easily identify the hot bins of a variable. We only use the access patterns of the hot bins to represent the access patterns of the whole variable. It is worth noting that selecting the number of bins for variables is important. A large number of bins for a variable can show fine-grained hot ranges but may ignore some important patterns. Currently, our tool divides a variable with an address range larger than five pages into five bins by default; one can change this number via an environment variable.

The aforementioned approach for maintaining address ranges merges them online to keep profiles compact. However, different memory accesses experience different latencies. For that reason, when analyzing access ranges for variables at different levels of abstraction (statement, loop, procedure, and various levels in the call path), one should not give equal weight to access ranges in all contexts. One can

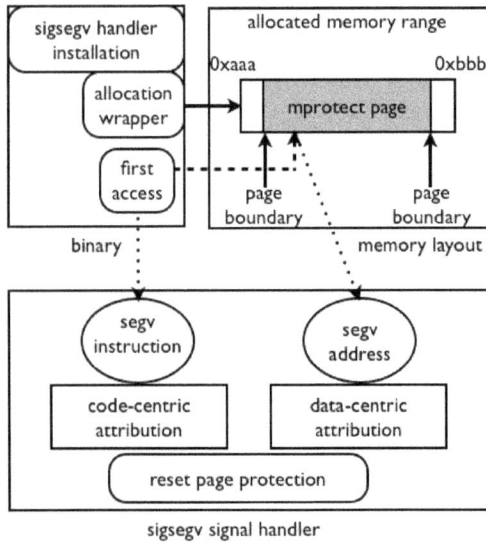

Figure 2. Identifying the first touch context for each heap variable. Our NUMA profiler applies both code-centric and data-centric attribution for first touches.

use aggregate latency measurements attributed to a context as a guide to identify what program contexts are important to consider for NUMA locality optimization, and then use address range information for those contexts as a guide to understand what changes to data and/or code mappings will be needed to improve NUMA performance.

6. Pinpointing first touches

As discussed in Section 2, identifying the source code *first touching* variables associated with NUMA performance losses is essential for optimization. However, manually identifying code performing first touches to variables is often difficult for complex programs. To automatically identify first touches, our tool uses a novel approach that employs page protection in Linux. Our strategy does not require any instrumentation of memory accesses, so it has low runtime overhead.

Figure 2 shows how we trap a first touch access to a large variable, e.g., an array. Our tool first installs a SIGSEGV handler before a monitored program begins execution. Then, our tool monitors memory allocations in the program using wrappers for allocation functions. Inside the wrapper, our tool masks off the read and write permission of the allocated memory range between the first and last page boundaries within the variable's extent. When the monitored executable accesses the protected pages, the OS delivers a SIGSEGV signal. Our tool's SIGSEGV handler catches the signal and does three things. First, it uses the signal context to perform code-centric attribution. Second, it uses the data address that caused the fault (available in the signal info structure) to perform data-centric attribution. With both code- and data-centric attribution of the SIGSEGV signal, one knows the

location of first touches to every monitored variable. Finally, it restores read and write permissions for the variable's monitored pages. It is worth noting that multiple threads may initialize a variable concurrently in a parallel loop, so more than one thread may enter the SIGSEGV handler. Thus, multiple threads may concurrently identify first touches and record code- and data-centric attributions. Call paths of first touches to the same variable from different threads are merged postmortemly.

7. Tool implementation

Our tool is implemented as extensions to HPCToolkit [1]—an open-source performance tool for call path profiling of parallel programs. HPCToolkit accepts a compiled binary executable as its input. The binary can be compiled by any compiler with any level of optimization. HPCToolkit launches an executable and then collects per-thread call path profiles, which it attributes to both code and data addresses. HPCToolkit uses an offline analyzer to merge profiles from multiple threads and attribute performance metrics to source code, static variables, and call paths of heap allocated data. Finally, HPCToolkit provides a graphical user interface for exploring performance data. In the rest of this section, we describe how we extended HPCToolkit's measurement, analysis, and presentation tools to support analysis of NUMA performance problems. We refer to our modified version of HPCToolkit for pinpointing and analyzing NUMA bottlenecks as HPCToolkit-NUMA.

7.1 Online profiler

Our extensions to HPCToolkit for NUMA performance analysis perform three tasks. First, they configure PMU hardware for address sampling. We extended HPCToolkit to leverage Perfmon [5] to control PMUs that employ IBS, PEBS and DEAR. Our extensions use Linux `Perf_events` [31] to configure PMUs for architectures that support MRK and PEBS-LL. For software-based sampling, we extended HPCToolkit to override callbacks for instrumentation hooks inserted for loads and stores by LLVM; these instrumentation callbacks record information each time a predefined threshold of accesses occurs.

Second, HPCToolkit's `hpcrun` utility captures these address samples and attributes them to code and data, recording them in augmented calling context trees (CCTs) [21]. The augmented CCT our NUMA extensions record is a mixture of variable allocation paths, memory access call paths, and first touch call paths. Dummy nodes in the augmented CCT separate segments of calling context sequences recorded for different purposes.

Third, the profiler collects NUMA metrics including M_l, M_r, metrics that show the number of sampled accesses touching each NUMA domain, latency metrics, and address-centric metrics that summarize each thread's variable accesses in each subtree of the CCT.

Sampling mechanisms	Processors	Threads	Events	Sampling periods
Instruction-based sampling (IBS)	AMD Magny-Cours	48	IBS op	64K instructions
Marked event sampling (MRK)	IBM POWER 7	128	PM_MRK_FROM_L3MISS	1
Precise event-based sampling (PEBS)	Intel Xeon Harpertown	8	INST_RETIRED:ANY_P	1000000
Data event address registers (DEAR)	Intel Itanium 2	8	DATA_EAR_CACHE_LAT4	20000
PEBS with load latency (PEBS-LL)	Intel Ivy Bridge	8	LATENCY_ABOVE_THRESHOLD	500000
Software-supported IBS (Soft-IBS)	AMD Magny-Cours[1]	48	memory accesses	10000000

Table 1. Configurations of different sampling mechanism on different architectures.

7.2 Offline analyzer and viewer

Adapting HPCToolkit's `hpcprof` offline profile analyzer for NUMA measurement was trivial. The only enhancement needed was the ability to perform [min, max] range computations when merging different thread profiles. Instead of accumulating metric values associated with the same context, [min, max] merging requires a customized reduction function.

We added an address-centric view to HPCToolkit's `hpcviewer` interface to display address-centric measurements for all threads. The view plots the minimum and maximum address accessed for a variable vs. the thread index. The address range for a variable is normalized to the interval [0, 1]. The upper right pane in Figure 3 shows an example of this view for a heap-allocated variable. In the next section, we show how this novel view provides insight that helps guide optimization for NUMA platforms.

8. Experiments

We tested HPCToolkit-NUMA on five different architectures to evaluate its functionality using different hardware and software support for address sampling. Table 1 shows our choices for events and sampling periods for evaluating each of the address sampling mechanisms. The criteria for choosing events is based on (1) sampling every memory access (not only NUMA-related events or instructions) to avoid biased results for access patterns and (2) sampling all instructions (if possible) to support computing NUMA latency per instruction. For the tests we ran, the sampling period we chose for each event except MRK gives 100–1000 samples per second per thread.[2] To evaluate the tool, we used four multi-threaded benchmarks:

- LULESH [16] is a shock hydrodynamics application benchmark from Lawrence Livermore National Laboratory (LLNL) written in C++ and parallelized with OpenMP.

- AMG2006 is an algebraic multi grid benchmark from LLNL's Sequoia benchmark suite [18]. AMG2006 is

Methods	LULESH	AMG2006	Blacksholes
IBS	295s (+24%)	89s (+37%)	192s (+6%)
MRK	93s (+5%)	27s (+7%)	132s (+4%)
PEBS	65s (+45%)	96s (+52%)	82s(+25%)
DEAR	90s (+7%)	120s (+12%)	73s (+4%)
PEBS-LL	35(+6%)	57s (+8%)	67s (+3%)
Soft-IBS	604s (+200%)	220s (+180%)	270s (+30%)

Table 2. Runtime overhead measurement of HPCToolkit-NUMA. The number outside the parenthesis is the execution time without monitoring and the percentage in the parenthesis is the monitoring overhead. The absolute execution time on different architectures is incomparable because we adjust the benchmark inputs according to the number of cores in the system.

written in C and parallelized with MPI and/or OpenMP. In this study, we used OpenMP but not MPI.

- Blacksholes is a benchmark from PARSEC benchmark suite [3]. It performs option pricing with Black-Scholes Partial Differential Equation (PDE). It is coded in C and parallelized using OpenMP.

- UMT2013 is a benchmark from LLNL Coral benchmark suite [17]. It performs three-dimensional, non-linear, radiation transport calculations using deterministic methods. UMT2013 is coded in hybrid C, C++, Fortran and parallelized with MPI and OpenMP. Like AMG2006, we only used OpenMP but not MPI in this study.

Some NUMA optimization of LULESH and AMG2006 has previously been described in the literature [21]. Guided by insights from HPCToolkit-NUMA, we were able to develop significantly better NUMA-aware optimizations for both LULESH and AMG2006, advancing the state of the art.

Table 2 shows the measurement overhead when running HPCToolkit-NUMA with different architectures with different sampling methods. From the table, we can see that the overhead of HPCToolkit-NUMA differs using different sampling methods. Soft-IBS incurs the highest runtime overhead because it is based on software instrumentation; PEBS incurs the second highest overhead because we compensate for for off-by-1 attribution by the PMU using online binary analysis to identify the previous instruction, which is diffi-

---

[1] Soft-IBS works on all of listed platforms; we choose AMD Magny-Cours for testing.

[2] Marked event sampling on POWER7 with the fastest sampling rate under user control generates less than 100 samples/second per thread.

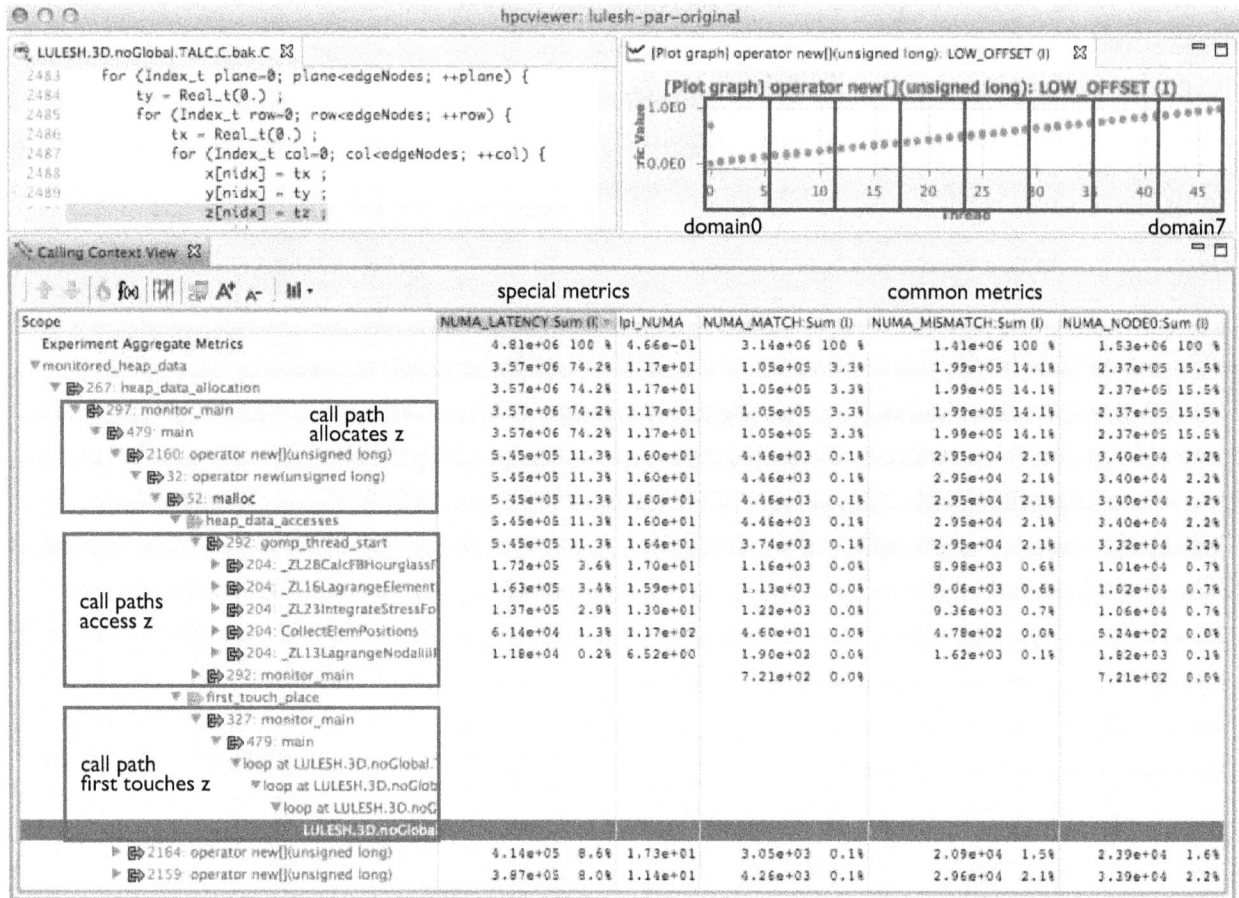

Figure 3. Identifying NUMA bottlenecks in LULESH using code-centric, data-centric and address-centric attributions.

cult for x86 code;[3] IBS has the third highest overhead because it samples all kinds of instructions and its sampling rate is high; and other sampling methods incur very low runtime overhead. At runtime, the aggregate runtime footprint of HPCToolkit-NUMA's data structures was less than 40MB for any sampling method on any of the architectures.

In the case studies that follow, we only show measurements obtained using IBS and MRK because HPCToolkit-NUMA can provide similar analysis results using any sampling method. Moreover, IBS is one of the two PMU hardware types that supports the lpi_{NUMA} metric, while MRK can show how we analyze NUMA bottlenecks using NUMA metrics we derived without the help of latency information. For experiments using IBS, we use a system with four 12-core AMD Magny-Cours processors. Overall, the system has 48 cores and 128GB memory, which is evenly divided into eight NUMA domains. For experiments using MRK, we use a system with four eight-core POWER7 processors. Overall, the system has 128 SMT hardware threads and 64GB memory. In this study, we consider each socket a NUMA domain. We run LULESH, AMG2006 and Blacksholes on all hard-

ware threads; we run UMT2013 with 32 threads because its standard input size is limited to 32 threads.

8.1 LULESH

We first measure LULESH with IBS on the AMD machine. Figure 3 shows the results of our NUMA performance analysis result displayed in a modified version of HPCToolkit's `hpcviewer`. The top left pane shows the source code of the monitored program. The top right pane shows the address-centric view, which represents memory ranges accessed by individual threads. The bottom left pane shows the program structure of synthetic CCTs. Annotations in this pane show a mixture of call paths in the CCT. The bottom right pane shows our NUMA metrics.

The overall program's NUMA latency per instruction (lpi_{NUMA}) is 0.466. This is significantly larger than our 0.1 rule of thumb, which means the NUMA problems in LULESH are significant enough to warrant optimization. We first investigate the heap-allocated variables and then other kinds of variables. The heap-allocated variables have a lpi_{NUMA} of 11.7 and 74.2% of the total latency is caused by remote NUMA domain accesses. We drill down the call path in the bottom left pane for the call sites (`operator`

---

[3] It would be better to perform this correction during post-mortem analysis.

new[] in the figure) of variable allocations, discovering three variables with more than 8% of total latency caused by NUMA accesses. One can identify the variable names from the source code pane by clicking their allocation sites (marked as 2160, 2164 and 2159 respectively to the left of operator new[]). Here, we study the variable z, which causes the most significant NUMA losses.

Overall, z accounts for 11.3% of the total latency caused by remote accesses. We observe two facts (1) M_r (labeled as NUMA_MISMATCH in the metric pane) is roughly seven times of M_l (labeled as NUMA_MATCH in the metric pane); and (2) all accesses to z come from NUMA domain 0 ($NUMA\_NODE0$ equals to the sum of M_l and M_r). Therefore, we infer that pages for z are all allocated in NUMA domain 0 but accessed by threads in other domains. The top right pane in Figure 3 plots the min and max addresses accessed in z by each thread. From the figure, we can see that other than thread 0, each thread touches a subset of z. Threads with higher ranks touch higher address intervals in z. Visualizing the results of address sampling provides the key insight about how to adjust the layout of heap data to improve performance, namely by co-locating data and computation upon it in the same NUMA domain.

Based on this address-centric view, it is clear that one could improve the NUMA performance of LULESH by dividing the memory range allocated for z into eight continuous regions, segmented by rectangles shown in the top right pane of Figure 3. One should allocate each block to the appropriate NUMA domain so it will be co-located with the threads that access it. We implemented this strategy by adjusting the code that first touches z, identified by our tool, and shown in the top left pane of Figure 3. This optimization exploits the higher bandwidth and lower latency of local memory. It also reduces the bandwidth consumed between NUMA domains. We similarly optimize other heap-allocated variables, including x, y, xd, yd and zd.

LULESH also makes heavy use of a stack-allocated variable nodelist. Since our tool does not currently provide detailed NUMA analysis of stack data, we modified the source code for the program to declare nodelist as a static variable. HPCToolkit-NUMA's data-centric analysis shows that nodelist accounts for 20.3% of total latency caused by remote accesses and 13.3% mismatching of memory accesses (M_r). There is high lpi_{NUMA} associated with nodelist, meaning that it has high NUMA latency that warrants optimization. The M_r metric associated with nodelist is about seven times as large as M_l and all accesses come from NUMA domain 0, which means that nodelist is initialized by the master thread but accessed by worker threads of other NUMA domains in parallel. Address-centric analysis identifies that nodelist has the same access pattern per thread as z does shown in Figure 3. Like optimization for z, such an access pattern reveals that a block-wise distribution of pages

allocated for nodelist would be appropriate, as before for z.

Guided by our tool, the block-wise data distribution we implemented for both heap-allocated and stack variables, we were able to speedup LULESH by 25% on our AMD system. Using with the page interleaving strategy suggested by our prior work [21] gave only a 13% improvement over the original code not tuned for NUMA architectures.

Measuring LULESH with MRK on POWER7 showed similar NUMA problems. 66% of L3 cache misses access remote memory. Heap allocated arrays, such as x, y, z, xd, yd and zd, account for 65% of remote accesses, while the stack variable nodelist accounts for 31%. On our POWER7 system, HPCToolkit-NUMA's address-centric view showed that these variables have access patterns similar to those we observed on our AMD system. Using a block-wise page distribution for these variables improved execution time for LULESH by 7.5% on our POWER7 system. In contrast, using an interleaved page allocation (as suggested by prior work [21]) degraded performance on POWER7 by 16.4%.

8.2 AMG2006

We ran AMG2006 with 48 threads on our AMD system, measuring it using IBS. HPCToolkit-NUMA showed that AMG2006 has a lpi_{NUMA} of more than 0.92, which means it has significant NUMA problems (more severe than LULESH) and worthy of investigation. The heap-allocated variables of AMG2006 account for 61.8% of the total memory latency caused by remote accesses. By looking at heap variable allocation call paths, we identified one problematic variable RAP_diag_data. RAP_diag_data accounts for 18.6% of total latency, with a lpi_{NUMA} of 15.9 and 8.1% of total M_r. By examining the sampled accesses and the first-touch access to RAP_diag_data, we found that RAP_diag_data was allocated and initialized by the master thread but accessed by all worker threads in other NUMA domains.

The address-centric view in Figure 4 shows the access patterns of RAP_diag_data across all 48 threads aggregated over the whole program. However, these threads do not show an obvious access pattern that can guide page distribution for this variable. We further investigate threads' access patterns for RAP_diag_data in individual OpenMP parallel regions rather than the whole program. The most interesting parallel region shown in the call path is hypre_boomerAMGRelax._omp, which accounts for 74.2% (13.8/18.6) of NUMA access latency caused by RAP_diag_data. Figure 5 shows the access patterns of RAP_diag_data in this parallel region. Obviously, threads have a regular access pattern of RAP_diag_data in this parallel region. Because accesses in hypre_boomerAMGRelax._omp dominate the costs of accessing RAP_diag_data, we can use this access pattern to direct the data distribution. Like optimization for LULESH, we apply block-wise distribution at the first touch place iden-

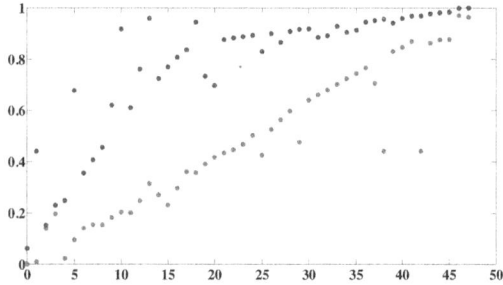

Figure 4. Address-centric view showing the overall access patterns of RAP_diag_data in AMG2006 across all threads.

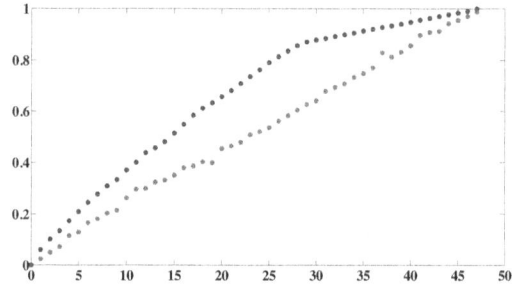

Figure 5. Address-centric view for the accesses to RAP_diag_data in the most significant loop in AMG2006.

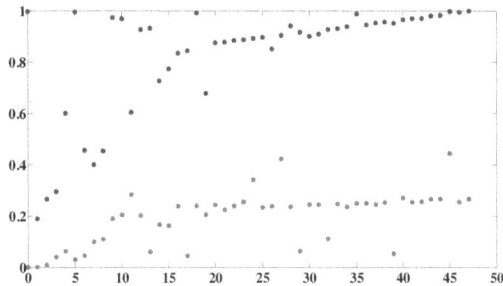

Figure 6. Address-centric view showing the overall access patterns of RAP_diag_j in AMG2006 across all threads

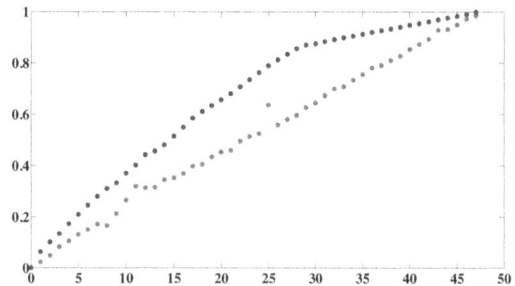

Figure 7. Address-centric view for the accesses to RAP_diag_j in the most significant loop in AMG2006.

tified by our tool to evenly allocate RAP_diag_data across the NUMA domains.

If we analyze the source code through the code-centric attribution, we find that accesses to RAP_diag_data in hypre_boomerAMGRelax._omp use the values of another array as indices (i.e., RAP_diag_data[A_diag_i[i]]), leading to indirect memory accesses. Without our address-centric analysis analysis, one cannot determine where data layout changes are needed and how to refine them to improve performance.

We examined other hot variables and found another NUMA bottleneck: RAP_diag_j accounts for 10.6% of total latency caused by NUMA accesses. Figure 6 and Figure 7 show its address-centric analysis results by considering all accesses and accesses in the most significant parallel region respectively. Obviously, the access patterns on the bottom are much more regular than the one on the top. As memory accesses in this parallel region account for 73.6% of total latency for RAP_diag_j in the whole program, we use its regular access pattern to allocate pages of RAP_diag_j in a block-wise fashion at its first touch location.

Besides these two variables, there are other three heap-allocated variables suffering from high remote access latency. According to access patterns from address-centric analysis, one of them can be optimized using block-wise distribution as for RAP_diag_data and RAP_diag_j. The other two show that each thread accesses the whole range of the variable, leading to an optimization of using interleaved page allocation. Our optimizations achieve a 51% re-

duction in the running time of the solver phase of AMG2006. In production codes that employ this software, the running time of the solver is most important. Without guidance from our address-centric analysis, prior NUMA optimization of AMG2006 used interleaved allocation for every problematic variable [21] , which only improved the solver phase performance of AMG2006 by 36%.

8.3 Blackscholes

We measured Blackscholes on our AMD system using IBS. HPCToolkit-NUMA shows a much smaller lpi_{NUMA} value (0.035 cycle per instruction) than the threshold (0.1) over the entire program, indicating that Blackscholes would not benefit from NUMA optimization. To validate this assessment, we eliminated NUMA bottlenecks in Blackscholes and showed that this optimization barely improved the program's performance.

HPCToolkit-NUMA identified that heap-allocated variables account for 66.8% of total latency caused by NUMA accesses and 51.6% of the latency associated with the variable buffer. With the values of M_l and M_r, together with the data source metrics, we identified that buffer is allocated in only one NUMA domain by the master thread and evenly accessed by all threads in the system.

HPCToolkit-NUMA's address-centric analysis in Figure 8 shows a regular access pattern across all threads. Each thread touches a sub-range of buffer in an ascending order, with large overlaps. To understand why the program reveals such pattern, we analyzed the source code. The top of Fig-

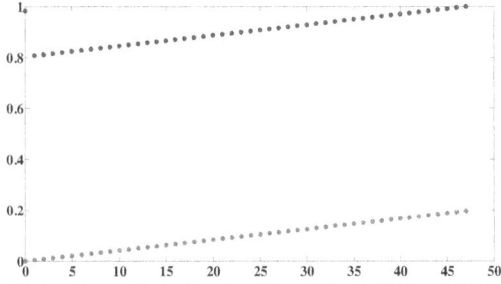

Figure 8. Address-centric view showing the access patterns of `buffer` across all threads.

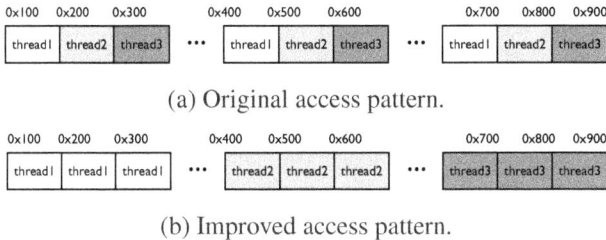

(a) Original access pattern.

(b) Improved access pattern.

Figure 9. Memory access patterns across threads in BlackScholes.

ure 9 shows the memory layout for `buffer`. The program sets five pointers to point different sections of `buffer`. All threads access to each section in parallel, leading to the access pattern shown in Figure 9a. According to our address-centric analysis, the three example threads in the figure touch the address ranges of (0x100, 0x700), (0x200, 0x800) and (0x300, 0x900) respectively, matching the pattern revealed by address-centric results shown in Figure 8.

As threads show non-local accesses to `buffer`, we re-group these sections into an array of structures as shown in Figure 9b. With this optimization, the three example threads touch (0x100, 0x300), (0x400, 0x600), (0x700, 0x900) respectively, with no overlap.

To allocate data block-wise, we changed the `buffer` initialization loop that our tool identified as the first touch location. Originally, only the master thread initializes `buffer`. We parallelized the initialization loop using OpenMP to make sure that each thread first touches its own data. With this optimization, there is no longer any latency related to `buffer` caused by remote accesses.

Although we largely eliminated the NUMA latency in the program by co-locating data and computation, the execution time of Blackscholes improves less than 0.1%. The trivial improvement proves that our derived metric lpi_{NUMA} reflects the severity of NUMA problems. One can estimate potential gains from NUMA optimization by examining lpi_{NUMA}.

8.4 UMT2013

We ran UMT2013 on our POWER7 system with 32 threads, sampling instructions that cause L3 data cache misses. We

```
do c=1,nCorner
  do ig=1,Groups
    source=Z%STotal(ig,c)+Z%STime(ig,c,Angle)
  enddo
enddo
```

Figure 10. A loop kernel in UMT2013 that has many remote accesses to `STime`.

bounded each thread to each hardware core in each of four NUMA domains. According to M_l and M_r, HPCToolkit-NUMA showed that 86% L3 cache misses lead to remote memory accesses and 47% of remote accesses due to the references of heap allocated variables.

Using HPCToolkit-NUMA, we identified the allocation call path of a hot variable – `STime`, which is a three-dimensional array that accounts for 18.2% of total remote accesses. Code-centric analysis in HPCToolkit-NUMA associates all remote accesses to `STime` with the reference shown in Figure 10. The reason for the high remote access ratio is that `STime` is allocated in one NUMA domain but accessed by threads in all NUMA domains. With address-centric analysis, HPCToolkit-NUMA identifies that `STime` has a staggered access pattern across threads, similar to the variable `buffer` in BlackScholes, shown in Figure 8. A deep analysis of the source code showed that the nested loop iterating over `STime` shown in Figure 10 is in an OpenMP parallel region. Two-dimensional planes of `STime` indexed by `Angle` are assigned to threads in a round-robin fashion. To ensure the data is co-located with its computation, we parallelized the initialization loop of `STime` identified by first touch analysis. This strategy has each thread initialize the part of `STime` that it accesses in the computation stage. This optimization eliminates most remote accesses to `STime` and yielded a 7% speedup for the program as a whole.

9. Related work

Several performance tools provide support for analyzing NUMA performance issues with multi-threaded programs. These tools mainly use two kinds of methods: simulation and measurement. The simulation tools such as MACPO [25] and NUMAgrind [32] collect memory traces and feed into a cache simulator. The simulator simulates an architecture with NUMA memory hierarchies to analyze the memory traces. However, such simulation-based tools incur high runtime overhead to the monitored program. For example, MACPO slows the program by 2x–5x and NUMAgrind has more than 100x runtime overhead.

On the other hand, measurement-based tools can provide insights with low overhead. For example, Memphis [24] uses AMD instruction-based sampling (IBS) to capture remote accesses and associates them with static variables. It compares IBS with the traditional hardware counters, showing that address sampling gives deeper insights into a program's NUMA bottlenecks.

MemProf [15], another measurement-based tool also uses AMD IBS to measure a program's NUMA bottlenecks. MemProf associates NUMA metrics with heap-allocated variables and partially supports attribution to static variables by coarsely aggregating metrics incurred by static variables in the same load module (executable or shared libraries).

Prior work on data-centric analysis in HPCToolkit used both IBS and MRK hardware support to attribute NUMA latency to both code and data [21]. Here, we extended that work with support for both address-centric and first-touch analysis. While our prior work enabled us to identify variables with the most remote accesses, it didn't provide insight into access patterns, which a code developer needs to reorganize data layout to co-locate it with computation.

Besides NUMA profilers, some previous work improves NUMA locality and performance using support from libraries [4], compilers [23] and operating systems [6, 7]. Unlike our approach, which is designed to help programmers fix NUMA problems in their code, these approaches aim to ameliorate NUMA problems to the greatest extent possible without source code changes. While these approaches require developers to use specific libraries, compilers, or OS kernels, our tool guides offline optimization of the source code which yields better code that can be run anywhere without any restrictions.

10. Conclusions and future work

In this paper, we present a profiling tool that identifies and analyzes NUMA bottlenecks in multi-threaded programs and helps guide program performance tuning by providing new metrics and insights into data access patterns. Using PMU support in modern microprocessors, our measurement-based tool can gather the information it needs with low run-time overhead. We demonstrate the utility of our tool and the information it provides to optimize four well-known benchmarks. While one code didn't warrant NUMA optimization (according to our metrics) or benefit significantly when it was applied anyway, our tool delivered insight and guidance that enabled us to significantly improve the performance of the other three codes.

In our experiments using different hardware for address sampling, we observed that not all mechanisms are equally-suited for our analysis. Although both IBS and MRK sample instructions, IBS samples all kinds of instructions, so one needs to filter out samples not of interest in software, which adds extra overhead. With IBS it is trivial to compute the load/store fraction in the whole instruction stream to assess the performance impact of memory instructions. In contrast, MRK can only sample instructions causing specific events (such as L3 cache misses or remote accesses). Consequently, MRK can highlight problematic memory instruction with low overhead. DEAR, PEBS and PEBS-LL sample events.

PEBS and PEBS-LL can directly sample NUMA events, while DEAR does not support NUMA events. Both instruction sampling and event sampling can effectively identify problematic memory accesses. Finally, IBS and PEBS-LL can measure latency for sampled load instructions. This information can be used to derive the metrics described in Section 4.

Our future work is five-fold. First, we plan to add full support for monitoring stack variables instead of requiring them to be changed to static or heap allocated ones for detailed measurements. Second, we plan to extend our tool to analyze more complex access patterns. Third, we plan to collect trace-based measurements to study time-varying NUMA patterns in addition to profiles. Fourth, we plan to augment hpcviewer with a new view to better present code-and data-centric measurements. Finally, our strategy for pinpointing first touches is only implemented at present for heap-allocated variables. We plan to extend it for static variables by protecting their pages when the executable or libraries are loaded before execution begins.

Acknowledgments

We thank Laksono Adhianto, Mike Fagan, and Mark Krentel for their contributions to HPCToolkit. Without their efforts, this work would not have been possible. This research was supported in part by Lawrence Livermore National Laboratories by subcontract B602160 of prime contract DE-AC52-07NA27344.

References

[1] L. Adhianto et al. HPCToolkit: Tools for performance analysis of optimized parallel programs. *Concurrency and Computation: Practice and Experience*, 22:685–701, 2010.

[2] Advanced Micro Devices. AMD Code-Analyst performance analyzer. http://developer.amd.com/tools-and-sdks/heterogeneous-computing/archived-tools/amd-codeanalyst-performance-analyzer/. Last accessed: Jan. 6, 2013.

[3] C. Bienia. *Benchmarking Modern Multiprocessors*. PhD thesis, Princeton University, January 2011.

[4] F. Broquedis, N. Furmento, B. Goglin, P.-A. Wacrenier, and R. Namyst. ForestGOMP: An efficient OpenMP environment for NUMA architectures. *Intl. Journal of Parallel Programming*, 38(5-6):418–439, 2010.

[5] H.-P. Corporation. Perfmon kernel interface. http://perfmon2.sourceforge.net/. Last accessed: Dec. 12, 2013.

[6] A. Cox and R. Fowler. The implementation of a coherent memory abstraction on a NUMA multiprocessor: experiences with PLATINUM. In *Proc. of the 12th ACM Symp. on Operating Systems Principles*, SOSP '89, pages 32–44, New York, NY, USA, 1989.

[7] M. Dashti et al. Traffic management: a holistic approach to memory placement on NUMA systems. In *Proc. of the*

18th *Intl. Conf. on Architectural Support for Programming Languages and Operating Systems*, ASPLOS '13, pages 381–394, New York, NY, USA, 2013.

[8] L. DeRose, B. Homer, D. Johnson, S. Kaufmann, and H. Poxon. Cray performance analysis tools. In *Tools for High Performance Computing*, pages 191–199. Springer Berlin Heidelberg, 2008.

[9] P. J. Drongowski. Instruction-based sampling: A new performance analysis technique for AMD family 10h processors. `http://developer.amd.com/Assets/AMD_IBS_paper_EN.pdf`, November 2007. Last accessed: Dec. 13, 2013.

[10] IBM Corporation. IBM Visual Performance Analyzer User Guide, version 6.2. `http://bit.ly/ibm-vpa-62`. Last accessed: Dec. 12, 2013.

[11] Intel VTune Amplifier XE 2013. `http://software.intel.com/en-us/intel-vtune-amplifier-xe`, April 2013. Last accessed: Dec. 12, 2013.

[12] Intel Corporation. Intel 64 and IA-32 architectures software developer's manual, Volume 3B: System programming guide, Part 2, Number 253669-032, June 2010.

[13] Intel Corporation. Intel Itanium Processor 9300 series reference manual for software development and optimization, Number 323602-001, March 2010.

[14] A. Kleen. A NUMA API for Linux. `http://developer.amd.com/wordpress/media/2012/10/LibNUMA-WP-fv1.pdf`, 2005. Last accessed: Dec. 12, 2013.

[15] R. Lachaize, B. Lepers, and V. Quéma. MemProf: a memory profiler for NUMA multicore systems. In *Proc. of the 2012 USENIX Annual Technical Conf.*, USENIX ATC'12, Berkeley, CA, USA, 2012.

[16] Lawrence Livermore National Laboratory. Livermore Unstructured Lagrangian Explicit Shock Hydrodynamics (LULESH). `https://codesign.llnl.gov/lulesh.php`. Last accessed: Dec. 12, 2013.

[17] Lawrence Livermore National Laboratory. LLNL Coral Benchmarks. `https://asc.llnl.gov/CORAL-benchmarks`. Last accessed: Dec. 12, 2013.

[18] Lawrence Livermore National Laboratory. LLNL Sequoia Benchmarks. `https://asc.llnl.gov/sequoia/benchmarks`. Last accessed: Dec. 12, 2013.

[19] X. Liu and J. Mellor-Crummey. Pinpointing data locality problems using data-centric analysis. In *Proc. of the 9th IEEE/ACM Intl. Symp. on Code Generation and Optimization*, pages 171–180, Washington, DC, 2011.

[20] X. Liu and J. Mellor-Crummey. Pinpointing data locality bottlenecks with low overheads. In *Proc. of the 2013 IEEE Intl. Symp. on Performance Analysis of Systems and Software*, Austin, TX, USA, April 21-23, 2013.

[21] X. Liu and J. M. Mellor-Crummey. A data-centric profiler for parallel programs. In *Proc. of the 2013 ACM/IEEE Conference on Supercomputing*, Denver, CO, USA, 2013.

[22] LLVM Compiler Infrastructure. `http://www.llvm.org`. Last accessed: Jan. 7, 2013.

[23] Z. Majo and T. R. Gross. Matching memory access patterns and data placement for NUMA systems. In *Proc. of the 10th IEEE/ACM Intl. Symp. on Code Generation and Optimization*, pages 230–241, New York, NY, USA, 2012.

[24] C. McCurdy and J. S. Vetter. Memphis: Finding and fixing NUMA-related performance problems on multi-core platforms. In *Proc. of 2010 IEEE Intl. Symp. on Performance Analysis of Systems Software*, pages 87–96, Mar. 2010.

[25] A. Rane and J. Browne. Enhancing performance optimization of multicore chips and multichip nodes with data structure metrics. In *Proc. of the 12th IEEE Intl. Conf. on Parallel Architectures and Compilation Techniques*, Minneapolis, MN, USA, 2012.

[26] Rogue Wave Software. ThreadSpotter manual, version 2012.1. `http://www.roguewave.com/documents.aspx?Command=Core_Download&EntryId=1492`, August 2012. Last accessed: Dec. 12, 2013.

[27] S. Shende and A. D. Malony. The TAU parallel performance system. *International Journal of High Performance Computing Applications, ACTS Collection Special Issue*, 2005.

[28] B.-W. Silas et al. Corey: an operating system for many cores. In *Proc. of the 8th USENIX conference on Operating Systems Design and Implementation*, pages 43–57, Berkeley, CA, USA, 2008.

[29] B. Sinharoy et al. IBM POWER7 multicore server processor. *IBM JRD*, 55(3):1:1–29, May 2011.

[30] M. Srinivas et al. IBM POWER7 performance modeling, verification, and evaluation. *IBM JRD*, 55(3):4:1–19, May/June 2011.

[31] V. Weaver. The unofficial Linux Perf Events web-page. `http://web.eece.maine.edu/~vweaver/projects/perf_events`. Last accessed: Dec. 12, 2013.

[32] R. Yang et al. Profiling directed NUMA optimization on Linux systems: A case study of the Gaussian computational chemistry code. In *Proc. of the 2011 IEEE Intl. Parallel & Distributed Processing Symposium*, pages 1046–1057, 2011.

Towards Fair and Efficient SMP Virtual Machine Scheduling

Jia Rao   Xiaobo Zhou

Department of Computer Science
University of Colorado at Colorado Springs
{jrao, xzhou}@uccs.edu

Abstract

As multicore processors become prevalent in modern computer systems, there is a growing need for increasing hardware utilization and exploiting the parallelism of such platforms. With virtualization technology, hardware utilization is improved by encapsulating independent workloads into virtual machines (VMs) and consolidating them onto the same machine. SMP virtual machines have been widely adopted to exploit parallelism. For virtualized systems, such as a public cloud, fairness between tenants and the efficiency of running their applications are keys to success. However, we find that existing virtualization platforms fail to enforce fairness between VMs with different number of virtual CPUs (vCPU) that run on multiple CPUs. We attribute the unfairness to the use of per-CPU schedulers and the load imbalance on these CPUs that incur inaccurate CPU allocations. Unfortunately, existing approaches to reduce unfairness, e.g., dynamic load balancing and CPU capping, introduce significant inefficiencies to parallel workloads.

In this paper, we present *Flex*, a vCPU scheduling scheme that enforces fairness at VM-level and improves the efficiency of hosted parallel applications. Flex centers on two key designs: (1) dynamically adjusting vCPU weights (*FlexW*) on multiple CPUs to achieve VM-level fairness and (2) flexibly scheduling vCPUs (*FlexS*) to minimize wasted busy-waiting time. We have implemented Flex in Xen and performed comprehensive evaluations with various parallel workloads. Results show that Flex is able to achieve CPU allocations with on average no more than 5% error compared to the ideal fair allocation. Further, Flex outperforms Xen's credit scheduler and two representative co-scheduling approaches by as much as 10X for parallel applications using busy-waiting or blocking synchronization methods.

Categories and Subject Descriptors   D.4.1 [*Operating Systems*]: Process Management—Scheduling, Synchronization; D.4.8 [*Operating Systems*]: Performance—Measurements

Keywords   Virtual Machine Scheduling; Multicore Systems; Parallel Program Optimization

1. Introduction

Cloud computing, unlocked by virtualization technologies, is bringing a transformative change in enterprise architectures. By consolidating multiple independent workloads, each in a virtual machine (VM), onto a fewer number of machines, enterprises benefit from improved hardware utilizations and significant energy savings. On the other hand, virtualization provides important flexibilities to end users. Virtual servers can be on-the-fly reconfigured to meet the growth of hosted applications. Public infrastructure-as-a-service (IaaS) clouds such as Amazon EC2 [1] and Microsoft Azure [35] allow users to lease virtual servers from cloud providers with a pay-as-you-go charging model. However, cloud providers are facing a dilemma – consolidating more VMs on their hardware infrastructure to generate more revenue and achieving good performance for hosted applications to avoid the loss of customers. Since it is a common practice in today's cloud providers to multiplex VMs onto hardware resources, e.g., CPU cores, the question left to providers is how to provide guaranteed performance to users.

Performance guarantee has twofold meanings in a public cloud service: *fairness* and *efficiency*. First, performance should be predictable and proportional to user payments. At least, users belonging to the same service category with the same pay rate should receive a fair amount of shared resources. Second, the overhead introduced by virtualization should be minimized to approximate the execution efficiency in dedicated systems. There is existing work addressing the unfairness issue due to shared CPU caches [12, 17, 22], network I/O interface [3, 19] and shared storage [23]. Other work attempted to improve the efficiency for virtualized I/O processing [37, 38]. With the prevalence of parallel programming, symmetric multiprocessing (SMP) VMs with multiple virtual CPUs (vCPUs) are widely adopted in cloud ser-

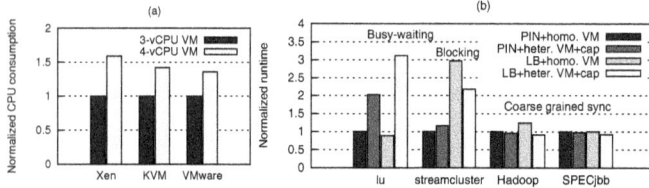

Figure 1. (a) VM-level unfairness for two heterogeneous VMs sharing 4 pCPUs. (b) Effect of fairness mechanisms, load-balancing (LB) and CPU capping (cap), on parallel performance.

vices. Literature has identified the synchronization overhead in SMP VMs as the major performance bottleneck for parallel programs in virtualized environments. Lock-holder preemption (LHP) [32] and vCPU stacking [27] are two unique issues arise with SMP scheduling. To mitigate these issues, researchers have proposed relaxed scheduling [29], balance scheduling [27], demand-based coordinated scheduling [11], and scheduling approaches based on spinlock-detection [7, 9, 32, 34].

In this work, we discover a hidden issue in consolidating SMP VMs – the scalable design of having independent schedulers on individual CPUs makes it difficult to achieve fair CPU allocation for SMP VMs. Existing mechanisms to enforce fairness, e.g., dynamic load balancing and CPU capping, however exacerbate SMP synchronization overhead. Figure 1(a) shows the actual CPU allocations for two heterogeneous VMs sharing four CPUs. SMP VMs can become heterogeneous in the number of vCPUs if some vCPUs are idle and go offline. The workloads running in the VMs are simply infinite loops that fully utilize a VM's processor resources. VMs were assigned the same weights and vCPUs were grouped together (e.g., using Linux `cgroup` in KVM) sharing the per-VM share. As shown in Figure 1(a), popular virtualization platforms, such as Xen [36], KVM [6] and VMware [33], are unable to achieve fair allocation at the VM level. The VM with a larger number of vCPUs gain advantages in getting more CPU resources. We attribute the unfairness to the use of per-CPU schedulers and the load imbalance on individual CPUs that leads to inaccurate CPU allocations. Load-balancing (LB) and CPU capping (cap) are popular approaches to enforce fairness, but introduce significant synchronization overhead to parallel workloads with different synchronization methods.

Figure 1(b) shows the performance of parallel workloads under different fairness mechanisms in Xen. Parallel workloads ran in the 4-vCPU VM and was co-located with a homogeneous (`homo.`) 4-vCPU VM or a heterogeneous (`heter.`) 3-vCPU VM. Details of the workloads are explained in Section 5. The baseline is when two homogeneous (`homo.`) VMs are co-located and their vCPUs are pinned (`PIN`) to CPUs. From the figure, we can see that when CPU capping is in place, heterogeneity in VM configuration incurs significant slowdowns (as much as 3X) to workloads

with busy-waiting synchronization (e.g., spinlocks). When LB is used for fairness, it penalizes workloads with non-busy-waiting synchronization (e.g., mutexes). In addition, workloads with coarse-grained synchronization are resilient to these fairness mechanisms.

In this work, we propose a unified approach, *Flex*, for enforcing VM-level fairness and improving the execution efficiency of parallel programs in virtualized environments. Flex relies on two independent components: (1) *FlexW* achieves VM-level fairness by dynamically adjusting VM weights to account for the allocation inaccuracies caused by load imbalance on individual CPUs; (2) *FlexS* improves parallel execution efficiency by eliminating busy-waiting time and accelerating sequential portions of parallel programs. FlexS employs a novel vCPU migration algorithm to prioritize vCPUs doing useful work without compromising VM-level fairness. To identify busy-waiting vCPUs, we also devise a simple but effective hardware metric-based approach. We find that branches per instruction (BPI) and branch miss prediction rate (BMPR) together accurately pinpoint the spin loops in different implementations of busy-waiting-based synchronization.

We have implemented Flex in Xen and performed comprehensive evaluations with various parallel workloads. Experimental results show that Flex achieves fairness between heterogeneous VMs with on average no more than 5% deviation from the ideal fair allocation. Further, Flex is able to realize a reasonably good level of differentiation and proportional allocation between VMs with different weights. Finally, Flex effectively reduces spinning time for busy-waiting-based workloads and avoids vCPU stacking for blocking-based workloads. Compared to default Xen, Flex achieves similar performance for VMs with advantages in CPU allocation and significantly boosts the performance of VMs with disadvantages. Flex performs closely to two representative co-scheduling and demand-based scheduling approaches in optimizing a single workload. When simultaneously optimizing a mix of two parallel workloads, Flex significantly outperforms both approaches by 30.4% and 35%, respectively. Moreover, Flex only incurs less than 1% of overhead to the critical execution path of Xen.

The rest of the paper is organized as follows. Section 2 introduces the basics of SMP VM scheduling and parallel synchronization, discusses challenges in attaining VM-level fairness and parallel efficiency. Section 3 and Section 4 describe the design and implementation of Flex, respectively. Section 5 presents the experiment results. Section 6 discusses related work and Section 7 concludes this paper.

2. Background and Motivation

In this section, we first describe the basics of SMP virtual machine scheduling and discuss parallel workloads with different synchronization mechanisms. Then, we demonstrate the difficulty of attaining fairness between SMP VMs in a multicore scenario. Finally, we show that existing scheduling strategies for fairness are inaccurate and introduce significant inefficiencies to parallel workloads.

2.1 SMP Virtual Machine Scheduling

Symmetric MultiProcessing (SMP) VMs, each configured with two or more virtual CPUs (vCPUs), allow users to simultaneously access multiple processors. Therefore, SMP VMs are widely used for hosting parallel workloads. In a virtualized environment, there exists a double scheduling scenario [25], where a guest operating system (OS) schedules processes on vCPUs and the hypervisor schedules vCPUs on physical CPUs (pCPUs). In systems with co-located VMs, multiple vCPUs could run on the same pCPU and the hypervisor allocates CPU cycles according to the *share* of each vCPU. To enforce fairness between VMs, the hypervisor assigns equal shares to individual VMs and the shares are further evenly distributed to vCPUs. Thus, VMs with a smaller number of vCPUs will receive a larger per-vCPU share. When a vCPU finishes running, its share is updated based on how long it ran on the pCPU.

Besides CPU shares, most systems also use an upper bound (e.g., a cap) to limit the maximum amount of CPU a VM is able to consume, even if the systems have idle CPU cycles. Such a resource limit effectively prevents rogue VMs from monopolizing all the resources and realizes performance isolation between VMs. In multicore systems, for scalability considerations, CPUs run independent copies of the scheduler. Load imbalance on different CPUs compromises the overall throughput and responsiveness. Thus, the schedulers perform load-balancing to evenly distribute vCPUs onto pCPUs. In general, there are two approaches to load balancing: *push migration* and *pull migration*. In push migration, the load-balancer periodically checks load balance in the memory hierarchy and pushes vCPUs from a busy node (e.g., a scheduling domain in Linux CFS scheduler) to a less-busy one if an imbalance is found. Pull migrations occur when a pCPU becomes idle and steals (or pulls) a waiting vCPU from a busy pCPU.

2.2 Parallel Program

Parallel programs break large problems into smaller tasks and solve them concurrently. The performance of parallel programs depends critically on the efficiency of task synchronization. We introduce different synchronization methods and discuss their issues in virtualized environments.

2.2.1 Task Synchronization

Task synchronization is needed to ensure correctness if multiple tasks share data with each other. There are many synchronization primitives designed for different purposes, such as `mutex`/`semaphore`, `spinlock` and `barrier`, typically

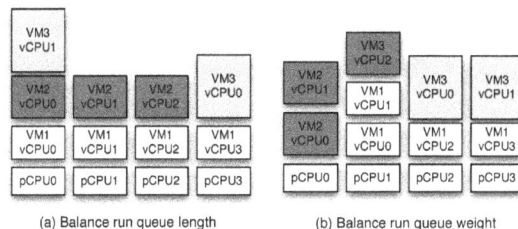

(a) Balance run queue length   (b) Balance run queue weight

Figure 2. vCPU-to-pCPU mappings for three heterogeneous VMs under different load-balancing policies. All VMs have the same share and the size of each vCPU represents the per-vCPU share.

there are two ways [1] to deal with a task that waits to access the critical section.

Busy-waiting (spinning). The task simply stays in a busy loop and repeatedly checks if the lock is available. Spinning is efficient if synchronization is expected to be very short and the task remains active to avoid expensive context switches. However, long spinning will lead to wasted CPU cycles that would be otherwise used by other tasks. Programs using busy-waiting synchronization are more susceptible to lock-holder preemptions (LHP) in virtualized environments.

Non-busy-waiting (blocking). The task voluntarily goes to sleep when fails to acquire the lock and is later awoken by the scheduler once the lock is released. Blocking effectively avoids wasted CPU cycles but requires frequent context switches. As shown in [11], spinlocks are also used to protect the queue that holds sleeping tasks when the lock is released and the scheduler dequeues (awakes) one task from the queue. Thus, blocking synchronizations are not immune to the inefficiencies in virtualized environments.

2.3 Challenges

Next, we discuss the challenges in attaining fairness and efficiency when scheduling SMP VMs in multicore systems.

2.3.1 Enforcing VM-level Fairness

Fair SMP VM scheduling requires that the aggregate CPU allocation to all vCPUs of a VM be proportional to its weight (share) in competition with other VMs sharing the same set of pCPUs. If all VMs have the same weight, each VM should receive the same amount of CPU time no matter how many vCPUs a VM has. As shown in Figure 1(a), existing VM schedulers fail to enforce VM-level fairness between heterogeneous VMs with different numbers of vCPUs. Although vCPU weights determine the relative CPU allocations on a pCPU, the absolute allocation depends on the total weight on the pCPU. In Figure 2, we demonstrate how the divergence on pCPU total weights leads to unfair allocation at VM level. We place three heterogeneous VMs, each with 4vCPU, 3vCPU and 2vCPU, respectively, on four pCPUs.

---

[1] Although a hybrid approach is possible, e.g., `spin-then-block`, we treat it as an application of the two fundamental approaches.

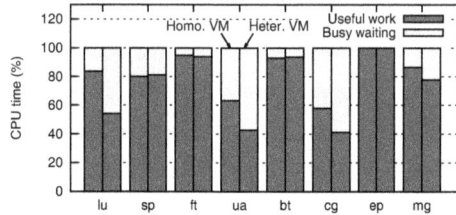

Figure 3. Imbalanced vCPU time allocation due to the co-location of heterogeneous VMs. Fairness capping introduces excessive busy-waiting time for NPB applications.

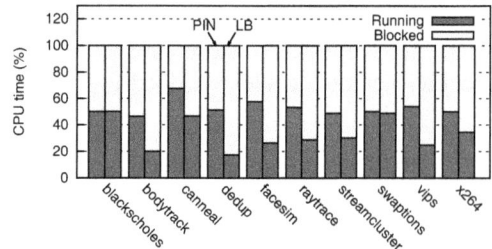

Figure 4. Dynamic load balancing (LB) penalizes PARSEC applications with blocking synchronization.

Figure 2(a) shows a typical vCPU mapping policy that balances the run queue size on each pCPU. For fairness, all VMs are given equal shares and their per-vCPU weights are inversely proportional to their vCPU counts.

Since there is an odd number of vCPUs on an even number of pCPUs, load imbalance inevitably exists. Thus, CPU allocations on vCPUs are no longer proportional to their weights. For example, VM3-vCPU1 receives less CPU time than VM3-vCPU0 because its allocation is diluted by a larger total weight on pCPU0. More importantly, the allocations on VM3-vCPU1 , VM1-vCPU1 and VM2-vCPU1 are not proportional to their weights, breaking VM-level fairness. A possible solution is to balance the run queue weight (as shown in Figure 2(b)) to minimize vCPU weight dilution. However, perfect weight balance on different pCPUs is not always possible and such balancing may introduce the vCPU stacking issue [27], which limits the effective parallelism and increases the synchronization latency in SMP VMs. In production systems, VM management software often pre-calculates the fair share of individual VMs and applies a resource *cap* to each VM, preventing it from consuming excessive CPU time. With a cap, vCPUs are stopped if the total CPU allocation of a VM exceeds its fair share. However, the use of resource cap turns the system into non-work-conserving mode and may lead to wasted resources.

2.3.2 Maximizing Parallel Efficiency

Synchronization overhead has been accused of limiting the scalability and performance of parallel programs in a virtualized environment [7, 11, 27, 32]. Lock-holder preemption (LHP) [32] and vCPU stacking [27] are two uniques issues that arise with SMP VM scheduling. We show that mechanisms for enforcing fairness inadvertently exacerbate these synchronization issues.

The LHP issue refers to the preemption of the vCPU that holds an important lock in the guest OS. Such preemptions seriously increase synchronization latency to milliseconds as opposed to a few microseconds in physical systems. In the case of spinlock holder preemption, CPU time is wasted when other sibling vCPUs busy-wait for the preempted vCPU to release the lock. We find that fairness mechanisms, such as vCPU capping, can lead to excessive busy-waiting or wasted CPU time. We ran the NASA paral-

lel benchmark (NPB) [5] in a 4-vCPU VM co-located with a heterogeneous 3-vCPU VM on four pCPUs. The background 3-vCPU VM ran three while(1) loops to burn CPU time. To enforce fairness, we applied a cap equivalent to the time of two CPUs to each VM. The OpenMP version of NPB was used and compiled with option OMP_WAIT_POLICY set to active. With this setting, threads stay in spin loops while waiting for other threads. For comparison, we also ran the NPB benchmark with a homogeneous 4-vCPU VM in the background. In this setting, no vCPU capping is needed. We instrumented NPB source code to calculate the total busy-waiting time spent by all threads.

Figure 3 shows that the co-location of heterogeneous VMs caused excessive busy-waiting in NPB applications. In heterogeneous co-location, the vCPU that had less contention on CPU time spent significant portion of time waiting for other slower vCPUs. When vCPU capping is in place, such wasted time is counted towards the fair share of the VM. As such, busy-waiting wastes the time could otherwise be used by useful work. Note that applications that dynamically adjust work assignment for application threads (e.g., ft, bt, sp) and applications without synchronization (e.g., ep) are resilient to such imbalance caused by vCPU capping.

As discussed in Section 2.3.1, load-balancing helps enforce VM-level fairness by averaging the run queue size or weight on different pCPUs so that actual CPU consumptions approximate VM weights. For example, pCPUs with less load will become idle earlier and steal (pull) runnable vCPUs from busier pCPUs. However, our findings reveal that such vCPU migrations cause severe slowdowns to parallel applications with blocking synchronization. We ran the PARSEC [30] benchmark in a 4-vCPU VM along with a 3-vCPU background VM running while(1) loops. PARSEC is composed of multithreaded programs that use Pthread blocking synchronization primitives. If failing to enter the critical section, a thread blocks itself and goes to sleep. Figure 4 draws the time that threads spent in running and blocked states under two scheduling policies. PIN binds vC-PUs to pCPUs and ensures that no vCPUs belonging to the same VM reside on one pCPU. It is similar to *balance scheduling* [27] and may incur imbalanced CPU allocation. Load-balancing (LB) allows vCPU migrations for fairness. From the figure, we can see that LB incurs excessive vCPU blocking to PARSEC applications. When PARSEC threads block themselves, the vCPUs that carry these threads become idle and also get blocked by the hypervisor. Thus, the corresponding pCPUs become idle and start to steal vC-PUs from other pCPUs. Since vCPU migrations only steal runnable (not actually running) vCPUs on the run queue, it is likely that vCPUs belonging to PARSEC applications are stolen as vCPUs running the `while(1)` loop never block and are likely in the running state during the steal. As a result, load-balancing causes severe vCPU stacking issues for application with blocking synchronization.

[**Summary**] In this section, we have shown that it is difficult to achieve VM-level fairness in multicore systems and existing solutions are likely to cause LHP and vCPU stacking issues. These findings motivated us to develop a SMP VM scheduling scheme that separates fairness enforcement from the rest of the scheduler and is carefully designed for improving parallel efficiency. To this end, we design FlexW, a vCPU accounting scheme that dynamically adjusts VM weights to realize fair allocation at the VM level, and FlexS, a flexible vCPU scheduling algorithm that eliminates wasted busy-waiting time.

3. Flex Scheduling for Fairness and Efficiency

Based on our findings, we attribute the unfairness in a heterogeneous VM co-location scenario to the inaccurate CPU allocation caused by diluted vCPU weights. We also find that excessive busy-waiting and vCPU stacking are the culprits of parallel performance slowdowns. Therefore, we try to answer the following questions when designing Flex. (1) *How to adaptively change vCPU weights to achieve VM-level fairness?* (2) *How to schedule vCPUs to eliminate busy-waitings?* (3) *How to avoid vCPU stacking?*

3.1 Overview

Flex centers on two key designs: flexible vCPU weight adjustment (FlexW) and flexible vCPU scheduling (FlexS). FlexW is a system-wide CPU accounting daemon that periodically monitors the actual CPU consumptions of all VMs. It calculates the desired fair share of individual VMs based on their weights. If there is a difference between actual allotted CPU time and the fair share, FlexW adjusts VM weights to compensate the discrepancy. FlexS is part of the vCPU scheduling module running on individual pCPUs. It nonintrusively detects busy-waiting vCPUs according to hardware metrics and preempts such vCPUs to avoid wasted CPU time. Before scheduling a vCPU from other VMs, FlexS tries to steal a sibling vCPU that is doing useful work from other pCPUs' run queues. In the following subsections, we present the details of each design.

Algorithm 1 Flexible vCPU Weight Adjustment

1: **Variables:** Virtual CPU v; Weight of the i_{th} VM w_i; Real-time weight of the i_{th} VM w_i^r; Number of shared CPUs P;
2:
3: /* System-wide accounting for period (t_1, t_2) */
4: **procedure** CPU_ACCOUNTING($void$)
5:     $acct\_count$++
6:     **for each** VM **do**
7:         **for each** vCPU **do**
8:             $cpus\_and(workers, workers, v \rightarrow cpu\_affinity)$
9:         **end for**
10:    **end for**
11:    $P = cpus\_weight(workers)$
12:    **for each** VM **do**
13:        $S_{i,GPS}(t_1, t_2) = \frac{w_i}{\sum w_j}(t_2 - t_1) \cdot P$
14:        $lag_i(t_1, t_2) = \frac{S_{i,GPS}(t_1, t_2) - S_i(t_1, t_2)}{S_{i,GPS}(t_1, t_2)}$
15:        $w_i^r = w_i^r + w_i \cdot lag_i(t_1, t_2)$
16:        **if** $acct\_count >$ FAIR_WINDOW **then**
17:            $acct\_count = 0$
18:            $w_i^r = w_i$
19:        **end if**
20:    **end for**
21: **end procedure**

3.2 Flexible vCPU Weight Adjustment

Algorithm 1 shows the flexible vCPU weight adjustment algorithm. For each accounting period, FlexW first determines the number of pCPUs shared by all VMs. Note that VMs may share different sets of pCPUs and form multiple accounting groups, each of which requires fair allocation within the group. In this work, we assume a single accounting group that shares the same set of pCPUs and leave enforcing fairness in multiple groups to future work. Then the total CPU time for shared P CPUs during time period (t_1, t_2) becomes $(t_2 - t_1) \cdot P$. Next, FlexW calculates the fair allocation $S_{i,GPS}(t_1, t_2)$ (line 12) under the idealized *Generalized Processor Sharing (GPS)* [21] algorithm using a VM's original weight w_i. The *lag* of a vCPU is the normalized difference between the fair allocation $S_{i,GPS}(t_1, t_2)$ and its actual consumed CPU time $S_i(t_1, t_2)$ (line 13). A positive lag indicates that the vCPU has received less time than under GPS [14] and vice versa. Finally, FlexW determines the real-time weight w_i^r of the VM based on its lag (in percentage) relative to the fair allocation and uses the adjusted weight in the next accounting interval. Note that we bring the lag to the same scale of weights by multiplying it with the original weight w_i.

There are many practical issues FlexW needs to deal with. The work-conserving property still needs to be preserved when enforcing fairness. Before calculating the fair share for each VM, FlexW checks if the total consumed CPU time equals to the available time (i.e., $(t_2 - t_1) \cdot P$). If VMs do not consume all CPU time, FlexW simply quits the weight adjustment process and set the real-time weights to the original weights. As such, the CPU time a VM could use is only limited when the system is overcommitted. Another issue is *infeasible weight* [21], where a VM's peak CPU consumption is smaller than its fair share. For example, a 2-vCPU VM's weight becomes infeasible if the fair share for this VM is equivalent to the time of 3 CPU. To this end, FlexW only calculates the fair share of VMs with feasible weight and uses the peak consumption as the fair share of VMs with infeasible weight.

Although FlexW resets VMs' real-time weights once the total CPU demand is below the available CPU time, it is possible that some VMs demand less than their fair share and others consume more than their share. In this case, FlexW still considers the system under work-conserving mode and keeps updating VMs' real-weights. As a result, the VMs that voluntarily demand less CPU will have ever-increasing real weights and will monopolize the CPU once their demands increase. Our solution is to keep a limited history of allocations and enforce fairness within a FAIR_WINDOW. All real-time weights are reset to original weights when switching to the next fair window (line 16). This design effectively prevents VMs from occupying the CPU for too long, but still gives frequent idling VMs higher shares within a fair window when they wake up.

3.3 Flexible vCPU Scheduling

While FlexW enforces fairness between VMs, it does not guarantee efficient SMP VM scheduling. It even introduces load imbalance as some vCPUs receive less CPU time than their siblings. As discussed in Section 2.3.2, load imbalance leads to excessive spin time for busy-waiting-based workloads and vCPU stacking for blocking-based workloads. Co-scheduling [20] has been considered most effective in minimizing synchronization latency, but suffers CPU fragmentation and priority inversion issues. Scheduling and de-scheduling vCPUs together is even harder under fairness constraints. When designing FlexS, we do not attempt to explicitly co-schedule vCPUs. Instead, we believe that synchronization efficiency is maximized if CPU time is only used for useful work during an accounting period. Thus, the objectives of FlexS are to de-schedule busy-waiting vCPUs and schedule vCPUs doing useful work as much as possible.

3.3.1 Identifying Busy-waiting vCPUs

Since busy-waiting avoids expensive context switches, it is widely used in application libraries and OS kernels. There is existing work detecting excessive busy-waiting by instrumenting Linux kernel to report spinning statistics [34] or by non-intrusively monitoring user-kernel mode switches [32] or by counting store instructions [7]. Besides kernel instrumentation being not always possible, existing non-intrusive approaches are not applicable to user-level busy-waiting implementations [32] or not accurate for different workloads [7]. For example, it is difficult to set a threshold for store-based spin detection and some applications (e.g., lu)

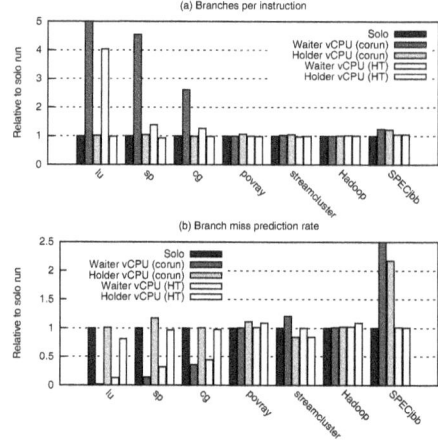

Figure 5. Branches per instruction (BPI) and Branch miss prediction rate (BMPR) together accurately identify busy-waiting vCPUs.

have inherent differences in the frequency of issuing stores on different threads (e.g., the master thread issues 20X times more stores than others). To this end, we design a simple but effective mechanism for busy-waiting detection.

Similar to hardware-assisted spin detection [9], which identifies busy-waiting vCPUs as ones execute excessive PAUSE instructions, our approach also finds a common pattern that spans across different spin implementations. We find that spin loops are usually designed to be highly efficient and contain only a few instructions. Such short loops are executed many times until the lock is acquired. Compared to other loops at both user and kernel levels, spin loops show a high branch per instruction (BPI) rate. Further, as the loops are repeatedly executed, the hardware branch predictor has a low branch miss prediction rate (BMPR). More importantly, spin loops always accompany with a lock-holder who is running the normal code. Thus, high BPI rates and low BMPR values along with distinctive behaviors from other vCPUs are good indicators of busy-waiting vCPUs. To validate our spin detection design, we created scenarios that one vCPU is slower than others. When executing parallel workloads, the slower vCPU is likely the lock/mutex *holder* and the faster ones are likely the *waiters*. We made a vCPU slower by running a while(1) loop on the same pCPU (i.e., corun) or running the loop on the pCPU's hyperthread (i.e., HT). Solo (without contention) was used as the baseline. We ran different 4-thread workloads to study the correlation between branch related hardware metrics and high-level synchronization. Details of parallel workloads are explained in Section 5. Besides parallel workloads, we also included a multiprogrammed workload with 4 copies of povray from the SPEC CPU2006 benchmark [31].

Figure 5(a) and (b) show that BPI climbs and BMPR plummets on spinning vCPUs (e.g., waiters in lu, sp and cg). Interestingly, BPI and BMPR not only qualitatively identify busy-waiting vCPUs but also quantitatively re-

Algorithm 2 Flexible vCPU Scheduling

1: **Variables:** Virtual CPU v; Maximum BPI (max_bpi) in v's VM; Minimum BMPR (min_bmpr) in v's VM.
2:
3: /* Periodic local vCPU accounting*/
4: **procedure** VCPU_ACCOUNTING(v)
5:     Burn_credits(v)
6:     Update v's BPI and BMPR values
7:     /* If vCPU is busy waiting, call Sschedule() and yield to others */
8:     **if** (Is_busy_waiting(v)) **then**
9:         $v \rightarrow yield = \text{TURE}$
10:         $raise\_softirq(\text{SCHEDULE\_SOFTIRQ})$
11:     **else**
12:         $v \rightarrow yield = \text{FALSE}$
13:     **end if**
14: **end procedure**
15:
16: **procedure** IS_BUSY_WAITING(v)
17:     /*BPI close to max and BMPR close to min indicate spinning*/
18:     **if** $\frac{(max\_bpi - v \rightarrow bpi)*10}{max\_bpi} == 0$ and $\frac{(v \rightarrow bmpr - min\_bmpr)*10}{min\_bmpr} == 0$ **then**
19:         return TRUE
20:     **else**
21:         return FALSE
22:     **end if**
23: **end procedure**
24:
25: **procedure** SCHEDULE($void$)
26:     /* If just yielded, switch this vCPU with a sibling on another CPU. Otherwise, follow the regular path. */
27:     **if** $curr \rightarrow yield ==$ TRUE **then**
28:         $next = $ Load_balance($curr$, SWITCH)
29:     **else**
30:         **if** load is balanced **then**
31:             $next = $ next vCPU in local run queue
32:         **else**
33:             $next = $ Load_balance($curr$, STEAL)
34:         **end if**
35:     **end if**
36:     Context switch to $next$
37: **end procedure**

---

flect the level of contention. For example, BPI is lower and BMPR is higher in HT than in Corun as the loop in HT does not contend CPU cycles but only shared resources like the reservation station and caches. Because synchronization contributes most to the dynamic portion of program execution, the number of branches executed per instruction stays relatively stable for programs with no or little synchronization no matter there is contention or not. As shown in Figure 5(a), independent copies of povray have similar BPI values in all scenarios. Similar conclusions can also be made for workloads with blocking synchronization (e.g., streamcluster and SPECjbb) as spinlocks are only used when operating on the queue of waiting threads [11]. Since

Hadoop workload embraces the embarrassing parallel model and its map tasks are largely independent of each other, its BPI also does not change with contentions. Figure 5(b) shows that BMPR changes more significantly than BPI for blocking workloads. One possible explanation is that the frequent switches between vCPUs due to voluntary vCPU blocking pollute the history of branch predictors leading to higher BMPRs. Nevertheless, due to the lack of short spin loops, BMPR never drops dramatically for these workloads.

Based on our observations, we use a simple heuristic to identify busy-waiting vCPUs – *If some vCPUs have the highest BPIs and the lowest BMPRs among their siblings, they are spinning*. FlexS maintains the maximum BPI and minimum BMPR among all vCPUs in a VM. When deciding a vCPU's busy-waiting status, FlexS calculates the distances of its BPI and BMPR to the VM-wide maximum and minimum. If being close enough (within 10%, line 18 in Algorithm 2), FlexS considers the vCPU a busy-waiter and performs flexible scheduling to eliminate busy-waiting time. It is possible that there may exist false-positive detections as FlexS infers busy-waiting vCPUs based on cross-vCPU comparisons. During program initialization or execution phase changes, some vCPUs can show considerably different behaviors than others and be mistakenly identified as spinning. To this end, FlexS clears BPI and BMPR values when a fair window expires so that program phases could be detected and false positives would not affect next detection windows.

3.3.2 Eliminating Busy-waiting Time

The key to eliminating busy-waiting is to stop spinning vCPUs and run vCPUs with useful work. Algorithm 2 shows the design of flexible vCPU scheduling. During periodic local vCPU accounting, FlexS updates a vCPU's BPI and BMPR values with new performance monitoring unit (PMU) readings. If FlexS identifies the vCPU as busy-waiting (function Is_busy_waiting), it raises a soft IRQ interrupt (line 10) on this pCPU and forces a call to the main Schedule function, where the current vCPU will be de-scheduled and the next-to-run vCPU is selected. Since the de-scheduled vCPU voluntarily yields to others, its unfinished time slice should be used to by its sibling vCPUs with useful work. Thus, the Schedule function has two paths when scheduling vCPUs. If a vCPU just yielded (line 27), FlexS pulls a runnable but not busy-waiting sibling (with a false yield flag) of this vCPU from another pCPU. Otherwise, follow the regular path.

To **avoid vCPU stacking**, Flex integrates balance scheduling into its design. When performing load balancing, we ensure that no vCPUs from the same VM will be stacked on one pCPU. For the yielded vCPU path, FlexS switches two vCPUs on two pCPUs so that no stacking could happen. For the regular path, if load is imbalanced (line 33), only vCPUs that have no siblings on the current pCPU could be stolen. However, frequent vCPU migrations will likely violate the fairness enforced by FlexW. This is because switching vCPUs (usually with different weights) changes the total weights of pCPUs. As discussed in Section 2.3.1, such a divergence in pCPU weights causes unfairness. We find that VMs that migrate vCPUs frequently tend to gain advantage in CPU allocation. To **preserve fairness**, we ensure that vCPU migrations do not affect the total weight on individual pCPUs. Specifically, FlexS exchanges the weights of two vCPUs when switching them. Besides the weight, a vCPU's relative position in its run queue also affects its CPU allocation. To this end, FlexS does not insert the switched out vCPU onto another pCPU's run queue, which will always put the vCPU on the tail of the run queue. Instead, the run queue pointers of the switching vCPUs are exchanged. As such, no run queue operations are needed on both pCPUs and the run queue positions are preserved.

4. Implementation

We implemented Flex in Xen (version 4.0.2) and patched Xen with *Perfctr-Xen* [18] to access low-level hardware performance counters. Perfctr-Xen maintains a per-vCPU data structure to store the values of hardware counters. We updated counter values every time (every 10 ms) Xen performs vCPU accounting. Xen uses *credit* to represent weight. For every 10 ms, a per-pCPU accounting routine burns the current running vCPU's credit. A system-wide master routine fires up every 30 ms to replenish credits for VMs based on their weights. The higher the weight, the more credits a VM receives per master accounting period. To calculate BPI and BMPR, we calculated the ratio of hardware events BR_INST_EXEC and INST_RETIRED, BR_MISP_EXEC and BR_INST_EXEC, respectively.

FlexW is implemented in the system-wide master accounting routine csched_acct(), where it iterates over all VMs and vCPUs. The iteration determines the total credit for the pCPUs shared by vCPUs, the max_bpi and min_bmpr of each VM, and the total consumed credits for each VM. FlexW computes the credits to be assigned to individual VMs in the next interval based on their real time weights. We added a global flag in Xen to record VM creation/termination and vCPU affinity changes. If nothing has changed since last accounting, we avoid the iteration that calculates the total available credit (Algorithm 1, line 6-9). We empirically set FAIR_WINDOW to 10 seconds, after which we reset VMs' real-time weights. To catch program phase changes, we also clear a VM's max_bpi and min_bmpr when a fair window expires.

The key to the effectiveness of FlexS in minimizing busy-waiting time is to find vCPUs with useful work on remote pCPUs. A per-pCPU run queue lock needs to be acquired from a remote pCPU before any vCPU can be stolen. Both a stealing pCPU and the main schedule function on a remote pCPU can contend for the lock. Note that the per-pCPU accounting timers have the same 10 ms interval and the per-

pCPU schedule timers have intervals of 30 ms (exactly three times of the accounting timers). Thus, a stealing pCPU is likely to collide with another stealing pCPU or the local schedule function. We make the per-pCPU accounting timer dynamic to avoid the lock contention. FlexS keeps a counter for each vCPU to record how many times it failed to steal a remote vCPU. FlexS sets the next vCPU accounting timer by subtracting its counter value from the default 10 ms. The counter is cleared when a vCPU succeeds in the stealing. Therefore, vCPUs wait for different amount of time before they try to steal again. vCPUs with higher failure counts will perform the stealing earlier than the ones recently succeeded in stealing. This effectively increases the success rate of stealing and leads to less wasted busy-waiting time. Iterating over all pCPUs for the stealing is not scalable as the number of shared pCPUs increases. To bound the steal time, we borrow the idea of the power of two choices [16]. That is, a vCPU iterates over two pCPUs for stealing before it quits.

5. Evaluation

In this section, we present an evaluation of Flex using various parallel workloads. We study the effectiveness of Flex in enforcing fairness and realizing differentiation in a multicore scenario (Section 5.1). Then we compare the performance of Flex with Xen's default credit scheduler and two representative co-scheduling approaches (Section 5.2). Finally, we study the overhead of Flex (Section 5.3).

We implemented Flex in Xen 4.0.2 and deployed our prototype on Dell PowerEdge T420, equipped with two quad-core Intel Xeon E5620 2.4GHz processors and 16GB memory. To evaluate the fairness and performance of Flex, we created two heterogeneous Xen VMs with 4 vCPUs and 3 vCPUs, respectively. Both VMs were configured with 6GB memory and set to the default weight (256 in Xen). We ran Linux kernel 2.6.32 with para-virtualized spinlocks as the guest OS. Both VMs were set to share four cores in one of the two processors. This setting ensures that all vCPUs share the same last-level cache and NUMA node so that the performance of parallel workloads only depends on the allocation of CPU time. For overhead study, we created up to 8 VMs, each with 4 vCPUs.

We selected the following parallel workloads and measured their performance with different approaches.

- **NASA parallel benchmarks (NPB)** [5] include 9 parallel programs derived from computational fluid dynamics applications. We used the OpenMP implementation of the benchmarks and set the problem size to class C. Environment variable OMP_WAIT_POLICY was set to active to use busy-waiting synchronization.

- **PARSEC** [30] is a multithreaded shared memory benchmark. Its contains 13 emerging programs that model after divergent application domains. Pthread non-busy-waiting primitives (e.g., mutexes, condition variables and barri-

280

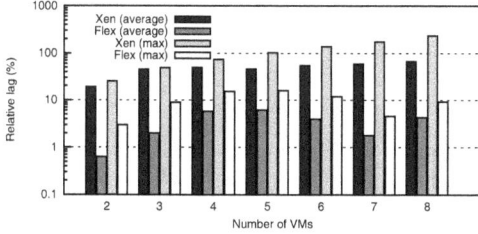

Figure 6. The average and maximum lag of Xen and Flex for different number of VMs.

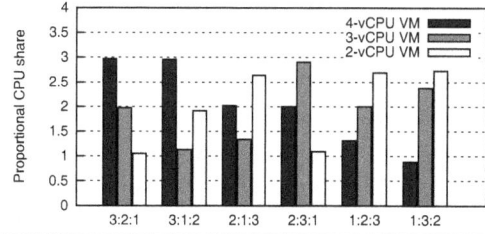

Figure 7. Flex realizes proportional share of CPU between VMs with different numbers of vCPU.

ers) are used for thread synchronization and the native input size was used.

- **Hadoop** is a popular implementation of the MapReduce framework for running data-parallel jobs. We selected a Bayesian classification job in the Hadoop Mahout machine learning library [28]. The job classifies 20,000 newsgroup documents into 20 categories. It consists of three phases of execution, each of which contains multiple map tasks and one reduce task. During each phase, the map tasks are independent of each other with no communications. The next phase starts only when the reduce task finishes in the previous phase.

- **SPECjbb2005** [26] evaluates the performance of server side Java by emulating a three-tier client/server system. It spawns multiple threads to emulate active users posting transaction requests in multiple warehouses within a wholesale company. Synchronization is needed when customer requests and company internal management operations both work on the same database table. Synchronized methods in Java are used to block waiting threads.

If not otherwise stated, we matched the number of threads/maps in these workloads with the number of vCPUs in the VMs.

For comparison, we evaluated three scheduling strategies:

- `Xen`: The default credit scheduler without mechanisms for VM-level fairness.

- `Balance+cap+CO`: For busy-waiting workloads, we used *balance scheduling* [27] with fairness capping. We also set the VM running parallel workloads to a higher priority to co-schedule its vCPUs.

- `Demand+cap`: For non-busy-waiting workloads, we implemented *demand-based coordinated scheduling* [11] with fairness capping. We monitored Xen event channel to prevent the preemption of sender vCPUs of interprocessor interrupts (IPI). Recipients of IPIs are by default prioritized by Xen as wakeup vCPUs are temporally elevated to the `boost` priority [19].

5.1 Fairness and Differentiation

In this subsection, we show the effectiveness of Flex in VM-level fairness and differentiation. We used the *absolute relative lag*, $|\frac{S_{i,GPS}(t_1,t_2) - S_i(t_1,t_2)}{S_{i,GPS}(t_1,t_2)}|$, to measure fairness. We

created four types of VMs with 4 vCPUs, 3 vCPUs, 2vCPUs and 1 vCPU, respectively. We changed the number of VMs sharing four cores and ensured that the mix contained heterogeneous VMs as many as possible. Figure 6 shows the maximum and average lag of individual VMs under Xen and Flex. From the figure, we can see that the default credit scheduler fails to enforce fairness at VM-level and the unfairness in terms of both maximum and average lag goes unboundedly to as much as 235% and 67%, respectively. In contrast, Flex achieves one order of magnitude (log scale in the y axis) less lag than Xen. The maximum lag of Flex is bounded by 15% and on average Flex incurs no more than 5% unfairness.

We are also interested in whether Flex can realize service differentiation, where VMs receive CPU time proportional to their weights. We consolidated three VMs, each with 4, 3, 2 vCPUs, respectively, onto four cores. Figure 7 shows the CPU allocation of the three VMs with different combinations of weight. Flex realized almost perfect proportional allocations for weight combination 3:2:1. However, allocations were not accurate when VMs with fewer vCPUs have large weights and VMs with more vCPUs have small weights, e.g., combinations 1:2:3 and 1:3:2. The reason is that Flex enforces proportional allocations for individual fair windows. Once VM real-time weights are reset, VMs with more vCPUs are likely to consume more CPU time, violating the proportionality. It is a trade-off between keeping a limited history of CPU allocation and perfect proportionality. Although not being always accurate, we conclude that Flex realizes a reasonably good level of differentiation.

5.2 Parallel Execution Efficiency

As discussed in Section 2.3.2, imbalanced CPU allocation in SMP VMs incurs excessive busy-waiting or severe vCPU stacking. In this subsection, we show that Flex is able to mitigate such issues and achieve good parallel efficiency. We first study the performance of one SMP VM in two imbalanced scenarios and then evaluate the performance of two SMP VMs with a mix of parallel workloads.

5.2.1 Imbalanced Allocation

We created two imbalanced scenarios, where two heterogeneous VMs, one with 4 vCPUs and one with 3 vCPUs, were co-located on four cores. As shown in Figure 1(a), the VM with more vCPUs gains advantage in getting more

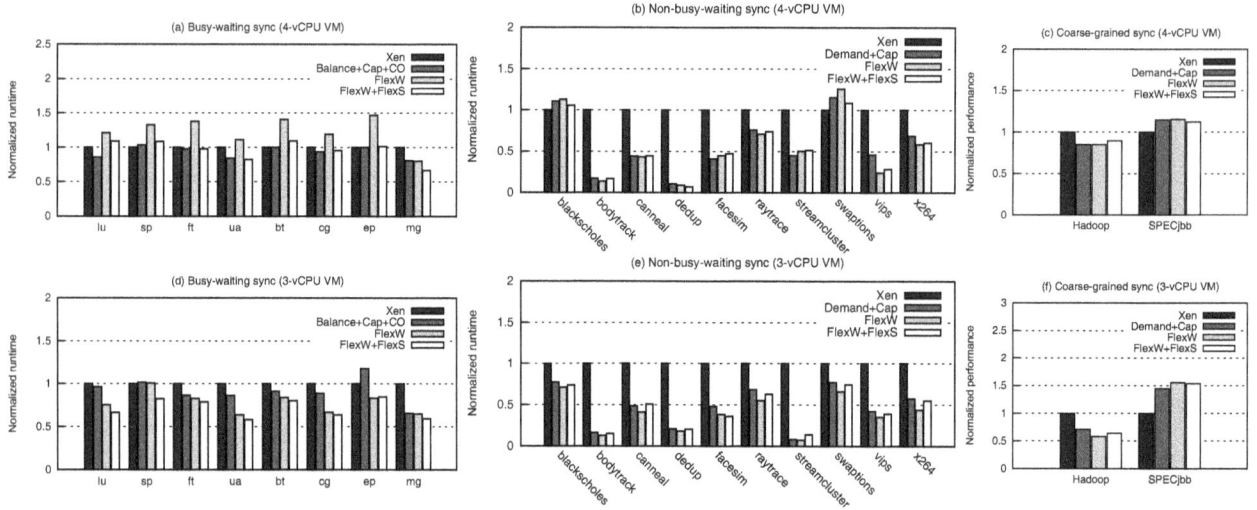

Figure 8. The performance of parallel workloads running with background `while(1)` loops under different policies. Runtime is normalized to baseline Xen and the lower the better. SPECjbb is measured using business operations per second (bops), the higher the better.

CPU time. We ran our parallel workloads in the two VMs in turn and measured their performance under different approaches. We studied two Flex variations: Flex without flexible scheduling (FlexW) and Flex with complete functionalities (FlexW+FlexS). To isolate performance from other factors, e.g., shared cache contention, we ran `while(1)` loops in the other VM.

Figures 8 (a) and (d) show the performance of NPB programs when running in the 4-vCPU and 3-vCPU VMs, respectively. The performance of different approaches is normalized to `Xen`. It is expected that default `Xen` delivered good performance in the 4-vCPU VM scenario because the VM attained more than its fair share. With balance scheduling and co-scheduling, `balance+cap+CO` achieved better performance (e.g., `lu`, `ua` and `mg`) than Xen using less CPU time (i.e., fair share). However, `balance+cap+CO` realizes co-scheduling by elevating the priority of the parallel workload, which inevitably hurts the performance of co-running workloads. We will show that this strategy performs badly when optimizing a mix of parallel workloads. Figure 8(a) also shows that `FlexW+FlexS` performed closely to `balance+cap+CO` except for `lu`. An examination of `lu` source code revealed that `lu` statically assigns work to threads and is sensitive to load imbalance. Unfortunately, `FlexW` alone was unable to deliver good performance with as much as 50% slowdown compared to `balance+cap+CO`. It indicates that only guaranteeing fair CPU share is not sufficient to achieve good performance. The key is to make efficient use of the fair share.

Figure 8(d) shows that both `FlexW` and `FlexW+FlexS` outperformed `Xen` and `balance+cap+CO` when NPB ran in the 3-vCPU VM. Similar to Xen, `balance+cap+CO` al-

located CPU time less than the fair share to the VM. Although capping effectively limited the co-running VM with `while(1)` loops to its fair share, the VM with parallel workloads was unable to consume its fair share as the imbalance diluted its weight and affected the actual CPU allocation. In contrast, both `FlexW` and `FlexW+FlexS` guaranteed fair share by using flexible weights. `FlexW+FlexS` performed consistently better than `FlexW` except for `ep`, which is an embarrassing parallel benchmark with no synchronizations. Thus, we conclude that `FlexS` effectively improved performance by reducing busy-waiting time.

Figures 8(b) and (e) show the performance of PARSEC benchmarks. As discussed in Section 2.3.2, default Xen incurs severe vCPU stacking issues to non-busy-waiting workloads when these workloads co-run with `while(1)` loops. Except for Xen, all the other three approaches avoids vCPU stacking. Therefore, their performance improvement over Xen was quite significant (as much as 10X for `bodytrack`). Because `blackscholes` and `swaptions` had little communication between threads, the vCPUs running these threads were less frequently blocked. The load-balancer in Xen effectively spread the vCPUs and avoided vCPU stacking. Thus, Xen outperformed other approaches in these two benchmarks (in Figure 8(b)) as the VM consumed more than its fair share under Xen. Similarly, the fairness capping in `demand+cap` stopped the `while(1)` VM from monopolizing CPU time and helped the load-balancer spread vCPUs. Among the best-performing approaches, Flex-based approaches outperformed `demand+cap` in the 3-vCPU VM scenario because `demand+cap` also had similar issues (as discussed above) attaining the fair share for the 3-vCPU VM. For the 4-vCPU VM scenario, `demand+cap` outperformed

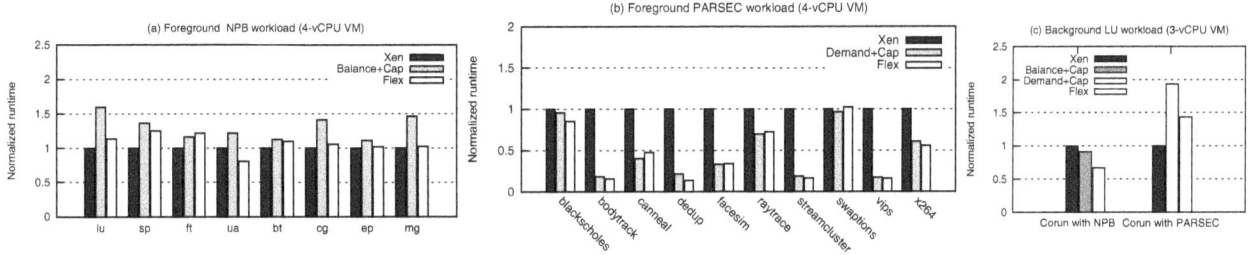

Figure 9. The performance of two parallel workloads running together. NPB and PARSEC run in the foreground and a copy of `lu` benchmark from NPB runs repeatedly in the background.

Flex-based approaches in `facesim` and `streamcluster`. These workloads are communication-intensive and IPI signals used by `demand+cap` provide more useful information about IPI senders and recipients than the hardware-level metrics. Another important observation is that `FlexW` achieved better performance than `FlexW+FlexS` in most workloads. The overhead of frequent vCPU migrations in `FlexS` outweighed its benefit of reducing busy-waiting as spinning only contributes to a small portion of thread synchronization in non-busy-waiting workloads.

Figures 8(c) and (f) show the performance of `Hadoop` and `SPECjbb`. These workloads have coarse-grained synchronization and do not benefit a lot from communication-aware scheduling schemes. The performance improvement of Flex-based approaches and `demand+cap` over Xen was due to the avoidance of vCPU stacking. Interestingly, `FlexW` outperformed `demand+cap` by 15% for Hadoop in the 3-vCPU VM scenario. The reason is that Flex kept increasing the VM's weight during the reduce phase as the CPU demand is below the fair share. This effectively accelerated the reduce task. In contrast, although the vCPU running the reduce task received all the share of the VM (other vCPUs were idle) in `demand+cap`, the actual CPU allocation was less than that in `Flex`. Therefore, Flex is able to accelerate the sequential portion of the `Hadoop` workload.

5.2.2 Mix of Parallel Workloads

In this experiment, we study a more practical scenario, where both co-located VMs ran parallel workloads. In this scenario, a scheduling scheme needs to optimize the performance of both workloads. As discussed above, `lu` employs static work assignment and is sensitive to the scheduling scheme. We used `lu` as the background workload and ran it repeatedly in the 3-vCPU VM. The foreground VM ran the NPB and PARSEC benchmarks in turn. We measured the performance of a scheme by averaging the performance relative to Xen for both foreground and background benchmarks. Since it is not possible to manually prioritize both workloads, we used `balance+cap` in this experiment. We use `Flex` to represent Flex with complete functionalities.

Figures 9(a), (b) and (c) show the performance of the foreground and background workloads. As expected, Xen

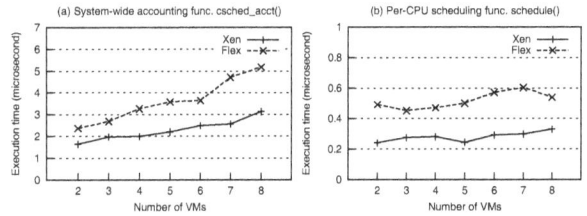

Figure 10. Overhead of Flex.

performed best for the foreground NPB workload as it allocated more than the fair share to it. However, this scarified the performance of `lu` in the background. Compared to `Flex`, Xen incurred 40% performance degradation to `lu` in Figure 9(c). Figures 9(a) and (c) also show that `Flex` achieved consistently better performance than `Balance+cap` in both foreground and background workloads. This confirms the observations in [11] that balance scheduling is not sufficient to optimize parallel performance in virtualized environments. In Figure 9(b), `Flex` performed closely to `demand+cap` in most workloads. However, `demand+cap` performed badly for the background `lu` as it is not designed for workload with busy-waiting loops. Overall, `Flex` outperformed `Balance+cap` and `demand+cap` by 30.4% and 35%, respectively.

5.3 Overhead

The overhead of Flex comes from two main sources: (1) the time required to adjust VM weights in the system-wide accounting function `csched_acct`; (2) the time required to perform vCPU stealing in the per-pCPU `schedule` function. Figures 10(a) and (b) show the execution time (in microsecond) of these two functions under Xen and Flex as the number of VMs increases. Since calculating VM weights requires the iteration over all vCPUs, the execution time of `csched_acct` in Flex increases faster than in Xen. However, the increase does not incur overhead to parallel programs as the global accounting is performed by the hypervisor's *idle* VM. The overhead in the main `schedule` function on individual pCPUs can be more significant to parallel performance. A prolonged `schedule` function will take up the time that can be used to run vCPUs. Figure 10 (b) shows that the distance between the execution time of `schedule` in Flex and in Xen does not increase with the number of VMs. Recall that Flex only tries to steal a vCPU from remote pCPUs for two times, its overhead compared to Xen in `schedule` is constant. Considering a scheduling interval of 30ms, Flex only adds less than 1% overhead to Xen.

6. Related Work

An important aspect of resource management is enforcing fairness across different entities. Fairness becomes even more critical for resource allocations in public cloud services because as a metered service, users expect the outcome of a cloud proportionate to their payment. It is believed that fairness in allocating computing resources like CPU cycles is well understood [3]. Thus, most work focused on addressing the unfairness in shared CPU caches [17], network I/O interface [3, 19] and shared storage [23]. Li *et al.* [14] were the first to find that scheduling algorithms based on per-CPU run queues are weak in fairness in a multicore scenario. For such algorithms, the allocation error relative to the ideal Generalized Processor Sharing [21] grows unboundedly with the number of threads and CPUs in the system. Li *et al.* proposed distributed weighted round robin (DRWW) which uses inter-CPU thread migrations to approximate GPS with a constant error. DRWW does not consider fairness for a group of threads thus is not applicable to scheduling SMP VMs. Linux `cgroup` [15] is designed for the fairness of a group of processes. However, as shown in Figure 1(a), it is weak in fairness when load is imbalanced on multiple CPUs. In contrast, Flex continuously monitors the actual CPU allocation for each VM and calculates the corresponding lag to the ideal allocation. Based on the lags, Flex adjusts VM weights accordingly. Although Flex does not explicitly address weight dilution due to load imbalance, it uses feedbacks of actual allocations to reduce unfairness.

There is a large body of work dedicated to addressing the synchronization overhead in parallel programs. Coscheduling of threads [20] refers to the scheme that schedules and de-schedules theads belonging to the same parallel application synchronously. Although it maximizes synchronization efficiency, it suffers from CPU fragmentation and priority inversion issues [13]. Demand-based scheduling, a less strict form of coscheduling, only involves the scheduling of communicating threads [4, 8, 24]. In a virtualized environment, there is a semantic gap between the hypervisor and guest OSes. Weng *et al.* [34] proposed to instrument the guest OS to report the statistics of spinlock holders and dynamically schedule them in the hypervisor. Because intrusive approaches are not always possible, work has been done to infer lock holders from user-kernel mode switches [32] or from low-level hardware statistics about store instructions [7]. However, these approaches are not applicable to all scenarios. For example, libraries with synchronization entirely in user mode (e.g., OpenMP) do not incur any user-

kernel mode switches or involve blocking. The frequency of store instructions may not be a good indicator of spinning for workloads with inherently different store issue rates in different threads. We found that the spin loops, no matter implemented at what levels, are shorter iterations compared to loops in regular code. Thus, our approach using BPI and BMPR to identify busy-waiting vCPUs is generic and applicable to a wide variety of workloads.

Modern CPUs provide hardware-assisted schemes (e.g., Intel's Pause Loop Exit (PLE) [10] and AMD's Pause Filter [2]) to detect excessive spinning by monitoring the `PAUSE` instruction in a busy-wait loop. Excessive spinning on a vCPU causes a transition from the guest OS to the hypervisor (e.g., via VMEXIT) and relinquishes the CPU to other VMs. However, hardware-based spin detection is only applicable to fully virtualized VMs and incurs frequent expensive VMEXITs to the hypervisor. In contrast, Flex uses a generic and lightweight spin detection mechanism based on hardware performance counters. It is applicable to both fully and para-virtualized VMs and does not require hardware virtualization support or traps into the hypervisor. Further, all the scheduling strategies in our experiments were configured with para-virtualized spinlocks, a software-based spin-then-block mechanism similar to PLE. Our results showed that Flex significantly outperformed the these approaches due to flexible vCPU scheduling.

Flex is closely related to demand-based coordinated scheduling [11], which infers synchronizing threads by observing IPI signals. This approach also addressed the load imbalance issue with load concious balance scheduling. However, it is only applicable to IPI-based synchronization and can not detect spin-based synchronization. Although Flex is designed for eliminating excessive spinning time, its enforcement of short term fairness during the fair window is likely to prioritize the active vCPUs in blocking-based workloads. Moreover, unlike load conscious scheduling [11], which only avoids overloaded CPUs, Flex takes one step forward to coordinate multiple CPUs in switching useful work.

7. Conclusion

Fairness-efficiency trade-offs have always been important issues in resource allocations. In this work, we find the deficiencies of existing hypervisors in enforcing fairness between SMP VMs. Straightforward solutions lead to low efficiency for parallel workloads. This paper proposes a holistic solution, *Flex*, to the fairness and efficiency issues. Flex separates its design into two independent parts. FlexW periodically monitors per-VM actual CPU allocation and adjusts VM weights to approximate the ideal fair allocation. FlexS eliminates excessive busy-waiting in guest OSes by detecting spinning vCPUs from hardware-level branch instruction metrics. FlexS stops busy-waiting vCPUs and opportunistically looks for vCPUs with useful work on other CPUs.

Experiments with Xen and various parallel workloads show that Flex is able to achieve allocations close to the ideal fair allocation and realizes a certain level of differentiation. Flex also shows good performance with parallel workloads using different synchronization methods.

Acknowledgements

We are grateful to the anonymous reviewers for their constructive comments. This research was supported in part by the U.S. National Science Foundation under grants CNS-1320122, CNS-1217979 and CNS-0844983.

References

[1] Amazon Elastic Compute Cloud. http://aws.amazon.com/ec2/.

[2] AMD Corporation. *AMD64 architecture programmers manual volume 2: System programming.* 2010.

[3] M. B. Anwer, A. Nayak, N. Feamster, and L. Liu. Network i/o fairness in virtual machines. In *Proc. of VISA*, 2010.

[4] A. C. Arpaci-Dusseau. Implicit coscheduling: coordinated scheduling with implicit information in distributed systems. *ACM Trans. Comput. Syst.*, 19(3), 2001.

[5] D. H. Bailey, E. Barszcz, J. T. Barton, D. S. Browning, R. L. Carter, L. Dagum, R. A. Fatoohi, P. O. Frederickson, T. A. Lasinski, R. S. Schreiber, H. D. Simon, V. Venkatakrishnan, and S. K. Weeratunga. The nas parallel benchmarkssummary and preliminary results. In *Proc. of SC*, 1991.

[6] K. based virtual machine. http://www.linux-kvm.org/.

[7] K. Chakraborty, P. M. Wells, and G. S. Sohi. Supporting overcommitted virtual machines through hardware spin detection. *IEEE Trans. Parallel Distrib. Syst.*, 23(2), Feb. 2012.

[8] A. C. Dusseau, R. H. Arpaci, and D. E. Culler. Effective distributed scheduling of parallel workloads. In *Proc. of SIGMETRICS*, 1996.

[9] Intel Corporation. *Intel® 64 and IA-32 Architectures Software Developer's Manual.* December 2009.

[10] Intel Corporation. *Intel® 64 and IA-32 Architectures Software Developer's Manual.* December 2009.

[11] H. Kim, S. Kim, J. Jeong, J. Lee, and S. Maeng. Demand-based coordinated scheduling for smp vms. In *Proc. of ASPLOS*, 2013.

[12] P. Lama and X. Zhou. NINEPIN: Non-invasive and energy efficient performance isolation in virtualized servers. In *Proc. of DSN*, 2012.

[13] W. Lee, M. Frank, V. Lee, K. Mackenzie, and L. Rudolph. Implications of i/o for gang scheduled workloads. In *Proc. of IPPS*, 1997.

[14] T. Li, D. Baumberger, and S. Hahn. Efficient and scalable multiprocessor fair scheduling using distributed weighted round-robin. In *Proc. of PPoPP*, 2009.

[15] P. B. Menage. Adding generic process containers to the linux kernel. In *Proc. of OLS*, 2010.

[16] M. Mitzenmacher. The power of two choices in randomized load balancing. *IEEE Trans. Parallel Distrib. Syst.*, 12(10), 2001.

[17] R. Nathuji, A. Kansal, and A. Ghaffarkhah. Q-clouds: managing performance interference effects for qos-aware clouds. In *Proc. of EuroSys*, 2010.

[18] R. Nikolaev and G. Back. Perfctr-xen: a framework for performance counter virtualization. In *Proc. of VEE*, 2011.

[19] D. Ongaro, A. L. Cox, and S. Rixner. Scheduling i/o in virtual machine monitors. In *Proc. of VEE*, 2008.

[20] J. Ousterhout. Scheduling techniques for concurrent systems. In *Proc. of ICDCS*, 1982.

[21] A. K. Parekh and R. G. Gallager. A generalized processor sharing approach to flow control in integrated services networks: the single-node case. *IEEE/ACM Trans. Netw.*, 1(3), 1993.

[22] J. Rao, K. Wang, X. Zhou, and C.-Z. Xu. Optimizing virtual machine scheduling in numa multicore systems. In *Proc. of HPCA*, 2013.

[23] D. Shue, M. J. Freedman, and A. Shaikh. Performance isolation and fairness for multi-tenant cloud storage. In *Proc. of OSDI*, 2012.

[24] P. Sobalvarro, S. Pakin, W. E. Weihl, and A. A. Chien. Dynamic coscheduling on workstation clusters. In *Proc. of JSSPP*, 1998.

[25] X. Song, J. Shi, H. Chen, and B. Zang. Schedule processes, not vcpus. In *Proc. of APSys*, 2013.

[26] SPEC Java Server Benchmark. http://www.spec.org/jbb2005/.

[27] O. Sukwong and H. S. Kim. Is co-scheduling too expensive for smp vms? In *Proc. of EuroSys*, 2011.

[28] The Apache Mahout machine learning library. http://mahout.apache.org/.

[29] The CPU Scheduler in VMware vSphere 5.1. http://www.vmware.com/files/pdf/techpaper/VMware-vSphere-CPU-Sched-Perf.pdf.

[30] The Princeton Application Repository for Shared-Memory Computers (PARSEC) . http://parsec.cs.princeton.edu/.

[31] The SPEC CPU2006 Benchmarks. http://www.spec.org/cpu2006/.

[32] V. Uhlig, J. LeVasseur, E. Skoglund, and U. Dannowski. Towards scalable multiprocessor virtual machines. In *Proc. of VM*, 2004.

[33] VMware. http://www.vmware.com.

[34] C. Weng, Q. Liu, L. Yu, and M. Li. Dynamic adaptive scheduling for virtual machines. In *Proc. of HPDC*, 2011.

[35] Windows Azure Open Cloud Platform. http://www.windowsazure.com.

[36] Xen. http://www.xen.org/.

[37] C. Xu, S. Gamage, P. N. Rao, A. Kangarlou, R. R. Kompella, and D. Xu. vslicer: latency-aware virtual machine scheduling via differentiated-frequency cpu slicing. In *Proc. of HPDC*, 2012.

[38] C. Xu, S. Gamage, H. Lu, R. R. Kompella, and D. Xu. vturbo: Accelerating virtual machine i/o processing using designated turbo-sliced core. In *Proc. of USENIX ATC*, 2013.

Efficient Deterministic Multithreading Without Global Barriers

Kai Lu[1,2]   Xu Zhou[1,2]   Tom Bergan[3]   Xiaoping Wang[1,2]

1.Science and Technology on Parallel and Distributed Processing Laboratory, National University of Defense
Technology, Changsha, PR China
2.College of Computer, National University of Defense Technology, Changsha, PR China
3.University of Washington, Computer Science and Engineering
{kailu, zhouxu, xiaopingwang}@nudt.edu.cn, tbergan@cs.washington.edu

Abstract

Multithreaded programs execute nondeterministically on conventional architectures and operating systems. This complicates many tasks, including debugging and testing. *Deterministic multithreading* (DMT) makes the output of a multithreaded program depend on its inputs only, which can totally solve the above problem. However, current DMT implementations suffer from a common inefficiency: they use frequent global barriers to enforce a deterministic ordering on memory accesses. In this paper, we eliminate that inefficiency using an execution model we call *deterministic lazy release consistency* (DLRC). Our execution model uses the Kendo algorithm to enforce a deterministic ordering on synchronization, and it uses a deterministic version of the lazy release consistency memory model to propagate memory updates across threads. Our approach guarantees that programs execute deterministically even when they contain data races. We implemented a DMT system based on these ideas (RFDet) and evaluated it using 17 parallel applications. Our implementation targets C/C++ programs that use POSIX threads. Results show that RFDet gains nearly 2x speedup compared with DThreads—a start-of-the-art DMT system.

Categories and Subject Descriptors   D.1.3 [*Programming Techniques*]: Concurrent Programming—Parallel programming;   D.3.4 [*Programming Languages*]: Processors—Runtime environments

Keywords   deterministic execution, multithreading, lazy release consistency

PPoPP '14,   February 15–19, 2014, Orlando, Florida, USA.
Copyright © 2014 ACM 978-1-4503-2656-8/14/02. . . $15.00.
http://dx.doi.org/10.1145/2555243.2555252

1.   Introduction

Multithreaded programs execute nondeterministically on conventional systems: a program may produce different outputs in different executions even when provided with exactly the same input. This complicates development in many aspects: debugging is difficult because bugs may disappear on subsequent executions, and testing, fault-tolerant replication, and intrusion analysis become more difficult as well [3, 17, 26, 30]. Deterministic multithreading (DMT) has been recently proposed as a solution. DMT systems constrain execution so that multithreaded programs always execute the same thread interleavings and produce the same output when provided with the same input. Due to its many applications, DMT has become an increasingly attractive goal [3, 4, 7, 9, 11, 17, 18, 30, 37].

Prior general-purpose DMT systems take one of two basic approaches. First, systems like Kendo [30] enforce a deterministic order on synchronization *only*. In Kendo, the basic idea is that a thread cannot perform synchronization until all other threads have executed more instructions. This approach, known as *weak determinism*, can be implemented very efficiently in software, but it provides few guarantees for programs with data races—such programs may execute nondeterministically. The second approach is to enforce a deterministic order on *all* memory operations. This approach, known as *strong determinism*, typically proceeds by executing threads in bulk-synchronous quanta [4, 7, 17, 18, 21, 28, 37]. Within each quantum, threads are isolated. Each quantum ends with a *global barrier*, followed by a short phase in which threads communicate memory updates in a deterministic fashion. Strong DMT systems are attractive because they guarantee determinism even in the presence of data races. However, strong DMT systems are not yet practical: hardware-supported approaches cannot run on commodity architectures, while software-only implementations suffer from prohibitive overhead [6].

The strong DMT systems proposed previously all suffer from a common source of overhead: global barriers. These barriers provide a convenient place to make deterministic decisions, but they force all threads to synchronize even

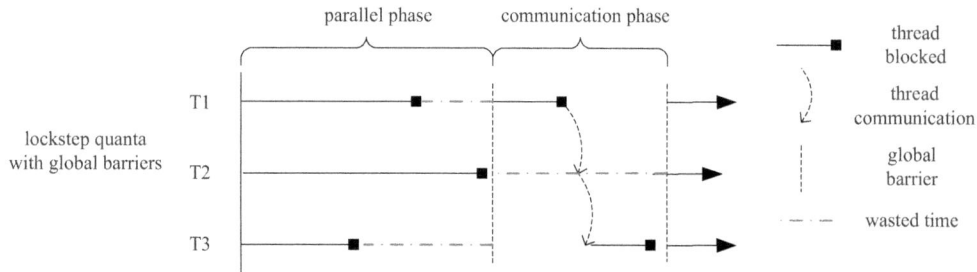

Figure 1. Global barriers in deterministic multithreading.

when such synchronization is unnecessary. This paper proposes a way to provide strong determinism without introducing *any* global barriers. Our insight is to combine the Kendo algorithm for deterministic synchronization with the *lazy release consistency* (LRC) memory model, which was first described in the context of distributed shared memory [24]. Hence, we call our approach *deterministic lazy release consistency* (DLRC). At a high-level, DLRC works in two parts. First, we use the Kendo algorithm [30] to ensure that synchronization operations happen in a deterministic order. Second, we give each thread a private memory space and enforce the following rule: a memory modification performed by thread $T1$ is made visible in thread $T2$ *if and only if* the modification *happens before* $T2$'s currently executing instruction. DLRC guarantees strong determinism but does not require global barriers.

We have implemented DLRC in a software runtime system called RFDet. Our implementation targets C/C++ programs that use POSIX threads (`pthreads`). We use page protection to give each thread a private memory space so that local modifications will not be immediately visible to other threads. We provide our own implementation of the `pthreads` library that is responsible for ensuring a deterministic order of synchronization (using the Kendo algorithm) and for propagating memory updates to other threads (following DLRC). A key challenge is propagating memory updates efficiently. We partition each thread's execution into synchronization-free *slices*, and for each slice we use page-diffing to compute the set of updates performed within that slice. We use copy-on-write techniques to minimize the number of pages that must be diffed. We evaluated RFDet on a range of parallel applications, including the deterministic stress test *racey* and 16 other programs from the SPLASH-2, Phoenix, and Parsec suites. Our evaluation shows that RFDet is deterministic and improves performance over DThreads [28]—a state of the art DMT system—by nearly 2x.

The rest of this paper is organized as follows. Section 2 provides background in DMT systems and summarizes related work. Section 3 describes deterministic lazy release consistency in detail. Section 4 describes our implementation of the RFDet runtime system. Section 5 describes our evaluation, and Section 6 concludes.

2. Background and Related Work

Strong Determinism with Lockstep Quanta. Strong determinism is a style of DMT that ensures deterministic results even in the presence of data races. There have been many recent attempts to provide efficient strong determinism. We leave a detailed discussion of that prior work to the survey by Bergan et al. [6] and to our bibliography [4, 7, 9, 17, 18, 21].

For this paper, we observe that all prior strong DMT systems use the same basic formula that is illustrated in Figure 1: execution is partitioned into quanta, where each quantum includes a parallel phase in which threads are isolated, followed by a short communication phase in which communication is resolved deterministically. A parallel phase ends after each thread has performed a deterministic amount of work, where "work" is usually measured by counting instructions, and phases are separated by global barriers. Note that DThreads [28] adopts a different mechanism: in DThreads, a parallel phase ends after each thread encounters any system-provided synchronization operation.

Global barriers introduce two sources of overhead. First, they introduce unnecessary serialization. Suppose threads $T1$ and $T3$ need to communicate, perhaps by writing to a shared queue. Following the formula in Figure 1, $T1$ and $T3$ must wait for the communication phase before their writes can proceed. Unfortunately, $T2$ must stop at the quantum barriers as well, *even though it has no need to communicate*—this serialization is unnecessary. Second, although all threads perform a deterministic amount of work per quantum, they might perform uneven amounts of work, leading to imbalance. This potential for imbalance is illustrated in Figure 1, and it has been shown to be a real performance issue that requires careful tuning [4, 17].

Prior authors have observed that some performance can be recovered by exploiting relaxed memory models. For example, the first system to provide strong determinism used sequentially consistent memory models [17]. Subsequent systems used a relaxed memory model derived from total-store-order (TSO) [4, 21], and most recently, RCDC proposed a new memory model called DMP-HB [18]. We continue this trend by introducing deterministic lazy release consistency (DLRC). DLRC is most similar to DMP-HB, but is more relaxed, as DLRC does *not* require global barriers. As we will argue in Section 3, DLRC relaxes memory consistency and improves the efficiency of strong determinism *without* breaking the semantics of the original program.

Prior systems use a variety of implementation strategies, including compiler instrumentation [4], page protection tricks [3, 7, 9, 28, 29], and even custom hardware [17, 18, 21]. Our system, RFDet, uses implementation techniques that are most similar to DThreads [28], so our evaluation will use DThreads as a comparison point.

Weak Determinism. Kendo [30] was the first system to provide determinism for race-free programs by serializing all synchronization operations in a deterministic order. The basic idea is to let each thread run until it reaches a synchronization operation, at which point the thread must wait until all other threads have executed more instructions. We refer to the Kendo paper for details [30].

Note that this algorithm does not use global barriers: threads do not block until they attempt to perform synchronization, and even then they are allowed to proceed immediately if they have the lowest instruction count. Our DLRC memory model makes use of the Kendo algorithm as explained in Section 3.

Parrot [14] also provides weak determinism, but rather than serializing synchronization via instruction counting as in Kendo, Parrot schedules threads in a deterministic round-robin order and uses programmer annotations to guide the scheduler towards efficient schedules. However, even with programmer annotations, Parrot cannot always find an efficient deterministic schedule and must occasionally resort to nondeterminism. In contrast, Kendo's (and DLRC's) use of instruction counting provides efficient and deterministic schedules without requiring programmer annotations.

Strong vs. Weak Determinism. It is useful to compare the guarantees of strong and weak determinism. Both ensure determinism for race-free programs, but their guarantees differ in the presence of data races. *Weak* systems such as Kendo do not resolve data races deterministically, and thus, they provide determinism *up to the first data race, only*. In contrast, *strong* systems such as DMP resolve *all* data races in a deterministic way, and thus provide determinism for entire executions.

Kendo can help debug the first race encountered on a given execution. This is useful, as all data races should be considered bugs [12]. However, in practice, not all data races are equally harmful—some races lead to severe crashes, while others go relatively unnoticed [22]—and developers need to prioritize their debugging effort towards those severe bugs. Hence, we consider it vital to resolve *all* races deterministically to ensure that the most severe races are reproducible, and thus, debuggable.

Schedule Memoization. Tern [15] and Peregrine [16] memorize schedules encountered during testing and reuse those schedules during deployment when possible. This provides high reliability guarantees in cases where tested sched-

ules can be reused. However, it is not possible to reuse tested schedules in all cases, so these systems must occasionally resort to nondeterministic execution. Hence, they provide *best-effort* determinism only.

A recent system by Bergan et al. [5] attempts to extend the approach introduced by Tern and Peregrine to use *input-covering schedules*. The idea is to compute a set of schedules S that is sufficiently large so that program execution can follow at least one schedule in S when given any input. However, this approach requires an expensive symbolic execution that has not been shown to scale to large systems.

Distributed Shared Memory (DSM) systems provide a logically shared memory space for distributed systems [23, 24] that does not share physical memory between nodes. In RFDet, we use similar techniques to implement memory modification propagation. There are two major differences: 1) RFDet ensures determinism while DSM systems do not (see Section 3); and 2) RFDet manages threads with physically shared memory, while DSM operates on distributed machines that do not share a physical address space.

Record and Replay systems (R+R) can deterministically replay a multithreaded execution that was recorded previously [25, 27, 32, 33]. These systems record a trace of thread interleavings in addition to program inputs. DMT systems like RFDet have two advantages over R+R systems. First, DMT systems guarantee that there is *one* possible execution for each input, so they can achieve deterministic replay by recording program inputs *only*—this can result in significantly lower recording overheads compared to R+R systems, which must record thread interleavings as well [7].

Second, while R+R systems can replay a specific execution for a given input, DMT systems ensure that *all* executions behave the same way for that given input. This allows DMT systems to provide benefits for program testing (by ensuring that a program behaves the same way in production as during testing) and for fault-tolerant state-machine replication (by ensuring that all state machine replicas make the same sequence of state changes when given the same sequence of inputs) [6, 15].

3. Deterministic Lazy Release Consistency

In deterministic lazy release consistency (DLRC), we divide program operations into two categories: synchronization operations (such as `pthread_mutex_lock`) and ordinary memory accesses (reads and writes). First, we use the Kendo algorithm to ensure that synchronization operations happen in a deterministic total order. Second, we give each thread a private memory space and enforce the following rule: a memory modification performed by thread $T1$ is made visible in thread $T2$ *if and only if* the modification *happens before* $T2$'s currently executing instruction. This has two implications: (1) if a modification happens before the currently executing instruction, the modification should be visible; and

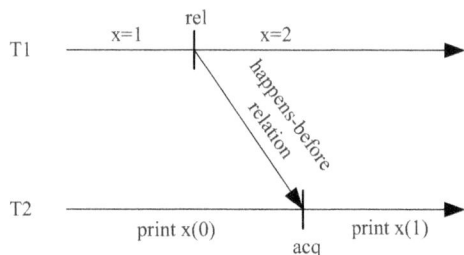

Figure 2. Deterministic lazy release consistency.

(2) any modification that does not happen before the currently executing instruction *must not* be visible.

More formally, the definition of DLRC depends on the happens-before relation. We use $\rightarrow$ to denote the happens-before relation, so $A \rightarrow B$ means operation A happens before operation B. The happens-before relation is the irreflexive transitive closure of program order and synchronization order, where $A \rightarrow B$ in program order if operations A and B are performed by the same thread and A appears in the program before B,[1] and where $A \rightarrow B$ in synchronization order if A and B are synchronization operations on the same object (e.g., the same lock) and A completes before B.

Now suppose that R and W are read and write operations, respectively, where R and W access the same location and may be performed by different threads. In DLRC, R reads the value written by W *only if* $W \rightarrow R$ and there does not exist another write $W2$, to the same location, such that $W \rightarrow W2$ and $W2 \rightarrow R$. If there exists a third write to the same location, $W3$, such that $W \rightarrow R$ and $W3 \rightarrow R$ but there is no happens-before relation between W and $W3$, then R may read the value written by *either* W or $W3$, as long as that choice is made deterministically. One strategy is to use thread creation order as a tie breaker.

As shown in Figure 2, the first `print` in $T2$ must not see the two modifications of $T1$ as there is no happens-before relation between them. Meanwhile, the second `print` must see the modification of x=1 but must not see the modification of x=2 because only x=1 happens before that `print` due to a previous synchronization between $T1$ and $T2$. Note that in each case there is a data race that DLRC has resolved in a deterministic fashion.

DLRC differs from LRC [23, 24] in two respects. First, synchronization happens deterministically in DLRC due to Kendo, but synchronization order is unspecified (nondeterministic) in LRC. Second, although LRC guarantees that a write W is visible to a read R if $W \rightarrow R$, as in DLRC, it may also allow a write W to be visible to R *even when* $W \nrightarrow R$. In contrast, DLRC guarantees that W *must not* be visible to R when $W \nrightarrow R$. For the example in Figure 2, x=2 *may* be visible to the second `print` in $T2$ in LRC, while this visibility *must* be disabled in DLRC. This limitation helps us to guar-

antee determinism but also makes the memory modification propagation procedure more complicated than that of LRC (see Section 4).

3.1 Advantages Over Prior Approaches

We have already said that DLRC improves prior approaches to determinism by eliminating global barriers. The following example illustrates our argument further. Suppose that in some program fragment, threads $T1$ and $T3$ attempt to acquire the same lock while thread $T2$ does not perform any synchronization. With DLRC, $T2$ executes in isolation and does not block. The only delays are, first, a small delay while $T1$ and $T3$ use Kendo to deterministically arbitrate the order of lock acquisition, and second, the unavoidable delay in which one thread waits for the other to release the lock.

In contrast, prior systems insert extra delays due to global barriers. In systems such as DMP [17], CoreDet [4], and Calvin [21], execution may proceed as shown in Figure 1. In these systems, synchronization cannot occur in the parallel phase, so $T1$ and $T3$ must wait for $T2$ to arrive at the global quantum barrier before they can synchronize. Due to imbalance, this delay can be significant [4, 6]. Further, even though $T2$ is not synchronizing, $T2$ must still wait for $T1$ and $T3$ to synchronize in the communication phase before it can continue execution. RCDC [18] improves this somewhat by allowing at most one thread to acquire a given lock in the parallel phase without waiting for the global barrier. However, two threads cannot acquire the same lock without a global barrier, as in our current example. In DThreads, the problem is potentially even worse as neither $T1$ or $T3$ can acquire the lock until $T2$ reaches some synchronization operation, which may be far in the future.

Even if no thread performs synchronization, many systems still require global barriers, leading to the potential for imbalance and wasted delays [4, 17, 18, 21]. DLRC requires no global barriers, and, as we argue in Section 5, this leads to improved performance.

3.2 Determinism

We demonstrate determinism with an informal argument by induction over an execution trace. In the base case, all threads execute for some time without performing synchronization. This is trivially deterministic since each thread is constrained to a private memory space. In the inductive case, some thread executes a synchronization operation. Our use of Kendo ensures that synchronization operations are ordered deterministically. Hence, the happens-before relation is updated deterministically, and from this fact and the inductive hypothesis, it follows that memory updates are propagated deterministically. Another way to argue determinism is the following: DLRC defines memory modification propagation as a deterministic function over the happens-before relation, and since our use of Kendo produces a deterministic happens-before relation, it follows that execution as a whole is deterministic.

---

[1] In the C++, this is the *sequenced-before* relation [1, 13].

3.3 Correctness

As our implementation is targeted to C and C++, we must show that source programs written in C and C++ can legally execute under DLRC. Here, we argue that DLRC correctly executes C++ programs that do not use low-level atomics—we will return to low-level atomics in Section 4.6. The C++ memory model requires that all program executions adhere to the following rule (see Section 6 of Boehm and Adve [1, 13]): If the program has a data race, its behavior is undefined; otherwise, the program's execution must be *consistent*. Boehm and Adve give a five-part definition of *consistent* in Section 6 of their paper. Below, we summarize the three parts of that definition that do not refer to low-level atomics, and we argue that, for race-free programs, DLRC preserves semantics:

1. *Execution respects single-threaded semantics.* This trivially holds as single-threaded semantics are not affected by DLRC.

3. *Each memory read R reads from a write W to the same location such that $W \to R$ and there does not exist another write $W2$ such that $W \to W2$ and $W2 \to R$.* DLRC follows this rule exactly (see above). Note that if there exists a third write, $W3$, where $W3 \to R$ and $W3$ is concurrent with W, then there is a data race and the C++ semantics allow R to read any arbitrary value.

5. *Lock and unlock operations on each individual lock are totally ordered by happens-before.* This property holds because, first, DLRC uses Kendo to order synchronization, and second, Kendo orders all synchronization operations in a (deterministic) total order.

Boehm and Adve further argue that the above rules guarantee sequentially consistent execution of race-free programs (see Section 7 of their paper). Thus, DLRC preserves sequential consistency for race-free programs, and we conclude that DLRC does not violate C++ semantics.

3.4 Discussion

Guarantees. DLRC guarantees that execution of a given program with a given input will produce *arbitrary but deterministic and semantically-valid results*, even in the presence of data races. Essentially, DLRC achieves determinism in the presence of data races by sequencing conflicting (racing) accesses in a deterministic order—note that this deterministic order depends on input, meaning that DLRC may resolve the same race in two different orders on two different inputs.

Inputs. We assume a broad definition of the term *input*. Namely, in addition to the usual notions of input such as commandline flags, user actions, and data read from files or the network, our notion of input includes environmental parameters such as psuedorandom seeds, number of processors, and system load. Particularly, if a program is designed to adjust its number of threads according to the current system load, then we consider the current system load an *input*,

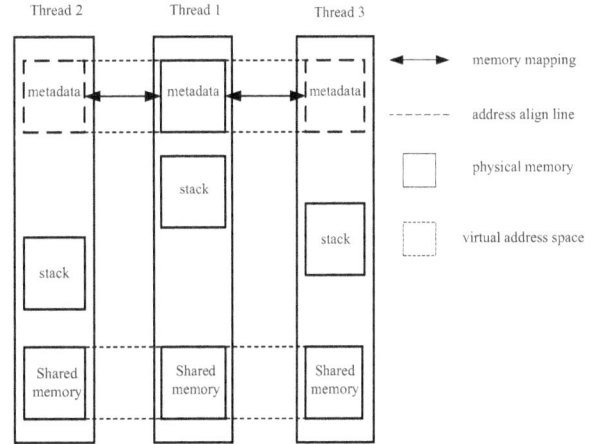

Figure 3. Memory spaces in FPDet. Between different threads, *metadata* spaces share both virtual addresses and physical memory, *shared memory* spaces share virtual addresses only, and *stacks* share neither of them.

and as a result, our system may produce different executions in environments with different system loads.

Other Languages. We see no reason why DLRC could not be implemented for other languages, such as Java. However, our specific implementation merges conflicting (racing) updates in a way that can violate the Java memory model (see Section 4.6), so, for Java, an alternative implementation is needed.

4. Implementation

This section presents our implementation of a DMT system (RFDet) based on DLRC. The first issue is to make local memory modifications invisible to other threads. To this end, we use processes to replace threads so that the memory spaces are separated, as shown in Figure 3. In Linux, this is implemented by using the `clone` system call so that processes share everything (file descriptors, sockets, etc.) except for a memory address space [28]. As a result, we have to provide our own memory allocator to avoid address conflicts (Section 4.4). To implement inter-process communication, we reserve a *metadata* space which is a shared memory region between these processes.

Based on these *isolated threads*, we implement thread communication according to DLRC in the following way. We provide our own implementation for the standard synchronization operations in POSIX `pthreads` (Section 4.1). We dynamically cut thread execution into slices using these synchronizations. For each slice, we monitor its modifications, record them into the metadata space, and use a vector clock timestamp to describe its happens-before relation with other slices (Section 4.2). In each synchronization operation that induces a happens-before relation with another thread, we propagate the memory modifications of all slices that happen before the synchronization operation to the local thread, and merge them into the local memory to make them visible (Section 4.3). We perform four optimizations to reduce the overhead in both time and space (Section 4.5).

4.1 Synchronization

We divide the standard POSIX `pthreads` synchronizations into *acquire* operations and *release* operations. Specifically, the acquire operations include *lock*, *conditional wait*, *thread entry*, *thread join* and *barrier*. The corresponding release operations are *unlock*, *conditional signal/broadcast*, *thread create*, *thread exit* and *barrier* respectively. Note that *barrier* is both an acquire and a release operation.

Deterministic Synchronization. As stated, we use the Kendo algorithm [30] to make synchronization deterministic. Briefly, in Kendo, a thread is allowed to perform synchronization only if it has executed fewer instructions than all other threads. We count instructions using compile-time instrumentation. Specifically, we insert a call to `instrTick(k)` in each basic block, where k is the number of memory instructions in that basic block. When `instrTick` is invoked at runtime, we increment the current thread's instruction count.

By contrast, the original Kendo implementation used performance counters to count instructions. We did not adopt this method because the determinism of performance counters is not proven [34]. We otherwise follow the Kendo algorithm as described, and we refer to the Kendo paper for further details [30].

Internal Synchronization Variables. Synchronization variables, such as mutexes, must be updated atomically across all threads. However, we cannot update the application's memory atomically because each thread has an isolated memory space. Our approach is to map each synchronization variable to an *internal synchronization variable* that is allocated in the metadata space. At each synchronization operation, we lookup the corresponding internal variable in the metadata space and operate on that internal variable directly.

Additionally, we add two fields to each internal synchronization variable: *lastTid* and *lastTime*. These represent, respectively, the ID of the last thread to *release* the synchronization variable, and the time at which that *release* occurred. We represent times using vector clocks [19] as explained in Section 4.2.

Mutexes and Condition Variables. At each *acquire* operation, such as `pthread_mutex_lock` or `pthread_cond_wait`, we check the *lastTid* field of the synchronization variable. If the last *release* was performed by a different thread, we propagate all memory modifications that happen before *lastTime* into the current (acquiring) thread as explained in Section 4.3. Otherwise, if the last *release* was performed by the same thread, we merge the current thread's previous slice and new slice for efficiency, as explained in Section 4.5. At each *release* operation, such as `pthread_mutex_unlock` or `pthread_cond_signal/pthread_cond_broadcast`, we

set the *lastTid* and *lastTime* fields before we release the synchronization variable.

Barriers. Barriers are special synchronizations as they perform both *acquire* and *release*. At each barrier, we first select the arriving thread with the smallest thread ID (call it thread T), and then merge all modifications that happened-before the barrier into T's local memory. The merging order is determined by thread ID (the thread with the smallest ID merges its modifications first) to ensure determinism. All threads are given a copy of T's local memory (using copy-on-write) after the merging completes.

Thread Create and Join. In `pthread_create`, we use the `clone` system call to implement threads so that each thread is actually a lightweight process. We assign each new thread a deterministic thread ID—calling `pthread_self` will return this ID instead of the ID assigned by the operating system. Note that there is a happens-before relation between thread creation and the child thread's entry point. However, we do not need to propagate memory modifications at this moment as the child process will inherit the memory of its creating process automatically. Further, we do not need to monitor memory modifications in the main thread before the first child thread is created. To implement `pthread_join`, we map the deterministic thread ID to the process ID returned by `clone`, and use `waitpid` to wait for the specified process. Note that we have to propagate all the modifications of the joined thread to the main thread at this moment.

4.2 Slices

A *slice* refers to a period of single-threaded execution between two consecutive synchronizations. In other words, each slice is immediately preceded and succeeded by synchronization and there is no synchronization within the slice itself. Hence, at each synchronization operation, we should end the previous slice and begin a new slice. Slices have a useful *atomic property*: **all memory accesses inside a slice will have the same happens-before relation to any instruction outside the slice.** This property enables us to make slices our basic unit for memory modification propagation.

Each slice is a triple *<tid, modifications, timestamp>*, where *tid* is a thread ID, *modifications* describes the ordered sequence of memory updates made by thread *tid* during the slice, and *timestamp* is a vector clock timestamp for the slice.

Vector Clocks. We can easily know the happens-before relation between any two slices by comparing their vector clock timestamps. Namely, given two slices A and B, $A \rightarrow B$ if and only if $Time(A) < Time(B)$ [19]. We maintain a vector clock for each thread and increase it in the standard way: 1) before each synchronization operation, we increase the vector clock so that the next slice is older than the previous slice; and 2) at each *acquire* that synchronizes with a *release* in a different thread, we update the vector clock to *timestamp* $\sqcup Time(R)$, where *timestamp* is the vector clock

```
1  void RecordStore(void *addr, size_t len) {
2      foreach pageid in pagesTouchedBy(addr, len) {
3          if (isInSharedMemory(pageid) &&
4              !currentSlice.hasPageSnapshot(pageid)) {
5              void *pagedata = metadata->allocOnePage();
6              memcpy(pagedata, PageAddr(pageid), PAGE_SIZE);
7              curentSlice.addPageSnapshot(pageid, pagedata);
8          }
9      }
10 }
```

Figure 4. Algorithm for Store instrumentation.

just before the *acquire*, $Time(R)$ is the vector clock of the release, and $\sqcup$ is a least-upper-bound.

Monitoring Memory Modifications. We represent *modifications* using a list of pairs $<addr, data>$, where each pair represents a write of the value *data* to address *addr*. The granularity of *data* is one byte. We need to collect the modifications performed during each slice. As in DThreads [28], our approach is to use page diffing: the first time a page is written in a slice, we take a snapshot of the page and add it to a *modified pages list*. Then, at the end of the slice, we compare the snapshot pages with the corresponding modified pages byte-by-byte to compute the modifications.

We collect modified pages by instrumenting all *Store* instructions at compile time. We instrument each *Store* instruction as shown in Figure 4. Specifically, we check if the page written by the *Store* is in shared memory (recall Figure 3) and if this is the first time the page has been written in the current slice. If so, we take snapshot of the page and add it to the *modified pages list* of the current slice.

We assume that stack variables are not shared across threads. At compile time, we use a conservative static escape analysis to filter out *Stores* to stack variables, similarly to prior work [4]. At runtime, we ignore stores to stack pages (line 3 of Figure 4). Further, our compiler instrumentation assumes the entire source code is available, including for libraries. If the source is not available for library L, then we assume that either (a) library L does not write to shared memory locations, in which case instrumentation is not needed, or (b) the shared memory locations written by library L can be determined from its interface, in which case we can instrument calls to L directly. Note that case (b) holds for standard C library functions such as `memset`, `memcpy`, and `strcpy`.

Another way to collect the modified pages is to use the `mprotect` system call to protect shared memory with no write permission at the beginning of each slice, and then use copy-on-write to collect the snapshot pages modified by the slice. We experimented with this approach, as it is the approach taken by DThreads [28], but we observed that this approach was less efficient than compile-time instrumentation due to the high frequency of page faults and `mprotect` system calls for programs with frequent synchronization (see our evaluation in Section 5).

```
1  void DoMemoryModificationPropagation(thread from,
2                                       vtime upperlimit,
3                                       vtime lowerlimit){
4      foreach slice in from.slicepointers {
5          if(slice.time < upperlimit &&
6              ! (slice.time < lowerlimit) ) {
7              copyToLocalMemory(slice.modifications);
8              localthread.slicepointers->append(slice);
9          }
10     }
11 }
```

Figure 5. Algorithm for memory modification propagation.

4.3 Memory Modification Propagation

To do memory modification propagation, each thread maintains a list of *slice pointers* that contains pointers to all slices that happen-before the thread's current program counter. The slice pointers are organized in the happens-before order of these slices. Concurrent slices are organized in a deterministic order that is defined below (see "handling conflicts"). As shown in Figure 5, when we need to do propagation at an *acquire*, we collect the slices that happen before the *release* in the remote thread and append them to the *slice pointers* list of the local thread. As each new slice is appended to this list, we write the slice's modifications to local memory to make those modifications visible.

When deciding *which* slices to propagate, four issues must be considered. The first issue is to **propagate only happens-before slices**—that is, slices should be propagated only if they happen-before the current operation. For example, in the first propagation between $T1$ and $T2$ in Figure 6, $T1$ may already have produced the modification x=3, which is contained in the second slice of $T1$, but this slice should not be propagated as, according to DLRC, the modification x=3 is not yet visible in $T2$. We set the vector time of the slice that succeeds the current *acquire* (the first lock in $T2$ for this example) as an *upperlimit* time to filter out these slices (line 5 of Figure 5).

The second issue is **transitive propagation**. Memory modification propagation must be transitive as the happens-before relation is transitive. Specifically, a slice of modifications can be propagated along several happens-before edges. As shown in Figure 6, x=1 is propagated from $T1$ to $T2$ at the first synchronization, and is also propagated from $T2$ to $T3$ at the second synchronization. Since we copy all slices into the local *slice pointers* list during propagation, the slice containing x=1 will be appended into the *slice pointers* list for $T2$ when $T2$ acquires the lock. That is, the *slice pointers* list for thread $T2$ contains all slices that must be propagated from $T2$ to $T3$, so transitive propagation will happen naturally.

The third issue is to avoid **redundant propagation**. Redundant propagation happens when the modifications of a slice are propagated to a thread which has already seen those modifications. In Figure 6, x=1 is redundant in the propaga-

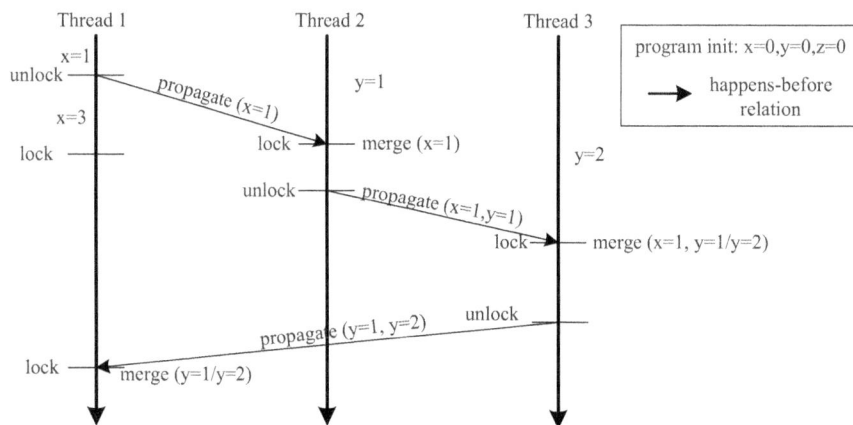

Figure 6. An example showing modification propagations in RFDet. The operation 'y=1/y=2' indicates modification y=1 overwrites modification y=2.

tion from $T3$ to $T1$. One way to identify a redundant slice is to check if it already exists in the set of local slice pointers. This method may be inefficient if the set of local slice pointers is large. A better method is to set a *lowerlimit* time to filter out the slices that have already been seen (line 6 of Figure 5), where *lowerlimit* is simply the vector timestamp of the slice that precedes the current *acquire* operation. Hence, any slice whose timestamp is smaller than *lowerlimit* must have been seen by the local thread (due to DLRC), and thus should be filtered out in propagation.

The last issue is **handling conflicts**. There are modification conflicts between threads due to W/W data races. As shown in Figure 6, y=1 performed by $T2$ and y=2 performed by $T3$ is a modification conflict, as they are not ordered by any happens-before relation. We resolve conflicts deterministically as follows. For barrier synchronizations, we sort modifications as described in Section 4.1. For all other synchronizations there is a unique "remote" thread, so we resolve these conflicts deterministically by always overwriting the local modifications with the remote modifications. So, in Figure 6, y=1 overwrites y=2. The exception to this policy is that we prefer "local" writes when the "remote" write is redundant—the reason for this policy is subtle and will be explained in Section 4.6.

4.4 Memory Allocation

Since threads are implemented in processes, the default memory allocator in Linux (e.g., `malloc` in glibc) is invalid— dynamic memory allocations in different threads may cause *memory address conflicts*. For example, if `malloc` is called twice from two threads, it may return the same virtual address for these two newly allocated heap objects. These addresses will conflict in memory modification propagation. To avoid address conflicts, we modified the Hoard [8] memory allocator to store allocation information in the metadata space so it is shared among threads. Therefore, when a thread tries to allocate a memory region, we also reserve

the virtual addresses of the memory region in other threads, which solves address conflicts. Note that these reserved virtual addresses may not be mapped with physical memory until they are touched by the local threads.

4.5 Optimizations

Garbage Collection. A slice stored in the metadata space becomes garbage when it has been propagated to every thread. We have to collect these garbage slices to prevent them from exhausting the metadata space. Therefore, we trigger garbage collection (GC) to reclaim unused slices when the metadata space usage reaches a predefined threshold. A slice is garbage when the timestamp of the slice is less than the current vector clock of every thread—such slices have already been merged into the local memory spaces of all threads.

Slice Merging. If we encounter an *acquire* operation that acquires a synchronization variable which was released by the same thread previously, we do not end the current slice. By continuing the current slice, we can avoid taking page snapshots and we reduce the number of pages that must be diffed. This optimization effectively merges the slices on both sides of the *acquire*. Note that this merging preserves the atomic property of slices stated in Section 4.2: all memory accesses in the merged slice will have the same happens-before relation to any instruction outside the slice. We omit the proof due to space limitation.

Prelock. In each critical section within a *lock/unlock* pair, we should propagate memory modifications according to the happens-before relation. However, memory propagation enlarges the original critical sections, leading to poor performance when lock contention is heavy. We cannot move memory propagation entirely out of the critical section as we cannot confirm the happens-before relation before the lock is acquired.

The *prelock* optimization is designed to shorten these long critical sections. The idea of *prelock* is to reserve the lock first. The reservation phase defines the order in which threads will enter user's critical section. For example, suppose thread $T1$ attempts to acquire a heavily contended lock currently held by thread $T2$. $T1$ first adds itself to the reservation order. We do not yet know the complete happens-before relation for $T1$'s eventual acquire operation. However, we know that acquire must happen-after the current vector times of $T2$ and of every thread before $T1$ in the reservation order. Thus, $T1$ can begin merging memory updates that must happen-before its eventual acquire. It can do this in parallel with $T2$, even before $T2$ releases the lock. When $T1$ finally gets the token to enter the lock's critical section, it should first finish the unhandled memory modification propagations. After the critical section, it passes the token to the next thread according to the reservation order. This optimization can move a large percentage of propagation work into parallel mode (almost 80% in our experiment). Note that the reservation order is determined by the Kendo algorithm to ensure determinism.

Lazy Writes. This optimization reduces the number of unnecessary memory writes performed during memory propagation. We leverage the observation that not all the propagated memory modifications are needed by the local thread, thus we could postpone the write of these modifications until they are actually read by the local thread.

This optimization could reduce memory accesses in two ways. First, if the modifications are not used at all, then the writes for these modifications are omitted. Second, if the modifications are not accessed by the local thread for a long time, eager modification propagation would make multiple updates to the location before the first access, while lazy propagation makes just one update (containing the most-recent value). For example, suppose a thread executes 20 critical sections between two accesses of memory location X. In the worst case, the thread may receive 20 updates for location X (one at each critical section). With the lazy writes optimization, only the *last* update will be written.

When the lazy writes optimizations is enabled, we do not write the propagated modifications into the local memory directly. Instead, given a set of local pages to modify, we use page protection to protect each local page with no *Read* or *Write* permissions. Afterwards, when a memory access hits one of these pages, we write the modifications of the page into the local memory and unprotect the page.

4.6 Discussion

Correctness of Page Diffing to Accumulate Modifications. We are careful to store modifications at *byte* granularity (Section 4.2). The C++ memory model defines all memory actions as operations over scalars [13], and since the smallest scalar value in C++ is a byte, we must track memory modifications at byte granularity for correctness.

Recall that we construct modification lists for a slice by diffing each modified page with a snapshot containing the page's original values. It is not obvious that this diffing pro-

cedure produces correct modification lists. Specifically, what happens when a thread overwrites a memory location with the *same* value? For example, suppose x==0 at the beginning of a slice, and suppose the slice executes the redundant assignment x=0. Because the final value of x is the same as its initial value, we do not include a modification for x in the slice's modification list, which means that the update x=0 will not be propagated to other threads. Perhaps surprisingly, this is both deterministic and semantically correct. Consider two cases:

First, suppose the program is race-free. In this case, each read R of location x should read the value written by a unique write operation, W_1, where W_1 happens-before R. Specifically, there must a sequence of writes $\{W_1, W_2, \ldots\}$, where each W_i writes to x, and where each write is progressively older according to the happens-before relation. Suppose that $W_1 \ldots W_k$ all write x=0, and suppose that W_{k+1} wrote some value to x other than 0. In this case, W_k is the youngest write that is not redundant, and the slice containing W_k will have the modification x=0. Hence, we guarantee that R reads the correct value (x=0) due to transitive propagation from the slice containing W_k to the slice containing R (recall Section 4.3).

Second, suppose the program has a data race. We must resolve all races deterministically. Our policy is to prefer writes that are *not* redundant. For example, in Figure 6, suppose that the initial value of y is y=2, making the write y=2 in $T3$ a redundant write. The first slice in $T3$ will be empty, so when $T3$ acquires the lock, it will merge the write y=1 from $T2$—this is effectively the same "remote write wins" policy that we described in Section 4.4. Now suppose that the initial value of y is y=1, making the write y=1 in $T2$ a redundant write. The first slice in $T2$ is now empty, so the write y=1 will not be propagated from $T2$ to $T3$. The result is that y=2 will be kept in $T3$ and propagated to $T1$. Hence, our page diffing procedure effectively implements the following conflict-resolution policy: we prefer the "local" writes when the "remote" writes are redundant.

This policy can lead to unexpected results in programs with data races. For example, continuing with Figure 6, suppose that y is a 32-bit integer initialized to y=0, and suppose that $T2$ writes y=256 while $T3$ writes y=255. Due to our policy of preferring non-redundant modifications combined with the fact that we compute page diffs at byte granularity, the final value merged in $T3$ will be y=511 (as 255=0x00ff, 256=0x0100, and 0x01ff=511). Of course, this result is deterministic, and it is also semantically valid, as the behavior of a C++ execution is undefined in the presence of a data race.

Ad Hoc and Lock-Free Synchronization. As in implementations of LRC [23], we assume that programs use system-provided synchronization operations only. Our implementation does not support ad hoc synchronization, such as via shared variable flags or lock-free algorithms. Pro-

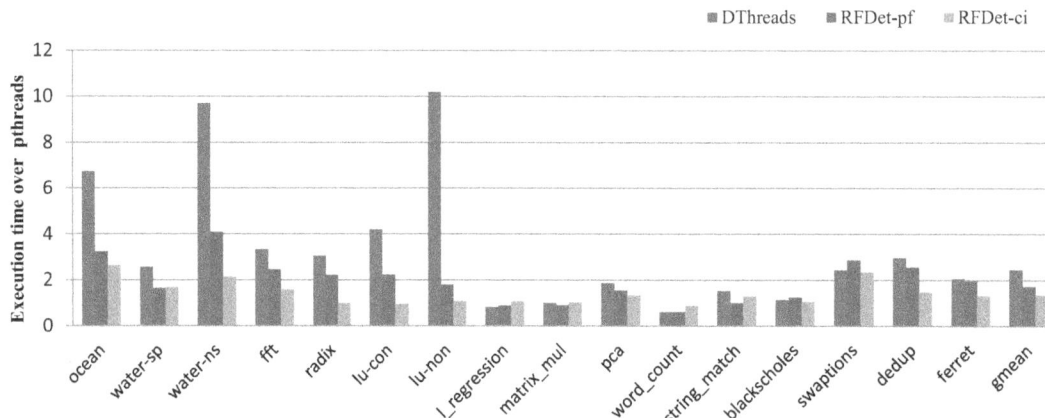

Figure 7. Execution time normalized to `pthreads`. All applications are running with 4 threads. RFDet-pf uses `mprotect` to monitor modifications, while RFDet-ci uses compile-time instrumentation to monitor modifications.

grams using ad hoc synchronization may be incorrect in DLRC (e.g., they may deadlock or violate atomicity) as the happens-before relations implied by ad hoc synchronization are not monitored and thus missed. There are two ways to remedy this. First, the programmer can wrap ad hoc synchronizations with a global lock to ensure they are serialized [36]. Second, we could extend our implementation to include an interface for ad hoc or lock-free synchronization, similarly to the new interface for low-level atomic operations in C++ [1, 2, 13], which we currently do not support. This new interface includes support for operations such as *atomic increment* and *atomic compare-and-swap*.

Totally supporting ad hoc synchronization and lock-free algorithms is future work. However, we do not foresee any major problems. To support C++ low-level atomics, we must use the Kendo algorithm to ensure that atomic operations happen in a deterministic order, and we must propagate memory modifications as described in Section 4.1, depending on whether the atomic operation being executed is an *acquire* and/or a *release*.

5. Evaluation

In this section, we present our evaluation results. All experiments were conducted on an AMD server with a 2.2 GHz, 12-core CPU (AMD Opteron 6174) and 16 GB physical memory, running Linux kernel version 2.6.31.5.

5.1 Methodology

To test whether RFDet can ensure determinism for multithreaded programs, we stressed it with *racey*—a parallel program which is designed to contain numerous data races to expose nondeterminism [20]. We verified the determinism of RFDet by running *racey* 1000 times with 2, 4 and 8 threads respectively. For each configuration, we got the same output for all the 1000 executions.

In the performance evaluation, we compare RFDet with DThreads [28]—a state-of-the-art DMT system, and `pthreads`—the conventional nondeterministic multithreading library. To test performance, we chose 16 parallel programs from three different benchmark suites, which are SPLASH-2 [35], Phoenix [31], and Parsec [10]. The SPLASH-2 suite was configured with c.m4.null.POSIX. This configuration uses *lock* and *unlock* to implement *barrier*. We use this configuration to make applications execute more synchronizations to stress performance. Moreover, successfully running benchmarks with this configuration shows that RFDet could support C/C++ codes as long as they correctly use these system-provided synchronization operations. Since RFDet does not support ad hoc synchronizations, we omit some benchmarks that contain complex ad hoc synchronizations in our experiments—they either cause deadlock (e.g., *fmm*) or violate atomicity (e.g., *canneal*). Note that DThreads does not support ad hoc synchronizations either [28].

5.2 Performance

To test performance, we ran each application 10 times with RFDet, DThreads and `pthreads` respectively, and gather their mean execution times, as shown in Figure 7. We provide two versions of RFDet which use different methods to monitor memory modifications. RFDet-ci uses compile-time instrumentation to monitor memory modifications, while RFDet-pf adopts the page protection method (recall the discussion in Section 4.2). As we can see, RFDet-ci and RFDet-pf incur an overhead of 35.2% and 72.9% respectively compared with `pthreads`. RFDet-ci performs better than RFDet-pf as it eliminates the overhead of page faults and system calls such as `mprotect` (as discussed in Section 4.2). Compared with DThreads, whose performance overhead is about 2.5x, both RFDet-ci and RFDet-pf have a smaller overhead—the performance improvements

Table 1. Profiling data of benchmark executions with 4 threads. In this table, *wait* refers to `pthread_cond_wait`, *signal* refers to both `pthread_cond_signal` and `pthread_cond_broadcast`, and *fork* refers to `pthread_create`. These programs normally execute equal number of *lock* and *unlock*, and execute equal number of *fork* and *join*, so we just show one number in these two columns.

benchmark	sync ops			memory ops				memory footprint & GC			
	lock/ unlock	wait/ signal	fork/ join	mem	load	store	store w/ copy	pthreads (MB)	RFDet (MB)	DThreads (MB)	GC
ocean	1100	671/199	6	36078529	29797587	6280942	77477	27	77.8	34.8	0
water-ns	6314	60/20	6	39256331	27183299	12073032	128983	5.9	53.3	11.0	9
water-sp	1103	90/30	6	89898824	64170352	25728472	13164	0.9	22.6	4.4	0
fft	54	21/7	6	163328252	87957717	75370535	49199	384	1012	450	0
radix	96	39/25	6	19087619	11675872	7411747	9422	40.5	295	107	0
lu-con	550	393/131	6	286770015	195163260	91606755	55806	16	60.1	25.7	0
lu-non	550	393/131	6	281461557	189840962	91620595	67364	8	100	43.9	0
linear_regression	0	0	16	35173933	19185782	15988151	2	0.004	4.0	1.6	0
matrix_multiply	0	0	16	3830399	3808551	21848	18	0.06	5.6	1.7	0
pca	816	0	32	3930114	3911170	18943	2034	1.5	76.9	1.7	0
wordcount	0	0	60	3607902	3215400	392502	149	2.1	56.6	3.8	0
string_match	0	0	8	15769972	12348432	3421540	2	0.02	4.1	1.6	0
blackscholes	24	0/1	4	1171467	1084629	86838	5	0.4	5.1	2.0	0
swaptions	24	0/1	4	28848349	21900213	6948136	2671	97.6	264	99.5	0
dedup	9304	152/3599	12	3345249	3327108	18141	12511	1310	5602	1506	5
ferret	43025	1/16	18	488092	419263	68834	4562	45.9	353	49.8	2

of RFDet-ci and RFDet-pf over DThreads are 81.6% and 42% respectively. Moreover, we noticed that the performance of RFDet is more stable than that of DThreads. As shown in Figure 7, the worst-case performance of RFDet is 2.6x slowdown (*ocean*), while the worst-case performance for DThreads is about 10x slowdown (*lu-non*).

Note that the major difference between DThreads and RFDet-pf is that we remove global barriers. DThreads introduces global barriers that may lead to poor synchronization schedules, thus causing load imbalance problems. Since RFDet does not introduce global barriers, it is more adaptable to a variety of synchronization patterns and has more stable performance overheads.

5.3 Performance in Detail

To analyze the performance results, we collected the profiling data of these program running in RFDet, as shown in Table 1. In this table, we provide the number of synchronization operations (we omit the number of barriers as none of the programs execute barriers in our configuration), the number of memory operations and the memory footprint for each benchmark application.

Theoretically, the performance of RFDet should be sensitive to the synchronization frequency of the user program. We have two reasons for this: 1) each synchronization may cause RFDet to perform memory modification propagation, which is the major overhead of RFDet; and 2) as we record memory modifications for each slice, higher synchronization frequency indicates more slices need to be recorded, which results in larger overhead. We can confirm this assumption from the profiling data of synchronization operations. For those applications that execute only a few synchronizations, such as *linear_regression*, *matrix_multiply* and *wordcount* in

the Phoenix suite, the runtime overheads are small—they even improve performance over `pthreads` due to better cache behavior [28]. On the other hand, most applications in the SPLASH-2 suite execute a large number of synchronizations, thus their performance overheads are more significant.

The frequency of memory operations may also affect performance, especially for *Store* operations. As we can see from Table 1, the number of *Store* instructions is much smaller than the number of *Load* instructions. Moreover, in the common case for most *Store* instructions, our added instrumentation (Figure 4) performs only a few branch instructions to check if the *Store* hits a new page. Hence, only a small portion of these *Store* instructions will trigger a memory copy (see Column 9 in Table 1).

5.4 Memory Usage

One limitation of RFDet is that it consumes much more memory than `pthreads`, as shown in Table 1. The extra memory consumption comes from two sources. First, the isolated threads maintain a local copy of each shared variable, thus incurring an extra memory usage of $(N-1) * SharedMemory$, where N is the number of threads and $SharedMemory$ is the amount of non-stack memory allocated by the application. Second, the metadata space consumes extra memory. Memory consumption is shown in the last three columns of Table 1. Column 10 is the memory usage of the application alone, and Column 11 is the memory usage of the application running with RFDet. Specifically, we define Column 10 and Column 11 as the equations below, where N and $SharedMemory$ are defined above, and where $StackMemory$ is equal to total memory used by all stacks and $MetadataSpaceMemory$ is equal to total memory used in the metadata space.

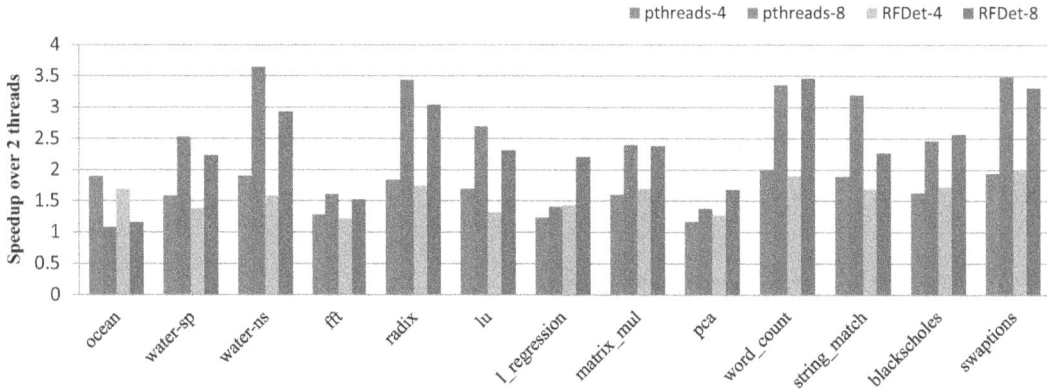

Figure 8. Scalability of RFDet-ci compared to `pthreads`.

$$Column10 = (SharedMemory + StackMemory)$$
$$Column11 = (N * SharedMemory + StackMemory$$
$$+ MetadataSpaceMemory)$$

Note that the memory consumption of the metadata space can affect the frequency of garbage collection, so we show the garbage collection count in the last column. We allocate memory in the metadata space when we either take a snapshot of a page (recall Figure 4) or convert these page snapshots to memory modification lists. The memory for storing a snapshot page is released immediately after we construct a byte-granularity modification list via page diffing. The memory for storing modification lists is released when we perform garbage collection. In our experiments, we set the size of the metadata space to 256MB and the threshold for GC to 90% metadata space usage, thus the corresponding GC count is shown in Table 1. However, when we set the metadata space to 512MB, there will be no GC for all these applications.

In pathological cases, even with garbage collection enabled, the slices in our metadata space can grow unboundedly large—this can happen if two threads execute for a long time without synchronizing. A specific example of this phenomenon is *linear_regression*: this benchmark has the least amount of communication (as it uses simple fork/join) but has the highest relative memory overheads. We could improve RFDet by using programmer annotations to identify threads that never communicate—this would enable eager collection of garbage slices and reduce the memory overheads of *linear_regression*, though we have not yet explored this idea.

Our Space/Time Tradeoff. Our approach investigates a space/time tradeoff in DMT. A fundamental cost of strong DMT is isolating threads' memory, which is often done using store buffers (CoreDet [4], RCDC [18], Calvin [21]) or memory protection (RFDet, DThreads, Conversion [29]).

Previous systems use global barriers to limit the growth of isolated memory. Specifically, at each global barrier, isolated memory regions (e.g., store buffers) are flushed into a *global store*, which is then read-only during the next parallel phase (recall Figure 1). Hence, global barriers reduce memory pressure in these previous systems.

In contrast, RFDet eliminates the need for global barriers by giving each thread an isolated memory space *and eliminating the global store entirely*—since there is no global store to update, there is never any need for global communication, beyond that already required by the program's explicit synchronization pattern, and we can eliminate those global barriers required by previous DMT systems. The downside, as we have just seen, is that isolated memory regions can grow arbitrarily large in RFDet, in the worst case. Hence, while previous systems trade lower memory pressure for lesser-performance, we make the opposite tradeoff.

5.5 Scalability and Optimizations

We also tested the scalability of RFDet-ci. In this experiment, we ran each application with 2, 4 and 8 threads respectively, and calculated the speedups of the 4-thread and 8-thread executions with respect to the 2-thread execution. Currently, we cannot run *dedup* and *ferret* with 8 threads due to running out of memory, so they are not included in this experiment. We also use *lu-con* to represent *lu-non* as the results of these two applications are similar. As shown in Figure 8, RFDet scales well for most applications (its scalability is comparable to that of `pthreads`). Note that *ocean* does not scale from 4 threads to 8 threads for both RFDet and `pthreads` in our platform due to poor parallelism.

We used applications in the SPLASH-2 suite to test the effectiveness of our *prelock* and *lazy write* optimizations. We chose these applications because they use plenty of synchronization operations, so the effect of these optimizations is magnified. In this experiment, we first disable both optimizations (the baseline execution). Then we enable one of

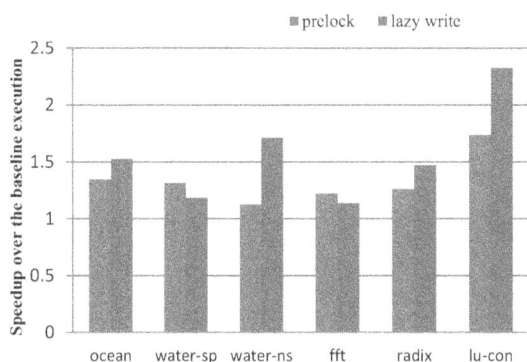

Figure 9. Optimization of *prelock* and *lazy write*.

the two optimizations each time and test the performance improvement over the baseline execution. Figure 9 shows the results of this experiment. As we can see, both optimizations improve performance, sometimes considerably.

6. Conclusion and Future Work

In this paper, we propose a new memory consistency model—deterministic lazy release consistency for C/C++ programs. In DLRC, only those modifications that happen before the current instruction should be visible. We use DLRC to implement an efficient deterministic multithreading system (RFDet) that, unlike prior systems, does not require global barriers. Our evaluation shows that RFDet ensures determinism with low overhead (35.2% on average, for the 16 parallel applications we tested). In the future, we will work on solutions for ad hoc synchronizations, e.g., providing interfaces for using ad hoc synchronizations or developing an automated tool for identifying and processing ad hoc synchronizations.

Acknowledgments

We thank our reviewers for their comments, which helped improve this paper greatly. This work is partially supported by National High-tech R&D Program of China (863 Program) under Grants 2012AA01A301 and 2012AA010901, by program for New Century Excellent Talents in University and by National Science Foundation (NSF) China 61272142, 61103082, 61003075, 61170261 and 61103193.

References

[1] S. V. Adve and J. K. Aggarwal, "A Unified Formalization of Four Shared-Memory Models," IEEE Trans. Parallel Distrib. Syst., vol. 4, pp. 613-624, 1993.

[2] S. V. Adve and M. D. Hill, "Weak ordering—a new definition," presented at the Proceedings of the 17th annual international symposium on Computer Architecture, Seattle, Washington, USA, 1990.

[3] A. Amittai, W. Shu-Chun, H. Sen, and F. Bryan, "Efficient system-enforced deterministic parallelism," presented at the Proceedings of the 9th USENIX conference on Operating systems design and implementation, Vancouver, BC, Canada, 2010.

[4] T. Bergan, O. Anderson, J. Devietti, L. Ceze, and D. Grossman, "CoreDet: a compiler and runtime system for deterministic multithreaded execution," presented at the Proceedings of the fifteenth edition of ASPLOS on Architectural support for programming languages and operating systems, Pittsburgh, Pennsylvania, USA, 2010.

[5] T. Bergan, L. Ceze, and D. Grossman, "Input-Covering Schedules for Multithreaded Programs," in Proceedings of the Conference on Object Oriented Programming, Systems, Languages, and Applications (OOPSLA), Indianapolis, Indiana, USA, 2013.

[6] T. Bergan, J. Devietti, N. Hunt, and L. Ceze, "The Deterministic Execution Hammer: How Well Does it Actually Pound Nails?," in WoDET, 2011.

[7] T. Bergan, N. Hunt, L. Ceze, and S. D. Gribble, "Deterministic process groups in dOS," in Proceedings of the 9th USENIX conference on Operating systems design and implementation, 2010.

[8] E. D. Berger, K. S. McKinley, R. D. Blumofe, and P. R. Wilson. "Hoard: A scalable memory allocator for multithreaded applications," in Proceedings of the International Conference on Architectural Support for Programming Languages and Operating Systems (ASPLOS-IX), pages 117-128, Cambridge, MA, Nov. 2000.

[9] E. D. Berger, T. Yang, T. Liu, and G. Novark, "Grace: Safe multithreaded programming for C/C++," in OOPSLA, 2009, pp. 81-96.

[10] C. Bienia, S. Kumar, J. P. Singh, and K. Li, "The PARSEC Benchmark Suite: Characterization and Architectural Implications," in Proceedings of the 17th international conference on Parallel architectures and compilation techniques, 2008.

[11] R. L. Bocchino Jr, V. S. Adve, S. V. Adve, and M. Snir, "Parallel programming must be deterministic by default," in Proceedings of the First USENIX conference on Hot topics in parallelism, 2009, pp. 4-4.

[12] H.-J. Boehm, "Position Paper: Nondeterminism is Unavoidable, but Data Races are Pure Evil," in Proceedsing of the 2012 ACM workshop on Relaxing synchronization for multicore and manycore scalability (RACES), 2012.

[13] H.-J. Boehm and S. V. Adve, "Foundations of the C++ concurrency memory model," presented at the Proceedings of the 2008 ACM SIGPLAN conference on Programming language design and implementation, Tucson, AZ, USA, 2008.

[14] H. Cui, J. Simsa, H. Li, B. Blum, X. Xu, J. Yang, G. A. Gibson, and R. E. Bryant, "Parrot: A Practical Runtime for Deterministic, Stable, and Reliable Threads," in Proceedings of the Twenty-Fourth ACM Symposium on Operating Systems Principles, Farmington, PA, USA, 2013.

[15] H. Cui, J. Wu, and J. Yang, "Stable deterministic multithreading through schedule memoization," in Proceedings of the 9th USENIX conference on Operating systems design and implementation, 2010.

[16] H. Cui, J. Wu, J. Gallagher, H. Guo, and J. Yang, "Efficient Deterministic Multithreading through Schedule Relaxation," in Proceedings of the Twenty-Third ACM Symposium on Operating Systems Principles, Cascais, Portugal, 2011.

[17] J. Devietti, B. Lucia, L. Ceze, M. Oskin, "DMP: deterministic shared memory multiprocessing,"presented at the Proceeding of the 14th international conference on Architectural support for programming languages and operating systems, Washington, DC, USA, 2009.

[18] J. Devietti, J. Nelson, T. Bergan, L. Ceze, and D. Grossman, "RCDC: a relaxed consistency deterministic computer," in Proceedings of the sixteenth international conference on Architectural support for programming languages and operating systems, Newport Beach, California, USA, 2011, pp. 67-78.

[19] C. J. Fidge., "Partial orders for parallel debugging," in ACM SIGPLAN/SIGOPS Workshop on Parallel and Distributed Debugging, January 1989, pp. 24(1): 183-194.

[20] M. Hill and M. Xu. Racey: A Stress Test for Deterministic Execution. Available: http://www.cs.wisc.edu/ markhill/racey.html

[21] D. R. Hower, P. Dudnik, M. D. Hill, and D. A. Wood, "Calvin: Deterministic or not? Free will to choose," in High Performance Computer Architecture (HPCA), 2011, pp. 333-334.

[22] B. Kasikci, C. Zamfir, and G. Candea. "Data Races vs. Data Race Bugs: Telling the Difference with Portend," in Proceedings of the Seventeenth International Conference on Architectural Support for Programming Languages and Operating Systems (ASPLOS), 2012.

[23] P. Keleher, A. L. Cox, and W. Zwaenepoel, "Lazy release consistency for software distributed shared memory," SIGARCH Comput. Archit. News, vol. 20, pp. 13-21, 1992.

[24] P. Keleher, A. L. Cox, S. Dwarkadas, and W. Zwaenepoel, "TreadMarks: distributed shared memory on standard workstations and operating systems," presented at the Proceedings of the USENIX Winter 1994 Technical Conference on USENIX Winter 1994 Technical Conference, San Francisco, California, 1994.

[25] T. J. LeBlanc and J. M. Mellor-Crummey, "Debugging parallel programs with instant replay," Computers, IEEE Transactions on, vol. 100, pp. 471-482, 1987.

[26] E. A. Lee, "The problem with threads," Computer, vol. 39, pp. 33-42, 2006.

[27] D. Lee, P. M. Chen, J. Flinn, and S. Narayanasamy, "Chimera: Hybrid Program Analysis for Determinism," presented at the Proceedings of the 2012 ACM SIGPLAN conference on Programming language design and implementation, Beijing, China, 2012.

[28] T. Liu, C. Curtsinger, and E. D. Berger, "DTHREADS: Efficient Deterministic Multithreading," in Proceedings of the 22nd ACM Symposium on Operating Systems Principles, 2011.

[29] T. Merrifield, and J. Eriksson, "Conversion: Multi-Version Concurrency Control for Main Memory Segments," in EuroSys, 2013.

[30] M. Olszewski, J. Ansel, and S. Amarasinghe, "Kendo: efficient deterministic multithreading in software," in Proceeding of the 14th international conference on Architectural support for programming languages and operating systems, 2009, pp. 97-108.

[31] C. Ranger, R. Raghuraman, A. Penmetsa, G. Bradski, and C. Kozyrakis, "Evaluating MapReduce for Multi-core and Multiprocessor Systems," in Proceedings of the 13th International Symposium on High Performance Computer Architecture, Washington, DC, USA, 2007, pp. 13-24.

[32] D. Subhraveti and J. Nieh, "Record and transplay: partial checkpointing for replay debugging across heterogeneous systems," in SIGMETRICS 2011, pp. 109-120.

[33] K. Veeraraghavan, D. Lee, B. Wester, J. Ouyang, P. M. Chen, J. Flinn, et al., "DoublePlay: Parallelizing Sequential Logging and Replay," in Proceedings of the sixteenth international conference on Architectural support for programming languages and operating systems, Newport Beach, California, USA, 2011.

[34] V. M. Weaver and S. A. McKee, "Can hardware performance counters be trusted?," in IISWC, 2008, pp. 141-150.

[35] S. C. Woo, M. Ohara, E. Torrie, J. P. Singh, and A. Gupta, "The SPLASH-2 programs: Characterization and methodological considerations," in Proceedings of the 22nd annual international symposium on Computer architecture, 1995, pp. 24-36.

[36] W. Xiong, S. Park, J. Zhang, Y. Zhou, and Z. Ma, "Ad hoc synchronization considered harmful," in Proceedings of the 9th USENIX conference on Operating Systems Design and Implementation, 2010, pp. 163-176.

[37] X. Zhou, K. Lu, X. Wang, and X. Li, "Exploiting parallelism in deterministic shared memory multiprocessing," J. Parallel Distrib. Comput., pp. 72(2012)716-727, 2012.

Race Directed Scheduling of Concurrent Programs

Mahdi Eslamimehr

UCLA, University of California, Los Angeles

mahdi@cs.ucla.edu

Jens Palsberg

UCLA, University of California, Los Angeles

palsberg@ucla.edu

Abstract

Detection of data races in Java programs remains a difficult problem. The best static techniques produce many false positives, and also the best dynamic techniques leave room for improvement. We present a new technique called race directed scheduling that for a given race candidate searches for an input and a schedule that lead to the race. The search iterates a combination of concolic execution and schedule improvement, and turns out to find useful inputs and schedules efficiently. We use an existing technique to produce a manageable number of race candidates. Our experiments on 23 Java programs found 72 real races that were missed by the best existing dynamic techniques. Among those 72 races, 31 races were found with schedules that have between 1 million and 108 million events, which suggests that they are rare and hard-to-find races.

Categories and Subject Descriptors D.2.5 Software Engineering [*Testing and Debugging*]

Keywords concurrency; race detection

1. Introduction

Concurrent programming with shared memory offers both the benefit of efficient execution and the pitfall of data races. Efficiency can be achieved when we let multiple processors run in parallel and exchange data via the shared memory. A data race arises when two processes simultaneously access a shared memory location and at least one of the two accesses is a write operation. Data races often result in hard-to-detects bugs and usually the programmers of concurrent software should try to avoid data races.

One reason for why data races are problematic can be found in a seminal paper by Adve, Hill, Miller, and Netzer [10]. Their observation is that on suitable hardware, every

PPoPP '14, February 15–19, 2014, Orlando, Florida, USA.
Copyright © 2014 ACM 978-1-4503-2656-8/14/02... $15.00.
http://dx.doi.org/10.1145/2555243.2555263

execution of a data-race-free program is *sequentially consistent*. Sequential consistency was introduced by Lamport in 1979 and means that "the result of any execution is the same as if the operations of all the processors were executed in some sequential order, and the operations of each individual processor appear in this sequence in the order specified by its program" [31]. Sequential consistency provides a useful memory model that simplifies the task of producing correct concurrent programs. If programmers can avoid data races, they can use sequential consistency as their memory model.

Researchers have developed many techniques to help programmers detect data races. Some of those techniques require program annotations that typically must be supplied by a programmer; examples include [9, 15]. Other techniques work with unannotated programs and thus they are easier to use. In this paper we focus on techniques that work with unannotated Java programs. We use 23 open-source benchmarks that have a total of more than 4.5 million lines of code, which we use "straight of the box" without annotations.

We can divide race-detection techniques into three categories: static, dynamic, and hybrid. A static technique examines the text of a program without running it; a dynamic technique runs a program, possibly multiple times, and gathers information during those executions; and a hybrid technique does both.

The advantage of a static technique is that if it is sound, then it will report every possible race, though it may also report false positives. We will show via experiments that the best existing static technique reports a large number of false positives that would be daunting to examine by hand. For our benchmarks, the Chord tool [34] reports a total 127,136 data races. So, current static techniques are of little use to working programmers. Potentially, a sound static technique can be valuable, particularly because if it reports zero races for a benchmark then indeed that benchmark has no races.

The advantage of a dynamic technique is that it reports only real races. For example, for our benchmarks, the Fast-Track, Goldilocks, RaceFuzzer, and Pacer tools together report a total 304 data races. So, current dynamic techniques give programmers valuable help, yet our experiments show that they leave many races to be discovered.

The advantage of a hybrid technique is that it may be able to combine the best of both worlds, static and dynamic. The best existing hybrid technique appears to be a technique by O'Callahan and Choi [35] that we call Hybrid, which for our benchmarks report a total 405 data races. This technique may produce both false positives and false negatives, yet the tool provides programmers with output of a fairly manageable size.

In this paper we focus on dynamic techniques. We will present a dynamic technique that reports significantly more real races than the previous techniques.

The main shortcoming of the existing dynamic techniques is that when they search for an execution that leads to a real race, they often come up empty handed. We present a novel approach to execution search that gives much better results. The central concept in our approach is the standard notion of *schedule*, which is a sequence of events that must be executed in order.

The challenge. Find an execution that leads to a real race.

Our result. We present *race directed scheduling* that for given a race candidate searches for an input and a schedule that lead to the race. The search iterates a combination of concolic execution and schedule improvement.

We have implemented race directed scheduling in a tool called Racageddon that does race detection for Java programs. We use an existing hybrid technique to produce a manageable number of race candidates.

For our benchmarks, our tool found 72 real races that were missed by the best existing dynamic techniques. Among the 304 real races found by the existing dynamic techniques, our technique found 272 of them. Our tool is fully automatic and its user needs no expertise on data races. Once our tool reports a race, our tool can replay the execution that leads to the race.

In summary, the two main contributions of this paper are:

- an effective and useful dynamic race detector and

- an experimental comparison of seven race detectors.

The rest of the paper. In the following section we discuss two techniques from previous work that we use as "black-box" components of Racageddon. In Section 3 we present our new approach, in Section 4 we present our experimental results, and in Section 5 we discuss related work.

2. Two Techniques from Previous Work

Racageddon uses two techniques from previous work [35, 41]. In both cases, Racageddon uses those techniques as "black boxes", that is, as unmodified components for which we rely only on their input-output behavior. We implemented both techniques ourselves after a careful study of the seminal papers [35, 41].

Generation of race candidates. We use a hybrid race detector by O'Callahan and Choi [35] that we call Hybrid. Hybrid combines lockset-based detection and happens-before-based detection into a single efficient technique that can pro-

duce both false positives and false negatives. We view the output of Hybrid as *race candidates* that deserve further attention. Hybrid provides a rather small number of race candidates, namely a total of 405 for our benchmarks of more than 4.5 million lines of code. Those 405 race candidates are an excellent starting point for our search for real races.

Schedule improvement. We use an approach to schedule improvement by Said, Wang, Yang, and Sakallah [41]. Their method maps a schedule to a permutation of the schedule. The idea is that a user supplies both a schedule that represents a trace of a program execution and also a race candidate, and then in return gets a schedule that has a better chance to lead to the race. The method has "memory": it takes advantage of the schedules that have been submitted in all previous calls. Together, all those schedules provide a wealth of information about happens-before relationships in a specific program. The method uses an SMT-solver and is highly efficient, even for the schedules of lengths beyond length 10^8 that we encountered in our experiments.

3. Race Directed Scheduling

We now present our approach to data race detection. We will use pseudo-code to describe both our approach and the data types that we use.

3.1 Data Types

Here are six data types that we use in Racageddon.

$$
\begin{array}{rcl}
\text{Program} & = & \text{a Java 6 program} \\
\text{Input} & = & \text{input to a Java 6 program} \\
\text{Event} & = & \text{threadId} \times \text{statementLabel} \\
\text{EventPair} & = & \text{Event} \times \text{Event} \\
\text{Schedule} & = & \text{Event sequence} \\
\text{Race} & = & \text{EventPair} \times \text{Input} \times \text{Schedule}
\end{array}
$$

Racageddon works for Java 6 programs, which have the type Program. The input to such programs is a vector of values; we use Input to denote the type of input vectors.

When a program execution executes a particular statement in a particular thread, we refer to that as an *event* that has type Event. In the context of race detection, the key data type is EventPair that we use to describe two events that may form a race.

The standard notion of *schedule* is here the data type Schedule, which is a sequence of events.

A Race is the type of information that we need to replay an execution that leads to a race. A Race has three components, namely the EventPair that is the race, the Input that we should supply at the beginning of the execution, and the Schedule that the execution should follow to reach the race.

3.2 Two Tools

Let us describe the interfaces to the two off-the-shelf tools from Section 2 in terms of the data types listed above.

hybrid : Program $\rightarrow$ (EventPair set)
improve : (Schedule $\times$ EventPair) $\rightarrow$ (Schedule $\oplus$ {none})

Here hybrid stands for O'Callahan and Choi's technique, while improve stands for Said, Wang, Yang, and Sakallah's technique. Notice that hybrid maps a Java program to a set of event pairs, that is, a set of race candidates. Notice also that improve maps a schedule to a better schedule or else to none if no better schedule was found. We leave implicit that improve has "memory" and takes advantage of the schedules that have been submitted in all previous calls. Notice finally that improve is idempotent in the sense that if $improve(trace, c) \neq$ none, then

$$improve(improve(trace, c), c) = improve(trace, c)$$

3.3 Concolic Execution

Racageddon uses concolic execution as one of its components. We will summarize the idea of concolic execution and we will introduce a slight generalization of the approach that we use in Racageddon.

Concolic execution [17, 18, 27, 32, 45–48], executes code with concrete and symbolic values simultaneously and uses the result to generate inputs for another execution. The term "concolic" combines the words "concrete" and "symbolic". Each execution collects constraints from the symbolic values and the conditions in the control-flow. Those constraints represent the executed control-flow path and they have *the concrete input to the run* as solution.

Suppose we want to execute a particular event, that is, a particular statement in a particular thread. We can execute a sequence of concolic runs that successively get closer and closer to execute the desired event. The idea is to do a minor modification of the constraints collected from conditions of branches. Imagine that a prefix of the concolic run made progress towards the desired event but at a particular branch B went off in a direction that appears to lead away from the desired event. We take the constraints from the prefix plus the *negation* of B. The solution to those constraints is an input that will steer the next concolic execution a little closer to the desired event by going off in the other direction at branch B.

Experience shows that concolic execution achieves better branch coverage with fewer test cases than testing with random inputs. In the first round of concolic execution, the input is chosen randomly.

We can generalize the standard approach to pursue execution of an entire schedule, that is, an event sequence. For example, suppose we want execution of the schedule (e_1, e_2, e_3). Some rounds of concolic execution may lead to execution of e_1. We can refer to those rounds together as a super-round. Now we can use the constraints that lead to execution of e_1 and continue with a second super-round that leads to execution of first e_1 and later e_2. Finally, we can do a third super-round and achieve execution of the entire schedule.

The above method generalizes easily to schedules of any length.

If we manage to execute an entire given schedule, we continue to explore additional schedules that have the given schedule as prefix.

We describe our interface to concolic execution in the following way.

$$concolic : \quad (Program \times Schedule) \rightarrow$$
$$((Race\ set) \times Schedule)$$

The input to concolic is a program and a schedule, and concolic will execute one super-round per element in the schedule. A run of concolic has two outputs. The first output is a set of all races that were found by any of the individual concolic executions. The second output is a schedule that represents the trace of final concolic execution, irrespectively of whether the given schedule was executed. We emphasize that each call to concolic may do many concolic executions, hence have many opportunities to collect races.

3.4 Helper functions

We use three helper functions:

$$present : \quad (EventPair \times Schedule) \rightarrow boolean$$
$$swap : \quad (Race\ set) \rightarrow (Race\ set)$$
$$\uplus : \quad ((Race\ set) \times (Race\ set)) \rightarrow (Race\ set)$$

Informally, present checks that the two elements of an event pair occur consecutively in a schedule. Additionally, swap makes a change to each element $((e', e''), v, s)$ of a race set, namely to swap e' and e'' both in the first component of the triple and also where they first occur consecutively in s. Finally, $\uplus$ does something akin to a union of two race sets, namely to do the union based only on the event pair of each race. We will maintain the invariant that for a given $c \in EventPair$, a race set contains at most one race of the form (c, v, s). The idea of $X \uplus Y$ is that if X contains a race of the form (c, v', s'), and Y contains a race of the form (c, v'', s''), then $X \uplus Y$ will, somewhat arbitrarily, contain the first race (c, v', s') (and leave out (c, v'', s'')). Formally,

$$present((e', e''), (e_1, \ldots, e_n)) =$$
$$\begin{cases} true & \text{if } \exists i : e' = e_i \land e'' = e_{i+1} \\ false & \text{otherwise} \end{cases}$$

$$swap(X) =$$
$$\{ ((e'', e'), v, (e_1, \ldots, e_{i-1}, e_{i+1}, e_i, e_{i+2}, \ldots, e_n)) \mid$$
$$((e', e''), v, (e_1, \ldots, e_n)) \in X \land$$
$$i \in 1..(n-1) \text{ is the smallest index such that:}$$
$$e' = e_i \land e'' = e_{i+1} \}$$

For every $X \in (Race\ set)$, we assume that if $(c', v', s') \in X$ and $(c'', v'', s'') \in X$ and $c' = c''$, then $v' = v''$ and $s' = s''$. The following definition of $\uplus$ maintains this property.

$$X \uplus Y = X \cup \{ ((e', e''), v, s) \in Y \mid$$
$$\forall (e_x, v_x, s_x) \in X : e_x \neq (e', e'') \}$$

3.5 Racageddon Overview

Racageddon iterates a combination of concolic execution and schedule improvement. We begin with a run of hybrid to produce candidate races and then we do two phases of search for races. In the Phase 1 we do a separate search for each of the candidate races. In the Phase 2 we do a search based on the races found in Phase 2. For our benchmarks, our experiments with Racageddon found 291 real races in Phase 1 and 53 additional real races in Phase 2.

In Phase 1 we interleave calls to concolic and improve. The idea is to turn the search for a race into a search for a schedule that leads to the race. Each call to concolic will produce a schedule that gets closer to execute the race, after which a call to improve will further improve that schedule. In more detail, each call to concolic will both try to execute the given schedule *and* continue execution beyond that schedule, typically until termination of the program. Part of the continued execution may make progress towards the desired race. The call to improve will permute some events in the schedule to make the next concolic run have a better chance to succeed. Notice that because improve is idempotent, we apply improve just once.

In Phase 2 we consider each race found in Phase 1 and do a swap of the two racing events in the schedule that lead to the race. The "swapped" schedule leads to a race of the same two events, which in itself provides nothing new. The interesting aspect of the "swapped" schedule is that a concolic execution will continue after the race and may proceed in a different way than the execution in Phase 1. Our experience is that those continued executions may find races that Phase 1 missed. Once Phase 2 finds a new race, we also do a swap of the schedule that led to that new race.

The alternation of improve and concolic steps is considerably more powerful than either one alone. For our benchmarks, our technique finds 344 races, while improve alone (applied to the trace of an initial run) finds only 151 races, and concolic alone finds only 47 races.

3.6 Racageddon Pseudo-code

Figure 1 shows pseudo-code for Racageddon. We will now go over the pseudo-code in detail. We hope our pseudo-code and explanation will enable a better understanding of the approach and enable practitioners to implement Racageddon easily.

The input to the Racageddon procedure is a program while the output is a set of races. The first four lines of Racageddon declares these four variables: (1) a set of race candidates, called *candidates*, that we initialize by a call to hybrid, (2) a set of races, called *races*, that initially is the empty set and that we eventually return as the result of the procedure, (3) a set of races, called r, that we use to hold intermediate results, and (4) a schedule, called *trace*, that holds each trace produced by concolic.

Phase 1 consists of a for-each-loop that tries each of the event pairs in the set of candidates. For each event pair we use a while-loop to do iterations that each does one call to improve and one call to concolic. We use the integer variable i to count the number of iterations and we bound i by 1000

```
(Race set) Racageddon(Program p) {
    (EventPair set) candidates = hybrid(p)
    (Race set) races = ∅
    (Race set) r
    Schedule trace

    /* Phase 1: try the candidates */
    for each EventPair c ∈ candidates do {
        boolean done = false
        int i = 0
        traces = ε
        while (¬ done) ∧ (i ≤ 1000) {
            case improve(trace, c) of
                Schedule s : {
                    (r, trace) = concolic(p, s)
                    races = races ⊎ r
                    done = present(c, trace)
                }
                none : {done = true}
            }
            i = i + 1
        }
    }

    /* Phase 2: try swaps of the races */
    (Race set) workset = swap(races)
    for each Race (c, v, s) ∈ workset do {
        (r, trace) = concolic(p, s)
        races = races ⊎ r
        workset = workset ⊎ swap(r)
    }

    return races
}
```

Figure 1. Racageddon.

to ensure that the search terminates, even if the search found no races. In practice, the highest number of calls to improve and concolic we did for any of our benchmarks was 197. So, none of our experiments exercised the condition $i \leq 1000$. We initialize *trace* to the empty schedule, denoted by ϵ, such that the initial call to improve can work correctly; that call will return ϵ.

The while-loop uses a Boolean-variable *done* to keep track of whether the search for a particular candidate can be terminated before i reaches 1000. We have two reasons for terminating the search early, which we do by setting *done* to true. If the candidate pair c is present in the *trace* executed by concolic, as found by the call present($e, trace$), then we can declare success and terminate the search. If the call to improve($e, trace$) returns none, then the search has stalled, and we abandon the search. While abandoning a search may seem sad, our experiments do it in some cases. One of the

304

reasons may be that the race candidate actually isn't a real race!

Notice how each iteration of the while-loop begins with $trace$, improves it to a schedule s (unless improve returns none), which then after execution of concolic turns into a new value for $trace$.

Phase 2 is a workset algorithm that uses the variable $workset$ that holds a set of races. The $workset$ variable holds a set of races still to be processed. Initially $workset$ is the set of races found in Phase 1, but swapped, in the sense that we now want to search for the "swapped" race. The main part of Phase 2 is a for-each-loop that iterates over the elements of $workset$. We use an advanced for-each-loop that works correctly even if elements are added to $workset$ during a run of the for-each-loop. Here, "works correctly" means that the for-each-loop does one iteration per element of $workset$, even if an element is added to $workset$ multiple times or added after the execution of the for-each-loop begins.

For each element of $workset$, Phase 2 makes one call to concolic and collects any races that may be found. For each new race found in Phase 2, we add the race to $workset$ such that we eventually can say that we tried the "swapped" version of every race that we found.

3.7 Example

We now present an example in which we walk through a run of Racageddon on this program with three shared variables and two threads:

x,y,z are shared variables
z has an initial value received from user input

Thread 1:   Thread 2:
l_1: x = 6 l_4: x = 2
l_2: if (z>4) l_5: if ($z^2 + 5 < x^2$)
l_3:   y = 5 l_6:   y = 3

We use these abbreviations for events: $e_1 = (1, l_1)$, $e_2 = (1, l_2)$, $e_3 = (1, l_3)$, $e_4 = (2, l_4)$, $e_5 = (2, l_5)$, $e_6 = (2, l_6)$,

The call to hybrid produces two race candidates:

$$candidates = \{(e_1, e_4), (e_1, e_5)\}$$

Now we begin Phase 1 of Racageddon. Suppose the for-each loop first considers the candidate (e_1, e_4).

Now we run the first iteration of the while-loop. Initially $trace$ is the empty schedule so improve returns the empty schedule. Now we run concolic on the empty schedule. Suppose that the initial random input, which becomes the values of the shared variable z, is 0. Nondeterminism can lead to several traces; suppose we get

$$trace = e_1, e_2, e_4, e_5$$

Notice here that we don't get to e_3 because the condition in e_2 fails due to $0 < 4$, and we don't get to e_6 because the

condition in e_5 fails due to $z^2 + 5 = 5$ and $x^2 = 4$ and $5 > 4$.

Now we run the second iteration of the while-loop. First we run improve on (e_1, e_4) and $trace$, which produces this permutation of $trace$:

$$trace = e_1, e_4, e_2, e_5$$

Now we run concolic on $trace$, and like above, let us suppose the initial random input leads to z = 0. The execution of concolic finds the race for which we are searching, so we can add that race to $races$:

$$races = \{((e_1, e_4), 0, (e_1, e_4, e_2, e_5))\}$$

Like above, we don't get to execute e_3 or e_6; the conditions in e_2 and e_5 fails for the same reasons as above.

Next the for-each-loop in Phase 1 considers the candidate (e_1, e_5).

Now we run the first iteration of the while-loop. Let us assume that this iteration proceeds like the first iteration for (e_1, e_4) so we get:

$$trace = e_1, e_2, e_4, e_5$$

Now we run the second iteration of the while-loop. First we run improve on (e_1, e_5) and $trace$, which produces this permutation of $trace$:

$$trace = e_4, e_5, e_1, e_2$$

Notice that even though e_5 and e_1 occur consecutively, we won't terminate the search because we are looking for (e_1, e_5). Now we run concolic on $trace$, and which leads to an execution with this trace:

$$trace = e_4, e_5, e_1, e_2, e_3$$

for which z had the initial value 10. (We skip the constraints and merely note that they have solution 10, among other solutions.) Note that $trace$ contains e_3 because the condition in e_2 succeeds due to $10 > 4$.

Now we run the third iteration of the while-loop. First we run improve on (e_1, e_5) and $trace$, which produces this permutation of $trace$:

$$trace = e_4, e_1, e_5, e_2, e_3$$

Next, the execution of concolic finds the race for which we are searching, so we can add that race to $races$:

$$races = \{((e_1, e_4), 0, (e_1, e_4, e_2, e_5)), \\ ((e_1, e_5), 10, (e_4, e_1, e_5, e_2, e_3))\}$$

We don't get to execute e_6 because the condition in e_5 fails due to $z^2 + 5 = 105$ and $x^2 = 36$ and $105 > 36$.

Now the for-each-loop has processed both elements of the set $candidates$, so we are done with Phase 1 and can move

305

Name	LOC	# threads	Brief description
Sor	1270	5	A successive order-relaxation benchmark
TSP	713	10	Traveling Salesman Problem solver
Hedc	30K	10	A web-crawler application kernel
Elevator	2840	5	A real-time discrete event simulator
ArrayList	5866	26	ArrayList from `java.util`
TreeSet	7532	21	TreeSet from `java.util`
HashSet	7086	21	HashSet from `java.util`
Vector	709	10	Vector from `java.util`
RayTracer	1942	5	Measures the performance of a 3D raytracer
MolDyn	1351	5	N-Body code modeling dynamic
MonteCarlo	3619	4	A financial simulator, using Monte Carlo techniques to price products
Derby	1.6M	64	Apache RDBMS
Colt	110K	11	Open Source Libraries for High Performance Scientific and Technical Computing
ChordTest	62	11	Mini-benchmark; comes with the Chord race detector
Avrora	140K	6	AVR microcontroller simulator
Tomcat	535K	16	Tomcat Apache web application server
Batic	354K	5	Produces a number of Scalable Vector Graphics (SVG) images based on Apache Batic
Eclipse	1.2M	16	Non-GUI Eclipse IDE
FOP	21K	8	XSL-FO to PDF converter
H2	20K	16	Executes a JDBCbench-like in-memory benchmark
PMD	81K	4	Java Static Analyzer
Sunflow	108K	16	Tool for rendering image with raytracer
Xalan	355K	9	XML to HTML transformer
TOTAL	4587K		

Figure 2. Our benchmarks.

on to Phase 2. Notice that we found both candidate races to be real races.

In Phase 2 we consider swapped versions of the two races found in Phase 1:

$$workset = \{ ((e_4, e_1), 0, (e_4, e_1, e_2, e_5)),$$
$$((e_5, e_1), 10, (e_4, e_5, e_1, e_2, e_3)) \}$$

Let us here focus on the run with the schedule (e_4, e_1, e_2, e_5). The call to concolic eventually executes $(e_4, e_1, e_2, e_5, e_3)$ and collects these constraints:

$$x = 6 \ \wedge \ z > 4 \ \wedge \ z^2 + 5 < x^2$$

that have solution z = 5. The next concolic execution therefore executes $(e_4, e_1, e_2, e_5, e_3, e_6)$, which contains the race (e_3, e_6). We add that race to *races*:

$$races = \{ ((e_1, e_4), 0, (e_1, e_4, e_2, e_5)),$$
$$((e_1, e_5), 10, (e_4, e_1, e_5, e_2, e_3)),$$
$$((e_3, e_6), 5, (e_4, e_1, e_2, e_5, e_3, e_6)) \}$$

In summary, hybrid produced two candidates races, Phase 1 found both candidates to be real races, and Phase 2 found one additional race. The key reason why we detected the additional race (e_3, e_6) is that the swapping of events lead the concolic execution to a new program state that was not previously reached.

4. Experimental Results

We use the Lime concolic execution engine; Lime is open source, `http://www.tcs.hut.fi/Software/lime`. In our implementation, events are at the Java bytecode level; we use Soot [53] to instrument bytecodes. We ran all our experiments on a Linux CentOs machine with two 2.4 GHz Xeon quad core processors and 32 GB RAM.

4.1 Benchmarks

Figure 2 lists our 23 benchmarks which we have collected from seven sources:

- From ETH Zurich [1, 54]: Sor, TSP, Hedc, Elevator.
- From `java.util`, Oracle's JDK 1.4.2 [2–4, 36]: ArrayList, TreeSet, HashSet, Vector.
- From Java Grande [5, 51]: RayTracer, MolDyn, MonteCarlo.
- From the Apache Software Foundation: [6, 25]: Derby.
- From European Org. for Nuclear Research (CERN) [4, 24]: Colt.
- From the Chord distribution [7]: ChordTest.
- From DaCapo [8, 12]: Avrora, Tomcat, Batic, Eclipse, FOP, H2, PMD, Sunflow, Xalan.

The sizes of the benchmarks vary widely: we have 2 huge (1M+ LOC), 10 large (20K–1M LOC), 8 medium (1K–8K LOC), and 3 small (less than 1K LOC) benchmarks.

Figure 2 also lists the high watermark of how many threads each benchmark runs.

4.2 Race Detectors

We compare Racageddon with one static race detector, namely Chord [34], one hybrid race detector, namely the one that we call Hybrid [35], and four dynamic race detectors, namely FastTrack [23], Goldilocks [21], RaceFuzzer [47], and Pacer [14]. Additionally we compare with a combined dynamic technique that we call FGRP.

Chord is a static technique, and by design it may report false positives; its main objective is to report all real races (or as many as possible).

We discussed Hybrid in Section 2.

FastTrack, Goldilocks, RaceFuzzer, Pacer, and Racageddon are all dynamic techniques that report only real races.

FastTrack and Goldilocks are based on the observation that a race happens if two accesses to a memory location (of which at least one access is a write) are not ordered by the happens-before relation. FastTrack uses a clever representation of the happens-before relation to achieve constant-time overhead for almost all monitored operations. Goldilocks uses a lockset-based algorithm to improve the precision of the computation of the happens-before relation.

RaceFuzzer performs random testing by choosing thread schedules at random and stopping a thread when it is about to execute a statement in a candidate race pair. RaceFuzzer and Racageddon have the following key similarities and differences. The main similarity is that both use Hybrid to generate race candidates and then they guide execution towards those race candidates. The main difference is that RaceFuzzer guides execution with a custom thread scheduler that controls thread interleaving, while Racageddon 1) uses the improve function get a better schedule ahead of execution and 2) interleaves calls to improve and concolic.

Pacer is a sampling-based data race detector that detects any race at a rate equal to the sampling rate. In our experiments, the sampling race was 100% and for each benchmark we used 100 trials. We used a sampling rate of 100% to make Pacer report as many races as possible, even though performance will be the slowest possible.

We use FGRP to stand for the union of FastTrack, Goldilocks, RaceFuzzer, and Pacer in following sense. We can implement FGRP as a tool that for a given benchmark starts runs of FastTrack, Goldilocks, RaceFuzzer, and Pacer in four separate threads, and if any one of them reports a race, then FGRP reports a race.

We implemented Hybrid and RaceFuzzer ourselves according to the published papers that describe them, while we got the implementations of Chord, FastTrack, Goldilocks, and Pacer from webpages and from their authors.

4.3 How we handle Reflection

Many of the benchmarks use reflection, yet each of the race detectors listed above either doesn't support reflection or supports reflection poorly. We overcome this problem with a the help of the tool chain TamiFlex [13].

The core of the problem is that all the race detectors do either a static analysis or some form of ahead-of-time instrumentation. Reflection tends to make static analysis unsound and to load uninstrumented classes. TamiFlex solves these problems in a manner that is sound with respect to a set of recorded program runs. If a later program run deviates from the recorded runs, TamiFlex issues a warning.

We have combined each of the race detectors with Tami-Flex and we have run all our experiments without warnings. As a result, the race detectors all handle reflection correctly and in the same way.

4.4 Race Siblings

The seven race detectors differ in how they report race *siblings*. We define that two event pairs are siblings if they have one event in common. Our versions of Hybrid and Race-Fuzzer may report race siblings, and also Chord, Pacer, and Racageddon may report race siblings. In contrast, FastTrack and Goldilocks report only one of two siblings. Intuitively, FastTrack and Goldilocks reports zero or one race per memory location, while the other race detectors may report multiple races per memory location. The reader should be aware of this difference when reading the measurements below.

4.5 Measurements

Figure 3 shows the numbers of races found in 23 benchmarks by Racageddon, including whether the races were found in Phase 1 or in Phase 2.

Figure 4 shows, for each benchmark, the number of schedules tried by Racageddon, the length of the longest schedule that found a race, and the number of branches in that longest schedule. One way to understand "the number of branches" is as follows. Suppose, for a given benchmark, we have the longest schedule that found a race and we want to reconstruct the input that led to execution of that schedule. We do that by first generating constraints from the branches in the schedule, and then solving the constraints, which produces an input that will work. Figure 4 shows the number of constraints that were generated in this manner.

Figure 5 shows the numbers of races found in 23 benchmarks by 7 techniques.

Figure 6 shows the time each of the runs took in minutes and seconds, and it shows the geometrical mean for each technique.

Some of the executions of Goldilocks crashed, which we indicate in Figure 5 and Figure 6 with "-". If we compare Figure 5 and Figure 6 we see that for ArrayList and Batic, we list that Goldilocks reported races while we list no execution times. The reason is that for ArrayList and Batic, our runs

	Number of races found		
Name	Total =	Phase 1 +	Phase 2
Sor	3	2	1
TSP	2	2	0
Hedc	11	9	2
Elevator	8	5	3
ArrayList	7	7	0
TreeSet	3	3	0
HashSet	8	7	1
Vector	4	4	0
RayTracer	4	3	1
MolDyn	6	4	2
MonteCarlo	3	2	1
Derby	18	15	3
Colt	10	7	3
ChordTest	2	2	0
Avrora	13	12	1
Tomcat	21	19	2
Batic	29	23	6
Eclipse	51	46	5
FOP	18	16	2
H2	39	30	9
PMD	13	12	1
Sunflow	30	22	8
Xalan	41	39	2
TOTAL	344	291	53

Figure 3. Races found by Racageddon.

Name	number of schedules	longest schedule	
		length	# branches
Sor	14	6,803	135
TSP	8	6,047	697
Hedc	28	249,268	4,084
Elevator	28	9,005	401
ArrayList	47	132,990	2,503
TreeSet	17	110,087	2,303
HashSet	38	139,553	2,979
Vector	40	6,308	108
RayTracer	9	71,084	520
MolDyn	188	4,680	362
MonteCarlo	24	12,061	994
Derby	105	108,302,900	39,103
Colt	63	948,033	9,418
ChordTest	2	505	10
Avrora	23	702,961	10,207
Tomcat	197	1,284,917	18,429
Batic	39	1,407,554	10,901
Eclipse	53	102,879,384	23,863
FOP	41	153,074	3,085
H2	35	297,655	7,310
PMD	48	310,049	7,201
Sunflow	37	1,624,320	8,821
Xalan	56	2,907,450	11,937

Figure 4. Schedules tried by Racageddon.

of Goldilocks crashed, yet the execution log contained some races that we report in Figure 5.

Figure 7 shows, for each benchmark, the lengths of the 72 schedules that lead to races found only by Racageddon.

Figure 8 shows, for each benchmark, how many of the races found by Hybrid are actually real races, as found by the combination of FGRP and Racageddon.

4.6 Evaluation

We now present our findings based both on the measurements listed above and on additional analysis of the races that were found.

Racageddon. We can see in Figure 3 that Racageddon found a total of 344 real races, including 291 races found in Phase 1 and 53 races found in Phase 2. The split between Phase 1 and Phase 2 demonstrates a subtlety of race directed scheduling: even when we have a schedule that finds a race, a swap of the race pair can lead to other races.

Number of schedules. We can see in Figure 4 that the number of schedules tried by Racageddon is rather modest and appears to be no worse than the product of a small constant and the number of race candidates. Note that in Racageddon, some runs of concolic finds multiple races. We can also see in Figure 4 that the longest schedules that found

races can have lengths that are more than 100,000,000. This shows that the improve method scales to long schedules.

Racageddon versus other Dynamic Techniques. We can see in Figure 5 that Racageddon finds the most races (344) of all the dynamic techniques. Among those 344 races, 72 races were found only by Racageddon and are entirely novel to this paper, while 272 were also found by FGRP. Dually, 32 races were found only by FGRP. In summary, we have that the combination of FGRP and Racageddon found 376 races in the 23 benchmarks.

Found only by FGRP:	32
Found by both:	272
Found only by Racageddon:	72
Total:	376

Let us consider races that Racageddon found but FGRP missed. One such race is a bug in Eclipse, specifically in the class HudsonSecurityManager in the package org.eclipse.hudson.security. The effect of the race is that a plug-in may fail to load and that the user may have to restart Eclipse.

Dually, let us consider races that FGRP found but that Racageddon missed. One such race is in Derby, specifically in the class Connection in the package org/apache/derby/client/am, where we find this code:

	Static	Hybrid	Dynamic							
benchmarks	Chord	Hybrid	FastTrack	Goldilocks	RaceFuzzer	Pacer	FGRP	Racageddon		
								total = new + FGRP		
Sor	3	8	0	0	0	3	3	3	3	0
TSP	17	3	1	1	0	1	1	2	1	1
Hedc	143	5	3	1	1	11	11	11	4	7
Elevator	54	13	1	-	0	4	4	8	4	4
ArrayList	8	14	0	1	5	6	6	7	1	6
TreeSet	11	13	0	-	6	8	9	3	0	3
HashSet	0	11	0	-	8	7	8	8	0	8
Vector	17	9	0	-	5	5	5	4	0	4
RayTracer	159	2	1	1	1	3	3	4	1	3
MolDyn	92	43	0	1	2	5	5	6	1	5
MonteCarlo	101	5	0	0	1	2	2	3	1	2
Derby	1110	21	1	-	2	14	15	18	4	14
Colt	549	13	0	0	3	7	7	10	3	7
ChordTest	2	2	1	1	2	2	2	2	0	2
Avrora	1887	9	3	3	6	11	12	13	1	12
Tomcat	110061	52	12	11	11	20	20	21	3	18
Batic	970	12	9	10	9	32	35	29	7	22
Eclipse	9401	77	14	-	13	39	43	51	8	43
FOP	34	21	5	5	8	13	15	18	3	15
H2	869	19	5	-	9	25	26	39	13	26
PMD	292	14	9	8	4	13	13	13	0	13
Sunflow	353	16	8	11	9	19	21	30	11	19
Xalan	1003	23	6	9	10	36	38	41	3	38
TOTAL	127136	405	79	63	115	286	304	344	72	272

Figure 5. The numbers of races found in 23 benchmarks by 7 techniques.

```
public void accumulateWarning(SqlWarning e) {
    if (warnings_ == null) {
        warnings_ = e;
    } else {
        warnings_.setNextException(e);
    }
}

public void clearWarningsX() throws SqlException {
    warnings_ = null;
    accumulated440ForMessageProcFailure_ = false;
    accumulated444ForMessageProcFailure_ = false;
    accumulatedSetReadOnlyWarning_ = false;
}
```

The accesses to warnings_ can form races. The effect of the race may be a null-pointer exception, which can happen in the following way. First a call to accumulateWarning sets warnings_ to e, and then a call to clearWarningsX sets warning_ to null, and finally the caller of the method accumulateWarning gets a null-pointer exception.

Race siblings. Are the 72 races found only by Racageddon genuinely new or are they merely siblings of other races found by Racageddon? As a step towards an answer to this question, let us define

B = the 272 races found by both Racageddon and FGRP

R = the 72 races found only by Racageddon

In terms of B and R, the question is whether the races in R have siblings in B or R. The answer is that 36 races in R have no siblings at all, each of 28 races in R has a sibling in B, and R contains 6 sibling pairs. Notice that the races in two of the sibling pairs in R also have siblings in B. We conclude that Racageddon finds 36+4 = 40 races that are genuinely new and don't have siblings among the other races found by Racageddon.

FastTrack versus Pacer. Pacer is based on FastTrack and as expected, every race found by FastTrack is also found by Pacer. Pacer finds many more races (286) than FastTrack (79) so our experiments confirm that Pacer is a highly worthwhile extension of FastTrack.

FGRP details. The combined dynamic technique FGRP found 304 races. Pacer was the biggest contributor to that collection of 304 races. Among those 304 races, Pacer found 286, some of which were also found by Goldilocks and RaceFuzzer. The remaining 304-286=18 races were found Goldilocks (10 races) and RaceFuzzer (8 races). In more detail, Goldilocks found additional races in Avrora (1), Batic

	Static	Hybrid	Dynamic				
benchmarks	Chord	Hybrid	FastTrack	Goldilocks	RaceFuzzer	Pacer	Racageddon
Sor	2:18	0:49	0:08	0:44	2:29	9:44	4:49
TSP	2:22	0:55	0:03	0:10	1:50	11:23	4:37
Hedc	4:07	1:00	0:08	0:25	2:01	5:00	3:08
Elevator	1:10	0:39	0:03	-	1:11	3:58	2:40
ArrayList	2:40	0:50	0:05	-	1:18	5:18	4:11
TreeSet	3:11	0:18	0:06	-	0:44	7:02	3:25
HashSet	2:58	0:21	0:06	-	0:59	4:57	2:43
Vector	0:43	0:15	0:01	-	0:38	5:05	2:52
RayTracer	1:24	0:09	0:03	0:38	0:26	4:18	2:22
MolDyn	0:38	1:42	0:02	1:08	2:49	15:36	6:45
MonteCarlo	2:31	2:02	0:04	1:16	4:01	16:31	6:58
Derby	35:09	1:26	0:13	-	1:50	11:34	5:02
Colt	4:37	0:04	0:10	0:23	0:09	4:48	2:23
Chord-Test	0:05	0:01	0:01	0:02	0:05	0:54	0:10
Avrora	19:37	2:40	0:39	4:57	3:19	23:03	11:17
Tomcat	12:01	3:57	0:41	4:11	6:01	45:12	19:00
Batic	27:29	3:01	0:18	-	3:55	30:01	14:54
Eclipse	41:11	3:50	0:35	-	4:14	48:46	19:15
FOP	6:50	0:17	0:12	0:36	0:25	13:21	4:49
H2	8:38	0:31	0:09	-	0:49	18:50	7:31
PMD	15:48	0:16	0:14	1:03	0:38	17:41	7:22
Sunflow	16:00	0:41	0:23	2:01	1:06	18:17	6:03
Xalan	33:11	2:39	0:20	3:00	3:47	30:37	13:19
geom. mean	4:36	0:40	0:08	-	1:16	10:41	4:51

Figure 6. Timings in minutes and seconds.

(3), FOP (2), SunFlow (2), and Xalan (2) (and RaceFuzzer found none of those 10 races). RaceFuzzer found additional races in TreeSet (1), HashSet (1), Derby (1), Eclipse (4), and H2 (1) (and GoldiLocks found none of those 8 races). We conclude that Goldilocks, RaceFuzzer, and Pacer are all worthwhile techniques that each finds races that the other techniques don't find. As a combined dynamic technique FGRP is highly powerful.

Chord. Chord is possibly the best current static race detector, yet our experiments strongly suggest that Chord finds a large number of false positives. We conclude that accurate static race detection continues to be an open problem.

Timings. The geometrical means of the execution times for each technique show that FastTrack and Hybrid are the fastest, while Pacer is the slowest. Racageddon is more than twice as fast as Pacer yet Racageddon finds significantly more races. Note that the timings for RaceFuzzer and Racageddon include the time to execute Hybrid. Note also that we implemented RaceFuzzer ourselves in a rather unoptimized fashion. As a result, our implementation of Race-Fuzzer is significantly slower than FastTrack, while the paper on RaceFuzzer [47] reported that the original implementation of RaceFuzzer is faster than FastTrack!

Rare races. Burckhardt, Kothari, Musuvathi, and Nagarakatte [16] characterized the depth of a bug as the minimum number of scheduling constraints required to find that bug. In the spirit of their characterization, Figure 4 lists the longest schedule that Racageddon used to find a race for each benchmark, along with the number of branches in that schedule. Six of those schedules have more than a million events, including one schedule with more than 100 million events. For 18 of those longest schedules, the result was that Racageddon found a race that FGRP didn't find. The exceptions are TSP, Elevator, Vector, MolDyn, and ChordTest, and we notice that those five benchmarks have some of the shortest "longest schedules" among the benchmarks.

Figure 7 lists the lengths of the 72 schedules that lead to races found only by Racageddon. We can groups those lengths as follows:

lengths	#
$10^3 - 10^4$	9
$10^4 - 10^5$	4
$10^5 - 10^6$	28
$10^6 - 10^7$	22
$10^7 - 10^8$	6
$10^8 - 10^9$	3

The table shows that many of those schedules are long. Specifically, 31 races were found with schedules that have

Name	Lengths
Sor	6462, 6661, 6803
TSP	5623
Hedc	57327, 224341, 236804, 249268
Elevator	6573, 7924, 8673, 8914
ArrayList	132990
TreeSet	-
HashSet	-
Vector	-
RayTracer	71084
MolDyn	4305
MonteCarlo	12061
Derby	58483566, 98555637, 105053813, 108302900
Colt	824877, 919592, 948033
ChordTest	-
Avrora	702961
Tomcat	1066481, 1169274, 1284917
Batic	182982, 323737, 760003, 1379402, 1393478, 1400516, 1407554
Eclipse	1697703, 3068331, 3429715, 16605080, 16785570, 77145639, 98049000, 102879384
FOP	134705, 150499, 153074
H2	32742, 116085, 217288, 232170, 241100, 264912, 273842,
	276819, 279795, 285748, 294678, 296133, 297655
PMD	-
Sunflow	374598, 730944, 1283212, 1348185, 1478131, 1494379, 1543108, 1575594, 1608075, 1620019, 1624320
Xalan	2674854, 2849301, 2907450

Figure 7. The lengths of the 72 schedules that lead to races found only by Racageddon.

between 1 million and 108 million events, which suggests that they are rare and hard-to-find races.

Hybrid. Both RaceFuzzer and Racageddon use Hybrid to produce race candidates. RaceFuzzer focuses solely on the race candidates, while Racageddon discovers additional race candidates. Overall, Hybrid produces a worthwhile starting point for those two dynamic techniques. We can see in Figure 8 that for our benchmarks, Hybrid reports 405 race candidates of which 238 (59%) are real races. Future work may be able to show that some of the remaining 405-238=167 race candidates are real races.

5. Related Work

In Section 2 we discussed two techniques for race detection, namely one by O'Callahan and Choi [35] and one by Said, Wang, Yang, and Sakallah [41], that we use in Racageddon. In Section 4 we discussed five additional techniques, namely Chord [34], FastTrack [23], Goldilocks [21], RaceFuzzer [47], and Pacer [14] that we have compared experimentally with Racageddon. The goal of this section is to highlight some other notable techniques and tools in the area of race detection and related areas.

Predictive race detectors. The technique in the paper by Said, Wang, Yang, and Sakallah [41] is an example of what some authors call *predictive* techniques. The terminology stems from that if a trace can be reordered into a trace that

leads to a deadlock, then the technique will do that. Smaragdakis et al. [50] presented a sound, predictive technique for race detection that works in polynomial time. We can view Smaragdakis et al.'s technique as an example of an improve function. Both the improve function of Said et al. [41] and by Smaragdakis et al. [50] are sound. So, we expect that if we replace one with the other, we will find the same number of races, and possibly faster. We leave experimental confirmation of this expectation to future work.

Swapping and flipping. Racageddon's notion of event swapping in Phase 2 is reminiscent of jCute's notion of flipping [48, 49]. While Racageddon simply swaps the order of two consecutive events, jCute does something more radical: it puts the second event in the position of the first event, and then it delays the thread that executes the first event as long as possible. We have found that a simple swap works well.

Dynamic race detectors. FastTrack, Goldilocks, RaceFuzzer, and Pacer were some of the best dynamic race detectors for Java until now. A predecessor of Pacer, namely LiteRace [33] was the seminal paper that showed how to do race detection in a way that samples and analyzes selected portions of a programs execution. Prior to LiteRace, a paper by Jump, Blackburn, and McKinley [30] presented a sampling technique that they applied in the context of memory management.

	Number of races	
Name	*reported*	*real*
Sor	8	3
TSP	3	1
Hedc	5	5
Elevator	13	7
ArrayList	14	6
TreeSet	13	8
HashSet	11	7
Vector	9	4
RayTracer	2	2
MolDyn	43	5
MonteCarlo	5	3
Derby	21	17
Colt	13	9
ChordTest	2	2
Avrora	9	9
Tomcat	52	20
Batic	12	11
Eclipse	77	46
FOP	21	15
H2	19	17
PMD	14	12
Sunflow	16	6
Xalan	23	23
TOTAL	405	238

Figure 8. Hybrid; *real* = found by FGRP ∪ Racageddon.

Some well known dynamic race detectors work for other languages than Java, including the seminal Eraser [44], and a tool by Sack et al. [40].

Arnold and M. Vechev and E. Yahav [11] presented the QVM run-time environment that continuously monitors an execution and potentially detects defects, including races.

Hybrid race detectors. The technique by O'Callahan and Choi [35] that we call Hybrid continues to be one of the best and most scalable hybrid techniques for race detection. Other hybrid techniques include one by von Praun and Gross [54], RaceTrack [56], and MultiRace [38]. We leave to future work to do a large-scale study of those three hybrid techniques like we did for Hybrid. In particular, future work should evaluate how well those techniques perform when we want to use their output as race candidates for other tools such as RaceFuzzer and Racageddon.

Static race detectors. Chord remains one of the best among the scalable static race detectors to date, hence it was our choice for experimental comparison in this paper. Among the other static race detectors, some use static analysis, including Warlock [52], RacerX [22], LockSmith [39], and Relay [55], some use model checking, including an approach by Henzinger, Jhala, and Majumdar [29], and some use type systems, including an approach based on ownership by Boyapati, Lee, and Rinard [15], and approaches that

capture common synchronization patterns by Freund [26] and later by Abadi, Flanagan, and Freund [9]. A related approach based on type systems by Sasturkar, Agarwal, Wang, and Stoller [43] enables specification and check of atomicity. Finally, Effinger-Dean, Boehm, Chakrabarti, and Joisha [20] presented a characterization of extended interference-free regions of C programs in which variables cannot be modified by other threads. All the static approaches may produce false positives and thus have a goal that is dual to our objective to find real races.

Other techniques. We implemented an early version of Racageddon as an extension of Java PathFinder [28]. Our Java PathFinder extension is effective at exploring all execution paths yet doesn't scale up to our current benchmarks.

Collingbourne et al. [19] presented a sound analysis technique for GPU-oriented languages like OpenCL and CUDA, which have concurrency models that are rather different from Java. One of the applications of their technique is to race detection. Intuitively, their main result is that a program has a race if and only a modified version of the program has a race when the threads are executed in lock step.

In the setting of distributed memory and distributed systems, Park et at. [37] presented a race detector for distributed memory along with an implementation for UPC, and Sasnauskas et al. [42] presented a technique for symbolic execution of distributed systems.

6. Conclusion

Racageddon implements a new technique that we call race directed scheduling. Our experiments show that race directed scheduling is efficient and useful, and ultimately that a combination of techniques is currently the best path to successful race detection.

For a large benchmark suite, our tool Racageddon found 72 real races that were missed by earlier techniques, including 31 races that were found with schedules that have between 1 million and 108 million events, which suggests that they are rare and hard-to-find races.

Our experiments also show that a combination of the four tools Goldilocks, Calfuzzer, Pacer, and Racageddon finds a total of 376 real races in our benchmarks. As far as we know, this is the most comprehensive list of real races for those benchmarks that is reported in the literature.

Our experiments validates Hybrid [35] as an excellent choice for producing race candidates. Across our benchmarks, Hybrid produces at most 41% false positives.

Our technique is applicable beyond Java, particularly to any language with a concurrency model based on threads and locks. The main requirements are that (1) the technique embodied in the Hybrid tool [35] applies, (2) the technique embodied in the improve function [41] applies (3) concolic execution [27] can be implemented. The main limitations of Racageddon are due to limitations of the constraint solvers used by concolic and improve.

Acknowledgments. We thank Michael Bond who gave us access to Pacer, and Can Bekar, Tayfun Elmas, Cormac Flanagan, Steve Freund, and Serdar Tasiran who gave us access to Goldilocks. We thank the PPOPP 2014 reviewers for a wealth of suggestions that helped us improve the paper.

References

[1] https://code.google.com/p/jchord/issues/attachmentText?id=53&aid=530000001&name=SOR.java&token=aYxeQMsIH8M6_VpOVEgmST9XHnw%3A1385586794467.

[2] http://grepcode.com/file/repository.grepcode.com/java/root/jdk/openjdk/6-b14/java/util/ArrayList.java.

[3] http://grepcode.com/file/repository.grepcode.com/java/root/jdk/openjdk/6-b14/java/util/TreeSet.java.

[4] http://web.engr.illinois.edu/~sorrent1/penelope/experiments.html.

[5] http://www2.epcc.ed.ac.uk/computing/research_activities/jomp/grande.html.

[6] http://db.apache.org/derby/derby_downloads.html.

[7] https://code.google.com/p/jchord/downloads/detail?name=chord-src-2.1.tar.gz.

[8] http://sourceforge.net/projects/dacapobench/files.

[9] M. Abadi, C. Flanagan, and S. N. Freund. Types for safe locking: Static race detection for Java. *ACM Transactions on Programming Languages and Systems*, 28(2):207–255, 2006.

[10] Sarita V. Adve, Mark D. Hill, Barton P. Miller, and Robert H. B. Netzer. Detecting data races on weak memory systems. In *Proceedings of ISCA, International Symposium on Computer Architecture*, pages 234–243, 1991.

[11] M. Arnold, M. Vechev, and E. Yahav. Qvm: An efficient runtime for detecting defects in deployed systems. In *OOPSLA, ACM Conference on Object-Oriented Programming, Systems, Languages, and Applications*, pages 143–162, 2008.

[12] Stephen M. Blackburn, Robin Garner, Chris Hoffmann, Asjad M. Khang, Kathryn S. McKinley, Rotem Bentzur, Amer Diwan, Daniel Feinberg, Daniel Frampton, Samuel Z. Guyer, Martin Hirzel, Antony Hosking, Maria Jump, Han Lee Intel, J. Eliot B. Moss, Aashish Phansalkar, Darko Stefanovic, Thomas VanDrunen, Daniel von Dincklage, and Ben Wiedermann. The DaCapo benchmarks: Java benchmarking development and analysis. In *OOPSLA'06, 21st annual ACM SIGPLAN conference on Object-Oriented Programming Systems, Languages, and Applications*, pages 169–190, 2006.

[13] Eric Bodden, Andreas Sewe, Jan Sinschek, Hela Oueslati, and Mira Mezini. Taming reflection: Aiding static analysis in the presence of reflection and custom class loaders. In *ICSE, 33rd International Conference on Software Engineering*, May 2011.

[14] Michael D. Bond, Katherine E. Coons, and Kathryn S. McKinley. Pacer: Proportional detection of data races. In *Proceedings of PLDI'10, ACM SIGPLAN Conference on Programming Language Design and Implementation*, pages 121–133, 2010.

[15] C. Boyapati, R. Lee, and M. Rinard. Ownership types for safe programming: Preventing data races and deadlocks. In *OOPSLA, ACM Conference on Object-Oriented Programming, Systems, Languages, and Applications*, pages 211–230, 2002.

[16] Sebastian Burckhardt, Pravesh Kothari, Madanlal Musuvathi, and Santosh Nagarakatte. A randomized scheduler with probabilistic guarantees of finding concurrency bugs. In *ASPLOS, International Conference on Architectural Support for Programming Languages and Operating Systems*, March 2010.

[17] J. Burnim and K. Sen. Heuristics for scalable dynamic test generation. In *Proc. 23rd IEEE/ACM International Conference on Automated Software Engineering*, pages 443–446, 2008.

[18] Cristian Cadar, Paul Twohey, Vijay Ganesh, and Dawson Engler. Exe: A system for automatically generating inputs of death using symbolic execution. In *Proceedings of 13th ACM Conference on Computer and Communications Security*, 2006.

[19] Peter Collingbourne, Alastair F. Donaldson, Jeroen Ketema, and Shaz Qadeer. Interleaving and lock-step semantics for analysis and verification of gpu kernels. In *Proceedings of ESOP, European Symposium on Programming*, pages 270–289. Springer-Verlag (*LNCS*), 2013.

[20] Laura Effinger-Dean, Hans-J. Boehm, Dhruva Chakrabarti, and Pramod Joisha. Extended sequential reasoning for data-race-free programs. In *ACM SIGPLAN Workshop on Memory Systems Performance and Correctness*, June 2011.

[21] Tayfun Elmas, Shaz Qadeer, and Serdar Tasiran. Goldilocks: Efficiently computing the happens-before relation using locksets. In *Proceedings of FATES/RV, Workshop on Formal Approaches to Testing and Runtime Verification*, pages 193–208, 2006.

[22] D. Engler and K. Ashcraft. RacerX: Effective, static detection of race conditions and deadlocks. In *SOSP, Nineteenth ACM Symposium on Operating Systems Principles*, pages 237–252, 2003.

[23] Cormac Flanagan and Stephen N. Freund. Fasttrack: Efficient and precise dynamic race detection. In *Proceedings of PLDI'09, ACM SIGPLAN Conference on Programming Language Design and Implementation*, pages 121–133, 2009.

[24] European Organization for Nuclear Research (CERN). Colt. http://acs.lbl.gov/software/colt/.

[25] Apache Software Foundation. Derby. http://db.apache.org/derby.

[26] S. N. Freund. Type-based race detection for Java. In *PLDI, ACM SIGPLAN 2000 Conference on Programming language design and implementation*, pages 219–232, 2000.

[27] Patrice Godefroid, Nils Klarlund, and Koushik Sen. Dart: directed automated random testing. In *Proceedings of PLDI'05, ACM SIGPLAN Conference on Programming Language Design and Implementation*, pages 213–223, 2005.

[28] Klaus Havelund and Thomas Pressburger. Model checking Java programs using Java pathfinder. *Software Tools for Technology Transfer*, 2(4):366–381, 2000.

[29] Thomas A. Henzinger, Ranjit Jhala, and Rupak Majumdar. Race checking by context inference. In *Proceedings of PLDI'04, ACM SIGPLAN Conference on Programming Language Design and Implementation*, pages 1–13, 2004.

[30] M. Jump, S. M. Blackburn, and K. S. McKinley. Dynamic object sampling for pretenuring. In *ICMM, ACM International Symposium on Memory Management*, pages 152–162, 2004.

[31] Leslie Lamport. How to make a multiprocessor computer that correctly executes multiprocess programs. *IEEE Trans. Comput.*, C–28,9:690–691, September 1979.

[32] Rupak Majumdar and Ru-Gang Xu. Directed test generation using symbolic grammars. In *Proceedings of the twenty-second IEEE/ACM International Conference on Automated Software Engineering*, 2007.

[33] Daniel Marino, Madanlal Musuvathi, and Satish Narayanasamy. Literace: Effective sampling for lightweight data-race detection. In *Proceedings of PLDI'09, ACM SIGPLAN Conference on Programming Language Design and Implementation*, pages 134–143, 2009.

[34] Mayur Naik, Alex Aiken, and John Whaley. Effective static race detection for Java. In *Proceedings of PLDI'06, ACM SIGPLAN Conference on Programming Language Design and Implementation*, 2006.

[35] Robert O'Callahan and Jong-Deok Choi. Hybrid dynamic data race detection. In *Proceedings of the ACM Conference on Principles and Practice of Parallel Programming*, pages 167–178, 2003.

[36] Oracle. JDK, 1.4.2. `http://www.oracle.com/technetwork/java/javase/index-jsp-138567.html`.

[37] Chang-Seo Park, Koushik Sen, Paul Hargrove, and Costin Iancu. Efficient data race detection for distributed memory parallel programs. In *Proceedings of IEEE Conference on Supercomputing*, 2011.

[38] E. Pozniansky and A. Schuster. MultiRace: Efficient on-the-fly data race detection in multithreaded C++ programs. *Concurrency and Computation: Practice and Experience*, 19(3):327–340, 2007.

[39] Polyvios Pratikakis, Jeffrey S. Foster, and Michael Hicks. LockSmith: Context sensitive correlation analysis for race detection. In *PLDI, ACM Conference on Programming Language Design and Implementation*, pages 320–331, 2006.

[40] P. Sack, B. E. Bliss, Z. Ma, P. Petersen, and J. Torrellas. Accurate and efficient filtering for the Intel thread checker race detector. In *ASID, 1st workshop on Architectural and System Support for Improving Software Dependability*, pages 34–41, 2006.

[41] Mahmoud Said, Chao Wang, Zijiang Yang, and Karem A. Sakallah. Generating data race witnesses by an SMT-based analysis. In *NASA Formal Methods*, pages 313–327, 2011.

[42] Raimondas Sasnauskas, Oscar Soria Dustmann, Benjamin Lucien Kaminski, Klaus Wehrle, Carsten Weise, and Stefan Kowalewski. Scalable symbolic execution of distributed systems. In *Proceedings of ICDCS, International Conference on Distributed Computing Systems*, pages 333–342, 2011.

[43] A. Sasturkar, R. Agarwal, L. Wang, and S. D. Stoller. Automated type-based analysis of data races and atomicity. In *PPoPP, Tenth ACM SIGPLAN Symposium on Principles and Practice of Parallel Programming*, pages 83–94, 2005.

[44] Stefan Savage, Michael Burrows, Greg Nelson, Patrick Sobalvarro, and Thomas Anderson. Eraser: A dynamic data race detector for multithreaded programs. *Transactions on Computer Systems*, 15(4):391–411, November 1997.

[45] Koushik Sen. Concolic testing. In *Proceedings of the twenty-second IEEE/ACM International Conference on Automated Software Engineering*, pages 571–572, 2007.

[46] Koushik Sen. Effective random testing of concurrent programs. In *IEEE/ACM International Conference on Automated Software Engineering*, pages 323–332, 2007.

[47] Koushik Sen. Race directed random testing of concurrent programs. In *Proceedings of PLDI'08, ACM SIGPLAN Conference on Programming Language Design and Implementation*, pages 11–21, Tucson, Arizona, June 2008.

[48] Koushik Sen and Gul Agha. Cute and jcute: Concolic unit testing and explicit path model-checking tools. In *Proc. 18th International Conference on Computer Aided Verification*, pages 419–423, 2006.

[49] Koushik Sen and Gul Agha. A race-detection and flipping algorithm for automated testing of multi-threaded programs. In *Proceedings of Haifa Verification Conference*, pages 166–182, 2006.

[50] Yannis Smaragdakis, Jacob Evans, Caitlin Sadowski, Jaeheon Yi, and Cormac Flanagan. Sound predictive race detection in polynomial time. In *Proceedings of POPL'12, SIGPLAN–SIGACT Symposium on Principles of Programming Languages*, pages 387–400, 2012.

[51] L. A. Smith, J. M. Bull, and J. Obdrzalek. A parallel Java grande benchmark suite. November 2001.

[52] N. Sterling. WARLOCK – a static data race analysis tool. In *USENIX Winter Technical Conference*, pages 97–106, 1993.

[53] Raja Vallé-Rai, Etienne Gagnon, Laurie Hendren, Patrick Lam, Patrice Pominville, and Vijay Sundaresan. Optimizing Java bytecode using the soot framework: Is it feasible? In *Proceedings of CC'00, International Conference on Compiler Construction*. Springer-Verlag (*LNCS*), 2000.

[54] C. von Praun and T. R. Gross. Object race detection. In *OOPSLA, ACM Conference on Object-Oriented Programming, Systems, Languages, and Applications*, pages 70–82, 2001.

[55] J. W. Voung, R. Jhala, and S. Lerner. RELAY: Static race detection on millions of lines of code. In *European Software Engineering Conference and ACM SIGSOFT International Symposium on Foundations of Software Engineering*, pages 205–214, 2007.

[56] Y. Yu, T. Rodeheffer, and W. Chen. RaceTrack: Efficient detection of data race conditions via adaptive tracking. In *SOSP, ACM Symposium on Operating Systems Principles*, pages 221–234, 2005.

Heterogeneous Computing - What Does It Mean for Compiler Research?

Norm Rubin

Nvidia Research
nrubin@nvidia.com

Abstract

The current trend in computer architecture is to increase the number of cores, to create specialized types of cores within a single machine, and to network such machines together in very fluid web/cloud computing arrangements. Compilers have traditionally focused on optimizations to code that improve performance, but is that the right target to speed up real applications? Consider loading a web page (like starting GMAIL) the page is transferred to the client, any JavaScript is compiled, the JavaScript executes, and the page gets displayed. The classic compiler model (which was first developed in the late 50's) was a great fit for single core machines but has fallen behind architecture, and language. For example how do you compile a single program for a machine that has both a CPU and a graphics coprocessor (a GPU) with a very different programming and memory model? Together with the changes in architecture there have been changes in programming languages. Dynamic languages are used more, static languages are used less. How does this effect compiler research?

In this talk, I'll review a number of traditional compiler research challenges that have (or will) become burning issues and will describe some new problems areas that were not considered in the past. For example language specifications are large complex technical documents that are difficult for non-experts to follow. Application programmers are often not willing to read these documents; can a compiler bridge the gap?

Categories and Subject Descriptors   D.3.4-compilers, C.1 processor architectures, D.2.11 software architectures

Bio

Norm Rubin has over thirty years of experience delivering commercial compilers for processors ranging from embedded (ARM), desktop (HP, ALPHA) and supercomputer (KSR), and is a recognized expert in th field. He was the architect and lead implementer for the widely used graphics compiler for AMD/ATI. That compiler is currently shipping on millions of machines including cell phones, consoles, and PCs. Norm was part of the AMD architecture team that designed GCN (Graphics core next). He was the lead designer of HSAIL, the virtual machine used in the HSA system architecture. Around a year ago he moved to NVIDA Research where he is working in algorithms and future programming models. Lately Norm has been looking at extending JavaScript to use GPUS and heterogeneous devices. Norm is also a visiting scholar at North Eastern Univ.

Dr. Rubin holds a PhD from the Courant Institute of NYU. Besides his work in compilers and architecture, he is well known for his work in GPU systems, compiler related parts of the tool chain, binary translators and dynamic optimizers.

PPoPP'14, February 15–19, 2014, Orlando, Florida, USA.
ACM 978-1-4503-2656-8/14/02.
http://dx.doi.org/10.1145/2555243.2558891

Fast Concurrent Lock-Free Binary Search Trees

Aravind Natarajan   Neeraj Mittal

Erik Jonsson School of Engineering and Computer Science
The University of Texas at Dallas
{aravindn, neerajm}@utdallas.edu

Abstract

We present a new *lock-free* algorithm for concurrent manipulation of a binary search tree in an asynchronous shared memory system that supports search, insert and delete operations. In addition to read and write instructions, our algorithm uses (single-word) compare-and-swap (CAS) and bit-test-and-set (BTS) atomic instructions, both of which are commonly supported by many modern processors including Intel 64 and AMD64. In contrast to existing lock-free algorithms for a binary search tree, our algorithm is based on marking *edges* rather than nodes. As a result, when compared to other lock-free algorithms, modify (insert and delete) operations in our algorithm (a) work on a smaller portion of the tree, thereby reducing conflicts, and (b) execute fewer atomic instructions (one for insert and three for delete). Our experiments indicate that our lock-free algorithm significantly outperforms all other algorithms for a concurrent binary search tree in many cases, especially when contention is high, by as much as 100%.

Categories and Subject Descriptors D.1.3 [*Programming Techniques*]: Concurrent Programming-Parallel Programming; E.1 [*Data Structures*]: Trees; D.3.3 [*Language Constructs and Features*]: Concurrent Programming Structures

Keywords Concurrent Data Structure, Lock-Free Algorithm, Binary Search Tree

1. Introduction

With the growing prevalence of multi-core, multi-processor systems, concurrent data structures are becoming increasingly important. In such a data structure, multiple processes may need to operate on overlapping regions of the data structure at the same time. Contention between different processes must be managed in such a way that all operations complete correctly and leave the data structure in a valid state.

Concurrency is most often managed through locks. However, locks are blocking; while a process is holding a lock, no other process can access the portion of the data structure protected by the lock. If a process stalls while it is holding a lock, then the lock may not be released for a long time. This may cause other processes to wait on the stalled process for extended periods of time. As a result, lock-based implementations of concurrent data structures are vulnerable to problems such as deadlock, priority inversion and convoying [20].

Non-blocking algorithms avoid the pitfalls of locks by using special (hardware-supported) *read-modify-write* instructions such as *load-link/store-conditional (LL/SC)* [18] and *compare-and-swap (CAS)* [20]. Non-blocking implementations of common data structures such as queues, stacks, linked lists, hash tables, search trees and tries have been proposed (*e.g.*, [1, 2, 12, 14, 15, 17, 18, 20, 22, 23, 25, 27–29, 29–31]).

Non-blocking algorithms may provide varying degrees of progress guarantees. Three widely accepted progress guarantees for non-blocking algorithms are: obstruction-freedom, lock-freedom, and wait-freedom. An algorithm is *obstruction-free* if any process that executes in isolation will finish its operation in a finite number of steps [22]. An algorithm is *lock-free* if some process will complete its operation in a finite number of steps [18]. An algorithm is *wait-free* if every operation executed by every process will complete in a finite number of steps [18].

Binary search trees are one of the fundamental data structures for organizing and storing *ordered* data that support search, insert and delete operations [9].

Several universal constructions exist which can be used to derive a concurrent non-blocking data structure from its sequential version [8, 13, 18–20]. Due to the general nature of these constructions, when applied to a binary search tree, the resultant data structures are quite inefficient. This is because universal constructions involve either: (a) applying operations to the data structure in a serial manner, or (b) copying the entire data structure (or parts of it that will change and

PPoPP '14, February 15–19, 2014, Orlando, Florida, USA.
Copyright © 2014 ACM 978-1-4503-2656-8/14/02. . . $15.00.
http://dx.doi.org/10.1145/2555243.2555256

any parts that directly or indirectly point to them), applying the operation to the copy and then updating the relevant part of the data structure to point to the copy. The first approach precludes any concurrency. The second approach, when applied to a tree, also precludes any concurrency since the root node of the tree indirectly points to every node in the tree.

Several customized non-blocking implementations of concurrent unbalanced search trees [4, 12, 23] and balanced search trees such as B-trees [1], B$^+$-trees [2], red-black trees [24, 27, 28], and tries [29, 30] have been proposed, which are more efficient than those obtained using universal constructions.

Ellen *et al.* proposed the first practical lock-free algorithm for a concurrent binary search tree in [12]. Their algorithm uses an external (or leaf-oriented) search tree in which only the leaf nodes store the actual keys; keys stored at internal nodes are used for routing purposes only. Howley and Jones proposed another lock-free algorithm for a concurrent binary search tree in [23]. Their algorithm uses an internal search tree in which both the leaf nodes as well as the internal nodes store the actual keys. As a result, search operations in Howley and Jones's algorithm are generally faster than those in Ellen *et al.*'s algorithm [23]. This is because the path traversed by a search operation in an external search tree always terminates at a leaf node, whereas the one in an internal search tree may terminate at an internal node. However, delete operations in an internal search tree are generally slower than those in an external search tree. This is because a delete operation in the former may involve replacing the key being deleted with the largest key in the left sub tree, which increases the likelihood of contention among operations.

Recently, Drachsler *et al.* proposed a lock-based internal binary search tree in which each node maintains pointers to its *logical* predecessor and successor nodes (based on the key order), in addition to maintaining pointers to its left and right children in the tree [11]. Modify operations update this logical information each time they add or remove keys from the tree. Further, search operations that do not find the key after traversing the tree from the root node to a leaf node traverse the logical chain induced by predecessor and successor pointers to handle the case in which the key may have "moved" to another node during the tree traversal. They have applied this idea to obtain lock-based algorithms for unbalanced binary search trees and relaxed AVL trees [11].

Brown *et al.* proposed general primitives for developing non-blocking algorithms for concurrent search trees, namely LLX, SCX and VLX [5]. These primitives, which operate on multiple words, are generalizations of the LL (load-linked), SC (store-conditional) and VL (validate) instructions, which operate on a single word. (An LL instruction reads the contents of a memory location. An SC instruction updates the contents of a memory location with a new value provided the location has not been modified since an LL instruction

was last performed on it. A VL instruction returns true if a memory location has not been modified since an LL instruction was last performed on it.) The LLX primitive operates on a single multi-word record, while the SCX and VLX primitives operate on multiple records. They also described an algorithm for implementing these primitives using single word CAS instruction [5]. Using the three primitives, they have developed efficient non-blocking algorithms for multi-sets [5] and relaxed red-black trees [6].

Observe that the lock-based algorithms for relaxed balanced binary search trees proposed in [3, 10] can be easily extended to work for unbalanced binary search trees by simply ignoring the balancing component of the algorithms. This is possible because, in these algorithms, the execution of an operation and the balancing of the tree are done in two separate steps. However, in the resulting algorithm, a key once added to the tree may never be "physically" removed from the tree. As a result, the size of the tree may become much larger than the number of keys stored in the tree.

Contributions: We present a new *lock-free* algorithm for concurrent manipulation of a binary search tree in an asynchronous shared memory system that supports search, insert and delete operations. In addition to read and write instructions, our algorithm uses (single-word) compare-and-swap (CAS) and bit-test-and-set (BTS) atomic instructions, both of which are commonly supported by many modern processors including Intel 64 and AMD64. (Our algorithm can be easily modified to use only CAS atomic instructions.) Like Ellen *et al.*'s algorithm, our algorithm is also based on external representation of a search tree. However, we use several ideas to reduce the contention among modify (insert and delete) operations as well as lower the overhead of a modify operation. They include: (i) marking edges rather than nodes for deletion, (ii) not using a separate explicit object for enabling coordination among conflicting operations, and (iii) allowing multiple keys being deleted to be removed from the tree in a single step. As a result, modify operations have a smaller contention window, allocate fewer objects and execute fewer atomic instructions than their counterparts in other lock-free algorithms [12, 23].

We have experimentally compared the performance of our concurrent algorithm with other concurrent algorithms for a binary search tree under a variety of conditions (different tree sizes, workload distributions and contention degrees). Our experiments indicate that our algorithm significantly outperforms all other algorithms in many cases by as much as 100%, especially when contention is high (tree size is small or workload is write-dominated).

Organization: The rest of the paper is organized as follows. We describe our system model in Section 2. Our lock-free algorithm for a binary search tree is described in Section 3. We present the results of our experimental evaluation of different concurrent algorithms for a search tree in Section 4. We discuss the qualitative differences between our lock-free algorithm and the lock-free algorithms proposed by Ellen *et al.* [12] and Howley and Jones [23] in more detail in Section 5. Finally, Section 6 concludes the paper and outlines directions for future research.

2. System Model

We assume an asynchronous shared memory system that, in addition to read and write instructions, also supports compare-and-swap (CAS) and bit-test-and-set (BTS) atomic instructions. A compare-and-swap instruction takes three arguments: *address*, *old* and *new*; it compares the contents of a memory location (*address*) to a given value (*old*) and, only if they are the same, modifies the contents of that location to a given new value (*new*). A bit-test-and-set instruction takes two arguments *address* and *position*; it sets a given bit (*position*) in the contents of a memory location (*address*) to 1. Both instructions are commonly available in many modern processors such as Intel 64 and AMD64.

We assume that a binary search tree (BST) implements a dictionary abstract data type and supports *search*, *insert* and *delete* operations [12]. For convenience, we refer to the insert and delete operations as *modify* operations. A search operation explores the tree for a given key and returns true if the key is present in the tree and false otherwise. An insert operation adds a given key to the tree if the key is not already present in the tree. Duplicate keys are not allowed in our model. A delete operation removes a key from the tree if the key is indeed present in the tree. In both cases, a modify operation returns true if it changed the set of keys present in the tree (added or removed a key) and false otherwise.

A binary search tree satisfies the following properties: (a) the left subtree of a node contains only nodes with keys less than the node's key, (b) the right subtree of a node contains only nodes with keys greater than or equal to the node's key, and (c) the left and right subtrees of a node are also binary search trees. As in [12], we use an *external* BST in our algorithm in which only the leaf nodes store the actual keys; keys stored at internal nodes are used for routing purposes only. Furthermore, every internal node has exactly two children.

To demonstrate the correctness of our algorithm, we use *linearizability* [21] as the safety property and *lock-freedom* [18] as the liveness property. Broadly speaking, linearizability requires that an operation should appear to take effect instantaneously at some point during its execution. Lock-freedom requires that some process be able to complete its operation in a finite number of its own steps (even if one or more processes have failed).

3. A Lock-Free Algorithm for Binary Search Tree

We first present the main idea behind our algorithm. We then present the details of the algorithm along with its pseudocode, followed by a brief proof of correctness.

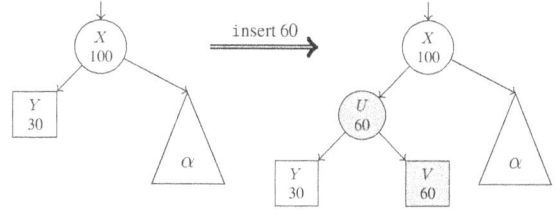

(a) An illustration of the insert operation. Nodes that are added to the tree have been shaded.

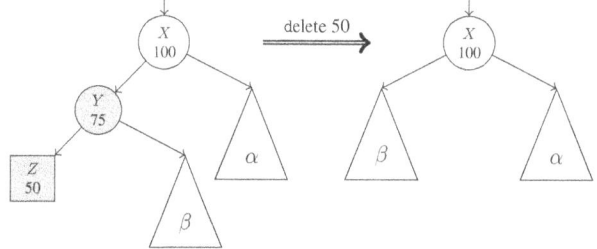

(b) An illustration of the delete operation. Nodes that are removed from the tree have been shaded.

Figure 1: Illustration of insert and delete operations. Numbers denote keys.

3.1 Overview of the Algorithm

Every operation in our algorithm starts with a *seek* phase in which the operation traverses the search tree starting from the root node until it reaches a leaf node. We refer to the path traversed by the operation in the seek phase as the *access path*. For convenience, we refer to the last three nodes on the access path as the grandparent, parent and leaf nodes, respectively. The operation then compares the given key with the key stored in the leaf node on the access path. Depending on the result of the comparison and the type of the operation, the operation either terminates or moves to the next phase. We now describe the next steps for each type of operation one-by-one.

For a search operation, if the two keys match, then the operation returns true (key was found); otherwise it returns false (key was not found).

For an insert operation, if the two keys match, then the operation returns false (the key already exists in the tree); otherwise it moves to the *execution* phase (the key does not exist in the tree). In the execution phase, the insert operation adds the key to the tree by adding two new nodes to the tree: an internal node and a leaf node. The new leaf node contains the key being inserted into the tree. The two children of the new internal node are the leaf node on the access path and the new leaf node. The insert operation then switches the pointer at the parent node that is pointing to the leaf node (on the access path) to point to the new internal node. As an illustration, consider Figure 1(a). In the example, to insert the key 60 into the tree, the operation creates an internal node U and a leaf node V, with Y and V as children of U. It then switches the pointer at node X, which is currently pointing to node Y, to point to node U.

For a delete operation, if the two keys do not match, then the operation returns false (the key does not exist in the tree); otherwise it moves to the *execution* phase (the key does exist in the tree). In the execution phase, the delete operation removes the key from the tree by removing the leaf and parent nodes on the access path from the tree. Specifically, it switches the pointer at the grandparent[1] node that is pointing to the parent node to point to the sibling node of the leaf node. As an illustration, consider Figure 1(b). In the example, to delete the key 50 from the tree, the operation switches the pointer at node X, which is currently pointing to node Y, to point to the sibling node of node Z (the root node of the subtree β).

For convenience, in the execution phase, we refer to the parent node on the access path as the *injection point* of the modify operation.

3.2 Details of the Algorithm

For ease of exposition, we assume that the memory allocated to nodes that are no longer part of the tree is not reclaimed. This allows us to assume that all new nodes have unique addresses and ignore the ABA problem that can occur otherwise [20]. A lock-free algorithm to reclaim memory allocated to objects that are no longer accessible by any process can be derived using the well-known notion of *hazard pointers* [26].

A tree node in our algorithm consists of three fields: (i) *key*, which contains the key stored in the node, (ii) *left*, which contains the address of the left child of the node, and (iii) *right*, which contains the address of the right child of the node. The *left* and *right* fields of a node are referred to as *child* fields.

An important feature of our algorithm is that it operates at the *edge* level, rather than at the node level. In contrast to [12, 23] in which a modify operation obtains "ownership" of the nodes it needs to work on, in our algorithm, a modify operation (specifically, a delete operation) obtains "ownership" of the edges it needs to work on. A delete operation obtains "ownership" of an edge by *marking* it. Note that every edge has a *tail* node and a *head* node. The marking of an edge indicates that either both its tail and head nodes or only its tail node will be removed from the tree. To distinguish between the two cases, we refer to the first type of marking as *flagging* and to the second type as *tagging*. As an illustration, consider the delete operation shown in Figure 1(b). Let U denote the root node of the subtree β. In the example, the edge (Y, Z) will be flagged whereas the edge (Y, U) will be tagged. Once an edge has been marked, it cannot be changed, that is, it cannot point to another node. So, once both the child edges of a node have been marked, it cannot

---

[1] It may be an ancestor node in general if multiple delete operations are in progress along the access path.

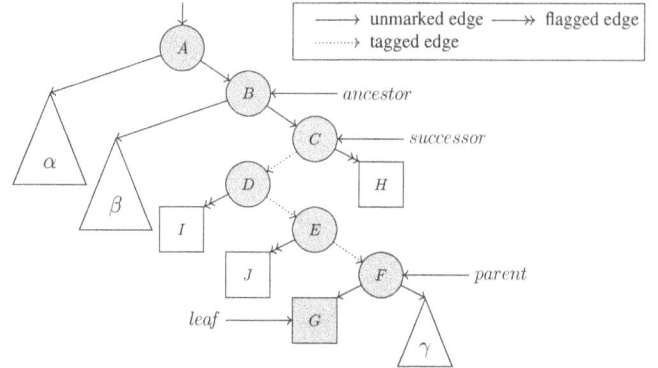

Figure 2: An illustration of the information returned by a seek phase. The figure shows an example of a suffix of an access path in the tree (consisting of shaded nodes).

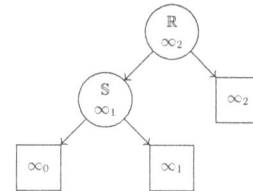

Figure 3: Sentinel nodes and keys used in our algorithm ($\infty_0 < \infty_1 < \infty_2$). The figure shows an empty tree. The two internal nodes are denoted $\mathbb{R}$ and $\mathbb{S}$.

be used as an injection point of another modify operation. This helps to coordinate between conflicting modify operations.

To enable the flagging or tagging of an edge, we steal two bits from each child address stored at a node; we denote the two bits by *flag* and *tag*. If *flag* (respectively, *tag*) bit in a child address has value 1, then we say that the (corresponding outgoing) edge has been flagged (respectively, tagged); otherwise we say that the edge is unflagged (respectively, untagged).

The pseudo-code of our algorithm is shown in Algorithm 1-Algorithm 4. In the pseudocode, we use the *addr()* function to obtain the address of a field and *read()* function to read the contents of a memory location. Also, if multiple subfields are packed into a single field (or word), then we use the symbol $\rightsquigarrow$ to refer to a specific subfield (*e.g.*, *left* $\rightsquigarrow$ *flag*, *left* $\rightsquigarrow$ *address*).

The structure of a tree node is shown in lines 1-5.

We next describe the details of the *seek* phase, which is executed by all operations after which we describe the search, insert and delete operations in detail.

3.2.1 Seek Phase

As explained earlier, in a seek phase, an operation traverses the tree along a simple path from the root node to a leaf node, which is referred to as the access path. At each internal node, the operation either follows the left pointer or the right pointer depending on how the given key compares with the node's key. The seek phase returns a *seek record*, which contains the addresses of *four* nodes encountered on the access path. Two of the nodes are the *leaf* node, which is the last node on the access path, and its *parent* node, which is the second-to-last node on the access path. Let (X, Y) denote the *last* untagged edge encountered by the operation on the access path *before* visiting the parent node. The other two nodes whose addresses are stored in the seek record are nodes X, referred to as the *ancestor* node, and Y, referred to as the *successor* node. The four fields of the seek record are named *leaf*, *parent*, *ancestor* and *successor*. For an illustration, please refer to Figure 2. Note that, if there is no conflicting delete operation in progress, then the successor node is the same as the parent node and the ancestor node is the same as the grandparent node (of the leaf node on the access path). Also note that all nodes on the access path starting from the successor node to the parent node (not inclusive) are in the process of being removed from the tree.

To ensure that all the addresses of a seek record are always well-defined, we assume the presence of three *sentinel* keys, ∞_0, ∞_1 and ∞_2, where $\infty_0 < \infty_1 < \infty_2$. The sentinel keys are greater than all other keys, and are never removed from the tree. For an illustration of a tree containing the sentinel keys, please refer to Figure 3. In the figure, $\mathbb{R}$ and $\mathbb{S}$ are two internal nodes, which are also never removed from the tree. As a result, the parent and grandparent nodes of the leaf node on the access path always exist. Also, note that none of the outgoing edges of $\mathbb{R}$ and $\mathbb{S}$ can ever be marked.

The structure of a seek record is shown in lines 6-11. The pseudo-code of the seek phase is given in lines 13-33. First, the seek record is initialized using the two internal sentinel nodes (lines 15-21). The *ancestor* pointer is initialized to the root node of the tree, $\mathbb{R}$, the *successor* and *parent* pointers to its left child, $\mathbb{S}$, and the *leaf* pointer to the left child of $\mathbb{S}$. Next, the tree is traversed using a loop (lines 22-32). In each iteration of the loop, if the access path can be extended (line 22), then the edge between the current *parent* and *leaf* nodes is examined. If it is untagged, the *ancestor* and *successor* pointers are advanced to point to the *parent* and *leaf* nodes, respectively (lines 24 & 25). Otherwise, the *ancestor* and *successor* pointers are not modified. Finally, the *parent* and *leaf* pointers are advanced (lines 26 & 27), thereby extending the access path. The loop terminates when the *leaf* pointer points to a leaf node, after which the seek function returns (line 33).

3.2.2 Search Operation

A search operation first executes the seek phase at the end of which it compares the given key with the key stored in the leaf node of the seek record. If the two keys match, then the operation returns true; otherwise, it returns false; The pseudo-code of the search operation is given in lines 34-39.

3.2.3 Insert Operation

An insert operation starts by executing the seek phase at the end of which it compares the given key with the key stored in the leaf node of the seek record. If the two keys match, then the operation simply returns false. Otherwise, it advances to the execution phase.

Let k denote the key to be inserted into the tree and $\mathcal{R}$ denote the seek record returned by the seek phase. Also, let k' denote the key stored in $\mathcal{R} \to leaf$. The insert operation first creates two new nodes: an internal node $newInternal$ and a leaf node $newLeaf$. The *key* field in $newLeaf$ is initialized to k. The *key* field in $newInternal$ is initialized to $\max(k, k')$. If $k < k'$, then $newLeaf$ becomes the left child of $newInternal$; otherwise it becomes the right child of $newInternal$. The sibling pointer of $newLeaf$ in $newInternal$ is set to $\mathcal{R} \to leaf$. Finally, the insert operation tries to replace the edge $(\mathcal{R} \to parent, \mathcal{R} \to leaf)$ with the edge $(\mathcal{R} \to parent, newInternal)$ using a CAS instruction on the appropriate *child* field of $\mathcal{R} \to parent$. If the CAS instruction succeeds, then the insert operation has completed. Otherwise, the insert operation performs helping if needed and then tries again by restarting from the seek phase.

We now describe how the insert operation determines if it needs to perform helping. The insert operation ascertains that the edge from $\mathcal{R} \to parent$ to $\mathcal{R} \to leaf$ still exists and has been marked (flagged or tagged). If yes, then clearly it implies that a concurrent delete operation is trying to remove $\mathcal{R} \to parent$ from the tree (assuming that $\mathcal{R} \to parent$ has not already been removed from the tree). In this case, the insert operation performs helping by executing the last two steps of a delete operation, which will result in $\mathcal{R} \to parent$ and one of its children being removed from the tree. Note that, if the edge from $\mathcal{R} \to parent$ to $\mathcal{R} \to leaf$ does not exist, then the injection point of the insert operation has changed and no helping is performed. After performing the helping if needed as described above, the insert operation restarts from the seek phase.

To summarize, the execution of an insert operation consists of an alternating sequence of seek and execution phases until the operation terminates.

The pseudo-code of the insert operation is given in lines 40-59. The pseudo-code of its execution phase is given in lines 44-59. The steps for creating and installing a new subtree are given in lines 50-51. In case the CAS instruction fails, the steps for helping a delete operation are given in lines 56-57. Helping, if needed, is performed by invoking a cleanup routine, which is given in lines 88-109 (explained in the next section).

3.2.4 Delete Operation

A delete operation has two modes: *injection* and *cleanup*. In the injection mode, its objective is to locate the leaf node that contains the given key and mark it by flagging its incoming edge. In the cleanup mode, its objective is to physically remove the leaf node that it flagged in the injection mode (and its parent) from the tree.

A delete operation starts by executing the seek phase at the end of which it compares its key with the key stored in the leaf node of the seek record. If the two keys do not match, then the operation simply returns false. Otherwise, it advances to the execution phase.

Let $\mathcal{R}$ denote the seek record returned by the seek phase. In the injection mode, the delete operation tries to flag the edge from $\mathcal{R} \to parent$ to $\mathcal{R} \to leaf$ using a CAS instruction; flagging the edge involves setting the $flag$ bit in the $child$ (*left* or *right*) field of $\mathcal{R} \to parent$ that points to $\mathcal{R} \to leaf$ to 1. If the CAS instruction succeeds, then the delete operation is guaranteed to complete eventually, and the operation enters the cleanup mode. However, if the CAS instruction fails, then the delete operation performs helping in the same way as discussed in the case of insert operation by invoking the cleanup routine if needed after which it tries again by restarting from the seek phase.

In the cleanup mode, the delete operation tries to remove nodes $\mathcal{R} \to parent$ and $\mathcal{R} \to leaf$ from the tree using the following two steps. For ease of exposition, without loss of generality, assume that $\mathcal{R} \to leaf$ is the left child of $\mathcal{R} \to parent$. The other case when $\mathcal{R} \to leaf$ is the right child of $\mathcal{R} \to parent$ is symmetric and can be easily derived. In the first step, the delete operation tags the sibling edge of $\mathcal{R} \to parent$, which points to the right child of $\mathcal{R} \to parent$, using a BTS instruction; tagging the edge involves setting the tag bit in the $right$ field of $\mathcal{R} \to parent$ to 1. Note that this step is guaranteed to succeed. Also, none of the children edges of $\mathcal{R} \to parent$ can now change (point to different nodes). This also implies that $\mathcal{R} \to parent$ can no longer act as the injection point of any modify operation from now on. Let S denote the right child of $\mathcal{R} \to parent$. In the second step, the delete operation tries to replace the edge $(\mathcal{R} \to ancestor, \mathcal{R} \to successor)$ with the edge $(\mathcal{R} \to ancestor, S)$ using a CAS instruction on the appropriate $child$ field of $\mathcal{R} \to ancestor$. Note that the edge $(\mathcal{R} \to parent, S)$ may have been concurrently flagged by another delete operation which is trying to remove the key stored in S from the tree (in this case S must be a leaf node and the edge must have been flagged before it was tagged). The value of the $flag$ bit in the $right$ field of $\mathcal{R} \to parent$ is copied to the new edge being created from $\mathcal{R} \to ancestor$ to S. This ensures that if the edge $(\mathcal{R} \to parent, S)$ is flagged, then the new edge $(\mathcal{R} \to ancestor, S)$ is also flagged. Note that after an edge has been tagged, it cannot be flagged. So the value of its $flag$ bit of the sibling edge cannot change after it has been tagged. If the CAS instruction succeeds, then the delete operation has completed. Otherwise, the delete operation executes the seek phase again.

Let S denote the seek record returned by the new seek phase. If $\mathcal{R} \to leaf$ and $S \to leaf$ do not match, then the

leaf node flagged for deletion has already been removed by another modify operation (via helping) and the delete operation terminates. Otherwise, it repeats the two steps described above (tag the sibling edge and switch the appropriate child pointer at the ancestor node) using the new seek record S. Again, if the second step of the clean up fails (since it involves performing a CAS instruction), then the operation repeats the seek phase to obtain a new seek record with a fresh set of the four node addresses. Note that the two steps for removing the nodes to clean up the tree may need to be repeated multiple times but the number of repetitions is guaranteed to be finite. This is because, once the edge to a leaf node has been flagged, the access path leading up to that leaf node cannot gain any new internal nodes. So every time, the clean up fails, it can be verified that either the access path has lost one or more internal nodes or the last untagged edge on the access path has moved closer to the root node.

To summarize, the execution of a delete operation consists of an alternating sequence of seek and execution phases until the operation terminates. It first executes the two phases in injection mode and then in cleanup mode.

As an illustration, consider Figure 2. Let K denote the root node of the subtree γ. In the example, to delete the key stored at G, a delete operation first flags the edge (F, G), then tags the edge (G, K) and finally replaces the edge (B, C) with the edge (B, K). Note that this will cause multiple leaf nodes (H, I and J all which are in the process of being deleted) to be removed from the tree in a single step.

The pseudo-code of the delete operation is given in lines 60-87. The pseudo-code of its execution phase is given in lines 73-87. The pseudo-code for flagging the edge to the leaf node that contains the given key is given in line 73. The pseudo-code for cleaning up the tree is given in lines 82-87. Since the code for cleaning up the tree may also be executed by another modify operation trying to the help the delete operation complete, its core steps are presented as a separate routine in lines 88-109, which may be invoked from line 57, line 76 or line 81.

3.3 Correctness Proof

To prove that our algorithm is correct, we show that it generates only linearizable executions and guarantees that some operation eventually completes. Due to space constraints, we only provide a proof sketch.

Linearizability: We start by making a few observations about our algorithm. First, the key stored at a node, once initialized, never changes. Second, an internal node always stays an internal node and a leaf node always stays a leaf node. Third, before an internal node is removed from the tree, both its child edges (or addresses) are marked after which the edges cannot change (point to another node). This implies that the first CAS instruction of a modify operation only succeeds if its injection point is still part of the tree at the time the CAS instruction is performed.

322

```
 1  struct Node {
 2      Key key;
        // each of the next two fields contains three
            sub-fields packed into a single word: one
            bit for flagging (flag), one bit for tagging
            (tag) and the remaining bits for a node
            address (address)
 3      {Boolean, Boolean, NodePtr} left;
 4      {Boolean, Boolean, NodePtr} right;
 5  };

 6  struct SeekRecord {
 7      NodePtr ancestor;
 8      NodePtr successor;
 9      NodePtr parent;
10      NodePtr leaf;
11  };
    // create a new seek record, which is used by all
        operations
12  struct SeekRecordPtr seekRecord := allocate a new seek record;

13  seek( key, seekRecord )
14  begin
        // initialize the seek record using the
            sentinel nodes
15      seekRecord → ancestor := R;
16      seekRecord → successor := S;
17      seekRecord → parent := S;
18      seekRecord → leaf := (S → left) ⤳ address;
        // initialize other variables used in the
            traversal
19      parentField := (seekRecord → parent) → left;
20      currentField := (seekRecord → leaf) → left;
21      current := currentField ⤳ address;

22      while current ≠ null do
            // move down the tree
            // check if the edge from the (current)
                parent node in the access path is tagged
23          if not (parentField ⤳ tag) then
                // found an untagged edge in the access
                    path; advance ancestor and successor
                    pointers
24              seekRecord → ancestor :=
                                seekRecord → parent;
25              seekRecord → successor :=
                                seekRecord → leaf;
            // advance parent and leaf pointers
26          seekRecord → parent := seekRecord → leaf;
27          seekRecord → leaf := current;
            // update other variables used in traversal
28          parentField := currentField;
29          if key < current → key then
30              currentField := current → left;
31          else currentField := current → right;
32          current := currentField ⤳ address;
        // traversal complete
33      return;
```

Algorithm 1: The definitions of the node structure and the seek record along with the pseudo-code of the seek routine.

It can be shown that the traversal of the tree during a seek phase never takes a "wrong turn". This means that the injection point of a modify operation as returned by a seek phase is always a "correct" node if the operation eventually completes. This, in turn, can be used to prove that our algorithm always maintains a legal binary search tree.

```
34  Boolean search( key )
35  begin
36      seek( key, seekRecord );
37      if (seekRecord → leaf) → key = key then
38          return true;         // key present in the tree
39      else return false;       // key not present in the tree

40  Boolean insert( key )
41  begin
42      while true do
43          seek( key, seekRecord );
44          if (seekRecord → leaf) → key ≠ key then
                // key not present in the tree
45              parent := seekRecord → parent;
46              leaf := seekRecord → leaf;
                // obtain the address of the child field
                    that needs to be modified
47              if key < parent → key then
48                  childAddr := addr( parent → left );
49              else childAddr := addr( parent → right );
50              create two nodes newInternal and
                    newLeaf and initialize them appropriately;
                // try to add the new nodes to the tree
51              result := CAS( childAddr, {0, 0, leaf},
                                {0, 0, newInternal});
52              if result then
53                  return true;     // insertion successful
54              else
                    // insertion failed; help the
                        conflicting delete operation
55                  {flag, tag, address} := read( childAddr );
56                  if (address = leaf) and (flag or tag) then
                        // address of the child has not
                            changed and either the leaf
                            node or its sibling has been
                            flagged for deletion
57                      cleanup( key, seekRecord );
58          else
                // key already present in the tree
59              return false;
```

Algorithm 2: The pseudo-code of the search and insert operations.

Now, to establish the linearizability property, we specify the *linearization point* of every operation. Note that modify operations that do not change the tree are treated as search operations. Also, search operations are partitioned into two types: those that find the key in the tree (search-hit) and those that do not (search-miss). The linearization point of an insert operation is defined to be the point at which it performs its CAS instruction successfully. The linearization point of a delete operation is defined to be the point at which the CAS instruction that removes its target key from the tree is performed. Note that this instruction may be performed by another operation. Also, if multiple keys are removed from the key by a single CAS instruction, then the linearization points of the corresponding delete operations can be ordered arbitrarily since all delete operations must have distinct target keys. For a search-hit operation, we consider two cases. If the leaf node returned by the seek phase of the operation is still part of the tree when the seek phase completes, then its

```
60  Boolean delete( key )
61  begin
        // start the operation in the injection mode
62      mode := INJECTION;
63      while true do
64          seek( key, seekRecord );
65          parent := seekRecord → parent;

            // obtain the address of the child field
                that needs to be modified
66          if key < parent → key then
67              childAddr := addr( parent → left );
68          else childAddr := addr( parent → right ) ;

69          if mode = INJECTION then
                // injection mode: check if the key is
                    present in the tree
70              leaf := seekRecord → leaf;
71              if leaf → key ≠ key then
                    // key not present in the tree
72                  return false;

                // inject the delete operation into the
                    tree
73              result := CAS( childAddr, {0, 0, leaf},
                                  {1, 0, leaf});
74              if result then
                    // advance to the cleanup mode and
                        try to remove the leaf node from
                        the tree
75                  mode := CLEANUP;
76                  done := cleanup( key, seekRecord );
77                  if done then return true;
78              else
79                  {flag, tag, address} := read( childAddr );
80                  if (address = leaf) and (flag or tag) then
                        // address of the child has not
                            changed and either the leaf
                            node or its sibling has been
                            flagged for deletion
81                      cleanup( key, seekRecord );

82          else
                // cleanup mode: check if the leaf node
                    that was flagged in the injection
                    mode is still present in the tree
83              if seekRecord → leaf ≠ leaf then
                    // leaf node no longer present in
                        the tree
84                  return true;
85              else
                    // the leaf node is still present in
                        the tree; remove it
86                  done := cleanup( key, seekRecord );
87                  if done then return true;
```

Algorithm 3: The pseudo-code of the delete operation.

```
88  Boolean cleanup( key, seekRecord )
89  begin
        // retrieve all addresses stored in the seek
            record for easy access
90      ancestor := seekRecord → ancestor;
91      successor := seekRecord → successor;
92      parent := seekRecord → parent;
93      leaf := seekRecord → leaf;

        // obtain the addresses on which atomic
            instructions will be executed
        // first obtain the address of the field of the
            ancestor node that will be modified
94      if key < ancestor → key then
95          successorAddr := addr( ancestor → left );
96      else successorAddr := addr( ancestor → right ) ;

        // now obtain the addresses of the child fields
            of the parent node
97      if key < parent → key then
98          childAddr := addr( parent → left );
99          siblingAddr := addr( parent → right );
100     else
101         childAddr := addr( parent → right );
102         siblingAddr := addr( parent → left );

103     {flag, _, _} := read( childAddr );
104     if not (flag) then
            // the leaf node is not flagged for
                deletion; thus the sibling node must be
                flagged for deletion
            // switch the sibling address
105         siblingAddr := childAddr;

        // tag the sibling edge; no modify operation
            can occur at this edge now
106     BTS( siblingAddr, TAG );
        // read the flag and address fields
107     {flag, _, address} := read( siblingAddr );
        // the flag field will be copied to the new
            edge that will be created
        // make the sibling node a direct child of the
            ancestor node
108     result := CAS( successorAddr, {0, 0, successor},
                          {flag, 0, address} );
109     return result;
```

Algorithm 4: The pseudo-code of the cleanup routine.

starts. It can be proved that, when the operations are ordered according to their linearization points, then the resulting sequence of operations is legal.

Lock-Freedom: Note that, if the system reaches a state after which no modify operation completes, then every search operation is guaranteed to complete after that because the tree will not undergo any further structural changes. Thus it suffices to prove that modify operations are lock-free. Assume, on the contrary, that the system can reach a state in which there is a process, say p, with a pending modify operation, say α, that takes an infinite number of steps but still no modify operation completes after that. This implies that there is a time, say t, after which the tree stops changing. This, in turn, means that every instance of the seek phase of α that starts after t traverses the *same* access path and returns the *same* node as the injection point for α. Assume that α is an insert operation. Since the tree does not change after t, the repeated failure of α is because α repeatedly finds

linearization point is defined to be the point at which the seek phase ends. Otherwise, its linearization point is defined to be the point just before the leaf node is removed from the tree. For a search-miss operation, we again consider two cases. If there is one or more delete operation on the same key whose linearization point overlaps with the search-miss operation, then the point just after the *last* such linearization point is taken to be the linearization point of the search-miss operation. Otherwise, the linearization point of the search-miss operation is defined to be the point at which the operation the last edge along its access path to be flagged or tagged, thereby implying that there is a delete operation β in progress that conflicts with α. Clearly, in our algorithm, every time p fails to inject α into the tree, it will try to help the conflicting delete operation complete. Thus, it can be verified that, after t, every time p fails to help β complete, the depth of the *ancestor* pointer returned by the subsequent seek phase of α will strictly decrease. Since the depth of the *ancestor* pointer can only decrease a finite number of times, eventually, β is guaranteed to complete. A similar argument can be given if α is a delete operation.

4. Experimental Evaluation

In this section, we describe the results of the comparative evaluation of different implementations of a concurrent BST, including that based on the algorithm described in this paper.

Other Concurrent Binary Search Tree Implementations: For our experiments, we considered three other implementations of concurrent BST besides our algorithm, denoted by NM-BST. They are: (i) the lock-based implementation based on Bronson *et al.*'s algorithm [3], denoted by BCCO-BST, and (ii) two lock-free implementations: one based on Ellen *et al.*'s algorithm [12], denoted by EFRB-BST, and one based on Howley and Jones's algorithm [23], denoted by HJ-BST, For a fair comparison, no memory reclamation is performed in any of the implementations.

Experimental Setup: We conducted our experiments on a 4-processor AMD Opteron 6276 2.3 GHz machine, with 16 cores per processor (yielding 64 cores in total), 256 GB of RAM, running the x86_64 version of Fedora release 16.

All implementations were written in C. The code for HJ-BST was obtained directly from the authors [23]. The code for EFRB-BST and BCCO-BST were derived from the C++ implementations of Wicht [7]. All implementations were compiled using g++ version 4.6.3 with optimization level set to O3. We used Google's TCMalloc library [16] for dynamic memory allocation because it has significantly lower overhead for dynamically allocating objects in a multithreaded program.

Our experimental setup is similar to the one used by Bronson *et al.* [3] and Howley and Jones [23]. To compare the performance of different implementations, we considered the following parameters:

1. **Maximum Tree Size:** This depends on the size of the key space. We consider four different key ranges: 1000 (1K), 10,000 (10K), 100,000 (100K) and 1 million (1M) keys. To ensure consistent results, as in [6], rather than starting with an empty tree, we *pre-populated* the tree prior to starting the simulation run.

2. **Relative Distribution of Various Operations:** As in [23], we considered three different workload distributions: (a) *write-dominated workload:* 0% search, 50%

insert and 50% delete. (b) *mixed workload:* 70% search, 20% insert and 10% delete, and (c) *read-dominated workload:* 90% search, 9% insert and 1% delete,

3. **Maximum Degree of Contention:** This depends on the number of threads. We conducted our experiments for 1, 2, 4, 8, 16, 32, 64, 128 and 256 threads.

We compared the performance of different implementations with respect to system throughput, given by the number of operations executed per unit time.

Simulation Results: Each simulation run was carried out for 30 seconds and the results were averaged over multiple runs. Figure 4 shows the results of our experiments.

It is clear that our algorithm has the best throughput for all the key space sizes under the write-dominated workload. For the 1K key space size, the NM-BST scheme performs 54%-113% better than the BCCO-BST scheme, 11%-228% better than the HJ-BST scheme, and 11%-122% better than the EFRB-BST scheme. This is due to the fact that modify operations in our algorithm allow greater concurrency and allocate fewer objects (discussed in detail in Section 5). For the 100K key space size, the NM-BST scheme outperforms the BCCO-BST scheme by 33%-67%, the HJ-BST scheme by 5%-187%, and the EFRB-BSTscheme by 9%-125% . Finally, for the 1M key space size, the NM-BST scheme outperforms the BCCO-BST scheme by 27%-74%, the HJ-BST scheme by 4%-135%, and the EFRB-BST scheme by 18%-80%. Note that our algorithm uses an external representation of the tree, which causes operations to traverse longer paths compared to the BCCO-BST and HJ-BST schemes. However, in spite of this, modify operations in our scheme are significantly faster than those in all the other schemes.

As the percentage of search operations is increased in the workload, however, the relative performance of the NM-BST scheme drops with an increase in the tree size. For the mixed workload, for the 10K key space size, the NM-BST scheme outperforms the next best HJ-BST scheme by 6%-80%, which falls to 2%-40% for the 100K key space size. For the 1M key space size, however, the HJ-BST scheme beats the NM-BST scheme by 4%-20%, for up to 16 threads. However, for this key space size, the NM-BST scheme still outperforms the BCCO-BST scheme by 6%-30%, and the EFRB-BST scheme by 3%-23%.

The impact that the external tree structure has on operations is clearly visible in the graphs for the read-dominated workload. Here, the NM-BST and EFRB-BST schemes outperform all the other schemes for the 1K and 10K key space sizes, but are beaten by the HJ-BST scheme for the 100K and 1M key space sizes. For the 1M key range, the HJ-BST scheme outperforms the next best NM-BST scheme by 2%-17%. The NM-BST scheme outperforms the EFRB-BST scheme by 12%-20% and the BCCO-BST scheme by 5%-50%.

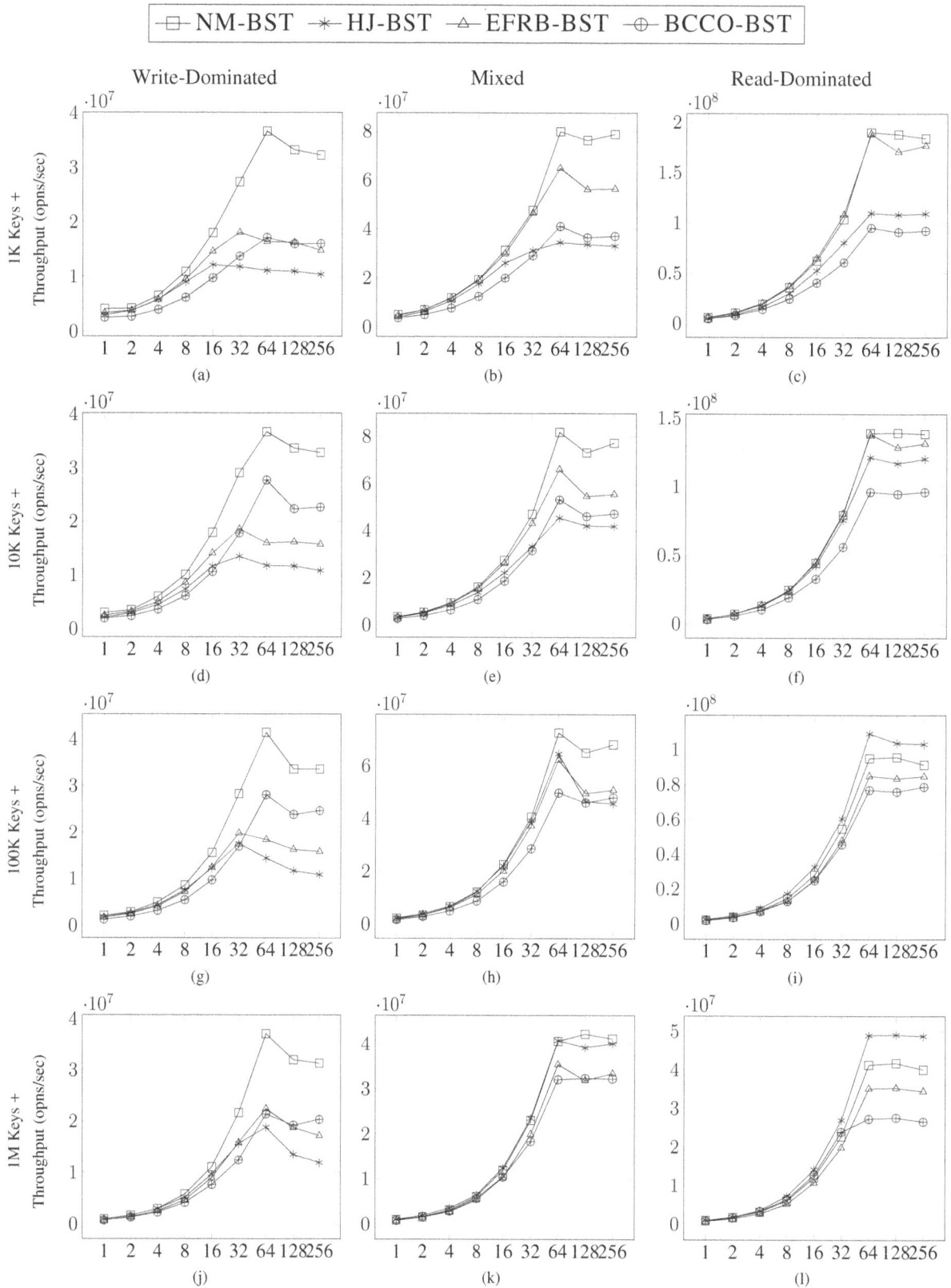

Figure 4: A comparison of the throughput of different algorithms. Each row of graphs represents a different key space size, and each column represents a different workload. Higher the throughput, better the performance of the algorithm.

Table 1: Comparison of different lock-free algorithms for a BST (in the absence of contention and with no memory reclamation).

Algorithm	Number of Objects Allocated		Number of Atomic Instructions Executed	
	Insert	Delete	Insert	Delete
Ellen *et al.*	4	1	3	4
Howley and Jones	2	1	3	up to 9
This work	2	0	1	3

5. Discussion

There are many reasons why our algorithm exhibited much better performance than other lock-free algorithms for a BST in our experiments. They are described as follows.

First, our algorithm has a smaller contention window than Ellen *et al.*'s algorithm. In fact, it can be verified that any two operations that can execute concurrently in Ellen *et al.*'s algorithm can also execute concurrently in our algorithm, but *not vice versa*. (For reference, in Ellen *et al.*'s algorithm, an insert operation needs to "lock" the parent node of the leaf node, and a delete operation needs to "lock" the parent and grandparent nodes of the leaf node.) One of the reasons for smaller contention window is that our algorithm operates at edge-level (marks edges) whereas Ellen *et al.*'s algorithm operates at node-level (marks nodes). For example, consider the tree in Figure 5. Some examples of operations that can be performed concurrently in our algorithm (because they involve disjoint set of edges) but not in Ellen *et al.*'s algorithm (because they involve one or more common nodes) are: `insert(40)` and `insert(60)`, and `delete(25)` and `delete(125)`. Comparing the contention window of our algorithm with that of Howley and Jones directly is not possible because the two algorithms use different internal representations (internal vs external BST).

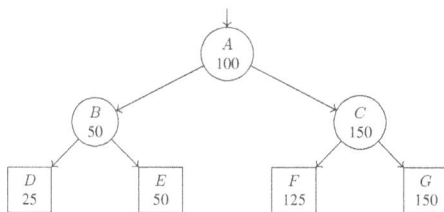

Figure 5: A sub-tree of a binary search tree.

Second, our algorithm allocates fewer objects and executes fewer atomic instructions per modify operation than the other two algorithms (see Table 1).

Third, a modify (insert as well as delete) operation has to successfully execute only a single atomic instruction to guarantee completion. (The remaining atomic instructions in a delete operation are required for "cleaning up" the tree and do not affect the outcome of the operation.) As a result, unlike as in Ellen *et al.*'s algorithm, there is no notion of

aborting a delete operation if the subsequent steps could not be performed successfully.

Fourth, our algorithm does not use explicit objects for coordination between conflicting operations ($DInfo$ and $IInfo$ objects in Ellen *et al.*'s algorithm and `ChildCASOp` and `RelocateOp` objects in Howley and Jones's algorithm). These objects are used for helping to ensure the lock-freedom property. In fact, in our algorithm, helping is performed for delete operations only; no helping is performed for insert operations. This is desirable since helping increases the overhead of an operation and may cause duplication of work. Furthermore, instead of using explicit objects for coordination, our algorithm steals a small number of bits from child addresses stored in a node to enable coordination between operations.

Finally, in our algorithm, multiple leaf nodes may be removed from the tree in a single step. For example, in Figure 2, when edge (B, C) is replaced with edge (B, K) at node B, where K is the root node of the subtree γ, then it not only removes the leaf node G from the tree but also removes the leaf nodes H, I and J along with it.

6. Conclusion and Future Work

In this paper, we have presented a new lock-free algorithm for concurrent manipulation of a binary search tree using single-word compare-and-swap and bit-test-and-set atomic instructions. Using a combination of several ideas (*e.g.*, marking an edge rather than a node, not using an explicit separate object for coordination among operations), we have not only reduced the contention between modify operations but also lowered the overhead of a modify operation. As we mentioned earlier, our algorithm can be easily modified to use only compare-and-swap instructions. Our experiments indicate that, when contention is high (tree size is small or workload is write-dominated), our algorithm significantly outperforms *all other existing* algorithms for a concurrent BST that we are aware of.

Ellen *et al.*'s lock-free algorithm for a BST has been extended to develop other lock-free tree-based data structures such as k-ary search trees [4] and binary tries [30]. As a future work, we plan to use the ideas in this work to develop more efficient lock-free algorithms for k-ary search trees and binary tries than those in [4, 30]. Further, we also plan to extend our lock-free algorithm to add support for other tree operations such as replace [30] and snapshot [29].

References

[1] M. A. Bender, J. T. Fineman, S. Gilbert, and B. C. Kuszmaul. Concurrent Cache-Oblivious B-Trees. In *Proceedings of the 17th ACM Symposium on Parallelism in Algorithms and Architectures (SPAA)*, pages 228–237, July 2005.

[2] A. Braginsky and E. Petrank. A Lock-Free B+tree. In *Proceedings of the 24th ACM Symposium on Parallelism in Algorithms and Architectures (SPAA)*, pages 58–67, 2012.

[3] N. G. Bronson, J. Casper, H. Chafi, and K. Olukotun. A Practical Concurrent Binary Search Tree. In *Proceedings of the 15th ACM SIGPLAN Symposium on Principles and Practice of Parallel Programming (PPoPP)*, pages 257–268, Jan. 2010.

[4] T. Brown and J. Helga. Non-Blocking k-ary Search Trees. In *Proceedings of the International Conference on Principles of Distributed Systems (OPODIS)*, pages 207–221, 2011.

[5] T. Brown, F. Ellen, and E. Ruppert. Pragmatic Primitives for Non-blocking Data Structures. In *Proceedings of the33rdACM Symposium on Principles of Distributed Computing (PODC)*, pages 207–221, 2013.

[6] T. Brown, F. Ellen, and E. Ruppert. A General Technique for Non-blocking Trees. In *Proceedings of the 19th ACM SIGPLAN Symposium on Principles and Practice of Parallel Programming (PPoPP)*, 2014.

[7] B.Wicht. Binary Trees Implementations Comparison for Multicore Programming. Technical report, Switzerland HES-SO University of Applied Science, June 2012. Code available at: `https://github.com/wichtounet/btrees/`.

[8] P. Chuong, F. Ellen, and V. Ramachandran. A Universal Construction for Wait-Free Transaction Friendly Data Structures. In *Proceedings of the 22nd ACM Symposium on Parallelism in Algorithms and Architectures (SPAA)*, pages 335–344, 2010.

[9] T. H. Cormen, C. E. Leiserson, and R. L. Rivest. *Introduction to Algorithms*. The MIT Press, 1991.

[10] T. Crain, V. Gramoli, and M. Raynal. A Contention-Friendly Binary Search Tree. In *Proceedings of the European Conference on Parallel and Distributed Computing (Euro-Par)*, pages 229–240, Aachen, Germany, 2013.

[11] D. Drachsler, M. Vechev, and E. Yahav. Practical Concurrent Binary Search Trees via Logical Ordering. In *Proceedings of the 19th ACM SIGPLAN Symposium on Principles and Practice of Parallel Programming (PPoPP)*, Orlando, Florida, USA, Feb. 2014.

[12] F. Ellen, P. Fatourou, E. Ruppert, and F. van Breugel. Non-Blocking Binary Search Trees. In *Proceedings of the 29th ACM Symposium on Principles of Distributed Computing (PODC)*, pages 131–140, July 2010.

[13] P. Fatourou and N. D. Kallimanis. A Highly-Efficient Wait-Free Universal Construction. In *Proceedings of the 23rd ACM Symposium on Parallelism in Algorithms and Architectures (SPAA)*, pages 325–334, 2011.

[14] M. Fomitchev and E. Ruppert. Lock-Free Linked Lists and Skiplists. In *Proceedings of the 23rd ACM Symposium on Principles of Distributed Computing (PODC)*, pages 50–59, July 2004.

[15] K. Fraser and T. L. Harris. Concurrent Programming Without Locks. *ACM Transactions on Computer Systems*, 25(2), May 2007.

[16] S. Ghemawat and P. Menage. TCMalloc: Thread-Caching Malloc. URL `http://goog-perftools.sourceforge.net/doc/tcmalloc.html`.

[17] T. Harris. A Pragmatic Implementation of Non-blocking Linked-lists. *Distributed Computing (DC)*, pages 300–314, 2001.

[18] M. Herlihy. Wait-Free Synchronization. *ACM Transactions on Programming Languages and Systems (TOPLAS)*, 13(1): 124–149, Jan. 1991.

[19] M. Herlihy. A Methodology for Implementing Highly Concurrent Objects. *ACM Transactions on Programming Languages and Systems (TOPLAS)*, 15(5):745–770, 1993.

[20] M. Herlihy and N. Shavit. *The Art of Multiprocessor Programming, Revised Reprint*. Morgan Kaufmann, 2012.

[21] M. Herlihy and J. M. Wing. Linearizability: A Correctness Condition for Concurrent Objects. *ACM Transactions on Programming Languages and Systems (TOPLAS)*, 12(3):463–492, July 1990.

[22] M. Herlihy, V. Luchangco, and M. Moir. Obstruction-Free Synchronization: Double-Ended Queues as an Example. In *Proceedings of the 23rd IEEE International Conference on Distributed Computing Systems (ICDCS)*, pages 522–529, 2003.

[23] S. V. Howley and J. Jones. A Non-Blocking Internal Binary Search Tree. In *Proceedings of the 24th ACM Symposium on Parallelism in Algorithms and Architectures (SPAA)*, pages 161–171, June 2012.

[24] J. H. Kim, H. Cameron, and P. Graham. Lock-Free Red-Black Trees Using CAS. *Concurrency and Computation: Practice and Experience*, pages 1–40, 2006.

[25] M. M. Michael. High Performance Dynamic Lock-Free Hash Tables and List-based Sets. In *Proceedings of the 14th ACM Symposium on Parallelism in Algorithms and Architectures (SPAA)*, pages 73–82, 2002.

[26] M. M. Michael. Hazard Pointers: Safe Memory Reclamation for Lock-Free Objects. *IEEE Transactions on Parallel and Distributed Systems (TPDS)*, 15(6):491–504, 2004.

[27] A. Natarajan and N. Mittal. Brief Announcement: A Concurrent Lock-Free Red-Black Tree. In *Proceedings of the 27th Symposium on Distributed Computing (DISC)*, Jerusalem, Israel, Oct. 2013.

[28] A. Natarajan, L. H. Savoie, and N. Mittal. Concurrent Wait-Free Red-Black Trees. In *Proceedings of the 15th International Symposium on Stabilization, Safety, and Security of Distributed Systems (SSS)*, pages 45–60, Osaka, Japan, Nov. 2013.

[29] A. Prokopec, N. G. Bronson, P. Bagwell, and M. Odersky. Concurrent Tries with Efficient Non-Blocking Snapshots. In *Proceedings of the 17th ACM SIGPLAN Symposium on Principles and Practice of Parallel Programming (PPoPP)*, pages 151–160, 2012.

[30] N. Shafiei. Non-blocking Patricia Tries with Replace Operations. In *Proceedings of the 33rd IEEE International Conference on Distributed Computing Systems (ICDCS)*, pages 216–225, JUL 2013.

[31] H. Sundell and P. Tsigas. Scalable and Lock-Free Concurrent Dictionaries. In *Proceedings of the 19th Annual Symposium on Selected Areas in Cryptography*, pages 1438–1445, Mar. 2004.

A General Technique for Non-blocking Trees

Trevor Brown and Faith Ellen
University of Toronto, Canada

Eric Ruppert
York University, Canada

Abstract

We describe a general technique for obtaining provably correct, non-blocking implementations of a large class of tree data structures where pointers are directed from parents to children. Updates are permitted to modify any contiguous portion of the tree atomically. Our non-blocking algorithms make use of the LLX, SCX and VLX primitives, which are multi-word generalizations of the standard LL, SC and VL primitives and have been implemented from single-word CAS [10].

To illustrate our technique, we describe how it can be used in a fairly straightforward way to obtain a non-blocking implementation of a chromatic tree, which is a relaxed variant of a red-black tree. The height of the tree at any time is $O(c + \log n)$, where n is the number of keys and c is the number of updates in progress. We provide an experimental performance analysis which demonstrates that our Java implementation of a chromatic tree rivals, and often significantly outperforms, other leading concurrent dictionaries.

Categories and Subject Descriptors   E.1 [*Data*]: Data Structures—Distributed data structures

Keywords   balanced binary search tree; non-blocking; chromatic tree; relaxed balance; red-black tree

1. Introduction

The binary search tree (BST) is among the most important data structures. Previous concurrent implementations of balanced BSTs without locks either used coarse-grained transactions, which limit concurrency, or lacked rigorous proofs of correctness. In this paper, we describe a general technique for implementing *any* data structure based on a down-tree (a directed acyclic graph of indegree one), with updates that modify any connected subgraph of the tree atomically. The

resulting implementations are non-blocking, which means that some process is always guaranteed to make progress, even if processes crash. Our approach drastically simplifies the task of proving correctness. This makes it feasible to develop provably correct implementations of non-blocking balanced BSTs with fine-grained synchronization (i.e., with updates that synchronize on a small constant number of nodes).

As with all concurrent implementations, the implementations obtained using our technique are more efficient if each update to the data structure involves a small number of nodes near one another. We call such an update *localized*. We use *operation* to denote an operation of the abstract data type (ADT) being implemented by the data structure. Operations that cannot modify the data structure are called *queries*. For some data structures, such as Patricia tries and leaf-oriented BSTs, operations modify the data structure using a single localized update. In some other data structures, operations that modify the data structure can be split into several localized updates that can be freely interleaved.

A particularly interesting application of our technique is to implement *relaxed-balance* versions of sequential data structures efficiently. Relaxed-balance data structures decouple updates that rebalance the data structure from operations, and allow updates that accomplish rebalancing to be delayed and freely interleaved with other updates. For example, a chromatic tree is a relaxed-balance version of a red-black tree (RBT) which splits up the insertion or deletion of a key and any subsequent rotations into a sequence of localized updates. There is a rich literature of relaxed-balance versions of sequential data structures [22], and several papers (e.g., [24]) have described general techniques that can be used to easily produce them from large classes of existing sequential data structures. The small number of nodes involved in each update makes relaxed-balance data structures perfect candidates for efficient implementation using our technique.

Our Contributions

- We provide a simple template that can be filled in to obtain an implementation of any update for a data structure based on a down-tree. We prove that any data structure that follows our template for all of its updates will automatically be linearizable and non-blocking. The template takes care of all process coordination, so the data structure designer is able to think of updates as atomic steps.

- To demonstrate the use of our template, we provide a complete, provably correct, non-blocking linearizable implementation of a chromatic tree [27], which is a relaxed-balanced version of a RBT. To our knowledge, this is the first provably correct, non-blocking balanced BST implemented using fine-grained synchronization. Our chromatic trees always have height $O(c + \log n)$, where n is the number of keys stored in the tree and c is the number of insertions and deletions that are in progress (Section 5.3).

- We show that sequential implementations of some queries are linearizable, even though they completely ignore concurrent updates. For example, an ordinary BST search (that works when there is no concurrency) also works in our chromatic tree. Ignoring updates makes searches very fast. We also describe how to perform successor queries in our chromatic tree, which interact properly with updates that follow our template (Section 5.5).

- We show experimentally that our Java implementation of a chromatic tree rivals, and often significantly outperforms, known highly-tuned concurrent dictionaries, over a variety of workloads, contention levels and thread counts. For example, with 128 threads, our algorithm outperforms Java's non-blocking skip-list by 13% to 156%, the lock-based AVL tree of Bronson et al. by 63% to 224%, and a RBT that uses software transactional memory (STM) by 13 to 134 times (Section 6).

2. Related Work

There are many lock-based implementations of search tree data structures. (See [1, 9] for state-of-the-art examples.) Here, we focus on implementations that do not use locks. Valois [32] sketched an implementation of non-blocking node-oriented BSTs from CAS. Fraser [17] gave a non-blocking BST using 8-word CAS, but did not provide a full proof of correctness. He also described how multi-word CAS can be implemented from single-word CAS instructions. Ellen et al. [15] gave a provably correct, non-blocking implementation of leaf-oriented BSTs directly from single-word CAS. A similar approach was used for k-ary search trees [11] and Patricia tries [28]. All three used the cooperative technique originated by Turek, Shasha and Prakash [31] and Barnes [4]. Howley and Jones [20] used a similar approach to build node-oriented BSTs. They tested their implementation using a model checker, but did not prove it correct. Natarajan and Mittal [25] give another leaf-oriented BST implementation, together with a sketch of correctness. Instead of marking nodes, it marks edges. This enables insertions to be accomplished by a single CAS, so they do not need to be helped. It also combines deletions that would

otherwise conflict. All of these trees are not balanced, so the height of a tree with n keys can be $\Theta(n)$.

Tsay and Li [30] gave a general approach for implementing trees in a wait-free manner using LL and SC operations (which can, in turn be implemented from CAS, e.g., [3]). However, their technique requires every process accessing the tree (even for read-only operations such as searches) to copy an entire path of the tree starting from the root. Concurrency is severely limited, since every operation must change the root pointer. Moreover, an extra level of indirection is required for every child pointer.

Red-black trees [5, 18] are well known BSTs that have height $\Theta(\log n)$. Some attempts have been made to implement RBTs without using locks. It was observed that the approach of Tsay and Li could be used to implement wait-free RBTs [26] and, furthermore, this could be done so that only updates must copy a path; searches may simply read the path. However, the concurrency of updates is still very limited. Herlihy et al. [19] and Fraser and Harris [16] experimented on RBTs implemented using software transactional memory (STM), which only satisfied obstruction-freedom, a weaker progress property. Each insertion or deletion, together with necessary rebalancing is enclosed in a single large transaction, which can touch all nodes on a path from the root to a leaf.

Some researchers have attempted fine-grained approaches to build non-blocking balanced search trees, but they all use extremely complicated process coordination schemes. Spiegel and Reynolds [29] described a non-blocking data structure that combines elements of B-trees and skip lists. Prior to this paper, it was the leading implementation of an ordered dictionary. However, the authors provided only a brief justification of correctness. Braginsky and Petrank [8] described a B+tree implementation. Although they have posted a correctness proof, it is very long and complex.

In a balanced search tree, a process is typically responsible for restoring balance after an insertion or deletion by performing a series of rebalancing steps along the path from the root to the location where the insertion or deletion occurred. Chromatic trees, introduced by Nurmi and Soisalon-Soininen [27], decouple the updates that perform the insertion or deletion from the updates that perform the rebalancing steps. Rather than treating an insertion or deletion and its associated rebalancing steps as a single, large update, it is broken into smaller, localized updates that can be interleaved, allowing more concurrency. This decoupling originated in the work of Guibas and Sedgewick [18] and Kung and Lehman [21]. We use the leaf-oriented chromatic trees by Boyar, Fagerberg and Larsen [7]. They provide a family of local rebalancing steps which can be executed in any order, interspersed with insertions and deletions. Moreover, an amortized *constant* number of rebalancing steps per INSERT or DELETE is sufficient to restore balance for any sequence of operations. We have also used our template to implement a non-blocking version of Larsen's leaf-oriented relaxed AVL tree [23]. In such a tree, an amortized *logarithmic* number of rebalancing steps per INSERT or DELETE is sufficient to restore balance.

There is also a node-oriented relaxed AVL tree by Bougé et al. [6], in which an amortized *linear* number of rebalancing steps per INSERT or DELETE is sufficient to restore balance. Bronson et al. [9] developed a highly optimized fine-grained locking implementation of this data structure using optimistic concurrency techniques to improve search performance. Deletion of a key stored in an internal node with two children is done by simply marking the node and a later insertion of the same key can reuse the node by removing the mark. If all internal nodes are marked, the tree is essentially leaf-oriented. Crain et al. gave a different implementation using lock-based STM [12] and locks [13], in which *all* deletions are done by marking the node containing the key. Physical removal of nodes and rotations are performed by one separate thread. Consequently, the tree can become very unbalanced. Drachsler et al. [14] give another fine-grained lock-based implementation, in which deletion physically removes the node containing the key and searches are non-blocking. Each node also contains predecessor and successor pointers, so when a search ends at an incorrect leaf, sequential search can be performed to find the correct leaf. A non-blocking implementation of Bougé's tree has not appeared, but our template would make it easy to produce one.

3. LLX, SCX and VLX Primitives

The load-link extended (LLX), store-conditional extended (SCX) and validate-extended (VLX) primitives are multi-word generalizations of the well-known load-link (LL), store-conditional (SC) and validate (VL) primitives and they have been implemented from single-word CAS [10]. The benefit of using LLX, SCX and VLX to implement our template is two-fold: the template can be described quite simply, and much of the complexity of its correctness proof is encapsulated in that of LLX, SCX and VLX.

Instead of operating on single words, LLX, SCX and VLX operate on Data-records, each of which consists of a fixed number of mutable fields (which can change), and a fixed number of immutable fields (which cannot). LLX(r) attempts to take a snapshot of the mutable fields of a Data-record r. If it is concurrent with an SCX involving r, it may return FAIL, instead. Individual fields of a Data-record can also be read directly. An SCX(V, R, fld, new) takes as arguments a sequence V of Data-records, a subsequence R of V, a pointer fld to a mutable field of one Data-record in V, and a new value new for that field. The SCX tries to atomically store the value new in the field that fld points to and *finalize* each Data-record in R. Once a Data-record is finalized, its mutable fields cannot be changed by any subsequent SCX, and any LLX of the Data-record will return FINALIZED instead of a snapshot.

Before a process invokes SCX or VLX(V), it must perform an LLX(r) on each Data-record r in V. The last such LLX by the process is said to be *linked* to the SCX or VLX, and the linked LLX must return a snapshot of r (not FAIL or FINALIZED). An SCX(V, R, fld, new) by a process modifies the data structure only if each Data-record r in V has not been changed since its linked LLX(r); otherwise the SCX fails. Similarly, a VLX(V) returns TRUE only if each Data-record r in V has not been changed since its linked LLX(r) by the same process; otherwise the VLX fails. VLX can be used to obtain a snapshot of a set of Data-records. Although LLX, SCX and VLX can fail, their failures are limited in such a way that we can use them to build non-blocking data structures. See [10] for a more formal specification of these primitives.

These new primitives were designed to balance ease of use and efficient implementability using single-word CAS. The implementation of the primitives from CAS in [10] is more efficient if the user of the primitives can guarantee that two constraints, which we describe next, are satisfied. The first constraint prevents the ABA problem for the CAS steps that actually perform the updates.

Constraint 1: Each invocation of SCX(V, R, fld, new) tries to change fld to a value new that it never previously contained.

The implementation of SCX does something akin to locking the elements of V in the order they are given. Livelock can be easily avoided by requiring all V sequences to be sorted according to some total order on Data-records. However, this ordering is necessary only to guarantee that SCXs continue to succeed. Therefore, as long as SCXs are still succeeding in an execution, it does not matter how V sequences are ordered. This observation leads to the following constraint, which is much weaker.

Constraint 2: Consider each execution that contains a configuration C after which the value of no field of any Data-record changes. There is a total order of all Data-records created during this execution such that, for every SCX whose linked LLXs begin after C, the V sequence passed to the SCX is sorted according to the total order.

It is easy to satisfy these two constraints using standard approaches, e.g., by attaching a version number to each field, and sorting V sequences by any total order, respectively. However, we shall see that Constraints 1 and 2 are *automatically* satisfied in a natural way when LLX and SCX are used according to our tree update template.

Under these constraints, the implementation of LLX, SCX, and VLX in [10] guarantees that there is a linearization of all SCXs that modify the data structure (which may include SCXs that do not terminate because a process crashed, but *not* any SCXs that fail), and all LLXs and VLXs that return, but do not fail.

We assume there is a Data-record *entry* which acts as the entry point to the data structure and is never deleted. This

Data-record points to the root of a down-tree. We represent an empty down-tree by a pointer to an empty Data-record. A Data-record is *in the tree* if it can be reached by following pointers from $entry$. A Data-record r is *removed from the tree* by an SCX if r is in the tree immediately prior to the linearization point of the SCX and is not in the tree immediately afterwards. Data structures produced using our template *automatically* satisfy one additional constraint:

Constraint 3: A Data-record is finalized when (and only when) it is removed from the tree.

Under this additional constraint, the implementation of LLX and SCX in [10] also guarantees the following three properties.

- If LLX(r) returns a snapshot, then r is in the tree just before the LLX is linearized.
- If an SCX(V, R, fld, new) is linearized and new is (a pointer to) a Data-record, then this Data-record is in the tree immediately after the SCX is linearized.
- If an operation reaches a Data-record r by following pointers read from other Data-records, starting from $entry$, then r was in the tree at some earlier time during the operation.

These properties are useful for proving the correctness of our template. In the following, we sometimes abuse notation by treating the sequences V and R as sets, in which case we mean the set of all Data-records in the sequence.

The memory overhead introduced by the implementation of LLX and SCX is fairly low. Each node in the tree is augmented with a pointer to a descriptor and a bit. Every node that has had one of its child pointers changed by an SCX points to a descriptor. (Other nodes have a NIL pointer.) A descriptor can be implemented to use only three machine words after the update it describes has finished. The implementation of LLX and SCX in [10] assumes garbage collection, and we do the same in this work. This assumption can be eliminated by using, for example, the new efficient memory reclamation scheme of Aghazadeh et al. [2].

4. Tree Update Template

Our tree update template implements updates that atomically replace an old connected subgraph in a down-tree by a new connected subgraph. Such an update can implement any change to the tree, such as an insertion into a BST or a rotation used to rebalance a RBT. The old subgraph includes all nodes with a field (including a child pointer) to be modified. The new subgraph may have pointers to nodes in the old tree. Since every node in a down-tree has indegree one, the update can be performed by changing a single child pointer of some node $parent$. (See Figure 1.) However, problems could arise if a concurrent operation changes the part of the tree being updated. For example, nodes in the old subgraph, or even $parent$, could be removed from the tree before $parent$'s child pointer is changed. Our template

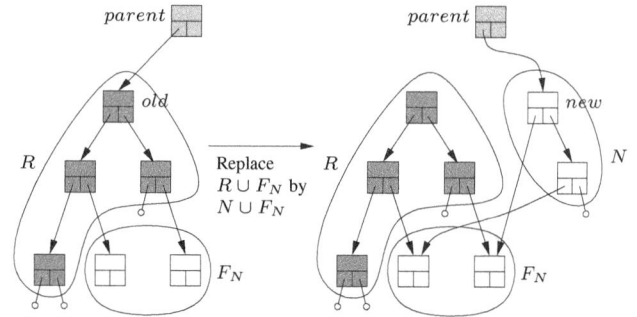

Figure 1. Example of the tree update template. R is the set of nodes to be removed, N is a tree of new nodes that have never before appeared in the tree, and F_N is the set of children of N (and of R). Nodes in F_N may have children. The shaded nodes (and possibly others) are in the sequence V of the SCX that performs the update. The darkly shaded nodes are finalized by the SCX.

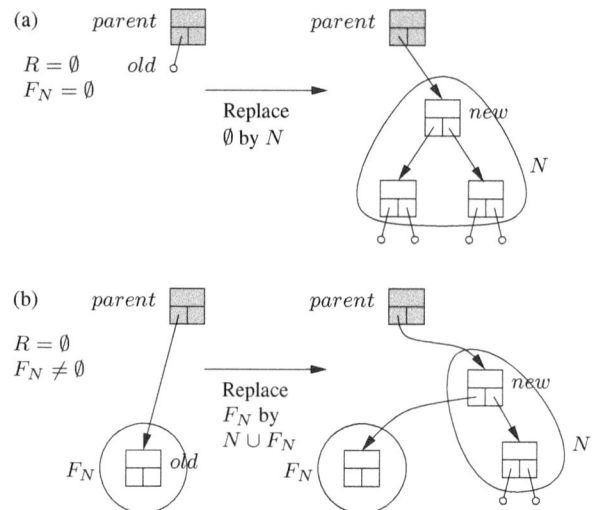

Figure 2. Examples of two special cases of the tree update template when no nodes are removed from the tree. (a) Replacing a NIL child pointer: In this case, $R = F_N = \emptyset$. (b) Inserting new nodes in the middle of the tree: In this case, $R = \emptyset$ and F_N consists of a single node.

takes care of the process coordination required to prevent such problems.

Each tree node is represented by a Data-record with a fixed number of child pointers as its mutable fields (but different nodes may have different numbers of child fields). Each child pointer points to a Data-record or contains NIL (denoted by $\multimap$ in our figures). For simplicity, we assume that any other data in the node is stored in immutable fields. Thus, if an update must change some of this data, it makes a new copy of the node with the updated data.

Our template for performing an update to the tree is fairly simple: An update first performs LLXs on nodes in a contiguous portion of the tree, including $parent$ and the set

```
1   TEMPLATE(args)
2      follow zero or more pointers from entry to reach a node n_0
3      i := 0
4      loop
5         s_i := LLX(n_i)
6         if s_i ∈ {FAIL, FINALIZED} then return FAIL
7         s'_i := immutable fields of n_i
8         exit loop when CONDITION(s_0, s'_0, ..., s_i, s'_i, args)
                    ▷ CONDITION must eventually return TRUE
9         n_{i+1} := NEXTNODE(s_0, s'_0, ..., s_i, s'_i, args)
                    ▷ returns a non-NIL child pointer from one of s_0, ..., s_i
10        i := i + 1
11     end loop
12     if SCX(SCX-ARGUMENTS(s_0, s'_0, ..., s_i, s'_i, args)) then
               return RESULT(s_0, s'_0, ..., s_i, s'_i, args)
13     else return FAIL
```

Figure 3. Tree update template. CONDITION, NEXTNODE, SCX-ARGUMENTS and RESULT can be filled in with any locally computable functions, provided that SCX-ARGUMENTS satisfies postconditions PC1 to PC8.

R of nodes to be removed from the tree. Then, it performs an SCX that atomically changes the child pointer as shown in Figure 1 and finalizes nodes in R. Figure 2 shows two special cases where R is empty. An update that performs this sequence of steps is said to *follow* the template.

We now describe the tree update template in more detail. An update UP($args$) that follows the template shown in Figure 3 takes any arguments, $args$, that are needed to perform the update. UP first reads a sequence of child pointers starting from $entry$ to reach some node n_0. Then, UP performs LLXs on a sequence $\sigma = \langle n_0, n_1, \ldots \rangle$ of nodes starting with n_0. For maximal flexibility of the template, the sequence σ can be constructed on-the-fly, as LLXs are performed. Thus, UP chooses a non-NIL child of one of the previous nodes to be the next node of σ by performing some deterministic local computation (denoted by NEXTNODE in Figure 3) using any information that is available locally, namely, the snapshots of mutable fields returned by LLXs on the previous elements of σ, values read from immutable fields of previous elements of σ, and $args$. (This flexibility can be used, for example, to avoid unnecessary LLXs when deciding how to rebalance a BST.) UP performs another local computation (denoted by CONDITION in Figure 3) to decide whether more LLXs should be performed. To avoid infinite loops, this function must eventually return TRUE in any execution of UP. If any LLX in the sequence returns FAIL or FINALIZED, UP also returns FAIL, to indicate that the attempted update has been aborted because of a concurrent update on an overlapping portion of the tree. If all of the LLXs successfully return snapshots, UP invokes SCX and returns a result calculated locally by the RESULT function (or FAIL if the SCX fails).

The full version of this paper describes an optimization to the template which does not require invocations of UP to always begin at $entry$. For example, an operation may backtrack from n_0 to try again from a nearby node after an invocation of UP returns FAIL.

UP applies the function SCX-ARGUMENTS to use locally available information to construct the arguments V, R, fld and new for the SCX. The postconditions that must be satisfied by SCX-ARGUMENTS are somewhat technical, but intuitively, they are meant to ensure that the arguments produced describe an update as shown in Figure 1 or Figure 2. The update must remove a connected set R of nodes from the tree and replace it by a connected set N of newly-created nodes that is rooted at new by changing the child pointer stored in fld to point to new. In order for this change to occur atomically, we include R and the node containing fld in V. This ensures that if any of these nodes has changed since it was last accessed by one of UP's LLXs, the SCX will fail. The sequence V may also include any other nodes in σ.

More formally, we require SCX-ARGUMENTS to satisfy nine postconditions. The first three are basic requirements of SCX.

PC1: V is a subsequence of σ.

PC2: R is a subsequence of V.

PC3: The node $parent$ containing the mutable field fld is in V.

Let G_N be the directed graph $(N \cup F_N, E_N)$, where E_N is the set of all child pointers of nodes in N when they are initialized, and $F_N = \{y : y \notin N$ and $(x, y) \in E_N$ for some $x \in N\}$. Let old be the value read from fld by the LLX on $parent$.

PC4: G_N is a non-empty down-tree rooted at new.

PC5: If $old =$ NIL then $R = \emptyset$ and $F_N = \emptyset$.

PC6: If $R = \emptyset$ and $old \neq$ NIL, then $F_N = \{old\}$.

PC7: UP allocates memory for all nodes in N, including new.

Postcondition PC7 requires new to be a newly-created node, in order to satisfy Constraint 1. There is no loss of generality in using this approach: If we wish to change a child y of node x to NIL (to chop off the entire subtree rooted at y) or to a descendant of y (to splice out a portion of the tree), then, instead, we can replace x by a new copy of x with an updated child pointer. Likewise, if we want to delete the entire tree, then $entry$ can be changed to point to a new, empty Data-record.

The next postcondition is used to guarantee Constraint 2, which is used to prove progress.

PC8: The sequences V constructed by all updates that take place entirely during a period of time when no SCXs change the tree structure must be ordered consistently according to a fixed tree traversal algorithm (for example, an in-order traversal or a breadth-first traversal).

Stating the remaining postcondition formally requires some care, since the tree may be changing while UP performs its LLXs. If $R \neq \emptyset$, let G_R be the directed graph $(R \cup F_R, E_R)$, where E_R is the union of the sets of edges representing child pointers read from each $r \in R$ when it was last accessed by one of UP's LLXs and $F_R = \{y :$

$y \notin R$ and $(x, y) \in E_R$ for some $x \in R$}. G_R represents UP's view of the nodes in R according to its LLXs, and F_R is the *fringe* of G_R. If other processes do not change the tree while UP is being performed, then F_R contains the nodes that should remain in the tree, but whose parents will be removed and replaced. Therefore, we must ensure that the nodes in F_R are reachable from nodes in N (so they are not accidentally removed from the tree). Let G_σ be the directed graph $(\sigma \cup F_\sigma, E_\sigma)$, where E_σ is the union of the sets of edges representing child pointers read from each $r \in \sigma$ when it was last accessed by one of UP's LLXs and $F_\sigma = \{y : y \notin \sigma \text{ and } (x, y) \in E_\sigma \text{ for some } x \in \sigma\}$. Since G_σ, G_R and G_N are not affected by concurrent updates, the following postcondition can be proved using purely sequential reasoning, ignoring the possibility that concurrent updates could modify the tree during UP.

PC9: If G_σ is a down-tree and $R \neq \emptyset$, then G_R is a non-empty down-tree rooted at *old* and $F_N = F_R$.

4.1 Correctness and Progress

For brevity, we only sketch the main ideas of the proof here. The full version of this paper, containing a complete proof, is available from http://www.cs.utoronto.ca/~tabrown. Consider a data structure in which all updates follow the tree update template and SCX-ARGUMENTS satisfies postconditions PC1 to PC9. We prove, by induction on the sequence of steps in an execution, that the data structure is always a tree, each call to LLX and SCX satisfies its preconditions, Constraints 1 to 3 are satisfied, and each successful SCX atomically replaces a connected subgraph containing nodes $R \cup F_N$ with another connected subgraph containing nodes $N \cup F_N$, finalizing and removing the nodes in R from the tree, and adding the new nodes in N to the tree. We also prove no node in the tree is finalized, every removed node is finalized, and removed nodes are never reinserted.

We linearize each update UP that follows the template and performs an SCX that modifies the data structure at the linearization point of its SCX. We prove the following correctness properties.

C1: If UP were performed atomically at its linearization point, then it would perform LLXs on the same nodes, and these LLXs would return the same values.

This implies that UP's SCX-ARGUMENTS and RESULT computations must be the same as they would be if UP were performed atomically at its linearization point, so we obtain the following.

C2: If UP were performed atomically at its linearization point, then it would perform the same SCX (with the same arguments) and return the same value.

Additionally, a property is proved in [10] that allows some query operations to be performed very efficiently using only READS, for example, GET in Section 5.

C3: If a process p follows child pointers starting from a node in the tree at time t and reaches a node r at time

$t' \geq t$, then r *was* in the tree at some time between t and t'. Furthermore, if p reads v from a mutable field of r at time $t'' \geq t'$ then, at some time between t and t'', node r was in the tree and this field contained v.

The following properties, which come from [10], can be used to prove non-blocking progress of queries.

P1: If LLXs are performed infinitely often, then they return snapshots or FINALIZED infinitely often.

P2: If VLXs are performed infinitely often, and SCXs are not performed infinitely often, then VLXs return TRUE infinitely often.

Each update that follows the template is wait-free. Since updates can fail, we also prove the following progress property.

P3: If updates that follow the template are performed infinitely often, then updates succeed infinitely often.

A successful update performs an SCX that modifies the tree. Thus, it is necessary to show that SCXs succeed infinitely often. Before an invocation of $\text{SCX}(V, R, fld, new)$ can succeed, it must perform an $\text{LLX}(r)$ that returns a snapshot, for each $r \in V$. Even if P1 is satisfied, it is possible for LLXs to always return FINALIZED, preventing any SCXs from being performed. We prove that any algorithm whose updates follow the template automatically guarantees that, for each Data-record r, each process performs at most one invocation of $\text{LLX}(r)$ that returns FINALIZED. We use this fact to prove P3.

5. Application: Chromatic Trees

Here, we show how the tree update template can be used to implement an ordered dictionary ADT using chromatic trees. Due to space restrictions, we only sketch the algorithm and its correctness proof. All details of the implementation and its correctness proof are in the full version of the paper. The ordered dictionary stores a set of keys, each with an associated value, where the keys are drawn from a totally ordered universe. The dictionary supports five operations. If *key* is in the dictionary, GET(*key*) returns its associated value. Otherwise, GET(*key*) returns $\bot$. SUCCESSOR(*key*) returns the smallest key in the dictionary that is larger than *key* (and its associated value), or $\bot$ if no key in the dictionary is larger than *key*. PREDECESSOR(*key*) is analogous. INSERT(*key*, *value*) replaces the value associated with *key* by *value* and returns the previously associated value, or $\bot$ if *key* was not in the dictionary. If the dictionary contains *key*, DELETE(*key*) removes it and returns the value that was associated immediately beforehand. Otherwise, DELETE(*key*) simply returns $\bot$.

A RBT is a BST in which the root and all leaves are coloured black, and every other node is coloured either red or black, subject to the constraints that no red node has a red parent, and the number of black nodes on a path from the root to a leaf is the same for all leaves. These properties guarantee that the height of a RBT is logarithmic in the

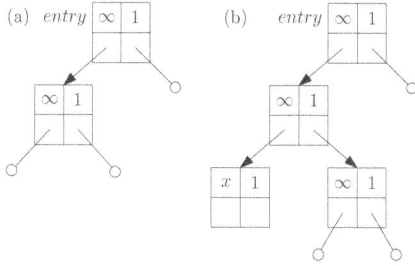

Figure 4. (a) empty tree, (b) non-empty tree.

number of nodes it contains. We consider search trees that are leaf-oriented, meaning the dictionary keys are stored in the leaves, and internal nodes store keys that are used only to direct searches towards the correct leaf. In this context, the BST property says that, for each node x, all descendants of x's left child have keys less than x's key and all descendants of x's right child have keys that are greater than *or equal to* x's key.

To decouple rebalancing steps from insertions and deletions, so that each is localized, and rebalancing steps can be interleaved with insertions and deletions, it is necessary to relax the balance properties of RBTs. A *chromatic tree* [27] is a relaxed-balance RBT in which colours are replaced by non-negative integer weights, where weight zero corresponds to red and weight one corresponds to black. As in RBTs, the sum of the weights on each path from the root to a leaf is the same. However, RBT properties can be violated in the following two ways. First, a red child node may have a red parent, in which case we say that a *red-red violation* occurs at this child. Second, a node may have weight $w > 1$, in which case we say that $w - 1$ *overweight violations* occur at this node. The root always has weight one, so no violation can occur at the root.

To avoid special cases when the chromatic tree is empty, we add sentinel nodes at the top of the tree (see Figure 4). The sentinel nodes and *entry* have key ∞ to avoid special cases for SEARCH, INSERT and DELETE, and weight one to avoid special cases for rebalancing steps. Without having a special case for INSERT, we automatically get the two sentinel nodes in Figure 4(b), which also eliminate special cases for DELETE. The chromatic tree is rooted at the leftmost grandchild of *entry*. The sum of weights is the same for all paths from the root of the chromatic tree to its leaves, but not for paths that include *entry* or the sentinel nodes.

Rebalancing steps are localized updates to a chromatic tree that are performed at the location of a violation. Their goal is to eventually eliminate all red-red and overweight violations, while maintaining the invariant that the tree is a chromatic tree. If no rebalancing step can be applied to a chromatic tree (or, equivalently, the chromatic tree contains no violations), then it is a RBT. We use the set of rebalancing steps of Boyar, Fagerberg and Larsen [7], which have a number of desirable properties: No rebalancing step increases the number of violations in the tree, rebalancing

steps can be performed in any order, and, after sufficiently many rebalancing steps, the tree will always become a RBT. Furthermore, in any sequence of insertions, deletions and rebalancing steps starting from an empty chromatic tree, the amortized number of rebalancing steps is at most three per insertion and one per deletion.

5.1 Implementation

We represent each node by a Data-record with two mutable child pointers, and immutable fields k, v and w that contain the node's key, associated value, and weight, respectively. The child pointers of a leaf are always NIL, and the value field of an internal node is always NIL.

GET, INSERT and DELETE each execute an auxiliary procedure, SEARCH(key), which starts at *entry* and traverses nodes as in an ordinary BST search, using READs of child pointers until reaching a leaf, which it then returns (along with the leaf's parent and grandparent). Because of the sentinel nodes shown in Figure 4, the leaf's parent always exists, and the grandparent exists whenever the chromatic tree is non-empty. If it is empty, SEARCH returns NIL instead of the grandparent. We define the *search path* for key at any time to be the path that SEARCH(key) would follow, if it were done instantaneously. The GET(key) operation simply executes a SEARCH(key) and then returns the value found in the leaf if the leaf's key is key, or $\perp$ otherwise.

At a high level, INSERT and DELETE are quite similar to each other. INSERT(key, $value$) and DELETE(key) each perform SEARCH(key) and then make the required update at the leaf reached, in accordance with the tree update template. If the modification fails, then the operation restarts from scratch. If it succeeds, it may increase the number of violations in the tree by one, and the new violation occurs on the search path to key. If a new violation is created, then an auxiliary procedure CLEANUP is invoked to fix it before the INSERT or DELETE returns.

Detailed pseudocode for GET, SEARCH, DELETE and CLEANUP is given in Figure 5. (The implementation of INSERT is similar to that of DELETE, and its pseudocode is omitted due to lack of space.) Note that an expression of the form P ? A : B evaluates to A if the predicate P evaluates to true, and B otherwise. The expression $x.y$, where x is a Data-record, denotes field y of x, and the expression $\&x.y$ represents a pointer to field y.

DELETE(key) invokes TRYDELETE to search for a leaf containing key and perform the localized update that actually deletes key and its associated value. The effect of TRYDELETE is illustrated in Figure 6. There, nodes drawn as squares are leaves, shaded nodes are in V, $\otimes$ denotes a node in R to be finalized, and $\oplus$ denotes a new node. The name of a node appears below it or to its left. The weight of a node appears to its right.

TRYDELETE first invokes SEARCH(key) to find the grandparent, n_0, of the leaf on the search path to key. If the grandparent does not exist, then the tree is empty (and

```
 1  GET(key)
 2      ⟨−, −, l⟩ := SEARCH(key)
 3      return  (key = l.k) ? l.v : NIL

 4  SEARCH(key)
 5      n_0 := NIL; n_1 := entry; n_2 := entry.left
 6      while  n_2 is internal
 7          n_0 := n_1; n_1 := n_2
 8          n_2 := (key < n_1.k) ? n_1.left : n_1.right
 9      return  ⟨n_0, n_1, n_2⟩

10  DELETE(key)
11      do
12          result := TRYDELETE(key)
13      while  result = FAIL
14      ⟨value, violation⟩ := result
15      if  violation  then  CLEANUP(key)
16      return  value

17  TRYDELETE(key)
18      ▷ If successful, returns ⟨value, violation⟩, where value is the
            value associated with key, or NIL if key was not in the
            dictionary, and violation indicates whether the deletion
            created a violation. Otherwise, FAIL is returned.
19      ⟨n_0, −, −⟩ := SEARCH(key)
20      ▷ Special case: there is no grandparent of the leaf reached
21      if  n_0 = NIL  then  return  ⟨NIL, FALSE⟩
22      ▷ Template iteration 0 (grandparent of leaf)
23      s_0 := LLX(n_0)
24      if  s_0 ∈ {FAIL, FINALIZED}  then  return  FAIL
25      n_1 := (key < s_0.left.k) ? s_0.left : s_0.right
26      ▷ Template iteration 1 (parent of leaf)
27      s_1 := LLX(n_1)
28      if  s_1 ∈ {FAIL, FINALIZED}  then  return  FAIL
29      n_2 := (key < s_1.left.k) ? s_1.left : s_1.right
30      ▷ Special case: key is not in the dictionary
31      if  n_2.k ≠ key  then  return  ⟨⊥, FALSE⟩
32      ▷ Template iteration 2 (leaf)
33      s_2 := LLX(n_2)
34      if  s_2 ∈ {FAIL, FINALIZED}  then  return  FAIL
35      n_3 := (key < s_1.left.k) ? s_1.right : s_1.left
36      ▷ Template iteration 3 (sibling of leaf)
37      s_3 := LLX(n_3)
38      if  s_3 ∈ {FAIL, FINALIZED}  then  return  FAIL
39      ▷ Computing SCX-ARGUMENTS from locally stored values
40      w := (n_1.k = ∞  or  n_0.k = ∞) ? 1 : n_1.w + n_3.w
41      new := new node with weight w, key n_3.k, value n_3.v, and
                children s_3.left, s_3.right
42      V := (key < s_1.left.k) ? ⟨n_0, n_1, n_2, n_3⟩ : ⟨n_0, n_1, n_3, n_2⟩
43      R := (key < s_1.left.k) ? ⟨n_1, n_2, n_3⟩ : ⟨n_1, n_3, n_2⟩
44      fld := (key < s_0.left.k) ? &n_0.left : &n_0.right
45      if  SCX(V, R, fld, new)  then  return  ⟨n_2.v, (w > 1)⟩
46      else  return  FAIL

47  CLEANUP(key)
48      ▷ Eliminates the violation created by an INSERT or DELETE of key
49      while  TRUE
50          ▷ Save four last nodes traversed
51          n_0 := NIL; n_1 := NIL; n_2 := entry; n_3 := entry.left
52          while  TRUE
53              if  n_3.w > 1  or  (n_2.w = 0  and  n_3.w = 0)  then
54                  ▷ Found a violation at node n_3
55                  TRYREBALANCE(n_0, n_1, n_2, n_3)     ▷ Try to fix it
56                  exit loop     ▷ Go back to entry and search again
57              else if  n_3 is a leaf  then return
58                  ▷ Arrived at a leaf without finding a violation
59              if  key < n_3.k  then
60                  n_0 := n_1; n_1 := n_2; n_2 := n_3; n_3 := n_3.left
61              else  n_0 := n_1; n_1 := n_2; n_2 := n_3; n_3 := n_3.right
```

Figure 5. GET, SEARCH, DELETE and CLEANUP.

it looks like Figure 4(a), so TRYDELETE returns successfully at line 21. TRYDELETE then performs $LLX(n_0)$, and uses the result to obtain a pointer to the parent, n_1, of the leaf to be deleted. Next, it performs $LLX(n_1)$, and uses the result to obtain a pointer to the leaf, n_2, to be deleted. If n_2 does not contain key, then the tree does not contain key, and TRYDELETE returns successfully at line 31. So, suppose that n_2 does contain key. Then TRYDELETE performs $LLX(n_2)$. At line 35, TRYDELETE uses the result of its previous $LLX(n_1)$ to obtain a pointer to the sibling, n_3, of the leaf to be deleted. A final LLX is then performed on n_3. Over the next few lines, TRYDELETE computes SCX-ARGUMENTS. Line 40 computes the weight of the node new in the depiction of DELETE in Figure 4, ensuring that it has weight one if it is taking the place of a sentinel or the root of the chromatic tree. Line 41 creates new, reading the key, and value directly from n_3 (since they are immutable) and the child pointers from the result of the $LLX(n_3)$ (since they are mutable). Next, TRYDELETE uses locally stored values to construct the sequences V and R that it will use for its SCX, ordering their elements according to a breadth-first traversal, in order to satisfy PC8. Finally, TRYDELETE invokes SCX to perform the modification. If the SCX succeeds, then TRYDELETE returns a pair containing the value stored in node n_2 (which is immutable) and the result of evaluating the expression $w > 1$.

DELETE can create an overweight violation (but not a red-red violation), so the result of $w > 1$ indicates whether TRYDELETE created a violation. If any LLX returns FAIL or FINALIZED, or the SCX fails, TRYDELETE simply returns FAIL, and DELETE invokes TRYDELETE again. If TRYDELETE creates a new violation, then DELETE invokes CLEANUP(key) (described in Section 5.2) to fix it before DELETE returns.

A simple inspection of the pseudocode suffices to prove that SCX-ARGUMENTS satisfies postconditions PC1 to PC9. TRYDELETE follows the template except when it returns at line 21 or line 31. In these cases, not following the template does not impede our efforts to prove correctness or progress, since TRYDELETE will not modify the data structure, and returning at either of these lines will cause DELETE to terminate.

We now describe how rebalancing steps are implemented from LLX and SCX, using the tree update template. As an example, we consider one of the 22 rebalancing steps, named RB2 (shown in Figure 6), which eliminates a red-red violation at node n_3. The other 21 are implemented similarly. To implement RB2, a sequence of LLXs are performed, starting with node n_0. A pointer to node n_1 is obtained from the result of $LLX(n_0)$, pointers to nodes n_2 and f_3 are obtained from the result of $LLX(n_1)$, and a pointer to node n_3 is obtained from the result of $LLX(n_2)$. Since node n_3 is to be removed from the tree, an LLX is performed on it, too. If any of these LLXs returns FAIL or FINALIZED, then this update

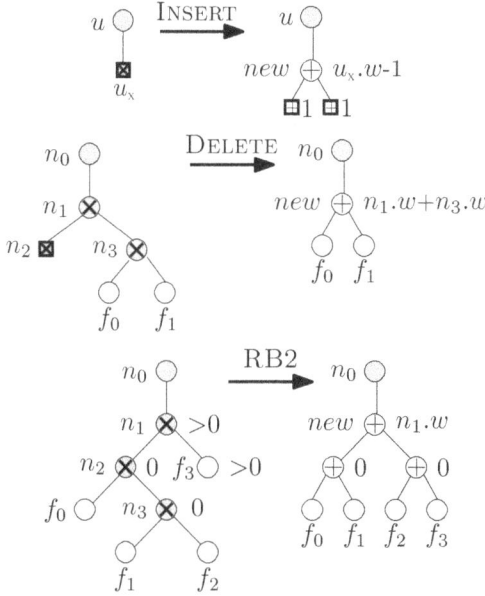

Figure 6. Examples of chromatic tree updates.

fails. For RB2 to be applicable, n_1 and f_3 must have positive weights and n_2 and n_3 must both have weight 0. Since weight fields are immutable, they can be read any time after the pointers to n_1, f_3, n_2, and n_3 have been obtained. Next, *new* and its two children are created. N consists of these three nodes. Finally, $\mathrm{SCX}(V, R, fld, new)$ is invoked, where fld is the child pointer of n_0 that pointed to n_1 in the result of $\mathrm{LLX}(n_0)$.

If the SCX modifies the tree, then no node $r \in V$ has changed since the update performed $\mathrm{LLX}(r)$. In this case, the SCX replaces the directed graph G_R by the directed graph G_N and the nodes in R are finalized. This ensures that other updates cannot erroneously modify these old nodes after they have been replaced. The nodes in the set $F_R = F_N = \{f_0, f_1, f_2, f_3\}$ each have the same keys, weights, and child pointers before and after the rebalancing step, so they can be reused. $V = \langle n_0, n_1, n_2, n_3 \rangle$ is simply the sequence of nodes on which LLX is performed, and $R = \langle n_1, n_2, n_3 \rangle$ is a subsequence of V, so PC1, PC2 and PC3 are satisfied. Clearly, we satisfy PC4 and PC7 when we create *new* and its two children. It is easy to verify that PC5, PC6 and PC9 are satisfied. If the tree does not change during the update, then the nodes in V are ordered consistently with a breadth-first traversal of the tree. Since this is true for all updates, PC8 is satisfied.

One might wonder why f_3 is not in V, since RB2 should be applied only if n_1 has a right child with positive weight. Since weight fields are immutable, the only way that this can change after we check $f_3.w > 0$ is if the right child field of n_1 is altered. If this happens, the SCX will fail.

5.2 The rebalancing algorithm

Since rebalancing is decoupled from updating, there must be a scheme that determines when processes should perform rebalancing steps to eliminate violations. In [7], the authors suggest maintaining one or more *problem queues* which contain pointers to nodes that contain violations, and dedicating one or more *rebalancing processes* to simply perform rebalancing steps as quickly as possible. This approach does not yield a bound on the height of the tree, since rebalancing may lag behind insertions and deletions. It is possible to obtain a height bound with a different queue based scheme, but we present a way to bound the tree's height without the (significant) overhead of maintaining any auxiliary data structures. The linchpin of our method is the following claim concerning violations.

> **VIOL:** If a violation is on the search path to key before a rebalancing step, then the violation is still on the search path to key after the rebalancing step, or it has been eliminated.

While studying the rebalancing steps in [7], we realized that most of them satisfy VIOL. Furthermore, any time a rebalancing step would violate VIOL another rebalancing step that satisfies VIOL can be applied instead. Hence, we always choose to perform rebalancing so that each violation created by an $\mathrm{INSERT}(key)$ or $\mathrm{DELETE}(key)$ stays on the search path to key until it is eliminated. In our implementation, each INSERT or DELETE that increases the number of violations cleans up after itself. It does this by invoking a procedure $\mathrm{CLEANUP}(key)$, which behaves like $\mathrm{SEARCH}(key)$ until it finds the first node n_3 on the search path where a violation occurs. Then, $\mathrm{CLEANUP}(key)$ attempts to eliminate or move the violation at n_3 by invoking another procedure TRYREBALANCE which applies one localized rebalancing step at n_3, following the tree update template. (TRYREBALANCE is similar to DELETE, and pseudocode is omitted, due to lack of space.) $\mathrm{CLEANUP}(key)$ repeats these actions, searching for key and invoking TRYREBALANCE to perform a rebalancing step, until the search goes all the way to a leaf without finding a violation.

In order to prove that each INSERT or DELETE cleans up after itself, we must prove that while an invocation of $\mathrm{CLEANUP}(key)$ searches for key by reading child pointers, it does not somehow miss the violation it is responsible for eliminating, even if a concurrent rebalancing step moves the violation upward in the tree, above where CLEANUP is currently searching. To see why this is true, consider any rebalancing step that occurs while CLEANUP is searching. The rebalancing step is implemented using the tree update template, and looks like Figure 1. It takes effect at the point it changes a child pointer fld of some node *parent* from a node *old* to a node *new*. If CLEANUP reads fld while searching, we argue that it does not matter whether fld contains *old* or *new*. First, suppose the violation is at a node that is removed from the tree by the rebalancing step, or a child of such a node. If the search passes through *old*, it will definitely reach the violation, since nodes do not change after they are removed from the tree. If the search passes through

337

new, VIOL implies that the rebalancing step either eliminated the violation, or moved it to a new node that will still be on the search path through *new*. Finally, if the violation is further down in the tree, below the section modified by the concurrent rebalancing step, a search through either *old* or *new* will reach it.

Showing that TRYREBALANCE follows the template (i.e., by defining the procedures in Figure 3) is complicated by the fact that it must decide which of the chromatic tree's 22 rebalancing steps to perform. It is more convenient to unroll the loop that performs LLXs, and write TRYREBALANCE using conditional statements. A helpful technique is to consider each path through the conditional statements in the code, and check that the procedures CONDITION, NEXTNODE, SCX-ARGUMENTS and RESULT can be defined to produce this single path. It is sufficient to show that this can be done for each path through the code, since it is always possible to use conditional statements to combine the procedures for each path into procedures that handle all paths.

5.3 Proving a bound on the height of the tree

Since we always perform rebalancing steps that satisfy VIOL, if we reach a leaf without finding the violation that an INSERT or DELETE created, then the violation has been eliminated. This allows us to prove that the number of violations in the tree at any time is bounded above by c, the number of insertions and deletions that are currently in progress. Further, since removing all violations would yield a red-black tree with height $O(\log n)$, and eliminating each violation reduces the height by at most one, the height of the chromatic tree is $O(c + \log n)$.

5.4 Correctness and Progress

As mentioned above, GET(key) invokes SEARCH(key), which traverses a path from $entry$ to a leaf by reading child pointers. Even though this search can pass through nodes that have been removed by concurrent updates, we prove by induction that every node visited *was* on the search path for key at some time during the search. GET can thus be linearized when the leaf it reaches is on the search path for key (and, hence, this leaf is the only one in the tree that could contain key).

Every DELETE operation that performs an update, and every INSERT operation, is linearized at the SCX that performs the update. Other DELETE operations (that return at line 21 or 31) behave like queries, and are linearized in the same way as GET. Because no rebalancing step modifies the set of keys stored in leaves, the set of leaves always represents the set of dictionary entries.

The fact that our chromatic tree is non-blocking follows from P1 and the fact that at most $3i + d$ rebalancing steps can be performed after i insertions and d deletions have occurred (proved in [7]).

5.5 SUCCESSOR queries

SUCCESSOR(key) runs an ordinary BST search algorithm, using LLXs to read the child fields of each node visited, until it reaches a leaf. If the key of this leaf is larger than key, it is returned and the operation is linearized at any time during the operation when this leaf was on the search path for key. Otherwise, SUCCESSOR finds the next leaf. To do this, it remembers the last time it followed a left child pointer and, instead, follows one right child pointer, and then left child pointers until it reaches a leaf, using LLXs to read the child fields of each node visited. If any LLX it performs returns FAIL or FINALIZED, SUCCESSOR restarts. Otherwise, it performs a validate-extended (VLX), which returns TRUE only if all nodes on the path connecting the two leaves have not changed. If the VLX succeeds, the key of the second leaf found is returned and the query is linearized at the linearization point of the VLX. If the VLX fails, SUCCESSOR restarts.

5.6 Allowing more violations

Forcing insertions and deletions to rebalance the chromatic tree after creating only a single violation can cause unnecessary rebalancing steps to be performed, for example, because an overweight violation created by a deletion might be eliminated by a subsequent insertion. In practice, we can reduce the total number of rebalancing steps that occur by modifying our INSERT and DELETE procedures so that CLEANUP is invoked only once the number of violations on a path from $entry$ to a leaf exceeds some constant k. The resulting data structure has height $O(k + c + \log n)$. Since searches in the chromatic tree are extremely fast, slightly increasing search costs to reduce update costs can yield significant benefits for update-heavy workloads.

6. Experimental Results

We compared the performance of our chromatic tree (Chromatic) and the variant of our chromatic tree that invokes CLEANUP only when the number of violations on a path exceeds six (Chromatic6) against several leading data structures that implement ordered dictionaries: the non-blocking skip-list (SkipList) of the Java Class Library, the non-blocking multiway search tree (SkipTree) of Spiegel and Reynolds [29], the lock-based relaxed-balance AVL tree with non-blocking searches (AVL-D) of Drachsler et al. [14], and the lock-based relaxed-balance AVL tree (AVL-B) of Bronson et al. [9]. Our comparison also includes an STM-based red-black tree optimized by Oracle engineers (RB-STM) [19], an STM-based skip-list (SkipListSTM), and the highly optimized Java red-black tree, java.util.TreeMap, with operations protected by a global lock (RBGlobal). The STM data structures are implemented using DeuceSTM 1.3.0, which is one of the fastest STM implementations that does not require modifications to the Java virtual machine. We used DeuceSTM's offline instrumentation ca-

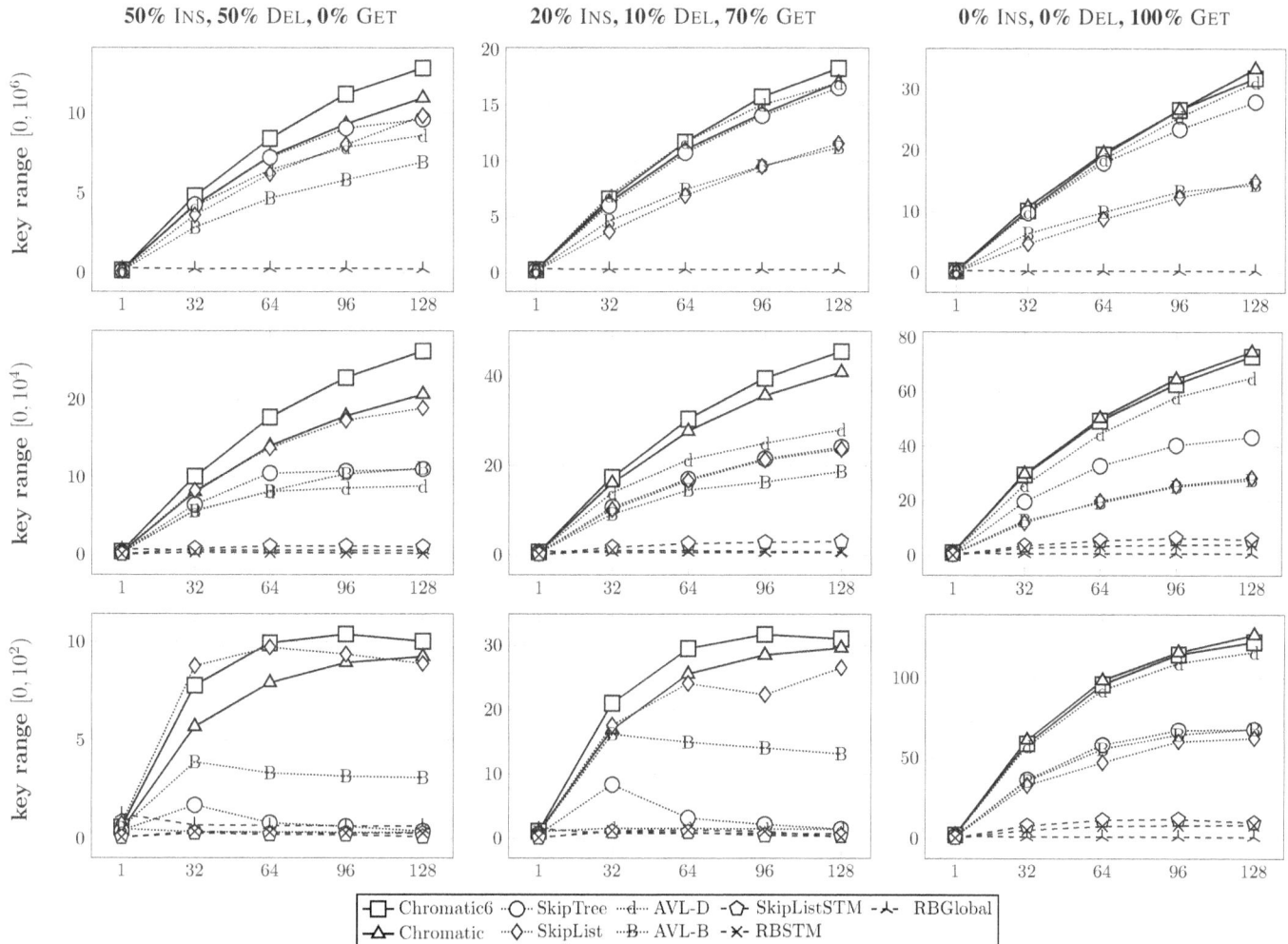

Figure 7. *Multithreaded* throughput (millions of operations/second) for 2-socket SPARC T2+ (128 hardware threads) on y-axis versus number of threads on x-axis.

pability to eliminate any STM instrumentation at running time that might skew our results. All of the implementations that we used were made publicly available by their respective authors. For a fair comparison between data structures, we made slight modifications to RBSTM and SkipListSTM to use generics, instead of hardcoding the type of keys as `int`, and to store values in addition to keys. Java code for Chromatic and Chromatic6 is available from http://www.cs.utoronto.ca/~tabrown.

We tested the data structures for three different operation mixes, 0i-0d, 20i-10d and 50i-50d, where xi-yd denotes $x\%$ INSERTs, $y\%$ DELETEs, and $(100 - x - y)\%$ GETs, to represent the cases when all of the operations are queries, when a moderate proportion of the operations are INSERTs and DELETEs, and when all of the operations are INSERTs and DELETEs. We used three key ranges, $[0, 10^2)$, $[0, 10^4)$ and $[0, 10^6)$, to test different contention levels. For example, for key range $[0, 10^2)$, data structures will be small, so updates are likely to affect overlapping parts of the data structure.

For each data structure, each operation mix, each key range, and each thread count in $\{1, 32, 64, 96, 128\}$, we ran five trials which each measured the total throughput (operations per second) of all threads for five seconds. Each trial began with an untimed prefilling phase, which continued until the data structure was within 5% of its expected size in the steady state. For operation mix 50i-50d, the expected size is half of the key range. This is because, eventually, each key in the key range has been inserted or deleted at least once, and the last operation on any key is equally likely to be an insertion (in which case it is in the data structure) or a deletion (in which case it is not in the data structure). Similarly, 20i-10d yields an expected size of two thirds of the key range since, eventually, each key has been inserted or deleted and the last operation on it is twice as likely to be an insertion as a deletion. For 0i-0d, we prefilled to half of the key range.

We used a Sun SPARC Enterprise T5240 with 32GB of RAM and two UltraSPARC T2+ processors, for a total of 16 1.2GHz cores supporting a total of 128 hardware threads. The Sun 64-bit JVM version 1.7.0_03 was run in server

339

mode, with 3GB minimum and maximum heap sizes. Different experiments run within a single instance of a Java virtual machine (JVM) are not statistically independent, so each batch of five trials was run in its own JVM instance. Prior to running each batch, a fixed set of three trials was run to cause the Java HotSpot compiler to optimize the running code. Garbage collection was manually triggered before each trial. The heap size of 3GB was small enough that garbage collection was performed regularly (approximately ten times) in each trial. We did not pin threads to cores, since this is unlikely to occur in practice.

Figure 7 shows our experimental results. Our algorithms are drawn with solid lines. Competing handcrafted implementations are drawn with dotted lines. Implementations with coarse-grained synchronization are drawn with dashed lines. Error bars are not drawn because they are mostly too small to see: The standard deviation is less than 2% of the mean for half of the data points, and less than 10% of the mean for 95% of the data points. The STM data structures are not included in the graphs for key range $[0, 10^6)$, because of the enormous length of time needed just to perform prefilling (more than 120 seconds per five second trial).

Chromatic6 nearly always outperforms Chromatic. The only exception is for an all query workload, where Chromatic performs slightly better. Chromatic6 is prefilled with the Chromatic6 insertion and deletion algorithms, so it has a slightly larger average leaf depth than Chromatic; this accounts for the performance difference. In every graph, Chromatic6 rivals or outperforms the other data structures, even the highly optimized implementations of SkipList and SkipTree which were crafted with the help of Doug Lea and the Java Community Process JSR-166 Expert Group. Under high contention (key range $[0, 10^2)$), Chromatic6 outperforms every competing data structure except for SkipList in case 50i-50d and AVL-D in case 0i-0d. In the former case, SkipList approaches the performance of Chromatic6 when there are many INSERTs and DELETEs, due to the simplicity of its updates. In the latter case, the non-blocking searches of AVL-D allow it to perform nearly as well as Chromatic6; this is also evident for the other two key ranges. SkipTree, AVL-D and AVL-B all experience negative scaling beyond 32 threads when there are updates. For SkipTree, this is because its nodes contain many child pointers, and processes modify a node by replacing it (severely limiting concurrency when the tree is small). For AVL-D and AVL-B, this is likely because processes waste time waiting for locks to be released when they perform updates. Under moderate contention (key range $[0, 10^4)$), in cases 50i-50d and 20i-10d, Chromatic6 significantly outperforms the other data structures. Under low contention, the advantages of a non-blocking approach are less pronounced, but Chromatic6 is still at the top of each graph (likely because of low overhead and searches that ignore updates).

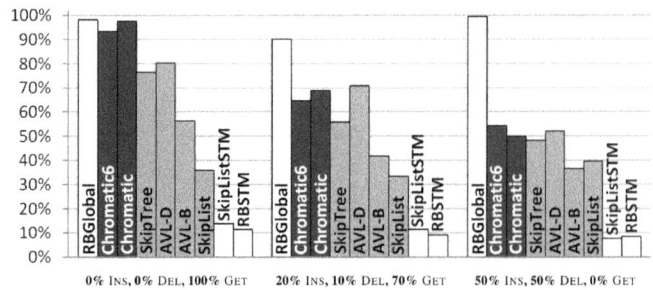

Figure 8. *Single threaded* throughput of the data structures relative to Java's sequential RBT for key range $[0, 10^6)$.

Figure 8 compares the single-threaded performance of the data structures, relative to the performance of the sequential RBT, `java.util.TreeMap`. This demonstrates that the overhead introduced by our technique is relatively small.

Although balanced BSTs are designed to give performance guarantees for worst-case sequences of operations, the experiments are performed using random sequences. For such sequences, BSTs without rebalancing operations are balanced with high probability and, hence, will have better performance because of their lower overhead. Better experiments are needed to evaluate balanced BSTs.

7. Conclusion

In this work, we presented a template that can be used to obtain non-blocking implementations of any data structure based on a down-tree, and demonstrated its use by implementing a non-blocking chromatic tree. To the authors' knowledge, this is the first provably correct, non-blocking balanced BST with fine-grained synchronization. Proving the correctness of a direct implementation of a chromatic tree from hardware primitives would have been completely intractable. By developing our template abstraction and our chromatic tree in tandem, we were able to avoid introducing any extra overhead, so our chromatic tree is very efficient.

Given a copy of [23], and this paper, a first year undergraduate student produced our Java implementation of a relaxed-balance AVL tree in less than a week. Its performance was slightly lower than that of Chromatic. After allowing more violations on a path before rebalancing, its performance was indistinguishable from that of Chromatic6.

We hope that this work sparks interest in developing more relaxed-balance sequential versions of data structures, since it is now easy to obtain efficient concurrent implementations of them using our template.

Acknowledgements

This work was supported by NSERC. We thank Oracle for providing the machine used for our experiments.

References

[1] Y. Afek, H. Kaplan, B. Korenfeld, A. Morrison, and R. Tarjan. CBTree: A practical concurrent self-adjusting search tree. In

Proc. 26th International Symposium on Distributed Computing, volume 7611 of *LNCS*, pages 1–15, 2012.

[2] Z. Aghazadeh, W. Golab, and P. Woelfel. Brief announcement: Resettable objects and efficient memory reclamation for concurrent algorithms. In *Proc. 32nd ACM Symposium on Principles of Distributed Computing*, pages 322–324, 2013.

[3] J. H. Anderson and M. Moir. Universal constructions for multi-object operations. In *Proc. 14th ACM Symposium on Principles of Distributed Computing*, pages 184–193, 1995.

[4] G. Barnes. A method for implementing lock-free data structures. In *Proc. 5th ACM Symposium on Parallel Algorithms and Architectures*, pages 261–270, 1993.

[5] R. Bayer. Symmetric binary B-trees: Data structure and maintenance algorithms. *Acta Informatica*, 1(4):290–306, 1972.

[6] L. Bougé, J. Gabarró, X. Messeguer, and N. Schabanel. Height-relaxed AVL rebalancing: A unified, fine-grained approach to concurrent dictionaries. Technical Report LSI-98-12-R, Universitat Politècnica de Catalunya, 1998. Available from http://www.lsi.upc.edu/dept/techreps/llistat_detallat.php?id=307.

[7] J. Boyar, R. Fagerberg, and K. S. Larsen. Amortization results for chromatic search trees, with an application to priority queues. *J. Comput. Syst. Sci.*, 55(3):504–521, Dec. 1997.

[8] A. Braginsky and E. Petrank. A lock-free B+tree. In *Proc. 24th ACM Symposium on Parallelism in Algorithms and Architectures*, pages 58–67, 2012.

[9] N. G. Bronson, J. Casper, H. Chafi, and K. Olukotun. A practical concurrent binary search tree. In *Proc. 15th ACM Symposium on Principles and Practice of Parallel Programming*, pages 257–268, 2010.

[10] T. Brown, F. Ellen, and E. Ruppert. Pragmatic primitives for non-blocking data structures. In *Proc. 32nd ACM Symposium on Principles of Distributed Computing*, 2013. Full version available from http://www.cs.utoronto.ca/~tabrown.

[11] T. Brown and J. Helga. Non-blocking k-ary search trees. In *Proc. 15th International Conf. on Principles of Distributed Systems*, volume 7109 of *LNCS*, pages 207–221, 2011.

[12] T. Crain, V. Gramoli, and M. Raynal. A speculation-friendly binary search tree. In *Proc. 17th ACM Symp. on Principles and Practice of Parallel Programming*, pages 161–170, 2012.

[13] T. Crain, V. Gramoli, and M. Raynal. A contention-friendly binary search tree. In *Euro-Par*, pages 229–240, 2013.

[14] D. Drachsler, M. Vechev, and E. Yahav. Practical concurrent binary search trees via logical ordering. In these proceedings, 2014.

[15] F. Ellen, P. Fatourou, E. Ruppert, and F. van Breugel. Non-blocking binary search trees. In *Proc. 29th ACM Symposium on Principles of Distributed Computing*, pages 131–140, 2010. Full version available as Technical Report CSE-2010-04, York University.

[16] K. Fraser and T. Harris. Concurrent programming without locks. *ACM Trans. on Computer Systems*, 25(2):5, 2007.

[17] K. A. Fraser. *Practical lock-freedom*. PhD thesis, University of Cambridge, 2003.

[18] L. J. Guibas and R. Sedgewick. A dichromatic framework for balanced trees. In *Proc. 19th IEEE Symposium on Foundations of Computer Science*, pages 8–21, 1978.

[19] M. Herlihy, V. Luchangco, M. Moir, and W. N. Scherer, III. Software transactional memory for dynamic-sized data structures. In *Proc. 22nd ACM Symposium on Principles of Distributed Computing*, pages 92–101, 2003.

[20] S. V. Howley and J. Jones. A non-blocking internal binary search tree. In *Proc. 24th ACM Symposium on Parallelism in Algorithms and Architectures*, pages 161–171, 2012.

[21] H. Kung and P. L. Lehman. Concurrent manipulation of binary search trees. *ACM Transactions on Database Systems*, 5(3):354–382, 1980.

[22] K. S. Larsen. Amortized constant relaxed rebalancing using standard rotations. *Acta Informatica*, 35(10):859–874, 1998.

[23] K. S. Larsen. AVL trees with relaxed balance. *J. Comput. Syst. Sci.*, 61(3):508–522, Dec. 2000.

[24] K. S. Larsen, T. Ottmann, and E. Soisalon-Soininen. Relaxed balance for search trees with local rebalancing. *Acta Informatica*, 37(10):743–763, 2001.

[25] A. Natarajan and N. Mittal. Fast concurrent lock-free binary search trees. In these proceedings, 2014.

[26] A. Natarajan, L. Savoie, and N. Mittal. Concurrent wait-free red black trees. In *Proc. 15th International Symposium on Stabilization, Safety and Security of Distributed Systems*, volume 8255 of *LNCS*, pages 45–60, 2013.

[27] O. Nurmi and E. Soisalon-Soininen. Chromatic binary search trees: A structure for concurrent rebalancing. *Acta Informatica*, 33(6):547–557, 1996.

[28] N. Shafiei. Non-blocking Patricia tries with replace operations. In *Proc. 33rd International Conference on Distributed Computing Systems*, pages 216–225, 2013.

[29] M. Spiegel and P. F. Reynolds, Jr. Lock-free multiway search trees. In *Proc. 39th International Conference on Parallel Processing*, pages 604–613, 2010.

[30] J.-J. Tsay and H.-C. Li. Lock-free concurrent tree structures for multiprocessor systems. In *Proc. International Conference on Parallel and Distributed Systems*, pages 544–549, 1994.

[31] J. Turek, D. Shasha, and S. Prakash. Locking without blocking: Making lock based concurrent data structure algorithms nonblocking. In *Proc. 11th ACM Symposium on Principles of Database Systems*, pages 212–222, 1992.

[32] J. D. Valois. Lock-free linked lists using compare-and-swap. In *Proc. 14th ACM Symposium on Principles of Distributed Computing*, pages 214–222, 1995.

Practical Concurrent Binary Search Trees
via Logical Ordering

Dana Drachsler

Technion

ddana@cs.technion.ac.il

Martin Vechev

ETH Zurich

martin.vechev@inf.ethz.ch

Eran Yahav

Technion

yahave@cs.technion.ac.il

Abstract

We present practical, concurrent binary search tree (BST) algorithms that explicitly maintain *logical ordering* information in the data structure, permitting clean separation from its physical tree layout. We capture logical ordering using intervals, with the property that an item belongs to the tree if and only if the item is an endpoint of some interval. We are thus able to construct efficient, synchronization-free and intuitive lookup operations.

We present (i) a concurrent non-balanced BST with a lock-free lookup, and (ii) a concurrent AVL tree with a lock-free lookup that requires no synchronization with any mutating operations, including balancing operations. Our algorithms apply on-time deletion; that is, every request for removal of a node, results in its immediate removal from the tree. This new feature did not exist in previous concurrent internal tree algorithms.

We implemented our concurrent BST algorithms and evaluated them against several state-of-the-art concurrent tree algorithms. Our experimental results show that our algorithms with lock-free contains and on-time deletion are practical and often comparable to the state-of-the-art.

Categories and Subject Descriptors D.1.3 [*Concurrent Programming*]; D.3.3 [*Programming Languages*]: Language Constructs and Features - Concurrent programming structures; E.1 [*Data Structures*]: Trees

Keywords Concurrency, Search Trees

1. Introduction

Concurrent data structures are a fundamental building block for leveraging modern multi-core processors. Recent years have seen rising interest in scalable and efficient concurrent algorithms for data structures. In this paper, we focus on concurrent algorithms for binary search trees (BST), important in a variety of applications. A BST data structure supports the operations `insert`, `remove`, and `contains` with their standard meaning. Any correct BST algorithm must preserve two invariants: (i) the BST does not contain duplicate keys, and (ii) the tree follows the standard BST structural layout.

A key challenge in designing correct and efficient concurrent BST algorithms is to devise a scalable design for the *lookup* operation. This operation is invoked by all three operations to check whether a given element exists in the tree. Because the lookup operation can execute concurrently with other mutating operations, the physical location of an element in the tree might change while the lookup operation is executing. A particularly tricky case arises when the lookup operation *does not find* the element it is looking for. The algorithm then needs to decide whether to continue searching for the element elsewhere in the tree, or to conclude that it is not present. It can be difficult to decide which of these decisions is correct.

To illustrate the difficulty of correctly performing lookups in a BST while the tree is being mutated by concurrent operations, consider an interleaving of two concurrent operations. Figure 1(a) shows an initial tree with two threads operating on it. First, T1 performs a `contains(7)` operation on the tree, reaches node 9 (one step away from reaching the target node 7), and is suspended. The resulting state is shown in Figure 1(b). Then, T2 performs the entire `remove(3)` operation, which results in swapping nodes 3 and 7, and removing node 3 from the tree. The resulting tree is shown in Figure 1(c). Finally, the suspended thread T1 is resumed and fails to find node 7, even though it is in the tree.

To address this challenge, some concurrent trees maintain all values in the leaves [7, 9, 11, 15], thus never changing the location of an element. Others provide no support for remove operations [4], and yet others use some form of notification such as version numbers [8] or node marking [10, 13] to detect concurrent updates during lookup. While these approaches differ on the exact details of how they synchronize, they all base their synchronization on the *tree layout*.

PPoPP '14, February 15–19, 2014, Orlando, Florida, USA.
Copyright is held by the owner/author(s). Publication rights licensed to ACM.
ACM 978-1-4503-2656-8/14/02... $15.00.
http://dx.doi.org/10.1145/2555243.2555269

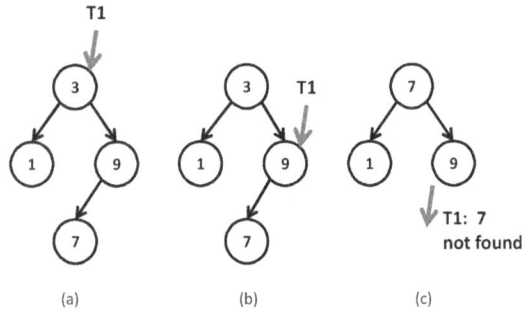

Figure 1: Concurrent lookup with mutating operations for two threads, T1: contains(7) ‖ T2: remove(3). The initial tree is shown in (a); the tree after T1 reaches node 9 and before 3 is removed in (b); and the tree after 3 is removed in (c) (3 is swapped with 7 and removed). Here, T1 fails to find 7 even though it is in the tree at the time T1 returns false.

In this paper, we present a fundamentally different approach to constructing concurrent BST algorithms, one which leads to a simple and intuitive lookup operation that also enjoys desirable progress guarantees (i.e., lock-freedom). Below, we informally explain the idea by means of example. We provide an elaborate description of the algorithms in Section 4.

Key Idea: Leveraging Logical Ordering   At the specification level, a binary search tree implements a set of elements such that a total order can be established between them. For instance, consider again the tree of Figure 1(a). This BST represents the set of integers $\{1, 3, 7, 9\}$, where elements can be ordered by the value of their keys: $1 < 3 < 7 < 9$. To avoid edge cases, we always add designated sentinel keys $-\infty$ and ∞ to any set, which for our example yields the set $\{-\infty, 1, 3, 7, 9, \infty\}$.

The *logical ordering* of elements can be *maintained explicitly* in the data structure, and this important property enables us to find the *successor* and *predecessor* of a node without traversing pointers along the tree layout. Because logical ordering is stable under layout manipulations (such as balancing), lookup operations can proceed concurrently with operations that mutate the layout.

Explicitly maintaining ordering information represents a different space-time-synchronization tradeoff than in other concurrent BSTs. In particular, we trade off the time for performing a lookup through traversal of layout pointers with the space required to explicitly maintain the ordering information (three pointers per node) and the time required to update the ordering information when it changes. This introduces some overhead for each individual operation, but allows lookup operations to operate without synchronization over the tree layout.

Lookups using Ordering   To see how ordering is leveraged, consider again our running example and the tree of Figure 1(c). This tree represents the set of elements $\{-\infty, 1, 7, 9, \infty\}$. Previously, contains was looking for key 7, which it missed due to concurrent interference caused by the remove(3) operation. However, when the tree is equipped with ordering, after contains reaches node 9 and learns that its left child is null, it looks up the *predecessor* of 9, finding that $7 < 9$ is in the ordered set, meaning that 7 is in the tree, and thus contains(7) correctly returns true.

It is natural to view the strict total order relation $<$ maintained by our algorithm as the pairs of elements in its transitive reduction. For our example, these are the pairs: $(-\infty, 1), (1, 7), (7, 9), (9, \infty)$. These pairs can be viewed as intervals where a key belongs to the set if it is an endpoint of some interval and does not belong to the set otherwise. Our algorithm can be viewed as explicitly maintaining these intervals and using them to answer lookup queries and to synchronize operations. That is, in our trees, each node keeps its successor endpoint and its predecessor endpoint (which are unique); the synchronization may also be performed on these endpoints as opposed to only on the tree layout as in previous algorithms.

Note that the logical ordering is independent of the physical tree layout, and a number of layouts represent the same ordered set. The conceptual separation between ordering of elements and the physical tree layout enables us to design concurrent algorithms where the balancing of the tree (which rearranges the physical layout) is independent of, and requires no synchronization with, the lookup queries, which use ordering information.

Note that in this example, remove changed the physical layout of the tree, yet this operation need not be synchronized with the lookup query issued by contains.

Main Contributions   The contributions of this paper are:

- Novel concurrent BST algorithms (both non-balanced and AVL), which leverage the idea of logical key ordering to obtain simple, intuitive, and robust lookup operations that also enjoy strong progress guarantees. By maintaining logical ordering we can cleanly separate operations that alter the tree layout (e.g., balancing) from those that require information about the presence of elements (e.g., lookup). Thus, balancing operations and lookup queries can proceed without synchronization.

- An implementation and evaluation of our algorithms – a non-balanced tree and an AVL tree. We evaluated our implementation with various loads and compared it to several state-of-the-art BSTs from the literature. The experimental results indicate that our trees (providing lock-free lookups) are practical and often comparable to state-of-the-art algorithms.

2. Background

A binary search tree (BST) is a data structure that consists of nodes, each associated with a unique *key* and having a parent, a *left* child and a *right* child. For every node, nodes in its left sub-tree have keys smaller than the node's key, and nodes in its right sub-tree have keys greater than the node's key. A BST supports three operations: `insert(k)`, `remove(k)` and `contains(k)`.

The `insert(k)` operation inserts k to the tree if k is not present. If k was inserted, the insertion is considered *successful*. In a successful insertion, the correct parent is located and the new node is connected to it as a child.

The `remove(k)` operation removes k from the tree if k is present. If k was removed, the removal is considered *successful*. Denote the node with key k by N_k. A successful removal has three possible scenarios:

- N_k is a leaf - remove it by updating N_k's parent to point to `null`.
- N_k has a single child - remove it by updating N_k's parent to point to N_k's child.
- N_k has two children - the node is removed in three steps: (i) locate N_k's successor node, denote it by N_s, (ii) remove N_s from its location, and (iii) update N_s to appear in N_k's location.

N_k's *successor*, N_s, is the left-most child of its right sub-tree, and it is guaranteed to have at most one child.

Removing a Node with Two Children (2C-removal) Because removing a node with two children involves N_k's successor, this type of removal often updates nodes which *are not adjacent, and many pointers may be traversed until N_s is reached*. Common implementations thus attempt to avoid 2C-removal. Some implementations provide external trees [7, 9, 11, 15] where the values are kept only at the leaves, and inner nodes serve only as routing nodes. Inner nodes cannot be requested (by the user) to be removed and thus 2C-removal never occurs. Other implementations do not support the remove operation [4]. Recent works cope with this challenge by not *physically* removing nodes in the case of 2C-removal [8, 10]. Instead, they mark these nodes as *logically* removed, and remove them only when these nodes have a single child. Avoiding physical 2C-removal can result in a large number of "zombie" nodes in a tree where a node has been logically deleted but cannot be removed. This has implications both for the space consumed by the tree, and for the extension of search paths. The authors of [13] never physically remove nodes that have no children. They apply 2C-removal by copying the successor's key to the removed node, and removing the successor if it has a child.

AVL Tree Balanced trees provide logarithmic worst-case time complexity. This guarantee becomes crucial as the tree grows or when the values for the operations are not picked uniformly. In balanced trees, the tree maintains a balancing invariant. In AVL trees [1] it holds that for each node the difference between the heights of its left sub-tree and its right sub-tree is less than two. This difference is often called the *balance factor*. Applying a mutating operation to the tree may result in breaking the invariant for multiple nodes. Upon a violation of the invariant, *rotation*s are applied. To detect the violation, and to decide which type of rotation is required, nodes save local information. Traditionally, nodes keep their balance factor. However, they can keep the heights of their left and right sub-trees instead. We use the latter approach since it allows for more concurrency.

Another balanced internal tree is the red-black tree [2]. Pfaff showed that in a sequential setting, there is no clear winner between the two trees [16]. However, AVL trees typically have shorter paths than red-black trees.

Relaxed Balanced Tree Maintaining the AVL invariant in a concurrent setting induces severe bottlenecks. This is because during rotations, the sub-trees of the violated nodes must not be updated. Thus, it is beneficial to consider a *relaxed balanced tree*, where the rebalance operations are decoupled from the mutating operations and may be delayed. Bougé et al. [6] proved that a concurrent tree which applies the AVL rotations using the local information of the node and its children achieves a relaxed balanced tree, guaranteed to be strictly balanced when there are no ongoing mutating operations. This should be contrasted with approaches such as [10] that perform rotations in a separate thread and thus can only guarantee some form of "eventual balance."

We follow Bougé et al.'s method and achieve a relaxed balanced tree which is strictly balanced at a quiescent state.

3. Concurrent Trees with Logical Ordering

In this section, we present the principles underlying our concurrent tree algorithms. In Section 3.1, we explain how we explicitly maintain logical ordering information in the BST. In Section 3.2, we show how logical ordering enables lock-free lookup queries. In Section 3.3, we show how it enables on-time 2C-removal. Finally, in Section 3.4, we provide the highlights of our synchronization method.

We deliberately present the operations without describing how they are synchronized. We provide synchronization details in Section 3.4 and in Section 4. To simplify presentation, we present our tree as implementing a set. However, our actual implementation and evaluation use a more general implementation of a map.

3.1 Adding Explicit Predecessors and Successors

We augment the tree to support *predecessor* and *successor* queries in $O(1)$. To this end, we extend each node with predecessor and successor pointers, denoted `pred` and `succ`. These pointers allow us to operate separately on the *tree layout* and the *tree ordering*, which is captured by the predecessor and successor relations. Roughly speaking, we implement the set semantics using the ordering, and achieve the time complexity using the tree layout.

The challenges introduced by the `remove` operation are resolved to local mutations with respect to the tree ordering, without a need to consult the tree layout. Specifically, the search for the successor in the case of 2C-removal can now be resolved by following a single pointer.

Maintaining the Predecessor and Successor   We now describe how `pred` and `succ` are maintained. In the following, we use N_k to denote a node with key k.

Insert   In a BST, a new node, N, is inserted as a child of either its predecessor, p, or its successor, s. Thus, N can access and set p and s using its parent's `pred` and `succ` pointers. Then, p's `succ` and s's `pred` are updated to point to N. For example, consider the tree in Figure 2(a). On a call to `insert(7)`, the parent will be N_9, which is N_7's successor. N_7's predecessor is N_9's old predecessor, N_3. During the insert, N_3's `succ` and N_9's `pred` are updated to point to N_7.

Remove   Upon a removal of a node N, N's predecessor and N's successor are set to point to each other. This update occurs regardless of how many children N has. N's predecessor and successor are accessed via N's `pred` and `succ`. This is illustrated by the tree in Figure 2(b). Upon applying `remove(3)`, the tree is updated to the tree of Figure 2(c). The removal of N_3 from the tree ordering is done by updating N_1's `succ` (i.e., N_3's predecessor) to point to N_7 (i.e., N_3's successor), and by updating N_7's `pred` to point to N_1.

3.2   Lock-Free Lookup Queries using Logical Ordering

In a sequential BST, whether a given value is present in the tree can be determined simply by following the child pointers until reaching a node with this value, or until reaching the end of a path in the tree. As shown in Section 1, in a concurrent setting, such traversal may lead to incorrect results due to concurrent mutations of the tree. To avoid this problem, we rely on the following observation: to determine whether k is present in the tree, it is enough to have two keys, k_1, k_2, such that (i) k_1 and k_2 are in the tree, (ii) for every $\tilde{k} \in (k_1, k_2)$, $\tilde{k}$ is not in the tree, and (iii) $k \in [k_1, k_2]$.

Using the logical ordering and the above observation, we can determine whether a key k is in the tree as follows:
- If k was found during traversal, then k is in the tree.
- If k was not found, then we must find two keys, k_1 and k_2, that are in the tree and such that $k \in (k_1, k_2)$. The search for k terminates when it reaches a node of value $\tilde{k}$ that lay at the end of the scanned path. If there are no concurrent updates, $\tilde{k}$ is either k's predecessor or successor; thus, one of the following holds: (i) $k \in (\text{pred}(\tilde{k}), \tilde{k})$, or (ii) $k \in (\tilde{k}, \text{succ}(\tilde{k}))$. In the presence of concurrent updates, k_1 and k_2 must be found, which will be done via the `pred` and `succ` pointers.

To illustrate this, consider the tree of Figure 2(a). Suppose that thread T is executing `contains(7)`, and has reached the end of the path, in which N_9 is the last node. Then, T reads N_9's `pred` and discovers that N_3 is N_9's predecessor. Thus, T infers that 7 does not appear in the tree.

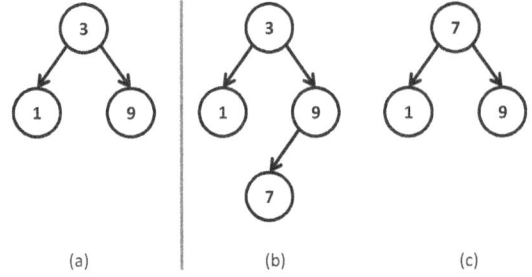

Figure 2: Lookup queries using intervals.

In contrast, suppose that T is executing `contains(7)` on the tree of Figure 2(b), and that T was suspended when it reached N_9. Then, another thread, T', applies `remove(3)`, which results in the tree that appears in Figure 2(c). Next, T resumes and discovers it has reached a leaf. Then, T checks N_9's `pred`, discovers N_7, and infers that 7 is in the tree. Note that T is not allowed to infer that 7 is not in the tree because 7 was present in the tree throughout T's traversal.

3.3   Removal using Logical Ordering

In a classic BST, a `remove` operation might have to scan an unbounded number of nodes to find the removed node's successor. This is because the search for the successor is done by searching for the left-most node in the removed node's right sub-tree. The height of the sub-tree is not bounded; thus, the search may scan an unbounded number of nodes. In concurrent algorithms, this means either blocking for a longer period or risking possible exposure to more concurrent updates. The latter might result in failure to find the key, even though it is present, and thus the search will incorrectly return a false result. In contrast, having the `succ` pointers allows the `remove` to find the successor using a single read.

3.4   Synchronization over the Logical Ordering

Our synchronization is based on locks, where each node can be locked in two separate layouts:
- The tree ordering layout
- The tree physical layout

Each update operation is applied in four steps:
1. Acquire ordering layout locks.
2. Acquire physical layout locks.
3. Update the ordering layout and release ordering locks.
4. Update the physical layout and release physical locks.

Locking the node in the tree's physical layout prevents concurrent updates to the node's physical layout information, that is, the node's children, parent and balance information. The synchronization over the physical layout is similar to previous approaches; see Section 4 for details.

Locking the node in the tree ordering layout prevents concurrent updates to the *intervals*. As described in Section 1, we capture the logical ordering via a set of intervals: $\{(p, s) \mid N_p, N_s \in tree \land \forall k \in (p, s), N_k \notin tree\}$. With each interval (p, s) we associate a lock. The intervals can be split, upon insertion, or merged, upon removal. Upon split-

```
class Node<K> {
    final K key;
    volatile boolean mark;
    volatile Node<K> left, right;
    volatile Node<K> parent;
    volatile int leftHeight, rightHeight;
    Lock treeLock;
    volatile Node<K> succ, pred;
    Lock succLock;
}
```

Figure 3: Fields of the node data structure.

ting an interval (p, s) to (p, k) and (k, s), we acquire (p, s)'s lock. Upon merging two intervals $(p, k), (k, s)$ to (p, s), we acquire (p, k)'s and (k, s)'s locks.

Technically, the intervals are captured via the `pred` and `succ` pointers, and (p, s)'s lock is kept in N_p. This lock can be reached from N_s by accessing N_p (via N_s's `pred`).

An update of (p, s) to $(p, k), (k, s)$ is applied as follows:
1. (p, s)'s lock is acquired.
2. N_k is created with `pred` set to N_p and `succ` set to N_s.
3. N_p's `succ` and N_s's `pred` are updated to N_k.

Note that even though (p, s)'s lock is kept in N_p, it prevents concurrent updates to N_s's `pred` as well.

For example, consider the tree in Figure 2(a). On a call to `insert(7)`, the interval $(3, 9)$ is locked (via N_3), after which, `pred` and `succ` are updated as described in Section 3.1. This results in the intervals $(3, 7), (7, 9)$.

An update of $(p, k), (k, s)$ to (p, s) is applied as follows:
1. (p, k)'s and (k, s)'s locks are acquired.
2. N_k is marked as removed (using a designated field). This also serves as an indication that (k, s) is removed.
3. N_p's `succ` is set to N_s and N_s's `pred` is set to N_p.

To illustrate this, consider the tree in Figure 2(b). Upon applying `remove(3)`, the intervals $(1, 3), (3, 7)$ are locked (via N_1 and N_3). Then, N_3 is marked as removed, which indicates that $(3, 7)$ is also removed. Next, `pred` and `succ` are updated as described in Section 3.1, which results in the interval $(1, 7)$. As an aside, we mention that only after these updates is the tree updated to the tree of Figure 2(c).

4. The Algorithm

In this section, we present the details of our implementation. The code is available at github.com/logicalordering/trees. We first present the basic data structure, and then describe the operations.

4.1 The Node Data Structure

Figure 3 shows the fields of a `Node` data structure in our tree. The `key` field is immutable; all other fields are mutable. Our node contains a `mark` field used to indicate whether the node was removed from the tree; this field is initially set to `false`. It maintains the heights of its sub-trees in `leftHeight` and `rightHeight` such that the AVL invariant can be checked and maintained. In addition to the fields of a standard BST node, it contains pointers to the predecessor, `pred`, and successor, `succ`, of the node. It also contains two locks:

Algorithm 1: search(k)

1   node = root
2   **while** *true* **do**
3   currKey = node.key
4   **if** *currKey == k* **then return** *node*
5   child = currKey < k ? node.right : node.left
6   **if** *child == null* **then return** *node*
7   node = child
8   **end**

- A `treeLock`: protects the tree's physical layout fields, `left`, `right`, `parent`, `leftHeight` and `rightHeight`.
- A `succLock`: protects the logical ordering layout fields, (i) the `succ` field, and (ii) the `pred` field of *the node pointed by* `succ`.

That is, for every node N, N's `succLock` protects the interval $(N, \text{succ}(N))$.

The Initial Tree The tree is initialized with two nodes, $N_{-\infty}$ and N_∞, with keys $-\infty$ and ∞, which are each other's predecessor and successor. The root is N_∞, and $N_{-\infty}$ is reachable only via the logical ordering layout (via the `pred` pointer).

4.2 The Search(k) and Contains(k) Operations

The `search` operation, shown in Algorithm 1, is the basic lookup operation that all other operations use. The `search` traverses once down the tree until the desired key is found or the end of the path is reached. It is oblivious to location updates caused by removals or rotations; thus, it may stray from its initial path. The `search` operation does not acquire any locks, and does not restart. Part of the beauty of our approach is the simplicity of this operation and the `contains` operation that follows.

The `contains` operation, which appears in Algorithm 2, begins by calling `search(k)`. If the returned node has key k, then `contains` returns `true` if the node's `mark` field is `false`, and `false` otherwise (as a marked node is logically removed). If the node has a key different than k, then two nodes are required to determine whether k is in the tree, N_{k_1} and N_{k_2}, that hold $k \in (k_1, k_2]$ and $\text{succ}(N_{k_1}) = N_{k_2}$. If $k_2 = k$ (i.e., k was found), the decision is made as described before. If $k_2 > k$, it can be concluded that k is not in the tree (actually it can be concluded that at *some* moment after the `contains` operation has started, k was not in the tree; see Section 5 for further details). To obtain N_{k_1} and N_{k_2}, the `contains` operation uses the node returned by `search`. It then traverses using the `pred` field until reaching the first node whose key is not greater than k. Once discovered, it scans nodes using the `succ` field, until reaching a node with a key equal to or greater than k. The last iteration of this loop reads N_{k_1}'s `succ` field and saves N_{k_2} as required. Note that `contains` does not acquire any locks, and does not restart. Also note that after calling `search`, it only traverses the `pred` and `succ` fields.

347

Algorithm 2: contains(k)

1 node = search(k)
2 **while** *node.key > k* **do** node = node.pred
3 **while** *node.key < k* **do** node = node.succ
4 **return** *(node.key == k && !(node.mark))*

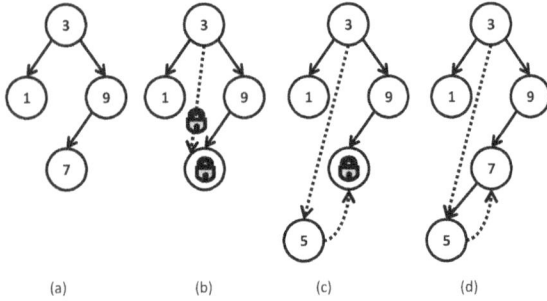

(a)   (b)   (c)   (d)

Figure 4: An example of the `insert(5)` operation. The initial tree is shown in (a); in (b) the tree after acquiring the `succLock` of 3 (5's predecessor), and after choosing and acquiring the `treeLock` of the parent, 7; the tree after updating the logical ordering layout in (c); and the tree after updating the tree's physical layout in (d).

4.3 The Insert(k) Operation

The `insert` operation, shown in Algorithm 3, begins by calling `search(k)` and then operates on the returned *node*. Provided that no changes were applied to the tree from the beginning of the operation, *node* is one of the following: (i) A node with key k, (ii) k's predecessor in the tree, or (iii) k's successor in the tree. At this point k's predecessor is stored in p, and there is an attempt to lock p's `succLock`. After locking, it needs to be checked that $k \in (p$'s key,$\text{succ}(p)$'s key$]$ and that the interval is not marked as removed. The latter is checked by confirming that p's `mark` field is `false`. If the interval is not removed, then it is guaranteed also that both p and $\text{succ}(p)$ are not logically removed: p is not removed, because it shares the same `mark` field with the interval, and $\text{succ}(p)$ is not removed, because at the end of every operation, intervals that were not removed do not include removed nodes as edge points.

If the validation succeeds, the insert takes place; otherwise, it restarts. If $\text{succ}(p)$'s key is greater than k, then this is a successful insertion, and k is inserted to the tree. Otherwise, $\text{succ}(p)$'s key is equal to k, and this is an unsuccessful insertion, in which case the tree remains unchanged.

A successful insertion begins with creating the new node with key k. Then, the parent is determined and locked via the `chooseParent` operation. Then, the update is applied, first by updating the logical ordering (lines 13–17) and then by updating the tree's physical layout (line 18). After that, balancing is applied, if needed. An example of the `insert` operation appears in Figure 4.

Algorithm 3: Insert(k)

1 **while** *true* **do**
2   node = search(k)
3   p = node.key > k ? node.pred : node
4   lock(p.succLock)
5   s = p.succ
6   **if** $k \in (p.key,s.key]$ && *!p.mark* **then**
7   **if** *s.key == k* **then**   // Unsuccessful insert
8   unlock(p.succLock)
9   **return** *false*
10   **end**
11   newNode = new Node(k) // Successful insert
12   parent = chooseParent(p, s, node)
13   newNode.succ = s
14   newNode.pred = p
15   s.pred = newNode
16   p.succ = newNode
17   unlock(p.succLock)
18   insertToTree(parent, newNode)
19   **return** *true*
20   **end**
21   unlock(p.succLock) // Validation failed, restart
22 **end**

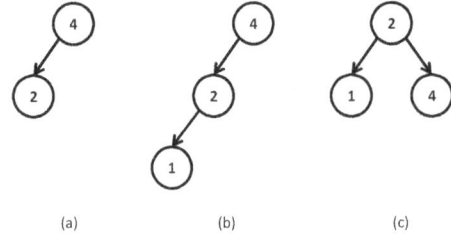

(a)   (b)   (c)

Figure 5: Choosing the correct parent for two concurrent threads, `T1: insert(1)` ∥ `T2: insert(3)`. The initial tree is shown in (a); the tree after T1 inserts 1 and T2 observes that 2 should be 3's parent in (b); the tree after rotation and T2's discovery that 4 should be the parent in (c).

Choosing the Correct Parent Whereas in a sequential BST, the node that was returned from `search` is the parent, in a concurrent AVL tree this is not necessarily the case. Consider the example of Figure 5, where two threads, T_1 and T_2, execute concurrently `insert(1)` and `insert(3)` to the tree of Figure 5(a). Both threads acquire the required `succLocks`: T_1 locks $-\infty$'s `succLock` and T_2 locks 2's `succLock`. Next, both threads observe that 2 should be their parent and T_2 is suspended. T_1 completes the insertion (Figure 5(b)), detects that 4 is not balanced and applies a rotation (Figure 5(c)). Then, T_2 resumes and observes that 2 cannot be the parent and 4 should be the new parent.

Thus, upon insertion, the correct parent must be chosen and concurrent rotations to it are prevented by acquiring its `treeLock`. This is done via the `chooseParent` operation that appears in Algorithm 4. In this operation, at every step,

---

Algorithm 4: chooseParent(p, s, firstCand)

1 candidate = firstCand == p || firstCand == s? firstCand : p
2 **while** *true* **do**
3   lock(candidate.treeLock)
4   **if** *candidate == p* **then**
5   **if** *candidate.right == null* **then return** *candidate*
6   unlock(candidate.treeLock)
7   candidate = s
8   **else**
9   **if** *candidate.left == null* **then return** *candidate*
10   unlock(candidate.treeLock)
11   candidate = p
12   **end**
13 **end**

Algorithm 5: insertToTree(parent, newNode)

1 newNode.parent = parent
2 **if** *parent.key < newNode.key* **then**
3   parent.right = newNode
4   parent.rightHeight = 1
5 **else**
6   parent.left = newNode
7   parent.leftHeight = 1
8 **end**
9 rebalance(lockParent(parent), parent)

Algorithm 6: lockParent(node)

1 **while** *true* **do**
2   p = node.parent
3   lock(p.treeLock)
4   **if** *node.parent == p* && *!p.mark* **then return** *p*
5   unlock(p.treeLock)
6 **end**

Algorithm 7: remove(k)

1 **while** *true* **do**
2   node = search(k)
3   p = node.key > k? node.pred : node
4   lock(p.succLock)
5   s = p.succ
6   **if** $k \in (p.key, s.key]$ && *!p.mark* **then**
7   **if** *s.key > k* **then**   // Unsuccessful remove
8   unlock(p.succLock)
9   **return** *false*
10   **end**
11   lock(s.succLock)   // Successful remove
12   hasTwoChildren = acquireTreeLocks(s)
13   s.mark = true
14   sSucc = s.succ
15   sSucc.pred = p
16   p.succ = sSucc
17   unlock(s.succLock)
18   unlock(p.succLock)
19   removeFromTree(s, hasTwoChildren)
20   **return** *true*
21   **end**
22   unlock(p.succLock) // Validation failed, restart
23 **end**

---

there is a node that is a candidate for the correct parent. Then, its `treeLock` is acquired and if it is validated as the correct parent, the operation returns it. The candidates for the correct parent are the new node's predecessor and successor. To validate that a candidate is the correct parent, it needs to be checked that the appropriate child pointer is empty. If the candidate is the predecessor, the right child should be empty, and if it is the successor, the left child should be empty. If the required child pointer is not empty, then the lock is released, and the other candidate is checked. Typically, the first candidate is the node that was returned from the `search` operation. However, concurrent updates might also occur before the `succLock` is acquired. Then, this node is no longer the predecessor or successor. In this case, we pick (arbitrarily) the predecessor to be the first candidate.

Updating the Physical Layout The physical update to the tree, which appears in Algorithm 5, connects the chosen parent to the new node and sets the height of this sub-tree to one. Afterwards, the `rebalance` operation is invoked, to update the heights of the parent's ancestors, and to apply rotations if necessary. This operation requires the parent and its parent to be locked, and thus the `lockParent` is called.

The `lockParent` operation, shown in Algorithm 6, receives a locked node and locks the node pointed by its `parent` field. If after acquiring the lock, this node is the correct parent and it is not marked as removed, it is returned. Otherwise, the operation restarts. Note that the node's parent may change while it is not locked. This is because in order

to change a node's parent, it is only necessary to acquire the `treeLocks` of its original and new parents, and there is no need to acquire the node's `treeLock`.

4.4 The Remove(k) Operation

The `remove` operation, shown in Algorithm 7, begins with a call to `search(k)` and then operates on the node that was returned. As in the `insert` operation, this operation tries to lock k's predecessor, denoted p, and applies the same validation. If validation succeeds, the operation checks whether this is a successful removal, in which case k will be removed, or an unsuccessful removal, in which case the operation will return without changing the tree.

A successful removal to a node, denoted n, is applied as follows. The first step is to acquire n's `succLock`, and then the required `treeLocks`. Next, the *mark* field is set to `true` to indicate that this node is logically removed from the tree. Then, the logical ordering is updated (lines 14–18) and finally, the tree's physical layout is updated (line 19). Here, the two `succLocks` are required to prevent concurrent updates to n's predecessor and successor.

Algorithm 8: acquireTreeLocks(n)

```
1  lock(n.treeLock)
2  lockParent(n)
3  if n.right == null || n.left == null then    // n is a leaf or
4      if n.right != null then           // has a single child
5          if !tryLock(n.right.treeLock) then restart
6      else if n.left != null then
7          if !tryLock(n.left.treeLock) then restart
8      end
9      return false
10 else                                 // n has two children
11     s = n.succ
12     if s.parent != n then
13         parent = s.parent
14         if !tryLock(parent.treeLock) then restart
15         if parent != s.parent || parent.mark then restart
16     end
17     if !tryLock(s.treeLock) then restart
18     if s.right != null then
19         if !tryLock(s.right.treeLock) then restart
20     end
21     return true
22 end
```

Algorithm 9: removeFromTree(n, hasTwoChildren)

```
1  if !hasTwoChildren then              // n is a leaf or has a
2      child = n.right == null ? n.left : n.right // single child
3      parent = n.parent
4      updateChild(parent, n, child)
5  else                                 // n has two children
6      s = n.succ
7      child = s.right
8      parent = s.parent
9      updateChild(parent, s, child)
10     copy n's left, right, leftHeight, rightHeight to s
11     n.left.parent = s
12     if n.right != null then          // n.right may be null if
13         n.right.parent = s           // s was the right child
14     end
15     updateChild(n.parent, n, s)
16     if parent == n then              // rebalance begins from s
17         parent = s
18     else             // rebalance begins from lower nodes
19         unlock(s.treeLock)
20     end
21     unlock(n.parent.treeLock)
22 end
23 unlock(n.treeLock)
24 rebalance(parent, child)
```

Algorithm 10: updateChild(parent, oldCh, newCh)

```
1  if parent.left == oldCh then
2      parent.left = newCh
3  else
4      parent.right = newCh
5  end
6  if newCh != null then newCh.parent = parent
```

Acquiring `treeLock`s The `acquireTreeLocks` operation, which appears in Algorithm 8, acquires all the required `treeLock`s for the removal. As discussed before, the removal of a node from the tree's physical layout is carried out differently when the node has two children than when it has less children. Thus, the operation's tasks are to determine how many children the node has, and acquire the set of required `treeLock`s accordingly. After the `treeLock`s are acquired, the number of children that the node has cannot change due to concurrent updates.

The `acquireTreeLocks` operation receives a node, n, acquires the required `treeLock`s, and returns `true` if n has two children and `false` otherwise. To guarantee the consistency of its response, it is enough to acquire n's `treeLock` (to block concurrent updates to its children by insertions, removals or rotations). However, the removal necessitates the acquisition of additional nodes' `treeLock`s. These nodes are located lower than n in the tree. As shall be described in Section 5, the locking order of the `treeLock`s is from the lower nodes in the tree to the higher ones. Thus, to acquire locks on these nodes, and to avoid deadlocks, the locking is not blocking, and if an attempt to lock fails, current locks are released and the operation restarts. This means that the number of children that n has may change. Thus, in each iteration, after acquiring n's `treeLock`, it is necessary to recheck the number of children n has.

The list of nodes whose `treeLock`s are acquired in this operation are:
- n and n's parent.
- If n has less than two children, n's child (if it exists).

- If n has two children, s, s's parent and s's child (if it exists), where s is n's successor.

Updating the Physical Layout The physical removal is done via the `removeFromTree` operation, which appears in Algorithm 9. If the node has at most one child, it is removed by connecting its parent to its child (which may be `null`). This update is applied via the `updateChild` operation (Algorithm 10).

A node with two children is removed by relocating n's successor, denoted s, to n's location in the tree. This is done in two steps: (i) s is detached from its current location, by updating its parent to point to its child (lines 7–9), (ii) s's location is updated to n's location, by setting s' tree fields (i.e., `parent`, `right`, `left`, `leftHeight`, `rightHeight`) to n's tree fields, and setting n's parent and children to point to s (lines 10–15).

During these updates, s is not reachable via the tree layout pointers. However, concurrent searches cannot miss its key, which remains reachable via the logical ordering.

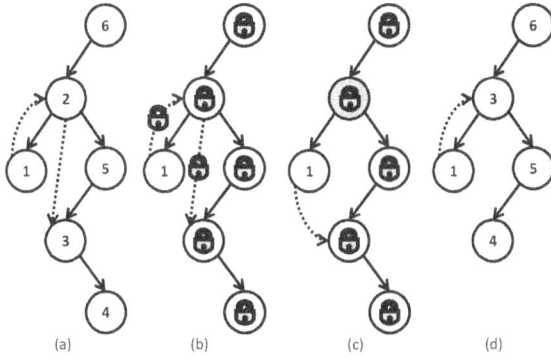

Figure 6: An example of the `remove(2)` operation. The initial tree is shown in (a); in (b) the tree after acquiring `succLocks` of 1 (2's predecessor) and 2, and the `treeLocks` of 2, 6 (2's parent), 3 (2's successor), 5 (3's parent) and 4 (3's child); in (c) the tree after marking 2 as removed and updating the logical ordering; in (d) the tree after relocating 3 to 2's location.

After n was removed, the heights are updated starting from the location of the removal. If n had less than two children, then the update begins from n's parent. Otherwise, it begins from s's original parent, or from s if n was its original parent. The heights are updated via the `rebalance` operation, which receives the nodes when they are locked.

An example of the `remove` operation appears in Figure 6.

4.5 Balancing the Tree

In AVL trees, after every update operation, a process of recovering the tree to a balanced state begins. The tree is balanced when all nodes are balanced. A node is balanced if the difference between the heights of its sub-trees is at most one. If it is imbalanced, the difference is two. Rotations are applied to rebalance imbalanced nodes. During the recovery process, multiple nodes may be examined, and any updates to these nodes or to their descendants must be blocked. Thus, a concurrent AVL may result in severe bottlenecks.

To avoid these bottlenecks, we apply a relaxed balancing. We use Bougé et al.'s algorithm [6] for relaxed balanced trees that guarantees the tree is balanced in a quiescent state. In their algorithm, nodes maintain two fields, denoted `leftHeight` and `rightHeight`, and an imbalanced node has a difference of *at least two* between the heights of its sub-trees. The decision of whether to apply a rotation, and if so, which type should be applied, is based on these fields. These heights may not reflect the current height of the left and right sub-trees. Thus, a rotation is not guaranteed to lead the node to a balanced state, nor is it guaranteed not to worsen the shape of the tree. However, as shown in [6], applying the AVL rotations on the basis of these heights leads to a strict AVL tree in a quiescent state.

Tree balance is validated from the node that was mutated by the `insert` or `remove` and up to the root. The root is a sentinel and thus it is not rotated. For each node that is

---

Algorithm 11: rotate(child, n, parent, leftRotation)

```
1  updateChild(parent, n, child)
2  n.parent = child
3  if leftRotation then
4      updateChild(n, child, child.left)
5      child.left = n
6      n.rightHeight = child.leftHeight
7      child.leftHeight = max(n.leftHeight, n.rightHeight) + 1
8  else Symmetric
```

---

scanned, its height is updated before checking whether it is balanced. If the traversal approached the node from the left child, then its `leftHeight` is updated, and otherwise its `rightHeight` is updated. If the height was not changed, and the node is balanced, then this operation did not cause a change in the height of its ancestors. In particular, the ancestors are balanced, and thus, the operation can terminate.

If the examined node is imbalanced, rotation is applied. Roughly speaking, a rotation switches the parent and child roles of the node and one of its children. That is, the child becomes the node's new parent, and the child's parent is the node's old parent. Switching the node with its left child is called a *right* rotation, and switching with the right child is called a *left* rotation. The decision of which rotation to apply is based on the node's *balance factor*, which is the difference between its `leftHeight` and `rightHeight`. In some cases, two consecutive rotations are required, first on the node's child and then on the node. The decision of whether to apply one or two rotations depends on the balance factor of the node's child. Algorithm 11 presents the code that applies a rotation, given a node, its child and its parent.

The `rebalance` operation (Algorithm 12), receives two locked nodes, *node* and its *child* (which may be `null`). After insertion, these nodes are the new node's grandparent and parent. After removal, if the removed node had less than two children, these nodes are its parent and child; otherwise, these are the parent and child of the node's successor. The `rebalance` begins with updating *node*'s height on the basis of *child*'s height (Algorithm 13). Then, it checks *node*'s balance factor. If the height of *node* has not changed and the balance factor is valid, the operation terminates. If the height has changed and the balance factor is valid, the traversal continues with the node's parent. Otherwise, if the balance factor is not valid, the rotation process begins.

The rotation process consists of several steps. First, a check is conducted to see whether *child* is the appropriate child to recover the balance factor. If not, *child*'s `treeLock` is released and *child* is set to the other child and attempted to be locked (lines 7–19). As in the `acquireTreeLocks` operation, this acquisition is against the locking order, and thus it is not blocking. If the lock acquisition fails, the `restart` operation (Algorithm 14) is called. In this operation, all `treeLocks` are released and reacquired. If after reacquiring the lock, *node* is marked as removed, the operation ter-

Algorithm 12: rebalance(node, child)

```
1  while node != root do
2      isLeft = (node.left == child)
3      updated = updateHeight(child, node, isLeft)
4      bf = node.leftHeight - node.rightHeight
5      if !updated && |bf| < 2 then return
6      while |bf| ≥ 2 do
7          if (isLeft && bf ≤ −2) || (!isLeft && bf ≥ 2) then
8              if child != null then unlock(child.treeLock)
9              child = isLeft? node.right : node.left
10             isLeft = !isLeft
11             if !tryLock(child.treeLock) then
12                 if !restart(node, parent) then return
13                 parent = null
14                 bf = node.leftHeight - node.rightHeight
15                 child = bf ≥ 2? node.left : node.right
16                 isLeft = (node.left == child)
17                 continue
18             end
19         end
20         chBF = child.leftHeight - child.rightHeight
21         if (isLeft && chBF <0) || (!isLeft && chBF >0) then
22             grandChild = isLeft? child.right : child.left
23             if !tryLock(grandChild.treeLock) then
24                 unlock(child.treeLock)
25                 if !restart(node, parent) then return
26                 <same code as in lines 13–17>
27             end
28             rotate(grandChild, child, node, isLeft)
29             unlock(child.treeLock)
30             child = grandChild
31         end
32         if parent == null then parent = lockParent(node)
33         rotate(child, node, parent, !isLeft)
34         bf = node.leftHeight - node.rightHeight
35         if |bf| ≥ 2 then
36             unlock(parent.treeLock)
37             parent = child
38             child = null
39             isLeft = bf ≥ 2? false: true
40             continue
41         end
42         temp = node; node = child; child = temp
43         isLeft = (node.left == child)
44         bf = node.leftHeight - node.rightHeight
45     end
46     if child != null then unlock(child.treeLock)
47     child = node
48     node = parent != null? parent: lockParent(node)
49     parent = null
50 end
```

Algorithm 13: updateHeight(ch, node, isLeft)

```
1  newH = ch == null? 0: max(ch.leftHeight, ch.rightHeight) + 1
2  oldH = isLeft? node.leftHeight : node.rightHeight
3  if isLeft then
4      node.leftHeight = newH
5  else
6      node.rightHeight = newH
7  end
8  return oldH == newH
```

Algorithm 14: restart(node, parent)

```
1  if parent != null then unlock(parent.treeLock)
2  while true do
3      unlock(node.treeLock)
4      lock(node.treeLock)
5      if node.mark then                // No need to balance
6          unlock(node.treeLock)
7          return false
8      end
9      bf = node.leftHeight - node.rightHeight
10     child = bf ≥ 2? node.left : node.right
11     if child == null then return true
12     if trylock(child.treeLock) then return true
13 end
```

A check is then performed to see whether two rotations are needed. If so, the `treeLock` of *child*'s child is acquired and the rotation is applied (lines 20–31). The acquisition of this lock is also non-blocking, and if it fails, `restart` is called. Next, the rotation to *node* is applied (lines 32–33). To this end, its parent's `treeLock` is acquired. After that, if the node is still not balanced, the process begins again (lines 34–41). Otherwise, we check whether its new parent (i.e., its old child) is balanced (lines 42–44). After both are balanced, the traversal continues upwards in the tree, with the node's old parent (lines 46–49).

Some of the lock releases are omitted from the code for brevity. We also note that there is an edge-case where *node* was not balanced, the `restart` operation was invoked, and afterwards *node* was detected as removed. If *node* was removed by relocating its successor, *s*, to *node*'s location, then *s* is not balanced. However, it is the responsibility of the thread that removed *node* to invoke `rebalance` on *s*. This happens in `removeFromTree`, after returning from `rebalance`. We omit this code for simplicity.

4.6   Binary Search Tree without Balancing

From the above description of the AVL tree, one can construct a BST without balancing. The BST is very similar to the AVL tree we presented, and it can be obtained by removing the balancing operation and applying minor optimizations (i.e., acquiring fewer `treeLocks`).

minates. Otherwise, *child* is set to one of its children, its `treeLock` is acquired, and the `rebalance` restarts.

4.7 Supporting Additional Operations

Our design can be used to support additional operations:

Retrieving the Minimal/Maximal Values Having the `pred` and `succ` fields in the nodes allows us to support the operations `min` and `max`. To access the minimal value, it is enough to read the `succ` field of $N_{-\infty}$ and check its `mark` field. If the latter is `false`, then the node's key can be returned; otherwise, the operation is restarted. The `max` operation is implemented similarly using N_∞'s `pred` field.

Iterating over Tree Elements Iteration requires implementation of: (i) `first()`, which returns the minimal node in the tree, and (ii) `next(node)`, which returns the successor of the given node. `first()` is similar to `minimal` with the exception that it returns the *node* and not its key. The `next(node)` operation can be implemented similarly by reading the `succ` field from *node* (instead of $N_{-\infty}$).

5. Correctness

In this section we discuss the correctness of our algorithm.

5.1 Lock Ordering and Deadlock Freedom

We now present the locking order that threads obey, and thus show that deadlocks cannot occur. There are two types of locks, `succLocks` and `treeLocks`, and we order them such that the `succLock` should be acquired first. Between two `succLocks` we order acquisition such that the lock of the node with the smaller key should be acquired first.

Between two `treeLocks` we order acquisition such that the lock of the node that appears lower in the tree should be acquired first. Whenever threads determine that one node appears lower (or higher) than another node in the tree, it cannot change due to concurrent operations. This follows since threads lock nodes that have an ancestor-descendant relation and determine that a node is lower than another node only after acquiring one of their `treeLocks`. The roles of ancestor-descendant can only be switched via the `rotate` operation, which requires both of their `treeLocks`.

When locking `treeLocks` against the locking order is required, threads optimistically attempt to acquire the lock (without blocking on it), and if they fail, all locks are released and the operation is restarted. When locking several `treeLocks` against the locking order, threads lock from the higher node to the lower one. That is, threads obey another locking order. This approach cannot result in a livelock. Livelock may occur when threads contend without blocking on the same set of locks and acquire them in a different order. Here, livelock cannot occur when two threads attempt to acquire locks against the locking order because they obey another locking order. Nor can livelock occur when two threads attempt to acquire locks, one obeying the locking order and the other not obeying it, since the first one will block on the locks until acquiring them.

The BST follows the same lock ordering as the AVL tree, and uses a subset of its locks; thus, it is also deadlock free.

5.2 Linearizability

To show linearizability, we provide the linearization points for each operation. The linearization points of unsuccessful inserts and removes (neither affects the tree) are where they return `false`, i.e. in lines 9 of `insert` and `remove`.

The linearization point of a successful `insert`(k) is in line 16, where p's `succ` field is updated to point to the new node. Any future `insert`(k) or `remove`(k) will observe k once it has acquired the `succLock` of k's predecessor, or once it has detected a different node n, acquired its `succLock` and observed that $k \notin (n$'s key, $\text{succ}(n)$'s key).

The linearization point of a successful `remove`(k) is in line 13, where n's `mark` field is set to `true`. Any future `insert`(k) or `remove`(k) will acquire the `succLock` of k's predecessor, and will observe that it has a different successor. Any future `contains`(k) that observes k will find its `mark` field set to `true`.

The linearization point of a successful `contains`(k) is when the `mark` field of the node with value k was observed to be `false`. The linearization point of an unsuccessful contains is more delicate. The simple case is when the node is marked as removed or when k is not in the tree. In this case the linearization point is when the `mark` field was observed as `true`, or upon observing that *node* has a bigger key in line 3. However, it may happen that the nodes read in line 2 were also removed from the tree (but the update was not completed yet). In this case, it is possible that another concurrent thread inserts k. Since this update was not observed in line 3, the insertion must have begun after the `contains` began. Thus, we linearize the unsuccessful `contains` just before the linearization point of the new insert.

5.3 Progress Guarantees

We now provide a sketch of the proof of the `contains`' progress guarantees. The `contains` consists of two phases:
- The traversal along the tree via the *right* and *left* fields.
- The traversal along the nodes via the *pred* and *succ* fields.

The first phase of the traversal is lock-free. A thread may stray from its path due to rotations or removals of nodes with two children. However, in these cases another thread has made progress (it successfully applied an insert or remove).

The second phase is also lock-free. If there are no concurrent updates, after a finite number of steps, the thread will find an unmarked node which is the predecessor of the key under search, or a node that precedes the predecessor. Then, if there are no concurrent updates, after a finite number of steps, the thread will find the predecessor and successor of the key under search. This traversal may only be delayed if the order layout is concurrently updated by another thread. In that case, the update operation was linearized (before or when the order layout was updated) and the other thread has made progress.

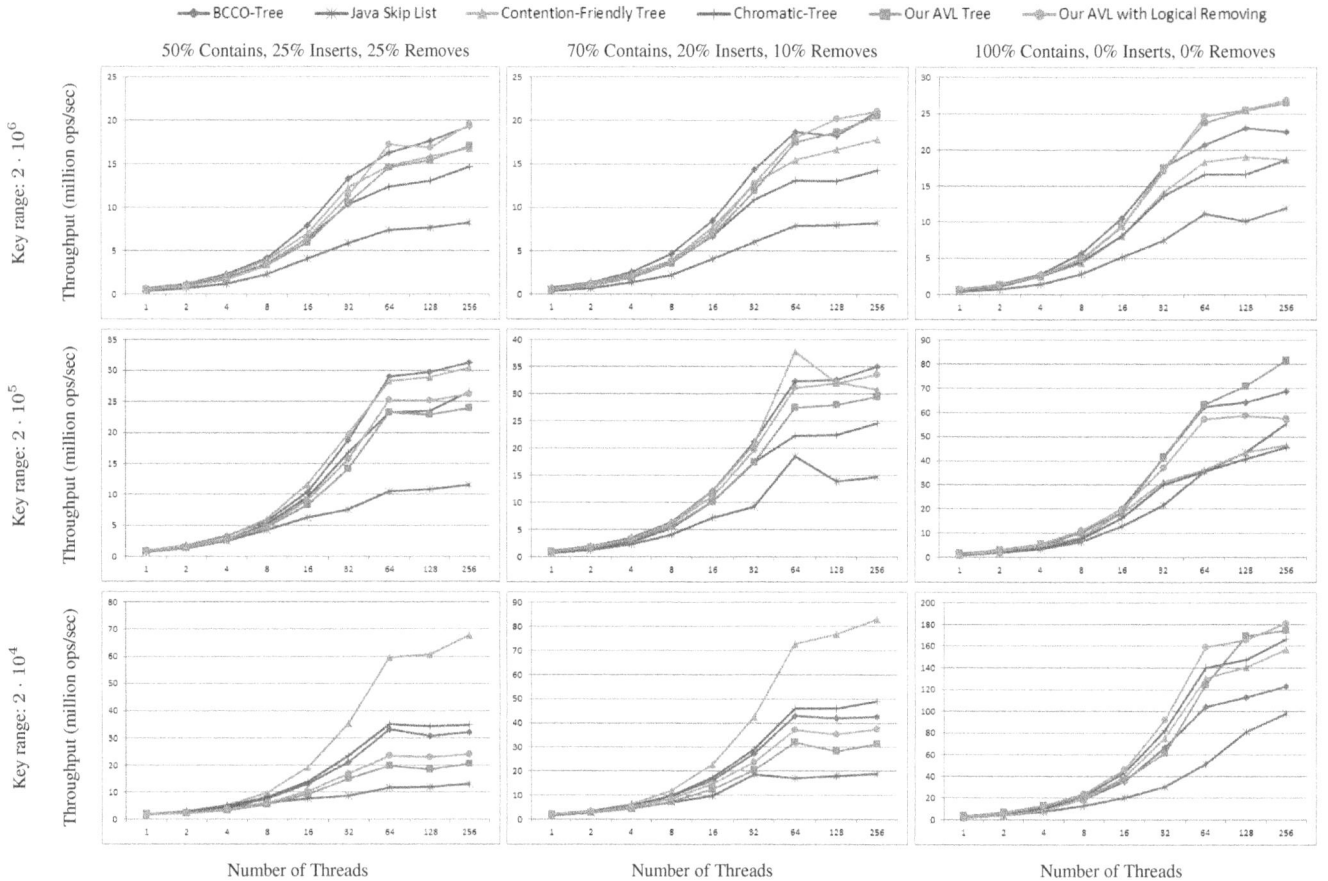

Table 1: Throughput for balanced tree implementations under different workloads on a 4-socket Opteron (64 h/w threads).

6. Evaluation

To evaluate the performance of our algorithms, we ran experiments on an AMD Opteron(tm) Processor 6376 with 128GB RAM and 64 cores: four processors with sixteen cores each and with hyper-threading support. We used Ubuntu 12.04 LTS and OpenJDK Runtime version 1.7.0_45 using the 64-bit Server VM (build 24.45-b08, mixed mode). We compared our algorithms to the following:

- BCCO Tree – The lock-based, relaxed AVL tree by Bronson et al. [8]. This is a variation of internal trees, referred to as *partially-external* trees.
- Contention-friendly tree – The lock-based, partially-external, relaxed AVL tree by Crain et al. [10], which delays rotations and removals and performs them in a separate maintenance thread.
- Java's Skip List – The non-blocking skip-list by Doug Lea, based on the work of Fraser and Harris [12], and included in the Java standard library.
- Chromatic Tree – The non-blocking, external, relaxed balance red-black tree, Chromatic6, by Brown et al. [9], which performs rotations only when the number of violations on a path is more than 6.

- EFRB-Tree – The non-blocking, external BST by Ellen et al. [11].

We also consider a variation of our trees, denoted *logical removing*, that implements a partially-external tree. In this variation, a node with two children is marked as logically removed via a designated flag, and it is not physically removed from the ordering layout or the physical layout. It will be physically removed only if its number of children reduces to one due to another removal or due to rotations. An insert can revive such a node by flipping this flag to false.

Differentiating Features Two key features distinguish our algorithms from past work on internal trees. First, our lookup operation is lock-free. This fault-tolerance property is important in large-scale systems where failure to guarantee some form of fault-tolerance makes reliability difficult to attain.

Second, in contrast to other approaches, our algorithms perform timely deletion. That is, they free the node upon removal (even when the deleted node is an internal node with two children), rather than keeping the node and physically deleting it later. This is useful as it keeps the memory consumption to what is expected by the programmer: a function of the keys which are *currently* in the tree. This is particu-

354

larly important in long-running applications where failure to remove deleted nodes can slowly lead to longer traversals.

The main performance question we wanted to address was the cost of these unique features: *would the throughput of our algorithms be comparable to that of existing algorithms which lack this combination?*

We focus our evaluation on workloads that make heavy use of `contains` operations:

- *100C-0I-0R*: 100% contains, 0% inserts, 0% removes.
- *70C-20I-10R*: 70% contains, 20% inserts, 10% removes.
- *50C-25I-25R*: 50% contains, 25% inserts, 25% removes.

We ran five-second trials, where each thread reported the number of operations it completed. We report the total number of operations applied by all threads, that is, the total throughput. The number of threads is 2^i where i varies between 0-8.

During the trial, each thread randomly chooses a type of operation with respect to the given distribution and then randomly chooses the value for that operation from a given range. The examined range sizes are: $2 \cdot 10^4$, $2 \cdot 10^5$ and $2 \cdot 10^6$. Before each trial, we prefilled the data structure as follows. For 100C-0I-0R and 50C-25I-25R, the data structures were prefilled to a size of $\frac{1}{2}$ of the key range. For 70C-20I-10R, the data structures were prefilled to a size of $\frac{2}{3}$ of the key range (the expected size at steady state). During prefilling, we ran the same workload as in the timed trials (i.e., same number of threads and same operations distribution), until reaching the desired size. We ran every experiment 8 times and report the arithmetic average. Each batch of 8 trials was run in its own JVM instance. To avoid HotSpot effects, we ran a warm-up phase before executing the trials. Table 1 compares balanced data structures, and Table 2 compares unbalanced data structures.

Throughput Evaluation In Table 1, it can be seen that under a heavy load of mutating operations (first column), and when the tree is quite small, our algorithms perform somewhat worse than the other trees. Under heavy load, threads spend more time waiting for locks. Also, since the lookup is optimistic, threads may progress along some path, and then due to rotations may find themselves scanning a different path. More changes result in more threads that stray from the correct path due to rotations. However, as the tree's size increases, even under heavy load of write operations our algorithm is comparable to the other implementations. When all of the operations are contains operations, our algorithm—while still providing lock-free contains—outperforms the state-of-the-art BSTs. In terms of space, the BCCO-tree may maintain up to 50% "zombie" nodes that have been logically, but not physically, removed. These nodes can be used to avoid allocation if a subsequent insert is attempting to insert the same key. This represents a different tradeoff than our approach, in which some allocations can be avoided by keeping "zombie" nodes in the tree after removal. The ability to avoid allocation using zombie nodes decreases as the key

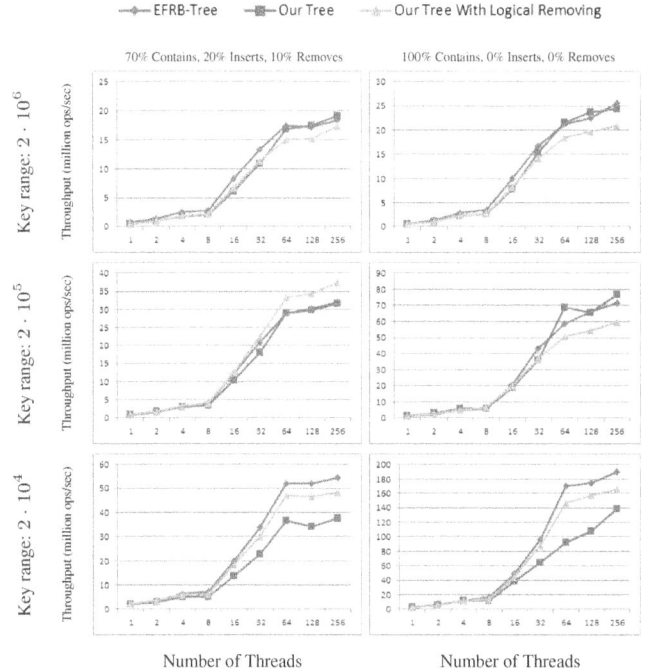

Table 2: Throughput for different BST implementations.

range increases and the probability for inserting a key that has been removed decreases. The benefit of saving allocation is also apparent when comparing our *logical removing* variation to our AVL under workloads that include update operations. In these workloads, the variation performs better than the AVL.

Table 2 presents the results for 70C-20I-10R and 100C-0I-0R of the unbalanced trees (50C-25I-25R produces similar results to 70C-20I-10R). It can be seen that our BST is often comparable to the *EFRB-Tree*. When all operations are contains operations, the comparison is between different implementations of lock-free contains for an internal tree (our tree), a partially-external tree (our variation), and an external tree (*EFRB-Tree*). When the operation mix includes update operations, threads may be blocked in both of our trees (waiting for locks), while in the *EFRB-Tree*, threads are never blocked. When the tree size is small, the external and partially-external trees have an advantage over our tree. Internal trees may suffer more contention in smaller trees since threads contend on nodes more frequently (since there could be up to two times fewer nodes in internal trees than in external trees). When the tree size is large, however, our tree is comparable to the *EFRB-Tree*.

7. Related Work

The literature contains many variants of concurrent trees that can be roughly classified according to the following characteristics:

Internal vs. External An internal tree (e.g., [8, 10, 13]) maintains values in inner nodes whereas an external tree

355

(e.g., [7, 9, 11, 15]) maintains values only at the leaves. One challenge in internal trees is removal of a node with two children. Bronson et al. [8] and Crain et al. [10] cope with this challenge by marking such a node as removed, and do not *physically* remove it until the node has a single child. Howley et al. [13] remove such a node by copying the value of its successor to the node, and then by removing the successor if it has a child (otherwise it is only logically removed).

Pessimistic vs. Optimistic   Most concurrent trees in the literature use optimistic concurrency [14], but it is also possible to use pessimistic locking protocols [3]. Optimistic trees are traversed without acquiring any lock, and locks are acquired when the required node is reached. One challenge in such trees is the validation that no other concurrent operation has occurred between detecting the required node after observing some state of the tree and the lock acquisition. Known algorithms [7, 8, 10, 11, 13] cope with this challenge by stamping the node with the ongoing operation or with a new *version* number.

Balanced vs. Unbalanced   Balancing might require additional synchronization, and the literature contains both unbalanced [11, 13, 15] and balanced trees with different balancing mechanisms, e.g., red-black trees [5, 9], and AVL [8, 10]. Concurrent trees are typically *relaxed balanced*, meaning that the mutating operations are decoupled from the rebalancing operations. That is, a mutating operation is first completed and only sometime afterwards the rebalance process begins. This process may be delayed, for example, while waiting to acquire locks. In [8] balance is applied after every mutating operation, whereas in [10] balance is applied by a single thread that runs in the background.

BST vs. Threaded BST   In a threaded BST, every node that normally had `null` in its right child pointer will have a pointer to the node's successor, and every node that normally had `null` in its left child pointer will have a pointer to the node's predecessor. In our approach, every node maintains this information and it is crucial for nodes that neither of their children is `null`. Pfaff [16] mentions the possibility of adding an in-order list to the sequential tree. This is done by extending each node to point to its predecessor and successor. Pfaff claims that it does not improve performance; no details are provided on the locking discipline used when this in-order list is added. In contrast, we show that using a locking that is based on logical-ordering is a sweet spot for simplifying the algorithm and obtaining performance better or comparable to state-of-the-art algorithms that use more complicated mechanisms.

8. Conclusion

We presented two practical concurrent binary search tree algorithms: a non-balanced tree and an AVL tree. The core idea behind our algorithms is the notion of logical ordering, which is explicitly maintained in the tree. Separating the log-

ical ordering from the tree layout enables clean separation between operations which update the tree layout, such as rotations, and those that look for elements. We leveraged this idea to design an intuitive, simple lookup operation, which is also lock-free. We have implemented our algorithms and showed that they are competitive with state-of-the-art balanced BST implementations.

Acknowledgements

We would like to thank Guy Gueta, Faith Ellen, Tim Harris, and Adam Morrison for their insightful comments.

References

[1] ADELSON-VELSKII, G., AND LANDIS, E. M. An algorithm for the organization of information. In *Proc. of the USSR Academy of Sciences,146:263-266* (1962).

[2] BAYER, R. Symmetric binary b-trees: Data structure and maintenance algorithms. *Acta Informatica 1*, 4 (1972), 290–306.

[3] BAYER, R., AND SCHKOLNICK, M. Concurrency of operations on b-trees. *Acta Informatica 9*, 1 (1977), 1–21.

[4] BENDER, M. A., FINEMAN, J. T., GILBERT, S., AND KUSZMAUL, B. C. Concurrent cache-oblivious b-trees. In *SPAA* (2005), pp. 228–237.

[5] BESA, J., AND ETEROVIC, Y. A concurrent red-black tree. *Journal of Parallel and Distributed Computing 73*, 4 (2013), 434 – 449.

[6] BOUGÉ, L., GABARRÓ, J., MESSEGUER, X., AND SCHABANEL, N. Height-relaxed avl rebalancing: A unified, fine-grained approach to concurrent dictionaries, 1998.

[7] BRAGINSKY, A., AND PETRANK, E. A lock-free b+tree. In *SPAA* (2012), pp. 58–67.

[8] BRONSON, N. G., CASPER, J., CHAFI, H., AND OLUKOTUN, K. A practical concurrent binary search tree. In *PPoPP* (2010), pp. 257–268.

[9] BROWN, T., ELLEN, F., AND RUPPERT, E. A general technique for non-blocking trees. In *Proc. 19th ACM Symposium on Principles and Practice of Parallel Programming* (2014).

[10] CRAIN, T., GRAMOLI, V., AND RAYNAL, M. A contention-friendly binary search tree. In *Euro-Par* (2013), pp. 229–240.

[11] ELLEN, F., FATOUROU, P., RUPPERT, E., AND VAN BREUGEL, F. Non-blocking binary search trees. In *PODC* (2010), pp. 131–140.

[12] FRASER, K. Practical lock-freedom. Tech. Rep. UCAM-CL-TR-579, University of Cambridge, Computer Laboratory, Feb. 2004.

[13] HOWLEY, S. V., AND JONES, J. A non-blocking internal binary search tree. In *Proc. 24th ACM Symposium on Parallelism in Algorithms and Architectures* (2012), pp. 161–171.

[14] KUNG, H. T., AND ROBINSON, J. T. On optimistic methods for concurrency control. *ACM Trans. Database Syst. 6*, 2 (June 1981), 213–226.

[15] NATARAJAN, A., AND MITTAL, N. Fast concurrent lock-free binary search trees. In *Proc. 19th ACM Symposium on Principles and Practice of Parallel Programming* (2014).

[16] PFAFF, B. Performance analysis of BSTs in system software. In *SIGMETRICS* (2004), ACM, pp. 410–411.

A Practical Wait-Free Simulation for Lock-Free Data Structures [*]

Shahar Timnat

Dept. of Computer Science, Technion
stimnat@cs.technion.ac.il

Erez Petrank

Dept. of Computer Science, Technion
erez@cs.technion.ac.il

Abstract

Lock-free data structures guarantee overall system progress, whereas wait-free data structures guarantee the progress of each and every thread, providing the desirable non-starvation guarantee for concurrent data structures. While practical lock-free implementations are known for various data structures, wait-free data structure designs are rare. Wait-free implementations have been notoriously hard to design and often inefficient. In this work we present a transformation of lock-free algorithms to wait-free ones allowing even a non-expert to transform a lock-free data-structure into a practical wait-free one. The transformation requires that the lock-free data structure is given in a normalized form defined in this work. Using the new method, we have designed and implemented wait-free linked-list, skiplist, and tree and we measured their performance. It turns out that for all these data structures the wait-free implementations are only a few percent slower than their lock-free counterparts, while still guaranteeing non-starvation.

Categories and Subject Descriptors   D.1.3 [*Programming Techniques*]: Concurrent Programming

Keywords   Wait-Freedom; Lock-Freedom

1. Introduction

Concurrent data structures are designed to utilize all available cores in order to achieve faster performance. One of the important properties of concurrent data structures is the progress guarantee they provide. Typically, the stronger the progress guarantee is, the harder it is to design the algorithm, and often, stronger progress guarantees come with a higher performance cost.

Standard progress guarantees include *obstruction-freedom*, *lock-freedom* (a.k.a. *non-blocking*), and *wait-freedom*. The strongest among these is wait-freedom. A wait-free algorithm guarantees that *every* thread makes progress (typically, completing a method) in a finite number of steps, regardless of other threads' behavior. This worst-case guarantee has its theoretical appeal and elegance, but is also important in practice for making concurrent data structures useable with real-time systems. For real-time, it is not enough that progress is made in almost all executions. Progress (i.e., meeting the deadline) must be proven to happen in *all* executions. However, very few wait-free algorithms are known, as they are considered notoriously hard to design, and largely inefficient. The weaker lock-freedom guarantee is more common. A lock-free algorithm guarantees that at least *one* thread makes progress in a finite number of steps. The downside of the lock-free guarantee is that all threads but one can starve in an execution, meaning that lock-freedom cannot suffice for a real-time scenario. As lock-free data structures are easier to design, constructions for many lock-free data structures are available in the literature, including the stack [17], the linked-list [14], the skiplist [17], and the binary search tree [7]. Furthermore, practical implementations for many lock-free algorithms are readily available in standard Java libraries and on the Web.

The existence of wait-free data structures has been shown by Herlihy [15] using universal simulations. Universal simulation techniques have evolved dramatically since then (e.g., [1, 4–6, 8, 12, 16]), but even the state-of-the-art universal construction is too slow compared to the lock-free or lock-based implementations and cannot be used in practice.

Recently, we have seen some progress with respect to practical wait-free data structures. A practical design of a wait-free queue relying on *compare and swap* (CAS) operations was presented in [18, 19]. Next, an independent construction of a wait-free stack and queue appeared in [9]. And finally, a wait-free algorithm for the linked-list has been shown in [24].[1]

---

[*] This work was supported by the Israeli Science Foundation grant No. 283/10.

---

[1] In fact, [9] also presented an entirely new universal construction. However, in the general case (i.e., except for the stack and the queue) this construction required each thread to create a local copy of the entire data structure for every operation, which makes it impractical.

To obtain a fast wait-free queue and linked-list, the fast-path-slow-path methodology has been adopted for use with wait-freedom in [19, 24]. The fast-path-slow-path methodology is ubiquitous in systems in general and in parallel computing particularly (e.g., [2, 3, 20, 22]). It is typically used to partitions slow handling of difficult cases from fast handling of the more typical cases.

The way the fast-path-slow-path methodology was used in [19] was to let an operation start executing using a fast lock-free algorithm, and only move to the slower wait-free path upon failing to make progress in the lock-free execution. It is often the case that an operation execution completes in the fast lock-free path, achieving good performance. But some operations fail to make progress in the fast path due to contention, and in this case, the execution moves to the slower wait-free path in which it is guaranteed to make progress. As many operations execute on the fast (lock-free) path, the performance of the combined execution is almost as fast as that of the lock-free data structure. It is crucial to note that even the unlucky threads, that do not manage to make progress in the fast path, are guaranteed to make progress in the slow path, and thus the strong wait-free guarantee can be obtained. The fast-path-slow-path methodology has been shown to make the wait-free queue [18] and linked-list of [24] almost as efficient as their lock-free counterpart.

The process of designing a fast wait-free algorithm for a new data structure is complex, difficult, and error-prone. One approach to designing new wait-free algorithms, which is also the one used in [18, 19, 24], is to start with a lock-free algorithm for the data structure, work (possibly hard) to construct a correct wait-free algorithm by adding a helping mechanism to the original algorithm, and then work (possibly hard) again to design a correct and efficient fast-path-slow-path combination of the lock-free and wait-free versions of the original algorithm. Designing a fast-path-slow-path algorithm is nontrivial. One must design the lock- and wait-free algorithms to work in sync to obtain the overall combined algorithm with the required properties.

In this work we ask whether this entire design can be done automatically, and so also by non-experts. Given a lock-free data structure, can we apply a generic method to add an adequate helping mechanism and obtain a wait-free version for it, and then automatically combine the original lock-free version with the obtained wait-free version to create a fast wait-free algorithm for the same data structure?

We answer this question in the affirmative and present an automatic transformation that takes a linearizable lock-free data structure in a normalized representation (that we define) and transforms it to a practical wait-free data structure, that is almost as efficient as the original lock-free algorithm.

We next claim that the normalized representation we propose is meaningful in the sense that important known lock-free algorithms for data structures can be easily specified in this form. In fact, all linearizable lock-free data structures

that we are aware of can be specified in a normalized form. We demonstrate the generality of the proposed normalized form by specifying several important lock-free data structures in their normalized form. We then obtain wait-free versions of them using the proposed transformation. In particular, we transform two linked-lists [11, 14], a skiplist [17], and a binary search tree [7] to create practical wait-free designs for them all. To the best of our knowledge, practical wait-free versions of the skiplist and the tree are not known in the literature and are presented here for the first time.

Next, in order to verify that the resulting algorithms are indeed efficient, we implemented all of the above wait-free algorithms and measured the performance of each. It turns out that the performance of all these implementations is only a few percent slower than the original lock-free algorithm from which they were derived. Given these results, it seems like wait-freedom can be adopted for general use, and not only for real-time systems. Similar to car airbags, they are seldom deployed but good to have in case of need.

The contributions of this work are the following:

1. A transformation from any normalized lock-free data structure to a wait-free data structure that (almost) preserves the original algorithm efficiency. This allows a simple creation of practical wait-free data structures.
2. A demonstration of the generality of the normalized representation, by showing the normalized representation for lock-free linked-list, skiplist and tree.
3. The first design of a practical wait-free skiplist.
4. The first design of a practical wait-free tree.
5. An implementation and reported measurements validating the efficiency of the proposed scheme.

The idea of transforming an algorithm to provide a practical algorithm with a different progress guarantee is not new. Taubenfeld [23], Ellen et al. [10] and Guerraoui et al. [13] are examples of such transformations. But none of them allows obtaining wait-free data structures in the standard asynchronous model.

The paper is organized as follows. In Section 2 we provide an overview of the proposed transfromation. In Section 3 we examine typical lock-free data structures, and characterize their properties in preparation to defining a normalized representation. The normalized representation is defined in Section 4, and the details of simulating normalized lock-free algorithms in a wait-free manner appear in Section 5. In Section 6 we give an example of how to apply our technique using Harris's linked-list. We give highlights of the correctness proof in Section 7, and our measurements are reported in Section 8.

2. Tranformation overview

The move from the lock-free implementation to the wait-free one is executed by simulating the lock-free algorithm in a wait-free manner. The simulation starts by simply running the original lock-free operation (with minor modifications that will be soon discussed). A normalized lock-free implementation has some mechanism for detecting failure to make progress (due to contention). When an operation fails to make progress it asks for help from the rest of the threads. Asking for help is done by enqueuing a succinct description of its current computation state on a wait-free queue (we use the queue of [18]). One modification to the fast lock-free execution is that each thread checks once in a while whether a help request is enqueued on the help queue. Threads that notice an enqueued request for help move to helping a single operation on the top of the queue. Help includes reading the computation state of the operation to be helped and then continuing the computation from that point, until the operation completes and its result is reported.

The major challenges are in obtaining a succinct description of the computation state, in the proper synchronization between the (potentially multiple) concurrent helping threads, and in the synchronization between helping threads and threads executing other operations on the fast lock-free path. The normalized representation is enforced in order to allow a succinct computation representation, to ensure that the algorithm can detect that it is not making progress, and to minimize the synchronization between the helping threads to a level that enables fast simulation.

The helping threads synchronize during the execution of an operation at critical points, which occur just before and just after a modification of the data structure. Assume that modifications of the shared data structure occur using a CAS operation. A helping thread runs the operation it attempts to help locally and independently until reaching a CAS instruction that modifies the shared structure. At that point, it coordinates with all helping threads which CAS should be executed. Before executing the CAS, the helping threads jointly agree on what the CAS parameters should be (address, expected value, and new value). After deciding on the parameters, the helping threads attempt to execute the CAS and then they synchronize to ensure they all learn whether the CAS was successful. The simulation ensures that the CAS is executed exactly once. Then each thread continues independently until reaching the next CAS operation and so forth, until the operation completes. Upon completing the operation, the operation's result is written into the computation state, the computation state is removed from the queue, and the *owner* thread (the thread that initiated the operation in the first place) can return.

There are naturally many missing details in the above simplistic description, but for now we will mention two major problems. First, synchronizing the helping threads before each CAS, and even more so synchronizing them again at the end of a CAS execution to enable all of them to learn whether the CAS was successful, is not simple. It requires adding version numbering to some of the fields in the data structure, and also an extra `modified bit`. We address this difficulty in Section 5.

The second problem is how to succinctly represent the computation state of an operation. An intuitive observation (which is formalized later) is that for a lock-free algorithm, there is a relatively light-weight representation of its computation state. This is because by definition, if at any point during the run a thread stops responding, the remaining threads must be able to continue to run as usual. This implies that if a thread modifies the data structure, leaving it in an "intermediate state" during the computation, then other threads must be able to restore it to a "normal state". Since this often happens in an execution of a lock-free algorithm, the information required to do so must be found on the shared data structure, and not (solely) in the thread's inner state. Using this observation, and distilling a typical behavior of lock-free algorithms, we introduce a normalized representation for a lock-free algorithm, as defined in Section 4. The normalized representation is built in a way that enables us to represent the computation state in a compact manner, without introducing substantial restrictions on the algorithm itself.

There is one additional key observation required. In the above description, we mentioned that the helping threads must synchronize in critical points, immediately before and immediately after each CAS that modifies the data structure. However, it turns out that with many of the CASes, which we denote *auxiliary CASes*, we do not need to use synchronization at all. As explained in Section 3, the nature of lock-free algorithms makes the use of auxiliary CASes common. Most of Section 3.2 is dedicated to formally define *parallelizable methods*; these are methods that only execute auxiliary CASes, and can therefore be run by helping threads without any synchronization. These methods will play a key role in defining normalized lock-free representation in Section 4.

3. Typical Lock-Free Algorithms

In this section we provide the intuition on how known lock-free algorithms behave, and set up some notation and definitions that are then used in Section 4 to formally specify the normalized form of lock-free algorithms.

3.1 Motivating Discussion

Let us examine the techniques frequently used within lock-free algorithms. We target linearizable lock-free data structures that employ CASes as the synchronization mechanism. A major difficulty that lock-free algorithms often need to deal with is that a CAS instruction executes on a single word (or double word) only, whereas the straightforward implementation approach requires simultaneous atomic modification of multiple (non-consecutive) words[2]. Applying a modification to a single-field sometimes leaves the data structure inconsistent, and thus susceptible to races. A commonly employed solution is to use one CAS that (implicitly) blocks any further changes to certain fields, and let any thread re-

---

[2] This is one of the reasons why transactional memories are so attractive.

move the blocking after restoring the data structure to a desirable consistent form and completing the operation at hand.

An elegant example is the delete operation in Harris's linked-list [14]. In order to delete a node, a thread first sets a special *mark* bit at the node's next pointer, effectively blocking this pointer from ever changing again. Any thread that identifies this "block" may complete the deletion by physically removing the node (i.e., execute a CAS that makes its predecessor point to its successor). The first CAS, which is executed only by the thread that initiates the operation, can be intuitively thought as an *owner CAS*.

In lock-free algorithms' implementations, the execution of the owner CAS is often separated from the rest of the operation (restoring the data structure to a "normal" form, and "releasing" any blocking set by the owner CAS) into different methods. Furthermore, the methods that do not execute the owner CAS but only restore the data structure can usually be safely run by many threads concurrently. This allows other threads to unblock the data structure and continue executing themselves. We call such methods *parallelizable methods*.

3.2 Notations and Definitions

In this section we formally define the essential concepts used in this work.

DEFINITION 3.1. (Futile CAS.) *A futile CAS is a CAS in which the expected value and the new value are identical.*

DEFINITION 3.2. (Equivalent Executions.) *Two executions E and E' of operations on a data structure D are considered equivalent if the following holds.*

- *(Results:) In both executions all threads execute the same data structure operations and receive identical results.*
- *(Relative Operation Order:) The order of invocation points and return points of all data structure operations is the same in both executions.*

Note that the second requirement does not imply the same timing for the two executions. It only implies the same relative order of operation invocations and exits. For example, if the ith operation of thread T_1 was invoked before the jth operation of T_2 returned in E, then the same must also hold in E'. Clearly, if E and E' are equivalent executions, then E is linearizable if and only if E' is linearizable.

In what follows we identify methods that can be easily run with help, i.e., can be executed in parallel by several threads without harming correctness and while yielding adequate output. To formalize parallelizable methods we first define a harmless, or *avoidable* parallel run of a method. Loosely speaking, a run of a method is avoidable, if each CAS executed in it is avoidable. By avoidable, we mean that either: 1) the CAS fails, or 2) the CAS is futile, or 3) there exists an equivalent execution in which the CAS fails. Normally, in the equivalent execution, the CAS fails because a different thread executes the same CAS (i.e., same address,

same expected-value, and same new-value), but this is not obligatory by the definition.

DEFINITION 3.3. (Avoidable method execution) *A run of a method M by a thread T on input I in an execution E is avoidable if each CAS that T attempts during the execution of M is avoidable in the following sense. Let S_1 denote the state of the computation right before the CAS is attempted by T. Then there exists an equivalent execution E' for E such that both executions are identical until reaching S_1, and in E' the CAS that T executes in its next step (after S_1) is either futile or unsuccessful. Also, in E' the first execution step from S_1 is executed by a thread who is the owner of an ongoing operation[3].*

We now move to defining parallelizable methods that can be executed on the data structure without "harming" its consistency. To this end, we conduct a mental experiment in which we consider additional parallel threads that execute methods concurrently with the run of the algorithm. This mental experiment creates executions that are not "legal". We will not have real executions in which a thread will just run a single method of an operation out of the blue with parameters supplied by some oracle. However, the resulting execution is well defined and we will use such "illegal" executions as hybrids for an argument that one real execution (the wait-free run) is equivalent to another real execution (an equivalent lock-free run).

DEFINITION 3.4. (Parallelizable method.) *A method M is a parallelizable method of a given lock-free algorithm, if for any execution in which M is called by a thread T with an input I the following two conditions hold. First, the execution of a parallelizable method depends only on its input, the shared data structure, and the results of the method's CAS operations. In particular, the execution does not depend on the executing thread's local state prior to the invocation of the parallelizable method. Second, at the point where M is invoked, if we create and run a finite number of parallel threads, each one executing M on the same input I concurrently with the execution of T, then in any possible resulting execution, all executions of M by the additional threads are avoidable.*

Loosely speaking, for every invocation of a parallelizable method M by one of the newly created threads, there is an *equivalent execution* in which this method's invocation does not change the data structure at all. This is because every CAS it attempts might be executed by one of the other (original) threads, thus making it fail (unless it is futile). For example, Harris's linked-list search method is parallelizable. The only CASes that the search method executes are those that physically remove nodes that are already logically deleted. Assume T runs the search method, and consider one such

---

[3] This implies that this owner thread is in the middle of executing some operation when arriving at S_1.

logically deleted node. Consider a CAS in which T attempts to physically remove this node from the list. We denote the state right before this attempt S_1. Now consider the thread T_1, which marked this node as logically deleted in the first place. This thread must currently be attempting to physically remove the node so that it can exit the delete operation. An alternative execution in which T_1 is given the time (at S_1) to physically remove the node, and only then does T attempt the considered CAS and fails, is equivalent.

Parallelizable methods play an important role in our construction, since helping threads can run them unchecked. If a thread cannot complete a parallelizable method, helping threads may simply execute the same method as well. By the definition, parallelizable methods may be run out of the blue by threads that do not execute actual operations on the data structure.

In the proof, we will claim the equivalence of the wait-free execution and the lock-free one via several equivalent executions, some of them being "illegal" executions that run parallelizable methods "out of the blue" by additional threads that only execute these methods and cease to exist. Such "illegal" executions will only be used to incrementally argue that two legal executions of the real protocols are equivalent.

We now focus on a different issue. In order to run the fast-path-slow-path methodology, there must be some means to identify the case that the fast path is not making progress on time, and then move to the slow path. To this end, we define the *Contention failure counter*. Intuitively, a contention failure counter is a counter associated with an invocation of a method (i.e. many invocations of the method imply separate counters), measuring how often the method is delayed due to contention.

DEFINITION 3.5. (Contention failure counter.) *A contention failure counter for a method M is an integer field C associated with an invocation of M (i.e. many invocations of M imply many separate contention failure counters). Denote by $C(t)$ the value of the counter at time t. The counter is initialized to zero upon method invocation, and is updated by the method during its run such that the following holds.*

- *(Monotonically increasing:) Each update to the contention failure counter increments its value by one.*
- *(Bounded by contention:) Assume M is invoked by Thread T and let $d(t)$ denote the number of data structure modifications by threads other than T between the invocation time and time t. Then it always hold that $C(t) \le d(t)$.* [4]
- *(Incremented periodically:) The method M does not run infinitely many steps without incrementing the contention failure counter.*

A lock-free method must complete within a finite number of steps if no modifications are made to the data structure outside this method. Otherwise, allowing this method to run solo results in an infinite execution, contradicting its lock-freedom. Thus, the requirements that the counter remains zero if no concurrent modifications occur, and the requirement that it does not remain zero indefinitely, do not contradict each other. The contention failure counter will be used to determine that a method in the fast-path is not making progress and so its executer should switch to the slow path.

For most methods, counting the number of failed CASes can serve as a good *contention failure counter*. However, more complex cases exist.

4. Normalized Lock-Free Algorithms

In this section, we specify what a normalized lock-free algorithm is. We later show how to simulate a normalized lock-free algorithm in a wait-free manner automatically.

4.1 The Normalized Representation

A normalized lock-free algorithm is one for which each operation can be presented in three stages, such that the middle stage executes the owner CASes, the first is a preparatory stage and the last is a post-execution step.

Using Harris's linked-list example, the delete operation runs a first stage that finds the location to mark a node as deleted, while sniping out of the list all nodes that were previously marked as deleted. By the end of the search (the first stage) we can determine the main CAS operation: the one that marks the node as deleted. Now comes the middle stage where this CAS is executed, which logically deletes the node from the list. Finally, in a post-processing stage, we attempt to snip out the marked node from the list and make it unreachable from the list head.

In a normalized lock-free algorithm, we require that: any access to the data structure is executed using a read or a CAS; the first and last stages be parallelizable, i.e., can be executed with *parallelizable methods*; and each of the CAS operations of the second stage be protected by versioning. This means that there is a counter associated with the field that is incremented with each modification of the field. This avoids potential ABA problems, and is further discussed in Section 5.

DEFINITION 4.1. *A lock-free algorithm is provided in a* normalized representation *if:*

- *Any modification of the shared data structure is executed using a CAS operation.*
- *Every operation of the algorithm consists of executing three methods one after the other and which have the following formats.*
  1) CAS Generator, *whose input is the operation's input, and its output is a list of CAS descriptors* [5]

---

[4] In particular, this implies that if no modifications were made to the data structure outside the method M since its invocation until time t, then $C(t) = 0$.

[5] A CAS descriptor is a triplet: $(address, expectedvalue, newvalue)$

2) CAS Executor, *which is a fixed method common to all data structures and all algorithms. Its input is the list of* CAS descriptors *output by the CAS generator method. The CAS executor method attempts to execute the CASes in its input one by one until the first one fails, or until all CASes complete. Its output contains the list of* CAS Descriptors *from its input and the index of the CAS that failed (which is zero if none failed).*

3) Wrap-Up, *whose input is the output of the* CAS Execution method *plus the operation's input. Its output is either the operation result, which is returned to the* owner thread, *or an indication that the* operation *should be restarted from scratch (from the* Generator method).

- *The* Generator *and the* Wrap-up *methods are parallelizable and they have an associated* contention failure counter.

- *Finally, we require that the CASes that the Generator method outputs be for fields that employ versioning (i.e., a counter is associated with the field to avoid an ABA problem).*

All lock-free algorithms for data structures that we are aware of today can be easily converted into this form. As an example, a normalized representation of Harris's linked-list is given in Section 6. We have also devised normalized representations for the binary-search-tree of Ellen et al. [7], the skiplist of Herlihy and Shavit [17], and the linked-list of Fomitchev and Ruppert [11]. This is probably the best indication that this normalized representation covers natural lock-free algorithms. We remark that all abstract data types can be implemented in a normalized lock-free algorithm, using a simplified version of the universal construction of Herlihy [15], but this construction is likely to be inefficient.

Intuitively, one can think of this normalized representation as separating owner CASes (those are the CASes that must be executed by the *owner thread* in the lock-free algorithm) from the other (denoted auxiliary) CASes. The auxiliary CASes can be executed by many helping threads and therefore create *parallelizable methods*. Intuitively, the first (generator) method can be thought of as running the algorithm without performing the owner CASes. It just makes a list of those to be performed by the executor method, and it may execute some auxiliary CASes to help previous operations complete.

As an example, consider the DELETE operation of Harris's linked-list. When transforming it to the normalized form, the generator method should call the search method of the linked-list. The search method might snip out marked (logically deleted) nodes; those are auxiliary CASes, helping previous deletions to complete. Finally, the search method returns the node to be deleted (if a node with the needed key exists in the list). The CAS that marks this node as logically deleted is the owner CAS, and it must be executed exactly once. Thus, the generator method does not execute this owner CAS but outputs it to be executed by the CAS

Executer method. If no node with the needed key is found in the list, then there are no owner CASes to be executed, and the generator method simply returns an empty list of CASes.

Next, the executor attempts to execute all these owner CASes. In Harris's linked list, like in most known algorithms, there is only one owner CAS. The CAS EXECUTOR method attempts the owner CAS (or the multiple owner CASes one by one), until completing them all, or until one of them fails. After the CAS EXECUTOR method is done, the operation might already be over, or it might need to start from scratch (typically if a CAS failed), or some other auxiliary CASes should be executed before exiting. The decision on whether to complete or start again (and possibly further execution of auxiliary CASes) is done in the WRAP-UP method. In Harris' linked-list example, if the GENERATOR method outputted no CASes, then it means that no node with the required key exists in the list, and the wrap-up method should return with failure. If a single CAS was outputted by the GENERATOR but its execution failed in the EXECUTER, then the operation should be restarted from scratch. Finally, if a single CAS was outputted by the GENERATOR and it was successfully executed by the EXECUTER, then the wrap-up method still needs to physically remove the node from the list (an auxiliary CAS), and then return with success. Removing the node from the list can be done similarly to the original algorithm, by calling the SEARCH method again.

5. Transformation Details

In this section, we provide the efficient wait-free simulation of any normalized lock-free algorithm. We start with an overview.

To execute an operation, a thread starts by executing the normalized lock-free algorithm with a *contention failure counter* checked occasionally to see if contention has exceeded a predetermined limit. If the operation completes, then we are done. Otherwise, the contention failure counter exceeded its threshold and the slow path must be taken. The slow path begins by the thread creating an *operation record* object that describes the operation it is executing. A pointer to this operation record is then enqueued in a wait-free queue called the *help queue*. Next, the thread helps operations on the *help queue* one by one according to their order in the queue, until its own operation is completed. Threads in the fast path that notice a non-empty *help queue* provide help as well, before starting their own fast-path execution.

To provide help, a thread examines the first operation record enqueued on the *help queue*. The operation record describes which operation should now be executed, and also which of its three methods needs to be run. Running the CAS GENERATOR method or the WRAP-UP method is easier, as they are parallelizable methods and they can be run by several threads concurrently at no risk. To execute one of these two, the helping thread executes their code using the input in the operation record. Upon completion, the helping thread creates a new updated operation record that includes the output of the method. It then tries (using an atomic CAS) to let the new operation record replace the original one, and become visible to all threads. If this CAS fails, then another thread has already completed the execution of this method and reported a (perhaps different) output, which has been publicly set as this method's output. The helping thread proceeds to help using the new publicly visible operation record, whether this operation record has been created by itself or by a different helping thread. It remains to describe helping the CAS EXECUTOR method.

The CAS EXECUTOR method is not parallelizable and therefore helping threads cannot simply run it concurrently. To support a concurrent execution of it, fields that can potentially be modified by the CAS EXECUTOR are paired with a versioning field and a `modified bit`. These additional fields allow executing each CAS exactly once, and publicly report success or failure. The success or failure of each CAS is reported in a special field on the CAS list. This controlled execution of the critical CASes requires care to ensure that: each CAS is executed exactly once, the success of the CAS gets published even if one of the threads stops responding, and an ABA problem is not created by letting several threads execute this sensitive CAS instead of the single thread that was supposed to execute it in the original lock-free algorithm. To achieve this careful execution, we first assume that each CAS is versioned, so that a belated CAS that occurs long after the original CAS completed, cannot foil the execution and it must fail. Furthermore, a common problem that appears when designing wait-free algorithms with helping threads naturally arises here. We need to execute the CAS in one memory location and report that the execution succeeded (or not) in a different memory location (in the CAS list pointed to by the operation record). To achieve this, we use, in addition to the version number (or in fact as part of the version number), an extra `modified bit` to signal whether the CAS has already been executed (successfully) or not. The details follow.

5.1 The Help Queue and the Operation Record

The description of operations that require help is kept in a wait-free queue, similar to the one proposed by Kogan and Petrank in [18]. The queue in [18] supports the standard ENQUEUE and DEQUEUE operations. We slightly modify it to support three operations: ENQUEUE, PEEK, and CONDITIONALLY-REMOVE-HEAD. The ENQUEUE operation just enqueues a value to the tail of the queue as usual. The new PEEK operation returns the current head of the queue, without removing it. Finally, the CONDITIONALLY-REMOVE-HEAD operation receives a value it expects to find at the head of the queue, and removes it (dequeues it) only if this value is found at the head. In this case it returns *true*. Otherwise, it does nothing and returns *false*. This queue is in fact simpler to design than the original queue, because DEQUEUE is not needed, because PEEK requires a single

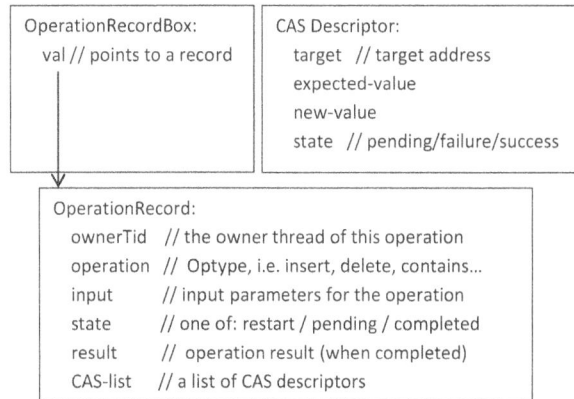

Figure 1. Operation Record

read, and the CONDITIONALLY-REMOVE-HEAD can be executed using a single CAS. (Therefore, CONDITIONALLY-REMOVE-HEAD can be easily written in a wait-free manner.) Some care is needed because of the interaction between ENQUEUE and CONDITIONALLY-REMOVE-HEAD, but a similar mechanism already appears in [18], and we simply used it in our case as well.

We use this queue as the `help queue`. If a thread fails to complete an *operation* due to contention, it asks for help by enqueuing a request on the `help queue`. This request is in fact a pointer to a small object (the operation record box) that is unique to the operation and identifies it. It is only reclaimed when the operation is complete. In this operation record box object there is a pointer to the `operation record` itself, and this pointer is modified by a CAS when the operation's status needs to be updated. We specify the content of this object and record in Figure 1.

5.2 Asking for Help and Giving Help

When a thread T starts executing a new operation, it first PEEKs at the head of the `help queue`. If it sees a non-null value, then T helps the enqueued operation before executing its own operation. After helping to complete one operation, T proceeds to execute its own operation (even if there are more help requests pending on the queue).

A thread starts executing its own operation by running the (normalized) lock-free version of the operation. As lock-freedom does not guarantee non-starvation, the thread may run for a long time without making progress. To obtain non-starvation, we make the thread check periodically that its *contention failure counter* does not exceed a predetermined limit. This check should be performed periodically, e.g., on each function call and each backward jump. If the operation completes while executing the lock-free (fast) path, then we are done. This must be the case when no contention occurs, because the given lock-free algorithm must make progress when no contention is encountered. Otherwise, the contention failure counter will notify that the operation is delayed due to contention. In this case, the thread creates

```
1:  void help (boolean beingHelped, OperationRecordBox myHelpBox)
    {
2:      while (true) {
3:          OperationRecordBox head = helpQueue.peekHead();
4:          if (head != null)
5:              helpOp(head);
6:          if (!beingHelped || myHelpBox.val.state == OpState.completed)
7:              return;
8:      }
9:  }
```

Figure 2. The help method

an operation record, encapsulates it with an operation record box and requests help by enqueuing the operation record box on the wait-free `help queue`. Next, the enqueuing thread starts helping the operations on the help queue one by one, until its own operation is completed (in practice, its own operation is likely to be the only one in the queue).

To participate in helping an operation, a thread calls the HELP method, telling it whether it is on the fast path, and so willing to help a single operation, or on the slow path, in which case it also provides a pointer to its own operation record box. In the latter case, the thread is willing to help all operations up to its own operation. The HELP method will PEEK at the head of the `help queue`, and if it sees a non-null operation record box, it will invoke the HELPOP method. A null value means the help queue is empty, and so no further help is needed.

The HELPOP, invoked by the HELP method, helps a specific *operation O*, until it is completed. Its input is *O*'s operation record box. This box may either be the current head in the `help queue` or it is an operation that has been completed and is no longer in the `help queue`. As long as the operation is not complete, HELPOP calls one of the three methods, PRECASES, EXECUTECASES, or POST-CASES, as determined by the operation record. If the operation is completed, HELPOP attempts to remove it from the queue using CONDITIONALLY-REMOVE-HEAD. When the HELPOP method returns, it is guaranteed that the operation record box in its input represents a completed operation and is no longer in the `help queue`.

The PRECASES method invokes the CAS GENERATOR method of the normalized lock-free algorithm, which generates the list of CAS descriptions for the CAS EXECUTOR. It runs a monitored version of the generator, which occasionally checks the contention counter in order to guarantee this method will not run forever. If the CAS GENERATOR completes its execution without being halted prematurely due to the contention failure counter, The PRECASES method allocates a new operation record that holds the result returned by the CAS GENERATOR. Then, the PRECASES method attempts to make its operation record the official global operation record for this operation by attempting to atomically change the operation record box to reference it. There is no need to check whether this attempt succeeded, any operation

```
1:  void helpOp(OperationRecordBox box) {
2:      OperationRecord record = null;
3:      do {
4:          record = box.val;
5:          if (record.state == OpState.restart) {
6:              preCASes(box, record);      ▷ CAS generator plus extras.
7:          }
8:          if (record.state == OpState.pending) {
9:              executeCASes(record);    ▷ carefully executes the CAS list.
10:             postCASes(box, record);   ▷ wrap-up method, plus extras.
11:         }
12:     } while (record.state == OpState.restart || record.state == Op-
    State.pending);
13:     helpQueue.conditionallyRemoveHead(box);
14: }
```

Figure 3. The helpOp method

```
1:  void preCASes(OperationRecordBox box, OperationRecord record) {
2:      ArrayList<ICasDesc> cas-list = MonitoredRun(Of Genera-
    torMethod on record);
3:      if (cas-list != null) {                                    ▷
4:          newRecord   =   new   OperationRecord(record.ownerTid,
    record.operation, record.input, OpState.pending, null, cas-list);
5:          box.val.compareAndSet(record, newRecord);
6:      }
7:  }
```

Figure 4. The preCASes method

record installed by any of the concurrently executing threads is a proper record that can be used to continue the operation.

If during the execution of the CAS GENERATOR method the contention counter reaches the predetermined threshold, the thread simply quits this method with null and reads the operation record box to see if another thread has made progress with this operation (if not, the HELPOP method will call the PRECASES method again.) If the `OperationRecord` is not replaced by a new one, then soon enough all threads will only run this CAS GENERATOR method, all helping the same operation.

Using the fact that the original algorithm is lock-free, it is possible to show that eventually some thread will successfully complete the operation without being interrupted by the contention failure counter. Intuitively, parallelizable methods can only execute a finite number of CASes while no owner CASes are executed[6]. For example, in the normalized form of Harris's linked list, given in Section 6, parallelizable methods can only execute physical deletions of logically deleted nodes. Thus, the number of CASes executed in the parallelizable methods is bounded by the number of logical deletions, and logical deletions are never executed inside parallelizable methods. Once the helping threads complete all the remaining physical deletions, they will execute no more CASes, and will not stop each other from completing.

---

[6] Formally, this is not accurate and some pathological exceptions exist. However, even in those cases some thread must successfully complete the operation eventually.

Next, we carefully execute the CASes obtained by the PRECASES method. This is done in the EXECUTECASES method (Figure 5). It receives as its input the operation record, which holds the list of CAS descriptions to be executed. Each CAS description is also associated with a `state` field, which describes the execution state of this CAS: succeeded, failed, or still pending. Ideally, we would have liked to execute three instructions atomically: (1) read the `state`, (2) attempt the CAS (if the `state` is pending), and (3) update the CAS `state`. Unfortunately, since these three instructions work on two different locations (the CASed memory address and the CAS state) we cannot run this atomically without using a heavy mutual exclusion machinery that foils wait-freedom (and is also costly).

We solve this atomicity problem and an additional ABA problem by adding the versioning mechanism to the fields that are being CASed. The ABA problem is introduced because a thread may be inactive for a while and then attempt to execute a CAS that was already executed. Returning to the atomicity issue, we must report the outcome of a CAS execution correctly, even if the thread that performed the successful CAS is delayed before reporting the success and all other threads fail to execute the CAS (as the field has already been modified). The ABA and the atomicity problems nicely represent two major standard problems that arise with the incorporation of a help mechanism to make a lock-free algorithm wait-free.

To solve the first ABA problem we employ versioning with all fields that require CASes. To solve the second problem we use an additional bit with each CASed field. (Practically, this would be one of the version bits.) This bit, denoted the `modified` bit, will signify that a successful CAS has been executed but (possibly) not yet reported. So when a CAS is executed, a successful execution will put the new value together with the `modified` bit set. All further attempts to modify this field must fail as the old value of any CAS never has this bit set. Thus, the operation that follows a successful CAS operation must be a CAS that clears this bit. However, before any thread attempts to clear this bit, the thread must first update the `state` of the CAS to reflect this success.

To summarize, the EXECUTECASES method goes over the CASes in the list one by one, and helps execute them as follows. First, it reads the CAS `state`. If it is successful and the `modified` bit is set, and if the version has not yet been incremented, then it uses a CAS to clear the modified bit and increment the version and moves on to help the next CAS. Otherwise, if the CAS `state` is currently set to failure, then the EXECUTECASES method immediately returns. Otherwise, the `state` is pending, and EXECUTECASES attempts to execute the listed CAS and set the `modified` bit atomically with it. Next, it checks whether the `modified` bit is set, and if it is, it sets the (separate) CAS `state` to success and only then attempts to clear the modified bit. Now if

```
 1: private void executeCASes(OperationRecord record) {
 2:     for (int i = 0; i < record.numOfCases(); i++) {
 3:         ICasDesc cas = record.list.get(i);
 4:         if (cas.GetState() == CasState.success) {
 5:             cas.ClearBit(); ▷ clears modified bit (if set). (See Remark 1)
 6:             continue;
 7:         }
 8:         if (cas.GetState() == CasState.failure)
 9:             return;
10:         cas.ExecuteCas();
11:         if (cas.ModifiedBitSet()) {       ▷ Checking not only that the
    modified bit is checked, but also that the version has not changed.
12:             cas.SetState(CasState.success);    ▷ Cas Succeeded. State is
    modified atomically with a CAS.
13:             cas.ClearBit();                    ▷ (See Remark 1)
14:         }
15:         if (cas.GetState() != CasState.success) {
16:             cas.SetState(CasState.failure);               ▷ Either
    this state change will fail because it has been previously updated, or
    the CAS really failed.
17:             return;
18:         }
19:     }
20: }
21: Remarks:
22: 1. Clearing the modified bit is done with a CAS. The expected value
    for this CAS instruction is the new value of the original CAS.
```

Figure 5. The executeCASes Method

the CAS `state` is not set to success, then EXECUTECASES sets this state to failure and returns. Otherwise, success is achieved and EXECUTECASES proceeds to the next CAS.

An invariant of this mechanism is that in the entire data structure, only a single `modified bit` might be set at any given moment. This is exactly the bit of the CAS that is currently being helped by all helping threads. Before clearing this `modified bit`, no other CAS execution can be helped.

The existence of the `modified bit` requires a minor modification to the fast-path. When a thread attempts a CAS and the CAS fails in the fast-path, it should check to see whether the CAS failed because the `modified bit` in the required field is set. If so, the thread should pause its current execution and call the help method to participate in helping the current operation to complete (clearing this bit in the process). Failing to do so will foil the lock-freedom property (and the wait-freedom property as well), because the thread may forever fail in attempts to modify that field, even when running solo.

After the CASes are executed, the HELPOP method calls the POSTCASES method (Figure 6), which invokes the WRAP-UP method of the original lock-free algorithm. If the WRAP-UP method fails to complete due to contention, the monitored run will return null and we will read again the `operation record` box. If the WRAP-UP method was completed without interruption, the POSTCASES method attempts to make its private operation record visible to all by atomically attempting to link it to the `operation record` box. Note that its private `operation record` may indicate a need to start the operation from scratch, or may indicate

```
1: void postCASes(OperationRecordBox box, OperationRecord record)
   {
2:   shouldRestart, operationResult = MonitoredRun(of Wrapup
     Method on record);
3:   if (operationResult == Null) Return
4:   if (shouldRestart)
5:     newRecord       =     new     OperationRecord(record.ownerTid,
       record.operation, record.input, OpState.restart, null, null);
6:   else
7:     newRecord       =     new     OperationRecord(record.ownerTid,
       record.operation, record.input, OpState.completed, operationResult,
       null);
8:   box.val.compareAndSet(record, newRecord);
9: }
```

Figure 6. The postCASes Method

that the operation is completed. When the control is returned to the HELPOP method, the record is read and the execution continues according to it.

6. Example: Harris's Linked-List

Harris designed a practical lock-free linked-list [14]. A Java implementation of it is available in [17]. Harris's list is a sorted list of nodes in which each node holds an integer key, and only one node with a given key may be in the list at any given moment. He employed a special `mark bit` in the `next` pointer of every node, used to mark the node as logically deleted. Thus, a node is deleted by first marking its next pointer using a CAS (in effect, locking this pointer from ever changing again) and then physically removing it from the list by a CAS of its predecessor's `next` field. Inserting a new node can be done using a single CAS, making the new node's designated predecessor point to the new node.

We start by noting that Harris's SEARCH method, which is used by both the INSERT and DELETE operations, is a *parallelizable method* as is (there is no need to change it to make it parallelizable). The SEARCH method's input is an integer key, and its output is a pair of adjacent nodes in the list, the first with a key smaller than the input value, and the second with a key greater than or equal to the input value. The SEARCH method might make changes to the list: it might physically remove marked nodes, those nodes that are logically deleted. The SEARCH method is restarted in practice anytime an attempted CAS fails. (Such an attempted CAS is always an *auxiliary CAS*, attempting to physically remove a logically deleted node.) A simple enough *contention failure counter* for this method can be implemented by counting the times this CAS failure happens.

We now specify a normalized form of Harris's linked-list.

- A *contention failure counter* for all of the methods in Harris's linked-list can be implemented by counting the number of failed CASes.
- The *parallelizable Generator* method is implemented as follows: For an insert(key) operation:

- Call the original search(key) method.
- If a node is found with the wanted key, return an empty list of CAS-descriptors. (The insert fails.)
- If a pair (pred, succ) is returned by the search method, create a new node n with the key, set n.next = succ, and return a list with a single CAS descriptor, describing a change of pred.next to point to n.

The generator method for a delete(key) operation is:
- Call the original search(key) method.
- If no node is found with the given key, return an empty list of CAS-descriptors.
- If a node n was found appropriate for deletion, return a list with a single CAS descriptor, describing a change of n.next to set its *mark bit*.

The generator method for a contains(key) operation is:
- return an empty list of CAS-descriptors.

- The *parallelizable Wrap-up* method is implemented as follows: For an insert(key) or a delete(key) operation:
- If the list of CAS-descriptors is empty, exit with result false (operation failed).
- If the CAS-descriptor was executed successfully, exit with result true (operation succeeded). For a delete operation, call the original search(key) prior to returning true, to ensure the node is physically removed.
- If the CAS-descriptor was not successful, indicate that a restart of the operation is required.

For a contains(key) operation:
- Call the original contains(key) method [17] (which is already a parallelizable method) and exit with the same result.

Note that there is a difference between calling the search method from inside the help mechanism via the GENERATOR method, and calling it from outside the help mechanism while executing the fast lock-free path. When calling from outside the GENERATOR method, if a thread tries to remove a logically deleted node and fails due to a checked `modified bit`, the thread switches to the help mechanism[7]. While when called from inside the Generator method, it is already inside the help mechanism, and thus recalling it should be avoided. For this reason, in the actual Java code, the search method receives a second parameter, a boolean that signifies whether the calling thread is already inside the slow path or not.

7. Correctness Highlights

We now discuss some key issues in the correctness proof for the simulation described in this paper. Assume that the given algorithm, denoted LF, is a linearizable lock-free algorithm presented in a normalized form for a certain abstract data

---

[7] As explained in Section 5.2, failing to do so will foil the lock-freedom property.

type, ADT. Let WF be the output algorithm as described in Section 5 with LF being the simulated lock-free algorithm. Then we claim that WF is a linearizable wait-free algorithm for the same abstract data type, ADT.

We show that for every execution of WF, there is an *equivalent execution* (Definition 3.2) of LF. Since we know that LF is correct and linearizable, it follows that WF is correct and linearizable as well. Consider any given execution of WF. We build an equivalent execution of LF in three steps.

Step 1: (Segregate generator and wrap-up.) Given an execution E_0 of WF we build an equivalent execution E_1 in which any operation executed in the slow path in E_0 by several helping threads is replaced by an operation that is executed by one single thread in the slow path. This single thread in E_1 executes the GENERATOR and WRAP-UP methods as they were performed by threads that successfully reported their respective results into the `operation record` box of this operation in E_0. Other threads may execute the GENERATOR or WRAP-UP *parallelizable methods* concurrently in E_1, but the output they produce is discarded and not used.

Step 2: (Move redundant help operations to auxiliary threads.) Given an execution E_1 output by Step 1, we build an equivalent execution E_2 in which all the extra executions of the GENERATOR or WRAP-UP *parallelizable methods*, whose output is discarded, are executed by new additional unrelated threads, each performing only one such extra method execution.

Step 3: (Drop auxiliary threads.) Given an execution E_2 output by Step 2, we construct an equivalent execution E_3 in which the additional unrelated threads are simply dropped. Using the fact that these additional threads execute *avoidable* methods, it can be shown that the resulting execution is equivalent. The execution E_3 is a legal linearizable execution of LF, which is equivalent to E and we are done.

Wait Freedom An easier yet critical part of the proof is showing that each operation in WF is completed after a finite number of steps. This is done in two steps. First, we show that if there is an operation in WF that takes an unbounded number of steps to complete, then from some point in the execution, no operation at all can be completed (since all the threads will be helping this single operation). Second, we use again the transition from an execution of WF (E_0) to an execution of LF (E_3). If for infinitely many steps no operation is linearized in E_0, then no operation is linearized in E_3 as well, in contradiction to the lock-free property of the original algorithm. Thus, WF is shown wait free by way of contradiction.

8. Performance

We chose four well-known lock-free algorithms of three widely-used data structures, and used the transformation described in this paper to derive a wait-free algorithm for each. In our implementation we applied a (generally applicable) optimization: we used the original (non-normalized) lock-free algorithm for the fast path with an additional contention failure counter for each of the methods of the original algorithm. This optimization is possible whenever the normalized algorithm and the original algorithm can safely run concurrently on the same data structure.

The performance of each wait-free algorithm was compared against the original lock-free algorithm. We stress that we compared against the original lock-free version of the algorithm without adding versioning to the CAS operations and without modifying it to fit a normalized representation.

The four lock-free algorithms we chose were Harris's linked-list [14], the binary-search-tree of Ellen et al. [7], the skiplist of Herlihy and Shavit [17], and the linked-list of Fomitchev and Ruppert [11]. All implementations were coded in Java. The Java implementations for Harris's linked-list and the skiplist were taken from [17]. We implemented the binary search tree and the list of Fomitchev and Ruppert in the most straightforward manner, following the papers.

In this work we do not specifically address the standard problem of memory management for lock-free (and wait-free) algorithms. If the original lock-free algorithm reclaims unused objects, then the obtained simulation works well with it, except that we need to reclaim objects used by the generated algorithm: the operation records, the operation record boxes, and the nodes of the help queue. This can be done using a few (constant) number of hazard pointers [21] per thread. The implementation is tedious, but does not introduce a significant difficulty.

All the tests were run on SUN's Java SE Runtime, version 1.6.0. We ran the measurements on 2 systems. The first is an IBM x3400 system featuring 2 Intel(R) Xeon(R) E5310 1.60GHz quad core processors (overall 8 cores) with a memory of 16GB and an L2 cache of 4MB per processor. The second system features 4 AMD Opteron(TM) 6272 2.1GHz processors, each with 8 cores (overall 32 cores), each running 2 hyper-threads (overall 64 threads), with a memory of 128GB and an L2 cache of 2MB per processor.

We used a micro-benchmark in which 50% of the operations are *contains*, 25% are *insert*, and 25% are *delete*. Each test was run with the number of threads ranging from 1 to 16 in the Xeon, and 1 to 32 in the Opteron. The keys were randomly and uniformly chosen in the range $[1, 1024]$. In each test, each thread executed 100,000 operations overall. We repeated each test 15 times, and performance averages are reported in the figures. The maximum standard deviation is less than 5%. The contention threshold was set to $k = 2$. In practice, this means that if one of the three simulation stages encounters k failed CASes, it gives up the fast path and moves to the slow path.

Figure 7 compares the four algorithms when running on the Opteron (the left graph of each couple) and on the Xeon (right). The figure shows the execution times (seconds) as a function of the number of threads. The performance of

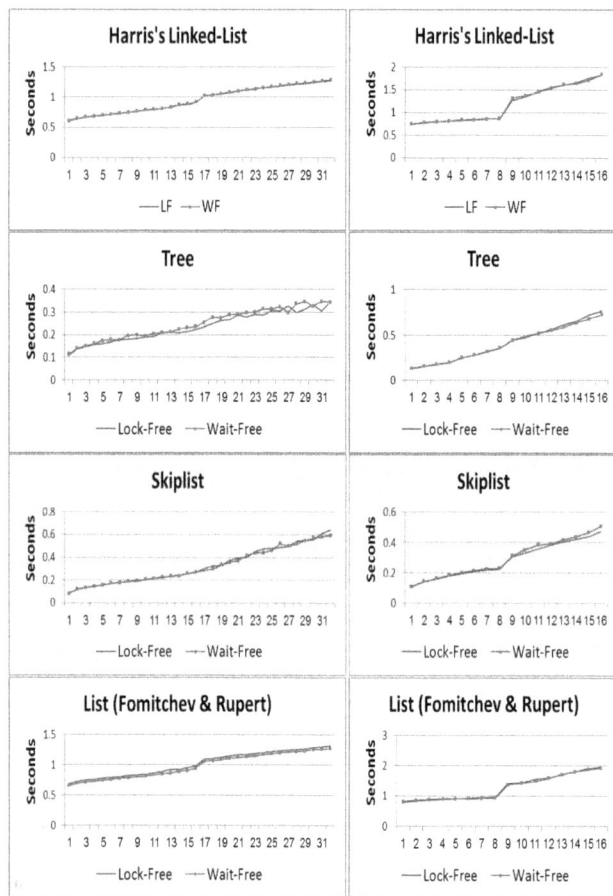

Figure 7. Lock-Free versus Wait-Free algorithms. Left: Opteron. Right: Xeon

the wait-free algorithms is comparable to the lock-free algorithms, the difference being 2% on average. We also measured how frequently the slow path was invoked. The fraction of operations running the slow path is small (up to 1/3,000). This allows the wait-free algorithms to retain similar performance to the lock-free algorithms. Still, a minority of the operations require the help mechanism to guarantee completion in a bounded number of steps, necessary for achieving wait-freedom.

References

[1] Yehuda Afek, Dalia Dauber, and Dan Touitou. Wait-free made fast. In *STOC*, pages 538–547, 1995.

[2] James H. Anderson and Yong-Jik Kim. Fast and scalable mutual exclusion. In *DISC*, pages 180–194, 1999.

[3] James H. Anderson and Yong-Jik Kim. Adaptive mutual exclusion with local spinning. In *DISC*, pages 29–43, 2000.

[4] James H. Anderson and Mark Moir. Universal constructions for large objects. *IEEE Trans. Parallel Distrib. Syst.*, 10(12):1317–1332, 1999.

[5] Phong Chuong, Faith Ellen, and Vijaya Ramachandran. A universal construction for wait-free transaction friendly data structures. In *SPAA*, pages 335–344, 2010.

[6] Tyler Crain, Damien Imbs, and Michel Raynal. Towards a universal construction for transaction-based multiprocess programs. In *ICDCN*, pages 61–75, 2012.

[7] Faith Ellen, Panagiota Fatourou, Eric Ruppert, and Franck van Breugel. Non-blocking binary search trees. In *PODC*, 2010.

[8] Panagiota Fatourou and Nikolaos D. Kallimanis. The redblue adaptive universal constructions. In *DISC*, pages 127–141, 2009.

[9] Panagiota Fatourou and Nikolaos D. Kallimanis. A highly-efficient wait-free universal construction. In *SPAA*, pages 325–334, 2011.

[10] Faith Ellen Fich, Victor Luchangco, Mark Moir, and Nir Shavit. Obstruction-free algorithms can be practically wait-free. In *DISC*, pages 78–92, 2005.

[11] Mikhail Fomitchev and Eric Ruppert. Lock-free linked lists and skip lists. In *PODC'04*, pages 50–59, 2004.

[12] Michael Greenwald. Two-handed emulation: how to build non-blocking implementation of complex data-structures using dcas. In *PODC*, pages 260–269, 2002.

[13] Rachid Guerraoui, Michal Kapalka, and Petr Kouznetsov. The weakest failure detectors to boost obstruction-freedom. *Distributed Computing*, 20(6):415–433, 2008.

[14] Timothy L. Harris. A pragmatic implementation of non-blocking linked-lists. In *DISC'01*, 2001.

[15] Maurice Herlihy. A methodology for implementing highly concurrent data structures. In *PPOPP*, pages 197–206, 1990.

[16] Maurice Herlihy. A methodology for implementing highly concurrent objects. *ACM TOPLAS*, 15(5):745–770, 1993.

[17] Maurice Herlihy and Nir Shavit. *The Art of Multiprocessor Programming*. Morgan Kaufmann, 2008.

[18] Alex Kogan and Erez Petrank. Wait-free queues with multiple enqueuers and dequeuers. In *PPOPP*, pages 223–234, 2011.

[19] Alex Kogan and Erez Petrank. A methodology for creating fast wait-free data structures. In *PPOPP*, pp. 141–150, 2012.

[20] Leslie Lamport. A fast mutual exclusion algorithm. *ACM Trans. Comput. Syst.*, 5(1):1–11, 1987.

[21] Maged M. Michael. Hazard pointers: Safe memory reclamation for lock-free objects. *IEEE Trans. Parallel Distrib. Syst.*, 15(6), 2004.

[22] Mark Moir and James H. Anderson. Wait-free algorithms for fast, long-lived renaming. *Sci. Comput. Program.*, 25(1):1–39, 1995.

[23] Gadi Taubenfeld. Contention-sensitive data structures and algorithms. In *DISC*, pages 157–171, 2009.

[24] Shahar Timnat, Anastasia Braginsky, Alex Kogan, and Erez Petrank. Wait-free linked-lists. In *OPODIS*, 2012.

Lock Contention Aware Thread Migrations

Kishore Kumar Pusukuri, Rajiv Gupta, Laxmi Narayan Bhuyan

University of California, Riverside

{kishore, gupta, bhuyan}@cs.ucr.edu

Abstract

On a cache-coherent multicore multiprocessor system, the performance of a multithreaded application with high lock contention is very sensitive to the distribution of application threads across multiple processors. This is because the distribution of threads impacts the frequency of lock transfers between processors, which in turn impacts the frequency of last-level cache (LLC) misses that lie on the critical path of execution. Inappropriate distribution of threads across processors increases LLC misses in the critical path and significantly degrades performance of multithreaded programs. To alleviate the above problem, this paper overviews a thread migration technique, which migrates threads of a multithreaded program across multicore processors so that threads seeking locks are more likely to find the locks on the same processor.

Categories and Subject Descriptors D.4.1 [*Process Management*]: Scheduling, Threads

Keywords Multicore, Lock contention, LLC miss, Migration, processor

1. Introduction

On a multicore multiprocessor system, the performance of a multithreaded application with *high lock contention* is highly sensitive to the distribution of threads across processors. In this paper, we demonstrate that the time spent on acquiring locks, as experienced by competing threads, can increase greatly depending upon the processors on which they are scheduled. When a lock is acquired by a thread, the time spent on acquiring it is longer if lock currently resides in a cache line of a remote processor as opposed to the processor on which the acquiring thread is running. In addition, once the thread acquires the lock, access to shared data protected by the lock is also likely to trigger LLC misses. This causes the thread to spend longer time in the critical section. When the competing threads of a multithreaded application are distributed across multiple processors, the above situation arises often and it increases lock transfers between processors. Frequent lock transfers between processors significantly increases long latency LLC misses that fall on the *critical path*. The larger the number of threads, the higher is the lock contention problem which causes LLC misses caused by inter-processor transfer of locks and the shared data they protect. Since the latency of LLC miss is high, the increase of LLC misses in the critical path increases both lock acquisition latency and critical section processing time, which leads to significant performance degradation.

To address the above problem, we propose a thread migration technique, which aims to reduce the variance in the lock arrival times of the threads scheduled on the same processor. The lock arrival times are the times at which threads arrive at the critical section just before they successfully acquire the lock. *By scheduling threads whose arrival times are clustered in a small time interval so that they can all get the lock without losing the lock to a thread on another processor.* Therefore, the thread migration technique ensures that once a thread releases the lock it is highly likely that another thread on the same processor will successfully acquire the lock and LLC misses will be avoided. Consequently, it reduces the lock acquisition time and speeds up the execution of shared data accesses in the critical section, ultimately reducing the execution time of the application.

2. Overview

The overview of the thread migration technique is provided in Algorithm 1. It is implemented by a daemon thread which executes throughout an application's lifetime repeatedly performing the following three steps: monitor threads; form thread groups; and affect thread grouping. The first step monitors the behavior of threads in terms of the percentage of elapsed time they spend on waiting for locks (i.e., lock times). The second step forms groups of similarly behaving threads using the lock times collected during the monitoring step. Finally the third step migrates threads across processors to ensure that threads belonging the same thread group are all moved to the same processor.

PPoPP '14, February 15–19, 2014, Orlando, Florida, USA.
Copyright is held by the owner/author(s).
ACM 978-1-4503-2656-8/14/02.
http://dx.doi.org/10.1145/10.1145/2555243.2555273

Algorithm 1: Lock Contention Aware Thread Migrations

Input: N: No. of threads; C: No. of processors.

repeat

    i. Monitor Threads -- sample lock times of N threads.

    if *lock times exceed threshold* **then**

        ii. Form Thread Groups -- sort threads according to lock times and divide them into C groups.

        iii. Affect Grouping -- migrate threads to establish newly computed thread groups.

    end

until *application terminates*;

The thread migration technique is designed to simultaneously reduce inter-processor lock transfers and preserve load balance across the processors – when some threads are migrated to a processor, others are migrated away from it. It is different from thread clustering [3], where contending threads are scheduled on the same processor. However, clustering of threads on the same processor reduces the cost of acquiring locks by sacrificing parallelism due to resulting load imbalance.

Operating system schedulers (e.g., Solaris) dynamically distribute threads across cores to balance the load across the cores but, as shown, they do not handle lock contention. In contrast, several works employ one-thread-per-core *binding* model for completely avoiding thread migrations and to maximizing performance of multithreaded programs running on multicore systems. However, on multiprocessor systems with a large number of cores, multithreaded programs that involve high lock contention exhibit poor performance with binding [2].

3. Preliminary Evaluation

We implemented the thread migration technique on a 64-core, 4-processor machine running Oracle Solaris 11 (each processor has 16 cores). We evaluated the thread migration technique with 20 multithreaded programs including SPEC jbb2005, PBZIP2, and programs from PARSEC, SPEC OMP2001, and SPLASH2 suites. Table 1 lists the programs and their short names. Figure 1 (a) shows LLC miss rates of the 20 programs. LLC miss rate is defined as last-level cache misses per thousand instructions (MPKI). As we can see, our thread migration technique reduces LLC miss rates compared to Solaris and thus improves performance. As Figure 1 (b) shows, our thread migration technique improves performance up to 54% (average 13%).

The key contributions of our work are as follows:

- We identify the important reasons for why modern OSes fail to achieve high performance for multithreaded applications with high lock contention running on multicore multiprocessor systems.

Table 1: Programs and their short names.

PARSEC: bodytrack (BT), fluidanimate (FA), facesim (FS), streamcluster (SC); SPEC OMP2001: applu (AL), ammp (AM), apsi (AS), equake (EQ), fma3d (FM), gafort (GA), galgel (GL), mgrid (MG), swim (SM), wupwise (WW); SPLASH2: ocean (OC), raytrace (RT), radix (RX), volrend (VL); PBZIP2 (PB); SPEC jbb2005 (JB).

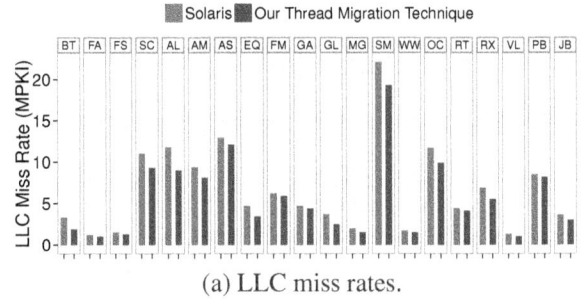

(a) LLC miss rates.

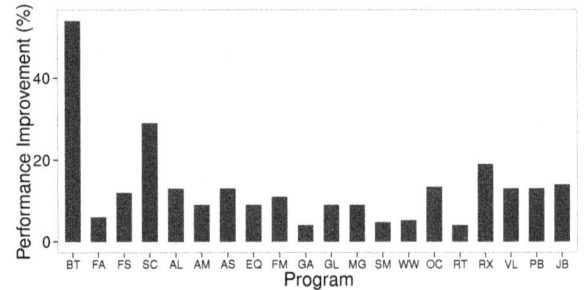

(b) Performance improvement (%).

Figure 1: Our thread migration technique reduces LLC misses and thus improves performance.

- We develop a thread migration technique, which orchestrates migration of threads between processors with the goal of simultaneously maintaining load balance and reducing lock transfers between processors to reduce LLC misses on the critical path.

- Our thread migration technique does not require any changes to the application source code or the OS kernel.

4. Acknowledgements

This work is supported by NSF grants CNS-1157377, CCF-0963996, and CCF-0905509.

References

[1] L. Jean-Pierre, D. Florian, T. Gaël, L. Julia and M. Gilles. Remote core locking: migrating critical-section execution to improve the performance of multithreaded applications. In *USENIX ATC*, 2012.

[2] K.K. Pusukuri and D. Johnson. Has one-thread-per-core binding model become obsolete for multithreaded programs running on multicore systems. In *USENIX HotPar*, 2013.

[3] F. Xian, W. Srisa-an, and H. Jiang. Contention-aware scheduler: unlocking execution parallelism in multithreaded java programs. In *OOPSLA*, 2008.

Infrastructure-Free Logging and Replay of Concurrent Execution on Multiple Cores

Kyu Hyung Lee   Dohyeong Kim   Xiangyu Zhang

Department of Computer Science, Purdue University, West Lafayette, IN, 47907, USA

{kyuhlee,kim1051,xyzhang}@cs.purdue.edu

Abstract

We develop a logging and replay technique for real concurrent execution on multiple cores. Our technique directly works on binaries and does not require any hardware or complex software infrastructure support. We focus on minimizing logging overhead as it only logs a subset of system calls and thread spawns. Replay is on a single core. During replay, our technique first tries to follow only the event order in the log. However, due to schedule differences, replay may fail. An exploration process is then triggered to search for a schedule that allows the replay to make progress. Exploration is performed within a window preceding the point of replay failure. During exploration, our technique first tries to reorder synchronized blocks. If that does not lead to progress, it further reorders shared variable accesses. The exploration is facilitated by a sophisticated caching mechanism. Our experiments on real world programs and real workload show that the proposed technique has very low logging overhead (2.6% on average) and fast schedule reconstruction.

Categories and Subject Descriptors   D.2.5 [*Software Engineering*]: Testing and Debugging—Debugging aids; Tracing

Keywords   Software reliability; Debugging; Replay

1.   Introduction

Logging and replay of concurrent execution in multi-core environment is very meaningful for debugging runtime failures and also very challenging. Much of the complexity stems from non-determinism that arises from the true parallel evaluation; the non-deterministic fine-grained interleavings are often difficult to precisely reproduce when replaying an erroneous execution.

In this paper, we aim to develop a logging and replay technique for execution on multiple cores, serving both software users and developers. It does not rely on any hardware or complex software infrastructure support, but rather operates directly on compiled binaries. It features a very low logging overhead as it does not try to log the precise non-deterministic access level interleavings. Replay is a cost-effective search process that produces a deterministic schedule leading to the failure.

2.   Related Works

The prior work most relevant to ours is PRES [4], which first tries to replay with syscall, synchronization, or even basic block log. If none of these succeeds, it tries to reverse shared memory access order. In comparison, PRES logs more information and it relies on a dynamic binary instrumentation framework, PIN [2], entailing higher logging overhead. Moreover, we introduce exploration window, two-layer exploration, and caching, which are critical for reducing search space and improving replay performance.

Another line of work is to record the order of instructions that access shared state, when they are executed in parallel on different cores. However the entailed instruction-level monitoring [1, 3] causes high logging overhead and often requires hardware or complex software infrastructure support, limiting its applicability.

3.   Design and Implementation

3.1   Logging

Minimizing logging overhead is one of our design goals. Therefore, we only log a subset of system calls (84 out of 326), signals and thread spawns which are the minimal set of information we need to replay a concurrent execution. A global order of these events is also recorded.

3.2   Replay with Incremental Schedule Exploration

In the replay phase, we combine I/O replay with schedule exploration to replay concurrency failures on a single core. We first try to follow only the event order in the log. If the replay fails to make progress due to schedule differences, we start a process that explores different sub-schedules *within a window* close to the point where the replay fails. We have two layers of exploration, one at the synchronized block level and the other at the fine-grained memory access level. Any new sub-schedule leading to some progress in replay is admitted to the final schedule. The process is iterative

PPoPP '14,   February 15–19, 2014, Orlando, Florida, USA.
Copyright is held by the owner/author(s).
ACM 978-1-4503-2656-8/14/02.
http://dx.doi.org/10.1145/2555243.2555274

Application Bugs	Original time(s)	Recording overhead (%)	PRES-like		Two-layer Exploration				Two-layer Exploration with caching					Replay time(s)
			FG Rep.	Time (sec)	CG Rep.	Log Mem	FG Rep.	Time (sec)	Cache Hit	CG Rep.	Log Mem	FG Rep.	Time (sec)	
Apache #1	12.43	3.22	28	301.21	24	1	1	40.21	10	14	1	1	29.85	1.64
Apache #2	7.14	3.78	22	615.42	32	1	1	281.42	8	10	1	1	92.59	6.12
Apache #3	10.89	2.94	16	196.73	27	1	1	43.85	9	14	1	1	31.23	1.28
MySQL #1	5.21	3.84	62	1342.6	46	1	2	137.1	17	24	1	2	81.47	2.47
MySQL #2	4.27	3.51	59	1429.1	39	1	1	151.82	15	22	1	1	92.5	3.71
PBZip2	9.87	1.11	8	1615.78	6	-	-	201.42	0	6	-	-	201.42	35.42
Transmission	1.58	0.63	2	4.61	3	-	-	1.32	0	3	-	-	1.32	0.43
Cherokee	120.42	2.11	15	684.29	12	1	3	61.51	2	7	1	3	42.11	4.15
Gftp	131.12	2.61	2	115	2	-	-	24.68	0	2	-	-	24.68	13.41

Table 1. Recording and replay performance. CG denotes coarse-grained and FG denotes fine-grained schedule exploration.

and terminates when the whole log, including the original failure, is successfully replayed.

3.2.1 Exploration Window

An important concept in our technique is *exploration window*, which defines the scope of sub-schedule exploration. Intuitively, we consider that an inconsistent event α_x is caused by state differences (compared with the original run) occur in between the preceding event α_p *in the same thread* and α_x. The state between α_p and α_x could be affected by any parallel execution in other threads. Hence, *the exploration window includes the execution durations of all threads that could happen in parallel with the duration from α_p to α_x*. We consider two durations could happen in parallel if the happens-before relation between the two cannot be inferred from the event log order.

3.2.2 Coarse-grained Exploration

The coarse-grained exploration aims to reorder the synchronized blocks within the window. At each preemption, the algorithm tries to select a thread based on the order of the threads' first events in the remaining log. The exploration is backward: priority is given to preemptions close to the end of the window.

3.2.3 Fine-grained Exploration

If the coarse-grained exploration fails to make progress, the algorithm resorts to reordering shared variable accesses within the window. The algorithm detects data races within the window and then selects a subset of races and reverses the order of the accesses in each race. We call the set of races to be reversed the *memory schedule*. The search of memory schedule is also backward, giving priority to accesses close to the end of the window. If fine-grained exploration cannot find a valid schedule in the current window, we continue to explore preceding windows.

3.3 Caching Replay Failures

According to our observation, the same replay failure tends to happen repetitively. To avoid redundant schedule exploration, we develop a caching mechanism. We have two caches, corresponding to the two possible replay failures, *unmatched events* and *deadlocks*.

4. Evaluation

We evaluate the performance of our technique over a set of real world bugs from 6 applications. We implemented PRES's replay algorithm according to the published paper [4]. We call it the PRES-like algorithm. Since PRES has multiple strategies, we only adapted one of the strategies such that it operates on our log, which mainly consists of system calls, signals and thread spawns. Upon replay failures, the PRES-like algorithm identifies all shared memory accesses, and then tries to reverse the order of the racy pairs.

Table 1 presents the results. Column 2 presents the original execution time without our logging tool for each application and column 3 shows recording overhead. Columns 4-5 show the number of schedule exploration attempts and the accumulated time for the PRES-like approach. Columns 6-9 show the cost of two-layer exploration without caching. Column 6 presents the number of tries for coarse-grained schedules, column 7 shows the number of times of collecting shared-memory access trace within the window. Column 8 shows the number of tries for fine-grained schedules and column 9 presents the accumulated time. Columns 10-14 show the cost of two-layer exploration with caching. Column 10 shows the number of cache hits. The last column shows the replay time when we have the correct schedule. It is significantly less than the original run except `Apache#2` and `PBZip2`. From the data, we make the following observations : (1) The logging overhead is very low, with the average of 2.6%. (2) Fine-grained exploration is rarely needed. (3) The caching mechanism is very effective in avoiding redundant exploration. (4) Our technique is more efficient than the PRES-like algorithm. Our schedule exploration with caching is an order of magnitude faster in most cases.

5. Conclusion

We have developed a logging and replay technique for real concurrent execution. The technique is self-contained, does not require any infrastructure support. Our results show that the technique is effective and practical, and substantially improves the state of the art.

References

[1] D. R. Hower and M. D. Hill. Rerun: Exploiting episodes for lightweight memory race recording. In *ISCA '08*.

[2] C. Luk, R. Cohn, R. Muth, H. Patil, A. Klauser, G. Lowney, S. Wallace, V. Reddi, and K. Hazelwood. Pin: building customized program analysis tools with dynamic instrumentation. In *PLDI '05*.

[3] S. Narayanasamy, C. Pereira, and B. Calder. Recording shared memory dependencies using strata. In *ASPLOS '06*.

[4] S. Park, Y. Zhou, W. Xiong, Z. Yin, R. Kaushik, K. Lee, and S. Lu. Pres: probabilistic replay with execution sketching on multiprocessors. In *SOSP '09*.

Parallelization Hints via Code Skeletonization

Cfir Aguston   Yosi Ben Asher
CS. University of Haifa, Israel
yosi@cs.haifa.ac.il

Gadi Haber
Intel Development Center, Haifa, Israel
gadi.haber@intel.com

Abstract

Tools that provide optimization hints for program developers are facing severe obstacles and often unable to provide meaningful guidance on how to parallelize real–life applications. The main reason is due to the high code complexity and its large size when considering commercially valuable code. Such code is often rich with pointers, heavily nested conditional statements, nested while–based loops, function calls, etc. These constructs prevent existing compiler analysis from extracting the full parallelization potential. We propose a new paradigm to overcome this issue by automatically transforming the code into a much simpler skeleton-like form that is more conductive for auto-parallelization. We then apply existing tools of source–level automatic parallelization on the skeletonized code in order to expose possible parallelization patterns. The skeleton code, along with the parallelized version, are then provided to the programmer in the form of an IDE (Integrated Development Environment) recommendation.

The proposed skeletonization algorithm replaces pointers by integer indexes and C-struct references by references to multi-dimensional arrays. This is because automatic parallelizers cannot handle pointer expressions. For example, $while(p \neq NULL)\{ p \to val++; p = p \to next; \}$ will be skeletonized to the parallelizable $for(Ip = 0; Ip < N; Ip++)\{ Aval[Ip]++; \}$ where $Aval[]$ holds the embedding of the original list. It follows that the main goal of the skeletonization process is to embed pointer-based data structures into arrays. Though the skeletonized code is not semantically equivalent to the original code, it points out a possible parallelization pattern for this code segment and can be used as an effective parallelization hint to the programmer. We applied the method on several representative benchmarks from SPEC CPU 2000 and reached up to 80% performance gain

after several sequential code segments had been manually parallelized based on the parallelization patterns of the generated skeletons. In a different set of experiments we tried to estimate the potential of skeletonization for a larger set of programs in SPEC 2000 and obtained an estimation of 27% additional loops that can be parallelized/vectorized due to skeletonization.

Categories and Subject Descriptors   D.1.3 [*PROGRAMMING TECHNIQUES*]: Parallel programming

Keywords   Skeletonization, Parallelization, Vectorization

1. Introduction

The emerging multi–core platforms and available vector operations have increased the demand for extracting more parallelism from applications. However, automatic parallelization of inherently sequential code remains a hard problem with limited success. One way to overcome the difficulties involved in parallelization is by using advisory tools [1–5]. These tools can analyze a piece of code and then provide the programmer with information on ways to refactor the code and by that to optimize it. However, this type of tools cannot handle commercially valuable applications which often include intense pointer use, complex control flow, frequent function calls, nesting, and more. In this work we propose a new advisory approach to address these issues called Skeletonization. The Skeletonization approach is a new analysis methodology for detecting parallelism that aims at software code containing pointer-intensive programs with complex control flow. It defines a set of rules for automatically transforming the code to a much simpler and basic form so that existing auto parallelizers can become more productive. The resulted simplified and parallelized code along with the log information produced by a compiler that analyzes it, are then used as a guidance for the programmer when coming to parallelize and optimize the original code. Overall, the skeletonized code has the following properties:

1. It is not necessarily semantically equivalent to the original code,

2. It is automatically generated from the original code.

PPoPP '14,   February 15–19, 2014, Orlando, Florida, USA.
Copyright is held by the owner/author(s).
ACM ACM 978-1-4503-2656-8/14/02..
http://dx.doi.org/10.1145/10.1145/2555243.2555275

3. It preserves the main or most critical data dependencies of the original code while ignoring potential data aliasing and ambiguities effects.

4. It replaces pointers and C-struct references by array references in an attempt to embed the program's data-structure (lists, trees, graphs) in multidimensional arrays so that they can be parallelized.

Figure 1 shows an example of a while loop that sequentially traverses two linked lists pointed by two pointers p, q and updates their $sval, tval$ fields. In general, a sequential traversal of a linked list can be parallelized if the linked list is replaced by an array-based representation. Thus, the skeleton version of this loop embeds the two linked lists value fields in two arrays $Msval[], Mtval[]$. Relative "distances" between pointers are reflected through index increments, e.g., $p \rightarrow snext \rightarrow sval$ is replaced by $Msval[Ip + 1]$ in which $p \rightarrow snext$ is transformed to $Ip + 1$. The auto parallelization applied to the skeletonized code uses loop-distribution that splits the for-loop into two separate loops. The first loop cannot be parallelized due to the output-dependency through $Msval[Ip] = Msval[Ip + 1] + Mtval[Iq]$. Yet the second loop has no cross-iteration dependencies and can be fully parallelized. The skeleton version of the loop and its parallel version form the recommendation given to the user showing a possible parallelization pattern for the original loop.

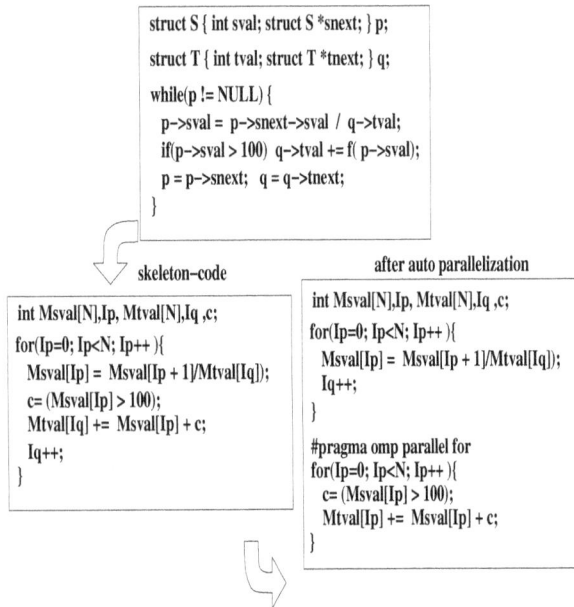

Figure 1. *Skeletonization example.*

Figure 2 shows how the user can implement the parallelization pattern suggested in figure 1. The idea is to use the first non-parallelizable loop to embed the two lists (pointed by p and q) into two arrays of pointers $AP[], AQ[]$ pointing to the elements of the two lists. By executing the first loop in its original form we can populate the two arrays and compute the number of elements that needs to be traversed by the second loop. Thus we can parallelize the second loop using the array-embedding of the two lists. Assuming that $f()$ is performing substantial work, the parallelization of the second loop can be beneficial.

```
#define Z = 1000   /* maximal list size */
struct S { int sval; struct S *snext; } p,shead,*AP[pr];
struct T { int tval; struct T *tnext; } q,thead,*AQ[pr];
p = shead; q = thead;   n =0;
while(p != NULL) {
  p->sval = p->snext->sval / q->tval;
  AP[n]= p;  AQ[n]=q;
  p = p->snext;   q = q->tnext; n++;
}
p = shead; q = thead;
#pragma omp parallel for
for(I=0; I<n; I++ ){
    if(AP[I]->sval > 100)  AQ[I]->tval += f( AP[I]->sval);
}
```

Figure 2. *Implementing the skeleton recommendation to the while-loop of figure 1.*

The experimental results, obtained by the skeletonizitaion system suggests a 30% improvement for SPEC benchmarks. For example, for the 179.ART benchmark: a total of 96 loops out of which 41 profiled loops identified, out of which 15 loops successfully auto-parallelized by ICC. Next, 14 loops (out of non-ICC parallelized loops) successfully parallelized after applying the Skeletonization recommendation. 6 loops (out of non-ICC vectorized loops) successfully vectorized after applying the Skeletonization recommendation. The overall improvement achieved between the original benchmark code and the fully optimized was 80% while the Skeletonization process contributed 37% speed-up.

References

[1] Intel advisor xe 2013. In *http://software.intel.com/en-us/intel-advisor-xe*.

[2] N. Jensen, P. Larsen, R. Ladelsky, A. Zaks, and S. Karlsson. Guiding programmers to higher memory performance. 2011.

[3] P. Larsen, R. Ladelsky, S. Karlsson, and A. Zaks. Compiler driven code comments and refactoring. In *Fourth Workshop on Programmability Issues for Multi-Core Computers (MULTIPROG-2011)*, page 64, 2011.

[4] P. Larsen, R. Ladelsky, J. Lidman, S. McKee, S. Karlsson, and A. Zaks. Automatic loop parallelization via compiler guided refactoring. Technical report, IMM-Technical Report-2011-12, DTU Informatics, 2011.

[5] J. Singh and J. Hennessy. An empirical investigation of the effectiveness and limitations of automatic parallelization. *The MIT Press, Cambridge, Mass*, pages 213–240, 1992.

Concurrency Bug Localization using Shared Memory Access Pairs

Wenwen Wang[1,2], Chenggang Wu[1], Pen-Chung Yew[3],
Xiang Yuan[1,2], Zhenjiang Wang[1], Jianjun Li[1], Xiaobing Feng[1]

[1]State Key Laboratory of Computer Architecture, Institute of Computing Technology, Chinese Academy of Sciences
[2]University of Chinese Academy of Sciences, Beijing, China
[3]Department of Computer Science and Engineering, University of Minnesota at Twin-Cities

[1,2]{wangwenwen, wucg, yuanxiang, wangzhenjiang, lijianjun, fxb}@ict.ac.cn, [3]yew@cs.umn.edu

Abstract

Non-determinism in concurrent programs makes their debugging much more challenging than that in sequential programs. To mitigate such difficulties, we propose a new technique to automatically locate buggy shared memory accesses that triggered concurrency bugs. Compared to existing fault localization techniques that are based on empirical statistical approaches, this technique has two advantages. First, as long as enough successful runs of a concurrent program are collected, the proposed technique can locate buggy memory accesses to the shared data even with only one single failed run captured, as opposed to the need of capturing multiple failed runs in other statistical approaches. Second, the proposed technique is more precise because it considers memory accesses in those failed runs that terminate prematurely.

Categories and Subject Descriptors D.2.5 [*Software Engineering*]: Testing and Debugging – Diagnostics

General Terms Reliability, Verification

Keywords Bug Localization, Shared Memory Access Pair

1. Introduction

The difficulties in debugging concurrent programs usually come from two main sources [2, 4]. First, concurrent programs have congenital non-determinism, i.e. even with the same program input, different runs of a concurrent program can exhibit different behavior due to different thread interleavings. Second, concurrency bugs are only triggered and manifested in some particular interleavings, which means concurrency bugs often cannot be deterministically reproduced without additional restrictions. This makes traditional single-stepping debugging techniques inapplicable.

This paper focuses on two types of concurrency bugs, *order violations* and *atomicity violations* (which includes single-variable and multi-variable atomicity violations). These two types of concurrency bugs account for 97% of common concurrency bugs [1]. We use a shared memory access pair, or an *access pair* for short, to specify the happen-before order of two consecutive shared memory accesses to the same shared variable from two different threads. During testing a concurrent program, our approach collects access pairs in program executions. If the program execution produces the expected output of the programmer, i.e. it is a *successful* run, the collected access pairs are accumulated. Otherwise, if the output is not expected, i.e. it is a *failed* run, our approach is applied to localize buggy access pairs triggering the concurrency bug. Our approach is composed by 3 *test procedures* (Section 3), which is based on *scenarios* (Section 2) that lead to concurrency bugs.

Compared to existing concurrency bug localization tools, our approach has two main advantages. First, as long as we get enough successful runs, this approach can accurately locate root causes of concurrency bugs even with only one single failed run captured. This can accommodate the limitation mentioned above in real practice. Second, this technique can more precisely localize the bugs compared to existing techniques because it takes into account the memory accesses in the failed runs that may have been terminated prematurely due to the manifestation of concurrency bugs.

2. Scenarios

Now, we describe different scenarios that cause access pairs to trigger a concurrency bug, i.e. *buggy access pairs*.

In the first scenario, denoted as Scenario I, buggy access pairs are only manifested in failed runs, but not in successful runs. These buggy access pairs can lead to order violation bugs and single-variable atomicity violation bugs.

PPoPP '14,   February 15–19, 2014, Orlando, Florida, USA.
Copyright is held by the owner/author(s).
ACM 978-1-4503-2656-8/14/02.
http://dx.doi.org/10.1145/2555243.2555276

Different from those in Scenario I, buggy access pairs in the second scenario, denoted as Scenario II, do not show up in both successful runs and failed runs. These buggy access pairs can lead to order violation bugs, single-variable atomicity violation bugs, and multi-variable atomicity violation bugs. The reason why these buggy access pairs are not manifested in failed runs is that programs are terminated after the manifestation of concurrency bugs. The latter accesses in buggy access pairs are not actually executed due to the premature termination of programs.

In the last scenario, denoted as Scenario III, buggy access pairs separately show up in both failed runs and successful runs. But, they never show up together in any successful run. The reason is that the bug involves multiple shared variables. Thus, these buggy access pairs can lead to multi-variable atomicity violation bugs. We consider these buggy access pairs as *coupled* buggy access pairs.

3. Test Procedures

To localize buggy access pairs, we design 3 test procedures, each of which is targeting buggy access pairs manifested in each scenario discussed in Section 2.

The first test procedure, denoted as Test Procedure I, aims to uncover buggy access pairs manifested with Scenario I. Thus, this test procedure can localize order violation bugs and single-variable atomicity violation bugs. Algorithm 1 describes the details of this test procedure, which consists of three steps. In `Step1` (line 1 through 6), we collect access pairs that show up in failed runs, but not in successful runs, denoted as $apSet$. In `Step2` (line 7 through 10), we filter out one type of false positives by identifying *predicable* access pairs in $apSet$. An access pair is predicable by another, if and only if the presence of the former one can be inferred by the presence of the latter one, but not vice versa. In `Step 3` (line 11), we filter out another type of false positives, which are caused by the execution of a rarely executed code region.

The second test procedure, denoted as Test Procedure II, aims to localize buggy access pairs manifested with Scenario II. These buggy access pairs cannot be directly localized as those manifested in Scenario I. To localize them, we need to first identify their *reversed* access pairs, which always show up in successful runs to guarantee the required order and atomicity constraints of shared memory accesses. After that, these buggy access pairs can be localized by reversing the heads and tails of their reversed access pairs.

The last test procedure, denoted as Test Procedure III, aims to localize buggy access pairs manifested with Scenario III. These buggy access pairs, or coupled buggy access pairs, never show up together in any successful run. To localize them, we firstly find out access pairs that show up in both failed runs and successful runs. Then, for any two of them that access different shared variables and are from two different threads, we check whether they are manifested together in successful runs.

Algorithm 1: Test Procedure I

Input: failed run: $FRun$; pass run set: $PSet$
Output: buggy access pairs manifested with Scenario 1

```
   // Step1: get access pairs that show up only
        in FRun
1  apSet ← FRun;
2  for access pair AP ∈ apSet do
3      for pass run PRun ∈ PSet do
4          if AP ∈ PRun then apSet ← apSet − {AP};
            break;
5      end
6  end
   // Step2: filter out predicable access pairs
7  for two access pairs APᵢ, APⱼ ∈ apSet do
8      if APᵢ is predicable by APⱼ then
            apSet ← apSet − {APⱼ};
9      else if APⱼ is predicable by APᵢ then
            apSet ← apSet − {APᵢ};
10 end
   // Step3: sort access pairs according to
        occurrence order
11 apList ← SortAccessPairs(apSet);
12 return apList;
```

To eliminate confusions introduced by dynamic instances of the same instruction when checking access pairs in successful runs, we append additional information to distinguish different dynamic instances. In the first level, denoted as *pc*, dynamic memory accesses are identified by their instruction addresses with no additional information. In the second level, denoted as *tid*, we add thread id and a global counter to identify each dynamic shared memory access. In the last level, denote as *loop*, we append loop information to each dynamic shared memory access [3].

4. Conclusion

This paper illustrates different scenarios that can lead to concurrency bugs. Based on these scenarios, this paper also presents a concurrency bug diagnosis framework, which consists of 3 test procedures to localize buggy shared memory access pairs manifested in different scenarios.

References

[1] S. Lu, S. Park, E. Seo, and Y. Zhou. Learning from mistakes – a comprehensive study on real world concurrency bug characteristics. In *ASPLOS*, 2008.

[2] S. Park, R. W. Vuduc, and M. J. Harrold. Falcon: Fault localization in concurrent programs. In *ICSE*, 2010.

[3] A. Muzahid, N. Otsuki, and J. Torrellas. AtomTracker: A comprehensive approach to atomic region inference and violation detection. In *MICRO*, 2010.

[4] J. Yu, S. Narayanasamy, C. Pereira, and G. Pokam. Maple: A converage-driven testing tool for multithreaded programs. In *OOPSLA*, 2012.

Task Mapping Stencil Computations for Non-Contiguous Allocations *

Vitus J. Leung[1]   David P. Bunde[2]   Johnathan Ebbers[2]   Stefan P. Feer[3,†]

Nickolas W. Price[2]   Zachary D. Rhodes[4,†]   Matthew Swank[2]

[1]Sandia National Laboratories   [2]Knox College   [3]3M Health Information Systems, Inc.   [4]Allstate Corporation

vjleung@sandia.gov   {dbunde,jebbers,nprice,mswank}@knox.edu   sfeer@mmm.com   rhodesz87@gmail.com

Abstract

We examine task mapping algorithms for systems that allocate jobs non-contiguously. Several studies have shown that task placement affects job running time. We focus on jobs with a stencil communication pattern and use experiments on a Cray XE to evaluate novel task mapping algorithms as well as some adapted to this setting. This is done with the miniGhost miniApp which mimics the behavior of CTH, a shock physics application. Our strategies improve average and single-run times by as much as 28% and 36% over a baseline strategy, respectively.

Categories and Subject Descriptors D. Software [*D.1 Programming Techniques*]: D.1.3 Concurrent Programming

Keywords Task mapping, stencil communication pattern, non-contiguous allocation, improved scalability

1. Introduction

We focus on improving the performance of parallel jobs by optimizing the placement of their tasks. This problem is called *task mapping* because the job's tasks are mapped to nodes. The goal is to map communicating tasks to nearby nodes, which benefits communication patterns other than all-to-all. Good mapping reduces bandwidth usage since messages consume bandwidth on each link used. The importance of mapping is being fueled by two ongoing trends. First, processors are improving faster than networks so bandwidth is increasingly limiting performance. Second, node counts are growing, increasing both the number of hops and the potential for hotspots. Several experiments have shown that improved mapping can significantly impact performance, including a speedup of 1.64 on a full application [5].

One way to classify prior work on task mapping is by the amount of structure assumed. At one extreme are graph-based approaches, which represent the problem as embedding a communication graph into a machine graph. They lose geometric information such as node coordinates. Thus, the problems are formally hard and cannot exploit the structure of practical applications. At the other extreme are whole-machine approaches that target systems such as Blue Gene that allocate jobs to contiguous groups of nodes. These approaches address structured communication patterns by folding one grid onto another. They cannot be used on systems with non-contiguous allocation, such as the Cray XE.

Our approach is in the middle. We map jobs with structured communication and non-contiguous allocations, using mesh-based algorithms. Specifically, we map jobs with a regular 3D nearest neighbor communication pattern onto a 3D mesh. This is the simplest case, but non-trivial because nodes allocated to other jobs interfere with the mapping.

2. Algorithms

Now we summarize our algorithms. As preprocessing, they rotate the job to match the relative order of the job dimensions with those of the nodes' bounding box. For example, a job with longer x dimension will rotate if assigned nodes whose bounding box has a longer y dimension. All algorithms except Baseline and GROUPING (prior work) do this.

We compare our algorithms against two from prior work:

- Baseline (provided by ALPS and Moab) numbers cores in allocation order, numbers tasks in row-major order, and maps corresponding elements.

---

* D.P. Bunde, J. Ebbers, S.P. Feer, N.W. Price, Z.D. Rhodes, and M. Swank were partially supported by contract 899808 from Sandia National Laboratories. Z.D. Rhodes also acknowledges support from a Post-baccalaureate Fellowship from Knox College. Sandia National Laboratories is a multi-program laboratory managed and operated by Sandia Corporation, a wholly owned subsidiary of Lockheed Martin Corporation, for the U.S. Department of Energy's National Nuclear Security Administration under contract DE-AC04-94AL85000.

† Work done while a student at Knox College.

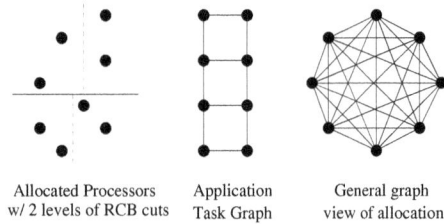

Allocated Processors   Application   General graph
w/ 2 levels of RCB cuts   Task Graph   view of allocation

Figure 1. Comparison of processor representations

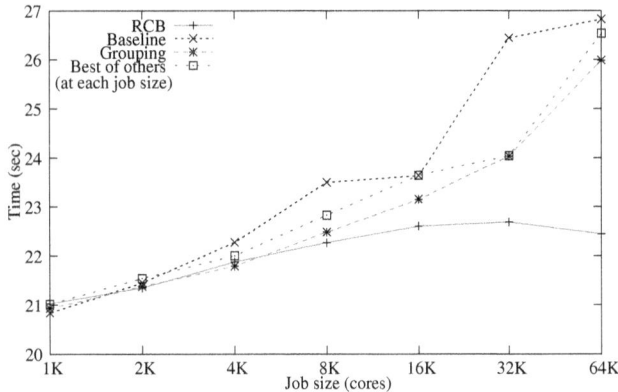

Figure 2. Running time as a function of job size

- GROUPING [2] follows Baseline after grouping tasks into 2 by 2 by 4 blocks, each mapped to a 16-core node.

We also adapted a couple of mapping algorithms that assume contiguous allocation [3]:

- CORNER ("Expand from corner") numbers tasks and cores by distance from $(0, 0, 0)$ and maps corresponding elements.

- ALLCORNERS ("Corners to center") rotates between corners, selecting from $(0, 0, 0)$, then from $(0, y_{max}, 0)$, etc.

We also implemented some completely new algorithms:

- COLMAJOR numbers tasks and nodes in column major order and maps corresponding elements.
- ROWMAJOR does this with row major numbering.
- ORDERED takes the order with the lowest average hops.
- OVERLAY defines a desired place for each task from its position relative to the front lower left corner. Each task is mapped to the unmapped node nearest its desired place.
- TWOWAYOVERLAY follows OVERLAY, but alternately maps tasks from opposite corners.
- RCB (Recursive Coordinate Bisection) bisects the job based on its longest dimension (X, Y, or Z), bisects the nodes using the same dimension, and recursively maps each half job onto the corresponding half of the nodes.

[6] also has a bisection heuristic, but they take a graph-based approach, forcing them to use lose problem geometry, as shown in Figure 1. RCB outperforms their approach [4].

3. Experiments

The experiments were run on Cielo (#26 on the Nov 2013 Top 500 list), a Cray XE6 with 143,104 compute cores in 8,944 dual socket compute nodes, connected in a 16x12x24 torus of Gemini ASICs, with 2 nodes per Gemini.

The application used in the experiments was miniGhost, a miniapp developed as part of the DOE exascale research program to represent major codes. MiniGhost is modeled on the computational core of CTH, a shock physics application with stencil communication. Experiments have shown that task mapping has more effect on CTH than miniGhost [1].

For a given job size (in cores), miniGhost can run with different numbers of cores per MPI rank (denoted cores/rank), which changes the number of ranks (but not nodes) to vary the mix of MPI and OpenMP. A trend we observed is that the worst mappers tend to perform best at 16 cores/rank (fewer messages) while better mappers favor intermediate values.

Figure 2 shows average running time (5 runs) by job size using 4 cores/rank, which balances message number and size. RCB does consistently well and is the best algorithm for most job sizes. Its outperformance of Baseline increases with job size, reaching just over 16%. It does even better with other values, reaching 24.1% with 2 cores/rank and 28.4% with 1 (5 run ave.; max of 35.5% on 1 run). These gains are fairly consistent, with standard deviations of 0.6, 0.4, and 0.2 seconds for 4, 2, and 1 cores/rank. The best running time for jobs with 8K+ cores was RCB with 2 cores/rank in 17 of the 20 trials (5 runs of 4 sizes). We also found

- The rotation step improves total time in ~60% of the runs, for 1–6% average improvement.
- Spearman rank correlation tests show ave hops correlates with running time. Also correlated (but not as highly) with time are maximum hops and variance.

Acknowledgments. We thank C. Vaughan and K. Hastings for helpful discussions.

References

[1] R. Barrett et al. Summary of Work for ASC L2 Milestone 4465: Characterize the Role of the Mini-Application in Predicting Key Performance Characteristics of Real Applications. Tech. Report SAND2012-4667, Sandia National Laboratories, 2012.

[2] R. Barrett et al. Navigating an evolutionary fast path to exascale. In *Proc. PMBS*, 2012.

[3] A. Bhatelé et al. Automated mapping of regular communication graphs on mesh interconnects. In *Proc. HiPC*, 2010.

[4] M. Deveci et al. Exploiting geometric partitioning in task mapping for parallel computers. In *Proc. IPDPS*, to appear.

[5] F. Gygi et al. Large-scale electronic structure calculations of high-Z metals on the BlueGene/L platform. In *Proc. SC*, 2006.

[6] T. Hoefler and M. Snir. Generic topology mapping strategies for large-scale parallel architectures. In *Proc. ICS*, 2011.

Data Structures for Task-based Priority Scheduling

Martin Wimmer   Francesco Versaci
Jesper Larsson Träff

Faculty of Informatics, Parallel Computing
Vienna University of Technology
1040 Vienna/Wien, Austria
{wimmer,traff,versaci}@par.tuwien.ac.at

Daniel Cederman   Philippas Tsigas

Computer Science and Engineering
Chalmers University of Technology
412 96 Göteborg, Sweden
{cederman,tsigas}@chalmers.se

Abstract

We present three lock-free data structures for priority task scheduling: a priority work-stealing one, a centralized one with ρ-relaxed semantics, and a hybrid one combining both concepts. With the single-source shortest path (SSSP) problem as example, we show how the different approaches affect the prioritization and provide upper bounds on the number of examined nodes. We argue that priority task scheduling allows for an intuitive and easy way to parallelize the SSSP problem, notoriously a hard task. Experimental evidence supports the good scalability of the resulting algorithm.

The larger aim of this work is to understand the trade-offs between scalability and priority guarantees in task scheduling systems. We show that ρ-relaxation is a valuable technique for improving the first, while still allowing semantic constraints to be satisfied: the lock-free, hybrid k-priority data structure can scale as well as work-stealing, while still providing strong priority scheduling guarantees, which depend on the parameter k. Our theoretical results open up possibilities for even more scalable data structures by adopting a weaker form of ρ-relaxation, which still enables the semantic constraints to be respected.

Categories and Subject Descriptors   D.4.1 [*Operating Systems*]: Process Management—Scheduling

Keywords   Task-parallelism, priority scheduling, k-priority data structure, work-stealing, parallel single-source shortest paths

PPoPP '14,   February 15–19, 2014, Orlando, Florida, USA.
Copyright is held by the owner/author(s).
ACM 978-1-4503-2656-8/14/02.
http://dx.doi.org/10.1145/2555243.2555278

1. Preliminaries

A `C++` implementation of our data structures and applications is available for download as part of the open source task-scheduling framework Pheet [3, 5][1]. Implementation details, proofs and further references are available in the accompanying technical report [4].

2. ρ-relaxation

In order to improve the scalability of the proposed data structures, we adopt a ρ-relaxation scheme, as introduced by Afek et al. [1], which allows up to ρ items in the data structure to be *ignored*, based on their recency. We say that an item in a priority queue is ignored whenever some other item with lower rank is returned by a pop.

The centralized k-priority queue satisfies ρ-relaxation in the following sense: a pop operation is allowed to ignore items added by the latest $\rho = k$ push operations (in the worst case, the top k by priority). In the hybrid k-priority queue pop operations are allowed to ignore the latest k items added by each thread, which implies that, being P the number of threads, up to $\rho = Pk$ items might be ignored.

3. Data structures

3.1 Work-stealing

We adapt work-stealing to priority scheduling, by using local priority queues per thread instead of deques [3]. This preserves the scalability of work-stealing, while imposing local prioritization on the tasks. Due to the decentralized nature of work-stealing, no global priority ordering can be imposed and thus no guarantees can be given on the priority of tasks that are being executed.

3.2 Centralized k-priority data structure

A global priority queue provides strong guarantees on the priority of tasks, but can suffer from congestion. We reduce congestion by adopting ρ-relaxation, which is realized by splitting the data structure into two components: (i) a local

---

[1] http://www.pheet.org

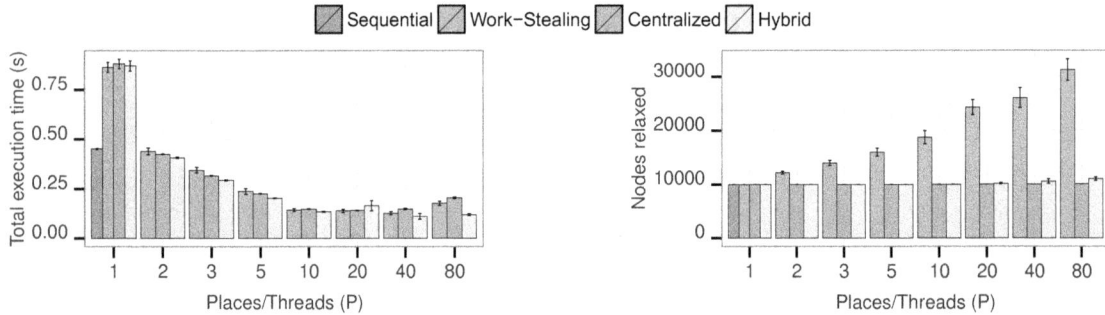

Figure 1. Total execution time and number of nodes relaxed for varying P ($n = 10000$, $k = 512$, $p = 50\%$).

priority queue per thread with references to tasks, and (ii) a global array of tasks. All the tasks stored in the global array at some index $i <$ `tail` are visible to all the threads and referenced in their local priority queues. Newly created tasks are stored in the global array at a random position in the range $\{$`tail`$, \dots,$ `tail` $+ k - 1\}$ (similarly to k-FIFO queues [2]), with the `tail` index being advanced whenever all the k positions are filled.

3.3 Hybrid k-priority data structure

The hybrid k-priority data structure combines the work-stealing and the ρ-relaxation ideas into a single data structure. It consists of three components: (i) a global list, storing tasks visible to all places, (ii) one local task list per thread, of length at most k, and (iii) one priority queue per thread, storing references to tasks in the global and local lists, ordered by priority. Newly created tasks are added to a local task list. When more than k tasks have been added to some local list, it is appended to the global one.

4. Evaluation

Our evaluation is based on a simple parallelization of Dijkstra's algorithm for SSSP, where nodes are speculatively relaxed to increase the available parallelism. Each thread selects the next node to relax based on its tentative distance value, by using the priority data structures presented in this work. Whenever a node is relaxed for which the tentative distance value is not final, this counts as *useless work*, since the node will have to be relaxed again. In our analysis using Erdős-Rényi random graphs we show that the useless work performed when using ρ-relaxed priority data structures can be bounded from above. The theoretical bounds are later verified by simulation.

We also performed an experimental evaluation of our three data structure implementations on an 80-core Intel Xeon system. We show the execution time and the total number of nodes relaxed for executions as a function of the number of threads P (Figure 1). The useless work can be computed by subtracting the number of nodes in the graph (10000) from the number of relaxed nodes. The ρ-relaxed data structures barely produce any useless work for $k \leq$

512, whereas for work-stealing the useless work exceeds the useful work for 20 threads and more.

The parallel implementations are also compared to a sequential implementation of Dijkstra's algorithm (shown only for one thread). Due to the small task granularity, the overhead for parallel execution on all data structures is relatively high, but for two or more threads the execution times drop below the sequential time.

5. Conclusion

We have developed three lock-free data structures for priority scheduling, each of them providing different trade-offs between scalability and guarantees concerning the execution order of tasks. We argue that the hybrid k-priority data structure offers the best compromise between scalability and amount of useless work performed.

Our evaluation shows that ρ-relaxation is a valuable technique to improve scalability, while still enabling strong guarantees. We understood more deeply which properties are required to obtain these guarantees and in future work we plan to further extend priority queues based on this insight: first results on such relaxed k-priority data structures look promising.

References

[1] Y. Afek, G. Korland, and E. Yanovsky. Quasi-linearizability: Relaxed consistency for improved concurrency. In *OPODIS*, pages 395–410, 2010.

[2] C. M. Kirsch, M. Lippautz, and H. Payer. Fast and scalable, lock-free k-FIFO queues. In *PaCT*, pages 208–223, 2013.

[3] M. Wimmer, D. Cederman, J. L. Träff, and P. Tsigas. Work-stealing with configurable scheduling strategies. In *18th ACM Symposium on Principles & Practice of Parallel Programming (PPoPP)*, pages 315–316, 2013.

[4] M. Wimmer, D. Cederman, F. Versaci, J. L. Träff, and P. Tsigas. Data structures for task-based priority scheduling. CoRR abs/1312.2501, 2013.

[5] M. Wimmer, M. Pöter, and J. L. Träff. The Pheet task-scheduling framework on the Intel®Xeon Phi™coprocessor and other multicore architectures. In *MTAAP (IPDPS) Workshop*, 2013.

Detecting Silent Data Corruption through Data Dynamic Monitoring for Scientific Applications

Leonardo Bautista Gomez and Franck Cappello

Argonne National Laboratory

Abstract

Parallel programming has become one of the best ways to express scientific models that simulate a wide range of natural phenomena. These complex parallel codes are deployed and executed on large-scale parallel computers, making them important tools for scientific discovery. As supercomputers get faster and larger, the increasing number of components is leading to higher failure rates. In particular, the miniaturization of electronic components is expected to lead to a dramatic rise in soft errors and data corruption. Moreover, soft errors can corrupt data silently and generate large inaccuracies or wrong results at the end of the computation. In this paper we propose a novel technique to detect silent data corruption based on data monitoring. Using this technique, an application can learn the *normal* dynamics of its datasets, allowing it to quickly spot anomalies. We evaluate our technique with synthetic benchmarks and we show that our technique can detect up to 50% of injected errors while incurring only negligible overhead.

Categories and Subject Descriptors C4 [*Performance of systems*]: Fault tolerance

Keywords Fault Tolerance; Supercomputers; Silent Data Corruption; Soft Errors; Bit Flips; Data Entropy.

1. Introduction

Computing-intensive scientific applications need post-petascale machines to achieve results in a reasonable amount of time. Unfortunately, the increasing number of components in such large machines leads to a decreasing mean time between failures (MTBF) for extreme-scale systems. In addition to hardware failures, soft errors can cause one or multiple bits to

PPoPP'14, February 15–19, 2014, Orlando, Florida, USA.
ACM 978-1-4503-2656-8/14/02.
http://dx.doi.org/10.1145/2555243.2555279

spontaneously flip to the opposite state. Although techniques such as error correcting codes (ECCs) have been proposed to tackle soft errors, the reality is that a significant number of bit flips still manage to pass undetected, this is called silent data corruption (SDC). Moreover, the constant need to reduce component size and voltage, limits the use of soft-error mitigation techniques, dramatically increasing the Soft Error Rate (SER) in the coming years [1, 3]. To guarantee correct results for scientific applications in the presence of SDC is one of the hardest challenges of extreme-scale computing. SDC, by definition, is not detected in the lower levels of the hardware/software stack. In contrast, higher-level software could leverage properties of the data dynamics in order to detect outliers that could suggest the presence of corruption. In this work, we propose a novel technique that leverages data entropy characteristics of scientific datasets to determine whether corruption has occurred. Experimental evaluation of our data dynamic monitoring technique on synthetic benchmarks show that our detector is able to reduce the number of SDC seen by the application, by up to 50% and can reach an accuracy of over 98% while incurring less than 1% of overhead to the application.

2. Ultra-light SDC detector

Our universe obeys a set of physical laws that dictate the behavior of matter and energy. These laws impose some limits (e.g., speed of light) that define what is physically possible and meaningful. These limits are inherited by the computational codes that simulate those phenomena, and they can be used to detect abnormalities. The presence of these physical limits in the computational codes executed on supercomputers provides us with our first insight into detecting data corruption. Unfortunately, when the interval of possible values is too large, corrupted data is likely to be inside this interval, decreasing the efficiency of such a strategy. Our second insight into detecting outliers in large HPC datasets is closely related to the notion of space. We notice that in a large number of physical phenomena, points that are close in space exhibit similar behavior. For instance, although the temperature on the Earth's surface can vary widely between the equator line and the poles, any two close points on the planet should have relatively close temperatures. The reason is that points close in space are subject to the same external factors and forces. This observation can be translated as a sort of *local regularity* of HPC datasets. Therefore, when the difference between neighbor elements in a HPC dataset is unusually high, it could be due to data corruption.

Based on these observations, we define a threshold t_d to trigger corruption suspicion. Each dataset d of the application has its own threshold t_d. When the difference between two neighbor elements of a dataset is higher than the threshold t_d, then the detector triggers a corruption suspicion alert. The threshold t_d can be defined as *the historical maximum of the absolute value of the finite difference between neighbor points*. Thus, our lightweight detector consists of a data dynamics monitor, DADYMO that scrubs the different datasets at the application level during runtime and that issues an alert every time the difference between two neighbor elements is higher than the threshold t_d of the particular dataset. Such lightweight test can be performed at high frequency without disturbing the application significantly.

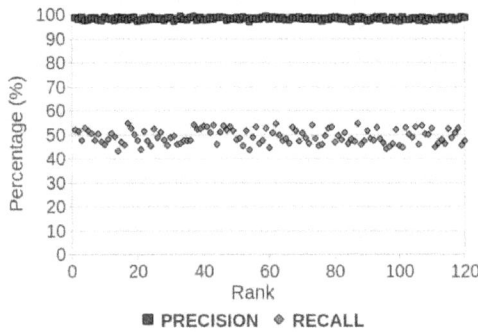

Figure 1. DADYMO Precision and Recall

3. Evaluation

In this section, we evaluate the accuracy of DADYMO with a synthetic benchmark. The accuracy of a SDC detector is quantified by using two measures: its *recall* and its *precision*. To evaluate our technique, we developed an error injector capable of making modifications in datasets at a binary level.

3.1 DADYMO Performance and Accuracy

We set up an experiment using a synthetic benchmark of a heat distribution simulation executed on over 100 MPI ranks. Each rank holds a temperature dataset with values in the range of [260.0, 360.0] kelvin in single precision and a maximum variation of 1.0 kelvin between neighbor cells. This configuration guarantees that from one value to its neighbor, only a maximum of 16 bits (out of 32) changes. Then, during the execution we inject over a thousand bit flips on each rank for a total of over $170,000$ injected random bit flips. During the whole execution, we execute DADYMO at high frequency in order to detect SDC.

First, we measure the throughput of DADYMO for each rank trough the simulation. We observed that all the ranks have the same throughput (700 MB/s). Thus, in a node with 16 MPI ranks the total node-level DADYMO throughput is 11 GB/s. The size of the dataset for each rank was 256 MBs; thus each DADYMO execution took just a fraction of a second, causing less than 1% overhead. After proving that DADYMO is a lightweight detector, we evaluate the accuracy of its detections. Thus, we count the number of detected bit flips and for each detection check whether the detected bit flip corresponds to an injection or not, so that we get the number of true positives and false positives. In this way we are able to get the precision and recall for each rank. We plot the results in Figure 2. As we can see, all processes have around 50% of recall and 98% of precision.

4. Related work

A large literature exists on soft errors rates [1, 4] and detection and correction techniques. Most of these techniques are implemented at the hardware level. Most of these strategies, however, target soft errors in general and do not focus on the particular case of SDC in parallel scientific applications. For some specific linear algebra algorithms, one of the most promising techniques against SDC is algorithm-based fault tolerance (ABFT). ABFT [2] is a technique that uses extra checksums to correct errors. However, ABFT has been implemented only on linear algebra kernels.

5. Conclusions

In this work we highlighted some properties of HPC datasets, such as low variations for close elements. Based on this property, we proposed to set a threshold t_d for each dataset to detect SDC. We evaluated our proposed scheme with synthetic benchmarks and our results show that our technique can detect over 50% of silent bit flips (recall) with a precision of 98% causing less than 1% overhead.

References

[1] Shekhar Borkar. Designing reliable systems from unreliable components: The challenges of transistor variability and degradation. *IEEE Micro*, 25:10–16, November 2005.

[2] Kuang-Hua Huang and Jacob A. Abraham. Algorithm-based fault tolerance for matrix operations. *Computers, IEEE Transactions on*, 100(6):518–528, 1984.

[3] Dong Li, Jeffrey S Vetter, and Weikuan Yu. Classifying soft error vulnerabilities in extreme-scale scientific applications using a binary instrumentation tool. In *Proceedings of the International Conference on High Performance Computing, Networking, Storage and Analysis*, page 57. IEEE Computer Society Press, 2012.

[4] Tezzaron Semiconductor. Soft errors in electronic memory-a white paper, 2004.

Fine-Grain Parallel Megabase Sequence Comparison with Multiple Heterogeneous GPUs

Edans F. de O. Sandes
University of Brasilia
edans@cic.unb.br

Guillermo Miranda
Barcelona Supercomputing Center
guillermo.miranda@bsc.es

Alba C. M. A. Melo
University of Brasilia
alba@cic.unb.br

Xavier Martorell
Universitat Politècnica de Catalunya
Barcelona Supercomputing Center
xavier.martorell@bsc.es

Eduard Ayguadé
Universitat Politècnica de Catalunya
Barcelona Supercomputing Center
eduard.ayguade@bsc.es

Abstract

This paper proposes and evaluates a parallel strategy to execute the exact Smith-Waterman (SW) algorithm for megabase DNA sequences in heterogeneous multi-GPU platforms. In our strategy, the computation of a single huge SW matrix is spread over multiple GPUs, which communicate border elements to the neighbour, using a circular buffer mechanism that hides the communication overhead. We compared 4 pairs of human-chimpanzee homologous chromosomes using 2 different GPU environments, obtaining a performance of up to 140.36 GCUPS (Billion of cells processed per second) with 3 heterogeneous GPUS.

Categories and Subject Descriptors D.1.3 [*Programming Techniques*]: Concurrent Programming; J.3 [*Life and Medical Sciences*]: Biology and Genetics

Keywords GPU; Biological Sequence Comparison; Smith-Waterman;

1. Introduction

Smith-Waterman (SW) [4] is an exact algorithm based on the longest common subsequence (LCS) concept, that uses dynamic programming to find local alignments between two sequences. SW is very accurate but it needs a lot of computational resources. GPUs (Graphics Processing Units) have been considered to accelerate SW, but very few GPU strate-

gies [1, 3] allow the comparison of Megabase sequences longer than 10 Million Base Pairs (MBP). SW#[1] uses 2 GPUs to execute a Myers-Miller [2] linear space variant of SW. CUDAlign [3] uses a single GPU to execute a combined strategy with SW and Myers-Miller. When compared to SW#(1 GPU), CUDAlign (1 GPU) presents better execution times for huge sequences [1].

In this work, we modified the most computational intensive stage of CUDAlign, parallelizing the computation of a single huge DP matrix among heterogeneous GPUs in a fine-grained way. In the proposed strategy, GPUs are logically arranged in a linear way so that each GPU calculates a subset of columns of the SW matrix, sending the border column elements to the next GPU. Experimental results collected in 2 different environments show performance of up to 140 GCUPS (Billion of cells processed per second) using 3 heterogeneous GPUS. With this performance, we are able to compare real megabase sequences in reasonable time.

2. Proposed Multi-GPU Strategy

We modified the first stage of CUDAlign [3] to parallelize computation of a single huge DP matrix among many heterogeneous GPUs. The parallelization is done using a multi-GPU wavefront method, where the GPUs are logically arranged in a linear way, i.e, the first GPU is connected to the second, the second to the third and so on. Each GPU computes a range of columns of the DP matrix and the GPUs transfer the cells of their last column to the next GPU. In a scenario composed of heterogeneous GPUs, assigning the same number of columns to all GPUs is not a good choice. In this case, the slowest GPU would determine the processing rate of the whole wavefront. To avoid this, we statically distribute the columns proportionally to the computational power of each GPU. This distribution can be obtained from sequence comparison benchmarks that determine each GPU

PPoPP '14,   February 15–19, 2014, Orlando, Florida, USA.
Copyright is held by the owner/author(s).
ACM 978-1-4503-2656-8/14/02.
http://dx.doi.org/10.1145/2555243.2555280

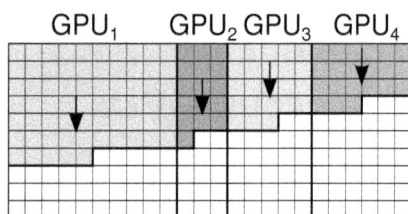

Figure 1. Columns distributions for 4 GPUs.

Table 1. Sequences used in the tests.

Chr.	Human		Chimpanzee		Score
	Accession	Size	Accession	Size	
chr19	NC_000019.9	59M	NC_006486.3	64M	17297608
chr20	NC_000020.10	63M	NC_006487.3	62M	40050427
chr21	NC_000021.8	48M	NC_006488.2	46M	36006054
chr22	NC_000022.10	51M	NC_006489.3	50M	31510791

computational power, in cells updated per second (CUPS). Then, the column distribution is defined proportionally to the computational power obtained in the comparisons. Figure 1 shows a possible column distribution for a 4-GPU configuration, where the faster GPUs are responsible to process more columns than the slower GPUs.

In our strategy, each GPU is bound to one process and each process has 3 CPU threads: one manager thread, that manages computation in GPU, and two communication threads, that handle inter-process communication overlapped with the computation. The inter-process communication is made by circular buffers and sockets, which transfer cells from one process to the next. In hosts with multiple attached GPUs, one process is created for each GPU, and the connection is handled by loopback sockets. In environments with different hosts, the connections are made using TCP sockets.

3. Experimental Results

We compared human and chimpanzee chromosomes 19 to 22, which sizes vary from 46MBP (Million Base Pairs) to 64MBP. As far as we know, this was the first time chromosomes 19, 20 and 22 were compared with SW. For validation purposes, the accession numbers, sizes and the optimal local scores obtained during our tests are presented in Table 1. The SW score parameters used in the tests were: match: $+1$; mismatch -3; first gap: -5; extension gap: -2.

The multi-GPU version of CUDAlign was tested in two heterogeneous multi-GPU environments: Panoramix and Laico. **Panoramix** is a single host connected to 1 Tesla K20c and 2 Tesla C2050. The column distribution was 46.10% to the K20c GPU and 26.95% to each C2050 GPU. **Laico** (LAboratory of Integrated and COncurrent systems) has several hosts with GPUs. For our tests, we selected one host with a GTX 580 GPU and two hosts with a GTX 680 GPU

each. The column distribution was 30.71% for the GTX 580 and 34.64% for each GTX 680.

Table 2 presents execution times and GCUPS for the comparisons in both heterogeneous environments. It shows that the relative performance ranged from 100.62 to 101.38 GCUPS (Billion of cells processed per second) in Panoramix and from 139.60 to 140.36 GCUPS in Laico. We can see that the results are very uniform, since the GCUPS varied in less than 0.76% in Panoramix and 0.55% in Laico. By dividing the GCUPS by the defined columns proportion in Panoramix, the K20c GPU was responsible for approximately 46 GCUPS and each C2050 GPU was responsible for approximately 27 GCUPS. For Laico, the GTX 580 was responsible for approximately 43 GCUPS and each the GTX 680 was responsible for 48 GCUPS.

Chr.	Size	Panoramix		Laico	
		Time	GCUPS	Time	GCUPS
chr19	59M×64M	37252s	101.02	26957s	139.60
chr20	63M×62M	38537s	100.96	27728s	140.31
chr21	48M×46M	22238s	100.62	16024s	139.63
chr22	51M×50M	25416s	101.38	18180s	140.36

Table 2. Execution Times and GCUPS.

4. Future Works

As future work, we intend to execute our parallel strategy in a dedicated cluster environment with several GPUs. In order to use the cluster resources in a reasonable way, we will develop a formal method to predict the execution time and speedup of a comparison given the size of the sequences and the number of GPUs.

Acknowledgments

We thankfully acknowledge the support of the grant SEV-2011-00067 of Severo Ochoa Program, awarded by the Spanish Government, the Spanish Ministry of Science and Technology (TIN2012-34557, CSD2007-00050) and the Generalitat de Catalunya (2009-SGR-980). This work is also partially supported by CNPq/Brazil (grants 242800/2012-2 and 211456/2013-6) and CAPES/PVE (grant 02/2012).

References

[1] M. Korpar and M. Sikic. SW#-GPU-Enabled Exact Alignments on Genome Scale. *Bioinformatics*, 29(19):2494–2495, 2013.

[2] E. W. Myers and W. Miller. Optimal Alignments in Linear Space. *Computer Applications in the Biosciences*, 4(1):11–17, 1988.

[3] E. Sandes and A. de Melo. Retrieving Smith-Waterman Alignments with Optimizations for Megabase Biological Sequences Using GPU. *IEEE Transactions on Parallel and Distributed Systems*, 24(5):1009–1021, 2013.

[4] T. F. Smith and M. S. Waterman. Identification of common molecular subsequences. *J Mol Biol*, 147(1):195–197, 1981.

Automatic Semantic Locking

Guy Golan-Gueta
Tel Aviv University
ggolan@tau.ac.il

G. Ramalingam
Microsoft Research
grama@microsoft.com

Mooly Sagiv
Tel Aviv University
msagiv@tau.ac.il

Eran Yahav
Technion
yahave@cs.technion.ac.il

Abstract

In this paper, we consider concurrent programs in which the shared state consists of instances of linearizable ADTs (abstract data types). We develop a novel automated approach to concurrency control that addresses a common need: the need to *atomically* execute a code fragment, which may contain multiple ADT operations on multiple ADT instances.

In our approach, each ADT implements ADT-specific semantic locking operations that serve to exploit the semantics of ADT operations. We develop a synthesis algorithm that automatically inserts calls to these locking operations in a set of given code fragments (in a client program) to ensure that these code fragments execute atomically without deadlocks, and without rollbacks.

We have implemented the synthesis algorithm and several general-purpose ADTs with semantic locking. We have applied the synthesis algorithm to several Java programs that use these ADTs. Our results show that our approach enables efficient and scalable synchronization.

Categories and Subject Descriptors D.1.3 [*Programming Techniques*]: Concurrent Programming

Keywords Compiler, Synchronization, Composition

1. The Problem

Atomic sections are a language construct that allow a programmer to declaratively specify that a given code fragment must (appear to) execute atomically, leaving it to a compiler and runtime to implement the necessary concurrency control. In this work we develop a methodology and automation support for realizing a restricted form of atomic sections.

The example in Fig. 1, inspired by the code of the *Intruder* benchmark (from [1]), illustrates the problem we ad-

```
atomic { set=map.get(id);
         if(set==null) { set=new Set(); map.put(id, set); }
         set.add(x);
         if(flag) { queue.enqueue(set); map.remove(id); }      }
```
Figure 1. Code that manipulates several linearizable ADTs.

dress in this paper. The shared state of this code fragment consists of three ADTs: (i) a Map ADT (pointed by the variable `map`); (ii) a Set ADT (pointed by the variable `set`); (iii) and a Queue ADT (pointed by the variable `queue`). (All program variables, such as `flag`, are thread-local.) Each of these ADTs is linearizable, and thus each individual ADT operation appears to execute atomically. However, in this case, we wish the entire code fragment to execute atomically: the individual ADTs cannot provide this guarantee.

We consider a Java multi-threaded program (also referred to as a *client*), which makes use of several linearizable ADT libraries. We assume that the only mutable state shared by multiple threads are *instances* of ADTs. We permit atomic sections as a language construct: a block of code may be marked as an atomic section. An execution of an atomic section is called a *transaction*. Our goal is to ensure that transactions appear to execute atomically and make progress (avoiding deadlocks), while exploiting the semantic properties of the ADT operations to achieve greater parallelism. We also wish to avoid the use of any rollbacks.

2. Overview

Our approach decomposes the responsibility for the task into two parts: one to be realized by the ADT implementations and one to be realized by a compiler (on behalf of the client code). We require each ADT implementation to provide a set of *semantic locking* operations. We show how a compiler can, given these ADT locking operations, automatically compile atomic sections in a given (client) program so as to provide the desired guarantees.

ADTs with Semantic Locking A *semantic locking operation* of an ADT is used by a client of the ADT to acquire permission to invoke a specific set of *base operations* on the ADT: in this case, we say that the client has a lock on the corresponding set of underlying ADT operations. It is the client transaction's responsibility to ensure that it has a lock on a

PPoPP '14, February 15–19, 2014, Orlando, Florida, USA.
Copyright is held by the owner/author(s).
ACM 978-1-4503-2656-8/14/02.
http://dx.doi.org/10.1145/2555243.2555281

```
// Standard API              // Synchronization API
void add(int i);             void lockAll();
void remove(int i);          void lockAdd();
boolean contains(int i);     void lockValue(int i);
int size();                  void unlockAll();
```

Figure 2. API of a Set with semantic locking.

base ADT operation before it invokes that operation. The ADT has the responsibility to ensure that two transactions are allowed to simultaneously hold locks on operations op_1 and op_2, respectively, only if op_1 and op_2 commute. Fig. 2 shows an example for an API of a Set ADT with semantic locking. In this example, an invocation of "lockAdd()" acquires locks on the add operations of the Set — hence, after transaction t invokes "lockAdd()", t is allowed to invoke the method "void add(int i)". For any integer v, an invocation of "lockValue(v)" acquires locks on all Set operations that refer to value v (e.g., "lockValue(7)" acquires locks on the operations: add(7), remove(7) and contains(7)). The method "lockAll()" acquires locks on all operations of the Set; and "unlockAll()" releases all locks owned by the current transaction.

We have used a simple annotation language (adopted from [4]) to specify the semantics of a locking operation (namely, the set of base operations it corresponds to); these annotations enable our compiler to take an ADT description as a parameter (our compiler is not aware of any specific ADT).

Automatic Atomicity We have developed a compiler for atomic sections. Given a client program and a specification of the semantic locking operations of the ADTs used by the client, the compiler inserts invocations of semantic locking operations into the atomic sections in the client program to guarantee atomicity and deadlock-freedom of these atomic sections. The synchronization generated by our compiler follows a semantics-aware two-phase locking protocol [3]. Fig. 3 shows the result of applying our compiler to the atomic section of Fig. 1. The basic idea is to consider every base ADT operation invocation (say "x.op()") in the transaction and insert a conditional call ("if (cond) x.lockY()") to a semantic locking operation before the base operation. The condition is used to dynamically check if the object has already been locked. A static analysis identifies the set S of all base operations that may be performed on the relevant object (x in the above example) in the future (by the transaction), and a semantic locking operation (lockY() in the above example) is chosen so that it obtains a lock on a superset of S. (An optimizing phase is used to identify when either the conditional check or the lock-acquisition is redundant and eliminate them.)

This basic scheme is modified by determining an order in which objects are locked (to avoid deadlocks) and by moving the semantic locking operations earlier in the transaction to respect the determined ordering. All locks are released at the end of the transaction to ensure two-phase-locking.

```
atomic {
    map.lockKey(id); set=map.get(id);
    if(set==null) { set=new Set(); map.put(id, set); }
    set.lockAdd(); set.add(x);
    if(flag) { queue.lockAll();
        queue.enqueue(set); queue.unlockAll(); map.remove(id); }
    map.unlockAll(); set.unlockAll();  }
```

Figure 3. The atomic section of Fig. 1 with semantic locking operations automatically inserted by our compiler.

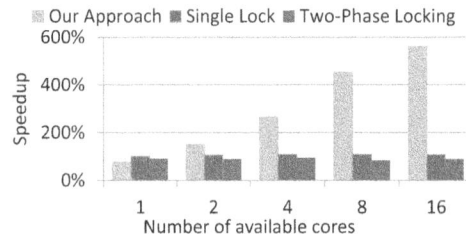

Figure 4. GossipRouter. Speedup over a single core.

A separate optimization phase it used to release locks on objects earlier when it is possible to do so safely.

Pointers and Limitations Our compiler handles programs in which pointers to ADTs are dynamically manipulated. For some of these programs, our compiler is unable to ensure deadlock-freedom by using only the semantic locking operations of the ADTs. These programs are handled using an additional specialized coarse-grain synchronization. However, our experimental evaluation shows that our compiler creates effective synchronization that benefits from semantic locking even in a program (the *GossipRouter* [2]) in which coarse-grained synchronization is used.

3. Performance Evaluation

We have applied our approach to 5 benchmarks. In 3 benchmarks we evaluate the performance of modules that are implemented using several general-purpose ADTs: a *Graph* (from [4]) a *ReferencesCounter* (reference counting module implemented using a Map and Counters) , and a specialized *Cache* (from [4]). In 2 benchmarks we evaluate the performance of Java applications: *Intruder* (from [1]) and *GossipRouter* (from [2]). The results show, for all benchmarks, that the our approach provides efficient and scalable performance. Fig. 4 shows the results for the *GossipRouter* application (in the figure, our approach is compared to a single lock and to a realization of the two-phase locking protocol).

References

[1] sites.google.com/site/deucestm/.

[2] http://www.jgroups.org.

[3] BERNSTEIN, P. A., HADZILACOS, V., AND GOODMAN, N. *Concurrency Control and Recovery in Database Systems.* Addison-Wesley, 1987.

[4] GOLAN-GUETA, G., RAMALINGAM, G., SAGIV, M., AND YAHAV, E. Concurrent libraries with foresight. In *PLDI* (2013).

Optimistic Transactional Boosting

Ahmed Hassan

Virginia Tech

hassan84@vt.edu

Roberto Palmieri

Virginia Tech

robertop@vt.edu

Binoy Ravindran

Virginia Tech

binoy@vt.edu

Abstract

Herlihy and Koskinen's transactional boosting methodology addressed the challenge of converting concurrent data structures into transactional ones. We present an optimistic methodology for boosting concurrent collections. Optimistic boosting allows greater data structure-specific optimizations, easier integration with STM frameworks, and lower restrictions on the boosted operations than the original boosting methodology.

Categories and Subject Descriptors D.1.3 [*Programming Techniques*]: Concurrent Programming – Parallel Programming; E.1 [*Data Structures*]: Concurrent Data Structures

Keywords STM, Transactional Boosting, Transactional Data Structures

1. Introduction

Concurrent collections of elements [3] are well optimized for preserving isolation of concurrent operations, but they do not support transactional accesses to objects. Software Transactional Memory (STM) [4] is increasingly becoming a promising technology for designing and implementing concurrent applications. STM can be trivially used for implementing transactional data structures and collections. However, the performance of STM-based transactional collections is significantly lower than their optimized, concurrent (non-transactional) counterparts.

As an alternative to using STM, Herlihy and Koskinen introduced the technique of *Transactional Boosting* [2], which converts concurrent data structures to transactional ones by providing a *semantic layer* of abstract locks on top of concurrent objects. However, it has some downsides. First, abstract lock acquisition and modifications in memory are eager. This does not natively provide opacity [1] at memory

level and contradicts with the methodology of most STM algorithms, which makes the integration between "boosted" data structures and any STM framework difficult. Second, the technique uses the underlying concurrent data structure as a black box, which prevents further optimizations. Finally, the methodology requires defining an inverse for each operation, which is not necessarily supported in all data structures.

Motivated by these observations, we present *Optimistic Transactional Boosting* (or OTB), an optimistic methodology for converting concurrent data structures into transactional ones. In OTB, transactional operations do not eagerly acquire the semantic locks and modify the shared data structure. Instead, they populate their changes in local logs during their execution, defering any physical modifications to commit time. This way, OTB combines the benefits of lazy concurrent data structures (i.e., un-monitored traversals), boosting (i.e., semantic validation), and transactional memory (i.e., optimistic concurrency control).

OTB gains significant advantages over Herlihy and Koskinen's boosting, which we call "pessimistic" boosting hereafter due to its pessimistic behavior on lock acquisition. First, it avoids the need for defining inverse operations. Second, it uses the concepts of validation, commit, and abort in the same way as general (optimistic) STM algorithms, but at the semantic layer, which enables easy integration with STM frameworks. Finally, it uses highly concurrent collections as white boxes (rather than black boxes as in pessimistic boosting) for designing new transactional versions of each concurrent (non-transactional) data structure, which allows more data structure-specific optimizations.

2. OTB Methodology

Each operation in OTB is divided into three steps:

Traversal. This step scans the objects and computes what the operation's results should be (its postcondition), and what it depends on (its precondition). This raises the need to define (in each transaction), what we call, *semantic read-set* and *semantic write-set*, which store these information.

Validation. This step checks the validity of preconditions. Specifically, the entities stored in the semantic read-set are validated in this step. The step is repeated after each new read (to guarantee opacity), and at commit time.

Commit. This step performs the modifications to the shared data structure. The step is not done at the end of each operation, but is deferred to commit time. All information needed for performing this step are maintained in the semantic write-sets during the first step (i.e., traversal). To publish write-sets, classical two-phase locking is used (but at the semantic layer). This semantic (or abstract) locking prevents semantic conflicts at commit.

Unlike the classical meaning of read-sets and write-sets in STM, not all memory reads and writes are saved in the semantic read-sets and write-sets. Instead, only those reads and writes that affect linearization of the object and consistency of the transaction are saved. This avoids *false conflicts* – i.e., concurrent operations that conflict at the memory level but are independent at the semantic level; thus, they do not require any abort, which degrades the performance of several STM-based data structures.

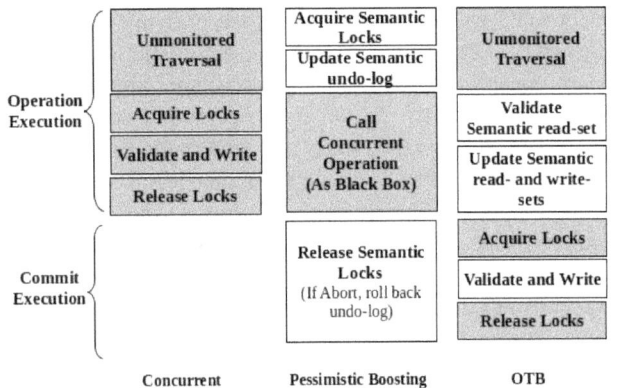

Figure 1. Execution flow of: concurrent (lock-based or lock-free) data structures; pessimistic boosting; OTB.

Figure 1 shows the execution flow of: concurrent (lazy) data structures, pessimistic boosting, and OTB.

Concurrent (non-transactional) data structures yield high performance because they traverse the data structure without instrumentation, and they only acquire locks (or use CAS operations in case of lock-free objects) at late phases.

To add transactional capabilities, pessimistic boosting acquires semantic locks eagerly, and saves the inverse operations in an undo-log (to rollback the transaction in case of abort). Then, it uses the underlying concurrent data structure as a black box without any modifications. (In both pessimistic boosting and OTB, dark blocks in Figure 1 are the same as the concurrent versions, while white blocks are added/modified.) At commit time, the only task to be accomplished is the release of semantic locks, because operations have already been executed eagerly.

In contrast to pessimistic boosting, OTB acquires semantic locks lazily, and uses the underlying data structure as a white box. Similar to concurrent data structures, OTB traverses objects without instrumentation. However, it differs from them in three aspects: *i)* lock acquisition and actual

writes are shifted to commit time; *ii)* the validation procedure is modified to satisfy the new transactional requirements; and *iii)* the necessary information is saved in local semantic read-sets and write-sets.

Thus, OTB gains the following benefits over pessimistic boosting. First, it does not require well defined commutativity rules or inverse operations. Second, integration with STM frameworks is easy, as OTB uses the same phases of validation and commit (with the same meaning as in STM). Third, it uses highly concurrent collections as white boxes to design new transactional versions of each concurrent (non-transactional) data structure. This allows greater optimizations according to the new transactional features, with minimal re-engineering overhead.

3. Example: OTB Set

Following the steps in Section 2, applying optimistic boosting on lazy linked list-based set [3] is straightforward. We briefly explain the guidelines for applying the three steps of optimistic boosting on set.

Traversal. Any operation (add, remove, or contains) on an item X traverses the list without instrumentation until it reaches the involved nodes. As in a lazy set, two nodes are involved in each operation: *pred*, the largest node lower than X; and *curr*, the successor of *pred*. These nodes are saved in the read-set (and the write-set if the operation is a successful add/remove operation). To cover the read-after-write hazard, the write-set is scanned before the list traversal.

Validation. List is validated in a similar way as its concurrent version [3]. The validity of *pred* and *curr* is checked: they should not have been deleted, and the reference of *pred* should point to *curr*. The only difference is that the entire read-set must be post-validated after each operation, and not just the current operation's nodes (to guarantee opacity).

Commit. Semantic locks on all *pred* and *curr* nodes in the write-set are acquired. Then, read-set is validated again, and the write-set is published. Finally, locks are released.

Acknowledgments

The authors would like to thank Maurice Herlihy for his comments and suggestions. This work is supported in part by US National Science Foundation under grant CNS 1116190.

References

[1] R. Guerraoui and M. Kapalka. On the correctness of transactional memory. In *PPoPP*, 2008.

[2] M. Herlihy and E. Koskinen. Transactional boosting: a methodology for highly-concurrent transactional objects. In *PPoPP*, 2008.

[3] M. Herlihy and N. Shavit. *The Art of Multiprocessor Programming, Revised Reprint*. Elsevier, 2012.

[4] N. Shavit and D. Touitou. Software transactional memory. *Distributed Computing*, 10(2), 1997.

Provably Good Scheduling for Parallel Programs that Use Data Structures through Implicit Batching

Kunal Agrawal

Washington University in Saint Louis

kunal@cse.wustl.edu

Jeremy T. Fineman

Georgetown University

jfineman@cs.georgetown.edu

Brendan Sheridan

Georgetown University

bss45@georgetown.edu

Jim Sukha

Intel Corporation

jim.sukha@intel.com

Robert Utterback

Washington University in Saint Louis

robert.utterback@go.wustl.edu

Abstract

This poster proposes an efficient runtime scheduler that provides provable performance guarantees to parallel programs that use data structures through the use of *implicit batching*.

Categories and Subject Descriptors F.2.2 [*Analysis of Algorithms and Problem Complexity*]: Nonnumerical Algorithms and Problems—*Sequencing and scheduling*; D.1.3 [*Programming Techniques*]: Concurrent Programming—*Parallel programming*

Keywords Batch data structures, Work stealing, Scheduler

Introduction

The goal of this research is to enable the use of data structures in parallel programs while providing theoretical performance guarantees to the program. A common approach when using data structures within parallel programs is to employ ***concurrent data structures*** — data structures that can cope with multiple simultaneous accesses. In general, designing concurrent data structure with low worst-case access cost is extremely challenging. It is often the case that the worst-case access has latency proportional to P, the number of processors. For example, the lock-free B^+-tree of [2] has a worst-case latency of $\Omega(P)$, exhibited by P concurrent insertions of contiguous keys. In this case, the total time to execute n data-structure operations on P processors is $\Omega(n)$, which means that the accesses are essentially sequential.

Concurrent data structures are in some sense overkill. Since the data-structure accesses belong to the same enclosing program, they can coordinate with each other to better cope with bad access patterns. A ***batch data structure*** takes as input a set of operations rather than one operation at a time. An advantage is that since the batch is known up front, operations can be combined and reorganized, and the batch can be parallelized. For example, a batch 2-3 tree [4] first sorts the keys being inserted by a batch, thus avoiding the bad case for B^+ trees mentioned above. Restructuring a parallel program to use batch data structure instead of a concurrent data structure can often be difficult or even infeasible, thereby limiting programmability.

Implicit Batching: We propose implicit batching, where the programmer provides two components: (1) a parallel program containing parallel accesses to a abstract data type A, and (2) a batch data-structure implementing the data structure A. The runtime scheduler then dynamically and transparently organizes the program's parallel accesses to the data structure into batches, and invokes the provided implementation of batch operations. Implicit batching provides several advantages. 1) Only one batch is active at a time, obviating the need for complicated concurrency control within the data structure. 2) The batches may use combining techniques to accelerate a set of operations. 3) Parallelism may be used to accelerate each batch. 4) Implicit batching coupled with a good scheduler yields a performance theorem.

Implicit batching resembles flat combining [3], which is more efficient than some of the best concurrent data structures under certain loads, but lacks a performance theorem guaranteeing good speedup. Implicit batching may be viewed as a generalization of flat combining in that it allows *parallel* implementations of batch operations, instead

This research is supported in part by NSF grants CCF-1218017, CCF-1150036, CCF-1218188, and CCF-1314633 of only a sequential one allowed by flat combining. Parallel batches are integral to a good performance theorem.

Scheduler and performance theorem: We focus on parallel programs expressed through ***dynamic multithreading***, which is common in parallel languages and libraries, such as Cilk dialects, Intel Threading Building Blocks, and Microsoft Task Parallel Library. The programmer expresses algorithmic parallelism, through linguistic constructs such as "spawn" and "sync," "fork" and "join," or parallel loops. The programmer does not provide any mapping from subcomputations to processors and the programs are typically scheduled using an efficient work-stealing scheduler (e.g., [1]) provided by the runtime system. A parallel program (without parallel data-structure accesses) having T_1 **work**—the running time on 1 processor, and T_∞ **span**—the length of the critical path, can be executed in $O(T_1/P + T_\infty)$ (expected) time on P processors using a work-stealing scheduler.

We designed a work-stealing scheduler, called *BATCHER*, that supports implicit batching and provides similar bounds for parallel programs that have data-structure accesses.

THEOREM 1. *Consider a dynamically multithreaded program with T_1 work, T_∞ span, n total data-structure operations, and m data-structure operations along any sequential chain of dependencies in the program. Let $W(n)$ be the worst-case total work of n data-structure operations grouped arbitrarily into batches. Let $s(n)$ be the worst-case span of a parallel size-P batch operation.[1] Then the expected running time of this program on P processors using BATCHER[2] is at most $O\left(\frac{T_1}{P} + T_\infty + \frac{W(n) + ns(n)}{P} + ms(n)\right)$.*

For concreteness, consider a search tree (a PRAM batch 2-3 tree [4] adapted to dynamic multithreading). For n operations, $W(n) = O(n \log n)$ and $s(n) = \max\{\lg n, \lg P \lg \lg P\}$. For large enough problems ($n = \Omega(P^{\lg \lg P})$), the run time reduces to $O\left(\frac{T_1 + n \lg n}{P} + T_\infty \lg n\right)$, which means that each operation costs $\Theta(\lg n)$; that is, BATCHER introduces no asymptotic overhead due to the use of concurrent operations.

Programming Interface: BATCHER provides distinct interfaces to the data-structure programmer, who implements the data structure, and the algorithm programmer, who uses the data structure; the runtime system stitches together these interfaces and does the scheduling. In order to perform a data-structure operation, the algorithm programmer calls the function BATCHIFY (provided by the BATCHER runtime)

BATCHIFY(BatcherDS *DS*, OpRecord *op*),

where *DS* points to the data structure, and *op* is the operation record for the data-structure operation to be performed. As

---

```
1   parallel_for i = 1 to n
2       do B[i] = INCREMENT(A[i])
```

Figure 1. A parallel loop that performs n parallel updates to a shared counter. Here, $A[1..n]$ is an array of values by which to increment (or decrement if negative) the counter, and $B[1..n]$ holds any return values from the INCREMENTs.

```
3   struct OpRecord {int value; int result;}

INCREMENT(int x)
4   OpRecord op
5   op.value = x
6   BATCHIFY(this, op)
7   return op.result

BOP(OpRecord D[1..size])
8   let v be the value of the counter
9   D[1]'s value field = v + D[1]'s value
10  perform parallel-prefix-sums on value fields of D[1..size],
         storing sums into result fields of D[1..size]
    // now D[i]'s result = ∑ᵢₖ₌₁ D[k]'s value
11  set the counter to D[size]'s result
```

Figure 2. A batch-counter implementation. Line 6 logically blocks until the *result* is available. The BOP procedure is called by the scheduler automatically.

---

far as the algorithm programmer is concerned, BATCHIFY resembles a normal procedure call to access a *concurrent data structure*, and the control flow blocks at this point until the operation completes. A BATCHER data structure inherits from a virtual BATCHERDS class, providing a single method BOP implementing the *parallel* batch operation:

BATCHERDS::BOP(OpRecord $D[1..size]$),

where D is an array of operation records for operations to be performed by this batch.

Figures 1 and 2 show a simple example program making n parallel increments to a shared counter. The batch increment is straightforward to implement through a parallel prefix-sums operation, without any atomic primitives in user code. Here, BATCHER guarantees a runtime of $O(n \lg P/P + \lg n)$ on P processors, i.e., nearly linear speedup.

References

[1] R. D. Blumofe and C. E. Leiserson. Scheduling multi-threaded computations by work stealing. *Journal of the ACM*, 46(5):720–748, 1999.

[2] A. Braginsky and E. Petrank. A lock-free B+tree. In *SPAA*, pages 58–67, 2012.

[3] D. Hendler, I. Incze, N. Shavit, and M. Tzafrir. Flat combining and the synchronization-parallelism tradeoff. In *SPAA*, pages 355–364, 2010.

[4] W. J. Paul, U. Vishkin, and H. Wagener. Parallel dictionaries in 2-3 trees. In *ICALP*, pages 597–609, 1983.

---

[1] We employ only binary forking, so $s(n) \geq \lg P$ implicitly.

[2] Just as in standard work-stealing results, our theoretical bounds assume that the only synchronization of the input algorithm occurs through "syncs" or "joins"; the algorithm or data-structure code itself does not use explicit synchronization primitives, e.g., locks or compare-and-swaps.

Theoretical Analysis of Classic Algorithms on Highly-threaded Many-core GPUs

Lin Ma, Kunal Agrawal, and Roger D. Chamberlain

Dept. of Computer Science and Engineering, Washington University in St. Louis

{lin.ma, kunal, roger}@wustl.edu

Abstract

The *Threaded many-core memory (TMM)* model provides a framework to analyze the performance of algorithms on GPUs. Here, we investigate the effectiveness of the TMM model by analyzing algorithms for 3 classic problems — suffix tree/array for string matching, fast Fourier transform, and merge sort — under this model. Our findings indicate that the TMM model can explain and predict previously unexplained trends and artifacts in experimental data.

Categories and Subject Descriptors Theory of computation [*Parallel algorithms*]

Keywords Threaded Many-core Memory (TMM) Model

1. Introduction

Asymptotic analysis allows one to compare the high-level performance characteristics of algorithms ignoring low level implementation details. The *Threaded Many-core Memory (TMM)* model [3] models GPUs as containing P cores grouped into a number of core groups; the cores in a core group share a fast local memory of size Z. Computation and access to fast memory takes unit time. A global memory is shared by all the core groups with ***memory latency*** of L time steps. Data is transferred from slow to fast memory in ***chunks*** of maximum size C. The hardware limit on the ***number of threads per core*** is represented by X; Given P total cores, the total number of threads supported on the machine is therefore bounded by XP.

An algorithm in the TMM model is analyzed using its computational complexity represented by its ***work*** T_1 — the total number of operations — and ***span*** T_∞ — the number of operations along the critical path. The memory complexity

Supported by NSF grants CNS-0905368, CNS-0931693 and Exegy, Inc.

is analyzed in terms of the ***total number of global memory transactions*** M. Up to C global memory accesses (if they are contiguous) may be grouped as a single memory transaction when we calculate M. In addition, $\mathcal{T}$ represents ***number of threads per core*** used by the algorithm; it depends on both the problem size and the hardware limit. Assuming that the program is scheduled perfectly, the performance of an algorithm in this model is described in Eq. (1) which calculates T_P, the running time of the algorithm on P cores:

$$T_P = O\left(\max(\frac{T_1}{P}, T_\infty, \frac{ML}{\mathcal{T}P})\right). \qquad (1)$$

We evaluate the TMM model through the analysis of 3 classic algorithms. By comparing TMM's predictions with empirical results from other investigators, we show that the TMM model is effective at explaining many kinds of empirical observations, and its analysis framework appears to be well suited to understanding and predicting the high-level characteristics of the performance of algorithms on GPUs.

2. Suffix Tree vs. Suffix Array

We investigate two algorithms that find all occurrences of a set of n ***query strings*** of length k in a given ***reference string*** of length m ($m \gg k$): ***suffix tree*** — a compressed trie containing all suffixes of the reference string as keys and the starting positions in the string as values, and ***suffix array*** — a lexicographically sorted array of all indices of suffixes. We analyze a particular GPU implementation of both [1].

Suffix Tree: Each thread takes a single query string, and checks at most k possible positions in the tree. The work and number of memory transfers is $O(nk)$. Therefore, the runtime, using Eq. (1), is

$$T_P = O\left(\max\left(\frac{nk}{P}, k, \frac{nkL}{\mathcal{T}P}\right)\right). \qquad (2)$$

Suffix Array: Again, each thread takes a single query and conducts a binary search on the suffix array. Each query takes $O(k \lg m)$ span with $O(k \lg m)$ work and $O(\frac{k \lg m}{C})$ memory transactions, since the suffix can be accessed in chunks of size C. Therefore, for n queries, using Eq. (1),

$$T_P = O\left(\max\left(\frac{nk \lg m}{P}, k \lg m, \frac{nk \lg m \cdot L}{C\mathcal{T}P}\right)\right). \qquad (3)$$

For Eq. (2) and Eq. (3), the last term (memory complexity term) can be refined into two terms depending on the relation between the batch size n and the thread limit XP. When

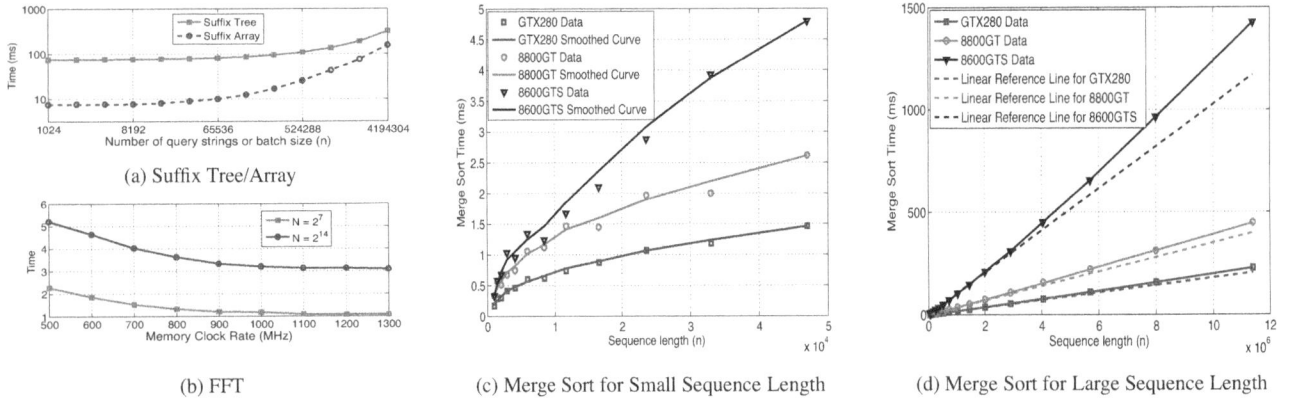

(a) Suffix Tree/Array

(b) FFT

(c) Merge Sort for Small Sequence Length

(d) Merge Sort for Large Sequence Length

Figure 1: (a) Runtime of suffix trees/arrays on NVIDIA GTX580 [1]. (b) Runtime of FFT with various memory frequencies on NVIDIA GTX280, two problem sizes $N = 2^7$ and $N = 2^{14}$. The y-axis is runtime on an arbitrary scale; the data are converted from GFLOPs from [2]. The x-axis shows increasing memory clock rate, denoting decreasing memory latency L. (c) Merge sort runtime for small sequence size [4]. (d) Merge sort runtime for large sequence size [4].

$n \leq XP$, each thread handles a single query; the number of threads $\mathcal{T}P$ increases with n, $n = O(\mathcal{T}P)$, and the two cancel out in the last term. When $n > XP$, we do not have sufficient threads to run all queries on separate threads, and the n queries are processed in $\lceil \frac{n}{XP} \rceil$ batches. As all available threads are used ($\mathcal{T} = X$), the third term becomes $\frac{nkL}{XP}$ for Eq. (2) and $\frac{nk \lg m \cdot L}{CXP}$ for Eq. (3). Considering both scenarios, Eq. (2) and (3) can be expressed respectively as:

$$T_P = O\left(\max\left(\frac{nk}{P}, k, kL, \frac{nkL}{XP}\right)\right)$$

$$T_P = O\left(\max\left(\frac{nk \lg m}{P}, k \lg m, \frac{k \lg m \cdot L}{C}, \frac{nk \lg m \cdot L}{CXP}\right)\right).$$

Theoretical Analysis vs. Empirical Validation: If we just consider computational complexity, suffix trees are clearly better than suffix arrays by a factor of $O(\lg m)$. However, in the TMM model, suffix arrays may be better if memory complexity dominates and as n increases, the running time goes from being independent of n to being linear in n for both algorithms, but the transitions happen at different values of n. Figure 1(a) shows the (replotted) empirical performance of these algorithms reported by [1] and qualitatively supports this prediction.

3. FFT

Fast Fourier Transform (FFT) computes the classic ***Discrete Fourier Transform (DFT)*** in $O(N \lg N)$ operations. At each of the $\lg N$ steps, it divides the DFT of size N into two interleaved DFTs of size $N/2$, followed by a combining stage of $N/2$ size-2 DFTs. On GPUs, those $N/2$ DFTs are computed in parallel, each by a thread. $T_1 = O(N \lg N)$, $T_\infty = O(\lg N)$, and $M = O(N \lg N/C)$ as memory accesses can be grouped. Using Eq. (1) and by the same logic of refining the last term as suffix trees/arrays, we get

$$T_P = O\left(\max\left(\frac{N \lg N}{P}, \lg N, \frac{\lg N \cdot L}{C}, \frac{N \lg N \cdot L}{CXP}\right)\right).$$

Theoretical Analysis vs. Empirical Validation: We highlight an interesting experiment, where the memory clock rate is varied [2]. Note that increasing the memory clock rate is equivalent to shrinking the memory latency L. We predict that after a certain point of increasing memory frequency, the algorithm runtime no longer depends on L. Figure 1(b) validates the above observation.

4. Merge Sort

In the merge sort algorithm on GPUs [4], we (1) divide the input sequence into $O(n/Z)$ blocks of size Z, (2) sort them in parallel locally within core groups using Batcher's odd-even merge sort with $O(\lg^2 Z)$ span, $O(n \lg^2 Z)$ work, and $O(n/C)$ memory transfers, and (3) then recursively merge them using pair-wise blocked merge in $\lg(n/Z)$ layers; each of which takes work $O(n \lg Z)$, span $O(\lg n)$ and memory complexity $O(n/C)$. We substitute into Eq. (1), and by refining the last term according to problem size, we get

$$T_P = O\left(\max(\frac{n \lg Z \lg \frac{n}{Z}}{P}, \lg n \lg \frac{n}{Z}, \frac{\lg \frac{n}{Z} \cdot L}{C}, \frac{n \lg \frac{n}{Z} \cdot L}{CXP})\right).$$

Theoretical Analysis vs. Empirical Validation: Results in Figures 1(c) and (d) are replotted from the data in [4]. As the analysis indicates, the experiments confirm that for small values of $n < XP$, the running time increases logarithmically (slower than linear), and as n gets larger, the running time increases with $n \lg \frac{n}{Z}$ (a little faster than linear).

References

[1] G. Encarnaijao, N. Sebastiao, and N. Roma. Advantages and GPU implementation of high-performance indexed DNA search based on suffix arrays. In *Proc. of HPCS*, 2011.

[2] N. K. Govindaraju et al. High performance discrete Fourier transforms on graphics processors. In *Proc. of SC*, 2008.

[3] L. Ma, K. Agrawal, and R. D. Chamberlain. A memory access model for highly-threaded many-core architectures. *Future Generation Computer Systems*, 30:202–215, January 2014.

[4] N. Satish et al. Designing efficient sorting algorithms for manycore GPUs. In *Proc. of IPDPS*, 2009.

SCCMulti

An Improved Parallel Strongly Connected Components Algorithm

Daniel Tomkins   Timmie Smith   Nancy M. Amato   Lawrence Rauchwerger

Parasol Laboratory
Department of Computer Science and Engineering
Texas A&M University
{kittsil,timmie,amato,rwerger}@cse.tamu.edu

Categories and Subject Descriptors   Software [*PROGRAM-MING TECHNIQUES*]: Concurrent Programming: Parallel programming

Keywords   Strongly Connected Components; Randomized Algorithms; Parallel Graph Algorithms

1. Overview

Graphs are used in social network analysis, motion planning, particle transport studies, and many other fields. We are able to efficiently analyze graph properties using sequential techniques, but many graphs, especially those used in scientific and social network applications, are so large that they do not fit in the memory available to a single processor. Unfortunately, graphs are difficult to analyze in parallel, and for many problems we are still unable to reach the theoretical bounds provided by sequential algorithms.

This work considers one such problem: finding the strongly connected components (SCCs) of a directed graph (digraph). An SCC is a maximal subgraph of a digraph such that there is a path from every node in the SCC to every other node in the SCC. SCCs are used in compiler analysis, data mining, physical reaction simulations, and scheduling [1], and to locate and collapse cycles in cyclic graphs [4].

The optimal sequential algorithm for finding SCCs is Tarjan's linear-time algorithm [6], which depends on depth-first search (DFS); however, DFS is P-complete. Parallel SCC algorithm research initially focused on using matrix multiplication techniques to compute the transitive closure of the graph, but this is costly in the total amount of work.

PPoPP '14,   February 15–19, 2014, Orlando, Florida, USA.
Copyright is held by the owner/author(s).
ACM 978-1-4503-2656-8/14/02.
http://dx.doi.org/10.1145/2555243.2555286

Other deterministic algorithms improved the total work, but only for certain types of graphs.

Randomized algorithms based on reachability queries (RQs) – which test the ability to get from one vertex to another along a directed path – greatly improve the work bound in the average case [1, 3–5]. However, these algorithms do not always perform well: e.g., Divide-and-Conquer Strong Components (DCSC) [1, 3] has good theoretical limits but performs poorly on graphs for which the maximum reachability is small; MULTIPIVOT [4] gives high probability guarantees on the total work but introduces a work overhead; and NSCC [5] offers fast, consistent performance in exchange for memory overhead and specialized data structures.

The main contributions of this work are SCCMULTI – a new algorithm which eliminates the drawbacks of the previous algorithms – and an experimental validation of SCC-MULTI on a range of graphs. A comparison of SCCMULTI and the previous algorithms is shown in the table below.

Algorithm	RQs	Weakness
NSCC [5]	$O(\log n)$	Large memory overhead
DCSC [1, 3]	$O(\log n)$	$O(n)$ RQs on some inputs
MULTIPIVOT [4]	$O(\log^2 n)$	$O(\log n)$ RQs per iteration
SCCMULTI	$O(\log n)$	

2. Algorithm

SCCMULTI is shown in Algorithm 1. On the kth iteration, SCCMULTI selects $\frac{2^k |V|}{n}$ nodes as pivots, where V is the set of vertices and n is the starting size of V. For any vertex v, call $SUCC(v)$ the set of nodes reached by v and $PRED(v)$ the set of nodes that reach v. Each pivot v_i marks all nodes in $SUCC(v_i)$ with s_i and all nodes in $PRED(v_i)$ with p_i. Nodes marked with both s_i and p_i form SCC_i and are removed. Finally, edges between nodes with different marks are removed, dividing the graph for the next iteration.

3. Experimental Results

We implemented DCSC, MULTIPIVOT, and SCCMULTI using C++ and the STAPL library, a parallel library which provides a distributed graph [2]. We did not implement NSCC because it uses a specific RQ algorithm that maintains com-

Algorithm 1 SCCMULTI

1: **for** k **from** 0 **to** $\log n$ **do**
2:     **for all** $i \leftarrow 1$ **to** $\frac{2^k |V|}{n}$ **do**
3:         $v_i \leftarrow random\_node(V)$
4:         **for all** $u \in SUCC(v_i)$ **do**
5:             $u.marks \leftarrow u.marks \cup s_i$
6:         **for all** $u \in PRED(v_i)$ **do**
7:             $u.marks \leftarrow u.marks \cup p_i$
8:         $SCC_i \leftarrow \{v \in V : s_i, p_i \in v.marks\}$
9:         $G = G \setminus SCC_i$
10:     **for all** $(u,v) \in E : u.marks \neq v.marks$ **do**
11:         $E \leftarrow E \setminus \{(u,v)\}$
12:     **for all** $v \in G$ **do**
13:         $v.marks \leftarrow \emptyset$

plex data structures, unlike the other algorithms. The results show that SCCMULTI is both fast and consistent.

Experiments were run on a Cray XE6m-200 with 24 nodes, each with one or two 16-core Opteron 6272 processors and 32 or 64GB RAM, and a Cray XE6 with 6,384 nodes, each with two 12-core Opteron 6172 processors and 32GB RAM. We ran each experiment 32 times and report the mean execution time and a 95% confidence interval.

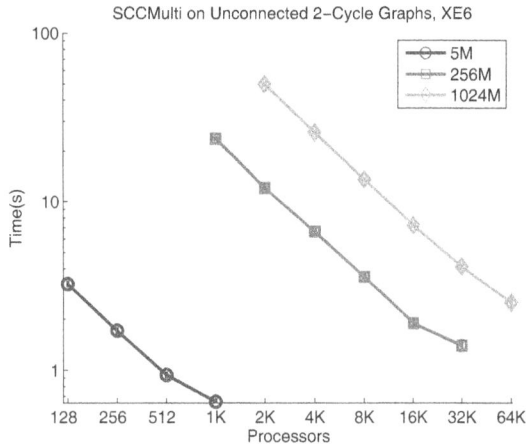

Figure 1. SCCMULTI Scalability for disconnected cycles.

Figure 1 shows the scalability of SCCMULTI using a graph of disconnected cycles. In experiments on lower core counts, MULTIPIVOT was an order of magnitude slower and DCSC three orders of magnitude slower. This is expected given MULTIPIVOT's extra $O(\log n)$ RQs per iteration and DCSC's inability to divide a graph with low reachability.

Figure 2 shows a comparison of the algorithms on two graphs. The Watts-Strogatz graph represents real-world, non-planar graphs, while the perturbed mesh with 20% random edge reversal simulates those used in particle transport studies. The results show that MULTIPIVOT is slower than SCCMULTI and DCSC. For Watts-Strogatz, SCCMULTI uses more pivots than DCSC, resulting in higher execution times on lower core counts. However, DCSC requires more

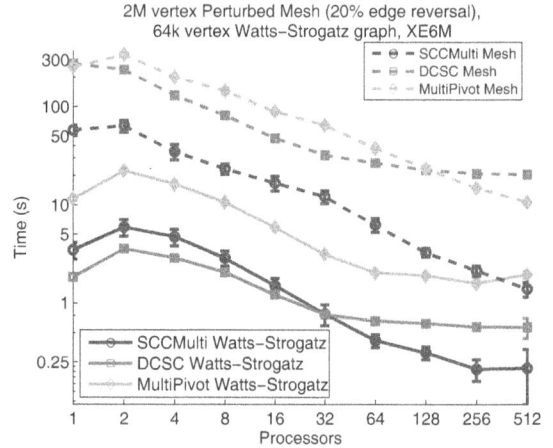

Figure 2. Perturbed mesh and small world graph results.

communication to maintain subgraph information, and, as a result, does not scale as well as SCCMULTI.

Acknowledgments

This research supported in part by NSF awards CNS-0551685, CCF-0833199, CCF-0830753, IIS-0916053, IIS-0917266, EFRI-1240483, RI-1217991, by NIH NCI R25 CA090301-11, by DOE awards DE-AC02-06CH11357, B575363, by Samsung, by Award KUS-C1-016-04, made by King Abdullah University of Science and Technology (KAUST). This research used resources of the National Energy Research Scientific Computing Center, which is supported by the Office of Science of the U.S. Department of Energy under Contract No. DE-AC02-05CH11231.

References

[1] L. Fleischer, B. Hendrickson, and A. Pinar. On Identifying Strongly Connected Components in Parallel. In J. D. P. Rolim, ed., *IPDPS Workshops*, volume 1800 of *Lec. Notes in Comp. Sci.*, pages 505–511. Springer, 2000. ISBN 3-540-67442-X.

[2] Harshvardhan, A. Fidel, N. M. Amato, and L. Rauchwerger. The STAPL Parallel Graph Library. In *Wkshp. on Lang. and Comp. for Par. Comp. (LCPC)*, Tokyo, Japan, Sep 2012.

[3] W. McLendon, III, B. Hendrickson, S. J. Plimpton, and L. Rauchwerger. Finding Strongly Connected Components in Distributed Graphs. *J. Par. Dist. Comp.*, 65:901–910, 2005.

[4] W. Schudy. Finding Strongly Connected Components in Parallel Using $O(\log^2 n)$ Reachability Queries. In *Proc. of the 20th Annual Symp. on Parallelism in Algorithms and Architectures*, SPAA '08, pages 146–151, New York, NY, USA, 2008. ACM. ISBN 978-1-59593-973-9.

[5] T. H. Spencer. More Time-Work Tradeoffs for Parallel Graph Algorithms. In *Proc. of the 3rd Annual Symp. on Parallelism in Algorithms and Architectures*, SPAA '91, pages 81–93, New York, NY, USA, 1991. ACM. ISBN 0-89791-438-4.

[6] R. E. Tarjan. Depth-First Search and Linear Graph Algorithms. *SIAM J. Comput.*, 1(2):146–160, 1972.

Initial Study of Multi-Endpoint Runtime for MPI+OpenMP Hybrid Programming Model on Multi-Core Systems *

Miao Luo, Xiaoyi Lu, Khaled Hamidouche, Krishna Kandalla, Dhabaleswar K. (DK) Panda

Dept. of Computer Science and Engineering
The Ohio State University
{luom, luxi, hamidouc, kandalla, panda}@cse.ohio-state.edu

Abstract

State-of-the-art MPI libraries rely on locks to guarantee thread-safety. This discourages application developers from using multiple threads to perform MPI operations. In this paper, we propose a high performance, lock-free multi-endpoint MPI runtime, which can achieve up to 40% improvement for point-to-point operation and one representative collective operation with minimum or no modifications to the existing applications.

1. Introduction

MPI/OpenMP hybrid programming model is widely regarded as suitable model for scaling parallel applications on emerging multi-/many-core computing architectures. In this model, applications can be deployed with one MPI process per compute node or CPU socket, with OpenMP "threads" running on other compute cores to accelerate computation. However, previous studies demonstrated that there are several challenges associated with combining these two models (MPI and OpenMP) to fully leverage the performance benefits of a hybrid model [2–4, 6]; including overhead from locks and waste of communication/computation resources. It is important to design a new MPI runtime and understand its impact in accelerating MPI/OpenMP hybrid applications on modern multi-core systems. In this paper, we propose a high performance, lock-free multi-endpoint MPI runtime and discuss how to deliver its benefits to applications for point-to-point and collective operations.

---

* This research is supported in part by National Science Foundation grants #OCI-0926691, #OCI-1148371 and #CCF-1213084

2. Design of Multi-endpoint MPI Runtime

2.1 Lock-free Communication Routines

In order to achieve lock-free communication routines, we identify the following two critical components that need to be re-designed according to multi-threading requirements:

Request Handling: Instead of sharing the same request memory region across different threads with locks, our proposed design pre-allocates request memory objects according to the number of threads that would be able to call MPI functions. Each thread is associated with a thread-ID as a thread local storage parameter (LST). Any request-related operations should access the corresponding request memory object according to a specific thread-ID.

Communication Resources Management: In order to launch send/receive operations without lock protection, the proposed multi-treading runtime establishes necessary connection resources according to the number of endpoints. These resources are stored in the form of a table. An Endpoint-ID serves as the index key for accessing the table. Particularly, the communication resources instantiate the concept of endpoint in the proposed runtime.

Based on the proposed multi-endpoint runtime, we are able to remove locks in the critical routines. However, it is not straight-forward to deliver the benefits of multi-endpoint runtime to applications. It is necessary to explore design alternatives to provide the benefits of the proposed multi-endpoint runtime to real applications, in a transparent manner, or with minimal modifications.

2.2 Optimization for Point-to-Point Operations

In the master-only model, MPI non-blocking send/receive operations are called after the OpenMP threads joined, or only the master thread makes MPI function calls through "pragma omp master" directive. Simple modifications are required for such programs in order to take advantage of the proposed multi-endpoint runtime. The application developers only need to add OpenMP pragma, "pragma omp parallel", outside of the MPI functions with the original input parameters. Inside the runtime, the number of endpoints E for communication requests is decided by the message size, according to a pre-defined tuning table. Each endpoint is responsible for sending its portion of size $\frac{n}{E}$ independently for the original message of size n. Threads that are not assigned with a communication task just bypass and wait at the barrier or continue with the next unrelated communication request.

2.3 Optimizations for Collective Operations

This section discusses our initial study of multi-endpoint based algorithm optimizations for the pair-wise exchange based MPI_Alltoallv operation, with no modification to applications.

Pair-wise exchange algorithm is widely utilized to implement the MPI_Alltoallv operation. $p - 1$ send/receive operations are required for every MPI rank with p processes. In the single-endpoint runtime, all the send/receive requests are handled by a single thread. The multi-endpoint runtime can optimize the algorithm by distributing these requests among a set of endpoints. In the new algorithm, all the p MPI ranks can be divided into E groups, where E is the number of active endpoints. In each node, the thread with Endpoint-ID equal to Group ID operates as the "receiver"; and, all the threads should perform as "sender" to the destinations with a Group ID equal to the Endpoint-ID of the "sender". The new "Group" algorithm successfully distributes the send requests from a single endpoint across multiple endpoints.

3. Experimental Results

We implement the new design based on MVAPICH2 1.9 [5] and use it for the comparison. We carry out the evaluations on the "Stampede" computing system from TACC [1]. Each compute node includes two Xeon E5-2680 processors with a total of 16 cores and 32GB memory per node. Nodes are interconnected with Mellanox FDR InfiniBand. We use 256 compute nodes (4,096 cores) for collective evaluations.

3.1 Point-to-Point Micro-Benchmark Evaluations

We compare the performance across different numbers of active endpoints with the default single-endpoint runtime in Figure 1. The best number of active endpoints varies according to message size. The multi-endpoint optimization can reduce the latency of the master-only mode by up to 40%. A tuning table inside the multi-endpoint runtime is configured according to the evaluation results. It helps the runtime to choose the most suitable number of active endpoints according to the message size.

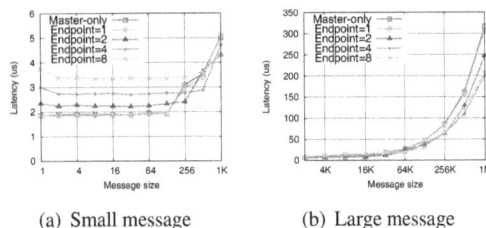

(a) Small message   (b) Large message

Figure 1. Evaluations for point-to-point

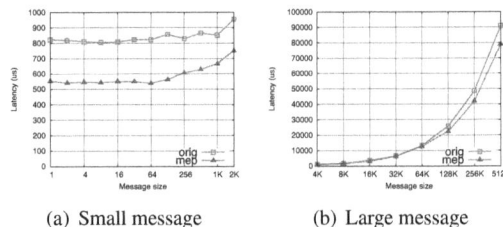

(a) Small message   (b) Large message

Figure 2. Evaluations: alltoallv

3.2 Collective Micro-Benchmark Evaluations

We compare our multi-endpoint optimized "Group" algorithm, with the process-based alltoallv operation ("orig") in Figure 2. The multi-endpoint runtime automatically adjusts the number of active endpoints according to the pre-defined tuning table. The multi-endpoint runtime ("mep") can achieve 30% improvement for small messages, which is mainly from the overlapped send startup time. For large messages, the new runtime can achieve up to 14% improvement from a better utilization of network bandwidth.

4. Conclusions and Future Work

This paper proposed an initial study of a lock-free, multi-endpoint runtime for MPI/OpenMP hybrid applications on emerging multi-core systems. This design can efficiently accelerate hybrid parallel applications with minimal modifications for point-to-point and no modification for collective operations. Preliminary results show that our framework can improve the performance of point-to-point and collective operations by up to 40% with 256 compute nodes (4,096 cores). For future work, we plan to investigate our multi-endpoint runtime design for heterogeneous architectures and explore more efficient collective algorithms based on the multi-endpoint design.

References

[1] Stampede at Texas Advanced Computing Center. http://www.tacc.utexas.edu/resources/hpc/stampede.

[2] P. Balaji, D. Buntinas, D. Goodell, W. Gropp, and R. Thakur. Fine-Grained Multithreading Support for Hybrid Threaded MPI Programming. *Int. J. High Perform. Comput. Appl.*, 24 (1):49–57, Feb. 2010.

[3] S. Bova, C. Breshears, H. Gabb, B. Kuhn, B. Magro, R. Eigenmann, G. Gaertner, S. Salvini, and H. Scott. Parallel Programming with Message Passing and Directives. *Computing in Science Engineering*, 3(5):22–37, 2001.

[4] Z. Lan, V. Taylor, and G. Bryan. Dynamic Load Balancing for Structured Adaptive Mesh Refinement Applications. In *International Conference on Parallel Processing*, 2001.

[5] MVAPICH2. http://mvapich.cse.ohio-state.edu/.

[6] R. Rabenseifner, G. Hager, and G. Jost. Hybrid MPI/OpenMP Parallel Programming on Clusters of Multi-Core SMP Nodes. In *Parallel, Distributed and Network-based Processing, 2009 17th Euromicro International Conference on*, pages 427–436, 2009.

Extracting Logical Structure and Identifying Stragglers in Parallel Execution Traces

Katherine E. Isaacs[*]   Todd Gamblin[†]   Abhinav Bhatele[†]   Peer-Timo Bremer[†]
Martin Schulz[†]   Bernd Hamann[*]

[*]Department of Computer Science, University of California, Davis
[†]Center for Applied Scientific Computing, Lawrence Livermore National Laboratory
keisaacs@ucdavis.edu, tgamblin,bhatele,ptbremer,schulzm@llnl.gov, hamann@cs.ucdavis.edu

Abstract

We introduce a new approach to automatically extract an idealized *logical structure* from a parallel execution trace. We use this structure to define intuitive metrics such as the *lateness* of a process involved in a parallel execution. By analyzing and illustrating traces in terms of logical steps, we leverage a developer's understanding of the happened-before relations in a parallel program. This technique can uncover dependency chains, elucidate communication patterns, and highlight sources and propagation of delays, all of which may be obscured in a traditional trace visualization.

Categories and Subject Descriptors   D.2.5 [*Software Engineering*]: Testing and Debugging – Tracing

Keywords   parallel execution trace; logical structure; visualization

1. Introduction

Analyzing the trace of a parallel execution is a powerful tool in identifying performance issues. Before specific problems have been identified, trace analysis typically starts with a visualization to obtain an overview and to form and test hypotheses about causes of observed slowdowns. Most visualizations align trace events by wall-clock time. Such a view rarely preserves the logical structure of the parallel code. Simple questions such as which messages arrived late are difficult to answer without the ability to identify logical phases or steps in a parallel program. As a result, a timeline view can be confusing even for small numbers of processes.

In contrast to existing approaches, we extract the underlying logical structure to show developers parallel traces in the context of their program's communication patterns. We then map timing information onto this structure. In this work, we

focus on MPI, a widely used message passing standard in high performance computing. We obtain our traces using VampirTrace [5] and store them in the Open Trace Format (OTF) [2]. Our approach is, however, generally applicable to any programming model based on message passing.

2. Extracting Logical Structure

The logical structure of a program is the ordering of events implied by that program. Ideally this structure reflects the developers' intended organization but may instead reflect the unintended result of the program. We describe the logical structure by assigning a *logical step* to each event. Events intended to happen simultaneously have the same step.

Our algorithm applies Lamport's *happened-before* relation [3] to derive structure from send and receive operations. Other operations are grouped into aggregate events occurring between the message events. We focus on sends and receives because they impose happened-before relations between processes. We first partition the send and receive events into related communication groups. Then we assign logical steps in each partition. The partitions themselves are partially ordered, imparting global steps on the events.

Partitions represent non-overlapping application phases. The partitioning may be pre-defined, but if not, we derive it from the trace. We first group events related by semantic or ordering constraints. Initially, each event is a partition. We build a graph over the partitions using happened-before relationships as edges. We then merge matching sends and receives as these must be related. Similarly, we merge partitions with events handled by the same `MPI_Waitall` call.

A merged partition maintains relations between its events and those in other partitions. This may introduce cycles into the partition graph, indicating that no absolute linear ordering exists. Therefore, partitions that form a strongly connected component must be related and are merged. Optionally, we attempt to merge partitions that logically belong together despite not having ordering constraints. In bulk synchronous codes, we expect each process to be active at any distance in the partition graph and merge accordingly.

We assign local steps in each partition following two principles. First, happened-before relationships must be maintained: events cannot change order and receives must oc-

PPoPP '14,   Feb 15–19, 2014, Orlando, FL, USA.
Copyright is held by the owner/author(s).
ACM 978-1-4503-2656-8/14/02.
http://dx.doi.org/10.1145/2555243.2555288

cur at least one step after their sends. Second, send events have a greater impact on structure. This is because the order messages are received is not always uniquely defined by the program and some events may contain multiple receives. We first determine simultaneous send groups by applying happened-before relationships while assuming receives are instantaneous. Then each event is assigned the least step possible based on these constraints. Global steps are offset by the maximum step in the preceding partitions. Finally, we insert aggregate events representing work done by a process between each pair of communication events.

3. Mapping Temporal Information

Traditional trace visualizations use the horizontal axis for recorded time. Visualizing the logical structure instead uses the horizontal axis to represent order. We restore the temporal information by coloring events with time-based metrics that take advantage of the logical structure.

We calculate how late an event was relative to its peers. We define the *lateness* of an event as the excess completion time over the earliest related event sharing the step. Figure 1 shows a portion of a 16-process MG [1] trace as visualized in Vampir [4] versus using logical steps and lateness. The latter shows a late aggregate event in the first process propagate lateness to other processes via message dependencies.

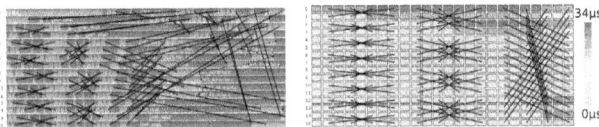

Figure 1: Vampir (left) and lateness-colored logical structure (right) visualization of a 16-process execution of MG.

We classify four situations contributing to event lateness (Figure 2). Two create lateness, through the event itself (2a) or a message for which the event is waiting (2d). The other two propagate lateness. Either the process is late in leaving the preceding event (2b) or a send is already late, causing the event to wait (2c). Figure 1 exhibits cases (a), (b), and (c).

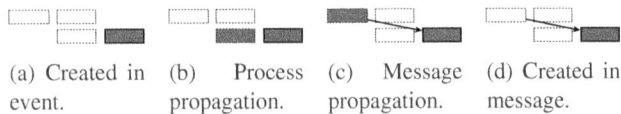

| (a) Created in event. | (b) Process propagation. | (c) Message propagation. | (d) Created in message. |

Figure 2: Initiation and propagation of lateness

We use this classification to narrow our focus to just the events where lateness originates, subtracting propagated lateness in each event to calculate *differential lateness*. By searching for events with high differential lateness, we can pinpoint areas of interest in the trace automatically.

4. Case Study

We analyze a massively parallel algorithm to compute *merge trees*. The algorithm relies on a global gather-scatter ap-

proach. Each process is assigned an equal portion of the data. All processes perform a local computation and send the results to their respective gather processes. These integrate the information and send the results both upwards to the next level merge and back downwards to the leaves. This repeats up the tree ending with the root performing the final gather.

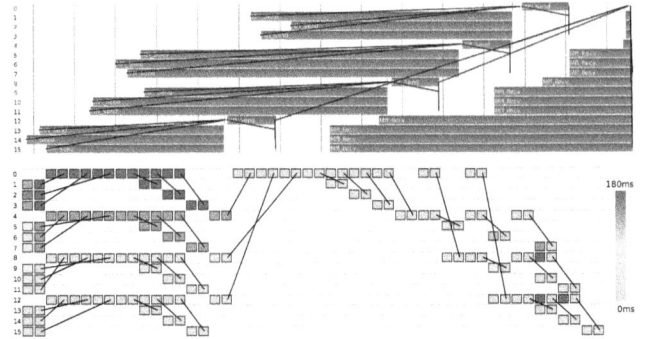

Figure 3: Vampir (top) and lateness-colored logical structure (bottom) visualization of a 16-process, 4-ary merge tree.

Figure 3 shows two visualizations of a complete 16-process, 4-ary merge tree. The logical step view exposes features not obvious in the traditional visualization. The late events reflect data-dependent load imbalance. The logical steps highlight the gather tree structure, revealing that the gather processes send back to the leaves before sending up to the root. This misses an opportunity for a more aggressive pipelining of the computation as no process can finish until the root has been reached and thus the gather should be prioritized over the scatter.

Acknowledgments

This research is supported by the U.S. Department of Energy Office of Science Graduate Fellowship administered by ORISE-ORAU under contract DE-AC05-06OR23100 and by Lawrence Livermore National Laboratory under contract DE-AC52-07NA27344 (LLNL-ABS-647655).

References

[1] D. H. Bailey et al. The nas parallel benchmarks. *Int. J. Supercomput. Appl.*, 5(3):63–73, 1991.

[2] A. Knüpfer, R. Brendel, H. Brunst, H. Mix, and W. E. Nagel. Introducing the open trace format (OTF). In *Proc. of 6th Int. Conf. on Comp. Sci.*, ICCS'06, pages 526–533. Springer-Verlag, 2006.

[3] L. Lamport. Time, clocks, and the ordering of events in a distributed system. *Commun. ACM*, 21(7):558–565, July 1978.

[4] W. E. Nagel, A. Arnold, M. Weber, H. C. Hoppe, and K. Solchenbach. VAMPIR: Visualization and analysis of MPI resources. *Supercomputer*, 12(1):69–80, 1996.

[5] TU Dresden Center for Information Services and High Performance Computing (ZIH). VampirTrace 5.14.2 user manual. http://www.tu-dresden.de/zih/vampirtrace, March 2013.

Author Index